Maine has lighthouses that prevent ships from crashing into its more than 3,000 miles of coastline. See chapter 13. © Kindra Clineff Photography

Faneuil Hall Marketplace lights up the nighttime skyline in Boston (top). Beacon Hill is home to many of the city's stateliest homes (bottom). See chapter 4. *Top photo © William Johnson/New England Stock; bottom photo © Chuck Pefley/Tony Stone Images.*

The Appalachian Trail crosses through sections of Maine, New Hampshire, Vermont, western Massachusetts (above), and Connecticut on its way to Georgia. But you don't have to hike the whole thing to enjoy the bucolic splendor; there are plenty of great day hikes. See chapters 8, 9, 10, 11, 12, and 13. © Kindra Clineff Photography.

Fall Foliage season brings every imaginable color to the region, whether it's the orange and yellow of the trees near Concord (above), or the crimson red of newly harvested cranberry bogs in Nantucket (opposite, top). See chapters 5 and 7. Both photos © Kindra Clineff Photography.

When should I travel to get the best airfare?
Where do I go for answers to my travel questions?
What's the best and easiest way to plan and book my trip?

frommers.travelocity.com

Frommer's, the travel guide leader, has teamed up with **Travelocity.com**, the leader in online travel, to bring you an in-depth, easy-to-use resource designed to help you plan and book your trip online.

At **frommers.travelocity.com**, you'll find free online updates about your destination from the experts at Frommer's plus the outstanding travel planning and purchasing features of Travelocity.com. Travelocity.com provides reservations capabilities for 95 percent of all airline seats sold, more than 47,000 hotels, and over 50 car rental companies. In addition, Travelocity.com offers more than 2,000 exciting vacation and cruise packages. Travelocity.com puts you in complete control of your travel planning with these and other great features:

    Expert travel guidance from Frommer's - over 150 writers reporting from around the world!

    Best Fare Finder - an interactive calendar tells you when to travel to get the best airfare

    Fare Watcher - we'll track airfare changes to your favorite destinations

    Dream Maps - a mapping feature that suggests travel opportunities based on your budget

    Shop Safe Guarantee - 24 hours a day / 7 days a week live customer service, and more!

Whether traveling on a tight budget, looking for a quick weekend getaway, or planning the trip of a lifetime, Frommer's guides and Travelocity.com will make your travel dreams a reality. You've bought the book, now book the trip!

A New Star-Rating System & Other Exciting News from Frommer's!

In our continuing effort to publish the savviest, most up-to-date, and most appealing travel guides available, we've added some great new features.

Frommer's guides now include a new **star-rating system.** Every hotel, restaurant, and attraction is rated from 0 to 3 stars to help you set priorities and organize your time.

We've also added **seven brand-new features** that point you to the great deals, in-the-know advice, and unique experiences that separate travelers from tourists. Throughout the guide look for:

Finds	Special finds—those places only insiders know about
Fun Fact	Fun facts—details that make travelers more informed and their trips more fun
Kids	Best bets for kids—advice for the whole family
Moments	Special moments—those experiences that memories are made of
Overrated	Places or experiences not worth your time or money
Tips	Insider tips—some great ways to save time and money
Value	Great values—where to get the best deals

We've also added a **"What's New"** section in every guide—a timely crash course in what's hot and what's not in every destination we cover.

Other Great Guides for Your Trip:

Frommer's Boston

Frommer's Cape Cod, Nantucket & Martha's Vineyard

Frommer's Portable Maine Coast

Frommer's Great Outdoor Guide to Vermont & New Hampshire

Frommer's Vermont, New Hampshire & Maine

Frommer's USA

New England
2002

by Wayne Curtis, Herbert Bailey Livesey,
Marie Morris & Laura M. Reckford

Here's what the critics say about Frommer's:

"Amazingly easy to use. Very portable, very complete."

—*Booklist*

"The only mainstream guide to list specific prices. The Walter Cronkite of guidebooks—with all that implies."

—*Travel & Leisure*

"Complete, concise, and filled with useful information."

—*New York Daily News*

"Hotel information is close to encyclopedic."

—*Des Moines Sunday Register*

Best-Selling Books • Digital Downloads • e-Books • Answer Networks •
e-Newsletters • Branded Web Sites • e-Learning
New York, NY • Cleveland, OH • Indianapolis, IN

About the Authors

Wayne Curtis (chapters 2, 3, 11 through 13, and the Appendix) is a freelance writer who's also the author of *Frommer's Nova Scotia, New Brunswick & Prince Edward Island*. He writes for the *Atlantic Monthly*, the *New York Times, Preservation*, and *Yankee*, among others. He lives on the Maine coast a few hundred yards from the Canadian border, and can be reached at curtis@maine.com.

Herbert Bailey Livesey (chapters 8 through 10) is a native New Yorker and a former NYU administrator. After leaving his career in higher education, he worked briefly as an artist before devoting himself to writing full time. He is the author of several travel guides, nine books on education and sociology, and a novel.

Marie Morris (chapters 4 and 5) is a native New Yorker and a graduate of Harvard, where she studied history. She has worked for the *New York Times, Boston* magazine, and the *Boston Herald*, and is also the author of *Frommer's Boston*. She lives in Boston.

Laura M. Reckford (chapters 6 and 7) is a writer and editor who lives on Cape Cod. Formerly the managing editor of *Cape Cod Life Magazine*, she has also been on the editorial staffs of *Good Housekeeping* magazine and *Entertainment Weekly*.

Published by:

Hungry Minds, Inc.

909 Third Ave.
New York, NY 10022

ISBN 0-7645-6446-3
ISSN 1044-2286

Editor: Leslie Shen
Production Editor: Cara L. Buitron
Photo Editor: Richard Fox
Cartographer: Nicholas Trotter
Production by Hungry Minds Indianapolis Production Services

Front cover photo: © Glen Allison/Tony Stone Images
Back cover photo: © Brooks Dodge/New England Stock

Special Sales

For general information on Hungry Minds' products and services please contact our Customer Care department; within the U.S. at 800-762-2974, outside the U.S. at 317-572-3993 or fax 317-572-4002. For sales inquiries and reseller information, including discounts, bulk sales, customized editions, and premium sales, please contact our Customer Care department at 800-434-3422.

Manufactured in the United States of America

5 4 3 2 1

Contents

List of Maps

An Invitation to the Reader

In researching this book, we discovered many wonderful places—hotels, inns, restaurants, shops, and more. We're sure you'll find others. Please tell us about them, so we can share the information with your fellow travelers in upcoming editions. If you were disappointed with a recommendation, we'd love to know that, too. Please write to:

Frommer's New England 2002
Hungry Minds, Inc. • 909 Third Avenue • New York, NY 10022

An Additional Note

Please be advised that travel information is subject to change at any time—and this is especially true of prices. We therefore suggest that you write or call ahead for confirmation when making your travel plans. The authors, editors, and publisher cannot be held responsible for the experiences of readers while traveling. Your safety is important to us, however, so we encourage you to stay alert and be aware of your surroundings. Keep a close eye on cameras, purses, and wallets, all favorite targets of thieves and pickpockets.

New! Frommer's Star Ratings & Icons

Every hotel, restaurant, and attraction listing in this guide has been ranked for quality, value, service, amenities, and special features using a star-rating scale. In country, state, and regional guides, we also rate towns and regions to help you narrow down your choices and budget your time accordingly. Hotels and restaurants in the Very Expensive and Expensive categories are rated on a scale of one (highly recommended) to three stars (exceptional). Those in the Moderate and Inexpensive categories rate from zero (recommended) to two stars (very highly recommended). Attractions, towns, and regions are rated according to the following scale: zero stars (recommended), one star (highly recommended), two stars (very highly recommended), and three stars (must-see).

In addition to the rating system, we also use seven icons to highlight insider information, useful tips, special bargains, hidden gems, memorable experiences, kid-friendly venues, places to avoid, and other useful information:

Finds *Fun Fact* *Kids* *Moments* *Overrated* *Tips* *Value*

The following abbreviations are used for credit cards:

AE American Express	DISC Discover	V Visa
DC Diners Club	MC MasterCard	

FROMMERS.COM

Now that you have the guidebook to a great trip, visit our website at **www.frommers.com** for travel information on nearly 2,000 destinations. With features updated regularly, we give you instant access to the most current trip-planning information available. At Frommers.com, you'll also find the best prices on air fares, accommodations, and car rentals—and you can even book travel online through our travel booking partners. At Frommers.com you'll also find the following:

- Daily Newsletter highlighting the best travel deals
- Hot Spot of the Month/Vacation Sweepstakes & Travel Photo Contest
- More than 200 Travel Message Boards
- Outspoken Newsletters and Feature Articles on travel bargains, vacation ideas, tips & resources, and more!

What's New in New England

BOSTON & CAMBRIDGE **Amtrak** (© 800/USA-RAIL; www. amtrak.com) has finally introduced high-speed rail service on the Northeast Corridor. **Acela Express** trains cover the 218 miles between Boston and New York in just over 3 hours; from Washington, the trip takes just under 6 hours.

The luxury boutique hotel **Fifteen Beacon,** 15 Beacon St., Beacon Hill (© 877/XV-BEACON), has attracted national attention for its over-the-top amenities and pampering. From a fireplace in every room to a little TV in every bathroom, the appointments are the latest in luxe, and service is of the your-wish-is-my-command variety.

The city's new (2000) museum of immigration isn't yet a must-see, but that's only because it isn't as well known as Boston's more established sights. **Dreams of Freedom,** 1 Milk St. (© 617/338-6022), is already a hit with families who have heard about it.

See chapter 4 for details.

SIDE TRIPS FROM BOSTON Louisa May Alcott's Concord home, **Orchard House,** 399 Lexington Rd. (© 978/369-4118), is about to launch an ambitious restoration project. Also under renovation is Salem's **Peabody Essex Museum,** East India Square (© 800/745-4054), which nevertheless continues to schedule intriguing special exhibitions. A major show of the work of photographer Edward S. Curtis begins in November 2001. While in Salem, check out the *Friendship,* a new three-masted tall ship anchored at the Salem Maritime

National Historic Site, 174 Derby St. (© 978/740-1660). A replica of a 1797 East Indiaman merchant vessel, the 171-footer is scheduled to open to the public in July 2001.

See chapter 5 for details.

CENTRAL & WESTERN MASSA-CHUSETTS It's easy to eat well in **Northampton,** and you can add the **Green Street Café,** 64 Green St. (© 413/586-5650), to the list of possibilities. Julia Child ate here and the chef is a grad of the French Culinary Institute, so expect Frenchified variations on contemporary American cooking.

Over in the **Berkshires,** the owner of **Salmon Run,** 78 Main St., in Lee (© 413/343-3900), has expressed his curious intention to cater not to tourists, but to local residents. We're spilling the news of his good eats at low cost, great for families.

The Mount, 2 Plunkett St. (© 413/637-1899), Edith Wharton's mansion in Lenox, remains in the throes of a $15-million restoration. Tours continue, but conflicts with the repertory **Shakespeare & Company** (© 413/637-3353), which has long staged its productions at the Mount, has caused the company to begin staged withdrawals until its lease expires in 2003.

In North Adams, that long-depressed former factory town, the ambitious new **Massachusetts Museum of Contemporary Art,** 87 Marshall St. (© 413/662-2111), is exceeding all hopes. Known as MASS MoCA, it has inspired other efforts to recycle the local building stock into restaurants, shops, and inns (including lodgings underwritten by the owners of the famed Red Lion in Stockbridge).

See chapter 8 for details.

CONNECTICUT Stamford has lost Kathleen's, a long-time favorite, but there are replacements. **Beacon,** 183 Harbor Dr. (℃ 203/327-4600), has been getting most of the ink, nearly all of it enormously enthusiastic. It's a massive operation, with an exhibition kitchen and tables spread over three levels and onto two decks. We prefer **Oceans 211,** 211 Summer St. (℃ 203/973-0494), quieter, more attentive, and presenting seafood in enchantingly inventive guises.

The **Westport Country Playhouse** (℃ 203/227-4177), one of the oldest summer theaters in the country, has gained new energy with the appointment of Joanne Woodward, a nearby resident, as a director. Well-known actors appear in almost every production.

In the **Litchfield Hills,** Woodbury's modest little Merryvale B&B has pushed out the walls of its 18th-century building to house a new 48-seat restaurant and renamed itself the **Longwood Country Inn,** on Main Street (℃ 203/266-0800). The guest rooms have been upgraded, too, some with fireplaces and whirlpool tubs for two.

Clinton Crossing, an upscale outlet mall at Exit 63 off Interstate 95, is fully operational. Among the designers represented are Calvin Klein, Donna Karan, Ralph Lauren, and Versace.

The **Mystic Aquarium,** 55 Coogan Blvd. (℃ 860/572-5955), has inaugurated a 1-acre outdoor habitat that contains a 750,000-gallon pool for white beluga whales and harbor seals, part of a $52-million expansion program.

See chapter 9 for details.

RHODE ISLAND *Money* magazine has dubbed **Providence** "The Best Place To Live In The East." The vitality of the "Renaissance City" is exemplified by downcity's **Waterplace Park & Riverwalk.** The artistic happening called **WaterFires** (℃ 401/272-3111) has proved so popular, it has expanded from its original one-time-only presentation to over 20 dates from July through October as well as on New Year's Eve.

The recent prosperity of Providence has fueled demand for downcity lodging. The latest response is the new **Courtyard by Marriott,** 32 Exchange Terrace (℃ 800/321-2211), near City Hall, the massive Providence Place mall, and the Fleet Skating Center.

In **Newport,** the owners of the exemplary **Cliffside Inn,** 2 Seaview Ave. (℃ 800/845-1811), have purchased an existing inn not far away and renamed it the **Adele Turner Inn.** There's every reason to believe it will be brought up to the lofty standards of its sister property. Small groups of visitors can now visit **Rough Point** (℃ 401/849-7300), heiress Doris Duke's 105-room mansion by the sea. Decorative touches include Ming Dynasty vases, Flemish tapestries, and paintings by Van Dyck and Gainsborough.

In **South County,** a good choice for a week's stay is the **Village Inn,** 1 Beach St., Narragansett (℃ 800/843-7437). A block from the beach, it's in a complex with a movie theater, a gas station, a Spanish restaurant, and a dozen shops. There's a heated indoor pool, too.

See chapter 10 for details.

VERMONT In **Manchester,** the **Southern Vermont Art Center,** on West Road (℃ 802/362-1405), opened a striking modern addition on its 400-acre grounds in 2000. The handsome new building, inspired by the region's barns, allows this well-regarded regional art museum to display more of its 800-piece permanent collection.

The **Palmer House Resort,** on Route 7A (℃ 800/917-6245), is an upscale motel just north of Manchester Center. In summer 2000, the owners added eight new spacious town house–style suites with gas fireplaces, wet bars, and private decks overlooking the stocked trout pond and the mountains west of town.

Right in the village of **Stowe,** the **Green Mountain Inn,** on Main Street (© **800/253-7302**), opened a new building in fall 2000 with luxe rooms and suites located directly behind the main inn. The new accommodations feature double Jacuzzis, marble baths, and 36-inch TVs.

The **Burlington Bikeway,** which runs northward along Lake Champlain from downtown Burlington to the Winooski River, got a nice boost in 2000 when some hurdles were cleared for a bike ferry across the mouth of the river. The ferry ran for several weekends, and plans call for an extended schedule in the future. This will eventually allow bikers to connect northward to the Champlain Islands. Ask at the Burlington visitor center for the current ferry status.

On the lodging front, a welcome new B&B opened in downtown Burlington in 2000. The **Lang House,** 360 Main St. (© **877/919-9799**), occupies an 1881 Queen Anne–style home on the hill between downtown and the university. It has nine handsome guest rooms, including a two-bedroom suite in the carriage house.

See chapter 11 for details.

NEW HAMPSHIRE Starting in 2000, discount airline **Pan Am** (© **800/359-7262**) started up operations out of a former military base on the outskirts of **Portsmouth.** This is the only airline that serves Portsmouth; it offers direct flights to a limited but growing roster of second-tier airports.

The **Inns at Mill Falls,** on Route 3, Meredith (© **800/622-6455**), just keeps on growing. This nicely managed complex at the northwest corner of **Lake Winnipesaukee** has more than 100 guest rooms spread among three buildings. Starting in 2002, it will have a fourth: The resort has acquired another property on a handsome point that juts into the lake.

In **North Conway,** the **Cranmore Inn,** 80 Kearsarge St. (© **800/526-5502**), added three new units in its stable building behind the main inn. Each unit has a kitchen, and one has two bedrooms.

See chapter 12 for details.

MAINE The **Portland** dining scene is in a state of permanent flux, and the past year has proved no different. The spot with the most buzz has been **Commissary,** in the Portland Public Market (© **207/228-2057**), which opened in November 2000. The restaurant was created by Maine native Matthew Kenney, who's developed a following with his three Manhattan restaurants: Matthew's, Mezze, and Monzu.

In **Brunswick,** the **Walker Art Building,** at Bowdoin College (© **207/725-327**), is slated for construction and expansion, which may briefly close or disrupt gallery visits into 2002. Call ahead.

In **Rockland,** April 2000 saw the opening of **Primo,** 2 South Main St. (©**207/596-0770**), to strong reviews and high-profile press. Executive chef Melissa Kelly has worked with legendary chefs Larry Forgione and Alice Waters, and won the 1999 James Beard Foundation award for "best chef in the Northeast."

In late 2000, the **American Skiing Corporation,** which owns and operates Sunday River Ski Resort as well as many other New England ski areas (including Mount Snow, Killington, and Sugarbush in Vermont) merged with a major resort management company and is now called Doral International. It's as yet unclear what this will mean over the long term for skiers, but no immediate changes are likely at any of the resorts.

See chapter 13 for details.

1

The Best of New England

One of the greatest challenges of traveling in New England is choosing from an abundance of superb restaurants, accommodations, and attractions. Where to start? Here's an entirely biased list of our favorite destinations and experiences. Over years of traveling through the region, we've discovered that these are places worth more than just a quick stop. They're all worth a major detour.

1 The Best of Small-Town New England

- **Marblehead** (Mass.): The "Yachting Capital of America" has major picture-postcard potential, especially in the summer, when the harbor fills with boats of all sizes. From downtown, a short distance inland, make your way toward the water down the narrow, flower-dotted streets. The first glimpse of blue sea and sky is breathtaking. See chapter 5.
- **Chatham** (Cape Cod, Mass.): Located on the "elbow" of the Cape, Chatham is proof that Main Street, U.S.A, is alive and well. Families throng here to enjoy the beach and to browse through shops brimming with upscale arts and crafts. In summer, visitors and locals come together every Friday night for great outdoor concerts, while the looming Chatham Lighthouse, built in 1828, keeps a close eye on the Atlantic. See chapter 6.
- **Edgartown** (Martha's Vineyard, Mass.): For many visitors, Edgartown *is* Martha's Vineyard, its regal captains' houses and manicured lawns a symbol of a more refined way of life. The old-fashioned Fourth of July parade harks back to small-town America, as

hundreds line Main Street cheering the loudest for the floats with the most heart. See chapter 7.
- **Stockbridge** (Mass.): Norman Rockwell made a famous painting of the main street of this, his adopted hometown. Facing south, it uses the southern Berkshires as backdrop for the sprawl of the Red Lion Inn and the other late–19th-century buildings that make up the commercial district. Then as now, they service a beguiling mix of unassuming saltboxes and Gilded Age mansions that have sheltered farmers, artists, and aristocrats since the days of the French and Indian Wars. See chapter 8.
- **Washington** (Conn.): A classic, with a Congregational church facing a green surrounded by clapboard colonial houses, all of them with black shutters. See chapter 9.
- **Essex** (Conn.): A widely circulated survey voted Essex tops on its list of the 100 best towns in the United States. That judgment is largely statistical, but a walk past white clapboard houses to the active waterfront on this unspoiled stretch of the Connecticut River rings all the bells. There is not an artificial note, a cookie-cutter

franchise, nor a costumed docent to muddy its near-perfect image. See chapter 9.

- **Grafton** (Vt.): Grafton was once a down-at-the-heels mountain town slowly being reclaimed by termites and the elements. A wealthy family took it on as a pet project, and has lovingly restored the village to its former self—even burying the electric lines to reclaim the landscape. It doesn't feel like a living-history museum; it just feels right. See chapter 11.

- **Woodstock** (Vt.): Woodstock has a stunning village green, a whole range of 19th-century homes, woodland walks leading just out of town, and a settled, old-money air. This is a good place to explore on foot or by bike, or to just sit and watch summer unfold. See chapter 11.

- **Montpelier** (Vt.): This is the way all state capitals should be: slow-paced, small enough so you can walk everywhere, and full of shops that still sell nails and strapping tape. Montpelier also shows a more sophisticated edge, with its Culinary Institute, an art-house movie theater, and several fine bookshops. But at heart it's a small town, where you just might run into the governor buying a wrench at the corner store. See chapter 11.

- **Hanover** (N.H.): It's the perfect college town: handsome brick buildings of Dartmouth College, a tidy green, a small but select shopping district, and a scattering of good restaurants. Come in the fall and you'll be tempted to join in the touch football on the green. See chapter 12.

- **Castine** (Maine): Soaring elm trees, a peaceful harborside setting, plenty of grand historic homes, and a few good inns make this a great spot to soak up some of Maine's coastal ambience off the beaten path. See chapter 13.

2 The Best Places to See Fall Foliage

- **Walden Pond State Reservation** (Concord, Mass.): Walden Pond is hidden from the road by the woods where Henry David Thoreau built a small cabin and lived from 1845 to 1847. When the leaves are turning and the trees are reflected in the water, it's hard to imagine why he left. See chapter 5.

- **Bash-Bish Falls State Park** (Mass.): Head from the comely village of South Egremont up into the forested hills of the extreme southwest corner of Massachusetts. The roads, which change from macadam to gravel to dirt and back, wind between crimson clouds of sugar maples and white birches feather-stroked against banks of black evergreens. The payoff is a three-state view from a promontory above a 50-foot cascade notched into a bluff, with carpets of russet and gold stretching all the way to the Hudson River. See chapter 8.

- **The Litchfield Hills** (Conn.): Route 7, running south to north through the rugged northwest corner of Connecticut, roughly along the course of the Housatonic River, explodes with color in the weeks before and after Columbus Day. It's something to see the fallen leaves whirling down the foaming river. See chapter 9.

- **I-91** (Vt.): An interstate? Don't scoff (the traffic can be terrible on narrow state roads). If you like your foliage viewing wholesale, cruise I-91 from Brattleboro to Newport. You'll be overwhelmed with gorgeous terrain, from the

Northern New England

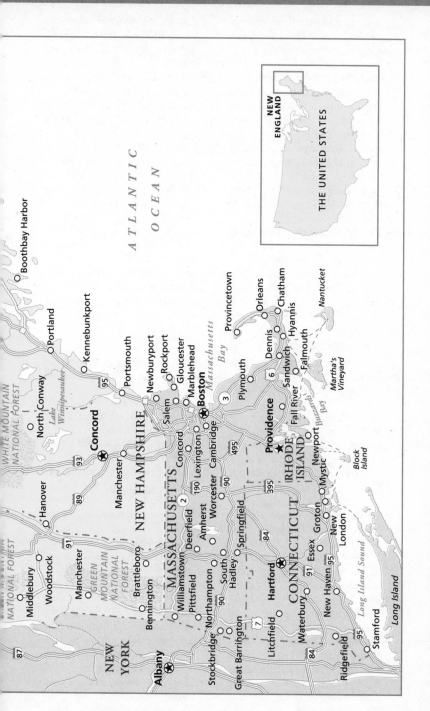

NEW ENGLAND

THE UNITED STATES

ATLANTIC OCEAN

Boothbay Harbor

Portland

Kennebunkport

WHITE MOUNTAIN NATIONAL FOREST

North Conway

Lake Winnipesaukee

Portsmouth

Newburyport

Rockport

Gloucester

Marblehead

Massachusetts Bay

Provincetown

Concord

Hanover

Manchester

NEW HAMPSHIRE

Salem

Concord

Boston

Plymouth

Orleans

Chatham

Hyannis

Dennis

Sandwich

Falmouth

Nantucket

Martha's Vineyard

Middlebury

Woodstock

Manchester

GREEN MOUNTAIN NATIONAL FOREST

Brattleboro

Bennington

Williamstown

Pittsfield

MASSACHUSETTS

Deerfield

Amherst

South Hadley

Northampton

Lexington

Cambridge

Worcester

Springfield

Providence

RHODE ISLAND

Newport

Fall River

Buzzards Bay

Block Island

NEW YORK

Albany

Stockbridge

Great Barrington

Litchfield

Waterbury

Hartford

CONNECTICUT

Essex

Groton

New London

Mystic

New Haven

Ridgefield

Stamford

Long Island Sound

Long Island

gentle Connecticut River Valley to the sloping hills of the Northeast Kingdom. See chapter 11.

- **Route 100** (Vt.): Route 100 winds the length of Vermont from Readsboro to Newport. It's the major north-south route through the center of the Green Mountains, and it's surprisingly undeveloped along most of its length. You won't have it to yourself along the southern stretches on autumn weekends, but as you head further north, you'll leave the crowds behind. See chapter 11.

- **The M/V *Mount Washington*** (N.H.): One of the more majestic views of the White Mountains is from Lake Winnipesaukee to the south. The vista is especially appealing as seen from the deck of the *Mount Washington,* an uncommonly handsome vessel that offers a variety of tours through mid-October, when the lake is trimmed with a fringe of fall color along the shoreline. See chapter 12.

- **Crawford Notch** (N.H.): Route 302 passes through this scenic valley, where you can see the brilliant red maples and yellow birches high on the hillsides. In fall, Mount Washington, in the background, is likely to be dusted with an early snow. See chapter 12.

- **Camden** (Maine): The dazzling autumn colors that cover the rolling hills are reflected in Penobscot Bay on the east side, and in the lakes on the west. Ascend the coastal peaks for views out to the color-splashed islands in the bay. Autumn is usually a week or two later on the coast, so you can stretch out your viewing pleasure. See chapter 13.

3 The Best Ways to View Coastal Scenery

- **Strolling Around Rockport** (Mass.): The town surrounds the small harbor and spreads out along the rugged, rocky coastline of Cape Ann. From the end of Bearskin Neck, the view is spectacular—fishing and pleasure boats in one direction, roaring surf in the other. See chapter 5.

- **Getting Back to Nature on Plum Island** (Mass.): The Parker River National Wildlife Refuge, in Newburyport, offers two varieties of coastal scenery: picturesque salt marshes packed with birds and other animals, and gorgeous ocean beaches where the power of the Atlantic is evident. See chapter 5.

- **Biking or Driving the Outer Cape** (Mass.): From Eastham through Wellfleet and Truro, all the way to Provincetown, Cape Cod's outermost towns offer dazzling ocean vistas and a number of exceptional bike paths, including the Province Lands, just outside Provincetown, that are bordered by spectacular swooping dunes. See chapter 6.

- **Heading "Up-Island" on Martha's Vineyard** (Mass.): Many visitors never venture beyond the port towns of Vineyard Haven, Oak Bluffs, and Edgartown. Though each has its charms, the scenery actually gets more spectacular "up-island," in towns like Chilmark, where you'll pass moorlike meadows and family farms surrounded by stone walls. Follow State Road and the scenic Moshup Trail to the westernmost tip of the island, where you'll experience the dazzling colored cliffs of Gay Head and the quaint fishing port of Menemsha. See chapter 7.

- **Cruising Newport's Ocean Drive** (R.I.): After a tour of the fabulously overwrought "cottages" of the hyper-rich that are strung along Bellevue Avenue, emerging onto the shoreline road that dodges the spray of the boiling Atlantic is a cleansing reminder of the power of nature over fragile monuments to the conceits of men. To extend the experience, take a 3½-mile hike along the Cliff Walk that skirts the edge of the bluff commanded by the largest mansions. See chapter 10.

- **Sitting in a Rocking Chair** (Maine): The views are never better than when you're caught unaware—such as suddenly looking up from an engrossing book on the front porch of an oceanside inn. Throughout the Maine chapter, look for mention of inns right on the water, such as Black Point Inn (Prouts Neck), Grey Havens (Georgetown Island), Samoset Resort (Rockport), Inn on the Harbor (Stonington), and the Claremont (Southwest Harbor). See chapter 13.

- **Hiking Monhegan Island** (Maine): The village of Monhegan is clustered around the harbor, but the rest of this 700-acre island is all picturesque wildlands, with miles of trails crossing open meadows and winding along rocky bluffs. See chapter 13.

- **Driving the Park Loop Road at Acadia National Park** (Maine): This is the region's premier ocean drive. You'll start high along a ridge with views of Frenchman Bay and the Porcupine Islands, then dip down along the rocky shores to watch the surf crash against the dark rocks. Plan to do this 20-mile loop at least twice to get the most out of it. See chapter 13.

- **Cruising on a Windjammer** (Maine): See Maine as it was first seen for centuries—from the ocean looking inland. A handsome fleet of sailing ships departs from various harbors along the coast, particularly Rockland and Camden. Spend from a night to a week exploring the dramatic shoreline. See chapter 13.

4 The Best Places to Rediscover America's Past

- **Paul Revere House** (Boston, Mass.): The history of the American Revolution is often told through stories of governments and institutions. At this little home in the North End, you'll learn about a real person. The self-guided tour is particularly thought-provoking, allowing you to linger on the artifacts that hold your interest. Revere had 16 children with two wives, supported them with his thriving silversmith's trade—and put the whole operation in jeopardy with his role in the events that led to the Revolutionary War. See chapter 4.

- **Old State House** (Boston, Mass.): Built in 1713, the once-towering Old State House is dwarfed by modern-day skyscrapers. It stands as a reminder of British rule (the exterior features a lion and a unicorn) and its overthrow—the Declaration of Independence was read from the balcony, which overlooks a traffic island where a circle of bricks represents the site of the Boston Massacre. See chapter 4.

- **Faneuil Hall** (Boston, Mass.): Although Faneuil Hall is best known nowadays as a shopping destination, if you head upstairs, you'll be transported back in time. The second-floor auditorium is in tip-top shape, and park rangers are on hand to talk about the building's role in the Revolution. Tune out the sound of sneakers squeaking across the floor, and you can almost hear Samuel Adams (his statue is out front) exhorting the Sons of Liberty. See chapter 4.

- **"Old Ironsides"** (Boston, Mass.): Formally named the USS *Constitution,* the frigate was launched in 1797 and made a name for itself battling Barbary pirates and seeing action in the War of 1812. Last used in battle in 1815, it was periodically threatened with destruction until a complete renovation in the late 1920s started its career as a floating monument. The staff consists of sailors on active duty who wear 1812 dress uniforms. See chapter 4.

- **North Bridge** (Concord, Mass.): British troops headed to Concord after putting down the uprising in Lexington, and the bridge (well, it's a replica) stands as a testament to the Minutemen who fought here. The Concord River and its peaceful green banks give no hint of the bloodshed that took place. On the path in from Monument Street, placards and audio stations provide a fascinating narrative. See chapter 5.

- **Plymouth Rock** (Plymouth, Mass.): Okay, it's a fraction of its original size and looks like something you might find in your garden. Nevertheless, Plymouth Rock makes a perfect starting point for exploration. Close by is the *Mayflower II,* a replica of the alarmingly small original vessel. The juxtaposition reminds you of what a dangerous undertaking the Pilgrims' voyage was. See chapter 5.

- **Sandwich** (Mass.): The oldest town on Cape Cod, Sandwich was founded in 1637. Glassmaking brought notoriety and prosperity to this picturesque town in the 19th century. Visit the Sandwich Glass Museum for the whole story, or tour one of the town's glassblowing studios. Don't leave without visiting the 76-acre Heritage Plantation, which has a working carousel, a sparkling antique-car collection, and a wonderful collection of Americana. See chapter 6.

- **Nantucket** (Mass): It looks like the whalers just left, leaving behind their grand houses, cobbled streets, and a gamut of enticing shops offering luxury goods from around the world. The Nantucket Historical Association owns more than a dozen properties open for tours, and the Whaling Museum is one of the most fascinating sites in the region. Tourism may be rampant, but not its tackier side effects, thanks to stringent preservation measures. See chapter 7.

- **Deerfield** (Mass.): Arguably the best-preserved colonial village in New England, Deerfield has scores of houses dating back to the 17th and 18th centuries. None of the clutter of modernity has intruded here. Fourteen houses on the main avenue can be visited through tours conducted by the organization known as Historic Deerfield. See chapter 8.

- **Newport** (R.I.): A key port of the clipper trade long before the British surrendered their colony, Newport retains abundant recollections of its maritime past. In addition to its great harbor, clogged with cigarette boats, tugs, ferries, and majestic sloops, the City by the Sea has kept three distinctive enclaves preserved: the waterside homes of colonial seamen, the hillside Federal houses of port-bound merchants, and the ostentatious mansions of America's post–Civil War industrial and financial grandees. See chapter 10.

- **Plymouth** (Vt.): President Calvin Coolidge was born in this high upland valley, and the state has done a superb job preserving his hometown village. You'll get a good sense of the president's roots, but also gain a greater understanding of how a New England village works. See chapter 11.
- **Shelburne Museum** (Shelburne, Vt.): Think of this sprawling museum as New England's attic. Located on the shores of Lake Champlain, the Shelburne features not only the usual exhibits of quilts and early glass, but also whole buildings preserved like specimens in formaldehyde. Look for the lighthouse, the railroad station, and the stagecoach inn. This is one of northern New England's "don't miss" destinations. See chapter 11.
- **Portsmouth** (N.H.): Portsmouth is a salty coastal city that just happens to boast some of the most impressive historic homes in New England. Start at Strawbery Banke, a historic compound of 42 buildings dating from 1695 to 1820. Then visit the many other grand homes in nearby neighborhoods, like the house John Paul Jones occupied while building his warship during the Revolution. See chapter 12.
- **Victoria Mansion** (Portland, Maine): Donald Trump had nothing on the Victorians when it came to material excess. You'll see Victorian decorative arts at their zenith in this elaborate Italianate mansion built during the Civil War years by a prosperous hotelier. It's open to the public for tours throughout the summer. See chapter 13.

5 The Best Literary Landmarks

- **Concord** (Mass.): Concord is home to a legion of literary ghosts. Homes of Ralph Waldo Emerson, Nathaniel Hawthorne, Henry David Thoreau, and Louisa May Alcott are popular destinations, and look much as they did during the "flowering of New England" in the mid–19th century. See chapter 5.
- **The Outer Cape** (Mass.): In the last century, the communities at the far end of the Cape—Wellfleet, Truro, and particularly Provincetown—were a veritable headquarters of bohemia. Henry David Thoreau walked the 28 miles from Eastham to Provincetown and wrote about it in his classic *Cape Cod*. Distinguished literati such as Edna St. Vincent Millay, Mary McCarthy, Edmund Wilson, Tennessee Williams, Norman Mailer, and many others have also taken refuge among the dunes here. See chapter 6.
- **The Frost Place** (Franconia Notch, N.H.): Two of the most famous New England poems— "The Road Not Taken" and "Stopping by Woods on a Snowy Evening"—were composed by Robert Frost at this farm just outside of Franconia. Explore the woods and read the verses posted along the pathways, then tour the farmhouse where Frost lived with his family. See chapter 12.
- **Salem** (Mass.): Native son Nathaniel Hawthorne might still feel at home here. A hotel and a boulevard bear his name, the Custom House where he found an embroidered scarlet *A* still stands, and his birthplace is open for tours. It has been moved into the same complex as the House of the Seven Gables, a cousin's home that inspired the classic novel. See chapter 5.

6 The Best Activities for Families

- **Exploring the Museum of Fine Arts** (Boston, Mass.): Parents hear "magnificent Egyptian collections," but kids think: "Mummies!" Even the most hyper youngster manages to take it down a notch in quiet, refined surroundings, and the collections at the MFA simultaneously tickle visitors' brains. See chapter 4.

- **Visiting the Museum of Science** (Boston, Mass.): Built around demonstrations, experiments, and interactive displays that never feel like homework, this museum is wildly popular with kids—and adults. Explore the exhibits, then take in a show at the planetarium or the Omni IMAX Theater. Before you know it, everyone will have learned something, painlessly. See chapter 4.

- **Catching a Free Friday Flick at the Hatch Shell** (Boston, Mass.): Better known for the Boston Pops' Fourth of July concert, the Esplanade is also famous for family films (*The Wizard of Oz* or *Pocahontas,* for example) shown on Friday nights in summer. The lawn in front of the Hatch Shell turns into a giant, carless drive-in movie as hundreds of people picnic and wait for the sky to grow dark. See chapter 4.

- **Learning about Sea Life at Woods Hole** (Cape Cod, Mass.): For junior oceanologists, this is the place to be. You can try the hands-on exhibits at the Woods Hole Oceanographic Institute, observe experiments at the Marine Biological Laboratory, explore the touch tanks at the country's oldest aquarium, and even collect crucial data with the "Ocean Quest" crew. See chapter 6.

- **Whale Watching off Provincetown** (Cape Cod, Mass.): Boats leave MacMillan Wharf for the 8-mile journey to Stellwagen Bank National Marine Sanctuary, a rich feeding ground for several types of whales. Nothing can prepare you for the thrill of spotting these magnificent creatures feeding, breaching, and even flipper slapping. Hands down, the best outfit in town is the **Dolphin Fleet** (✆ **800/826-9300**), which is affiliated with the Center for Coastal Studies. See chapter 6.

- **Deep-Sea Fishing:** Charter fishing boats these days usually have high-tech fish-finding gear—imagine how your kids will react to reeling in one big bluefish after another. The top spots to mount such an expedition are Barnstable Harbor or Rock Harbor in Orleans, on Cape Cod; Point Judith, at the southern tip of Rhode Island; and the Maine coast. See chapters 6, 10, and 13, respectively.

- **Riding the Flying Horses Carousel in Oak Bluffs** (Martha's Vineyard, Mass.; ✆ **508/693-9481**): Some say this is the oldest carousel in the country, but your kids might not notice the genuine horsehair, sculptural details, or glass eyes. They'll be too busy trying to grab the brass ring to win a free ride. After your ride, stroll around the town of Oak Bluffs. Children will be enchanted with the clustered "gingerbread" houses, a carryover from the 19th-century revivalist movement. See chapter 7.

- **Biking Nantucket** (Mass.): Short, flat trails crisscross the island, and every one leads to a beach. The shortest rides lead to Children's Beach, with its own playground, and Jetties Beach, with a skate park and water-sports equipment for rent; older kids will be able to make the few miles to Surfside and Madaket. See chapter 7.

- **Learning to Ski at Jiminy Peak** (Mass.): More than 70% of Jiminy Peak's trails are geared toward beginners and intermediates, making it one of the premier places to learn to ski in the East. The mountain is located in the heart of the Berkshires, near Mount Greylock. See chapter 8.

- **Visiting Mystic Seaport and Mystic Aquarium** (Conn.): The double-down winner in the family-fun sweepstakes has to be this combination: performing dolphins and whales, full-rigged tall ships, penguins and sharks, and river rides on a perky little 1906 motor launch. These are the kinds of G-rated attractions that have no age barriers. See chapter 9.

- **Exploring Burlington's Bikeway** (Vt.): A lovely bike path follows the shores of Lake Champlain on an abandoned railbed. Efforts to link up this trail with others to the north include two new bike ferries that span rivers and causeway gaps. Lakeshore beaches and leafy parks dot the route. See chapter 11.

- **Visiting the Montshire Museum of Science** (Norwich, Vt.): This handsome children's museum, in a soaring, barnlike space on the Vermont–New Hampshire border, has interactive exhibits that put the wonder back into science. Afterward, stroll the nature trails along the Connecticut River. See chapter 12.

- **Riding the Mount Washington Cog Railway** (Crawford Notch, N.H.): It's fun! It's terrifying! It's a great glimpse into history. Kids love this ratchety climb to the top of New England's highest peak aboard trains that were specially designed to scale the mountain in 1869. As a technological marvel, the railroad attracted tourists by the thousands a century ago. They still come to marvel at the sheer audacity of it all. See chapter 12.

- **Exploring Monhegan Island** (Maine): Kids from 8 to 12 especially enjoy overnight excursions to Monhegan Island. The mailboat from Port Clyde is rustic and intriguing, and the hotels are an adventure. Leave at least an afternoon to sit atop the high, rocky bluffs scouting the glimmering ocean for whales. See chapter 13.

7 The Best Country Inns

- **Hawthorne Inn** (Concord, Mass.; ℂ 978/369-5610): Everything here—the 1870 building, the garden setting a stone's throw from the historic attractions, the antique furnishings, the eclectic decorations, the accommodating innkeepers—is top of the line. See chapter 5.

- **Longfellow's Wayside Inn** (Sudbury, Mass.; ℂ 800/339-1776): A gorgeous inn, an unusual setting, excellent food, the imprimatur of a distinguished New England author, nearly 300 years

of history, and the schoolhouse the little lamb followed Mary to. What's not to like? See chapter 5.

- **Captain's House Inn** (Chatham, Cape Cod, Mass.; ℂ 800/315-0728): An elegant country inn positively dripping with good taste, this is among the best small inns in the region. Most rooms have fireplaces, elegant paneling, and antiques; they're sumptuous yet cozy. This could be the ultimate spot to enjoy Chatham's Christmas Stroll festivities. See chapter 6.

- **Charlotte Inn** (Edgartown, Martha's Vineyard, Mass.; ✆ **508/ 627-4751**): Edgartown tends to be the most formal enclave on Martha's Vineyard, and this compound of exquisite buildings is by far the fanciest address in town. The rooms are distinctively decorated: One boasts a baby grand, another its own thematic dressing room. The conservatory restaurant, L'étoile, is among the finest you'll find this side of France. See chapter 7.

- **Mayflower Inn** (Washington, Conn.; ✆ **860/868-9466**): Not a tough call at all for this part of the region: Immaculate in taste and execution, the Mayflower is as close to perfection as any such enterprise is likely to be. A genuine Joshua Reynolds hangs in the hall. See chapter 9.

- **Griswold Inn** (Essex, Conn.; ✆ **860/767-1776**): "The Griz" has been accommodating sailors and travelers as long as any inn in the country, give or take a decade. For all that time, it has been the focus of life and commerce in the lower Connecticut River Valley, always ready with a mug of suds, a haunch of beef, and a roaring fire. The walls are layered with nautical paintings and memorabilia, and there's music every night in the schoolhouse-turned-tavern. See chapter 9.

- **The Equinox** (Manchester Village, Vt.; ✆ **800/362-4747**): This is southern Vermont's grand resort, with nearly 200 rooms in a white clapboard compound that seems to go on forever. The rooms are pleasant enough, but the real draws are the grounds and the resort's varied activities—it's set on 2,300 acres with pools, tennis courts, an 18-hole golf course, and even its own mountainside. Tried

everything on vacation? How about falconry classes or backcountry driving at the Range Rover school? See chapter 11.

- **Windham Hill Inn** (West Townshend, Vt.; ✆ **800/944-4080**): New innkeepers have added welcome amenities like air-conditioning in the rooms and a conference room in the barn while still preserving the antique charm of this 1823 farmstead. It's at the end of a remote dirt road in a high upland valley, and guests are welcome to explore 160 private acres on a network of walking trails. See chapter 11.

- **Jackson House Inn** (Woodstock, Vt.; ✆ **800/448-1890**): The constant improvements and the meticulous attention to service have made this longtime favorite a solid addition to our "best of" list this edition. The meals are stunning, the guest rooms the very picture of antique elegance. The only downside? It fronts a sometimes noisy road. See chapter 11.

- **Twin Farms** (Barnard, Vt.; ✆ **800/894-6327**): Just north of Woodstock may be the most elegant inn in New England. Its rates are a tad breathtaking, but guests are certainly pampered here. Novelist Sinclair Lewis once lived on this 300-acre farm, and today it's an aesthetic retreat that offers serenity and exceptional food. See chapter 11.

- **The Pitcher Inn** (Warren, Vt.; ✆ **888/867-8424**): One of the newest New England inns (built in 1997) is also one of the best. It combines traditional New England form and scale with modern and luxe touches, plus a good dollop of whimsy. See chapter 11.

- **Basin Harbor Club** (Vergennes, Vt.; ✆ **800/622-4000**): Established in 1886, this lakeside resort has the sort of patina that only comes with age. It's a classic old-fashioned family resort, with golf, boating on Lake Champlain, jackets-required dining, evening lectures on the arts, and even a private airstrip. Bring books, board games, and relearn what summer's all about. See chapter 11.

- **Balsams Grand Resort Hotel** (Dixville Notch, N.H.; ℂ **800/ 255-0600**): The designation "country inn" is only half-correct. You've got plenty of country—it's set on 15,000 acres in far northern New Hampshire. But this historic resort is more castle than inn. The Balsams has been offering superb hospitality and gracious comfort since 1866. It has two golf courses, miles of hiking trails, and, in winter, its own downhill and cross-country ski areas. See chapter 12.

- **White Barn Inn** (Kennebunkport, Maine; ℂ **207/967-2321**): Much of the White Barn staff hails from Europe, and guests are treated with a continental graciousness. The rooms are a delight, and the meals (served in the barn) are among the best in Maine. See chapter 13.

- **The Claremont** (Southwest Harbor, Maine; ℂ **800/244-5036**). The 1884 Claremont is a Maine classic. This waterside lodge has everything a Victorian resort should, including sparely decorated rooms, creaky floorboards in the halls, great views of water and mountains, and a perfect croquet pitch. See chapter 13.

8 The Best Moderately Priced Accommodations

- **Newbury Guest House** (Boston, Mass.; ℂ **617/437-7666**) and **Harborside Inn** (Boston, Mass.; ℂ **617/723-7500**): These sister properties would be good deals even if they weren't ideally located—the former in Back Bay, the latter downtown. Rates even include breakfast. See chapter 4.

- **Harvard Square Hotel** (Cambridge, Mass.; ℂ **800/458-5886**): Smack in the middle of Cambridge's most popular destination, this hotel is a comfortable place to stay in a great location. See chapter 4.

- **John Carver Inn** (Plymouth, Mass.; ℂ **800/274-1620**): This hotel is centrally located, whether you're immersing yourself in Pilgrim lore or passing through on the way from Boston to Cape Cod. Ask about the "Destination Plymouth" packages for a good deal. See chapter 5.

- **Isaiah Hall B&B Inn** (Dennis, Cape Cod, Mass.; ℂ **800/736-0160**): Nestled amid oak trees in Dennis, this B&B has been welcoming visitors for more than 50 years. The inn and its gregarious owner are popular with actors starring in summer stock at the nearby Cape Playhouse. Guests enjoy country-cozy rooms and a communal breakfast. See chapter 6.

- **Nauset House Inn** (East Orleans, Cape Cod, Mass.; ℂ **508/255-2195**): This romantic 1810 farmhouse is like a sepia-toned vision of old Cape Cod. Recline in a wicker divan surrounded by fragrant flowers while the wind whistles outside. Better yet, stroll to Nauset Beach and take a quiet walk as the sun sets. Your genial hosts also prepare one of the finest breakfasts in town. See chapter 6.

- **Tollgate Hill Inn** (Litchfield, Conn.; ℂ **800/445-3903**): No sacrifices in comfort will be made when you stay here, and you'll enjoy the marvelously atmospheric 1745 tavern that serves thoroughly up-to-date eclectic cuisine. On weekends, there's live jazz, and Sunday brunch beside the fireplace in winter couldn't be more New England. See chapter 9.

- **Beech Tree Inn** (Newport, R.I.; © **800/748-6565**): Arrive on Friday afternoon at the Beech Tree, and the innkeepers sit you down to a complimentary bowl of chowder, fresh bread, and a glass of wine. Breakfast the next morning, huge and cooked to order, makes lunch irrelevant. Unlike many B&Bs, all rooms here have air-conditioning, TVs, and phones. See chapter 10.

- **Inn at the Mad River Barn** (Waitsfield, Vt.; © **800/631-0466**): It takes a few minutes to adapt to the spartan rooms and no-frills accommodations here. But you'll soon discover that the real action takes place in the living room and dining room, where skiers relax and chat after a day on the slopes, and share heaping helpings at mealtime. See chapter 11.

- **Thayers Inn** (Littleton, N.H.; © **800/634-8179**): This old-fashioned downtown inn has 48 eclectic rooms and a whole lot of relaxed charm. Ulysses S. Grant and Richard Nixon slept here, among others. Rooms start at just $40 if you're willing to share a bathroom; from $50 for private bathroom. See chapter 12.

- **Philbrook Farm Inn** (Shelburne, N.H.; © **603/466-3831**): Come here if you're looking for a complete getaway. The inn has been taking in travelers since the 1850s, and the owners know how to do it right. The farmhouse sits on 1,000 acres between the Mahoosuc Mountains and the Androscoggin River, and guests can hike with vigor or relax in leisure with equal aplomb. See chapter 12.

- **Maine Idyll Motor Court** (Freeport, Maine; © **207/865-4201**): The 20 vintage cottages have all the classic appeal of an old-time vacation, and are kept up spotlessly. No phones, no credit cards, and no frills, but solid value with rates ranging from $48 to $72. See chapter 13.

- **Driftwood Inn & Cottages** (Bailey Island, Maine; © **207/833-5461**): Where else can you find rooms at the edge of the rocky Maine coast for $70? This classic shingled compound dates from 1910 and mostly offers rooms with shared bathrooms—but it's worth that small inconvenience for the views alone. See chapter 13.

9 The Best Restaurants

- **Aujourd'hui** (Boston, Mass.; © **617/351-2071**): The exquisite setting, spectacular view, telepathic service, and, of course, marvelous food combine to transport you to a plane where you might not even notice (or care) how much it's costing. See chapter 4.

- **Rialto** (Cambridge, Mass.; © **617/661-5050**): This is a don't-miss destination if your plans include fine dining. The contemporary setting is a great match for chef Jody Adams's inventive cuisine, and the service is efficient without being too familiar—surely a draw for the visiting celebrities who flock here. See chapter 4.

- **The Mews** (Provincetown, Cape Cod, Mass.; © **508/487-1500**): Of Provincetown's many waterfront venues, this enduring favorite offers the most consistently excellent food and service at fair prices. The lower-level dining room, serving fusion cuisine with fresh fish a specialty, sits on the beach with bay and harbor views from every table. See chapter 6.

- **L'étoile** (Edgartown, Martha's Vineyard, Mass.; ℂ **508/627-5187**): The most exemplary dining experience on Martha's Vineyard can be found in this exquisite conservatory at the renowned Charlotte Inn. The nouvelle-cuisine offerings vary seasonally, but chef Michael Brisson continually dazzles with a menu of delicacies flown in from the four corners of the earth. See chapter 7.

- **Òran Mór** (Nantucket, Mass.; ℂ **508/228-8655**): Climb up the stairs of this historic building and prepare yourself for an extravagant dining experience. Chef/owner Peter Wallace has created an intimate setting for his creative international cuisine, served with utmost professionalism. The best sommelier on the island will assist you in choosing a wine to go with your elegant meal. See chapter 7.

- **Truc Orient Express** (West Stockbridge, Mass.; ℂ **413/232-4204**): The artists who live in this funky Berkshires hamlet deserve something out of the prevailing red-sauce and red-meat mode. They get it in this converted warehouse, with eye-opening Thai, Vietnamese, and Southeast Asian dishes that rarely emerge from kitchens this far west of Ho Chi Minh City. Tastes range from delicate to sinus-clearing. See chapter 8.

- **Union League Café** (New Haven, Conn.; ℂ **203/562-4299**): This august setting of arched windows and high ceilings is more than a century old and was long the sanctuary of an exclusive club. It still looks good, but the tone has been lightened into an approximation of a Lyonnaise brasserie. The menu observes the southern French tastes for curry, olive oil, pastas, lamb, and shellfish. See chapter 9.

- **Scales & Shells** (Newport, R.I.; ℂ **401/846-3474**): Ye who turn aside all pretension, get yourselves hence. There isn't a frill or affectation anywhere near this place, and since the wide-open kitchen is right at the entrance, there are no secrets, either. What we have here are marine critters mere hours from the depths, prepared and presented free of any but the slightest artifice. This might well be the purest seafood joint on the southern New England coast. See chapter 10.

- **Chantecleer** (Manchester Center, Vt.; ℂ **802/362-1616**): Swiss chef Michel Baumann has been turning out dazzling dinners here since 1981, and the kitchen hasn't gotten stale in the least. The dining room in an old barn is magical, the staff helpful and friendly. It's a great spot for those who demand top-notch continental fare but don't like the fuss of a fancy restaurant. See chapter 11.

- **T. J. Buckley's** (Brattleboro, Vt.; ℂ **802/257-4922**): This tiny diner on a dark Brattleboro side street serves up outsized tastes prepared by talented chef Michael Fuller. Forget about stewed-too-long diner fare; get in your mind big tastes blossoming from the freshest of ingredients prepared just right. See chapter 11.

- **Jackson House Inn** (Woodstock, Vt.; ℂ **800/448-1890**): Situated in a modern addition to an upscale country inn, the Jackson House Inn serves meals that are ingeniously conceived, deftly prepared, and artfully arranged. The three-course meals cost around

$50, and offer excellent value at that. See chapter 11.

- **Hemingway's** (Killington, Vt.; ☎ **802/422-3886**): Killington seems an unlikely place for a serious culinary adventure, yet Hemingway's will meet the loftiest expectations. The menu changes frequently to ensure only the freshest of ingredients. If it's available, be sure to order the wild mushroom and truffle soup. See chapter 11.

- **White Barn Inn** (Kennebunkport, Maine; ☎ **207/967-2321**): The setting, in an ancient, rustic barn, is magical. The tables are set with floor-length tablecloths, and the chairs feature imported Italian upholstery. The food? To die for. Enjoy entrees such as grilled duckling breast with ginger and sun-dried cherry sauce, or a roast rack of lamb with pecans and homemade barbecue sauce. See chapter 13.

- **Primo** (Rockland, Maine; ☎ **207/596-0770**): Primo opened its doors in 2000, and foodies have already beaten a rutted trail here. The New American menu changes nightly, reflects the seasons, and draws from the freshest local products. Even the informal dishes (like wood-fired pizza) are outstanding. See chapter 13.

10 The Best Local Dining Experiences

- **Durgin-Park** (Boston, Mass.; ☎ **617/227-2038**): A meal at this landmark restaurant might start with a waitress dropping a handful of cutlery in front of you, and saying, "Here, give these out." The surly service usually seems to be an act, but it's so much a part of the experience that some people are disappointed when the waitresses are nice (as they often are). In any case, it's worked since 1827. See chapter 4.

- **Woodman's of Essex** (Essex, Mass.; ☎ **800/649-1773**): This busy North Shore institution is not for the faint of heart—or the hard of artery, unless you like eating corn and steamers while everyone around you is gobbling fried clams and onion rings. The food at this glorified clam shack is fresh and delicious, and a look at the organized pandemonium behind the counter is worth the (reasonable) price. See chapter 5.

- **The Bite** (Menemsha, Martha's Vineyard, Mass.; ☎ **508/645-9239**): This is your quintessential "chowdah" and clam shack, serving up exceptional chowder, potato salad, and fried fish. Those in the know bring their picnic dinner over to nearby Menemsha Beach, where the sunsets are awesome. See chapter 7.

- **Abbott's Lobster in the Rough** (Noank, Conn.; ☎ **860/536-7719**): Places like this frill-free shack abound along more northerly reaches of the New England coast, but here's a little bit o' Maine a Sunday drive from Manhattan. Shore dinners rule, so roll up sleeves, tie on napkins and feedbags, dive into bowls of chowder and platters of boiled shrimp and steamed mussels, and dunk hot lobster chunks in pots of drawn butter. See chapter 9.

- **Louis' Lunch—The Very First (Well, Probably) Burgers** (New Haven, Conn.; ☎ **203/562-5507**): Not a lot of serious history has happened in New Haven, but boosters claim it was here that hamburgers were invented in 1900. This boxy little luncheonette lives on, moved from its original site in order to save it. The patties are freshly ground daily, thrust into vertical grills, and served on white toast. Garnishes are tomato, onion, and cheese. No ketchup and no fries, so don't even ask. See chapter 9.

- **Wooster Street Pizza** (New Haven, Conn.): New Haven's claim to America's first pizza is a whole lot shakier, but it has few equals as purveyor of the ultra-thin, charred variety of what they still call "apizza" in these parts, pronounced "ah-peetz." Old-timer **Frank Pepe's**, 157 Wooster St. (℡ **203/865-5762**), is usually ceded top rank among the local parlors, but it is joined at the summit by such contenders as **Sally's**, 237 Wooster St. (℡ **203/624-5271**) and the upstart **Brü Rm. at BAR**, 254 Crown St. (℡ **203/495-1111**). See chapter 9.

- **Johnnycakes and Stuffies** (R.I.): Sooner or later, most worthy regional food faves become known to the wider world (witness Buffalo wings). The Ocean State still clutches a couple of taste treats within its borders. "Johnnycakes" are flapjacks made with cornmeal, which come small and plump or wide and lacy, depending upon family tradition. "Stuffies" are the baby-fist-size quahog (*KWAH*-og or *KOE*-hog), clams barely known elsewhere in New England. The meat is chopped up, combined with minced bell peppers and bread crumbs, and packed back into both halves of the shell. See chapter 10.

- **Blue Benn Diner** (Bennington, Vt.; ℡ **802/442-5140**): This classic 1945 Silk City diner has a barrel ceiling, acres of stainless steel, and a vast menu. Don't overlook specials scrawled on paper and taped all over the walls. And leave room for a slice

of delicious pie, like blackberry, pumpkin, or chocolate cream. See chapter 11.

- **Al's** (Burlington, Vt.; ℡ **802/862-9203**): This is where Ben and Jerry go to eat french fries—as does every other potato addict in the state. See chapter 11.

- **Lou's** (Hanover, N.H.; ℡ **603/643-3321**): Huge crowds flock to Lou's, just down the block from the Dartmouth campus, for breakfast on weekends. Fortunately, breakfast is served all day here, and the sandwiches on fresh-baked bread are huge and delicious. See chapter 12.

- **Chauncey Creek Lobster Pier** (Kittery Point, Maine; ℡ **207/439-1030**): Chauncey's is one of the best lobster pounds in the state, with colorful picnic tables on the water, great crustaceans, and a liberal policy about brining in your own beer and side dishes. See chapter 13.

- **Becky's** (Portland, Maine; ℡ **207/773-7070**): Five different kinds of home fries on the menu? It's breakfast nirvana at this local institution on the working waterfront. It's a favored hangout of fishermen, high-school kids, businessmen, and just about everyone else. See chapter 13.

- **Silly's** (Portland, Maine; ℡ **207/772-0360**): Hectic and fun, this tiny, informal, kitschy restaurant serves up delicious finger food, like pita wraps, hamburgers, and pizza. The milkshakes alone are worth the detour. See chapter 13.

- **Fisherman's Friend** (Stonington, Maine; ℡ **207/367-2442**): This is a lively and boisterous kind of place, where you'll get your fill of both local color and what may be Maine's most succulent lobster stew. See chapter 13.

11 The Best of the Performing Arts

- **Symphony Hall** (Boston, Mass.; ✆ 617/266-1492): Home to the Boston Symphony Orchestra, the Boston Pops, and other local and visiting groups and performers, this is a perfect (acoustically and otherwise) destination for classical music. See chapter 4.

- **Hatch Shell** (Boston, Mass.; ✆ 617/727-9547, ext. 555): This amphitheater on the Charles River Esplanade plays host to free music and dance performances and films almost every night in the summer. Around the Fourth of July, the Boston Pops provide the entertainment. Bring a blanket to sit on. See chapter 4.

- **Boston's Theater District:** The area's performance spaces are in the midst of a nearly unprecedented boom, and this is the epicenter. Previews and touring companies of Broadway hits, local music and dance troupes, and other productions of every description make this part of town hop every night. See chapter 4.

- *The Nutcracker* (Boston, Mass.; ✆ 617/695-6955 for tickets): New England's premier family-oriented holiday event is Boston Ballet's extravaganza. When the Christmas tree grows through the floor, even fidgety preadolescents forget that they think they're too cool to be here. See chapter 4.

- **The Comedy Connection at Faneuil Hall** (Boston, Mass.; ✆ 617/248-9700): Even in the Athens of America, it's not all high culture. The biggest national names and the funniest local comedians take the stage at this Quincy Market hot spot. See chapter 4.

- **The Berkshire Theatre Festival** (Stockbridge, Mass.; ✆ 413/298-5576): An 1887 "casino" and converted barn mount both new and classic plays from June to late August in one of the prettiest towns in the Berkshires. Name artists on the order of Joanne Woodward and Dianne Wiest are often listed as actors and directors in the annual playbill. See chapter 8.

- **The Jacob's Pillow Dance Festival** (Becket, Mass.; ✆ 413/243-0745): Celebrated dancer/choreographer Martha Graham made this her summertime performance space for decades. Guest troupes are among the world's best, often including Dance Theatre of Harlem, the Merce Cunningham Dance Company, and the Paul Taylor Company, supplemented by repertory companies working with jazz, flamenco, or world music. See chapter 8.

- **Tanglewood Music Festival** (Lenox, Mass.; ✆ 617/266-1492 in Boston, 413/637-5165 in Lenox): By far the most dominating presence on New England's summer cultural front, the music festival that takes place on this magnificent Berkshires estate is itself in thrall to the Boston Symphony Orchestra and its director, Seiji Ozawa. While the BSO reigns, room is made for such guest soloists as Jessye Norman and Itzhak Perlman as well as practitioners of other forms, from jazz (Dave Brubeck) to folk (James Taylor) and the Boston Pops. See chapter 8.

- **The Williamstown Theatre Festival** (Williamstown, Mass.; ✆ 413/597-3400): Classic, new, and avant-garde plays are all presented during the June-through-August season at this venerable festival. There are two stages, one for works by established playwrights, the smaller second venue for less mainstream or experimental plays. There is usually a Broadway headliner on hand; Frank Langella has been a frequent presence. See chapter 8.

- **The Norfolk Chamber Music Festival** (Norfolk, Conn.; © **860/542-3000**): A century-old "Music Shed" on the Ellen Battell Stoeckel Estate in this Litchfield Hills town shelters such important chamber performance groups as the Tokyo String Quartet and the Vermeer Quartet. Young professional musicians perform morning recitals. See chapter 9.
- **Summer in Newport** (R.I.): From Memorial Day to Labor Day, only a scheduling misfortune will deny visitors the experience of an outdoor musical event.

In calendar order, the highlights (well short of all-inclusive) are the July Newport Music Festival, the August Ben & Jerry's Folk Festival and JVC Jazz Festival, and the Waterfront Irish Festival in September. See chapter 10.

- **The Marlboro Music Festival** (Marlboro, Vt.; © **215/569-4690** off-season, 802/254-2394 in summer): Pablo Casals participated in this highly regarded festival between 1960 and 1973. He's gone, but today you can hear accomplished masters and talented younger musicians in a 700-seat auditorium amid the rolling hills of southern Vermont. Performances are held weekends from mid-July to mid-August. See chapter 11.

12 The Best Destinations for Antiques Hounds

- **Charles Street** (Boston, Mass.): Beacon Hill is one of the city's oldest neighborhoods, and at the foot of the hill is a thoroughfare that's equally steeped in history. Hundreds of years' worth of furniture, collectibles, and accessories jam the shops along its 5 blocks. See chapter 4.
- **Main Street, Essex** (Mass.): The treasures on display in this North Shore town run the gamut, from one step above yard sale to one step below nationally televised auction. Follow Route 133 west of Route 128 through downtown and north almost all the way to the Ipswich border. See chapter 5.
- **Route 6A: The Old King's Highway** (Cape Cod, Mass.): Antiques buffs, as well as architecture and country-road connoisseurs, will have a field day along scenic Route 6A. Designated a Regional Historic District, this former stagecoach route winds through a half dozen charming Cape Cod

villages and is lined with scores of antiques shops. The largest concentration is in Brewster, but you'll find good pickings all along this meandering road, from Sandwich to Orleans. See chapter 6.

- **Sheffield** (Mass.): This southernmost town in the Berkshires is home to at least three dozen dealers in collectibles, Americana, military memorabilia, English furniture of the Georgian period, silverware, weather vanes, . . . even antique birdhouses. Most of them are strung along Route 7, with a worthwhile detour west along Route 23 in South Egremont. See chapter 8.
- **Brimfield Antique and Collectible Shows** (Brimfield, Mass.): This otherwise undistinguished town west of Sturbridge erupts with three monster shows every summer, in mid-May, mid-July, and early September. Upward of 6,000 dealers set up tented and tabletop shops in fields around

town. Call ℭ **800/628-8379** for details, and book room reservations far in advance. See chapter 8.

- **Woodbury** (Conn.): More than 30 dealers strung along Main Street offer a diversity of precious treasures, near-antiques, and simply funky old stuff. American and European furniture and other pieces are most evident, but there are forays into crafts and assorted whimsies as well. Pick up the directory of the Woodbury Antiques Dealers Association, available in most of the shops. See chapter 9.

- **Newfane and Townshend** (Vt.): A handful of delightful antiques shops are hidden in and around these picture-perfect towns. But the real draw is the Sunday flea market, held just off Route 30 north of Newfane, where you never know what might turn up. See chapter 11.

- **Portsmouth** (N.H.). Picturesque downtown Portsmouth is home to a half dozen or so antiques stores and some fine used-book shops. For more meaty browsing, head about 25 miles northwest on Route 4 to Northwood, where a dozen good-size shops flank the highway. See chapter 12.

- **Route 1, Kittery to Scarborough** (Maine). Antiques scavengers delight in this 37-mile stretch of less-than-scenic Route 1. Antiques minimalls and high-class junk shops alike are scattered all along the route, though there's no central antiques zone. See chapter 13.

Planning Your Trip to New England

by Wayne Curtis

This chapter covers the nuts-and-bolts travel information you'll need before setting off on your New England journey.

1 The Regions in Brief

BOSTON Oliver Wendell Holmes dubbed Boston the "Hub of the Universe," and the label stuck. Today, "The Hub" is the region's largest and most vibrant city. This alluring metropolis of historic and modern buildings, world-class museums, and topnotch restaurants is an important stop for travelers on any trip to New England.

CAPE COD & THE ISLANDS The ocean is writ large on Cape Cod, a low peninsula with miles of sandy beaches and grassy dunes that whisper in the wind. The carnival-like atmosphere of Provincetown is a draw, as are the genteel charms of Nantucket and Martha's Vineyard, two islands just offshore.

THE BERKSHIRES Massachusetts' rolling hills at the state's western edge are home to historic old estates, graceful villages, and an abundance of festivals and cultural events, including the Tanglewood Music Festival and Jacob's Pillow Dance Festival.

THE PIONEER VALLEY Extending through Massachusetts along the Connecticut River, the area takes its name from the early settlers who arrived here in the 17th century. Among the many picturesque towns is unspoiled Historic Deerfield.

THE LITCHFIELD HILLS The historic northwest corner of Connecticut has sleepy villages, hidden hiking trails, and a surfeit of New England charm—all just a couple of hours from New York City.

THE CONNECTICUT COAST The eastern coast is home to the historic towns of Mystic and New London, where you can get a glimpse of the shipbuilding trade at the Mystic Seaport Museum and the navy submarine base in nearby Groton.

NEWPORT, RHODE ISLAND AREA The lifestyles of the truly rich and famous are on parade in Newport, once home to the likes of Astors, Vanderbilts, and Auchinclosses. A tour of the oceanfront mansions never fails to astonish.

THE GREEN MOUNTAINS Extending the length of Vermont from Massachusetts to Canada, this mostly gentle chain of forested hills and low mountains offers great hiking, scenic back road drives, fantastic inns, and superb bicycling.

THE WHITE MOUNTAINS Since the mid–19th century, New Hampshire's White Mountains have drawn travelers to its rugged, windswept peaks and forests dotted with glacial boulders and clear, rushing streams. New England's best back-country hiking and camping are found here.

THE MAINE COAST Maine's rocky coast is the stuff of legend, art, and poetry. The southern coast features most of the state's beaches; farther "down east," you'll find rocky headlands and Acadia National Park, New England's only national park.

MAINE'S NORTH WOODS Consisting of millions of acres of uninhabited terrain, the North Woods is almost entirely owned by timber companies that harvest trees to feed their mills. Within this vast tree plantation are pockets of undisturbed wildlands that recall the era when Thoreau paddled and portaged his way north.

2 Visitor Information

In New England you're never far from a brochure. Shops, hotels, inns, museums, and even restaurants invariably feature crammed racks of colorful pamphlets touting local sights and accommodations. These mini-centers can be helpful in generating ideas for spur-of-the-moment excursions, but for a more comprehensive overview, you should head for the state information centers or local chambers of commerce. Addresses and phone numbers are provided for each region in the chapters that follow. Call in advance and ask for information to be mailed to you. All state websites feature links allowing you to request visitor packets online.

- **Connecticut Office of Tourism,** Department of Economic and Community Development, 505 Hudson St., Hartford, CT 06106 (© **800/282-6863** or 860/270-8080; www.ctbound.com).
- **Maine Tourism Association,** P.O. Box 2300, Hallowell, ME

04347 (© **800/533-9595** outside Maine, or 207/623-0363; www.visitmaine.com).
- **Massachusetts Office of Travel and Tourism,** State Transportation Building, 10 Park Plaza, Suite 4510, Boston, MA 02116 (© **800/227-6277** or 617/973-8500; www.mass-vacation.com).
- **New Hampshire Office of Travel and Tourism,** P.O. Box 1856, Concord, NH 03302 (© **800/386-4664** or 603/271-2343; www.visitnh.gov).
- **Rhode Island Department of Economic Development,** 1 West Exchange St., Providence, RI 02903 (© **800/556-2484** or 401/277-2601; www.visitrhodeisland.com).
- **Vermont Tourism and Marketing,** 6 Baldwin St., Montpelier, VT 05663 (© **800/837-6668** or 802/828-3237; www.1-800-vermont.com).

3 When to Go

THE SEASONS

The well-worn joke about New England's weather is that the region has just two seasons: winter and August. There's a kernel of truth to that, especially in the north, but it's mostly a canard to keep outsiders from moving here. In fact, the individual seasons are among those elements that make New England so distinctive.

SUMMER Peak summer season runs from July 4 to Labor Day. Crowds surge into New England's tourist areas in the mountains and along the coast for these two months, and activity remains frenetic through Labor Day evening, when calm begins to reclaim these regions. Summers are verdant and lush, and in the mountains, warm (rarely hot) days are the

New England's Regions

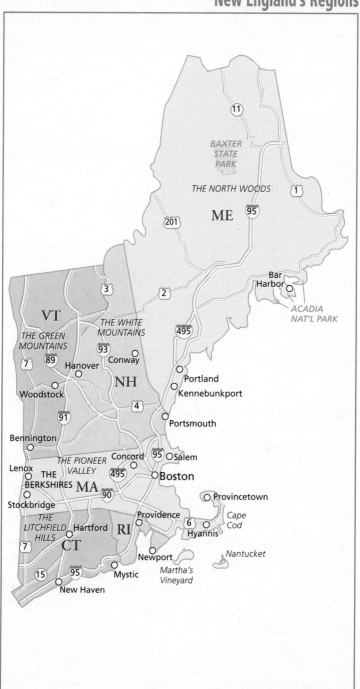

BAXTER STATE PARK

THE NORTH WOODS

ME

201   95

11

1

Bar Harbor

ACADIA NAT'L PARK

495

VT

THE GREEN MOUNTAINS

7   89   Hanover

Woodstock

91

Bennington

3

THE WHITE MOUNTAINS

93   Conway

NH

4

2

Portland

Kennebunkport

Portsmouth

Lenox

THE BERKSHIRES

Stockbridge

THE PIONEER VALLEY   Concord   95   Salem

495   Boston

MA   90

THE LITCHFIELD HILLS   Hartford   RI

7   CT

15   95   Mystic

New Haven

Providence

Newport

Martha's Vineyard

6   Cape Cod

Hyannis

Provincetown

Nantucket

rule, followed by cool nights. Along the coast, ocean breezes keep temperatures down; Cape Cod and the Islands, for example, are generally 10 degrees cooler than the mainland in summer.

The weather in summer typically follows the winds. Southerly breezes bring haze, heat, and humidity. Northwest winds bring cool weather and knife-sharp vistas. These systems tend to alternate, often with rain between them, and the change from hot to cool will sometimes occur in a matter of minutes. Rain is never far away—some days it's a quick afternoon thunderstorm; other times it's a steady drizzle that brings a 4-day soaking. Travelers should come prepared.

For most of the region, especially the coastal areas, midsummer is the prime season for travel. Expect to pay premium prices at hotels and restaurants except near the empty ski resorts of northern New England, where you can often find bargains. Also be aware that early summer (generally mid-May through June) brings out voracious black flies and mosquitoes, especially in the north country. Outdoorsy types are better off waiting until July before heading into the deep woods.

AUTUMN   In northern New England, don't be surprised to smell the tang of fall approaching as early as mid-August, a time when you'll also notice a few leaves turned blaze-orange in otherwise verdant trees at the edges of wetlands. Fall comes early here, puts its feet up on the couch, and stays for a time. The foliage season begins in earnest in the northern part of the region by the third week in September; in the south, it reaches its peak by the middle to end of October. The change in seasons in southern Connecticut runs three to four weeks behind northern Maine. And the higher elevations of the Green and White mountains likewise start to feel wintry a month or so before coastal locations.

Fall in New England is one of America's great natural spectacles, with miles of rolling hills blanketed with brilliant reds and stunning oranges. The season is garish in a way that seems determined to embarrass understated New England. Along winding country roads you'll find heaps of pumpkins for sale beneath blazing red sugar maples, and crisp apples available by the bushel. Take the time to scout out the farm stands, where you'll be amazed at the fertility of this seemingly flinty land.

Keep in mind that this is the most popular time of year to travel—bus tours fill the roads and available guest rooms throughout October. As a result, hotels are invariably booked solid and advance reservations are essential; you can also expect to pay a foliage premium of $20 or more per room at many inns and hotels.

WINTER   New England winters are like wine—some years are good, some are lousy. During a good season, plenty of light, fluffy snow covers the deep woods and ski slopes. A good New England winter offers a profound peace as the muffling qualities of fresh snow bring a thunderous silence to the landscape. During these winters, exploring the forest on snow-shoes or cross-country skis is a magical experience.

During the *other* winters, the lousy ones, the weather brings a nasty mélange of rain and sleet. It's bone-numbing cold, and bleak, bleak, bleak. Look into the eyes of the residents on the streets during this time. They are all thinking of the Caribbean.

The higher you go in the mountains, and the farther north you head, the better your odds of finding snow and avoiding rain. Winter coastal vacations can be spectacular (nothing beats cross-country skiing at the edge of the pounding surf), but it's a high-risk venture that could yield rain rather than snow.

Ski areas naturally are crowded during the winter months. They're especially so during school vacations, when most resorts tend to jack up their rates.

SPRING New England is famous for its elusive spring, which some residents claim lasts only a weekend or so, typically around mid-May, but sometimes as late as June. One day the ground is muddy, the trees are barren, and gritty snow is piled in shady hollows. The next day, temperatures are in the 80s, trees are blooming, and kids are swimming in the lakes. It's a little weird, frankly. Travelers must be very crafty and alert if they want to experience spring in New England. Spring is also known as the mud season, and a time when many innkeepers and restaurateurs close up for a few weeks for either vacation or renovation.

Also be aware that New England is home to hundreds of colleges, universities, and prep schools. As graduation nears (mid- to late May and early June), the region is afflicted with unusually high hotel occupancy rates in towns near schools. As always, it's best to book rooms well in advance.

Burlington, Vermont's Average Temperatures (°F/°C)

	Jan	Feb	Mar	Apr	May	June	July	Aug	Sept	Oct	Nov	Dec
Avg. High	25/-4	27/-3	38/3	53/12	66/19	76/24	80/27	78/26	69/21	57/14	44/7	30/-1
Avg. Low	8/-13	9/-13	21/-6	33/1	44/7	54/12	59/15	57/14	49/9	39/4	30/-1	15/-9

Boston's Average Temperatures (°F/°C)

	Jan	Feb	Mar	Apr	May	June	July	Aug	Sept	Oct	Nov	Dec
Avg. High	36/2	38/3	43/6	54/12	67/19	76/24	81/27	79/26	72/22	63/17	49/9	40/4
Avg. Low	20/-7	22/-6	29/-2	38/3	49/9	58/14	63/17	63/17	56/13	47/8	36/2	25/-4

NEW ENGLAND CALENDAR OF EVENTS

January

New Year's and First Night Celebrations, regionwide. Boston, Mass.; Portland, Maine; Providence, R.I.; Hartford, Conn.; Portsmouth, N.H.; Burlington, Vt.; and many other cities and towns, including on Cape Cod and Martha's Vineyard, celebrate the coming of the New Year with an abundance of festivities. Check with local chambers of commerce for details. New Year's Eve.

Wildflower Inn Sleigh Rally, East Burke, Vt. About a dozen sleighs, horse teams, and drivers trot their stuff at this 4-hour wintertime rally, which harkens back to the days before cars. Call the Wildflower Inn (✆ **800/627-8310**) for date and time. Late January.

February

U.S. National Toboggan Championships, Camden, Maine. This is a raucous and lively athletic event where being overweight is actually an advantage. Held at the toboggan chute of the Camden Snow Bowl. Call ✆ **207/236-3438.** Early February.

Dartmouth Winter Carnival, Hanover, N.H. Huge and elaborate ice sculptures grace the village green during this festive celebration of winter, which includes numerous sporting events and other winter-related activities. Call ℂ **603/646-1110.** Mid-February.

Stowe Derby, Stowe, Vt. The oldest downhill/cross-country ski race in the nation pits racers who scramble from the wintry summit of Mount Mansfield into the village on the Stowe Rec path. Call ℂ **802/253-3423** for details. Late February.

March

St. Patrick's Day/Evacuation Day. Parade, South Boston; celebration, Faneuil Hall Marketplace. The 5-mile parade salutes the city's Irish heritage and the day British troops left Boston in 1776. Head to Faneuil Hall Marketplace for music, dancing, food, and plenty of Irish spirit. Call ℂ **800/888-5515.** March 17.

New England Spring Flower Show, Dorchester, Mass. This annual harbinger of spring presented by the Massachusetts Horticultural Society (ℂ **617/536-9280**) draws huge crowds starved for a glimpse of green. Second or third week of the month.

Maine Boatbuilders Show, Portland. As winter fades, more than 200 exhibitors and 9,000 boat aficionados gather to make plans for the coming summer. A great place to meet boatbuilders and get ideas for your dream craft. Call ℂ **207/774-1067** for details. Mid- to late March.

April

Patriots' Day, Boston (Paul Revere House, Old North Church, Lexington Green, Concord's North Bridge). The events of April 18 and 19, 1775, which signified the start of the Revolutionary War, are commemorated and reenacted. Participants dressed as Paul Revere and William Dawes ride to Lexington and Concord to warn the Minutemen that "the regulars are out" (not that "the British are coming"—most colonists considered themselves British). Mock battles are fought at Lexington and Concord. Call the **Lexington Visitor Center** (ℂ **781/862-1450**) or the **Concord Chamber of Commerce** (ℂ **978/369-3120**). Third Monday of the month; a state holiday in Massachusetts and Maine.

Boston Marathon, from Hopkinton, Mass., to Boston. International stars and local amateurs run in the world's oldest and most famous marathon. The noon start means elite runners hit Boston around 2pm; weekend runners stagger across the Boylston Street finish line as late as 4 hours after that. Contact the **Boston Athletic Association** (ℂ **617/236-1652;** www.bostonmarathon.org) for details. Always run on Patriots' Day, the third Monday of the month.

Sugarbush Celebration, Waitsfield, Vt. Ski-related events herald the coming of spring and the most inviting season for skiing. Special events for kids are held. Call ℂ **802/583-2381.** Mid-April.

Daffodil Festival, Nantucket. Spring's arrival is heralded with masses of yellow blooms adorning everything in sight, including a cavalcade of antique cars. Call ℂ **508/228-1700.** Late April.

May

Lilac Festival, Shelburne, Vt. See the famed lilacs (more than 400 bushes) at the renowned Shelburne Museum when they're at their most beautiful. Call ℂ **802/985-3346** for details. Mid- to late May.

MooseMainea, Greenville, Maine. A variety of low-key events, from an antique-car show to a black-fly festival, are staged deep in the heart of moose territory. But the real attraction is the possibility of spotting one of the gangly beasts on a forest safari. Call © **207/695-2702.** Mid-May to mid-June.

Brimfield Antique Fair, Brimfield, Mass. Up to 6,000 dealers fill several fields near this Central Massachusetts town, with similar fairs in July and September. Call © **800/628-8379** or 508/347-2761, or go to www.brimfieldshow.com. Mid-May.

Cape Maritime Week, Cape Cod. A multitude of cultural organizations mount special events, such as lighthouse tours, highlighting the region's nautical history. Call © **508/362-3828.** Mid-May.

June

Old Port Festival, Portland, Maine. A 1-day block party in the heart of Portland's historic district with live music, food vendors, and activities for kids. Call © **207/772-2249.** Early June.

Yale-Harvard Regatta, on the Thames River in New London, Conn. One of the oldest collegiate rivalries in the country. Call © **617/495-4848.** Early June.

Taste of Hartford, Hartford, Conn. One of New England's largest outdoor festivals. Many area restaurants serve up their specialties. You'll also get a "taste" of local music, dance, magic, and comedy. Call © **860/728-3089.** Early June.

Market Square Weekend, Portsmouth, N.H. This lively street fair attracts 300 vendors and revelers from throughout southern New Hampshire and Maine into downtown Portsmouth to dance, listen to music, sample food, and enjoy summer's arrival. Call © **603/431-5388.** Second Saturday in June.

Motorcycle Week, Loudon and Weirs Beach, N.H. Tens of thousands of bikers descend on the Lake Winnipesaukee region early each summer to compare their machines and cruise the strip at Weirs Beach. The Gunstock Hill Climb and the Loudon Classic race are the centerpieces of the week's activities. Call © **603/783-4931.** Mid-June.

Boston Globe **Jazz & Blues Festival,** Boston. Big names and rising stars of the jazz world appear at lunchtime, after-work, evening, and weekend events, some of which are free. Call © **617/267-4301** or go to www.boston.com/jazzfestival for the current schedule. Third week of June.

Whatever Family Festival, Augusta, Maine. A community celebration to mark the cleaning up of the Kennebec River, culminating in a wacky race involving all manner of watercraft, some more seaworthy than others. Call © **207/623-4559.** Late June to early July.

Jacob's Pillow Dance Festival, Becket, Mass. The oldest dance festival in America features everything from ballet to modern dance and jazz. For a season brochure, call © **413/243-0745.** Late June through August.

Williamstown Theater Festival, Williamstown, Mass. This nationally distinguished theater festival presents everything from the classics to uproarious comedies and contemporary works. Scattered among the drama are literary readings and cabarets. Call © **413/597-3399.** Late June through August.

Stowe Flower Festival, Stowe, Vt. Nearly three-dozen events celebrate the joys of making the earth bloom, with offerings as diverse as garden tours and seminars by the experts. Call © **800/247-8693.** Last week in June.

July

Boston Harborfest, downtown (along Boston Harbor and the Harbor Islands). The city puts on its Sunday best for Fourth of July, which has become a gigantic week-long celebration of Boston's maritime history and an excuse to just get out and have fun. Events include concerts, guided tours, cruises, fireworks, the Boston Chowderfest, and the annual turn-around of the USS *Constitution*. Call © **617/227-1528.** First week in July.

Boston Pops Concert and Fireworks Display, Hatch Memorial Shell on the Esplanade. Independence Week culminates in the famous Boston Pops Fourth of July concert. People wait from dawn till dark for the music to start. The program includes Tchaikovsky's *1812 Overture* with actual cannon fire that segues into the fireworks. Call © **617/727-1300,** ext. 450, or go to www.july4th.org. July 4.

Independence Day, regionwide. Communities throughout New England celebrate the Fourth of July with parades, cookouts, road races, and fireworks. Contact local chambers of commerce for details. July 4.

Wickford Art Festival, Wickford, R.I. More than 200 artists gather in this quaint village for one of the East Coast's oldest art festivals. Wickford is the ancestral home of author John Updike and is said to be the setting for his book *The Witches of Eastwick*. Call © **401/294-6840** or go to www.wickfordart.org. Weekend after July 4.

Newport Music Festival, Newport, R.I. Chamber-music concerts are held inside Newport's opulent mansions. Call © **401/846-1133.** Second and third weeks of July.

Friendship Sloop Days, Rockland, Maine. This 3-day event is a series of boat races that culminates in a parade of sloops. Call © **207/596-0376.** Mid-July.

Vermont Quilt Festival, Northfield. Displays are only part of the allure of New England's largest (and oldest) quilt festival. You can also attend classes and have your heirlooms appraised. See class and event descriptions at www.vqf.org or call © **802/485-7092** for more information. Mid-July.

Barnstable County Fair, East Falmouth, Mass. (on Cape Cod). An old-time county fair complete with rides, food, and livestock contests. Call © **508/563-3200.** Late July.

Revolutionary War Days, Exeter, N.H. Learn all you need to know about the War of Independence during this historic community festival, which features a Revolutionary War encampment and dozens of reenactors. Call © **603/772-2622.** Third weekend in July.

Marlboro Music Festival, Marlboro, Vt. This is a popular 6-week series of classical concerts featuring talented student musicians and seasoned artists performing in the peaceful hills outside of Brattleboro. Call © **802/254-2394** (or 215/569-4690 in winter) for information. Weekends from July to mid-August.

Tanglewood, near Lenox, Mass. The Boston Symphony Orchestra makes its summer home at this fine estate, bringing symphonies, chamber concerts, and solo recitals to the Berkshire Hills. Tickets go on sale in April, and the best seats are usually gone by May or June. Call the Tanglewood Concert Line at © **413/637-1666** (July and August only) or Symphony Hall at © **617/266-1492;** or go to www.tanglewood.org. July to August.

Maine Lobster Festival, Rockland. Fill up on the local harvest at this event marking the importance and delectability of Maine's favorite crustacean. Enjoy a boiled lobster or two, and take in the ample entertainment during this informal waterfront gala. Call ✆ **800/ 562-2529** or 207/596-0376. Late July/early August.

August

Maine Festival, Brunswick. A 3-day festival showcasing Maine-made crafts, music, foods, and performers. It's boisterous, fun, and filling. Call ✆ **207/772-9012.** Early August.

Southern Vermont Crafts Fair, Manchester. More than 200 artisans show off their fine work at this popular festival, which also features creative food and good music. Held on the grounds of Hildene, a grand historic home. Call ✆ **802/ 362-1788.** Early August.

Newport Folk Festival. Newport, R.I. Thousands of music-lovers congregate at Fort Adams State Park for a heavy dose of performances on an August weekend. It's one of the nation's premier folk festivals. For information, call ✆ **401/847-3700** or go to www.newportfolk.com. Early August.

Annual Star Party, St. Johnsbury, Vt. The historic Fairbanks Museum and Planetarium hosts special events and shows, including night-viewing sessions during the Perseid Meteor Shower. Call ✆ **802/748-2372.** Mid-August.

Blueberry Festival, Machias, Maine. A festival marking the harvest of the region's wild blueberries. Eat to your heart's content. Call ✆ **207/794-3543.** Mid-August.

JVC Jazz Festival. Newport, R.I. This 3-day jazz festival brings together some of the best in the music industry to play for a sizzling weekend at Fort Adams State Park. Call ✆ **401/847-3700.** Mid-August.

Martha's Vineyard Agricultural Fair, West Tisbury, Mass. An old-fashioned country fair featuring horse pulls, livestock shows, musicians, and woodsman contests, along with plenty of carnival action. Call ✆ **508/693-4343.** Third weekend in August.

Blue Hill Fair, Blue Hill, Maine. A classic country fair just outside one of Maine's most elegant villages. Call ✆ **207/374-9976.** Late August to Labor Day.

September

Windjammer Weekend, Camden, Maine. Come visit Maine's impressive fleet of old-time sailing ships, which host open houses throughout the weekend at this scenic harbor. Call ✆ **207/236-4404.** Labor Day weekend.

Vermont State Fair, Rutland. All of Vermont seems to show up for this grand event, with a midway, live music, and plenty of agricultural exhibits. Call ✆ **802/775-5200** for details. Early September.

Providence Waterfront Festival, Providence, R.I. Musical performances, especially the jazz festival on Sunday, are the highlight of this weekend event. A food court and children's tent round out the activities. Call ✆ **401/621-1992.** Weekend after Labor Day.

Norwalk Oyster Festival, Norwalk, Conn. This waterfront festival celebrates Long Island Sound's seafaring past. Highlights include oyster-shucking and -slurping contests, harbor cruises, concerts, and fireworks. Call ✆ **203/838-9444.** Weekend after Labor Day.

Convergence International Festival of the Arts, Providence, R.I.

Various Providence arts organizations pull together for this week-long citywide event, which includes sculptural installations, musical performances, and other arts events. Call © **401/621-1992.** Mid-September.

Eastern States Exposition, West Springfield, Mass. "The Big E" is New England's largest agricultural fair, with a midway, games, rides, rodeo and lumberjack shows, country-music stars, and lots of eats. Call © **413/737-2443.** Mid- to late September.

Provincetown Arts Festival, Provincetown (Cape Cod), Mass. One of the country's oldest art colonies celebrates its past and present with local artists opening their studios. It's a great opportunity for collecting contemporary works. Call © **508/487-3424.** Late September.

Common Ground Fair, Windsor, Maine. A sprawling, old-time state fair with a twist: the emphasis is on organic foods, recycling, and wholesome living. Call © **207/623-5115.** Late September.

October

Northeast Kingdom Fall Foliage Festival, Northeast Vermont. A cornucopia of events staged in towns and villages throughout Vermont's northeast corner heralds the arrival of the fall foliage season. Be the first to see colors at their peak. Call © **802/748-3678.** Early October.

Fryeburg Fair, Fryeburg, Maine. Cotton candy, tractor pulls, live music, and huge vegetables and barnyard animals at Maine's largest agricultural fair. There's also harness racing in the evening. Call © **207/985-3278.** One week in early October.

Mystic Chowderfest, Mystic, Conn. A festival of soup served from bubbling cauldrons set on wood fires. Call © **860/572-5315.** Mid-October.

Harvest Day, Canterbury, N.H. A celebration of the harvest season, Shaker style. Lots of autumnal exhibits and children's games. Call © **603/783-9511.** Mid-October.

Cranberry Harvest Festival, Nantucket. Tour scenic cranberry bogs and local inns just when foliage is at its burnished prime. Call © **508/228-1700.** Mid-October.

Head of the Charles Regatta, Boston and Cambridge. High school, college, and post-collegiate rowing teams and individuals—some 4,000 in all—race in front of hordes of fans along the banks of the Charles River. This event always seems to fall on the crispest, most picturesque Sunday of the season. Call the Metropolitan District Commission Harbor Master (© **617/727-0537**) for information. Late October.

November

Thanksgiving Celebration, Plymouth, Mass. The holiday that put Plymouth on the map is observed with a "stroll through the ages," showcasing 17th- and 19th-century Thanksgiving preparations in historic homes. Nearby Plimoth Plantation, where the colony's first years are re-created, wisely offers a Victorian Thanksgiving feast (reservations required). Call the Plymouth Visitors Center (© **800/872-1620**) or the Plimoth Plantation (© **508/746-1622**). Thanksgiving Day.

Brookfield Holiday Craft Exhibition & Sale, Brookfield, Conn. Thousands of unique, elegant, and artful gifts are displayed in gallery settings on three floors of a restored gristmill. Call © **203/775-4526.** Mid-November to end of December.

Victorian Holiday, Portland, Maine. From late November until Christmas, Portland decorates its Old Port in a Victorian Christmas theme. Enjoy the window displays, take a free hayride, and listen to costumed carolers sing. Call ℂ **207/772-6828** for details.

December

Christmas Tree Lighting, Prudential Center, Boston. Carol singing precedes the lighting of a magnificent tree from Nova Scotia—an annual expression of thanks from the people of Halifax for Bostonians' help in fighting a devastating fire more than 70 years ago. Call the Greater Boston Convention and Visitors Bureau at ℂ **617/536-4100.** Early December.

Christmas Prelude, Kennebunkport, Maine. This scenic coastal village greets Santa's arrival in a lobster boat, and marks the coming of Christmas with street shows, pancake breakfasts, and tours of the town's splendid inns. Call ℂ **207/967-3286.** Early December.

Candlelight Stroll, Portsmouth, N.H. Historic Strawbery Banke gets in a Christmas way with old-time decorations and more than 1,000 candles lighting the 10-acre grounds. Call ℂ **603/433-1100** for information. First two weekends of December.

Boston Tea Party Reenactment, Congress Street Bridge, Boston. Chafing under British rule, the colonists rose up on December 16, 1773, to strike a blow where it would cause real pain—in the pocketbook. Call ℂ **617/338-1773.** Mid-December.

Woodstock Wassail Celebration, Woodstock, Vt. Enjoy classic English grog, along with parades and dances at this annual event. Call ℂ **802/457-3555.** Mid-December.

Christmas Eve and Christmas Day. Special festivities throughout New England. In Newport, R.I., several of the great mansions have special tours; Mystic, Conn., has a special program of Christmas festivities; Nantucket, Mass., features carolers in Victorian garb, art exhibits, and tours of historic homes. December 24 to 25.

4 The Active Vacation Planner

Don't let New England's outsized reputation for quaint villages and pastoral landscapes obscure another fact: it's also a superb destination for those who like outdoor adventure woven into their vacation itinerary.

Of course, New England isn't the Rockies or western Canada—you won't find endless acres of wilderness populated by grizzlies and bighorn sheep. But you may be surprised at the amount of undeveloped terrain available for outdoor activities. While the three northern states are the least densely populated and offer the best chances for slipping away from the crowds—Maine, for example, has one-third the population of Connecticut living on nearly seven times the land— you'll still find plenty of outdoor opportunities such as canoeing, hiking, and bicycling throughout the region, even in the southernmost reaches.

The state and regional chapters that follow offer a number of tips on specific outdoor adventures (such as bicycling trips and sea-kayaking tours). This section offers a general overview, as well as contact information for guided tours and recreation specialists.

For more detailed information on where to go and what to do in New England's backcountry, see *Frommer's Great Outdoor Guide to New England.*

OUTFITTERS & ORGANIZED TOURS Reputable resources for New England excursions include the following:

Appalachian Mountain Club (© 603/466-2727; www.outdoors.org), New England's largest outdoor club, hosts numerous workshops and tours throughout the year, many based out of its Pinkham Notch compound in New Hampshire's White Mountains. (Other workshops are held at Mount Greylock in the Massachusetts Berkshires, as well as in the Catskills of New York and the Delaware Water Gap of New Jersey.) 1- to 5-day classes range from introductory rock climbing to identifying wild mushrooms to tracking wild animals; tours include backcountry canoeing and hiking trips throughout the region.

Away.com (© 800/843-5630; www.away.com), one of the best managed of the outdoor-adventure websites, has extensive trip-planning information for those seeking thrills; packaged tours are also available online. Adventure specialists promptly answer any queries you might have. You can search by state and activity.

Backroads (© 800/462-2848 or 510/527-1555; www.backroads.com), the venerable Berkeley-based retailer of packaged soft-adventure trips, offers multisport trips to Maine (biking, walking, and sea kayaking), as well as biking and walking excursions through Vermont and Martha's Vineyard. This is one of the higher-end outfitters; accommodations typically consist of luxe inns.

Elderhostel (© 877/426-8056; www.elderhostel.org), has a large number of excellent programs in New England (and throughout the world) for those over 55 (or traveling with someone who is); many offerings focus on learning about the outdoors through hiking, kayaking, canoeing, and more. Accommodations vary, but the price is right—averaging $500 for 6 days, including meals and instruction. Browse the website or ask to be put on the mailing list. Courses are so popular that catalogs are distributed via a lottery system to ensure that everyone gets an even shot at signing up for the classes most in demand.

Gorp Travel (© 877/532-4677; www.gorptravel.com), one of the first online resources for outdoor adventure, also offers dozens of adventure packages around the globe. More than 100 New England trips are listed, ranging from 1-day canoe excursions in Connecticut to 6-day kayaking and hiking trips along the Maine coast. Overnights typically find travelers at upscale inns. A colorful printed catalog is free for the asking.

L.L.Bean (© 888/552-3261; www.llbean.com), the region's premier outdoor retailer, also offers frequent workshops on activities ranging from ice climbing to sporting clays. The outdoor discovery program features a 3-day fly-fishing school, 3-day canoe and kayak symposiums, and a weekend cross-country ski workshop. A free catalog of programs is available.

Sierra Club (© 415/977-5500; www.sierraclub.org/chapters), the venerable environmental organization, has chapters in all six New England states. All host outings ranging from area hikes and bike rides to ice-skating parties open to nonmembers. To view a schedule of upcoming events, visit the website and follow links by state.

Zoar Outdoor (© 800/532-7483; www.zoaroutdoor.com), an all-purpose adventure center on Route 2 (the Mohawk Trail) in western Massachusetts, is a great destination for river sports, including white-water rafting and kayaking, as well as rock climbing. The center also features camping and offers canoe and kayak rentals. Ask about the family adventure packages.

ALPINE SKIING New England's most challenging alpine ski resorts are located in the three northernmost states, although western Massachusetts also offers skiing that's popular with families. All of the major ski areas offer vacation packages (including accommodations and lift tickets); see the state or regional chapters that follow for resort contact information.

Moguls Ski and Snowboard Tours (© 800/666-4857; www.skimoguls. com) sells packaged ski vacations in Maine, New Hampshire, and Vermont. You can compare options on the firm's easy-to-navigate website.

For information on resorts and current ski conditions, contact **Ski Vermont** (© 800/837-6668; www. skivermont.com), **Ski Maine Association** (© 207/761-3774; www. skimaine.com), or **Ski New Hampshire** (© 800/887-5464, or 603/745-9396 in N.H.; www.skinh.com).

BACKPACKING Contact the **Appalachian Mountain Club** (see above) for information on trail guidebooks and organized group backpacking trips in the White Mountains and beyond. Contact information for ranger stations in the Green and White mountains national forests is in the New Hampshire and Vermont chapters.

Appalachian Trail Conference (© 304/535-6331; www.atconf.org) is the best single source for information on hiking New England's premier long-distance pathway, which passes through five of the region's six states (Rhode Island is the exception). This nonprofit organization publishes detailed trail guides for every step along the route.

Green Mountain Club, on Route 100 between Waterbury and Stowe (© 802/244-7037; www.green mountainclub.org), is the best source of information on Vermont's Long Trail, the oldest long-distance hiking trail in the nation. The club publishes the definitive *Long Trail Guide.* The information center and bookstore are open Monday through Friday, usually until about 4:30pm.

Baxter State Park (© 207/723-5140) consists of more than 200,000 wild acres in the north-central part of Maine. The park maintains about 180 miles of backcountry hiking trails and more than 25 backcountry sites, some accessible only by canoe. Most hikers coming to the park are intent on ascending 5,267-foot Mount Katahdin, but dozens of other peaks are well worth scaling, and just traveling through the deep woods hereabouts is a sublime experience. Reservations, which can be made by mail or in person (but not by phone), are required for backcountry camping; many of the best spots fill up shortly after the first of the year.

Note that backcountry camping is not permitted at Acadia National Park in Maine.

BIKING With its human scale and quiet back roads, New England offers great opportunities for road bikers and mountain bikers alike. Bikes are easy to rent throughout the region (just look in the local Yellow Pages under "bicycle"), and bike shops are great sources of information on the best routes. Look for tips in the regional chapters that follow.

Organized inn-to-inn bike tours through the rolling hills of Vermont are a great way to see the countryside by day while relaxing in luxury at night. Tours are typically self-guided, with luggage transferred for you each day by vehicle. Try **Bike Vermont** (© 800/257-2226; www.bikevt. com), **Country Inns Along the Trail** (© 800/838-3301; www.inntoinn. com), or **Vermont Bicycle Touring** (© 800/245-3868; www.vbt.com). VBT also offers three trips in Maine, including a 6-day Acadia trip with some overnights at the grand Claremont Hotel.

The **Massachusetts Bicycle Coalition** (© 617/542-2453; www.massbike.org) strives to improve the biking experience around the state through the development of bikeways. The group's website offers information on state bikeways and numerous links to local bike groups.

Bike the Whites (© 800/448-3534; www.bikethewhites.com) offers self-guided biking tours between three inns in the White Mountains, with each day involving a relaxed 20 miles of biking. Luggage is shuttled from inn to inn.

BIRDING Each state has one or more birding hot lines, which offer recorded announcements of recent unusual sightings: Connecticut (© 203/254-3665); Rhode Island (© 401/949-3870); Cape Cod (© 508/349-9464); Western Massachusetts (© 413/253-2218); Eastern Massachusetts (© 781/259-8805); Vermont (© 802/457-2779); New Hampshire (© 603/224-9900); and Maine (© 207/781-2332).

Many experienced birders sign up for whale-watching trips to view pelagic birds; some birder-only trips are scheduled, usually in conjunction with a statewide birding group. For tips on upcoming offshore birding expeditions in Massachusetts, see **www.neseabirds.com**.

The **Maine Audubon Society** (© 207/781-2330) offers a series of superb in-depth bird-watching workshops each summer on a beautiful 333-acre island in Mucongus Bay, just northeast of Pemaquid Point. The highlight of the workshops is a boat trip to an offshore island to see nesting puffins.

CANOEING The **Allagash Wilderness Waterway** in Maine is considered by many to be the region's premier canoe trip. Some 80 campsites are spaced along the nearly 100-mile route, which includes a 9-mile stretch of Class I-II white water. For a map and brochure, contact the Bureau of Parks and Recreation, Maine Department of Conservation, State House Station #22, Augusta, ME 04333 (© 207/287-3821). The Allagash is also served by several outfitters, including **Allagash Canoe Trips** (© 207/695-3668; www.allagash canoetrips.com), which leads 5- to 7-day excursions. Bring a sleeping bag; everything else is taken care of.

Battenkill Canoe Ltd. (© 800/421-5268 or 802/362-2800; www.battenkill.com) runs guided canoeing and walking excursions of between 2 and 6 nights' duration in Vermont (as well as abroad). Nights are spent at inns.

Upper Valley Land Trust (© 603/643-6626; www.uvlt.org) has established a network of primitive campsites along the Connecticut River; canoeists can paddle and portage its length and camp along the riverbanks. Two of the campsites are accessible by car. Call for a brochure or visit the group's website.

See also Appalachian Mountain Club and Zoar Outdoor, above.

CROSS-COUNTRY SKIING Catamount Trail Association (© 802/864-5794; www.catamount trail.together.com) oversees the 200-mile Catamount Trail, a cross-country ski trail that runs the length of Vermont.

Maine Nordic Council (© 800/754-9263) prepares a recorded guide to conditions at cross-country ski areas throughout the state; it's updated Fridays in winter.

Ski New Hampshire (© 800/887-5464, or 603/745-9396 in N.H.; www.skinh.com) offers current information on conditions at cross-country ski resorts, as well as assistance in finding a ski resort that's suited to your skills and interests.

Vermont Department of Travel and Tourism (© 802/828-3239; www.1-800-vermont.com) updates a recorded cross-country ski report for the state each Thursday.

Western Massachusetts Cross Country Ski Areas Association (no phone; www.xcskimass.com) produces a website with current ski conditions, a list of upcoming events, and information on the association's eight members.

DEEP-SEA FISHING Ports all up and down the New England coast are home to charter fishing boats; inquire with the chamber of commerce at your destination for more information. Other resources include the following:

Cape Cod Charter Association (© **508/945-6052**; www.capecod outdoors.com) books fishing trips on various charter boats sailing from the Cape and the islands.

Rhode Island Party & Charter-boat Association (© **401/737-5812**) is a good contact for setting up trips from this state. Many of the boats sail from bustling Port Judith.

Fish-Maine.com (© **207/273-3474**; www.fish-maine.com) manages a handy website featuring information and links to about three dozen charter boats based along the Maine coast and rivers.

FRESHWATER   FISHING **Housatonic Anglers** (© **860/672-4457**; www.housatonicanglers.com) offers 3-day fly-fishing classes in the summer and fall on the scenic and bountiful Housatonic River in Connecticut. Ask also about guide services (the rate includes a gourmet lunch) and the guest cottages located on 14 private acres along the river.

Orvis Catalog Store, in Manchester, Vermont (© **802/362-3750;** www.orvis.com), sells the company's well-regarded flyrods and equipment and features small ponds to try out gear before you buy. Orvis also offers top-rated fly-fishing classes, in which an expert will critique your technique and offer pointers.

Maine Professional Guides Association (© **207/549-5631;** www. maineguides.org) represents dozens of registered Maine guides, who pass stringent proficiency tests before being licensed. The association's website features links to numerous Maine guide services.

Maine Sporting Camp Association, P.O. Box 89, Jay, ME 04239 (no phone; www.mainsportingcamps. com), represents some 50 traditional backcountry lodges scattered in the more remote sections of the state. Fishing guides are often available for hire by the day. Write for a free brochure, or check the website.

See also Maine's L.L.Bean, above, for fly-fishing equipment and workshops.

HIKING Hikers have dozens of specialized guides to choose from, each offering detailed information on thousands of trails that wind through New England hills and mountains. Local bookstores are amply stocked with guides, which can also be ordered in advance through Amazon.com or other online booksellers. See also "Backpacking," above, for information on regional trails.

Country Walkers (© **800/464-9255** or 802/244-1387; www. countrywalkers.com) has a glorious color catalog (more like a wishbook) outlining supported walking trips around the world. Among them: walking tours in coastal Maine and north-central Vermont. Trips run 4 or 5 nights, and include all meals and lodging at appealing inns.

New England Hiking Holidays (© **800/869-0949;** www.nehiking holidays.com) offers an extensive inventory of options, including weekend trips in the White Mountains as well as more extended excursions to the Maine coast and Vermont. Trips typically involve moderate day hiking coupled with nights at comfortable lodges.

HORSEBACK RIDING

Horserentals.com (© 877/446-7730; www.horserentals.com) features a directory of stables that offer horse rentals and guided trail rides in all six New England states.

Kedron Valley Stables (© 802/457-1480) runs 4- to 6-day trips in the Green Mountain National Forest of Vermont. You'll be guided through secluded woods and historic towns like South Woodstock, Tyson, and Window, staying at inns and eating at wonderful country restaurants.

Vermont Icelandic Horse Farm (© 802/496-7141) leads trips on tiny Icelandic ponies, which move at a steady gait without much rocking—much like driving with good shocks. Owner Christina Calabrese offers half-day to 3-day trips for experienced riders.

SAILING

JWorld Sailing School (© 800/343-2255 or 401/849-5492; www.jworldschool.com) is a performance sailing school founded in Newport, Rhode Island, in 1981. (It also has locations in Key West, Annapolis, and San Diego.) Offerings include a 5-day learn-to-sail course; each class has just four students and includes 6-hour days on the water.

School of Ocean Sailing (© 800/732-6281; www.sailingschool.com) offers classes in open-water sailing and navigation (technical as well as celestial) aboard a 52-foot steel ketch. The 5-day classes begin and end in Portland, and cruise along the scenic mid-coast area of Maine.

Maine Windjammer Association (© 800/807-9463; www.midcoast.com/sailmwa) is a consortium of handsome vintage and new sailing ships that take passengers on crewed trips of between 1 and 7 days. Most are based in the Camden and Rockland area, and range in size from 53 to 132 feet. An array of excursions are available, from simple day sails to weeklong expeditions gunkholing among Maine's thousands of scenic islands and coves.

Hinckley Yacht Charters (© 800/492-7245; www.acadia.net/hyc) is on the southwestern shores of Mount Desert Island in Maine, and features more than 20 of the internationally famous boats available for weekly rental (from $2,250) to qualified sailors. Those without experience should contact **Hinckley Crewed Charters** (© 800/504-2305 or 207/244-0122; www.hinckleyyacht.com) for information on fully outfitted charters.

Winds of Ireland (© 800/458-9301 or 802/863-5090; www.windsofireland.com), in South Burlington, Vermont, on "New England's West Coast," charters seven Hunters, ranging from 28 to 41 feet.

SEA KAYAKING

Adventure Learning (© 800/649-9728 or 978-346-9728; www.adventure-learning.com) offers 1-day sea-kayaking workshops and tours, including a whale-watching paddle that departs from Newburyport, Massachusetts.

Collinsville Canoe & Kayak (© 860/693-6977; www.cckstore.com) leads 4- to 6-hour guided trips around some of the more appealing lakes and estuaries of coastal Connecticut. Lessons and rentals are also available.

Maine Island Trail Association (© 207/596-6456 or 207/761-8225, www.mita.org) oversees the nation's first long-distance water trail. Established in 1987, this 325-mile waterway winds along the coast from Portland to Machias, and incorporates some 70 state- and privately-owned islands along the route. Members of the association, a private nonprofit group, help maintain and monitor the islands and in turn are granted permission to visit and camp on them provided they follow certain restrictions. Membership is $40 per year.

Spas for Sybarites

New England's Puritan work ethic and its inhabitants' preference for austere forms of recreation (fly-fishing in April, ice-skiing in January) don't necessarily mean that sybarites will be left out in the cold. Spas have made some inroads in New England, and now offer guests the sort of pampering that the Pilgrims would have found altogether bewildering. Below is a sampling of some reputable spas in New England.

Canyon Ranch, 165 Kemble St., Lenox, MA 01240 (ℂ **800/742-9000;** www.canyonranch.com), is the region's premier spa. It's located in the Berkshires at the Bellefontaine mansion, an extraordinary 1897 replica of a palace at Versailles. The spa mixes athletic and outdoor endeavors with nutritional dining, and tops it all off with massages and other body work, including mud treatments, relexology, shiatsu, and herbal wraps. The rates are not for the budget-minded (a 3-night stay for two typically runs more than $2,000), but they do include treatments, gratuities, and other activities that are priced separately at many other spas.

Norwich Inn & Spa, 607 W. Thames St., Route 32, Norwich, CT 06369 (ℂ **800/ASK-4-SPA;** www.norwichinnandspa.com), is an intimate retreat in a brick Georgian mansion on 40 acres not far from Mystic that offers a long list of services like invigorating loofah scrubs, clay wraps, and thalassotherapy, a seawater-based treatment. It also has tennis courts and an 18-hole golf course next door.

Topnotch at Stowe, Mountain Road, Stowe, VT 05672 (ℂ **800/ 451-8686;** www.topnotch.com), is considered a resort spa rather than a destination spa, but it has an attractive indoor pool and fitness facility situated on 120 acres a short drive from Stowe's ski area and near great summer hiking trails. A variety of treatments are available, and there's easy access to year-round outdoor activities, like hiking in the Green Mountains and horseback riding on superb local trails. Spa and non-spa meals are served in the elegant on-site restaurant.

Northern Pines Health Resort, 559 State Rte. 85, Raymond, ME 04071 (ℂ **207/655-7624;** www.maine.com/norpines), is 40 minutes west of Portland and is less extravagant than other spas. Located on 70 acres that border a lovely Maine lake (it's a former girls' summer camp), this intimate bed-and-breakfast/resort emphasizes a holistic approach to stress control and weight loss. Meals are vegetarian, and teatime is yoga time.

Kripalu Center for Yoga and Health, P.O. Box 793, Lenox, MA 01240 (ℂ **800/967-3577;** www.kripalushop.org), is a superb destination for those who use "quest" as a verb. The emphasis is on spirit and soul, with weekend retreats offering programs such as "Raw Juice Fasting" and "The Practice of Thai Yoga Massage." It's located in the Berkshires on the grounds of a former Jesuit seminary, and the accommodations range from dormitories to rather spartan private rooms (make your own bed). The center publishes an extensive bulletin of classes and events; you can browse upcoming programs on the website.

Maine Island Kayak Co. (℡ 207/766-2373; www.sea-kayak.com) has a fleet of seaworthy kayaks it employs on camping trips up and down the Maine coast, as well as to Canada and Belize. The firm has a number of 2- and 3-night expeditions each summer, and the staff has plenty of experience training novices.

Maine Sports Outfitters (℡ 800/244-8799 or 207/236-8797) offers rentals and guided tours from a convenient Penobscot Bay location.

See also L.L.Bean, above, for information on the store's kayak classes and symposia.

SNOWMOBILING   The **Maine Snowmobile Association** (℡ 207/622-6983; www.mesnow.com) has information on the more than 12,000 miles of maintained snowmobile trails in the largest and most northerly of New England states. The website has loads of information, including current snow conditions, a directory of sled-friendly accommodations, and a list of outfitters who rent snowmobiles.

The **New Hampshire Snowmobile Association** (℡ 603/224-8906; www.nhsa.com) provides information on the nearly 6,000 miles of groomed, scenic snowmobile trails that lace the state, including information on how to register your snowmachine (mandatory) through any of the 248 off-highway recreational-vehicle agents. For current trail conditions, call ℡ 603/ 743-5050 or go to the website.

Snowmobile Vermont (℡ 860/916-0937; www.snowmobilevt.com) runs a website with everything you need to know to plan a trip here—where to rent, where to stay, how to contact area snowmobile clubs, what regulations are in force, and more. There's also a message board to post your own questions.

WHITE-WATER RAFTING   The region's big-water rivers are in northern and western Maine, but white-water rafting trips are available in Massachusetts, Vermont, and Connecticut as well.

Raft Maine (℡ 800/723-8633 or 207/824-3694; www.raftmaine.com) is a trade association of white-water outfitters running descents on Maine's popular rivers, including the Penobscot, the Kennebec, and the Dead. See the Maine chapter for more information on the rivers.

North American Whitewater Expeditions (℡ 800/727-4379) runs early-spring trips on Connecticut's Housatonic River and Vermont's West River, as well as summer-long trips in Maine and Massachusetts.

See also Zoar Outdoor, above, for information on rafting rivers in western Massachusetts.

5 Health & Insurance

STAYING HEALTHY

A few things to watch for when venturing off the beaten track:

POISON IVY   The shiny, three-leafed plant is common throughout the region. If touched, you may develop a nasty, itchy rash, which should be treated with calamine lotion or similar salves available at pharmacies (without prescription). The reaction tends to be worse in some people than others. It's safest to simply avoid it. If you're unfamiliar with what it looks like, ask at a ranger station or visitor information booth.

GIARDIA   That crystal-clear stream coursing down a high backcountry peak may seem as pure as it gets, but consider the possibility that it may be contaminated with animal feces. Giardia cysts may be present in some streams and rivers; when ingested by humans, the cysts can result in diarrhea and weight loss. Symptoms may not surface until well after you've left the backcountry and returned home. Carry your own water for day trips, or bring a small filter (available at most sporting-goods shops) to treat backcountry water. Failing that, at least boil water or treat it with iodine before using it for cooking, drinking, or washing. If you detect symptoms, see a doctor immediately.

LYME DISEASE Lyme disease has been a growing problem in New England since 1975, when the disease was identified in the town of Lyme, Connecticut. The disease is transmitted by tiny deer ticks—smaller than the more common, relatively harmless wood tick that you're more likely to encounter. Look for a bull's-eye-shaped rash (3 to 8 inches in diameter); it may feel warm but usually doesn't itch. Symptoms include muscle and joint pain, fever, and fatigue. If left untreated, heart damage may occur. It's more easily treated in early phases than later, so it's best to seek medical attention as soon as any symptoms are noted.

RABIES Since 1989, rabies has been spreading northward from New Jersey into New England. The disease is spread by animal saliva, and is prevalent in skunks, raccoons, bats, and foxes. It is always fatal if left untreated in humans. Infected animals tend to display erratic and aggressive behavior. The best advice is to keep a safe distance between yourself and any wild mammal you encounter. If bitten, wash the wound as soon as you

can and immediately seek medical attention. Treatment is no longer as painful as it once was, but it still involves an unpleasant series of shots.

INSURANCE
There are three kinds of travel insurance: trip cancellation, medical, and lost luggage coverage. Trip cancellation insurance is a good idea if you have paid a large portion of your vacation expenses up front. Check your existing policies before you buy any additional coverage. For independent-travel health-insurance providers, see below. Your homeowner's insurance should cover stolen luggage. For information on car renter's insurance, see "Getting Around," below.

Some credit cards (American Express and certain gold and platinum Visa and MasterCards) offer automatic flight insurance against death or dismemberment in case of an airplane crash.

Among the reputable issuers of travel insurance:

- **Access America,** 6600 W. Broad St., Richmond, VA 23230 (© **800/284-8300**)
- **Travel Guard International,** 1145 Clark St., Stevens Point, WI 54481 (© **800/826-1300**)
- **Travel Insured International, Inc.,** 11717 Burt St., Suite 202, Omaha, NE 68154 (© **800/243-3174**)
- **Travelex Insurance Services,** P.O. Box 9408, Garden City, NY 11530-9408 (© **888/457-4602**)

6 Choosing an Inn or B&B

What's the difference between an inn and a B&B? The difference narrows by the day. Until recently, inns were always full-service affairs, whereas B&Bs consisted of private homes with an extra bedroom or two and a homeowner looking for some extra income. A few of these old-style B&Bs still

exist, but they seem to be fading to the margins, in large part driven by the fact that Americans generally don't want to share bathrooms with other guests.

Today, the only difference between an inn and a B&B is that inns serve dinner (and sometimes lunch), whereas B&Bs provide breakfast only. At least that's the distinction we employ for this guide. Readers shouldn't infer that B&Bs in this guide are necessarily more informal or in any way inferior to a full-service inn. Indeed, many of the B&Bs listed have the air of gracious inns that have accidentally overlooked dinner.

B&Bs today are by and large professionally run affairs, where guests have private baths, a common area that's separate from the owner's living quarters, and attentive service. The owners prepare sumptuous breakfasts and offer a high level of service. All of the B&Bs in this guide are of the more professionally run variety, although many still have a few rooms that share bathrooms (we note where that's the case).

As innkeeping evolves into the more complex and demanding "hospitality industry," you're bound to bump up against more restrictions, rules, and regulations. It's always best to ask in advance to avoid unpleasant surprises. A few notes on recent trends:

SMOKING A majority of inns and B&Bs have banned smoking indoors, and some have even exiled smokers from the property, front lawn included. Frommer's has stopped mentioning whether or not smoking is allowed in inns because it has rapidly become a nonissue—it's banned almost everywhere. Assume that no smoking is allowed at any of the accommodations listed in this guide. (The larger, more modern hotels—such as Radisson or Holiday Inn—may have guest rooms set aside for smokers.) If being able to smoke indoors is important to you, be sure to inquire first.

CHILDREN A good many inns cater to couples and strongly prefer children over a certain age only. We note the recommended age where restrictions apply, but it's still best to ask first just to be safe. Don't assume that all places are able to accommodate children. The guest rooms at many inns are quite cozy, and would lack space for a cot even if the innkeeper had an extra one on the premises.

ADDITIONAL GUESTS The room rates published in this guide are for two people sharing a room. Many places charge $10 or more for each extra guest sharing the room. Don't assume that children traveling with you stay free; ask first about extra charges.

MINIMUM STAY It's become increasingly common for inns to require that you book a minimum of 2 nights or more during busy periods. These typically include weekends in summer (or in winter near ski areas), holidays, and the fall foliage season. These policies are mentioned in the following pages when known, but they're in constant flux, so don't be surprised if you're told you need to reserve an extra day when you make reservations.

Note that minimum-stay policies typically apply only to those making advance reservations. If you stop by an inn on a Saturday night—or call a couple of days before you arrive—and find a room available, innkeepers won't insist on the second night.

DEPOSITS Many establishments now require guests to provide a credit-card number to hold a room. Cancellation policies vary widely. Some places have a graduated refund—the further in advance you cancel, the less you'll be charged—while other places are quite generous about refunding your deposit. Most inns will scrupulously spell out the cancellation policy when you make reservations. Always ask before you divulge your credit-card number, and, if possible, have the policy e-mailed, faxed, or mailed to you before you agree to anything.

PETS We've noted inns that allow pets, but we still don't recommend showing up with a pet in tow unless you've cleared it in advance. Note that many establishments have only one or two rooms (often a cottage or room with exterior entrance) set aside for guests traveling with pets. Also, it's increasingly common for a cleaning fee of $10 or $20 to be charged to pet owners.

SERVICE CHARGES Rather than increase room rates, hotels, inns, and B&Bs are increasingly adopting the strategy of tacking on unpublicized fees to guests' bills. Most innkeepers will tell you about these when you reserve or check in; the less scrupulous will surprise you at checkout. This is an unfortunate trend, but there you have it.

The most common surcharge is an involuntary "service charge" of 10% or 15%, coupled with state lodging taxes (even "sales-tax-free" New Hampshire hits tourists with an 8% levy) that can bump up the cost of a bed by 20% or 25% (or even more in Connecticut, which has a 12% lodging tax). Note that the rates listed in this guide don't include service charges or sales tax.

Other charges might include a foliage-season surcharge ($10 or more per room), a "resort fee" (there's a 13% to 15% levy at hotels in Waterville Valley, N.H., to underwrite guest access at the local athletic club), a pet fee (see above), or a daily fee for the in-room safe, whether or not you choose to use it. Ask about extra fees when you book.

7 Tips for Travelers with Special Needs

FOR TRAVELERS WITH DISABILITIES Prodded by the Americans with Disabilities Act, a growing number of inns and hotels are retrofitting some of their rooms for people with special needs. Improvements may include rooms with barrier-free entrances, wheelchair-accessible showers, and fire alarms equipped with strobe lights. Outdoor recreation areas, especially on state and federal lands, are also providing more trails and facilities for those who've been effectively barred in the past because of seemingly small barriers. Accessibility is improving regionwide, but improvements are far from universal. When in doubt, call ahead to ensure that you'll be accommodated.

Many of the major car-rental companies now offer hand-controlled cars for disabled drivers. **Avis** (© 800/331-1212) can provide such a vehicle at any U.S. location with 48-hour advance notice; **Hertz** (© 800/654-3131) requires between 24 and 72 hours advance reservation at most of its locations. **Wheelchair Getaways** (© 800/642-2042; www.wheelchair-getaways.com) rents specialized vans with wheelchair lifts and other features for the disabled in more than 100 cities. Delivery can be arranged to all New England states.

Wilderness Inquiry (© 800/728-0719 or 612/676-9400; www.wildernessinquiry.org) offers adventure-travel packages for travelers with disabilities nationwide, including lake and river canoe trips in Maine.

FOR SENIORS New England is well suited for older travelers, with a wide array of activities for seniors that are often available at discounts. It's wise to request a discount at hotels or motels when booking the room, not when you arrive. An identification card from the **American Association of Retired Persons (AARP),** 601 E St. NW, Washington, DC 20049 (© 202/434-2277; www.aarp.com), can be invaluable in obtaining discounts.

Reasonably priced educational programs for people over 55 are offered by **Elderhostel,** 75 Federal St., Boston, MA 02110 (© **617/426-7788;** www.elderhostel.org). Rates include lodging and meals.

The Mature Traveler, a monthly newsletter on senior travel, is a valuable resource. It is available by subscription ($29.95 a year) from GEM Publishing Group, Box 50400, Reno, NV 89513-0400. GEM also publishes *The Book of Deals,* a collection of more than 1,000 senior discounts on airlines, lodging, tours, and attractions around the country; it's available for $9.90 by calling © **800/460-6676.**

FOR FAMILIES Be sure to ask about family discounts when visiting attractions. Many places offer a flat family rate that costs less than paying for each ticket individually.

Recommended destinations for families include Boston, with its plethora of museums; Cape Cod, with its miles of famous beaches and dunes; and Martha's Vineyard, with bike paths, beaches, and kid-scaled architecture in the cottage section of Oak Bluffs. Other destinations good for kids are Weirs Beach on New Hampshire's Lake Winnipesaukee, Hampton Beach on New Hampshire's tiny coast, and York Beach and Acadia National Park in Maine.

North Conway, N.H., also makes a good base for exploring with younger kids. The town has lots of motels with pools, and there are nearby train rides, aquaboggans, streams for splashing around, easy hikes, and the always-entertaining StoryLand. Excellent children's museums are located in Mystic, Boston, Portsmouth, Portland, and Norwich.

Several specialized guides offer more detailed information for families on the go. Try *Best Hikes with Children in Vermont, New Hampshire & Maine,* by Cynthia and Thomas Lewis (Mountaineers, 2000); *Best Hikes with Children in Connecticut, Massachusetts & Rhode Island,* also by Cynthia and Thomas Lewis (Mountaineers, 1998); *Fun Places to Go with Children in New England,* by Pamela Wright and Diane Bair (Chronicle Books, 1998), and *Great Family Vacations Northeast,* by Candyce Stapen (Globe Pequot, 1999).

FOR GAY & LESBIAN TRAVELERS
Provincetown, on the tip of Cape Cod, is one of the first and still one of the most famous gay resort communities. Gay entrepreneurs and politicians are well represented in the town's businesses and politics, and much of the nightlife revolves around gay culture. Gay travelers in Provincetown can easily relax and enjoy themselves with aplomb.

Outside of Provincetown, New England isn't exactly a hotbed of gay culture, although there are noted pockets, like Ogunquit, Maine. The cities, especially Providence, Boston, and Burlington, tend to be very welcoming to alternative lifestyles. For a small city, Portland, Maine, has an active gay population and three or four gay bars and clubs (they tend to fluctuate from year to year), attracting refugees from Boston and New York. Portland also hosts a sizable gay pride festival early each summer.

Outside metropolitan areas, attitudes toward homosexuality vary widely, but New Englanders tend to be fairly tolerant of people of all persuasions, provided they're not trying to impose a new tax on them.

As of July 2000, Vermont became the first state in the nation to permit couples of the same sex to be joined in civil union—at this point, the closest thing to gay marriage available. One needn't be a resident of Vermont to establish a civil union; many same-sex couples have traveled here, paid their $20 fee to a town clerk, and exchanged legally recognized vows before a judge or clergy member, even though such unions generally aren't recognized outside of Vermont. A good guide to the civil union law is found on the state's website at www.sec.state.vt.us/pubs/civilunions. htm. Note that the law has provoked a backlash among some Vermonters, who are agitating to have it repealed—you may see "Take Back Vermont" signs posted on some barns and trees.

Vermont has a fine monthly newsletter covering gay, lesbian, and bisexual issues and happenings called *Out in the Mountain,* P.O. Box 1078, Richmond, VT 05477 (www.mountainpridemedia.org). The newsletter is available free at many Vermont bookstores and other shops, or for $23 per year by mail from the address above.

For a more detailed directory of gay-oriented enterprises in New England, track down a copy of *The Pink Pages,* published by KP Media, 66 Charles St., #283, Boston, MA 02114. The price is $8.95 (plus $2.05 for shipping and handling). Call © 800/338-6550 or go to www.pinkweb.com.

More adventurous souls should consider linking up with the **Chiltern Mountain Club,** P.O. Box 407, Boston, MA 02117 (© **888/831-3100** or 617-/556-7774; www.chiltern.org/chiltern). This is an outdoor-adventure club for gays and lesbians; about two-thirds of its 1,200 members are men. The club organizes trips to northern New England throughout the year. Membership is $20 per year (or $25 per couple).

8 Getting There

BY CAR   From the south, I-95 is the major interstate highway serving Connecticut, Rhode Island, Massachusetts, and Maine. The least stressful route (with fewer tractor-trailers) from New York to Boston is via Hartford, Conn., using I-84 and the Massachusetts Turnpike. The easiest approach to northern New England from southern New England is along one of the three main interstate highway corridors. I-91 heads more or less due north from Hartford along the Vermont–New Hampshire border, then angles through northern Vermont. Another major interstate is I-93, which departs from I-95 near Boston, then cuts through New Hampshire to connect with I-91 near St. Johnsbury, Vt. For Maine, take I-95 north; it parallels the southern Maine coast before veering inland.

If scenery is your priority, the most picturesque way to enter New England is from the west. The most scenic way to arrive in northern Vermont is to drive I-87 to Exit 34 near Port Kent on Lake Champlain, then catch the car ferry across the lake to Burlington. For a more southern route, take any of a half-dozen smaller state highways that cross from New York State into Connecticut and Massachusetts. These routes, while often slow, take you through rolling hills and farmland and are exceptionally scenic.

Be aware that the interstates out of Boston can be sluggish on Friday afternoons and evenings in the summer, especially along the routes leading to Cape Cod and Maine. A handful of choke points (particularly the Bourne Bridge to Cape Cod and the Maine tollbooths on I-95) can back up for miles. North Conway, N.H., is also famed for its nightmarish weekend traffic, especially during the foliage season.

BY PLANE   Airlines serving New England include **American** (© 800/433-7300), **Continental** (© 800/525-0280), **Delta** (© 800/221-1212),

Tips Airport Alternatives

Ongoing airport construction, chronic overscheduling, and poor management of some of the commuter airlines can make connections through Boston's Logan Airport a frustrating experience. If your destination is Burlington, Portland, Bangor, or one of the other regional airports, try very hard to line up flights that avoid changing planes in Boston. **BY BUS** Bonanza (© **800/556-3815** or 617/720-4110) operates largely in Connecticut and Rhode Island. **Concord Trailways** (© **800/639-3317** or 617/426-8080) serves New Hampshire and Maine, including some smaller towns in the Lake Winnipesaukee and White Mountains areas. **Greyhound** (© **800/231-2222** or 617/526-1810; www.greyhound.com) serves destinations throughout New England; its easy-to-use website has detailed schedule and fare information. **Peter Pan** (© **800/343-9999** or 617/426-7838) serves western Massachusetts and Connecticut. **Plymouth & Brockton** (© **508/746-0378**) serves Massachusetts's south shore and onward to Cape Cod. And **Vermont Transit** (© **800/451-3292**) is affiliated with Greyhound and serves Vermont, New Hampshire, and Maine with frequent departures from Boston.

Jet Blue (© 800/538-2583), **Northwest** (© 800/225-2525), **Pan Am** (© 800/359-7262), **Southwest** (© 800/435-9792), **TWA** (© 800/221-2000), **United** (© 800/241-6522), and **US Airways** (© 800/428-4322).

Carriers to Cape Cod and the Islands include several of the above, plus **Cape Air/Nantucket Airlines** (© **800/352-0714** or 508/771-6944) and **Island Airlines** (© **800/248-7779** or 508/775-6606). Charter flights throughout the region are offered by Cape Air and Nantucket Airlines, as well as by **Cape Flight Limited** (© **508/775-8171**) and **King Air Charters** (© **800/247-2427**).

The traditional gateways to New England have been Boston, New York City, and Montreal. Major commercial carriers also serve Hartford, Conn. (Bradley International); Burlington, Vt.; and Bangor and Portland, Maine. Note that if you're heading to southwest Vermont (the Bennington or Manchester areas), the closest major airport is Albany, N.Y.

In the last few years, however, Providence, R.I., and Manchester, N.H., have grown in prominence thanks to the arrival of **Southwest Airlines,** which has brought competitive, low-cost airfares and improved service. Manchester in particular has gone from a sleepy backwater airport to a bustling destination, recently eclipsing Portland in numbers of passengers served.

Another discount carrier is **Pan Am,** once a dominant (then bankrupt) air carrier, and now back to life (under the auspices of entrepreneurs who purchased the name) and operating out of Portsmouth, N.H., also serving Bangor. Pan Am is the only airline that serves Portsmouth; it connects to a limited but growing roster of second-tier airports, including Gary, Ind.; Sanford, Fla.; and Allentown, Penn.

Upstart discounter **Jet Blue** offers direct service between Burlington, Vt., and New York City.

Feeder airlines and charter companies serve several smaller airports in the region (see regional chapters for

Driving Distances

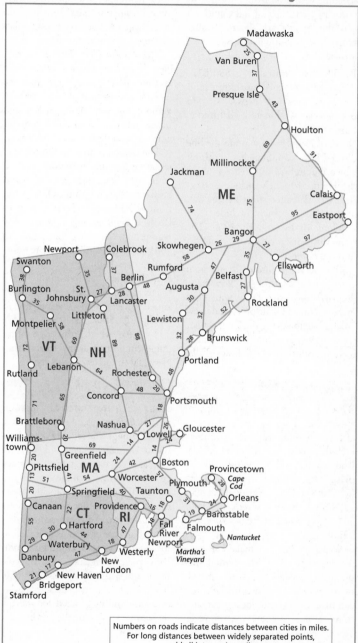

Numbers on roads indicate distances between cities in miles.
For long distances between widely separated points,
add all intervening mileages.

more information). Many of the scheduled flights from Boston to northern New England and Cape Cod and the Islands are aboard smaller prop planes; inquire if this is an issue for you.

BY TRAIN   Amtrak (© **800/872-7245**) operates Northeast Direct service from Newport News, Va., to Boston via Washington, Baltimore, Philadelphia, and New York City. North of New Haven, Conn., the line divides into two branches, both of which reunite in Boston. Stops along the Hartford branch include Springfield and Worcester; stops on the Providence, R.I., branch include New London, Mystic, and Kingston. The route through Providence is about 15 minutes faster.

Train service is limited in northern New England. Amtrak's *Vermonter* departs Washington, D.C., with stops in Baltimore, Philadelphia, and New York before following the Connecticut River northward. Stops in Vermont include Brattleboro, Bellows Falls, Claremont (N.H.), White River Junction, Randolph, Montpelier, Waterbury, Burlington/Essex Junction, and St. Albans. A bus connection takes passengers on to Montreal.

The *Ethan Allen Express* departs New York and travels north up the Hudson River Valley and into the Adirondacks before veering over to Vermont and terminating at Rutland. Buses continue on to Killington and north to Middlebury and Burlington.

The nation's first high-speed rail service went into operation in 2000 with Amtrak's *Acela* making stops between Washington, D.C., and Boston. Rail service from Boston to Portland and serving seacoast New Hampshire was slated to resume in 2001. Contact Amtrak for more information on both services (© **800/872-7245;** www.amtrak.com).

For rail service between New York and Connecticut, try cheaper **Metro North** (© **800/223-6052** or 212/532-4900), which runs commuter trains connecting many towns from New Haven to New York City.

9 Getting Around

BY CAR   The major New England airports all host national car-rental chains. Useful phone numbers include: **Avis** (© 800/831-2847), **Budget** (© 800/527-0700), **Enterprise** (© 800/325-8007), **Hertz** (© 800/654-3131), **National** (© 800/227-7368), **Rent-A-Wreck** (© 800/535-1391), and **Thrifty** (© 800/367-2277).

Web resources can make comparison shopping easier. **Microsoft Expedia** (www.expedia.com) and **Travelocity** (www.travelocity.com) help you compare prices and locate bargains from various companies nationwide. You can make reservations online once you've found the best deal.

Before you drive off in a rental car, be sure you're insured. The basic insurance coverage offered by most car rental companies, known as the **Loss/Damage Waiver** (LDW) or **Collision Damage Waiver** (CDW), can cost $20 per day or more. It usually covers the full value of the vehicle with no deductible if an outside party causes damage to the car. In all states but California, you will probably be covered in case of theft as well. Liability coverage varies according to company policy and state law, but the minimum is usually at least $15,000. If you are at fault in an accident, however, you will be covered for the full replacement value of the car but not for liability.

Most major credit cards provide some degree of coverage as well—provided they were used to pay for the rental. Terms vary widely, however, so be sure to call your credit-card company directly before you rent. The credit card will cover damage or theft of a rental car for the full cost of the vehicle. If you already have insurance, your credit card will provide secondary coverage—which basically covers your deductible. Credit cards will not cover liability.

The **speed limit** on interstate highways in the region is generally 65 miles per hour, although this is reduced to 55 miles per hour near cities. State highways are a less formal network, and the speed limits (and the conditions of the roads) vary widely. Watch for speed limits to drop in one or two stages as you approach a town; that's where the local police often lurk in search of speeders.

BY BUS   See "Getting There," above, for a list of bus companies serving New England. While express bus service to major cities and tourist areas is quite good, quirky schedules and routes between regional destinations (for instance, from North Conway to Portland) may send you miles out of the way and increase trip time significantly.

 FAST FACTS: **New England**

AAA Members can get help with trip planning, road service, and discount tickets to events and attractions. AAA also offers excellent free maps to members. Call ℂ **800/564-6222** for more information on membership and branch locations throughout New England.

American Express American Express offers travel services, including check cashing and trip planning, through a number of affiliated agencies in the region. Call ℂ **800/221-7282.**

Emergencies In the event of fire, crime, or medical emergency, dial ℂ **911.**

Internet Access Many public libraries have free terminals with Web access, allowing travelers to check their e-mail through a Web-based e-mail service such as Yahoo! or Hotmail. Internet cafes have come and gone in the last few years; it's best to ask around locally, or try visiting www.netcafeguide.com or www.cybercafe.com.

Liquor Laws The legal age to consume alcohol is 21. In Maine, New Hampshire, and Vermont, liquor is sold at government-operated stores only; in Connecticut, Massachusetts, and Rhode Island, liquor is sold in privately owned shops. Restaurants that don't have liquor licenses sometimes allow patrons to bring in their own. Ask first.

Maps Maps of the region and individual states are available at convenience stores and supermarkets. Some states also offer free road maps at official tourist information centers. For more detailed coverage, consider purchasing one or more of the **DeLorme** atlases, now available for all 50 states. These are sold at most book and outdoors stores around the region. DeLorme's corporate headquarters is in Yarmouth, Maine, where it stocks a wonderful store full of atlases, maps, and CD-ROMs.

Newspapers/Magazines The *Boston Globe, Wall Street Journal,* and *New York Times* are distributed throughout New England, although they can sometimes be hard to find in smaller, more remote villages. Almost every small town has a daily or weekly newspaper covering local happenings. These are good sources of information for events and restaurant specials.

Taxes The state sales taxes as of 2001 are: Connecticut, 6% (12% on lodging); Maine, 5% (7% on meals and lodging); Massachusetts, 5% (local sales taxes may also apply on lodging); New Hampshire, no general sales tax but 8% tax on lodging and meals; Rhode Island, 7% (plus 5% surtax on lodging); and Vermont, 5% (9% on meals and lodging).

Time Zone All New England states are in the Eastern time zone, as is the Canadian province of Quebec to the north. The provinces of New Brunswick, Nova Scotia, and Prince Edward Island are in the Atlantic time zone, which is 1 hour ahead.

For Foreign Visitors

by Wayne Curtis

Most of the information you'll need to ensure a pleasant trip can be found in chapter 2. Some aspects of U.S. laws, customs, and culture that might be perplexing to visitors from overseas are covered in this chapter.

1 Preparing for Your Trip

ENTRY REQUIREMENTS

DOCUMENTS Of the many people from around the world who visit the United States, Canadian citizens may have it easiest. Canadians need only present some form of identification at the border (often proof of citizenship); a passport isn't necessary unless you plan to stay more than 90 days, although it may be helpful as identification for certain transactions, especially financial.

More than two dozen countries currently participate in the Visa Waiver Pilot program, which allows travelers from these countries to enter the United States for up to 90 days with just a valid passport and a visa waiver form. Travelers under this program generally must also have a return ticket and proof of solvency. Check with your travel agency for the program's current status and the participating airlines and cruise lines. (The countries in this program as of 2001 are Andorra, Argentina, Australia, Austria, Belgium, Brunei, Denmark, Finland, France, Germany, Iceland, Ireland, Italy, Japan, Liechtenstein, Luxembourg, Monaco, the Netherlands, New Zealand, Norway, Portugal, San Marino, Singapore, Slovenia, Spain, Sweden, Switzerland, the United Kingdom, and Uruguay.)

Other foreign visitors should apply for a U.S. visa at the embassy or consulate with jurisdiction over their permanent residence. You may apply for a visa in any country, but it's generally easier to get a visa at home. Applicants must have a passport that's valid for at least 6 months beyond the dates they propose to visit, a passport-size photo (1½-inch square), and some indication that they have a residence outside the United States to which they plan to return. Applicants must also fill out a Form OF-156 (available free at all U.S. embassies and consulates). If you have a letter of invitation from a U.S. resident, that's sometimes helpful. Drug addicts and anarchists need not apply.

Bear in mind that the U.S. government assumes that everyone visiting the U.S. plans to immigrate here illegally. Regard this as presumptuous and cynical if you want, but that's how the system works under U.S. law. Therefore, it's up to the traveler to convince American authorities otherwise. The more evidence one assembles to that effect, the easier it will be to obtain a visa. Especially helpful is an indication of how one's trip will be financed.

Once in the country, foreign visitors come under the jurisdiction of the

Immigration and Naturalization Service (INS). If you'd like to change the length or the status of your visa (for instance, from nonimmigrant to immigrant), contact the nearest INS office. Look in the local phone book under "U.S. Government."

Be sure to carefully check the valid dates on your visa. If you overstay 1 or 2 days, it's probably not a problem. If it's more than that, you may be on the receiving end of an interrogation by customs officials on your way out of the country, and it may hinder efforts to get another visa the next time you apply.

MEDICAL REQUIREMENTS

Unless you've recently been in an area suffering from an epidemic (such as yellow fever or cholera), you don't need any inoculations to enter the United States. Not all prescription drugs that are sold overseas are necessarily available in the United States. If you bring your own supplies of prescription drugs (and especially syringes), it's wise to carry a physician's prescription in case you need to convince customs officials that you're not a smuggler or drug addict.

CUSTOMS REQUIREMENTS

Jet and ship passengers will be asked to fill out a customs form declaring what goods you are bringing into the country. Visitors planning to spend at least 72 hours in the United States may bring 1 liter of alcohol, 200 cigarettes *or* 4.4 pounds of smoking tobacco *or* 50 cigars (but no Cuban cigars), and $100 worth of gifts without paying any duties. Anything over these amounts will be taxed.

Many types of food are restricted (baked goods and cured cheese are among the exceptions). For details on what foods are allowed, see www.aphis.usda.gov/oa/travel.html. Live plants are also prohibited. Up to U.S.$10,000 in cash may be brought in or out of the country without any formal notification. If you are carrying more than that amount, you must notify customs officials when either entering or departing the country. For more information, visit the official website of the U.S. Customs Service at www.customs.gov/travel/travel.htm.

MONEY

The basic unit of U.S. currency is the dollar, which consists of 100 cents. Common coins include the penny (1¢), nickel (5¢), dime (10¢), and quarter (25¢). You may come across a 50¢ or $1 coin, but these are relatively rare. Dollar bills and coins are accepted everywhere, but some smaller shops won't accept larger bills ($50 or $100) because they lack sufficient change or are fearful of counterfeit bills. It's best to travel with a plentiful supply of $10 and $20 bills.

CURRENCY EXCHANGE Foreign-exchange bureaus, which are common in many countries, are rare in the United States. Many banks will exchange foreign currency for dollars, but it's often a time-consuming and expensive process, especially for less common currencies. It's best to plan ahead and obtain dollars or dollar-based traveler's checks in your own country before departure.

Canadian dollars are often accepted in shops and restaurants that cater to travelers in the border states of Maine, New Hampshire, and Vermont, although it's harder to use Canadian currency the farther you are from the border. Many hotels and restaurants will accept Canadian currency at a discount close to its current trading value; to avoid unpleasant surprises, ask what the rate is before buying.

ATMS Check with your bank as to whether you can use automatic teller machines (ATMs) in the United States. The most popular American ATM networks are **PLUS** (© 800/843-7587) and **Cirrus** (© 800/424-7787).

TRAVELER'S CHECKS Traveler's checks are considered as good as cash in most U.S. shops and banks. Widely recognized brands include American Express, Barclay's, Thomas Cook, and Visa. With other types of checks, you might meet with some resistance, particularly in smaller towns. Some shops may resist cashing checks of $100 or more if they have insufficient change; it's best to cash these at hotels or banks. Most banks will cash traveler's checks denominated in U.S. dollars without charge.

CREDIT CARDS Credit cards are a common form of payment throughout the United States for everything from expensive hotel rooms to inexpensive gifts. It's not entirely impractical to travel the country with no cash, just a credit card in your back pocket. Among the most commonly accepted cards are American Express, Discover, MasterCard, and Visa. Because American Express charges a higher rate for processing its transactions, some hotels and restaurants may decline to accept the card.

It's highly recommended that you have at least one credit card (fully paid up) when you travel in the United States. Credit cards are commonly accepted in lieu of deposits when reserving a car rental or hotel room. Many ATMs (automatic teller machines) will debit your credit card and provide cash on the spot. Don't ever give your card to anyone as a deposit; they should always record the information from it and return it to you. Also, put your credit-card receipts in a safe place—the information on them may be used by the unscrupulous to make purchases.

INSURANCE

Foreign visitors who are not insured are strongly urged to take out a traveler's insurance policy to cover any emergencies that may arise during their stay here. The United States does not offer national medical coverage for its residents; medical services are paid for either in cash or, more commonly, by an individual's insurance company. Be aware that hospital and doctors' fees are extremely high in the United States, and even a minor medical emergency could result in a debilitating expense for those traveling without insurance.

Comprehensive policies available in your country may also cover other disasters, including bail (in the event that you are arrested), automobile accidents, theft or loss of baggage, and emergency evacuation to your country in the event of a dire medical situation. Check with your local automobile association (if there is one) or insurance company for detailed information on travelers' insurance.

Packages such as "European Worldwide Services" in Europe are sold by automobile clubs and travel agencies at attractive rates. **Travel Assistance International (TAI)** (© 800/821-2828; www.travelassistance.com) is the agent for European Assistance Worldwide, so holders of this company's policies can contact TAI for assistance while in the United States.

Canadians should check with their provincial health offices or call **HealthCanada** (© 613/957-2991) to find out the extent of their coverage and what documentation and receipts they must take home in case they are treated for a medical emergency in the United States.

SAFETY

New England—with the notable exception of parts of Boston—has some of the lowest crime rates in the country. The odds of anything untoward happening during your visit here are very slight. But all travelers are advised to take the usual precautions against theft, robbery, and assault.

Travelers should avoid any unnecessary public displays of wealth. Don't bring out fat wads of cash from your pocket, and save your best jewelry for private occasions. If you are approached by someone who demands money, jewelry, or anything else from you, do what most Americans do: Hand it over. Don't argue. Don't negotiate. Just comply. Afterwards, immediately contact the police (see "Emergencies," in "Fast Facts," below).

The crime you're statistically most likely to encounter is theft of items from your car. Break-ins can occur any time of the day or night. Don't leave anything of value in plain view. At the least, lock valuables in your trunk. Better still, keep them with you at all times.

Late at night, you should look for a well-lighted area if you need gas or you need to step out of your car for any reason. Also, it's not advisable to sleep in your car late at night at highway rest areas, which can leave you vulnerable to robbers.

Take the usual precautions against leaving cash or valuables in your hotel room when you're not present. Many hotels have safe-deposit boxes. Smaller inns and hotels often do not, although it can't hurt to ask to leave small items in the house safe. Some small inns don't even have locks on guest-room doors. Don't be alarmed; if anything, this is a good sign, indicating that there have been no problems here in the past. If you're feeling at all nervous about this, lock your valuables in your car's trunk.

2 Getting to the United States

Most international travelers come to northern New England from Canada, via Boston's Logan Airport, or via one of the three New York City–area airports. Boston offers the easiest access to northern New England. Portland, the White Mountains, and the southern Green Mountains are 2 to 3 hours away by car. If you're headed to southern New England, both New York and Boston serve as convenient gateways.

Dozens of airlines serve New York and Boston airports from overseas. But because New York gets far more air traffic from abroad, the fares there and back are often more competitive. Some helpful numbers include (all numbers in London): **Air Canada** (© 0181/759-2636), **American Airlines** (© 0181/572-5555), **British Airways** (© 0345/222-111), **Continental** (© 01293/776-464), **Delta** (© 0800/414-767), **United** (© 0845/844-4747), and **Virgin Atlantic** (© 0293/747-747).

Those coming from Latin America, Asia, Australia, or New Zealand will probably arrive in New England

through gateway cities like Miami, Los Angeles, or San Francisco, clearing customs before connecting onward. Airports with regularly scheduled flights into the region include—in addition to Boston—Hartford, Conn.; Providence, R.I.; Portland, Maine; Manchester, N.H.; and Burlington, Vt. Albany, N.Y., is another option, especially if your destination is southern Vermont.

Bus service is fairly extensive throughout the region, and you can connect to all major cities and many smaller ones through hubs in Boston or New York. Most buses leave Boston from the **South Station,** 700 Atlantic Ave., and New York from the **Port Authority Bus Terminal,** Eighth Avenue and 42nd Street.

Travelers seeking to explore more remote regions like the Litchfield Hills, the Berkshires, or the White Mountains are advised to rent a car. Cars may be easily rented at most airports and at many in-town locations in larger cities. See chapter 2 for a listing of phone numbers for car-rental firms.

FAST FACTS: **For the Foreign Traveler**

Automobile Organizations Becoming a member of an automobile club is handy for obtaining maps and route suggestions, and can be helpful should an emergency arise with your car. The nation's largest automobile club is the American Automobile Association (AAA) (© **800/222-4357**), which has nearly 1,000 offices nationwide. AAA offers reciprocal arrangements with many overseas automobile clubs; if you're a member of a club at home, find out whether your privileges extend to the United States.

Business Hours Most offices are open from 8 or 9am to 5 or 6pm. Shops usually open around 9:30 or 10am. Banks typically close at 3 or 4pm, but most have ATMs available 24 hours. Post offices in larger cities may be open past 5pm, but it's best to call ahead before going out of your way. A few supermarkets are open 24 hours a day, but rarely is this the case in smaller towns. If you need quick provisions, look for one of the brightly lit convenience stores, which are usually open until at least 10 or 11pm.

Climate See "When to Go," in chapter 2.

Currency See "Money," above.

Drinking Laws You must be 21 years old to drink alcohol legally in most of the United States. No matter what your age, state laws in New England are notoriously harsh on those who drive drunk. Know your tolerance. If you plan to exceed that, allow enough time for the effects to wear off, or imbibe within walking distance of your hotel or inn.

Driving A current overseas license is valid on U.S. roads. If your license is in a language other than English, we recommend getting an International Driver's Permit from the American Automobile Association affiliate or other automobile organization in your own country prior to departure (see "Automobile Organizations," above).

Drivers may make a right turn at a red light, provided that they first stop fully and confirm that no other driver is approaching from the left. At some intersections (often in cities), signs prohibit such a turn.

Electricity Electrical incompatibility makes it tricky to use appliances manufactured for Europe in the United States. The current here is 110 to 120 volts, 60 cycles, compared to the 220 to 240 volts, 50 cycles used in much of Europe. If you're bringing an electric camera flash, laptop, or other gadget that requires electricity, be sure to bring the appropriate converter and plug adapter.

Embassies/Consulates Embassies for countries with which the United States maintains diplomatic relations are located in Washington, D.C. Call directory assistance (© **202/555-1212**) and request the phone number.

A handful of countries maintain consulates in Boston. Among English-speaking countries, these include **Canada,** 3 Copley Place, Suite 400 (© 617/262-3760); **Great Britain,** Federal Reserve Plaza, 600 Atlantic Ave., 25th floor (© 617/248-9555); **Ireland,** 535 Boylston St. (© 617/267-9330); and **Israel,** 1020 Statler Office Building, 20 Park Plaza (© 617/535-0200). For other countries, contact directory assistance (© 617/555-1212).

Emergencies In the event of any type of emergency—whether medical, fire, or if you've been the victim of a crime—simply dial © **911** from any phone. You do not need a coin to make this call from pay phones. A dispatcher will immediately send medics, police, or the fire department to assist you. If 911 fails to work, dial 0 (zero, not the letter *O*) and report your situation to the operator.

Gasoline Gasoline is widely available throughout New England, with the exception of the North Woods region of Maine, where you can travel many miles without seeing a filling station. Gas prices vary throughout the region because of varied state taxes. In general, you're better off filling up in larger cities or towns before setting off to remote or rural areas. Gas is available in several different grades at each station; the higher the octane, the more expensive it is. Rental cars will take any grade.

Many of the filling stations in New England have both "self-serve" and "full-serve" pumps; look for signs as you pull up. The full-service pumps cost a few cents more per gallon, but an attendant will pump your gas and check your oil (you might have to ask for this). The self-serve pumps often have simple directions posted on them. If you're at all confused, ask anyone who happens to be around for instructions.

Holidays With some important exceptions, national holidays usually fall on Mondays to allow workers to enjoy a 3-day weekend. The exceptions are New Year's Day (January 1), Independence Day (July 4), Veterans Day (November 11), Thanksgiving (fourth Thursday in November), and Christmas (December 25). Other holidays include Martin Luther King, Jr., Day (third Monday in January), Presidents' Day (third Monday in February), Easter (first Sunday following the first full moon after March 21), Memorial Day (last Monday in May), Labor Day (first Monday in September), and Columbus Day (second Monday in October). In Maine, Massachusetts, and Rhode Island, Patriots' Day is celebrated on the third Monday in April. Banks, government offices, and post offices are closed on these holidays. Shops are sometimes open, but assume that virtually everything will be closed on Thanksgiving and Christmas.

Languages Some of the larger hotels may have multilingual employees, but don't count on it. Outside of the cities, English is the only language spoken. The exception is along the Canadian border and in some Maine locales (including Old Orchard Beach), where French is commonly spoken, or at least understood.

Legal Aid If a foreign tourist accidentally breaks a law, it's most likely to be for exceeding the posted speed limit on a road (it's the law U.S. residents most frequently run afoul of). If you are pulled over by a police officer, don't attempt to pay the fine directly—that may be interpreted as a bribe, and you may find yourself in deeper trouble. You'll be issued a summons with a court date and a fine listed on it; if you pay the fine by mail, you won't have to appear in court. If you are arrested for a more serious infraction, you'll be allowed one phone call from jail. It's advisable to contact your embassy or consulate.

Mail Virtually every small town and village has a post office, and larger cities will have several branch offices. Mail within the United States costs 34¢ for a 1-ounce letter, and 21¢ for each additional ounce; postcards are 20¢. Overseas mail to Europe, Australia, New Zealand, Asia, and South America is 80¢ for a half ounce, 70¢ for a postcard. Letters to Mexico or

Canada (up to 1 ounce) are 60¢. If in doubt about weight or costs, ask the postal clerk. Mail may also be deposited at blue mailboxes with the inscription "U.S. MAIL" or "United States Postal Service," located on many streets.

If you need to receive mail during your travels, have your correspondents address it to your name, "[c/o] General Delivery" at the city or town you are visiting. Go in person to the main post office to collect it; you'll be asked for identification (a passport is ideal) before it's given to you.

Newspapers/Magazines Overseas newspapers and magazines are commonly found in Boston and Cambridge, but are harder to track down elsewhere in New England. Your best bet is to check in the phone book for Borders or Barnes & Noble, two of the largest chain bookstores in New England. These offer a selection of the overseas press.

Taxes Visitors to the United States are assessed a $10 Customs tax upon entering the country, and a $6 tax on departure. The United States does not have a value-added tax (VAT), so you won't be able to get a refund on taxes. The tax you most commonly come across is a sales tax (usually 5% to 6%) added on to the price of goods and some services. New Hampshire does not have a sales tax on goods, but does levy an 8% tax on hotel rooms and meals at restaurants.

Telephone & Fax Pay phones are not hard to find except in the more remote regions. Shops that have public phones inside often display a blue sign featuring a bell within a circle outside the store. Telephone numbers beginning with "800," "877," or "888" are toll-free. Press "1" before dialing a toll-free number. Don't confuse these with "900" numbers, which carry a substantial per-minute charge and are often used for phone-sex lines.

Local pay-phone calls typically cost 35¢. How far you can call on a local call varies from place to place, and the boundaries will often seem arbitrary. If you're uncertain whether a call is long distance or not, try to place it as a local call. If your coins are returned and a recorded voice comes on telling you to deposit more money for the first 3 minutes, that means it's a long-distance call.

Phone directories include the Yellow Pages (stores and services, listed by category) and the White Pages (names, listed alphabetically). Some White Pages are divided into commercial and residential listings. Phone books are sometimes found at pay phones; failing that, ask to see one at a shop or restaurant. To find a specific local phone number, dial 411 and an operator will take your request. Sometimes this is a free call from a pay phone; sometimes it's not.

Long-distance calls at pay phones tend to be very expensive, and you'll need a lot of coins. There are other options. At some phones, you can use your credit card. The least expensive choice is usually to use prepaid long-distance phone cards, which are sold at many convenience stores and other outlets, typically for $5 or $10. Follow the instructions on the card (you'll call a toll-free number first, then punch in a code and the number you wish to call). Long-distance charges using the cards are usually about 15¢ to 35¢ per minute, which is less expensive and more convenient than feeding coins into a pay phone. Some cards offer generous rates on overseas calls, but rates vary widely; ask before you buy.

Be aware that many hotels (notably the more expensive chain hotels) tack on a surcharge for local and long-distance calls made from your room. Even toll-free calls can cost $1 or more. Ask about these charges when you check in. If your hotel does add a high surcharge and you plan to make a lot of calls, you're better off using a pay phone in the lobby.

To charge the phone call to the person receiving your call, dial 0 (zero, not the letter O) and then the area code and the number you're calling. An operator (or computer) will come on the line and ask your name, and will then call the number to ask permission to reverse the charges. If the person you're calling accepts, the call will be put through.

If you need to send or receive a fax (facsimile), ask at your hotel or look in the Yellow Pages under "Fax Transmission Service." Many photocopy shops will provide this service for you.

Time Zone All of New England is in the eastern time zone—the same as New York and the rest of the Eastern seaboard. All states shift to daylight saving time (1 hour ahead) on the first Sunday in April, and back to standard time on the last Sunday in October. "Spring forward, fall back" is how most Americans remember how to adjust their clocks.

Eastern Standard Time is 5 hours behind Greenwich Mean Time; when it's noon in London or Paris, it's 7am in Boston.

Tipping Tipping is commonly practiced in the United States to recognize good service. Be aware that in restaurants, servers are paid a bare minimum and depend on tips for their wage. Tipping isn't usually considered optional; it's skipped only when the service is deplorable. For decent to good service, tip 15%; for outstanding service, 20%. Other suggestions for tipping include: bartenders, 10% to 15%; bellhops, $1 per bag; cab drivers, 10% to 15% of the fare; chambermaids, $1 per day; checkroom attendants, $1 per garment; parking attendants, $1. No tipping is expected at gas stations, or at fast-food or other self-service restaurants.

Toilets Public toilets (commonly called "rest rooms") are increasingly scarce in the United States, and the ones that do exist are often not fit for use. Restaurants have rest rooms for their customers; some will let the public use them, but many have signs indicating FOR PATRONS ONLY. This is remedied by buying a pack of gum or a cup of coffee. Fast-food restaurants (like McDonald's or Burger King) are a good bet for reasonably clean toilets when traveling on the highways.

4

Boston & Cambridge

by Marie Morris

The turn of the century found Boston where it had been at the turn of the other 3 centuries of its existence: in the middle of a transformation. As the 1700s dawned, the town was growing into a center of colonial commerce; 100 years later, flush with post-Revolutionary prosperity, it was becoming a city. The late 19th century saw the rise of the "Athens of America" and the rich cultural tradition that endures today.

In the new millennium, the city is undergoing a dramatic physical change. The elevated expressway that slashes through downtown is moving underground, development is spreading along the waterfront, and Boston is preparing to show off. When the "Big Dig" highway-construction project ends (in 2004 or 2005), it will leave behind a peerless blend of high technology and history. The building

boom may overshadow the famous 18th- and 19th-century architecture, but even rampant development can't change the colonial character that makes the central city appealing to residents and visitors alike.

Cambridge and Boston are so close that many people believe they're the same—a notion both cities' residents and politicians are happy to dispel. Cantabrigians are often considered more liberal and better educated than Bostonians, which is another idea that's sure to get you involved in a heated discussion. Harvard dominates Cambridge's history and geography, but there's more to see than just the university.

Take a few days (or weeks) to get to know the Boston area, or use it as a gateway to the rest of New England. Here's hoping your experience is memorable and delightful.

1 Orientation

ARRIVING

BY PLANE The major domestic carriers that serve Boston's Logan International Airport are **AirTran** (© 800/247-8726), **American** (© 800/433-7300), **America West** (© 800/235-9292), **Continental** (© 800/523-3273), **Delta** (© 800/221-1212), **Frontier** (© 800/432-1359), **Midway** (© 800/446-4392), **Northwest** (© 800/225-2525), **TWA** (© 800/221-2000), **United** (© 800/241-6522), and **US Airways** (© 800/428-4322). Many major international carriers also fly into Boston.

Southwest (© 800/435-9792) serves **T. F. Green Airport,** in the Providence suburb of Warwick, R.I. (© **888/268-7222;** www.pvd-ri.com), and New Hampshire's **Manchester International Airport** (© **603/624-6556;** www.flymanchester.com). Several other major carriers serve both, and prices often undercut fares to Boston. **Bonanza** (© **800/556-3815;** www.bonanzabus.com) offers bus service from T. F. Green to Boston's South Station; the fare is $16 one-way, $29 round-trip. Allow at least 90 minutes. From Manchester, **Vermont**

Transit (© 800/552-8737; www.vermonttransit.com) runs buses to South Station; some continue to Logan. The fare is $12 one-way, $23.50 round-trip. Allow 60 to 90 minutes.

The regional commuter airline **Shuttle America** (© 888/999-3273; www. shuttleamerica.com) serves **Hanscom Field,** off Route 2A in Bedford (© 781/ 869-8000; www.massport.com). Hanscom is handy if you're visiting the western suburbs, but handles only propeller aircraft, no jets.

Boston's **Logan International Airport,** in East Boston at the end of the Sumner, Callahan, and Ted Williams tunnels, is 3 miles across the harbor from downtown. All five terminals have ATMs, Internet kiosks, pay phones with dataports, fax machines, and information booths (near baggage claim). Terminals C and E have bank branches that handle currency exchange; A and C have children's play spaces. Ongoing construction at the airport is near completion but still causes detours and delays. If you're returning a rental car, allow extra time to negotiate the often-confusing layout.

The Massachusetts Port Authority, or **MassPort** (© 800/23-LOGAN; www.massport.com), coordinates airport transportation. Access to the city is by subway, cab, bus, and boat. The **subway** is fast and cheap—10 minutes to Government Center and $1 for a token (good for one ride). Free **shuttle buses** run from each terminal to the Airport station on the MBTA (or "T") Blue Line daily from 5:30am to 1am. The Blue Line stops at State Street and Government Center, downtown points where you can exit or transfer (free) to the other lines.

A **cab** from the airport to downtown or the Back Bay costs about $18 to $24. The ride into town takes 10 to 45 minutes, depending on traffic and the time of day. If you must travel during rush hour or on Sunday afternoon, allow extra time, or plan to take the subway or water shuttle (and pack accordingly).

The trip to the downtown waterfront (near cab stands and several hotels) in a weather-protected **boat** takes 7 minutes, dock to dock. The free no. 66 shuttle bus connects all terminals to the Logan ferry dock. The **Airport Water Shuttle** (© 617/330-8680) runs to Rowes Wharf on Atlantic Avenue Monday through Friday from 6am to 8pm, Saturday and Sunday from 10am to 8pm. The one-way fare is $10 for adults, $5 for seniors, and free for children under 12. **Harbor Express** (© 617/376-8417; www.harborexpress.com) runs from the airport to Long Wharf Monday through Friday from 6:30am to 9pm (to 11pm on Friday), and less frequently on weekends. (The return trip goes through Quincy, so the Airport Water Shuttle is much faster.) The one-way fare is $10.

MassPort (see above) coordinates **minibus service** between the airport and South Station Sunday through Friday from 6am to 8pm. The one-way fare for the "Logan Dart" is $5. Some hotels have **limousines** or **shuttle vans;** ask when you make your reservations. To arrange private service, call ahead for a reservation, especially at busy times. Your hotel can recommend a company, or try **Carey Limousine Boston** (© 800/336-4646 or 617/623-8700) or **Commonwealth Limousine Service** (© 800/558-LIMO outside Mass., or 617/ 787-5575).

BY CAR   Boston is 218 miles from New York; driving time is about 4½ hours. From Washington, it takes about 8 hours to cover the 468 miles; the 992-mile drive from Chicago takes around 21 hours.

Driving to Boston is not difficult, but between the cost of parking and the hassle of downtown traffic, the savings on airfare may not be worth the aggravation.

Tips **Out of Order**

Aquarium, the first Blue Line stop on the downtown side of the harbor, was closed for Big Dig construction at press time. If your destination is along the waterfront or in the North End, call ahead to see which station to use.

The **Big Dig** dominates the area near the Central Artery, which is being moved underground without being closed. If you're thinking of using the car to get around town, think again.

The major highways are **I-90,** the Massachusetts Turnpike ("Mass. Pike"), an east-west toll road that leads to the New York State Thruway; **I-93/U.S. 1,** extending north to Canada and leading to the Northeast Expressway, which enters downtown; and **I-93/Route 3,** the Southeast Expressway, which connects with the south, including Cape Cod. **I-95** (Mass. Route 128) is a beltway about 11 miles from downtown that connects to I-93 and to highways in Rhode Island, Connecticut, and New York to the south and New Hampshire and Maine to the north.

The **Mass. Pike** extends into the city and connects with the **Central Artery** (the John F. Fitzgerald Expressway), which meets the Northeast Expressway. To avoid Big Dig construction, exit at Cambridge/Allston or Prudential Center in the Back Bay.

To reach Cambridge, take **Storrow Drive** or **Memorial Drive** (on either side of the Charles River). The Mass. Pike's Allston/Brighton exit connects with Storrow Drive. It has a Harvard Square exit; cross the Anderson Bridge to John F. Kennedy Street to reach the square. Memorial Drive intersects with Kennedy Street; turn away from the bridge to reach the square.

The **American Automobile Association** (© 800/AAA-HELP; www.aaa. com) provides members with maps, itineraries, and other information, and arranges free towing if you break down. The privately operated Mass. Pike arranges its own towing; if you break down, wait in your car until a patrol arrives.

BY TRAIN   Boston has three rail centers: **South Station,** on Atlantic Avenue; **Back Bay Station,** on Dartmouth Street across from the Copley Place mall; and **North Station,** on Causeway Street near the FleetCenter. Each train station is also a rapid transit station. See the "Boston Transit & Parking" map on p. 67.

Amtrak (© 800/USA-RAIL or 617/482-3660; www.amtrak.com) serves South Station, Back Bay Station, and Route 128. Its new Acela Express high-speed service has cut trip time from New York to just over 3 hours and from Washington to about 6. Standard Northeast Corridor service takes 4 to 5 hours and 8 hours, respectively. Travel time from Chicago is 22 hours (sleepers are available). During slow times, excursion fares may be available. Discounts are not offered on Friday and Sunday afternoons. Always remember to ask for the discounted rate; also remember that for longer trips, it may be easier than you think to find an airfare that's cheaper than the train.

South Station is a stop on the Red Line, which runs to Cambridge by way of Park Street, the hub of the **subway** (© 617/222-3200; www.mbta.com). At Park Street you can connect to the Green, Blue, and Orange Lines. The Orange Line links Back Bay Station with Downtown Crossing (where there's a walkway

---

Tips Area Code Alert

As of April 2001, you must dial all 10 digits—area code plus number—to complete a local call in eastern Massachusetts. (If you accidentally dial "1" first, the call still goes through as a local call.) The area codes for Boston and the immediate suburbs are **617** and **857**; for nearby suburbs, **781** and **339**; for northern and western suburbs, **978** and **351**; and for southern suburbs, **508** and **774**.

---

to Park Street station) and other points. The **commuter rail** serves Ipswich, Rockport, and Fitchburg from North Station, and points south and west of Boston, including Plymouth, from South Station.

BY BUS   The **South Station Transportation Center,** on Atlantic Avenue next to the train station, is the city's bus-service hub. It's served by regional and national lines, including **Greyhound** (© **800/231-2222** or 617/526-1801; www.greyhound.com), **Bonanza** (© **800/556-3815** or 617/720-4110; www.bonanzabus.com), and **Peter Pan** (© **800/237-8747** or 617/426-8554; www.peterpanbus.com).

VISITOR INFORMATION

BEFORE YOU LEAVE HOME   Contact the **Greater Boston Convention & Visitors Bureau,** 2 Copley Place, Suite 105, Boston, MA 02116-6501 (© **888/ SEE-BOSTON** or 617/536-4100; 0171/431-3434 in the U.K.; fax 617/ 424-7664; www.bostonusa.com). It offers a comprehensive visitor information kit ($6.25) with a planner, guidebook, map, and coupon book; and a *Kids Love Boston* guide ($3.25) for families. Free smaller planners for specific seasons or events are often available.

The **Massachusetts Office of Travel and Tourism,** 10 Park Plaza, Suite 4510, Boston, MA 02116 (© **800/227-6277** or 617/973-8500; fax 617/973-8525; www.massvacation.com) distributes the *Getaway Guide,* a free magazine with information on attractions and lodgings, a map, and a seasonal calendar.

The **Cambridge Office for Tourism,** 18 Brattle St., Cambridge, MA 02138 (© **800/862-5678** or 617/441-2884; fax 617/441-7736; www.cambridge-usa. org), distributes information about Cambridge.

An excellent resource for travelers with disabilities is **Very Special Arts Massachusetts,** 2 Boylston St., Boston, MA 02116 (© **617/350-7713;** TTY 617/ 350-6836; www.vsamass.org). Its comprehensive website includes general access information and specifics on more than 200 arts and entertainment facilities.

IN PERSON   The **Boston National Historic Park Visitor Center,** 15 State St. (© **617/242-5642;** www.nps.gov/bost), across the street from the Old State House and the State Street T, is a good place to start exploring. National Park Service rangers staff the center, dispense information, and lead free tours of the Freedom Trail. The audiovisual show about the trail provides basic information on 16 historic sites. The center is wheelchair accessible and has rest rooms. Open daily from 9am to 5pm.

The Freedom Trail begins at the **Boston Common Information Center,** 146 Tremont St., on the Common. The center is open Monday through Saturday from 8:30am to 5pm, Sunday from 9am to 5pm. The **Prudential Information**

Center, on the main level of the Prudential Center, is open Monday through Saturday from 9am to 8pm, Sunday from 11am to 6pm. The **Greater Boston Convention & Visitors Bureau** (✆ **888/SEE-BOSTON** or 617/536-4100) operates both centers.

There's an outdoor information booth at **Faneuil Hall Marketplace** between Quincy Market and the South Market Building. It's staffed in the spring, summer, and fall from 10am to 6pm Monday through Saturday, noon to 6pm Sunday.

In Cambridge, there's an **information kiosk** (✆ **617/497-1630**) in the heart of Harvard Square, near the T entrance at the intersection of Mass. Ave., John F. Kennedy Street, and Brattle Street. It's open Monday through Saturday from 9am to 5pm, Sunday from 1 to 5pm.

CITY LAYOUT

Parts of Boston reflect the city's original layout, a seemingly haphazard plan that leaves even longtime residents tearing their hair. Old Boston abounds with alleys, dead ends, one-way streets, streets that change names, and streets named after extinct geographical features. On the plus side, every "wrong" turn **downtown,** in the **North End,** or on **Beacon Hill** is a chance to see something you might otherwise have missed.

Nineteenth-century landfill projects transformed much of the landscape, altering the shoreline and creating the **Back Bay,** where the streets run parallel. After some frustrating time in the older part of the city, this simple plan will seem ingenious.

FINDING AN ADDRESS   There's no rhyme or reason to the street pattern, compass directions are virtually useless, and there aren't enough street signs. The best way to find an address is to call ahead and ask for directions, including landmarks, or leave time for wandering around. If the directions involve a T stop, be sure to ask which exit to use—most stations have more than one.

STREET MAPS   Free maps of downtown Boston and the transit system are available at visitor information centers around the city. *Where* and other

---

 It's a Big, Big, Big, Big Dig

In a city with glorious water views, historic architecture, and gorgeous parks, the most prominent physical feature is a giant highway-construction project. The Central Artery/Third Harbor Tunnel Project, better known as the "Big Dig," is a $14-billion undertaking that will move Interstate 93 underground—without closing the road—and connect the Mass. Pike to the airport. It encompasses a new bridge over the Charles River (north of North Station), reconfigured Mass. Pike access (south of South Station), and a giant construction site in between.

If it stays on schedule, the Big Dig will be complete in late 2004 or early 2005; meanwhile, it's causing countless traffic nightmares and making engineering history. Many of the construction techniques are so unusual that professionals come from all over the world just to see them in action. To learn more, visit www.bigdig.com, or just go for a walk downtown.

tourism-oriented magazines, available free at most hotels, include maps of central Boston and the T. *Streetwise Boston* ($5.95), and *Artwise Boston* ($5.95) are sturdy, laminated maps available at most bookstores. Less detailed but more fun is MapEasy's *GuideMap to Boston* ($5.95), a hand-drawn map of the central areas and major attractions.

BOSTON NEIGHBORHOODS IN BRIEF

See the map on p. 67 to locate these areas, which visitors are most likely to frequent. When Bostonians say "**downtown**," they usually mean the first six neighborhoods defined here.

The Waterfront   This narrow area along **Atlantic Avenue** and **Commercial Street,** once filled with wharves and warehouses, now boasts luxury condos, marinas, restaurants, offices, and hotels. Also here are the New England Aquarium, at the foot of **State Street,** and departure points for harbor cruises and whale-watching expeditions.

The North End   One of the city's oldest neighborhoods has been an immigrant stronghold for much of its history. It's now less than half Italian American, but you'll still hear Italian spoken and find many Italian restaurants, *caffès*, and shops. **Hanover Street** is the main street of the North End, which lies across **I-93** from the rest of downtown. Clubs and restaurants cluster on and near **Causeway Street** in the **North Station** area (between North Washington Street and Beacon Hill), but it's not a good place to wander alone at night.

Faneuil Hall Marketplace & Haymarket   Employees aside, Boston residents tend to be scarce at Faneuil Hall Marketplace (also called Quincy Market). An irresistible draw for out-of-towners and suburbanites, the cluster of restored market buildings across **I-93** from the North End is the city's most popular attraction. **Haymarket,** along Blackstone Street, is home to an open-air produce market on Friday and Saturday. **Congress Street** separates the marketplace from Government Center.

Government Center   Here, modern design strays into the red-brick facade of traditional Boston architecture. Across **Cambridge Street** from Beacon Hill, Government Center is home to state and federal office towers, Boston City Hall, and a central T stop.

Financial District   In the city's banking, insurance, and legal center, skyscrapers surround the landmark Custom House Tower. This area is frantic during the day and practically empty in the evening. **State Street** separates the Financial District from Faneuil Hall Marketplace.

Downtown Crossing   The Freedom Trail runs through this shopping and business district east of Boston Common, which hops during the day and slows considerably at night. The intersection that gives Downtown Crossing its name is where Winter Street becomes Summer Street at **Washington Street**, the most "main" street downtown.

Beacon Hill   Narrow, tree-lined streets and architectural showpieces make up this residential area near the State House. **Charles Street** is the main drag of "the Hill." Louisburg (say "Lewis-burg") Square and Mount Vernon Street, two of the loveliest and most exclusive spots in Boston, are on Beacon Hill. It's also home to Massachusetts General Hospital, off **Cambridge Street** on the nominally less fashionable north side. On the south side, **Beacon Street** borders **Boston Common,** as does **Park Street,** which is just 1 block long (but looms large in the geography of the T).

Charlestown One of the oldest areas of Boston is where you'll see the Bunker Hill Monument, USS *Constitution* ("Old Ironsides"), and one of the city's best restaurants, Olives (see "Dining," below). Yuppification has brought some diversity to the mostly white residential neighborhood, but pockets remain that have earned their reputation for insularity. To get here, follow **North Washington Street** from the North End.

South Boston Waterfront (Seaport District) The city's newest neighborhood has had several names; these are the most popular. Across **Fort Point Channel** from downtown, it's where you'll find the World Trade Center, Seaport Hotel, Fish Pier, federal courthouse, Museum Wharf, and a lot of construction.

Chinatown The fourth-largest Chinese community in the country is a small but growing area jammed with Asian restaurants, groceries, and other businesses. As the "Combat Zone," or red-light district, has nearly disappeared, Chinatown has expanded to fill the area between Downtown Crossing and the Mass. Pike extension. Its main street is **Beach Street.** Also in this neighborhood, the tiny **Theater District** extends about 1½ blocks in each direction from the intersection of **Tremont** and **Stuart streets;** be careful here at night after the crowds thin out.

South End Cross **Huntington Avenue** or Stuart Street to reach this landmark district packed with Victorian row houses and little parks. Known for its ethnic, economic, and cultural diversity, as well as its galleries and boutiques, the South End has a large gay community and

some of the city's best restaurants. Main thoroughfares include **Tremont** and **Washington streets,** which originate downtown, and **Columbus Avenue.** *Note:* Don't confuse the South End with South Boston, a residential neighborhood on the other side of I-93.

Back Bay Fashionable since its creation out of landfill over a century ago, the Back Bay overflows with gorgeous architecture and chic shops. It extends from **Arlington Street,** in the plush area near the **Public Garden,** to the student-dominated sections near Massachusetts Avenue, or **Mass. Ave.** Unlike downtown, it's laid out in a grid. The main streets include the prime shopping areas of **Boylston** and **Newbury streets** and largely residential Commonwealth Avenue, or **Comm. Ave.,** and **Beacon Street.** The cross streets go in alphabetical order.

Huntington Avenue Landmarks dot the honorary "Avenue of the Arts" (or, with a Boston accent, "Otts"). Not a formal neighborhood, Huntington Avenue is where you'll find Symphony Hall (at the corner of **Mass. Ave.**), Northeastern University, and the Museum of Fine Arts.

Kenmore Square The landmark white-and-red Citgo sign above the intersection of **Comm. Ave., Beacon Street,** and **Brookline Avenue** tells you you're approaching Kenmore Square. Boston University students throng its shops, bars, restaurants, and clubs. The college-town atmosphere goes out the window when the Red Sox are in town and baseball fans flock to Fenway Park, 3 blocks away.

Cambridge The backbone of Boston's neighbor across the Charles River is Mass. Ave., which originates in Roxbury and extends into Cambridge, Arlington, and

Lexington, 9 miles away. The Red Line subway parallels Mass. Ave. in the areas you're likeliest to visit, where the T stops bear the names of the neighborhoods: Kendall Square (Kendall/MIT), Central Square, Harvard Square, and Porter Square.

2 Getting Around

It's impossible to say this often enough: When you reach your hotel, *leave your car in the garage* and *walk* or *use public transportation.* If you must drive in town, ask at the front desk for a route around or away from Big Dig construction.

BY PUBLIC TRANSPORTATION

The **Massachusetts Bay Transportation Authority,** or **MBTA** (℡ **800/392-6100** outside Mass., or 617/222-3200; www.mbta.com), is known as the "T," and its logo is the letter in a circle. It runs subways, trolleys, buses, and ferries in Boston and many suburbs, along with the commuter rail. Its website includes maps, schedules, and other information.

Newer stations on the Red, Blue, and Orange Lines are wheelchair accessible; the Green Line is being converted. All T buses have lifts or kneelers; call ℡ **800/LIFT-BUS** for more information. To learn more, call the **Office for Transportation Access** (℡ **617/222-5438** or TTY 617/222-5854).

The **Boston Visitor Pass** (℡ **877/927-7277** or 617/222-5218; www.mbta.com) includes unlimited travel on the subway and local buses, in commuter rail zones 1A and 1B, and on two ferries, plus discounts on attractions. The cost is $6 for 1 day (so tokens are cheaper for fewer than six trips), $11 for 3 consecutive days, and $22 for 7 consecutive days. If the timing works, a new commuter pass may be a better deal: The $12.50 **weekly combo pass** covers subways and buses but not ferries, and is good from Sunday through Saturday only. You can buy a pass in advance by phone or online (there's a shipping fee), or when you arrive at the Airport T, South Station, Back Bay Station, or North Station. They're also for sale at the Government Center and Harvard T stations; the Boston Common, Prudential Center, and Faneuil Hall Marketplace information centers; and some hotels.

BY SUBWAY & TROLLEY   Red, Blue, and Orange Line trains and Green Line trolleys make up the **subway** system, which runs partly aboveground. The local fare is $1—you'll need a token—and can be as much as $2.50 for some surface line extensions. Transfers are free. Route and fare information and timetables are available through the website and at centrally located stations. Service begins around 5:15am and ends around 12:30am. The exception is New Year's Eve, when closing time is 2am and service is free after 8pm. A sign on the token booth in every station gives the time of the last train in either direction.

The oldest system in the country, the T dates to 1897. The ancient Green Line is the most unpredictable—leave extra time if you're taking it to a vital appointment. Note that downtown stops are so close together that walking is often faster.

BY BUS   T buses and "trackless trolleys" (buses with electric antennae) provide service around town and to and around the suburbs. The local bus fare is 75¢; express buses are $1.50 and up. Exact change is required. You can use a token, but you won't get change. Important local routes include **no. 1** (Mass. Ave. from Dudley Square in Roxbury through the Back Bay and Cambridge to Harvard Square); **92** and **93** (between Haymarket and Charlestown); and **77** (Mass. Ave. north of Harvard Square to Porter Square, North Cambridge, and Arlington).

BY FERRY   Two useful ferries (both included in the T visitor pass) run from **Lovejoy Wharf,** off Causeway Street behind North Station and the FleetCenter. One goes to **Long Wharf** (near the Aquarium T stop) and the **Charlestown Navy Yard**—it makes a good final leg of the Freedom Trail. The other serves the **World Trade Center,** on Northern Avenue. The fare is $1.25. Call ℰ **617/ 227-4321** for more information. Service between Lovejoy Wharf and **Russia Wharf,** near South Station, is in the works; call the T or check www.mbta.com for details.

BY TAXI

Taxis are expensive and not always easy to flag—find a cab stand or call a dispatcher. Stands are usually near hotels. There are also busy ones at Faneuil Hall Marketplace (on North Street), South Station, Back Bay Station, and on either side of Mass. Ave. in Harvard Square, near the Coop and Au Bon Pain.

To call ahead, try the **Independent Taxi Operators Association** (ℰ **617/ 426-8700**), **Boston Cab** (ℰ **617/536-5010** or 617/262-2227), **Metro Cab** (ℰ **617/242-8000**), or **Town Taxi** (ℰ **617/536-5000**). In Cambridge, call **Ambassador Brattle** (ℰ **617/492-1100**) or **Yellow Cab** (ℰ **617/547-3000**). Boston Cab can dispatch a wheelchair-accessible vehicle; advance notice is recommended. If you want to report a problem or have lost something in a cab, call the police department's **Hackney Hot Line** (ℰ **617/536-8294**).

The fare structure: the first quarter mile (when the flag drops), $1.50; each additional eighth of a mile, 25¢. Wait time is extra, and the passenger pays tolls as well as the $1.50 airport fee on trips entering and leaving Logan. Charging a flat rate is not allowed in the city; the police department publishes a list (available on the Logan website, www.massport.com/logan) of distances to the suburbs that establishes the flat rate for those trips.

BY CAR

If you plan to visit only Boston and Cambridge, *you do not need a car.* With the Big Dig, outrageously expensive parking, and confusing geography, Boston in particular is a motorist's nightmare. If you arrive by car, park at the hotel and walk or use public transit. For day trips, you'll probably want a car (yours or a rental).

RENTALS   The major car-rental firms have offices at Logan Airport and in Boston; some have other area branches. Boston levies a $10 surcharge on car rentals that goes toward the construction of a new convention center. If you're traveling at a busy time, especially during foliage season, reserve well in advance. Most companies set aside cars for nonsmokers, but you have to request one. Most agencies offer shuttle service from the airport to their offices.

Companies with offices at the airport include **Alamo** (ℰ 800/327-9633), **Avis** (ℰ 800/831-2847), **Budget** (ℰ 800/527-0700), **Dollar** (ℰ 800/ 800-4000), **Hertz** (ℰ 800/654-3131), and **National** (ℰ 800/227-7368). **Enterprise** (ℰ 800/325-8007) and **Thrifty** (ℰ 800/367-2277) are nearby but not on the grounds; leave time for the shuttle-bus ride.

PARKING   It's difficult to find your way around Boston and practically impossible to park in some areas. Most spaces on the street are metered (and patrolled until 6pm on the dot Monday through Saturday), have strict time limits, or both. In some areas, parking is allowed only at certain hours. Rates vary (usually $1 an hour downtown); bring plenty of quarters. Time limits range from 15 minutes to 2 hours. The penalty is a $25 ticket, but should you blunder into a tow-away zone, retrieving the car will take at least $100 and a lot of running around. The city tow lot (✆ **617/635-3900**) is at 200 Frontage Rd., South Boston. Take a taxi, or ride the Red Line to Andrew and flag a cab.

It's usually best to leave the car in a garage or lot and walk. A full day at most lots costs no more than $25 (in other words, cheaper than a parking ticket), but some downtown facilities charge as much as $30. Many lots charge a lower flat rate if you enter and exit before certain times or park in the evening. Some restaurants offer discounts at nearby garages; ask when you make reservations.

The reasonably priced city-run **Boston Common Garage,** off Charles Street (✆ **617/954-2096**), accepts vehicles under 6 feet, 3 inches tall. The **Prudential Center Garage** (✆ **617/267-1002**) has entrances on Boylston Street, Huntington Avenue, and Exeter Street, and at the Sheraton Boston Hotel. Parking is discounted if you buy something at the Shops at Prudential Center and have your ticket validated. The **Copley Place Garage,** off Huntington Avenue (✆ **617/375-4488**), offers a similar deal. Many businesses in Faneuil Hall Marketplace validate parking at the **75 State St. Garage** (✆ **617/742-7275**).

Good-size garages downtown are at **Government Center,** off Congress Street (✆ **617/227-0385**); **Sudbury Street** off Congress Street (✆ **617/973-6954**); the **New England Aquarium** (✆ **617/723-1731**); and **Zero Post Office Square,** in the Financial District (✆ **617/423-1430**). In the Back Bay, there's a large garage near the Hynes Convention Center on **Dalton Street** (✆ **617/247-8006**).

DRIVING RULES   When traffic permits, you may turn right at a red light after stopping, unless a sign is posted saying otherwise. Seat belts are mandatory for adults and children, children under 12 may not ride in the front seat, and infants and children under 5 must be in car seats. Two pertinent state laws: Pedestrians in the crosswalk and vehicles already in a rotary (traffic circle or roundabout) have the right of way.

 FAST FACTS: Boston & Cambridge

American Express   The main local office is at 1 State St. (✆ **617/723-8400**), opposite the Old State House. It's open Monday through Friday from 8:30am to 5:30pm. The Back Bay office, 222 Berkeley St. (✆ **617/236-1334**), at Boylston Street, is open Monday through Friday from 9am to 5:30pm. The Cambridge office, 39 John F. Kennedy St., Harvard Square (✆ **617/868-2600**), is open Monday through Friday from 8:30am to 5pm, Saturday from 11am to 5:30pm, and Sunday from noon to 5pm.

Area Code   Eastern Massachusetts has eight area codes, two for each of four regions: Boston proper, **617** and **857**; immediate suburbs, **781** and **339**; northern and western suburbs, **978** and **351**; southern suburbs, **508** and **774**. To complete a local call, no matter the distance, you must dial the whole 10-digit number.

Car Rentals   See "Getting Around," earlier in this chapter.

Dentists   Ask at the front desk of your hotel or try the **Massachusetts Dental Society** (✆ **800/342-8747** or 508/651-7511; www.massdental.org).

Doctors Your hotel concierge should be able to help you. Hospital referral services include **Brigham and Women's** (© 800/294-9999), **Massachusetts General** (© 800/711-4MGH), and **New England Medical Center** (© 617/636-9700). An affiliate of Mass. General, **MGH Back Bay** (formerly the Boston Evening Medical Center), 388 Commonwealth Ave. (© 617/267-7171), offers walk-in service and honors most insurance plans.

Embassies/Consulates See "Fast Facts: For the Foreign Traveler," in chapter 3.

Emergencies Call © **911** for fire, ambulance, or police. For the state police, call © **617/523-1212.**

Hospitals **Massachusetts General Hospital,** 55 Fruit St. (© 617/726-2000), and **New England Medical Center,** 750 Washington St. (© 617/636-5000), are closest to downtown. In Cambridge are **Mount Auburn Hospital,** 330 Mt. Auburn St. (© 617/492-3500), and **Cambridge Hospital,** 1493 Cambridge St. (© 617/498-1000).

Hot Lines AIDS Hotline (© 800/590-2437 or 617/451-5155); Poison Control (© 800/682-9211); Rape Crisis (© 617/492-7273); Travelers Aid Society (© 617/542-7286).

Information See "Visitor Information," earlier in this chapter. For directory assistance, dial © **411.**

Internet Access The ubiquitous **Kinko's** charges 10¢ to 20¢ a minute. Locations include 2 Center Plaza, Government Center (© 617/973-9000); 187 Dartmouth St., Back Bay (© 617/262-6188); and 1 Mifflin Place, off Mount Auburn Street near Eliot Street, Harvard Square (© 617/497-0125).

Liquor Laws The legal drinking age is 21. In many bars, particularly near college campuses, and at sporting events, you may be asked for ID. Retail liquor outlets are closed on Sunday. Some suburban towns, notably Rockport, are "dry."

Newspapers/Magazines The daily papers are the *Boston Globe* and *Boston Herald.* The "Calendar" section of the Thursday *Globe* contains extensive cultural listings. The Friday *Herald* has a similar, smaller insert called "Scene." Both papers briefly list weekend events in their Saturday editions. The arts-oriented *Boston Phoenix,* published on Thursday, has entertainment and restaurant listings.

Where, a free monthly magazine, contains information on shopping, nightlife, attractions, museums, and galleries. Newspaper boxes around both cities dispense the free weeklies *Phoenix* and *Tab* and biweeklies *Improper Bostonian* and *Stuff@Night. Boston* magazine, available at newsstands, is a lifestyle-oriented monthly.

Pharmacies Downtown Boston has no 24-hour drugstore. The pharmacy at the **CVS** in the Porter Square Shopping Center, off Mass. Ave. in Cambridge (© 617/876-5519), is open 24 hours. The **CVS** at 155–157 Charles St. (© 617/523-1028), next to the Charles/MGH Red Line T stop, is open until midnight. Some emergency rooms can fill your prescription at the hospital's pharmacy.

Police Call © **911** for emergencies.

Rest Rooms The visitor center at 15 State St. has public rest rooms, as do most tourist attractions, hotels, department stores, and public buildings.

The CambridgeSide Galleria, Copley Place, Prudential Center, and Quincy Market shopping areas and most Starbucks branches have clean rest rooms. In 2001, Boston announced plans to install free-standing, self-cleaning pay toilets in eight areas downtown, including City Hall Plaza, near the Government Center T. Expected to cost 25¢, they should be in place by the time you read this.

Safety On the whole, Boston and Cambridge are safe cities for walking. As in any urban area, stay out of parks (including Boston Common, the Public Garden, and the Esplanade) at night unless you're in a crowd. Areas to avoid at night include Boylston Street between Tremont and Washington, and Tremont Street from Stuart to Boylston. Try not to walk alone late at night in the Theater District and around North Station. Public transportation is busy and safe, but service stops between 12:30 and 1am.

Taxes The 5% sales tax does not apply to food, prescription drugs, newspapers, or clothing that costs less than $175. The lodging tax in Boston and Cambridge is 12.45%; the tax on meals and takeout food is 5%.

Taxis See "Getting Around," earlier in this chapter.

Transit Info Call ☎ 617/222-3200 for the T (subways, local buses, commuter rail), and ☎ 800/23-LOGAN for MassPort (airport transportation).

3 Accommodations

Boston has one of the busiest hotel markets in the country, with some of the highest prices. The cooling economy may lessen the demand for rooms, but the supply is limited, so you'll still need to do some planning. Rates at most downtown hotels are lower on weekends than on weeknights, when business and convention travelers fill rooms; leisure hotels offer discounts during the week. If you don't mind cold and the possibility of snow, aim for January through March, when you'll find great deals, especially on weekends. It helps to be flexible with scheduling—a hotel that's full of conventioneers one week may be courting business a few days later.

It's always a good idea to make a reservation, especially during fall foliage season. The spring and fall convention seasons, the vacation months of July and August, and college graduation time (May and early June) are busy and crowded, too.

Before you rule out a hotel because of its location, consult a map. Especially downtown, neighborhoods are so small that the borders are somewhat arbitrary. The division to consider is **downtown vs. Back Bay vs. Cambridge** (and not, say, the waterfront vs. the adjoining Financial District). For example, if your interests lie primarily in Cambridge, Back Bay is not the most convenient place to stay. But if you're with a companion whose business is downtown, and you have the Back Bay shopping bug, the Theater District may be a good compromise.

The state **hotel tax** is 5.7%. Boston and Cambridge (like Worcester and Springfield) add a 2.75% convention-center tax to the 4% city tax, bringing the total tax to 12.45%.

The Convention & Visitors Bureau **Hotel Hot Line** (☎ 800/777-6001) can help make reservations even during the busiest times. It's staffed Monday through Friday until 8pm, Saturday and Sunday until 4pm. If you're driving

Boston Accommodations

**Massachusetts
Institute of
Technology**

Vassar St.

Memorial Drive

Amherst Alley

Charles River Basin

Boston City Limits

Harvard Bridge

Longfellow Bridge

Back St.

Beacon St.

Fairfield St.

Gloucester St.

Exeter St.

Marlborough St.

Dartmouth St.

Clarendon St.

Berkeley St.

Memorial Drive

James J. Storrow

Bay State Road

Raleigh St.

Deerfield St.

Charlesgate W.

Charlesgate E.

Hereford St.

Commonwealth Ave.

Newbury St.

Boylston St.

Copley

Copley
Square

St. James Ave.

Boston
Univ.

Kenmore

Kenmore
Square

Hynes/ICA

BACK BAY

Back Bay
Station

←To Brookline

Newbury St.

90

MASS. TPK.

**Fenway
Park**

Van Ness St.

Massachusetts Ave.

Dalton St.

Prudential

Harcourt St.

Garrison St.

Back Bay/
South End

Yarmouth St.

Dartmouth

Holyoke St.

W. Canton St.

Yawkey Wy.

Boylston St.

**Back Bay
Fens**

Norway St.

Burbank St.

Westland Ave.

Huntington Ave.

W. Newton St.

Braddock Pkwy.

Cumberland St.

Greenwich St.

W. Botolph St.

Warren Ave.

W. Brookline

Pembroke St.

Peterborough St.

Queensberry St.

Agassiz Rd.

Symphony Rd.

Gainsborough St.

Symphony

Albemarle St.

Claremont
Pkwy.

Wellington St.

Columbus Ave.

Concord St.

W. Newton St.

W. Springfield St.

Worcester St.

Rutland St.

W. Haven St.

Tremont St.

Newland Pl.

Haven

Park Dr.

Fenway

Hemenway Ave.

Forsyth Way

Spear St. Pl.

Northeastern

Massachusetts Ave.

Museum
Rd.

Museum

Huntington Ave.

Greenleaf
St.

**Northeastern
University**

*Wm. E. Carter
Playground*

Northampton St.

Camden
St.

Cumston St.

2nd St.

1st St.

from the west, stop at the Mass. Pike's Natick rest area and try the **reservation service** at the visitor information center.

BED-AND-BREAKFASTS Call as soon as you start planning your trip, especially if you'll be visiting during foliage season. Most places require a minimum stay of at least 2 nights. The following organizations can help you find a B&B:

- **Bed and Breakfast Agency of Boston** (© **800/248-9262** or 617/720-3540, © **0800/89-5128** from the U.K.; fax 617/523-5761; www.boston-bnbagency.com).
- **Bed and Breakfast Associates Bay Colony Ltd.** (© **800/347-5088** or 781/449-5302; fax 781/449-5958; www.bnbboston.com).
- **Bed & Breakfast Reservations North Shore/Greater Boston/Cape Cod** (© **800/832-2632** outside Mass., © **617/964-1606** or 978/281-9505; fax 978/281-9426; www.bbreserve.com).
- **Host Homes of Boston** (© **800/600-1308** or 617/244-1308; fax 617/244-5156; www.hosthomesofboston.com).
- **New England Bed and Breakfast** (© **617/244-2112**).

THE WATERFRONT & FANEUIL HALL MARKETPLACE

These areas are convenient to the Financial District and other downtown destinations, but not as handy if you plan to spend a lot of time in Back Bay or Cambridge. Remember to **ask for a room on a high floor**—you'll want to be as far as possible from the noise and disarray of the Big Dig.

VERY EXPENSIVE

Boston Harbor Hotel ✦✦✦ The Boston Harbor Hotel is one of the finest in town, an excellent choice for both business and leisure travelers. The 16-story brick building is within walking distance of downtown and the waterfront attractions; the Airport Water Shuttle stops behind the hotel. The plush guest rooms were renovated in 1999 and 2000. Each is a luxurious combination of bedroom and living room, with mahogany furnishings that include an armoire, a desk, and comfortable chairs. Rooms with city views are less expensive than those that face the harbor, but just now we'd opt for the savings and an up-close look at the Big Dig—the water will always be there, but the construction won't. If you don't share our fascination with the project, the best units are suites with private terraces and dazzling water vistas.

Rowes Wharf (entrance on Atlantic Ave.), Boston, MA 02110. © **800/752-7077** or 617/439-7000. Fax 617/330-9450. www.bhh.com. 230 units. $365–$555 double; from $455 suite. Extra person $50. Children under 18 stay free in parents' room. Weekend packages available. AE, DC, DISC, MC, V. Valet parking $28 weekdays, $20 weekends; self-parking $26 weekdays, $15 weekends. T: Red Line to South Station (or Blue Line to Aquarium, if it's open). Pets accepted. **Amenities:** Restaurant (New England), cafe, bar; 60-foot indoor lap pool; well-appointed health club and spa; concierge; courtesy car; state-of-the-art business center; salon; 24-hour room service; in-room massage; baby-sitting available; laundry service; dry cleaning; video rentals. *In room:* A/C, TV, dataport, minibar, hair dryer.

Boston Marriott Long Wharf ✦ The chief appeal of this standard-issue Marriott is its location, a stone's throw from the New England Aquarium. It attracts business travelers with its proximity to the Financial District, and families with its easy access to downtown and waterfront attractions. Guest rooms and bathrooms underwent renovation in 2000 and 2001; each large unit has either one king or two double beds. Big Dig construction is directly under the windows of the rooms near the street. Ask to be as close to the water as possible, and you'll have good views of the wharves and waterfront without the attendant noise.

296 State St. (at Atlantic Ave.), Boston, MA 02109. ✆ **800/228-9290** or 617/227-0800. Fax 617/227-2867. www.marriotthotels.com/BOSLW. 400 units. Apr–Nov $379–$450 double, Dec–Mar $269–$379 double; $450–$490 suite year-round. Weekend packages from $179 per night. AE, DC, DISC, MC, V. Parking $30. T: Blue or Orange Line to State (or Blue Line to Aquarium, if it's open). **Amenities:** Restaurant (seafood), cafe and lounge, bar and grill; indoor pool; exercise room; Jacuzzi; sauna; game room; concierge; business center; room service until 1am; laundry service; dry cleaning. *In room:* A/C, TV, dataport, coffeemaker, hair dryer.

Millennium Bostonian Hotel ★★ The relatively small Bostonian offers excellent service and features that make it competitive with larger hotels. It's popular with business travelers who want a break from convention-oriented giants, and with vacationers who enjoy the boutique atmosphere. The traditionally appointed guest rooms vary in size and contain top-of-the-line furnishings and amenities. They're soundproofed, an important feature in this busy location. Half of the units have French doors that open onto small private balconies; the plushest rooms are good-sized suites with working fireplaces or Jacuzzis. Three brick 19th-century buildings make up the hotel; the 38 units in the new wing, added in 1999, include a suite and four rooms on the glass-enclosed top floor.

At Faneuil Hall Marketplace, 40 North St., Boston, MA 02109. ✆ **800/343-0922** or 617/523-3600. Fax 617/523-2454. www.millennium-hotels.com/boston. 201 units. $245–$420 double; $265–$450 deluxe double; $500–$775 suite. Extra person $20. Children under 18 stay free in parents' room. Weekend and other packages available. AE, DC, DISC, MC, V. Valet parking $30. T: Green or Blue Line to Government Center, or Orange Line to Haymarket. **Amenities:** Restaurant (contemporary American), lounge; access to nearby health club with pool; small fitness room; concierge; morning limo service; secretarial services available; 24-hour-room service; in-room massage; baby-sitting available; laundry service; dry cleaning. *In room:* A/C, TV w/ movies, dataport, minibar, hair dryer, iron, safe, exercise equipment delivery on request.

MODERATE

Harborside Inn ★★ Under the same management as the Newbury Guest House in Back Bay, the Harborside Inn offers a similar combination of location and (for this neighborhood) value. The renovated 1858 warehouse is near Faneuil Hall Marketplace, the harbor, the Financial District, and the Big Dig. The nicely appointed guest rooms have queen-size beds, hardwood floors, Oriental rugs, and Victorian-style furniture. They surround a skylit atrium; city-view units are more expensive but can be noisier. Still, they're preferable to the interior rooms, whose windows open only to the atrium. Units on the top floors of the eight-story building have lower ceilings but better views. Rates include free local phone calls.

185 State St. (between I-93 and the Custom House Tower), Boston, MA 02109. ✆ **617/723-7500.** Fax 617/670-2010. www.hagopianhotels.com. 54 units. $165–$225 double; $215–$325 suite. Extra person $15. Rates may be higher during special events. AE, DC, DISC, MC, V. No parking available. T: Blue or Orange Line to State (or Blue Line to Aquarium, if it's open). **Amenities:** Restaurant (international bistro); access to nearby health club ($15 charge); limited room service; laundry service; dry cleaning. *In room:* A/C, TV, dataport, hair dryer.

AT THE AIRPORT
EXPENSIVE

Hilton Boston Logan Airport ★★ This new (1999) hotel smack in the middle of the airport draws most of its guests from meetings, conventions, and canceled flights. Walkways lead directly to Terminals A (close) and E (distant). The hotel is convenient and well equipped for business travelers, and an excellent fall-back for vacationers who don't mind a short commute to downtown. Guest rooms are large and tastefully furnished; the best units, on higher floors of the 10-story building, afford sensational views. Soundproofing throughout the building is excellent. The closest competition, the Hyatt Harborside, is less convenient to the T but right at the ferry dock.

85 Terminal Rd., Logan International Airport, Boston, MA 02128. (℃ **800/HILTONS** or 617/568-6700. Fax 617/568-6800. www.hilton.com. 599 units. $149–$399 double; from $500 suite. Children under 19 stay free in parents' room. Weekend and other packages from $159 per night. AE, DC, DISC, MC, V. Valet parking $20; self-parking $18. T: Blue Line to Airport, then take shuttle bus. **Amenities:** Restaurant (American), Irish pub, coffee counter; indoor lap pool; health club and spa; 24-hour shuttle bus to airport destinations (including car-rental offices and ferry dock); well-equipped business center; 24-hour room service; laundry service; dry-cleaning. *In room:* A/C, TV, high-speed Internet access, minibar, coffeemaker, hair dryer, iron.

MODERATE

Opened in March 2001, the **Hampton Inn Boston Logan Airport,** 2300 Lee Burbank Hwy., Revere (℃ **800/426-7866** or 781/286-5665; www.hampton-inn.com), is about 3 miles north of the airport. A free shuttle bus serves the 227-room hotel, which has a pool; rates start at about $129 for a double and include continental breakfast.

FINANCIAL DISTRICT
VERY EXPENSIVE

Wyndham Boston ★★   This meticulously designed luxury hotel (a complete rehab of the 1928 Batterymarch Building) opened in 1999. Like other downtown lodgings, it draws business travelers during the week and leisure travelers on weekends. The 14-story building is near Faneuil Hall Marketplace and the waterfront, but not all that close (by downtown standards) to the T. The spacious guest rooms have 9½-foot ceilings that make them feel even larger. The best units, on the upper floors, have great views of the harbor and downtown. Soundproofing throughout makes the whole building exceptionally quiet. The closest competitor, literally and figuratively, is Le Meridien, which is less convenient to public transit but has a swimming pool.

89 Broad St., Boston, MA 02110. (℃ **800/WYNDHAM** or 617/556-0006. Fax 617/556-0053. www.wyndham. com. 362 units. $189–$395 double weekdays, $139–$295 double weekends; $265–$465 suite weekdays, $179–$365 suite weekends. Children under 13 stay free in parents' room. Weekend, holiday, and other packages available. AE, DC, DISC, MC, V. Valet parking $30 weekdays, $16 weekends. T: Blue or Orange Line to State, or Red Line to South Station. **Amenities:** Restaurant (California-Italian), bar; fitness center; sauna; concierge; business center; 24-hour room service; baby-sitting available; laundry service; dry cleaning. *In room:* A/C, TV, high-speed Internet access, minibar, coffeemaker, hair dryer, iron.

DOWNTOWN CROSSING & BEACON HILL

The **Holiday Inn Select Boston Government Center,** 5 Blossom St., at Cambridge Street (℃ **800/HOLIDAY** or 617/742-7630), offers all the features you'd expect of the international chain, including a heated outdoor pool. It was under renovation at press time; be sure to ask for a refurbished room.

VERY EXPENSIVE

Fifteen Beacon ★★   Nonstop pampering, high-tech appointments, and outrageously luxurious rooms make this boutique hotel *the* name to drop with the expense-be-hanged set. The high-flying business clientele appears (at the moment) impervious to the whims of the stock market, and curious leisure travelers have flocked here since the hotel opened in 2000. Management bends over backward to keep them returning, with attentive service and lavish perks—for instance, at check-in, guests receive personalized business cards listing the direct phone and fax numbers they'll have during their stay. The individually decorated rooms are opulent yet understated—no chintz or fussy antiques here. All units contain queen-size canopy beds with Italian linens (300 thread count, of course), surround-sound stereo systems, gas fireplaces, and Kiehl's toiletries and 4-inch TVs in the bathrooms. The lobby restaurant, though overpriced and a bit cramped, is one of the best places in the city to see (or be) movers and shakers, especially at breakfast.

15 Beacon St., Boston, MA 02108. ℭ **877/XV-BEACON** or 617/670-1500. Fax 617/670-2525. www.xvbeacon. com. 61 units. From $395 double. Valet parking available. T: Red or Green Line to Park. **Amenities:** Restaurant (New England/continental), bar; fitness room; access to nearby health club (with Jacuzzi and sauna); concierge; in-town courtesy car; 24-hour room service; massage available; laundry service; dry cleaning. *In room:* A/C, TV w/ movies, fax/copier/printer, high-speed Internet access, minibar, hair dryer, safe.

Swissôtel Boston ★★ *Value*   This centrally located 22-story hotel lives two lives. It's a busy convention and business destination during the week, and the excellent weekend packages make it popular with sightseers. The plain exterior contrasts with the elegant European style and luxurious appointments that take over in the second-floor lobby. Guest rooms cluster around four atriums with semiprivate lobbies, creating the effect of several small hotels in one. Rooms are large enough to hold sitting areas, desks, and settees; they have king or European twin beds. Ask for a room on a high floor; this neighborhood was ugly even before construction on Millennium Place began on nearby Washington Street.

1 Avenue de Lafayette (off Washington St.), Boston, MA 02111. ℭ **888/73-SWISS** or 617/451-2600. Fax 617/451-0054. www.swissotel.com. 501 units. $329–$379 double; $399–$449 deluxe double; $499–$699 suite or Swiss Butler Executive Level; $2,500 Presidential Suite. Extra person $25. Children under 12 stay free in parents' room. Weekend packages from $139 per night. AE, DC, DISC, MC, V. Valet parking $30; self-parking $26. T: Red Line to Downtown Crossing, or Green Line to Boylston. Small pets accepted. **Amenities:** Restaurant (international), lounge; 52-foot indoor pool; health club; sauna; concierge; high-tech business center; 24-hour room service; laundry service; dry cleaning. *In room:* A/C, TV, fax, dataport, minibar, coffeemaker, hair dryer.

EXPENSIVE

Omni Parker House ★   The Parker House offers a great combination of nearly 150 years of history and extensive renovations. It has been in continuous operation longer than any other hotel in America, since 1855. A massive overhaul begun when the detail-oriented Omni chain took over the hotel, upgrading it throughout and adding a business center and exercise facility. Guest rooms aren't huge, but they are thoughtfully laid out and nicely appointed; many have views of Old City Hall or Government Center.

60 School St., Boston, MA 02108. ℭ **800/THE-OMNI** or 617/227-8600. Fax 617/742-5729. www.omnihotels. com. 552 units (some with shower only). $189–$295 double; $249–$375 superior double; $279–$435 one-bedroom suite. Children under 18 stay free in parents' room. Weekend packages available. AE, DC, DISC, MC, V. Valet parking $27; self-parking $20. T: Green or Blue Line to Government Center, or Red Line to Park St. **Amenities:** Restaurant (New England), 2 bars; health club; concierge; staffed business center; 24-hour room service; in-room massage; laundry service; dry cleaning. *In room:* A/C, TV, dataport, minibar, hair dryer, iron.

CHINATOWN/THEATER DISTRICT
EXPENSIVE

Radisson Hotel Boston ★★   The Radisson chain isn't prominent in the Northeast and the location isn't the sexiest, so this hotel can be a pleasant surprise. For starters, its guest rooms are among the largest in the city. Each has a private balcony (with great views from the higher floors), sitting area, and one king or two queen beds. Regular updates since a complete renovation in 1997 have made the hotel as popular with business travelers as it already was with tour groups and families. The best units are the executive-level rooms on the top five floors of the 24-story building.

200 Stuart St. (at Charles St. S.), Boston, MA 02116. © **800/333-3333** or 617/482-1800. Fax 617/451-2750. www.radisson.com/bostonma. 356 units (some with shower only). $159–$359 double. Extra person $20; cot $20; cribs available free. Children under 18 stay free in parents' room. Weekend, theater, and other packages available. AE, DC, DISC, MC, V. Valet parking $21; self-parking $19. T: Green Line to Boylston, or Orange Line to New England Medical Center. **Amenities:** Restaurant (traditional American); cafe; Stuart Street Playhouse (© **617/426-4499**); a small theater that often books one-person shows; heated indoor pool; exercise room; concierge; staffed business center; limited room service; laundry service; dry cleaning. *In room:* A/C, TV, dataport, coffeemaker, hair dryer, iron.

BACK BAY/SOUTH END
VERY EXPENSIVE

The **Ritz-Carlton, Boston** was in transition at press time, preparing to close for extensive renovations that were expected to last nearly a year. The **Ritz-Carlton, Boston Common,** a new 155-room hotel in the Millennium Place development on Washington Street near the Theater District, was scheduled to open in mid-2001. The new location will take up some of the slack until the 278-room Back Bay hotel reopens (in March 2002, if it's on schedule) after a top-to-bottom overhaul. For information on the legendary original or its stylish sibling, call the chain's main number (© **800/241-3333**) or check out **www.ritzcarlton.com**.

Eliot Hotel ★★★   This exquisite hotel combines the flavor of Yankee Boston with European-style service and amenities. On tree-lined Commonwealth Avenue, it feels more like a classy apartment building than a hotel, with a romantic atmosphere that belies the top-notch business features. Every unit is a spacious suite with antique furnishings, traditional English-style chintz fabrics, and authentic botanical prints. French doors separate the living rooms and bedrooms, and bathrooms are outfitted in Italian marble. Many suites have pantries with microwaves. The hotel is near Boston University and MIT (across the river), and the location contrasts pleasantly with the bustle of Newbury Street, a block away.

370 Commonwealth Ave. (at Mass. Ave.), Boston, MA 02215. © **800/44-ELIOT** or 617/267-1607. Fax 617/536-9114. www.eliothotel.com. 95 units. $315–$435 one-bedroom suite for two; $570–$780 two-bedroom suite. Extra person $20. Children under 18 stay free in parents' room. AE, DC, MC, V. Valet parking $28. T: Green Line B, C, or D to Hynes/ICA. Small pets accepted. **Amenities:** Restaurant (New England/French); access to nearby health club; concierge; business center; 24-hour room service; baby-sitting; laundry service; dry cleaning. *In room:* A/C, TV/VCR, fax/copier/printer, high-speed Internet access, minibar, hair dryer.

Fairmont Copley Plaza Hotel ★★   The "grande dame of Boston" is a true grand hotel, an old-fashioned lodging that recalls the days when an out-of-town trip (by train, of course) was an event, not an ordeal. Built in 1912, the six-story Renaissance Revival building faces Copley Square, with Trinity Church and the Boston Public Library on either side. Already known for superb service, the Copley Plaza has enjoyed a renaissance of its own since becoming a Fairmont property in 1996. Extensive renovations included restoration of the spacious guest rooms, which contain reproduction Edwardian antiques. The traditional furnishings reflect the elegance of the opulent public spaces. Rooms that face the lovely square or Clarendon Street afford better views than those that overlook busy Dartmouth Street.

138 St. James Ave., Boston, MA 02116. © **800/441-1414** or 617/267-5300. Fax 617/247-6681. www.fairmont. com. 379 units. From $249 double; from $429 suite. Extra person $30. Weekend and other packages available. AE, DC, MC, V. Valet parking $30. T: Green Line to Copley, or Orange Line to Back Bay. Pets up to 20 lbs. accepted ($25 per day). **Amenities:** 2 restaurants (steakhouse, American), bar, lounge; fitness center; access to nearby health club; concierge; car-rental desk; well-equipped business center; salon; 24-hour room service; in-room massage; baby-sitting; laundry service; dry cleaning. *In room:* A/C, TV/VCR, fax, dataport, minibar, hair dryer, iron.

Four Seasons Hotel ⭐⭐⭐   Many hotels offer exquisite service, a beautiful location, elegant guest rooms and public areas, a terrific health club, and wonderful restaurants. No other hotel in Boston—indeed, in New England—combines every element of a luxury hotel as seamlessly as the Four Seasons. If we were traveling with someone else's credit cards, we'd head straight here. Overlooking the Public Garden, the 16-story brick-and-glass building (the hotel occupies eight stories) incorporates the traditional and the contemporary. Each spacious room is elegantly appointed and has a striking view. The best accommodations overlook the Public Garden; city views from the back of the hotel aren't as desirable but can be engaging, especially from the higher floors. Children receive bedtime snacks and toys, and can ask at the concierge desk for duck food to take to the Public Garden. Small pets even enjoy a special menu and amenities.

200 Boylston St., Boston, MA 02116. ℂ 800/332-3442 or 617/338-4400. Fax 617/423-0154. www. fourseasons.com. 274 units. $535–$775 double; $1,450–$1,950 one-bedroom suite; $2,050–$2,300 two-bedroom suite. Weekend packages available. AE, DC, DISC, MC, V. Valet parking $27. T: Green Line to Arlington. Pets accepted. **Amenities:** Restaurant (see Aujourd'hui in "Dining," below), lounge; heated 51-foot pool and whirlpool; well-equipped health club and spa; concierge; limo to downtown; excellent business center; 24-hour room service; in-room massage; baby-sitting; laundry service; dry cleaning. *In room:* A/C, TV/VCR with free videos, fax, high-speed Internet access, minibar, hair dryer, safe.

EXPENSIVE

Hilton Boston Back Bay ⭐⭐   Across the street from the Prudential Center complex, the Hilton is primarily a business hotel, but vacationing families also find it convenient and comfortable. A recently completed $19-million renovation added 44 executive units and spruced up the entire 26-story tower. Rooms are large, soundproofed, and furnished in modern style. The weekend packages, especially in winter, can be a great deal. The closest competitor is the Sheraton, across the street. It's three times the Hilton's size (which generally means less personalized service), has a better pool, and books more vacation and function business.

40 Dalton St., Boston, MA 02115. ℂ 800/874-0663, 800/HILTONS, or 617/236-1100. Fax 617/867-6104. www.hilton.com. 385 units (some with shower only). $179–$295 double; $450 minisuite; $650 one-bedroom suite; $850 two-bedroom suite. Packages and AAA discount available. Extra person $20; rollaway $20. Children stay free in parents' room. AE, DC, DISC, MC, V. Valet parking $24; self-parking $17. T: Green Line B, C, or D to Hynes/ICA. Small pets accepted. **Amenities:** Restaurant (steakhouse); bar; nightclub; heated indoor pool; well-equipped fitness center; business center; concierge; room service until 1am; laundry service; dry cleaning. *In room:* A/C, TV, dataport, coffeemaker, hair dryer, iron.

Sheraton Boston Hotel ⭐⭐   Its central location, range of accommodations, lavish convention and function facilities, and huge pool make this newly refurbished 29-story hotel one of the most popular in the city. It attracts both business and leisure travelers with direct access to the Hynes Convention Center and the Prudential Center complex; because it's so big, it often has rooms available when smaller properties are full. A $100-million overhaul completed in 2001 upgraded the entire property, including the lobby and meeting facilities. The fairly large guest rooms are decorated in sleek contemporary style. Units on higher floors afford gorgeous views, especially to the west and north.

39 Dalton St., Boston, MA 02199. ℂ 800/325-3535 or 617/236-2000. Fax 617/236-1702. www. sheraton.com. 1,215 units. $149–$369 double; from $400 suite. Children under 17 stay free in parents' room. Weekend packages available. 25% discount for students, faculty, and retired persons with ID, depending on availability. AE, DC, DISC, MC, V. Valet $28; self-parking $25. T: Green Line E to Prudential, or B, C, or D to Hynes/ICA. Small pets accepted. **Amenities:** Restaurant (New England), lounge; heated indoor/outdoor pool; well-equipped health club; Jacuzzi; sauna; concierge; car-rental desk; courtesy car; 24-hour room service; in-room massage; laundry service; dry cleaning. *In room:* A/C, TV, dataport, coffeemaker, hair dryer, iron.

Westin Copley Place Boston ★★   Towering 36 stories in the air above Copley Square, the Westin attracts conventiongoers, sightseers, and dedicated shoppers. Skybridges link the hotel to Copley Place and the Prudential Center complex, and Copley Square is across the street from the pedestrian entrance. The multilingual staff emphasizes quick check-in. The spacious guest rooms—all on the eighth floor or higher—have traditional oak and mahogany furniture, two phones, and windows that open. They're scheduled to be spruced up and outfitted with even more comfortable beds by early 2001. But you might not even notice at first, because you'll be captivated by the view. Qualms you might have had about choosing a huge chain hotel will fade as you survey downtown Boston, the airport and harbor, or the Charles River and Cambridge.

10 Huntington Ave., Boston, MA 02116. ℂ **800/WESTIN-1** or 617/262-9600. Fax 617/424-7483. www.westin.com. 800 units. $229–$499 double; $269–$2,200 suite. Extra person from $25. Weekend packages available. AE, DC, DISC, MC, V. Valet parking $28. T: Green Line to Copley, or Orange Line to Back Bay. Pets under 20 lbs. accepted. **Amenities:** 2 restaurants (steakhouse, seafood), bar; indoor pool; health club; sauna; concierge; tour desk; car-rental desk; well-equipped business center; 24-hour room service; laundry service; dry cleaning. *In room:* A/C, TV, dataport, minibar, coffeemaker, hair dryer, safe.

MODERATE

Chandler Inn Hotel ★ *Value*   The Chandler Inn is a bargain for its location, just 2 blocks from Back Bay. It underwent $1 million in renovations in 2000, and even with the accompanying price hike, the comfortable, unpretentious hotel is a deal. The revamped guest rooms have individual climate controls and tasteful contemporary-style furniture, including desks, small wardrobes, and TV armoires. Each holds either a queen or double bed or two twin beds, without enough room to squeeze in a cot. Bathrooms are tiny, and the one elevator in the eight-story inn can be slow, but the staff is welcoming and helpful. This is a gay-friendly hotel—Fritz, the bar next to the lobby, is a neighborhood hangout—that often books up early. Plan ahead.

26 Chandler St. (at Berkeley St.), Boston, MA 02116. ℂ **800/842-3450** or 617/482-3450. Fax 617/542-3428. www.chandlerinn.com. 56 units. Apr–Dec $145–$155 double; Jan–Mar $125–$135 double. Rates include continental breakfast. Children under 12 stay free in parent's room. AE, DC, DISC, MC, V. No parking available. T: Orange Line to Back Bay. Pets accepted with prior approval. *In room:* A/C, TV, hair dryer.

The MidTown Hotel ★★ *Value*   Even without free parking and a pool (open seasonally), this centrally located two-story hotel would be a good deal for families and budget-conscious businesspeople; it also books a lot of tour groups. It's on a busy street within easy walking distance of Symphony Hall and the Museum of Fine Arts. The well-maintained rooms are large, bright, and attractively outfitted, although bathrooms are on the small side. Some units have connecting doors that allow families to spread out. The best rooms are on the side of the building that faces away from Huntington Avenue. For business travelers, many rooms have two-line phones; photocopying and fax services are available at the front desk.

220 Huntington Ave., Boston, MA 02115. ℂ **800/343-1177** or 617/262-1000. Fax 617/262-8739. www. midtownhotel.com. 159 units. Apr–Aug $149–$209 double; Sept to mid-Dec $189–$269, mid-Dec to Mar $119–$169. Extra person $15. Children under 18 stay free in parents' room. AAA, AARP, and government employees' discount available, subject to availability. AE, DC, DISC, MC, V. Free parking. T: Green Line E to Prudential, or Orange Line to Mass. Ave. **Amenities:** Restaurant (breakfast only); heated outdoor pool (seasonal); baby-sitting; dry cleaning; video rentals. *In room:* A/C, TV, high-speed Internet access, coffeemaker, hair dryer.

Newbury Guest House ★★ *Value*   After just a little shopping in Back Bay, you'll appreciate what a find this cozy inn is: a bargain on Newbury Street. It's a pair of brick town houses built in the 1880s and combined into a refined guesthouse. It offers comfortable furnishings, a pleasant staff, nifty architectural details, and a buffet breakfast served in the ground-level dining room, which adjoins a brick patio. Rooms are modest in size, but nicely appointed and well maintained. The Hagopian family opened the B&B in 1991, and it operates near capacity all year, drawing business travelers during the week and sightseers on weekends. At these prices in this location, there's only one caveat: Reserve early.

261 Newbury St. (between Fairfield and Gloucester sts.), Boston, MA 02116. © 617/437-7666. Fax 617/ 262-4243. www.hagopianhotels.com. 32 units (some with shower only). Winter $115–$160 double; rest of year $125–$170. Extra person $15. Rates include continental breakfast. Rates may be higher during special events. 2-night minimum stay on weekends. AE, DC, DISC, MC, V. Parking $15 (reservation required). T: Green Line B, C, or D to Hynes/ICA. *In room:* A/C, TV, hair dryer.

INEXPENSIVE

Hostelling International–Boston   This hostel near the Berklee College of Music and Symphony Hall caters to students, youth groups, and other travelers in search of comfortable, no-frills lodging. Accommodations are dorm-style, with three to six beds per room. It has two full dine-in kitchens, 19 bathrooms, and a large common room. The recently remodeled public areas contain meeting and workshop space. The hostel provides a "sheet sleeping sack," or you can bring your own; sleeping bags are not permitted. The enthusiastic staff organizes free and inexpensive cultural, educational, and recreational programs. The first-floor rooms and bathrooms are wheelchair accessible, and there's a wheelchair lift at the building entrance.

Note: To get a bed in summer, you must be a member of Hostelling International–American Youth Hostels. For information, contact HI–AYH, P.O. Box 37613, Washington, DC 20013 (© 202/783-6161; www.hiayh.org). If you are not a U.S. citizen, apply to your home country's hostelling association.

12 Hemenway St., Boston, MA 02115. © 888/HOST222 or 617/536-9455. Fax 617/424-6558. www. bostonhostel.org. 205 beds. Members $24 per bed; nonmembers $27 per bed. MC, V. T: Green Line B, C, or D to Hynes/ICA. **Amenities:** Coin-op laundry. *In room:* No phone.

OUTSKIRTS & BROOKLINE

Staying in this area means becoming a commuter to downtown Boston (unless you're in town only to visit Fenway Park or the Longwood Medical Area). It's not a great choice if your destination is Cambridge, due to the unwieldy public transit connections.

EXPENSIVE

Doubletree Guest Suites ★★ *Value*   This hotel is one of the best deals in town—every unit is a two-room suite with a living room, bedroom, and bathroom. Business travelers can entertain in their rooms, and families can spread out. Overlooking the Charles River, the hotel is near Cambridge and the recreational path along the river, although not in an actual neighborhood. There's complimentary van service to and from attractions and business areas in Boston and Cambridge, making the somewhat inconvenient location easier to handle. The large, attractively furnished suites surround a 15-story atrium. Most bedrooms have a king-size bed and writing desk. Each living room contains a full-size sofa bed, a dining table, and a good-size refrigerator. The Hyatt Regency Cambridge, the hotel's nearest rival, is more convenient but generally more expensive.

400 Soldiers Field Rd., Boston, MA 02134. © **800/222-TREE** or 617/783-0090. Fax 617/783-0897. www.
doubletreehotels.com. 308 units. $139–$259 double. Extra person $20. Children under 18 stay free in par-
ents' room. Weekend packages $154–$264. AARP and AAA discounts available. AE, DC, DISC, MC, V. Parking
$15–$18. **Amenities:** Restaurant (American), lounge, Scullers Jazz Club (see below); heated indoor pool;
exercise room; whirlpool; sauna; concierge; car-rental desk; van service; business center; 24-hour room service; baby-sitting; coin-op laundry; laundry service; dry cleaning. *In room:* A/C, TV, minibar, coffeemaker.

MODERATE
Many options in this price range and area are chain hotels, including the **Holi-
day Inn Boston Brookline,** 1200 Beacon St., Brookline (© **800/HOLIDAY** or
617/277-1200); the **Howard Johnson Hotel Kenmore,** 575 Commonwealth
Ave., Boston (© **800/654-2000** or 617/267-3100); and the **Howard Johnson
Inn,** 1271 Boylston St., Boston (© **800/654-2000** or 617/267-8300).

INEXPENSIVE
Anthony's Town House   The Anthony family has operated this four-story
brownstone guesthouse since 1944, and a stay here feels like a night at
Grandma's. Many patrons are Europeans accustomed to guesthouse accommodations with shared bathrooms, but budget-minded Americans won't be disappointed. Each floor has three high-ceilinged rooms furnished in Queen Anne or
Victorian style, and a bathroom with enclosed shower. Smaller rooms (one per
floor) have twin beds; the large front rooms have bay windows. Guests have the
use of two refrigerators. The guesthouse is 1 mile from Kenmore Square, about
15 minutes from downtown by subway, and 2 blocks from a busy commercial
strip.

1085 Beacon St., Brookline, MA 02446. © **617/566-3972.** Fax 617/232-1085. www.anthonystownhouse.
com. 12 units (none with private bathroom). $68–$98 double. Extra person $10. Weekly rates and winter dis-
counts available. No credit cards. Limited free parking. T: Green Line C to Hawes St. *In room:* A/C, TV, hair
dryer, no phone.

Longwood Inn   In a residential area 3 blocks from the Boston–Brookline border, this three-story Victorian guesthouse offers comfortable accommodations at
modest rates. Guests have the use of a fully equipped kitchen, common dining
room, and TV lounge. There's one apartment with a private bathroom, kitchen,
and balcony. Tennis courts, a running track, and a playground at the school next
door are open to the public. Public transportation is easily accessible, and the
Longwood Medical Area and busy Coolidge Corner neighborhood are within
walking distance.

123 Longwood Ave., Brookline, MA 02446. © **617/566-8615.** Fax 617/738-1070. http://go.boston.
com/longwoodinn. 22 units, 17 with bathroom (some with shower only). Apr–Nov $79–$109 double,
Dec–Mar $65–$89 double; $89–$119 one-bedroom apt (sleeps four or more). Weekly rates available. No
credit cards. Free parking. T: Green Line D to Longwood, or C to Coolidge Corner. **Amenities:** Coin-op laundry. *In room:* A/C.

CAMBRIDGE
VERY EXPENSIVE
The Charles Hotel ★★★   This nine-story brick hotel a block from Harvard
Square has been *the* place for business and leisure travelers to Cambridge since
it opened in 1985. Much of its fame derives from its excellent restaurants, jazz
bar, and day spa, and the service is, if anything, equally exalted. In the posh
guest rooms, the style is contemporary country, with custom adaptations of
Early American Shaker furniture. The austere design contrasts with the indul-
gent amenities, which include down quilts and state-of-the-art Bose Wave
radios; bathrooms contain telephones and TVs.

1 Bennett St., Cambridge, MA 02138. © **800/882-1818** outside Mass., or © **617/864-1200.** Fax 617/864-5715. www.charleshotel.com. 293 units. $380–$460 double; $500–$3,000 suite. Extra person $20. Weekend packages available. AE, DC, MC, V. Valet and self-parking $20. T: Red Line to Harvard. Pets accepted. **Amenities:** 2 restaurants (including Rialto, see below), bar, Regattabar jazz club (see below); access to adjacent health club (with glass-enclosed pool, Jacuzzi, and exercise room); access to adjacent spa and salon; concierge; car-rental desk; business center; 24-hour room service; in-room massage; baby-sitting; laundry service; same-day dry cleaning; video rentals. *In room:* A/C, TV, high-speed Internet access, minibar, hair dryer, iron.

Royal Sonesta Hotel ★★ *(Kids)*   This luxurious hotel is in a curious location—it's close to only a few things but convenient to everything, making it a good choice for both businesspeople and families. The CambridgeSide Galleria mall is across the street, and the Museum of Science is around the corner on the bridge to Boston, which is closer than Harvard Square. In the other direction, MIT and the techno hotbed of Kendall Square are 10 minutes away on foot. Most of the spacious rooms have lovely views of the river or the city (higher prices are for better views). Everything is custom designed and renovated regularly—all units have been completely revamped in the past 5 years. Original contemporary artwork, including pieces by Andy Warhol and Frank Stella, hangs throughout the public spaces and guest rooms.

5 Cambridge Pkwy., Cambridge, MA 02142. © **800/SONESTA** or 617/806-4200. Fax 617/806-4232. www.sonesta.com/boston. 400 units. $239–$279 standard double, $259–$299 superior double, $279–$319 deluxe double; $329–$950 suite. Extra person $25. Children under 18 stay free in parents' room. Weekend and other packages available. AE, DC, DISC, MC, V. Valet parking $20; self-parking $18. T: Green Line to Lechmere; 10-min. walk. Pets accepted with prior approval. **Amenities:** Restaurant (northern Italian), cafe; heated indoor/outdoor pool with retractable roof; well-equipped health club and spa; business center; concierge; room service until 1am; laundry service; dry cleaning. *In room:* A/C, TV, high-speed Internet access, minibar, coffeemaker, hair dryer, safe.

EXPENSIVE

The Inn at Harvard ★★   At first glance, the red-brick Inn at Harvard looks almost like a college dorm—it's adjacent to Harvard Yard, and its Georgian-style architecture would fit nicely on campus. Inside, there's no mistaking it for anything other than an elegant hotel, popular with business travelers and university visitors. The elegantly decorated guest rooms have cherry furniture; each holds a lounge chair or two armchairs around a table, a work area, and an original painting from the Fogg Art Museum. Some units have dormer windows and window seats. The four-story skylit atrium holds the "living room," a huge, well-appointed guest lounge that's suitable for meeting with a visitor if you don't want to conduct business in your room.

1201 Mass. Ave. (at Quincy St.), Cambridge, MA 02138. © **800/458-5886** or 617/491-2222. Fax 617/491-6520. www.theinnatharvard.com. 109 units (some with shower only). $199–$359 double; $650 presidential suite. Extra person $10. Children under 19 stay free in parents' room. Packages and senior, AAA, and AARP discounts available. AE, DC, DISC, MC, V. Valet parking $30. T: Red Line to Harvard. **Amenities:** Restaurant (New England), dining privileges at the nearby Harvard Faculty Club; access to nearby health club; concierge; car-rental desk; limited room service; laundry service; dry cleaning. *In room:* A/C, TV, dataport, hair dryer.

Sheraton Commander Hotel ★   This six-story hotel in the heart of Cambridge's historic district opened in 1927, and it's exactly what you'd expect of a traditional hostelry within sight of the Harvard campus. The colonial-style decor begins in the elegant lobby and extends to the decent-size guest rooms, which are attractively furnished and well maintained. Ask the pleasant front-desk staff for a room facing Cambridge Common; even if you aren't on a (relatively) high floor, you'll have a decent view. Suites have two TVs, and some have

Cambridge Accommodations & Dining

To Ⓣ Davis

Porter Square Ⓣ

Harvard Square

Harvard Ⓣ

HARVARD UNIVERSITY

Widener Library

Longfellow House

Cambridge Common

Radcliffe College

Fresh Pond

Mt. Auburn Cemetery

Cambridge Cemetery

Charles River

Soldiers Field/ Harvard Stadium

Anderson Bridge

Harvard Business School

Western Ave. Bridge

River St. Bridge

Magazine Beach

Memorial Drive

ACCOMMODATIONS ■

Best Western
  Homestead Inn **1**
A Cambridge House
  Bed & Breakfast Inn **2**
The Charles Hotel **5**
Harvard Square Hotel **7**
Holiday Inn Express
  Hotel and Suites **18**
The Inn at Harvard **10**
Royal Sonesta Hotel **16**
Sheraton Commander Hotel **4**

DINING ◆

The Blue Room **14**
Border Cafe **8**
Dalí **11**
The Helmand **17**
Legal Sea Foods **15**
Mr. Bartley's Burger
  Cottage **9**
Oleana **13**
Rialto **6**
S&S Restaurant **12**
Tea-Tray in the Sky **3**

wet bars, refrigerators, and whirlpools. The Sheraton Commander doesn't have the cachet and amenities of the Charles—but with the money you save, you can buy your own cachet.

16 Garden St., Cambridge, MA 02138. © **800/325-3535** or 617/547-4800. Fax 617/868-8322. www. sheratoncommander.com. 175 units. $139–$385 double; $295–$750 suite. Extra person $20. Children under 18 stay free in parents' room. Weekend packages and AAA and AARP discounts available. AE, DC, DISC, MC, V. Valet parking $18. T: Red Line to Harvard. **Amenities:** Restaurant and cafe (American); small fitness center; concierge; limited room service; baby-sitting; laundry room; laundry service; dry cleaning. *In room:* A/C, TV, dataport, coffeemaker, hair dryer, iron.

MODERATE

The **Holiday Inn Express Hotel and Suites,** 250 Msgr. O'Brien Hwy., Cambridge (© **888/887-7690** or 617/577-7600; fax 617/354-1313; www. bristolhotels.com), is a limited-service lodging on a busy street a 5-minute walk from Lechmere station on the Green Line. The neighborhood is busy and noisy, but the hotel is convenient.

Best Western Homestead Inn 🌟 The busy commercial neighborhood is no prize, but this four-story motel is comfortable and convenient for motorists. Guest rooms are spacious, with contemporary or reproduction colonial furnishings, and are at least one floor up from the busy street. The pool and free parking and breakfast help make up for the less-than-scenic location, and a 2½-mile jogging trail around Fresh Pond is across the street. There's a restaurant next door, and a shopping center with a 10-screen movie theater nearby. Boston is about a 15-minute drive or a 30-minute T ride away; Lexington and Concord are less than 30 minutes away by car.

220 Alewife Brook Pkwy., Cambridge, MA 02138. © **800/491-4914** or 617/491-8000. Fax 617/491-4932. www.bwhomestead.com. 69 units. Mid-Mar to Oct $129–$219 double; Nov to mid-Mar $129–$159 double. Extra person $10. Rates include continental breakfast. Rates may be higher during special events. Children under 16 stay free in parents' room. AE, DC, MC, V. Free parking. T: Red Line to Alewife, 10-min. walk. **Amenities:** Indoor pool; Jacuzzi; access to nearby health club; dry cleaning. *In room:* A/C, TV, fax, dataport, coffeemaker, hair dryer, iron.

A Cambridge House Bed & Breakfast Inn 🌟🌟 A Cambridge House feels almost like a country inn, but is on a busy stretch of Cambridge's main street (Mass. Ave.), set back from the sidewalk by a lawn. The three-story building is a beautifully restored 1892 Victorian. The well-maintained rooms vary widely in size; they're warmly decorated with Waverly–Schumacher fabrics and period antiques. Most contain fireplaces and four-poster canopy beds with down comforters. The best units face away from the street. The inn serves a generous breakfast and afternoon refreshments.

2218 Mass. Ave., Cambridge, MA 02140. © **800/232-9989** or 617/491-6300, or 800/96-2079 in the U.K. Fax 617/868-2848. www.acambridgehouse.com. 15 units (some with shower only). $139–$350 double. Extra person $35. Rates include buffet breakfast. AE, DISC, MC, V. Free parking. T: Red Line to Porter. **Amenities:** Concierge. *In room:* A/C, TV, fax, dataport, hair dryer.

Harvard Square Hotel 🌟 Smack in the middle of Harvard Square, this six-story brick hotel is a favorite with visiting parents and budget-conscious business travelers. The unpretentious guest rooms were renovated in early 2000 and outfitted with new furniture and carpeting. They're relatively small but comfortable; some overlook Harvard Square. The front desk handles fax and copy services.

110 Mount Auburn St., Cambridge, MA 02138. © **800/458-5886** or 617/864-5200. Fax 617/864-2409. www.doubletreehotels.com. 73 units. $129–$209 double. Extra person $10. Children under 17 stay free in

parents' room. Corporate rates and AAA and AARP discounts available. AE, DC, DISC, MC, V. Parking $20. T: Red Line to Harvard. **Amenities:** Dining privileges at the Harvard Faculty Club; car-rental desk; laundry service; dry cleaning. *In room:* A/C, TV, dataport, fridge, hair dryer, iron.

4 Dining

Travelers from around the world relish the variety of skillfully prepared seafood available in the Boston area. Lunch is an excellent, economical way to check out a fancy restaurant without breaking the bank. At restaurants that accept reservations, it's always a good idea to make them, particularly for dinner.

WATERFRONT
EXPENSIVE

The **Legal Sea Foods,** at 255 State St. (℮ **617/227-3115**), sits, somewhat disconcertingly, across from the New England Aquarium. See "Back Bay," below.

Sel de la Terre ★★ PROVENÇAL   Side-by-side with the Big Dig, Sel de la Terre is a peaceful taste of southern France. The subtly flavorful food—scallops handled so gently that they're still sweet, juicy roasted chicken, haddock infused with rosemary—relies on fresh local ingredients. The relaxing atmosphere belies the mayhem outside as well as the go-go business-lunch crowd (dinner is calmer). The unusual pricing structure feels like a deal when you're tucking into a generous portion of roasted lamb, less of a bargain if you're eating pasta. Whatever you're eating, try the sublime pommes frites. There's a boulangerie at the entrance, which is handy, because the breads are out of this world.

255 State St. ℮ **617/720-1300.** www.seldelaterre.com. Reservations recommended. Main courses $14 lunch, $21 dinner. Children's menu $7. AE, DISC, MC, V. Daily 11:30am–2:30pm and 5:30–10pm. T: Orange or Blue Line to State (or Blue Line to Aquarium, if it's open).

MODERATE

Billy Tse Restaurant CHINESE/PAN-ASIAN/SUSHI   This casual, affordable spot on the edge of the Italian North End serves excellent renditions of the usual Chinese dishes and especially good fresh seafood. The Thai- and Vietnamese-influenced pan-Asian selections are just as enjoyable. Main dishes range from seven kinds of fried rice to the house special noodles, topped with shrimp, calamari, and scallops in a scrumptious sauce. Lunch specials, served until 4pm, include vegetable fried rice or vegetable lo mein.

240 Commercial St. ℮ **617/227-9990.** Reservations recommended at dinner on weekends. Main courses $5–$20; lunch specials $5.50–$7.50. AE, DC, DISC, MC, V. Mon–Thurs 11:30am–11:30pm; Fri–Sat 11:30am–midnight; Sun 11:30am–11pm. T: Green or Orange Line to Haymarket (or Blue Line to Aquarium, if it's open).

THE NORTH END & CHARLESTOWN

Many North End restaurants don't serve dessert, but you can satisfy your sweet tooth at a *caffè.* Our favorites include **Caffè dello Sport,** 308 Hanover St., and **Caffè Vittoria,** 296 Hanover St. There's also table service at **Mike's Pastry,** 300 Hanover St., which is better known for its bustling take-out business.

VERY EXPENSIVE

Mamma Maria ★★★ NORTHERN ITALIAN   In a town house overlooking North Square and the Paul Revere House, this traditional-looking restaurant offers innovative seasonal cuisine and a level of sophistication that's unusual for the casual North End. The excellent entrees are unlike anything else in this neighborhood, except in size—portions are more than generous. Fork-tender osso buco, a limited-quantity nightly special, is almost enough for two, but

Boston Dining

Aujourd'hui **13**
The Bay Tower **23**
Billy Tse Restaurant **28**
Brasserie Jo **6**
Buddha's Delight **15**
Café Jaffa **4**
Caffè dello Sport **34**
Caffè Vittoria **33**
China Pearl **17**
Cosí Sandwich Bar (Federal St.) **20**
Cosí Sandwich Bar (Milk St.) **21**
Cosí Sandwich Bar (State St.) **22**
Daily Catch **30**
Durgin-Park **26**
The Elephant Walk **1**
Empire Garden Restaurant **16**
Galleria Umberto **36**
Giacomo's Ristorante **37**
Golden Palace Restaurant **18**
Grillfish **11**

Grill 23 & Bar **12**
Hamersley's Bistro **8**
Icarus **10**
La Summa **31**
Legal Sea Foods (Copley Place) **7**
Legal Sea Foods (Park Square) **14**
Legal Sea Foods (Prudential Center) **3**
Legal Sea Foods (Waterfront) **25**
Le Gamin Café **9**
Les Zygomates **19**
Mamma Maria **29**
Mike's Pastry **32**
Olives **39**
Piccola Venezia **35**
Pizzeria Regina **38**
Sel de la Terre **24**
Tapéo **5**
Top of the Hub **2**
Ye Olde Union Oyster House **27**

you'll want it all for yourself. You can't go wrong with main-course pastas, either, and the fresh seafood specials are uniformly marvelous. The pasta, bread, and desserts are homemade, and the shadowy, whitewashed rooms make this a popular spot for getting engaged.

3 North Sq. ✆ 617/523-0077. www.mammamaria.com. Reservations recommended. Main courses $19–$35. AE, DC, DISC, MC, V. Sun–Thurs 5–9:30pm; Fri–Sat 5–10:30pm. Closed 1 week in Jan. Valet parking available. T: Green or Orange Line to Haymarket.

Olives ★★ ECLECTIC   This informal bistro, the flagship of celebrity chef Todd English's growing empire, is a perennial hotspot with an infuriating reservations policy. A line often forms shortly after 5pm; if you don't arrive by 5:45pm, expect the charm-free front-desk staff to send you away for at least 2 hours. Once you're seated, you'll find the noise level high, the service uneven, and the ravenous customers festive. Happily, the food is worth the ordeal. "Olives Classics" on the regularly changing menu include a delicious tart of olives, caramelized onions, and anchovies, and spit-roasted chicken flavored with herbs and garlic over mashed potatoes. Grilling is a justifiably popular technique—yellowfin tuna, atop parsley mashed potatoes and accented with perfect mussels, holds up beautifully, and any lamb dish is sure to please. When you order your entree, the server will ask if you want falling chocolate cake for dessert. Say yes.

10 City Sq. ✆ **617/242-1999.** Reservations accepted for parties of six or more. Main courses $19–$32. AE, DC, MC, V. Mon–Fri 5:30–10pm; Sat 5–10:30pm. Valet parking available. T: Orange or Green Line to North Station; 15-min. walk.

MODERATE

Daily Catch ★ SOUTHERN ITALIAN/SEAFOOD   This storefront restaurant is about the size of a large kitchen (it seats just 20), but it packs a wallop—of garlic. It's a North End classic, with excellent food, chummy service, and very little elbowroom. The surprisingly varied menu includes Sicilian-style calamari (squid stuffed with bread crumbs, raisins, pine nuts, parsley, and garlic), fresh clams, squid-ink pasta puttanesca, and a variety of broiled, fried, and sautéed fish and shellfish. Calamari comes any number of ways—even the garlic-and-oil pasta sauce has ground-up squid in it. Fried calamari makes an excellent appetizer. All food is prepared to order, and some dishes are served in the frying pans in which they were cooked.

323 Hanover St. ✆ **617/523-8567.** www.dailycatch.com. Reservations not accepted. Main courses $12–$19. No credit cards. Sun–Thurs 11:30am–10pm; Fri–Sat 11:30am–11pm. T: Green or Orange Line to Haymarket.

Giacomo's Ristorante ★★ ITALIAN/SEAFOOD   The line snakes out the door and down the street, especially on weekends. No reservations, cash only, a tiny dining room with an open kitchen—what's the secret? Terrific food, plenty of it, and the we're-all-in-this-together atmosphere. To start, try fried calamari or mozzarella with excellent marinara sauce. Take the chef's advice or put together your own main dish from the list of daily ingredients on a board on the wall. The best suggestion is salmon and sun-dried tomatoes in tomato cream sauce over fettuccine. Nonseafood offerings such as butternut-squash ravioli are equally memorable. Service is friendly but incredibly swift. After a 40-minute dinner, dessert at a caffè is practically a necessity.

355 Hanover St. ✆ **617/523-9026.** Reservations not accepted. Main courses $11–$22. No credit cards. Mon–Thurs 5–10pm; Fri–Sat 5–10:30pm; Sun 4–10pm. T: Green or Orange Line to Haymarket.

La Summa ⚜ SOUTHERN ITALIAN Away from the restaurant rows of Hanover and Salem streets, La Summa maintains a cozy neighborhood atmosphere. It's worth seeking out for wonderful homemade pasta and desserts; the more elaborate entrees are scrumptious, too. Try any seafood special, lobster ravioli, *pappardelle e melanzane* (eggplant strips tossed with ethereal fresh pasta), or the aptly named "house special"—veal, chicken, sausage, shrimp, artichokes, pepperoncini, olives, and mushrooms in white-wine sauce. Desserts, especially tiramisu, are terrific.

30 Fleet St. ⓒ **617/523-9503.** Reservations recommended. Main courses $11–$21. AE, DC, DISC, MC, V. Mon–Sat 4:30–10:30pm; Sun 2–10:30pm. T: Green or Orange Line to Haymarket. ITALIAN.

Piccola Venezia Piccola Venezia's glass front wall faces the Freedom Trail—a touristy location with a neighborhood feel. Portions are large and the homey food tends to be heavy on red sauce; more sophisticated dishes are available, often as daily specials. Spaghetti and meatballs, chicken parmigiana, eggplant rolatini, and pasta puttanesca are always on the menu. This is a good place to try traditional Italian-American favorites such as polenta (home-style, not the yuppie croutons available at so many other places), *baccala* (reconstituted salt cod), or the house specialty, tripe.

263 Hanover St. ⓒ **617/523-3888.** Reservations recommended at dinner. Main courses $10–$20; lunch specials $5–$8. AE, DISC, MC, V. Daily 11am–10pm (lunch Mon–Fri until 4pm). T: Green or Orange Line to Haymarket.

INEXPENSIVE

An excellent eat-and-run spot just off the Freedom Trail is the cafeteria-style **Galleria Umberto,** 289 Hanover St. (ⓒ **617/227-5709**). Join the line for fresh, tasty, cheap pizza, *arancini* (a rice ball filled with ground beef, peas, and cheese), potato croquettes, or calzones—ham and cheese, spinach, spinach and cheese, or spinach and sausage. Lunch is served Monday through Saturday; cash only.

Pizzeria Regina ⚜⚜ PIZZA Regina's may look like a movie set, but it's the real thing. Busy waitresses weave through the boisterous dining room, delivering peerless pizza steaming hot from the brick oven. Nouveau ingredients like sun-dried tomatoes appear on the list of toppings, but that's not authentic. House-made sausage, maybe some pepperoni, and a couple of beers—now, *that's* authentic.

⌒*Overrated* **Sky-High Dining: The Lowdown**

First, a disclaimer: This is not to disparage the food at either of the following elegant places, which is quite good. But the fact is, you're paying for the view. Make a reservation, and if you can't get a table *by the window* (the odds are better at the Bay Tower), have a drink in the lounge, then eat somewhere else.

The **Bay Tower** (ⓒ **617/723-1666**; www.baytower.com) is on the 33rd floor of 60 State St., overlooking Faneuil Hall Marketplace, the waterfront, and the airport. It serves international fusion cuisine at dinner Monday through Saturday. The service and desserts are exquisite.

Top of the Hub (ⓒ **617/536-1775**) is on the 52nd floor of the Prudential Tower, 800 Boylston St. It serves lunch Monday through Saturday, Sunday brunch, and dinner daily. The contemporary American menu includes excellent clam chowder.

11½ Thacher St. ℂ 617/227-0765. www.pizzeriaregina.com. Reservations not accepted. Pizza $9–$16. No credit cards. Mon–Thurs 11am–11:30pm; Fri–Sat 11am–midnight; Sun noon–11pm. T: Green or Orange Line to Haymarket.

FANEUIL HALL MARKETPLACE & FINANCIAL DISTRICT

The **food court** at Faneuil Hall Marketplace is a great place to pick up picnic food. Eat there, or cross under the Expressway and pass the Marriott to reach the plaza at the end of Long Wharf. Or head to the left of the hotel and dine in Christopher Columbus Park.

EXPENSIVE

Les Zygomates ✦✦ FRENCH/ECLECTIC   The construction maze near South Station surrounds this delightful bistro and wine bar. It offers a great selection of wine by the bottle, glass, and 2-ounce "taste." The efficient staff will guide you toward a good accompaniment for chef and co-owner Ian Just's delicious cuisine, which is hearty and filling but not heavy. Roasted salmon fillet is toothsome; flank steak with garlic mashed potatoes and sautéed vegetables is succulent. For dessert, try not to fight over the lemon mousse. There's live music nightly (rock and alternative on Monday, jazz Tuesday through Saturday).

129 South St. ℂ 617/542-5108. www.winebar.com. Reservations recommended. Main courses $15–$25; prix-fixe $15 lunch, $19 dinner (Mon–Thurs). AE, DC, DISC, MC, V. Mon–Fri 11:30am–1am (lunch until 2pm, dinner until 10:30pm); Sat 6pm–1am (dinner until 11:30pm). Valet parking available at dinner. T: Red Line to South Station.

Ye Olde Union Oyster House ✦ NEW ENGLAND/SEAFOOD   America's oldest restaurant in continuous service, the Union Oyster House opened in 1826. Its tasty, traditional New England fare is popular with both savvy locals and tourists on the adjacent Freedom Trail. They're not here for anything fancy; the best bets are simple, classic preparations. Try the oyster stew or cold seafood sampler of oysters, clams, and shrimp. Follow with a broiled or grilled dish such as scrod or salmon, or perhaps fried seafood or grilled pork loin. A shore dinner (chowder, steamers, lobster, corn, and dessert) is an excellent introduction to local favorites. Ask to be seated at John F. Kennedy's favorite booth (no. 18), which is marked with a plaque.

41 Union St. (between North and Hanover sts.). ℂ 617/227-2750. www.unionoysterhouse.com. Reservations recommended. Main courses $9.50–$20 lunch; $15–$31 dinner. Children's menu $5–$10. AE, DC, DISC, MC, V. Sun–Thurs 11am–9:30pm (lunch until 5pm); Fri–Sat 11am–10pm (lunch until 6pm). Union Bar daily 11am–midnight (lunch until 3pm, late-supper fare until 11pm). Valet and validated parking available. T: Green or Orange Line to Haymarket.

MODERATE

Durgin-Park ✦✦ Kids NEW ENGLAND   For huge portions of delicious food, a rowdy atmosphere where CEOs share tables with students, and famously cranky waitresses, Bostonians have flocked to Durgin-Park since 1827. Politicians rub shoulders with grandmothers, and everyone's disappointed when the waitresses are nice (as they often are). Approximately 2,000 people a day find their way to the line that stretches down a flight of stairs to the first floor of Faneuil Hall Marketplace's North Market building. They come for prime rib the size of a hubcap, giant lamb chops, piles of fried seafood, fish dinners broiled to order, and bounteous portions of roast turkey. Steaks and chops are broiled on an open fire over wood charcoal. Vegetables come a la carte—now is the time to try Boston baked beans. For dessert, the strawberry shortcake is justly celebrated.

340 Faneuil Hall Marketplace. © 617/227-2038. www.durginpark.com. Reservations accepted for parties of 15 or more. Main courses $6.25–$19; specials $16–$25. AE, DC, DISC, MC, V. Daily 11:30am–2:30pm; Mon–Thurs 2:30–10pm; Fri–Sat 2:30–10:30pm; Sun 2:30–9pm. Validated parking available. T: Green or Blue Line to Government Center or Orange Line to Haymarket.

INEXPENSIVE

Cosí Sandwich Bar ✦ ECLECTIC   Flavorful fillings on delectable bread make Cosí a downtown lunch favorite. This location, right on the Freedom Trail, makes a fantastic refueling stop. Tasty Italian flatbread, baked fresh all day, gets split open and filled with your choice of meat, fish, vegetables, cheese, and spreads. Other branches are at 14 Milk St., near Downtown Crossing (© 617/426-7565), and 133 Federal St. (© 617/292-2674), which has patio seating in warm weather.

53 State St. (at Congress St.). © 617/723-4447. Sandwiches $5.75–$8.25; soups and salads $2.95–$6.50. AE, DC, MC, V. Mon–Thurs 7am–6pm; Fri 7am–5pm. T: Orange or Blue Line to State.

CHINATOWN/THEATER DISTRICT

The best way to sample Chinese food is by trying **dim sum,** the traditional mid-day meal featuring a variety of appetizer-style dishes. It's especially popular with families on weekends, when the variety of offerings is greatest. Our favorite dim sum is at **Empire Garden Restaurant,** also known as Emperor's Garden, 690–698 Washington St., 2nd floor (© 617/482-8898); other good destinations are **Golden Palace Restaurant,** 14 Tyler St. (© 617/423-4565), and **China Pearl,** 9 Tyler St., 2nd floor (© 617/426-4338).

INEXPENSIVE

Buddha's Delight ✦ VEGETARIAN/VIETNAMESE   Fresh and healthful meet cheap and filling on the menu here. It lists "chicken," "pork," and even "lobster"—in quotes because the chefs substitute fried and barbecued tofu and gluten for meat, poultry, fish, or dairy (some beverages have condensed milk) to create more-than-reasonable facsimiles of traditional dishes. Between pondering how they do it and savoring the strong, clear flavors, you might not miss your usual protein. Try spring rolls—"fresh" (in paper-thin mung-bean wrappers) are better than fried—then "shrimp" or "pork" with rice noodles, or excellent chow fun.

5 Beach St., 2nd floor. © 617/451-2395. Main courses $6–$12. MC, V. Sun–Thurs 11am–9:30pm; Fri–Sat 11am–10:30pm. T: Orange Line to Chinatown.

SOUTH END
VERY EXPENSIVE

Hamersley's Bistro ✦✦ ECLECTIC   This is the place that put the South End on Boston's culinary map, a pioneering restaurant that's both classic and contemporary. One of its many claims to fame is its status as a Julia Child favorite. The menu changes seasonally and offers about a dozen entrees noted for their emphasis on taste and texture. The signature roast chicken, flavored with garlic, lemon, and parsley, comes with roasted potato, onions, and whole cloves of sweet baked garlic. Salmon au poivre with sorrel, leeks, and fingerling potatoes is delicious, as are short ribs braised in beer and served with mashed potatoes. The wine list is excellent.

553 Tremont St. © 617/423-2700. www.hamersleysbistro.com. Reservations recommended. Main courses $23–$38. Tasting menu varies. AE, DISC, MC, V. Mon–Fri 6–10pm; Sat 5:30–10pm; Sun 5:30–9:30pm. Closed 2 weeks in Jan. Valet parking available. T: Orange Line to Back Bay.

Icarus ⋆⋆⋆ AMERICAN　This shamelessly romantic subterranean restaurant offers every element of a great dining experience. Chef/owner Christopher Douglass uses choice local ingredients to create imaginative dishes that often seem more like alchemy than cooking. The menu changes regularly—you might start with braised exotic mushrooms on polenta, or succulent lobster salad. Move on to pine-nut-and-lemon-crusted lamb chops served with lamb osso bucco, or lemony grilled chicken with garlic mashed potatoes so good you'll want to ask for a plate of them. Don't—save room for an unbelievable dessert. The seasonal fruit sorbets are especially delicious.

3 Appleton St. ✆ 617/426-1790. www.icarusrestaurant.com. Reservations recommended. Main courses $21–$32.50. AE, DC, DISC, MC, V. Mon–Thurs 6–10pm; Fri 6–10:30pm; Sat 5:30–10:30pm; Sun 5:30–10pm. Valet parking available. T: Green Line to Arlington or Orange Line to Back Bay.

MODERATE

Grillfish SEAFOOD　A splash of Florida style in conservative Boston, this sassy interloper specializes in reasonably priced seafood. An open-fire grill and a PG-13-rated mural over the bar dominate the high-ceilinged room. Shrimp scampi (an unusual version, with tomatoes) is available as an appetizer or entree. Grilled fish—from a regular roster augmented with specials—comes with sweet onion or garlic-tomato sauce. Sautéed dishes have marsala or piccata sauce, and several types of shellfish are available over pasta. Diners shout to be heard over the loud music; sit near the windows or on the small patio (open seasonally) if you prefer a quieter atmosphere. Grillfish is a small chain with branches in the Miami and Washington areas.

162 Columbus Ave. ✆ 617/357-1620. www.grillfish.com. Reservations accepted for parties of six or more. Main courses $10–$22. AE, DISC, MC, V. Sun–Mon 5:30–10pm; Tues–Thurs 5:30–11pm; Fri–Sat 5:30–midnight.

INEXPENSIVE

Le Gamin Café ⋆ FRENCH　The waiter has a heavy French accent. The posters on the walls do, too. The signature sandwiches—with three fillings mixed and matched from a list of more than a dozen—are splendid. The perfect crêpes include an orange-filled version with swooningly good homemade caramel sauce. The tuna in the salade Niçoise is a tad dry and the room a bit noisy, but everything else is just so. Part of a small chain that originated in Manhattan, this is the perfect spot for lingering over morning coffee or a midafternoon glass of wine.

550 Tremont St. ✆ 617/654-8969. www.legamin.com. Main courses $5–$11.50; crêpes $3–$9.50. MC, V. Daily 8am–midnight. T: Orange Line to Back Bay.

BACK BAY
VERY EXPENSIVE

Aujourd'hui ⋆⋆⋆ CONTEMPORARY AMERICAN　On the second floor of the city's premier luxury hotel, the most beautiful restaurant in town offers incredible service and food to its special-occasion and expense-account clientele. Yes, the cost is astronomical, but how often is it true that you get what you pay for? Here, it is. The regularly changing menu encompasses basic hotel dining room offerings and creations that characterize an inventive kitchen, and the wine list is excellent. Entrees might include loin of veal stuffed with Swiss chard, pine nuts, and crayfish, or grilled beef sirloin; there's always a lobster option. The dessert menu includes picture-perfect soufflés and homemade sorbets. "Alternative Cuisine" offerings slash calories, cholesterol, sodium, and fat, but not flavor.

In the Four Seasons Hotel, 200 Boylston St. ℂ 617/351-2071. Reservations recommended (required on hol-idays). Main courses $19–$23.50 lunch, $35–$45 dinner; Sun buffet brunch $58 adults, $28 children. AE, DC, DISC, MC, V. Mon–Fri 6:30–11am; Sat–Sun 7–11am; Mon–Fri 11:30am–2:30pm; Sun brunch 11:30am–2:30pm; Mon–Sat 5:30–10:30pm; Sun 6–10:30pm. Valet parking available. T: Green Line to Arlington.

Grill 23 & Bar ★★ AMERICAN   This wood-paneled, glass-walled restaurant attracts a briefcase-toting clientele, but it's more than just a steakhouse. Traditional dishes such as steak au poivre and lamb chops coexist with bolder, more creative options such as pot pie with filet mignon and lobster, and sirloin-and-chorizo meatloaf. If the fish dishes aren't quite as memorable—hey, it's a steakhouse. The bountiful a la carte side dishes include out-of-this-world garlic mashed potatoes. Desserts are luscious but (horrors!) don't always include cheesecake. The service is exactly right for the setting, helpful yet not familiar, but the noise level soars as the evening progresses.

161 Berkeley St. ℂ 617/542-2255. www.grill23.com. Reservations recommended. Main courses $21–$40. AE, DC, DISC, MC, V. Mon–Thurs 5:30–10:30pm; Fri–Sat 5:30–11pm; Sun 5:30–10pm. Valet parking available. T: Green Line to Arlington.

EXPENSIVE

The Spanish tapas restaurant **Dalí,** 415 Washington St. (see "Cambridge," below), has a Back Bay outpost called **Tapéo,** at 266 Newbury St., in Boston (ℂ 617/267-4799).

Legal Sea Foods ★★★ SEAFOOD   The food at Legal Sea Foods ("Legal's," to Bostonians) isn't the fanciest, cheapest, or trendiest. It's the freshest, and management's commitment to that policy has produced a thriving chain. The menu includes regular selections (scrod, haddock, bluefish, salmon, shrimp, calamari, and lobster, among others) plus whatever looked good at the market that morning, prepared in every imaginable way. It's all splendid. The clam chowder is famous, the fish chowder lighter but equally good. We suggest the Prudential Center branch because it takes reservations (at lunch only), a deviation from a long tradition. Equally annoying but equally traditional is the policy of serving each dish when it's ready, instead of one table at a time.

In the Prudential Center, 800 Boylston St. ℂ 617/266-6800. www.legalseafoods.com. Reservations recom-mended at lunch, not accepted at dinner. Main courses $7–$15 lunch, $14–$35 dinner; lobster priced daily. AE, DC, DISC, MC, V. Mon–Thurs 11am–10:30pm; Fri–Sat 11am–11:30pm; Sun noon–10pm. T: Green Line B, C, or D to Hynes/ICA or E to Prudential. Other locations include: 255 State St. ℂ 617/227-3115. T: Orange or Blue line to State (or Blue Line to Aquarium, if it's open). 36 Park Sq. (between Columbus Ave. and Stuart St.). ℂ 617/426-4444. T: Green Line to Arlington. Copley Place, 2nd level. ℂ 617/266-7775. T: Orange Line to Back Bay or Green Line to Copley. 5 Cambridge Center, Cambridge. ℂ 617/864-3400. T: Red Line to Kendall/MIT.

MODERATE

Brasserie Jo ★ REGIONAL FRENCH   One of the most discriminating diners we know lit up like a marquee on hearing that Boston has a branch of this Chicago favorite. The food is classic—house-made pâtés, fresh baguettes, salade Niçoise, Alsatian onion tart, *choucroute,* coq au vin—but never boring. The house beer, an Alsace-style draft, is a good accompaniment. This casual, all-day French brasserie and bar is a good bet before or after the symphony or during a shopping break. The only drawbacks are the noise level, which can be high when the spacious room is full, and the uneven service, which ranges from solicitous to forgetful.

120 Huntington Ave. ℂ 617/425-3240. Reservations recommended at dinner. Main courses $6–$15 lunch, $6–$25 dinner. AE, DC, DISC, MC, V. Mon–Fri 6:30am–11pm; Sat 7am–11pm; Sun 7am–10pm; late-night menu daily until 1am. T: Green Line E to Prudential.

INEXPENSIVE

Café Jaffa MIDDLE EASTERN   A long, narrow brick room with a glass front, Café Jaffa looks more like a snazzy pizza place than the excellent Middle Eastern restaurant it is. Reasonable prices, high quality, and large portions draw hordes of young people for traditional Middle Eastern offerings such as falafel, baba ghanoush, and hummus, as well as burgers and steak tips. Lamb, beef, and chicken kabobs come with Greek salad, rice pilaf, and pita bread. For dessert, try the baklava if it's fresh (give it a pass if not).

48 Gloucester St. ℂ 617/536-0230. Main courses $5–$13. AE, DC, DISC, MC, V. Mon–Thurs 11am–10:30pm; Fri–Sat 11am–11pm; Sun 1–10pm. T: Green Line B, C, or D to Hynes/ICA.

KENMORE SQUARE
MODERATE

The Elephant Walk ★★ FRENCH/CAMBODIAN   France meets Cambodia on the menu at this madly popular spot 4 blocks from Kenmore Square. Many Cambodian dishes have part-French names, such as *poulet dhomrei* (chicken with Asian basil, bamboo shoots, fresh pineapple, and kaffir lime leaves) and *curry de crevettes* (shrimp curry with picture-perfect vegetables). Or try *loc lac,* fork-tender beef cubes in addictively spicy sauce. On the French side, you'll find classics like filet mignon with pommes frites. The pleasant staff will help out if you need guidance.

900 Beacon St., Boston. ℂ 617/247-1500. Reservations recommended at dinner Sun–Thurs, not accepted Fri–Sat. Main courses $7–$19 lunch, $10–$25 dinner. AE, DC, DISC, MC, V. Mon–Sat 11:30am–2:30pm; Mon–Thurs 5–10pm; Fri 5–11pm; Sat 4:30–11pm; Sun 4:30–10pm. Valet parking available at dinner. T: Green Line C to St. Mary's St.

CAMBRIDGE

The Red Line runs from downtown Boston to the heart of Harvard Square. Many of the restaurants listed here can be reached on foot from there. If inexpensive ethnic food is more your speed, head for Central and Inman squares.

   Note: See the "Cambridge Accommodations & Dining" map on p. 84 for the locations of the restaurants reviewed below.

VERY EXPENSIVE

Rialto ★★★ MEDITERRANEAN   This is our favorite Boston-area restaurant. It attracts a chic crowd, but it's not a "scene" in the sense that out-of-towners will feel left behind. The dramatic but comfortable room has floor-to-ceiling windows overlooking Harvard Square. Chef Jody Adams's menu changes regularly, and main courses are so good that you might as well close your eyes and point. Seared duck breast with foie gras, squash raviolis, and quince is wonderful, and any fish is a guaranteed winner—say, seared tuna in mustard seeds with wild rice and olive vinaigrette. For dessert, seasonal sorbets are a great choice.

In the Charles Hotel, 1 Bennett St. ℂ 617/661-5050. Reservations recommended. Main courses $20–$33. AE, DC, MC, V. Sun–Thurs 5:30–10pm; Fri–Sat 5:30–11pm. Bar Sun–Thurs 4:30pm–midnight; Fri–Sat 5pm–1am. Valet and validated parking available. T: Red Line to Harvard.

EXPENSIVE

There's a **Legal Sea Foods** branch in Kendall Square; see "Back Bay," above.

The Blue Room ★★★ ECLECTIC   The Blue Room sits below plaza level in an office-retail complex, a slice of foodie paradise in high-tech heaven. The cuisine is a rousing combination of top-notch ingredients and layers of aggressive flavors, the service excellent, and the crowded dining room not as noisy as it looks. Main courses tend to be roasted, grilled, or braised. Roast chicken, served with garlic mashed potatoes, is world-class. Grilled tuna appears often, and pork loin with cider glaze will make you think twice the next time you skip over pork on a menu to get to steak. In warm weather, there's seating on the brick patio.

1 Kendall Sq. ☎ **617/494-9034**. www.blueroom.net. Reservations recommended. Main courses $16–$22. AE, DC, DISC, MC, V. Sun–Thurs 5:30–10pm; Fri–Sat 5:30–11pm; Sun 11am–2:30pm. Validated parking available. T: Red Line to Kendall/MIT, 10-min. walk.

Dalí Restaurant & Tapas Bar ★★★ SPANISH   Dalí is a festive spot where the bar fills with people cheerfully waiting an hour or more for a table. The payoff is authentic Spanish food, notably tapas, little plates of flavorful hot or cold creations. Entrees include excellent paella, but most people come in a group and explore the three dozen or more tapas offerings, all perfect for sharing. They include delectable garlic potatoes, salmon balls with not-too-salty caper sauce, pork tenderloin with blue goat cheese and mushrooms, and delicious sausages. The staff sometimes seems overwhelmed, but never fails to supply bread for sopping up juices, and sangria for washing it all down. Finish with excellent flan, or try the rich *tarta de chocolates*.

The owners of Dalí also run **Tapéo** (☎ **617/267-4799**), at 266 Newbury St., between Fairfield and Dartmouth streets in Boston's Back Bay.

415 Washington St., Somerville. ☎ **617/661-3254**. www.dalirestaurant.com. Reservations not accepted. Tapas $3.50–$8; main courses $19–$24. AE, DC, MC, V. Daily winter 5:30–11pm; summer 6–11pm. T: Red Line to Harvard; follow Kirkland St. to intersection of Washington and Beacon sts. (20-min. walk).

Oleana ★★ MEDITERRANEAN   Both casual neighborhood eatery and culinary travelogue, Oleana made one of the most promising debuts of 2001. Chef and co-owner Ana Sortun creates cuisine typical of and inspired by the Mediterranean. The seasonal menu might include traditional Portuguese clams *cataplana*, with sausage in an aromatic tomatoey broth; almond-fried chicken, a great contrast of crunchy crust and juicy flesh; and spicy tuna, in a perfectly matched peppery sauce that trades intense heat for intense flavor. Service is polished, portions generous, and the dessert menu heavy on house-made ice cream. In warm weather, there's seating on the patio.

134 Hampshire St. ☎ **617/661-0505**. Reservations recommended. Main courses $17–$24. AE, MC, V. Sun–Thurs 5:30–10pm; Fri–Sat 5:30–11pm. Free parking. T: Red Line to Central; 10-min. walk.

MODERATE

Border Cafe TEX-MEX/CAJUN   This unbelievably crowded restaurant has been a Harvard Square favorite for over 15 years. Patrons loiter at the bar while waiting for a table, enhancing the festival atmosphere. Portions are generous, and the beleaguered staff keeps the chips and salsa coming. Try the excellent chorizo appetizer, seafood enchiladas, tacos, or popcorn shrimp. Fajitas for one or two, sizzling noisily in a large iron frying pan, are also popular.

32 Church St. ☎ **617/864-6100**. Reservations not accepted. Main courses $7–$15. AE, MC, V. Mon–Thurs 11am–1am; Fri–Sat 11am–2am; Sun noon–11pm. T: Red Line to Harvard.

The Helmand ★★ AFGHAN   Unusual cuisine, an elegant setting, and reasonable prices make this spacious spot near the CambridgeSide Galleria mall something of an open secret. Distinctly Middle Eastern with Indian and Pakistani influences, Afghan food is vegetarian friendly; many non-veggie dishes use meat as one element rather than the centerpiece. *Aushak*, pasta pockets filled with leeks or potatoes and topped with split-pea-and-carrot sauce, also comes with meat sauce. Other entrees include stews like *deygee kabob*, an excellent mélange of lamb, yellow split peas, onion, and red peppers. For dessert, don't miss the Afghan version of baklava.

143 First St. ✆ 617/492-4646. Reservations recommended. Main courses $9–$16. AE, MC, V. Sun–Thurs 5–10pm; Fri–Sat 5–11pm. T: Green Line to Lechmere.

INEXPENSIVE

Mr. Bartley's Burger Cottage ★★ AMERICAN   Great burgers and the best onion rings in the world make Bartley's a perennial favorite with a cross section of Cambridge. The 40-year-old family business is a high-ceilinged, crowded room plastered with signs and posters. Burgers bear the names of local and national celebrities, notably political figures; the names change, but the ingredients stay the same. Anything you can think of to put on ground beef is available, from American cheese to béarnaise sauce. There are also some good dishes that don't involve meat, notably veggie burgers and creamy, garlicky hummus.

1246 Mass. Ave. ✆ 617/354-6559. Most items under $9. No credit cards. Mon–Wed and Sat 11am–9pm; Thurs–Fri 11am–10pm. T: Red Line to Harvard.

S&S Restaurant ★★ DELI   *Es* is Yiddish for "eat," and this Cambridge classic is as straightforward as its name ("eat and eat"). Founded in 1919 by the great-grandmother of the current owners, the wildly popular brunch spot draws huge crowds at busy times on weekends. It looks contemporary, but the brunch offerings are traditional: pancakes, waffles, fruit salad, fantastic omelets. After noon, you can order an excellent bloody Mary. You'll also find traditional deli items (corned beef, pastrami, tongue, potato pancakes, and blintzes), and breakfast anytime. Be early for brunch, or plan to spend a good chunk of your Saturday or Sunday people-watching and getting hungry. Or dine on a weekday and soak up the neighborhood atmosphere.

1334 Cambridge St., Inman Sq. ✆ 617/354-0777. www.sandsrestaurant.com. Main courses $4–$12. AE, MC, V. Mon–Wed 7am–11pm, Thurs–Fri 7am–midnight, Sat 8am–midnight, Sun 8am–10pm; brunch Sat–Sun until 4pm. T: Red Line to Harvard, then no. 69 (Harvard–Lechmere) bus to Inman Sq. Or Red Line to Central, 10-min. walk on Prospect St.

Tea-Tray in the Sky ★ AMERICAN/TEAROOM   This cozy little storefront is a perfect stop for a meal or snack on a shopping expedition north of Harvard Square. Lavishly decorated with tea-related accessories and original art (much of it for sale), the room seats just 20. The encyclopedic tea menu, both familiar and exotic (white tea, several kinds of chai), accompanies an extensive food menu. The baked goods are made in-house, and the salads, soups, and sandwiches (including a superb tuna melt) are so delectable that you might forget to save room for cakes, tarts, scones, and other pastries. Try anything involving chocolate, and be prepared to share. The name is a tribute to *Alice's Adventures in Wonderland*—check out the mural.

1796 Mass. Ave. ✆ 617/492-8327. www.teatray.com. Reservations not accepted. Main courses $5–$12.75. AE, DC, DISC, MC, V. Tues–Fri 10am–10pm, Sat 10am–11pm, Sun 10am–7pm. Closed Sun in summer. T: Red Line to Porter.

5 Seeing the Sights in Boston

If you'll be in town for more than a couple of days, make your first stop a **BosTix** (✆ **617/262-8632;** www.boston.com/artsboston) booth for a coupon book that offers discounts on admission to many area museums and attractions. It's not worth the money (currently $9) for single travelers, as many of the coupons offer two-for-one deals, but couples and families can take good advantage. For

Kids Up, Up & Away: Great Views

The **John Hancock Observatory** ★★, 200 Clarendon St. (© 617/
572-6429; www.cityviewboston.com), has a sensational 60th-floor
view. Powerful binoculars (bring quarters) allow long-distance views.
Admission is $6 for adults, $4 for seniors and children 5 to 15. Hours
from April through October are daily from 9am to 11pm; November
through March, Monday through Saturday from 9am to 11pm, Sunday
from 9am to 6pm. T: Green Line to Copley or Orange Line to Back Bay.
   The **Prudential Center Skywalk** ★, on the 50th floor of 800 Boylston
St. (© 617/859-0648), offers the only 360-degree view of Boston and
beyond. When it's clear, you can see as far as the mountains of southern New Hampshire or the beaches of Cape Cod. The exhibits here are
less interesting than at the Hancock Observatory, but the view is a little better, especially at sunset. Hours are Monday through Saturday
from 10am to 10pm, Sunday from noon to 10pm. Admission is $6 for
adults, $4 for seniors and children 2 to 10. T: Green Line E to Pruden-
tial or B, C, or D to Hynes/ICA.

locations, see "Boston & Cambridge After Dark," below. Books are also available
by phone, online, and by mail, subject to a handling charge.
   A **CityPass** offers great savings—in money and time. It's a booklet of tickets
to the Harvard Museum of Natural History, John Hancock Observatory,
Kennedy Library, Museum of Fine Arts, Museum of Science, and New England
Aquarium. The price (at press time, $28.25 for adults, $21.75 for seniors, and
$18 for children 3 to 17) represents a 50% savings if you visit all six attractions,
and having a ticket means you can go straight to the entrance without waiting
in line. The passes, good for 9 days from the date of purchase, are on sale at participating attractions, the Boston Common and Prudential Center visitor information centers, through the **Greater Boston Convention & Visitors Bureau**
(© 800/SEE-BOSTON; www.bostonusa.com), and from www.citypass.com.

THE TOP ATTRACTIONS

Boston Tea Party Ship & Museum Kids   On December 16, 1773, a public
meeting of independent-minded Bostonians led to the symbolic act of resistance
commemorated here. The brig *Beaver II* is a full-size replica of one of the three
merchant ships loaded with tea that stood at anchor that night. The colonists,
protesting the royal government's tax on tea, emptied the vessels' cargo into the
harbor. The ship sits alongside a museum with exhibits on the "tea party." The
audio and video displays (including a 15-minute film), dioramas, and information panels tell the story of the uprising. You can dump a bale of tea into Boston
Harbor—a museum staffer retrieves it—and drink some complimentary tax-free
tea (iced in summer, hot in winter). A visit takes about an hour and makes a
good stop on the way to or from the Children's Museum.

Congress Street Bridge. © 617/338-1773. www.bostonteapartyship.com. Admission $8 adults, $7 students,
$4 children 4–12. Mar–Nov daily 9am–dusk (about 6pm summer, 5pm spring and fall). Closed Thanksgiving,
Dec–Feb. T: Red Line to South Station. Walk north on Atlantic Ave. 1 block, pass the Federal Reserve Bank,
turn right onto Congress St., and walk 1 block.

Boston Attractions

BosTix (Copley Square) **7**
BosTix (Faneuil Hall) **22**
Boston Common **10**
Boston Duck Tours **6**
Boston Massacre Site **21**
Boston Tea Party Ship & Museum **30**
Bunker Hill Monument **24**
Charlestown Navy Yard **24**
Children's Museum **31**
Copp's Hill Burying Ground **25**
Dreams of Freedom Center **18**
Faneuil Hall Marketplace **22**
Foster's Rotunda **29**
Frog Pond **11**
Institute of Contemporary Art **5**
Isabella Stewart Gardner Museum **1**
John F. Kennedy Library and Museum **32**
John Hancock Observatory **8**
King's Chapel **15**

Mapparium **3**
Massachusetts State House **12**
Museum of Fine Arts **2**
Museum of Science **23**
New England Aquarium **28**
Old Granary Burying Ground **14**
Old North Church **26**
Old South Meeting House **19**
Old State House **20**
Park Street Church **13**
Paul Revere House **27**
Prudential Center **6**
Public Garden **9**
Site of the First Public School/
  Benjamin Franklin statue **16**
Symphony Hall **4**
3 School St. **17**
USS Constitution **24**

Dreams of Freedom Center ★ *Kids*   The Freedom Trail isn't just about colonial Boston. If you need proof, detour from the trail to the city's new museum of immigration. Boston native Ben Franklin is the "host" of a multimedia show about the changing face of the city's population. It's an interactive experience unlike the city's typically low-tech attractions—a plus if you're traveling with wired (in both senses) kids. You'll have your passport stamped as you make your way through the thought-provoking exhibits. They include a gallery of bags and suitcases that offers a look at what people brought with them on their long journey to the New World, and the interiors of two important modes of transportation: an early-20th-century ship and a jet liner. Allow about an hour.

1 Milk St., off Washington St. © 617/338-6022. www.dreamsoffreedom.org. Admission $7.50 adults, $3.50 children 6–17. April–Dec daily 10am–6pm; Jan–March Tues–Sun 10am–5pm. T: Green or Blue Line to State, or Red or Orange Line to Downtown Crossing.

Faneuil Hall Marketplace ★★ *Kids*   Since Boston's most popular attraction opened, in 1976, cities all over the country have imitated the "festival market" concept. The complex of shops, food stands, restaurants, bars, and public spaces is such a magnet for tourists and suburbanites that you could be forgiven for thinking that the only Bostonians in the crowd are employees.

The three central buildings of the five-structure complex sit on brick-and-stone plazas that teem with crowds shopping, eating, performing, watching performers, and people-watching. In warm weather, it's busy from just after dawn until well past dark. **Quincy Market** (you'll hear the whole complex called by that name) is the central three-level Greek Revival–style building; its central corridor, the **Colonnade,** is an enormous food court. On either side, under glass canopies, pushcarts hold everything from crafts created by New England artisans to hokey souvenirs. In the plaza between the **South Canopy** and the South Market building is an **information kiosk,** and throughout the complex you'll find an enticing mix of chain stores and unique shops. On summer evenings, the tables that spill outdoors from the restaurants and bars are filled with people. One constant since the year after the market—the *original* market—opened is **Durgin-Park,** a traditional New England restaurant with traditionally crabby waitresses (see "Dining," above). **Faneuil Hall** ★ itself—nicknamed the "Cradle of Liberty"—sometimes gets overlooked, but it's well worth a visit. National Park Service rangers give free 20-minute talks every half hour from 9am to 5pm in the second-floor auditorium.

Between North, Congress, and State sts. and I-93. © 617/338-2323. www.faneuilhallmarketplace.com. Marketplace Mon–Sat 10am–9pm; Sun noon–6pm. Food court opens earlier; some restaurants open early for Sun brunch and close at 2am daily. T: Green or Blue Line to Government Center, Orange Line to Haymarket, or Blue or Orange Line to State (or Blue Line to Aquarium, if it's open).

The Institute of Contemporary Art ★   Across from the Hynes Convention Center, the ICA mounts rotating exhibits of 20th- and 21st-century art, including painting, sculpture, photography, and video and performance art. The institute also offers films, lectures, music, video, poetry, and educational programs for children and adults. "Docent Teens"—participants in the institute's nationally recognized program for urban youth—lead tours on Thursday afternoons, and staff members lead tours on Fridays at 12:30pm. Check at this location for updates on the ICA's new home, at Fan Pier on the South Boston waterfront, scheduled to open in 2004.

955 Boylston St. © 617/266-5152. www.icaboston.org. Admission $6 adults, $4 students and seniors, free for children under 12; free to all Thurs 5–9pm. Wed noon–5pm; Thurs noon–9pm; Fri–Sun noon–7pm. Closed major holidays. T: Green Line B, C, or D to Hynes/ICA.

Isabella Stewart Gardner Museum ★★   Isabella Stewart Gardner (1840–1924) was an incorrigible individualist long before such behavior was acceptable for a woman in polite Boston society, and her iconoclasm has paid off for art lovers. "Mrs. Jack" designed her exquisite home in the style of a 15th-century Venetian palace and filled it with European, American, and Asian painting and sculpture. You'll see works by Titian, Botticelli, Raphael, Rembrandt, Matisse, and Mrs. Gardner's friends James McNeill Whistler and John Singer Sargent. Titian's magnificent *Europa,* which many scholars consider his finest work, is one of the most important Renaissance paintings in the nation. If you enjoy representational art and ornate architecture, run right over; if not, you'll probably be happier at the nearby Museum of Fine Arts.

The building, which opened to the public after Mrs. Gardner's death, holds a hodgepodge of furniture and architectural details imported from European churches and palaces. The pièce de résistance is the magnificent skylit courtyard, filled year-round with fresh flowers from the museum greenhouse. Although the terms of Mrs. Gardner's will forbid changing the arrangement of the museum's content, there has been some evolution: A special exhibition gallery features two or three changing shows a year, often by contemporary artists in residence.

280 The Fenway. ⓒ **617/566-1401.** www.boston.com/gardner. Admission $11 adults Sat–Sun, $10 adults Mon–Fri; $7 seniors; $5 college students with ID; free for children under 18. Tues–Sun and some Mon holidays 11am–5pm. Closed Thanksgiving, Christmas. T: Green Line E to Museum.

John F. Kennedy Library and Museum ★★ *Kids*   The Kennedy era springs to life at this dramatic library, museum, and educational research complex overlooking Dorchester Bay. It captures the 35th president's accomplishments and legacy in sound and video recordings and fascinating displays of memorabilia and photos. Far from being a static experience, it changes regularly, with temporary shows and reinterpreted displays that highlight and complement the permanent exhibits. A visit begins with a 17-minute film about Kennedy's early life. The exhibits start with the 1960 campaign and end with a tribute to Kennedy's legacy. There's a film about the Cuban Missile Crisis, and displays on the civil-rights movement, the Peace Corps, the space program, and the Kennedy family. Expanded exhibits focus on First Lady Jacqueline Bouvier Kennedy and Attorney General Robert F. Kennedy. As the tour winds down, you pass through a darkened chamber where news reports of John Kennedy's assassination and funeral play.

A special separate-admission exhibition, ***Jacqueline Kennedy: The White House Years,*** will run from September 12, 2001, to February 28, 2002. Using items from the museum's collections, the show will focus on the First Lady's influence on fashion and explore her other interests, including art and historic preservation. Mrs. Kennedy is a perennial favorite with museum visitors. Tickets are being sold in advance and you will need a reservation. Ticket for this exhibit prices are $16 adults, $14 seniors and students, and $13 for youths ages 13 to 17.

Columbia Point. ⓒ **877/616-4599** or 617/929-4500. www.jfklibrary.org. Admission $8 adults; $6 seniors and students with ID; $4 youths 13–17; free for children under 13. Daily 9am–5pm (last film begins at 3:55pm). T: Red Line to JFK/UMass, then take free shuttle bus, which runs every 20 min. By car, take Southeast Expressway (I-93/Rte. 3) south to Exit 15 (Morrissey Blvd./JFK Library), turn left onto Columbia Rd., and follow signs to free parking lot.

Museum of Fine Arts ★★★ *Kids*   One of the world's great museums, the MFA works constantly to become even more accessible and interesting. The museum's not-so-secret weapon in its quest is a powerful one: its magnificent collections. Every installation reflects a curatorial attitude that makes even those who go in with a sense of obligation leave with a sense of discovery and wonder. That includes children, who can launch a scavenger hunt, admire the mummies, or participate in family-friendly programs scheduled year-round, with extra offerings during school vacations.

The MFA is especially noted for its **Impressionist paintings** ★★★ (including 43 Monets—the largest collection outside Paris), Asian and Old Kingdom Egyptian collections, classical art, Buddhist temple, and medieval sculpture and tapestries. The American and European paintings and sculpture are a remarkable assemblage of timeless works that may seem as familiar as the face in the mirror or as unexpected as a comet. There are also magnificent holdings of prints, photography, furnishings, and decorative arts, including the finest collection of Paul Revere silver in the world. The museum has two restaurants, a cafe, and a cafeteria. Pick up a floor plan at the information desk, or take a free **guided tour** (weekdays except Monday holidays at 10:30am and 1:30pm, Wednesday at 6:15pm, Saturday at 10:30am and 1pm).

Two separate-admission shows may be worth planning for; you'll need advance tickets. *Impressionist and Post-Impressionist Still Life Painting* will run from February 17, 2001, to June 9, 2002. Assembled from around the world in collaboration with the Phillips Collection, it should be the latest in a series of MFA blockbusters. *The Look: Photographs by Horst and Hoyningen-Huene,* a celebration of the work of two of *Vogue* magazine's best-known photographers, will run from October 21, 2001, to January 6, 2002.

Tip: The Huntington Avenue entrance is usually much less busy than the West Wing lobby—and farther from the gift shop, restaurants, garage, and access to special exhibits. If you're making a lengthy visit (which generally involves lots of walking anyway), walk back along Huntington Avenue when you leave the T, enter from the driveway, and stop to take in the recently restored John Singer Sargent murals.

465 Huntington Ave. ℰ **617/267-9300.** www.mfa.org. Adults $12; students and seniors $10 when entire museum is open ($10 and $9 respectively when only West Wing is open); children 7–17 $5 on school days before 3pm, otherwise free. Voluntary contribution Wed 4–9:45pm. Surcharges may apply for special exhibitions. Free admission for Museum Shop, library, restaurants, and auditoriums. Entire museum Mon–Tues 10am–4:45pm; Wed 10am–9:45pm; Thurs–Fri 10am–5pm; Sat–Sun 10am–5:45pm. West Wing only Thurs–Fri 5–9:45pm. Closed Thanksgiving, Christmas. T: Green Line E to Museum or Orange Line to Ruggles.

Museum of Science ★★★ (Kids)   For the ultimate pain-free educational experience, head to the Museum of Science. The demonstrations, experiments, and interactive displays introduce facts and concepts so effortlessly that everyone winds up learning something. Take a couple of hours or a whole day to explore the permanent and temporary exhibits, most of them hands-on and all of them great fun. Among the 600-plus exhibits, you might meet an iguana or a dinosaur, find out how much you'd weigh on the moon, or climb into a space module. Activity centers and exhibits focus on fields of interest—light and optics, computers, the human body—as well as interdisciplinary approaches. **Investigate!** teaches visitors to think like scientists, analyzing questions through activities such as sifting through an archaeological dig. The **Science in the Park** uses familiar tools such as playground equipment and skateboards to look at Newtonian physics. And there's a **Discovery Center** especially for preschoolers.

The separate-admission theaters are worth planning for, even if you're skipping the exhibits. If you're making a day of it, buy all your tickets at once, not only because it's cheaper but also because shows sometimes sell out. Tickets are for sale in person and, subject to a service charge, over the phone and online (www.tickets.mos.org).

The **Mugar Omni Theater** ✰✰✰, which shows IMAX movies, is an intense experience. It bombards you with images on a five-story domed screen and sounds from a state-of-the-art digital system. Films, which usually focus on adventure and the natural world, change every 4 to 6 months. The **Charles Hayden Planetarium** ✰✰ takes you into space with daily star shows as well as shows on special topics that change several times a year. On weekends, rock-music laser shows take over.

In 1999, the Museum of Science joined forces with the Computer Museum and acquired its fascinating interactive exhibits. The first to open in its new home, the wildly popular **Virtual FishTank** ✰✰✰, uses 3-D computer graphics and character-animation software to allow visitors to program their own virtual fish. You can even "build" fish on your home computer (through www.virtualfishtank.com) and launch them at the museum.

Science Park. 🕐 **617/723-2500.** www.mos.org. Admission to exhibit halls $10 adults, $7 seniors and children 3–11. Mugar Omni Theater, Hayden Planetarium, or laser shows $7.50 adults, $5.50 seniors and children 3–11. Discounted tickets to two or three parts of the complex available. July 5–Labor Day Sat–Thurs 9am–7pm; Fri 9am–9pm. Day after Labor Day to July 4 Sat–Thurs 9am–5pm; Fri 9am–9pm. Closed Thanksgiving, Christmas. T: Green Line to Science Park.

New England Aquarium ✰ (Kids) This entertaining complex is home to more than 7,000 fish and aquatic mammals. At busy times in the summer, it seems to contain at least that many people—in July and August, especially on weekends, try to make this your first stop of the day. You'll want to spend at least half a day, and huge afternoon crowds can make just getting around painfully slow. Also consider investing in a Boston CityPass (see p. 99); it allows you to skip the ticket line, which can be uncomfortably long.

The focal point of the main building is the four-story, 200,000-gallon **Giant Ocean Tank.** It holds a replica of a Caribbean coral reef, a vast assortment of sea creatures, and, five times a day, scuba divers who plunge in to feed the sharks. Other exhibits show off freshwater and tropical specimens, sea otters, the Aquarium Medical Center, denizens of the Amazon, and the ecology of Boston Harbor. The hands-on **Edge of the Sea** exhibit contains a tide pool with resident sea stars, sea urchins, and horseshoe crabs. The complex is scheduled to gain an **IMAX theater** with 3-D capability in late 2001; call for admission fees. The aquarium runs naturalist-led **harbor tours** that teach "Science at Sea" daily in the spring, summer, and fall. Discounts are available when you combine a visit to the aquarium with a harbor tour or a whale watch (see "Organized Tours," below).

Central Wharf. 🕐 **617/973-5200.** www.neaq.org. Admission summer weekends and holidays $14.50 adults, $12.50 seniors, $8 children 3–11; weekdays year-round and off-season weekends $13 adults, $11 seniors, $7 children. Harbor tours $13 adults, $10 seniors and college students with ID, $9 youths 12–18, $8.50 children 3–11. Free admission for outdoor exhibits, cafe, and gift shop. July–Labor Day Mon–Tues and Fri 9am–6pm; Wed–Thurs 9am–8pm; Sat–Sun and holidays 9am–7pm. Day after Labor Day to June Mon–Fri 9am–5pm; Sat–Sun and holidays 9am–6pm. T: Blue Line to Aquarium.

THE FREEDOM TRAIL ✰✰✰

A line of red paint or red brick on the sidewalk, the 3-mile Freedom Trail links 16 historical sights. Markers identify the stops, and plaques point the way from one to the next. The trail begins at **Boston Common,** where the Information Center, 146 Tremont St., distributes pamphlets that describe a self-guided tour. For a preview, visit the Freedom Trail Foundation's website at **www.thefreedomtrail.org**.

You can also explore the **Black Heritage Trail** ✿✿ from here. Stops include stations on the Underground Railroad and homes of famous citizens as well as the African Meeting House, the oldest standing black church in the country. A 2-hour guided tour of this trail starts at the Visitor Center, 46 Joy Street (© **617/742-5415**; www.nps.gov/boaf).

As you progress along the Freedom Trail, you'll come to another information center, the **Boston National Historic Park Visitor Center,** 15 State St. (© **617/242-5642**; www.nps.gov/bost). From here, rangers lead free guided tours of the "heart" of the trail. An audiovisual show provides basic information on the stops. The wheelchair-accessible center has rest rooms and a bookstore. It's open daily from 9am to 5pm (except Thanksgiving, Christmas, and New Year's Day).

The hard-core history fiend who peers at every artifact and reads every plaque along the trail will wind up at Bunker Hill some 4 hours later, weary but rewarded. The family with restless children will probably appreciate the enforced efficiency of the 90-minute ranger-led tour.

Space doesn't permit us to detail every stop on the Trail, but here's a concise listing:

- **Boston Common.** In 1634, when their settlement was just 4 years old, the town fathers paid the Rev. William Blackstone £30 for this property. In 1640, it was set aside as common land. Be sure to stop at Beacon and Park streets, where a **memorial** ✿✿✿ designed by Augustus Saint-Gaudens celebrates the deeds (indeed, the very existence) of Col. Robert Gould Shaw and the Union Army's 54th Massachusetts Colored Regiment, who fought in the Civil War. You may remember the story of the first American army unit made up of free black soldiers from the movie *Glory.*
- **Massachusetts State House** (© **617/727-3676**). Charles Bulfinch designed the "new" State House, and Gov. Samuel Adams laid the cornerstone of the state capitol in 1795. Free guided tours leave from the second floor Monday through Saturday from 10am to 3:30pm.
- **Park Street Church,** 1 Park St. (© **617/523-3383**; www.parkstreet.org). The plaque at the corner of Tremont Street describes this Congregational church's storied past. From late June through August, it's open Tuesday through Saturday from 9am to 3pm. Sunday services are at 10:45am and 5:30pm in summer; 8:30am, 11am, and 5:30pm in winter.
- **Old Granary Burying Ground.** This cemetery, established in 1660, contains the graves of—among other notables—Samuel Adams, Paul Revere, John Hancock, and the wife of Isaac Vergoose, believed to be the "Mother Goose" of nursery-rhyme fame. It's open daily from 9am to 5pm (until 3pm in winter).
- **King's Chapel,** 58 Tremont St. (© **617/523-1749**). Completed in 1754, this church was built by erecting the granite edifice around the existing wooden chapel. The **burying ground** (1630), facing Tremont Street, is the oldest in Boston. It's open daily from 8am to 5:30pm (until 3pm in winter).
- **Site of the First Public School.** Founded in 1634, the school is commemorated with a colorful mosaic in the sidewalk on (of course) School Street. Inside the fence is the 1856 statue of **Benjamin Franklin,** the first portrait statue erected in Boston.
- **3 School St.** This is the former Old Corner Bookstore. Built in 1712, it's on a plot of land that was once home to the religious reformer Anne Hutchinson.

- **Old South Meeting House,** 310 Washington St. (© **617/482-6439**). Originally built in 1670 and replaced by the current structure in 1729, it was the starting point of the Boston Tea Party. It's open daily from 9am to 5pm. Admission is $3 for adults, $2.50 for seniors, and $1 for children 6 to 12. When you finish exploring, cross the street to the **Dreams of Freedom** center (see "The Top Attractions," above).

- **Old State House** ★, 206 Washington St. (© **617/720-3290**; www. bostonhistory.org). Built in 1713, it served as the seat of colonial government in Massachusetts before the Revolution, and as the state capitol until 1797. It houses the Bostonian Society's fascinating museum of the city's history, open daily from 9am to 5pm. Admission is $3 for adults, $2 for seniors and students, and $1 for children 6 to 18.

- **Boston Massacre Site.** On a traffic island in State Street, across from the T station under the Old State House, a ring of cobblestones marks the place where the skirmish took place on March 5, 1770.

- **Faneuil Hall** ★. Built in 1742 (and enlarged using a Charles Bulfinch design in 1805), it was a gift to the city from the merchant Peter Faneuil. National Park Service rangers give free 20-minute talks every half hour from 9am to 5pm in the second-floor auditorium.

- **Paul Revere House** ★★, 19 North Sq. (© **617/523-2338**; www. paulreverehouse.org). The oldest house in downtown Boston (built around 1680) presents history on a human scale. Revere bought it in 1770, and it became a museum in the early 20th century. It's open November 1 to April 14 from 9:30am to 4:15pm, and April 15 to October 31 from 9:30am to 5:15pm; closed Thanksgiving, Christmas, New Year's Day, and Mondays from January through March. Admission is $2.50 for adults, $2 for seniors and students, and $1 for children 5 to 17.

- **Old North Church,** 193 Salem St. (© **617/523-6676**; www. oldnorth.com). Paul Revere saw a signal in the steeple and set out on his "midnight ride." Officially named Christ Church, this is the oldest church building in Boston; it dates to 1723. It's open daily from 9am to 5pm; Sunday services (Episcopal) are at 9am, 11am, and 5pm. The quirky gift shop and museum, in a former chapel, are open daily from 9am to 5pm; proceeds go to support the church. Donations are appreciated.

- **Copp's Hill Burying Ground,** off Hull Street. The second-oldest cemetery (1659) in the city, it contains the graves of Cotton Mather and his family and of Prince Hall, who established the first black Masonic lodge. It's open daily from 9am to 5pm (until 3pm in winter).

- **USS** *Constitution* ★★, Charlestown Navy Yard (© **617/242-5670**). Active-duty sailors in 1812 dress uniforms give free tours of "Old Ironsides" daily between 9:30am and 3:50pm. The **USS** *Constitution* **Museum** ★ (© **617/426-1812**; www.ussconstititionmuseum.org) is open daily, May

---

(*Tips* **Out to Sea**

A fun way to return to downtown from Charlestown is on the **ferry** that connects Long Wharf (near the Aquarium), the Navy Yard, and Lovejoy Wharf (near North Station). It costs $1.25 (free if you have an MBTA Boston Visitor Pass).

through October from 9am to 6pm, November through April from 10am to 4pm; it's closed Thanksgiving, Christmas, and New Year's Day. A program that makes admission free to all has been extended until further notice.

- **Bunker Hill Monument** (© **617/242-5644**), Charlestown. The 221-foot granite obelisk honors the memory of the men who died in the Battle of Bunker Hill (actually fought on Breed's Hill) on June 17, 1775. The top is 295 stairs up. National Park Service rangers staff the monument, which is open daily from 9am to 4:30pm. Admission is free.

PARKS & GARDENS

The best-known park in Boston is the spectacular **Public Garden** ★★★, bordered by Arlington, Boylston, Charles, and Beacon streets. Something lovely is in bloom at the country's first botanical garden at least half of the year. For 5 months, the lagoon is home to the celebrated **swan boats** (© **617/522-1966;** www.swanboats.com). The pedal-powered vessels—the attendants pedal, not the passengers—come out of hibernation on the Saturday before Patriots Day (the third Monday of April). Although they don't move fast, they'll transport you. They operate in summer daily from 10am to 5pm; in spring daily from 10am to 4pm; and from Labor Day to mid-September Monday through Friday from noon to 4pm and Saturday and Sunday from 10am to 4pm. The 15-minute ride costs $1.75 for adults, $1.50 for seniors, and 95¢ for children under 13.

The most spectacular garden is the **Arnold Arboretum** ★★, 125 Arborway, Jamaica Plain (© **617/524-1718;** www.arboretum.harvard.edu). One of the oldest parks in the United States, founded in 1872, it is open daily from sunrise to sunset. Admission is free. Its 265 acres contain more than 15,000 ornamental trees, shrubs, and vines from all over the world. Lilac Sunday, in May, is the only time picnicking is allowed in the arboretum. This is definitely a place to take a camera. To get here, take the Orange Line to Forest Hills and follow signs to the entrance. The visitor center is open Monday through Friday from 9am to 4pm, Saturday and Sunday from noon to 4pm.

The world-famous **Emerald Necklace,** Frederick Law Olmsted's vision for a loop of green spaces, threads through the city. See "Organized Tours," below, for information on seeing part or all of the Emerald Necklace with a Boston Park Ranger.

ORGANIZED TOURS

WALKING TOURS ★★ **Boston by Foot** ★★, 77 N. Washington St. (© **617/367-2345,** or 617/367-3766 for recorded info; www.boston byfoot.com), offers excellent tours. From May through October, the nonprofit

---

Finds **Eye in the Sky**

For a smashing view of the airport, the harbor, and the South Boston waterfront, stroll along the water (or Atlantic Avenue) to the Boston Harbor Hotel complex. Above the landmark arch is Foster's Rotunda. Enter through the lobby of 30 Rowes Wharf, immediately turn right, and take the elevator that runs straight to the ninth-floor rotunda. Step out onto the balcony and soak up the scenery. There's no admission charge, but open hours are limited: Monday through Friday from11am to 4pm.

educational corporation conducts historical and architectural tours that focus on neighborhoods or themes. The rigorously trained volunteer guides encourage questions. Buy tickets ($8) from the guide; reservations are not required. The 90-minute tours take place rain or shine. Call for offerings and schedules.

The **Society for the Preservation of New England Antiquities** (© 617/ 227-3956; www.spnea.org) offers a fascinating 2-hour tour that describes life in the mansions and garrets of Beacon Hill in 1800. "Magnificent and Modest" costs $10 and starts at the Harrison Gray Otis House, 141 Cambridge St., at 11am on Saturdays and Sundays from May through October. The price includes a tour of the Otis House; reservations are recommended.

The **Boston Park Rangers** (© 617/635-7383; www.ci.boston.ma.us/parks) periodically offer free guided walking tours of the Emerald Necklace, a loop of green spaces designed by pioneering American landscape architect Frederick Law Olmsted. The tours highlight the city's major parks and gardens, including Boston Common, the Public Garden, the Commonwealth Avenue Mall, the Muddy River in the Fenway, Olmsted Park, Jamaica Pond, the Arnold Arboretum, and Franklin Park. Check ahead for schedules.

The nonprofit **Boston History Collaborative** (© 617/574-5950) coordinates several new heritage trails. Presented as guided and self-guided walking tours, longer excursions by bus and boat, and copiously documented websites, they focus on maritime history (www.bostonbysea.org), literary history (www.Lit-Trail.org), immigration (www.BostonFamilyHistory.org), and inventions (www.innovationtrail.org). For information on the seaborne version of Boston by Sea, see "Sightseeing Cruises," below.

TROLLEY TOURS   Because Boston is so pedestrian friendly, this isn't the best choice for the able-bodied and unencumbered making a long visit. But if you're short on time, unable to walk long distances, or traveling with children, a trolley tour can be worth the money. The narrated tours can give you an overview of the sights before you focus on specific attractions, or you can use your all-day pass to hit as many places as possible in 8 hours or so.

The various companies cover the major attractions and offer informative narratives and anecdotes in their 90- to 120-minute tours. Most offer free reboarding if you want to visit the sites. Tickets cost $18 to $24 for adults, $12 or less for children. Boarding spots are at hotels, historic sites, and tourist information centers.

Each company paints its cars a different color. Orange-and-green **Old Town Trolleys** (© 617/269-7150; www.historictours.com) are the most numerous. Minuteman Tours' **Boston Trolley Tours** (© 617/269-3626; www.historictours. com) are blue; **Beantown Trolleys** (© 800/343-1328 or 781/968-6100; www.bostontrolley.com) say "Gray Line" but are red; and **CityView Luxury Trolleys** (© 800/525-2489 outside the 617 area code, or 617/363-7899) are silver. The **Discover Boston Multilingual Trolley Tours** (© 617/742-0767) vehicle is white, and conducts tours in Japanese, Spanish, French, German, and Italian.

SIGHTSEEING CRUISES ★★   The season runs from April through October, with spring and fall offerings often restricted to weekends. If you're prone to seasickness, check the size of the vessel (larger equals more comfortable) before buying tickets.

Boston Harbor Cruises, 1 Long Wharf (© 617/227-4321; www. bostonharborcruises.com), is the largest company. Ninety-minute **historic**

sightseeing cruises, which tour the Inner and Outer harbors, depart daily at 11am and 7pm (the sunset cruise), with extra excursions at busy times. Tickets are $15 for adults, $12 for seniors, and $10 for children under 12. The 45-minute *Constitution* cruise takes you around the Inner Harbor and docks at the Charlestown Navy Yard so you can visit "Old Ironsides." Tours leave Long Wharf hourly from 10:30am to 4:30pm, and on the hour from the navy yard from 11am to 5pm. Tickets are $8 for adults, $7 for seniors, and $6 for children. The same company offers service to **Georges Island,** where free water-taxi service to the rest of the Boston Harbor Islands is available (see "A Vacation in the Islands," below).

Massachusetts Bay Lines (© 617/542-8000; www.massbaylines.com) offers 55-minute harbor tours from Memorial Day to Columbus Day. Cruises leave from Rowes Wharf on the hour from 10am to 6pm; the price is $8 for adults, $5 for children and seniors. The 90-minute sunset cruise, at 7pm, costs $15 for adults, $10 for children and seniors.

The **Charles Riverboat Company** (© 617/621-3001; www.charlesriverboat. com) offers 55-minute narrated cruises around the lower Charles River basin and in the opposite direction, through the Charles River locks to Boston Harbor. Boats depart from the CambridgeSide Galleria mall; river tours leave on the hour from noon to 5pm, harbor tours once a day at 10:30am. Tickets for either tour are $8 for adults, $6 for seniors, and $5 for children 2 to 12.

The Boston History Collaborative's **Boston by Sea** tour (www.BostonBySea. org) is available as an entertaining but pricey 90-minute boat trip around the harbor. Subtitled "Living History in Story, Sites, and Songs," the excursion includes a thorough account of the city's maritime legacy, video clips, and even some tunes (namely, sea chanteys). Tickets cost $25 for adults, $20 for seniors and students, and $10 for children under 13. Tours leave Long Wharf daily at 1 and 3pm in warm weather. For reservations, call Boston Harbor Cruises (© 617/227-4321).

WHALE WATCHING 🐋🐋   For information on Cape Ann excursions, see "A Whale of an Adventure," in chapter 5.

The **New England Aquarium** (see "The Top Attractions," above) runs whale watches (© 617/973-5277) daily from May to mid-October and on weekends in April and late October. They travel several miles out to Stellwagen Bank, the feeding ground for whales as they migrate from Newfoundland to Province-town. Allow 3½ to 5 hours. Tickets are $27 for adults, $21.50 for seniors and college students, $19.50 for youths 12 to 18, and $17 for children 3 to 11. Children must be 3 years old and at least 30 inches tall. Reservations are strongly recommended.

Boston Harbor Whale Watch (© 617/345-9866; www.bostonwhale.com) promises more time watching whales than trying to find them. Tours depart from Rowes Wharf. In late June, they operate Fridays, Saturdays, and Sundays. From July to early September, there's service Monday through Friday at 10am, Saturday and Sunday at 9am and 2pm. Expect to spend about 4½ hours at sea. Tickets are $21 for adults, $18 for seniors and children under 13. Reservations are suggested.

ESPECIALLY FOR KIDS

Destinations with something for every family member include **Faneuil Hall Marketplace** (© 617/338-2323) and the **Museum of Fine Arts** (© 617/

Kids Boston by Duck

The most unusual way to see Boston is with **Boston Duck Tours** ★★★ (© **800/226-7442** or 617/723-DUCK; www.bostonducktours.com). The tours, offered only April through November, are pricey but great fun. Sightseers board a "duck," a reconditioned Second World War amphibious landing craft, on the Boylston Street side of the Prudential Center. The 80-minute narrated tour begins with a quick but comprehensive jaunt around the city. Then the duck lumbers down a ramp, splashes into the Charles River, and takes a spin around the basin. Tickets cost $22 for adults, $19 for seniors and students, $12 for children 4 to 12, and 25¢ for children under 4. Tours run every 30 minutes from 9am to 1 hour before sunset. You can buy tickets online or in person (inside the Pru or outside the New England Aquarium). Try to buy same-day tickets early in the day, or ask about the limited number of tickets available 2 days in advance. Reservations are not accepted (except for groups of more than 15). No tours are offered December through March.

267-9300), which offers special weekend and after-school programs. Hands-on exhibits are a big draw at the **Boston Tea Party Ship & Museum** (© **617/ 338-1773**), the **New England Aquarium** (© 617/973-5200), and the **USS *Constitution* Museum** (© 617/426-1812). The **Museum of Science** (© 617/ 723-2500) is not only hands-on paradise but also home to the **Charles Hayden Planetarium** and the **Mugar Omni Theater.** A **Red Sox game** (see "Spectator Sports," below) is another sure-fire kid pleaser.

The allure of seeing people the size of ants draws young visitors to the **John Hancock Observatory** (© 617/572-6429) and the **Prudential Center Skywalk** (© 617/236-3318). And they can see actual ants—though they might prefer the dinosaurs—at the Museum of Comparative Zoology, part of the **Harvard Museum of Natural History** (© **617/495-3045;** see "Exploring Cambridge," below).

Older children who have studied modern American history will enjoy a visit to the **John F. Kennedy Library and Museum** (© 617/929-4523). Middleschoolers who enjoyed Esther Forbes's *Johnny Tremain* might get a kick out of the **Paul Revere House** (© **617/523-2338**). Young visitors who have read Robert McCloskey's children's classic *Make Way for Ducklings* will relish a visit to the Public Garden, as will fans of E. B. White's *The Trumpet of the Swan,* who certainly will want to ride on the **swan boats.** Considerably less tame and much longer are **whale watches** (see "Organized Tours," above, and "A Whale of an Adventure," in chapter 5); **sightseeing cruises** fall somewhere in the middle.

The walking-tour company **Boston by Foot** ★★, 77 N. Washington St. (© **617/367-2345,** or 617/367-3766 for recorded info; www.bostonbyfoot. com), has a special program, **Boston by Little Feet,** geared to children 6 to 12 years old. The 1-hour walk gives a child's-eye view of the architecture along the Freedom Trail and of Boston's role in the American Revolution. Children must be accompanied by an adult. Tours ($6 per person) run May through October and meet at the statue of Samuel Adams on the Congress Street side of Faneuil Hall, Saturday at 10am, Sunday at 2pm, and Monday at 10am, rain or shine.

The **Historic Neighborhoods Foundation,** 99 Bedford St. (© **617/ 426-1885;** www.historic-neighborhoods.org), offers a 90-minute "Make Way for Ducklings" tour ($5 per person age 5 or older). Popular with children and adults, it follows the path of the Mallard family described in Robert McCloskey's famous book, and ends at the Public Garden.

Children's Museum ★★ *Kids*   A delightful destination for kids under 11, the Children's Museum is great fun for adults, too. Children can stick with the family or wander on their own, learning, doing, and role-playing. The centerpiece of the renovated warehouse building is a two-story-high maze, the **New Balance Climb,** which incorporates motor skills and problem-solving. The hands-on exhibits include, among many others, **Grandparents' Attic,** a souped-up version of playing dress-up at Grandma's; **Under the Dock,** an environmental exhibit that teaches about the Boston waterfront and allows kids to dress up in a crab suit; hands-on physical experiments (such as creating giant soap bubbles); and **Boats Afloat,** which has an 800-gallon play tank and a replica of the bridge of a working boat. Children under 4 and their caregivers have a special room, **Playspace,** that's packed with toys and activities. Check ahead for information on traveling exhibitions, participatory plays, and other special programs.

300 Congress St. (Museum Wharf). © 617/426-8855. www.bostonkids.org. Admission $7 adults; $6 children 2–15 and seniors; $2 children age 1; free for children under 1; $1 for all Fri 5–9pm. Sat–Thurs 10am–5pm; Fri 10am–9pm. Closed Thanksgiving, Christmas, and until noon on New Year's Day. T: Red Line to South Station. Walk north on Atlantic Ave. 1 block (past Federal Reserve Bank), turn right onto Congress St., walk 2 blocks (across bridge). Call for information on discounted parking.

6 Exploring Cambridge

Harvard Square ★ is a people-watching paradise of students, instructors, commuters, and sightseers. Restaurants and stores pack the three streets that radiate from the center of the square and the streets that intersect them. On weekend afternoons and evenings year-round, you'll hear music and see street performers. To get away from the urban bustle, stroll down to the paved paths along the Charles River.

From Boston, take the Red Line toward Alewife. In Cambridge, the subway stops at Kendall/MIT, and Central, Harvard, and Porter squares. If you're staying in or visiting Back Bay, a longer and more colorful route is the no. 1 bus (Harvard–Dudley), which runs along Mass. Ave.

By car from Boston, follow Mass. Ave., or take Storrow Drive along the south bank of the river to the Harvard Square exit. Memorial Drive runs along the north side of the river near MIT, Central Square, and Harvard. Traffic in and around Harvard Square is almost as bad as in downtown Boston. Once you get to Cambridge, park the car and walk.

HARVARD UNIVERSITY

Harvard is the oldest college in the country, and if you suggest aloud that it's not the best, you may encounter the attitude that inspired the saying, "You can always tell a Harvard man, but you can't tell him much." The university encompasses the college and 10 graduate and professional schools in more than 400 buildings around Boston and Cambridge. Free student-led tours of the main campus leave from the **Events & Information Center,** in Holyoke Center, 1350 Mass. Ave. (© **617/495-1573**), during the school year twice a day during the week and once on Saturday, except during vacations, and during the summer

Harvard Square & Environs

Arthur M. Sackler Museum **20**	Harvard Museum of Natural History **4**	Massachusetts Hall **11**
Busch–Reisinger Museum **21**	Harvard Square **8**	Memorial Church **17**
Cambridge Common **2**	Harvard Yard **14**	Memorial Hall **7**
Carpenter Center for the Visual Arts **22**	Hollis and Stoughton Halls **13**	Peabody Museum of Archaeology & Ethnology **5**
Christ Church **3**	Holyoke Center **23**	Science Center **6**
Fogg Art Museum **21**	John F. Kennedy Park **25**	Sever Hall **18**
Harvard Hall **9**	John Harvard Statue **15**	University Hall **16**
Harvard Lampoon Castle **24**	Johnston Gate **10**	Wadsworth House **12**
	Longfellow National Historic Site **1**	Widener Library **19**

four times a day Monday through Saturday and twice on Sunday. Call for exact times; reservations aren't necessary. You're also free to wander on your own. The Events & Information Center has maps, illustrated booklets, and self-guided walking-tour directions. You might want to check out the university's website at www.harvard.edu.

Harvard University Art Museums ✦ The Harvard art museums house a total of about 150,000 works in three collections. The exhibit spaces also serve as teaching and research facilities. You can take a 1-hour guided tour on weekdays September through June, and Wednesdays only in July and August.

The **Fogg Art Museum,** 32 Quincy St., near Broadway, centers on an impressive 16th-century Italian stone courtyard. Each of the 19 galleries holds something different—17th-century Dutch and Flemish landscapes, 19th-century British and American paintings and drawings, French paintings and drawings from the 18th century through the Impressionist period, contemporary sculpture, and changing exhibits.

The **Busch-Reisinger Museum,** in Werner Otto Hall (enter through the Fogg), is the only museum in North America devoted to the painting, sculpture, and decorative art of northern and central Europe, specifically Germany. The early-20th-century collections include works by Klee, Feininger, Kandinsky, and artists and designers associated with the Bauhaus.

The **Arthur M. Sackler Museum,** 485 Broadway, at Quincy Street, houses the university's collections of Asian, ancient, and Islamic art. They include internationally renowned Chinese jades and cave reliefs, superb Roman sculpture, Korean ceramics, Greek vases, and Persian miniature paintings and calligraphy.

32 Quincy St. and 485 Broadway. © 617/495-9400. www.artmuseums.harvard.edu. Admission to all three museums $5 adults, $4 seniors, $3 students, free for children under 18; free to all Wed 10am–5pm, Sat 10am–noon. Mon–Sat 10am–5pm; Sun 1–5pm. Closed major holidays. T: Red Line to Harvard. Cross Harvard Yard diagonally from the T station and cross Quincy St.

Harvard Museum of Natural History and Peabody Museum of Archaeology & Ethnology ⭐ *Kids* These fascinating museums house the university's collections of items and artifacts related to the natural world. The world-famous academic resource offers interdisciplinary programs and exhibitions that tie in elements of all the associated fields. You'll certainly find something interesting here, be it a dinosaur skeleton, a hunk of meteorite, a Native American artifact, or the world-famous Glass Flowers.

The Museum of Natural History comprises three institutions. The best-known museum is the **Botanical Museum,** and the best-known display is the **Glass Flowers** ⭐⭐⭐, 3,000 models of more than 840 plant species devised between 1887 and 1936 by the German father-and-son team of Leopold and Rudolph Blaschka. You may have heard about them, and you may be skeptical, but it's true: They look real. Children love the **Museum of Comparative Zoology** ⭐⭐, where dinosaurs share space with preserved and stuffed insects and animals that range in size from butterflies to giraffes. The **Mineralogical & Geological Museum** is the most specialized—hold off unless there's an interesting interdisciplinary display or you're really into rocks.

Young visitors enjoy the dollhouse-like "Worlds in Miniature" display at the **Peabody Museum** ⭐, which represents people from all over the world in scaled-down homes. The Peabody also boasts the **Hall of the North American Indian,** where 500 artifacts representing 10 cultures are on display.

Museum of Natural History: 26 Oxford St. © 617/495-3045. www.hmnh.harvard.edu. Peabody Museum: 11 Divinity Ave. © 617/496-1027. www.peabody.harvard.edu. Admission to both $5 adults, $4 seniors and students, $3 children 3–13; free to all Sat 9am–noon. Mon–Sat 9am–5pm; Sun 1–5pm. Closed July 4, Thanksgiving, Christmas, New Year's Day. T: Red Line to Harvard. Cross Harvard Yard, keeping John Harvard statue on right, and turn right at Science Center. First left is Oxford St.

A HISTORIC HOUSE

Longfellow National Historic Site ⭐ By the time you visit, this ravishing yellow mansion should have reopened after 2 years of refurbishment. The books and furniture have remained intact since the poet Henry Wadsworth Longfellow died here in 1882. Now a unit of the National Park Service, during the siege of Boston in 1775 to 1776 the house served as the headquarters of Gen. George Washington, with whom Longfellow was fascinated. The poet first lived in the house as a boarder in 1837; when he and Fanny Appleton married in 1843, her father made it a wedding present. On the absorbing tour— the only way to see the house—you'll learn about the history of the building and its famous occupants.

105 Brattle St. ℭ **617/876-4491**. www.nps.gov/long. Guided tour $2 adults, free for seniors and children under 17. Call ahead to confirm times. Tours June–Oct Wed–Sun and mid-Mar to May and Nov to mid-Dec Sat–Sun 10:45am, 11:45am, 1pm, 2pm, 3pm, and 4pm. Mid-Mar to May and Nov to mid-Dec Wed–Fri 12:30pm, 1:30pm, 2:30pm, and 3:30pm. Closed mid-Dec to mid-Mar. T: Red Line to Harvard, then follow Brattle St. about 7 blocks; house is on the right.

A CELEBRATED CEMETERY

Dedicated in 1831, **Mount Auburn Cemetery** ⚘, 580 Mt. Auburn St. (ℭ **617/ 547-7105**), was the first of America's rural, or garden, cemeteries. Since the day it opened, Mount Auburn has been a popular place to retreat and reflect. The graves of Henry Wadsworth Longfellow, Oliver Wendell Holmes, James Russell Lowell, and Winslow Homer are here. In season, you'll see gorgeous flowering trees and shrubs. The cemetery is open daily from 8am to dusk; there is no admission fee. Animals, picnicking, and jogging are not allowed. Bus routes 71 and 73 start at Harvard station and stop near the gates; they run frequently on weekdays, less often on weekends. From Harvard Square by car (5 minutes) or on foot (30 minutes), take Mount Auburn Street or Brattle Street west; just after they intersect, the gate is on the left. Stop at the office to pick up brochures and a map or to rent the 60-minute audio tour ($5; a $12 deposit is required), which you can play in your car or on a portable tape player. The **Friends of Mount Auburn Cemetery** (ℭ **617/864-9646**) conducts workshops and coordinates walking tours. Call for topics, schedules, and fees.

A STROLL AROUND CAMBRIDGE

To explore Harvard and the surrounding area, begin your walk in **Harvard Square.** Town and gown meet at this lively intersection, where you'll get a taste of the improbable mix of people drawn to the crossroads of Cambridge.

Start at the Harvard T station, with the **Harvard Coop** at your back. Walk half a block, crossing Dunster Street. To your right is **Holyoke Center,** an administration building designed by the Spanish architect Josep Luis Sert, the dean of the university's Graduate School of Design from 1953 to 1969, and a disciple of Le Corbusier.

Across the street is **Wadsworth House,** 1341 Mass. Ave., a yellow wood structure built in 1726 as a residence for Harvard's fourth president. Stop us if you've heard this one: George Washington slept here. Turn left and follow the outside of the brick wall along Mass. Ave. to another T entrance. Pass through **Johnston Gate,** which guards the oldest part of **Harvard Yard.** "The Yard" was just a patch of grass with grazing animals when Harvard College was established in 1636 to train young men for the ministry. The Continental Army, under Washington's command, spent the winter of 1775–76 here.

With Johnston Gate at your back, to your right is **Massachusetts Hall** (1720), the university's oldest surviving building. It houses the president's office and rooms for first-year students. To your left is **Harvard Hall** (1765), a classroom building. The matching side-by-side buildings behind Harvard Hall are **Hollis** and **Stoughton halls.** Hollis dates to 1763 and has been home to many students who went on to great fame, among them Ralph Waldo Emerson, Henry David Thoreau, and Charles Bulfinch.

Across the Yard is **University Hall,** the college's main administration building, designed by Bulfinch and constructed in 1812 and 1813. It's the backdrop of the **John Harvard statue** ⚘⚘, one of the most photographed objects in the Boston area. Designed by Daniel Chester French in 1884, it's known as the

"Statue of Three Lies" because the inscription reads "John Harvard—Founder—1638." In fact, the college was established in 1636; Harvard (one of many people involved) wasn't the founder, but donated money and his library; and this isn't John Harvard, anyway. No portraits of him survive, so the model was, according to various accounts, either his nephew or a student. Walk over to the statue and join the throng of tourists posing for pictures with the benevolent-looking gentleman.

Walk around University Hall into the adjoining quadrangle; you're leaving the "Old Yard" for the "New Yard," where commencement and other university-wide ceremonies take place. On your right is **Widener Library,** the centerpiece of the world's largest university library system. It was built in 1913 as a memorial to Harry Elkins Widener, a 1907 Harvard graduate who died when the *Titanic* sank in 1912. Legend has it that he was unable to swim 50 yards to a lifeboat, and his mother donated $2 million for the library on the condition that every undergraduate pass a 50-yard swimming test.

Facing the library is **Memorial Church,** built in 1931 and topped with a tower and weather vane 197 feet tall. You're welcome to look around this Georgian Revival–style edifice unless services are going on. The entrance is on the left. The south wall, toward the Yard, lists the names of Harvard graduates who died in the world wars, Korea, and Vietnam. One is Joseph P. Kennedy, Jr., '38, the president's brother.

Continue across the Yard onto Quincy Street. To your right is the curvilinear **Carpenter Center for the Visual Arts,** 24 Quincy St. Designed by the Swiss-French architect **Le Corbusier,** along with the team of Sert, Jackson, and Gourley, it was constructed from 1961 to 1963. It's the only building in North America designed by Le Corbusier.

Reenter the Yard, pass Memorial Church, and turn right. Follow the path out of the Yard to the **Science Center,** Zero Oxford St. The 10-story monolith supposedly resembles a Polaroid camera (Edwin H. Land, founder of Cambridge-based Polaroid Corporation, was one of its main benefactors). Sert also designed this structure, which was built from 1970 to 1972.

To your right as you face the Science Center is **Memorial Hall,** a Victorian structure built from 1870 to 1874. The hall of memorials (enter from Kirkland or Cambridge streets) is a transept where you can read the names of the Harvard men who died fighting for the Union during the Civil War—but not those who died for the Confederacy.

With the Science Center behind you and "Mem Hall" to your left, turn right, and follow the walkway for the equivalent of a block and a half as it curves around to the right. The **Harvard Law School** campus is on your right. Carefully cross Mass. Ave. to **Cambridge Common.** Memorials and plaques dot this well-used plot of greenery and bare earth. Turn left and head back toward Harvard Square; after a block or so you'll walk near or over **horseshoes** embedded in the concrete. This is the path William Dawes, Paul Revere's fellow alarm-sounder, took from Boston to Lexington on April 18, 1775.

Turn right onto Garden Street and find **Christ Church,** Zero Garden St. The oldest church in Cambridge, it was designed by Peter Harrison of Newport, R.I. (also the architect of King's Chapel in Boston), and opened in 1761. Note the square wooden tower. Inside the vestibule you can still see bullet holes made by British muskets.

With the church at your back, turn right and return to Mass. Ave. Turn right again, then walk 2 blocks into the middle of the square and 1 more block on

John F. Kennedy Street. Turn left onto Mount Auburn Street. Stay on the left-hand side of the street as you cross Dunster, Holyoke, and Linden streets.

The corner of Mount Auburn and Linden streets is a good vantage point for viewing the **Harvard Lampoon Castle,** designed by Wheelwright & Haven in 1909. Listed on the National Register of Historic Places, this is the home of Harvard's undergraduate humor magazine, the *Lampoon.* The main tower looks like a face, with windows as the eyes, nose, and mouth, topped by what looks like a miner's hat.

Follow Mount Auburn Street back to John F. Kennedy Street and turn left. Cross the street at some point, and follow it toward the Charles River, almost to Memorial Drive. On your right is **John F. Kennedy Park** and the adjacent Graduate School of Government. Walk away from the street to the fountain, engraved with excerpts from the president's speeches. This is an excellent place to take a break and plan the rest of your day.

7 Spectator Sports & Outdoor Pursuits

SPECTATOR SPORTS

Boston's reputation as a great sports town derives in part from the days when at least one pro team was one of the world's best. With the exception of the Patriots, who lost the 1997 Super Bowl, none of them has done much lately. But passions still run deep: Insult a local team and be ready to defend yourself. That enthusiasm also applies to college sports, particularly hockey, in which the Division I schools are fierce rivals.

BASEBALL   No other experience in sports matches watching the **Boston Red Sox** play at **Fenway Park** ★★★, which they do from April to early October, and later if they make the playoffs. The organization has announced ambitious (and coolly received) plans to demolish most of the current park—nothing is official, except the sense that if you've been planning to visit "sometime," you'd better make some plans. Adding to the Fenway mystique is the quirkiness of the oldest park in the major leagues (1912) and the fact that (as of press time) the team last won the World Series in 1918.

The Fenway Park **ticket office** (ⓒ **617/267-8661** for info, ⓒ **617/267-1700** for tickets, 617/482-4SOX for touch-tone ticketing; www.redsox.com) is at 4 Yawkey Way, near the corner of Brookline Avenue. Tickets go on sale in January; order early. Forced to choose between tickets for a low-numbered grandstand section (say, 10 or below) and less expensive bleacher seats, go for the bleachers and the better view. Throughout the season, a limited number of standing-room tickets go on sale the day of the game; also check to see whether returned tickets are for sale. Prices start at $16. Tickets for people with disabilities and for no-alcohol sections are available. Smoking is not allowed in the park. Games usually begin at 6 or 7pm on weeknights and 1pm on weekends. Take the Green Line B, C, or D to Kenmore or D to Fenway.

Tours (ⓒ **617/236-6666**) are offered May through September, Monday through Friday at 10am, 11am, noon, and 1pm, plus 2pm when the team is away. There are no tours on weekends, holidays, or before day games. Admission is $5 for adults, $4 for seniors, and $3 for children under 16.

BASKETBALL   Sixteen NBA championship banners hang in the FleetCenter, testimony to the glorious history of the **Boston Celtics.** Unfortunately, the most recent is from 1986. The Celtics play from early October to April or May; when a top contender is visiting, you may have trouble buying tickets. Prices are as low as $10 for some games and top out at $70. For information, call the **FleetCenter** (© 617/624-1000; www.nba.com/celtics); for tickets, call **Ticketmaster** (© 617/931-2000; www.ticketmaster.com). To reach the FleetCenter, take the Green or Orange Line or commuter rail to North Station.

FOOTBALL The **New England Patriots** (© 800/543-1776; www.patriots. com) were playing to sellout crowds even before they won the conference title in 1997 (and lost the Super Bowl). The Patriots play August through December, or January if they make the playoffs, at Foxboro Stadium on Route 1 in Foxboro, about a 45-minute drive south of the city. Call or check the website for public-transit options. Tickets ($25 to $65) almost always sell out. Plan as far in advance as you can.

HOCKEY The **Boston Bruins** are in roughly the same condition as the Celtics—burdened by history and looking to the future. Their games are exciting, especially if you happen to be in town at the same time as the archrival Montreal Canadiens, but among the priciest ($43 to $70) in the league. For information, call the **FleetCenter** (© 617/624-1000; www.bostonbruins.com); for tickets, call **Ticketmaster** (© 617/931-2000; www.ticketmaster.com). To reach the FleetCenter, take the Green or Orange Line or commuter rail to North Station.

Economical fans who don't have their hearts set on seeing a pro game will be pleasantly surprised by the quality of local **college hockey** ✿. Even for sold-out games, standing-room tickets are usually available shortly before game time. Local teams regularly hit the national rankings; they include **Boston College,** Conte Forum, Chestnut Hill (© 617/552-3000); **Boston University,** Walter Brown Arena, 285 Babcock St. (© 617/353-3838); **Harvard University,** Bright Hockey Center, North Harvard Street, Allston (© 617/495-2211); and **Northeastern University,** Matthews Arena, St. Botolph Street (© 617/ 373-4700).

HORSE RACING **Suffolk Downs** ✿, 111 Waldemar Ave., East Boston (© 617/567-3900; www.suffolkdowns.com), is one of the best-run smaller tracks in the country. The season runs from late September to early June, and there are extensive simulcasting options during and after the live season. The day's entries appear in the *Globe* and the *Herald.* The track is off Route 1A, about a mile from Logan Airport; the Blue Line of the T has a Suffolk Downs stop.

THE MARATHON Every year on Patriots Day (the third Monday in April), the **Boston Marathon** ✿✿✿ rules the roads from Hopkinton to Copley Square in Boston. Cheering fans line the entire route. An especially nice place to watch is tree-shaded Comm. Ave. between Kenmore Square and Mass. Ave., but you'll be in a crowd wherever you stand, particularly near the finish line in front of the Boston Public Library. For information about qualifying, contact the **Boston Athletic Association** (© 617/236-1652; www.bostonmarathon.org).

ROWING In late October, the **Head of the Charles Regatta** ✿ (© 617/ 864-8415; www.hocr.org) attracts some 4,000 oarsmen and oarswomen. They race against the clock for 4 miles, from the Charles River basin to the Eliot Bridge in west Cambridge. The largest crew event in the country draws tens of thousands of prepsters who socialize and occasionally even watch the action.

OUTDOOR PURSUITS

The incredibly helpful site maintained by the **Metropolitan District Commission** (© 617/727-9547; www.magnet.state.ma.us/mdc) includes descriptions

Jugglers, dancers and an assortment of acrobats fill the street.

She shoots you a wide-eyed look as a seven-foot cartoon character approaches.

What brought you here was wanting the kids

to see something magical while they still believed in magic.

America Online Keyword: Travel

With 700 airlines, 50,000 hotels and over 5,000 cruise and vaca-

tion getaways, you can now go places you've always dreamed of.

Travelocity.com
A Sabre Company
Go Virtually Anywhere.

WORLD'S LEADING TRAVEL WEB SITE, 5 YEARS IN A ROW" WORLD TRAVEL AWARDS

I HAVE TO CALL THE TRAVEL AGENCY AGAIN. DARN, OUT TO LUNCH. NOW HAVE TO CALL THE AIRLINE. I HATE CALLING THE AIRLINES. I GOT PUT ON HOLD AGAIN. "INSTRUMENTAL TOP 40" ... LOVELY. I HATE GETTING PUT ON HOLD. TICKET PRICES ARE ALL OVER THE MAP. HOW DO I DIAL INTERNA TIONALLY? OH SHOOT, FORGOT THE RENTAL CAR. I'M STILL ON HOLD. THIS MUSIC IS GIVING ME A HEADACHE. WONDER IF SOMEONE ELSE HAS CHEAPER FLIGHTS. FORGET IT, CAN' TAKE IT ANYMORE ... I'M HANGING UP

YAHOO! TRAVEL
100% MUZAK-FREE

Booking your trip online at Yahoo! Travel is simple. You compare the best prices. You click. You go have fun. Tickets, hotels, rental cars, cruises & more. Sorry, no muzak.

Finds A Vacation in the Islands

Majestic ocean views, hiking trails, historic sites, rocky beaches, nature walks, campsites, and picnic areas abound in New England. The **Boston Harbor Islands** 🐾🐾 (📞 617/223-8666; www.bostonislands.com) have them all. Their unspoiled beauty makes a welcome break from the urban landscape 45 minutes to the west, but they're not well known, even to many longtime Bostonians. Bring a sweater or jacket, and note that fresh water is available only on Georges Island (management suggests that you bring your own).

There are 30 islands in the Outer Harbor, and at least a half dozen are open to the public. Ferries run to the most popular, **Georges Island,** home of Fort Warren (1834), which held Confederate prisoners during the Civil War. You can investigate on your own or take a ranger-led tour. The island has a visitor center, refreshment area, fishing pier, picnic area, and wonderful view of Boston's skyline. Allow at least half a day, longer if you plan to take the free water taxi to **Lovell, Gallops, Peddocks, Bumpkin,** or **Grape Island,** all of which have picnic areas and campsites.

Administered as a National Park Partnership, the Boston Harbor Islands National Recreation Area (www.nps.gov/boha) is the focus of a public-private project designed to make the islands more interesting and accessible. For more information, visit the website, consult the staff at the **kiosk on Long Wharf,** stop at the **Discovery Center** in the courthouse on Fan Pier (on Northern Avenue across the Fort Point Channel from the Boston Harbor Hotel), or contact the **Friends of the Boston Harbor Islands** (📞 617/740-4290; www.fbhi.org).

Boston Harbor Cruises (📞 617/227-4321; www.bostonharborcruises. com) serves Georges Island from Long Wharf; the trip takes 45 minutes, and tickets cost $8 for adults, $7 for seniors, and $6 for children under 12. Cruises depart at 10am, noon, and 2pm on spring and fall weekends, and daily on the hour from 10am to 4pm in the summer. Water taxis and admission to the islands are free.

of properties and activities, and has a planning area to help you make the most of your time.

BEACHES   The beaches in Boston proper are not worth the trouble. The Boston Harbor water is not only bone-chilling, but also subject to being declared unsafe for swimming. If you want to swim, book a hotel with a pool. If you want the sand-between-your-toes experience, add some time to your excursion to the North Shore or to Walden Pond in Concord. See chapter 5 for information on suburban beaches.

BIKING   Even expert cyclists who feel comfortable with Boston's layout will be better off in Cambridge, which has bike lanes, or on the area's many bike paths. The 17¾-mile **Dr. Paul Dudley White Charles River Bike Path** loops from the Museum of Science to Watertown and back. You can enter and exit at many points along the way. Bikers share the path with lots of pedestrians, joggers, and in-line skaters. On summer Sundays from 11am to 7pm, **Memorial Drive** from Central Square to west Cambridge is closed to cars.

State law requires that children under 12 wear helmets. Bicycles are forbidden on buses and the Green Line, and on other lines during rush hours.

Most rental shops charge around $5 an hour, with a minimum of 2 hours, or a flat daily rate of $20 to $25. They include **Back Bay Bikes & Boards,** 333 Newbury St., near Mass. Ave. (© 617/247-2336), and **Community Bicycle Supply,** 496 Tremont St., near East Berkeley Street (© 617/542-8623). Across the river, try **Cambridge Bicycle,** 259 Mass. Ave., near MIT (© 617/ 876-6555), or **Ata Bikes,** 1771 Mass. Ave., near Porter Square (© 617/ 354-0907; www.atabike.com). For more information, contact **MassBike** (© 617/491-7433; www.massbike.org).

GOLF   The **Massachusetts Golf Association,** 175 Highland Ave., Needham (© 781/449-3000; www.mgalinks.org), represents more than 310 golf courses around the golf-mad state. Given a choice, play on a weekday, when you'll find lower prices and smaller crowds than on weekends.

One of the best public courses in the area, **Newton Commonwealth Golf Course,** 212 Kenrick St., Newton (© 617/630-1971; www.sterlinggolf.com), is a challenging 18-hole Donald Ross design. It's 5,305 yards from the blue tees, par is 70, and greens fees are $23 weekdays, $30 weekends. Within the city limits is the legendary 6,099-yard **William J. Devine Golf Course,** in Franklin Park, Dorchester (© 617/265-4084; www.sterlinggolf.com). As a Harvard student, Bobby Jones sharpened his game on the 18-hole, par-70 course, which emerged from a state of decrepitude in time to catch the golf boom of the '90s. Greens fees are $23 weekdays, $26 weekends. Less challenging but with more of a neighborhood feel is 9-hole, par-35 **Fresh Pond Golf Course,** 691 Huron Ave., Cambridge (© 617/349-6282; www.freshpondgolf.com). The 3,161-yard layout adjoins the Fresh Pond Reservoir (there's water on four holes) and charges $17, or $26 to go around twice, on weekdays; $20 and $35 on weekends.

GYMS   The concierge or front desk staff at your hotel can recommend a health club. The hotels with the best health clubs (see "Accommodations," above) include the Four Seasons Hotel, the Boston Harbor Hotel, the Royal Sonesta Hotel, and the Hilton Boston Logan Airport. The best combination of facilities and value is at the **Central Branch YMCA,** 316 Huntington Ave., near Symphony Hall (© 617/536-7800). A $10 one-day pass includes the use of the pool, gym, weight room, fitness center, and indoor track. Closer to downtown, **Fitcorp** (© 617/375-5600; www.fitcorp.com) charges $12 for a guest pass that includes well-equipped facilities but no pool. It has locations at 1 Beacon St. (© 617/248-9797), near Government Center; 133 Federal St. (© 617/ 542-1010), in the Financial District; and in the Prudential Center (© 617/ 262-2050).

ICE-SKATING   The rink at the Boston Common **Frog Pond** (© 617/ 635-2197) is an extremely popular cold-weather destination. It's an open surface with an ice-making system and a clubhouse where you can rent skates for $5; admission is $3 (free for children under 14). Try to go on a weekday; huge crowds descend on weekends.

IN-LINE SKATING   Unless you're confident of your ability and your knowledge of Boston traffic, stay off the streets. A favorite car-free spot is the **Esplanade,** between Back Bay and the Charles River. It continues onto the bike path that runs to Watertown and back, but once you leave the Esplanade, the pavement isn't totally smooth—your best bet is to wait for a Sunday in the summer, when **Memorial Drive** in Cambridge is closed to cars. It's a perfect surface.

The **InLine Club of Boston** offers event and safety information on its website (www.sk8net.com).

For rentals, visit the **Beacon Hill Skate Shop,** 135 Charles St. S. (© 617/482-7400), not far from the Esplanade, or **Blades Boards & Skates,** at 349A Newbury St. (© 617/437-6300), near Mass. Ave., or 38 John F. Kennedy St., Cambridge (© 617/491-4244), near Memorial Drive.

JOGGING   The **Dr. Paul Dudley White Charles River Bike Path** (see "Biking" above) is the area's busiest jogging trail. The 17¾-mile loop along the water is so popular because it's car-free (except at intersections), scenic, and generally safe. The bridges along the river allow for circuits of various lengths, but be careful around abutments, where you can't see far ahead. Don't jog at night, and try not to go alone. Visit the MDC website (www.magnet.state.ma.us/mdc) to view a map that gives distances. If the river's not convenient, check with the concierge or desk staff at your hotel for a map with suggested routes.

SAILING   The best deal in town is **Community Boating, Inc.,** 21 Embankment Rd., on the Esplanade (© 617-523-1038; www.community-boating.org). It's open April through November, and the fleet includes 13- to 23-foot sailboats as well as windsurfers and kayaks. Visitors pay $50 for 2 days of unlimited use in the Charles River Basin, a gorgeous but congested patch of water between Back Bay and Cambridge's Kendall Square.

TENNIS   Public courts maintained by the **Metropolitan District Commission** (© 617/727-5114) are available throughout the city at no charge. To find the one nearest you, call the MDC or ask the concierge or desk staff at your hotel. Well-maintained courts near downtown that seldom get busy until after work are on the Southwest Corridor Park in the South End (there's a nice one near **West Newton Street**) and off **Commercial Street** near the North Washington Street bridge in the North End. The courts on **Boston Common** and in **Charlesbank Park,** overlooking the river next to the State Police barracks on the bridge to the Museum of Science, are more crowded during the day.

8 Shopping

Boston-area shopping represents a harmonious blend of classic and contemporary. Both Boston and Cambridge boast tiny boutiques and sprawling malls, esoteric bookshops and national chain stores, classy galleries and snazzy secondhand-clothing outlets.

Note: Massachusetts has no sales tax on clothing priced below $175 or on food. All other items are taxed at 5% (as are restaurant meals and take-out food). The state no longer prohibits stores from opening before noon on Sunday, but many still wait until noon or don't open at all—call ahead before setting out.

BACK BAY   This is the area's premier shopping district. Dozens of classy galleries, shops, and boutiques make Newbury Street a world-famous destination. Nearby, a weatherproof walkway across Huntington Avenue links upscale **Copley Place** (© 617/375-4400) and the **Shops at Prudential Center** (© 800/SHOP-PRU). This is where you'll find the tony department stores **Neiman Marcus** (© 617/536-3660), **Lord & Taylor** (© 617/262-6000), and **Saks Fifth Avenue** (© 617/262-8500).

If you're passionate or just curious about art, try to set aside a couple of hours for strolling along **Newbury Street** ★★★. Besides being a prime location for upscale boutiques, it boasts an infinite variety of styles and media in the dozens of art galleries at street level and on the higher floors (remember to look up). Browsers and questions are welcome. Most galleries are open Tuesday through Sunday from 10 or 11am to 5:30 or 6pm. For specifics, pick up a copy of the free monthly *Gallery Guide* at businesses along Newbury Street, or check with the **Newbury Street League** (© 617/267-7961; www.newbury-st.com).

DOWNTOWN   **Faneuil Hall Marketplace** (© 617/338-2323) is the busiest attraction in Boston not only because of its smorgasbord of food outlets, but also for its shops, boutiques, and pushcarts, filled with everything from rubber stamps to costume jewelry, cookies to souvenirs. Although it has more upscale chain outlets than only-in-Boston shops, the latter category is a fun one. The best example is the **Boston City Store** (© 617/635-2911), on the lower level of Faneuil Hall. It sells the equivalent of the municipal attic and basement—clothing, office equipment, even old street signs and mounted-police horseshoes. The stock changes regularly according to what has outlived its usefulness or been declared surplus.

If the hubbub here is too much for you, stroll over to **Charles Street,** at the foot of Beacon Hill. A short but commercially dense (and picturesque) street, it's home to perhaps the best assortment of gift and antiques shops in the city. Be sure to check out the contemporary home accessories at **Koo De Kir**, 34 Charles St. (© 617/723-8111), the well-edited selection at **Upstairs Downstairs Antiques,** 93 Charles St. (© 617/367-1950), and engagingly funky gifts at **Black Ink**, 101 Charles St. (© 617/723-3883).

One of Boston's oldest shopping areas is **Downtown Crossing.** Now a traffic-free pedestrian mall along Washington, Winter, and Summer streets near Boston Common, it's home to two major department stores (**Filene's** and **Macy's**); tons of smaller clothing, shoe, and music stores; food and merchandise pushcarts; and outlets of two major bookstore chains, **Barnes & Noble** and **Borders.**

Downtown Crossing is where you'll find **Filene's Basement** ✸✸✸, 426 Washington St. (© 617/542-2011), a New England legend. The famed automatic markdown policy (25% off the already-discounted price after 2 weeks on the selling floor, up to 75% after 7 weeks) applies only here, at the flagship store. We happen to love this sort of place, but others find that battling the crowds isn't worth the payoff—the selling floors are pretty wild at busy times.

CAMBRIDGE   The bookstores, boutiques, and T-shirt shops of **Harvard Square** lie about 15 minutes from downtown Boston by subway. Despite the neighborhood association's efforts, chain stores have swept over "the Square." You'll find a mix of national and regional outlets, and more than a few persistent independent retailers. They include the delightful children's store **Calliope,** 33 Brattle St. (© 617/876-4149); **Colonial Drug,** 49 Brattle St. (© 617/864-2222), which stocks hard-to-find perfume and other high-end cosmetics; **Oona's,** 1210 Mass. Ave. (© 617/491-2654), a trove of lovely "experienced" clothing and accessories; and the **Harvard Shop,** 52 John F. Kennedy St. (© 617/864-3000), which carries excellent souvenirs.

For a less generic experience, walk along **Mass. Ave.** in either direction to the next T stop. The stroll takes about an hour. Heading north toward **Porter Square,** be sure to stop at **Joie de Vivre,** 1792 Mass. Ave. (© 617/864-8188), a top-notch gift shop. Going southeast to **Central,** pop into board-game central, **The Games People Play,** 1100 Mass. Ave. (© 800/696-0711 or 617/492-0711), and **Pearl Art & Craft Supplies,** 579 Mass. Ave. (© 617/547-6600), an excellent link in the national discount chain.

Finds **By the Book**

Bookworms flock to Cambridge; Harvard Square in particular caters to general and specific audiences. Check out the basement of the **Harvard Book Store**, 1256 Mass. Ave. (© **800/542-READ** outside of 617 area code, or 617/661-1515; www.harvard.com), for great deals on remainders and used books; and **WordsWorth Books**, 30 Brattle St. (© **800/899-2202** or 617/354-5201; www.wordsworth.com), for a huge discounted selection. Up the street, children's books have their own store at **Curious George Goes to WordsWorth**, 1 John F. Kennedy St. (© **617/498-0062**; www. curiousg.com). Barnes & Noble runs the book operation at the **Harvard Coop**, 1400 Mass. Ave. (© **617/499-2000**; www.thecoop.com), which stocks textbooks, academic works, and a large general selection. Two excellent Boston stores with huge selections of used merchandise are the **Avenue Victor Hugo Bookshop**, 339 Newbury St. (© **617/266-7746**; www. avenuevictorhugobooks.com), in Back Bay, and the **Brattle Book Shop**, 9 West St. (© **800/447-9595** or 617/542-0210; www.brattlebookshop.com), near Downtown Crossing. Also near Downtown Crossing are **Barnes & Noble**, 395 Washington St. (© **617/426-5184**; www.barnesandnoble. com), and **Borders Books & Music**, 24 School St. (© **617/557-7188**; www. borders.com).

And if you just can't manage without a trip to a mall, head to East Cambridge. Take the Green Line to Lechmere, or the Red Line to Kendall/MIT and the free shuttle bus to the **CambridgeSide Galleria,** 100 CambridgeSide Place (© **617/ 621-8666**).

9 Boston & Cambridge After Dark

For up-to-date entertainment listings, consult the "Calendar" section of the Thursday *Boston Globe,* the "Scene" section of the Friday *Boston Herald,* and the Sunday arts sections of both papers. Three free publications, available at newspaper boxes around town, publish nightlife listings: the *Boston Phoenix,* the *Stuff@Night* (a *Phoenix* offshoot), and the *Improper Bostonian.* The *Phoenix* website (www.bostonphoenix.com) archives the paper's season preview issues; especially before a summer or fall visit, it's a worthwhile planning tool.

GETTING TICKETS   Some companies and venues sell tickets over the phone or online; many will refer you to a ticket agency. The major agencies that serve Boston, **Ticketmaster** (© **617/931-2000;** www.ticketmaster.com), **Next Ticketing** (© **617/423-NEXT;** www.nextticketing.com), and **Tele-charge** (© **800/447-7400** or TTY 888/889-8587; www.telecharge.com), calculate service charges per ticket, not per order. To avoid the fee, visit the box office in person. If you wait until the day before or day of a performance, you'll sometimes have access to tickets that were held back for one reason or another and have just gone on sale.

DISCOUNT TICKETS   Visit a BosTix (© **617/482-2849;** www.boston. com/artsboston) booth at Faneuil Hall Marketplace (on the south side of Faneuil Hall) or in Copley Square (at the corner of Boylston and Dartmouth streets). Same-day tickets to musical and theatrical performances are half price, subject to availability. Credit cards are not accepted, and there are no refunds or exchanges. Check the board for the day's offerings. BosTix also sells coupon books offering discounted and two-for-one admission to many area museums; full-price advance tickets; and tickets to museums, historic sites, and attractions in and around town. The booths, which are also Ticketmaster outlets, are open Tuesday through Saturday from 10am to 6pm (half-price tickets go on sale at 11am), Sunday from 11am to 4pm. The Copley Square location is open Monday from 10am to 6pm.

THE PERFORMING ARTS

The city's premier classical performance hall is **Symphony Hall,** 301 Mass. Ave. (© **617/266-2492;** www.bso.org), which turned 100 in 2000. It plays host to other notable groups and artists when the BSO and the Pops are away. The **Hatch Shell** on the Esplanade (© **617/727-9547,** ext. 450) is an amphitheater best known as the home of the Boston Pops' Fourth of July concerts. On summer nights, free music and dance performances and films take over the stage to the delight of crowds on the lawn.

Other venues that attract big-name visitors include the **Berklee Performance Center,** 136 Mass. Ave. (© **617/266-1400,** ext. 8820; www.berkleebpc.com); the **Boston Center for the Arts,** 539 Tremont St. (© **617/426-7700;** www. bcaonline.org); **Jordan Hall,** 30 Gainsborough St. (© **617/536-2412;** www. newenglandconservatory.edu/jordanhall); and **Sanders Theatre,** 45 Quincy St., Cambridge (© **617/496-2222;** www.fas.harvard.edu/~memhall).

THE MAJOR COMPANIES

In addition to the companies listed below, the **Boston Lyric Opera** (© **617/ 542-6772** or 617/542-4912; www.blo.org) performs classical and contemporary works. The season runs from October to March. Performances are at the **Shubert Theatre,** 265 Tremont St., and tickets cost $27.50 to $108.

Boston Symphony Orchestra   The Boston Symphony, one of the world's greatest, was founded in 1881. The repertoire includes contemporary music, but classical is the BSO's calling card—you might want to schedule your trip to coincide with a particular performance, or with a visit by a celebrated guest artist or conductor. The season runs from October to April, with performances most Tuesday, Thursday, and Saturday evenings; Friday afternoons; and some Friday evenings. Explanatory talks (included in the ticket price) begin 30 minutes before the curtain. If you can't get tickets in advance, check at the box office for returns from subscribers 2 hours before showtime. A limited number of rush tickets (one per person) are available on the day of the performance for Tuesday and Thursday evening and Friday afternoon programs. Some Wednesday evening and Thursday morning rehearsals are open to the public. Symphony Hall, 301 Mass. Ave. (at Huntington Ave.). © 617/266-1492 or 617/CONCERT (program information). SymphonyCharge © 888/266-1200 (outside 617) or 617/266-1200. www.bso.org. Tickets $25–$83. Rush tickets $8 (on sale 9am Fri, 5pm Tues and Thurs). Rehearsal tickets $14.50. T: Green Line E to Symphony, or Orange Line to Mass. Ave.

Boston Pops   From early May to early July, members of the Boston Symphony Orchestra lighten up. Tables and chairs replace the floor seats at Symphony Hall, and drinks and light refreshments are served. The Pops play a range of music from light classical to show tunes to popular music (hence the name), sometimes with celebrity guest stars. Performances are Tuesday through Sunday evenings. Special holiday performances in December ($19 to $72) usually sell out well in advance, but it can't hurt to check; tickets go on sale in late October. The regular season ends with a week of free outdoor concerts at the Hatch Shell on the Esplanade along the Charles River. It includes the traditional Fourth of July concert. Symphony Hall, 301 Massachusetts Ave. (at Huntington Ave.). ✆ 617/266-1492 or 617/CONCERT (program information). SymphonyCharge ✆ 888/266-1200 (outside 617) or 617/266-1200. www.bso.org/pops. Tickets $35–$55 for tables; $14–$35 for balcony seats. T: Green Line E to Symphony, or Orange Line to Mass. Ave.

Boston Ballet Boston Ballet's reputation seems to jump a notch every time someone says, "So it's not just *The Nutcracker.*" The country's fourth-largest dance company performs the holiday staple from Thanksgiving through New Year's. During the rest of the season (October through May), it presents an eclectic mix of classic story ballets and contemporary works. Because the Wang was originally a movie theater, the pitch of the seats makes the top two balconies less than ideal for ballet—paying more for a better seat is a good investment. 19 Clarendon St. ✆ 617/695-6955 or 800/447-7400 (Tele-charge). www.bostonballet.org. Performances at the Wang Theatre, 270 Tremont St. (box office Mon–Sat 10am–6pm). Tickets $23–$73. Student rush tickets (1 hr. before curtain) $12.50, except for The Nutcracker. T: Green Line to Boylston.

THEATER & PERFORMANCE ART

Boston is one of the last cities for pre-Broadway tryouts, allowing an early look at a classic (or classic flop) in the making. It's also a popular destination for touring companies of established Broadway hits. You'll find most of the shows headed to or coming from Broadway in the **Theater District,** at the **Colonial Theatre,** 106 Boylston St. (✆ 617/426-9366); the **Shubert Theatre,** 265 Tremont St. (✆ 617/482-9393); the **Wang Theatre,** 270 Tremont St. (✆ 617/482-9393; www.wangcenter.org); and the **Wilbur Theater,** 246 Tremont St. (✆ 617/423-4008).

The excellent local theater scene boasts the **Huntington Theatre Company,** which performs at the Boston University Theatre, 264 Huntington Ave. (✆ 617/266-0800; www.huntington.org), and the **American Repertory Theatre,** which makes its home at Harvard University's Loeb Drama Center, 64 Brattle St., Cambridge (✆ 617/547-8300; www.amrep.org).

The off-Broadway performance-art sensation **Blue Man Group** branched out from New York to Boston in 1995. The troupe of three cobalt-colored entertainers uses music, percussion, food, and audience participants—props include social commentary, Twinkies, marshmallows, breakfast cereal, toilet paper, and lots of blue paint. Older children and teenagers enjoy the mayhem as much as adults. Shows are at the **Charles Playhouse** (✆ 617/426-6912), 74 Warrenton St., in the Theater District, at 8pm Wednesday and Thursday, 7 and 10pm Friday and Saturday, and 3 and 6pm Sunday. Tickets are $53 and $43 at the box office and through Ticketmaster (✆ 617/931-ARTS).

CHURCH CONCERTS

Fridays at Trinity This landmark church features 30-minute organ recitals by local and visiting artists on Fridays at 12:15pm. Take advantage of the chance to look around the architectural showpiece. Trinity Church, Copley Sq. ✆ 617/536-0944. Donations accepted. T: Green Line to Copley or Orange Line to Back Bay.

King's Chapel Noon Hour Recitals Organ, instrumental, and vocal solos fill this historic building with music and make for a pleasant break along the Freedom Trail. Concerts are at 12:15pm on Tuesdays. 58 Tremont St. ✆ 617/227-2155. $2 donation requested. T: Red or Green Line to Park St.

THE CLUB & MUSIC SCENE

The Boston-area club scene changes constantly, and somewhere out there is a good time for everyone, regardless of age, clothing style, musical taste, or budget. Check the "Calendar" section of the Thursday *Globe*, the *Phoenix*, the "Scene" section of the Friday *Herald*, *Stuff@Night*, or the *Improper Bostonian* while you're planning.

Bars close at 1am, clubs at 2am. The T shuts down between 12:30 and 1am. The drinking age is 21; a valid driver's license or passport is required as proof of age. The law is strictly enforced, especially near college campuses (in other words, practically everywhere). Be prepared to show an ID if you appear to be younger than 35 or so, and try to be patient while the amazed 30-year-old ahead of you fishes out a license.

Big-name rock and pop artists play the **FleetCenter**, 150 Causeway St. (© **617/624-1000;** www.fleetcenter.com), when it's not in use by the Bruins (hockey), the Celtics (basketball), the circus (in October), and touring ice shows. Concerts are in the round or on the arena stage.

COMEDY

The Comedy Connection at Faneuil Hall A large room with a clear view from every seat, the oldest original comedy club in town (established in 1978) draws top-notch talent from near and far. Big-name national acts lure enthusiastic crowds, and the openers are often just as funny but not as famous—yet. Shows are nightly at 8pm, plus Friday and Saturday at 10:15pm. The cover seldom tops $15 during the week, but jumps for a big name appearing on a weekend. The Backstage restaurant-club next door, under the same ownership, offers dinner-show packages. Quincy Market. © **888/398-5100** or 617/248-9700. www. comedyconnectionboston.com. Cover $10–$37. T: Green or Blue Line to Government Center or Orange Line to Haymarket.

The Comedy Studio *(Finds* Nobody here is a sitcom star—yet. With a growing reputation for ferreting out undiscovered talent, the no-frills Comedy Studio draws connoisseurs, college students, and network scouts. It's not just setup-punchline-laugh, either; sketches and improv spice up the standup. At the Hong Kong restaurant, 1236 Mass. Ave., Cambridge. © **617/661-6507.** www.thecomedystudio. com. Cover $5–$7. T: Red Line to Harvard.

DANCE CLUBS

Avalon A cavernous space divided into several levels, with a full concert stage, private booths and lounges, large dance floors, and a spectacular light show, Avalon is either great fun or sensory overload. It recently expanded, allowing more concert bookings (They Might Be Giants, O-Town, and Elliott Smith have played recently); when the stage is not in use, DJs spin for the crowd of 20- and 30-somethings. Friday is "Avaland," with national names in the booth and costumed house dancers on the floor. On Saturday (suburbanites' night out), expect more mainstream dance hits. The dress code calls for jackets, shirts with collars, and no jeans or athletic wear. Open Thursday (international night) through Sunday (gay night) from 10pm to 2am. 15 Lansdowne St. © **617/262-2424.** Cover $5–$20. T: Green Line B, C, or D to Kenmore.

The Roxy This former hotel ballroom boasts excellent DJs and live music, a huge dance floor, a stage, and a balcony (perfect for checking out the action below). Occasional concerts and boxing cards take good advantage of the sight lines. Call for the latest schedule—offerings change regularly. The crowd tends to be a bit older than at Avalon. Open from 8pm (entertainment starts at 10pm) to 2am Thursday through Saturday, and some Wednesdays and Sundays. No jeans or athletic shoes. In the Tremont Boston hotel, 279 Tremont St. ℭ 617/338-7699. www.gbcx.com/roxy. Cover $10–$15. T: Green Line to Boylston.

FOLK & ECLECTIC

Club Passim   Passim has launched more folk careers than the mass production of acoustic guitars—Joan Baez, Suzanne Vega, and Tom Rush started out here. In a basement on the street between buildings of the Harvard Coop, this legendary coffeehouse (which doesn't serve alcohol) enjoys an international reputation built on more than 30 years of nurturing new talent and showcasing established musicians. There's live music nightly, and coffee and food until 10pm. Tuesday is open-mike night. Open Sunday through Thursday from 11am to 11pm, Friday and Saturday until 4am. 47 Palmer St., Cambridge. ℭ 617/492-7679. www.clubpassim.org. Cover $5–$25; most shows $12 or less. T: Red Line to Harvard.

Johnny D's Uptown Restaurant & Music Club *Finds*   This family-owned and -operated establishment is one of the best in the area. It draws a congenial postcollegiate-and-up crowd for acts on international tours as well as acts that haven't been out of eastern Massachusetts. The music ranges from zydeco to rock, rockabilly to jazz, blues to ska. This place is worth a long trip, but it's only two stops past Harvard Square on the Red Line (about a 15-minute ride at night). Open daily from 11:30am to 1am. Brunch starts at 9am on weekends; dinner runs from 4:30 to 9:30pm Tuesday through Saturday, with lighter fare until 11pm. 17 Holland St., Davis Sq., Somerville. ℭ 617/776-2004 or 617/776-9667 (concert line). www.johnnyds.com. Cover $2–$16, usually $5–$10. T: Red Line to Davis.

JAZZ & BLUES

On summer Fridays at 6:30pm, the **Waterfront Jazz Series** (ℭ 617/635-3911) brings amateurs and professionals to Christopher Columbus Park, on the waterfront, for a refreshing interlude of free music and cool breezes. On summer Thursdays at 6pm, the **Boston Harbor Hotel** (ℭ 617/439-7000) stages performances on the "Blues Barge," which floats in the water behind the hotel. The *Boston Globe* Jazz & Blues Festival (ℭ 617/267-4301; www.boston.com/jazzfest) is usually scheduled for the third week of June. Constellations of jazz and blues stars (large and small) appear, sometimes free, often outdoors. The festival wraps up with a free Sunday program at the Hatch Shell.

House of Blues *Kids*   The original House of Blues, near Harvard Square, packs 'em in every evening and on weekend afternoons. It attracts tourists, music buffs, and big names—Mighty Sam McClain, Junior Brown, Tom Tom Club, and the Fabulous Thunderbirds have played recently. The restaurant is open Monday through Saturday from 11:30am to 11pm, Sunday from 4:30 to 11pm; the music hall Sunday through Wednesday until 1am, Thursday through Saturday until 2am. **Sunday gospel buffet brunch** seatings are at 10am, noon, and 2pm; advance tickets ($26 for adults, $13 for children) are highly recommended. 96 Winthrop St., Cambridge. ℭ 617/491-2583, or 617/497-2229 for tickets. Dining reservations (ℭ 617/491-2100) accepted for parties of 25 or more. www.hob.com. Cover $7–$30; Fri–Sat matinee no cover. T: Red Line to Harvard.

Regattabar   The Regattabar's selection of local and international artists is often considered the best in the area—a title that Scullers (see below) is happy to dispute. Irma Thomas, Joe Lovano, McCoy Tyner, and Rebecca Parris have appeared recently. The large third-floor room holds about 200 and, unfortunately, sometimes gets a little noisy. Buy tickets in advance from Concertix (there's a service charge), or try your luck at the door an hour before showtime. Open Tuesday through Saturday and some Sundays, with one or two performances per night. In the Charles Hotel, 1 Bennett St., Cambridge. © **617/661-5000** or 617/876-7777 (Concertix). Tickets $8–$35. T: Red Line to Harvard.

Scullers Jazz Club Overlooking the Charles River, Scullers is a lovely, comfortable room that books top singers and instrumentalists—recent notables include Branford Marsalis, Abbey Lincoln, Chuck Mangione, and (quite a coup) Bobby Short. Patrons tend to be more hard-core and quieter than the crowds at the Regattabar, but it really depends on who's performing. There are usually two shows a night Tuesday through Saturday; the box office is open Monday through Saturday from 11am to 6:30pm. Ask about dinner packages, which include preferred seating and a four-course meal. In the Doubletree Guest Suites hotel, 400 Soldiers Field Rd. © **617/562-4111** or 617/931-2000 (Ticketmaster). www.scullersjazz.com. Tickets $10–$40. Validated parking available.

Wally's Cafe This Boston institution, near a busy corner in the South End, opened in 1947. It draws a notably diverse crowd—black, white, straight, gay, affluent, indigent—and features nightly live music by local ensembles, students and instructors from the Berklee College of Music, and (on occasion) internationally renowned musicians. 427 Mass. Ave. © **617/424-1408.** www.wallyscafe.com. No cover (one-drink minimum). T: Orange Line to Mass. Ave.

ROCK & ALTERNATIVE

Lilli's A classy, lounge-like space on a nondescript strip, Lilli's is relatively new and indisputably cool. It attracts a funky 20- to 40-something crowd—more grad student than law student, if you know what we mean. The co-owners include a respected local booker and a veteran DJ, so the recorded music is nearly as good as the top-notch local (and sometimes national) rock, folk, roots, and jazz artists. 608 Somerville Ave., Somerville. © **617/591-1661.** www.lillisclub.com. T: Red Line to Porter; 10-min. walk.

The Middle East The best rock club in the area books an impressive variety of progressive and alternative rock in two rooms (upstairs and downstairs) every night. Showcasing top local talent as well as bands with local roots and international reputations, it's a popular hangout that gets crowded, hot, and *loud.* Some shows are all ages (most are 18-plus); the age of the crowd varies with the performer. 472–480 Mass. Ave., Central Sq., Cambridge. © **617/864-EAST** or 617/931-2000 (Ticketmaster). www.mideastclub.com. Cover $7–$15. T: Red Line to Central.

Paradise Rock Club Hard by the Boston University campus, the medium-sized Paradise draws enthusiastic, student-intensive crowds for top local rock and alternative performers. You might see national names or others who aren't ready to headline a big show. Most shows are 18-plus. You must be 21 to drink alcohol, a policy that became nonnegotiable here after a months-long "vacation" courtesy of the Boston Licensing Board; don't forget your ID. 967 Commonwealth Ave. © **617/562-8804** or 617/423-NEXT for tickets. www.dlclive.com. T: Green Line B to Pleasant St.

Toad *(Value* Essentially a bar with a stage, this smoky, claustrophobic space (the high ceiling helps a little) attracts a savvy three-generation clientele with big local names and no cover. Toad enjoys good acoustics but not much elbow-room—a plus when restless musicians wander into the crowd. 1912 Mass. Ave., Cambridge. © **617/497-4950** (info line). No cover. T: Red Line to Porter.

T. T. the Bear's Place   This no-frills spot generally attracts a young crowd, but 30-somethings will feel comfortable, too. Bookings range from cutting-edge alternative rock and roots music to ska and funk shows to up-and-coming pop acts. New bands predominate early in the week, with more established artists on weekends. Open Monday from 7pm to midnight, Tuesday through Sunday from 6pm to 1am. 10 Brookline St., Cambridge. ℂ 617/492-0082 or 617/492-BEAR (concert line). www.mindspring.com/~ttthebears. Cover $3–$15, usually less than $10. T: Red Line to Central.

BARS & LOUNGES

The Bay Tower   This posh 33rd-floor lounge affords a mesmerizing view of the harbor, the airport, and Faneuil Hall Marketplace. There's dancing to live music Monday through Saturday (piano on weeknights, jazz quartet Friday and Saturday). No denim or athletic shoes. 60 State St. ℂ 617/723-1666. www. baytower.com. T: Orange or Blue Line to State.

The Black Rose   Purists might sneer at the Black Rose's touristy location, but performers don't. Sing along with the authentic entertainment at this jam-packed pub and restaurant at the edge of Faneuil Hall Marketplace. You might be able to make out the tune on a fiddle over the din. 160 State St. ℂ 617/742-2286. www.irishconnection.com. Cover $3–$5. T: Orange or Blue Line to State.

Brew Moon Restaurant & Microbrewery   Fresh, handcrafted beer meets tasty edibles at these popular spots. The Munich Gold has won more awards than Tom Hanks; for something lighter, try the out-of-this-world house-brewed root beer. Both locations feature live music at the **Sunday jazz brunch,** from 11am to 3pm. 115 Stuart St. ℂ 617/742-BREW. T: Green Line to Boylston. 50 Church St., Cambridge. ℂ 617/499-BREW. T: Red Line to Harvard.

Bristol Lounge   An elegant room with soft lounge chairs and a fireplace, the Bristol is an oasis anytime, and features a fabulous dessert buffet on weekend nights. There's live jazz every evening, and food until 11:30pm (12:30am on Friday and Saturday). In the Four Seasons Hotel, 200 Boylston St. ℂ 617/351-2053. T: Green Line to Arlington.

Bull & Finch Pub   If you're out to impersonate a native, try not to be shocked when you enter "the *Cheers* bar" and the inside looks nothing like the bar on the TV show. (The outside does, though—bring a camera.) The Bull & Finch really is a neighborhood bar, but today it's far better known for attracting legions of out-of-towners, who find good pub grub and plenty of souvenirs. 84 Beacon St. ℂ 617/227-9605. www.cheersboston.com. T: Green Line to Arlington.

Casablanca   Students and professors jam this legendary Harvard Square watering hole, especially on weekends. It offers an excellent jukebox, excellent food, and excellent eavesdropping. 40 Brattle St., Cambridge. ℂ 617/876-0999. T: Red Line to Harvard.

Grendel's Den   A vestige of pre-franchise Harvard Square, this cozy subterranean space reopened after lengthy renovations and quickly reclaimed its position as *the* place to celebrate turning 21. Recent grads and grad students dominate, but Grendel's has been so popular for so long that it also gets its share of Gen Y's parents. 89 Winthrop St., Cambridge. ℂ 617/491-1050. T: Red Line to Harvard.

Hard Rock Cafe *Kids*   This link in the chain is a fun one—just ask the other tourists in line with you. The bar is shaped like a guitar, and the stained-glass windows glorify rock stars. Memorabilia of Jimi Hendrix, Elvis Presley, Madonna, local heroes Aerosmith and the Cars, and others decorates the walls.

The restaurant menu favors salads, burgers, and sandwiches (including the legendary "pig sandwich"). 131 Clarendon St. ✆ **617/424-ROCK.** www.hardrock.com. T: Orange Line to Back Bay or Green Line to Copley.

John Harvard's Brew House   This subterranean Harvard Square hangout pumps out terrific English-style brews in a clublike setting and prides itself on its food. The beer selection changes regularly; it includes at least one selection from each "family" (ambers, porters, seasonals, and more), all brewed on the premises. 33 Dunster St., Cambridge. ✆ **617/868-3585.** www.johnharvards.com. T: Red Line to Harvard.

Mr. Dooley's Boston Tavern   Sometimes an expertly poured Guinness is all you need. If one of the nicest bartenders in the city pours it, so much the better. This Financial District bar, an after-work hot spot, offers many imported beers on tap, live music, and a menu of pub favorites. 77 Broad St. ✆ **617/338-5656.** www.somerspubs.com. Cover $3 Fri–Sat. T: Orange or Blue Line to State.

The Purple Shamrock   This rowdy, fun place near Faneuil Hall attracts wall-to-wall 20-somethings with DJs, cover bands, and, we're obliged to report, karaoke (on Tuesday). 1 Union St. ✆ **617/227-2060.** Cover $3–$6 Thurs–Sat. T: Green or Blue Line to Government Center, or Orange Line to Haymarket.

Samuel Adams Brew House   This dark, sometimes noisy spot boasts excellent pretzels, friendly service, and the signature local brew, guaranteed to be served fresh. Choose from the dozen beers on tap or order a sampler of four. In the Lenox Hotel, 710 Boylston St. ✆ **617/536-2739.** T: Green Line to Copley.

Top of the Hub   The 52nd-story view of greater Boston from this appealing lounge is especially lovely at sunset. There is music and dancing nightly. Dress is casual but neat. Prudential Center, 800 Boylston St. ✆ **617/536-1775.** T: Green Line E to Prudential.

5

Side Trips from Boston: Lexington & Concord, the North Shore & Plymouth

by Marie Morris

Besides being, in the words of Oliver Wendell Holmes, "the hub of the solar system," Boston is the hub of a network of wonderful day trips and longer excursions. The destinations in this chapter are lively communities where you'll find sights and attractions of great beauty and historical significance. Exploring can take as little as half a day or as long as a week (or more).

WEST OF BOSTON If time is short, combine a visit to Cambridge (see chapter 4) with a trip to **Lexington** 🎔 and **Concord** 🎔🎔🎔 for a hefty dose of American history. The route that Paul Revere took out of Boston on April 18, 1775, is tough to follow—he started by crossing the harbor in a rowboat, for one thing—but his fellow rider William Dawes cut through Harvard Square. Both proceeded to warn the colonists that British troops were on the march.

NORTH OF BOSTON Great prosperity came to eastern Massachusetts after the Revolution, as the new nation took advantage of the lifting of British trade barriers. Today, the spoils of the China Trade adorn mansions and public edifices in seaside locales such as **Marblehead** 🎔🎔🎔, **Salem** 🎔🎔, and **Cape Ann.** Fishing is still an important industry, but these days the area caters more to commuters and tourists than to those who make their living from the sea. A worthwhile detour from the north or west is **Lowell** 🎔, a once-decrepit mill town where tourism is now the largest industry.

SOUTH OF BOSTON The communities between Boston and Cape Cod are mostly commuter suburbs. The prime historical destination is **Plymouth,** one of the oldest permanent European settlements in North America. It's a pleasant place where you can walk in the footsteps of the Pilgrims—and of the countless out-of-towners who flock here in summer and at Thanksgiving. Farther south, the old whaling port of **New Bedford** makes an interesting detour.

1 Lexington 🎔

9 miles NW of downtown Boston, 6 miles NW of Cambridge, 6 miles E of Concord

A country village turned prosperous suburb, Lexington takes great pride in its history. It's a pleasant town with some engaging destinations, but it lacks the atmosphere and abundant attractions of nearby Concord. Being sure to leave time for a tour of the **Buckman Tavern,** you can schedule as little as a couple

> ### Tips Planning Pointers
>
> If you have a few days to explore and history is your main motivation,
> consider approaching the area in roughly chronological order. Start in
> Plymouth with the Pilgrims, then move on to Lexington and Concord to
> learn about the rebellious colonists. Finally, acquaint yourself with the
> North Shore and Cape Ann, which flourished after the Revolution. How-
> ever, if you lack the time or inclination to make your own arrangements,
> consider an escorted tour. One reliable company is Gray Line's **Brush Hill
> Tours,** 435 High St., Randolph (℡ **800/343-1328** or 781/986-6100;
> www.grayline.com).

of hours to explore downtown Lexington, possibly en route to Concord. A visit
can also fill a half or full day. The town contains part of **Minute Man National
Historical Park,** which is definitely worth a visit.

The shooting phase of the Revolutionary War started here, with a skirmish on
the town green. It began when British troops clashed with local militia members,
who were known as "Minutemen" for their ability to assemble on short notice.
British soldiers marched from Boston to Lexington late on April 18, 1775.
Tipped off, Paul Revere and William Dawes rode ahead to sound the warning.
They did their job so well that the alarm came long before the advancing forces.
The Lexington Minutemen, under the command of Capt. John Parker, got the
word shortly after midnight, but the redcoats were still several hours away. The
colonists repaired to their homes and the Buckman Tavern. Five hours later,
some 700 British troops under Major Pitcairn arrived.

A tense standoff ensued. Three times Pitcairn ordered them to disperse, but
the patriots—fewer than 100, and some accounts say 77—refused. Parker called:
"Stand your ground. Don't fire unless fired upon, but if they mean to have a war,
let it begin here!" Finally the captain, perhaps realizing as the sky grew light how
badly outnumbered his men were, gave the order to fall back.

As the Minutemen began to scatter, a shot rang out. One British company
charged into the fray, and the colonists attempted to regroup as Pitcairn tried
unsuccessfully to call off his troops. Nobody knows who started the shooting,
but when it was over, eight militia members, including a drummer boy, lay dead,
and 10 were wounded.

ESSENTIALS
GETTING THERE   Take Route 2 from Cambridge through Belmont, exit at
Route 4/225, and follow signs to downtown. (To reach Route 2 from downtown
Boston, take Storrow or Memorial Drive.) Or take Route 128 (I-95) to Exit 31A
and follow signs. If it's not rush hour, allow about 35 minutes. Mass. Ave. (the
same street as in Boston and Cambridge) runs through the center of town.
There's metered parking on the street and in several municipal lots.

The **MBTA** (℡ **617/222-3200;** www.mbta.com) runs bus routes 62 (Bedford) and 76 (Hanscom) to Lexington from Alewife station, the last stop on the
Red Line. The one-way fare is 75¢, and the trip takes about 25 minutes. Buses
operate Monday through Saturday every hour during the day and every half
hour during rush periods. There's no Sunday service, and no public transportation between Lexington and Concord.

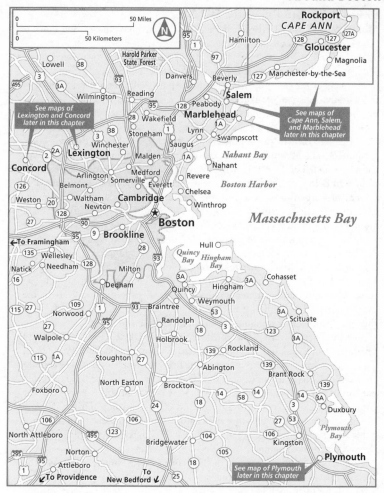

See maps of Lexington and Concord later in this chapter

See maps of Cape Ann, Salem, and Marblehead later in this chapter

See map of Plymouth later in this chapter

VISITOR INFORMATION   The Chamber of Commerce **Visitor Center,** 1875 Mass. Ave., Lexington (⟨ **781/862-1450;** www.lexingtonchamber.org), distributes maps and information. The community website (**www.lexington web.com**) has some visitor information. You can also contact the **Greater Merrimack Valley Convention & Visitors Bureau,** 9 Central St., Suite 201, Lowell (⟨ **800/443-3332** or 978/459-6150; www.merrimackvalley.org).

GETTING AROUND   Downtown Lexington is easily negotiable on foot, and most of the attractions are within walking distance. If you prefer not to walk to the Munroe Tavern and the Museum of Our National Heritage (see below), buses 62 and 76 pass by on Mass. Ave.

SPECIAL EVENTS   **Patriots Day,** a state holiday observed on the third Monday in April, commemorates the start of the Revolution. Celebrations include a re-enactment of the battle and other festivities. Make your Patriots Day reservations well in advance: It's the day of the Boston Marathon and the start of a school vacation week.

EXPLORING THE HISTORIC SITES

Minute Man National Historical Park is in Lexington, Concord, and Lincoln (see "Concord," below).

Start your visit to Lexington at the **visitor center,** on the town common or "Battle Green," next to a bustling business district. It's open daily from 9am to 5pm (October through June from 10am to 4pm). A **diorama** and accompanying narrative illustrate the Battle of Lexington. The **Minuteman statue** (1900) on the green is of Capt. John Parker, who commanded the militia. The **Old Revolutionary Monument** (1799) marks the grave of seven of the eight colonists who died in the conflict, which the **Line of Battle Boulder** commemorates. The **Memorial to the Lexington Minutemen** bears the names of the men who fell in the battle. Across Massachusetts Avenue, near Clarke Street, is the **Old Belfry,** a reproduction of the freestanding bell that sounded the alarm the day of the battle. **Ye Olde Burying Ground,** at the west end of the green, dates to 1690 and contains Parker's grave. A stop at the visitor center and a walk around the monuments takes about half an hour, and gives a good sense of what went on here and why the participants are still held in such high esteem.

Three important destinations in Lexington were among the country's first "**historic houses**" when their restoration began in the 1920s. The **Lexington Historical Society** (② 781/862-1703; www.lexingtonhistory.org) operates all three. Currently headquartered in the Munroe Tavern, the society is in the process of restoring a building on Depot Square (downtown, off Mass. Ave. near the Battle Green) that will hold exhibits, offices, and a gift shop.

The **Buckman Tavern** ⭐⭐, 1 Bedford St. (② 781/862-5598), built around 1710, is the only building still on the green that was here on April 19, 1775. If time is short and you have to pick just one house to visit, this is it. The interior has been restored to its appearance on the day of the battle. You'll see the original bar and front door, which has a hole in it from a British musket ball. The Minutemen gathered here to wait for word of British troop movements, and brought their wounded here after the conflict. On the excellent tour, costumed guides describe the history of the building and its inhabitants, explain the battle, and discuss colonial life.

Within easy walking distance is the **Hancock-Clarke House,** 36 Hancock St. (② 781/861-0928). Samuel Adams and John Hancock, who had left Boston several days earlier upon learning that the British were after them, were sleeping here (or trying to) when Revere arrived. They fled to nearby Woburn. Built around 1698 by Hancock's grandfather and lavishly improved by his uncle, the house, restored and furnished in colonial style, contains the Historical Society's museum of the Revolution.

The British took over the **Munroe Tavern** ⭐, 1332 Mass. Ave. (about 1 mile east of the green), to use as their headquarters and field hospital. The taproom ceiling still has a bullet hole made by a careless soldier. The 1690 building holds

---

Tips **Poetry in Motion**

Before you set out for Lexington and Concord, you might want to read *Paul Revere's Ride,* Henry Wadsworth Longfellow's classic but historically questionable poem that dramatically chronicles the events of April 18 and 19, 1775.

ATTRACTIONS ●
Battle Green **3**
Buckman Tavern **2**
Hancock-Clarke House **1**
Munroe Tavern **7**
Museum of our National Heritage **8**

DINING ◆
Aesop's Bagels **6**
Bertucci's **4**
Lemon Grass **5**

many fascinating artifacts. The furniture, carefully preserved by the Munroe family, includes the table and chair where President Washington dined in 1789. The historically accurate **gardens** at the rear (free admission) are beautifully planted and maintained.

All three houses are open for guided tours Monday through Saturday from 10am to 5pm and Sunday from 1 to 5pm, April through October. The Buckman Tavern is also open in late March and November, Monday through Saturday from 11am to 3pm and Sunday from 1 to 3pm. Admission for adults is $5 per house, $8 for two houses, $10 for all three; for seniors, $7 for two houses, $11 for all three; for children 6 to 16, $3 per house, $5 for two or three. The last tour starts 30 minutes before closing time; tours take 30 to 45 minutes. Call for information about group tours, which are offered by appointment.

Museum of Our National Heritage ★ Kids   This museum explores history through popular culture. It makes an entertaining complement to the colonial focus of the rest of the town. The installations in the six exhibition spaces change regularly; you can start with another dose of the Revolution, the permanent exhibit *Let It Begin Here.* Other topics have ranged from Route 66 to George Washington, Frank Lloyd Wright to American circus posters. Lectures, concerts, and family programs are also offered. The Scottish Rite of Freemasonry sponsors the museum.

33 Marrett Rd., Rte. 2A (at Mass. Ave.). ✆ 781/861-6559 or 781/861-9638. www.mnh.org. Free admission. Mon–Sat 10am–5pm, Sun noon–5pm. Closed Thanksgiving, Christmas, New Year's Day. T: Bus 62 or 76 from downtown Lexington to Rte. 2A.

WHERE TO STAY

Bedford is 15 minutes from downtown Lexington along Route 4/225 on the other side of I-95. The **Ramada Sovereign Inn,** 340 Great Rd., Bedford (✆ **888/298-2054** or 781/275-6700), is a pleasant motor inn with an indoor pool. The high-season rate is about $109 to $129.

Renaissance Bedford Hotel ★   The sights in Lexington and Concord are convenient to this three-story, lodge-style hotel, which neatly makes the transition from a weekday business destination to a weekend family resort. There's also plenty to do without leaving the property. The well-maintained guest rooms contain oversize work desks; larger units have king-size beds. The hotel shuttle transports guests to destinations within 5 miles, including the Burlington Mall.

44 Middlesex Tpk., Bedford, MA 01730. ✆ 800/HOTELS-1 or 781/275-5500. Fax 781/275-3042. www.renaissancehotels.com/BOSSB. 284 units. Sun–Thurs $199–$249 double; Fri–Sat $99–$229. Extra person $15. Children under 19 stay free in parents' room. Weekend packages and senior discounts available. AE, DC, DISC, MC, V. **Amenities:** Restaurant (eclectic); lounge; indoor pool; indoor and outdoor tennis courts; fitness center; whirlpool; sauna; shuttle; business center; 24-hour room service; laundry service; dry cleaning. *In room:* A/C, TV, dataport, minibar, coffeemaker, hair dryer, iron.

Sheraton Lexington Inn   Overlooking the interstate, but sheltered from the noise by a stand of trees, this two-story hotel is 5 minutes from downtown by car. It offers the usual chain amenities—reliable, if generic. Rooms are large enough to hold a wing chair or couch, and some have balconies. It's a decent choice for families, and popular with travelers who have business on the Route 128 high-tech corridor.

727 Marrett Rd. (Exit 30B off I-95), Lexington, MA 02173. ✆ 800/325-3535 or 781/862-8700. Fax 781/863-0404. 119 units. $119–$199 double; $199–$369 suite. Extra person $10. AAA and AARP discounts available. AE, DC, DISC, MC, V. **Amenities:** Restaurant (American); outdoor pool; exercise room; access to nearby health club. *In room:* A/C, TV, dataport, coffeemaker, hair dryer, iron.

WHERE TO DINE

Bertucci's, 1777 Mass. Ave. (✆ 781/860-9000), a branch of the family-friendly pizzeria chain, also serves salads and pasta dishes. **Aesop's Bagels,** 1666 Mass. Ave. (✆ 781/674-2990), is a good place to pick up a light meal.

Lemon Grass THAI   This popular restaurant is a former coffee shop disguised with bamboo decorations and the aroma of Asian spices. You might start with satay (skewers of meat served with delectable peanut sauce) or chicken coconut soup, with a kick of pepper. Entrees include a tasty rendition of traditional pad Thai and excellent curry dishes. The accommodating staff will adjust the heat and spice to suit your taste.

1710 Mass. Ave. ✆ 781/862-3530. Main courses $5.75–$8.50 lunch, $7.50–$16 dinner. AE, DISC, MC, V. Mon–Fri 11:30am–3pm; Mon–Thurs 5–9:30pm; Fri–Sat 5–10pm; Sun 4–9pm.

2 Concord ★★★

18 miles NW of Boston, 15 miles NW of Cambridge, 6 miles W of Lexington.

Concord (say "conquered") revels in its legacy as a center of groundbreaking thought and its role in the country's political and intellectual history. A visit can easily fill a day; if your interests are specialized or time is short, a half-day excursion is reasonable. For an excellent overview of town history, start your explorations at the **Concord Museum.**

After just a little time in this lovely town, you may find yourself adopting the local attitude toward two of its most famous residents: Ralph Waldo Emerson, who comes across as a well-respected uncle figure, and Henry David Thoreau, everyone's favorite eccentric cousin. Long before they wandered the countryside, the first official battle of the Revolutionary War took place at the **North Bridge,** now part of Minute Man National Historical Park. By the middle of the 19th century, Concord was the center of the Transcendentalist movement. Homes of **Emerson, Thoreau, Nathaniel Hawthorne,** and **Louisa May Alcott** are open to visitors, as is the authors' final resting place, Sleepy Hollow Cemetery.

ESSENTIALS

GETTING THERE   From Lexington (10 min.), take Route 2A west from Mass. Ave. (Route 4/225) at the Museum of Our National Heritage; follow the BATTLE ROAD signs. From Boston and Cambridge (30–40 min.), take Route 2 into Lincoln and stay in the right lane. Where the main road makes a sharp left, go straight onto Cambridge Turnpike, and follow signs to HISTORIC CONCORD. To go straight to Walden Pond, use the left lane, take what's now Route 2/2A another mile or so, and turn left onto Route 126. There's parking throughout town and at the attractions.

The **commuter rail** (© 617/222-3200; www.mbta.com) takes about 45 minutes from North Station in Boston, with a stop at Porter Square in Cambridge. The round-trip fare is $8. The station is about three-quarters of a mile over flat terrain from the town center. There is no bus service from Boston to Concord, and no public transportation between Lexington and Concord.

VISITOR INFORMATION   The **Chamber of Commerce,** 2 Lexington Rd., Concord (© 978/369-3120; www.ultranet.com/~conchamb), maintains an information booth on Heywood Street, 1 block southeast of Monument Square. It's open from 9:30am to 4:30pm on Saturdays and Sundays in April, daily May through October. One-hour tours are available starting in May on Saturdays, Sundays, and Monday holidays. Weekday and group tours are available by appointment. The community (**www.concordma.com**) and town (**www. concordnet.org**) websites include visitor information. You can also contact the **Greater Merrimack Valley Convention & Visitors Bureau,** 9 Central St., Suite 201, Lowell (© 800/443-3332 or 978/459-6150; www.merrimackvalley.org).

Value Let's Make a Deal

A **"Ticket to History"** includes admission to the Concord Museum, the Old Manse, and Orchard House. You don't have to visit all three in one day: The ticket is good any time (except during special events) from April 15 to October 31. It costs $17 for adults, $14 for seniors and students, $8 for children, and $45 for families.

GETTING AROUND   Major attractions are within walking distance of downtown. If you're trying to stop everywhere in a day or are visiting Walden Pond or Great Meadows, you'll need a car.

SEEING THE SIGHTS
LITERARY LANDMARKS & HISTORIC ATTRACTIONS

Concord Museum ★★ *Kids*   Just when you're (understandably) suspecting that everything interesting in this area started on April 18, 1775, and ended the next day, this superb museum sets you straight. It's a great place to start your visit to the town. The **History Galleries** ★★ explore the question "Why Concord?" Artifacts, murals, films, maps, documents, and other presentations illustrate the town role as a Native American settlement, Revolutionary War battleground, 19th-century intellectual center, and focal point of the 20th-century historic preservation movement. One of the lanterns that signaled Paul Revere from the Old North Church is on display. You'll also see the contents of Ralph Waldo Emerson's study and a large collection of Henry David Thoreau's belongings. Pick up a **family activity pack** ★ as you enter and use the games and reproduction artifacts (including a quill pen and powder horn) to give the kids a hands-on feel for life in the past. The museum also offers changing exhibits in the New Wing.

200 Lexington Rd. (at Cambridge Tpk.). 🌀 **978/369-9609** for recorded info, or 978/369-9763. www.concordmuseum.org. Admission $7 adults, $6 seniors and students, $3 children under 16, $16 per family. Ticket to History (includes Old Manse and Orchard House) $17 adults, $14 seniors and students, $8 children, $45 per family. Apr–Dec Mon–Sat 9am–5pm, Sun noon–5pm; Jan–Mar Mon–Sat 11am–4pm, Sun 1–4pm. Parking allowed on road. Follow Lexington Rd. out of Concord Center and bear right at museum onto Cambridge Tpk.; entrance is on left.

The Old Manse ★   The history of this engaging old home touches on the military and the literary, but it's mostly the story of a family. The Rev. William Emerson built the Old Manse in 1770 and watched the Battle of Concord from his yard. For almost 170 years, the house was home to his widow, her second husband, their descendants, and two famous friends. Nathaniel Hawthorne and his bride, Sophia Peabody, moved in after their marriage in 1842 and stayed for 3 years. As a wedding present, Henry David Thoreau sowed the vegetable garden for them. This is also where William's grandson Ralph Waldo Emerson wrote the essay "Nature." Today, you'll see mementos and memorabilia of the Emerson and Ripley families and of the Hawthornes, who scratched notes on two windows with Sophia's diamond ring.

269 Monument St. (at North Bridge). 🌀 **978/369-3909.** www.thetrustees.org. Guided tour $6.50 adults, $5.50 seniors and students, $4.50 children 6–12. Ticket to History (includes Concord Museum and Orchard House) $17 adults, $14 seniors and students, $8 children, $45 per family. Mid-Apr to Oct Mon–Sat 10am–5pm; Sun and holidays noon–5pm (last tour at 4:30pm). Closed Nov to mid-Apr. From Concord Center, follow Monument St. to North Bridge parking lot (on right); Old Manse is on left.

Orchard House ★★★ *Kids*   *Little Women* (1868), Louisa May Alcott's best-known and most popular work, was written and set at Orchard House. Seeing the family home brings the Alcotts to life for legions of female visitors and their pleasantly surprised male companions. Fans won't want to miss the excellent tour, copiously illustrated with heirlooms. Serious buffs can check ahead for information on holiday programs and many other special events, some of which require reservations.

Louisa's father, the writer and educator Amos Bronson Alcott, created Orchard House by joining and restoring two homes. The family lived here from 1858 to 1877, socializing in the same circles as Emerson, Thoreau, and

Hawthorne. Other family members served as the models for the characters in *Little Women*. Anna ("Meg"), the eldest, was an amateur actress, and May ("Amy") a talented artist. Elizabeth ("Beth"), a gifted musician, died before the family moved to this house. Their mother, the social activist Abigail May Alcott, frequently assumed the role of breadwinner—Bronson, Louisa wrote in her journal, had "no gift for money making."

Note: Call before visiting; an extensive preservation project is under way and will extend through June 2002.

399 Lexington Rd. ✆ **978/369-4118.** www.louisamayalcott.org. Guided tours $7 adults, $6 seniors and students, $4 children 6–17, $16 per family. Ticket to History (includes Concord Museum and Old Manse) $17 adults, $14 seniors and students, $8 children, $45 per family. Apr–Oct Mon–Sat 10am–4:30pm, Sun 1–4:30pm; Nov–Mar Mon–Fri 11am–3pm, Sat 10am–4:30pm, Sun 1–4:30pm. Closed Jan 1–15, Easter, Thanksgiving, Christmas. Follow Lexington Rd. out of Concord Center and bear left at Concord Museum; house is on the left. Overflow parking lot is across the street.

Ralph Waldo Emerson House   This house offers an instructive look at the days when a philosopher could attain the status we now associate with rock stars. Emerson, also an essayist and poet, lived here from 1835 until his death, in 1882. He moved here after marrying his second wife, Lydia Jackson, whom he called "Lydian"; she called him "Mr. Emerson," as the staff still does. The tour gives a good look at his personal side and at the fashionably ornate interior decoration of the time. You'll see original furnishings and some of Emerson's personal effects.

28 Cambridge Tpk. ℂ **978/369-2236.** Guided tours $6 adults, $4 seniors and students. Call to arrange group tours (10 people or more). Mid-Apr to Oct Thurs–Sat 10am–4:30pm; Sun 2–4:30pm. Closed Nov to mid-Apr. Follow Cambridge Tpk. out of Concord Center; just before Concord Museum, house is on right.

Sleepy Hollow Cemetery 🏛   Follow the signs for AUTHOR'S RIDGE and climb the hill to the graves of some of the town's literary lights, including the Alcotts, Emerson, Hawthorne, and Thoreau. Emerson's grave, fittingly, bears no religious symbols, just an uncarved quartz boulder. Thoreau's grave is nearby; at his funeral, in 1862, his old friend Emerson concluded his eulogy with these words: ". . . wherever there is knowledge, wherever there is virtue, wherever there is beauty, he will find a home."

Entrance on Rte. 62 W. ℂ **978/318-3233.** Daily 7am to dusk. Call ahead for wheelchair access.

The Wayside 🏛   The Wayside was Nathaniel Hawthorne's home from 1852 until his death, in 1864. The Alcotts also lived here (the girls called it "the yellow house"), as did Harriett Lothrop, who wrote the *Five Little Peppers* books under the pen name Margaret Sidney and owned most of the current furnishings. The fascinating 45-minute ranger tour (the house is part of Minute Man National Historical Park) illuminates the occupants' lives and the house's crazy-quilt architecture. The exhibit in the barn (free admission) consists of audio presentations and figures of the authors.

455 Lexington Rd. ℂ **978/369-6975.** www.nps.gov/mima. Guided tours $4 adults, free for children under 17. May–Oct Thurs–Tues 10am–4:30pm. Closed Nov–Apr. Follow Lexington Rd. out of Concord Center past Concord Museum and Orchard House. Park across the street.

MINUTE MAN NATIONAL HISTORICAL PARK ★★

This 900-acre national park preserves the scene of the first Revolutionary War battle, on April 19, 1775. Encouraged by victory in Lexington, the British continued to Concord in search of stockpiled arms (which the colonists had already moved). Warned of the advance, the Minutemen crossed the North Bridge, evading the "regulars" standing guard, and awaited reinforcements on a hilltop. The British searched nearby homes and burned any guns they found, and the Minutemen, seeing the smoke, mistakenly thought the soldiers were burning the town. The gunfire that ensued, the opening salvo of the Revolution, is remembered as **"the shot heard 'round the world."**

    The park is open daily year-round. A visit can take as little as half an hour—for a jaunt to the North Bridge—or as long as half a day (or more) if you stop at both visitor centers and perhaps participate in a ranger-led program. To reach the bridge (a reproduction) from Concord Center, follow Monument Street until you see the parking lot on the right. Walk a short distance to the bridge, stopping along the unpaved path to read and hear the narratives. On one side of the bridge is a plaque commemorating the British soldiers who died in the Revolutionary War. On the other side is Daniel Chester French's **Minute Man** statue, engraved with a stanza of the poem Emerson wrote for the dedication ceremony in 1876.

    You can also start at the **North Bridge Visitor Center** 🏛, 174 Liberty St., off Monument Street (ℂ **978/369-6993;** www.nps.gov/mima), which overlooks the Concord River and the bridge. A diorama and video illustrate the Battle of Concord; exhibits include uniforms, weapons, and tools of colonial and British soldiers. Park rangers lead programs and answer questions. Outside, picnicking is allowed, and the scenery (especially the fall foliage) is lovely. The bridge isn't far; you'll want to see the exhibits here, too. The center is open daily from 9am to 5:30pm (until 4pm in winter).

At the Lexington end of the park, the **Minute Man Visitor Center** ✿, off Route 2A, 1 mile west of I-95, Exit 30B (✆ **781/862-7753;** www.nps.gov/mima), is open daily from 9am to 5pm (until 4pm in winter). The park includes the first 4 miles of the Battle Road, the route the defeated British troops took as they left Concord. At the visitor center, you'll see a fascinating multimedia program on the Revolution, informational displays, and a 40-foot mural illustrating the battle. On summer weekends, rangers lead tours of the park—call ahead for times. A new 5½-mile interpretive path, the **Battle Road Trail,** carries pedestrian, wheelchair, and bicycle traffic. Panels and granite markers display information about the area's military, social, and natural history and point the way along the trail.

Also on the park grounds, on Old Bedford Road, is the **Hartwell Tavern.** Costumed interpreters demonstrate daily life on a farm and in a tavern in colonial days. It's not Disney, but it is interesting. It's open from 9:30am to 5pm, daily June through August and on Saturdays and Sundays in April, May, September, and October. Admission is free.

NEARBY SIGHTS

DeCordova Museum and Sculpture Park ✿✿ Indoors and out, the DeCordova shows the work of American contemporary and modern artists, with an emphasis on living New England residents. The main building, on a leafy hilltop, overlooks a pond and the area's only outdoor public sculpture park. The museum also has a roof garden and a sculpture terrace; the latter displays the work of one sculptor per year. Picnicking is allowed in the sculpture park; bring your lunch or buy it at the cafe (open Wednesday through Sunday from 11am to 4pm). Free guided tours of the main galleries start at 2pm Wednesday and Sunday, year-round; sculpture-park tours run May through October on Saturday and Sunday at 1pm.

51 Sandy Pond Rd., Lincoln. ✆ **781/259-8355.** www.decordova.org. Museum $6 adults; $4 seniors, students, and children 6–12. Tues–Sun and Mon holidays 11am–5pm. Free admission to sculpture park, daily 8am–10pm. Closed New Year's Day, July 4, Thanksgiving, Christmas. From Rte. 2 E., take Rte. 126 to Baker Bridge Rd. (first left after Walden Pond). When it ends, go right onto Sandy Pond Rd.; museum is on left. From Rte. 2 W., take I-95 to Exit 28B, follow Trapelo Rd. 2½ miles to Sandy Pond Rd., then follow signs.

Gropius House ✿ Architect Walter Gropius (1883–1969), founder of the Bauhaus school of design, built this home for his family in the prosperous suburb of Lincoln in 1937. Having taken a job at the Harvard Graduate School of Design, he worked with Marcel Breuer to design the hilltop house, now maintained by the Society for the Preservation of New England Antiquities. They used traditional materials such as clapboard, brick, and fieldstone, with components then seldom used in domestic architecture, including glass blocks and welded steel. Breuer designed many of the furnishings, which were made for the family at the Bauhaus. Decorated as it was in the last decade of Gropius's life, the house affords a revealing look at his life, career, and philosophy. Call for information on special tours and workshops.

68 Baker Bridge Rd., Lincoln. ✆ **781/259-8843** or 617/227-3957, ext. 300. www.spnea.org. Guided tours $5. Tours on the hour June–Oct 15 Wed–Sun 11am–4pm; Oct 16–May Sat–Sun 11am–4pm. Take Rte. 2 to Rte. 126 south to left on Baker Bridge Rd.; house is on the right. From I-95, Exit 28B, follow Trapelo Rd. to Sandy Pond Rd., go left onto Baker Bridge Rd.; house is on the left.

WILDERNESS RETREATS

The titles of Henry David Thoreau's first two published works can serve as starting points: *A Week on the Concord and Merrimack Rivers* (1849) and *Walden* (1854).

To see the area from water level, there's no need to take a week; 2 hours or so should suffice. Rent a **canoe** 🛶 at the **South Bridge Boathouse,** 496 Main St. (© **978/369-9438;** www.sbridge.qpg.com), about seven-tenths of a mile west of the center of town, and paddle to the North Bridge and back. Rates are about $11 per hour on weekends, less on weekdays.

At the **Walden Pond State Reservation** 🛶🛶, 915 Walden St., Route 126 (© **978/369-3254;** www.state.ma.us/dem/parks/wldn.htm), a pile of stones marks the site of the cabin where Thoreau lived from 1845 to 1847. Today, the picturesque reservation is an extremely popular destination for walking (a path circles the pond), swimming, and fishing. Although crowded, it's well preserved and insulated from development, making it less difficult than you might expect to imagine Thoreau's experience. Call for the schedule of interpretive programs. No dogs or bikes are allowed. From Memorial Day to Labor Day, a daily parking fee is charged and the lot fills early every day—call before setting out, because the rangers turn away visitors if the park has reached capacity (1,000). To get here from Concord Center, take Walden Street (Route 126) south, cross Route 2, and follow signs to the parking lot.

Another Thoreau haunt, an especially popular destination for birders, is **Great Meadows National Wildlife Refuge** 🛶, Weir Hill Road, Sudbury (© **978/443-4661;** northeast.fws.gov/ma/grm.htm). The Concord portion of the 3,400-acre refuge includes 2½ miles of walking trails around man-made ponds that attract abundant wildlife. More than 200 species of native and migratory birds have been recorded. The refuge is open daily from sunrise to sunset; admission is free. Follow Route 62 (Bedford Street) east out of Concord Center for 1⅓ miles, then turn left onto Monsen Road.

WHERE TO STAY

About 2 miles from the center of town, the two-story **Best Western at Historic Concord,** 740 Elm St., Concord (© **800/528-1234** or 978/369-6100), is just off Route 2. The motel has a fitness room and a seasonal outdoor pool; doubles go for $125 in season.

Colonial Inn 🛶   The main building of the Colonial Inn has overlooked Monument Square since 1716. Like many historic inns, it's not luxurious, but it's comfortable, centrally located—and possibly home to a ghost. Additions since it became a hotel in 1889 have left the inn large enough to offer modern conveniences and small enough to feel friendly. It's popular with local businesspeople as well as vacationers, especially during foliage season. The 12 original guest rooms—one of which (room 24) supposedly is haunted—are in great demand. Reserve early if you want to stay in the main inn, which is decorated (surprise, surprise) in colonial style. Rooms in the Prescott wing are larger, with country-style decor; an annex holds two good-sized apartments.

The dining options are pleasant, though hardly exciting—you're here for the atmosphere, not the cuisine. Two lounges serve light meals; sit on the porch and you'll have a front-row seat for the action on Monument Square. The lovely restaurant serves salads, sandwiches, and pasta at lunch, and traditional American fare at dinner. Afternoon tea is served Wednesday through Sunday; reservations required (© **978/369-2373**).

48 Monument Sq., Concord, MA 01742. ℭ **800/370-9200** or 978/369-9200. Fax 978/369-2170. www.concordscolonialinn.com. 45 units (some with shower only). Apr–Oct $185–$195 main inn, $149–$189 Prescott wing, $295–$350 cottage; Nov–Mar $155 main inn, $135 Prescott wing, $250 cottage. AE, DC, DISC, MC, V. **Amenities:** Restaurant (American), 2 lounges, bar with live jazz and blues on weekends; laundry service; dry cleaning. In room: A/C, TV.

Hawthorne Inn ★★ This is the quintessential country inn. Built around 1870, it sits on a tree-shaded property across the street from Nathaniel Hawthorne's home, the Wayside. Antiques and handmade quilts enhance the rooms, which aren't huge but are meticulously maintained and gorgeously decorated. Original art is on display throughout, and there's a small pond in the peaceful garden. Personable innkeepers Gregory Burch and Marilyn Mudry, who have been in business for more than 20 years, acquaint interested guests with the philosophical, spiritual, military, and literary aspects of Concord's history.

462 Lexington Rd., Concord, MA 01742. ℭ **978/369-5610.** Fax 978/287-4949. www.concordmass.com. 7 units (some with shower only). $185–$285 double. Off-season discounts available. Extra person $20. Rates include continental breakfast. AE, DISC, MC, V. From Concord Center, take Lexington Rd. a quarter of a mile east; inn is on right. In room: A/C, TV.

A NEARBY HISTORIC INN

Longfellow's Wayside Inn ★★ Worth a visit even if you're not spending the night, this local institution dates to 1716 and got its name when Henry Wadsworth Longfellow published *Tales of a Wayside Inn* in 1863. Part of a nonprofit educational and charitable trust, it claims to be the country's oldest operating inn. All 10 guest rooms are attractively decorated and furnished with antiques, but only two (the most popular, of course) are in the original building. Reserve as early as possible.

In addition to being a popular wedding and honeymoon destination, the inn is the centerpiece of what amounts to a tiny theme park. Buildings on the 106-acre property include the Redstone School of **"Mary Had a Little Lamb"** fame, a wedding chapel, and a working gristmill. The mill stone-grinds the wheat flour and cornmeal used in the inn's baked goods. Old grindstones dot the lawn, a pleasant spot for sunbathing.

In the rambling **dining rooms** ★, costumed staff members dish up generous portions of traditional New England fare, which often incorporates produce grown at the inn. The menu changes daily; favorite choices include prime rib, lobster casserole, and strawberry shortcake. You'll see lots of families—this seems to be *the* place for grandparents' birthdays. Food is served Monday through Saturday from 11:30am to 3pm and 5 to 9pm, Sunday from noon to 8pm (dinner menu only). Main courses are $8.50 to $15 at lunch, $15 to $30 at dinner. Reservations are recommended, especially on weekends.

Wayside Inn Rd., Sudbury, MA 01776. ℭ **800/339-1776** or 978/443-1776. Fax 978/443-8041. www.wayside.org. 10 units (some with shower only). Summer $110–$130 double; off-season $80–$110. Extra person $15. Rates include breakfast. AE, DC, DISC, MC, V. Closed July 4, Christmas. From Main St. in Concord, follow Sudbury Rd. to Rte. 20 west; 11 miles after passing I-95, bear right onto Wayside Inn Rd. The inn is on the right. In room: A/C.

WHERE TO DINE

For basic to lavish picnic provisions, stop in downtown Concord at the **Cheese Shop,** 25–31 Walden St. (ℭ **978/369-5778**), before setting out. See also the **Colonial Inn** and **Longfellow's Wayside Inn,** above.

Tips   **Road Trips North of Boston**

For convenience and flexibility, **drive** if you can. The drive from Boston to Cape Ann on I-93 and Route 128 takes about an hour. A more leisurely excursion on Routes 1A, 129, and 114 allows you to explore Marblehead and Salem on your way to Gloucester and Rockport. You can also follow Route 1 to I-95 and 128, but during rush hour the traffic is unbearable. To take Route 1A, check a map or ask at the front desk of your hotel for directions to the Callahan Tunnel. If you miss the tunnel and wind up on I-93, follow signs to Route 1 and pick up Route 1A in Revere. The **North of Boston Convention & Visitors Bureau,** 17 Peabody Sq., Peabody (*©* **800/742-5306** or 978/977-7760; www.northofboston.org), publishes a visitor guide that covers many destinations in this chapter.

Nashoba Brook Bakery & Café *☆* AMERICAN   The enticing variety of fresh artisan breads, baked goods, pastries, and from-scratch soups, salads, and sandwiches makes this airy cafe a popular destination throughout the day. It offers a good break from the sightseeing circuit. The industrial-looking building off West Concord's main street backs up to little Nashoba Brook, which is visible through the glass back wall. Order and pick up at the counter, then grab a seat along the window or near the children's play area. Or order takeout—this is great picnic food—or a fresh loaf of crusty bread.

152 Commonwealth Ave., West Concord. *©* **978/318-1999.** www.slowrise.com. Sandwiches $5–$6; salads $6–$8 per pound. Mon–Sat 8am–8pm. From Concord Center, follow Main St. (Rte. 62) west, across Rte. 2; bear right at traffic light in front of train station and go 3 blocks.

3 Marblehead *☆☆☆*

15 miles NE of Boston, 4 miles SE of Salem

Scenery, history, architecture, and shopping combine to make Marblehead one of the area's most popular day trips, for locals and visitors alike. The narrow streets of the historic district, **"Old Town"** *☆☆☆*, lead down to the magnificent harbor that helps make this the self-proclaimed "Yachting Capital of America." The homes along the way have plaques bearing the dates of construction as well as the names of the builders and original occupants—a history lesson without any studying.

Many of the houses have stood since before the Revolutionary War, when Marblehead was a center of merchant shipping. Two historic homes are open for tours. Allow at least a full morning to visit Marblehead, but be flexible, because you may want to hang around.

ESSENTIALS

GETTING THERE   From Boston, take Route 1A north until you see signs in Lynn for Swampscott and Marblehead. Take Lynn Shore Drive to Route 129, and follow it into Marblehead. Or take I-93 or Route 1 to Route 128, then Route 114 through Salem into Marblehead. Except at rush hour, allow 35 to 40 minutes.

MBTA (*©* **617/222-3200;** www.mbta.com) bus route 441/442 runs from Haymarket (Orange or Green Line) in Boston to downtown Marblehead. During rush periods Monday through Friday, bus 448/449 connects Marblehead to Downtown Crossing. The trip takes about an hour; the one-way fare is $2.75.

VISITOR INFORMATION The **Marblehead Chamber of Commerce,** 62 Pleasant St. (© **781/631-2868;** www.marbleheadchamber.org), is open Monday through Friday from 9am to 5pm. The **information booth** (© **781/639-8469**) on Pleasant Street near Spring Street is open May through October, daily from 10am to 6pm. The chamber publishes a visitor guide and a map that includes an event calendar; ask for a business directory if you want a description of a walking tour. Marblehead has a community website at **www.marblehead.com.**

GETTING AROUND Wear good walking shoes—the car or bus can get you to Marblehead, but it can't negotiate many of the narrow streets of Old Town. The downtown area is fairly compact and moderately hilly.

SPECIAL EVENTS Sailing regattas take place all summer. **Race Week,** in mid- to late July, draws competitors from across the country. During the **Christmas Walk,** on the first weekend in December, Santa Claus arrives by lobster boat.

EXPLORING THE TOWN

A stroll through the winding streets of Old Town invariably leads to shopping, snacking, or gazing at something picturesque, be it the harbor or a beautiful home. If you prefer more structure, consult the Chamber of Commerce's business directory, which includes a walking tour. Regardless, pass by the **Lafayette House,** a private home at the corner of Hooper and Union streets. Legend has it that one corner of the first floor was chopped off in 1824 to allow Lafayette's carriage to negotiate the corner. In Market Square on Washington Street, near the corner of State Street, is the **Old Town House,** a public meeting and gathering place since 1727.

Be sure to spend some time in **Crocker Park** ★★, on the water off Front Street. Especially in the warmer months, when boats jam the harbor, the view is breathtaking. There are benches and a swing, and picnicking is allowed. You may not want to leave, but snap out of it—the view from **Fort Sewall,** at the other end of Front Street, is just as mesmerizing. The ruins of the fort, built in the 17th century and rebuilt late in the 18th, are another excellent picnic spot.

By car or bicycle, the swanky residential community of **Marblehead Neck** ★ is worth a look. Follow Ocean Avenue across the causeway and visit the **Audubon Bird Sanctuary** (look for the tiny sign at the corner of Risley Avenue), or continue to **Castle Rock** for another eyeful of scenery. At the end of "the Neck," at Harbor and Ocean avenues, is **Chandler Hovey Park,** which has a (closed) lighthouse and a panoramic view. Many inns and B&Bs provide bikes for guests' use; to rent, visit **Marblehead Cycle,** 25 Bessom St., 1 block off Pleasant Street (② **781/631-1570**). Bikes go for $14 for a half day, $20 for a full day.

Abbot Hall   A 5-minute stop here (look for the clock tower) is just the ticket if you want to be able say you did some sightseeing. The town offices and Historical Commission share Abbot Hall with Archibald M. Willard's famous painting *The Spirit of '76* ★, on display in the Selectmen's Meeting Room. The thrill of recognizing the ubiquitous drummer, drummer boy, and fife player is the main reason to stop here. Cases in the halls contain objects and artifacts from the Historical Society's collections.

Washington Sq. ② 781/631-0528. Free admission. Year-round Mon–Tues and Thurs 8am–5pm, Wed 7:30am–7:30pm, Fri 8am–1pm; May–Oct Fri 8am–5pm, Sat 9am–6pm, Sun 11am–6pm. From the historic district, follow Washington St. up the hill.

Jeremiah Lee Mansion ★★   The prospect of seeing original hand-painted wallpaper in an 18th-century home is reason enough to visit this house, built in 1768 for a wealthy merchant and considered an outstanding example of pre-Revolutionary Georgian architecture. Original rococo carving and other details complement historically accurate room arrangements, and ongoing restoration and interpretation by the Marblehead Historical Society place the 18th- and 19th-century furnishings and artifacts in context. The friendly guides welcome questions and are well versed in the history of the home. The **lawn and gardens** are open to the public.

The Historical Society's headquarters, across the street, house the **J. O. J. Frost Folk Art Gallery** and a changing exhibition gallery. Frost, a noted primitivist painter, was a Marblehead native. The society occasionally offers candlelight tours of the house and walking tours of the town. Call ahead for schedules.

Mansion: 161 Washington St. ② 781/631-1768. Guided tours $5 adults, $4.50 seniors and students, free for children under 11. June to mid-Oct Mon–Sat 10am–4pm; Sun 1–4pm. Closed mid-Oct to May. Historical

Society: 170 Washington St. Free admission. Year-round Mon–Fri 10am–4pm; mid-May to Dec Sat 10am–4pm; June–Aug Sun 1–4pm. Follow Washington St. until it curves right and heads uphill toward Abbot Hall; mansion is on right.

King Hooper Mansion   Shipping tycoon Robert Hooper got his nickname because he treated his sailors so well, but it's easy to think he was called "King" because he lived like royalty. Around the corner from the home of Jeremiah Lee (whose sister was the second of Hooper's four wives), the 1728 King Hooper Mansion gained a Georgian addition in 1745. The period furnishings, although not original, give a sense of the life of an 18th-century merchant prince, from the wine cellar to the third-floor ballroom. The building houses the headquarters of the **Marblehead Arts Association,** which stages monthly exhibits and runs a gift shop that sells members' work. The mansion has a lovely **garden;** enter through the gate at the right of the house.

8 Hooper St. (℃) 781/631-2608. Donation requested for tour. Mon–Sat 10am–4pm, Sun 1–5pm. Call ahead; no tours during private parties. Where Washington St. curves at the foot of hill near Lee Mansion, look for the colorful sign.

SHOPPING ★★
One of Marblehead's claims to fame is its excellent retail scene. Because it's a year-round community and not just a summer destination, it offers more variety than a typical touristy town. Shops, boutiques, and galleries abound in **Old Town** and on **Atlantic Avenue** and the east end of **Pleasant Street.**

Jewelry aficionados can't miss **Antiquewear,** 82 Front St. (℃ **781/639-0070;** http://users.primushost.com/~antiquew), near the town pier. It sells 19th-century buttons ingeniously fashioned into women's and men's jewelry of all descriptions.

WHERE TO STAY
The accommodations listings of the **Chamber of Commerce,** 62 Pleasant St. (℃ **781/631-2868;** www.marbleheadchamber.org), include many of the town's innumerable inns and B&Bs. Contact the chamber or consult one of the agencies listed in chapter 4 under "Accommodations."

Harbor Light Inn ★★   A stone's throw from the Old Town House, two Federal-era mansions make up this gracious inn. From the wood floors to the 1729 beams (in a third-floor room) to the swimming pool, it's both historical and relaxing. Rooms are comfortably furnished in period style, with some lovely antiques; most have canopy or four-poster beds. Eleven have working fireplaces, and five of those have double Jacuzzis. VCRs and free video rentals are available. The best rooms, on the top floor at the back of the building (away from the street), have gorgeous harbor views. If you don't book one, you can still take in the scenery from the rooftop observation deck, which is open to all guests. Undeniably romantic, the inn also attracts business travelers (often for off-site meetings) during the week.

58 Washington St., Marblehead, MA 01945. (℃ **781/631-2186.** Fax 781/631-2216. www.harborlightinn.com. 21 units (some with shower only). $125–$195 double; $175–$295 suite. Rates include breakfast. Corporate rate available midweek. 2- to 3-night minimum stay on weekends and holidays. AE, MC, V. Free parking. **Amenities:** Heated outdoor pool. *In room:* A/C, TV, dataport, hair dryer.

Marblehead Inn ★ *Kids*   This three-story Victorian mansion just outside the historic district underwent extensive restoration and reopened in 1998 as an all-suite inn. It's not as convenient and romantic as the Harbor Light Inn, but offers better amenities and a more family-friendly atmosphere. Each attractively decorated unit contains a living room, bedroom, and workstation. This is a good choice for businesspeople making an extended stay as well as parents traveling with children, who can make good use of the self-catering kitchenette (the inn supplies breakfast provisions). Most suites have Jacuzzis, and some have working fireplaces and small patios. The 1872 building has been an inn since 1923, and once played host to Amelia Earhart.

264 Pleasant St. (Rte. 114), Marblehead, MA 01945. (✆ **800/399-5843** or 781/639-9999. Fax 781/639-9996. www.marbleheadinn.com. 10 units (some with shower only). $129–$209 double. Extra person $25. Rates include continental breakfast. Winter discounts and long-term rates available. 2-night minimum stay on busy weekends, 3-night minimum on holiday weekends. AE, MC, V. Free parking. *In room:* A/C, TV, fax, dataport, kitchenette, coffeemaker, hair dryer.

Spray Cliff on the Ocean 🌟   Spray Cliff, a three-story Victorian Tudor built in 1910 on a cliff overlooking the ocean, is 5 minutes from town and a world away. It books honeymooners, vacationers in search of isolation, and some midweek business travelers. The most desirable of the large, sunny rooms are the five that face the water. Three units have fireplaces, and all are luxuriously decorated in contemporary style with bright accents. Roger and Sally Plauché have run their romantic inn on a quiet residential street 1 minute from the beach since 1994.

25 Spray Ave., Marblehead, MA 01945. (✆ **800/626-1530** or 781/631-6789. Fax 781/639-4563. www.spraycliff.com. 7 units (some with shower only). May–Oct $200–$250 double. Extra person $25. Rates include continental breakfast and evening refreshments. Off-season discounts available. 2- to 3-night minimum stay on weekends and holidays. AE, MC, V. Free parking. Take Atlantic Ave. (Rte. 129) to traffic light at Clifton Ave. and turn east (right driving north, left driving south); parking is at end of street. No children accepted. **Amenities:** Bikes (free). *In room:* No phone.

A NEARBY SEASIDE INN

Lynn offers travelers the same attribute that draws property buyers: value. The ocean views are as breathtaking as those elsewhere on the North Shore, without the breathtaking expense of those posh communities. Marblehead is 10 minutes away.

Diamond District Bed and Breakfast 🌟🌟   This comfortable B&B is a three-story Georgian-style mansion built in 1911 as a private home, and innkeepers Jerry and Sandra Caron court both business and leisure travelers. The Atlantic is a block away; the 3-mile public beach (a good place to burn off the inn's generous breakfast) is popular for jogging, skating, and biking as well as swimming. It's visible from many of the good-sized rooms, tastefully decorated with elaborate Victorian touches. The best are third-floor units with ocean views and Jacuzzis. All rooms have down comforters, and two have cozy electric fireplaces. The large living room and porch overlook houses on Lynn Shore Drive and, just past them, the ocean. The whirlpool spa, on the back lawn, also has a water view.

The Carons also own the **1882 Stewart House,** across the street (away from the water). It contains a common living room, a double room, two doubles that share a bathroom (a good choice for families), and a tiny single room.

142 Ocean St., Lynn, MA 01902. (✆ **800/666-3076** or 781/599-4470. Fax 781/599-5122. www.diamonddistrictinn.com. 15 units, 13 with bathroom (some with shower only). $135–$265 double. Winter discounts available. Extra person $20. Rates include breakfast. 2-night minimum stay on holiday, summer, and fall weekends. AE, DC, DISC, MC, V. Take Rte. 1A north to signs for Swampscott/Marblehead; after rotary, take Lynn Shore Dr. north 9/10 mile, past 2 traffic lights and Christian Science Church. Turn left onto Wolcott Rd., then right onto Ocean St.; inn is on the right. **Amenities:** Outdoor whirlpool spa. *In room:* A/C, TV, dataport.

WHERE TO DINE

At a number of places in Old Town, you can stock up for a picnic along the water. The best is **Iggy's Bread of the World** ⭐⭐, 5 Pleasant St. (𝄡 781/639-4717), which serves fabulous gourmet baked goods and coffee. It has a small seating area—but really, go outside.

The Barnacle SEAFOOD   This unassuming spot affords a shorebird's-eye view of the harbor from the deck, the counter facing the windows, and the crowded dining room. The food is tasty and plentiful. It's not innovative, but it is fresh—the restaurant's lobster boat delivers daily—and popular with local residents, which is always a good sign. The chowder and fried seafood, especially clams, are terrific. This is an agreeable place to quaff a beer and watch the boats sail by.

141 Front St. 𝄡 781/631-4236. Reservations not accepted. Main courses $5–$15 lunch, $13–$18 dinner. No credit cards. Daily 11:30am–4pm; Sun–Thurs 5–9pm, Fri–Sat 5–10pm. Closed Tues in winter.

Driftwood Restaurant ⭐ DINER/SEAFOOD   At the foot of State Street next to Clark Landing (the town pier) is an honest-to-goodness local hangout. Join the crowd at a table or the counter for generous portions of breakfast (served all day) or lunch. Try pancakes or hash, chowder or a seafood "roll" (a hot-dog bun filled with, say, fried clams or lobster salad). The house specialty, served on weekends and holidays, is fried dough, which is exactly as delicious and indigestible as it sounds.

63 Front St. 𝄡 781/631-1145. Main courses $2–$10; breakfast items under $6. No credit cards. Summer daily 6:30am–5pm; winter daily 6:30am–2pm.

King's Rook ⭐ CAFE/WINE BAR   This cozy spot serves coffees, teas, hot chocolate, soft drinks, and more than 20 wines by the glass, and the food has a sophisticated flair. The intimate side-street atmosphere and racks of newspapers and magazines make this a great place to linger over a pesto pizza, excellent spinach soup, a tasty salad, or a rich dessert—and, of course, a beverage.

12 State St. 𝄡 781/631-9838. Reservations not accepted. Main courses $5–$10. DISC, MC, V. Mon–Fri noon–2:30pm; Tues–Fri 5:30–11:30pm; Sat–Sun noon–11:30pm. Closed Mon in winter.

4 Salem ⭐⭐

16 miles NE of Boston, 4 miles NW of Marblehead

Settled in 1626 (4 years before Boston) and later known around the world as a center of merchant shipping, Salem is internationally famous today for a 7-month episode in 1692. The witchcraft trials led to 20 deaths, 3 centuries of notoriety, countless lessons on the evils of prejudice, and innumerable bad puns ("Stop by for a spell" is a favorite slogan). Today, the city abounds with witch-associated attractions. Most are historically accurate, but you'll also see a fair number of goofy souvenirs and opportunistic tourist traps. (An excellent antidote to the latter is the **Peabody Essex Museum**.) Salem is a family-friendly destination that's worth at least a half-day visit, perhaps after a stop in Marblehead; it can easily fill a day.

Visitors concentrating on wall-to-wall witches will miss another important part of the city's history. Salem's merchant vessels circled the globe in the 17th and 18th centuries, returning laden with treasures. The city peaked between the Revolutionary War and the War of 1812, with the opening of the China Trade—many overseas merchants even believed that Salem was an independent country. One reminder of that era, a replica of the 1797 East Indiaman tall ship *Friendship,* is anchored near the Salem Maritime National Historic Site.

ESSENTIALS

GETTING THERE   From Marblehead, take Route 114 west into downtown Salem. From Boston, take Route 1A north to Salem, being careful in Lynn, where the road turns left and immediately right. Or take I-93 or Route 1 to Route 128, then Route 114 east. There's metered street parking and a reasonably priced garage opposite the visitor center.

From Boston, the **MBTA** (© 617/222-3200; www.mbta.com) runs commuter trains from North Station and bus route 450 from Haymarket (Orange or Green Line). The train is more comfortable, but runs less frequently. It takes 30 to 35 minutes; round-trip fare is $5.50. The station is about 5 blocks from the downtown area. The one-way fare for the 35- to 55-minute bus trip is $2.75. During warm weather and Halloween festivities, **ferries** (© 617/227-4321; www.bostonharborcruises.com) run from Long Wharf in Boston to the Blaney Street Ferry Terminal, off Derby Street. Call ahead for schedules and other details, such as access to downtown from the terminal. The 75-minute trip costs about $10 for adults, less for seniors and children.

VISITOR INFORMATION   A good place to start is the **National Park Service Visitor Center,** 2 New Liberty St. (© 978/740-1650; www.nps.gov/sama), open daily from 9am to 5pm. Exhibits highlight early settlement, maritime history, and the leather and textiles industries. The center distributes brochures and pamphlets, including one that describes a walking tour of the historic district, and has an auditorium where a free film on Essex County provides an overview.

Destination Salem (the city's Office of Tourism & Cultural Affairs), 10 Liberty St. (© 877/SALEM-MA or 978/744-3663; www.salem.org), collaborates with the Chamber of Commerce to publish a free visitor guide that includes a good map. The **Salem Chamber of Commerce,** 32 Derby Sq. (© 978/744-0004; www.salem-chamber.org), maintains a rack of brochures and pamphlets at its office on the first floor of Old Town Hall. It's open Monday through Friday from 9am to 5pm. Salem has an excellent community website at **www.salemweb.com**.

GETTING AROUND   In the congested downtown area, walking is the way to go. If it's hot or you plan to visit more than three or four places, you might prefer to ride. At the Essex Street side of the visitor center, you can board the **Salem Trolley** (© 508/744-5469) for a 1-hour narrated tour, and you can reboard as often as you'd like at any of the 15 stops. It operates from 10am to 5pm (last tour at 4), daily April through October, Saturdays and Sundays in March and November. Tickets ($10 for adults, $9 for seniors, $5 for children 5 to 12, $25 per family) are good all day. It's a good deal if you're spending the day and don't want to keep moving the car or carrying leg-weary children.

SPECIAL EVENTS   The city's 3-week Halloween celebration, **Haunted Happenings** 🎃🎃 (www.salemhauntedhappenings.com), includes parades, parties, tours, and a ceremony on the big day. During **Heritage Days,** a weeklong event in mid-August, the city celebrates its multicultural history with musical and theatrical performances, a parade, and fireworks.

Salem

ATTRACTIONS ●

Central Wharf **15**
Custom House **18**
Derby Wharf **16**
The *Friendship* **17**
Harbor Sweets **5**
The House of the Seven Gables **21**
Moby Duck Tours **11**
Peabody Essex Museum **8**
Pickering Wharf **14**
Salem Maritime National Historic Site **17**
Salem Trolley **9**
Salem 1630: Pioneer Village **6**
Salem Willows Amusement Park **22**
Salem Witch Museum **11**
West India Goods **20**

ACCOMMODATIONS ■

Coach House Inn **7**
Hawthorne Hotel **12**
Salem Inn **1**

DINING ◆

Lyceum Bar & Grill **2**
Red's Sandwich Shop **4**
Rockmore Restaurant **13**
Stromberg's **3**

Post Office
Church
Information
Pedestrian Mall
Station Stop

EXPLORING SALEM

The historic district extends well inland from the waterfront. Many 18th-century houses, some with original furnishings, still stand. Ship captains lived near the water at the east end of downtown, in relatively small houses crowded close together. The captains' employers, the shipping-company owners, built their homes away from the water (and the accompanying aromas). Many lived on **Chestnut Street** ★★, a grand thoroughfare that is a National Historic Landmark. Ask at the visitor center for the pamphlet that describes a walking tour of the historic district.

By car or trolley, the **Salem Willows** amusements are 5 minutes away; many signs point the way. The strip of rides and snack bars has a honky-tonk air, and the waterfront park is a good place to bring a picnic and wander along the shore. Admission is free; metered parking is available. To enjoy the great view without the arcades and rides, have lunch one peninsula over at **Winter Island Park.**

The House of the Seven Gables ★ Nathaniel Hawthorne's cousin lived here, and stories and legends of the house and its inhabitants inspired his 1851 book of the same name. If you haven't read the eerie novel, don't let that keep you away—begin your visit with the audiovisual program, which tells the story. The house, built by Capt. John Turner in 1668, holds six rooms of period furniture, including pieces referred to in the book, along with a secret staircase. Tours include a visit to Hawthorne's birthplace and descriptions of what life was like for the house's 18th-century inhabitants. The costumed guides can get a little silly as they mug for young visitors, but they're well versed in the history of the buildings and eager to answer questions. Also on the grounds, overlooking Salem Harbor, are period gardens, the **Retire Beckett House** (1655), the **Hooper-Hathaway House** (1682), and a **counting house** (1830).

54 Turner St. ℂ **978/744-0991.** www.7gables.org. Guided tours $8 adults, $5 children 6–17, free for children under 6. Tour and Salem 1630 admission $13 adults, $9 children 6–17. May–Dec daily 10am–5pm; Jan–Apr Mon–Sat 10am–5pm, Sun noon–5pm. Closed Thanksgiving, Christmas, New Year's Day. From downtown, follow Derby St. east 3 blocks past Derby Wharf.

Peabody Essex Museum ★★ Kids The Peabody Essex Museum is a treasure trove of art and cultural history peeking out from behind a figure wearing a pointy black hat. Though sometimes overshadowed by Salem's every-witch-way reputation, the museum's encyclopedic collections offer an engaging look at nearly 4 centuries in a fascinating seaport (yes, including the witchcraft trials). The museum is in the midst of a huge expansion; some areas may be closed during your visit, but call or surf ahead, because many won't change.

Visitors may want to plan around two special exhibitions: *The Master Prints of Edward S. Curtis: Portraits of Native America,* an important show of more than 60 original prints by the legendary photographer, will run from November 2001 to March 2002. In the summer of 2002, *Treasures of the Musé National de la Marine* will include some 200 objects from the French maritime museum, plus 33 ship models.

The permanent collections blend "the natural and artificial curiosities" Salem's sea captains and merchants brought back from around the world with the local artifacts of the county historical society. The well-planned displays help you understand the significance of each item, and interpretive materials (including interactive and hands-on activities) get children involved. You might see objects related to the history of the port of Salem (including gorgeous furniture), the whaling trade, the witchcraft trials, and East Asian art. Portraits of area residents include Charles Osgood's omnipresent rendering of Nathaniel Hawthorne.

Sign up for a fascinating tour of one or more of the museum's nine historic houses—the 1804 **Gardner-Pingree House** ★★, a magnificent Federal mansion where a notorious murder was committed in 1830, has been meticulously restored. You can also take a gallery tour or select from about a dozen pamphlets for self-guided tours on various topics.

East India Sq. ✆ **800/745-4054** or 978/745-9500. www.pem.org. Admission $10 adults, $8 seniors and students, free for children under 17. House tour only $6. Apr–Oct Mon–Sat 10am–5pm, Sun noon–5pm; Nov–March Tues–Sat 10am–5pm, Sun noon–5pm. Closed Thanksgiving, Christmas, New Year's Day. Take Hawthorne Blvd. to Essex St., following signs for visitor center. Enter on Essex St. or New Liberty St.

Salem Maritime National Historic Site ★ *Kids*
The historic site is a 9-acre finger of parkland extending into the harbor, plus an entertaining introduction to Salem's seagoing history: a real live ship. A full-size replica of a 1797 East Indiaman merchant vessel, the *Friendship* ★★ is a three-masted 171-footer. The tall ship is a faithful replica with some concessions to the modern era, such as diesel engines and accessibility for people with disabilities. The hull was laid in Albany, N.Y., and towed to Massachusetts, where construction was completed from 1999 to 2001. After being commissioned in July 2001, the *Friendship* finally opened to the public. Fees for visitors were not set at press time, but a tour of the ship likely will be included in the **guided ranger tour** ★.

Central Wharf holds a warehouse (ca. 1800) that houses the orientation center. Tours, which vary seasonally, expand on Salem's maritime history. Yours might include the **Derby House** (1762), a wedding gift to shipping magnate Elias Hasket Derby from his father, and the **Custom House** (1819). Legend (myth, really) has it that this is where Nathaniel Hawthorne was working when he found an embroidered scarlet *A*. If you prefer to explore on your own, you can see the free film at the orientation center and wander around Derby Wharf, the West India Goods Store, the Bonded Warehouse, the Scale House, and Central Wharf.

Derby Wharf, 174 Derby St. ✆ **978/740-1660.** www.nps.gov/sama. Free admission. Guided tours $3 adults, $2 seniors and children 6–16. Daily 9am–5pm. Closed Thanksgiving, Christmas, New Year's Day. Take Derby St. east; just past Pickering Wharf, Derby Wharf is on the right.

Salem 1630: Pioneer Village *Kids*
This is a popular destination for school and day-camp field trips; adults traveling alone may feel out of place. A re-creation of life in Salem just 4 years after European settlement, the Puritan village is staffed by costumed interpreters who lead tours, demonstrate crafts, and tend farm animals. They escort visitors around the various dwellings—wear sneakers, as the village isn't paved—and explain their activities. As with any undertaking of this nature, it takes a while to get used to the atmosphere, but once you do, it's great fun.

Forest River Park, off West Ave. ✆ **978/744-0991.** www.7gables.org. Admission $7 adults, $5 children 6–17. Admission and House of the Seven Gables tour $13 adults, $9 children 6–17. Late Apr to late Nov Mon–Sat 10am–5pm, Sun noon–5pm. Closed late Nov to late Apr. Take Lafayette St. (Rtes. 114 and 1A) south from downtown to West Ave., turn left, and follow signs.

Salem Witch Museum ★★ *Kids*
This is one of the most memorable attractions in eastern Massachusetts—it's both interesting and scary. The main draw of the museum (a former church) is a three-dimensional audiovisual

Trying Times: The Salem Witch Hysteria

The Salem witch trials took place in 1692, a product of superstition that originated in Europe, religious control of government, and plain old boredom.

The crisis began quietly in the winter of 1691–92 in Salem Village (now the town of Danvers). The Rev. Samuel Parris's household included his 9-year-old daughter, Elizabeth, her cousin Abigail, and a West Indian slave named Tituba who told stories to amuse the girls during the long, harsh winter. Entertained by tales of witchcraft, sorcery, and fortune-telling, the girls and their friends began to act out the stories, claiming to be under a spell, rolling on the ground and wailing. The settlers—aware that thousands of people in Europe had been executed as witches in the previous centuries—took the behavior seriously.

At first, only Tituba and two other women were accused of casting spells. Soon, though, the infighting typical of the Puritan theocracy came to the fore, and an accusation of witchcraft became a handy way to settle a score. Anyone "different" was a potential target, from the elderly to the deaf to the poor. A special court convened in Salem proper, and although the girls recanted, the trials began. Defendants had no counsel, and pleading not guilty or objecting to the proceedings was considered equivalent to a confession. From March 1 to September 22, of the more than 150 people who were accused, 27 were convicted.

In the end, 19 people went to the gallows, and one man who refused to plead, Giles Corey, was pressed to death by stones piled on a board on his chest. Finally, cooler heads prevailed. Leading cleric Cotton Mather and his father, Harvard president Increase Mather, led the call for tolerance. With the jails overflowing, the court called off the trials and freed the remaining prisoners, including Tituba.

The episode's lessons about open-mindedness and tolerance have echoed through the years since. Salem was the backdrop for Arthur Miller's *The Crucible*. The 1953 play is both a story about the witch trials and an allegory about the McCarthy Senate hearings of the 1950s— another kind of witch hunt in a time when those lessons needed to be taught again.

presentation with life-size figures. The show takes place in a huge room lined with displays that are lighted in sequence. The 30-minute narration tells the story of the witchcraft trials and the accompanying hysteria. The well-researched presentation tells the story accurately, if somewhat overdramatically. One of the victims was crushed to death by rocks piled on a board on his chest—smaller kids may need a reminder that he's not real.

19½ Washington Sq., on Route 1A. ✆ **978/744-1692.** www.salemwitchmuseum.com. Admission $6.50 adults, $6 seniors, $4.50 children 6–14. Daily July–Aug 10am–7pm; Sept–June 10am–5pm. Closed Thanksgiving, Christmas, New Year's Day. Follow Hawthorne Blvd. to the northwest corner of Salem Common.

ORGANIZED TOURS & CRUISES

Salem Trolley (see "Getting Around," above) offers the best value, but it's land-locked. **Moby Duck Tours** ⚓ ((C) **508/741-4386;** www.mobyduck.com) leave from New Liberty Street in front of the visitor center. The amphibious tour vehicle cruises the streets of the city, then plunges into the harbor, delighting the kids on board. Tickets for the 55-minute (25 minutes on land, 30 on water) tours are $14 for adults, $12 for seniors, and $8 for children under 12. Tours operate on Saturdays and Sundays in May, daily from Memorial Day to Halloween.

SHOPPING

Snazzy gift shops throughout New England sell the chocolate confections of **Harbor Sweets** ⚓⚓. You can go to the source at Palmer Cove, 85 Leavitt St., off Lafayette Street ((C) **508/745-7648**). The deliriously good sweets are expensive, but candy bars and small assortments are available. Open Monday through Friday from 8:30am to 4:30pm, Saturday from 9am to 3pm, with extended hours around candy-centered holidays.

Pickering Wharf, at the corner of Derby and Congress streets, is a cluster of shops, boutiques, restaurants, and condos near a marina. The waterfront setting makes it a popular place for strolling, snacking, and shopping.

If you can't get witchcraft off your mind, several shops specialize in the necessary accessories. Do bear in mind that Salem is home to many practicing witches who take their beliefs very seriously. The **Broom Closet,** 3–5 Central St. ((C) **978/741-3669**), and **Crow Haven Corner,** 125 Essex St. ((C) **978/745-8763**), sell everything from crystals to clothing and cast a modern-day light on age-old customs.

WHERE TO STAY

The busiest and most expensive time of year is **Halloween week;** reserve well in advance.

Most major hotel and motel chains are represented on or near Route 1 north of I-95, within 30 minutes of downtown Salem. In Salem, the **Clipper Ship Inn,** 40 Bridge St./Rte. 1A ((C) **978/745-8022**), is a comfortable, modern motel northeast of downtown. A double in high season runs $110 to $150.

Coach House Inn   Built in 1879 for a ship's captain, this inn is 2 blocks from the harbor. It's a good choice if you don't mind the 20-minute walk or 5-minute drive from downtown Salem. In addition to sightseers, it books travelers with business at nearby Salem State College. The three-story mansion was redecorated in 1998. The good-size guest rooms are elegantly furnished in traditional style. All have high ceilings, and most have (nonworking) fireplaces. Breakfast arrives at your door in a basket.

284 Lafayette St. (Rtes. 1A and 114), Salem, MA 01970. (C) **800/688-8689** or 978/744-4092. Fax 978/745-8031. www.coachhousesalem.com. 11 units, 9 with bathroom (1 with shower only). $80–$98 double with shared bathroom; $95–$145 double with private bathroom; $150–$185 suite. Rates include continental breakfast. 2- to 3-night minimum stay on weekends and holidays. AE, DISC, MC, V. Free parking. *In room:* A/C, TV, coffeemaker.

Hawthorne Hotel ⚓   This historic hotel, built in 1925, is both convenient and comfortable. It attracts vacationers and business travelers, and is popular for functions. The six-story building is centrally located and well maintained, with a traditional atmosphere. The guest rooms, renovated between 1997 and 1999, are attractively furnished and adequate in size. The best units, on the Salem Common (north) side of the building, have better views than rooms that face the street. Ask to be as high up as possible, as the neighborhood is busy.

18 Washington Sq. (at Salem Common), Salem, MA 01970. © 800/729-7829 or 978/744-4080. Fax 978/745-9842. www.hawthornehotel.com. 89 units (some with shower only). $99–$199 double; $199–$309 suite. Extra person $12. Children under 16 stay free in parents' room. Off-season discounts, senior discounts, and weekend and other packages available. 2-night minimum stay on holiday weekends. AE, DC, DISC, MC, V. Limited self-parking. Small pets accepted ($15). **Amenities:** Restaurant (American), cafe; exercise room; limited room service; laundry service; dry cleaning. *In room:* A/C, TV, dataport.

Salem Inn ★★   The Salem Inn, which consists of three properties, occupies a comfortable niche between too-big hotel and too-small B&B. Its clientele includes honeymooners as well as sightseers and families, and the variety of rooms means the innkeepers can make a good match of guest and accommodations. The best units are the luxury and family suites in the 1874 Peabody House, a recently restored mansion. Guest rooms are large and tastefully decorated; some have fireplaces, canopy beds, and whirlpool baths. Family suites have kitchenettes. Guests of all three houses can relax in the peaceful rose garden at the rear of the main building.

7 Summer St. (Rte. 114), Salem, MA 01970. © 800/446-2995 or 978/741-0680. Fax 978/744-8924. www.SalemInnMA.com. 39 units (some with shower only). Nov–Sept $129–$229 double; Oct $180–$290. Rates include continental breakfast. 2- to 3-night minimum stay during special events and holidays. AE, DC, DISC, MC, V. Free parking. Pets accepted by prior arrangement ($15 per night). *In room:* A/C, TV, coffeemaker, hair dryer.

WHERE TO DINE

Pickering Wharf has a food court as well as a link in the **Victoria Station** (© 978/744-7644) chain, whose deck has a great view of the marina.

Lyceum Bar & Grill ★★ CONTEMPORARY AMERICAN   The elegance of the Lyceum's dining rooms matches the quality of the food, which attracts local businesspeople and out-of-towners. Grilling is a favorite cooking technique—try the signature marinated grilled portobellos. They're available as an appetizer and scattered throughout the menu—say, in delectable pasta with chicken, red peppers, and Swiss chard in wine sauce, or with beef tenderloin, red pepper sauce, and garlic mashed potatoes. Spicy vegetable lasagna is also tasty. Try to save room for one of the traditional yet sophisticated desserts—the brownie sundae is out of this world.

43 Church St. (at Washington St.). © 978/745-7665. www.lyceumsalem.com. Reservations recommended. Main courses $6–$10 lunch, $16–$22 dinner. AE, DISC, MC, V. Mon–Fri 11:30am–3pm; Sun brunch 11am–3pm; daily 5:30–10pm.

Red's Sandwich Shop NEW ENGLAND   Locals and visitors feel equally comfortable at this no-frills hangout. Hunker down at the counter or a table and be ready for your waitress to call you "dear" as she brings you pancakes and eggs at breakfast, or soup (opt for chicken over chowder) and a burger at lunch. **Red's Winter Island Grille** (© 978/744-0203), under the same management, is open seasonally at Winter Island Park.

15 Central St. © 978/745-3527. www.redssandwichshop.com. Most items under $7. No credit cards. Mon–Sat 5am–3pm, Sun 6am–1pm.

Rockmore Restaurant ★ SEAFOOD/AMERICAN   If you're going to eat at a restaurant with a gimmick, it might as well be a good one. This is: It's on a float in the middle of Salem Harbor. The Rockmore serves burgers, sandwiches, and fresh seafood in an extremely casual atmosphere, usually to local boaters.

Milling Around: A Trip to Lowell

A 19th-century textile center that later fell into disrepair, **Lowell** is a 21st-century success story. A city built around restored mills and industrial canals will never be a glamorous vacation spot, but thousands of visitors a year find Lowell a fascinating and rewarding destination. The sights concentrate on the history of the Industrial Revolution and the textile industry. They include boardinghouses where the "mill girls" lived; the workers, some as young as 10 years old, averaged 14-hour days weaving cloth on power looms.

Start at the **Lowell National Historical Park Visitor Center,** 246 Market St. (© **978/970-5000**; www.nps.gov/lowe), open daily from 9am to 5pm. Rangers lead free programs and tours, and canal cruises and free trolley tours operate in summer. Ask for a map of the area, and use it to find your way around downtown. Two interesting museums are within easy walking distance: the **American Textile History Museum,** 491 Dutton St. (© **978/441-0400**; www.athm.org), and the **New England Quilt Museum** ★, 18 Shattuck St. (© **978/452-4207**; www.nequilt museum.org). For more information, consult the **Greater Merrimack Valley Convention & Visitors Bureau,** 9 Central St., Suite 201, Lowell (© **800/443-3332** or 978/459-6150; www.merrimackvalley.org).

To drive to Lowell, take Route 3 or I-495 to the Lowell Connector and follow signs north to Exit 5B and the historic district. The **commuter rail** (© **617/222-3200**; www.mbta.com) from Boston's North Station takes about 45 minutes and costs $8.50 round-trip.

The food is fine, but nobody's here for the food. (Did we mention it's on a *float*?) If you're not traveling by boat, ferry service is available from 94 Wharf St., Pickering Wharf.

Salem Harbor. © **978/740-1001.** www.rockmoreco.com. Main courses $7–$15. AE, DISC, MC, V. Memorial Day to Labor Day daily 11am–10pm, weather permitting.

Stromberg's ★ *Kids* SEAFOOD   For generous portions of well-prepared seafood and a view of the water, seek out this popular spot at the foot of the bridge to Beverly, which draws both locals and out-of-towners. You won't care that Beverly Harbor isn't the most exciting spot, especially if it's summer and you're out on the deck. The fish and clam chowders are excellent, daily specials are numerous, and there are more chicken, beef, and pasta options than you might expect. Crustacean lovers in the mood to splurge will fall for the world-class lobster roll.

2 Bridge St. (Rte. 1A). © **978/744-1863.** www.strombergs.com. Reservations recommended at dinner. Main courses $6–$11 lunch, $11–$17 dinner; children's menu $5. AE, DISC, MC, V. Sun, Tues–Thurs 11am–9pm, Fri–Sat 11am–10pm.

5 Cape Ann

Gloucester, Rockport, Essex, and Manchester-by-the-Sea make up Cape Ann, a rocky peninsula so enchantingly beautiful that when you hear the slogan "Massachusetts's *other* Cape," you may forget what the first one was. Cape Ann and Cape Cod do share some attributes—scenery, shopping, seafood, and traffic.

The smaller cape's proximity to Boston and manageable scale make it a wonderful day trip and a good choice for a longer stay. With the decline of the fishing industry that brought great prosperity to the area in the 19th century, Cape Ann has played up its long-standing reputation as a haven for artists. Along with galleries and crafts shops, you'll find historical attractions, beaches—and oh, that scenery!

Be aware that this is hardly a four-season destination. Many establishments close in the fall or early winter through April or May; some open on weekends in December.

The **Cape Ann Transportation Authority,** or CATA (✆ **978/283-7916**), runs buses from town to town on Cape Ann and operates special routes in summer.

The **Cape Ann Chamber of Commerce,** 33 Commercial St., Gloucester (✆ **800/321-0133** or 978/283-1601; www.capeannvacations.com), and the **North of Boston Convention & Visitors Bureau,** 17 Peabody Sq., Peabody (✆ **800/742-5306** or 978/977-7760; www.northofboston.org), provide abundant visitor information and advice.

MANCHESTER-BY-THE-SEA

The scenic route to Gloucester from points south is Route 127, which runs through Manchester-by-the-Sea, a lovely village incorporated in 1645. Now a prosperous suburb of Boston, Manchester is probably best known for **Singing Beach** (see "Life's a Beach," below). In 2000, it masqueraded as a Vermont village and became a movie backdrop for David Mamet's *State and Main*. The **commuter rail** (✆ **617/222-3200;** www.mbta.com) from Boston costs $8.50 round-trip and stops in the center of the compact downtown area, where there are many shops and restaurants. Nearby **Masconomo Park** overlooks the harbor.

The home of the Manchester Historical Society is the **Trask House,** 10 Union St. (✆ **978/526-7230**), a 19th-century sea captain's home. Tours show off the period furnishings, including pieces produced in Manchester, and the society's costume collections. It's specialized, but intriguing to devotees of house tours. Open late June through August, Saturday from 10am to 4pm, Sunday from noon to 4pm, and by appointment. A donation is requested.

MAGNOLIA

Pay close attention as you head north from Manchester or south from Gloucester on Route 127—Magnolia is easy to miss, but the village (technically part of Gloucester) is worth a detour. Notable for its lack of waterfront commercial property, the village center is unremarkable. The homes surrounding it, many of them former summer residences now occupied through the winter, are magnificent.

Just up the coast are two notable geological formations. **Rafe's Chasm** is a huge cleft in the shoreline rock, opposite the reef of **Norman's Woe,** which figures in Henry Wadsworth Longfellow's scary poem "The Wreck of the Hesperus." About three-quarters of a mile out of the center, look for a small parking area on the right. After a quarter-mile walk through the woods, you'll find a gorgeous panorama of stone and surf.

The **Hammond Castle Museum,** 80 Hesperus Ave. (✆ **978/283-2080** or 978/283-7673; www.hammondcastle.org), is a medieval-style edifice designed by eccentric inventor John Hays Hammond, Jr. Constructed of Rockport granite from 1926 to 1929, the castle cost more than $6 million. Guided tours aren't offered, so you're on your own with a pamphlet to direct you—not the best way to explore such a peculiar place, but if you like the medieval era, you'll definitely enjoy this. It has 85-foot towers, battlements, stained-glass windows, and a great hall 60 feet high. Many 12th-, 13th-, and 14th-century furnishings, tapestries, paintings, and architectural fragments fill the rooms. Admission is $6.50 for adults, $5.50 for seniors and students, and $4.50 for children 4 to 12. It's open year-round on Saturdays and Sundays from 10am to 3pm; June to December, it's also open Monday through Friday from 10am to 6pm.

ESSEX ✮

West of Gloucester (past Route 128) on Route 133 lies a beautiful little town known for Essex clams, salt marshes, a long tradition of shipbuilding, a plethora of antiques shops, and one celebrated restaurant.

Life's a Beach

Paradoxically, Cape Ann is almost as well known for its sandy beaches as for its rocky coastline. Two things to know: (1) The water is *cold,* and (2) Parking can be scarce, especially on weekends, and pricey—as much as $15 per car. If you can't set out early, wait until midafternoon and hope that the people who arrived first have had enough. During the summer, lifeguards are on duty from 9am to 5pm at larger public beaches. Surfing is generally permitted outside of those hours. The beaches listed here all have bathhouses and snack bars. Watch out for greenhead flies at North Shore beaches in July and August. They don't sting—they take little bites of flesh. Plan to bring or buy insect repellent.

The best-known North Shore beach is **Singing Beach** ★★, off Masconomo Street in Manchester-by-the-Sea. Because it's accessible by public transportation, it attracts the most diverse crowd—carless singles, local families, and other beach bunnies of all ages. They walk two-thirds of a mile on Beach Street from the train station to find sparkling sand and lively surf. Take the commuter rail (© 617/222-3200; www.mbta.com) from Boston's North Station.

Nearly as famous and popular is **Crane Beach** ★, off Argilla Road in Ipswich, part of a 1,400-acre barrier beach reservation. Fragile dunes and a white-sand beach lead down to Ipswich Bay. The surf is calmer than that at less sheltered Singing Beach, but still quite chilly. Pick up Argilla Road south of Ipswich Center near the intersection of Routes 1A and 133. Also on Ipswich Bay is Gloucester's **Wingaersheek Beach** ★, on Atlantic Street off Route 133. From Exit 13 off Route 128, the beach is about 15 minutes away (mind the speed limits). When you finally arrive, you'll find beautiful white sand, a glorious view, and more dunes. Because these beaches are harder to get to, they attract more locals—but also lots of day-tripping families.

Most other good beaches in Gloucester have almost no nonresident parking. Two exceptions are **Half Moon Beach** and **Cressy's Beach,** at Stage Fort Park, off Route 127 near Route 133 and downtown. Because they're easy to reach, the sandy beaches and the park snack bar are popular local hangouts.

Legend has it that **Woodman's of Essex** ★★★, on Main Street (© 800/649-1773 or 978/768-6451; www.woodmans.com), was the birthplace of the fried clam in 1916. Today, the thriving family business is a great spot to join legions of locals and visitors from around the world for lobster "in the rough," chowder, steamers, corn on the cob, onion rings, and (you guessed it) superb fried clams. Expect the line to be long, even in winter, but it moves quickly and offers a view of the regimented commotion in the food-preparation area. Eat in a booth, upstairs on the deck, or out back at a picnic table. You'll want to be well fed before you set off to explore the numerous antiques shops along Main Street.

The water views in town are of the Essex River, a saltwater estuary. Narrated 90-minute sightseeing tours that put you in prime birding territory are available

through **Essex River Cruises** ✮, Essex Marina, 35 Dodge St. (© **800/
748-3706** or 978/768-6981; www.essexcruises.com), daily April through October. The pontoon boat, which allows for excellent sightseeing, is screened and
has rest rooms. Call for reservations.

GLOUCESTER ✮✮
The ocean has been Gloucester's lifeblood since long before the first European
settlement in 1623. The most urban of Cape Ann's communities, Gloucester
(which rhymes with "roster") is a working city, not a cutesy tourist town. Miles
of gorgeous coastline surround the densely populated downtown area. If you
read or saw *The Perfect Storm,* you'll have some sense of what to expect. Gloucester is home to one of the last commercial fishing fleets in New England, an internationally celebrated artists' colony, a large Portuguese-American community,
and just enough historic attractions. Allow at least half a day, perhaps combined
with a visit to the tourist magnet of Rockport; a full day would be better, especially if you plan a cruise or whale watch.

ESSENTIALS
GETTING THERE   From Boston, the quickest route is I-93 (or Route 1, if
it's not rush hour) to Route 128, which ends at Gloucester. The slower but pret-
tier approach from downtown Salem is Route 1A across the bridge at Beverly to
Route 127. It runs through Manchester to Gloucester. Route 128 exits for Manchester allow access to Route 127. There's street parking and a free lot on the
causeway to Rocky Neck. Gloucester is 33 miles northeast of Boston, 16 miles
northeast of Salem, and 7 miles south of Rockport.

   The **commuter rail** (© **617/222-3200;** www.mbta.com) runs from Boston's
North Station. The trip takes about an hour; round-trip fare is $9. The station
is across town from downtown, about 10 blocks, so allow time for getting to the
waterfront. The **Cape Ann Transportation Authority,** or CATA (© **978/
283-7916**), runs buses from town to town on Cape Ann.

VISITOR INFORMATION   The **Gloucester Tourism Commission,** 22
Poplar St. (© **800/649-6839** or 978/281-8865; www.gloucesterma.com), operates an excellent **Visitors Welcoming Center** at Stage Fort Park, off Route 127
near the intersection with Route 133. It's open in summer, daily from 9am to
5pm. The **Cape Ann Chamber of Commerce** information center, 33 Commercial St. (© **800/321-0133** or 978/283-1601; www.capeannvacations.com),
is open year-round—in summer, Monday through Friday from 8am to 6pm,

---

⎛Finds *The Perfect Storm*
Sebastian Junger's best-selling book *The Perfect Storm,* a thrilling but
tragic nonfiction account of the "no-name" hurricane of 1991, became a
blockbuster movie in 2000. Even before that, fans of the book were arriving in Gloucester and asking to be pointed toward the neighborhood tavern that co-stars in both accounts. The **Crow's Nest,** 334 Main St. (© **978/
281-2965**), a bit east of downtown, is a no-frills place with a horseshoe-
shaped bar and a crowd of regulars who seem amused that their favorite
hangout is a tourist attraction. The Crow's Nest plays a major role in
Junger's story, but its ceilings aren't high enough for it to be a movie set—
so the crew built an exact replica nearby.

Saturday from 10am to 6pm, Sunday from 10am to 4pm; in winter, Monday through Friday from 8am to 5pm. Call or write for a brochure.

GETTING AROUND   Downtown is fairly compact and walkable, but there's more to Gloucester than that. If you can manage it, travel by car. You'll be able to make the best use of your time, especially if you plan several stops. The **Cape Ann Transportation Authority** (see above) serves most of Gloucester on its regular routes and operates special loops in summer.

SPECIAL EVENTS   Gloucester holds summer festivals and street fairs at the drop of a hat. They honor everything from clams to schooners. The best known is **St. Peter's Fiesta,** a colorful 4-day event at the end of June. The Italian-American fishing colony's enormous festival has more in common with a carnival midway than a religious observation, but it's great fun. There are parades, rides, music, food, sporting events, and, on Sunday, the blessing of the fleet. On summer Sunday nights, the **Concerts in the Park** (© **978/281-0543**) series brings live jazz, country, and traditional music to Stage Fort Park.

EXPLORING THE TOWN

Start at the water, as visitors have done for centuries. The French explorer Samuel de Champlain called the harbor "Le Beauport" in 1604—some 600 years after the Vikings first visited—and its configuration and proximity to good fishing gave it the reputation it enjoys to this day. The **Gloucester Maritime Trail** brochure, available at visitor centers, describes four excellent self-guided tours.

On Stacy Boulevard west of downtown is a reminder of the sea's danger. Leonard Craske's bronze statue of the **Gloucester Fisherman,** known as "The Man at the Wheel," bears the inscription "They That Go Down to the Sea in Ships 1623–1923." As you take in the glorious view, consider this: More than 10,000 fishermen lost their lives during the city's first 300 years.

To reach **East Gloucester,** follow signs as you leave downtown or go directly from Route 128, Exit 9. On East Main Street, you'll see signs for the world-famous **Rocky Neck Art Colony** ★★, the oldest continuously operating art colony in the country. Park in the lot on the tiny causeway and head west along Rocky Neck Avenue, which abounds with studios, galleries, restaurants, and people. The attraction is the presence of working artists, not just shops that happen to sell art. Most galleries are open daily from 10am to 10pm in summer. Another place to see local artists' creations is the prestigious **North Shore Arts Association** ★, 197 E. Main St. (© **978/283-1857;** www.cape-ann.com/nsaa), founded in 1922. It's open late May through October, Monday through Saturday from 10am to 5pm, Sunday from 1 to 5pm. Admission is free.

Stage Fort Park, off Route 127 near the intersection with Route 133, offers an excellent view of the harbor and has a busy seasonal snack bar. It's a good spot for picnicking, swimming, or just playing on the cannons in the Revolutionary War fort.

Beauport (Sleeper-McCann House) ★★   The Society for the Preservation of New England Antiquities, which operates Beauport, describes it as a "fantasy house," and that's putting it mildly. Interior designer Henry Davis Sleeper accumulated vast stores of American and European decorative arts and antiques in his summer home. From 1907 to 1934, he decorated the 40 rooms, 26 of which are open to the public, to illustrate literary and historical themes. The entertaining tour concentrates more on the house in general than on the countless objects. You'll see architectural details from other buildings, magnificent arrangements of colored glassware, an Early American kitchen, the "Red Indian Room" (with a majestic view of the harbor), and "Strawberry Hill," the master bedroom. Note that the house is closed on summer weekends.

75 Eastern Point Blvd. ℂ **978/283-0800**. www.spnea.org. Guided tour $6 adults, $5.50 seniors, $3 students and children 6–12. Tours on the hour May 15–Sept 14 Mon–Fri 10am–4pm; Sept 15–Oct 15 daily 10am–4pm. Closed Oct 16–May 14 and summer weekends. Take E. Main St. south to Eastern Point Blvd. (a private road), continue half a mile to house, park on left.

Cape Ann Historical Museum ⭑ This meticulously curated museum makes an excellent introduction to Cape Ann's history and artists. It devotes an entire gallery to the extraordinary work of **Fitz Hugh Lane** ⭑⭑⭑, the Luminist painter whose light-flooded canvases show off the best of his native Gloucester. The nation's single largest collection of his paintings and drawings is here. Other galleries feature works on paper by 20th-century artists such as Maurice Prendergast and Milton Avery, work by other contemporary artists, and granite-quarrying tools and equipment. There's also an outdoor sculpture court. The **maritime and fisheries galleries** display entire vessels, exhibits on the fishing industry, ship models, and historic photographs and models of the Gloucester waterfront. The **Capt. Elias Davis House** (1804), decorated and furnished in Federal style with furniture, silver, and porcelains, is part of the museum.

27 Pleasant St. ℂ **978/283-0455**. www.cape-ann.com/historical-museum. Admission $5 adults, $4.50 seniors, $3.50 students, free for children under 6. Mar–Jan Tues–Sat 10am–5pm. Closed Feb. Follow Main St. west through downtown and turn right onto Pleasant St.; the museum is 1 block up on right. Metered parking on street or in lot across street.

ORGANIZED TOURS & CRUISES

For information on whale watches, see "A Whale of an Adventure," below.

Moby Duck Tours ⭑ (ℂ **978/281-3825**; www.mobyduck.com) are 55-minute sightseeing expeditions that travel on land (20 minutes) before plunging into the water (35 minutes). They're just the right length for kids, who delight in the transition from street to sea. The amphibious vehicles leave from Harbor Loop downtown. Tickets cost $14 for adults, $12 for seniors, and $8 for children under 12. Tours operate on Saturdays and Sundays from Memorial Day to June, daily from July to Labor Day.

Also at Harbor Loop, you can tour the two-masted schooner ***Adventure*** ⭑⭑ (ℂ **978/281-8079**; www.schooner-adventure.org), a 121-foot fishing vessel built in Essex in 1926 and undergoing extensive restoration. It doesn't move, so it's not as thrilling as the *Thomas E. Lannon* (see below), but it's quicker and cheaper and can be much more interesting, depending on what's being worked on. The "living museum," a National Historic Landmark, is open to visitors from Memorial Day to Labor Day, Thursday through Sunday from 10am to 4pm. The suggested donation is $5 for adults, $4 for children. The *Adventure* serves **breakfast** every Sunday from 9:30am to 1pm. The hearty meal includes typical American breakfast items, plus whatever the volunteer cooks decide to add to the menu. This is a great way to check out the ship, fuel up for sightseeing, and—most important—mingle with the locals. Adults pay $8, children $5; reservations are recommended.

The schooner ***Thomas E. Lannon*** ⭑ (ℂ **978/281-6634**; www.schooner.org) is a lovely reproduction of a Gloucester fishing vessel. The 65-foot tall ship sails from Seven Seas Wharf downtown; 2-hour excursions ($30 for adults, $25 for seniors, $20 for children under 17) leave about four times a day May through

Kids A Whale of an Adventure

The waters off the Massachusetts coast are prime **whale-watching** ★★ territory, and Gloucester is a center of cruises. Stellwagen Bank, which runs from Gloucester to Provincetown about 27 miles east of Boston, is a rich feeding ground for the magnificent mammals, who dine on sand eels and other fish that gather on the ridge. The most commonly sighted species are finback, humpback, and minke whales; you might also see rare right whales. The whales often perform for their audience by jumping out of the water, and dolphins occasionally join the show. Naturalists on board narrate the trip for the companies listed here, pointing out the whales and describing birds and fish that cross your path.

Whale watching is not particularly time- or cost-effective, especially if restless children are along, but it's so popular for a reason: The payoff is, literally and figuratively, huge. This is an "only in New England" experience that kids (and adults) will remember for a long time.

The season runs from May through October. Dress warmly—it's much cooler at sea than in town—and wear a hat and rubber-soled shoes; pack sunglasses, sunscreen, a camera, and plenty of film. If you're prone to motion sickness, take precautions, because you'll be at sea for 4 to 6 hours.

This is an extremely competitive business—they'd deny it, but the companies are virtually indistinguishable. Most guarantee sightings, offer morning and afternoon cruises and deep-sea fishing excursions, honor other firms' coupons, and offer AARP and AAA discounts. Check ahead for sailing times, prices ($26 to $28 for adults, less for children and seniors), and reservations, which are always a good idea. In downtown Gloucester, **Cape Ann Whale Watch,** Rose's Wharf, 415 Main St. (© **800/877-5110** or 978/283-5110; www.caww.com), is the oldest and best-known operation. Also downtown are **Captain Bill's Whale Watch,** 33 Harbor Loop (© **800/33-WHALE** or 978/283-6995; www.cape-ann.com/captbill.html), and **Seven Seas Whale Watch,** Seven Seas Wharf (© **800/238-1776** or 978/283-1776; www.7seas-whalewatch.com). At the Cape Ann Marina, off Route 133, is **Yankee Whale Watch** (© **800/WHALING** or 978/283-0313; www.yankee-fleet.com/whale.htm).

October. Reservations are recommended. The company offers music and dining cruises and "storytelling sails."

WHERE TO STAY

The 40-unit **Vista Motel,** 22 Thatcher Rd. (Rte. 127A), Gloucester (© **866/VISTA-MA** or 978/281-3410; www.vistamotel.com), is a comfortable establishment on a hilltop near the Rockport border. It has a heated outdoor pool. Summer rates run $110 to $120 double.

Atlantis Oceanfront Motor Inn   This motor inn sits across the street from the water, affording stunning views from every window. It's more basic than the neighboring Bass Rocks Ocean Inn, but the views are the same. The good-size guest rooms are decorated in comfortable, contemporary style. Every unit has a terrace or balcony. Second-floor accommodations are slightly preferable, because the view is a little better.

125 Atlantic Rd., Gloucester, MA 01930. ℂ 800/732-6313 or 978/283-0014. Fax 978/281-8994. www. cape-ann.com/atlantis.html. 40 units (some with shower only). Late June to Labor Day $120–$140 double; spring and fall $80–$115. Extra person $8. Closed Nov to mid-Apr. 2-night minimum stay on spring and fall weekends, 3-night minimum on holiday and summer weekends. AE, MC, V. Follow Rte. 128 to the end (Exit 9, East Gloucester), turn left onto Bass Ave. (Rte. 127A), and follow it half a mile. Turn right and follow Atlantic Rd. **Amenities:** Coffee shop (breakfast only); heated outdoor pool. *In room:* A/C, TV.

Best Western Bass Rocks Ocean Inn   A family operation since 1946, the Bass Rocks Ocean Inn offers gorgeous ocean views and modern accommodations in a traditional setting. The spacious guest rooms take up a sprawling, comfortable two-story motel across the road from the rocky shore. A Colonial Revival mansion built in 1899 and known as the "wedding-cake house" holds the office and public areas, including a billiards room and a library. The inn has larger rooms and more of a resort feel than the neighboring Atlantis. Each unit has a balcony or patio. Second-floor rooms have slightly better views. In the afternoon, the staff serves coffee, tea, lemonade, and chocolate-chip cookies.

107 Atlantic Rd., Gloucester, MA 01930. ℂ 800/528-1234 or 978/283-7600. Fax 978/281-6489. www. bestwestern.com. 48 units. Late June to Labor Day $165–$210 double. Spring and fall discounts available. Extra person $8; rollaway $12. Children under 12 stay free in parents' room. Rates include continental breakfast. 3-night minimum stay on summer weekends and some spring and fall weekends. Closed Nov to late Apr. AE, DC, DISC, MC, V. Follow Rte. 128 to the end (Exit 9, East Gloucester), turn left onto Bass Ave. (Rte. 127A), and follow it ¹⁄₂ mile. Turn right and follow Atlantic Rd. **Amenities:** Heated outdoor pool; bikes for guests' use. *In room:* A/C, TV, fridge.

WHERE TO DINE

See "Essex," above, for information about **Woodman's of Essex,** which is about 20 minutes from downtown Gloucester.

Boulevard Oceanview Restaurant ✮ PORTUGUESE/SEAFOOD   This is a friendly neighborhood place in a high-tourist-traffic location. Across the street from the waterfront promenade just west of downtown, it's a dinerlike spot with water views from the front windows and the small deck. It serves ultra-fresh seafood (crane your neck and you can almost see the processing plants) and lunch-counter sandwiches. Try "Seafood Portuguese style"—shrimp *a la plancha* (in irresistible lemon-butter sauce)—or one of the several unusual casseroles.

25 Western Ave. (Stacy Blvd.). ℂ 978/281-2949. Reservations recommended at dinner in summer. Sandwiches $3.50–$7.50; main courses $7–$15.50; lobster priced daily. DISC, MC, V. Summer daily 11am–10pm; winter daily 11am–9:30pm.

The Gull Restaurant ✮✮ *Kids* SEAFOOD/AMERICAN   Floor-to-ceiling windows show off the Annisquam River from almost every seat at the Gull. The big, welcoming restaurant is known for prime rib as well as seafood. It draws locals, visitors, boaters, and families for large portions at reasonable prices. The seafood chowder is famous (with good reason), appetizers tend toward bar food, and fish is available in just about any variety and style. Daily specials run from simple lobster (market price) to sophisticated fish and meat dishes. At lunch, there's an extensive sandwich menu.

75 Essex Ave. (Rte. 133), at Cape Ann Marina. ℂ 978/281-6060. Reservations recommended for parties of eight or more. Main courses $5–$13 lunch, $8–$22 dinner; breakfast $3.45–$7.95. DISC, MC, V. Late Apr to Oct daily 6am–9pm. Closed Nov to late Apr. Take Rte. 133 west from intersection with Rte. 127, or take Rte. 133 east from Rte. 128.

Halibut Point Restaurant ⭐ SEAFOOD/AMERICAN   A local legend for its chowders and burgers, Halibut Point is a friendly tavern that serves generous portions of good food. The "Halibut Point Special"—10 bucks for a cup of chowder, a burger, and a beer—hits the high points. Although the clam chowder is terrific, spicy Italian fish chowder is so good that some people come to Gloucester just for that. There's also a raw bar if you prefer to start with shellfish. Main courses are simple (mostly sandwiches) at lunch, somewhat more elaborate at dinner. Be sure to check the specials board—you didn't come all this way to a fishing port not to have fresh fish, did you?

289 Main St. ⓒ **978/281-1900.** Main courses $5–$9 lunch, $9–$16 dinner. AE, DISC, MC, V. Daily 11:30am–11pm.

The Rudder Restaurant SEAFOOD/INTERNATIONAL   A meal at the Rudder (also known as Evie's Rudder) isn't just a meal—it's a party. Overlooking Smith Cove, in the heart of the Rocky Neck Art Colony, the 40-year-old restaurant is packed with gadgets, colored lights, antiques, photos, menus from around the world, and other collectibles. Ask for a seat on the deck (if it's not low tide) and be prepared for "spontaneous entertainment." You might hear live piano music or see Susan's invisible flaming baton twirling act. Yes, it's pricey, but you're also paying for the floor show. The chefs are creative, too—try the shrimp farcis appetizer. Main-course offerings run the gamut from shrimp scampi over fresh linguine to chicken piccata.

73 Rocky Neck Ave., E. Gloucester. ⓒ **978/283-7967.** Reservations required on weekends. Main courses $15–$25; children's menu $8. DISC, MC, V. Memorial Day to Labor Day daily noon–10:30pm; call for spring and fall hours. Closed Dec to mid-Apr.

ROCKPORT ⭐

This lovely little town at the tip of Cape Ann was settled in 1690. Over the years, Rockport has been an active fishing port, a center of granite excavation and cutting, and a thriving summer community whose specialty seems to be selling fudge and refrigerator magnets to out-of-towners. But there's more to Rockport than just gift shops. It's home to a lovely state park, and popular with photographers, sculptors, jewelry designers, and painters. Winslow Homer, Fitz Hugh Lane, and Childe Hassam are among the famous artists who have captured the local color. Rockport makes an entertaining half-day trip, perhaps combined with a visit to Gloucester.

ESSENTIALS

GETTING THERE   Rockport is north of Gloucester along Route 127 or 127A. At the end of Route 128, turn left at the signs for Rockport to take 127, which is shorter but more commercial. To take 127A, continue until you see the sign for East Gloucester and turn left. Parking is next to impossible, especially on summer Saturday afternoons. Make one loop around downtown, then head to the free parking lot on Upper Main Street (Route 127). The shuttle bus to downtown costs $1. Rockport is 40 miles northeast of Boston, 7 miles north of Gloucester.

The **commuter rail** (ⓒ **617/222-3200;** www.mbta.com) runs from Boston's North Station. The trip takes 60 to 70 minutes; the round-trip fare is $10. The station is about 6 blocks from the downtown waterfront. The **Cape Ann Transportation Authority,** or CATA (ⓒ **978/283-7916**), runs buses from town to town on Cape Ann.

VISITOR INFORMATION The **Rockport Chamber of Commerce and Board of Trade,** 3 Main St. (© **978/546-6575;** www.rockportusa.com), is open in summer daily from 9am to 5pm, in winter Monday through Friday from 10am to 4pm. From mid-May to mid-October, the chamber operates an information booth on Upper Main Street (Route 127), about a mile from the town line and a mile from downtown—look for the WELCOME TO ROCKPORT sign. At either location, ask for the pamphlet *Rockport: A Walking Guide,* which has a good map and three short walking tours. Off-season, Rockport closes up almost as tight as an Essex clam; from January to mid-April, it's pretty but somewhat desolate.

GETTING AROUND For traffic and congestion, downtown Boston has nothing on Rockport on a summer weekend afternoon. If you can schedule only one weekday trip, make it this one. When you arrive, park and walk, especially downtown. The Cape Ann Transportation Authority (see above) runs within the town.

SPECIAL EVENTS The **Rockport Chamber Music Festival** (© **978/546-7391**) takes place over several weeks in June and early July at the Rockport Arts Association, 12 Main St. Events include performances, family concerts, lectures, and discussions. The annual **Christmas pageant,** held on Main Street in early December, is a crowded, kid-friendly event with carolers and live animals.

EXPLORING THE TOWN

The most famous sight in Rockport has something of an "Emperor's New Clothes" aura—it's a wooden fish warehouse on the town wharf, or T-Wharf, in the harbor. The barn-red shack known as **Motif No. 1** is the most frequently painted and photographed object in a town surrounded by rocky coastline and filled with lovely buildings. The color certainly catches the eye in the neutrals of the surrounding seascape, but you may find yourself wondering what the big deal is. Originally constructed in 1884 and destroyed during the blizzard of 1978, Motif No. 1 was rebuilt using donations from the local community and visitors. It stands again on the same pier, duplicated in every detail, reinforced to withstand storms.

Nearby is **Bearskin Neck,** named after an unfortunate ursine visitor who washed ashore in 1800. It holds perhaps the highest concentration of gift shops anywhere. The narrow peninsula has one main street (South Road) and several alleys crammed with galleries, snack bars, antiques shops, and ancient houses. Dozens of little stores carry clothes, gifts, toys, inexpensive novelties, and expensive handmade crafts and paintings. The peninsula ends in a plaza with a magnificent water view.

Throughout the town, more than two dozen **galleries** ✿ display the work of local and nationally known artists. The **Rockport Art Association,** 12 Main St. (© **978/546-6604**), open daily year-round, sponsors major exhibitions and special shows throughout the year.

The 1922 **Paper House,** 52 Pigeon Hill St., Pigeon Cove (© **978/546-2629**), is an unusual experience. Everything in it (walls, furniture, even a piano) was built entirely out of 100,000 newspapers. Every item is made from papers of a different period. It's open May through October, daily from 10am to 5pm. Admission is $1.50 for adults, $1 for children. Follow Route 127 north from downtown until you see signs at Curtis Street pointing to the left.

Don't fight the craving for fudge that overwhelms travelers when they get their first whiff of saltwater. Give in to temptation, then watch taffy being made at **Tuck's Candy Factory,** 7 Dock Sq. (© **800/569-2767** or 978/546-6352), a local landmark since the 1920s.

A TRIP TO THE EDGE OF THE SEA

The very tip of Cape Ann is accessible to the public, and worth the 2½-mile trip north on Route 127 to **Halibut Point State Park** ★★ (© **978/546-2997;** www.state.ma.us/dem/parks/halb.htm). The surf-battered point got its name not from the fish, but because sailing ships heading for Rockport and Gloucester must "haul about" when they reach the jutting promontory.

About 10 minutes from the parking area, you'll come to a huge water-filled quarry next to a visitor center, where staffers dispense information, brochures, and bird lists. Swimming in the water-filled quarry is absolutely forbidden. There are walking trails, tidal pools, a World War II observation tower that's open to visitors, and a rocky beach where you can climb around on giant boulders. Guided tours ($2.50) are available on Saturday mornings in summer, and there are also bird, wildflower, and tidal-pool tours; call the park for information and schedules. This is a great place to just wander around and admire the scenery. On a clear day, you can see Maine.

WHERE TO STAY

When Rockport is busy, it's *very* busy, and when it's not, it's practically empty. If you haven't made summer reservations well in advance, cross your fingers and call the Chamber of Commerce to ask about cancellations. For those not driving, most innkeepers will arrange for guests to be picked up at the train station; be sure to ask about this service when you reserve.

On Route 127 between Route 128 and downtown is the **Sandy Bay Motor Inn,** 173 Main St. (© **800/437-7155** or 978/546-7155; fax 978/546-9131; www.sandybaymotorinn.com). A modern building overlooking the road, it has an indoor pool and accepts pets with a $50 deposit. In summer, doubles start at $110.

In Town

Captain's Bounty Motor Inn   This modern, well-maintained motor inn is on the water. In fact, it's almost *in* the water, and nearly as close to the center of town as to the harbor. Each rather plain unit in the three-story building overlooks the water and has its own balcony. Rooms are spacious and soundproofed, with good cross-ventilation but no air-conditioning. The best units are on the adults-only top floor. Kitchenette units are available. Although it's hardly plush, and the pricing structure is a bit peculiar (note the charge for children), you can't beat the location.

1 Beach St., Rockport, MA 01966. © **978/546-9557.** www.cape-ann.com/capt-bounty. 24 units. May to mid-June $83 double, $87 efficiency, $95 efficiency suite; mid-June to early Sept $110 double, $130 efficiency, $145 efficiency suite; early Sept–Oct $90 double, $95 efficiency, $100 efficiency suite. Extra person $10; $5 for each child over 5. 2- to 3-night minimum stay on weekends and holidays. DISC, MC, V. Closed Nov–Apr. *In room:* TV.

Inn on Cove Hill ★   This three-story inn was built in 1791 using the proceeds of pirates' gold found nearby. It's an attractive Federal-style home just 2 blocks from the town wharf. Although it's close to downtown, the inn is set back from the road and has a hideaway feel. The guest rooms are decorated in period style, with at least one antique piece in each. Most units have colonial furnishings and handmade quilts, and some have canopy beds. In warm weather, breakfast (with home-baked breads and muffins) is served on china at the garden tables; in inclement weather, breakfast in bed arrives on individual trays.

37 Mt. Pleasant St., Rockport, MA 01966. ℂ **888/546-2701** or 978/546-2701. Fax 978/546-1095. www.cape-ann.com/covehill. 9 units, 7 with bathroom (some with shower only). $90–$135 double with private bathroom; $55 double with shared bathroom. Extra person $25. Rates include continental breakfast. 2-night minimum stay June–Oct weekends. AE, MC, V. *In room:* A/C, no phone.

Peg Leg Inn   The Peg Leg Inn consists of five Early American houses with front porches, attractive living rooms, and well-kept flower-bordered lawns that run down to the ocean's edge. (Guests can use the sandy beach across the road.) It's not luxurious, but is convenient and comfortable. Vacationing couples make up much of the clientele; rowdy families will probably be more comfortable at a more relaxed establishment (such as the Sandy Bay Motor Inn, above). Rooms are good-size and neatly furnished in colonial style. The best units open onto excellent ocean views. Breakfast is served in the main building's dining room.

2 King St., Rockport, MA 01966. ℂ **800/346-2352** or 978/546-2352. www.pegleginn.com. 29 units (some with shower only). Mid-June to Labor Day and holiday and fall weekends $90–$150 double; $160 two-bedroom. Extra person $15. Rates include continental breakfast. Off-season discounts available. 2- to 3-night minimum stay on summer and holiday weekends. AE, MC, V. Closed Nov–Mar. *In room:* TV, no phone.

On the Outskirts

Rockport's most luxurious hotel changed hands in 2001. You can expect to be pampered at the **Yankee Clipper Inn,** 96 Granite St. (Rte. 127), P.O. Box 2399, Rockport (ℂ **800/545-3699** or 978/546-3407; www.yankeeclipperinn.com). Doubles run $219 for an ocean-view room, $319 for a deluxe ocean-view room.

Emerson Inn by the Sea ★★   Somewhere in an old guest register, you might find Ralph Waldo Emerson's name—the philosopher stayed at the original (1840) inn. He wouldn't recognize it today: The oceanfront building expanded in 1912, and innkeepers Bruce and Michele Coates have transformed it into a miniresort. Still, the inn retains a relaxing old-fashioned feel, with modern conveniences like a heated outdoor saltwater pool. Traditional furnishings such as four-poster beds grace the rooms, which are nicely appointed but not terribly large. If you can manage the stairs, the view from the top-floor units is worth the exertion. The best units have private balconies, fireplaces, or hot tubs; the regular ocean-view rooms offer the same scenery. Public areas include a lounge with a wide-screen TV and a selection of videos. The dining room and the independently owned **Wisteria** (ℂ **978/546-0077**) day spa are open to the public.

1 Cathedral Ave., Rockport, MA 01966. ℂ **800/964-5550** or 978/546-6321. Fax 978/546-7043. www.emersoninnbythesea.com. 35 units (some with shower only). May–Oct $235–$295 "best" double, $175–$195 ocean-view double, $135–$165 double without view; Nov–Apr $175–$245 "best," $135–$165 with view, $95–$125 without view. Extra person $25; crib or cot $25. Spa packages available. Rates include breakfast from spring through fall, continental breakfast in winter. Weekly rates available. 2-night minimum stay on weekends mid-May to Oct. AE, DC, DISC, MC, V. Follow Rte. 127 north from the center of town for 2 miles; turn right at Phillips Ave. **Amenities:** Dining room; outdoor pool; whirlpool; sauna. *In room:* A/C.

WHERE TO DINE

Rockport is a "dry" community—no alcoholic beverages can be sold or served—but you can bring your own bottle, sometimes subject to a corking fee.

The birthplace of the fried clam, **Woodman's of Essex** (see "Essex," above), is about half an hour from Rockport.

Brackett's Oceanview Restaurant *Kids* SEAFOOD/AMERICAN   The dining room at Brackett's has a gorgeous view of the water. The nautical decor suits the seafood-intensive menu, which offers enough variety to make this a good choice for families—burgers are always available. The service is friendly and the fresh seafood quite good, if not particularly adventurous. Try the moist, plump codfish cakes if you're looking for a traditional New England dish, or something with Cajun spices for variety. The most exciting offerings are on the extensive dessert menu, where anything homemade is a great choice.

29 Main St. ✆ 978/546-2797. www.bracketts.com. Reservations recommended at dinner. Main courses $6–$20 lunch, $9–$26 dinner. AE, DC, DISC, MC, V. Mid-Apr to Memorial Day Thurs–Sun 11:30am–8pm; Memorial Day to Oct Sun–Fri 11:30am–8pm, Sat 11:30am–9pm. Closed Nov to mid-Apr.

The Greenery ✦ SEAFOOD/AMERICAN   The Greenery could get away with serving so-so food because of its great location at the head of Bearskin Neck—but it doesn't. The cafe at the front serves light fare to stay or go; the dining rooms, at the back, boast great views of the harbor. The food ranges from tasty crab salad quiche at lunch to lobster at dinner to steamers and fresh-caught fish anytime. As in any town with working fisherman, check out the daily specials. All baking is done in-house, which explains the lines at the front counter for muffins and pastries. When the restaurant is busy, the cheerful service tends to drag. This is a good place to launch a picnic lunch on the beach, and an equally good spot for lingering over coffee and dessert while watching the action around the harbor.

15 Dock Sq. ✆ 978/546-9593. Reservations recommended at dinner. Main courses $6.25–$12 lunch, $9.25–$22 dinner; breakfast items $1.50–$7. AE, DC, DISC, MC, V. Apr–Dec Mon–Fri 11am–11pm, Sat–Sun 7am–11pm. Closed Jan–Mar.

My Place By-the-Sea SEAFOOD   The lure of My Place By-the-Sea is its location at the very end of Bearskin Neck, where its touristy clientele finds Rockport's only outdoor oceanfront deck. The two decks and shaded patio afford excellent views of Sandy Bay. The menu is reliable, with many options dictated by the daily catch. The baked fish and seafood pasta entrees are good choices.

68 South Rd., Bearskin Neck. ✆ 978/546-9667. Reservations recommended at dinner; accepted same day after noon. Main courses $7–$13 lunch, $15–$22 dinner. AE, DC, DISC, MC, V. Apr–Nov daily 11:30am–9:30pm. Closed Dec–Mar.

Portside Chowder House CHOWDER/SEAFOOD   The crowds at this busy restaurant are here for chowder—clam and whatever else looked good that day. It comes by the cup, pint, and quart, to go or to eat in. You can also get seafood platters and surprisingly good burgers and lobster rolls, but the real reason to come here (even the locals do) is for tasty chowder to carry to the edge of the sea for a picnic.

Tuna Wharf, off Bearskin Neck. ✆ 978/546-7045. Reservations not accepted. Most menu items less than $8. No credit cards. Late June to Labor Day daily 11am–8pm; Labor Day to late June daily 11am–3pm. Closed Thanksgiving, Christmas.

6 Newburyport, Ipswich & Plum Island

The area between Cape Ann and the New Hampshire border is magnificent, with outdoor sights and sounds that can only be described as natural wonders, and enough impressive architecture to keep any city slicker happy.

In a part of the world where the word "charming" is used almost as often as "hello," **Newburyport** is a singular example of a picturesque waterfront city. Downtown Newburyport is on the Merrimack River. On the town's Atlantic coast, **Plum Island** contains one of the country's top nature preserves. On the other side of Ipswich Bay, **Ipswich** is a lovely town that's home to **Crane Beach,** on another wildlife reservation.

NEWBURYPORT ★★

To get here directly from Boston, take I-93 (or Route 1 if it's not rush hour) to I-95—*not* Route 128, as for most other destinations in this chapter—and follow it to Exit 57, a solid 45-minute ride. Signs point to downtown, where you can park and explore. The **commuter rail** (© 617/222-3200; www.mbta.com) from North Station takes about 75 minutes and costs $10 round-trip.

Newburyport has a substantial year-round population that lends it a less touristy atmosphere than its appearance might suggest. Start your visit at the **Greater Newburyport Chamber of Commerce and Industry,** 29 State St. (© 978/462-6680; www.newburyportchamber.org), in the heart of the red-brick downtown shopping district. It also runs a seasonal information booth on Merrimac Street near Green Street.

Market Square, at the foot of State Street near the waterfront, is the center of a neighborhood packed with boutiques, gift shops, plain and fancy restaurants, and antiques stores. You can also wander to the water, take a stroll on the boardwalk, and enjoy the action on the river. Architecture buffs will want to climb the hill to High Street, where the **Charles Bulfinch**–designed building (1805) that houses the Superior Court is only one of several Federal-era treasures. Ask at the Chamber of Commerce for the walking-tour map.

If you haven't gone out to sea yet, now is a good time, and here's a good place: **Newburyport Whale Watch** ★★, Hilton's Dock, 54 Merrimac St. (© 800/848-1111 or 978/499-0832; www.newburyportwhalewatch.com), offers 4½-hour cruises on a 100-foot boat with on-board marine biologists as guides. Tickets are $27 for adults, $22 for seniors, and $18 for children 4 to 16; reservations are suggested. (See "A Whale of an Adventure," above, for more information.)

Or, head to the ocean using an inland route. From downtown, take Water Street south until it becomes Plum Island Turnpike and follow it to the Parker River National Wildlife Refuge.

PARKER RIVER NATIONAL WILDLIFE REFUGE ★★

The 4,662-acre refuge (© 978/465-5753; northeast.fws.gov/ma/pkr.htm) on **Plum Island** is a complex of barrier beaches, dunes, and salt marshes, one of the few remaining in the Northeast. The refuge is flat-out breathtaking, whether you're exploring the marshes or the seashore. More than 800 species of plants and animals (including more than 300 bird species) visit or make their home on the narrow finger of land between Broad Sound and the Atlantic Ocean.

The refuge offers some of the best **birding** ★★★ anywhere, as well as observation of mammals and plants. Wooden boardwalks with observation towers and platforms wind through marshes and along the shore—most lack handrails, so this isn't an activity for rambunctious children. You might see native and migratory species such as owls, hawks, martins, geese, warblers, ducks, snowy egrets, swallows, monarch butterflies, Canada geese, foxes, beavers, and harbor seals.

The ocean beach closes April 1 to allow piping plovers, listed by the federal government as a threatened species, to nest. The areas not being used for nesting will reopen July 1; the rest open in August, when the birds are through. The currents are strong and can be dangerous, and there are no lifeguards—swimming is allowed but not encouraged. Surf fishing is popular, though; striped bass and bluefish are found in the area. A permit is required for night fishing and vehicle access to the beach.

The refuge is open from dawn to dusk year-round. There's a daily entrance fee of $5 for motorists, $2 for bikers and pedestrians. The seven parking lots fill quickly on weekends when the weather is good, so plan to arrive early. South of lot 4 (Hellcat Swamp), the access road isn't paved; although it's flat and well maintained and the speed limit is low, this isn't the place for your brand-new sports car.

IPSWICH

Across Ipswich Bay from Plum Island is the town of Ipswich. It's accessible from Route 1A (which you can pick up in Newburyport or at Route 128 in Hamilton) and from Route 133 (which intersects with Route 128 in Gloucester and I-95 in Georgetown). The **visitor center,** in the Hall Haskell House on South Main Street (Route 133), is open daily in summer. Visitor information is also available from the **Ipswich Community Chamber of Commerce,** 46 Newmarch St. (© **978/356-3231**), and the business association's website (**www.ipswichma.com**).

Settled in 1630, Ipswich is dotted with **17th-century houses**—reputedly the largest concentration in the United States. Many are private homes; ask at the visitor center for a map of a tour that passes three dozen of them. House-tour aficionados can go inside the **John Whipple House,** 1 South Village Green (© **978/356-2811**). Built between 1655 and 1700, it's decorated with period furnishings and decorative objects. May through October, tours ($7) start on the hour from 10am to 3pm Wednesday through Saturday, noon to 3pm on Sunday.

Ipswich is also known for two more contemporary structures. The **Clam Box,** 206 High St., Route 1A/133 (© **978/356-9707**), is a restaurant shaped like—what else?—a red-and-white-striped take-out clam box. This is a great place to try Ipswich clams, and not an easy place to sneak past if you have children in the car. Heading south from Newburyport, it's on the right.

South of Ipswich Center, near the intersection of Routes 1A and 133, look carefully for the Argilla Road sign (on the east side of the street). If you're traveling west on Route 133 from Gloucester and Essex, watch for a sign on the right pointing to Northgate Road, which intersects with Argilla Road. Follow it east to the end, where you'll find the 1,400-acre Crane Estate.

The property is home to **Crane Beach** (see "Life's a Beach," on p. 160), the **Crane Wildlife Refuge**, a network of hiking trails, and **Castle Hill,** 290 Argilla Rd. (© **978/356-4351;** www.thetrustees.org). One of the Boston area's most popular wedding locations, the exquisite Stuart-style seaside mansion known as the Great House was built by Richard Teller Crane, Jr., who made his fortune in plumbing and bathroom fixtures early in the 20th century. If you can't wangle an invitation to a wedding, tours of the house ($7 for adults, $5 for seniors and children) are given on Wednesday and Thursday in summer and two Sundays a year, spring and fall. They're also offered with afternoon tea on the last Thursday of the month May through October. Call for reservations.

Children who can't get excited about a tour might be pacified by a stop just before Castle Hill. **Russell Orchards Store and Winery**, 143 Argilla Rd. (© **978/356-5366;** www.russellorchardsMA.com), is open daily May through November. It has a picnic area, farm animals, and an excellent country store. Depending on the season, you might go on a hayride or taste fruit wines. Be sure to try some cider and doughnuts.

More Whale Tales: A Trip to New Bedford

The masses that flock to eastern Massachusetts aren't yet swarming the cobblestone streets of New Bedford, which makes it a good destination for families on the verge of crowd-phobia. The **New Bedford Whaling National Historical Park,** which encompasses the downtown historic district, commemorates the city's past as the world's leading whaling port.

The downtown area near the waterfront has been restored, and the attractions are reasonably close together. Start your visit at the **National Park Service Visitor Center,** 33 William St. (© **508/996-4095;** www.nps. gov/nebe), open daily from 9am to 4pm. The exhibits will gain a new film about whaling and the city in mid-2002. Take a guided walking tour (daily in summer, some off-season weekends) or pick up a brochure that describes self-guided excursions around the historic district.

The centerpiece of the Historical Park is the **New Bedford Whaling Museum** ⭐, 18 Johnny Cake Hill (© **508/997-0046;** www. whalingmuseum.org). It's the world's premier whaling museum, which sounds terribly specialized but is actually quite absorbing. The newest display is the skeleton of a 65-foot juvenile blue whale, Kobo (short for "king of the blue ocean"), in the newly expanded lobby. Admission to the lobby is free, but the rest of the museum is worth a visit. Children love the half-scale model of the whaling bark *Lagoda,* the world's largest ship model. The museum is open daily from 9am to 5pm, until 9pm on the second Thursday of each month. Admission is $6 for adults, $5 for seniors and students, and $4 for children 6 to 14.

The **Seamen's Bethel,** 15 Johnny Cake Hill (© **508-992-3295**), a nondenominational chapel described in Herman Melville's classic novel *Moby-Dick,* is across the street. Up the hill from the water, the **Rotch-Duff-Jones House & Garden Museum,** 396 County St. (© **508/997-1401**), is an 1834 Greek Revival mansion with magnificent formal gardens.

By car, take the Southeast Expressway south to I-93 (Route 128), then Route 24 south. Follow signs to Route 140 south to I-195. From Plymouth, take Route 44 west to Route 24 south. **American Eagle** (© **800/453-5040** or 508/993-5040) runs buses from Boston's South Station; the 75-minute trip costs $10 one-way, $18 round-trip. For more information, contact the **Bristol County Convention & Visitors Bureau,** 70 N. Second St., New Bedford (© **800/288-6263** or 508/997-1250; www.bristol-county.org). It distributes a vacation guide with a section on outlet shopping.

7 Plymouth

Everyone educated in the United States knows at least a little about Plymouth—about how the Pilgrims, fleeing religious persecution, left England on the *Mayflower* and landed at **Plymouth Rock** in 1620. Many also know that the Pilgrims endured disease and privation, and that just 51 people from the original group of 102 celebrated the first Thanksgiving in 1621 with Squanto, a Pawtuxet Indian associated with the Wampanoags, and his cohorts.

What you won't know until you visit is how small everything was. The *Mayflower* (a replica) seems perilously tiny, and when you contemplate how dangerous life was at the time, it's hard not to be impressed by the settlers' accomplishments. The *Mayflower* passengers weren't even aiming for Plymouth—and at first, they didn't wind up here. They originally set out for what they called "Northern Virginia," near the mouth of the Hudson River. On November 11, 1620, rough weather and high seas forced them to make for Cape Cod Bay and anchor at Provincetown. The captain then announced that they had found a safe harbor, and refused to continue to their original destination. On December 16, Provincetown having proven an unsatisfactory location, the weary travelers landed at Plymouth.

Today, Plymouth is in many ways a model destination, where the 17th-century coexists with the 21st, and most historic attractions are both educational and fun. Tourists jam the downtown area in summer, but the year-round population is so large that Plymouth feels more like the working community it is than like a warm-weather day-trip destination. It's a manageable 1-day excursion from Boston, particularly enjoyable if you're traveling with children. It also makes a good stop between Boston and Cape Cod.

ESSENTIALS

GETTING THERE By car, follow the Southeast Expressway (I-93) from Boston to Route 3. From Cape Cod, take Route 3 north. Take Exit 6A to Route 44 east, and follow signs to the historic attractions. The 40-mile trip from Boston takes 45 to 55 minutes if it's not rush hour. Take Exit 5 to the **Regional Information Complex** for maps, brochures, and information. Take Exit 4 to go directly to **Plimoth Plantation.**

The **commuter rail** (© 617/222-3200; www.mbta.com) serves Cordage Park, on Route 3A north of downtown, from South Station. The round-trip fare is $10. The **Plymouth Area Link** bus (75¢) runs between the train station and downtown.

Plymouth & Brockton buses (© 617/773-9401 or 508/746-0378; www.p-b.com) are more frequent and more expensive: $9 one-way, $17 round-trip. The ride takes about an hour from South Station.

VISITOR INFORMATION If you haven't visited the Regional Information Complex (see "Getting There," above"), you'll want to stop in and at least pick up a map at the **visitor center** (© 508/747-7525), open seasonally at 130 Water St., across from the town pier. To plan ahead, contact **Destination Plymouth** (also known as Plymouth Visitor Information), 510 Water St., Suite 10C, Plymouth (© 800/USA-1620 or 508/747-7525; www.visit-plymouth.com).

GETTING AROUND The downtown attractions are accessible on foot. A shallow hill slopes from the center of town to the waterfront. **Plymouth Rock Trolley Company** (© 800/286-2241 or 508/747-2240) offers a 40-minute narrated tour and unlimited reboarding daily Memorial Day through October and weekends through Thanksgiving. It serves marked stops downtown (every 20 minutes) and Plimoth Plantation (once an hour in summer). Tickets are $7 for adults, $3 for children 3 to 12.

EXPLORING THE HISTORIC SITES

No matter how often you suffered through elementary-school pageants wearing a big black hat and paper buckles on your shoes, you can still learn something

Plymouth

Nelson St. Recreation Area

Town Wharf

State Pier

Plymouth Harbor

Cape Ann

Salem

Lexington

Marblehead

Concord

Boston

Plymouth

(i) Information

ACCOMODATIONS ■
Cold Spring Motel **2**
Governor Bradford
  on the Harbour **8**
John Carver Inn **14**
Pilgrim Sands Motel **22**
Sheraton Inn Plymouth **4**

DINING ◆
Lobster Hut **6**
Run of the Mill Tavern **19**

ATTRACTIONS ●
Harlow Old Fort House **20**
Hedge House **3**
Jabez Howland House **15**
Jenney Grist Mill **18**
Mayflower II **9**
Mayflower Society
  Museum **11**
National Monument
  to the Forefathers **1**

Ocean Spray Cranberry
  World **5**
Pilgrim Hall Museum **7**
Plimoth Plantation **21**
Plymouth National
  Wax Museum **13**
Plymouth Rock **12**
Sparrow House **16**
Spooner House **10**
Town Brook Park **17**

about Plymouth and the Pilgrims. The logical place to begin is where the Pilgrims first set foot—at **Plymouth Rock** ⚑⚑. The rock, accepted as the landing place of the *Mayflower* passengers, was originally 15 feet long and 3 feet wide. It was moved on the eve of the Revolution, when it broke in two, and several times thereafter. In 1867, it assumed its present position at tide level. The Colonial Dames of America commissioned the portico around the rock, designed by McKim, Mead & White and erected in 1920. The rock itself isn't much to look at, but the accompanying descriptions are interesting, and the atmosphere curiously inspiring.

To get away from the bustle of the waterfront, make your way to **Town Brook Park,** at Jenney Pond, across Summer Street from the John Carver Inn. Near the tree-bordered pond is the **Jenney Grist Mill,** 6 Spring Lane (✆ **508/747-3715**). It's a working museum where you can see a reconstructed water-powered mill that operates in summer, daily from 10am to 5pm. Admission is $2.50 for adults, $2 for children 5 to 12. The specialty shops in the complex, including the ice-cream shop, are open year-round, daily from 10am to 6pm. Ducks and geese live in the pond, and there's room to run around.

Also removed from the waterfront is the **National Monument to the Forefathers** (✆ 508/746-1790), a granite behemoth inscribed with the names of the *Mayflower* passengers. Heading away from the harbor on Route 44, look carefully on the right for the turn onto Allerton Street, and climb the hill. The 81-foot-high monument is elaborately decorated with figures representing moral and political virtues and scenes of Pilgrim history—a style of public statuary so unfashionable that it seems quite rebellious. The monument is incongruous in its little park in a residential neighborhood, but it's also quite impressive. The view from the hilltop is excellent.

Mayflower II ⚑ *(Kids)* Berthed a few steps from Plymouth Rock, *Mayflower II* is a full-scale reproduction of the type of ship that brought the Pilgrims from England to America in 1620. Even at full scale, the 106½-foot vessel seems remarkably small. Although little technical information about the original *Mayflower* survives, William A. Baker, designer of *Mayflower II,* incorporated the few references in Governor Bradford's account of the voyage with other research to re-create the ship as authentically as possible. Costumed guides provide interesting first-person narratives about the vessel and voyage, while other interpreters provide a contemporary perspective. Displays describe and illustrate the journey and the Pilgrims' experience, including 17th-century navigation techniques.

State Pier. ✆ **508/746-1622**. www.plimoth.org. Admission $8 adults, $6 children 6–12. *Mayflower II* and Plimoth Plantation admission $22 adults, $20 seniors, $14 children 6–12. Apr–Nov daily 9am–5pm.

Pilgrim Hall Museum ⚑ This is a great place to get a sense of the day-to-day lives of Plymouth's first European residents. Many original possessions of the early Pilgrims and their descendants are on display, including one of Myles Standish's swords, Governor Bradford's Bible, and an uncomfortable chair (you can sit in a replica) that belonged to William Brewster. Regularly changing exhibits explore aspects of the settlers' lives, such as home construction or the history of prominent families. Through May 2002, *Patriots and Pilgrims* will focus on Plymouth's role in the Revolution. Among the permanent exhibits is the skeleton of the *Sparrow-Hawk,* a ship wrecked on Cape Cod in 1626 that lay buried in the sand until 1863.

75 Court St. ℂ **508/746-1620.** www.pilgrimhall.org. Admission $5 adults, $4.50 seniors and AAA members, $3 children 5–17. Feb–Dec daily 9:30am–4:30pm. Closed Christmas. From Plymouth Rock, walk north on Water St. and up the hill on Chilton St.

Plimoth Plantation ★★ *Kids*   Allow at least half a day to explore this re-creation of the 1627 Pilgrim village, which children and adults find equally interesting. Enter by the hilltop fort that protects the "villagers" and walk down the hill to the farm area, visiting homes and gardens constructed with careful attention to historic detail. Once you get over the feeling that the whole opera-tion is a bit strange (we heard someone mention Pompeii), talking to the "Pil-grims" is great fun. They're actors who, in speech, dress, and manner, assume the personalities of members of the original community. You can watch them fram-ing a house, splitting wood, shearing sheep, preserving foodstuffs, or cooking a pot of fish stew over an open hearth, all as it was done in the 1600s, and using only the tools and cookware available then. Wear comfortable shoes—you'll be walking a lot, and the plantation isn't paved.

The plantation is as accurate as research can make it. Accounts of the original colony were combined with archaeological research, old records, and the history written by the Pilgrims' leader, William Bradford (who often used the spelling "Plimoth"). There are daily militia drills with matchlock muskets that are fired to demonstrate the community's defense system. In fact, little defense was needed, because the Native Americans were friendly. Local tribes included the Wampanoags, who are represented near the village at **Hobbamock's Homesite** (included in plantation admission). Museum staffers show off native foodstuffs, agricultural practices, and crafts.

At the main entrance are two modern buildings with an interesting orienta-tion show, exhibits, a gift shop, a bookstore, and a cafeteria. There's also a pic-nic area. Call for information on the numerous special events, lectures, tours, workshops, theme dinners, and children's and family programs offered through-out the season.

Rte. 3. ℂ **508/746-1622.** www.plimoth.org. Admission $20 adults, $12 children 6–12. Plimoth Plantation and *Mayflower II* admission $22 adults, $20 seniors, $14 children 6–12. Apr–Nov daily 9am–5pm. From Rte. 3, take Exit 4, Plimoth Plantation Hwy.

Plymouth National Wax Museum ★★ *Kids*   Adults who visited this enter-taining museum as children can still tell you all about the Pilgrims. The galleries hold more than 180 life-size figures arranged in scenes. Dramatic soundtracks tell the story of the move to Holland to escape persecution in England, the harrow-ing trip across the ocean, the first Thanksgiving, and even the tale of Myles Stan-dish, Priscilla Mullins, and John Alden. This museum is a must if children are in your party, and adults will enjoy it, too. On the hill outside is a monument at the gravesite of the Pilgrims who died during the settlement's first winter.

16 Carver St. ℂ **508/746-6468.** Admission $6 adults, $5.50 seniors, $2.75 children 5–12. Daily Mar–May 9am–5pm; June 9am–7pm; July–Aug 9am–9pm; Sept–Oct 9am–7pm; Nov 9am–5pm. Closed Dec–Feb. From Plymouth Rock, turn around and walk up the hill or the steps.

Ocean Spray Cranberry World   Cranberries aren't just for Thanksgiving dinner, as this interesting center will remind you. Displays include outdoor demonstration bogs, antique harvesting tools, a scale model of a cranberry farm, and interactive exhibits. There are daily cooking demonstrations and free cran-berry refreshments. September and October are harvest time.

158 Water St. ℂ **508/747-2350.** Free admission. May–Nov daily 9:30am–5pm. Guided tours available; call for reservations. From Plymouth Rock, walk north along the waterfront.

ORGANIZED TOURS & CRUISES

To follow in the Pilgrims' footsteps, take a **Colonial Lantern Tour** 🐾🐾
(© **800/698-5636** or 508/747-4161; www.lanterntours.com). Participants
carry pierced-tin lanterns on a 90-minute walking tour of the original settlement
under the direction of a knowledgeable guide. It might seem a bit hokey at first,
but it's fascinating. Tours run nightly April through Thanksgiving. Tickets are
$10 for adults and $8 for children; check the meeting place when you call for
reservations.

Narrated cruises run April or May through November. **Splashdown
Amphibious Tours** 🐾 (© 508/747-7658; www.ducktoursplymouth.com) take
you around town on land and water. The kid-friendly 1-hour excursions (half
on land, half on water) leave from two stops on Water Street—Harbor Place,
near the Governor Bradford motor inn, and Village Landing, near the
Sheraton—and wind up in the harbor. They cost $16 for adults, $10 for children 3 to 12, and $3 for children under 3. **Capt. John Boats,** Town Wharf
(© **800/242-2469** or 508/746-2643; www.captjohn.com), offers several tours.
The most eye-catching option is the *Pilgrim Belle* paddle-wheeler. Its 75-minute
narrated tours of the harbor ($9 for adults, $7 for seniors, $6 for children) leave
from State Pier; dining and entertainment cruises are also available.

THE HISTORIC HOUSES

You can't stay in Plymouth's historic houses, but they're worth a visit to see the
changing styles of architecture and furnishings since the 1600s. Costumed
guides explain the homemaking and crafts of earlier generations. Most of the
houses are open Memorial Day through Columbus Day, during Thanksgiving
celebrations, and around Christmas; call for schedules.

Tip: Unless you have a sky-high tolerance for house tours, pick just one or
two from eras that you find particularly interesting. This advice applies especially if you're sightseeing with children.

Six homes are open to visitors. The 1640 **Sparrow House,** 42 Summer St.
(© **508/747-1240;** admission $1), and the 1666 **Jabez Howland House,** 33
Sandwich St. (© **508/746-9590;** $4 adults, $2 children), are most engaging for
those curious about the original settlers. The other houses are the 1677 **Harlow
Old Fort House,** 119 Sandwich St. (© **508/746-0012;** $4 adults, $2 children);
the 1749 **Spooner House,** 27 North St. (© **508/746-0012;** $4 adults, $2 children); the 1754 **Mayflower Society Museum,** 4 Winslow St. (© **508/
746-2590;** $2.50 adults, 75¢ children); and the 1809 **Hedge House,** 126 Water
St. (© **508/746-0012;** $4 adults, $2 children).

A LEGENDARY ATTRACTION NEARBY

The **Edaville Railroad** 🐾🐾 (© **877/EDAVILLE** or 508/866-8190;
www.edaville.org) reopened in 1999 after being shuttered for 7 years. The
narrow-gauge railroad, originally opened in 1947, is a great favorite with young
New Englanders. The main attraction is the entertaining 45-minute train ride
on a 5½-mile loop of tracks that takes you past the bogs of a working cranberry
plantation. Also on the premises are kiddie rides, a carousel, a railroad museum,
and a cafe. This is a retro experience—no high-tech multimedia stuff, just good
clean fun.

The railroad is extremely crowded when the weather is good; we strongly suggest arriving when it opens. Edaville currently operates Memorial Day weekend
through Labor Day weekend plus Columbus Day weekend, Friday through

Monday from 10am to 5pm. During the Christmas Light Festival from early November to early January, hours are Monday through Friday from 4 to 9pm, Saturday and Sunday from 2 to 9pm. Admission is $12.50 for adults, $10.50 for seniors, and $7.50 for children 3 to 12. The railroad is in South Carver. From Plymouth, follow Route 44 west to Route 58 south, continue about 3 miles to Rochester Road, and turn right.

WHERE TO STAY

Just about every establishment in town participates in a Destination Plymouth program that piles on the deals and discounts. Especially in the off-season, this can represent great savings. Check Destination Plymouth's website (www. visit-plymouth.com), or ask the reservations staff at the individual lodgings.

On busy summer weekends, it's not unusual for every room in town to be taken. Make reservations well in advance.

Cold Spring Motel ★ *Value*   Convenient to downtown and the historic sights, this pleasant, fastidiously maintained motel and the adjacent cottages surround a landscaped lawn. A $2-million project completed in 2001 updated the existing accommodations and added 30 units. Rooms are pleasantly decorated and big enough for a family to spread out; if the adults want privacy, book a two-bedroom cottage. The location, a bit removed from the water, makes the Cold Spring a good deal. The two-story building is 2 blocks inland, set back from the street in a quiet part of town.

188 Court St. (Rte. 3A), Plymouth, MA 02360. © **800/678-8667** or 508/746-2222. Fax 508/746-2744. www.coldspringmotel.com. 62 units (some with shower only). $69–$119 double; $109–$169 suite; $99–$119 cottage. Extra person $10. Off-season discounts available. Mid-May to Oct rates include continental breakfast. AE, DISC, MC, V. Closed Dec–Mar. *In room:* A/C, TV, dataport, fridge, coffeemaker, hair dryer.

Governor Bradford on the Harbour   This well-maintained three-story motor inn occupies a great location across the street from the waterfront and only a block from Plymouth Rock, the *Mayflower II,* and the center of town. Each attractively decorated room contains modern furnishings; all were redone in 2000. The more expensive units on the top floor offer excellent water views—if that's what you care about, they're definitely worth the money.

98 Water St., Plymouth, MA 02360. © **800/332-1620** or 508/746-6200. Fax 508/747-3032. www. governorbradford.com. 94 units (some with shower only). $108–$159 double. Extra person $10. Children under 16 stay free in parents' room. Off-season and AAA discounts available. AE, DC, DISC, MC, V. **Amenities:** Small heated outdoor pool; coin-op laundry. *In room:* A/C, TV, dataport, fridge.

John Carver Inn ★ *Kids*   A three-story colonial-style building with a landmark portico, this hotel offers comfortable, modern accommodations and plenty of amenities, including two swimming pools. The new indoor "theme pool," a big hit with families, has a large water slide and Pilgrim ship model. Business features make this the Sheraton's main competition for corporate travelers. The good-size guest rooms are regularly renovated and decorated in colonial style. The best units are the lavishly appointed two-room suites, with two TVs and private Jacuzzis.

25 Summer St., Plymouth, MA 02360. © **800/274-1620** or 508/746-7100. Fax 508/746-8299. www.johncarverinn.com. 85 units. Mid-Apr to mid-June and mid-Oct to Nov $99–$149 double, $209 suite; mid-June to mid-Oct $129–$179 double, $239 suite; Dec to mid-Apr $89–$129 double, $189 suite. Extra person $15; rollaway $15. Children under 19 stay free in parents' room. Packages, senior discounts, and AAA discounts available. AE, DC, DISC, MC, V. **Amenities:** Restaurant (American/seafood); outdoor pool; indoor pool; room service; laundry service; dry cleaning. *In room:* A/C, TV, dataport.

Pilgrim Sands Motel ★★ *(Kids)*   This attractive motel is on its own private beach 3 miles south of town, within walking distance of Plimoth Plantation. If you want to avoid the bustle of downtown and still be near the water, it's an excellent choice. The good-size rooms are tastefully furnished and well maintained. If you can swing it, book a beachfront unit—the view is worth the money, especially when the surf is rough.

150 Warren Ave. (Rte. 3A), Plymouth, MA 02360. ℂ 800/729-SANDS or 508/747-0900. Fax 508/746-8066. www.pilgrimsands.com. 64 units. Summer $115–$155 double, spring and early fall $94–$125, Apr and late fall $77–$97, Dec–Mar $70–$85; $130–$250 suite year-round. Extra person $6–$8 ($10–$15 in suite). 2-night minimum stay on holiday weekends. Rates may be higher on holiday weekends. AE, DC, DISC, MC, V. **Amenities:** Coffee shop; indoor pool; outdoor pool; Jacuzzi. *In room:* A/C, TV, dataport, fridge, hair dryer.

Sheraton Inn Plymouth   If you need the amenities of a chain and want to be near the historic sights, this is your only choice. Happily, it's a good one. The four-story hotel sits on a hill across the street from the waterfront. Vacationers enjoy the central location, and the facilities for business travelers are the most extensive in town. Rooms are tastefully furnished in contemporary style; some have small balconies that overlook the indoor pool. The best units, facing the harbor on the top two floors, afford excellent views.

180 Water St., Plymouth, MA 02360. ℂ 800/325-3535 or 508/747-4900. Fax 508/746-2609. www.sheraton plymouth.com. 175 units. Apr–Oct $145–$190 double; Nov–Mar $115–$135. Extra person $15. Children under 18 stay free in parents' room. AE, DC, DISC, MC, V. **Amenities:** Restaurant (American), pub; indoor pool; exercise room; whirlpool; sauna; laundry service; dry cleaning. *In room:* A/C, TV, dataport, coffeemaker, hair dryer.

WHERE TO DINE

Lobster Hut ✦ SEAFOOD   The Lobster Hut is a busy self-service restaurant with a great view. It's popular with both locals and sightseers. Order and pick up at the counter, then head to an indoor table or out onto the large deck that overlooks the bay. To start, try clam chowder or lobster bisque. The seafood "rolls" (hot-dog buns with your choice of filling) are excellent. The many fried-seafood options include clams, scallops, shrimp, and haddock. There are also boiled and steamed items, burgers, chicken tenders—and lobster, of course. Beer and wine are served, but only with meals.

25 Town Wharf. ℂ 508/746-2270. Reservations not accepted. Luncheon specials $5–$8; main courses $6–$14; sandwiches $3–$7; lobster priced daily. MC, V. Summer daily 11am–9pm; winter daily 11am–7pm. Closed Jan.

Run of the Mill Tavern ✦ AMERICAN   This friendly restaurant sits 3 blocks inland, across from Town Brook Park. You won't mind not having a water view—the food is not only tasty but also reasonably priced, and the comfortable wood-paneled tavern is a popular hangout. The unconventional clam chowder, made with red potatoes, is fantastic. Other appetizers include nachos, potato skins, and mushrooms. Entrees are well-prepared versions of familiar meat, chicken, and fish dishes, plus sandwiches, burgers, and fresh seafood specials (fried, broiled, or baked).

Jenney Grist Mill Village, off Summer St. ℂ 508/830-1262. Reservations not accepted. Main courses $6–$12; children's menu $3–$3.50. AE, DC, DISC, MC, V. Sun–Thurs 11:30am–10pm; Fri–Sat 11:30am–11pm. Bar closes at 1am.

Cape Cod

by Laura M. Reckford

Only 75 miles long, Cape Cod is a curling peninsula encompassing miles of beaches, hundreds of freshwater ponds, more than a dozen richly historic New England villages, scores of classic clam shacks and ice-cream shops—and it's just about everyone's idea of the perfect summer vacation spot.

More than 13 million visitors flock to the Cape from around the world to enjoy summertime's nonstop carnival. In full swing, the Cape is, if anything, perhaps a bit too popular for some tastes. Connoisseurs are discovering the subtler appeal of off-season, when prices plummet along with the population. For some select travelers, the prospect of sunbathing en masse on sizzling sand can't hold a candle to a long, solitary stroll on a windswept beach with only the gulls as company. Come Labor Day, the crowds clear out—even the stragglers are gone by Columbus Day—and the whole place hibernates until Memorial Day weekend, the official start of "the season."

We've listed mostly summer rates for the accommodations in this chapter, since that's when the vast majority of travelers plan their trips, but if you decide to explore the Cape off-season, you'll get the added benefit of lower rates everywhere you go.

The **Cape Cod Chamber of Commerce,** Routes 6 and 132, Hyannis (© **888/332-2732** or 508/862-0700; fax 508/362-2156; www.capecodchamber.org), is a clearinghouse of information. Stop in at the **Cape Cod Chamber of Commerce Information Center,** at the Sagamore Bridge rotary (open seasonally), or the chamber's **Route 25 Visitors Center,** open year-round daily (© **508/759-3814**).

1 The Upper Cape

Because the Upper Cape towns are so close to Boston by car (just over an hour), they've become bedroom as well as summer communities. They are perhaps a bit more staid than those towns further east, but they are also spared some of the fly-by-night qualities that come with a transient populace. Shops and restaurants—many catering to an older, affluent crowd—tend to stay open year-round.

SANDWICH ✦✦

Sandwich is both the oldest town in this part of the Cape and the most quaint. Towering oak trees, 19th-century churches, and historic houses line its Main Street. A 1640 gristmill still grinds corn beside bucolic Shawme Pond. There is still an element of peacefulness in this little town just a few miles from the Sagamore Bridge.

Sandwich is a popular choice for families, who can take advantage of several nearby activities (Heritage Plantation, Thornton Burgess Homestead, and Green

Cape Cod

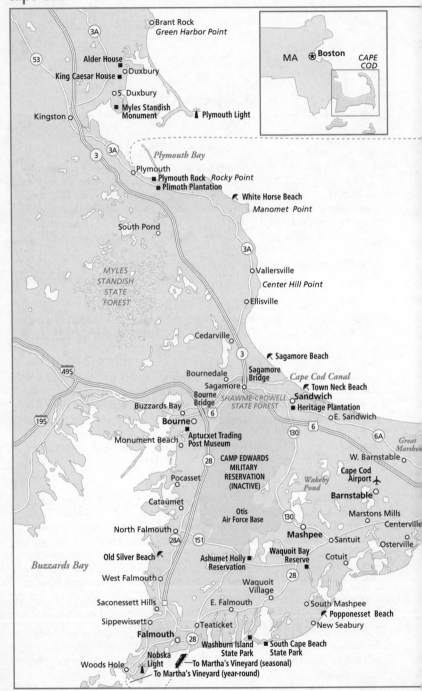

Brant Rock
Green Harbor Point

53

3A

Alder House
King Caesar House
Duxbury
S. Duxbury
Myles Standish
Monument

Kingston

Plymouth Light

MA ⊛ Boston
CAPE COD

3

3A

Plymouth Bay

Plymouth
Plymouth Rock *Rocky Point*
Plimoth Plantation

White Horse Beach
Manomet Point

South Pond

3A

Vallersville
Center Hill Point

Ellisville

MYLES STANDISH STATE FOREST

Cedarville

3

Sagamore Beach

495

Bournedale
Sagamore
Bridge
Sagamore
Cape Cod Canal

Town Neck Beach
Sandwich
Heritage Plantation
E. Sandwich

Buzzards Bay
Bourne
Bridge
6
SHAWME-CROWELL STATE FOREST

195

Bourne

Monument Beach
Aptucxet Trading
Post Museum

130

6

6A

Great Marshes

W. Barnstable

28

CAMP EDWARDS
MILITARY
RESERVATION
(INACTIVE)

Wakeby Pond

Cape Cod
Airport

Barnstable

Pocasset

Cataumet

Otis
Air Force Base

130

Marstons Mills
Centerville

North Falmouth

28A

151

Mashpee
Santuit

Osterville

Old Silver Beach

Ashumet Holly
Reservation

Waquoit Bay
Reserve

28

Cotuit

Buzzards Bay

West Falmouth

Waquoit
Village

Saconessett Hills

E. Falmouth

South Mashpee
Popponesset Beach

Sippewissett

Falmouth

Teaticket

28

Washburn Island
State Park

New Seabury

South Cape Beach
State Park

Nobska
Light

To Martha's Vineyard (seasonal)

Woods Hole

To Martha's Vineyard (year-round)

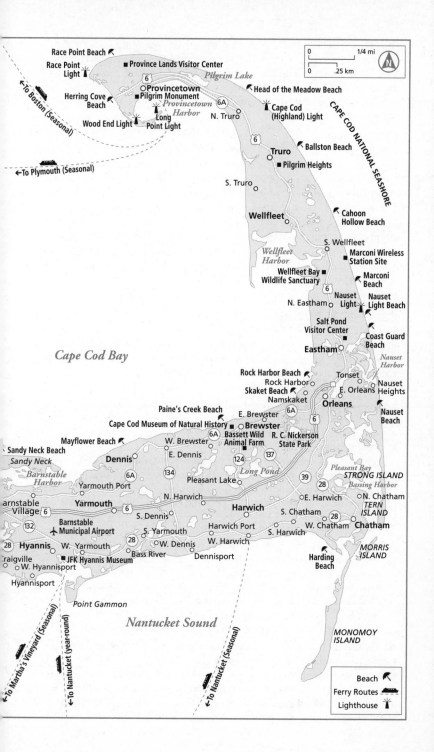

Briar Nature Center) as well as pristine Sandy Neck, one of the Cape's best bay beaches. It is also a good choice for nature buffs who will find excellent places for hiking (Shawme Crowell State Forest), biking (Cape Cod Canal bike path), and canoeing (Old Sandwich Harbor, Scorton Creek). The town is a convenient base for exploring other parts of the Cape, like the nightlife of Hyannis or the ocean beaches of Wellfleet.

ESSENTIALS

GETTING THERE   Cross the Cape Cod Canal on either the Bourne or Sagamore bridges. At the Bourne Bridge rotary, take Sandwich Road along the canal; it turns into Route 6A as it nears Sandwich Center. If you cross the Sagamore Bridge, take Exit 1 or 2, and follow Sandwich Road/Route 6A or Route 130, respectively, to Sandwich Center. It's 3 miles east of Sagamore, 16 miles northwest of Hyannis.

VISITOR INFORMATION   The **Cape Cod Canal Region Chamber of Commerce,** 70 Main St., Buzzards Bay (© **508/759-6000;** fax 508/759-6965; www.capecodcanalchamber.org), is open year-round daily from 10am to 5pm. A consortium of Sandwich businesses has put together a walking guide (with map) available at most inns in town.

BEACHES & OUTDOOR PURSUITS

BEACHES   For the Sandwich beaches listed below, nonresident parking stickers—$20 for the length of your stay—are available at **Sandwich Town Hall Annex,** 145 Main St. (© **508/833-8012**). Note that there's no swimming allowed within the Cape Cod Canal—currents are much too swift and dangerous.

- **Sandy Neck Beach** 🌟🌟🌟, off Sandy Neck Road in East Sandwich: This 6-mile stretch of silken barrier beach with low, rounded dunes is one of the Cape's most beautiful beaches; its parking lot tends to fill up early in summer. It's also popular with endangered piping plovers—and, unfortunately, their nemesis, off-road vehicles (ORV). ORV permits ($80 per season for nonresidents) can be purchased at the gatehouse (© **508/362-8300**) as long as it's not nesting season. ORV drivers must be equipped with supplies like a spare tire, jack, shovel, and tire-pressure gauge. Parking costs $10 per day in season; up to 3 days of camping in self-contained vehicles is permitted at $10 per night.

- **Town Neck Beach,** off Town Neck Road in Sandwich: A bit rocky but ruggedly pretty, this narrow beach offers a busy view of passing ships, plus rest rooms and a snack bar, but no lifeguards. Parking costs $4 per day, or you could hike from town (about 1½ miles) and then over the community-built **boardwalk** 🌟, which offers picturesque salt-marsh views.

- **Wakeby Pond,** Ryder Conservation Area, John Ewer Road (off South Sandwich Road on the Mashpee border): This beach, on the Cape's largest freshwater pond, has lifeguards, rest rooms, and parking ($4 per day).

BICYCLING   The **Cape Cod Canal bike path** 🌟🌟🌟 is a flat, 14-mile loop maintained by the U.S. Army Corps of Engineers (© **508/759-5991**). It is equally well suited to bikers, skaters, and runners. Park free at the Bourne Recreation Area, north of the Bourne Bridge, on the Cape side. The closest rentals are available at **Cape Cod Bike Rental,** 40 Rte. 6A, Sandwich (© **508/833-2453**), which charges around $22 per day.

BOATING   **Paddle Cape Cod** (✆ **888/226-6393** or 508/564-4051; www. paddlecapecod.com) runs naturalist-guided trips throughout the Cape. If you want to explore on your own by canoe, you can rent one in Falmouth (see below) and paddle around Old Sandwich Harbor, Sandy Neck, or the salt-marsh maze of Scorton Creek, which leads out to Talbot Point.

FISHING   Sandwich has eight fishable ponds; for details and a license, inquire at **Town Hall,** in the center of town (✆ **508/888-0340**). No permit is required for fishing from the banks of the Cape Cod Canal. Call the **Army Corps of Engineers** (✆ **508/759-5991**) for canal tide and fishing information. Local deep-water charters include the *Tigger Two,* docked in the Sandwich Marina (✆ **508/888-8372**).

NATURE & WILDLIFE AREAS   The **Shawme-Crowell State Forest,** off Route 130 in Sandwich (✆ **508/888-0351**), offers 285 campsites and 742 acres to roam. Entrance is free; parking costs $2. The **Sandwich Boardwalk** 🐾 links the town and Town Neck Beach by way of salt marshes that attract a great many birds, including great blue herons. The 57-acre **Green Briar Nature Center & Jam Kitchen** 🐾, off Route 6A, Sandwich (✆ **508/888-6870**), has a mile-long path crossing marsh and stands of white pine.

To obtain a map of other conservation areas in Sandwich (some 16 sites encompassing nearly 1,300 acres), stop by the **Sandwich Conservation Commission,** 16 Jan Sebastian Dr., off Route 130 (✆ **508/888-4200**).

MUSEUMS

Heritage Plantation of Sandwich ★★★ *Kids*   This is one of those rare museums that appeal equally to adults and children. All ages have the run of 76 beautifully landscaped acres, crisscrossed with walking paths and riotous with color in late spring, when the towering rhododendrons are in bloom. Scattered buildings house a wide variety of collections, from Native American artifacts to Early American weapons. The art holdings, especially the primitive portraits, are outstanding. The high point for most children will be a ride on the 1912 carousel. There's also a replica Shaker round barn packed with gleaming antique automobiles. Call ahead for a schedule of the outdoor summer concerts usually held Sundays at 2pm.

Grove and Pine sts. (about ½ mile southwest of the town center). ✆ **508/888-3300.** Admission $9 adults, $8 seniors, $4.50 children 6–18. Mid-May to mid-Oct daily 10am–5pm; no tickets sold after 4:15pm. Closed late Oct to mid-May.

Sandwich Glass Museum 🐾🐾   Even if you don't consider yourself a glass fan, make an exception for this fascinating museum, which captures the history of the town above and beyond its legendary industry. A brief video introduces Deming Jarves's brilliant 19th-century endeavor: bringing glassware—a hitherto rare commodity available only to the rich—within reach of the middle classes. All went well until Midwestern factories undercut Jarves by using coal to fire their furnaces. Unable to keep up with their level of mass production, Jarves switched back to hand-blown techniques just as his workforce was ready to revolt. An excellent gift shop stocks Sandwich-glass replicas as well as original glassworks. During the summer season, volunteers demonstrate glassmaking techniques.

129 Main St. (in the center of town). ✆ **508/888-0251.** Admission $3.50 adults, $1 children 6–16. Apr–Dec daily 9:30am–5pm; Feb–Mar Wed–Sun 9:30am–4pm. Closed Jan, Thanksgiving, and Christmas.

WHERE TO STAY

Bay Beach ★★★   As Sandwich's only beachfront inn, Bay Beach offers immaculate, modern rooms perfect for romantic interludes. These two homes, overlooking Town Neck Beach with a view of the Sagamore Bridge and the boat traffic along the canal, are filled with amenities. Some units even have fireplaces and double Jacuzzis.

1–3 Bay Beach Lane. (on Town Beach), Sandwich, MA 02563. ✆ **800/475-6398** or 508/888-8813. Fax 508/888-5416. www.baybeach.com. 7 units. Summer $175–$345 double. Rates include breakfast. MC, V. Closed Nov–Apr. No children under 16 accepted. **Amenities:** Exercise room. *In room:* A/C, TV, CD player, fridge, hair dryer.

Belfry Inne & Bistro ★★   This Victorian rectory and the former church next door have been converted into Sandwich's most stylish lodging option. Rooms in the rectory have retrofitted queen-size antique beds, claw-foot tubs (or Jacuzzis), and a scattering of fireplaces and private balconies. The third floor, with its single attic rooms and delightful *Alice in Wonderland* mural leading up to the belfry, is perfect for families with children. Next door in the Abbey are six deluxe guest rooms and a very fine restaurant (see "Where to Dine," below). The Abbey rooms are painted vivid colors and tucked cleverly into sections of this old church; all have Jacuzzis. One room features a stained-glass window; another has angel windows.

8 Jarves St. (in the center of town), Sandwich, MA 02563. ✆ **800/844-4542** or 508/888-8550. Fax 508/888-3922. www.belfryinn.com. 14 units. Summer $95–$165 double. Rates include breakfast. AE, MC, V. **Amenities:** Restaurant (new American).

The Dan'l Webster Inn ★★   This popular lodging and dining spot in the center of Sandwich village is a dependable bet for a comfortable stay or a hearty meal. The inn encompasses a modern main building, designed to look historic, as well as several historic homes nearby that have been outfitted with modern amenities. The main building sits on the site of a colonial tavern favored by Daniel Webster, the famous orator and prominent Boston lawyer, who enjoyed fishing on the Cape. All rooms are ample and nicely furnished with reproductions. Especially appealing are the suites in the historic houses, which feature fireplaces and canopy beds. There are also eight deluxe one-room suites in the main building, with perks like balconies, gas fireplaces, oversize whirlpool baths, and heated tile bathroom floors. The inn's common spaces are convivial, if bustling; the restaurant is a tour-bus lunch stop that turns out surprisingly sophisticated fare.

149 Main St. (in the center of town), Sandwich, MA 02563. ✆ **800/444-3566** or 508/888-3622. Fax 508/888-5156. www.danlwebsterinn.com. 54 units. Summer $149–$189 double; $219–$349 suite. AE, DC, DISC, MC, V. **Amenities:** Restaurant (international); small heated pool; access to local health club; limited room service. *In room:* A/C, TV.

Spring Hill Motor Lodge ★   Of the many motels on Route 6A, this one boasts the most amenities and improvements. Most impressive are the oversize night-lit tennis court and large, heated pool. The interiors are cheerfully contemporary, the grounds elegantly landscaped. In addition to the motel rooms, there are four cottages that are light, airy, and comfortable.

351 Rte. 6A (about 2½ miles east of the town center), East Sandwich, MA 02537. ✆ **800/647-2514** or 508/888-1456. Fax 508/833-1556. www.sunsol.com/springhill. 28 units. Summer $95–$125 double; $160 efficiency; $1100 per week for 1-bedroom cottage; $1,400 per week for 2-bedroom cottage. AE, DC, DISC, MC, V. **Amenities:** Heated pool; tennis court. *In room:* A/C, TV, fridge, coffeemaker.

The Village Inn at Sandwich ★★   Why envy the guests relaxing in rockers on the wraparound porch of this 1837 Federal house when you could be among them? You'll enjoy light and airy sleeping quarters with gleaming bleached floors and California-esque splashes of colorful fabric. From the French country–style dining room to the cozy dormer attic, the mood is one of carefree comfort. Innkeeper Susan Fehlinger, an artist, runs a program called Sandwich Artworks with workshops by well-known Cape Cod artists.

4 Jarves St. (in the center of town), Sandwich, MA 02563. ✆ **800/922-9989** or 508/833-0363. Fax 508/833-2063. www.capecodinn.com. 8 units (2 with shared bathroom). Summer $85–$105 double. Rates include breakfast. Packages available. AE, DISC, MC, V. *In room:* No phone.

WHERE TO DINE

Aquagrille ★ SEAFOOD   Overlooking Sandwich's picturesque marina and not-so-picturesque power plant, this spot wants to be the premier place for fish in Sandwich. All the elements are in place: a spacious, attractive dining room with a glass-enclosed harborview deck; a long, curving bar; and an attentive staff. The food is delicious, with fish (grilled or fried) the obvious choice, plus lots of pasta dishes. The towering lobster salad with haricot vert, tomato, avocado, chives, and crème fraîche is the perfect antidote to a steamy summer night. Those with larger appetites may want to choose their grilled fish (tuna, salmon, swordfish, or scrod) and sauce (Cajun rémoulade, chipotle aioli, béarnaise, dill mayonnaise, roasted red bell pepper, or tomato-and-basil stew). Ask for a table that doesn't face the power plant.

14 Gallo Rd. (next to Sandwich Marina). ✆ **508/888-8889.** Reservations recommended. Main courses $7–$20. AE, MC, V. May–Oct Mon–Fri noon–2:30pm and 5–9pm; Sat–Sun noon–9pm; call for off-season hours.

The Bee-Hive Tavern ★★ INTERNATIONAL   A cut above the rather characterless restaurants clustered along this stretch of road, this modern-day tavern employs some atmospheric old-time touches: Green-shaded bankers' lamps illuminate the dark wooden booths, and vintage prints convey a clubby feel. The food is straightforward but tasty. Steaks, chops, and fresh-caught fish are among the pricier choices, while burgers, sandwiches, and salads cater to lighter appetites (and wallets). This is a great option for lunch, when you should try the lobster roll, one of the Cape's best.

406 Rte. 6A (about ½ mile east of the town center), East Sandwich. ✆ **508/833-1184.** Main courses $7–$16. MC, V. Mon–Fri 11:30am–9pm; Sat–Sun 8am–9pm.

The Belfry Bistro ★★★ NEW AMERICAN   Sandwich's most romantic dining option is located in a restored 19th-century church (see the Belfry Inne under "Where to Stay," above). Entrees range from shrimp scampi with artichoke hearts to filet mignon served with garlic and leek mashed potatoes. Chef Michael Arbarchuk's menu changes seasonally; his appetizers might include a lobster, scallop, and leek strudel wrapped in phyllo and served on a bed of sautéed leeks and scallions. Desserts are clearly a specialty; especially good is the Victorian gingerbread with fresh berries.

8 Jarves St. (in the center of town). ✆ **508/888-8550.** Reservations recommended. Main courses $14–$25. AE, MC, V. Apr to mid-Oct Tues–Sat 5–10pm; Sun 11am–2pm; call for off-season hours.

Marshland Restaurant ★ DINER   Locals have been digging this diner for 2 decades. This is home-cooked grub, slung fast and cheap. You'll gobble up the hearty breakfast and be back in time for dinner.

109 Rte. 6A. ✆ **508/888-9824.** Most items under $10. No credit cards. Tues–Sat 6am–9pm; Sun 7am–1pm; Mon 6am–2pm. Open year-round.

FALMOUTH ★★ & WOODS HOLE ★★★

Falmouth is a classic New England town, complete with church steeples encircling the town green and a walkable and bustling Main Street. With over 20,000 year-round residents, it's the second-largest town on the Cape, after Barnstable.

Woods Hole, one of nine villages in Falmouth, has been a world-renowned oceanic research center since 1871, when the U.S. Commission of Fish and Fisheries set up a primitive collection station. Today the various scientific institutes—the National Marine Fisheries Service, the Marine Biological Laboratory, and the Woods Hole Oceanographic Institute—employ thousands of scientists. They offer a unique opportunity to get in-depth—and often hands-on—exposure to marine biology.

The Woods Hole community is also among the hipper ones on the Cape, with a number of restaurants, bars, and shops making crowded Water Street (don't even think of parking here in summer) a very pleasant place to stroll.

Falmouth Heights, a cluster of shingled Victorian summerhouses on a bluff east of Falmouth's harbor, is as popular as it is picturesque; its narrow ribbon of beach is a magnet for all, especially the younger crowd.

ESSENTIALS

GETTING THERE   After crossing the Bourne Bridge, take Route 28 south. It's 18 miles south of Sagamore, 20 miles southwest of Hyannis.

The **Sea Line Shuttle** (© 800/352-7155) connects Woods Hole, Falmouth, and Mashpee with Hyannis year-round Monday through Saturday (except holidays). The fare ranges from $1 to $3.50, depending on distance; children under 5 ride free.

VISITOR INFORMATION   Contact the **Falmouth Chamber of Commerce,** Academy Lane, Falmouth (© **800/526-8532** or 508/548-8500; fax 508/548-8521; www.falmouth-capecod.com).

BEACHES & OUTDOOR PURSUITS

BEACHES   While Old Silver Beach, Surf Drive Beach, and Menauhant Beach will sell a 1-day pass for $10, most other Falmouth public beaches require a parking sticker. Renters can obtain temporary beach parking stickers, for $50 per week or $75 per month, at **Falmouth Town Hall,** 59 Town Hall Sq. (© **508/548-7611**), or in season at the **Surf Drive Beach Bathhouse** (© **508/548-8623**). The town beaches for which a parking fee is charged all have rest rooms and concession stands. Here is a list of some of Falmouth's public shores:

- **Falmouth Heights Beach** ★★, off Grand Avenue in Falmouth Heights: Once a rowdy spot, this is primarily a family beach these days. Parking is sticker-only. This neighborhood supported the Cape's first summer colony; the grand Victorian mansions still overlook the beach.
- **Menauhant Beach,** off Central Avenue in East Falmouth: A bit off the beaten track, Menauhant is a little less mobbed than Falmouth's other public beaches and better protected from the winds. Parking costs $10 per day.
- **Old Silver Beach** ★★, off Route 28A in North Falmouth: Western-facing (great for sunsets) and relatively calm, this warm Buzzards Bay beach is a popular, often crowded place. It's the chosen spot for the college crowd. Families cluster on the opposite side of the street, where a shallow pool is perfect for toddlers. Parking costs $10.

• **Surf Drive Beach** ☝, off Shore Street in Falmouth: About a mile from downtown, and appealing to families, this is an easy-to-get-to choice with limited parking ($10).

BICYCLING   The **Shining Sea Bicycle Path** ☝☝☝ (© 508/548-8500) is a 3⅓-mile beauty following the coast from Falmouth village to Woods Hole with plenty of swimmable beach along the way. (Unfortunately, the beach here has mainly rocks instead of sand.) You can park at the trailhead on Locust Street in Falmouth, or any spot in town (parking in Woods Hole is scarce). The closest bike shop—near the village green—is **Corner Cycle,** at Palmer Avenue and North Main Street (© **508/540-4195**).

BOATING   **Patriot Party Boats,** 227 Clinton Ave. (at Scranton Avenue on the harbor), Falmouth (© **800/734-0088** or 508/548-2626), offers scenic cruises past the Elizabeth Islands on a sleek replica 1750s schooner, the *Liberte.* Two-hour sails cost $20 for adults. Also offered are trips to Cuttyhunk Island for hiking, birding and/or beaching.

   Paddle Cape Cod (© **888/226-6393** or 508/564-4051) runs naturalist-guided trips throughout the Cape. **Cape Cod Kayak** (© **508/540-9377**) rents kayaks (free delivery) by the day or week, and offers lessons and ecotours. If you want to explore on your own, **Edward's Boat Yard,** 1209 E. Falmouth Hwy., East Falmouth (© **508/548-2216**), rents canoes for exploring Waquoit Bay (see "Nature & Wildlife Areas," below).

FISHING   Falmouth has six fishable ponds. Freshwater fishing and shellfishing licenses can be obtained at **Falmouth Town Hall,** 59 Town Hall Sq. (© **508/548-7611,** ext. 219). Surf Drive Beach is a great spot for surf casting, once the crowds have dispersed. To go after bigger prey, head out on one of the **Patriot Party Boats,** based in Falmouth's Inner Harbor (© **800/734-0088** or 508/548-2626). For sport fishing, call Captain Bob MacGregor of the **Hop-Tuit** (© **508/540-7642**).

NATURE & WILDLIFE AREAS   **Ashumet Holly and Wildlife Sanctuary** ☝, operated by the Massachusetts Audubon Society at 186 Ashumet Rd., off Route 151 (© **508/362-1426**), is an intriguing 49 acres of more than 1,000 holly trees, along with 130 species of birds and a kettle pond that's covered with a carpet of Oriental lotus blossoms in summer. The trail fee is $3 for adults and $2 for seniors and children under 16.

   Near the center of Falmouth (just follow Depot Road to the end) is the 650-acre **Beebe Woods** ☝, a treasure for hikers and dog walkers. From here, you can wind your way to the town-owned, 90-acre **Peterson Farm** (entrance off Woods Hole Road; take a right at the Quisset farmstand), with paths through woods and fields, as well as a flock of sheep grazing in a meadow near historic farm buildings.

   The 2,250-acre **Waquoit Bay National Estuarine Research Reserve,** 149 Waquoit Hwy., East Falmouth (© **508/457-0495**), maintains a 1-mile, self-guided nature trail. Also inquire about the boat ride over to **Washburn Island** ☝ on Saturdays in season (by reservation only). After the 20-minute boat trip, naturalist-led guided walks are offered. The reserve also holds a number of walks and interpretive programs.

WATER SPORTS   Falmouth is something of a sail-boarding mecca, prized for its unflagging southwesterly winds. While Old Silver Beach in North Falmouth is the most popular spot for windsurfing, it is allowed here only prior to 9am

and after 5pm. Windsurfers are allowed during the day at the Trunk River area
on the west end of Falmouth's Surf Drive Beach.

SEA SCIENCE

National Marine Fisheries Service Aquarium ★★ (Kids) A little beat up
after 1¼ centuries of service and endless streams of eager schoolchildren, this
aquarium—the first such institution in the country—may not be state-of-the-
art, but it's a treasure nonetheless. The displays, focusing on local waters, might
make you think twice before taking a dip. Children show no hesitation, though,
in getting up to their elbows in the touch tanks. A key exhibit concerns the effect
of plastic trash on the marine environment. You might time your visit to coincide with the feeding of two seals, Coco and Sandy, who live here. The fish fly
at 11am and 4pm.

Albatross St. (off the western end of Water St.), Woods Hole. ℂ **508/495-2001.** Free admission. Mid-June
to early Sept daily 10am–4pm; mid-Sept to mid-June Mon–Fri 10am–4pm.

Woods Hole Oceanographic Institution Exhibit Center and Gift Shop
★ (Kids) This world-class research organization—locally referred to by its
acronym, WHOI (pronounced "Hooey")—is dedicated to the study of marine
science. At this small but interactive exhibit center, kids might enjoy looking
through microscopes at organisms or listening to sounds of marine animals on
a computer. *Titanic* fans will enjoy the brief video, displays, and life-size model
of the submersible that discovered the wreck. One-hour walking tours of WHOI
are offered twice a day Monday through Friday in July and August; reservations
required (ℂ **508/289-2252**).

15 School St. (off Water St.), Woods Hole. ℂ **508/289-2663.** $2 donation requested. Late May to early Sept
Mon–Sat 10am–4:30pm; Sun noon–4:30pm. Call for off-season hours. Closed Jan–Mar.

WHERE TO STAY
Expensive
Coonamessett Inn ★ A gracious inn built around the core of a 1796 homestead, the Coonamessett Inn is Falmouth's most traditional lodging choice. Set
on 7 lushly landscaped acres overlooking a pond, it has the feel of a country
club. Some of the bedrooms, decorated in reproduction antiques, can be a bit
somber, so try to get one with good light. The dining room is unabashedly formal and fairly good, though inconsistent. A better choice is the adjoining tavern
Eli's, where a jazz combo holds forth on weekends.

Jones Rd. and Gifford St. (about ½ mile north of Main St.), Falmouth, MA 02540. ℂ **508/548-2300.** Fax
508/540-9831. www.capecodrestaurants.org. 28 units. Summer $180–$260 double. Rates include continental breakfast. AE, MC, V. **Amenities:** Restaurant, tavern. *In room:* A/C, TV.

Inn at West Falmouth ★★ One of the loveliest small inns on the Cape and
the most stylish in Falmouth, this Shingle-style house is set high on a wooded
hill with distant views to Buzzards Bay. The cozy living room with fireplace has
heaps of bestsellers begging to be borrowed, while the spacious guest rooms are
lavished with unusual antiques. Some units have small balconies and whirlpool
tubs. After a leisurely breakfast, you might carry off a tome to the sparkling
heated pool set in the deck, or wander the landscaped grounds. Chappaquoit
Beach is about a 10-minute walk away.

66 Frazar Rd. (off Rte. 28A), West Falmouth, MA 02574. ℂ **800/397-7696** or 508/540-7696.
www.innatwestfalmouth.com. 8 units. Summer $175–$300 double. Rates include continental breakfast. AE,
MC, V. **Amenities:** Small heated pool; clay tennis court.

Moderate

Grafton Inn ☆☆   Reminiscent of a more leisurely age, this turreted Victorian grande dame has a front-row seat on Falmouth Heights's lively beach. All rooms have thoughtful touches like extra pillows, homemade chocolates, and fresh flowers—as well as coveted ocean views. An elaborate breakfast is served at individual tables on the screened porch. In the afternoon, wine and cheese are served. The ferry to Martha's Vineyard, leaving from Falmouth Harbor, is a 15-minute walk away.

261 Grand Ave. S., Falmouth Heights, MA 02540. ℂ 800/642-4069 or 508/540-8688. Fax 508/540-1861. www.graftoninn.com. 10 units. Summer $164–$210 double. Rates include breakfast. AE, MC, V. Closed mid-Nov to mid-Feb. No children under 16 accepted. *In room:* A/C, TV, hair dryer, no phone.

Inn on the Sound ☆☆☆   The ambience here is as breezy as the setting, high on a bluff beside Falmouth's premier sunning beach, with a sweeping view of Nantucket Sound from the large front deck. Innkeeper Renee Ross is an interior decorator, and it shows: There's none of the usual frilly/cutesy stuff in these well-appointed guest rooms, most of which have ocean views. Several have private decks. The breakfasts, especially the surprise French toast and the crab-and-cream-cheese soufflé, offer incentive to dawdle.

313 Grand Ave., Falmouth Heights, MA 02540. ℂ 800/564-9668 or 508/457-9666. Fax 508/457-9631. www.innonthesound.com. 10 units. Summer $95–$195 double. Rates include breakfast. AE, DISC, MC, V. No children under 16. *In room:* TV, no phone.

Sands of Time Motor Inn & Harbor House ☆   This property, across the street from the ferry terminal, consists of two buildings, a two-story motel in front of a shingled 1879 Victorian mansion. The motel rooms feature crisp, above-average decor, plus private porches overlooking the harbor. The bedrooms in the Harbor House are more lavish—some with four-poster beds, working fireplaces, wicker furnishings, and harbor views.

549 Woods Hole Rd., Woods Hole, MA 02543. ℂ 800/841-0114 or 508/548-6300. Fax 508/457-0160. www.sandsoftime.com. 36 units (2 with shared bathroom). Summer $120–$170 double. Rates include continental breakfast. AE, DC, DISC, MC, V. Closed Nov–Mar. **Amenities:** Small heated pool; tennis court on motel property. *In room:* A/C, TV, dataport.

Wildflower Inn ☆   Though located on a busy stretch of road, this B&B is immaculately appointed and filled with welcoming touches, like the row of wooden rocking chairs lining the front porch. The guest rooms are creatively decorated with wicker furnishings and country quilts. There's even a safari room with an iron canopy bed draped with decorative mosquito netting. Two dormer rooms on the top floor come with whirlpool baths, and the attached apartment features a loft bedroom reached by a spiral staircase. The five-course breakfast, served on the wraparound porch, might include such treats as apple-pie French toast garnished with edible flowers. The inn is across the street from the satellite parking lot for the Martha's Vineyard ferries, so you can easily hop a bus down to the terminal in Woods Hole.

167 Palmer Ave. (2 blocks north of Main St.), Falmouth, MA 02540. ℂ 800/294-5459 or 508/548-9524. Fax 508/548-9524. www.wildflower-inn.com. 6 units. Summer $140–$195 double; $225 cottage. Rates include breakfast. AE, MC, V. **Amenities:** Bikes for guests' use. *In room:* A/C, no phone.

Inexpensive

Inn at One Main   Though a centenarian (built in 1892), this shingled house with Queen Anne flourishes has a crisp, youthful air. The bedrooms embody barefoot romance, rather than the Victorian brand. Lace, chintz, and wicker

have been laid on lightly, leaving plenty of space to kick about. The Turret
Room, with its brass bed, is perhaps the most irresistible. Breakfasts feature gingerbread pancakes, orange-pecan French toast, homemade scones—it's a good
thing the Shining Sea Bikeway is right at hand.

1 Main St. (1 block northwest of village green), Falmouth, MA 02540. ✆ 888/281-6246 or 508/540-7469.
Fax 603/462-5680. www.bbonline.com/ma/onemain. 6 units. Summer $110–$150 double. Rates include
breakfast. AE, DISC, MC, V. *In room:* A/C, hair dryer, no phone.

WHERE TO DINE

Betsy's Diner ★★ AMERICAN   We once had the best piece of baked scrod
ever at this vintage 1950s diner. The menu features turkey dinner, breakfast all
day, and homemade soups. Many people come here for the large selection of
scrumptious homemade pies, which are the best on Cape Cod. Each red vinyl
booth is equipped with its own jukebox with retro hits.

457 Main St. (in the center of town). ✆ 508/540-0060. Main courses $4–$10. AE, MC, V. Daily 6am–8pm.

Chapaquoit Grill ★★ NEW AMERICAN   The only dining spot in sleepy
West Falmouth, this roadside bistro has California aspirations, wood-grilled
slabs of fish accompanied by trendy salsas, and personal pizzas delivered straight
from the brick oven. A no-reservations policy means long waits nightly in season and weekends year-round.

410 Rte. 28A, West Falmouth. ✆ 508/540-7794. Reservations not accepted. Main courses $8–$16. MC, V.
Daily 5–10pm.

Fishmonger's Cafe ★★ NATURAL FOODS   This sunny cafe attracts local
young people, scientists, and tourists for an array of imaginatively prepared
dishes, with vegetarian choices a specialty. The chefs change the eclectic menu
every few days and have added some Thai entrees. Regulars sit at the counter to
enjoy a bowl of the Fisherman's Stew. Newcomers usually go for the tables by
the window, where you can watch boats come and go from Eel Pond. Lunch
could be a tempeh burger or a regular beef version.

56 Water St. (at the Eel Pond drawbridge), Woods Hole. ✆ 508/540-5376. Main courses $10–$19. AE, MC,
V. Mid-June to Oct Mon–Fri 7–11am, 11:30am–4pm, and 5–10pm; Sat–Sun 7–11:30am, noon–4:30pm, and
5:30–10:30pm. Call for off-season hours. Closed mid-Dec to mid-Feb.

The Flying Bridge ★ Kids AMERICAN/CONTINENTAL   Seafood, appropriately enough, predominates at this harborside mega-restaurant (capacity:
some 600). With three bars tossed into the mix and live music upstairs on weekends, things can get a bit crazy; you'll find comparative peace and quiet—as well
as tip-top views—out on the deck. In addition to basic bar food (Buffalo wings
and the like), you'll find fish in many guises, from fish-and-chips to appealing
blackboard specials. The kids will enjoy wandering onto the attached dock to
watch the ducks in the harbor.

220 Scranton Ave. (about ½ mile south of Main St.). ✆ 508/548-2700. Main courses $8–$20. AE, MC, V.
Apr–Dec daily 11:30am–10pm; call for off-season hours.

Regatta of Falmouth-by-the-Sea ★★★ INTERNATIONAL   This place
has it all: harbor views, polished yet innovative cuisine, and superb service. The
decor features rose-petal pale walls and custom Limoges china. The excellence
continues in the kitchen. Favorites include the Menemsha Bay scallop bisque
with fresh chervil and, for a main course, grilled lobster basted with lime buerre
blanc sauce and served with hand-cut tarragon fettuccine, baby eggplant, and
asparagus. For dessert, nothing beats the caramelized banana puff pastry tart
filled with chocolate ganache.

217 Clinton Ave. (end of Scranton Ave. on Falmouth Harbor, about 1 mile south of Main St.). © **508/548-5400.** Reservations recommended. Main courses $20–$30. AE, MC, V. Late May to mid-Sept daily 4:30–10pm; call for off-season hours. Closed mid-Oct to Apr.

FALMOUTH AFTER DARK

God knows whom you'll meet in the rough-and-tumble old **Cap'n Kidd,** 77 Water St., Woods Hole (© **508/548-9206**): maybe a lobsterwoman, maybe a Nobel Prize winner. Good grub, too. Grab a stool at the **British Beer Company,** 263 Grand Ave., Falmouth Heights (© **508/540-9600**), and choose from a revolving selection of over 18 drafts from the British Isles as you ponder views of the beach across the street. Everyone heads to **Liam McGuire's Irish Pub,** 273 Main St., Falmouth (© **508/548-0285**), for a taste of the Emerald Isle.

2 The Mid Cape

Visitors who want to be centrally located on the Cape choose the Mid Cape, which is just over an hour from Boston (without traffic), an easy (less than an hour) drive to the Outer Cape, and a 1-hour ferry ride from Nantucket. This is the Cape's most populous area and also the prime location for its cheapest motels, which line Route 28 from Hyannis through Dennis.

Hyannis is the Cape's unofficial capital. It's a sprawling concrete jungle of strip malls and chain stores where the Kennedy mystique of the 1960s had the unfortunate side effect of spurring heedless development over the ensuing decades—a period during which the Cape's year-round population doubled to more than 200,000. The summer population is about three times that, and you'd swear every single person had daily errands to run in Hyannis. And yet this overrun town still has pockets of charm, especially the waterfront area and Main Street.

But the real beauty of the Mid Cape lies in its smaller places: old-money hideaways like **Osterville** 🌟 to the west, and charming villages like **West Barnstable** 🌟🌟 and **Yarmouth Port** 🌟🌟🌟, which can be found along the **Old King's Highway** 🌟🌟🌟 (Route 6A) on the bay side of the Cape. A drive along this winding two-lane road reveals the early architectural history of the region, from humble colonial saltboxes to ostentatious captains' mansions. Scores of intriguing antiques shops subtly compete to draw a closer look, and each village seems a throwback to a kinder, gentler era.

HYANNIS & ENVIRONS

Hectic Hyannis is the commercial center and transportation hub of the Cape, with the enormous Cape Cod Mall and Barnstable Airport, one of the busiest airports in the region during the summer months. It also has a diverse selection of restaurants, bars, and nightclubs. But if you were to confine your visit to this one town, you'd get a warped view of the Cape. Along Routes 132 and 28, you could be visiting Anywhere, USA: The roads are lined with the standard chain stores and restaurants, and mired with maddening traffic.

While Hyannis's impersonal hotels and motels have more beds at better prices than anywhere else on the Cape, there's little reason to choose them unless you happen to have missed the last ferry out. We recommend staying in Hyannisport or heading due north to Barnstable Village, where you'll find a myriad of charming B&Bs in historic houses along the scenic Old King's Highway. Once you're settled, you can visit Hyannis to sample some of the Cape's best restaurants and nightlife. See below for details on Barnstable Village and environs.

ESSENTIALS

GETTING THERE After crossing the Sagamore bridge, head east on Route 6 or 6A. The latter passes through Barnstable Village; Route 132 south of Route 6A leads to Hyannis. You can also fly into Hyannis, and there's good bus service from Boston and New York.

VISITOR INFORMATION Contact the **Hyannis Area Chamber of Commerce,** 1481 Rte. 132, Hyannis (*C* **800/449-6647,** 877/492-6647, or 508/362-5230; fax 508/362-9499; www.hyannis.com).

BEACHES & OUTDOOR PURSUITS

BEACHES Most of the Nantucket Sound beaches are fairly protected and offer little in the way of surf. Beach parking costs $10 a day, usually payable at the lot; for a weeklong parking sticker ($40), visit the **Recreation Department,** 141 Basset Lane, at the Kennedy Memorial Skating Rink (*C* **508/790-6345**).

- **Craigville Beach** ⭐⭐, off Craigville Beach Road in Centerville: This broad expanse of sand boasts lifeguards and rest rooms. A destination for the bronzed and buffed, it's known as "Muscle Beach." It's a short walk to Craigville Village, a former Methodist camp meeting site with Carpenter Gothic cottages that is still used for religious retreats.
- **Kalmus Beach,** off Gosnold Street in Hyannisport: This 800-foot spit of sand stretching toward the mouth of the harbor makes an ideal launching site for windsurfers. The surf is tame, the slope shallow, and the conditions ideal for kids. There are lifeguards, a snack bar, and rest rooms to facilitate family outings.
- **Orrin Keyes Beach** (Sea Beach), at the end of Sea Street in Hyannis: This little beach at the end of a residential road is popular with families.
- **Veterans Beach,** off Ocean Street in Hyannis: A small stretch of harborside sand adjoining the John F. Kennedy Memorial (a moving tribute from the town), this spot is not tops for swimming, unless you're very young and easily wowed. Parking is usually easy, though, and it's walkable from town. The snack bar, rest rooms, and playground will see to a family's needs.

FISHING The **Tightlines Sport Fishing Service,** 65 Camp St., Hyannis (*C* **508/790-8600**), conducts saltwater fly-fishing expeditions. **Hy-Line Cruises** (*C* **508/790-0696**) offers seasonal sonar-aided "bottom" or blues fishing from its Ocean Street dock in Hyannis. **Helen H Deep-Sea Fishing,** 137 Pleasant St., Hyannis (*C* **508/790-0660**), offers year-round expeditions aboard a 100-foot boat with a heated cabin and full galley. For a smaller, more personalized expedition, get in touch with Capt. Ron Murphy of **Stray Cat Sportfishing Charters** (*C* **508/428-8628**).

GOLF Open year-round, the **Hyannis Golf Club,** Route 132 (*C* **508/362-2606**), offers a 46-station driving range, as well as an 18-hole championship course. Smaller, but scenic, is the 9-hole **Cotuit High Ground Country Club,** 31 Crockers Neck Rd., Cotuit (*C* **508/428-9863**).

WATER SPORTS **Eastern Mountain Sports,** 1513 Iyannough Rd./Rte. 132 (*C* **508/362-8690**), offers rental kayaks, tents, and sleeping bags, and sponsors free clinics and walks, such as a full-moon hike.

TOURS BY STEAMER & SLOOP

The Hesperus Offering an elegant means of exploring the harbor (while sneaking a peak at the Kennedy compound), the 50-foot *John Alden* sloop

Hyannis Inn Motel **2**
Inn on Sea Street **6**
Radisson Inn Hyannis **1**
Sea Breeze Inn **5**
Sheraton Hyannis Resort **3**
Simmons Homestead Inn **4**

accommodates only 22 passengers, who are welcome to help trim the sails or even steer. Most opt to luxuriate in the sparkling sun and cooling breezes.

Pier 16, Ocean St. Dock, Hyannis. ℂ **508/790-0077**. Tickets $25 adults, $20 seniors and children 12 and under. Late May to mid-Oct daily 12:30pm, 3pm, and 5:30pm; call for off-season schedule. Closed Nov–Apr.

Hyannisport Harbor Cruises   For a fun and informative introduction to the harbor and its residents, take a leisurely 1- to 2-hour narrated tour aboard the Hy-Line's 1911 steamer replicas *Patience* and *Prudence*. Five family trips a day offer free passage for children under 12, but for a real treat, take the Sunday "Ice-Cream Float," which includes a design-your-own Ben & Jerry's sundae, or the Thursday "Jazz Boat," accompanied by a Dixieland band. The latest offering is a lobster luncheon cruise on Mondays and Wednesdays.

Ocean St. Dock, Hyannis. ℂ **508/790-0696**. www.hy-linecruises.com. Tickets $10–$16 adults, free–$8 children 12 and under. Late June to Sept 16 departures daily; call for schedule. Closed Nov to mid-Apr.

THE KENNEDY LEGACY

For a lovely sightseeing drive, mosey around the moneyed sound shore to the west. Don't even bother tracking down the Kennedy Compound in Hyannisport; it's effectively screened from view, and you'll see more at the John F. Kennedy Hyannis Museum in town. Or if you absolutely must satisfy your curiosity, take a harbor cruise (see above).

John F. Kennedy Hyannis Museum ✸✸ This photographic and multimedia display captures the Kennedys during the glory days from 1934 to 1963. The death of John F. Kennedy, Jr., in a plane crash in the summer of 1999 saw visitation jump five times higher than average. A special exhibit of photos of John, Jr., will be on display at least through the end of 2001.

397 Main St., Hyannis. ⓒ 508/790-3077. Admission $3 adults, free for children under 17. Apr–Oct Mon–Sat 10am–4pm; Sun and holidays 1–4pm; last admission at 3:30pm. Call for off-season hours.

SHOPPING

Although Hyannis is the commercial center of the Cape, the stores here are fairly standard. Head for the wealthy enclaves west of Hyannis, and along the Old King's Highway (Route 6A) to the north, to locate the real gems.

The 1742 **Farmhouse,** 1340 Main St. (about 1 mile south of Route 28), Osterville (ⓒ **508/420-2400**), is filled with rooms of antiques and reproductions set up like a well-decorated antique home.

Ex-Nantucketer Bob Marks fashions the only authentic Nantucket lightship baskets crafted off-island; as aficionados know, they don't come cheap. You'll find them at **Oak and Ivory,** 1112 Main St. (about 1 mile south of Route 28), Osterville (ⓒ **508/428-9425**).

If you like potato chips, don't miss **Cape Cod Potato Chips,** Breed's Hill Road (at Independence Way, off Route 132), Hyannis (ⓒ **508/775-7253**). Free factory tours are offered in July and August, Monday through Friday from 9am to 5pm and Saturday from 10am to 4pm.

WHERE TO STAY

There are a variety of generic but convenient hotels and motels in Hyannis. Within strolling distance of restaurants, shops, and the ferries is the 77-unit **Hyannis Inn Motel,** 473 Main St. (ⓒ **800/922-8993** or 508/775-0255; www.hyannisinnmotel.com), with an indoor pool and summer rates of $88 to $135. If you need a full health club, try the **Radisson Inn Hyannis,** 287 Iyannough Rd./Rte. 28 (ⓒ **800/333-3333** or 508/771-1700; www.radisson.com/capecod); it has an uninspiring location, but is within spitting distance of the airport. Rooms start at $145. Another option is the **Sheraton Hyannis Resort,** at the West End Circle off Main Street (ⓒ **800/598-4559** or 508/775-7775; www.sheraton.com), which boasts a golf course, tennis courts, pools, and restaurants. Doubles start at $189.

Inn on Sea Street Just a short walk from Sea Street beach, this establishment comprises two historic houses and a tiny cottage. The main house is more formally decorated in a Victorian style. Some of its rooms have four-poster or canopy beds and claw-foot tubs. The house across the street, mansard-roofed with a wraparound porch, has larger rooms decorated with English country antiques. All units in this house have TVs and air-conditioning. The elaborate breakfast might feature such treats as rhubarb coffeecake and breakfast quiche with cheese and bacon.

358–363 Sea St., Hyannis, MA 02601. ℭ **508/775-8030.** Fax 508/771-0878. www.capecod.net/innonsea.
10 units (2 with shared bathroom). Summer $85–$135 double; $130 cottage. Rates include breakfast. AE,
DISC, MC, V. In room: No phone.

Sea Breeze Inn ✮   The coast used to be lined with superior guest houses of
this sort, and to find one still in its prime is a real treat. Within whistling distance of the beach, this classic shingled beach house has been decked out with
the totems of small-town America: a picket fence, exuberant plantings, and even
a wooden rocker built for two couples. Also on the grounds are four cottages,
including one with a double Jacuzzi.

270 Ocean Ave. (about 1 mile south of the West End rotary), Hyannis, MA 02601. ℭ **508/771-7213.** Fax
508/862-0663. www.seabreezeinn.com. 18 units. Summer $80–$140 double; $1,200–$2,500 per week for
cottage. Rates include continental breakfast (except in large cottages). AE, DISC, MC, V. In room: A/C, TV.

Simmons Homestead Inn ✮✮   Innkeeper Bill Putman has decorated his
place with a sense of humor. Each room in this rambling 1820s manse has an
animal theme represented by stuffed toys, sculptures, even needlepoint and wallpaper. Those who prefer privacy may book the spiffily updated "servants' quarters," a spacious wing with its own private deck. Outside, Putman's classic car
collection is housed in two large garages. This is the kind of place where you'll
find everyone mulling around the hearth sipping complimentary wine while
they compare notes and nail down dinner plans. To help guests plan their days
and evenings, Putman has typed up extensive notes on day trips (including the
islands), bike routes, and his own personal, quirky restaurant reviews. There's a
regulation billiards parlor (one foot on the floor and no spitting), and in accor-
dance with the permissive (i.e., fun) atmosphere here, dogs are allowed, and so
is smoking in the common room.

288 Scudder Ave. (about ¼ mile west of the West End rotary), Hyannisport, MA 02647. ℭ **800/637-1649**
or 508/778-4999. Fax 508/790-1342. www.capecodtravel.com/simmonsinn. 14 units. Summer $180–$220
double; $325 two-bedroom suite. Rates include breakfast. AE, DISC, MC, V. Dogs welcome. **Amenities:** Out-
door hot tub; bikes (free); billiards room. In room: Hair dryer, iron, no phone.

Tradewinds Inn ✮   Many rooms in this attractive motel have wonderful
views of Craigville Beach. And since it's hard to see the sand once the summer
crowds hit, this property also has its own 500-foot stretch of private beach. On
cloudy days, guests may enjoy strolling up to the Craigville Campground next
door, a compound of 19th-century cottages that still serve as a Methodist camp
meeting preserve. The motel also abuts tiny Lake Elizabeth, where young Jack
and Ted Kennedy learned to sail.

780 Craigville Beach Rd. (across the street from Craigville Beach), Centerville, MA 02632. ℭ **877/444-7966**
or 508/775-0365. www.twicapecod.com. 46 units. Summer $119–$189 double; $199–$235 suite. Rates
include continental breakfast in season. AE, MC, V. Closed Oct–Apr. In room: A/C, TV.

WHERE TO DINE
Very Expensive

The Regatta of Cotuit at the Crocker House ✮✮✮ NEW AMERICAN
One of the best restaurants on Cape Cod, this year-round cousin of the Regatta
of Falmouth-by-the-Sea (see section on Falmouth, above) serves fine cuisine in
the formal Federal-era rooms of a 1790 Cape. Nightly specials might include
sautéed fillet of halibut with a citrus buerre blanc, lobster mashed potatoes, and
a marinated vegetable salad. The cuisine is exquisitely prepared and presented,
fortified by herbs and vegetables plucked fresh from the kitchen garden. You're
likely to experience the best service on Cape Cod at this enchanting locale.

4631 Rte. 28 (near the intersection of Rte. 130), Cotuit. ✆ **508/428-5715.** Reservations recommended. Main courses $22–$35. AE, MC, V. Apr–Dec daily 5–10pm; Jan–Mar Tues–Sun 5–10pm.

Expensive

The Black Cat ✪ NEW AMERICAN   Located less than a block from the Hy-Line ferries, this is a fine place to catch a quick bite while you wait for your boat to come in. The menu is pretty basic—steak, pasta, and, of course, fish—but attention is paid to the details; the onion rings, for instance, are made fresh. The dining room, with its bar of gleaming mahogany and brass, will appeal to chilled travelers on a blustery day; in fine weather, you might prefer the porch. There's live jazz on weekends in season.

165 Ocean St. (opposite the Ocean St. Dock), Hyannis. ✆ **508/778-1233.** Main courses $15–$29. AE, DC, DISC, MC, V. Apr–Oct daily 11:30am–10pm; call for off-season hours.

Penguin SeaGrill ✪✪ INTERNATIONAL   The versatile menu here bounces from Asian influences, like "Thai Jumpin' Squid," to mussels Portuguese style. The focus is definitely seafood; pay attention to the specials and you can't go wrong. Large lobsters are served nightly, meats and fish are wood-grilled, and the wine list is impressive. The setting is contemporary, with brick walls, mirrored accents, and mammoth carved fish. There's entertainment on Friday nights in season. For years, this has been considered one of the top restaurants on the Cape.

331 Main St. (in the center of town), Hyannis. ✆ **508/775-2023.** Reservations recommended. Main courses $15–$24. AE, DC, DISC, MC, V. June–Sept Sun–Thurs 5–10pm; Fri–Sat 5–11pm; call for off-season hours. Closed Jan.

Ristorante Barolo ✪✪✪ NORTHERN ITALIAN   This is the best Italian restaurant in town. Part of a smart-looking brick office complex, this place does everything right, from offering extra-virgin olive oil for dunking the crusty bread to getting those pastas perfectly al dente. Entrees include a number of tempting veal choices, like *Vitello alla Sorrentina* (Provimi veal, mozzarella, and basil with plum-tomato sauce), as well as such favorites as *Linguine al Frutti di Mare,* with littlenecks, mussels, shrimp, and calamari. The desserts are brought in daily from Boston's famed North End.

1 Financial Place (297 North St., just off the West End rotary), Hyannis. ✆ **508/778-2878.** Reservations recommended. Main courses $8–$26. AE, DC, MC, V. June–Sept Sun–Thurs 4:30–10pm; Fri–Sat 4:30–11pm; call for off-season hours.

Roadhouse Cafe ✪✪✪ AMERICAN/NORTHERN ITALIAN   The humble name belies the culinary caliber of this intimate but ambitious restaurant. This is not the hybrid "Italian-American" fare that so poorly represents both. Instead, the extensive menu is pretty much split between American standards, such as oysters Rockefeller, and real Italian cooking. There's also a lighter-fare menu served in the snazzy bistro in back. Among the appetizers are beef carpaccio with fresh-shaved Parmesan, and vine-ripened tomatoes and buffalo mozzarella drizzled with balsamic vinaigrette. The latter also makes a tasty marinade for native swordfish headed for the grill. The signature dessert, a distinctly non-Italian cheesecake infused with Bailey's Irish Creme, is itself an excuse to come check out the live jazz in the bistro (see "Hyannis & Environs After Dark," below).

488 South St. (off Main St., near the West End rotary), Hyannis. ✆ **508/775-2386.** Reservations recommended. Main courses $12–$25. AE, DC, DISC, MC, V. Daily 4–11pm.

Moderate

Tugboats ☆ AMERICAN   Yet another harborside perch for munching and ogling, this one's especially appealing: The two spacious decks are angled just right to catch the sunset. Forget fancy dining and chow down on blackened swordfish bites or lobster fritters. Among the desserts is a Key lime pie purportedly lifted straight from Papa's of Key West.

21 Arlington St. (at the Hyannis Marina, off Willow St.), Hyannis. ✆ 508/775-6433. Main courses $11–$15. AE, DC, MC, V. Late May to late Oct daily 11:30am–10:30pm; mid-Apr to late May Tues–Sun 11:30am–10:30pm. Closed Nov to mid-Apr.

Inexpensive

Baxter's Boat House *Kids* SEAFOOD   A shingled shack on a jetty jutting out into the harbor, Baxter's has catered to the boating crowd since the mid-1950s with Cape classics such as fried clams and fish virtually any way you like it, served on paper plates on picnic tables.

177 Pleasant St. (near the Steamship Authority ferry), Hyannis. ✆ 508/775-7040. Main courses $8–$14. AE, MC, V. Late May to early Sept Mon–Sat 11:30am–10pm; Sun 11:30am–9pm; call for off-season hours. Closed mid-Oct to Mar.

Mayflower Cape Cod Diner ☆ *Kids* DINER   In the tradition of great diners, this one has a tin ceiling, comfy booths, and a shiny counter. It also serves breakfast all day and has sassy waitresses who pour really good coffee. Wash down a tuna melt with a root-beer float or splurge on the roast turkey dinner.

50 Sea St. (at the corner of South St., 1 block from Main St.). ✆ 508/771-3554. All items under $9. AE, MC, V. Late May to Sept Mon–Sat 7am–8pm; Sun 7am–1pm; call for off-season hours.

Ying's ☆☆ THAI/JAPANESE/KOREAN   This is the best Asian food in town, and the atmosphere provides a much-needed dose of tranquility in hectic Hyannis. There's a water garden at the entrance and an eight-seat sushi bar in addition to tables. While specializing in three distinct Asian cuisines may seem risky, Ying's handles the challenge with aplomb. The sushi menu is extensive, but there are also Thai and Korean specialties, including many vegetarian dishes.

59 Center St. (at Center Plaza, 1 block north of Main St.), Hyannis ✆ 508/790-2432. All items under $15. AE, MC, V. Daily 11:30am–10:30pm.

HYANNIS & ENVIRONS AFTER DARK

From July to early September, try to catch a show at the **Cape Cod Melody Tent,** West End rotary, Hyannis (✆ 508/775-9100). Built as a summer theater in 1950, this billowy big-top proved even better suited to variety shows. A nonprofit venture since 1990, the Melody Tent has hosted the major performers of the past 50 years, from jazz greats to comedians, crooners to rockers. Every seat is a winner in this grand oval, only 20 banked aisles deep. There's also a children's theater program Wednesdays at 11am.

The congenial lounge at **Baxter's Boat House,** 177 Pleasant St. (see "Where to Dine," above), Hyannis (✆ 508/775-7040), with low-key blues piano, draws an attractive crowd. **Roo Bar,** 586 Main St., Hyannis (✆ 508/778-6515), feels very Manhattan, with ultracool servers, a long sleek bar area, and lots of attitude. The bistro food is good, too.

A good place for after-dinner entertainment is **Roadhouse Cafe,** 488 South St. (see "Where to Dine," above), Hyannis (✆ 508/775-2386), a dark-paneled bar that stocks 48 boutique beers. Insiders know to show up Monday nights to hear local jazz great Dave McKenna.

The cramped dance floor makes for instant camaraderie at **Harry's,** 700 Main St., Hyannis (© **508/778-4188**). This intimate space features classic blues that really demands to be absorbed. Cover ranges from $3 to $5.

With a whimsically decorated setting and a sassy staff, **Starbuck's,** 645 Rte. 132, Hyannis (© **508/778-6767**), has had a hopping bar scene for decades. There's no cover for the acoustic acts and soft-rock bands, and the drinks range from silly (Grape Crush) to serious (27-ounce margaritas).

BARNSTABLE VILLAGE & ENVIRONS ★★

Just a couple miles from Hyannis, the bucolic village of Barnstable houses the county courthouse and government offices for the region. In this peaceful setting are some of the most charming and well-managed B&Bs around. The bay area along historic Route 6A, the Old King's Highway, unfolds in a blur of greenery and well-kept colonial houses.

OUTDOOR PURSUITS

BEACHES   Barnstable's primary bay beach is Sandy Neck, accessed through East Sandwich (see the Sandwich section, above).

BOATING   Paddle Cape Cod (© **888/226-6393** or 508/564-4051; www.paddlecapecod.com) runs naturalist-guided trips throughout the Cape. If you want to explore on your own, you can rent a kayak from Eastern Mountain Sports (see "Water Sports" under Hyannis, above) and paddle around Scorton Creek, Sandy Neck, and Barnstable Harbor.

FISHING   The township of Barnstable has 11 ponds for freshwater fishing; for information and permits, visit **Town Hall,** 367 Main St., Hyannis (© **508/790-6240**), or **Sports Port,** 149 W. Main St., Hyannis (© **508/775-3096**). Shellfishing permits are available from the **Department of Natural Resources,** 1189 Phinneys Lane, Centerville (© **508/790-6272**). Surf casting, without a license, is permitted on Sandy Neck. Among the charter boats berthed in Barnstable Harbor is the *Drifter* (© **508/398-2061**), a 36-foot boat offering ½- and 1-day trips.

SHOPPING

Of the hundreds of antiques shops scattered through the region, perhaps a dozen qualify as destinations for well-schooled collectors. **Harden Studios,** 3264 Rte. 6A (in the center of town), Barnstable Village (© **508/362-7711**), is one of them. Some items, such as the primitive portraits and mourning embroidery, are all but extinct outside of museums. **Tao Water Art Gallery,** 1989 Rte. 6A, West Barnstable (© **508/375-0428**), is a Zen-like space featuring paintings by Chinese artists as well as museum reproductions of Chinese antiques and jade.

WHERE TO STAY

The Acworth Inn ★★   Innkeepers Cheryl and Jack Ferrell know that it's the small touches that make a stay memorable, from the cranberry spritzer offered on arrival to the handmade chocolates that take the place of pillow mints. Cheryl, who does baking demonstrations locally, even grinds the whole grains that go into her home-baked breakfasts, in the form of cranberry-orange rolls or whole-wheat pancakes. Those looking to avoid the excess of Victorian furnishings in many B&Bs will delight in the simple, fresh, decor here, mainly in shades of white and beige. Two rooms in the carriage house have been combined into a romantic luxury suite with whirlpool bath, TV/VCR, working fireplace, air-conditioning, and fridge. The inn is close to Barnstable Village and popular Cape Cod Bay beaches.

4352 Rte. 6A (near the Yarmouth Port border), Cummaquid, MA 02637. ℂ 800/362-6363 or 508/362-3330. Fax 508/375-0304. www.acworthinn.com. 5 units. Summer $115–$150 double; $185 suite. Rates include breakfast. AE, DC, DISC, MC, V. No children under 12 accepted. **Amenities:** Bikes for guests' use. *In room:* A/C, hair dryer, iron, no phone.

Beechwood Inn ★★   Look for a butterscotch 1853 Queen Anne Victorian all but enshrouded in weeping beeches. Admirers of late-19th-century decor are in for a treat: The interior remains dark and rich, with a red-velvet parlor and tin-ceilinged dining room, where innkeeper Debbie Traugot serves a three-course breakfast that features home-baked delights such as applesauce pancakes. Two of the upstairs bedrooms embody distinctive period styles from the 1860s and 1880s. Each affords a distant view of the bay. Rooms range from spacious (the Lilac) to snug (the Garret).

2839 Rte. 6A (about 1½ miles east of Rte. 132), Barnstable, MA 02630. ℂ 800/609-6618 or 508/362-6618. Fax 508/362-0298. www.beechwoodinn.com. 6 units. Summer $140–$180 double. Rates include breakfast. AE, DISC, MC, V. *In room:* A/C, fridge, no phone.

WHERE TO DINE

Dolphin Restaurant ★★ NEW AMERICAN   It looks like just another run-of-the-mill roadside eatery, so it's easy to miss. Never mind the corny decor (pine paneling and clunky captains' chairs) that dates from the 1950s. The finesse is to be found in the menu, where amid the more typical fried fish you'll find such delicacies as Chilean sea bass with roasted corn salsa and lime vinaigrette, or roast duck with mango glaze and toasted coconut.

3250 Rte. 6A (in the center of town), Barnstable. ℂ 508/362-6610. Main courses $14–$21. AE, DC, MC, V. May–Oct Mon–Sat 11:30am–3pm; daily 5–9:30pm; call for off-season hours.

Mattakeese Wharf ★ SEAFOOD   This place, with great views and average food, is always packed; don't even bother on summer weekends. The outdoor seating fills up first—the broad decks jut out into the harbor and afford sunset views to Sandy Neck. The fish is fresh but preparations are bland. The bouilla-baisse, however, is always good. And you can't go wrong if you stick to the varied combinations of pasta, seafood, and sauce, from Alfredo to *fra diavolo*. There's live piano music most nights in season.

271 Mill Way (about ½ mile north of Rte. 6A), Barnstable. ℂ 508/362-4511. Reservations recommended. Main courses $12–$25. AE, MC, V. June–Oct daily 11:30am–10pm; call for off-season hours. Closed Nov–Apr.

YARMOUTH

Yarmouth represents the Cape at its best—and worst. **Yarmouth Port** ★★★, on Cape Cod Bay, is an enchanting village, whereas the sound-side "villages" of West to South Yarmouth are a lesson in unbridled development run amuck. This section of Route 28 is a nightmarish strip of mostly tacky accommodations and "attractions."

ESSENTIALS

GETTING THERE   After crossing either the Bourne or the Sagamore bridge, head east on Route 6 or 6A. Route 6A (north of Route 6, Exit 7) passes through the village of Yarmouth Port. The villages of West Yarmouth, Bass River, and South Yarmouth are located along Route 28, east of Hyannis; to reach them from Route 6, take Exit 7 south (Yarmouth Road) or Exit 8 south (Station Street).

VISITOR INFORMATION   Contact the **Yarmouth Area Chamber of Commerce,** 657 Rte. 28, West Yarmouth (© **800/732-1008** or 508/778-1008; fax 508/778-5114; www.yarmouthcapecod.com).

BEACHES & OUTDOOR PURSUITS

BEACHES   Yarmouth boasts 11 saltwater and two pond beaches open to the public. The body-per-square-yard ratio can be pretty intense along the sound, but so's the social scene, so no one seems to mind. The beachside parking lots charge $10 a day and sell weeklong stickers for $40.

- **Bass River Beach,** off South Shore Drive in Bass River (South Yarmouth): Located at the mouth of the largest tidal river on the eastern seaboard, this sound beach offers rest rooms, a snack bar, and a wheelchair-accessible fishing pier. The beaches along the south shore (Nantucket Sound) tend to be clean and sandy with comfortable water temps (kids will want to stay in all day), but they can also be quite crowded during peak times. You'll need a beach sticker to park here.

- **Grays Beach,** off Center Street in Yarmouth Port: This isn't much of a beach, but tame waters make the tiny spit good for young children; it adjoins the Callery-Darling Conservation Area (see "Nature & Wildlife Areas," below). The Bass Hole boardwalk offers one of the most scenic walks in the Mid Cape. Parking is free, and there's a picnic area.

- **Parker's River Beach,** off South Shore Drive in Bass River: This choice has the usual amenities like rest rooms and a snack bar, plus a 20-foot gazebo for the sun-shy.

- **Seagull Beach,** off South Sea Avenue in West Yarmouth: Rolling dunes, a boardwalk, and all the necessary facilities, like rest rooms and a snack bar, attract a young crowd. Bring bug spray, though: Greenhead flies get the munchies in July.

FISHING   Of the five fishing ponds in the Yarmouth area, **Long Pond,** near South Yarmouth, is known for its largemouth bass and pickerel; for details and a license (shellfishing is another option), visit **Town Hall,** 1146 Rte. 28, South Yarmouth (© **508/398-2231**), or **Riverview Bait and Tackle,** 1273 Rte. 28, South Yarmouth (© **508/394-1036**). Full-season licenses for state residents cost $28.50; for out-of-staters, $38.50. You can cast for striped bass and bluefish off the pier at Bass River Beach (see above).

NATURE & WILDLIFE AREAS   In Yarmouth Port, follow Centre Street about a mile north and bear northeast on Homers Dock Road; from here, a 2½-mile trail through the **Callery-Darling Conservation Area** leads to Grays Beach, where you can continue across the Bass Hole Boardwalk.

MUSEUMS

Winslow Crocker House ★★   The only property on the Cape currently preserved by the prestigious Society for the Preservation of New England Antiquities, this house, built around 1780, deserves every honor. Not only is it a lovely example of the shingled Georgian style, but it's also packed with outstanding antiques—Jacobean to Chippendale—collected in the 1930s by Mary Thacher, a descendent of the town's first land grantee. Anthony Thacher and his family had a rougher crossing than most: Their ship foundered off Cape Ann in 1635, and though their four children drowned, Thacher and his wife were able to

make it to shore, clinging to the family cradle. You'll come across a 1690 replica
in the parlor.

250 Rte. 6A (about ½ mile east of the town center), Yarmouth Port. ✆ 508/362-4385. Admission $4 adults,
$3.50 seniors, $2 children 6–12, free to Cape Cod residents. June to mid-Oct hourly tours Sat–Sun 11am–5pm
(last tour at 4pm). Closed mid-Oct to May.

SHOPPING

Driving Route 6A, the Old King's Highway, in Yarmouth Port, you'll pass a
number of antiques stores and fine shops for the home. Ron Kusins's pewter
designs range from the traditional to the contemporary. You can watch this
nearly extinct art in action at **Pewter Crafters of Cape Cod,** 933 Rte. 6A (near
the Dennis border), Yarmouth Port (✆ **508/362-3407**).

The most colorful bookshop on the Cape is **Parnassus Books,** 220 Rte. 6A,
Yarmouth Port (✆ **508/362-6420**), housed in an 1858 Swedenborgian church.
Relevant new stock, including the Cape-related reissues published by Parnassus
Imprints, is offered alongside the older treasures; don't expect much hand-hold-
ing on the part of the gruff proprietor. The outdoor racks, maintained on an
honor system, are open 24 hours a day.

WHERE TO STAY

Captain Farris House ★★   Sumptuous is the only way to describe this 1845
inn, improbably set amid a peaceful garden a block off bustling Route 28. Fine
antiques and striking contemporary touches lift this inn's interiors way above the
average B&B decor. Some suites are apartment-size, with fireplaces and
whirlpool-tub bathrooms. Welcoming touches include chocolates and fresh
flowers. Next door, the 1825 Elisha Jenkins House contains an additional large
suite with its own deck. Breakfast consists of three courses served in the formal
dining room or the sunny courtyard.

308 Old Main St. (just west of the Bass River Bridge), Bass River, MA 02664-4530. ✆ 800/350-9477 or
508/760-2818. Fax 508/398-1262. www.captainfarris.com. 10 units. Summer $110–$160 double; $175–$225
suite. Rates include breakfast. AE, DISC, MC, V. In room: A/C, TV/VCR, dataport, hair dryer, iron.

Red Jacket ★★   Of the huge resort motels lining Nantucket Sound in South
Yarmouth, Red Jacket has the best location. It's at the end of the road and borders Parker's River on the west, so sunsets are particularly fine. Families who
want all the fixings will find them, though the atmosphere can be a bit impersonal. All rooms have a balcony or porch; you'll want one overlooking the private beach on Nantucket Sound or looking out towards the river. Some rooms
have Jacuzzis. Off-season rates can be as low as $85.

S. Shore Dr. (Box 88), South Yarmouth, MA 02664. ✆ 800/672-0500 or 508/398-6941. Fax 508/398-1214.
www.redjacketinns.com/redjacket. 150 units, 13 cottages. Summer $185–$280 double; $350–$570 cottages.
MC, V. Closed Nov to mid-Apr. **Amenities:** Restaurant, bar/lounge; indoor and outdoor heated pools; tennis
court; exercise rooms; whirlpool; sauna; basketball; volleyball; putting green; equipment rental (parasailing,
kayaks, paddleboats, sailboats); children's programs; concierge; catamaran cruises. In room: A/C, TV, fridge.

Wedgewood Inn ★★   This elegant 1812 Federal house sits atop its undulating lawn with unabashed pride. Innkeeper Gerrie Graham provides a warm welcome, complete with tea delivered to your room. In the main house, the formal
and spacious front bedrooms have pencil-post beds, Oriental rugs, antique
quilts, and wood-burning fireplaces, while the downstairs rooms have private
screened porches. The two romantic hideaways under the eaves are decorated in
a cheerful country style. The picturesque barn contains three very private suites,

with canopy beds, fireplaces, and decks. These suites also include telephones and TVs cleverly tucked into painted cabinets.

83 Main St./Rte. 6A (in the center of town), Yarmouth Port, MA 02675. ✆ **508/362-5157** or 508/362-9178. Fax 508/362-5851. www.wedgewood-inn.com. 9 units. Summer $140–$205 double. Rates include breakfast. AE, MC, V. *In room:* A/C, hair dryer, no phone (except in barn units).

WHERE TO DINE

Unsuspecting passersby invariably do a double take when they happen upon **Hallet's,** 139 Rte. 6A, Yarmouth Port (✆ **508/362-3362**), an 1889 drugstore where you can get a float from the original marble soda fountain.

abbicci ★★ NORTHERN ITALIAN Many consider this sophisticated venue *the* place to eat on Cape Cod. While the exterior is a modest 18th-century Cape, the interior features mosaic floors and mural-covered walls in several cozy rooms. The knowledgeable staff delivers delicious, artfully prepared seafood dishes as well as veal, lamb, and, of course, pasta. A taste of the veal *nocciole* (with toasted hazelnuts and a splash of balsamic vinegar), and you'll be transported straight to Tuscany. This small restaurant can get overburdened on summer weekends; expect a wait even with a reservation.

43 Main St./Rte. 6A (near the Cummaquid border), Yarmouth Port. ✆ **508/362-3501.** Reservations recommended. Main courses $16–$28. AE, DC, DISC, MC, V. Daily 5–10pm.

Inaho ★★ JAPANESE What better application of the Cape's oceanic bounty than fresh-off-the-boat sushi? From the front, Inaho is a typical Cape Cod cottage, but park in the back so you can enter through the Japanese garden. Inside, it's a veritable *shibui* sanctuary, with minimalist decor softened by tranquil music and service. On chilly days, opt for the tempura or a steaming bowl of shabu-shabu.

157 Main St./Rte. 6A (in the village center), Yarmouth Port. ✆ **508/362-5522.** Reservations not accepted. Main courses $12–$20; sushi and rolls $4–$9. MC, V. Tues–Sun 5–10pm; call for off-season hours.

Jack's Out Back ★★ *Kids* AMERICAN   This neighborhood cafe is hyperactive and full of fun. Chef/owner Jack Braginton-Smith makes a point of dishing out good-natured insults along with the home-style grub, which you bus yourself from the open kitchen. This is a perfect place for impatient children, who'll find lots of familiar, approachable dishes.

161 Main St./Rte. 6A (behind Main St. buildings, in the center of town), Yarmouth Port. ✆ 508/362-6690. Most items under $7. No credit cards. Daily 6:30am–2pm.

DENNIS

In Dennis, as in Yarmouth, virtually all the good stuff—pretty drives, inviting shops, restaurants with real personality—are in the north, along Route 6A. Route 28 is chockablock with RV parks and generic motels. Spend most of your time in Dennis Village and not its southern offshoots.

ESSENTIALS

GETTING THERE   After crossing either the Bourne or the Sagamore bridge, head east on Route 6 or 6A. Route 6A passes through the villages of Dennis and East Dennis (which can also be reached via northbound Route 134 from Route 6, Exit 9). Route 134 south leads to the village of South Dennis; if you follow Route 134 all the way to Route 28, the village of West Dennis will be a couple of miles to your west, and Dennisport a couple of miles east.

VISITOR INFORMATION   Contact the **Dennis Chamber of Commerce,** 242 Swan River Rd., West Dennis (✆ **800/243-9920** or 508/398-3568; www.dennischamber.com).

BEACHES & OUTDOOR PURSUITS

BEACHES   Dennis harbors more than a dozen saltwater and two freshwater beaches open to nonresidents. The bay beaches are charming and a big hit with families, who prize the easygoing surf. The beaches on the sound also tend to attract wall-to-wall families, but the parking lots are usually not too crowded, since so many beachgoers choose accommodations within walking distance. The lots charge $10 per day; for a weeklong permit ($34), visit **Town Hall,** on Main Street in South Dennis (✆ **508/760-6159**).

- **Chapin Beach,** off Route 6A in Dennis: A nice, long bay beach pocked with occasional boulders and surrounded by dunes. No lifeguard, but there are rest rooms available.
- **Corporation Beach,** off Route 6A in Dennis: Before it filled in with sand, this bay beach—with a wheelchair-accessible boardwalk, lifeguards, snack bar, rest rooms, and children's play area—was once a packet landing owned by a shipbuilding corporation and donated to the town by Mary Thacher, owner of the Winslow Crocker House (see p. 202).
- **Mayflower Beach,** off Route 6A in Dennis: This 1,200-foot bay beach has the necessary amenities, plus an accessible boardwalk. The tidal pools attract lots of children.
- **Scargo Lake,** in Dennis: This large kettle-hole pond (formed by a melting fragment of a glacier) has two pleasant beaches: Scargo Beach, accessible right off Route 6A; and Princess Beach, off Scargo Hill Road, where there are rest rooms and a picnic area.
- **West Dennis Beach,** off Route 28 in West Dennis: This long (1½-mile) but narrow beach along the sound has lifeguards, a playground, a snack bar, rest rooms, and a special kite-flying area. The eastern end is reserved for residents; the west end tends to be less packed.

BICYCLING The 25-mile **Cape Cod Rail Trail** 🚴🚴🚴 (© **508/896-3491**) starts here, on Route 134, ½ mile south of Route 6, Exit 9. Once a Penn Central track, this 8-foot-wide paved bikeway extends all the way to Wellfleet (with a few on-road lapses), passing through woods, marshes, and dunes. At the trailhead is **Bob's Bike Shop,** 430 Rte. 134, South Dennis (© **508/760-4723**), which rents bikes and in-line skates. Rates are $10 for a couple hours, up to $22 for the full day. Another paved bike path runs along Old Bass Road, 3½ miles north to Route 6A.

FISHING Fishing is allowed in **Fresh Pond** and **Scargo Lake;** for a license (shellfishing is also permitted), visit **Town Hall,** on Main Street in South Dennis (© **508/394-8300**), or **Riverview Bait and Tackle,** 1273 Rte. 28 in South Yarmouth (© **508/394-1036**). Plenty of people drop a line off the **Bass River Bridge** along Route 28 in West Dennis. Several charter boats operate out of the Northside Marina in East Dennis's Sesuit Harbor, including the *Albatross* (© **508/385-3244**).

NATURE & WILDLIFE AREAS Behind the Town Hall parking lot on Main Street in South Dennis, a ½-mile walk along the **Indian Lands Conservation Trail** leads to the Bass River, where blue herons and kingfishers often take shelter. Dirt roads off South Street in East Dennis, beyond the Quivet Cemetery, lead to **Crow's Pasture,** a patchwork of marshes and dunes bordering the bay; this trail is about a 2½-mile round-trip.

WATER SPORTS Located on the small and placid Swan River, **Cape Cod Waterways,** 16 Rte. 28, Dennisport (© **508/398-0080**), rents canoes, kayaks, and paddleboats for exploring 200-acre Swan Pond (less than a mile north) or Nantucket Sound (2 miles south). A 1-day rental costs $35.

MUSEUMS

Cape Museum of Fine Arts 🚴 Part of the prettily landscaped Cape Playhouse complex, this small museum has done a great job of acquiring hundreds of works by area artists dating back to the turn of the 20th century.

60 Hope Lane (off Rte. 6A in the center of town). © **508/385-4477**. www.cmfa.org. Admission $5 adults, free for children under 16. May–Oct Mon–Sat 10am–5pm, Sun 1–5pm; Oct–May Tues–Sat 10am–5pm, Sun 1–5pm. Open year-round.

SHOPPING

There's a growing cluster of flea market–style shops in Dennisport, but you may want to save your time and money for the better antiques shops along Route 6A, where you'll also find fine contemporary crafts.

More than 136 dealers stock the co-op **Antiques Center of Cape Cod,** 243 Rte. 6A (about 1 mile south of Dennis Village center), Dennis (© **508/ 385-6400**); it's the largest such enterprise on the Cape.

Dennis Village along Route 6A has become a magnet for interesting small galleries. Among the finest is **Scargo Stoneware Pottery and Art Gallery** 🚴, 30 Dr. Lord's Rd. S. (off Route 6A, about 1 mile east of the town center), Dennis (© **508/385-3894**).

WHERE TO STAY

Corsair & Cross Rip Resort Motels 🚴 *Kids* Of the many family-oriented motels lining this part of the sound, these two neighbors are among the nicest, with fresh decor, two beach-view pools, and their own chunk of sand. As a

---

Kids **Especially for Kids**

Dennisport boasts a good rainy-day—or any-day—destination for little kids, the nonprofit **Cape Cod Discovery Museum & Toy Shop,** 444 Rte. 28 (✆ **508/398-1600**). Hours are daily from 9:30am to 5:30pm in season, 9:30am to 4:30pm off-season. For a nominal admission, the entire family will enjoy this educational play space equipped with a frozen-shadow wall, a transparent piano, a pretend diner, a dress-up puppet theater, a veterinary shop, and more.

On Friday mornings in season, the **Cape Playhouse,** 820 Rte. 6A, Dennis (✆ **508/385-3911**), hosts various visiting companies that mount children's theater geared toward kids 4 and up; at only $6, tickets go fast.

---

rainy-day backup, there's an indoor pool, a game room, and a toddler playroom equipped with toys. Some units have kitchenettes.

41 Chase Ave. (off Depot St., 1 mile southeast of Rte. 28), Dennisport, MA 02639. ✆ 800/201-1072 or 508/398-2279. Fax 508/760-6681. www.corsaircrossrip.com. 47 units. Summer $135–$155 double; $155–$245 efficiency. Special packages and family weekly rates available. AE, MC, V. **Amenities:** Two outdoor pools; indoor pool; game rooms; coin-op laundry. *In room:* A/C, TV w/ free movies, fridge, coffeemaker.

The Four Chimneys Inn ✯ Scargo Lake is directly across the street, and the village is a brief walk from this imposing 1880 Victorian. Opulent tastes are evident in the high ceilings and marble fireplace of the front parlor. Guest rooms vary in size, but all are appealing, with hand-painted stenciling and wicker furnishings. Three rooms have decks overlooking the lovely grounds. Six units are equipped with TVs; two also have air-conditioning.

946 Rte. 6A (about ½ mile east of the town center), Dennis, MA 02638. ✆ 800/874-5502 or 508/385-6317. Fax 508/385-6285. www.fourchimneysinn.com. 8 units. Summer $90–$155 double; $155 suite. Rates include continental breakfast. AE, MC, V. Closed mid-Oct to mid-Apr. *In room:* No phone.

Isaiah Hall B&B Inn ✯✯ This inn's location, on a quiet side street in a residential neighborhood, bodes well for a good night of sleep, but it's also just a short walk to restaurants and Corporation Beach on Cape Cod Bay. Your animated hostess, Marie Brophy, has been entertaining the entertainers from the nearby Cape Playhouse for over 15 years. Home-baked breakfasts are served at the long plank table that dominates the 1857 country kitchen. Bedroom styles range from 1940s knotty pine to spacious and spiffy.

152 Whig St. (1 block northwest of the Cape Playhouse), Dennis, MA 02638. ✆ 800/736-0160 or 508/385-9928. Fax 508/385-5879. www.isaiahhallinn.com. 10 units. Summer $102–$141 double; $171 suite. Rates include continental breakfast. AE, DISC, MC, V. Closed mid-Oct to late Apr. No children under 7 accepted. *In room:* A/C, TV/VCR.

Lighthouse Inn ✯✯ *Kids* Set smack dab on placid West Dennis Beach on Nantucket Sound, this popular resort has been welcoming families for over 60 years. In 1938, Everett Stone acquired a decommissioned 1885 lighthouse and built a charming inn and a 9-acre cottage colony around it. With amusements such as miniature golf right on the premises, there's plenty to do. The rooms aren't what you'd call fancy, but some have great views. The dining room is open to the public. Lunch is served on the deck overlooking Nantucket Sound, a delightful setting to enjoy a club sandwich.

1 Lighthouse Inn Rd. (off Lower County Rd., ½ mile south of Rte. 28), West Dennis, MA 02670. ✆ 508/398-2244. Fax 508/398-5658. www.lighthouseinn.com. 44 units, 24 cottages. Summer $206–$250

double; $405–$488 2-bedroom cottage. MC, V. Rates include breakfast and all gratuities. Closed mid-Oct to mid-May. **Amenities:** Restaurant, bar with cabaret-style entertainment; outdoor heated pool and pool house/changing rooms; miniature golf; tennis court; volleyball; children's programs (in July and August); game room; shuffleboard. *In room:* TV/VCR, fridge, hair dryer, safe.

WHERE TO DINE

Sundae School ✸, 387 Lower County Rd. (at Sea Street, about a third of a mile south of Route 28), Dennisport (✆ **508/394-9122**), features a turn-of-the-20th-century marble soda fountain.

Bob Briggs' Wee Packet Restaurant and Bakery ✸✸ SEAFOOD Since 1949, this tiny joint has served all the requisite seafood staples, plus steak and chicken dishes. Grab a Formica table for a traditional summer feast topped off by a timeless dessert such as blueberry shortcake.

79 Depot St. (at Lower County Rd., about ⅓ mile south of the town center), Dennisport. ✆ 508/398-2181. Main courses $6–$15. MC, V. Late June to early Sept daily 8am–8:30pm; May to late June daily 11:30am–8:30pm. Closed mid-Sept to Apr.

The Dog House ✸ HOT DOGS Hot dogs, cheese dogs, and chili dogs are the specialty at this tiny hut, but there are also hamburgers and salmon burgers. Onion rings are hand-battered, and the chili's homemade. Grab a picnic table in this pine glade, and wash it all down with fresh lemonade.

179 Lower County Rd. (about ½ mile from Nantucket Sound), Dennisport. ✆ 508/398-7774. All items under $10. No credit cards. Late May to mid-Sept daily 11am–8pm; call for off-season hours. Closed Nov–Apr.

Gina's by the Sea ✸✸ ITALIAN A landmark amid Dennis's "Little Italy" beach community since 1938, this intimate restaurant specializes in traditional Italian comfort food, such as homemade ravioli stuffed with smoked mozzarella. Save room for Mrs. Riley's Chocolate Rum Cake, made daily by the owner's mother. This popular place fills up fast, so if you want to eat before 8:30pm, arrive before 5:30pm.

134 Taunton Ave. (about 1½ miles northwest of Rte. 6A, off New Boston and Beach sts.). ✆ 508/385-3213. Reservations not accepted. Main courses $10–$23. AE, MC, V. June–Sept daily 5–10pm; Apr–May and Oct–Nov Thurs–Sun 5–10pm. Closed Dec–Mar.

The Marshside ✸✸ AMERICAN This is one of the Cape's best diners, a well-run establishment overlooking a picturesque marsh. There's a relaxed atmosphere that comes from having a year-round staff that knows what it's doing (a rarity on the Cape). The food is fresh, tasty, and cheap, be it a fried-fish platter, a burger, or a veggie melt. Save room for homemade desserts.

28 Bridge St. (at the junction of Routes 134 and 6A), East Dennis. ✆ 508/385-4010. Main courses $7–$15. AE, DC, DISC, MC, V. Daily 7am–9pm. Open year-round.

The Red Pheasant Inn ✸✸ CONTEMPORARY AMERICAN An enduring Cape favorite since 1977, this handsome space—an 18th-century barn turned chandlery—has managed not only to keep pace with trends, but also to remain a front-runner. Favorites include roast rack of lamb, boneless roast duckling, and sole meunière. In the fall, expect game specials like venison and ostrich. The signature cherrystone-and-scallop chowder gets its zip from fresh-plucked thyme. Two massive brick fireplaces tend to be the focal point in the off-season. In fine weather, sit out in the garden room.

905 Main St. (about ½ mile east of the town center), Dennis. ✆ 508/385-2133. Reservations recommended. Main courses $17–$27. DISC, MC, V. Apr–Dec daily 5–10pm; Jan–Mar Wed–Sun 5–10pm.

Scargo Cafe ✪ INTERNATIONAL   A richly paneled captain's house given a modernist reworking, this lively bistro deftly spans old and new with a menu neatly split into "traditional" and "adventurous" categories. Traditionalists will find the popular grilled lamb loins served with mint jelly; adventurous dishes include "wildcat chicken" (a sauté with sausage, mushrooms, and raisins, flambéed with apricot brandy). Lighter nibbles, such as burgers or Scallop Harpoon—a bacon-wrapped skewerful, served over rice—are available all day, a boon for beachgoers who tend to return ravenous. A kitchen that's open until 11pm makes this the perfect (and only) place in the neighborhood to go after a show at the Cape Playhouse.

799 Main St./Rte. 6A (opposite the Cape Playhouse). ℂ **508/385-8200**. Main courses $11–$21. AE, DISC, MC, V. Mid-June to mid-Sept daily 11am–3pm and 4:30–11pm; mid-Sept to mid-June 11am–10pm.

DENNIS AFTER DARK

The oldest continuously active straw-hat theater in the country and still one of the best, **The Cape Playhouse** ✪✪, 820 Rte. 6A (ℂ **877/385-3911** or 508/385-3911), was the 1927 brainstorm of Raymond Moore, who'd spent a few summers as a playwright in Provincetown and quickly tired of the strictures of "little theater." Salvaging an 1838 meetinghouse, he plunked it amid a meadow and got his New York buddy, designer Cleon Throckmorton, to turn it into a proper theater. It was an immediate success, and a parade of stars have trod the boards in the decades since, from Humphrey Bogart to Jane Fonda. Not all of today's headliners are quite as impressive, but the theater can be counted on for a varied season of polished work. Performances are staged from mid-June to early September. Tickets range from $15 to $35.

The **Cape Cinema** ✪✪✪, 36 Hope Lane, off Route 6A, in the center of town (ℂ **508/385-2503** or 508/385-5644), is an Art Deco surprise, with a Prometheus-themed ceiling mural. George Mansour, curator of the Harvard Film Archive, sees to the art-house programming. The setting and seating—black leather armchairs—may spoil you forever.

3 The Lower Cape

The Lower Cape towns tend to attract a more elite crowd of vacationers. Not surprisingly, the area supports the Cape's priciest shops, restaurants, inns, and rental cottages (many of which occupy prime locations on inlets and waterways).

Located on the easternmost portion of historic Route 6A, **Brewster** still enjoys much the same cachet that it boasted as a high roller in the maritime trade. But for a relatively recent incursion of condos—and with it, increased car traffic—it looks much as it might have in the late 19th century, with its general store still serving as a social centerpiece. Perhaps because excellence breeds competition, Brewster has spawned several fine restaurants and has become something of a magnet for gourmands.

Chatham ✪✪✪, the Cape's most chichi town, is touted by realtors as "the Nantucket of the Cape." Its Main Street offers appealing shops and eateries, complemented by a scenic lighthouse and plentiful beaches nearby.

As the gateway to the Outer Cape, where all roads merge, **Orleans** sports a bustling Main Street with a number of fine shops. Its nearby cousin, **East Orleans,** is on the upswing as a destination, offering a couple of fun restaurants and—best of all—a goodly chunk of magnificent, unspoiled Cape Cod National Seashore.

BREWSTER

With miles of placid Cape Cod Bay beach and 2,000 acres of state park, Brewster is an attractive place for vacationing families. Route 6A, the Old King's Highway, becomes Brewster's Main Street and houses a bevy of B&Bs, pricey restaurants, and the Cape's finest antiques shops. The town has also managed to absorb an intrusively huge development within its borders, the 380-acre condo complex known as Ocean Edge. Brewster also welcomes the tens of thousands of transient campers and day-trippers who arrive each summer to enjoy hiking and canoeing in Nickerson State Park.

ESSENTIALS

GETTING THERE   After crossing either the Bourne or the Sagamore bridge, head east on Route 6 or 6A. Route 6A passes through the villages of West Brewster, Brewster, and East Brewster. You can also reach Brewster by taking Route 6, Exit 10 north, along Route 124.

VISITOR INFORMATION   The **Visitor Center** is behind the Town Hall, 2198 Main St./Rte. 6A, Brewster (© **508/896-3500;** fax 508/896-1086; www.capecodtravel.com/brewster).

BEACHES & OUTDOOR PURSUITS

BEACHES   Brewster's eight bay beaches have minimal facilities. When the tide is out, the beach extends as much as 2 miles, leaving behind tidal pools to splash in and explore, and vast stretches of rippled, reddish sand. On a clear day, you can see the whole curve of the Cape, from Sandwich to Provincetown. You can purchase a beach parking sticker ($8 per day, $25 per week) at the **Visitor Center,** behind Town Hall, 2198 Main St./Rte. 6A (© **508/896-4511**).

- **Breakwater Beach,** off Breakwater Road, Brewster: Only a brief walk from the center of town, this calm, shallow beach (the only one with rest rooms) is ideal for young children.
- **Flax Pond** in Nickerson State Park (see "Nature & Wildlife Areas," below): This large freshwater pond, surrounded by pines, has a bathhouse and offers water-sports rentals. The park contains two more ponds with beaches—Cliff and Little Cliff. Access and parking are free.
- **Linnells Landing Beach,** on Linnell Road in East Brewster: This is a half-mile, wheelchair-accessible bay beach.
- **Paines Creek Beach,** off Paines Creek Road, West Brewster: With 1½ miles to stretch out on, this bay beach has something to offer sun lovers and nature lovers alike. Your kids will love it if you arrive when the tide's coming in—the current will give an air mattress a nice little ride.

BICYCLING   The **Cape Cod Rail Trail** 🚲🚲🚲 intersects with the 8-mile **Nickerson State Park** trail system at the park entrance, where there's plenty of free parking; you could follow the Rail Trail back to Dennis (about 12 miles) or onward toward Wellfleet (13 miles). In season, **Idle Times** (© **508/255-8281**) provides rentals within the park. Another good place to jump in is on Underpass Road about a half mile south of Route 6A. Here you'll find **Brewster Bicycle Rental,** 442 Underpass Rd. (© **508/896-8149**), and **Brewster Express,** which makes sandwiches to go. Just up the hill is the well-equipped **Rail Trail Bike & Blade,** 302 Underpass Rd. (© **508/896-8200**). Both shops offer free parking. Bicycle rentals start at around $12 for 4 hours and go up to about $18 for 24 hours.

Biking the Cape Cod Rail Trail

The 25-mile Cape Cod Rail Trail ★★★ is one of New England's longest and most popular bike paths. Once a bed of the Penn Central Railroad, the trail is relatively flat and straight. On weekends in summer months, you'll have to contend with dogs, in-line skaters, young families, and bikers who whip by you on their way to becoming the next Lance Armstrong. Still, if you want to venture away from the coast and see some of the Cape's countryside without having to deal with motorized traffic, this is one of the best ways to do it.

The trail starts in South Wellfleet on Lecount Hollow Road or in South Dennis on Mass. 134, depending on which way you want to ride. Beginning in South Wellfleet, the path cruises by purple wildflowers, flowering dogwood, and small maples, where red-winged blackbirds and goldfinches nest. In Orleans, you'll have to ride on Rock Harbor and West roads until the City Council decides to complete the trail. Fortunately, the roads provide a good view of the boats lining Rock Harbor. Clearly marked signs lead back to the Rail Trail. You'll soon enter Nickerson State Park bike trails, or you can continue straight through Brewster to a series of swimming holes—Seymour, Long, and Hinckley's ponds. A favorite picnic spot is the Pleasant Lake General Store in Harwich. Shortly afterward, you'll cross over Route 6 on Mass. 124 before veering right through farmland, soon ending in South Dennis.

—Stephen Jermanok

BOATING   April through October, **Paddle Cape Cod** (📞 **888/226-6393** or 508/564-4051; www.paddlecapecod.com) runs 3- to 3½-hour naturalist-guided trips daily, weather permitting. If you want to explore on your own by canoe, you can rent one at **Goose Hummock,** in Orleans (📞 **508/255-2620**), and paddle around Paines Creek and Quivett Creek, as well as Upper and Lower Mill ponds.

FISHING   Brewster offers more ponds for fishing than any other town: 14 in all. Among the most popular are Cliff and Higgins ponds (within Nickerson State Park), which are regularly stocked. For a license, visit the Town Clerk at **Town Hall,** 2198 Rte. 6A (📞 **508/896-4506**).

GOLF   The 18-hole championship **Ocean Edge Golf Course,** 832 Villages Dr. (📞 **508/896-5911**), is the most challenging in Brewster.

NATURE & WILDLIFE AREAS   Admission is free to the two trails maintained by the Cape Cod Museum of Natural History (see below). The **South Trail,** covering a three-quarter-mile round-trip, crosses a cranberry bog beside Paines Creek to reach a forest of beeches and tupelos; toward the end of the loop, you'll come upon a "glacial erratic," a huge boulder dropped by a receding glacier. Before heading out on the quarter-mile **North Trail,** stop at the museum for a free guide describing the local flora, including wild roses, cattails, and sumacs. Also accessible from the museum is the **John Wing Trail** ★★, a 1½-mile network traversing 140 acres of preservation land, including upland, salt marsh, and beach. (*Note:* This can be a soggy trip. Be sure to heed the posted warnings about high tides, especially in spring, or you might very well find yourself stranded.)

As it crosses Route 6A, Paines Creek Road becomes Run Hill Road. Follow it to the end to reach **Punkhorn Park Lands,** an undeveloped 800-acre tract popular with mountain bikers; it features several kettle ponds, a "quaking bog," and 45 miles of dirt paths composing three marked trails.

The 25-acre **Spruce Hill Conservation Area,** behind the Brewster Historical Society Museum, includes a 600-foot stretch of beach, reached by a former carriage road reportedly favored by Prohibition bootleggers.

Just east of the museum is the 1,955-acre **Nickerson State Park,** at Route 6 and Crosby Lane (© **508/896-3491**). This back-to-nature preserve encompasses 418 campsites (reservations pour in a year in advance, but some are held open for new arrivals willing to wait a day or two), eight kettle ponds, and 8 miles of bike paths.

WATER SPORTS Various small sailboats, kayaks, canoes, and even aqua bikes (also known as sea cycles) are available seasonally at **Jack's Boat Rentals,** on Flax Pond within Nickerson State Park (© **508/896-8556**).

MUSEUMS

Cape Cod Museum of Natural History ★ (Kids)
Long before "ecology" became a buzzword, noted naturalist writer John Hay helped to found a museum that works to preserve Cape Cod's unique landscape. Open since 1954, the museum has a number of interesting interactive exhibits. The children's exhibits include an animal-puppet theater and a "live hive"—like an ant farm, only with busy bees. Four marine-room tanks contain fish, turtles, frogs, crabs, lobster, starfish, and mollusks. The bulk of the museum is outdoors, where 85 acres invite exploration (see "Nature & Wildlife Areas," above). There's an on-site archaeology lab on Wing Island, thought to have sheltered one of Brewster's first settlers—the Quaker John Wing, driven from Sandwich in the mid–17th century by religious persecution—and before him, native tribes dating back 10 millennia. The museum sponsors lectures, concerts, marsh cruises, bike tours, and "eco-treks"—including a sleepover on uninhabited Monomoy Island off Chatham. Other activities include astronomy cruises and seal cruises.

869 Rte. 6A (about 2 miles west of the town center). © **800/479-3867** in eastern Mass., or 508/896-3867. www.ccmnh.org. Admission $5 adults, $4.50 seniors, $2 children 5–12. Mon–Sat 9:30am–4:30pm; Sun 11am–4:30pm. Closed major holidays. Open year-round.

SHOPPING

Brewster's stretch of Route 6A offers the best antiquing on the Cape. The artifacts at **Kingsland Manor Antiques,** 440 Rte. 6A, about 1 mile east of the Dennis border (© **800/486-2305** or 508/385-9741), tend to be on the flamboyant side—which makes browsing all the more fun. There's always an interesting variety at **Monomoy Antiques,** 3425 Rte. 6A (© **508/896-6570**), including finds from local estate sales. Specialties include rare books, English china, Native American artifacts, and decoys.

Imagine a town dump full of treasures, and you'll get an idea of what's in store at **Diane Vetromile's Antiques,** 3884 Rte. 6A (no phone). If the sign that reads ANTIQUES is out, it's open. This place is a tad kooky, but any junk aficionado will be thrilled by the pickings: hubcaps, iron rakes, wood shutters—the more peeled paint, the better. Owner Diane Vetromile is herself a sculptor, who works with (surprise) found objects; her work is on view at Jacob Fanning Gallery and Farmhouse Antiques, both in Wellfleet.

No one should miss the venerable **Brewster Store,** 1935 Main St. (© **508/ 896-3744**), built as a church in 1852. Inside, you'll find everything from penny candy to comics to the best-selling Brewster Store Coffee. Neighbors meet on the wide front porch to catch up on village gossip.

WHERE TO STAY

Candleberry Inn 🏛 The decor in this 18th-century Federal home is country but not cutesy, with wide-board floors, wainscoting, and windows with original glass. Some guest rooms have working fireplaces and canopy beds. Three rooms in the carriage house are decorated in a more contemporary style; two share a deck, and all have TVs. In season, the three-course breakfast is served on the sunny porch overlooking 2 acres of landscaped grounds. Guests love the view of Main Street from the glider rocking benches on the lawn. The innkeepers also rent two off-site cottages—one on the beach in Brewster, the other in Chatham with marsh views.

1882 Main St./Rte. 6A, Brewster, MA 02631. © **800/573-4769** or 508/896-3300. Fax 508/896-4016. www.candleberryinn.com. 9 units. Summer $95–$225 double. Rates include breakfast. AE, DISC, MC, V. In room: A/C, hair dryer.

Captain Freeman Inn 🏛🏛 This deluxe 1866 Victorian inn has a terrific location, right next to the Brewster Store and within walking distance of a pretty bay beach. The "luxury rooms"—each with fireplace and private porch with a hot tub for two—incorporate every extra you could hope for: a canopied, four-poster bed, a TV/VCR, even a little fridge prestocked with soda. The plainer rooms are just as pretty. Innkeeper Carol Edmondson teaches cooking classes here, so you can be sure breakfasts are top-notch.

15 Breakwater Rd. (off Rte. 6A, in the town center), Brewster, MA 02631. © **800/843-4664** or 508/896-7481. Fax 508/896-5618. www.captainfreemaninn.com. 12 units. Summer $135–$250 double. Rates include breakfast and afternoon tea. AE, MC, V. No children under 10 accepted. **Amenities:** Outdoor pool; badminton; croquet; bikes (free); video library.

Michael's Cottages (Kids) These family-friendly cottages are small but centrally located. Across the street is Brewster's Drummer Boy park, which hosts summer band concerts and has a playground, historic windmill, and antique house. The closest beach is Paine's Creek, about a mile away. The cottages have screened porches, fireplaces, and microwaves. The two-bedroom cottage also has a dishwasher and washer/dryer.

618 Main St./Rte. 6A, Brewster, MA 02631. © **800/399-2967** or 508/896-4025. Fax 508/896-3158. www.sunsol.com/michaels. 7 units. Summer $115 double. July–Aug, rentals are by the week only: $625–$700 double; $1,025 2-bedroom. AE, DISC, MC, V. Closed mid-Nov to late Apr. In room: A/C, TV.

Old Sea Pines Inn 🏛🏛 (Value) (Kids) In the main house, the parlor, the expansive porch lined with rockers, and the handful of rather minuscule bedrooms recall the inn's days as the Sea Pines School of Charm and Personality for Young Women. (These bargain rooms with shared bathrooms are the only ones in the house without air-conditioning, but at $65 per night, who cares?) The annex rooms are playful, with colorful accoutrements such as pink TVs. Sundays from mid-June to mid-September, Old Sea Pines is the site of a dinner-theater performance by the Cape Cod Repertory Theatre.

2553 Main St. (about 1 mile east of the town center), Brewster, MA 02631. © **508/896-6114**. Fax 508/896-7387. www.oldseapinesinn.com. 24 units (5 with shared bathroom). Summer $65–$135 double; $125–$155 suite. Rates include breakfast and afternoon tea. AE, DC, DISC, MC, V. Closed Jan–Mar. In room: No phone.

WHERE TO DINE
Very Expensive

The Bramble Inn Restaurant ★★★ INTERNATIONAL   Often named among the best restaurants on Cape Cod, the Bramble Inn is also one of the most expensive—but worth it for a special night out. Five dining rooms are each imbued with a distinct personality, from sporting (the Tack Room) to best-Sunday-behavior (the Elegant Parlor). But the highlight is Ruth Manchester's extraordinary cuisine. A four-course menu that evolves every few weeks gives her free rein to incorporate seasonal delicacies. Her assorted seafood curry (with lobster, cod, scallops, and shrimp in a light curry sauce with grilled banana, toasted almonds, coconut, and chutney) and rack of lamb (with deep-fried beet-and-fontina polenta, pan-seared zucchini, and mustard port cream) were written up in the *New York Times*.

2019 Main St. (about ⅓ mile east of Rte. 124). ✆ **508/896-7644.** Reservations suggested. Fixed-price dinner $48–$58. AE, DISC, MC, V. June to mid-Oct Tues–Sun 6–9pm; call for off-season hours. Closed Nov to mid-May.

Chillingsworth ★★ FRENCH   This longtime contender for the title of best restaurant on the Cape now has two dining options: fancy with jackets suggested for men, and more casual with no reservations. The fancy dining room boasts antique appointments and a six-course table d'hôte menu that will challenge the most shameless gourmands. Specialties include steamed lobster over spinach and fennel with sea beans and lobster-basil butter sauce; and seared and roasted boneless rib-eye of veal with fresh morels, mushroom torte, and asparagus. Finish with warm chocolate cake with pistachio ice cream and chocolate drizzle. Or try the moderately priced Bistro, which serves meals in the adjoining greenhouse or on the shady lawn.

2449 Main St. (about 1 mile east of the town center). ✆ **800/430-3640** or 508/896-3640. Reservations suggested. Jacket advised for men in fine-dining section. Fixed-price meals $50–$68. Bistro main courses $13–$24. AE, DC, MC, V. Mid-June to mid-Oct Tues–Sun 11:30am–2:30pm and 6–9:30pm; call for off-season hours. Closed late Nov to mid-May.

High Brewster ★★★ CLASSIC AMERICAN   By candlelight, the cozy rooms of this 1738 colonial are irresistibly romantic. Robert Hickey's sensual, sophisticated cuisine only serves to intensify the mood. Dishes tend to be bold—mushroom-filled ravioli, for instance, with fresh tomato salsa, or pan-seared salmon with sun-dried tomato vinaigrette—yet Hickey's good at adapting local ingredients with traditional preparations to create treats our ancestors could have imagined only in their dreams. What they would have given, heaven only knows, to be able to celebrate the harvest with apple crisp topped with homemade apple-rum ice cream.

964 Satucket Rd. (off Rte. 6A, about 2 miles southwest of the town center). ✆ **508/896-3636.** Reservations required. Fixed-price dinner $45–$65. AE, MC, V. Late May to mid-Sept daily 5:30–9pm; call for off-season hours. Closed Dec–Mar.

Moderate

The Brewster Fish House ★★ NEW AMERICAN   Spare and handsome as a Shaker refectory, this small restaurant bills itself as "nonconforming," and delivers on the promise. The approach to seafood borders on genius: Consider, for instance, squid delectably tenderized in a marinade of soy and ginger, or walnut-crusted ocean catfish accompanied by kale sautéed in Marsala. There are always beef and vegetarian options as well. No wonder the place is packed; better get here early if you want to get in.

2208 Main St. (about ½ mile east of the town center). ☎ **508/896-7867**. Reservations not accepted. Main courses $14–$25. MC, V. May–Aug Mon–Sat 11:30am–3pm and 5–10pm; Sun noon–3pm and 5–9:30pm; call for off-season hours. Closed Jan–Mar.

Inexpensive

Brewster Inn & Chowder House ⭐ ECLECTIC   To get the gist of the expression "chow down," just observe the crowd happily doing so at this plain-ish century-old restaurant. The draw is hearty, predictable staples—homemade chowder; fried, broiled, or baked fish—at prices geared to ordinary people rather than splurging tourists. This place also makes the best martinis in town, and there's a good old bar, the Woodshed, out back.

1993 Rte. 6A (in the center of town). ☎ **508/896-7771**. Main courses $12–$16. AE, DISC, MC, V. Late May to mid-Oct daily 11am–3pm; Sun–Thurs 5–9:30pm; Fri–Sat 5–10pm; call for off-season hours. Open year-round.

Cobie's AMERICAN   Accessible to cars whizzing along Route 6A and within collapsing distance for cyclists on the Rail Trail, this picture-perfect clam shack has been dishing out exemplary fried clams, lobster rolls, foot-long hot dogs, and all the other beloved staples of summer since 1948.

3260 Rte. 6A (about 2 miles east of Brewster center). ☎ **508/896-7021**. Most items under $10. No credit cards. Late May to mid-Sept daily 11am–9pm. Closed mid-Sept to late May.

CHATHAM ⭐⭐⭐

Chatham (say *Chatt*-um) is small-town America the way Norman Rockwell imagined it. Roses climb white picket fences in front of simple Cape cottages, all within a stone's throw of the ocean. The Cape's fanciest town is also its prettiest. As a result, inn rooms are pricier here and rentals are snapped up more quickly. But those looking for a picture-perfect New England town will love Chatham's winding Main Street, filled with pleasing shops and leading to a beautiful beach with lighthouse.

Sticking out from the peninsula like a sore elbow, Chatham was one of the first spots to attract early explorers. Samuel de Champlain stopped by in 1606, but got into a tussle with the prior occupants and left in a hurry. The first colonist to stick around was William Nickerson, who befriended a local *sachem* (tribal leader) and built a house beside his wigwam in 1656. To this day, listings for Nickersons still occupy a half page in the Cape Cod phone book.

Chatham is the only area on the Cape to support a commercial fishing fleet—against increasing odds. Overfishing has resulted in closely monitored limits to give the stock time to bounce back. Boats must now go out as far as 100 miles to catch their fill. Despite the difficulties, it's a way of life few locals would willingly relinquish.

ESSENTIALS

GETTING THERE   After crossing either the Bourne or the Sagamore bridge, head east on Route 6 and take Exit 11 south (Route 137) to Route 28. From this intersection, the village of South Chatham is about a half mile west, and West Chatham is about 1½ miles east. Chatham itself is about 2 miles farther east on Route 28. The town lies 32 miles east of Sandwich, 24 miles south of Provincetown.

VISITOR INFORMATION   Visit the **Chatham Chamber of Commerce,** 533 Main St., Chatham (☎ **800/715-5567** or 508/945-5199; www.chatham capecod.org), or the new **Chatham Chamber booth** (no phone) at the intersection of Routes 137 and 28.

BEACHES & OUTDOOR PURSUITS

BEACHES Chatham has an unusual array of beach styles, from the peaceful shores of Nantucket Sound to the treacherous, shifting shoals along the Atlantic. For information on beach stickers ($8 per day, $35 per week), call the **Permit Department,** on George Ryder Road in West Chatham (© 508/945-5180).

- **Chatham Light Beach:** Located directly below the lighthouse parking lot (where stopovers are limited to 30 minutes), this narrow stretch of sand is easy to get to: Just walk down the stairs. Currents here can be tricky and swift, so swimming is discouraged.
- **Cockle Cove Beach, Ridgevale Beach,** and **Hardings Beach** ✦✦: Lined up along the sound, each at the end of its namesake road south of Route 28, these family-pleasing beaches offer gentle surf suitable for all ages, as well as full facilities.
- **Forest Beach:** No longer an officially recognized town beach (there's no life-guard), this sound landing near the Harwich border is still popular, especially among surfboarders.
- **Oyster Pond Beach,** off Route 28: Only a block from Chatham's Main Street, this sheltered saltwater pond (with rest rooms) swarms with children.
- **South Beach:** A former island jutting out slightly to the south of the Chatham Light, this glorified sandbar can be dangerous, so heed posted warnings and content yourself with strolling or, at most, wading.
- **North Beach:** Extending all the way south from Orleans, this 5-mile barrier beach is accessible from Chatham only by boat; if you don't have your own, you can take the **Beachcomber** (© 508/945-5265), a water taxi, which leaves from the fish pier. The round-trip cost is $12 for adults, $8 for children 3 to 15.

BICYCLING Though Chatham has no separate paths per se, a demarcated bike/blading lane makes a scenic 8-mile circuit of town, heading south onto "The Neck," east to the Chatham Light, up Shore Road all the way to North Chatham, and back to the center of town. A brochure prepared by the **Chatham Chamber of Commerce** (© 800/715-5567 or 508/945-5199) shows the route. Rentals are available at **Bikes & Blades,** 195 Crowell Rd. (© **508/945-7600**).

FISHING Chatham has five ponds and lakes that permit fishing; Goose Pond off Fisherman's Landing is among the top spots. For saltwater fishing sans boat, try the fishing bridge on Bridge Street at the southern end of Mill Pond. First, though, get a license at **Town Hall,** 549 Main St., Chatham (© **508/945-5101**). If you hear the deep sea calling, sign on with the *Booby Hatch* (© **508/430-2312**), a 33-foot sport-fishing boat, or the 31-foot *Banshee* (© **508/945-0403**), both berthed in Stage Harbor. Sportfishing rates average around $550 to $600 for 8 hours. Shellfishing licenses are available at the **Permit Department,** on George Ryder Road in West Chatham (© **508/945-5180**).

NATURE & WILDLIFE AREAS Heading southeast from the Hardings Beach parking lot, the 2-mile round-trip **Seaside Trail** offers beautiful parallel panoramas of Nantucket Sound and Oyster Pond River. Access to 40-acre Morris Island, southwest of the Chatham Light, is easy: You can walk or drive across and start right in on a marked three-quarter-mile trail. Heed the high tides, though—they can come in quickly, leaving you stranded.

The **Beachcomber** (© **508/945-5265**) runs seal-watching cruises out of Stage Harbor. Parking is behind the former Main Street School just on the left before the rotary. The cruises cost $18 for adults, $12 for children 3 to 15.

Chatham's natural bonanza lies southward: The uninhabited **Monomoy Islands** ★★, 2,750 acres of brush-covered sand favored by some 285 species of migrating birds, is the perfect pit stop along the Atlantic Flyway. Harbor and gray seals are catching on, too. If you go out from late November to May, you won't have any trouble seeing them. Both the **Wellfleet Bay Wildlife Sanctuary,** operated by the Audubon Society (© **508/349-2615**), and Brewster's **Cape Cod Museum of Natural History** (© **508/896-3867**) offer guided trips. The Audubon's naturalist-guided trips take place April through November and cost $30 to $60. About a dozen times each summer, the museum organizes sleep-overs in the island's only surviving structure—a clapboard "keeper's house" flanked by an 1849 lighthouse.

WATER SPORTS   Seaworthy vessels, from sailboards to paddle craft, can be rented from **Monomoy Sail and Cycle,** 275 Rte. 28, North Chatham (© **508/945-0811**). Pleasant Bay, the Cape's largest bay, is best for those with experience; if the winds aren't going your way, try Forest Beach on the South Chatham shore. Kayaks and sailboards cost $45 for 24 hours.

SHOPPING

Chatham's tree-shaded Main Street offers a terrific opportunity to shop and stroll. **The Spyglass,** 618 Main St. (© **508/945-9686**), stocks nautical instruments like antique telescopes, sextants, barometers, captains' desks, and maps and charts. The **Artful Hand Gallery,** 459 Main St. (© **508/945-4933**), Boston's premier purveyor of superlative contemporary crafts, is always worth a visit for intriguing fine crafts and gifts. Also of note are **Chatham Glass,** 758 Main St., just west of the Chatham rotary (© **508/945-5547**), with handblown glassworks; and **Chatham Pottery,** 2058 Rte. 28, east of the intersection with Route 137 (© **508/430-2191**).

WHERE TO STAY

Chatham's accommodations tend to be more expensive than those of neighboring towns, as it's considered a fancy place to vacation. But for those allergic to fussy inns, Chatham has several decent motels. Practically across the street from the Chatham Bars Inn, the very basic **Hawthorne,** 196 Shore Rd. (© **508/945-0372;** www.thehawthorne.com), boasts one of the best locations in town: right on the water, with striking views of Chatham Harbor, Pleasant Bay, and the Atlantic. Rates are $150 to $170 double. The personable **Seafarer of Chatham,** 2079 Rte. 28, West Chatham (© **800/786-2772** or 508/432-1739; www.seafarerofchatham.com), lacks a pool, but is only a half mile from Ridgevale Beach. Doubles cost $120 to $145. The cheapest option is the **Chatham Motel,** 1487 Main St./Rte. 28 (© **800/770-5545** or 508/945-2630; www.chathammotel.com), 1½ miles from Hardings Beach. It has an outdoor pool; summer rates are $115.

Very Expensive

Chatham Bars Inn ★★★   Set majestically above the beach in Chatham with commanding views out to a barrier beach and the Atlantic beyond, the grand old Chatham Bars Inn is the premier hotel on Cape Cod. This colonnaded 1914 brick building—surrounded by 26 cottages on 20 acres—has recently undergone a multimillion-dollar renovation. Take in the sweeping views on the breezy veranda, where you can order a drink and recline in an Adirondack chair. Many guest rooms have private balconies with views of the beach or the landscaped grounds. Cottage rooms are cheery with painted furniture and Waverly fabrics.

(*Note:* A dozen or so units have not yet been renovated; inquire when you reserve.) Guests can take meals in the formal Main Dining Room (see "Where to Dine," below), the Tavern, or the seasonal Beach House Grill right on the quarter-mile private beach.

Shore Rd. (off Seaview St., about ½ mile northwest of the town center), Chatham, MA 02633. © 800/527-4884 or 508/945-0096. Fax 508/945-5491. www.chathambarsinn.com. 205 units. Summer $210–$420 double; $425–$540 1-bedroom suite; $580–$1,300 2-bedroom suite. AE, DC, MC, V. **Amenities:** Outdoor heated pool; putting green; nearby public nine-hole course; 3 all-weather tennis courts; basic fitness room; shuffleboard; croquet; volleyball; children's programs; concierge; complimentary launch to Nauset Beach; room service; baby-sitting; video library. *In room:* A/C, TV/VCR, fridge, hair dryer, iron.

Pleasant Bay Village ★★
Set across the street from Pleasant Bay, a few minutes' walk from the beach, this is one fancy motel. Over the past 25 years, owner Howard Gamsey has transformed this 6-acre property into a playful Zen paradise, where waterfalls cascade through rock gardens into a pool dotted with lily pads and koi. Guest rooms, done up in restful pastels, are unusually pleasant. Many bathrooms feature marble counters and stone floors; the suites have kitchenettes. The breakfast room is decorated with antique kilims. In summer, you can order lunch from the grill without having to leave your place at the pool. In July and August, dinner is also served.

1191 Orleans Rd./Rte. 28 (about 3 miles north of Chatham center), Chathamport, MA 02633. © 800/547-1011 or 508/945-1133. Fax 508/945-9701. www.pleasantbayvillage.com. 58 units. Summer $165–$255 double; $355–$455 suite. AE, MC, V. Closed Nov–Apr. **Amenities:** Outdoor heated pool. *In room:* A/C, TV, fridge, hair dryer.

Wequassett Inn Resort and Golf Club ★★★
Fans of golf, sailing, and tennis will enjoy this 22-acre resort occupying its own little peninsula sticking out into Pleasant Bay. Adjacent is the private Cape Cod National Golf Club, where inn guests enjoy exclusive privileges. Tucked amid the woods along the shore, 15 modest dwellings, built in the 1940s, harbor roomy quarters done up in an opulent country style. These cost a bit more than the more modern "villa" units, but, with their bay views, are worth it. The 18th-century Eben Ryder House is home to an elegant restaurant, open to the public (jackets preferred for men at dinner). The pool is set at the neck of Clam Point, a calm beach; Nauset Beach is a 15-minute ride via the inn's Power Skiff ($10). Bay tours and fishing charters can also be arranged.

2173 Rte. 28 (about 5 miles NW of the town center, on Pleasant Bay), Chatham, MA 02633. © 800/225-7125 or 508/432-5400. Fax 508/432-5032. www.wequassett.com. 104 units. Summer $315–$800 double. AE, DC, DISC, MC, V. Closed late Nov to mid-Apr. **Amenities:** Restaurant (regional); pool; complimentary van service to 2 public golf courses (in Harwich and in Brewster) and to the private Cape Cod National Golf Club; access to 4 all-weather Plexipave tennis courts (fee) and pro shop; fitness room; sailing and saltwater fly-fishing instruction; equipment rental (bikes, sailboards, Sunfish, Daysailers, Hobie Cats); croquet; volleyball; van service to Chatham and Orleans villages for shopping. *In room:* A/C, TV, minibar.

Expensive

Captain's House Inn ★★★
Set on 2 meticulously maintained acres, this 1839 Greek Revival house, along with a cottage and carriage house, is a shining example of 19th-century style. The rooms are richly furnished, with a preponderance of canopied four-posters, beamed ceilings, and, in some cases, brick hearths. Most have TV/VCRs, and some are equipped with Jacuzzis. Morning repast is served at noncommunal tables (a thoughtful touch for those of us slow to rev up, sociability-wise). The window-walled breakfast room is also the site of a traditional tea.

369–377 Old Harbor Rd. (about ½ mile north of the rotary), Chatham, MA 02633. ℂ **800/315-0728** or 508/945-0127. Fax 508/945-0866. www.captainshouseinn.com. 19 units. Summer $125 single; $165–$375 double. Rates include breakfast and afternoon tea. AE, DISC, MC, V. **Amenities:** Croquets; bikes for guests' use. *In room:* A/C, hair dryer, iron.

Chatham Wayside Inn 🏚🏚 Centrally located on Main Street, this 1860 stagecoach stop has undergone a thoroughly modern renovation. Don't expect any musty antique trappings amid the lush carpeting and reproduction furnishings, including four-poster beds. The prize rooms boast patios or balconies overlooking the town bandstand. The restaurant serves sophisticated fare, indoors and out. This is one of the few inns on the Cape whose rooms and restaurant are fully wheelchair-accessible.

512 Main St. (in the center of town), Chatham, MA 02633. ℂ **800/391-5734** or 508/945-5550. Fax 508/945-3407. www.waysideinn.com. 56 units. Summer $165–$265 double; $285–$365 suite. Off-season packages available. DISC, MC, V. **Amenities:** Restaurant (new American); outdoor heated pool. *In room:* A/C, TV/VCR.

Moderate

The Dolphin of Chatham 🏚 With an 1805 main building, motel units, and cottages, the Dolphin offers a wide range of options in the heart of town. Even on exquisitely groomed Main Street, this property's colorful gardens stand out. The main inn has seven rooms with romantic touches like beamed ceilings, canopied beds, and lacy curtains. The rest of the units are standard motel issue, except for the honeymoon suite, housed in a whimsical windmill. The pool bar offers lunch and drinks; the inn also has a terrific bar area, where guests can enjoy light dinner fare from a screened porch overlooking Main Street. Lighthouse Beach is a pleasant stroll away.

352 Main St. (at the east end), Chatham, MA 02633-2428. ℂ **800/688-5900** or 508/945-0070. Fax 508/945-5945. www.dolphininn.com. 37 units. Summer $149–$209 double; $209–$275 2-bedroom suite; $1,700 per week for cottage. Rates include continental breakfast. AE, DC, DISC, MC, V. **Amenities:** Outdoor heated pool; hot tub. *In room:* A/C, TV, fridge, hair dryer.

Moses Nickerson House 🏚 George and Linda Watts run this gem of a B&B with a sense of humor mixed with gracious hospitality. This grand 1839 captain's home is every inch devoted to stylish comfort. Whether you opt for a canopied bed or a ruggedly handsome, hunt-club–style room, rest assured you'll be pampered—with a home-baked breakfast in the solarium, and later an afternoon pick-me-up in the dazzling parlor.

364 Old Harbor Rd. (about ½ mile north of Main St.), Chatham, MA 02633. ℂ **800/628-6972** or 508/945-5859. Fax 508/945-7087. www.capecodtravel.com/mosesnickersonhouse. 7 units. Summer $139–$199 double. Rates include breakfast and afternoon tea. AE, DISC, MC, V. *In room:* A/C, TV.

WHERE TO DINE

Chatham Wayside Inn 🏚 NEW AMERICAN The Wayside's central location makes it a good spot for a reasonably priced meal in town. Diners have several seating choices depending on their mood (and the weather): the clubby tavern with gleaming wood tables and comfy Windsor chairs, the front room's cozy booths, or the screened terrace. More important, perhaps, is what's on the plate. Specialties include crab cakes and entrees like rack of lamb and pesto cod. For something a little different, try the chowder, prepared Portuguese style with double-smoked bacon, fresh quahogs, and red bliss potatoes. At lunchtime, the terrace is the perfect spot to watch Main Street's parade of shoppers.

512 Main St. (in the center of town). ℂ **508/945-5550.** Main courses $13–$22. DISC, MC, V. May–Oct daily 8–11am, 11:30am–4pm, and 5–9pm; Nov–Apr Tues–Sun 8–11am, 11:30am–4pm, and 5–9pm.

The Impudent Oyster 🌣 INTERNATIONAL   All but hidden off the main drag, this perennially popular 1970s-era eatery continues to cook up fabulous fish in exotic guises, ranging from Mexican to Szechuan, but mostly continental. The flavorful specialties are the *salmon piche* (baked with a Dijon and herb bread-crumb crust), the *steak au poivre,* and the *chicken Français.* There's also a children's menu.

15 Chatham Bars Ave. (off Main St., in the center of town). ℭ **508/945-3545.** Reservations recommended. Main courses $13–$23. AE, MC, V. Mon–Sat 11:30am–3pm; Sun noon–3pm; daily 5–10pm.

The Main Dining Room at the Chatham Bars Inn 🌣🌣🌣 NEW AMERI-CAN   If it's grandeur you're after, the setting here supplies a surplus. The dining room is vast, and the view of the Atlantic is of the million-dollar variety. Your fellow diners are decked out in their summer finery, and in the background a pianist tickles the ivories. Dinners consist of hearty traditional fare like roast duckling with orange mandarin ginger sauce and wild rice, or fillet of haddock with lobster stuffing and a Newburg sauce. This is not delicate food, but it is delicious—and the chowder may be the best on Cape Cod. Dessert choices are equally dense.

Shore Rd. (about 1/3 mile northwest of the town center). ℭ **508/945-0096.** Reservations recommended. Main courses $21–$35. AE, DC, MC, V. June–Nov daily 7:30–11am and 6:30–9:30pm; call for off-season hours.

Vining's Bistro 🌣🌣 FUSION   If you're looking for cutting-edge cuisine in a sophisticated setting, venture upstairs at Chatham's minimall and into this ineffably cool cafe. The film-noirish murals suggest a certain bohemian abandon, but the food is up-to-the-minute. The menu offers compelling juxtapositions such as the warm lobster tacos with salsa fresca and crème fraîche, or the spit-roasted chicken suffused with achiote-lime marinade and sided with a salad of oranges and jicama.

595 Main St. (in the center of town). ℭ **508/945-5033.** Reservations not accepted. Main courses $15–$20. AE, DC, MC, V. June to early Sept daily 5:30–10pm; call for off-season hours.

CHATHAM AFTER DARK

Chatham's free **band concerts** 🌣🌣🌣 are arguably the best on the Cape and attract crowds in the thousands. This is small-town America at its most nostalgic, as the band, made up mostly of local folks, plays old standards that never go out of style. Held in Kate Gould Park (off Chatham Bars Avenue) from July to early September, they kick off at 8pm every Friday. Better come early to claim your square of lawn (it's already checkered with blankets by late afternoon). Call ℭ **508/945-5199** for information.

A great leveler, the **Chatham Squire,** 487 Main St. (ℭ **508/945-0945**), attracts CEOs, seafarers, and collegiates alike. No cover.

The piano bar **Upstairs at Christian's,** 443 Main St. (ℭ **508/945-3362**), has the air of a vintage frat house with leather couches and purloined movie posters. Live music is offered nightly in season and on weekends year-round. Cinematically themed nibbles accompany the movie-motif drinks. No cover.

ORLEANS 🌣

Orleans is where the "Narrow Land" (the early Algonquin name for the Cape) starts to get very narrow indeed: From here on up—or "down," in paradoxical local parlance—it's never more than a few miles wide from coast to coast. But this is also where the ocean-side beaches open up into a glorious expanse some 40 miles long, framed by dramatic dunes and serious surf.

The Cape's three main roads (Routes 6, 6A, and 28) converge here, too, so on summer weekends it acts as a rather frustrating funnel. Nevertheless, Main Street boasts some appealing restaurants and shops. The village of East Orleans, near the entrance to Nauset Beach, may be the best place to base yourself. The 10-mile-long beach, which is the southernmost stretch of the Cape Cod National Seashore preserve, is a magnet for the young and buff.

ESSENTIALS

GETTING THERE   After crossing either the Bourne or the Sagamore bridge, head east on Route 6 or 6A (the long but scenic route); both converge with Route 28 in Orleans. The town is 31 miles east of Sandwich, 25 miles south of Provincetown.

VISITOR INFORMATION   Contact the **Orleans Chamber of Commerce,** 44 Main St. (Box 153), Orleans (✆ **800/865-1386** or 508/255-1386; www.capecod-orleans.com). There's an **information booth** at the corner of Route 6A and Eldredge Parkway (✆ **508/240-2484**).

BEACHES & OUTDOOR PURSUITS

BEACHES   From here all the way to Provincetown on the Cape's eastern side, you're dealing with the wild Atlantic. Current conditions are clearly posted at the entrance. Weeklong parking permits ($25 for renters, $40 for transients) may be obtained from **Town Hall,** on School Road (✆ **508/240-3775**). Day-trippers who arrive early enough—better make that before 9am—can pay at the gate (✆ **508/240-3780**).

- **Crystal Lake,** off Monument Road about three-quarters of a mile south of Main Street: Parking—if you can find a space—is free, but there are no facilities here.
- **Nauset Beach** ★★★, in East Orleans (✆ **508/240-3780**): Stretching southward all the way past Chatham, this 10-mile-long barrier beach, which is part of the Cape Cod National Seashore but is managed by the town, has long been one of the Cape's gonzo beach scenes—good surf, big crowds, lots of young people. Once you get past the swarms near the parking lot, you'll have about 9 miles of beach mostly to yourself. You'll see lots of birds and perhaps harbor seals off-season. Full facilities, including a terrific snack bar complete with fried-fish offerings, can be found within the 1,000-car parking lot; the in-season fee is $8 per car, which is also good for same-day parking at Skaket Beach (see below). Substantial waves make for good surfing in the special section reserved for that purpose. In July and August, concerts are held from 7 to 9pm in the gazebo.
- **Pilgrim Lake,** off Monument Road about 1 mile south of Main Street: This small freshwater beach is covered by a lifeguard in season. You must have a beach parking sticker.
- **Skaket Beach,** off Skaket Beach Road to the west of town (✆ **508/255-0572**): This peaceful bay beach is a better choice for families. After the tide recedes (as much as a mile), little kids enjoy splashing in the tide pools. Parking costs $8, and you'd better turn up early.

BICYCLING   Orleans presents the one slight gap in the 25-mile **Cape Cod Rail Trail** ★★★ (✆ **508/896-3491**): Just east of the Brewster border, the trail merges with town roads for about 1½ miles. The best way to avoid cars is to zigzag west to Rock Harbor. Rentals are available at **Orleans Cycle,** 26 Main St., in the center of town (✆ **508/255-9115**).

BOATING   In season, **Arey's Pond Boat Yard,** off Route 28 in South Orleans (© **508/255-7900**), offers sailing lessons on Little Pleasant Bay. Individual lessons are $60 per hour; weekly group lessons cost $160 to $250. The **Goose Hummock Outdoor Center,** 15 Rte. 6A, south of the rotary (© **508/ 255-2620;** www.goose.com), rents canoes, kayaks, and more, and the northern half of Pleasant Bay is the perfect place to use them.

FISHING   Fishing is allowed in Baker Pond, Pilgrim Lake, and Crystal Lake. For details and a license, visit **Town Hall,** at Post Office Square in the center of town (© **508/240-3700,** ext. 305), or **Goose Hummock** (see above). Surf casting—no license needed—is permitted on Nauset Beach South, off Beach Road. **Rock Harbor,** about 1¼ miles northwest of the town center, shelters New England's largest sport-fishing fleet: some 18 boats at last count. One call (© **800/287-1771** in Mass., or © **508/255-9757**) will get you information on them all—or go look them over in person.

WATER SPORTS   The **Pump House Surf Co.,** 9 Cranberry Hwy./Rte. 6A (© **508/240-2226**), rents and sells wet suits, body boards, and surfboards, in addition to providing up-to-date reports on where to find the best waves. **Nauset Sports,** at Jeremiah Square, Route 6A at the rotary (© **508/255-4742**), also rents surfboards, body boards, skim boards, and wet suits.

SHOPPING

Though shops are somewhat scattered, Orleans is full of great finds for browsers and grazers. The proprietor of **Countryside Antiques,** 6 Lewis Rd., south of Main Street in the center of East Orleans (© **508/240-0525**), roams the world in search of stylish furnishings, mostly old. Stop by **Kemp Pottery,** 9 Cranberry Hwy./Rte. 6A, south of the rotary (© **508/255-5853**), and check out Steve Kemp's turned and slab-built creations—from soup tureens to fanciful sculptures; they're remarkably colorful and one of a kind. **Tree's Place,** Route 6A at the intersection of Route 28, Orleans (© **888/255-1330** or 508/255-1330), is considered the premier gallery for contemporary realist work in the region.

WHERE TO STAY

The Cove ★   Sensibly turning its back on busy Route 28, this well-camouflaged motel complex focuses instead on placid Town Cove, where guests are offered a free minicruise in season. The interiors are adequate, if not dazzling, and a small pool and a restful gazebo overlook the waterfront.

13 S. Orleans Rd. (Rte. 28, north of Main St.), Orleans, MA 02653. © **800/343-2233** or 508/255-1203. Fax 508/255-7736. www.thecoveorleans.com. 47 units. Summer $109–$189 double; $169–$189 suite or efficiency. Open year-round. AE, DC, DISC, MC, V. **Amenities:** Small outdoor heated pool. *In room:* A/C, TV/VCR, microwave, fridge, coffeemaker, hair dryer.

Kadee's Gray Elephant ★★ *(Kids)*   These exuberantly decorated studio apartments are extremely cheery. Nauset Beach is a few miles down the road. There's a friendly restaurant/snack bar next door (see "Where to Dine," below), and the little minigolf course is geared just right for kids.

216 Main St., East Orleans, MA 02643. © **508/255-7608.** Fax 508/240-2976. kadees@capecod.net. 6 units. Summer $110–$140 double. Weekly rates available. Closed mid-Oct to Mar. MC, V. **Amenities:** Restaurant/snack bar (seafood); minigolf. *In room:* A/C, TV.

Nauset House Inn ★★   Just a half mile from Nauset Beach, this reasonably priced inn is for those seeking a quiet retreat. Several of the rooms in greenery-draped outbuildings feature such extras as a sunken bath or private deck. Most romantic is a 1907 conservatory appended to the 1810 farmhouse. Breakfast would seem relatively workaday, were it not for the setting—a rustic refectory—and the innkeeper's memorable muffins.

143 Beach Rd. (about 1 mile east of the town center), Box 774, East Orleans, MA 02643. ☎ **508/255-2195.** Fax 508/240-6276. www.nausethouseinn.com. 14 units (6 with shared bathroom). Summer $60–$140 double. Rates include breakfast. DISC, MC, V. Closed Nov–Mar. No children under 12. *In room:* No phone.

Nauset Knoll Motor Lodge ⭐⭐
You can't get any closer to Nauset Beach. Each room in this nothing-fancy motel has picture windows looking out over the dunes to the ocean. The simple accommodations are well maintained, and by staying here, you'll save on daily parking charges at the beach (one of the most popular on the Cape). The whole complex is owned by Uncle Sam and is under the supervision of the National Park Service.

237 Beach Rd. (at Nauset Beach, about 2 miles east of the town center), East Orleans, MA 02643. ☎ **508/255-2364.** 12 units. Summer $135 double. MC, V. Closed late Oct to mid-Apr. *In room:* TV, no phone.

The Orleans Inn ⭐
You can't miss this mansard-roofed 1875 beauty, perched right on the edge of Town Cove. The simple guest rooms, some with twin beds or sleeper sofas, are cheerful with modern amenities and extra touches like a box of chocolates on the bureau. Ask for one of the rooms facing the water. Downstairs is a bar and restaurant with wonderful views.

Rte. 6A/PO Box 188 (just south of the Orleans rotary), Orleans, MA 02653. ☎ **508/255-2222.** Fax 508/255-6722. www.orleansinn.com. 11 units. Summer $125–$250 double. Rates include continental breakfast. AE, MC, V. **Amenities:** Restaurant, bar. *In room:* TV, dataport, iron.

WHERE TO DINE

Stop by the charming **Fancy's Farm,** 199 Main St., East Orleans (☎ **508/255-1949**), for fresh pastries, sandwiches, and salads and soups to go.

The Barley Neck Inn ⭐⭐ FRENCH
This 1857 captain's house is the top place to eat in Orleans. The owners have recruited a superb chef in Franck Champely, who arrived from Taillevent and Maxim's by way of New York's Four Seasons. His background shines in straightforward yet subtle dishes such as grilled Atlantic salmon fillet with a red-pepper coulis and basil vinaigrette, or sautéed shrimp in a sauce of sweet garlic and Chablis atop lemon angel-hair pasta and shiitake mushrooms. For a less-expensive menu from the same kitchen, go next door to Joe's Beach Road Bar and Grille.

5 Beach Rd. (about ½ mile east of the town center). ☎ **800/281-7505** or 508/255-0212. Reservations recommended. Main courses $14–$24. AE, MC, V. June to early Sept daily 5–10pm; call for off-season hours. Open year-round.

Kadee's Lobster & Clam Bar ⭐⭐ SEAFOOD
This is the best clam shack in town, and also one of those cheerful businesses that you leave with a smile on your face. Fine weather calls for a lobster roll, or perhaps the Fisherman's Feed combo platter splurge. On the other hand, there's nothing like the classic chowders and stews or a healthy seafood kabob to take the chill off. There's also a raw bar with oysters, clams, and shrimp.

212 Main St., East Orleans. ☎ **508/255-6184.** Reservations not accepted. Main courses $7–$24; early-bird specials Mon–Thurs 4–5pm. MC, V. Late June to early Sept daily noon–9pm; late May to late June Mon–Thurs 5–9pm, Fri–Sun noon–9pm. Closed early Sept to late May.

The Lobster Claw Restaurant ⭐ Kids SEAFOOD
This sprawling, family-owned business has been serving up quality seafood for almost 30 years. Get the baked stuffed lobster with all the fixings.

Rte. 6A (just south of the rotary), Orleans. ☎ **508/255-1800.** Main courses $10–$19; early-bird specials daily 4–5:30pm. AE, DISC, MC, V. Daily 11:30am–9pm. Closed Nov–Mar.

Mahoney's Atlantic Bar & Grill ⭐ NEW AMERICAN   Seafood is the specialty at this casual bar/restaurant. Dishes like tuna sashimi, grilled sea bass, and pan-seared lobster are why you came to Cape Cod. There are also poultry, meat, pasta, and vegetarian options. Sixteen wines are available by the glass. Some nights in season, there's live jazz and blues.

28 Main St. (in the center of town), ℂ **508/255-5505.** Reservations recommended. Main courses $12–$21. AE, MC, V. Daily 8am–10pm.

Nauset Beach Club ⭐ NORTHERN ITALIAN   The first thing you may notice about this trattoria is the tantalizing aromas. Unfortunately, the next impression is apt to be a surfeit of attitude, when, for example, the maitre d' informs you that each person in your party must order an entree—no exceptions made for young diners. If you're willing to play by the rules, the reward is worth it: luscious pastas and other Italian-accented regional fare.

222 Main St. (about ½ mile east of the town center). ℂ 508/255-8547. Reservations suggested. Main courses $14–$19. AE, DISC, MC, V. Late May to mid-Oct daily 5:30–9:30pm; mid-Oct to late May Tues–Sat 5:30–9:30pm.

ORLEANS AFTER DARK

Joe's Beach Road Bar & Grille, at the Barley Neck Inn (ℂ **508/255-0212**), is a big old barn of a bar that might as well be town hall: It's where you'll find all the locals exchanging juicy gossip and jokes. On Sunday evenings in season, there's live "Jazz at Joe's." Other nights feature Jim Turner, a blind piano player who entertains with show tunes and boogie-woogie. There's never a cover. There's live music on weekends at the **Land Ho!** (ℂ **508/255-5165**), the best pub in town. There's usually no cover.

4 The Outer Cape ⭐⭐⭐

It's only on the Outer Cape that the landscape and even the air feel really beachy. You can smell the seashore just over the horizon—in fact, everywhere you go, because you're never more than a mile or two away from sand and surf. You won't find any high-rise hotels along the shoreline or tacky amusement arcades—just miles of pristine beaches and dune grass rippling in the wind. That's because in the early 1960s, 27,000 acres here became the federally protected Cape Cod National Seashore.

WELLFLEET ⭐⭐⭐

With the well-tended look of a classic New England village and surrounded by pristine beaches, Wellfleet is the chosen destination for artists, writers, off-duty psychiatrists, and other contemplative types. Distinguished literati such as Edna St. Vincent Millay and Edmund Wilson put this rural village on the map in the 1920s, in the wake of Provincetown's bohemian heyday.

To this day, Wellfleet remains remarkably unspoiled. Once you leave Route 6, commercialism is kept to a minimum, though the town boasts plenty of appealing shops, distinguished galleries, and a couple of excellent restaurants. It's hard to imagine any other community on the Cape supporting so sophisticated an undertaking as the Wellfleet Harbor Actors' Theatre, or hosting such a wholesome event as public square-dancing on the adjacent Town Pier. And where else could you find a thriving drive-in movie theater right next door to an outstanding nature preserve?

ESSENTIALS

GETTING THERE   After crossing either the Bourne or the Sagamore bridge, head east on Route 6 or 6A (the long but scenic route) to Orleans, and north on Route 6. Wellfleet is 42 miles northeast of Sandwich, 14 miles south of Provincetown.

VISITOR INFORMATION   Contact the **Wellfleet Chamber of Commerce,** off Route 6, Wellfleet (© **508/349-2510;** fax 508/349-3740; www.capecod.net/ wellfleetcc).

BEACHES & OUTDOOR PURSUITS

BEACHES   Wellfleet's fabulous ocean beaches tend to sort themselves demographically: LeCount Hollow is popular with families, Newcomb Hollow with high-schoolers, White Crest with the college crowd (including surfers and off-hour hang gliders), and Cahoon with 30-somethings. Only the latter two beaches permit parking by nonresidents ($10 per day). To enjoy the other two, as well as Burton Baker Beach on the harbor and Duck Harbor on the bay, plus three freshwater ponds, you'll have to walk or bike in, or see if you qualify for a sticker ($25 per week). Bring proof of residency to the seasonal Beach Sticker Booth on the Town Pier, or call the **Wellfleet Recreation Department** (© **508/ 349-9818**). Parking is free at all beaches and ponds after 4pm.

- **Marconi Beach** ☆☆, off Marconi Beach Road in South Wellfleet: A National Seashore property, this cliff-lined beach charges a fee of $7 per day, or $20 for the season. Rest rooms are available. *Note:* The bluffs are so high that the beach lies in shadow by late afternoon.
- **Mayo Beach,** Kendrick Avenue (near the Town Pier): Right by the harbor, facing south, this warm, shallow bay beach (with rest rooms) is hardly secluded but will please young waders. Parking is free. You can grab a bite at the Bookstore Restaurant across the street, which serves three meals a day and sells used books around back.
- **White Crest Beach** ☆☆ and **Cahoon Hollow Beach** ☆☆☆, off Ocean View Drive in Wellfleet: These two town-run ocean beaches—big with surfers—are open to all. Both have snack bars and rest rooms. Parking costs $10 per day.

BICYCLING   The end of the 25-mile **Cape Cod Rail Trail** ☆☆☆ (© **508/896-3491**), Wellfleet is also among its more desirable destinations: A country road off the path leads right to LeCount Hollow Beach. Located at the end of the trail, the **Black Duck Sports Shop,** 1446 Rte. 6 (© **508/349-9801**), stocks everything from rental bikes to inflatable boats; the deli at the adjoining **South Wellfleet General Store** (© **508/349-2335**) can see to your snacking needs.

BOATING   **Jack's Boat Rentals,** on Gull Pond off Gull Pond Road, about a half-mile south of the Truro border (© **508/349-9808**), rents canoes, kayaks, sailboards, and Sunfish, as well as sea cycles and surf bikes. Gull Pond connects to Higgins Pond by way of a placid, narrow channel lined with red maples and choked with yellow water lilies. Needless to say, it's a great place to paddle. If you'd like a canoe for a few days, you'll need to go to the Jack's Boat Rentals location on Route 6 in Wellfleet (next to the Cumberland Farms). In addition to watercraft to go, Jack's is also the place for information on **Eric Gustavson's guided kayak tours** (© **508/349-1429**) of nearby kettle ponds and tidal rivers.

The **Chequessett Yacht & Country Club,** on Chequessett Neck Road in Wellfleet (© **508/349-3704**), offers group sailing lessons. For experienced sailors, **Wellfleet Marine Corp.,** on the Town Pier (© **508/349-2233**), rents 14- to 20-foot sailboats in season.

FISHING   For a license to fish at Long Pond, Great Pond, or Gull Pond (all stocked with trout and full of native perch, pickerel, and sunfish), visit **Town Hall,** 300 Main St. (© **508/349-0301**), or the **Town Pier** (© **508/349-9818**). Surf casting, which doesn't require a license, is permitted at the town beaches. Shellfishing licenses—Wellfleet's oysters are world-famous—can be obtained from the **Shellfish Department,** on the Town Pier off Kendrick Avenue (© **508/349-0300**).

Also heading out from here, in season, is the 60-foot party fishing boat *Navigator* (© **508/349-6003**), and three smaller boats: the *Erin-H* (© **508/349-9663**), *Jac's Mate* (© **508/255-2978**), and *Snooper* (© **508/349-6113**).

NATURE & WILDLIFE AREAS   You'll find 6 miles of very scenic trails lined with lupines and bayberries—Goose Pond, Silver Spring, and Bay View— within the **Wellfleet Bay Wildlife Sanctuary** in South Wellfleet (see below).

Right in town, the picturesque boardwalk known as **Uncle Tim's Bridge,** off East Commercial Street, crosses Duck Creek to access a tiny island crisscrossed by paths.

The Cape Cod National Seashore maintains two spectacular self-guided trails. The 1¼-mile **Atlantic White Cedar Swamp Trail** ★★, off the parking area for the Marconi Wireless Station (see below), shelters a rare stand of the lightweight species prized by Native Americans as wood for canoes; the moss-choked swamp is a magical place, refreshingly cool even at the height of summer. A boardwalk will see you over the muck, but the return trip does entail a calf-testing half-mile trek through deep sand. Consider it a warm-up for magnificent **Great Island** ★★, jutting 4 miles into the bay (off the western end of Chequessett Neck Road) to cup Wellfleet Harbor. Before attaching itself to the mainland in 1831, Great Island harbored a busy whaling post; a 1970 dig turned up the foundations of an early-18th-century tavern. Be sure to cover up, wear sturdy shoes, bring water, and venture to **Jeremy Point**—the very tip—only if you're sure the tide is going out.

A spiffy eco-friendly visitor center serves as both introduction and gateway to the **Wellfleet Bay Wildlife Sanctuary** ★★★, off Route 6, a couple hundred yards north of the Eastham border, in South Wellfleet (© **508/349-2615;** fax 508/349-2632; www.wellfleetbay.org), a 1,000-acre refuge maintained by the Massachusetts Audubon Society. Passive solar heat and composting toilets are just a few of the waste-cutting elements incorporated into the $1.6-million building. You'll see redwing blackbirds and osprey as you follow 5 miles of trails through forests, salt marsh, and moors. The sanctuary offers naturalist-guided tours and special workshops for children; inquire about canoeing, birding, and seal-watching excursions. Trail use is free for Massachusetts Audubon Society members; the nonmember fee is $3 for adults and $2 for seniors and children. Trails are open July through August from 8am to 8pm, September through June from 8am to dusk. The visitor center is open from Memorial Day to Columbus Day, daily from 8:30am to 5pm; in the off-season, it's closed Mondays.

WATER SPORTS   Surfing is restricted to White Crest Beach, and sail-boarding to Burton Baker Beach at Indian Neck during certain tide conditions; ask for details at the Beach Sticker Booth on the Town Pier.

SHOPPING

A stroll from Main Street down Bank Street and then along Commercial Street will take you past a dozen galleries worth a look. Crafts make a strong showing in Wellfleet, too, as do women's clothing and eclectic home furnishings. But unlike Provincetown, Wellfleet pretty much closes up come Columbus Day, so buy while the getting's good.

The **Cove Gallery,** 15 Commercial St., by Duck Creek (© **508/ 349-2530**)—with a waterside sculpture garden—carries the work of many well-known artists, including Barry Moser and Leonard Baskin. John Grillo's annual show astounds with its boldly colored paintings. The **Left Bank Small Works & Jewelry Gallery,** 3 W. Main St., in the center of town (© **508/349-7939**), features an irresistible sampling of jewelry designs.

WHERE TO STAY

Aunt Sukie's Bayside Bed & Breakfast ⭐

Sue and Dan Hamar's 1830 house is perched on a bluff in an exclusive residential neighborhood overlooking Cape Cod Bay. Behind the house, a boardwalk takes you to a private bay beach. The Nickerson Suite has wide-board floors and a fireplace; the Chequessett and Billingsgate rooms are more contemporary. All units have sweeping bay views. In front of the house are beautiful gardens; out back is a large deck where guests can eat breakfast and sunbathe. The Hamars also own a two-bedroom cottage about a mile away in the pines.

525 Chequessett Neck Rd, Wellfleet, MA 02667. © **800/420-9999** or 508/349-2804. www.auntsukies.com. 4 units. Summer $150–$200 double; $1,200–$1,400 per week for cottage. Room rates include continental breakfast. MC, V. Closed mid-Jan. to mid-Mar. *In room:* Fridge.

Even'tide ⭐ 𝘒𝘪𝘥𝘴

Set back from busy Route 6, this well-run motel is a good base for families. In case of rain, there's a 60-foot indoor pool, unusual in this part of the Cape. On the property are seven cottages and four "apartment" units with kitchenettes. The Rail Trail goes right by the motel, and a 1-mile path through the woods leads to Marconi Beach.

650 Rte. 6 (about 1 mile north of the Eastham border), South Wellfleet, MA 02663. © **800/368-0007** in Mass., or 508/349-3410. Fax 508/349-7804. www.eventidemotel.com. 31 units. Summer $89–$120 double, $122–$149 efficiency. AE, DC, DISC, MC, V. **Amenities:** Indoor pool; self-service laundry. *In room:* A/C, TV, fridge.

The Inn at Duck Creeke

This historic complex consists of four buildings set on 5 woodsy acres overlooking a tidal creek and salt marsh. An 1880s captain's house features wide-board floors and charming but basic bedrooms, many with shared bathrooms; the carriage house contains a few light and airy cabin-style rooms; and the 1715 saltworks building has smaller cottage-type rooms with antique decor. In the main building, each shared bathroom adjoins two rooms, which might not suit those in search of privacy. The third-floor rooms in the main house have air-conditioning. The accommodations in the carriage house and saltworks building are quieter and can be downright romantic. But there's definitely a no-frills quality to this place—towels are thin, and so are walls. A big plus: two good on-site restaurants, Sweet Seasons (see "Where to Dine," below) and the publike Duck Creeke Tavern, with live entertainment in season.

70 Main St. (Box 364), Wellfleet, MA 02667. © **508/349-9333.** Fax 508/349-0234. www.capecod.net/ duckinn. 27 units (8 with shared bathroom). Summer $70–$100 double. Rates include continental breakfast. AE, MC, V. Closed Nov–Apr. **Amenities:** 2 restaurants (new American, pub fare). *In room:* No phone.

Surfside Cottages ★★ These cottages, fun in a 1960s way, are smack dab on a spectacular beach, within biking distance of Wellfleet Center, and a short drive to Provincetown for dinner. All have kitchens, fireplaces, and screened porches. Some have outdoor showers and roof decks. Bring your own sheets and towels—renting a set costs $10 per person.

Ocean View Dr. (at LeCount Hollow Rd.), Box 937, South Wellfleet, MA 02663. ℂ and fax **508/349-3959.** www.capecod.net/surfside. 18 cottages. Mid-May to Oct $750–$1,350 per week; off-season $70–$125 per day. MC, V. Pets allowed off-season. *In room:* Kitchen, microwave, coffeemaker.

WHERE TO DINE

A former fishing shack, **Hatch's Fish & Produce Market,** 310 Main St., behind Town Hall (ℂ **508/349-6734** for produce, or 508/349-2810 for fish market), is the unofficial heart of Wellfleet. You'll find the best of local bounty, from fresh-picked corn and fruit-juice Popsicles to steaming lobsters and home-smoked mussels. Closed late September to late May.

Aesop's Tables ★★ NEW AMERICAN This delightful restaurant—offbeat enough to stay interesting year after year—has it all: a historic setting; a relaxed atmosphere; and delectable food turned out by chef Patricia Worthington. Owner Brian Dunne oversees the sourcing of the superb local provender, even growing some of the edible flowers and delicate greens that go into the Monet's Garden salad. The scallops and oysters come straight from the bay. For dessert, try Clementine's Citrus Tart.

316 Main St. (in the center of town). ℂ **508/349-6450.** Reservations recommended. Main courses $15–$27. AE, DISC, MC, V. July–Aug Wed–Sun noon–3pm; daily 5:30–9:30pm; call for off-season hours. Closed Nov–Apr.

The Lighthouse ★ AMERICAN Nothing special in and of itself, this bustling institution is an off-season haven for locals and a beacon to tourists year-round. Except on Thursday's "Mexican Night," the menu is all-American, from the steak-and-eggs breakfast to the seafood dinners. Appreciative patrons usually keep up a dull roar throughout the day, revving up to a deafening clamor as the Bass and Guinness flow from the tap.

317 Main St. (in the center of town). ℂ **508/349-3681.** Main courses $9–$18. DISC, MC, V. May–Oct daily 7am–10pm; call for off-season hours. Closed Mar.

Mac's Seafood Market and Restaurant SEAFOOD This take-out shack with picnic tables on the town pier features fresh local seafood unloaded from the boats just steps away. Besides grilled fish dinners, there are homemade chowders, seafood salads, sushi, and a raw bar.

On the Wellfleet Town Pier. ℂ **508/349-0404.** Daily 11am–9pm. Closed Oct–May.

Painter's Restaurant ★★ NEW AMERICAN/ASIAN Kate Painter trained at some pretty fancy establishments: San Francisco's Stars, Boston's Biba, and Cape Cod's own Chillingsworth. Still, if she had her druthers—and now she does, having set up her own restaurant in a 1750 tavern—she'd prefer, in the words of her mission statement, "simple food in a funky place." The setting, a wood-beamed bistro dressed up with friends' artwork, is indeed funky, but her kitchen is turning out pretty sophisticated food. On the appetizer list, the crackling Asian cellophane shrimp with tomato coulis is a flavorful delight. Entrees include such dishes as Painter's Tuna, served with a lovely orange-ginger Asian dipping sauce and wasabi. Painter's sense of humor shows up in the desserts:

"Something Chocolate" and "Something Lemon" are just that, an intriguing cross between cake and soufflé.

50 Main St. (near Rte. 6). ℂ 508/349-3003. Main courses $8–$23. AE, MC, V. Late May to mid-Oct daily 6–10pm; mid-Oct to late May Wed–Sat 6–10pm.

Sweet Seasons Restaurant ✿ NEW AMERICAN   Judith Pihl's Mediterranean-influenced fare is still appealing after 20-plus years, as is this dining room's peaceful pond view. Some of the dishes can be a bit heavy by contemporary standards, but there's usually a healthy alternative: Wellfleet littlenecks and mussels in a golden, aromatic tomato-and-cumin broth, for instance, as opposed to Russian oysters with smoked salmon, vodka, and sour cream. Lighter fare is served in the adjoining Duck Creeke Tavern.

At the Inn at Duck Creeke, 70 Main St. (about ⅛ mile west of Rte. 6). ℂ 508/349-6535. Reservations recommended. Main courses $16–$23. AE, MC, V. Late June to mid-Sept daily 5:30–10pm. Closed mid-Sept to late June.

WELLFLEET AFTER DARK

The **Beachcomber,** 1220 Old Cahoon Hollow Rd., off Ocean View Drive (ℂ 508/349-6055), arguably the best dance club on Cape Cod, is definitely the most scenic. It's right on Cahoon Hollow Beach—so close, in fact, that late beachgoers on summer weekends can count on a free concert of reggae, blues, ska, or rock. The cover varies. Closed mid-September to late May.

Local talent—jazz, pop, folk, blues, and various hybrids—accompanies the light fare at **Duck Creeke Tavern,** at the Inn at Duck Creeke, 70 Main St. (ℂ 508/349-7369). Locally spawned blues and jazz usually inhabit the cozy attic at the **Upstairs Bar at Aesop's Tables,** 316 Main St. (ℂ 508/349-6450).

The **Wellfleet Drive-In Theater,** 51 Rte. 6, just north of the Eastham border (ℂ 800/696-3532 or 508/349-2520), clearly deserves National Landmark status: Built in 1957, it's the only drive-in left on Cape Cod and one of a scant half dozen surviving in the state. The rituals are unbending and every bit as endearing as ever: the cartoons, the countdown plugging the allures of the snack bar, and, finally, two full first-run features. It's open daily from late May to mid-September; showtime is at dusk. Call for off-season hours. Admission is $6 for adults and $3.50 for seniors and children 5 to 11.

The principals behind the **Wellfleet Harbor Actors' Theatre,** 1 Kendrick Ave., near the Town Pier (ℂ 508/349-6835), aim to provoke—and usually succeed, even amid this very sophisticated, seen-it-all summer colony. Performances are given from late May to October, daily at 8pm.

PROVINCETOWN ✿✿✿

You made it all the way to the end of the Cape, to one of the most unique spots on the eastern seaboard. Explorer Bartholomew Gosnold must have felt much the same thrill in 1602, when he and his crew happened upon a "great stoare of codfysshes" here. The Pilgrims, of course, were overjoyed when they slogged into the harbor 18 years later: Never mind that they'd landed several hundred miles off course.

And Charles Hawthorne, the painter who "discovered" this near-derelict fishing town in the late 1890s and introduced it to the Greenwich Village intelligentsia, was besotted by this "jumble of color in the intense sunlight accentuated by the brilliant blue of the harbor."

He'd probably be aghast at the commercial circus his enthusiasm has wrought—though pleased, no doubt, to find the Provincetown Art Association

& Museum, which he helped found in 1914, still going strong. The whole town, in fact, is dedicated to creative expression, both visual and verbal. The general atmosphere of open-mindedness plays a pivotal role, allowing a varied assortment of individuals to explore their creative urges.

That same open-mindedness may account for Provincetown's ascendancy as a gay and lesbian resort. In peak season, Provincetown's streets are a celebration of the individual's freedom to be as "out" as the imagination allows. But the street life also includes families who enjoy beaches, whale watching, and saltwater taffy; art lovers who stroll through the colorful galleries; and gourmands who appreciate fine restaurants and cafes. In short, Provincetown has something for just about everyone.

ESSENTIALS

GETTING THERE   After crossing either the Bourne or the Sagamore bridge, head east on Route 6 or 6A (the long but scenic route) to Orleans, then north on Route 6. Provincetown is 56 miles northeast of Sandwich, 42 miles northeast of Hyannis.

Bay State Cruises (© 617/748-1428; www.baystatecruisecompany.com) makes round-trips from Boston, daily from late June to early September and on weekends in the shoulder seasons. Their high-speed **Provincetown Express** boat makes two round-trips daily from mid-May to mid-October; it takes just under 2 hours. **Captain John Boats** (© 508/747-2400) connects Plymouth and Provincetown in summer.

VISITOR INFORMATION   Contact the **Provincetown Chamber of Commerce,** 307 Commercial St., Provincetown (© 508/487-3424; fax 508/ 487-8966; www.ptownchamber.com), or the gay-oriented **Provincetown Business Guild,** 115 Bradford St., Provincetown (© 800/637-8696 or 508/487-2313; fax 508/487-1252; www.ptown.org).

BEACHES & OUTDOOR PURSUITS

BEACHES   With nine-tenths of its territory (basically, all but the "downtown" area) protected by the Cape Cod National Seashore, Provincetown has miles of beaches. The 3-mile bay beach that lines the harbor, though certainly swimmable, is not all that inviting compared to the magnificent ocean beaches overseen by the National Seashore. The two official access areas (see below) tend to be crowded; however, you can always find a less densely populated stretch if you're willing to hike down the beach a bit. *Note:* Local activists have been lobbying for "clothing-optional" beaches for years, but the rangers, fearful of voyeurs trampling the dune grass, are firmly opposed and routinely issue tickets, so stand forewarned (and fully clothed).

- **Herring Cove** ★★: This popular west-facing National Seashore beach is known for its spectacular sunsets. The long stretches of pristine sand front a calmer beach than Race Point (see below), because Herring Cove faces Cape Cod Bay. Herring Cove is a haven for same-sex couples, who tend to sort themselves by gender and gather to the far left side of the beach. Parking costs $7 per day, $20 per season.
- **Long Point** ★: Trek out over the breakwater at the far west end of Commercial Street and walk about 1½ miles over sand, or catch a water shuttle ($10 round-trip) from Flyer's Boat Rental (see "Boating," below) to visit this very last spit of land, capped by an 1827 lighthouse. Shuttles run hourly in July and August.

Provincetown

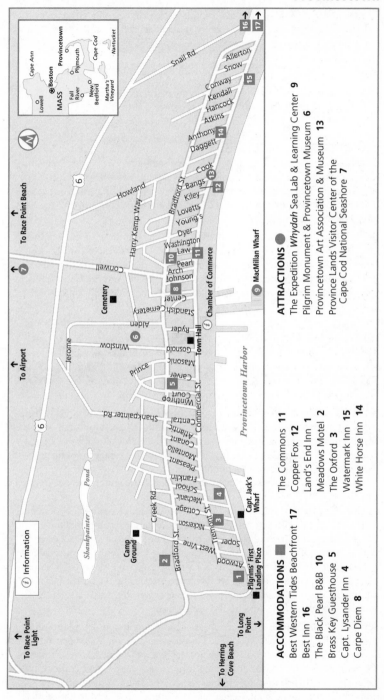

ATTRACTIONS ●

The Expedition *Whydah* Sea Lab & Learning Center **9**
Pilgrim Monument & Provincetown Museum **6**
Provincetown Art Association & Museum **13**
Province Lands Visitor Center of the
  Cape Cod National Seashore **7**

ACCOMMODATIONS ■

Best Western Tides Beachfront **17**
Best Inn **16**
The Black Pearl B&B **10**
Brass Key Guesthouse **5**
Capt. Lysander Inn **4**
Carpe Diem **8**
The Commons **11**
Copper Fox **12**
Land's End Inn **1**
Meadows Motel **2**
The Oxford **3**
Watermark Inn **15**
White Horse Inn **14**

231

• **Race Point** ✹✹✹: Facing the Atlantic Ocean, Race Point offers rougher surf than Herring Cove Beach, and you might actually spot whales en route to Stellwagen Bank.

BICYCLING   North of town, nestled amid the Cape Cod National Seashore preserve, is the spectacular 7-mile **Province Lands Trail** ✹✹✹, a heady swirl of steep dunes (watch out for sand drifts on the path) anchored by wind-stunted scrub pines. With its free parking, the **Province Lands Visitor Center** ✹✹ (✆ **508/487-1256**) is a good place to start: You can survey the landscape from the observation tower to try to get your bearings before setting off amid the dizzying maze. With any luck, you'll find a spur path leading to one of the beaches—Race Point or Herring Cove—lining the shore. Rentals are offered in season by **Nelson's Bike Shop,** 43 Race Point Rd. (✆ **508/487-8849**). It's also an easy jaunt from town, where you'll find plenty of good bike shops—such as the centrally located **Ptown Bikes,** 42 Bradford St. (✆ **508/487-8735**); reserve several days in advance.

BOATING   In addition to operating a Long Point shuttle from its own dock (see "Beaches," above), **Flyer's Boat Rental,** 131 Commercial St. in the West End (✆ **508/487-0898**), offers all sorts of craft, from kayaks and dinghies to sailboats; sailing lessons and fishing trips are also available. **Off the Coast Kayak Company,** 3 Freeman St., in the center of town (✆ **508/487-2692**), offers kayak tours and rentals in season.

FISHING   Surf casting is permitted at **Herring Cove Beach** (off Route 6) and **Race Point Beach** (near the Race Point Coast Guard Station); also, many people drop a hand-line or light tackle right off the West End breakwater. For low-cost deep-sea fishing via party boat, board the *Cee Jay* (✆ **800/675-6723** or 508/487-4330). For serious sport-fishing, sign on for the *Shady Lady II* (✆ **508/487-0182**). Both depart from MacMillan Wharf.

NATURE TRAILS   Within the Province Lands (off Race Point Road, a half mile north of Route 6), the National Seashore maintains the 1-mile, self-guided **Beech Forest Trail** ✹✹, a shaded path that circles a shallow freshwater pond blanketed with water lilies before heading into the woods. You can see the shifting dunes gradually encroaching on the forest.

Another wonderful walk is along the **West End breakwater** ✹✹ out to the end of Long Point, about 3 miles round-trip. The breakwater is located at the end of Commercial Street, next to the Provincetown Inn. It's about a 20-minute walk across the wide breakwater; then it's soft sand for the remainder of the hike. **Wood End Lighthouse** is directly across the spit of sand near the breakwater. It will take about another 40 minutes to reach **Long Point Light,** at the very tip of Cape Cod. Hikers determined to reach the end of Long Point will want to bring a hat, water, and sunscreen for this intense trek along the beach. The outside of the arm tends to be the more scenic route; the inside coast can be crowded with picnicking families and surf casters.

WHALE WATCHING ✹✹✹   Stellwagen Bank, 8 miles off Provincetown, is a rich feeding ground for whales. The **Dolphin Fleet** ✹, on MacMillan Wharf (✆ **800/826-9300** or 508/349-1900), was the first, and by most accounts is still the best, outfit running whale-watching trips to Stellwagen. Most cruises carry a naturalist to provide running commentary; on the *Dolphin,* these are scientists from the Center for Coastal Studies, out doing research crucial to the whales' survival, and part of the proceeds goes to further their worthwhile efforts. Tickets are $19 for adults, $17 for seniors, $16 for children 7 to 12, and free for children under 7. There are nine 3½-hour trips daily; call to reserve. Closed November through March.

Tips for first-timers: Dress very warmly, in layers (it's cold out on the water), and definitely take along a waterproof windbreaker. If you're prone to seasickness, consider taking a motion-sickness pill at the start of the trip (they're provided free as you board the vessel). It can get rough out here.

ORGANIZED TOURS & CRUISES

See also "Whale Watching," above, for information on trips to Stellwagen Bank.

Art's Dune Tours is at the corner of Commercial and Standish streets (© **800/894-1951** or 508/487-1950). In 1946, Art Costa started driving sightseers out to ogle the decrepit "dune shacks" where such transient luminaries as Eugene O'Neill, Jack Kerouac, and Jackson Pollock found their respective muses. The Park Service wanted to raze these eyesores, but luckily saner heads prevailed: They're now National Historic Landmarks. The tours typically take 1 to 1½ hours. Tickets are $12 for adults, $8 for children 4 to 11. Call for schedule and reservations.

Bay Lady II leaves from MacMillan Wharf in the center of town (© **508/ 487-9308**). The sunset trip aboard this 73-foot reproduction gaff-rigged Grand Banks schooner is especially spectacular. Trips cost $10 to $15 for adults, $5 for children under 12. There are four 2-hour sails daily from mid-May to mid-October. Call for schedule and reservations.

Board a 1931 Stinson Detroiter at **Willie Air Tours,** Provincetown Municipal Airport, on Race Point Road 2 miles northwest of town (© **508/487-9989**), to fathom the forces still shaping the land. Back-seat riders get to luxuriate on a red leather banquette, but the passenger next to the pilot gets the best view. The flight is smooth and gentle, an intoxicating way to experience the tip of the Cape. From late May to late October, 15-minute flights cost $50 for two adults, $15 for children 12 and under.

MUSEUMS

The Expedition Whydah Sea Lab & Learning Center ⚓   Cape Cod native Barry Clifford made headlines in 1984 when he tracked down the wreck of the 17th-century pirate ship *Whydah* (pronounced *Wid*-dah) 1,500 feet off the coast of Wellfleet, where it had lain undisturbed since 1717. Only 10% excavated to date, it has already yielded more than 100,000 artifacts. Visitors can observe the reclamation work as it's done.

MacMillan Wharf (just past the whale-watching fleet). © **508/487-8899**. www.whydah.com. Admission $5 adults, $3.50 children 6–12. June–Aug daily 10am–8pm; Sept–Dec and Apr–May daily 10am–5pm. Closed Jan–Mar.

Pilgrim Monument & Provincetown Museum ⭐⭐   Anywhere you go in town, this granite tower looms, ever ready to restore your bearings. Climb up the 60 ramps interspersed with 116 steps—a surprisingly easy lope—and you'll get a gargoyle's-eye view of the spiraling coast and, in the distance, Boston against a backdrop of New Hampshire's mountains. Definitely devote some time to the curious exhibits in the museum at the monument's foot, chronicling P-town's checkered past as both fishing port and arts nexus. Among the memorabilia, you'll find polar bears brought back from MacMillan's expeditions and early programs for the Provincetown Players.

High Pole Hill Rd. (off Winslow St., north of Bradford St.). © **508/487-1310**. Admission $6 adults, $3 children 4–12. July–Aug daily 9am–7pm; off-season daily 9am–5pm. Last admission 45 min. before closing. Closed Dec–Mar.

Province Lands Visitor Center of the Cape Cod National Seashore ✪

Though much smaller than the Salt Pond Visitor Center, this center also does a good job of explaining this special environment, where plant life must fight a fierce battle to maintain its toehold amid shifting sands buffeted by salty winds. After perusing the exhibits, circle the observation deck for great views of the dunes. Inquire about any special events scheduled, such as free guided walks and family campfires (reservations required). There are also canoe programs and surf-casting programs, both with equipment provided.

Race Point Rd. (about 1½ miles northwest of the town center). ✆ **508/487-1256**. Free admission. Mid-Apr to late Nov daily 9am–5pm. Closed late Nov to mid-Apr.

Provincetown Art Association & Museum ✪✪✪

This extraordinary cache of 20th-century American art began with five paintings donated by local artists, including Charles Hawthorne, the teacher who first "discovered" this picturesque outpost. Founded in 1914, only a year after New York's revolutionary Armory Show, the museum was the site of innumerable "space wars," as classicists and modernists vied for square footage; an uneasy truce was finally struck in 1927, when each camp was accorded its own show. In today's less competitive atmosphere, it's not unusual to see a tame still life sharing space with an unrestrained abstract. Fulfilling its charter to promote "social intercourse between artists and laymen," the museum sponsors a full schedule of concerts, lectures, readings, and classes.

460 Commercial St. (in the East End). ✆ **508/487-1750**. Suggested donation $3 adults, $1 seniors and children under 12. July–Aug daily noon–5pm and 8–10pm; call for off-season hours. Open year-round.

SHOPPING

ART GALLERIES   Of the several dozen galleries in town, only a handful are reliably worthwhile. In season, most of the galleries and even some of the shops open around 11am, then take a supper-time siesta from around 5 to 7pm, reopening and greeting visitors up to as late as 10 or 11pm.

Berta Walker represents a broad selection of artists' estates as well as current artists at **Berta Walker Gallery** ✪, 208 Bradford St., in the East End (✆ **508/487-6411**). Closed late October to late May. **DNA Gallery** ✪, 288 Bradford St. (✆ **508/487-7700**), has attracted such talents as photographer Joel Meyerowitz; sculptor Conrad Malicoat, whose free-form brick chimneys can be seen about town; and local conceptualist/provocateur Jay Critchley. Readings by cutting-edge authors add to the buzz. Closed mid-October to late May.

Julie Heller started collecting early P-town paintings as a child. She chose so incredibly well, her roster at **Julie Heller Gallery,** 2 Gosnold St. (✆ **508/487-2169**), reads like a who's who of local art. Hawthorne, Avery, Hofmann, Lazzell, Hensche—all the big names from Provincetown's past are here. Closed weekdays January through April; open winter weekends by chance or appointment. **Schoolhouse Center for Art and Design,** 494 Commercial St., in the East End (✆ **508/487-4800**), is an impressive setup with two galleries, studios, arts programs, and an events series.

DISCOUNT SHOPPING   **Marine Specialties,** 235 Commercial St., in the center of town (✆ **508/487-1730**), is packed to the rafters with useful stuff, from discounted Doc Martens to cut-rate Swiss Army knives and all sorts of odd nautical surplus. Be sure to look up: Hung from the ceiling are some real antiques, including several carillons' worth of ships' bells. **Provincetown Second Hand Store,** 389 Commercial St., in the center of town (✆ **508/487-9163**), is a local institution selling drag for Guys and Dolls.

FASHION **Mad as a Hatter,** 360 Commercial St., in the center of town
(© **508/487-4063**), has hats to suit every style, from folksy to downright diva-
esque. Closed January to mid-February. **Moda Fina,** 349 Commercial St.
(© **508/487-6632**), specializes in women's clothing and accessories, including
unique summer dresses. **Silk & Feathers,** 377 Commercial St., in the East End
(© **508/487-2057**), has seasonal styles, lingerie almost too pretty to cover up,
seaweed soaps, and statement jewelry.

WHERE TO STAY

Those on a budget can't do much better than the **Meadows Motel,** 122 Bradford St. Ext. (far west end of town), Provincetown (© **888/675-0880** or
508/487-0880; meadowsmtl@aol.com). Rooms have TVs and minifridges; rates
are $70 to $80 in season.

Very Expensive

Brass Key Guesthouse ★★★   Brass Key Guesthouse is the fanciest place to
stay in Provincetown. With Ritz-Carlton–style amenities and service in mind,
Michael MacIntyre and Bob Anderson have created a paean to luxury. These
innkeepers think of everything: down pillows, showers with jets, and gratis iced
tea and lemonade delivered poolside in season. While all rooms share top-notch
amenities like Bose radios, decorative styles vary according to the building. The
1828 Federal-style Captain's House and the Gatehouse are decorated in a playful country style—a loft is filled with teddy bears, for instance—while rooms in
the Victorian-era building are classically elegant, with materials like mahogany,
walnut, and marble. Most deluxe rooms have gas fireplaces and whirlpool tubs;
some bathrooms even have phones and TVs. In the center of it all is the extensively landscaped multilevel patio with heated pool and whirlpool. In high season, the clientele here is primarily gay men, though all are made to feel welcome.

67 Bradford St. (in the center of town), Provincetown, MA 02657. © 800/842-9858 or 508/487-9005. Fax
508/487-9020. www.brasskey.com. 33 units. Summer $195–$395 double; $285–$395 cottage. Rates include
continental breakfast and afternoon wine and cheese. AE, DISC, MC, V. Closed mid-Nov to early Apr. No children under 18 accepted. **Amenities:** Outdoor heated pool; 17-foot whirlpool; video library. *In room:* A/C,
TV/VCR, dataport, fridge, hair dryer, safe.

Expensive

Best Western Tides Beachfront ★★ *Kids*   Families will be delighted with
this beachfront motel, set on 6 acres well removed from Provincetown's bustle
and North Truro's ticky-tacky congestion. Every inch of this complex has been
groomed to the max, including the ultragreen grounds, the breakfast room that
seems to have been lifted whole from a country inn, and the spotless guest rooms
decorated in a soothing palette of pastels.

837 Commercial St. (near the Truro border), Provincetown, MA 02657. © 800/528-1234 or 508/487-1045.
Fax 508/487-1621. www.bwprovincetown.com. 64 units. Summer $139–$199 double, $249–$269 suite. AE,
DC, DISC, MC, V. Closed Nov to mid-May. **Amenities:** Outdoor heated pool; shuffleboard. *In room:* A/C, TV,
dataport, fridge, safe.

Land's End Inn ★★   Enjoying a prime 2-acre perch atop Gull Hill in the far
West End, this magical 1907 bungalow is stuffed to bursting with rare and often
outlandish antiques. In the dark-paneled living room, it's always Christmas: The
ornate decorations never come down. In other words, the place is quite unique,
in a way that will delight some guests and overwhelm others. The loft suite,
entered through a cabinet (very Narnia), must be one of the most unusual
accommodations on the Cape. From the spacious living room, you climb the
spiral stairway to the bedroom, where an immense stained-glass window serves

as your headboard. Some of the other rooms are tiny, but all are positively drip-ping with kitschy style. Though the clientele is predominantly gay, all visitors will feel welcome. The inn is part of a trust that donates its profits to the per-forming arts, in particular the Provincetown Repertory Theatre and the Provincetown Academy for the Performing Arts.

22 Commercial St. (in the West End), Provincetown, MA 02657. ℂ 800/276-7088 or ℂ and fax 508/487-0706. www.landsendinn.com. 17 units (1 with shared bathroom). Summer $125–$210 double; $145–$155 apartment; $285 suite. Rates include continental breakfast. MC, V. Open year-round.

Watermark Inn ⭐⭐⭐ If you'd like to experience P-town without being stuck in the thick of it (the carnival atmosphere can get tiring at times), this con-temporary inn at the peaceful edge of town is the perfect choice. The beachfront manor contains 10 dazzling suites; the prize ones, on the top floor, have picture windows and sweeping views from their decks. Pastel handmade quilts brighten up the clean, monochromatic rooms.

603 Commercial St. (in the East End), Provincetown, MA 02657. ℂ 508/487-0165. Fax 508/487-2383. www.watermark-inn.com. 10 units. Summer $160–$320 suite. Mid-May to mid-Sept, suites rent by the week only. AE, MC, V. Open year-round. *In room:* TV, kitchenette.

Moderate

Best Inn ⭐ Formerly the Holiday Inn, this is a good choice for first-timers not quite sure what they're getting into. It's a no-surprises motel at the eastern edge of town, a bit far from the action but congenial enough. An in-season shut-tle will whisk you down Commercial Street or to the beaches.

698 Commercial St. (at Rte. 6A, in the East End), Provincetown, MA 02657. ℂ 800/422-4224 or 508/487-1711. Fax 508/487-3929. www.capeinn.com. 78 units. Summer $139–$179 double. Rates include continental breakfast. AE, DC, DISC, MC, V. Closed Nov–Apr. Dogs allowed. **Amenities:** Pool bar and grill; out-door pool; lounge. *In room:* A/C, TV, fridge, coffeemaker, hair dryer, iron.

Carpe Diem ⭐⭐ Rainer and Jurgen, two young, urbane Germans, run this stylish 1884 house whose theme is "seize the day." The location, a quiet side street right in the center of town, suits most P-town habitués to a T. The rooms are exquisitely outfitted with European antiques, brightly painted walls, and down comforters; most have minifridges as well. Two deluxe garden suites boast private entrances, Jacuzzis, and fireplaces. The cottage has a two-person whirlpool. Breakfasts feature homemade German bread and muffins served at the family-size dining-room table. On clear days, sun worshippers choose the patio, where there's an eight-person hot tub.

12 Johnson St. (in the center of town), Provincetown, MA 02657. ℂ 800/487-0132 or 508/487-4242. Fax 508/487-4242. www.carpediemguesthouse.com. 13 units. Summer $125–$165 double; $195 suite, $235 cot-tage. Rates include continental breakfast. AE, MC, V. **Amenities:** Hot tub. *In room:* A/C, TV/VCR, dataport.

The Commons ⭐ Right in the thick of town, but removed from the hurly-burly by a street-side bistro (see "Where to Dine," below) and peaceful patio, this venerable guest house has received a stylish renovation. The bedrooms offer marble-look bathrooms and (in most cases) bay views. At the pinnacle is a beamed attic studio with its own deck overlooking MacMillan Wharf. All the delights of town are within easy reach, including—right on the property—one of Provincetown's best up-and-coming restaurants.

386 Commercial St. (in the center of town), Provincetown, MA 02657. ℂ 800/487-0784 or 508/487-7800. Fax 508/487-6114. www.capecod.net/commons. 14 units. Summer $105–$160 double; $160 suite. Rates include continental breakfast. AE, MC, V. Closed Jan–Mar. Pets allowed. **Amenities:** Restaurant (eclectic/French bistro). *In room:* TV.

Copper Fox ⭐ This majestic 1856 Federal-style captain's house is set well back from the road and just a short walk from the galleries and restaurants of the East End. The expansive lawn, unusual in Provincetown where space is at a premium, is dotted with urns and a birdbath. The inn has a large wraparound porch and a second-floor deck, which offers a perfect view of the harbor across the street. Several of the spacious rooms also have bay views. Two apartments have private entrances and kitchens; one has a private garden, and the other is large enough to accommodate six people. Bathrooms have been thoroughly modernized, but some have stylish claw-foot tubs.

448 Commercial St. (in the East End), Provincetown, MA 02657. ℂ and fax 508/487-8583. www. provincetown.com/copperfox. 7 units. Summer $140–$169 double; $185 apartment. Rates include continental breakfast and afternoon tea. MC, V. Open year-round. **Amenities:** Video library. *In room:* A/C, TV.

The Oxford ⭐⭐ In the far West End, this restored 1853 house offers truly affordable elegance. One downstairs room is quite large, with 8-foot windows overlooking the landscaped grounds. Accommodations with shared bathrooms are smaller. A new one-bedroom cottage is in the works. The drawing room is especially cozy, with sofas arranged in front of the fireplace. In the morning, the inn fills with the scrumptious aroma of home-baked breads and coffeecake. You may want to enjoy your coffee out on the veranda overlooking the courtyard's fountain and pond.

8 Cottage St. (in the West End), Provincetown, MA 02657. ℂ 888/456-9103 or 508/487-9103. www.oxfordguesthouse.com. 6 units (2 with shared bathroom). Summer $100–$275 double. Rates include continental breakfast. AE, DISC, MC, V. Pets allowed in apartment. *In room:* A/C, TV/VCR, CD player, dataport, fridge, hair dryer.

Inexpensive

The Black Pearl Bed & Breakfast ⭐ Every room in this cheery captain's house has a look all its own, from bold Southwestern to fanciful Micronesian murals; several boast skylights and private decks. The fully muralled Connemara Cottage takes the cake, with an antique bedstead, wood-burning fireplace, and double Jacuzzi, plus such niceties as air-conditioning, phone, and TV/VCR. The Lullwater suite consists of two rooms with TV/VCR, phone, air-conditioning, fridge, microwave, fireplace, and separate entrance with French doors to a private deck with hot tub.

11 Pearl St. (off Commercial St., near the center of town), Provincetown, MA 02657. ℂ 508/487-6405. Fax 508/487-7412. www.provincetown.com/blackpearl/index.html. 6 units. Summer $95–$105 double; $190 suite; $165 cottage. Rates include continental breakfast. MC, V. Closed Jan–Mar. *In room:* TV, hair dryer.

Captain Lysander Inn ⭐ This 1840 Greek Revival house has definite curb appeal: Set back from the street in the quiet West End, it's fronted by a flower-lined path leading to a sunny patio. The conservatively furnished rooms are quite nice for the price, and some have lovely water views. Tall windows make these rooms feel light and airy; they're also spotlessly clean.

96 Commercial St. (in the West End), Provincetown, MA 02657. ℂ 508/487-2253. Fax 508/487-7579. 14 units (6 with shared bathroom). Summer $95 double with shared bathroom, $105 double with private bathroom; efficiency $125 per day, $1,400 per week; apartment $200 per day, $1,200 per week; cottage $250 per day, $1,400 per week. Rates include continental breakfast. MC, V. Open year-round. *In room:* No phone.

White Horse Inn ⭐ Look for the house with the bright yellow door in the far East End of town. The rates are terrific, especially given the fact that this inn is the very embodiment of Provincetown's bohemian mystique. Frank Schaefer has been tinkering with this late-18th-century house since 1963; the rooms may be a bit austere, but each is enlivened by some of the 300-plus paintings he has collected over the decades. A number of his fellow artists helped him out in cobbling together the studio apartments out of salvage: There's an aura of beatnik improv about them still. Guests over the past 35 years have embodied a range of high and low art—cult filmmaker John Waters stayed here often, as did poet laureate Robert Pinsky.

500 Commercial St. (in the East End), Provincetown, MA 02657. (©) **508/487-1790.** 24 units (10 with shared bathroom). Summer $60 single with shared bathroom; $70–$80 double; $125–$140 efficiency. No credit cards. *In room:* No phone.

WHERE TO DINE

You must peruse the scrumptious meat pies and pastries at the beloved **Provincetown Portuguese Bakery,** 299 Commercial St., in the center of town ((©) **508/487-1803**). Closed November through March.

Spiritus, 190 Commercial St., in the center of town ((©) **508/487-2808**), is an extravagant pizza parlor open until 2am. The pizza's good, as are the fruit drinks, coffees, and premium ice cream. For a peaceful morning repast, check out the little garden in back. Closed November through March.

Very Expensive

Chester ★★★ NEW AMERICAN   Step through the colonnaded portico for a singular dining experience. Chester specializes in local seafood, meats, and vegetables prepared simply and with a flourish. The candlelit dining room is decorated with bright paintings by local artists. Service is exceptional, the food is beautifully presented, and the portions are hearty. Starters like spinach and scallop risotto take advantage of local provender, as does the entree Chatham cod with prosciutto and sage. The extensive wine list has won *Wine Spectator* awards. For dessert, look no further than the warm chocolate cake or homemade ice cream.

404 Commercial St. (©) **508/487-8200.** Reservations recommended. Main courses $19–$32. AE, MC, V. July to early Sept daily 6–10pm; May–June and mid-Sept to Dec Thurs–Sun 6–10pm; call for off-season hours. Closed Jan–Apr.

The Dancing Lobster Cafe Trattoria ★★★ MEDITERRANEAN Chef/owner Nils "Pepe" Berg's establishment is a popular place—expect to wait a half hour, even with a reservation. The food is excellent, featuring seafood from local fishermen and Venetian specialties in particular. Start with the grilled squid bruschetta, saffrony Venetian fish soup, or crab ravioli. Main courses may include steak al "Pepe" with green and black peppercorns, brandy, demiglace, and cream.

373 Commercial St. (in the center of town). (©) **508/487-0900.** Reservations recommended. Main courses $17–$30. MC, V. July–Sept Tues–Sun 11:30am–5pm and 5:30–11pm; May–June and Oct 6–9pm. Closed Nov–Apr.

Martin House ★★ FUSION   Easily one of the most charming restaurants on the Cape, this snuggery of rustic rooms happens to contain one of the Cape's most forward-thinking kitchens. The chef favors regional delicacies, such as the local littlenecks that appear in a kafir-lime-tamarind broth with Asian noodles. Main courses might include local-lobster-stuffed squash blossoms with a warm porcini-saffron vinaigrette, or grilled rack of pork with mango salsa and cactus-pear demiglace on spicy masa. The peaceful, softly lit rooms make an optimal setting for exploring new tastes. In season, sit in the rose-choked garden terrace beside the small fountain.

157 Commercial St. (©) **508/487-1327.** Reservations recommended. Main courses $14–$30. AE, DC, DISC, MC, V. May–Oct daily 6–11pm; Jan–May and Nov–Dec Thurs–Mon 6–10pm. Closed mid-Dec.

Expensive

The Commons Bistro & Bar ✩✩ ECLECTIC/FRENCH BISTRO   It's a toss-up: The sidewalk cafe provides a prime opportunity for studying P-town's inimitable street life, whereas the plum-colored dining room, adorned with an extraordinary collection of original Toulouse-Lautrec prints, affords a welcome refuge. Either way, you'll get to partake of Chach Breseno's tasty and creative fare. At lunchtime, her overstuffed lobster club sandwich on country bread is unbeatable. The Commons boasts the only wood-fired oven in town to date, which comes in handy in preparing the popular gourmet pizzas with toppings like smoked salmon, crème fraîche, and golden caviar. At dinner, you must try the gingered and smoked salmon with scallion basmati rice and orange-soy vinaigrette. For dessert, go for the crème brûlée.

386 Commercial St. (see "Where to Stay," above). ✆ 508/487-7800. Reservations recommended. Main courses $14–$23. AE, MC, V. Late June to early Sept daily 6–10:30pm; call for off-season hours. Closed Jan.

The Mews ✩✩✩ FUSION/INTERNATIONAL   Bank on fine food and suave service at this beachfront restaurant, an enduring favorite since 1961. Upstairs is the cafe, with its century-old carved mahogany bar. The dining room downstairs sits right on the beach. The best soup in the region is the Mews' scrumptious summertime special, chilled cucumber miso bisque with curry shrimp timbale. Perennial pleasures include the Marsala-marinated portobello mushrooms and a mixed seafood carpaccio. Among the showier entrees is "captured scallops": prime Wellfleet specimens enclosed with a shrimp-and-crab mousse in a crisp won-ton pouch and served atop a petite filet mignon with chipotle aioli. Desserts and coffees—take them upstairs in the cafe, to the accompaniment of soft-jazz piano—are delectable. Awash in sea blues that blend with the view, Cafe Mews offers a lighter menu and serves as an elegantly informal community clubhouse almost year-round.

429 Commercial St. ✆ 508/487-1500. Reservations recommended. Main courses $18–$27. AE, DC, DISC, MC, V. Late May to mid-Oct Mon–Fri 6–10pm, Sat–Sun 11am–2:30pm and 6–10pm; mid-Feb to late May and mid-Oct to late Dec Thurs–Mon 6–10pm, Sun 11am–2:30pm. Open year-round.

Moderate

Bubala's by the Bay ✩✩ ECLECTIC   Once a nothing-special seaside restaurant, this trendy bistro—miraculously transformed with a gaudy yellow paint job and Picassoesque murals—promises "serious food at sensible prices." And that's what it delivers: from buttermilk waffles to creative focaccia sandwiches to pad Thai. This is the only place on Cape Cod that offers ostrich, served with a grilled pepper crust and a caramelized onion and balsamic glaze. In season, there's entertainment nightly.

183 Commercial St. (in the West End). ✆ 508/487-0773. Main courses $10–$21. AE, DISC, MC, V. Apr–Oct daily 8am–11pm. Closed Nov–Mar.

Little Fluke Cafe ✩ NEW AMERICAN   This tiny cafe with outdoor tables is a perfect people-watching spot at breakfast or lunch. In the morning, try the famous blueberry cornmeal pancakes. Dinner is a bit pricey for this very casual atmosphere, but the small menu offers tasty choices for fish lovers, meat eaters, and vegetarians. Good choices are the pan-seared salmon with a soy-ginger reduction and wasabi cream, or the grilled marinated portobello mushroom with sautéed baby spinach and seasonal vegetables.

401½ Commercial St. (in the East End). ✆ 508/487-4773. Reservations not accepted. Main courses $15–$24. No credit cards. July–Aug daily 8am–1pm; Wed–Sun 6–10pm; call for off-season hours. Closed Oct–Apr.

The Lobster Pot ⭐ SEAFOOD   Snobbish foodies might turn their noses up at a venue so flagrantly Olde Cape Coddish, but for Provincetown regulars, no season seems complete without at least one pilgrimage. The line, which starts near the aromatic, albeit frantic, kitchen, often snakes into the street. A lucky few will make it all the way to the outdoor deck, but most tables, indoors and out, still afford nice views of MacMillan Wharf. By all means spring for a jumbo lobster—boiled or broiled, sauced or simple. And definitely start off with the chowder, a perennial award-winner.

321 Commercial St. (in the center of town). ℂ 508/487-0842. Reservations not accepted. Main courses $14–$21. AE, DC, DISC, MC, V. Mid-June to mid-Sept daily 11:30am–10:30pm; mid-Feb to mid-June and mid-Sept to Dec 11:30am–9:30pm. Closed Jan to mid-Feb.

Lorraine's ⭐⭐⭐ MEXICAN/NEW AMERICAN   Some are calling this the town's best restaurant. Even those who shy away from Mexican restaurants should try it; the cuisine of chef Lorraine Najar is truly unique. Abandon all caution and begin with *chile relleno de queso,* fresh chile peppers stuffed with the chef's choice nightly, rolled in corn meal and corn flour, and lightly deep-fried. For a main course, consider *viere verde*—sea scallops sautéed with tomatillos, flambéed in tequila, and cloaked in a green-chili sauce. On Fridays and Saturdays, tapas are served until midnight. This place is hopping; there's entertainment nightly in season.

463 Commercial St. (in the East End). ℂ 508/487-6074. Reservations suggested. Main courses $15–$22. MC, V. June–Sept daily 6–10pm. Call for off-season hours. Closed Jan–Mar.

Napi's ⭐⭐ INTERNATIONAL   Restaurateur Napi Van Dereck can be credited with bringing P-town's restaurant scene up to speed—back in the early 1970s. His namesake restaurant still reflects that Zeitgeist, with its rococo-hippie carpentry, select outtakes from his sideline in antiques, and some rather outstanding art. The cuisine is a lot less granola than it once was, or maybe we've just caught up—hearty peasant fare never really goes out of style. And these peasants really get around, culling dumplings from China, falafel from Syria, and, from Greece, shrimp feta flambéed with ouzo and Metaxa. A lower-priced tavern menu is available on weeknights.

7 Freeman St. (at Bradford St.). ℂ 800/571-6274 or 508/487-1145. Reservations recommended. Main courses $12–$24. AE, DC, DISC, MC, V. May–Oct daily 5–10pm; Nov–Apr daily 11:30am–4pm and 5–9pm.

Inexpensive

Café Crudité VEGETARIAN   With its tiny deck overlooking Provincetown's main drag, this health-conscious vegetarian/macrobiotic/vegan hideaway is a great place to sit out the hype and its empty-caloric enticements. In addition to the basic macrobiotic breakfast (a bowl of miso-and-rice soup), morning options include an unusual "Egg Saag"—two eggs poached and served atop seven-grain bread spread with Indian-spiced spinach. Cold sesame noodles are available throughout the day, as are double-bean burritos. Coffees, including a wicked frozen cappuccino, represent the only departure from the straight and narrow.

336 Commercial St. (upstairs). ℂ 508/487-6237. Most items under $10. No credit cards. June to early Sept daily noon–10pm; call for off-season hours. Closed Dec–Mar.

Take-Out & Picnic Fare

At **Clem and Ursie's** ⭐⭐, 85 Shankpainter Rd., off Bradford Street (ℂ **508/487-2333**), grab a picnic table for a dinner of fried seafood, barbecued chicken, and ribs. There are also more elaborate choices like bouillabaisse, *fra diavolo,* and Japanese udon. Closed November to April.

Mojo's, 5 Ryder St. Ext. (℃ **508/487-3140**), a fried-seafood shack on Fisherman's Wharf, is known for its lightly breaded fried fish. There are also veggie burgers, burritos, and chicken tenders. Eat at one of the six picnic tables on the patio or take it to the beach. Closed October to May.

The best gourmet take-out shop is **Angel Foods,** 467 Commercial St., in the East End (℃508/487-6666), which offers Italian specialties. The rollwiches—pita bread packed with a wide range of fillings—at **Box Lunch,** 353 Commercial St., in the center of town (℃ **508/487-6026**), are ideal for a strolling lunch. Stop at **Fresh from the Oven,** 129 Bradford St., in the center of town (℃ **508/487-9331**), for more elaborate fixings like homemade hummus and curried chicken-salad pita. Closed November to May.

PROVINCETOWN AFTER DARK

There's so much going on in season on any given night that you might want to simplify your search by calling or stopping in at the **Provincetown Reservations System office,** 293 Commercial St., in the center of town (℃ **508/487-6400**).

The hottest club in town for the last few years, **Antro,** 258 Commercial St., 2nd floor, beside Town Hall (℃ **508/487-8800**), is the current home of "Two Fags and a Drag" and the ever-popular all-star musical comedy drag revue "Big Boned Barbies," starring Kandi Kane. Closed October to May.

Perhaps the nation's premier gay bar, the **Atlantic House,** 6 Masonic Place, off Commercial Street (℃ **508/487-3821**), is open year-round. The "A-house" also welcomes straight folks, except in the leather-oriented Macho Bar upstairs. In the little fireplaced bar downstairs, check out the Tennessee Williams memorabilia, including a portrait *au naturel.*

Come late afternoon, if you're wondering where all the beachgoers have gone, it's a safe bet that a number are attending the gay-lesbian tea dance held daily in season from 3:30 to 6:30pm on the pool deck at the **Boatslip Beach Club,** 161 Commercial St. (℃ **508/487-1669**). The action then shifts to the Pied (see below), but returns here later in the evening for disco.

Crown & Anchor, 247 Commercial St., in the center of town (℃ **508/487-1430**), houses a number of bars spanning leather, disco, comedy, drag shows, and cabaret. Facilities include a pool bar and game room.

On early evenings in season, a "parade" of gay revelers descends from the Boatslip to the **Pied** ⚡, 193A Commercial St., in the center of town (℃ **508/487-1527**), for its After Tea T-Dance from 6:30 to 10pm. The late-night wave consists of a fair number of women, or fairly convincing simulacra thereof. For a glimpse of stars-in-the-making, check out "Putting on the Hits," a sampling of local talent held Tuesdays at 10pm. Call for schedule.

CAPE COD NATIONAL SEASHORE ⚡⚡⚡

No trip to Cape Cod would be complete without a visit to the Cape Cod National Seashore on the Outer Cape. Take an afternoon barefoot stroll along the "The Great Beach," and see why the Cape attracts so many artists and poets. On August 7, 1961, President John F. Kennedy signed a bill designating 27,000 acres in the 40 miles from Chatham to Provincetown as the Cape Cod National Seashore, a new national park. However, as early as the 1930s, the National Park Service had been interested in Cape Cod's Great Beach; back then the land would have cost taxpayers about $10 an acre! Unusual in a national park, the Seashore includes 500 private residences, the owners of which lease land from

Recommended Reading
Henry David Thoreau's *Cape Cod* is an entertaining account of the author's journeys on the Cape in the late 19th century. The writer/naturalist walked along the beach from Eastham to Provincetown, and you can follow in his footsteps. Henry Beston's *The Outermost House* describes a year of living on the beach in Eastham in a simple one-room dune shack. The shack washed out to sea about 20 years ago, but "The Great Beach" remains.

the park service. Convincing residents that a National Seashore would be a good thing for Cape Cod was an arduous task back then, and Provincetown still grapples with Seashore officials over town land issues.

ESSENTIALS
GETTING THERE   Take Route 6, the Mid-Cape Highway, to Eastham (about 45 miles from the Sagamore Bridge).

VISITOR INFORMATION   Pick up a map of the Cape Cod National Seashore at the **Salt Pond Visitor Center,** in Eastham (✆ **508/225-3421**). It's open daily, late May to early September from 9am to 5pm, early September to late May from 9am to 4:30pm. There is also the **Province Lands Visitor Center,** a smaller site, in Provincetown. Both centers have ranger activities, maps, gift shops, and bathrooms. Seashore beaches are all off Route 6 and are clearly marked. Additional beaches along this stretch are run by individual towns, and you must have a sticker or pay a fee to park.

BEACHES & OUTDOOR PURSUITS
BEACHES   The Seashore's claim to fame is its spectacular beaches—in reality, one long beach—with dunes 50 to 150 feet high. This is the Atlantic Ocean, so the surf is rough (and cold), but a number of the beaches have lifeguards. A $20 pass will get you into all of them for the season, or you can pay a daily rate of $7. Most of the Seashore beaches have large parking lots, but you'll need to arrive early (before 10am) on busy summer weekends to claim a spot. If the beach you want to go to is full, try the one next door—most of the beaches are 5 to 10 miles apart. Don't forget your beach umbrella; the sun exposure here can get intense.

- **Coast Guard and Nauset Light Beaches** 🦀🦀🦀, off Ocean View Drive, Eastham: Connected to outlying parking lots by a free shuttle, these pristine National Seashore beaches have lifeguards and rest rooms.
- **Head of the Meadow Beach** 🦀🦀, off Head of the Meadow Road, Truro: Among the more remote National Seashore beaches, this spot (with rest rooms) is known for its excellent surf. Because beachgoers don't have to traverse steep dunes to get here, Head of the Meadow is easier for seniors or those with disabilities to access.
- **Marconi Beach** 🦀🦀, off Marconi Beach Road in South Wellfleet: The bluffs are so high at this National Seashore property that the beach lies in shadows by late afternoon. Rest rooms are available.
- **Race Point and Herring Cove Beaches** 🦀🦀🦀, off Route 6, Provincetown: Race Point has rough surf, and you might even spot a whale on its way to Stellwagen Bank, a breeding ground. Herring Cove, with much calmer waters, is a good place to watch sunsets, and is popular with same-sex couples.

BICYCLING   The best path on Cape Cod is the **Province Lands Trail,** 5 swooping and invigorating miles at Race Point Beach. There is also a 2-mile, relatively flat path linking Head of the Meadow Beach to High Head.

FISHING   Surf casting is allowed from the ocean beaches. Race Point is a popular spot.

NATURE TRAILS   The Seashore also has a number of walking trails—all free, all picturesque, and all worth a trip. In Eastham, **Fort Hill** ✿✿✿ (off Route 6) has one of the best scenic views on Cape Cod as well as a popular boardwalk trail through a red maple swamp. Following the trail markers around Fort Hill, you'll pass "Indian Rock" (bearing the marks of untold generations who used it to sharpen their tools) and enjoy scenic vantage points overlooking the channel-carved marsh and out to sea. Keep an eye out for egrets and great blue herons. The Fort Hill Trail hooks up with the half-mile Red Cedar Swamp Trail, offering boardwalk views of an ecology otherwise inaccessible.

The **Nauset Marsh Trail** ✿ is accessed from the Salt Pond Visitor Center on Route 6 in Eastham. **Great Island** ✿✿, on the bay side in Wellfleet, is surely one of the finest places to have a picnic; you could spend the day hiking the trails. On **Pamet Trail** ✿ off North Pamet Road in Truro, hikers pass the decrepit old cranberry-bog building (restoration is in the works) on the way to a trail through the dunes. Don't try the old boardwalk trail over the bogs here; it has flooded and is no longer in use. The **Atlantic White Cedar Swamp Trail** ✿✿ is located at the Marconi Station site (described below). **Small Swamp** ✿ and **Pilgrim Spring** ✿ trails are found at Pilgrim Heights Beach. **Beech Forest Trail** ✿✿ is located at Race Point in Provincetown.

SEASHORE SIGHTS   The **Old Harbor Lifesaving Station** ✿, Race Point Beach off Race Point Road, Provincetown (© **508/487-1256**), was one of 13 lifesaving stations mandated by Congress in the late 19th century. This shingled shelter with a lookout tower was part of a network responsible for saving some 100,000 lives. Before the U.S. Lifesaving Service was founded in 1872 (it became part of the Coast Guard in 1915), shipwreck victims lucky enough to be washed ashore were still doomed unless they could find a "charity shed"—a hut supplied with firewood—maintained by the Massachusetts Humane Society. The six valiant "Surfmen" manning each life-saving station took a more active approach, patrolling the beach at all hours and rowing out into the surf to save all they could. Their old equipment is on view at this museum. Free admission; parking fee for Race Point Beach (see "Beaches," above). It's open daily from 3 to 5pm in July and August; call for off-season hours. Closed November to April.

The **Marconi Wireless Station** ✿, on Marconi Park Site Road (off Route 6), South Wellfleet (© **508/349-3785**), tells the story of the first international telegraphic communication. It's from this spot that inventor Guglielmo Marconi sent the world's first wireless communiqué: "Cordial greetings from President Theadore [sic] Roosevelt to King Edward VII in Poldhu, Wales." It was also here, in 1912, that news of the *Titanic* first reached these shores. There's scarcely a trace left of this extraordinary feat of technology (the station was dismantled in 1920); still, the outdoor displays convey the leap of imagination that was required.

The **Captain Edward Penniman House** ✿, at Fort Hill off Route 6 in Eastham, is a grandly ornate 1868 Second Empire mansion. It's open for tours in season, but the exterior far outshines the interior. Call the visitor center

(© 508/255-3421) for times. Check out the huge whale jawbone gate before crossing the street to the trails (see "Nature Trails," above).

Five lighthouses, all automated now, dot the Seashore. In 1996, both Nauset Light, in Eastham, and Highland Light, in Truro, were successfully moved from precarious positions on the edge of dunes in order to save the beloved lighthouses. **Nauset Light** ★, with its cheerful red stripe, was moved from Chatham in 1923. The lighthouse flashes an alternating red and white light that can be seen for 23 miles; public tours are offered.

Highland Light ★★, also known as **Cape Cod Light,** is the site of the first light in this area, dating back to 1798. The present structure was built in 1857. Follow signs from Route 6 in North Truro to the end of Highland Road. This lighthouse, set high on a cliff, was the first light seen by ships traveling from Europe. Now that the structure has been moved back from the eroding cliff, the National Seashore allows visitors to climb the winding staircase to the top with a tour guide. Nearby is the 1907 **Highland House** ★★, home of the collections of the Truro Historical Society. Take a look at the antique nautical items, as well as the fascinating Early Americana. Admission to both the museum and lighthouse is $5 for adults, free for children under 12. (*Note:* There's a minimum 4-foot height requirement for climbing to the top of the lighthouse.) Both the lighthouse and the Highland House are open June through September, daily from 10am to 5pm.

Wood End Light, on Long Point in Provincetown, is an unusual square lighthouse built as a "twin" to Long Point Light in 1873. Hearty souls can hike first across the breakwater at the west end of Commercial Street and then about a half mile over soft sand to see this lighthouse.

Long Point Light, in Provincetown, established in 1827, is isolated at the very tip of Cape Cod. It's about an hour's walk from the breakwater, or a short boat ride from the center of town. Its fixed green light can be seen for 8 miles. This lighthouse was once the center of a thriving fishing community in the 1800s. Storms and erosion led the community to float their houses across the bay to Provincetown's west end, where a couple of the houses—some of the oldest in town—are still standing.

7

Martha's Vineyard & Nantucket

by Laura M. Reckford

Megastars and CEOs, vacationing families, and penniless students all seek refuge on Martha's Vineyard and Nantucket, two picturesque islands off the coast of Cape Cod. Both islands have much to offer families with children and couples seeking a romantic getaway. Their fame as summer resorts doesn't begin to take into account their rich history, diverse communities, and artistic traditions. But the popularity of these islands means that if you must go in the middle of summer, expect crowds and even—yikes!—traffic jams.

While only about 25 nautical miles apart, each island has its own distinct personality. Martha's Vineyard, large enough to support a year-round population spanning a broad socio-economic spectrum, is not quite as rarefied as Nantucket. Vineyarders pride themselves on their liberal stances. True, a prime oceanside estate might fetch millions here, but the residents still dicker over the price of zucchini at the local farmers' market. Nantucket, flash-frozen in the mid–19th century through zealous zoning, has long been considered a Republican haven. It's rich and traditional. Social scene aside, Nantucket has more pristine public shores than the Vineyard, as well as the best upscale shopping in the region. But there's something for everyone on both islands, and an island vacation is bound to be one that's cherished for many years.

1 Martha's Vineyard ✸✸✸

With 100 square miles, Martha's Vineyard is New England's largest island, yet each of its six communities is blessed with endearing small-town charm. When the former First Family vacationed here, locals joked that the Clintons tested their reputed nonchalance toward famous faces. But don't visit the Vineyard for the celebrities. Instead, savor the decidedly laid-back pace of this unique place.

Most visitors never take the time to explore the entire island, staying in the down-island towns of **Vineyard Haven** ✸ (officially called Tisbury), **Edgartown** ✸✸✸, and **Oak Bluffs** ✸✸✸. The "up-island" towns—**West Tisbury** ✸✸, **Chilmark** ✸ (including the fishing village of **Menemsha** ✸✸✸), and **Aquinnah** ✸✸ (formerly known as Gay Head)—tend to be far less touristy.

By all means, admire the regal sea captains' homes in Edgartown. Stroll down Circuit Avenue in Oak Bluffs with a Mad Martha's ice-cream cone, then ride the Flying Horses Carousel, said to be the oldest working carousel in the nation. Check out the cheerful "gingerbread" cottages behind Circuit Avenue, where the echoes of 19th-century revival meetings still ring out from the imposing tabernacle.

But don't forget to journey "up-island" to marvel at the red clay cliffs of Aquinnah, a national historic landmark. Or bike the country roads of West

Tisbury and Chilmark. Buy a lobster roll in the fishing village of Menemsha. There's a surprising degree of diversity here, for those who take the time to discover it.

ESSENTIALS
GETTING THERE
BY FERRY   Most visitors take ferries from the mainland to the Vineyard. You'll most likely catch a boat from Woods Hole on Cape Cod; however, boats do run from Falmouth, Hyannis, New Bedford, and Nantucket. A state-of-the-art catamaran ferry makes the trip from New London, Conn. It's easy to get a passenger ticket on almost any of the ferries, but space for cars is extremely limited, especially on summer weekends, when reservations must be made months in advance. Unless you absolutely must have your car with you, you'll probably want to leave it on the mainland. Traffic and parking on the island can be brutal in summer, and it's easy to take the shuttle buses (see below) from town to town or simply bike around.

From Woods Hole   The state-run **Steamship Authority** (© **508/477-8600** from mid-April to mid-September daily from 6am to 9pm, or 508/693-9130 daily from 8am to 5pm; off-season office hours vary; www.islandferry.com) operates daily year-round, weather permitting. It maintains the only ferries that accommodate cars. These large ferries make the 45-minute trip to Vineyard Haven throughout the year; some boats go to Oak Bluffs from late May to late October (call for seasonal schedules). The cost of a round-trip car passage from mid-May to mid-October is $104; off-season, it drops to $62.

Many people prefer to leave their cars on the mainland, take the ferry (often with their bikes), and then rent a car, Jeep, or bicycle on the island. You can park your car at the Woods Hole lots (always full in summer) or at one of the many lots in Falmouth that absorb the overflow of cars. Parking costs $10 per day. Free shuttle buses (some equipped for bikes) run regularly from the outlying lots to the Woods Hole ferry terminal. If you're leaving your car on the mainland, plan to arrive at the parking lots in Falmouth at least 45 minutes before sailing time.

The cost of a round-trip passenger ticket on the ferry is $10 for adults and $5 for children 5 to 12 (kids under 5 ride free). If you're bringing your bike along, it's an extra $6 round-trip, year-round. You do not need a ferry reservation if you're traveling without a car, and there are no reservations needed for parking. Car rates do not include drivers or passengers; you must buy a ticket for each person going to the island.

From Falmouth   You can board the *Island Queen* (© **508/548-4800;** www.islandqueen.com) at Falmouth Harbor for a 35-minute cruise to Oak Bluffs (passengers only). The boat runs from late May to mid-October; round-trip fare costs $10 for adults, $5 for children under 13, and an extra $6 for bikes. There are seven crossings a day in season (eight on Friday and Sunday), and no reservations are needed. Parking will run $10 or $12 a day.

The **Falmouth-Edgartown Ferry Service** (© **508/548-9400**) operates a 1-hour passenger ferry called the *Pied Piper,* from Falmouth Harbor to Edgartown. The boat runs from late May to mid-October; reservations are required. In season, there are five crossings a day (six on Friday). Round-trip fares are $22 for adults and $16 for children under 12 ($6 round-trip for bikes). Parking is $10 per day.

Martha's Vineyard

For accommodations in Edgartown, see "Edgartown" map

ACCOMMODATIONS ▪

Attleboro House **6**
The Captain R. Flanders House **3**
Crocker House Inn **5**
The Dockside Inn **7**
Duck Inn **1**
Martha's Place **4**
Menemsha Inn and Cottages **2**
The Oak House **8**

Beach 🏖️ Ferry ⛴️ Lighthouse

Nantucket Sound

Ferry to Hyannis (Seasonal)

Ferry to Nantucket (Seasonal)

Ferry to Falmouth (Seasonal)

Ferry to Woods Hole (Year-round)

Ferry to New Bedford (Seasonal)

Cape Pogue Wildlife Refuge

East Beach (Wasque)

Dyke Bridge

Wasque Point

Norton Point

Cape Pogue Bay

Chappaquiddick Island

Chappaquiddick Rd.

Litchfield Rd.

Pacha Pond

Katama Bay

Katama Beach

South Beach

Edgartown Harbor

Edgartown Harbor Lighthouse Beach

Edgartown

Katama Rd.

Herring Creek Rd.

Main St.

Edgartown–W. Tisbury Rd.

Meeting House Rd.

Joseph A. Sylvia State Beach

Oak Bluffs Town Beach

East Chop

Seaview Ave.

Oak Bluffs

Owen Park Beach

West Chop

Tashmoo Lake

Vineyard Haven

Lake Tashmoo Town Beach

Main St.

Beach Rd.

Lagoon Pond

Barnes Rd.

County Rd.

Felix Neck Wildlife Sanctuary

Sengekontacket Pond

Airport Rd.

Martha's Vineyard Airport

MANUEL F. CORRELLUS STATE FOREST

Oyster Pond

Edgartown Great Pond

Atlantic Ocean

Cape Cod

Nantucket

Martha's Vineyard

Lamberts Cove Rd.

Lamberts Cove

Vineyard Sound

Cedar Tree Neck Sanctuary

Old County Rd.

North Tisbury

State Rd.

West Tisbury

South Rd.

State Rd.

North Rd.

Middle Rd.

Tisbury Great Pond

Chilmark Pond

Lucy Vincent Beach (restricted to residents)

Squibnocket Beach (restricted to residents)

Chilmark

Menemsha

Menemsha Beach

Menemsha Harbor Beach

Lobsterville Beach

Menemsha Pond

State Rd.

Moshup Trail

Squibnocket Pond

South Rd.

Gay Head Cliffs & Light

Aquinnah (formerly Gay Head)

Aquinnah Beach (Moshup Beach)

N

0   2 Mi
0   2.5 Km

247

> **Tips** **Reservations Policy for Car Passage to the Vineyard**
>
> Reservations are required to bring your car to Martha's Vineyard on Friday, Saturday, Sunday, and Monday from mid-June to mid-September, plus Memorial Day weekend. During these months, standby is in effect only on Tuesday, Wednesday, and Thursday. Technically, reservations can be made up to 1 hour in advance of ferry departure, but in summer ferries are almost always full, and you certainly cannot depend on a cancellation. Be aware that your space may be forfeited if you have not checked into the ferry terminal 30 minutes prior to sailing time. Reservations may be changed to another date and time with at least 24 hours' notice; otherwise, you'll have to pay for an additional ticket for your car. If you arrive without a reservation on a day that allows standby, come early and be prepared to wait in line for hours. Your passage is guaranteed if you're in line by 2pm on designated standby days. For up-to-date **Steamship Authority** information, go to **www.islandferry.com**.

From Hyannis May through October, **Hy-Line** (© **508/778-2600;** www.hy-linecruises.com) operates from the Ocean Street dock to Oak Bluffs. It runs three trips a day; travel time is about 1 hour and 45 minutes. A round-trip costs $26 for adults and $13.50 for children 5 to 12 ($10 extra for bikes). In July and August, it's a good idea to reserve a parking spot in Hyannis; the all-day fee is $10.

From Nantucket From early June to late September, **Hy-Line** (© **508/778-2600;** www.hy-linecruises.com) runs three passenger ferries to Oak Bluffs. There is no car-ferry service between the islands. Trip time is 2 hours and 15 minutes. The one-way fare is $12.50 for adults, $6.25 for children 5 to 12 ($5 extra for bikes).

From New Bedford The *Schamonchi,* at Billy Woods Wharf (© **508/997-1688;** www.mvferry.com), makes runs to Vineyard Haven from mid-May to mid-October. Trip time is 1½ hours. A 1-day/round-trip ticket is $17 for adults, $9 for children under 12 ($5 extra for bikes). If you're staying overnight, the fare is a dollar more and parking is $8 per calendar day. No reservations are needed. This is a great way to avoid Cape traffic.

From New London, Conn. The *Tatobam* (© **888/SAILFOX;** www.foxnavigation.com) is a high-speed catamaran that makes the trip to Vineyard Haven in just over 2 hours. Fox Navigation, a subsidiary of the Mashantucket Pequot Tribal Nation, which runs Foxwoods Casino in Ledyard, Conn., owns the boat. It leaves the Admiral Harold E. Shear State Pier in New London on Friday, Saturday, Sunday, and Monday at 9am and arrives at West Dock in Vineyard Haven at 11:15am. It departs West Dock in Vineyard Haven at 4pm and arrives in New London at 6:15pm. A round-trip ticket is $89 first class, $59 clipper class. Parking at the state pier is free.

BY PLANE You can fly into **Martha's Vineyard Airport,** also known as Dukes County Airport (© **508/693-7022**), in West Tisbury, about 5 miles outside Edgartown.

Airlines serving the Vineyard include **Cape Air/Nantucket Airlines** (© **800/352-0714** or 508/771-6944), which connects the island year-round with Boston (trip time is 33 minutes; hourly shuttle service in summer costs about $240 round-trip), Hyannis (20 minutes; $80), Nantucket (15 minutes; $76), and New Bedford (20 minutes; $83); **Continental Express/Colgan Air** (© **800/525-0280**), which offers seasonal nonstop flights from Newark (75 minutes; $240); and **US Airways Express** (© **800/428-4322**), which flies from Boston for about $100 round-trip and also has seasonal weekend service from La Guardia (80 minutes; $300 round-trip). The only company offering year-round charter service is **Direct Flight** (© **508/693-6688**). **Westchester Air** (© **800/759-2929**) also runs some charters from White Plains, N.Y.

BY BUS **Bonanza Bus Lines** (© **800/556-3815**) connects the Woods Hole ferry port with Boston (from South Station), New York City, and Providence, R.I. The trip from South Station in Boston takes about 1 hour and 35 minutes and costs about $15 one-way; from Boston's Logan Airport, it's $20 each way; from New York, it's about a 6-hour bus trip to Hyannis or Woods Hole, costing approximately $47 each way or $84 round-trip.

BY LIMO   **Cape Cod Livery** (© **800/235-5669** or 508/563-5669) will pick you up at Boston's Logan Airport and take you to meet your ferry in Woods Hole (or anywhere else in the Upper Cape area). The trip takes about 1 hour and 45 minutes depending on traffic, and costs about $115 each way for a car-load of people. Book the service a couple of days in advance.

GETTING AROUND
BY BICYCLE & MOPED   The best way to explore the Vineyard is on two wheels, even if only for a couple of hours. There's a little of everything for cyclists, from paved paths to hilly country roads (see "Exploring the Vineyard on Two Wheels," below, for details on where to ride).

Mopeds are also a popular way to navigate Vineyard roads, but remember that some roads tend to be narrow and rough—the number of accidents involving mopeds seems to rise every year, and many islanders are opposed to these vehicles. (The renting of mopeds is banned in Edgartown.) You'll need a driver's license to rent one.

Bike-, scooter-, and moped-rental shops are clustered throughout all three down-island towns. Bike rentals cost about $15 to $30 a day (the higher prices are for suspension mountain bikes); scooters and mopeds, $30 to $80. In Vineyard Haven, try **Strictly Bikes,** Union Street (© **508/693-0782**). In Oak Bluffs, there's **Anderson's** (© **508/693-9346**), which rents bikes only, and **DeBettencourt's Bike Shop** (© **508/693-0011**), both on Circuit Avenue Extension. In Edgartown, you'll find **Wheel Happy,** 204 Upper Main St. and 8 S. Water St. (© **508/627-5928**), which rents only bikes.

BY CAR   If you're staying for a long visit or want to do some exploring up-island, you may want to bring your car or rent one on the island. Keep in mind that car-rental rates can soar during peak season, and gas is also more expensive here. Representatives of the national car-rental chains are located at the airport and in Vineyard Haven and Oak Bluffs. Local agencies also operate out of all three port towns, and many of them rent Jeeps, mopeds, and bikes as well.

The national chains include **Budget** (© **800/527-0700** or 508/693-1911), **Hertz** (© **800/654-3131**), and **Thrifty** (© **800/874-4389**). Local agencies include **Adventure Rentals,** Beach Road, Vineyard Haven (© **508/693-1959**);

All Island Rent-a-Car, at the airport (© **508/693-6868**); and **AAA Island Rentals,** with locations at 141 Main St., Edgartown (© **508/627-6800**), and Five Corners, Vineyard Haven (© **508/696-5300**).

BY SHUTTLE BUS & TROLLEY   In season, shuttle buses run often enough to make them a practical means of getting around. Connecting Vineyard Haven (across from the ferry terminal), Oak Bluffs (near the Civil War statue in Ocean Park), and Edgartown (Church Street, near the Old Whaling Church), the **Island Transport** (© **508/693-0058**) yellow school buses cost about $1.50 to $4, depending on distance. From late June to early September, they run from 6am to midnight every 15 minutes or half hour. Hours are reduced in spring and fall. Late June through August, buses go out to Gay Head (via the airport, West Tisbury, and Chilmark), leaving every couple of hours from down-island towns.

In season, the **Martha's Vineyard Transit Authority** (© **508/627-7448** or 508/627-9663) operates several shuttle buses (white buses with a purple "Come ride with us" logo). The Edgartown downtown shuttle and the South Beach buses circle throughout town or out to South Beach every 20 minutes. They also stop at the free parking lots just north of the town center. Parking here and shuttling into town is a great way to avoid circling the streets in search of a vacant spot on busy weekends. A one-way trip in town is just 50¢; a trip to South Beach (leaving from Edgartown's Church Street visitor center) is $1.50.

BY TAXI   Upon arrival, you'll find taxis at all ferry terminals and at the airport, and there are permanent taxi stands in Oak Bluffs (at the Flying Horses Carousel) and Edgartown (next to the Town Wharf). Most taxi companies operate cars as well as vans for larger groups and travelers with bikes. Options on the island include **Accurate Cab** (© **888/557-9798** or 508/627-9798) which is the only all-night service; **Adam Cab** (© **800/281-4462** or 508/693-3332); **All Island Taxi** (© **800/693-TAXI** or 508/693-2929); and **Martha's Vineyard Taxi** (© **508/693-9611** or 508/693-8660). In summer, rates from town to town are generally flat fees based on where you're headed and the number of passengers. A trip from Vineyard Haven to Edgartown would cost around $15 for two people. Rates double from after midnight until 7am.

BY CHAPPAQUIDDICK FERRY   The **On-Time ferry** (© **508/627-9427**) runs the 5-minute trip from Memorial Wharf on Dock Street in Edgartown to **Chappaquiddick Island** 🚗🚗 from June to mid-October, every 5 minutes from 7am to midnight. Passengers, bikes, mopeds, dogs, and cars (three at a time) are all welcome. The one-way fare costs $1 per person, $4 for one car and one driver, $2.50 for one bike and one person, and $3.50 for one moped or motorcycle and one person.

VISITOR INFORMATION

Contact the **Martha's Vineyard Chamber of Commerce,** at Beach Road, Vineyard Haven (© **508/693-0085;** fax 508/693-7589; www.mvy.com). Its office is just 2 blocks up from the ferry terminal in Vineyard Haven. There are also information booths at the ferry terminal in Vineyard Haven, across from the Flying Horses Carousel in Oak Bluffs, and on Church Street in Edgartown. For information on current events, check the two local newspapers, the *Vineyard Gazette* and the *Martha's Vineyard Times.*

In case of an **emergency,** call © **911** and/or head for the **Martha's Vineyard Hospital,** Linton Lane, Oak Bluffs (© **508/693-0410**), which has a 24-hour emergency room.

Edgartown

ACCOMMODATIONS

The Arbor **1**
Charlotte Inn **10**
Colonial Inn of
  Martha's Vineyard **12**
Edgartown Inn **13**
Harbor View Hotel **14**

Hob Knob Inn **3**
Inn at 148 Main **2**
The Jonathan Munroe
  House **5**
The Point Way Inn **4**
Victorian Inn **11**

ATTRACTIONS

Dr. Daniel Fisher House **6**
Old Whaling Church **7**
Vincent House Museum **8**
Vineyard Museum **9**

A STROLL AROUND EDGARTOWN ✦✦✦

A good way to get acclimated to the pace and flavor of the Vineyard is to walk the streets of Edgartown. This walk starts at the Dr. Daniel Fisher House and meanders along for about a mile; depending on how long you linger at each stop, it should take about 2 to 3 hours. If you're driving, park at the free lots at the edge of town (you'll see signs on the roads from Vineyard Haven and West Tisbury), and bike or take the shuttle bus (50¢) to the Edgartown visitor center on Church Street.

The **Dr. Daniel Fisher House** ✦, 99 Main St. (© **508/627-8017**), is a prime example of Edgartown's trademark Greek Revival opulence. A key player in the 19th-century whaling trade, Dr. Fisher amassed a fortune sufficient to found the Martha's Vineyard National Bank. Built in 1840, his prosperous and proud mansion boasts such classical elements as colonnaded porticos, as well as a delicate roof walk.

Note: The only way to view the interior (now headquarters for the Martha's Vineyard Preservation Trust) is on a guided **Vineyard Historic Walking Tour** (© **508/627-8619**). This tour, which also takes in the neighboring Old Whaling Church, originates next door at the Vincent House Museum. Tours are offered June through September, Monday through Saturday from 10:30am to 3pm. The cost is $7 to $10 for adults, free for children 12 and under.

The **Vincent House Museum** ⚘, off Main Street between Planting Field Way and Church Street, a transplanted 1672 full Cape, is considered to be the oldest surviving dwelling on the island. The **Old Whaling Church** ⚘⚘, 89 Main St., a magnificent 1843 Greek Revival edifice designed by local architect Frederick Baylies, Jr., was built as a whaleboat would have been, out of massive pine beams. With its 27-foot windows and 92-foot tower (a landmark easily spotted from the sea), this is a building that knows its place in the community. Maintained by the Preservation Trust and still supporting a Methodist parish, the building is now used primarily as a performance venue.

Continuing down Main Street and turning right onto School Street, you'll pass another Baylies monument, the 1839 **Baptist Church,** which, having lost its spire, was converted into a private home with a rather grand, column-fronted facade. Two blocks farther, on your left, is the **Vineyard Museum** ⚘⚘, 59 School St. (© **508/627-4441**), a fascinating complex assembled by the Dukes County Historical Society. An absorbing display of island history, this cluster of buildings contains exhibits of early Native American crafts; an entire 1765 house; an extraordinary array of maritime art; a carriage house to catch odds and ends; and the Gay Head Light Tower's decommissioned Fresnel lens.

Give yourself enough time to explore the museum's curiosities before heading south 1 block on Cooke Street. Cater-corner across South Summer Street, you'll spot the first of Baylies's impressive endeavors, the 1828 **Federated Church.** One block left are the offices of the *Vineyard Gazette,* 34 S. Summer St. (© **508/627-4311**). Operating out of a 1760 house, this exemplary small-town newspaper has been going strong since 1846.

Walk down South Summer Street to Main Street and take a right toward the water, stopping in at any inviting shops along the way. Veer left on Dock Street to reach the **Old Sculpin Gallery,** 58 Dock St. (© **508/627-4881**), open late June to early September. The output of the Martha's Vineyard Art Association displayed here tends to be amateurish, but you might happen upon a find. The real draw is the stark old building itself, which started out as a granary (part of Dr. Fisher's vast holdings) and spent the better part of the 20th century as a boat-building shop.

Cross the street to survey the harbor from the deck at Town Wharf. It's from here that the tiny On-Time ferry makes its 5-minute crossing to **Chappaquiddick Island** ⚘⚘. (Don't bother looking for the original **Dyke Bridge,** infamous scene of the Kennedy/Kopechne debacle; it has been dismantled and, at long last, replaced.)

Stroll down North Water Street to admire the many formidable captains' homes, several of which have been converted into inns. Each has a tale to tell. The 1750 **Daggett House** (no. 59), for instance, expanded upon a 1660 tavern, and the original beehive oven is flanked by a "secret" passageway. Nathaniel Hawthorne holed up at the **Edgartown Inn** (no. 56) for nearly a year in 1789 while writing *Twice Told Tales*—and, it is rumored, romancing a local maiden who inspired *The Scarlet Letter.* On your way back to Main Street, you'll pass the **Gardner-Colby Gallery** (no. 27), filled with beautiful island-inspired paintings.

After all that walking, you can stop for lunch or a drink at **Newes from America,** 23 Kelley St., at the Kelley House off North Water Street (℃ **508/ 627-4397**), a colonial-style basement pub with hearty food.

BEACHES & OUTDOOR PURSUITS

BEACHES   Most down-island beaches in Vineyard Haven, Oak Bluffs, and Edgartown are open to the public and just a walk or a short bike ride from town. In season, shuttle buses make stops at **State Beach,** between Oak Buffs and Edgartown. Most of the Vineyard's magnificent up-island shoreline is privately owned or restricted to residents, and thus off-limits to visitors. Renters in up-island communities, however, can obtain a beach sticker (around $35 to $50 for a season sticker) for those private beaches by applying with a lease at the relevant **town hall:** West Tisbury (℃ **508/696-0147**), Chilmark (℃ **508/645-2113** or 508/645-2100), or Aquinnah (℃ **508/645-2300**). Also, many up-island inns offer the perk of temporary passes to the beautiful up-island beaches. In addition to the public beaches listed below, you might want to track down a few hidden coves by requesting a map of conservation properties from the **Martha's Vineyard Land Bank** (℃ **508/627-7141**). Below is a list of visitor-friendly beaches:

- **Aquinnah Beach** ★★ (Moshup Beach), off Moshup Trail: Parking costs $15 a day in season at this peaceful half-mile beach just east (Atlantic side) of the colorful cliffs. Although it is against the law, nudists tend to gravitate toward this beach. Because of rapid erosion, climbing the cliffs or stealing clay for a souvenir here is forbidden. Rest rooms are near the parking lot, which is a 10-minute walk from the beach; lifeguards patrol the beach.
- **Joseph A. Sylvia State Beach** ★★★, midway between Oak Bluffs and Edgartown: Stretching a mile and flanked by a paved bike path, this placid beach on Nantucket Sound has views of Cape Cod and is prized for its gentle and (relatively) warm waves, which make it perfect for swimming. The wooden drawbridge is a local landmark, and visitors and islanders alike have been jumping off it for years. Be aware that State Beach is one of the Vineyard's most popular; come midsummer, it's packed. The shuttle bus stops here, and roadside parking is also available—but it fills up fast, so stake your claim early. There are no rest rooms, and only the Edgartown end of the beach, known as Bend-in-the-Road Beach, has lifeguards.
- **Lake Tashmoo Town Beach,** off Herring Creek Road, Vineyard Haven: The only spot on the island where lake meets the ocean, this tiny strip of sand is good for swimming and surf casting but is somewhat marred by limited parking and often brackish waters. Nonetheless, this is a popular spot, as beachgoers enjoy a choice between the Vineyard Sound beach with mild surf or the placid lake beach. Bikers will have no problem reaching this beach from Vineyard Haven; otherwise, you have to have access to a car to get to this beach.
- **Menemsha Beach** ★★, next to Dutchers Dock in Menemsha Harbor: The gentle surface of this small but well-trafficked strand, with lifeguards and rest rooms, is quite popular with families. In season, it's virtually wall-to-wall colorful umbrellas and beach toys. Nearby food vendors in Menemsha— selling everything from ice cream and hot dogs to steamers and shrimp cocktail—are also a plus here.
- **Oak Bluffs Town Beach,** Seaview Avenue: This sandy strip extends from both sides of the ferry wharf, which makes it a convenient place to linger while waiting for the next boat. This is an in-town beach, within walking

distance for visitors staying in Oak Bluffs. The surf is consistently calm and the sand smooth, so it's also ideal for families with small children. Public rest rooms are available at the ferry dock, but there are no lifeguards.

- **Owen Park Beach,** off Main Street in Vineyard Haven: A tiny strip of harborside beach adjoining a town green with swings and a bandstand will suffice for young children, who, by the way, get lifeguard supervision. There are no rest rooms, but this is an in-town beach, so it's probably a quick walk from your Vineyard Haven inn.

- **South Beach** ☆☆☆ (Katama Beach), about 4 miles south of Edgartown on Katama Road: If you have time for only one trip to the beach and you can't get up-island, go with this popular 3-mile barrier strand that boasts heavy wave action (check with lifeguards for swimming conditions), sweeping dunes, and, most important, relatively ample parking space. It's also accessible by bike path or shuttle. Lifeguards patrol some sections of the beach, and there are sparsely scattered toilet facilities. The rough surf here is popular with surfers. *Tip:* Families tend to head to the left, college kids to the right.

- **Wasque Beach** ☆☆, Wasque Reservation, Chappaquiddick: You'll find some sandy roads on the way to this half-mile beach, but few crowds. Take the On-Time ferry to Chappy, go straight 2 miles, and veer right on School Street for ⅘ miles and left on Wasque Road for 1⅕ miles. Bikers will have to dismount in places along the 4-mile trip. There's a rest room at the parking lot. Pay at the gatehouse ($3 per car and $3 per person) in season.

- **East Beach** ☆, Wasque (pronounced *Way*-squee) Reservation, Chappaquiddick: Relatively few people go to the bother of biking or hiking (or four-wheel driving) this far, so you should be able to find all the privacy you crave. Take the On-Time Ferry to Chappy, then go straight 2½ miles and continue straight for another half mile on a dirt road. Biking on Chappaquiddick is one of the great Vineyard experiences, but the roads can be quite sandy, and you will have to dismount for the final half mile to Wasque. Because of its exposure on the east shore of the island, the surf is rough here. Still, it's one of the Vineyard's best-kept secrets and an ideal spot for bird watching. Pack a picnic; there are no stores on Chappy. There is a portable toilet in the parking lot. Pay at the gatehouse ($3 per car and $3 per person) for access in season.

FISHING   To fish for shellfish, you'll need to get information and a permit from the appropriate town hall (for the phone numbers, see "Beaches," above). Popular spots for surf casting include Wasque Point on Chappaquiddick, South Beach, and the jetty at Menemsha Pond.

The party boat *Skipper* (☎ **508/693-1238**) offers half-day trips out of Oak Bluffs harbor in season. The cost is $25 for adults and $15 for children 12 and under. Bring your own poles and bait. Deep-sea excursions can be arranged aboard **Big Eye Charters** (☎ **508/627-3649**) out of Edgartown, and **Summer's Lease** (☎ **508/693-2880**) out of Oak Bluffs. Up-island, there's **North Shore Charters** (☎ **508/645-2993**) and **Flashy Lady Charters** (☎ **508/645-2462**) out of Menemsha, locus of the island's commercial fishing fleet.

IGFA world-record holder Capt. Leslie S. Smith operates **Backlash Charters** (☎ **508/627-5894**; backlash@tiac.net), specializing in light tackle and fly-fishing, out of Edgartown. Cooper Gilkes III, proprietor of **Coop's Bait & Tackle,** 147 W. Tisbury Rd., Edgartown (☎ **508/627-3909**), which offers rentals as well as supplies, is another acknowledged authority. He's available as an instructor or charter guide.

Exploring the Vineyard on Two Wheels

Biking on the Vineyard is a memorable experience, not just for the smooth, well-maintained paths but also for the long stretches of virtually untrafficked up-island roads that reveal breathtaking country landscapes and sweeping ocean views.

A triangle of paved bike paths, roughly 8 miles to a side, links the down-island towns of Oak Bluffs, Edgartown, and Vineyard Haven. The Vineyard Sound portion along Beach Road, flanked by water on both sides, is especially enjoyable. From Edgartown, you can also follow the bike path to South Beach. For a more woodsy ride, there are paved paths and mountain-biking trails in the **Manuel F. Correllus State Forest** (© **508/693-2540**), a vast spread of scrub oak and pine in the middle of the island. The bike paths are accessible off Edgartown–West Tisbury Road.

The up-island roads leading to West Tisbury, Chilmark, Menemsha, and Aquinnah are a cyclist's paradise, with sprawling, unspoiled pastureland, old farmhouses, and brilliant sea views reminiscent of Ireland's countryside. But keep in mind that the terrain is often hilly, and the roads are narrow and a little rough around the edges. From West Tisbury to Chilmark Center, try **South Road**—about 5 miles—which passes stone walls rolling over moors, clumps of pine and wildflowers, verdant marshes and tidal pools, and, every once in awhile, an Old Vineyard farmhouse. **Middle Road** is another lovely ride with a country feel, taking you from West Tisbury to Chilmark (it's usually less trafficked, too).

Our favorite up-island route is the 6-mile stretch from Chilmark Center out to Aquinnah via **State Road** and **Moshup Trail** ✦. The ocean views along this route are spectacular. Don't miss the **Quitsa Pond Lookout,** about 2 miles down **State Road,** which provides a panoramic vista of Nashaquitsa and Menemsha ponds, beyond which you can see Menemsha, Vineyard Sound, and the Elizabeth Islands. A bit farther, just over the Aquinnah town line, is the Aquinnah spring, a roadside iron pipe where you can refill your water bottle with the freshest and coldest water on the island. At the fork after the spring, turn left on Moshup Trail—in fact, a regular road—and follow the coast, which offers gorgeous views of the ocean and sweeping sand dunes. You'll soon wind up in Aquinnah, where you can explore the red clay cliffs and pristine beaches. On the return trip, you can take the handy bike ferry ($7 round-trip) from Aquinnah to Menemsha. It runs daily in summer and on weekends in May.

There are lots of bike-rental operations near the ferry landings in Vineyard Haven and Oak Bluffs, and there are also a few outfitters in Edgartown. For information on bike-rental shops, see "Getting Around," above.

A very good outfitter out of Boston called **Bike Riders** (© **800/ 473-7040**; www.bikeriderstours.com) runs 6-day island-hopping tours of Martha's Vineyard and Nantucket. The cost is $1,395 per person, plus $60 if you need to borrow a bike. It's a perfect way to experience both islands.

GOLF   President Clinton helped to publicize the nine-hole **Mink Meadows Golf Course,** off Franklin Street, Vineyard Haven (✆ **508/693-0600**), which occupies a top-dollar chunk of real estate but is open to the general public, as well as the semiprivate, championship-level 18-hole **Farm Neck Golf Club,** off Farm Neck Road, Oak Bluffs (✆ **508/693-3057**).

IN-LINE SKATING   In-line skaters are everywhere on the island's paved paths. You'll find rentals at **Jamaikan Jam,** Post Office Square off Circuit Avenue, Oak Bluffs (✆ **508/693-5003**). Another source is **Sports Haven,** 5 Beach St., Vineyard Haven (✆ **508/696-0456**). Rates are about $20 to $25 per day, including pads.

NATURE TRAILS   About a fifth of the Vineyard's land mass has been set aside for conservation, and it's all accessible to energetic bikers and hikers. The **West Chop Woods,** off Franklin Street in Vineyard Haven, comprise 85 acres with marked walking trails. Midway between Vineyard Haven and Edgartown, the **Felix Neck Wildlife Sanctuary** ★★ includes a 6-mile network of trails over varying terrain, from woodland to beach.

The 633-acre **Long Point Wildlife Refuge** ★★, off Waldron's Bottom Road in West Tisbury (✆ **508/693-7392** for gatehouse), offers heath and dunes, freshwater ponds, a popular family-oriented beach, and interpretive nature walks for children.

Up-island, along the sound, the **Menemsha Hills Reservation** ★, off North Road in Chilmark (✆ **508/693-7662**), encompasses 210 acres of rocks and bluffs, with steep paths, lovely views, and even a public beach. **Cedar Tree Neck Sanctuary,** off Indian Hill Road southwest of Vineyard Haven (✆ **508/ 693-5207**), offers some 300 forested acres that end in a stony beach. Swimming and sunbathing are prohibited here.

Some remarkable botanical surprises can be found at the 20-acre **Polly Hill Arboretum** ★★, 809 State Rd., West Tisbury (✆ **508/693-9426**). Legendary horticulturist Polly Hill has developed this property over the past 40 years and allows the public to wander the grounds Thursday through Tuesday from 7am to 7pm. This is a magical place, particularly from mid-June to July, when the Dogwood Allee is in bloom. Wanderers will pass old stone walls on the way to the Tunnel of Love, an arbor of plaited hornbeam. There are also witch hazels, camellias, magnolias, and rhododendrons. To get here from Vineyard Haven, go south on State Road, bearing left at the junction of North Road. The Arboretum entrance is 0.4 miles on the right. There's a requested donation of $5 for adults, $3 for children under 12.

WATER SPORTS   **Wind's Up,** 199 Beach Rd., Vineyard Haven (✆ **508/ 693-4252**), rents out canoes, kayaks, and various sailing craft, including windsurfers, and offers on-site instruction, on a placid pond. Canoes and kayaks rent for $18 to $20 per hour. Surfboards and boogie boards are available as well.

MUSEUMS & HISTORIC LANDMARKS

Cottage Museum ★   This little museum, a cottage in the center of Oak Bluffs' famous "campground," displays 19th-century artifacts: bulky black bathing costumes and a melodeon used for hymnal singalongs. The campground is a 34-acre circle with more than 300 multicolored, elaborately trimmed Carpenter Gothic cottages, which look very much the way they might have more than a hundred years ago. These adorable little houses were loosely modeled on the revivalists' canvas tents that inspired them. In 1867, when this cottage was built, campers typically attended three lengthy prayer services daily.

Opportunities for worship remain: within the park at the 1878 Trinity Methodist Church, or just outside, on Samoset Avenue, at the nonsectarian 1870 Union Chapel, a magnificent octagonal structure with superb acoustics.

At the very center of the campgrounds is the striking Trinity Park Tabernacle. Built in 1879, the open-sided chapel is the largest wrought-iron structure in the country. Thousands can be accommodated on its long wooden benches, which are usually filled to capacity for the Sunday-morning services in summer, as well as for community sings (Wednesdays in July and August) and occasional concerts.

1 Trinity Park (within the Camp Meeting Grounds), Oak Bluffs. © 508/693-7784. Admission $1 (donation). Mid-June to Sept Mon–Sat 10am–4pm. Closed Oct to mid-June.

Flying Horses Carousel ★★★ *Kids*   You don't have to be a kid to enjoy the colorful mounts adorning what is considered to be the oldest working carousel in the country. Built in 1876 at Coney Island, this National Historic Landmark predates the era of horses that "gallop." Lacking the necessary gears, these merely glide smoothly in place to the joyful strains of a calliope. The challenge lies in going for the brass ring that entitles the lucky winner to a free ride. Take a moment to admire the intricate hand-carving and real horsehair manes, and gaze into the horses' glass eyes for a surprise: tiny animal charms glinting within.

33 Circuit Ave. (at Lake Ave.), Oak Bluffs. © 508/693-9481. Tickets $1 per ride, or $8 for 10 rides. Late May to early Sept daily 9:30am–10pm; call for off-season hours. Closed mid-Oct to mid-Apr.

The Martha's Vineyard Historical Society/Vineyard Museum ★★   All of Martha's Vineyard's colorful history is captured here, in a compound of historic buildings. To acclimate yourself chronologically, start with the pre-colonial artifacts—from arrowheads to colorful Gay Head clay pottery—displayed in the 1845 **Captain Francis Pease House.** The **Gale Huntington Reference Library** houses rare documentation of the island's history, from genealogical records to whale-ship logs. Some extraordinary memorabilia, including scrimshaw and portraiture, are on view in the adjoining **Francis Foster Maritime Gallery.**

To get a sense of daily life during the era when the waters of the East Coast were the equivalent of a modern highway, visit the **Thomas Cooke House,** a shipwright-built colonial built in 1765, where the Customs collector lived and worked. The Fresnel lens on display outside the museum was lifted from the Gay Head Lighthouse in 1952, after nearly a century of service. Though it no longer serves to warn ships of dangerous shoals (that light is automated now), it still lights up the night every evening in summer, just for show.

59 School St. (at Cook St., 2 blocks southwest of Main St.), Edgartown. © 508/627-4441. Fax 508/627-4436. Admission in season $6 adults, $4 children 6–15. Early June to mid-Oct Tues–Sat 10am–5pm. Off-season Wed–Fri 1–4pm; Sat 10am–4pm.

ORGANIZED TOURS & CRUISES

Hugh Taylor (James's brother) alternates with a couple of other captains in taking the helm of *Arabella,* docked in Menemsha Harbor at the end of North Road (© 508/645-3511). This swift 50-foot catamaran makes daily trips to Cuttyhunk and offers sunset cruises around the Aquinnah cliffs. Zipping along at 15 knots, it's a great way to see lovely coves and vistas otherwise denied the ordinary tourist. Evening sails are $40 for adults, $20 for children under 12. Day sails are $60 for adults, $30 for children. From mid-June to mid-September, departures are daily at 10:30am and 6pm. Reservations are required.

The Trustees of Reservations, a statewide land conservation group, offers fascinating 2½-hour **Natural History Tours** (© 508/627-3599) by safari vehicle or canoe around Cape Pogue on Chappaquiddick Island. The canoe tour on Poucha Pond and Cape Pogue Bay is designed for all levels. The cost for the safari tour is $12 for adults and $6 for children; the canoe tour is $30 for adults, $15 for children. Call for reservations.

SHOPPING

ANTIQUES & COLLECTIBLES   For the most exquisite Asian furniture, lamps, porcelains, and jewelry, visit **All Things Oriental,** 123 Beach Rd., Vineyard Haven (© **508/693-8375**). The treasures here are handpicked in China by owner Shirley Seaton.

You don't have to be a bona fide collector to marvel over the museum-quality marine antiques at **C. W. Morgan Marine Antiques,** Beach Road, just east of the town center, Vineyard Haven (© **508/693-3622**). Frank Rapoza's collection encompasses paintings and prints, intricate ship models, nautical instruments, sea chests, and scrimshaw.

ARTS & CRAFTS   No visit to Edgartown would be complete without a peek at the wares of scrimshander Thomas J. DeMont, Jr., at **Edgartown Scrimshaw Gallery,** 43 Main St. (© **508/627-9439**). All the scrimshaw in the gallery is hand-carved using ancient mammoth ivory or antique fossil ivory.

The **Field Gallery,** State Road (in the center of town), West Tisbury (© **508/ 693-5595**), set in a rural pasture, is where Marc Chagall meets Henry Moore and where Tom Maley's playful figures have enchanted locals and passersby for decades. You'll also find drawings and cartoons by Jules Feiffer. The Sunday-evening openings are high points of the summer social season. Closed from mid-October to mid-May.

Don't miss the **Granary Gallery at the Red Barn,** Old County Road (off Edgartown–West Tisbury Road, about a quarter mile north of the intersection), West Tisbury (© **800/472-6279** or 508/693-0455), which displays astounding prints by the late longtime summer resident Alfred Eisenstaedt and dazzling color photos by local luminary Alison Shaw.

Another rather unique local artisans' venue is **Martha's Vineyard Glass Works,** State Road, North Tisbury (© **508/693-6026**). The three resident artists—Andrew Magdanz, Susan Shapiro, and Mark Weiner—have shown nationwide to considerable acclaim.

FASHION   Treading a comfortable middle ground between functional and fashionable, the varied women's and men's labels at **LeRoux,** 89 Main St. (in the center of town), Vineyard Haven (© **508/693-6463**), include some nationally known names.

GIFTS & HOME DECOR   Our favorite place for gifts in Oak Bluffs is **Craftworks,** 149 Circuit Ave. (© **508/693-7463**), which is filled to the rafters with whimsical, colorful contemporary American crafts, some by local artisans. **Paper Tiger,** 29 Main St., Vineyard Haven (© **508/693-8970**), is an old-fashioned stationery store with wonderful papers and cards.

Carly Simon's **Midnight Farm,** 18 Water-Cromwell Lane, Vineyard Haven (© **508/693-1997**), offers a world of high-end, imaginative gift items, from soaps and candles to children's clothes and toys to furniture and glassware.

WHERE TO STAY

Before deciding where to stay on Martha's Vineyard, consider the type of vacation you prefer. The down-island towns of Vineyard Haven, Oak Bluffs, and Edgartown provide shops, restaurants, beaches, and harbors all within walking distance, and frequent shuttles to get you all over the island. But all three can be overly crowded on busy summer weekends. Vineyard Haven is the gateway for most of the ferry traffic; Oak Bluffs is a raucous town with most of the Vineyard's bars and nightclubs. And many visitors make a beeline to Edgartown's manicured Main Street. Up-island inns provide more peace and quiet, but you'll probably need a car to get around. Also, you may not be within walking distance of the beach.

We've provided only summer rates below, since the Vineyard is so seasonal. If you do visit in the off-season, you may find substantial discounts at establishments that remain open year-round.

EDGARTOWN
Very Expensive

Charlotte Inn ★★★   Ask anyone to recommend the best inn on the island, and this is the name you're most likely to hear. It's one of only two Relais & Châteaux properties on the Cape and Islands. Owners Gery and Paula Conover have been tirelessly fine-tuning this cluster of 18th- and 19th-century houses since 1971. Linked by formal gardens, each house has a distinctive look and feel, though the predominant mode is English country. Some guest rooms have VCRs; the bathrooms are luxurious, and some are bigger than most standard hotel rooms. However sterling the accommodations here, the restaurant may actually gather more laurels: L'étoile is one of the island's finest (see "Where to Dine," below).

27 S. Summer St. (in the center of town), Edgartown, MA 02539. ℂ **508/627-4751.** Fax 508/627-4652. 25 units. Summer $295–$525 double; $695–$850 suite. Rates include continental breakfast; full breakfast offered for extra charge. AE, MC, V. Open year-round. No children under 14 accepted. **Amenities:** Restaurant (French). *In room:* A/C, TV (except one room), hair dryer, no phone.

Harbor View Hotel ★   The grand exterior of this Gilded Age hotel unfortunately masks a rather bland interior with motel-style generic rooms. Nevertheless, it does have a rather fine location; its 300-foot veranda overlooks Edgartown Harbor and the lighthouse. Front bedrooms with that pretty view cost quite a bit more; in back, there's a large pool surrounded by newer annexes, where some rooms and suites have kitchenettes. The hotel is just far enough from "downtown" to avoid the traffic hassles, but close enough for a pleasant walk past regal captains' houses. The Coach House (see "Where to Dine," below) serves three meals in an elegant, romantic setting.

131 N. Water St. (about ½ mile northwest of Main St.), Edgartown, MA 02539. ℂ **800/255-6005** or 508/627-7000. Fax 508/627-8417. www.harbor-view.com. 124 units. Summer $285–$475 double; $485–$675 suite. AE, DC, MC, V. Open year-round. **Amenities:** 2 restaurants (seafood, casual); heated outdoor pool; 2 tennis courts; concierge; room service; baby-sitting; laundry service. *In room:* A/C, TV, hair dryer, iron, safe.

Hob Knob Inn ★★★   Owner Maggie White has reinvented this 19th-century Gothic Revival as an exquisite destination now vying for top honors as one of the Vineyard's best places to stay. Her style is peppy/preppy, with crisp floral fabrics and striped patterns creating a clean and comfortable look. The full farm breakfast is a delight, and is served at beautifully appointed individual tables in the sunny, brightly painted dining rooms. Bovine lovers will enjoy the agrarian theme, a decorative touch throughout the inn. The staff will pack guests a splendid picnic basket or plan a charter fishing trip on Maggie's 27-foot Boston Whaler.

128 Main St. (on upper Main St., in the center of town), Edgartown, MA 02539. ℂ **800/696-2723** or 508/627-9510. Fax 508/627-4560. www.hobknob.com. 20 units. Summer $200–$525 double. Rates include breakfast and afternoon tea. AE, MC, V. Open year-round. **Amenities:** Gym with top-notch equipment; bike rental; business center; limited room service; massage. *In room:* A/C, TV, dataport, hair dryer.

The Inn at 148 Main ★★   This is a luxurious small inn, consisting of three buildings, two recently restored and one new. Though built in the 1840s, the main inn's interior is light and airy, and the spacious guest rooms are outfitted with every amenity. The luxurious carriage-house suite, with gas fireplace and tiled Jacuzzi tub for two, is exceptional. By the way, this is the only small lodging establishment on the Vineyard with an outdoor heated pool and hot tub.

148 Main St. (on upper Main St.), Edgartown, MA 02539. © **508/627-7248.** Fax 508/627-9505. one48@vineyard.net. 8 units. Summer $250–$400 double. Rates include continental breakfast. AE, DISC, MC, V. No children under 12 accepted. Open year-round. **Amenities:** Outdoor heated pool; hot tub. *In room:* A/C, TV/VCR, hair dryer.

The Point Way Inn ★★   This lovely inn has just undergone a multimillion-dollar freshening up and is just as pretty as can be. While some of the bedrooms are on the small side, they're cheerfully decorated in a contemporary style with cozy bedding and amenities. Some units have hair dryers and VCRs. Guests staying in the garden room, which has a separate entrance, are allowed to bring a well-behaved pooch. Hearty morning meals, which might include crepes, stuffed French toast, or quiche, are served in the sunlit breakfast room. In the afternoons, there are homemade cookies, and in the evenings, wine and cheese.

104 Main St. (on upper Main St.), Edgartown, MA 02539. © **888/711-6633** or 508/627-8633. Fax 508/627-3338. www.pointway.com. 12 units. Summer $225–$325 double; $375 suite. Rates include breakfast. AE, DISC, MC, V. Closed Jan to mid-Feb. Pets allowed in 1 room ($50). *In room:* A/C, TV, no phone.

Expensive

Colonial Inn of Martha's Vineyard ★★★   This 1911 inn in the center of town has been transformed into a fine modern hotel, and recent renovations have elevated it to what can accurately be described as "affordable luxury." Its lobby serves as a conduit to the Nevins Square shops beyond. Guest rooms, decorated in soothing, contemporary tones (with pine furniture, hardwood floors, beadboard wainscoting, and four-poster beds), offer all one could want in the way of conveniences. Many rooms have hair dryers and dataports; suites have VCRs (free videos) and kitchenettes; and some units have private balconies and awesome harbor views. All guests are free to enjoy the scenery and a cocktail on one of the four common harborview decks. Be sure to visit the roof deck around sunset or, if you're up for it, sunrise.

38 N. Water St., Edgartown, MA 02539. © **800/627-4701** or 508/627-4711. Fax 508/627-5904. www.colonialinnmvy.com. 43 units. Summer $170–$325 double; $350 suite or efficiency. Rates include continental breakfast. AE, MC, V. Closed Dec–Mar. **Amenities:** 2 fine restaurants. *In room:* A/C, TV.

The Jonathan Munroe House ★   With its graceful wraparound, colonnaded front porch, the Jonathan Munroe House stands out from the other inns and captains' homes on this stretch of upper Main Street. Almost directly across the street is the famous Old Whaling Church, with its hourly tolls. Guest rooms are immaculate, antique-filled, and dotted with clever details. Many rooms have fireplaces and baths with whirlpool jets. At breakfast, don't miss the homemade waffles and pancakes, served on the sunny porch. Request the garden cottage, with its flowering window boxes, if you're in a honeymooning mood.

100 Main St., Edgartown, MA 02539. © **508/627-5536.** Fax 508/627-5536. www.jonathanmunroe.com. 8 units. Summer $185–$250 double; $350 cottage. Rates include breakfast. AE, MC, V. No children under 12 accepted. Open year-round. *In room:* A/C, no phone.

Victorian Inn ⭐⭐⭐   Do you ever long to stay at a quaint, reasonably priced inn that is bigger than a B&B but smaller than a Marriott? In the center of Edgartown, the Victorian Inn is a freshened-up version of those old-style hotels that used to exist in every New England town. There are enough rooms here so you don't feel like you're trespassing in someone's home, yet there's a personal touch. With three floors of long, graceful corridors, the Victorian could serve as a stage set for a 1930s romance. Several guest rooms have canopy beds and balconies with a harbor view. Each year, innkeepers Stephen and Karen Caliri have improved and refined the inn, and they are always quick to dispense helpful advice with good humor.

24 S. Water St. (in the center of town), Edgartown, MA 02539. ☎ 508/627-4784. www.thevic.com. 14 units. Summer $165–$350 double. Rates include breakfast and afternoon tea. MC, V. Open year-round. Pets welcome Nov–Mar. *In room:* A/C, no phone.

Moderate

The Arbor ⭐   This unassuming-looking house, hugging the bike path at the edge of town, packs surprising style: Innkeeper Peggy Hall tacked a lovely cathedral-ceilinged living room onto her 1880 farmhouse to add light and liveliness. And that's what you'll find as you compare notes with other travelers, or peruse a fine collection of coffee-table books from the comfort of an overstuffed chintz couch. The bedrooms range from tiny to spacious, but all are nicely appointed, largely with antiques—and the rates are singularly gentle, especially considering the fresh-baked breakfast served on fine china.

222 Upper Main St. (on the western edge of town, about ¾ mile from the harbor), Edgartown, MA 02539. ☎ 508/627-8137. www.mvy.com/arborinn. 11 units (2 with shared bathroom). Summer $135–$185 double. Rates include continental breakfast. MC, V. Closed Nov–Apr. *In room:* A/C, no phone.

Edgartown Inn ⭐⭐ *Value*   This centrally located historic inn offers perhaps the best value on the island. Nathaniel Hawthorne holed up here for nearly a year, and Daniel Webster also spent time here. It's a lovely 1798 Federal manse, a showplace even here on captains' row. Guest rooms are no-frills but pleasantly traditional; some have TVs. Some units in the front of the house have harbor views. Modernists may prefer the two cathedral-ceilinged quarters in the annex out back, which offer lovely light and a sense of seclusion. Breakfast is available in the dining room for an extra charge. Service is excellent here; be sure to say hello to Henry King, who has been on staff for 50 years.

56 N. Water St., Edgartown, MA 02539. ☎ 508/627-4794. Fax 508/627-9420. www.edgartowninn.com. 20 units (4 with shared bathroom). Summer $100–$225 double. No credit cards. Closed Nov–Mar. *In room:* A/C, no phone.

OAK BLUFFS

Those looking for a basic motel with a central location can try **Surfside Motel,** across from the ferry dock on Oak Bluffs Avenue (☎ **800/537-3007** or 508/693-2500). Doubles are $150 to $160 and come with air-conditioning, TVs, fridges, and phones; well-behaved pets are allowed.

Expensive

The Oak House ⭐⭐   This 1872 Queen Anne bay-front beauty has preserved all the luxury and leisure of the Victorian age. Innkeeper Betsi Convery-Luce trained at Johnson & Wales; her pastries are sublime. The common rooms are furnished in an opulent Victorian mode, as are the 10 guest rooms. Those toward the back are quieter, but those in front have Nantucket Sound views. This inn is very service-oriented, and requests for feather beds, down pillows, and nonallergenic pillows are accommodated. Anyone intent on decompressing is sure to benefit from this immersion into another era—the one that invented the leisure class.

75 Seaview Ave. (on the sound), Oak Bluffs, MA 02557. © **800/245-5979** or 508/693-4187. Fax 508/696-7385. www.vineyard.net/inns. 10 units. Summer $180–$220 double; $275–$280 suite. Rates include continental breakfast and afternoon tea. AE, DISC, MC, V. Closed late Oct to early May. *In room:* A/C, TV.

Moderate

The Dockside Inn ★★ *(Kids)*   Set close to the harbor, the Dockside is perfectly located for exploring the town of Oak Bluffs and is geared toward families. The welcoming exterior, with its colonnaded porch and balconies, duplicates the inns of yesteryear. Once inside, the whimsical Victorian touches will transport you immediately into the spirit of this rollicking town. Most of the cheerfully decorated, standard-size rooms have either a garden or a harbor view. Suites have kitchenettes, and some have private decks. Location, charm, and flair mean this is a popular place, so book early.

9 Circuit Ave. Extension (Box 1206), Oak Bluffs, MA 02557. © **800/245-5979** or 508/693-2966. Fax 508/696-7293. 22 units. Summer $150–$200 double; $250–$350 suite. Rates include continental breakfast. AE, DISC, MC, V. Closed late Oct to early Apr. *In room:* A/C, TV, hair dryer.

Inexpensive

Attleboro House   As old-fashioned as the afghans that proprietor Estelle Reagan crochets for every bed, this harborside guest house—serving Camp Meeting visitors since 1874—epitomizes the simple, timeless joys of summer. None of the rooms is graced with a private bathroom, but the rates are so retro that you may not mind. What was good enough for 19th-century tourists more than suffices today.

42 Lake Ave. (on the harbor), Oak Bluffs, MA 02557. © **508/693-4346.** 11 units (all with shared bathroom). Summer $75–$95 double; $105–$175 suite. Rates include continental breakfast. MC, V. Closed Oct–May. *In room:* No phone.

VINEYARD HAVEN (TISBURY)
Very Expensive

Martha's Place ★★   Martha's Place is exceptional for its elegance in the heart of this bustling port town. Owners Richard Alcott and Martin Hicks lovingly restored and refurbished this stately Greek Revival home and surrounded it with rosebushes. Swags and jabots line the windows; every knob has a tassel, every fabric a trim. If you enjoy admiring a neoclassical armoire or an antique bed draped in blue velvet, Martha's is the place. The spacious guest rooms feature antique beds with excellent mattresses, Egyptian cotton linens, and down comforters. The bathrooms are quite luxurious—ever seen one with a fireplace? Most units have harbor views. Breakfast is served at the large dining-room table set with china and silver, or you can have your meal in bed, if you prefer. The innkeepers also run a luxury boat charter business that guests can book for a fee.

114 Main St. (across from Owen Park, in the center of town), Vineyard Haven, MA 02568. © **508/693-0253.** Fax 508/693-1890. www.marthasplace.com. 6 units. Summer $175–$425 double. Rates include continental breakfast. DISC, MC, V. **Amenities:** Mountain bikes (free). *In room:* A/C, TV on request, hair dryer.

Expensive

Crocker House Inn ★   Jynell and Jeff Kristal have recently renovated this 1920s home near the harbor into a comfortable and casually elegant place to stay. Rooms are particularly light and airy here; they've all been completely redone with new linens, beds, and furniture with a country flavor. Jynell has

Marriott experience, and it shows in the room details and service-oriented hospitality. Jeff bakes the blueberry muffins in the morning, and guests rave about his chocolate-chip cookies set out with iced tea and lemonade in the afternoon.

12 Crocker Ave./P.O. Box 1658 (off Main St.), Vineyard Haven, MA 02568. ℭ **800/772-0206** or 508/693-1151. Fax 508/693-1123. www.crockerhouseinn.com. 8 units. Summer $195–$285 double, $385 suite. Rates include continental breakfast. AE, MC, V. Open year-round. Children over 12 welcome. *In room:* A/C, TV on request.

CHILMARK (INCLUDING MENEMSHA), WEST TISBURY & AQUINNAH
Expensive

Menemsha Inn and Cottages ✪   There's an almost Quaker-like plainness to this weathered waterside compound set in the pines near Menemsha Harbor, though many of the rooms are quite inviting. Mostly it's a place to revel in the outdoors (on 11 seaside acres) without distractions. The late *Life* photographer Alfred Eisenstaedt summered here for 4 decades, and the interior aesthetics would please any artist. There's no restaurant—just a restful breakfast room. Cottages have hair dryers, TV/VCRs, outdoor showers, barbecue grills, and kitchenettes. The most luxurious suites are located in the Carriage House, which has a spacious common room with a fieldstone fireplace. All units have private decks, most with water views. Guests have access to complimentary passes and shuttle bus service to the Lucy Vincent and Squibnocket private beaches.

Off North Rd. (about ½ mile northeast of harbor), Menemsha, MA 02552. ℭ **508/645-2521.** Fax 508/645-9500. www.menemshainn.com. 27 units. Summer $175–$215 double; $275 suite; $1,800–$2,200 per week for cottage. Rates for rooms and suites include continental breakfast. No credit cards. Closed Dec–Apr. **Amenities:** Tennis court; workout room. *In room:* TV.

Moderate

The Captain R. Flanders House ✪   Set amid 60 acres of rolling meadows crisscrossed by stone walls, this late-18th-century farmhouse, built by a whaling captain, has remained much the same for 2 centuries. The living room, with its broad-plank floors, is full of astonishing antiques, but there's none of that "for show" feel that's prevalent in more self-conscious B&Bs. Two new countrified cottages overlook the pond. Breakfasts include homemade muffins and island-made honey. The owners will provide guests with a coveted pass to nearby Lucy Vincent Beach.

North Rd. (about 1 mile northeast of Menemsha), Chilmark, MA 02535. ℭ **508/645-3123.** 7 units (2 with shared bathroom). Summer $165 double; $250 cottage. Rates include continental breakfast. AE, DISC, MC, V. Closed mid-Nov to Apr. *In room:* No phone.

Duck Inn   Elise LeBovit knows that some guests will find her farmhouse B&B over the top, and that's fine with her. Others will find it just right, a place with real personality and glorious ocean views at every turn. Set on a meadow above the Gay Head cliffs, it's like a post-hippie pension, complete with hot tub. The five rooms, including one tucked into the 200-year-old stone foundation, are fancifully decorated (one is arrayed with antique kimonos) and runaway romantic. The pink-stucco living room is agreeably cluttered and comfy, and LeBovit dishes out "gourmet organic" breakfasts, such as pear couscous muffins and chocolate-raspberry crepes.

10 Duck Pond Way (off State Rd. about ½ mile east of the lighthouse), Aquinnah, MA 02535. ℭ **508/645-9018.** Fax 508/645-2790. 5 units. Summer $105–$195 double. Rates include breakfast. MC, V. Closed Nov–Apr. **Amenities:** Hot tub. *In room:* No phone.

WHERE TO DINE

Outside Oak Bluffs and Edgartown, all of Martha's Vineyard is "dry," including Vineyard Haven, so bring your own bottle; some restaurants charge a small fee for uncorking.

EDGARTOWN
Very Expensive

L'étoile ✦✦✦ FRENCH   Every signal (starting with the price) tells you that this is going to be one very special meal. To get to the restaurant, you first pass through a pair of sitting rooms before coming to a summery conservatory, sparkling with the light of antique brass sconces and fresh with the scent of potted citrus trees. Everything is perfection, from the table settings (gold-rimmed Villeroy & Boch) to a nouvelle-cuisine menu that varies seasonally. Chef Michael Brisson is determined to dazzle, with an ever-evolving menu of delicacies flown in from the four corners of the earth. Sevruga usually makes an appearance—perhaps as a garnish for chilled leek soup. An étouffée of lobster with cognac and chervil sauce might come with littlenecks, bay scallops, and roasted corn fritters.

Charlotte Inn, 27 S. Summer St. (off Main St.). ✆ **508/627-5187.** Reservations required. Jackets recommended for men. Fixed-price menus from $68. AE, MC, V. July–Aug daily 6:30–9:45pm; call for off-season hours. Closed Jan to mid-Feb.

Expensive

Alchemy ✦ FRENCH BISTRO   This spiffy new restaurant is a little slice of Paris on Main Street. Such esoteric choices as oyster brie soup and Burgundy Vintners salad share the bill with escargot and chantarelle fricassee. As befits a true bistro, there's also a large selection of cocktails, liqueurs, and wines. In addition to lunch and dinner, a bar menu is served from 2:30 to 11pm. This choice isn't for everyone, but sophisticated diners will enjoy the continental flair here.

71 Main St. (in the center of town). ✆ **508/627-9999.** Reservations not accepted. Main courses $22–$33. AE, MC, V. Apr–Nov daily noon–11pm; call for off-season hours. Open year-round.

The Coach House ✦✦ NEW AMERICAN   With wraparound windows and views of the harbor and the lighthouse, this restaurant in Edgartown's grand hotel is an elegant place to dine. The mirrored bar is the swankiest place in town for a drink. The menu is simple but stylish. To start, there's softshell crab with

---

Finds **The Quintessential Lobster Dinner**

When the basics—a lobster and a sunset—are what you crave, head to **The Home Port** ✦✦, on North Road in Menemsha (✆ **508/645-2679**). At first glance, prices for the lobster dinners may seem a bit high, but note that they include an appetizer (go with the stuffed quahog), salad, amazing fresh-baked breads, nonalcoholic beverage (remember, it's BYOB in these parts), and dessert. The decor is on the simple side, but who really cares? It's the riveting harbor views that have drawn fans to this family-friendly place for over 60 years. Locals not keen on summer crowds order takeout (less than half price), then head down to Menemsha Beach for a private sunset supper. Fixed-price platters range from $25 to $45. Reservations are required. Open mid-May to mid-October daily from 6 to 10pm.

arugula and teardrop tomatoes. As a main course, try the caramelized sea scallops with a salad of Asian pear and apple. Service here is excellent; these are trained waiters, not your usual college surfer dudes. At the end of your meal, you may want to sit on the rockers on the hotel's porch and just watch the lights twinkling in the harbor.

Harbor View Hotel, 131 N. Water St. ✆ **508/627-7000**. Reservations recommended. Main courses $22–$36. AE, MC, V. Mon–Sat 7–11am and noon–2pm; Sun 8am–1:30pm; daily 6–10pm. Call for off-season hours. Open year-round.

La Cucina Ristorante at the Tuscany Inn ✿✿ NORTHERN ITALIAN Chef Marco Canora is the genius behind this exceptional Italian restaurant set in an elegant inn. Seating is outdoors under a verdant arbor, or indoors in the tiled dining rooms. Specialties of the house are a bit more refined than at most local venues: marinated quail salad; roasted salmon with fennel, red onion, and mint salad; or rosemary- and lavender-marinated lamb chops with cannelini beans, oven-dried tomatoes, sage, and lamb jus. If you're unable to pop over to Tuscany this year, La Cucina will tide you over just fine.

22 N. Water St. (in the center of town). ✆ **508/627-8161**. Reservations recommended. Main courses $28–$42. MC, V. Late May to late Sept Wed–Mon 6–10pm. Closed Oct–May.

Lattanzi's ✿✿ NORTHERN ITALIAN   Some say Al Lattanzi cooks the best veal chops on Martha's Vineyard. Lattanzi's would be the ideal place to eat in the dead of winter, by the glow of the paneled living room's handsome fireplace. Service is exceptional, and the wine list has a wide range of well-priced bottles. Back to the veal chop. You have two choices: *Piccolo Fiorentina*, which is hickory-grilled with black peppercorns and lemon, or *Lombatina di Vitello al Porcini*, which is served with porcini-mushroom cream. If it's July, get the striped-bass special; from local waters, it's luscious.

Lattanzi also owns the very good brick-oven pizza joint next door (✆ **508/ 627-9084**).

19 Church St. (Old Post Office Sq., off Main St. in the center of town). ✆ **508/627-8854**. Reservations recommended. Main courses $22–$38. AE, DC, DISC, MC, V. June–Sept daily 6–10pm; call for off-season hours. Open year-round.

Moderate
Among the Flowers Cafe ✿ AMERICAN   Everything's fresh and appealing at this outdoor cafe near the dock. The breakfasts are the best around, and all the crepes, waffles, and eggs are available at lunch as well. The comfort-food dinners (chicken and black pepper sauté over pasta, butter-and-crumb-crusted baked haddock with a sautéed lobster-and-shallot-butter cream) are among the most affordable options in this pricey town. There's almost always a wait, not just because it's so picturesque, but also because the food is homey, hearty, and kind on the wallet.

Mayhew Lane. ✆ **508/627-3233**. Main courses $14–$26. AE, DC, MC, V. July–Aug daily 8am–10pm; May–June and Sept–Oct daily 8am–4pm. Closed Nov–Apr.

Chesca's ✿✿ ITALIAN   Chesca's is a solid entry, with yummy food at reasonable prices. You're sure to find favorites like paella (with roasted lobster and other choice seafood), risotto (with roasted vegetables), and ravioli (with portobello mushrooms and asparagus). Smaller appetites can fill up on homemade soup and salad.

Colonial Inn, 38 N. Water St. ✆ **508/627-1234**. Main courses $13–$32. AE, MC, V. Reservations not accepted. Late June to early Sept daily 5:30–10pm; call for off-season hours. Closed Nov–Mar.

Inexpensive

Main Street Diner AMERICAN   A solid choice for a cheap breakfast or lunch, with no-nonsense selections that seem straight out of the 1950s.

Old Post Office Sq. (off Main St. in the center of town). ✆ **508/627-9337**. Most items under $10. MC, V. Daily 7am–9pm year-round.

The Newes from America PUB FARE   The food is better than average at this subterranean tavern, built in 1742. Locals love the French onion soup here. Beers are a specialty: Try a rack of five esoteric brews, or let your choice of food—from a wood-smoked oyster "Island Poor Boy" sandwich to an 18-ounce porterhouse steak—dictate your draft; the menu comes handily annotated with recommendations. Don't miss the seasoned fries, accompanied by a savory Southwestern dipping sauce.

The Kelley House, 23 Kelley St. ✆ **508/627-4397**. Main courses $7–$10. AE, MC, V. Daily 11am–11pm. Open year-round.

OAK BLUFFS

Few can resist the two dozen enticing ice-cream flavors at **Mad Martha's** ⭐, 117 Circuit Ave. (✆ **508/693-9151**), in the center of Oak Bluffs.

Expensive

Sweet Life Cafe ⭐⭐⭐ FRENCH/AMERICAN   Locals are crazy about this pearl of a restaurant, set in a restored Victorian house on upper Circuit Avenue. In season, the most popular seating is outside in the gaily lit garden. Fresh Island produce is featured, with seafood specials an enticing draw. The menu changes often, and everything's terrific. If the roasted lobster with potato-Parmesan risotto, roasted yellow beets, and smoked-salmon chive fondue is offered, order it.

63 Circuit Ave. ✆ **508/696-0200**. Reservations recommended. Main courses $20–$32. AE, DISC, MC, V. Mid-May to mid-Sept daily 5:30–10pm; Apr to mid-May and mid-Sept to Dec Thurs–Mon 5:30–9:30pm. Closed Jan–Apr.

Moderate

Jimmy Seas Pan Pasta Restaurant ⭐ MEDITERRANEAN   If you're wondering why the luncheonette-level decor at this restaurant, where Frank Sinatra's crooning resounds at all times, doesn't quite match up with the menu prices, it's because chef Jimmy Cipolla gives his all to his one-pot pasta dishes, served right in the pan. Pasta comes in such intriguing guises as pumpkin tortellini in a creamy sage sauce, and everything's fair game for toppings, from chicken and shrimp with fresh pesto to swordfish in a balsamic vinaigrette. Portions are enormous.

32 Kennebec Ave. ✆ **508/696-8550**. Reservations not accepted. Main courses $16–$23. MC, V. May–Oct daily 5–10pm; call for off-season hours. Open year-round.

Zapotec MEXICAN/SOUTHWESTERN   Look for the chili-pepper lights entwining the porch of this clapboard cottage: They're a beacon leading to tasty regional Mexican cuisine, from mussels Oaxaca (with chipotle peppers, cilantro, lime, and cream) to crab cakes Tulum (mixed with grilled peppers and cilantro, served with dual salsas), plus the standard chicken and beef burritos. There are also tasty fish tacos, topped with a creamy yogurt dressing. A good mole is hard to find this far north; here you can accompany it with Mexico's unbeatable beers, refreshing sangria, or perhaps a hand-picked, well-priced wine.

14 Kennebec Ave. (in the center of town). ✆ **508/693-6800**. Reservations not accepted. Main courses $14–$18. AE, MC, V. June–Oct daily noon–2pm and 5–10pm; call for off-season hours. Closed Nov–Apr.

Inexpensive
Papa's Pizza *(Kids)* PIZZA   The pizza at this vintage-look parlor is on the tame side; nevertheless, some call it the best on the Vineyard. For families with kids, it's ideal. Stop in if only to see the vintage photos of one-time "campers."

53 Circuit Ave. ℃ 508/693-1400. Most items under $8. MC, V. June–Aug Sun–Thurs 11am–9pm; Fri–Sat 11am–10pm; call for off-season hours. Open year-round.

VINEYARD HAVEN (TISBURY)
Just around the corner from the Black Dog Tavern, on Water Street near the ferry terminal, is the **Black Dog Bakery** (℃ 508/693-4786). The doors open at 5am, and from midmorning on, it's elbowroom only as customers line up for freshly baked breads, muffins, and desserts that can't be beat. Don't forget some homemade doggie biscuits for your pooch.

Expensive
Black Dog Tavern ★★ NEW AMERICAN   How does a humble harbor shack come to be a national icon? Location helps. So do cool T-shirts. Soon after *Shenandoah* captain Robert Douglas decided, in 1971, that this hard-working port could use a good restaurant, vacationers, stuck waiting for the ferry, began to wander in to tide themselves over with a bit of "blackout cake" or peanut-butter pie. The food is still home cooking, though the prices are high at dinner time. Seafood is a specialty, of course, like grilled swordfish with banana, basil, and lime—and the blackout cake has lost none of its appeal. Though the lines grow ever longer, nothing much has changed at this beloved spot. Eggs Galveston for breakfast at the Black Dog Tavern is still one of the ultimate Vineyard experiences—go early, when it first opens, and sit on the porch, where the views are perfect.

Beach St. Extension (on the harbor), Vineyard Haven. ℃ 508/693-9223. Reservations not accepted. Main courses $14–$27. AE, MC, V. June to early Sept Mon–Sat 7–11am, 11:30am–2:30pm, and 5–10pm; Sun 7am–1pm and 5–10pm. Call for off-season hours. Open year-round.

CHILMARK (INCLUDING MENEMSHA) & WEST TISBURY
For picnic fixings, check out **Alley's General Store,** on State Road in the center of West Tisbury (℃ 508/693-0088).

Moderate
The Bite ★★ SEAFOOD   It's usually places like "The Bite" that we crave when we think of New England. This is your quintessential "chowdah" and clam shack, flanked by picnic tables and serving up superlative chowder, potato salad, fried fish, and so forth.

Basin Rd. (off North Rd., about ¼ mile northeast of the harbor), Menemsha. ℃ 508/645-9239. Main courses $18–$30. No credit cards. July–Aug daily 11am–9pm; call for off-season hours. Closed Oct–Apr.

MARTHA'S VINEYARD AFTER DARK
BARS & CLUBS   All towns except for Oak Bluffs and Edgartown are dry, and last call at bars and nightclubs is at midnight. Hit Oak Bluffs for the rowdiest bar scene and best nighttime street life. In Edgartown, you may have to hop around before you find the evening's most happening spot.

People have been known to dance on the tables at **David Ryans,** 11 N. Water St., Edgartown (℃ 508/627-4100). The bartender decides the canned tunes, from Sinatra to the Smashing Pumpkins. There's no cover.

Young and loud are the watchwords at the **Lampost** and the **Rare Duck,** 111 Circuit Ave., Oak Bluffs (℃ 508/696-9352), a pair of clubs in the center of town. The Lamppost features live bands and a dance floor; the Rare Duck (down in the basement), acoustic acts. Entertainment includes such prospects as "'80s night" and "male hot-body contest." Cover varies from $1 to $5.

The Vineyard's first and only brewpub, **Offshore Ale Company,** 30 Kennebec Ave., Oak Bluffs (℗ **508/693-2626**), is an attractively rustic place, with high ceilings, oak booths, and peanut shells strewn on the floor. Local acoustic performers entertain several nights a week in season; cover varies.

The **Ritz Cafe,** 1 Circuit Ave., Oak Bluffs (℗ **508/693-9851**), is a down-and-dirty blues club that features live music every night in season and on weekends year-round. The cover's $2 to $3.

THE PERFORMING ARTS Attend a concert, play, or lecture at the **Old Whaling Church,** 89 Main St., Edgartown (℗ **508/627-4442**). This magnificent 1843 Greek Revival church functions primarily as a 500-seat performing-arts center offering lectures and symposia, films, plays, and concerts. Ticket prices vary. Call for schedule.

The **Vineyard Playhouse,** 24 Church St., Vineyard Haven (℗ **508/ 696-6300** or 508/693-6450), is an intimate (112-seat) black-box theater, where Equity professionals put on a rich season of favorites and challenging new work, followed, on summer weekends, by musical or comedic cabaret in the gallery/lounge. Children's theater selections are performed on Saturdays at 10am. Townspeople often get involved in the outdoor Shakespeare production, a 3-week run starting in mid-July at the Tashmoo Overlook Amphitheatre about 1 mile west of town. The season runs June through September; call for off-season hours.

2 Nantucket ✦✦✦

Once the whaling capital of the world, this tiny island, 30 miles off the coast of Cape Cod, still counts its isolation as a defining characteristic. At only 3½ by 14 miles in size, Nantucket is smaller and more insular than Martha's Vineyard. But charm-wise, Nantucket stands alone, providing 21st-century luxury and amenities wrapped in an elegant 19th-century package.

Sophisticated Nantucket Town features bountiful stores, quaint inns, cobblestone streets, interesting historic sites, and pristine beaches. The rest of the island is mainly residential, but for a couple of notable villages. **Siasconset** ✦✦✦ (nicknamed 'Sconset), on the east side of the island, is a tranquil community with picturesque, rose-covered cottages and a handful of businesses, including a pricey French restaurant. Sunset aficionados head to **Madaket** ✦, on the west coast of the island, for the evening spectacular.

The lay of the land on Nantucket is rolling moors, heathlands, cranberry bogs, and miles of exquisite public beaches. The vistas are honeymoon-romantic: an operating windmill, three lighthouses, and a skyline dotted with church steeples.

ESSENTIALS
GETTING THERE
BY FERRY From Hyannis Ferry service to Nantucket is fairly hassle-free, unless you're bringing a car in summer. But first-time visitors to the island will find a car more of a nuisance than a convenience, unless they're staying outside of Nantucket Town. From Hyannis (South Street Dock), the **Steamship Authority** (℗ **508/477-8600,** or 508/228-3274 from Nantucket; www. islandferry.com) operates year-round ferry service (including cars, passengers,

ACCOMMODATIONS ■

The Wauwinet **1**

See the "Nantucket Town" map to locate the accommodations discussed in this section

and bicycles) to Steamship Wharf in Nantucket. No advance reservations are needed for passengers. But if you bring your car in summer, you must reserve months in advance—only six boats make the trip daily, and they fill up fast. If you arrive without a reservation, there is no guarantee you will get to the island that day. Arrive at least 1 hour before departure to avoid having your space being released to standbys. There's a $10 processing fee for canceling reservations entirely with 2 weeks' notice.

Total trip time is 2 hours and 15 minutes. A round-trip fare for a car costs $316 from mid-May to mid-October; $194 from mid-October to mid-May. Car rates do not include drivers or passengers; you must get tickets for each person going to the island. For passengers, a one-way ticket is $12.50 ($25 round-trip) for adults, $6.25 one-way ($12.50 round-trip) for children 5 to 12, and $10 round-trip for bikes. Remember that parking at the ferry dock costs $8 to $10 per day; you do not need to make parking reservations.

The Steamship Authority's fast ferry to Nantucket, the *Flying Cloud* (© **508/495-3278**), is for passengers only. It takes 1 hour and runs five to six times a day in season. The cost is $23 one-way ($42 round-trip) for adults and $17.25 one-way ($31.50 round-trip) for children. AAA members get a $4 discount. Parking costs $8 to $10. Watch for the parking signs on Route 6; if lots next to the dock are full, you'll need to take Exit 6 for a satellite lot, instead of Exit 7 for the main lot. Passenger reservations are highly recommended.

Tips **Planning Ahead: Ferry Parking**

For all **Hy-Line** ferry service, Ocean Street Dock (© **888/778-1132** or 508/778-2602), in July and August, it's a good idea not only to reserve tickets in advance, but also to reserve a parking spot ahead of time. The all-day parking fee is $10 in season. Travelers on **Steamship Authority** (© **508/477-8600**) vessels do not need a parking reservation, but when the lots near the ferry terminal are full, satellite lots are used and passengers must take shuttle buses to the terminal. Be sure to arrive at least an hour before sailing time to allow for parking.

Hy-Line Cruises, Ocean Street Dock (© **888/778-1132** or 508/778-2600; for high-speed ferry reservations, 800/492-8082 or 508/778-0404; www.hy-linecruises.com), offers two types of passenger-only ferries from the Ocean Street dock in Hyannis to Nantucket's Straight Wharf. The *Grey Lady II*, a year-round high-speed passenger catamaran, makes the trip in 1 hour. The one-way fare costs $31.50 for adults ($56 round-trip), $25.50 for children 1 to 12 ($41 round-trip), and $5 extra for bicycles ($10 round-trip). The boat seats 70 and makes six round-trips daily in season—reserve in advance.

Early May through October, Hy-Line runs its standard, 1-hour-and-50-minute ferry service. Round-trip tickets are $26 for adults, $13 for children 4 to 12, and $10 extra for bikes. On busy holiday weekends, the slow ferry fills up, too, so order tickets in advance. Buy or pick up your tickets at least half an hour before your boat leaves the dock.

Three of the slow crossings, on the **MV** *Great Point,* have a first-class section with a private lounge, bathrooms, bar, and snack bar. One-way fare is $21 for adults and children ($42 round-trip). If you're taking the slow boat, consider spending the extra $10 on first class at least one-way. The large, comfortable seats here are a far cry from the unforgiving benches otherwise available. No pets are allowed on the *Great Point.*

Hy-line's "Around the Sound" cruise is a 1-day round-trip excursion from Hyannis with stops in Nantucket and Martha's Vineyard. It runs from early June to late September. The price is $36 for adults, $18 for children 4 to 12, and $15 extra for bikes.

From Martha's Vineyard From Oak Bluffs on Martha's Vineyard, Hy-Line runs three passenger-only ferries daily to Nantucket from early June to late September (there's no car-ferry service between the islands). The trip time from Oak Bluffs is 2 hours and 15 minutes. The one-way fare is $12 for adults, $6 for children 5 to 12, and $5 extra for bikes.

From Harwich Port You can avoid the summer crowds in Hyannis and by boarding a **Freedom Cruise Line** (© **508/432-8999**) passenger-only ferry to Nantucket. From mid-May to mid-October, boats leave from Saquatucket Harbor in Harwich Port; the trip takes 1½ hours. A round-trip ticket is $39 for adults, $34 for children 2 to 12, $5 for children under 2, and $10 extra for bikes. Parking is free for the first 24 hours; $12 per night thereafter. Advance reservations are highly recommended.

BY PLANE You can fly into **Nantucket Memorial Airport** (© **508/325-5300**), about 3 miles south of Nantucket Road on Old South Road. The flight to Nantucket takes about 30 to 40 minutes from Boston, 15 minutes from Hyannis, and a little more than an hour from New York City airports.

Airlines providing service to Nantucket include **Business Express/Delta Connection** (℡ **800/221-1212**), from Boston (year-round) and New York (seasonally); **Cape Air/Nantucket Air** (℡ **800/352-0714**), year-round from Hyannis, Boston, Martha's Vineyard ($76 round-trip), and New Bedford ($71 round-trip); **Continental Express** (℡ **800/525-0280**), seasonally from Newark; **Island Airlines** (℡ **508/228-7575**), year-round from Hyannis; and **US Airways Express** (℡ **800/428-4322**), year-round from Boston. Island Airlines and Nantucket Airlines both offer year-round charter service.

GETTING AROUND

Nantucket is easily navigated by bike, by moped, or on foot, and also by shuttle bus or taxi. The chamber of commerce strongly suggests that visitors leave their cars behind, in order to minimize congestion and environmental impact. If you're staying outside of Nantucket Town, however, or if you plan to explore the outer reaches of the island, you might want to bring your own car or rent one here. Keep in mind, in-town traffic can reach gridlock in peak season, and parking can be a nightmare.

BY BICYCLE & MOPED When we head to Nantucket for a few days, we prefer to get around by bike. The island is relatively flat, and paved bike paths abound—they'll get you from Nantucket Town to Siasconset, Surfside, and Madaket. There are also many unpaved back roads to explore, which make mountain bikes a wise choice. Mopeds are also available, but be aware that local rules and regulations are strictly enforced. Mopeds are not allowed on sidewalks or bike paths. You'll need a driver's license to rent a moped, and state law requires that you wear a helmet.

You can bring your own bike over on the ferries for a small additional charge. Otherwise, shops that rent bikes and mopeds (all within walking distance of the ferries) include **Cook's Cycle Shop, Inc.,** 6 S. Beach St. (℡ **508/228-0800**); **Nantucket Bike Shop,** at Steamboat Wharf and Straight Wharf (℡ **508/228-1999**); and **Young's Bicycle Shop,** at Steamboat Wharf (℡ **508/228-1151**), which also does repairs. **Holiday Cycle,** 4 Chester St. (℡ **508/228-3644**), rents bikes only.

BY SHUTTLE BUS June through September, inexpensive shuttle buses, with bike racks and wheelchair lifts, make a loop through Nantucket Town and to a few outlying spots; for routes and stops, contact the **Nantucket Regional Transit Authority** (℡ **508/228-7025;** www.nantucket.net/trans/nrta) or pick up a map and schedule at the visitor center on Federal Street or the Chamber Office on Main Street. The cost is 50¢ to $1, and exact change is required. A 3-day pass can be purchased at the visitor center for $10. Dogs are allowed on the bus as long as they are relatively clean and dry.

BY CAR & JEEP We recommend a car if you'll be here for more than a week, or if you're staying outside Nantucket Town. Remember, though, there are no in-town parking lots; parking, although free, is limited.

Rental agencies on the island include **Affordable Rentals of Nantucket,** 6 S. Beach Rd. (℡ **508/228-3501**); **Budget,** at the airport (℡ **800/527-0700** or 508/228-5666); **Hertz,** at the airport (℡ **800/654-3131** or 508/228-9421); **Nantucket Windmill Auto Rental,** at the airport (℡ **800/228-1227** or 508/228-1227); **Thrifty Car Rental,** at the airport (℡ **508/325-4616**); and

Young's 4 X 4 & Car Rental, Steamboat Wharf (© **508/228-1151**). A four-wheel-drive rental costs about $180 per day (including an over-sand permit).

BY TAXI   You'll find taxis (many are vans that can accommodate large groups or those traveling with bikes) waiting at the airport and at all ferry ports. During the busy summer, we recommend reserving a taxi in advance to avoid a long wait upon arrival. Rates are flat fees, based on one person riding before 1am, with surcharges for additional passengers, bikes, and dogs. A taxi from the airport to Nantucket Town hotels will cost about $10. Reliable cab companies on the island include **A-1 Taxi** (© **508/228-3330**), **Aardvark Cab** (© **508/728-9999**), **All Point Taxi** (© **508/228-5779**), and **Lisa's Taxi** (© **508/228-5779**).

VISITOR INFORMATION

Contact the **Nantucket Island Chamber of Commerce,** 48 Main St., Nantucket (© **508/228-1700;** www.nantucketchamber.org). When you arrive, also stop by the **Nantucket Visitors Service and Information Bureau,** in Nantucket Town at 25 Federal St. (© **508/228-0925**). It's open daily from June to September, Monday through Saturday from October to May. There are also information booths at Steamboat Wharf and Straight Wharf.

Check the island's newspaper, the *Inquirer & Mirror,* for information on current events and activities around town.

Nantucket Accommodations (© **508/228-9559;** fax 508/325-7009; www.nantucketaccomodations.com), a 29-year-old private service, arranges reservations for inns, B&Bs, and hotels; it has access to 95% of the island's lodging facilities, in addition to houses and cottages available by the night or week (as opposed to most realtors, who will only handle rentals for 2 weeks or more). The charge for the service is $15—a fee assessed only when a reservation is made. Last-minute travelers should keep in mind that **Nantucket Visitors Service** (© **508/228-0925**), a daily referral service for available rooms rather than a booking service, always has the most updated list of lodging availability and cancellations.

ATMs can be difficult to locate on Nantucket. **Nantucket Bank** (© **508/228-0580**) has three locations: 2 Orange St., 104 Pleasant St., and the airport lobby, all open 24 hours. **Pacific National Bank** has four locations: the A&P supermarket (next to the wharves), the Stop & Shop (open 24 hours seasonally), the Steamship Wharf Terminal, and Pacific National Bank lobby (open during bank hours only).

In case of a medical emergency, the **Nantucket Cottage Hospital,** 57 Prospect St. (© **508/228-1200**), is open 24 hours.

BEACHES & OUTDOOR PURSUITS

BEACHES   In distinct contrast to Martha's Vineyard, virtually all of Nantucket's 110-mile coastline is open to the public.

- **Children's Beach:** This small beach is a protected cove just west of busy Steamship Wharf. Appealing to families, it has a park, playground, rest rooms, lifeguards, snack bar, and even a bandstand for free weekend concerts.
- **Cisco Beach** (⚐): About 4 miles from town, in the southwestern quadrant of the island (from Main Street, turn onto Milk Street, which becomes Hummock Pond Road), Cisco enjoys vigorous waves—great for the surfers who flock here. Rest rooms and lifeguards are available.

- **Coatue Beach** 🏖: This fishhook-shaped barrier beach, on the northeastern side of the island at Wauwinet, is Nantucket's outback, accessible only by four-wheel-drive vehicles, water craft, or the very strong legged. Swimming is strongly discouraged because of fierce tides.

- **Dionis Beach** 🏖🏖: About 3 miles out of town (take the Madaket bike path to Eel Point Road) is Dionis, which enjoys the gentle sound surf and steep, picturesque bluffs. It's a great spot for swimming, picnicking, and shelling, and you'll find fewer children than at Jetties or Children's beaches. Stick to the established paths to prevent further erosion. Lifeguards patrol here and rest rooms are available.

- **Jetties Beach** 🏖🏖🏖: Located about a half mile west of Children's Beach on North Beach Street, Jetties is about a 20-minute walk, or even shorter bike ride, shuttle-bus ride, or drive, from town (there's a large parking lot, but it fills up early on summer weekends). It's another family favorite, for its mild waves, lifeguards, bathhouse, and rest rooms, and relatively affordable restaurant, the Jetties Cafe & Grille (✆ **508/325-6347**). Facilities include the town tennis courts, volleyball nets, a skate park, and a playground; water-sports equipment and chairs are available for rent. Every August, Jetties hosts an intense sand-castle competition, and the Fourth of July fireworks are held here as well.

- **Madaket Beach** 🏖: Accessible by Madaket Road, the 6-mile bike path that runs parallel to it, and by shuttle bus, this westerly beach is narrow and subject to pounding surf and sometimes serious crosscurrents. Unless it's a fairly tame day, you might content yourself with wading. It's the best spot on the island for admiring the sunset. Facilities include rest rooms, lifeguards, and mobile food service.

- **Siasconset Beach:** The easterly coast of 'Sconset is as pretty as the town itself and rarely, if ever, crowded, perhaps because of the water's strong sideways tow. You can reach it by car, by shuttle bus, or via a less scenic and somewhat hilly 7-mile bike path (Polpis path or Milestone path). There are usually lifeguards on duty, but the closest facilities (rest rooms, grocery store, cafe) are back in the center of the village.

- **Surfside Beach** 🏖🏖🏖: Three miles south of town via a popular bike/skate path, broad Surfside—equipped with lifeguards, rest rooms, and a surprisingly accomplished little snack bar—is appropriately named and commensurately popular. It draws thousands of visitors a day in high season, from college students to families, but the free parking lot can fit only about 60 cars—you do the math or, better yet, ride your bike or take the shuttle bus.

BICYCLING 🏖🏖🏖   Several lovely, paved bike paths radiate out from the center of town to outlying beaches. The main paths run about 6⅕ miles west to Madaket, 3½ miles south to Surfside, and 8⅕ miles east to Siasconset. To avoid backtracking from Siasconset, continue north through the charming village, and return on the **Polpis Road bike path** 🏖🏖, which passes cranberry bogs and other scenic vistas. Strong riders could do a whole circuit of the island in a day, but most will be content to combine a single route with a few hours at a beach. You'll find picnic benches and water fountains at strategic points along all the paths.

Lighthouse enthusiasts will want to stop by **Brant Point Light** at the end of Easton Street. Located next to the Coast Guard station, this squat lighthouse is still used by boats maneuvering in and out of the harbor. It's a scenic spot to take a break and enjoy the view; you'll see ferries chugging by, and immense yachts competing for prize berths along the wharves.

For a free map of the island's bike paths (and a list of Nantucket's bicycle rules), stop by **Young's Bicycle Shop,** at Steamboat Wharf (© **508/228-1151**). It's definitely the best place for bike rentals. See "Getting Around," above, for more rental options.

FISHING   To fish for shellfish, you'll need a permit from the **harbormaster's office,** 34 Washington St. (© **508/228-7261**). You'll see surf casters all over the island (no permit is required); for a guided trip, try Mike Mont of **Surf & Fly Fishing Trips** (© **508/228-0529**). Deep-sea charters heading out of Straight Wharf include Captain Josh Eldridge's *Monomoy* (© **508/228-6867**) and Captain David Martin's *Flicka* (© **508/325-4000**).

NATURE TRAILS   Through preservationist foresight, about a third of Nantucket's 42 square miles are protected from development. Contact the **Nantucket Conservation Foundation,** 118 Cliff Rd. (© **508/228-2884**), for a map of its holdings ($3), which include the 205-acre **Windswept Cranberry Bog** (off Polpis Road), where bogs are interspersed amid hardwood forests, and a portion of the 1,100-acre **Coskata-Coatue Wildlife Refuge** 🐾🐾, comprising the barrier beaches beyond Wauwinet (see "Organized Tours & Cruises," below). The **Maria Mitchell Association** (see "Museums & Historic Landmarks," below) also sponsors guided birding and wildflower walks in season.

WATER SPORTS   **Nantucket Community Sailing** manages the concession at **Jetties Beach** (© **508/228-5358**), which offers lessons and rents out kayaks, sailboards, sailboats, and more. **Sea Nantucket,** on tiny Francis Street Beach off Washington Street (© **508/228-7499**), also rents kayaks; it's a quick sprint across the harbor to beautiful Coatue.

MUSEUMS & HISTORIC LANDMARKS

Hadwen House 🐾🐾   During Nantucket's most prosperous years, whaling merchant Joseph Starbuck built the "Three Bricks" (nos. 93, 95, and 97 Main St.) for his three sons. His daughter married successful businessman William Hadwen, owner of the candle factory that is now the Whaling Museum, and Hadwen built this grand Greek Revival home across the street from his brothers-in-law in 1845. Although locals (mostly Quakers) were scandalized by the opulence, the local outrage spurred Hadwen on, and he decided to make the home even grander than he had originally intended. The home soon became a showplace for entertaining the Hadwens' many wealthy friends. Hadwen then built the matching home next door for his niece. The Historical Association has done a magnificent job restoring the home and furnishing it with period pieces, fabrics, porcelains, and wallpapers. The gardens are maintained in period style by the Nantucket Garden Club.

96 Main St. (at Pleasant St., a few blocks southwest of the town center). © 508/228-1894. Admission $4 adults, $3 children 5–14; also included in Nantucket Historical Association pass ($10 adults, $5 children). June–Sept daily 10am–5pm; call for off-season hours. Closed mid-Oct to late May.

Jethro Coffin House 🐾   Built around 1696, this saltbox is the oldest building left on the island. A National Historical Landmark, the brick design on its central chimney has earned it the nickname "The Horseshoe House." It was struck by lightning and severely damaged (in fact, nearly cut in two) in 1987, prompting a long-overdue restoration. Dimly lit by leaded glass diamond-pane

Nantucket Town

Anchor Inn **5**
Cliff Lodge **3**
Cliffside Beach Club **2**
Jared Coffin House **7**
Martin House Inn **4**

The Nesbitt Inn **8**
The Pineapple Inn **9**
Sherburne Inn **6**
Union Street Inn **10**
White Elephant **1**

See the "Nantucket" map to locate the Wauwinet Hotel.

windows, it's filled with period furniture such as lathed ladder-back chairs and a clever trundle bed on wooden wheels. Nantucket Historical Association tour guides will fill you in on all the related lore.

Sunset Hill Rd. (off W. Chester Rd., about ½ mile northwest of the town center). © **508/228-1894.** Admission $3 adults, $2 children 5–14; also included in Nantucket Historical Association pass ($10 adults, $5 children). Mid-June to early Sept daily 10am–5pm; call for off-season hours. Closed mid-Oct to late May.

The Maria Mitchell Association ★★   This is a group of six buildings organized and maintained in honor of distinguished astronomer and Nantucket native Maria Mitchell (1818–89). The science center consists of astronomical observatories, with a lecture series, children's science seminars, and stellar observation opportunities (when the sky is clear) from the **Loines Observatory,** 59 Milk St. (© **508/228-8690**), and the **Vestal Street Observatory,** 3 Vestal St. (© **508/228-9273**).

The **Hinchman House Natural Science Museum,** 7 Milk St. (© **508/ 228-0898**), houses a visitor center and offers evening lectures, bird watching, wildflower and nature walks, and discovery classes for children and adults. The **Mitchell House,** 1 Vestal St. (© **508/228-2896**), the astronomer's birthplace, features a children's history series and adult-artisan seminars, and has wildflower and herb gardens as well. The **Science Library** is at 2 Vestal St. (© **508/228-9219**), and the tiny, child-oriented **aquarium** at 28 Washington St. (© **508/228-5387**).

4 Vestal St. (at Milk St., about ½ mile southwest of the town center). © **508/228-9198**. www.mmo.org. Museum pass (for birthplace, aquarium, science museum and Vestal Street Observatory) $7 adults, $5 seniors and children age 6–14. Early June to late Aug Tues–Sat 10am–4pm; call for off-season hours.

Nantucket Life-Saving Museum 🌟   Housed in a replica of the Nantucket Lifesaving Station (the original serves as the island's youth hostel), the museum has loads of interesting exhibits, including historic photos and newspaper clippings, as well as one of the last remaining Massachusetts Humane Society surf boats and its horse-drawn carriage.

158 Polpis Rd. © **508/228-1855**. Admission $3 adults, $2 children. Mid-June to mid-Oct daily 9:30am–4pm.

Whaling Museum 🌟🌟🌟   Housed in a former spermaceti (a waxy fluid extracted from sperm whales) candle factory, this museum is a must-visit, if not for the awe-inspiring skeleton of a 43-foot finback whale (stranded in the 1960s), then for the exceptional collections of scrimshaw and nautical art. Check out the action painting *Ship Spermo of Nantucket in a Heavy Thunder-Squall on the Coast of California 1876,* executed by a captain who survived the storm. The price of admission includes daily lectures on the brief and colorful history of the industry, like the beachside "whalebecue" feasts that natives and settlers once enjoyed.

13 Broad St. (in the center of town). © **508/228-1894**. Admission $5 adults, $3 children 5–14; also included in the Nantucket Historical Association pass ($10 adults, $5 children). Late May to mid-Oct daily 10am–5pm; call for off-season hours. Closed early Dec to mid-Apr.

ORGANIZED TOURS & CRUISES

Built in 1926, the *Christina,* at Slip 19, Straight Wharf (© **508/325-4000**), is a classic solid mahogany cat boat. It makes seven 1½-hour trips daily in season; the sunset trips tend to sell out a day or two in advance. A sail around the harbor ($20 per person; sunset sails $30 per person) is probably the best entertainment bargain on Nantucket. No sailings November through April.

Endeavor Sailing Excursions, at Slip 15, Straight Wharf (© **508/ 228-5585**), offers jaunts across the harbor into Nantucket Sound on the *Endeavor,* a spirited 31-foot replica Friendship sloop. Skipper James Genthner will gladly drop you off for a bit of sunbathing or beachcombing. Rates are $22.50 to $35 for a 1½-hour sail (highest rates are in July and August); reservations recommended. No sailings November through April.

The Trustees of Reservations, a private statewide conservation organization, runs the 3-hour guided **Coskata-Coatue Wildlife Refuge Natural History Tour** (© **508/228-6799**). The trip, via Ford Expedition, takes you over sand dunes and through rare habitat out to the **Great Point Lighthouse,** a partly solar-powered replica of the 1818 original. Those interested can tour the inside of the lighthouse. On the way, you might spot snowy egrets, ospreys, terns, and oystercatchers. Tours are offered from mid-May to mid-October, daily at

9:30am and 2:30pm. The cost is $30 for adults, $15 for children 15 and under. Call to make a reservation.

SHOPPING ★★★

All of the shops listed below are located right in the center of Nantucket Town.

ANTIQUES & COLLECTIBLES **Tonkin of Nantucket,** 33 Main St. (© **508/228-9697**), specializes in English and French antiques. Antiques hounds will be in heaven browsing through the 9,000 square feet of silver, china, marine paintings, ship models, fireplace equipment, and Majolica.

ARTS & CRAFTS The **Artists' Association of Nantucket** has the widest selection of work by locals, and the gallery at 19 Washington St. (© **508/228-0294**) is impressive. Closed February and March. Exquisite pieces can be found at **Nantucket Glassworks**, 28 Centre St. (© **508/228-7779**), where owners Robert and Jayne Dane show top-quality work.

Definitely poke your head into **Sailor's Valentine,** in the Macy Warehouse on lower Main Street (© **508/228-2011**), which houses an international collection of contemporary fine art, sculpture, folk art, and "outsider art." There are also new versions of the namesake craft, a boxed design of colorful shells, which 19th-century sailors used to bring back from the Caribbean for their sweethearts at home.

FASHION Martha's Vineyard may have spawned "Black Dog" fever, but this island boasts the inimitable "Nantucket reds"—cotton clothing that starts out tomato-red and washes out to salmon-pink. The fashion originated at **Murray's Toggery Shop,** 62 Main St. (© **800/368-2134** or 508/228-0437).

HOME DECOR Although certain influences are evident (from Queen Anne to Shaker), the hand-fashioned furniture at **Stephen Swift,** 34 Main St. (© **508/228-0255**), is far too individualized to pass as reproduction.

WHERE TO STAY

As with Martha's Vineyard, we've only given summer rates here, since Nantucket is so seasonal. However, if you do visit in the off-season, you can find substantial discounts on hotel rates at any of the places that remain open. Note, though, that lodging rates on Nantucket are at high-season levels during the popular Christmas Stroll in December and Daffodil Festival in April.

VERY EXPENSIVE

Cliffside Beach Club ★★★ Right on the beach, and within walking distance (about a mile) of town, this is surely the premier lodging on the island. It may not be as fancy as some, but there's a sublime beachy-ness to the whole setup, from the simply decorated rooms and the cheerful, youthful staff to the blue, yellow, and green umbrellas lined up on the beach. All bedrooms have such luxuries as French milled soaps, thick towels, and exceptional linens. Guests receive an umbrella, chairs, and beach towels. A very good continental breakfast is served in the large clubhouse room, its beamed ceilings draped with colorful quilts. Lucky guests on the Fourth of July get a front-row seat for the fireworks staged at nearby Jetties Beach.

46 Jefferson Ave. (about 1 mile from town center), Nantucket, MA 02554. © **508/228-0618.** Fax 508/325-4735. www.cliffsidebeach.com. 28 units. Summer $335–$535 double; $655–$1,310 suite; $655 apartment; $870 cottage. Rates include continental breakfast. AE. Closed mid-Oct to late May. **Amenities:** Restaurant (bistro/seafood); health club with Cybex equipment and on-staff trainer; indoor hydrotherapy spa; sauna; massage room. *In room:* A/C, TV, fridge, hair dryer.

The Wauwinet ✦✦✦   This ultradeluxe beachfront retreat, situated next to a wildlife sanctuary, is the most luxurious lodging choice on the island. Each of the lovely rooms—all with a cozy nook from which to gaze out across the water—has a unique decorating scheme, with pine armoires, plenty of wicker, exquisite Audubon prints, handsome fabrics, and a lovely array of antique accessories. Extras include Egyptian cotton bathrobes, bottled water, and a personalized set of engraved note cards. If you order up a video from the extensive library, it is delivered on a tray with a couple of boxes of complimentary popcorn. The staff goes to great lengths to please, ferrying you into town, for instance, in a 1946 "Woody," or dispatching you on a 21-foot launch across the bay to your own private strip of beach.

120 Wauwinet Rd. (about 8 miles east of Nantucket center), Wauwinet, MA 02554. ✆ **800/426-8718** or 508/228-0145. Fax 508/228-6712. www.wauwinet.com. 30 units. Summer $540–$890 double; $850–$1,500 cottage. Rates include breakfast and afternoon wine and cheese. AE, DC, MC, V. Closed Nov–May. **Amenities:** Restaurant (regional); 2 clay tennis courts with pro shop; croquet lawn; boats and bikes for guests' use. *In room:* A/C, TV/VCR, CD player, hair dryer, iron.

White Elephant ✦✦   This luxury property, right on the harbor, is the ultimate in-town lodging and has been newly renovated by the owners of the Wauwinet (see above). Guest rooms, distributed among one main building and 12 cottages, are mostly spacious, airy suites (the most spacious rooms on Nantucket), with country-chic decor. About half the rooms have working fireplaces, and most have harbor views. The pleasant common rooms include a library. The same company owns Breakers, a 25-room hotel next door that offers a less bustling atmosphere.

Easton and Willard sts. (Box 1139), Nantucket, MA 02554. ✆ **800/ISLANDS** or 508/228-2500. Fax 508/325-1195. www.whiteelephanthotel.com. 66 units. Summer $400–$750 double; $350–$1,160 cottage. Rates include breakfast. AE, DC, DISC, MC, V. Closed Nov–Apr. **Amenities:** Restaurant (lobster/steakhouse; see Brant Point Grill, below); outdoor heated pool; fitness center; concierge; business lounge; room service; laundry service, dry cleaning; extensive video library. *In room:* A/C, TV, VCR or DVD player, stereo, high-speed Internet access, hair dryer, iron, safe.

EXPENSIVE

Jared Coffin House ✦✦   This grand brick manse built in 1845 is the social center of town, as well as a mecca for visitors. Accommodations range from well-priced singles (rare in these parts) to spacious doubles. Rooms in the neighboring annex houses are equally grand. The central location does have drawbacks: The front rooms can be quite noisy, and 20-minute waits for breakfast are not unusual since the locals come here, too. It's the best breakfast in town, though not included in the room rate; we recommend calling ahead to get your name put on the list.

29 Broad St. (at Centre St.), Nantucket, MA 02554. ✆ **800/248-2405** or 508/228-2400. Fax 508/228-8549. www.jaredcoffinhouse.com. 60 units. Summer $175–$325 double. AE, DC, DISC, MC, V. Open year-round. **Amenities:** Restaurant. *In room:* TV.

The Pineapple Inn ✦✦   This newly renovated historic inn has quickly become one of the premier places to stay on the island. The graceful Quaker entrance of the 1838 home leads to spacious guest rooms decorated in a colonial style with fine reproductions and antiques, including handmade Oriental rugs, marble bathrooms, and many four-poster canopy beds. The smaller, less expensive units are on the third floor. The continental breakfast features fresh baked goods, espresso, cappuccino, and fresh-squeezed orange juice. The garden patio with climbing roses is a fine place to enjoy an afternoon cocktail and contemplate dinner plans.

10 Hussey St. (in the center of town), Nantucket, MA 02554. ℂ **508/228-9992.** Fax 508/325-6051. www.pineappleinn.com. 12 units. Summer $160–$295 double. Rates include continental breakfast. AE, MC, V. Closed early Dec to mid-Apr. Children 8 and over welcome. *In room:* A/C, TV, dataport, hair dryer.

Sherburne Inn ✿

You'd never guess from the gracious foyer of this 1835 house that it was once the headquarters of the Atlantic Silk Company, a short-lived 19th-century enterprise. Now it's an elegant and comfortable inn offering quiet comforts in the heart of Nantucket village. Guest rooms vary in size, with smaller units a good value at lower rates. Ask for one on the sunny side of the house. Innkeeper Susan Gasparich's recipes for baked goods like butterscotch coffeecake have been featured in *Gourmet* magazine.

10 Gay St. (in the center of town), Nantucket, MA 02554. ℂ **888/577-4425** or 508/228-4425. Fax 508/228-8114. www.sherburneinn.com. 8 units. Summer $150–$275. Rates include continental breakfast. AE, DISC, MC, V. Open year-round. Children 6 and over welcome. *In room:* A/C, TV.

Union Street Inn ✿✿

Sophisticated innkeepers Deborah and Ken Withrow have a terrific location for their historic 1770s property, just steps from Main Street but in a quiet, residential section. Ken's experience in big hotels shows in the amenities and full concierge service offered. Many guest rooms have canopied or four-poster beds made up with Egyptian linens; half have working fireplaces. All are outfitted with antique furniture and fixtures. Unlike many Nantucket inns whose zoning laws forbid them to serve a full breakfast, this inn's location allows a superb complete breakfast on the garden patio. If you're hanging around in the afternoon, there are usually home-baked cookies or other goodies to sample as well.

7 Union St. (in the center of town), Nantucket, MA 02554. ℂ **800/225-5116** or 508/228-9222. Fax 508/325-0848. www.union-street-inn.com. 12 units. Summer $150–$295 double; $325 suite. Rates include breakfast. AE, MC, V. Closed Jan–Feb. **Amenities:** Concierge. *In room:* A/C, TV, hair dryer, no phone.

MODERATE

Anchor Inn ✿

Innkeepers Ann and Charles Balas have a historic gem in this sea captain's home located next to the Old North Church. Authentic details can be found throughout the house, in the antique hardware and paneling and period furnishings. Guests enjoy continental breakfast with homebaked muffins at individual tables on the enclosed porch.

66 Centre St. (in the center of town), P.O. Box 387, Nantucket, MA 02554. ℂ **508/228-0072.** www.anchor-inn.net. 11 units. Summer $175–$195. Rates include continental breakfast. AE, MC, V. Closed Jan–Feb. *In room:* A/C (in season), TV, hair dryer.

Cliff Lodge ✿✿

Debby and John Bennett have freshened up this charming 1771 whaling captain's house with their own countrified style. The cheerful interiors feature colorful quilts and splatter-painted floors. Rooms range from a first-floor beauty with king-size bed, paneled walls, and fireplace to the tiny third-floor units tucked into the eaves. All are spotlessly clean and blessed with quality beds and linens. The spacious apartment in the rear of the house is a sunny delight. The continental breakfast, home-baked breads and muffins served on the garden patio, is congenial. Chat with Debby for a wealth of island info and the latest goings-on, then climb up to the roof walk for a bird's-eye view of the town and harbor.

9 Cliff Rd. (a few blocks from the center of town), Nantucket, MA 02554. ℂ **508/228-9480.** Fax 508/228-6308. www.nantucket.net/lodging/clifflodge. 12 units. Summer $115 single; $155–$195 double; $375 apartment. Rates include continental breakfast. MC, V. Open year-round. Children 12 and over welcome. *In room:* A/C, TV.

Martin House Inn ★★ *Value*   This is one of the lower-priced B&Bs in town, but also one of the most stylish, with a formal parlor and dining rooms and a spacious side porch, complete with hammock. Charming innkeeper Debbie Wasil, who also owns the nearby Centerboard, keeps this historic 1803 mariner's home in shipshape condition. The garret single rooms with a shared bathroom are a bargain. Higher-priced rooms have four-poster beds and working fireplaces. The extensive continental breakfast includes Martin's famous granola, as well as home-baked breads, muffins, and fresh fruits.

61 Centre St. (between Broad and Chester sts.; a couple blocks from town center), Nantucket, MA 02554. 🕾 **508/228-0678.** Fax 508/325-4798. www.nantucket.net/lodging/martinn. 13 units (4 with shared bathroom). Summer $75–$85 single; $125–$295 double. Rates include continental breakfast. MC, V. Open year-round. *In room:* No phone.

INEXPENSIVE

The Nesbitt Inn   This Victorian-style inn in the center of town has been run by the same family for 95 years. It's quite old-fashioned, and a bargain for Nantucket. All rooms have sinks and share bathrooms, which are in the hall. There's a friendly, family atmosphere to the place, and beloved innkeepers Dolly and Nobby Noblit are salt-of-the-earth Nantucketers, who will cheerfully fill you in on island lore.

21 Broad St., Box 1019, Nantucket, MA 02554. 🕾 **508/228-0156** or 508/228-2446. 13 units (all with shared bathroom), 2 apartments. Summer $75 single; $85–$125 double; apartment $1,150 per week. Rates include continental breakfast. MC, V. Closed mid-Dec to Feb. *In room:* No phone.

WHERE TO DINE
VERY EXPENSIVE

Chanticleer Inn ★★ FRENCH   A contender for the priciest restaurant on the Cape and Islands, this rose-covered cottage-turned-French-auberge has fans who insist they'd have to cross an ocean to savor the likes of the classic cuisine. Unfortunately, along with the French cuisine, the restaurant has also imported some Gallic attitude; service here can be haughty. A few glamorous options on the prix-fixe menu include *gateau de grenouilles aux pommes de terre* (a frogs' legs "cake" in a potato crust); *tournedos de lotte marinée au gingembre, sauce au rhum, croquettes d'ail* (a gingered monkfish scaloppini with a lemon-rum sauce and sweet garlic fritters); and *pain perdu, glace au chocolat blanc, coulis d'abricots secs* (a bread pudding with white-chocolate ice cream and apricot sauce). The restaurant's stellar wine cellar is stocked with 38,000 bottles.

9 New St., Siasconset. 🕾 **508/257-6231** or 508/257-9756. Reservations recommended. Jacket required for men. Main courses $42–$45; prix-fixe dinner $70. AE, DC, MC, V. Mid-May to mid-Oct Tues–Sun noon–2:30pm and 6:30–9:30pm. Closed mid-Oct to mid-May.

Club Car ★★★ CONTINENTAL   For decades one of the top restaurants on Nantucket, this posh venue is popular with locals, many of whom particularly enjoy beef-Wellington night on autumn Sundays. Executive chef Michael Shannon is chummy with Julia Child, and the menu has classic French influences. Interesting offerings include a first course of Japanese octopus in the style of Bangkok (with mixed hot peppers, tiparos fish sauce, mint, cilantro, lime, and tomato concassee) and an entree of roast rack of lamb Club Car (with fresh herbs, honey-mustard glaze, and minted Madeira sauce). Some nights, seven-course tasting menus are available for $65 per person. The lounge area is within an antique first-class car from the old Nantucket railroad; you'll want to have a drink while cuddled in the red leather banquettes before or after dinner. Lunch at the Club Car is a great deal for those on a budget.

1 Main St. ℂ **508/228-1101.** Reservations recommended. Main courses $32–$38. MC, V. July–Aug daily 11am–3pm and 6–10pm; call for off-season hours. Closed Jan–May.

The Pearl ⟵⟶ NEW AMERICAN   It's Miami Beach on Nantucket at the newest and swankiest fine-dining establishment on the island. The contemporary look here features bluish lighting and large fish tanks. There are numerous stylish touches: appetizers and desserts served in martini glasses, local seafood prepared in innovative ways, an extensive champagne list. Skip the *grande deluxe plateau de mer;* it's not a lot of shellfish for a lot of money. But do choose the wild mushroom galette with white truffle cream. As a main course, look no further than the pan-roasted striped bass with citrus tomato infusion and local lobster.

12 Federal St. ℂ **508/228-9701.** Reservations recommended. Main courses $34–$40. AE, MC, V. Late June to early Sept daily 6:30–9:30pm; call for off-season hours. Closed mid-Oct to Apr.

The Summer House ⟵⟶ NEW AMERICAN   The classic Nantucket atmosphere, 'Sconset style, distinguishes this fine-dining experience from others on the island: wicker and wrought iron, roses and honeysuckle. A pianist plays nightly—often Gershwin standards. The pounding Atlantic Ocean is just over the bluff. Service is wonderful, and the food excellent, though expensive. Specialties of the house include fresh, locally caught seafood delicately prepared and stylishly presented. The distinctive main courses include roast saddle of lamb with rosemary caponatina port and feta mashed potatoes; the unusual and tasty lobster cutlets with coconut-jasmine risotto timbale and mint-tomato relish; and the grilled rib-eye with wild mushrooms, foie gras, and cabernet. Desserts are bountiful—order the blueberry pie if it's in season.

17 Ocean Ave., Siasconset. ℂ **508/257-9976.** Reservations recommended. Main courses $30–$42. AE, MC, V. July–Aug daily 6–10pm; mid-May to June and Sept to mid-Oct Wed–Sun 6–10pm. Closed mid-Oct to Apr.

EXPENSIVE

American Seasons ⟵⟶ REGIONAL AMERICAN   This romantic little restaurant has a great theme: Choose your region (New England, Pacific Coast, Wild West, or Down South) and select creative offerings. You can mix or match your appetizers and entrees. For instance, start with Louisiana crawfish risotto with fire-roasted onion and fried parsnips in a sweet corn puree from Down South; then from the Pacific Coast, an aged beef sirloin with caramelized shallot and Yukon potato hash served with an Oregon blue-cheese salad with white-truffle oil and fried onions.

80 Centre St. (2 blocks from the center of town). ℂ **508/228-7111.** Reservations recommended. Main courses $24–$27. AE, MC, V. Apr–Nov daily 6–9pm. Closed Dec–Mar.

Brant Point Grill ⟵ NEW AMERICAN   This pretty dining room on the harbor is a lobster, steak, and chops house. If you can't sit on the terrace, try to snag a seat near one of the windows where you can watch the twilight fade over the harbor. The candlelight and white, airy dining room make for a perfectly romantic setting. However, dinner at this establishment is an expensive proposition. For instance, the appetizer list includes Kobe Beef Tartare, "the caviar of beef," for $35. Prime New York strip steak runs $35 to $39. There are also a range of fish dishes. You may want to stick to lunch, when prices are more reasonable.

White Elephant Hotel (Easton and Willard sts.). ℂ **508/325-1320.** Reservations recommended. Jacket requested for men. Main courses $26–$39. AE, DC, DISC, MC, V. Mid-May to mid-Oct daily noon–2:30pm and 6–10pm. Closed mid-Oct to mid-May.

Company of the Cauldron ✸✸ CONTINENTAL   This is one of the island's most romantic restaurants. It's an intimate candlelit dining room where, several nights a week in season, a classical harpist plays. There is one intricate and distinct three- to four-course prix-fixe meal offered each night, so check the menu out front or call ahead to see which night to go. Dietary preferences, like vegetarianism, can be accommodated with advance notice. Don't miss the soft-shell crab appetizer, offered in season. The main course could be seafood, such as a special swordfish preparation, or a meat dish, like rack of lamb or beef Wellington.

5 India St. (between Federal and Centre sts.). ✆ **508/228-4016.** Reservations required. Prix-fixe $48–$50. MC, V. Tues–Sun seatings at 7 and 9pm; call for off-season hours. Closed late Oct to mid-May.

DeMarco ✸✸ NORTHERN ITALIAN   This frame house carved into a cafe/bar and loft is where to get the best northern Italian food on the island. A forward-thinking menu and attentive service ensure a superior meal, which might include *antipasto di salmone* (house-smoked salmon rollantini, lemon-herb cream cheese, cucumber-and-endive salad with chive vinaigrette) and the delicate *capellini con scampi* (capellini with rock shrimp, tomato, black olives, capers, and hot pepper).

9 India St. (between Federal and Centre sts.). ✆ **508/228-1836.** Reservations recommended. Main courses $18–$32. AE, MC, V. Mid-June to Sept daily 6–10pm; call for off-season hours. Closed mid-Oct to mid-May.

Òran Mór ✸✸✸ INTERNATIONAL   Renowned chef Peter Wallace runs this second-floor waterfront venue, which has quickly become the premier restaurant on the island. The unusual name is Gaelic and means "great song"; it's the name of Wallace's favorite single-malt scotch. Climb up the stairs of this historic building and prepare yourself for a somewhat extravagant experience. The menu changes nightly; standouts are the appetizer lobster risotto and the entree roast loin of elk with oven-roasted tomato bruschetta. There are always local seafood specials. Some say the grilled breast of duck with savory tapioca and local nectar jus is the best duck dish on the island. An excellent sommelier is on hand to assist wine lovers. On Sundays off-season, a scrumptious brunch is sometimes served; call to check.

2 S. Beach St. (in the center of town). ✆ **508/228-8655.** Reservations recommended. Main courses $26–$32. AE, MC, V. July–Aug daily 6–10pm; Sept–June Mon–Sat 6–9pm, Sun noon–8pm. Open year-round.

21 Federal ✸✸ NEW AMERICAN   Agreeable host Chick Walsh has created an institution popular with locals, particularly for the happening bar scene. With many *Wine Spectator* awards to its credit, 21 Federal features about 11 carefully selected wines available by the glass each night. Chef Russell Jaehnig seems to get better and more refined every year. Don't fill up on the cheddar-cheese bread sticks: There's a lot of good food to come. For melt-in-your-mouth pleasure, start with the tuna tartare with wasabi crackers and cilantro aioli. The fish entrees are most popular here, although you might opt for the fine breast of duck accompanied by pecan wild rice and shiitake mushrooms. We love the pan-crisped salmon with champagne cabbage and beet-butter sauce, which has been a staple on the menu for years. Desserts are tantalizing.

21 Federal St. (in the center of town). ✆ **508/228-2121.** Reservations recommended. Main courses $24–$34. MC, V. June–Oct daily 6–10pm; call for off-season hours. Closed Jan–Mar.

MODERATE

Arno's ✸ ECLECTIC   A storefront facing the passing parade of Main Street, this institution packs surprising style between its bare-brick walls. The internationally influenced menu yields tasty, bountiful platters. Specialties include grilled sirloin steaks and fresh grilled fish. Generous servings of specialty pasta dishes like shrimp and scallop scampi Florentine are featured nightly.

41 Main St. ✆ 508/228-7001. Reservations recommended. Main courses $16–$23. AE, DC, DISC, MC, V. Apr–Dec daily 8am–9pm. Closed Jan–Mar.

Black Eyed Susan's ★★ ETHNIC ECLECTIC   This is supremely exciting food in a funky bistro atmosphere. It's small, popular with locals, and packed. Reservations are accepted for the 6pm seating only, and these go fast. Others must line up outside the restaurant (the line starts forming around 5:30pm), and the hostess will assign you a time to dine. Inside, it may seem a bit too cozy, but that's all part of the charm. The menu is in constant flux, as chef Jeff Worster's mood and influences change biweekly. We always enjoy the spicy Thai fish cake and the tandoori chicken with green mango chutney. There's usually a South-western touch like the Dos Equis beer-battered catfish quesadilla with mango slaw and jalapeño; mop up the sauce with the delectable organic sourdough bread. There's no liquor license, but you can BYOB.

10 India St. (in the center of town). ✆ 508/325-0308. Reservations accepted for 6pm seating only. Main courses $17–$23. No credit cards. Apr–Oct daily 7am–1pm; Mon–Sat 6–10pm; call for off-season hours. Closed Nov–Mar.

Le Languedoc Cafe ★★ NEW AMERICAN   There's also an expensive din-ing room upstairs, but locals prefer the casual bistro atmosphere downstairs and out on the terrace. There's a clubby feel here as diners come and go, greeting each other and enjoying themselves. Soups are superb, as are Angus-steak burgers. More elaborate dishes include the roasted tenderloin of pork stuffed with figs and pancetta, berlotti bean stew, and the napoleon of grilled tuna, tape-nade, and roasted vegetables with pesto sauce.

24 Broad St. ✆ 508/228-2552. Reservations not accepted for cafe; recommended for main dining room. Main courses $9–$19. AE, MC, V. June–Sept Tues–Sun noon–2pm; daily 6–10pm; call for off-season hours. Closed Jan to late May.

INEXPENSIVE

Espresso Cafe INTERNATIONAL   This reliable self-service cafe is in the heart of town. Pastries, sandwiches, soups, and international dishes are afford-ably priced, delicious, and made on site. The cafe has some of the best coffee in Nantucket village. In good weather, enjoy a leisurely snack on the sunny patio out back.

40 Main St. ✆ 508/228-6930. Most items under $10. No credit cards. Late May to Oct daily 7:30am–10pm; Nov to late May daily 7:30am–4:30pm.

Fog Island Cafe ★ NEW AMERICAN   You'll be wowed by the creative breakfasts and lunches at this sassy cafe; they're reasonably priced and made with super-fresh ingredients. Homemade soups and salads are healthy and yummy. The dinner menu features fresh seafood, pasta dishes, and vegetarian alternatives.

7 S. Water St. ✆ 508/228-1818. Main courses $10–$20. MC, V. July–Aug Mon–Sat 7am–2pm and 5–10pm; Sun 7am–1pm and 5–10pm; call for off-season hours. Open year-round.

TAKE-OUT & PICNIC FARE

Something Natural, 50 Cliff Rd. (✆ **508/228-0504**), a terrific value on pricey Nantucket, turns out gigantic sandwiches. Save room for the addictive chocolate-chip cookies. Stock up for a day at the beach, or eat your lunch right at the picnic tables on the grounds.

You can get fresh-picked produce right in town from **Bartlett's Ocean View Farm,** 33 Bartlett Farm Rd. (© **508/228-9403**). The truck's parked on Main Street in season.

Juice Guys, 4 Easy St. (© **508/228-4464**), is the spot to get your Nantucket Nectars fix. High-tech blenders mix potent combinations of fresh juice with vitamins, sorbet, yogurt, nuts, fruit, and holistic enhancers. Closed late December to April.

The **Juice Bar,** 12 Broad St. (© **508/228-5799**), is a humble hole-in-the-wall that scoops up some of the best homemade ice cream and frozen yogurt around, complemented by superb homemade hot fudge. Closed late December to March.

NANTUCKET AFTER DARK

Acoustic performers from all over the country hold forth in the **Brotherhood of Thieves,** 23 Broad St., in the center of Nantucket Town (no phone), an atmospheric pub where you'll find live folk music just about every night in season; no cover. It's closed in February. The **Chicken Box,** 12 Dave St. (© **508/228-9717**), is the rocking spot for the 20-something crowd. Depending on the band or theme, it sometimes seems like the entire population of the island is shoving their way in here. Jimmy Buffett shows up late at night about once a summer, unannounced, and jams with the band. The cover varies. The **Rose & Crown,** 23 S. Water St. (© **508/228-2595**), features live, loud music for dancing, and all ages show up for the fun. Closed January through March. The **Hearth Pub and Patio,** at the Harbor House, 23 S. Water St. (© **508/228-1500**), is a handsome hall with elegant appointments. There's live music most nights in season from 5pm to midnight; no cover.

The **Nantucket Arts Alliance** (© **800/228-8118** or 508/228-8118) operates Box Office Nantucket, offering tickets for all sorts of cultural events around town. It operates out of the Macy Warehouse on Straight Wharf, in season daily from 10am to 4pm.

Theater buffs will want to spend an evening at the **Actors' Theatre of Nantucket,** Methodist Church, 2 Centre St. (© **508/228-6325**). Drawing on some considerable local talent of all ages, this shoe-box theater assays thought-provoking plays as readily as summery farces. The season runs from mid-May to mid-September; call for off-season hours. Tickets are $15. You can catch the children's productions ($10) from mid-July to mid-August.

8

Central & Western Massachusetts

by Herbert Bailey Livesey

While Boston and its maritime appendages of Cape Ann and Cape Cod face the sea and embrace it, inland Massachusetts turns in upon itself. Countless ponds and lakes shimmer in its folds and hollows, often hidden by deep forests and granite outcroppings. Farming and industry grew along the north-south valleys of the Connecticut and Housatonic rivers.

The heartland Pioneer Valley, bordering the Connecticut River, earned its name in the early 18th century, when European trappers and farmers first began to push west from the colonies clinging to the edges of Massachusetts Bay. They were followed by ambitious capitalists who erected red-brick mills along the river for the manufacture of textiles and paper. Most of those enterprises failed or faded in the post–World War II movement to the milder climate and cheaper labor of the South, leaving a miasma of economic hardship that has yet to be remedied. But those

industrialists also helped fund several distinguished colleges for which the valley is now known; their educated populations provide much energy and a rich cultural life.

Roughly the same pattern applied in the Berkshires, the twin ranges of rumpled hills that define the western band of the state. There is only one college of note here, however, and the development of this region in the 19th century was prompted mainly by the construction of the railroad from New York and Boston. Artistic and literary folk made a favored summer retreat of it, followed by wealthy urbanites attracted by the region's reputation for creativity and bohemianism. Many of their extravagant mansions, dubbed "Berkshire Cottages," still survive, and to this day the region attracts the Town-and-Country crowd, who support a vibrant summer schedule of the arts, then steal away as the crimson leaves fall and the Berkshires grow quiet beneath six months of snow.

1 Sturbridge & Old Sturbridge Village

18 miles SW of Worcester, 32 miles E of Springfield

First things first: Sturbridge and Old Sturbridge Village aren't a single entity. The former is an organic community, populated by working people with real lives. But why are there so many motels and restaurants in a town of fewer than 8,000 residents? That's because of the latter, a fabricated early-19th-century village comprised of authentic buildings moved here from other locations and peopled by docents pretending to follow the pursuits of 170 years past. It is deservedly popular, one of the two most prominent tourist destinations in central Massachusetts.

ESSENTIALS
GETTING THERE   Take the east-west Massachusetts Turnpike (I-90) to Exit 9, or take I-84 to Exit 3B.

VISITOR INFORMATION   The **Sturbridge Area Visitors Center,** 380 Main St. (© **508/347-2761**), is open Monday through Friday during regular business hours.

SPECIAL EVENTS   Highly popular annual occasions are the **Brimfield Antique and Collectible Shows** ⚘, when over 6,000 dealers gather along a mile-long strip for up to 6 days (Tuesday through Sunday) in mid-May, mid-July, and early September. Call © **800/628-8379** or 508/347-2761, or go to www.brimfieldshow.com for details. Brimfield is an otherwise sleepy village adjoining Sturbridge on the west. Since it has so few hotels, most of the dealers and seekers stay in Sturbridge, so you'll need to reserve your room at least 6 months in advance during show periods.

   Thanksgiving and Christmas weeks at Old Sturbridge Village bring traditional New England dinners, concerts, and candlelit nights. Call © **800/733-1830** or 508/347-3362 for details.

EXPLORING A 19TH-CENTURY VILLAGE
There is only one sight of significance in this otherwise pleasantly unremarkable town. Expect crowds on long holiday weekends in summer and during the October foliage season.

Old Sturbridge Village ⚘⚘⚘   Only one of the more than 40 restored structures in the complex stands on its original site—the Oliver Wight House, now part of the Old Sturbridge Village Lodges (see below), beside the entrance road. The rest were transported here from as far away as Maine, starting 50 years ago. All are authentic buildings, not re-creations, and they represent the living quarters and places of trade and commerce of a settlement of the 1830s. Among these are a Quaker meetinghouse, a sawmill, a bank, shops, a pottery, a blacksmith shop, a school, a cider mill, a cooperage, and a printing office. At the edges of the village are a working farm and an extensive herb garden.

   Costumed docents perform carefully researched demonstrations of blacksmithing, hearth cooking, sheep shearing, maple sugaring, musketry, printing, basket weaving, carpentry, and more. Visitors are welcome to question them as they go about their tasks. "Residents" include children who roll hoops and play games true to the period. These change with the seasons, and special events and activities mark such dates as Washington's Birthday, Mother's Day, Thanksgiving, Christmas, and the Fourth of July. Town meetings, weddings, militia drills, and a harvest fair are staged. The boat ride on the adjacent Quinebaug River is only 20 minutes long, but is especially popular with younger visitors.

1 Old Sturbridge Rd. © **800/733-1830** or 508/347-3362. Fax 508/347-0375. www.osv.org. Admission (2-day pass) $20 adults, $18 seniors, $10 children 6–15, free for children under 6. Apr–Oct daily 9am–5pm; Nov–Dec and Mar daily 10am–4pm; schedule varies Jan–Feb, call ahead. Closed Dec 25. Take Exit 3B off I-84 or Exit 9 off I-90, drive west on Rte. 20, and bear right into the turnaround just before the entrance to the village.

WHERE TO STAY
When the choices below are full, try the **EconoLodge,** 262 Main St. (© **508/347-2324**), the **Colonial Quality Inn,** on Route 20 (© **508/347-3306**), or the **Sturbridge Coach Motor Lodge,** 408 Main St. (© **508/347-7327**). The first

Central & Western Massachusetts

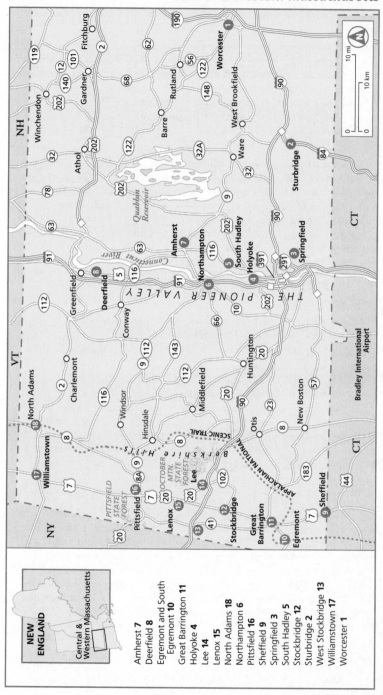

two are located near Exit 9 off I-84, the third near the entrance to Old Sturbridge Village.

Old Sturbridge Village Lodges ⭐ Apart from the centerpiece Oliver Wight House, which is more than 200 years old, these six barnlike structures arranged around a common green and pool are of post–World War II origin. Rooms are fresh, spacious, and straightforward, outfitted with colonial reproductions. Free morning coffee is available in the office.

Rte. 20 E., Sturbridge, MA 01566. ✆ **508/347-3327.** Fax 508/347-3018. www.osv.org. 59 units. May–Oct $85–$130 double; Nov–Apr $80–$95 double. Extra person $5. AE, DISC, MC, V. **Amenities:** Heated outdoor pool. *In room:* A/C, TV.

Publick House ⭐⭐ This four-building complex is the high-profile lodging in the Sturbridge area. The main structure is a tavern built in 1771. Rooms are rustic, some with canopied beds, rag rugs, and farmhouse colonial reproductions. A 1786 Federal-style farmhouse called the Colonel Ebenezer Crafts Inn, a mile from the hotel, has its own pool.

Rte. 131 (P.O. Box 187), Sturbridge, MA 01566. ✆ **800/782-5425** or 508/347-3313. Fax 508/347-5073. www.publickhouse.com. 126 units. $75–$160 double. AE, DC, DISC, MC, V. From Exit 3B off I-84, drive 1½ miles south of Rte. 20 on Rte. 131. Pets accepted in some rooms of Country Motor Lodge ($5 per night). **Amenities:** 3 restaurants (American), 2 bars; 3 heated outdoor pools; tennis courts; dry cleaning. *In room:* A/C, TV, hair dryer.

WHERE TO DINE

In addition to the establishments listed below, you might sample any of the three restaurants associated with the **Publick House** (see above).

Rom's ⭐ ITALIAN/AMERICAN This was once a hot-dog and fried-clam roadside stand that has grown over nearly 50 years like a multigenerational New England farmhouse. Today, it can seat 750 diners on two levels and remains a near-ideal family restaurant, with something to please everyone, from home-made pastas and pizzas to full seafood dinners. The lobster roll is twice the size but about the same price as those offered on the coast. All-you-can-eat buffets at Wednesday dinner and Thursday lunch are crowd pleasers, for quality is high and portions are generous. A takeout window ladles "buckets of rigatoni," fish-and-chips, and shrimp in a basket.

Rte. 131 (2 miles S. of Rte. 20). ✆ **800/ROM-1952** or 508/347-3349. Main courses $8.50–$16.50. AE, DISC, DC, MC, V. Daily 11:30am–9pm.

The Whistling Swan/Ugly Duckling ⭐ CONTINENTAL/AMERICAN This 1855 Greek Revival mansion houses two restaurants that share a kitchen. On the main floor is the Whistling Swan, with widely spaced tables, wall sconces, and Sheraton-style chairs. The menu lists dishes like frogs' legs Provençale, sole with orange-lime sauce, even surf-and-turf. The execution is safe and careful, and the service efficient if often unsophisticated. Upstairs, the Ugly Duckling packs tables together under the rough-cut board roof. Patrons strive to be heard over the live piano—it's loud, even boisterous. The food is simple and hearty. Which venue to choose? We'd mount the stairs, in a New York minute.

502 Main St. (Rte. 20). ✆ **508/347-2321.** Reservations suggested on weekends. Main courses $12.95–$24.95. AE, DC, MC, V. Whistling Swan Mon–Fri 11:30am–2:30pm and 5:30–9:30pm; Sat 11:30am–2:30pm and 5:30–10pm; Sun noon–8pm. Ugly Duckling Tues–Thurs 11:30am–11pm; Fri–Sat 11:30am–11:30pm.

2 Springfield

89 miles W of Boston, 32 miles N of Hartford

Times have been tough in this once-prosperous manufacturing city on the east bank of the Connecticut River. But its loyal citizens haven't given in to the consequences of job flight and high unemployment, and there is evidence of redevelopment throughout downtown, with recycled loft and factory buildings standing beside modern glass towers. Springfield remains the most important city in western Massachusetts and has enjoyed some success in attracting new enterprises, notably in plastics, toolmaking, and electronic equipment. Vacationers can pass a few hours in its small museums and the Old Storrowtown Village of restored 18th-century buildings, but Springfield is primarily a stop on the way north or south.

ESSENTIALS

GETTING THERE Springfield is located near the juncture of the east-west Massachusetts Turnpike (I-90), a toll highway, and north-south I-91, and is readily accessible from every city in the Northeast.

Bradley International (© 203/627-3000), in Windsor Locks, Conn., is the nearest major airport, about 20 miles to the south. Rent a car here from any of the major companies or catch a bus, cab, or limo into Springfield. Major airlines serving Bradley include **American** (© 800/433-7300), **Continental** (© 800/ 525-0280), **Delta** (© 800/221-1212), **Northwest** (© 800/225-2525), **United** (© 800/241-6522), and **US Airways** (© 800/247-8786).

Amtrak (©800/USA-RAIL; www.northeast.amtrak.com) trains stop daily both ways in Springfield on routes between Boston and Chicago; Boston and Washington, D.C.; and New York and St. Albans, Vt. (where there are connecting buses from Montréal), with intermediate stops in Philadelphia, New York, and Hartford, among others.

VISITOR INFORMATION The **Greater Springfield Convention and Visitors Bureau** (© 413/787-1548) is at 1500 Main St.

SPECIAL EVENTS The **Eastern States Exposition** is a huge old-fashioned agricultural fair with games, rides, a midway, and entertainment. It's held on a fairground on the opposite side of the Connecticut River in West Springfield in mid-September. Call © 413/737-2443 for details. Also on the grounds is the **Old Storrowtown Village,** a collection of restored colonial buildings, accessible by guided tour Monday through Saturday from June to Labor Day, and by appointment the rest of the year.

MUSEUMS & HISTORIC SITES

Basketball Hall of Fame ★★ Dr. James Naismith invented basketball in Springfield in 1891, providing the logic for this memorial and entertainment center. A must for fans, it is painless even for those who regard the game as a blur of 7-foot armpits. Take the elevator to the third floor and work your way down. Up here are the inductees (227 to date) and displays recalling the history of the game. Remember the Waterloo Hawks? The Indianapolis Kautskys? Or the Philadelphia Hebrews? The Hall covers every aspect of the game, from high school to the NBA to the Olympics, as well as such offshoots as wheelchair leagues and the Harlem Globetrotters. On the ground floor is a shooting court with 15 baskets at various heights, and next to it a virtual-reality display, in which visitors can insert themselves on a large viewing screen and play against the pros.

W. Columbus Ave. (at Union St.). ℂ **413/781-6500.** Fax 413/781-1939. Admission $10 adults, $6 seniors and children 7–15, free for children under 7. Daily 9:30am–5:30pm. Closed Thanksgiving, Christmas, New Year's Day.

Springfield Museums at the Quadrangle ⭐ *Kids*   Four museums and a library surrounding a single inner quadrangle constitute this worthwhile resource, much of it built by the generosity of industrialists who flourished in Springfield during the 19th and early 20th centuries. Begin a tour by entering the library from State Street and walking through to the back. On the right is the first museum; the others around the quad make a counterclockwise circuit. Before setting out, note the limited hours below.

The **George Walter Vincent Smith Art Museum's** eponymous donor, a wealthy carriage manufacturer, installed his eclectic collection in this 1896 Italian Renaissance–style mansion. Upstairs is a gallery of largely sentimental pastoral scenes, with a few small landscapes by George Inness, Thomas Cole, and Albert Bierstadt. On the main floor are cases of Japanese samurai weaponry surrounding a heavily carved 1805 Shinto shrine.

Likely to be the biggest winner with children, the **Science Museum** contains a planetarium (showtime at 2:45pm), dioramas of large African animals, and the Monsanto Eco-Center. This new section strives for cohesion with some interactive devices, aquariums with native and tropical fish, a boa and poisonous frogs, and scattered other exhibits.

Enter the **Connecticut Valley Historical Museum** through a gateway that is a representation of the headgear worn by Dr. Seuss's famous Cat in the Hat. (The children's author grew up in Springfield.) There are examples of weapons made by the city's firearms manufacturers, including a blunderbuss and an unusual 1838 rifle with a revolving cartridge chamber.

The strongest and most professionally organized repository of the lot is the **Museum of Fine Arts** ⭐, which has 20 galleries with canvases by European and American artists, including examples of colonial paintings through Gilbert Stuart and John Copley to early-20th-century realists George Bellows and Reginald Marsh, culminating with both magic realists and Abstract Expressionists of recent decades—Frank Stella, Helen Frankenthaler, Don Eddy, and George Sugarman. Make a particular effort to view the remarkable serigraph of lower Manhattan by Richard Estes.

220 State St. (at Chestnut St.). ℂ **413/263-6800.** www.quadrangle.com. Combined admission for all four museums $4 adults, $1 children 6–18, free for children under 6; $1 extra for the planetarium. Wed–Sun noon–4pm.

WHERE TO STAY

Marriott Springfield ⭐⭐   Directly across the street from the Sheraton (see below), this representative of the widespread chain shares, even duplicates, most of its rival's attributes. Free coffee is available in the lobby, and there's food service at poolside. In-room fridges are available.

1500 Main St., Springfield, MA 01105. ℂ **800/228-9290** or 413/781-7111. Fax 413/731-8932. 264 units. $139–$149 double. AE, DC, DISC, MC, V. **Amenities:** Restaurant (continental), two bars; heated indoor pool; exercise room; whirlpool; sauna; limited room service; same-day dry cleaning. *In room:* A/C, TV w/ pay movies, dataport, coffeemaker, hair dryer.

Sheraton Springfield Monarch ⭐⭐   Easy to find, just off the Springfield Center exit of I-91, this can be a treat after a few nights in idiosyncratic New

And to Think That I Saw It on Mulberry Street

Interest in the man who called himself Dr. Seuss spiked with the opening last year of a new Broadway show, *Seussical,* and the hit movie *The Grinch.* The grandparents of Theodor Seuss Geisel lived on Springfield's Mulberry Street, and in 1937, the writer and illustrator named the first of his dozens of children's books for the neighborhood. He followed up with such classics as *The Cat in the Hat* and *How the Grinch Stole Christmas.* Over 100 million copies of his books have been sold, and every title is still in print.

Geisel spent most of his adult life in California, the result of a nearly two-decade career in documentary films, during which he won two Academy Awards. But much of his inspiration for the children's books to which he returned can be traced to Springfield. His drawing of Bartholomew Cubbins's castle bears a strong resemblance to the Howard Street Armory, now a community center, and certain of his landscapes look as if they were recalled from his playtimes in Forest Park, near his boyhood home at 74 Fairfield St.

Alas, Mulberry Street is no longer the august avenue it once must have been, its Victorian manses now crowded by undistinguished apartment blocks and commercial strips—and the former Central High School from which Geisel graduated is now a condonimium.

England bed-and-breakfasts. Predictable, yes, but curl up in a room with all these conveniences, and lack of charm can suddenly seem unimportant—especially when it's combined with room service, a friendly bar, and a capable restaurant. Due to quirks in seasonal pricing, executive-level rooms are sometimes cheaper than standard units, so be sure to inquire.

1 Springfield Center, Springfield, MA 01114. © **800/426-9004** or 413/781-1010. Fax 413/734-3249. 310 units. $139–$169 double. AE, DC, DISC, MC, V. **Amenities:** Restaurant (continental); bar; heated indoor pool; exercise room; whirlpool; sauna; business center; shopping arcade; limited room service; same-day dry cleaning; executive-level rooms. *In room:* A/C, TV w/ pay movies, dataport, coffeemaker, hair dryer, iron.

WHERE TO DINE

Pioneer Valley Brew Pub ✪ ECLECTIC AMERICAN   This "Deco diner" is a welcome exception to the largely forlorn dining scene. The main room is spacious, and a second one in the back adjoins a terrace. The ales and lagers on tap (try Armory Amber) will wash down such tasty dishes as grilled pork loin with apple-raisin chutney or sautéed duck breast with wild-rice pancakes and warm fruit compote. Main courses come with bread, vegetable, and a salad that has stayed too long in the fridge. Subtlety isn't a strong suit, not with flavors and portions this big.

5159 Taylor St. (near Dwight St.). © **413/732-2739.** Main courses $11.95–$17.95. AE, DISC, MC, V. Tues–Fri 11:30am–9pm; Sat 5–10pm.

Student Prince and The Fort ✪ GERMAN/AMERICAN   In 1935, German immigrants opened the Student Prince and began serving beer in steins along with schnitzels, sauerbraten, and hasenpfeffer. That might not have seemed the precise historical moment to ensure the success of such an enterprise, but it thrived. In 1946, they added a dining room next door, which they chose to call the Fort. The result is the most popular place in town. Monster portions are the rule, with veal shanks as thick as a linebacker's forearm and plates heaped high with sausages, boiled potatoes, and sauerkraut. On draft are seven German brews.

8 Fort St. (west of Main St.). ✆ **413/734-7475.** Main courses $9.75–$23.75. AE, DC, DISC, MC, V. Daily noon–10pm.

SPRINGFIELD AFTER DARK

Springfield Symphony Hall, at Court Street and East Columbus Avenue (✆ **413/787-6600;** tickets@citystage.symphonyhall.com), is the principal facility for one-night stands of touring performers and musicals, as well as productions meant for children. Think *Fiddler on the Roof* and *Cinderella.*

A strip of beer-and-pool joints, music bars, and hip eateries has developed along downtown Worthington Street. Check out the food and weekend live jazz at **Caffeine's,** 54 Worthington St. (✆ **413/788-6646**), or puff an hour away in its adjacent cigar lounge, **Nicotine's** (✆ **413/781-0386**). On weekends, the **Fat Cat Bar & Grill** (✆ **413/734-0554**) presents live ska, rock, funk, and whatever; all ages are welcome Sundays at 7pm.

3 The Pioneer Valley

Low hills and quilted fields channel the Connecticut River as it runs south toward Long Island Sound, forming the Pioneer Valley. The earliest European settlers came here for what proved to be uncommonly fertile soil and were followed in the 19th century by men who harnessed the power of the river and became wealthy textile and paper manufacturers.

These industrialists took the lead in funding the institutions of higher learning that are now the pride of the region. Prestigious Smith, Mount Holyoke, and Amherst are here, as are innovative Hampshire College and the sprawling main campus of the University of Massachusetts, with its enrollment of more than 25,000 students. All five contribute mightily to the cultural life of the valley, and the towns of **Northampton, Amherst,** and **South Hadley** are invigorated by the vitality of thousands of college-age young people.

In the north, near Vermont, the living village of **Deerfield** preserves the architecture and atmosphere of colonial New England, but without the whiff of sterility that often afflicts artificial gatherings of old buildings with costumed docents.

Interstate 91 and Route 5 both traverse the valley from south to north. The trip from edge to edge on the interstate takes less than an hour, while Route 5 tenders more of the flavor of pastoral vistas and colorful mill towns.

There are ample numbers of motels along the way, but if you're looking for lodgings more representative of the character of the region, contact the **Folkstone Bed & Breakfast Reservation Service** (✆ **800/762-2751** or 508/480-0380).

ESSENTIALS

GETTING THERE   From Boston and upstate New York, take the Massachusetts Turnpike (I-90), a toll highway, to Springfield, then follow I-91 or Route 5 north. While there are local buses, you'll want a car.

The nearest major airport is **Bradley International** (✆ **203/627-3000**), just south of Springfield, in Windsor Locks, Conn. (See the Springfield section, above, for a list of airlines that serve Bradley.) **Valley Transporter** (✆ **800/ 872-8752** or 413/549-1350) offers van shuttles between the airport and Amherst, Northampton, Hadley, Holyoke, and Deerfield.

Amtrak (© 800/USA-RAIL; www.northeast.amtrak.com) *Vermonter* trains stop in Amherst and Northampton on the route between St. Albans, Vt., and Washington, D.C.

VISITOR INFORMATION The **Pioneer Valley Tourist Information Center** (© 413/665-7333) is at the intersection of Routes 5 and 10 in South Deerfield, at Exit 24 of I-91.

HOLYOKE

Once an important paper-manufacturing center, Holyoke (8 miles north of Springfield, 88 miles west of Boston) has suffered a long economic slide since World War II. Abandoned factories and the dissolute air of the commercial center don't bolster first impressions. Still, there are a couple of modestly worthwhile sights.

Canals dug during the city's heyday as a paper-manufacturing center still cut through the downtown area (they were intended to allow access to the mills). Long and narrow **Heritage State Park,** with its entrance at 221 Appleton St. (© 413/534-1723), runs beside one of the canals, and has an interpretive center that offers walking tours and exhibits revisiting the industrial glory days. On most Sundays from mid-June to late August, the ancient locomotive of the **Heritage Park Railroad** pulls train buffs on a 2-hour trip downriver from the park to Holyoke Mall at Ingleside. Times and fares vary. Call Heritage State Park for more information.

WHERE TO STAY & DINE

Yankee Pedlar Inn ✻ If you're looking for a sedate, tranquil country inn, this isn't it. Business is thriving, and it bustles with weddings, tour groups, and corporate get-togethers. The dining room is highly popular with locals as well as travelers. Near-constant redecorating covers the inevitable signs of wear. Of the five buildings in the largely Victorian complex, the 1850 House has the most modern rooms, while the Carriage House has the least expensive. Some units have canopied beds and/or kitchenettes. Live musical entertainment is presented on weekends.

1866 Northampton St. (Rte. 5), Holyoke, MA 01040. © 413/532-9494. Fax 413/536-8877. www.yankeepedlar.com. 30 units. $79–$109 double; $115–$139 suite. Rates include breakfast. AE, DC, MC, V. Take Exit 16 off I-91 and head east 5 blocks. **Amenities:** Restaurant (American); bar; access to nearby health club. *In room:* TV/VCR, video rentals.

SOUTH HADLEY

Pioneer educator Mary Lyon founded Mount Holyoke Female Seminary, one of the Seven Sisters group, here in 1836. Strung along the eastern side of Route 116 (College Street), the college is the essential reason for the existence of this small town (pop. 13,600), although it was settled in the late 17th century. It lies 15 miles north of Springfield and 7 miles south of Amherst.

On the campus is a worthy **Art Museum** ✻ (© 413/538-2245), which focuses on art of the Orient, Egypt, and the Mediterranean, but also mounts temporary exhibits on a considerable range of topics. Hours are Tuesday through Friday from 11am to 5pm, Saturday and Sunday from 1 to 5pm. Admission is free. It's closed during school holidays, but not in summer. To find it, take Park Street from the east side of the Y intersection in the center of town and follow the signs.

Joseph Skinner State Park (© 413/586-0350) straddles the border between South Hadley and Hadley. On its 390 acres are miles of walking trails, picnic grounds, and the historic Summit House with panoramic views of the valley. The building (open Saturdays and Sundays May through October) was erected in a single day in 1821 by a group of energetic male friends who wanted a place to party.

NORTHAMPTON ★★

Smith College, with its campus sprawling along Main Street slightly west of the commercial center, is Northampton's dominating physical and spiritual presence. One of the original Seven Sisters, Smith is the largest female liberal-arts college in the United States.

Northampton was long the home of Calvin Coolidge, who pursued his law practice here before and after his monosyllabic occupancy of the Oval Office. A room maintained by the **Forbes Library,** 20 West St. (𝒞 **413/584-6037**) contains many of his papers. Coolidge lived in houses at 21 Massasoit St. and on Hampton Terrace, but the homes are not open to the public.

Much else is open and available to visitors, however, and Northampton supplies many of the diversions of a thriving New England college town. Cultural events range from chamber music and dance recitals to theatrical productions and art exhibitions, the number and diversity of restaurants and bars are far greater than most cities its size can flaunt, and its many stores and galleries are as unusual and kicky as any devout shopper might ask. Try to allow at least a long day and overnight in the area.

A well-received book by Tracy Kidder, *Home Town* (Random House; 1999), profiles Northampton and a number of its townspeople.

SEEING THE SIGHTS

Note: The Words & Pictures Museum has closed permanently. The **Smith College Museum of Art,** with its permanent collection of paintings by Degas, Monet, Seurat, Picasso, and Winslow Homer, closed in the spring of 2000 for major renovations and isn't expected to reopen before the fall of 2002. Call 𝒞 **413/585-2760** for updates.

Historic Northampton ★   Among Northampton's most popular attractions are the Museum Houses, three historic homes still standing on their original sites (although lately looking in need of maintenance). They are the 1730 Parsons House, the 1796 Shepherd House, and the 1812 Isaac Damon House, which contains a furnished parlor true to 1820.

46 Bridge St. (east of the railroad bridge). 𝒞 **413/584-6011**. www.historic-northampton.org. Exhibit Center Tues–Fri 10am–4pm; Sat–Sun noon–4pm. Donations welcome. House tours $3 adults, $2 seniors and students, $1 children 12 and under. Tours given Sat–Sun noon–4pm.

Smith College ★   To a considerable extent, the campus buildings that line Elm Street are a testament to the excesses of late-19th-century architecture. Their often egregious admixtures of Gothic, Greco-Roman, Renaissance, and medieval esthetic notions lend a Teutonic sobriety to the west end of town. On the other hand, Frederick Law Olmsted, famed for his design of New York's Central Park, laid out much of the original landscaping, and the campus contains many wooded walks and gardens.

Elm St. 𝒞 **413/584-2700**.

OUTDOOR PURSUITS

Three miles southwest of town on Route 10 in Easthampton is **Arcadia Nature Center and Wildlife Sanctuary** (𝒞 **413/584-3009**), a 700-acre preserve operated by the Massachusetts Audubon Society. It contains a mixed ecology of marshes and woods bordering the Connecticut River, with 5 miles of trails. The sanctuary is open Tuesday through Sunday from dawn to dusk. Admission is $3 for adults, $2 for seniors and children 3 to 15.

The 8½-mile **Norwottuck Trail Bike Path** follows a former railroad bed running between Northampton and Amherst. Access is via Damon Road and at Mount Farms Mall. Bikes can be rented at **Valley Bicycles,** 319 Main St. (© **413/256-0880**), across the river in Amherst.

Look Memorial Park, 300 N. Main St. (© **413/584-5457**), is northwest of town off Route 9, with 157 acres of woods, a 5-acre lake, picnic grounds, and a small zoo of native animals. Boats are available for rent. Musical and theatrical events, including puppet shows, are held in summer.

SHOPPING

For browsing bibliophiles, one of the pleasures of college towns is the larger than usual number of bookstores, often dealing in exotica not found in the big chains. In a town with a bookstore at every other corner, **Raven Used Books,** 4 Old South St. (© **413/584-9868**), shines. Along with the usual categories, it has shelves devoted to shamanism, prophecy, and erotica. The store is carved out of a basement a few steps down the hill from Main Street.

In addition to the abundance of bookstores, Northampton enjoys the most diverse shopping in the valley. The **Antiques Center of Northampton,** 9½ Market St. (© **413/584-3600**), contains the stalls of more than 60 independent dealers on three floors; closed Wednesdays. **Ten Thousand Villages,** 82 Main St. (© **413/582-9338**), is part of a widespread nonprofit Mennonite program selling handicrafts from more than 30 Third World countries. In stock are baskets from the Philippines, textiles from Bangladesh, and pottery, toys, instruments, and jewelry from five continents.

A former department store has been reconfigured into **Thorne's Marketplace,** 150 Main St. (© **413/584-5582**), now containing more than 30 specialty boutiques offering furniture, clothing, folk art, kitchenware, toys, candy, jewelry, CDs, books, and a box office for theatrical and music events. Next to the side entrance of the marketplace is **Herrell's,** 7 Old South St. (© **413/ 586-9700**), home base of a minichain of New England ice-cream emporia. It tempts with over 100 flavors, all made on the premises.

Northampton has a reputation as a small town with an unusually vigorous arts community. Burnishing that image is the prestigious **R. Michelson Gallery,** 132 Main St. (© **413/586-3964**), which occupies a grandly proportioned former bank. The gallery is the sole representative of the prolific sculptor and graphic artist Leonard Baskin, who lived in the area until his death in 2000.

WHERE TO STAY

This is a college town, with frequent influxes of parents and alumnae during graduation, homecoming, and other events, so anticipate higher rates and limited vacancies at those times, in addition to the usual holiday weekends.

Autumn Inn   A genteel motel with a vaguely Georgian style, the Autumn is conveniently situated opposite the quieter northern end of the Smith campus. The restaurant has a huge wood-burning fireplace.

259 Elm St., Northampton, MA 01060. © **413/584-7660.** Fax 413/586-4808. 30 units. Apr–Nov $88–$112 double, $150 suite; Dec–Mar $78–$88 double, $120 suite. AE, DC, MC, V. **Amenities:** Restaurant (American; breakfast and lunch only); unheated outdoor pool (summer only). *In room:* A/C, TV, dataport.

Hotel Northampton ⭐   Built in 1927, this brick building at the center of town looks older. Recent restoration has brought it up to date, with rooms of varying sizes containing lots of wicker and colonial reproductions, feather duvets, and assorted Victoriana. Many front rooms have balconies overlooking King Street; some have canopied beds, coffeemakers, and fridges; and a few have Jacuzzis. Downstairs, Wiggins Tavern is an authentic colonial watering hole with dark beams and stone fireplaces.

36 King St., Northampton, MA 01060. ℂ 800/547-3529 or 413/584-3100. Fax 413/584-9455. www.hotel northampton.com. 99 units. $105–$235 double. Rates include continental breakfast. AE, DISC, MC, V. Free parking. **Amenities:** 2 restaurants (American), 2 bars; exercise room; business center; limited room service; laundry; dry cleaning. *In room:* A/C, TV, dataport.

Inn at Northampton ⭐   The entrance isn't clearly marked, and the inn is hidden behind a Mobil gas station. Renovations have elevated it from a standard motel to something closer to a modest resort and conference center.

Rte. 5 and I-91 (just west of Exit 18), Northampton, MA 01060. ℂ 800/582-2929 or 413/586-1211. Fax 413/586-0630. www.hampshirehospitality.com. innhoho@javanet.com. 122 units. $109–$139 double; $149 suite. Rates include continental breakfast Mon–Fri. AE, DC, DISC, MC, V. **Amenities:** Restaurant (steakhouse), bar; heated indoor pool; outdoor pool; lighted tennis court; whirlpool; business center; limited room service. *In room:* A/C, TV, dataport, coffeemaker, hair dryer.

WHERE TO DINE

Eastside Grill ⭐⭐ REGIONAL AMERICAN   The consensus choice for tops in town, this white clapboard building with a nautical look is a retreat for the 40-plus set from the prevailing collegiate tone of Northampton. The far-reaching menu has bayou riffs, such as duck étouffée and shrimp and andouille jambalaya, as well as a gumbo of the day. But while the Cajun/Creole dishes absorb much of the kitchen's attention, there are ample alternatives. Seafood is impressive, especially the pan-blackened scallops and caramelized tuna, and the "cowboy steak" has an herb-chipotle rub.

19 Strong Ave. (1 block south of Main St.). ℂ 413/586-3347. Reservations recommended. Main courses $9.95–$15.95. AE, DC, DISC, MC, V. Mon–Thurs 5–10pm; Fri 5–10:30pm; Sat 4–10:30pm; Sun 4–9pm.

Fitzwilly's ⭐ AMERICAN   Occupying a building constructed in 1898, this ingratiating pub makes the most of its high stamped-tin ceilings and ample space. Copper brewing kettles signal an intriguing selection of beers, some from regional microbreweries, including draft Smuttynose Lager and Berkshire Pale Ale. Beyond the two bars are curtained booths where patrons dive into grilled pizzas, ribs, pastas, and such pub faves as blooming onion, Buffalo shrimp, and fried calamari. Everything is available for take-out.

23 Main St. (near Pleasant St.). ℂ 413/584-8666. Reservations not accepted. Main courses $8.95–$14.95. AE, DC, DISC, MC, V. Daily 11:30am–1am.

Green Street Café ⭐⭐ NEW AMERICAN   Julia Child dined here, and the chef is a graduate of the French Culinary Institute. That accounts for the Gallic tilt of the menu and the excellent baguettes, baked right here, served with both butter and tapenade. Don't overdose on the bread, though, for there are any number of delectables emerging from the kitchen—salmon in parchment and chicken in sauternes with späetzle, for two. The restaurant grows its own vegetables in season, and the emphasis throughout the year is on fresh ingredients. All that, and a fireplace, too. *Note:* An odd state blue law restricts its sale of wine and beer to the months of April through January.

64 Green St. ℭ **413/586-5650.** Reservations recommended. Main courses $16–$26. MC, V. Mon–Fri noon–2pm and 5:30–10pm; Sat 5:30–10pm; Sun 10:30am–2:30pm and 5:30–10pm. Follow Main St. toward the Smith campus, straight into West St., turning right on Green St.

La Cazuela ✦✦ SOUTHWESTERN/MEXICAN   The menu at this restaurant mixes recipes of the American Southwest with those of Mexico, and while the kitchen takes its job seriously, strict authenticity isn't the point. In addition to the predictable enchiladas and chimichangas, dinner specials explore regional cuisines with such dishes as *pollo en adobo:* chicken chunks marinated in a chili and garlic paste charbroiled with peppers and onions. La Cazuela is in an 1850 building, with folkloric artifacts, cacti, and adobe-red walls that give the interior a Santa Fe look.

7 Old South St. (down the hill from Main St.). ℭ **413/586-0400.** Reservations recommended. Main courses $8.25–$13.95. AE, DISC, MC, V. Sun–Thurs 5–9pm; Fri–Sat 5–10pm.

Vermont Country Deli & Cafe ✦ ECLECTIC   Appetizing sights glimpsed through the window drag people inside. A long case is crowded with tantalizing salads and main courses, like Hunan orange chicken, sesame noodles, and spinach knishes. Fat focaccia sandwiches are made to order. On the opposite side of the room are plump sticky buns, lemon muffins, sourdough baguettes, and urns of various coffees.

48 Main St. (near Pleasant St.). ℭ **413/586-7114.** Main courses $5.50–$8.95. MC, V. Sun–Wed 7am–7pm; Thurs–Sat 7am–8pm.

NORTHAMPTON AFTER DARK

The presence of Smith and four other area colleges only partially accounts for the large number of bars and clubs in town, making Northampton the nightlife magnet of the valley. In April, the **Loud Music Festival** rattles walls with more than 250 alternative rock bands from around the country. For a rundown of what's happening, pick up a copy of *The Valley Advocate.*

Still thriving after 105 years, the **Academy of Music,** 74 Main St. (ℭ **413/ 584-8435**), shows big-screen films and provides a venue for opera, ballet, and pop performers on tour.

Another old favorite, the **Iron Horse Music Hall,** 20 Center St. (ℭ **413/ 586-8686**), has played host to an enormous variety of artists, from Bonnie Raitt to Dave Brubeck to grunge rockers. It's open nightly from 5:30pm to 1am, usually with 7 and 9pm shows. Covers vary, so call ahead.

Live bluegrass, jam rock, and soul-funk alternate with DJs at the **Pearl Street Nightclub,** 10 Pearl St. (ℭ **413/584-0610**). There are often dance nights targeted at teenagers as well as gay nights. Nearby is the funky bar of the **Bay State Hotel,** 41 Strong Ave. (ℭ **413/584-8513**). It's a refuge for smokers, with live rock Thursday through Saturday.

The **Calvin Theatre and Performing Arts Center,** 19 King St. (ℭ **401/ 586-0851**), offers touring performers and groups as diverse as Sonny Rollins, the Kronos String Quartet, flamenco troupes, and children's theater.

AMHERST

Yet another Pioneer Valley town defined by its educational institutions, this one has an even larger student population than most, with distinguished Amherst College occupying much of its center, the large University of Massachusetts campus to its immediate northwest, and Hampshire College off South Pleasant Street. All three—and Smith College and Mount Holyoke, on the other side of the Connecticut River—combine to provide a full September-to-June slate of artistic and musical events. UMass alone has six galleries, while Amherst has a pair of small museums.

On the edge of the town green is a seasonal **information booth.** Its hours vary, but if it's closed, visitors can call the **Chamber of Commerce** (�C **413/ 253-0700**) for information

HISTORIC HOMES & COLLEGES

Most of the historic homes are within a few blocks of the Amity/Main/Pleasant street crossing. **Amherst College** lies mostly along the east side of the town green. At the northeast corner is the **Town Hall,** another fortress-like Romanesque Revival creation of Boston's H. H. Richardson.

Amherst College   Named for Baron Jefferey Amherst, a British general during the last of the French and Indian Wars, the illustrious liberal-arts college maintains a cooperative relationship with Smith, Mount Holyoke, the University of Massachusetts, and the experimental Hampshire College. It was founded in 1821, with Noah Webster on its first board of trustees. Robert Frost was a member of the faculty for more than a decade.

Amherst's campus cuts through the heart of the town and contains two museums open to the public. The **Pratt Museum of Natural History** ✦ (℃ **413/542-2165**), at the southeast corner of the main quad, contains dinosaur tracks collected from sedimentary rocks of the valley, as well as fossils, a mastodon skeleton, and indigenous rocks and minerals. The **Mead Art Museum** ✦ (℃ **413/542-2335**), at Routes 116 and 9, displays varied collections of sculptures, paintings, photographs, and antiquities. Its strengths lie in the works of 19th- and 20th-century American artists and French Impressionists.

S. Pleasant and College sts. ℃ **413/542-2000.** www.amherst.edu. Free admission to both museums.

Dickinson Homestead ✦   Designated a National Historic Monument, this is the house where Emily Dickinson was born in 1830 and where she lived until her family moved in 1840. They returned in 1855, and the famous poet stayed here until her death 31 years later. The "Belle of Amherst" was the granddaughter and daughter of local movers and shakers, the source of her support while she produced the poetry that was to be increasingly celebrated even as she withdrew into near-total seclusion.

280 Main St. (2 blocks east of the Town Hall). ℃ **413/542-8161.** Admission $5 adults, $4 seniors and students, $3 children 6–11, free for children under 6 and students from the five area colleges. Guided tours only, Mar and Nov to]mid-Dec Wed and Sat 1–4pm on the hour; Apr–May and Sept–Oct Wed–Sat 1–4pm on the hour; June–Aug Wed–Sun 1–4pm on the half hour, Sat 10:30 and 11:30am. Reservations recommended.

University of Massachusetts   Though the university was founded in 1863, this sprawling 1,200-acre campus north of the town center dates mainly from the 1960s. Several of its buildings top out at over 20 stories. Its 25,000 students study for degrees in 90 academic fields. Art is given a high priority by the administration, with six galleries scattered around the campus. Foremost among these is the University Gallery in the **Fine Arts Center** ✦, beside the pond in the quadrangle. It focuses on works of 20th-century artists. The center also mounts productions in dance, music, and theater. Call the box office at ℃ **413/ 545-2511** for information on current and upcoming performances.

Rte. 116. ℃ **413/545-4237** for tour information. Campus tours available daily at 11am and 1:15pm, except Sat–Sun in June–July, Mar break, and most holidays.

OUTDOOR PURSUITS

An 8½-mile bicycle trail follows an old railroad bed from Warren Wright Road in Belchertown, passing through Amherst, and on to Elder Island in the Connecticut River adjacent to Northampton. Bikes can be rented at **Valley Bicycles,** 319 Main St., Amherst (✆ **800/831-5437** or 413/256-0880). It operates a seasonal shop, **Valley Bicycles Trailside,** 8 Railroad St. (✆**584-4466**), directly on the trail.

SHOPPING

Atticus/Albion Bookstore, 8 Main St. (✆ **413/256-1547**), has a rumpled aspect that is catnip for readers who like to poke among the piles of books and take a seat on the window sofa to skim their finds. The nearby **Jefferey Amherst Bookshop,** 55 S. Pleasant St. (✆ **413/253-3381**), is tidier, specializing in Emily Dickinson and academic texts.

WHERE TO STAY

Allen House Victorian Inn ✦

The colorful exterior paint job makes this Queen Anne–style Victorian, built in 1886, easy to spot. The interior is fitted out in the manner of the Aesthetic artistic movement, which lasted barely 10 years. In any event, the parlor and bedrooms are lovingly decorated, embellished with tracery and curlicues that are somehow Arabic in feel. The carriage house in back serves as bicycle storage for guests who want to take advantage of the nearby Norwottuck Trail.

599 Main St. (5 blocks east of the Town Hall), Amherst, MA 01002. ✆ 413/253-5000. www.allenhouse.com. 7 units. $75–$175 double. Rates include breakfast. AE, DISC, MC, V. No children under 10 accepted. *In room:* A/C, TV, dataport, hair dryer.

Lord Jeffery Inn ✦✦

It's a running battle to keep the principal lodging in a college town from looking a little battered. At the moment, the Lord Jeff is winning, thanks to almost constant renovation and redecorating. So despite the wear and tear of more than 70 years of graduations, homecomings, and conferences, the inn offers an environment that is as warm as its several fireplaces. The Sorbonne-trained chef has turned the Windowed Hearth into Amherst's event restaurant, open for dinner and Sunday brunch.

30 Boltwood Ave. (next to the Town Hall), Amherst, MA 01002. ✆ 800/742-0358 or 413/253-2576. Fax 413/256-6152. www.pinnacle-inns.com/lordjefferyinn. 48 units. $69–$128 double; $109–$173 suite. AE, MC, V. Pets accepted ($10). **Amenities:** 2 restaurants (eclectic); bar; limited room service. *In room:* A/C, TV, dataport.

WHERE TO DINE

Another option is the **Windowed Hearth,** at the Lord Jeffery Inn, above.

Judie's ✦✦ ECLECTIC AMERICAN

You don't want to leave Amherst without eating at Judie's. The vivacious owner does her best to suit every taste. Just to keep things ticking, for example, there's a "Munchie Madness" period from 3 to 6pm, with a half-price snacks menu. Throughout the day, folks drop by for a cup of seafood bisque and one of the trademark popovers. Typical of the dinner entrees is the seafood gumbo with shrimp, sausage, scallops, salmon, and lobster with peppers, onions, artichoke hearts, and roasted red peppers. This being a college town, portions run from really big to immense, the better to assuage raging young metabolisms. A glass-enclosed porch fronts the converted house.

51 N. Pleasant St. (north of Amity and Main sts.). ✆ 413/253-3491. Main courses $9–$16.50. AE, DISC, MC, V. Sun–Thurs 11:30am–10pm; Fri–Sat 11:30am–11pm.

AMHERST AFTER DARK

Students and other young adults tend to gravitate toward the livelier music scene in Northampton, but Amherst does offer some nighttime entertainment. Close at hand is the **Black Sheep Cafe,** 79 Main St. (℗ **413/253-3442**), which is active nightly with folk and blues singers, poetry readings, chamber music—a broad, unpredictable selection. There's usually no cover.

The beer is good, the food indifferent, and the music varied at the **Amherst Brewing Company,** 36 N. Pleasant St. (℗ **413/253-4400**). Reggae, soul, and R&B are some of the forms on stage, usually at least Thursday through Saturday nights at 10pm.

Amherst College's **Buckley Recital Hall** (℗ **413/542-2195**) and the **Mullins Center** (℗ **413/733-2500**) at UMass mount a variety of pop, classical, dance, and theatrical performances that might include, for example, the Cincinnati Symphony, Mummenschantz, or Elton John.

DEERFIELD ★★★

Meadows cleared and plowed more than 300 years ago still surround this historic town between the Connecticut and Deerfield rivers. Every morning, tobacco and dairy farmers leave houses fronting the main street to work their land nearby. Students attend the distinguished prep school, Deerfield Academy, founded in 1797. Lawyers maintain offices here, while other residents commute to jobs elsewhere. Deerfield is an invaluable fragment of American history, and it isn't one of those New England village exhibits with costumed performers who go home to their condos at night.

A town still exists here, 16 miles north of Northampton and 16 miles northwest of Amherst, because the earliest English settlers were determined to thrive despite their status as a frontier pressure point in the wars that tormented colonial America. Massacres of Deerfield's settlers by the French and Indian enemies of the British nearly wiped out the town in 1675 and again in 1704. In the latter raid, 47 people were killed and another 112 were taken prisoner and marched to French Québec.

The main thoroughfare, simply called "The Street," is lined with more than 80 houses built in the 17th, 18th, and 19th centuries. Most are private, but 14 of them can be visited through tours conducted by Historic Deerfield, a local tourism organization (see below).

MUSEUMS & HISTORIC HOMES

"The Street" is a mile long, with most of the museum houses concentrated along the long block north of the central town common. There are two buildings operated by organizations other than Historic Deerfield. One is Memorial Hall Museum, east of the town common on Memorial Street, for which a separate admission is charged. (For the slightly larger fee of $12 adults, $5 children and students, tours of the 14 museum houses can be combined with a visit to Memorial Hall through Historic Deerfield.) The other is the Indian House Memorial, north of the Deerfield Inn, also maintained by a separate organization. Since it is only a 1929 reproduction of an earlier house, it is of less interest than the other structures.

Special celebrations in the town are held on Patriots' Day (the third Monday in April), Washington's Birthday, Thanksgiving, and the Christmas holidays. In summer, there is an antique and classic car show; call the information center (℗ **413/774-5581;** see below) for details.

Historic Deerfield ★★★ Begin with a visit to the Hall Tavern, opposite the post office, where tickets are sold and maps and brochures are available. A particularly useful booklet provides a walking tour of 88 historic locations in the village. This is also the departure point for guided tours, which customarily leave on the half hour during busier times between April and October, and according to demand during the slower months. While there are no charges for simply strolling the Street, the only way to get inside the museum houses is by tour.

The 14 houses on the tour were constructed between 1720 and 1850. They contain more than 20,000 furnishings, silver and pewter pieces, textiles, ceramics, and implements used from the early 17th century to 1900. Included are imports from China and Europe as well as items made in the Connecticut River Valley during its prominence as an industrial center.

The **Museum Store** (© 413/774-5581) is in a weathered shack between the post office and the Deerfield Inn. Apart from a few T-shirts, its judicious selections include weather vanes, hand-dipped candles, books, fruit preserves, and reproductions of light fixtures found in the village houses.

A stone building behind the Dwight House contains the **Flynt Center of Early American Life** ★, with galleries for changing exhibitions of paintings, textiles, and decorative arts relevant to the local history.

A free attraction is the **Channing Blake Meadow Walk.** Open from 8am to 6pm in good weather, the trail begins beside the Rev. John Farwell Moors House, a Historic Deerfield holding on the west side of the Street. The walk is marked by interpretive tablets and goes through a working farm, past the playing fields of Deerfield Academy, and through pastures beside the Deerfield River. Along the trail you can see sheep and cattle up close; for that reason, dogs aren't allowed on the trail.

Information Center, Hall Tavern, The Street. © 413/774-5581. Admission to all museum houses (good for 2 consecutive days) $12 adults, $6 children 6–17, free for children under 6. Daily 9:30am–4:30pm.

Memorial Hall Museum ★ Deerfield Academy's original 1798 classroom building was converted into this museum of village history in 1880. A popular, if suggestively grisly, exhibit is the preserved door of a 1698 home that shows the gashes made by weapons of the French and Indian raiders in 1704. Should the point be too muted, a hatchet is also embedded in the door. Five period rooms are also on view, and other exhibits display colonial furniture, vintage clothing, quilts, paintings, pottery, pewter, and Native American weapons and tools. Special events—plays, crafts fairs, recitals, lectures, and even ice-cream socials—are held monthly.

8 Memorial St. (between the Street and Rtes. 5 and 10). © 413/774-3768. or 413/774-7476 off-season. Admission $6 adults, $3 children and students, free for children under 6. May–Oct daily 10am–4:30pm.

Yankee Candle Car Museum ★★ The Yankee Candle Company has been a prominent retail presence in New England for decades. This complex, a few miles south of historic Deerfield, sprawls over several acres with offices, warehouses, a giant store selling the primary product, and, best of all, this repository of fabulous vehicles dating back to 1897. There is room on the floor for 85 cars and a dozen motorcycles. Here are "steamers" from 1903 and 1910, one of Ford's "Tin Lizzies," a 1966 Ferrari, Jerry Seinfeld's VW Beetle, the gull-winged '81 DeLorean roadster of the type featured in *Back to the Future,* and many more, all in pristine condition.

Rte. 5 (¼ mile north of Exit 24 off I-91), South Deerfield. © 877/636-7707. Admission $5 adults, $2 children 4–11. Daily 9:30am–6pm (longer hours in Dec).

WHERE TO STAY & DINE

Deerfield Inn ★★   Even if it had any significant competition, this inn would attract more than its share of guests. Built in 1884, it's located in the middle of the Street and is one of the stellar stopping places in the valley. The innkeepers restlessly scour the establishment, over the last few years replacing all the bathroom fixtures, refinishing the older furniture, and installing new carpeting. Six of the guest rooms, named after people who lived in the village, have four-posters. Antiques and reproductions of early-19th-century styles are judiciously mixed throughout.

81 Old Main St., Deerfield, MA 01342. © **800/926-3865** or 413/774-5587. Fax 413/775-7221. www. deerfieldinn.com. 23 units. May–Oct $235–$255 double; Nov–Apr $188–$201. Midweek discounts available. Rates include breakfast and afternoon tea. AE, DC, MC, V. **Amenities:** Restaurant (American), cafeteria, bar. *In room:* A/C, TV.

4 The Berkshires

They are more than hills, but less than mountains, so the Taconic and Hoosac ranges that define this region at the western end of the state go by the collective name "The Berkshires." The hamlets, villages, and two small cities that have long drawn sustenance from the region's kindly Housatonic River and its tranquil tributaries are as New England as New England can be.

Mohawks and Mohegans lived and hunted here, and while white missionaries established settlements at Stockbridge and elsewhere in an attempt to Christianize the native tribes, the Indians eventually moved on west. Farmers, drawn to the narrow but fertile floodplains of the Housatonic, were supplanted in the 19th century by manufacturers, who erected the brick mills that drew their power from the river.

At the same time, artists and writers were drawn to the mild summers and seclusion that these hills and lakes offered. Nathaniel Hawthorne, Herman Melville, and Edith Wharton were among those who put down temporary roots. By the last decades of the 19th century and the arrival of the railroad, wealthy New Yorkers and Bostonians had discovered the region and began to erect extravagant summer "cottages." With their support, culture and the performing arts found a hospitable reception. By the 1930s, theater, dance, and music performances had established themselves as regular summer fixtures. Tanglewood, Jacob's Pillow, and the Berkshire and Williamstown Theatre festivals draw tens of thousands of visitors every summer.

Note that many inns routinely stipulate minimum 2- or 3-night stays in summer and over holiday weekends and often require advance deposits.

ESSENTIALS

GETTING THERE   The Massachusetts Turnpike (I-90) runs east-west from Boston to the Berkshires, with an exit near Lee and Stockbridge. From New York City, the scenic Taconic State Parkway connects with I-90 not far from Pittsfield.

Amtrak (© **800/USA-RAIL;** www.northeast.amtrak.com) operates several trains daily between Boston and Chicago, stopping in Pittsfield each way.

VISITOR INFORMATION   The **Berkshire Visitors Bureau,** Berkshire Common (off South Street, near the entrance to the Hilton), Pittsfield (© **800/237-5747** or 413/443-9186), provides brochures and assists with lodging reservations. In addition, local chambers of commerce maintain information

The Berkshires

Bartholomew's Cobble **20**
Berkshire Botanical Garden **13**
Berkshire Scenic Railway Museum **8**
Berkshire Theatre Festival **12**
Bousquet Ski Area **6**
Brodie Mountain Ski Area **3**
Butternut Basin Ski Area **18**
Catamount Ski Area **19**
Chesterwood **14**
Hancock Shaker Village **5**
Jacob's Pillow Dance Festival **11**
Jiminy Peak Ski Area **4**
Massachusetts Museum of
   Contemporary Art (MASS MoCA) **2**
Monument Mountain **17**
The Mount, Edith Wharton
   Restoration **10**
Naumkeag **16**
Norman Rockwell Museum **15**
Pleasant Valley Wildlife Sanctuary **7**
Shakespeare and Company **10**
Tanglewood Music Festival **9**
Williamstown Theatre Festival **1**

VERMONT

NEW YORK

Williamstown
North Adams

SAVOY MTN.
STATE
FOREST

MT. GREYLOCK
STATE
RESERVATION

Adams

Cheshire

Lanesborough

PITTSFIELD
STATE
FOREST

Dalton

MASSACHUSETTS

Pittsfield

PERU
STATE
FOREST

South
Mountain

Lenox

Becket

OCTOBER MTN.
STATE
FOREST

Stockbridge
Bowl

Lee

West
Stockbridge

Stockbridge

BEARTOWN
STATE
FOREST

Housatonic

OTIS
STATE
FOREST

Great
Barrington

EAST MTN.
STATE
FOREST

Egremont
New
Marlborough

SANDISFIELD
STATE
FOREST

Sheffield

Ashley Falls

BASH-BISH
FALLS
STATE PARK

CONNECTICUT

0   5 mi
0   5 km

303

booths at central locations in Great Barrington, Lee, Lenox, Pittsfield, Stock-bridge, and Williamstown (see the sections that follow). Also check out **www.berkshires.com** and **www.westernmassvisit.net**.

SHEFFIELD ⟨⟩

The first settlement of any size encountered when approaching from Connecticut on Route 7 is Sheffield, known as the "Antiques Capital of the Berkshires." It occupies a floodplain beside the Housatonic River, 11 miles south of Great Barrington, with the Berkshires rising to the west.

Agriculture has been the principal occupation of its residents, and still is, to a degree. Everyone else sells antiques, or so it might seem driving along Route 7 (also known as Main Street or Sheffield Plain). The meticulously maintained houses cultivate an impression of prosperous tranquility.

May through October, stop by the **Colonel Ashley House,** Cooper Hill Road (© **413/229-8600**), in Ashley Falls. Built in 1735, this modified saltbox is believed to be the oldest house in Berkshire County. Ashley was a person of considerable repute in colonial western Massachusetts, a pioneer settler, an officer in one of the French and Indian Wars, and later a lawyer and a judge. The house is open from 1 to 5pm on Saturday, Sunday, and holiday Mondays in June, September, and October; Wednesday through Sunday from July to Labor Day. To find it, drive south from Sheffield on Route 7, then veer off onto Route 7A toward Ashley Falls. Bear right on Rannapo Road. At the Y intersection, turn right on Cooper Hill Road.

OUTDOOR PURSUITS

The 278-acre nature reservation called **Bartholomew's Cobble** ⟨⟩, on Route 7A (© **413/229-8600**), lies beside an oxbow bend in the Housatonic. Its 6 miles of trails, for hiking or cross-country skiing, cross pastures, penetrate forests, and provide vistas of the river valley from the area's high point, Hurlburt's Hill. Picnicking is permitted. Birders should take binoculars. The requested donations are $3 for adults and $1 for children 6 to 12. To get to Bartholomew's Cobble, follow the directions for the Colonel Ashley House (see above), except at the end of Rannapo Road, bear left on Weatogue Road and follow it to the reservation entrance.

ANTIQUING

Sheffield lays justifiable claim to the title of "Antiques Capital of the Berkshires"—no small feat, given what seems to be an effort by half the population of the Berkshires to sell collectibles, oddities, and true antiques to the other half. These are canny, knowledgeable dealers who know exactly what they have, so expect high quality and few bargains. Of the many possibilities, here is a slender sampling, driving north on Route 7.

The **Antiques Center of Sheffield,** 33 S. Main St. (© **413/229-3400**), is not afflicted by excessive tidiness, but offers a diverse stock, including railroad lanterns, military mementos, and wildly varied Americana. In pristine contrast is the well-ordered **Darr Antiques,** 34 S. Main St. (© **413/229-7773**), which specializes in formal 18th- and 19th-century English and American furniture, with some Chinese accessories.

Farther north along Route 7, **Dovetail Antiques,** 440 Sheffield Plain (© **413/229-2628**), specializes in American clocks, primarily those made in Connecticut in the last century. Some have gears and cogs made of wood.

Sheffield on Stage

From late June to late August, the **Barrington Stage Company** mounts musicals, comedies, and dramas at the **Consolati Performing Arts Center,** on Berkshire School Road. For information, call © **413/528-8888** or go to www.barringtonstageco.org. On five Saturday evenings in July and August, the **Berkshire Choral Festival,** 245 N. Undermountain Rd. (© **413/ 229-8526;** www.choralfest.org), performs classical works at the Berkshire School in Sheffield.

Continuing along Route 7, on the left at the edge of town, is **Susan Silver** (© **413/229-8169**), with meticulously restored 18th- and 19th-century English library furniture—desks, reading stands—and French accessories.

There are at least two dozen other dealers along this route. Most of them stock the **free directory** of the Berkshire County Antiques Dealers Association, which lists member dealers from Sheffield to Cheshire and across the border in Connecticut and New York. Look, too, for the pamphlet called *The Antique Hunter's Guide to Route 7.*

SOUTH EGREMONT

If you're coming to the Berkshires from the Taconic Parkway in New York, you can't help but drive through the town of Egremont. Its larger, busier half is South Egremont, a diverting village that was once a stop on the stagecoach route between Hartford and Albany. It retains many structures from that era, including mills that utilized the stream that still rushes by. Those circumstances make it a magnet for antiques dealers and restaurateurs.

OUTDOOR PURSUITS

HIKING   Scenic **Bash-Bish Falls State Park** ⛰⛰, on Route 23 (© **413/ 528-0330**), makes a rewarding day outing for hiking, birding, and fishing (no camping or picnicking, though). To get here, drive west on Route 23 from town, turning south on Route 41, and immediately right on Mount Washington Road. Watch for signs directing the way to Mount Washington State Forest and Bash-Bish Falls. After 8 miles, a sign indicates a right turn toward the falls. Look for it opposite a church with an unusual steeple. The road begins to follow the course of a mountain stream, going downhill. In about 3 miles is a large parking place next to a craggy promontory.

The sign also points off to a trail down to the falls, which should be negotiated only by reasonably fit adults. First, mount the promontory for a splendid view across the plains of the Hudson Valley to the pale-blue ridgeline of the Catskill Mountains. The falls can be heard, but not yet seen, down to the left. If this trail seems too steep, continue driving down the road to another parking area, on the left. From here, a gentler trail a little over a mile long leads to the falls. The falls themselves are quite impressive, crashing down from more than 50 feet. The park is open from dawn to dusk.

SKIING   At the western edge of the township, touching the New York border, is the **Catamount Ski Area,** on Route 23 (© **413/528-1262;** www. catamountski.com). About 2 hours from Manhattan, it is understandably popular with New Yorkers. It has 24 trails, including the daunting Catapult, the steepest run in the Berkshires (experts only), and four double chairlifts. There is night skiing on 13 trails. Rentals are available.

WHERE TO STAY

Egremont Inn ✛ Slip into this friendly former stagecoach stop as easily as into a favorite old flannel robe. Thousands of travelers have preceded you, for the Egremont has been a tavern and inn since 1780. That longevity shows, in tilting floors and lintels and a grand brick fireplace constructed over an ancient blacksmithing hearth. Dinner is served Wednesday through Sunday year-round. A singer-guitarist performs Thursday nights, a jazz ensemble Saturday evenings.

Old Sheffield Rd. (1 block off Rte. 23), South Egremont, MA 01258. © 413/528-2111. Fax 413/528-3284. www.egremontinn.com. 19 units. Weekdays $90–$145 double; weekends $105–$170 double. Weekend packages available. Rates include breakfast. AE, DISC, MC, V. **Amenities:** 2 restaurants (American), bar; outdoor pool; 2 tennis courts. *In room:* A/C.

Weathervane Inn An affectionate cat welcomes new arrivals to a building that began as a 1735 farmhouse, but was renovated in Greek Revival style in 1835. Many of the guest rooms have four-poster beds with quilts; fireplaces have been added to two units. The new innkeepers, who took over in 1998, are gradually upgrading all the rooms.

Rte. 23, South Egremont, MA 01258. © 800/528-9580 or 413/528-9580. Fax 413/528-1713. www. weathervaneinn.com. 10 units. A/C. $125–$165 double; $225–$245 suite. Rates include breakfast and afternoon tea. AE, DC, MC, V. **Amenities:** Unheated outdoor pool; public golf course next door. *In room:* A/C, dataport.

WHERE TO DINE

Mom's Cafe ECLECTIC This informal drop-in place perks from early breakfast to late espresso every day of the week. That and its low prices are the cafe's greatest virtues. Mom's menu runs from omelets and pancakes to pastas and pizzas with toppings as diverse as avocado and pineapple. In good weather, eat on the deck over the stream that runs behind the building.

Main St. © 413/528-2414. Main courses $3.95–$8.95. MC, V. Daily 6:30am–10pm.

GREAT BARRINGTON

Even with a population well under 8,000, this pleasant commercial and retail center, 7 miles south of Stockbridge, is the largest town in the southernmost part of the county. Rapids in the Housatonic provided power for a number of mills in centuries past, most of which are now gone, and in 1886 it was one of the first communities in the world to have electricity on its streets and in its homes.

Great Barrington has no sights of particular significance, leaving time to browse its many antiques galleries and growing number of specialty shops. Convenient as a home base for excursions to such nearby attractions as Monument Mountain, Bash-Bish Falls, Butternut Basin, Tanglewood concerts, and the museums and historic houses of Stockbridge, it has a number of unremarkable but entirely adequate motels north of the center along or near Route 7 that tend to fill up more slowly on weekends than the better-known inns in the area. It is something of a dining destination, too, compared with other Berkshire towns.

The **Southern Berkshire Chamber of Commerce** maintains an information booth at 362 Main St. (© 413/528-1510; www.greatbarrington.org), near the town hall. It's open Tuesday through Saturday from 9am to 5pm.

OUTDOOR PURSUITS

The **Egremont Country Club,** on Route 23 (© 413/528-4222), is open to the public. Its facilities include an 18-hole golf course, tennis courts, and an Olympic-size pool.

Butternut Basin, also on Route 23, 2 miles east of town (© 413/528-2000, or 800/438-7669 for snow conditions; www.butternutbasin.com), is known for its strong family ski programs. A children's center provides day care for kids 2½ to 6 from December 23 until the end of the season, and the SKIwee program for children 4 to 12 offers full- and half-day programs that include lunch, ski instruction, and lift tickets. Six double and quad chairlifts provide access to 22 trails. There are also 5 miles of cross-country trails. On weekends, lift tickets cost $39 for adults, $28 for seniors and children 7 to 14, and $10 for children 6 and under.

A little over 4 miles north of town, west of Route 7, is **Monument Mountain,** with two trails to the summit. The easier route is the Indian Monument Trail, about an hour's hike to the top; the more difficult one, the Hickey Trail, isn't much longer but takes the steep way up. The summit, called Squaw Peak, offers splendid panoramic views.

SHOPPING

Head straight for **Railroad Street,** the town's best shopping strip. Start on the corner with Main Street, at **T. P. Saddle Blanket & Trading Co.** (© 413/ 528-6500). An unlikely emporium that looks as if it had been lifted whole from the Colorado Rockies, it's packed with country furniture and western gear— boots, hats, Indian jewelry, jars of salsa, and blankets.

Mistral's, 6 Railroad St. (© 413/528-1618), stocks Gallic tableware, linens, fancy foods, furniture, and night wear. Nearby, **Nahuál,** 9 Railroad St. (© 413/ 528-2423), offers colorful and imaginative folk arts and handicrafts, primarily from Africa and Latin America. **Church Street Trading Company,** 4 Railroad St. (© 413/528-6120), defies easy categorization, what with walking sticks, dog collars, and candles all on display. The primary wares are sturdily stylish North Country sweaters, shirts, and pants.

Around the corner, **The Chef's Shop,** 290 Main St. (© 413/528-0135), features a bounty of kitchen gadgets, cookware, and cookbooks. Periodically, chefs from several of the restaurants recommended in these pages will conduct 3-hour cooking classes.

In town, just before Route 7 turns right across a short bridge, Route 41 goes straight, toward the village of Housatonic. In about 4 miles you'll see a long shed that houses the kiln and workrooms of **Great Barrington Pottery** (© 413/ 274-6259). Owner Richard Bennett has been throwing pots according to ancient Japanese techniques for more than 30 years.

WHERE TO STAY

North of town on U.S. 7 is **Monument Mountain Motel,** 249 Stockbridge Rd. (© 413/528-3272; fax 413/528-3132), which has a pool, tennis courts, and a riverside location. The **Chamber of Commerce** operates a lodging hot line at © 800/269-4825 or 413/528-4006.

The Old Inn on the Green & Gedney Farm 🌴🌴   This establishment is comprised of a former 1760 tavern/general store and the newly renovated 18th-century Thayer House, both on the village green, and a pair of converted dairy barns down the road. Most desirable are the luxury units in Thayer House, some with fireplaces and all with air-conditioning, and in the barn, where contemporary furnishings and accessories are combined with Oriental rugs. The restaurant, which has built a reputation based on the creativity of its kitchen, is open for dinner only. All five intimate dining rooms have fireplaces; reservations are advised.

Rte. 57, New Marlborough, MA 01230. © 800/286-3139 or 413/229-3131. Fax 413/229-8236. www.oldinn.com. 26 units. $175–$245 double; $245–$285 suite; $325–$365 Thayer House room. Mon–Wed

25% discount. Rates include breakfast. AE, MC, V. Take Rte. 23 east from Great Barrington, picking up Rte. 57 after 3.4 miles. After 5.7 miles, the Old Inn is on the left. Continue another ¼ mile to the barns on the left. Registration is on the ground floor of the gray barn. **Amenities:** Restaurant (creative American); courtyard pool at Thayer House. *In room:* Hair dryer, no phone.

Windflower Inn ⚐   A roadside lodging built in the middle of the last century in Federal style, the Windflower commands a large plot of land opposite the Egremont Country Club on Route 23 between Great Barrington and South Egremont. Six rooms have fireplaces; four have canopied beds.

684 S. Egremont Rd. (P.O. Box 25), Great Barrington, MA 01230. ☎ **800/992-1993** or 413/528-2720. Fax 413/528-5147. www.windflowerinn.com. 13 units. $100–$200 double. Children stay in parents' room for $25. Rates include breakfast and afternoon tea. AE. **Amenities:** Unheated outdoor pool. *In room:* A/C, TV, dataport.

WHERE TO DINE

In addition to the places listed below, you might check out the restaurant at the **Old Inn on the Green & Gedney Farm** (see above).

Barrington Brewery ⚐ ECLECTIC AMERICAN   Nothing detracts from the primary function of this brewery in a converted barn. All its beers and ales are made upstairs and funneled directly to the taps in the tavern. They are good enough to distract even devoted oenophiles (although interesting wines are also available). Grub, of the burger and nacho variety, is secondary but tasty enough. Breads and desserts are made on the premises.

Rte. 7 (in the Jennifer House complex, north of town). ☎ **413/528-8282.** Main courses $10.95–$16.95. AE, DISC, MC, V. Daily 11:30am–10pm (bar open later, depending on business).

Castle Street Cafe ⚐⚐ NEW AMERICAN   This storefront bistro has ruled the Great Barrington roost for some time now, and recently expanded into the next building, installing what it calls a "Celestial Bar," with live jazz piano 6 nights a week in summer and on weekends the rest of the year. While a Francophilic inclination is apparent in the main room, it isn't overpowering. Pasta servings are so large that smaller portions are available. Have a drink at the short bar in the new room while you're checking out the night's menu, or stay there for such casual eats as burritos, burgers, spareribs, and pizzas. An award-winning wine list is another reason to stop in. The dining room is smoke-free, but addicts are welcome to light up in the bar.

10 Castle St. (near the Town Hall). ☎ **413/528-5244.** Main courses $9–$22. AE, DISC, MC, V. Daily 5–10pm (until 11pm Fri–Sat).

Union Bar & Grill ⚐ NEW AMERICAN   A sculptor designed the industrial-chic interior, with the exposed ceiling ducts and brushed metal trim associated with New York's TriBeCa. The menu might have been transplanted, too, given, for one example, the herb-crusted snowy halibut and its accompanying scallion pancake with tomato-ginger jam. At lunch, even the usually prosaic steak sandwich turns out to be a grilled pita wrapped around caramelized red onion, beef slices, melted cheese, and a piquant sauce. The young and hip mingle easily with seniors and families.

293 Main St. ☎ **413/528-6228.** Main courses $14.95–$19.95. MC, V. Thurs–Tues 11:30am–11pm (bar until 1am).

GREAT BARRINGTON AFTER DARK

The **Aston Magna Festival** features classical music performed on period instruments. Concerts are held on five Sundays in July and August at the St. James

Church, Main Street and Taconic Avenue (© **800/875-7156** or 413/528-3595).

The **Triplex Cinema,** 70 Railroad St. (© **413/528-8886**), shows a mixed bag of independent and foreign flicks as well as major studio releases.

STOCKBRIDGE ★★

Stockbridge's ready accessibility to Boston and New York (about 2½ hours from each and reachable by rail since the mid–19th century) transformed the original frontier settlement into a Gilded Age summer retreat for the rich. The town has long been popular with artists and writers as well. Norman Rockwell, who lived here for 25 years, rendered the Main Street of his adopted town in a famous painting. Along and near Main Street are a number of historic homes and other attractions, enough to fill up a long weekend, even without the Tanglewood concert season in nearby Lenox. One of the Berkshires' hottest destinations, Stockbridge is inevitably jammed in the warmer months, especially on weekends and during foliage season.

Stockbridge lies 7 miles north of Great Barrington and 6 miles south of Lenox. The **Stockbridge Chamber of Commerce** (© **413/298-5200;** www.stockbridgechamber.org) maintains a seasonal information booth opposite the row of stores depicted by Rockwell. It's open, sometimes with an attendant, May through October.

SEEING THE SIGHTS

Norman Rockwell Museum ★★   This striking building opened in 1993, at a cost of $4.4 million, to house the works of Stockbridge's favorite son. The beloved illustrator used both his neighbors and the town where he lived to tell stories about an America rapidly fading from memory. Most of Rockwell's paintings adorned covers of the weekly *Saturday Evening Post:* warm and often humorous depictions of homecomings, first proms, and visits to the doctor. He addressed serious concerns, too, notably with his poignant portrait of a little African-American girl being escorted by U.S. marshals into a previously segregated school. Art critics long derided his paintings as saccharine and sentimental, but today a revision of sorts has led to widespread appreciation for his deft brushwork. A major retrospective of his works, *Norman Rockwell: Pictures for the American People,* is touring the country until February 2002, when it closes with a flourish at the Guggenheim in New York. The lovely 36-acre grounds also contain Rockwell's last studio (closed November through April).

Rte. 183. © **413/298-4100.** www.nrm.org. Admission $9 adults, $2 children 6–18; $20 per family. May–Oct daily 10am–5pm; Nov–Apr Mon–Fri 10am–4pm, Sat–Sun 10am–5pm. Take Main St. (Rte. 102) west to the junction with Rte. 183, then turn left (south) at the traffic signal. In about half a mile, you'll see the entrance to the museum on the left.

Chesterwood ★   Sculptor Daniel Chester French, best known for the Lincoln Memorial in Washington, D.C., used this estate as his summer home and studio for more than 30 years. His *Minute Man* statue at the Old North Bridge in Concord, completed in 1875 at the age of 25, launched his highly successful career. The grounds of the 122-acre estate are used for an annual show of contemporary sculpture.

4 Williamsville Rd. © **413/298-3579.** www.chesterwood.org. Admission $8.50 adults ($5.50 for grounds only), $5 children 13–18, $3 children 6–12. May–Oct daily 10am–5pm. Drive west on Main St., south on Rte. 183 about 1 mile to the Chesterwood sign.

Naumkeag ✦ In 1886, architect Stanford White designed this 26-room house for Joseph Hodge Choate, who served as U.S. ambassador to the Court of St. James. The client dubbed it "Naumkeag," a Native American name for Salem, Mass., his childhood home. His house of many gables and chimneys is largely of the New England Shingle style, surrounded by impressive gardens. Admission is by guided tour only, but worth it for the glimpses of the rich interior, fully furnished and decorated in the manner of the period.

Prospect Hill. ✆ **413/298-3239**. www.thetrustees.org. Admission $8 adults, $2.50 children. Memorial Day to Columbus Day daily 10am–5pm. From the Cat & Dog Fountain in the intersection next to the Red Lion Inn, drive north on Pine St. to Prospect Hill Rd. about ¹/₂-mile.

Berkshire Botanical Garden ✦ These 15 acres of flower beds, shrubs, ponds, and raised vegetable and herb gardens are an inviting destination for strollers and picnickers. The first weekend in October is devoted to a harvest festival, which features jugs of cider, displays of pumpkins, and hayrides.

Rtes. 102 and 183. ✆ **413/298-3926**. www.berkshirebotanical.org. Admission $5 adults, $4 seniors, $3 students, free for children under 12. May–Oct daily 10am–5pm. Tours offered Sat–Sun June–Aug. Drive west from downtown Stockbridge on Main St., picking up Church St. (Rte. 102) northwest for about 2 miles.

Mission House ✦ The Rev. John Sergeant had the most benevolent, if paternalistic, of intentions: He sought to build a house among the members of the Housatonic tribe, hoping to convert them to civilized (i.e., English) ways through proximity to his godly self and his small band of settlers. The weathered Mission House, built in 1739, was the site of this Christianizing process, and it was moved to its current location in 1928.

Main and Sergeant sts. (Rte. 102). ✆ **413/298-3239**. Admission $5 adults, $2.50 children. Memorial Day to Columbus Day daily 10am–5pm. Visits are by guided tour.

The Berkshire Theatre Festival ✦✦ From June to August, and occasionally at other times during the year, the Berkshire Theatre Festival holds its season of classic and new plays, often with marquee names starring or directing. Dianne Wiest and Joanne Woodward have been participants. Its venue is a "casino" built in 1887 to plans by architect Stanford White. A second venue, the Unicorn Theatre, opened in 1996. Tickets are usually fairly easy to get, unless you're trying for a weekend night or a performance with a name star.

P.O. Box 797, Main St. ✆ **413/298-5576**. www.berkshiretheatre.org. Tickets $22–$40 Main Stage, $18 Unicorn Theatre.

WHERE TO STAY

Inn at Stockbridge ✦✦ A mile north of Stockbridge center, this 1906 building with a grandly columned porch is set well back from the road on 12 acres. The innkeepers are eager to please, serving full breakfasts by candlelight and afternoon spreads of cheese and wine. Ask for the Terrace Room, one of the charming older units, with a deck, private entrance, and Jacuzzi. Four new rooms have fireplaces and whirlpools.

30 East St. (Rte. 7), Stockbridge, MA 01262. ✆ **888/466-7865** or 413/298-3337. Fax 413/298-3406. www.stockbridgeinn.com. 12 units. June–Oct $125–$275 double; Nov–May $115–$225 double. Rates include breakfast and afternoon refreshments. AE, DISC, MC, V. No children under 12 accepted. **Amenities:** Outdoor pool. *In room:* A/C, TV, hair dryer.

The Red Lion Inn ✦✦ So well known that it serves as a symbol of the Berkshires, this busy inn had its origins as a stagecoach tavern in 1773. That original building is long gone, and the hotel that grew up on the site burned to the ground in 1896. It was quickly rebuilt into what is essentially the structure you see today. Many of the antiques arranged in both public and private rooms survived the fire. The rocking chairs on the porch are the perfect place to while away an hour reading or people-watching. The Lion's Den has nightly live entertainment, usually of the folk-rock variety. Jackets are required for men in the pricey main dining room, but not in the casual Widow Bingham Tavern, nor, in good weather, in the courtyard out back. The wine cellar has been recognized with important awards. Make reservations even further in advance than is recommended for other Berkshire inns.

Main St., Stockbridge, MA 01262. (C) 413/298-5545. Fax 413/298-5130. www.redlioninn.com. 110 units (16 share bathrooms). Mid-Apr to late May $115–$185 double, $185–$285 suite; June to late Oct $169–$209 double, $259–$375 suite; late Oct to mid-Apr $107–$167 double, $175–$325 suite. AE, DC, DISC, MC, V. **Amenities:** 3 restaurants (eclectic/American), 2 bars; outdoor pool; golf and tennis privileges nearby; exercise room; limited room service; massage; baby-sitting; laundry; dry cleaning. *In room:* A/C, TV/VCR, dataport, hair dryer.

Taggart House ★★ Ordinarily, an inn with only four guest rooms wouldn't merit space here. But what rooms! The decor of this outwardly sedate 1850 Victorian/colonial mansion provides guests with a breathtaking immersion in the Gilded Age. Start with the theatrical main floor—the inlaid mahogany dining table was once a centerpiece in an Argentine palace and is now the site of candlelight breakfasts. There's a paneled library, a ballroom, a harpsichord, and nine beguiling fireplaces. And upstairs, beds are decorated with fur throws, East Indian silk coverlets, or velvet canopies.

Main St. (a block west of the Red Lion), Stockbridge, MA 01262. (C) and fax 413/298-4303. www.taggart-house.com. 4 units. July–Oct $235–$355 double; Nov–June $195–$275. Rates include breakfast. 2- to 3-night minimum stays summer and fall weekends. AE, DC, DISC, MC, V. Young children not accepted. *In room:* A/C, dataport.

WHERE TO DINE

See also the dining options at the **Red Lion Inn,** reviewed above.

Michael's ★ ELECTIC AMERICAN This tavern with a sports tilt is one of the few nearby alternatives to the Red Lion Inn. Bar snacks served around the 60-inch TV are of the nachos variety, while entrees in the dining room run to steaks, chicken Dijon, and scallops marinara. The food is pretty good, the greeting friendly, and the place stays open throughout the day.

9 Elm St. (off Main St.). (C) 413/298-3530. Main courses 9.95–$16.95. AE, DC, MC, V. Mon–Sat 11:30am–9pm (bar until 1am); Sun noon–10pm.

WEST STOCKBRIDGE

The hills around this Stockbridge satellite (it's just 5 miles northwest) are alive with creativity. Potters, painters, writers, sculptors, weavers, and glass blowers pursue their compulsions, selling the results from their studios and several galleries. A pamphlet called *The Art of West Stockbridge,* available in display racks throughout the area, describes the work of some of the more important artisans and where it can be found.

One of the most ambitious enterprises is the **Berkshire Center for Contemporary Glass** ★, 6 Harris St. ((C) 413/232-4666), in the heart of the village. Kids find the process fascinating and are even allowed to participate. The center is open daily from 10am to 10pm May through October, from 10am to 6pm November through April.

WHERE TO STAY

The Inn at Richmond ⭐ This used to be a horse farm, and animals are still boarded in the barns at the back of the property. The book-lined library is irresistible, with its fireplace, piano, and waiting bottles of port and sherry; an adjoining room has a fridge stocked with soft drinks. All guest rooms have wall-to-wall carpeting and large beds; some have sleeper sofas, five have working fireplaces, and two have whirlpools. Three housekeeping cottages feature equipped kitchens, costing $750 a week in winter, $1,200 a week in summer and fall. The inn is about 5 miles north of West Stockbridge, and Tanglewood and Hancock Shaker Village are only 20 minutes away.

802 State Rd. (Rte. 41), Richmond, MA 01254. ℂ 888/968-4748 or 413/698-2566. Fax 413/698-2100. www.innatrichmond.com. 10 units. Memorial Day–Oct $125–$325 double, $205–$265 suite; Nov–May $110–$215 double, $155–$195 suite. Rates include breakfast. AE, MC, V. Children 10 and over welcome. *In room:* A/C, TV, dataport, hair dryer, iron.

WHERE TO DINE

La Bruschetta ⭐⭐ NEW ITALIAN The chef/owners create splendidly aromatic dishes that require care and advanced technique. Pre-appetizers are bruschetta and a basket of warm bread with a saucer of olive oil, so you might want to skip first courses. Rich, long-simmered sauces characterize the main courses, whether pasta, meat, or fowl, demanding to be sopped up to the last drop. Wines are as carefully selected as the ingredients.

1 Harris St. ℂ 413/232-7141. Reservations advised. Main courses $17.50–$22. AE, MC, V. May–June Thurs–Sun 6–9pm; July to early Sept Thurs–Mon 5–9pm; late Sept to Oct Thurs–Mon 6–9pm, Sun 5:30–8:30pm; Nov–April Fri–Sun 6–9pm.

Truc Orient Express ⭐⭐ VIETNAMESE The menu is full of revelatory taste sensations. *Mai tuyet nhi* is a soup adrift with snow mushrooms and lobster meat, a suitable lead-in to the extravaganza called *lauthap cam-chap pin loo*, a hot pot crowded with meatballs, shrimp, squid, scallops, and assorted veggies simmered tableside in a shiny brass pot and ladled over rice noodles. Tables are set up on the deck in summer.

2 Harris St. ℂ 413/232-4204. Main courses $7.50–$18. AE, DISC, MC, V. Summer daily 11am–10pm; winter Wed–Mon 5–9:30pm.

LEE

While Stockbridge and Lenox were developing into luxurious recreational centers for the upper crust of Boston and New York, Lee was a thriving paper-mill town. That meant that it was shunned by the wealthy summer people and thus remained essentially a town of workers and merchants. It has a somewhat raffish though not unappealing aspect, its center bunched with shops and offices and few of the stately homes and broad lawns that characterize neighboring communities.

The town's contribution to the Berkshire cultural calendar is the Jacob's Pillow Dance Festival, which first thrived as "Denishawn," a fabled alliance between founders Ruth St. Denis and Ted Shawn.

Lee is located 5 miles southeast of Lenox. In summer and early fall, the **Lee Chamber of Commerce** (ℂ 413/243-0852; www.leechamber.org) operates an information center on the town common, Route 20 (ℂ 413/243-4929). It can help you find lodging, often in guest houses and B&Bs—rarely as grand as those in neighboring Lenox, but nearly always significantly cheaper. That's something to remember when every other place near Tanglewood is either booked or quoting prices of $200 a night.

The Jacob's Pillow Dance Festival ★★★   In 1931, Ted Shawn and Ruth St. Denis decided to put on a show in the barn, and so was born Jacob's Pillow. After decades of advance and retreat and evolution, Jacob's Pillow is now to dance what Tanglewood is to classical music. Once a regular summer venue for Shawn and famed dancer and choreographer Martha Graham, one of his early disciples, the theater has long welcomed troupes of international reputation, including of late the Mark Morris Dance Group, the Trisha Brown Company, and the Paul Taylor Dance Company.

The more prominent companies are seen in the main Ted Shawn Theatre, while other troupes are assigned to the Doris Duke Studio Theatre, where tickets are cheaper. Admission is free to the Simon Performance Space, an outdoor stage. The growing campus includes a store, a pub, a dining room, a tent restaurant, and exhibition space. Picnic lunches can be pre-ordered 24 hours in advance and picked up at the Pub.

The season runs from late June to late August, and tickets go on sale May 1 (the summer's program is usually announced by February; call the number below to request a schedule by mail). Tickets are usually readily available, unless the performance in question is a big-name event, or you've decided to go at the last minute. They can be ordered any time at www.jacobspillow.org.

P.O. Box 287, George Carter Rd., Becket. ©413/243-0745. www.jacobspillow.org. Tickets $20–$50. From Lee, take Route 20 east about 5 miles, then turn north on Route 8 toward Becket.

Santarella ★   With no obligatory historic homes or museums to see, visitors often make the short excursion to an odd fairy-tale structure called Santarella, but known by most as the "Gingerbread House." At the front wall are jagged limestone outcroppings, conical turrets top towers, and the shingled roof rolls like waves on the ocean. Erected at the turn of the 20th century, it served as a studio for sculptor Henry Hudson Kitson from 1930 to 1947. It now houses galleries showcasing the works of Berkshire artists.

Tyringham Rd. © 413/243-3260. May–Oct daily 10am–4:30pm. Admission $3.75 adults, free for children. Take Rte. 20 south from Lee to Rte. 102, near the no. 2 interchange of the Massachusetts Tpk. Following the signs through the complicated intersection, pick up Tyringham Rd. on the other side and drive south about 4 miles.

OUTDOOR PURSUITS

October Mountain State Forest offers 50 campsites (with showers) and more than 16,000 acres for hiking and walking, canoeing and other nonmotorized boating, cross-country skiing, and snowmobiling. To get here, drive northwest on Route 20 into town, turn right on Center Street, and follow the signs.

WHERE TO STAY

A lakeside motel on the road to Lenox, the **Best Western Black Swan,** 435 Laurel St. (Rte. 20) (© 413/243-2700; fax 413/243-2700; www.travelweb.com), has a pool and restaurant; some rooms have fireplaces.

Applegate ★   This B&B utilizes a gracious 1920s Georgian colonial manse to full advantage. The top unit has a canopied bed, Queen Anne reproductions, sunlight filtering through gauzy curtains, a steam shower, and a fireplace (with real wood). Four additional units are under construction; each will have a TV, whirlpool, and gas fireplace. The sun porch contains a large TV with VCR. Breakfast is by candlelight, and the innkeepers set out wine and cheese in the afternoon.

279 W. Park St., Lee, MA 01238. © 800/691-9012 or 413/243-4451. www.applegateinn.com. 8 units. June–Oct $125–$260 double; Nov–May $95–$225. MC, V. From Stockbridge, drive north on Rte. 7 about

½ mile; take a right on Lee Rd. The inn is 2¼ miles ahead. No children under 12 accepted. **Amenities:** Outdoor pool; 9-hole golf course across the street; bikes. *In room:* A/C, no phone.

Chambéry Inn ⭑   This was the Berkshires' first parochial school (1885), named for the French hometown of the nuns who ran it. That accounts for the extra-large bedrooms, which were formerly classrooms. Seven of them, with 13-foot ceilings and the original woodwork and blackboards, are equipped with whirlpool baths and gas fireplaces. A breakfast tray is delivered to your door each morning.

199 Main St., Lee, MA 01238. © 413/243-2221. Fax 413/243-0039. www.berkshireinns.com. 9 units. July–Aug and Oct $99–$160 double, $135–$259 suite; Sept and last 2 weeks in June $85–$220 double, $129–$195 suite; Nov to mid-June $85–$220 double, $119–$179 suite. Rates include breakfast. AE, DISC, MC, V. No children under 18 accepted. **Amenities:** Limited room service from the neighboring restaurant. *In room:* A/C, TV, coffeemaker, hair dryer.

Federal House ⭑   Built in 1824 in the Federal style, including a portico with fluted columns, this distinguished inn still sports antiques belonging to the original family in its bedrooms, which are perfectly nice if pricey. Four have TVs. The Federal House made a name for itself with sumptuous "event" and holiday meals. Both dining rooms have fireplaces. The food is complemented by an impressive wine cellar.

Main St. (Rte. 102), South Lee, MA 01260. © 800/243-1824 or 413/243-1824. www.berkshireweb.com. 10 units. July–Aug and Oct $145–$225 double; Sept and Nov–May $100–$155 double. Rates include breakfast. AE, MC, V. Children over 12 welcome. **Amenities:** Restaurant (contemporary French). *In room:* A/C.

WHERE TO DINE

Another dining option is the restaurant at the **Federal House** (see above).

Salmon Run SEAFOOD/AMERICAN   The sign from the 1940s restaurant this used to be still hangs from the outside wall, and apart from a few requisite nautical touches, the inside rooms still look pretty much as they must have back then. Never mind. The owner has geared this to the local family trade, not tourists. The area abounds with more ambitious restaurants, but if you hanker for a fairly priced lunch of lobster bisque and an honest sandwich overflowing with fried whole clams, you aren't likely to do better this far from the Atlantic.

78 Main St. © 413/343-3900. Main courses $7.95–$17.95. AE, DC, MC, V. Sun–Thurs 11am–9pm; Fri–Sat 11am–10pm.

LENOX ⭑⭑ & TANGLEWOOD

Stately homes and fabulous mansions mushroomed in this former agricultural settlement from the 1890s until 1913, when the 16th Amendment, authorizing income taxes, put a severe crimp in that impulse. But Lenox remains a repository of extravagant domestic architecture surpassed only in such fabled resorts of the wealthy as Newport and Palm Beach. And since many of the cottages have been converted into inns and hotels, it is possible to get inside some of these beautiful buildings, if only for a cocktail or a meal.

The reason for so many lodgings in a town with a population of barely 5,000 is Tanglewood, a nearby estate where a series of concerts by the Boston Symphony Orchestra are held every summer. While the performances of the BSO are the big draw, there are also solo recitals, chamber concerts, and appearances by the young musicians who study at the prestigious Tanglewood Music Center.

Lenox lies 7 miles south of Pittsfield. The **Lenox Chamber of Commerce** (© 413/637-3646; www.lenox.org) provides visitor information.

Tanglewood Music Festival ★★★   Lenox is filled with music every summer, and the undisputed headliners are the Boston Symphony Orchestra. Concerts are given at the famous Tanglewood estate, usually beginning the first weekend in July and ending the weekend before Labor Day. The estate is on West Street (actually in Stockbridge township, although it's always associated with Lenox). From Lenox, take Route 183 1½ miles southwest of town.

While the BSO is Tanglewood's 800-pound cultural gorilla, the program features a menagerie of other performers and musical idioms. These run the gamut from popular artists (past performers have included James Taylor and Bonnie Raitt) and jazz vocalists and combos (including Dave Brubeck and Wynton Marsalis) to such guest soloists as Itzhak Perlman and Yo-Yo Ma.

The Koussevitzky Music Shed is an open-ended auditorium that seats 5,000, supplemented by a surrounding lawn where an outdoor audience lounges on folding chairs and blankets. This is the venue for orchestral and other large concerts. Chamber groups and solo performers appear in the smaller Ozawa Hall. Major performances are on Friday and Saturday nights and Sunday afternoon.

Tentative programs are available after the New Year; the summer schedule is usually locked in by March. *Note:* Tickets, especially to the most popular performances, can sell out quickly, so it's a good idea to get yours as far in advance as possible. If you do decide to go at the last minute, take a blanket or lawn chair and get tickets for the lawn, which are almost always available. You can also attend open rehearsals during the week, as well as the rehearsal for the Sunday concert on Saturday morning.

The estate itself (✆ **413/637-5165** June–Aug), with more than 500 acres of manicured lawns and gardens, much of it overlooking the lake called Stockbridge Bowl, was put together starting in 1849 by William Aspinwall Tappan. Admission to the grounds is free when concerts aren't scheduled.

In 1851, a structure on the property called the Little Red Shanty was rented to Nathaniel Hawthorne, who stayed here long enough to write a children's book, *Tanglewood Tales,* and meet Herman Melville, who lived in nearby Dalton and became a close friend. The existing Hawthorne Cottage is a replica (and isn't open to the public). On the grounds is the original Tappan mansion, with fine views.

West St., Stockbridge. For recorded information on concert programs, call ✆ 617/266-1492 from Sept–June 10 (note that information about coming Tanglewood concerts is not available until the program is announced in Mar or Apr). www.bso.org (tentative program info available after Jan 1). Tickets $14–$85 Shed and Ozawa Hall, $13–$16 lawn. Lawn tickets for children under 12 are free; children under 5 not allowed in the Shed or Ozawa Hall. Higher prices apply for some special appearances. To order tickets by mail before June, write the Tanglewood Ticket Office at Symphony Hall, Boston, MA 02115. After June 1, write the Tanglewood Ticket Office, Lenox, MA 01240. Tickets can be charged to a credit card through **Symphony Charge** (✆ 888/266-1200 outside Boston, or ✆ 617/266-1200) or at www.bso.org.

The Mount, Edith Wharton Restoration ★   Wharton, who won a Pulitzer for her novel *The Age of Innocence,* was singularly equipped to write that deftly detailed examination of the upper classes of the Gilded Age and the first decades of this century. She was born into that stratum of society in 1862 and traveled in the circles that made the Berkshires a regular stop on their restless movements between New York, Florida, Newport, and the Continent. Wharton had her villa built on this 130-acre lakeside property in 1902 and lived here 10 years before leaving for France, never to return. She took an active hand in the creation of the Mount; the mansion is a notable rarity—one of the few designated

National Historic Landmarks designed by a woman. Wharton was, after all, the author of an upscale 1897 how-to guide called *The Decoration of Houses.* A $15-million restoration campaign is under way, with work so far completed on the exterior terrace and greenhouse and continuing on the interior and extensive gardens.

2 Plunkett St. (at the intersection of Rtes. 7 and 7A). © 413/637-1899. www.edithwharton.org. Guided tours given Memorial Day to Oct daily 9am–5pm. Admission $6 adults, $5.50 seniors, $4.50 children 13–18, free for children under 13.

Shakespeare & Company ✪   The repertory company has long used buildings and outdoor amphitheaters on the grounds of the Mount (see above) to stage its May-to-October season of plays by the Bard, works by Edith Wharton and George Bernard Shaw, and efforts by new American playwrights. After increasingly bitter conflict with the custodians of the Wharton property relating to the restoration project described above, officials of the company have made an offer to purchase the National Music Foundation on Kemble Street. This is expected to take place in a series of staggered moves up until 2003, when the lease at the Mount expires. In the meantime, performances take place Tuesday through Sunday (weekends only after Labor Day), usually at 3, 5, or 8pm. Tickets are generally easy to get. The summer schedule is announced by February or March. Lunch and dinner picnic baskets can be purchased on site.

Plunkett St. © 413/637-3353. www.shakespeare.org. Tickets $14.50–$33.50.

Frelinghuysen Morris House & Studio ✪   Built on 46 acres of land next to the Tanglewood property in the early 1940s, this Bauhaus-influenced house was the home of abstract artists Suzy Frelinghuysen and George L. K. Morris. Their chosen style was Cubism, which they persisted in pursuing long after it had been abandoned by better-known practitioners. Works by some of those artists—Braque, Léger, Gris, and Picasso—can be viewed alongside the canvases of the owners. On the grounds is a monumental sculpture by Gaston Lachaise. Visits are by tour only.

92 Hawthorne St. © 413/637-0166. Admission $8 adults, $3 children 5–16. July 4–Labor Day Thurs–Sun 10am–4pm; Sept–Oct Thurs–Sat 10am–4pm. Drive south from Tanglewood on Rte. 183, turn left on Hawthorne Rd., then left again on Hawthorne St. (note 2 different streets).

OUTDOOR PURSUITS

Pleasant Valley Wildlife Sanctuary, 472 West Mountain Rd. (© **413/637-0320**), has a small museum and 7 miles of hiking and snowshoeing trails crossing its 1,500 acres. Beaver lodges and dams can be glimpsed from a distance, and waterfowl and other birds are found in abundance—bring binoculars. Hours are Tuesday through Sunday from dawn to sunset; admission is $3 for adults and $2 for children 3 to 15. To get here, drive north 6.6 miles on Routes 7 and 20 and turn left on West Dugway Road.

In town, **Main Street Sports & Leisure,** 48 Main St. (© **413/637-4407**), rents bicycles, canoes, skates, snowshoes, cross-country skis, tennis rackets, and related equipment. The staff can recommend routes and trails, give you preprinted driving directions to area state parks and forests, and arrange guided trips. **Kennedy Park,** right down the street from the store, is a favorite spot for cross-country skiing in winter, or for a ramble in any season. Dogs are allowed off-leash throughout the 12 miles of trails.

More extensive hiking trails can be found at **October Mountain State Forest** (see "Outdoor Pursuits" under the section on Lee, above) or at **Beartown**

State Forest, in nearby Monterey. The Appalachian Trail, which runs from Maine to Georgia, connects with a loop trail around a small pond with a nice swimming area. To get here, take Route 7 South for 3½ miles, then turn left onto West Road. After 2½ miles, turn left at the T intersection onto Route 102 East. Turn right over the bridge onto Meadow Street, then turn right onto Pine Street and follow the signs from there.

WHERE TO STAY

The list of lodgings below is only partial, and most can accommodate only small numbers. The Tanglewood concert season is a powerful draw, so prices are highest in summer as well as the brief fall foliage season. Rates are of Byzantine complexity, set according to wildly varying combinations of seasons and days of the week as well as facilities offered. Minimum 2- or 3-night stays are usually required during the Tanglewood weeks, foliage, and holidays. *Note:* For visits during the Tanglewood concert season, reserve far in advance—February isn't too soon.

Given the substantial number of lodgings and limited space to describe them, admittedly arbitrary judgments have been made to winnow the list. Some inns, for example, are so rule-ridden and facility-free they come off as crabby—no kids, no pets, no phones, no TV, no credit cards, no breakfast before 9am, shared bathrooms—and they cost twice as much as nearby motels that have all those conveniences. Let them seek clients elsewhere.

Others are open only 6 or 7 months a year and charge the world for a bed or a meal. In this latter category, though, one place demands at least a mention: **Blantyre,** 16 Blantyre Rd. (© 413/637-3556 in summer, 413/298-3806 in winter), in its 1902 Tudor-Norman mansion, cossets its guests with a soak in undeniable luxury, both in dining room and bedchamber.

If all the area's inns are booked or if you want to be assured the full quota of 21st-century conveniences, Routes 7 and 20 north and south of town harbor a number of motels, including the **Mayflower Motor Inn** (© **413/443-4468**), the **Susse Chalet** (© **413/637-3560**), the **Lenox Motel** (© **413/499-0324**), and the **Comfort Inn** (© **413/443-4714**).

Very Expensive

Canyon Ranch in the Berkshires ✦✦✦   Resorts successfully melding turn-of-the-last-century opulence and contemporary impulses for fitness and healthy living are rare, so for those with the discretionary income or others who'd like to splurge just once, this is the place. A guard turns away the unconfirmed at the gate, so there's no popping in for a look around. The core facility is the 1897 mansion modeled after Le Petit Trianon at Versailles. A fire in 1949 left only the magnificent library untouched, but that loss has been offset by major renovations. Sweat away the pounds in the huge spa complex, with 40 exercise classes a day, weights, an indoor track, racquetball, squash, and all the equipment you might want. Canoeing and hiking are added possibilities. Guest rooms are in contemporary New England style, with all the hotel conveniences except tempting minibars. After being steamed, exhausted, pummeled, and showered, the real events of each day are mealtimes: "nutritionally balanced gourmet," naturally.

165 Kemble St., Lenox, MA 01240. © **800/726-9900** or 413/637-4100. Fax 413/637-0057. www.canyonranch. com. 127 units. All-inclusive 3-night packages from $1,030–$2,045 double; 7-night packages $3,275–$3,909 double. Rates include all meals and allowances of $105–$210 for health, beauty, and fitness services. Taxes and 18% service charge extra. AE, DISC, MC, V. **Amenities:** Restaurant (spa cuisine); heated indoor and outdoor pools; tennis courts; health club and spa; bicycles, massage. *In room:* A/C, TV/VCR, hair dryer.

Cranwell Resort & Golf Club ★★★ The main building of this all-season resort looks like a castle in the Scottish Highlands, but no 17th-century laird lived this well. It stands at the center of a 380-acre resort, ringed by views of the surrounding hills. That's where the most expensive rooms are; the rest are in four smaller outlying buildings. Accommodations are outfitted with less concern for adherence to a particular style than for surrounding guests in immediate comfort. In addition to the lovely grounds (which serve as cross-country ski trails in winter), there is a 60-acre golf school. Three dining rooms range from formal to pubby, and live jazz is featured Friday and Saturday nights. Construction of a 35,000-square-foot spa with pool should be complete by the time of your visit.

55 Lee Rd. (Rte. 183), Lenox, MA 01240. ℂ **800/272-6935** or 413/637-1364. Fax 413/637-4364. www. cranwell.com. 107 units. July–Aug $209–$459 double; Sept–Oct $209–$459; Nov–Apr $99–$239. Golf and ski packages available. AE, DC, DISC, MC, V. From Lenox Center, go north to Rte. 20 E. The resort is on the left. **Amenities:** 3 restaurants (eclectic); bar; heated outdoor pool; golf course; 2 tennis courts; extensive new health club. *In room:* A/C, TV, dataport, fridge, coffeemaker, hair dryer, iron.

Wheatleigh ★★ Glamorous young New Yorkers and Europeans drape themselves in Gatsbyesque poses around the lavishly appointed great hall. Much of the time, they look elaborately bored, no easy feat in this persuasive 1893 replica of a 16th-century Tuscan palazzo, which aspires to the highest standards of the moneyed Berkshires. Wheatleigh has always been very expensive, even though the cheapest rooms average only 11 by 13 feet. But other places are catching up, and the manager is striving to give requisite value. The dining room rounds out the experience, with painstakingly conceived food in superb presentation.

Hawthorne Rd., Lenox, MA 01240. ℂ **413/637-0610.** Fax 413/637-4507. www.wheatleigh.com. 19 units. $215–$725 double. AE, DC, MC, V. **Amenities:** Restaurant, lounge; heated outdoor pool; tennis court; exercise room; bike rental; concierge; in-room massage; baby-sitting; laundry service; dry cleaning service. *In room:* A/C, TV/VCR, fax, hair dryer.

Expensive

Cliffwood Inn ★ One of the relatively compact manses of the Vanderbilt era, this inn has a long veranda in back overlooking the outdoor pool. Antiques and convincing reproductions of many styles and periods fill the common and private spaces. Six of the seven guest rooms have working fireplaces (including one in a bathroom!). Only two units have TVs.

25 Cliffwood St., Lenox, MA 01240. ℂ **800/789-3331** or 413/637-3330. Fax 413/637-0221. www. cliffwood.com. 7 units. July to Labor Day and foliage season $146–$240 double; May 15–June 30 and Sept after Labor Day $123–$182; Nov–May 14 $100–$146. Rates include breakfast daily in high season, Sat–Sun only in shoulder season, Sun and holiday weekends only in low season. No credit cards. Children over 10 welcome. **Amenities:** Outdoor pool and indoor counter-current workout pool; whirlpool. *In room:* A/C.

Gateways Inn ★★ Harley Procter, who hitched up with a man called Gamble and made a bundle, had this house built in 1912. Its most impressive feature is the staircase that winds down into the lobby. Designed by McKim, Mead & White, it's a stunner, just the thing for a grand entrance. Equally impressive is the suite named for conductor Arthur Fiedler, with not one but two fireplaces, a big four-poster on the sun porch, and a Jacuzzi. Eight rooms now have working fireplaces. Dining here is one of Lenox's greater pleasures, especially since a new chef came on board. The tiny bar is being expanded and a terrace added for after-concert light meals and desserts.

51 Walker St., Lenox, MA 01240. ℂ **800/492-9466** or 413/637-2532. Fax 413/637-1432. www. gatewaysinn.com. 11 units. June–Oct $120–$260 double, $275–$400 suite; Nov–May $100–$180 double, $230–$320 suite. Rates include breakfast. AE, DC, DISC, MC, V. Children over 12 accepted. **Amenities:** Restaurant, bar. *In room:* A/C, TV.

Whistler's Inn   Both innkeepers are compulsive travelers who bring things back from every trip, filling the cavernous rooms of their Tudor mansion with cut glass, painted screens, assorted Victoriana, grandfather clocks, Persian rugs, and shelf after shelf of books. The result: rooms that are not so much decorated as gathered, without a single boring corner. Most have TVs, some have fireplaces. A carriage house, open in summer, has one room decked in African style, the other suggesting Santa Fe. Breakfast is suitably proportioned, and a bottle of sherry or port is kept in the library for guests to enjoy along with tea and cookies. Facilities for children are limited.

5 Greenwood St., Lenox, MA 01240. ✆ 413/637-0975. Fax 413/637-2190. www.whistlersinnlenox.com. 14 units. June 16–Oct $130–$275 double; Nov–June 15 $100–$200. Rates include breakfast. AE, DISC, MC, V. *In room:* A/C, TV.

Moderate

Note that **Amadeus,** long recommended here, has closed.

Brook Farm Inn   "There is poetry here," insist the owners of this picture-pretty 1870 farmhouse, and an afternoon idle in the hammock overlooking the pool or a curled-up read by the fireplace will have you agreeing. Six rooms have wood-burning fireplaces. Breakfast is an ample buffet.

15 Hawthorne St., Lenox, MA 01240. ✆ 800/285-7638 or 413/637-3013. Fax 413/637-4751. www. brookfarm.com. 12 units. July to Labor Day $140–$215 double; Labor Day to Oct $100–$170; Nov–June $105–$150. Rates include breakfast and afternoon tea. MC, V. From the town center, go south 1 block on Old Stockbridge Rd. Turn right. No children under 15 accepted. **Amenities:** Outdoor pool. *In room:* A/C.

Candlelight Inn   A folksy gathering place for locals as well as guests, the bar in this 1885 Victorian enjoys a convivial nightly trade, and the dining rooms are often full. In winter, sit beside a crackling fire; in summer, lunch out in the courtyard. While the Candlelight does most of its business on the restaurant side, the upstairs rooms are homey and unpretentious.

35 Walker St., Lenox, MA 01240. ✆ 800/428-0580 or 413/637-1555. www.candlelightinn-lenox.com. 8 units. $69–$189 double. Rates include breakfast. AE, DISC, MC, V. Often closed for a week or so in Jan. No children under 10 accepted. *In room:* A/C, no phone.

Gables Inn ★★   Edith Wharton, who spent more than two decades in Lenox, made this Queen Anne mansion her home for 2 years while her house, The Mount, was being built. That may be enough to interest fans of the novelist, but there's much more to appeal to potential guests, including the canopied four-poster in Edith's bedroom. Meticulously maintained Victoriana and related antiques are found in every corner. Many rooms have wood-burning fireplaces, and suites have VCRs and fridges.

81 Walker St., Lenox, MA 01240. ✆ 800/382-9401 or 413/637-3416. Fax 413/637-3416. www.gableslenox.com. 19 units. $90–$200 double; $160–$250 suite. Rates include breakfast. DISC, MC, V. No children under 12 accepted. **Amenities:** Heated indoor pool, tennis court. *In room:* A/C, TV.

Village Inn   An inn off and on since 1775, this place hasn't a whiff of pretense. Its large number of rooms come in considerable variety and are categorized as Deluxe, Superior, Standard, or Economy. That means four-posters in the high-end rooms, some of which have fireplaces and/or whirlpool baths, and constricted quarters with double beds at the lower prices. Claw-foot tubs are common in rooms in all categories. Ask about rooms on the renovated third floor. Afternoon tea and dinner are served in the restaurant, light meals in the tavern (where smoking is allowed).

16 Church St., Lenox, MA 01240. © **800/253-0917** or 413/637-0020. Fax 413/637-9756. www.villageinn-lenox.com. 32 units. Summer–fall $115–$235 double, $375–$455 suite; winter–spring $65–$185 double, $255–$295 suite. Discount of 30% applies during midweek in winter/spring. AE, DC, DISC, MC, V. No children under 6 accepted. **Amenities:** Restaurant, bar; free video library. *In room:* A/C, TV/VCR.

WHERE TO DINE

See also "Where to Stay," above, since many inns have dining rooms. In particular, **Blantyre** (© **413/637-3556**) is worth a splurge. In high season, **Spigalina,** 80 Main St. (© **413/637-4455**), serves imaginative Mediterranean cooking. Note that three of the restaurants listed below serve lunch, in a region where most restaurants don't open until evening.

Café Lucia ★★ REGIONAL ITALIAN   Here on Lenox's Restaurant Row, the post-preppie crowd of regulars and weekend refugees from the city is attired in country-casual cashmere and tweed, a taste no doubt honed at campuses of the Ivy League and Seven Sisters. The waitresses display a professionalism rarely experienced in these hills, bringing satisfying, if commonplace, starters—carpaccio, bruschetta, and the like—followed by superior renditions of *saltimbocca alla Romana* and eight pastas. The house specialty is *osso buco con risotto,* although northern Italy is not the only inspiration here. Dine out on the broad deck in warmer months.

80 Church St. © 413/637-2640. Reservations recommended. Main courses $19–$32. AE, DC, DISC, MC, V. Tues–Sun 5:30–10pm. Closed 3 weeks Mar or Apr. Winter hours fluctuate, especially around holiday weekends; call ahead.

Church Street Cafe ★★ ECLECTIC AMERICAN   The most popular place in town delivers fanciful combinations that please the eye and pique the taste buds. Creative appearances on the menu include a pizza topped with lobster and mascarpone drizzled with white truffle oil, and a dinner plate of grilled miso-marinated salmon on Asian eggplant with braised greens and scallion rice. A large deck fills up whenever the weather allows.

65 Church St. © 413/637-2745. Reservations recommended on weekends. Main courses $17.50–$28.50. MC, V. May–Oct daily 11:30am–2pm and 5:30–9pm. Nov–Apr Tues–Sat 11:30am–2pm and 5:30–9pm.

Roseborough Grill ★ AMERICAN/GLOBAL   Inside the rambling old farmhouse are plain wooden tables and chairs unadorned at lunch but dressed with linen and candles at night. Serious jazz drifts out of the stereo, and often-surprising food issues from the kitchen. Past dishes have included grilled mahi-mahi in a Moroccan pesto fish broth, Thai shrimp linguine, and Asian short ribs, all of which demonstrate that the co-chefs gambol in many scented fields, usually emerging with dignity intact.

71 Church St. © 413/637-2700. Main courses $16.95–$26. AE, DC, DISC, MC, V. Thurs–Mon 11:30am–3pm and 5–9pm (until 10pm Fri–Sat). Call ahead in winter.

Zinc ★★ CONTEMPORARY BISTRO   With its eponymous zinc bar, butcher paper over white tablecloths, mirrored walls, tile floor, and waitresses in ankle-length aprons, this new entry leaps to the upper echelon of Berkshires dining. That is, if you admire not only the setting but also a cuisine and wine list that adhere with some rigor to the French bistro canon. The menu lists such appetizers as roasted boneless quail stuffed with polenta and continues with steak frites and seared tuna with braised bok choy. A remarkable 24 wines are available by the glass, some of the most refreshing hailing from the Loire Valley. Apart from the disappointingly ordinary cheese plate, a meal here is as satisfying as can be found in these parts.

56 Church St. © **413/637-8800.** Reservations suggested. Main courses $16–$21. AE, MC, V. Wed–Mon 11:30am–3pm and 5:30–10pm (bar until 12:30am).

SHOPPING

The Bookstore, 9 Housatonic St. (© **413/637-3390**), helps fill a yawning need in the Berkshires, which are curiously lacking in comprehensive bookstores. Those in pursuit of art and antiques, on the other hand, cannot easily exhaust the possibilities. Among them: **La Vie en Rose,** 67 Church St. (© **413/637-3663**), known for its hand-painted furniture and vintage jewelry; the **Ella Lerner Gallery,** 17 Franklin St. (© **413/637-3315**), which specializes in European and American painters of the 19th and 20th centuries; and the **Hoadley Gallery,** 21 Church St. (© **413/637-2814**), which shows American crafts and ceramics. Out on Route 7, heading toward Pittsfield, serious cooks should watch for **The Cook's Resource,** 374 Pittsfield Rd. (© **413/637-0606**).

PITTSFIELD

Berkshire County's largest city (pop. 48,000) gets little attention in most tourist literature, and for good reason. A commercial and industrial center, it presents little of the charm that marks such popular destinations as Stockbridge and Lenox. Still, it is a convenient base for day excursions to attractions elsewhere in the region, including several ski centers, Tanglewood, and Hancock Shaker Village, a few miles to the west. In summer, the Pittsfield Mets play minor-league baseball at Wahconah Park, a 1919 stadium with real wooden box seats. Pittsfield is also home to the house where Herman Melville wrote *Moby Dick.*

The **Berkshire Visitors Bureau** (© **800/237-5747** or 413/443-9186; www.berkshires.org) is located in the same block of buildings as the Crowne Plaza Hotel, on Berkshire Common. Pittsfield lies 137 miles west of Boston, 7 miles north of Lenox.

SEEING THE SIGHTS

Arrowhead   Herman Melville bought this 18th-century house in 1850 and lived here until 1863. It was during this time that he wrote his masterpiece, *Moby Dick.* In truth, however, the house is of limited interest to visitors other than literature students and avid readers. In celebration of the 150th anniversary of publication of *Moby Dick,* there are continuing special exhibits and programs in 2001.

780 Holmes Rd. © **413/442-1793.** www.mobydick.org. Admission $5 adults, $4.50 seniors, $3 ages 16–25, $1 children 6–15. From Fri before Memorial Day to Oct 31 daily 9:30am–5pm, rest of year by appointment only. Visits are by guided tour only, given on the hour starting at 10am and ending at 4pm. Drive east from Park Sq. on East St., turn right on Elm St., and turn right on Holmes Rd.

Berkshire Museum ✦   It began in 1903 as the "Museum of Natural History and Art," words chiseled in stone above the entrance. The holdings bounce from Babylonian cuneiform tablets to stuffed birds to tanks of live fish in the basement aquarium. An auditorium seating 300 serves as the "Little Cinema," which has a season of art and foreign films during the warmer months. Apart from the aquarium, the greatest interest may be generated by the art and archaeological artifacts assembled on the second floor, including a delicate necklace from Thebes dating to at least 1500 B.C.

39 South St. (Rte. 7, 1 block south of Park Sq.). © **413/443-7171.** www.berkshiremuseum.org. Admission $7 adults; $5 seniors, students, and Monday matinee; $4 children 3–18. Tues–Sat 10am–5pm; Sun noon–5pm (open daily July–Aug).

Movers & Shakers

Mother Ann arrived in 1774 with eight disciples just as the disgruntled American colonies were about to burst into open rebellion. The former Ann Lee, once imprisoned in England for her excess of religious zeal, had anointed herself leader of the United Society of Believers in Christ's Second Coming. The austere Protestant sect was dedicated to simplicity, equality, and celibacy. They were popularly known as "the Shakers" for their spastic movements when in the throes of religious ecstasy. By the time of her death in 1784, Mother Lee had made many converts, who then fanned out across the country to form communal settlements from Maine to Indiana. One of the most important Shaker communities, Hancock, edged the Massachusetts–New York border, near Pittsfield.

Shaker society produced dedicated, highly disciplined farmers and craftspeople whose products were much in demand in the outside world. They sold seeds, invented early agricultural machinery and hand tools, and erected large buildings of several stories and exquisite simplicity. Their spare, clean-lined furniture and accessories anticipated the so-called Danish Modern style by a century and in recent years have drawn astonishingly high prices at auction.

All of these accomplishments required a verve owed at least in part to sublimation of sexual energy, for a fundamental Shaker tenet was total celibacy for its adherents. They kept going with converts and adoption of orphans (who were free to leave, if they wished). But by the 1970s, the inevitable result of this policy left the movement with a bare handful of believers. The string of Shaker settlements and museums that remain is testament to their dictum, "Hands to work, hearts to God."

Hancock Shaker Village ★★★   Of the 20 restored buildings that make up the village, its signature structure is easily the 1826 round stone barn. The Shaker preoccupation with functionalism joined with purity of line and respect for materials has never been clearer than it is in the design of this building—its round shape expedited the chores of feeding and milking livestock by arranging cows in a circle, and the precise joinery of the roof beams and support pillars is a joy to observe.

The second must-see is the brick dwelling that contained the communal dining room, kitchens, and upstairs sleeping quarters. Sexes were separated at meals, work, and religious services, and such features as the opposing staircases leading to male and female "retiring rooms" served equality.

While artisans and docents labor in gardens and in shops demonstrating Shaker crafts and techniques, they are not in costume, nor do they pretend to be Shaker inhabitants. They are knowledgeable about their subject, though, and dispense such nuggets as explanations of the Shaker discipline that required members to dress the right side first, to button from right to left, and to step with the right foot first.

The museum shop is excellent, and a cafe serves lunches in summer and fall, with some dishes based on Shaker recipes. On Saturday nights July through

October, the village presents tours and Shaker four-course dinners by candle-light at a cost of about $40. Reservations for these are essential.

Rtes. 20 and 41, Pittsfield. ℭ 800/817-1137 or 413/443-0188. www.hanckshakervillage.org. Admission Memorial Day to late Oct $13.50 adults, $5.50 children 6–17, $33 per family (two adults and children under 18); rest of year (by guided tour only) $10 adults, $5 children 6–17, $25 per family. Memorial Day to late Oct daily 9:30am–5pm; rest of year daily 10am–3pm (tours on the hour). Call ahead in winter for hours and events.

OUTDOOR PURSUITS
Plaine's Bike, Ski, Snowboard, 55 W. Housatonic St. (ℭ **413/499-0294**), rents bikes and carries equipment for all the sports its name suggests. It's on Route 20, west of downtown, at the corner of Center Street.

A prime recreational preserve is **Pittsfield State Forest,** entered on Cascade Street (ℭ **413/442-8992**), a little over 3 miles west of the center of town. Its 10,000 acres have 31 campsites, boat ramps, streams for canoeing and fishing, and trails for hiking, horseback riding, and cross-country skiing. It's open daily from 8am to 8pm. Admission is $2 per car.

BOATING   Onota Boat Livery, 463 Pecks Rd. (ℭ **413/442-1724**), rents canoes and motorboats for use on Onota Lake, conveniently located at the western edge of the city.

SKIING   South of the city center, off Route 7 near the Pittsfield city limits, is the **Bousquet Ski Area,** Dan Fox Drive (ℭ **413/442-8316** business office, 413/442-2436 snow phone; www.bousquets.com). Bousquet (pronounced "Bos-kay") has 21 trails, with a vertical drop of 750 feet, two double lifts and two rope tows. Night skiing is available Monday through Saturday. Rentals and lessons are available. Lift tickets cost $25.

About 10 miles north of Pittsfield on Route 7, in the town of New Ashford, is **Brodie Mountain Ski Area** (ℭ **413/443-4752;** www.skibrodie.com), with a vertical drop of 1,250 feet. Night skiing is available, and in summer the ski area offers racquetball, tennis, 150 campsites, and a heated pool. Lift tickets are $24 to $39 for adults, $20 to $30 for seniors and juniors.

Alternatively, turn west a mile short of Brodie Mountain on Brodie Mountain Road and continue about 2 miles to **Jiminy Peak** ✦, Hancock (ℭ **413/738-5500,** or 413/738-7325 for ski reports). This expanding resort aspires to four-season activity, so skiing on 28 trails (18 open at night) with seven lifts is supplemented the rest of the year by horseback riding, trapshooting, fishing in a stocked pond, six tennis courts, mountain biking, pools, and golf at the nearby Waubeeka Springs course.

WHERE TO STAY
The Country Inn at Jiminy Peak ✦   This is one of the better lodging deals in the Berkshires, if your idea of luxury is space. All units are one-bedroom suites with full kitchens and pullout sofas, suitable for families. The furnishings are a bit worn, and guests could probably live without the constant reminders that they, too, "could be part of the Jiminy Peak family" by buying a condo. But these shortcomings pale beside the on-site downhill skiing and abundant recreational facilities (see "Outdoor Pursuits," above).

Brodie Mountain Rd. (near Rte. 43), Hancock, MA 01237. ℭ 800/882-8859 or 413/738-5500. Fax 413/738-5513. www.jiminypeak.com. 105 units. $150–$330 suite. Winter rates include lift tickets. AE, DC, DISC, MC, V. **Amenities:** Restaurant; bar; outdoor pool and indoor pool (both heated); six tennis courts; exercise room; whirlpool; sauna; children's programs; game room; baby-sitting; coin-op washers and dryers. *In room:* A/C, TV/VCR, kitchenette, coffeemaker.

WILLIAMSTOWN ★★ & NORTH ADAMS

This community and its prestigious liberal-arts college were both named for Col. Ephraim Williams, who was killed in 1755 in one of the French and Indian Wars. He bequeathed the land for creation of a school and a town. His college grew, spreading east from the central common along both sides of Main Street (Route 2). Over the town's 200-year history, buildings have been erected in several styles of the times. That makes Main Street a virtual museum of institutional architecture, with representatives of the Georgian, Federal, Gothic Revival, Romanesque, and Victorian modes and a few that are yet to be labeled. They stand at dignified distances from one another, so what might have been a tumultuous visual hodgepodge is a stately lesson in historical design. The impressive Clark Art Institute is the best reason to make a special trip, perhaps in conjunction with a performance at the increasingly ambitious Williamstown Theatre Festival.

A free weekly newspaper, the *Advocate,* produces useful guides to both the northern and southern Berkshires. For a copy, write to the *Advocate,* P.O. Box 95, 38 Spring St., Williamstown, MA 01267. An unattended **information booth** at the corner of North Street (Route 7) and Main Street (Route 2) has an abundance of pamphlets and brochures free for the taking.

ART MUSEUMS

Sterling and Francine Clark Art Institute ★★★   Within these walls are canvases by Renoir (34 of them), Degas, Gauguin, Toulouse-Lautrec, Pissarro, and their predecessor, Corot. Also on display is the famed Degas sculpture *Little Dancer,* believed to be his only three-dimensional piece and a signature work of the Institute. While they are the stars, there are also 15th- and 16th-century Dutch portraitists, English and European genre and landscape painters, and Americans Sargent and Homer, as well as fine porcelain, silverware, and antique furnishings. This qualifies as one of the great cultural resources of the Berkshires and the state.

Apart from the collection itself, Clark's farsighted endowment funded the modern wing added to the original neoclassical building and has covered all acquisitions, upkeep, and renovations. His stipulation that there be no admission fee was finally breached, but the charge applies only to adults, four months a year. A substantial bookstore in the lobby has been joined by a snack counter and an attractive cafe.

225 South St., Williamstown. ℂ **413/458-2303**. www.clarkart.edu. Admission July–Oct $5 adults, free for students and children under 18; free to all Tues and Nov–June. Sept–June Tues–Sun 10am–5pm; July–Aug daily 10am–5pm.

Massachusetts Museum of Contemporary Art ★   A lot of excitement and anticipation has surrounded this ambitious project, the conversion of an abandoned 27-building textile factory complex into a center for the visual and

---

Pittsfield on Stage

The **Berkshire Opera Company,** 297 North St. (ℂ **413/443-7400**), stages its July and August productions of both established and new operas at the Koussevitzky Arts Center of Berkshire Community College in Pittsfield. That venue is also employed by the **Albany Berkshire Ballet,** 51 North St. (ℂ **413/445-5382**), with up to 14 performances of two ballets from early July to mid-August.

performing arts. Even before its official opening, it had a nickname—MASS MoCA—and hosted performances by David Byrne, Patti Smith, and the Merce Cunningham Dance Company. Its creators and the residents of North Adams nurture fervent hopes that it will be an attraction to reverse the slide of the depressed mill town and enhance the tourist and commercial desirability of the northern Berkshires. While is too soon to tell whether those ambitions will be fulfilled, the museum has already attracted more than 140,000 visitors and is certainly worth the short detour east from neighboring Williamstown. Its chief virtue—from the standpoint of those contemporary artists who choose to work on a grand scale—is the vastness of the spaces available.

87 Marshall St., North Adams. (C) 413/662-2111. www.massmoca.org. Admission $8 adults, $3 children 6–16. Lower prices in winter. (A dual ticket for $15 includes admission to the Norman Rockwell Museum in Stockbridge.) Summer daily 10am–6pm; winter Wed–Mon 11am–5pm.

Williams College Museum of Art ★   The second leg of Williamstown's two prominent art repositories exists in large part thanks to the college's collection of almost 400 paintings by the American modernists Maurice and Charles Prendergast. The museum also has works by Juan Gris, Fernand Léger, James Whistler, Pablo Picasso, Andy Warhol, and Edward Hopper.

15 Lawrence Hall Dr., Williamstown. (C) 413/597-2429. www.williams.edu/WCMA. Free admission. Tues–Sat (and some Mon holidays) 10am–5pm; Sun 1–5pm.

OUTDOOR PURSUITS
Waubeeka Golf Links, Routes 7 and 43, South Williamstown ((C) **413/ 458-5869**), is open to the public, with weekend greens fees of $35.

   Mount Greylock State Reservation ★ contains the highest peak (3,487 feet) in Massachusetts as well as a section of the Appalachian Trail. A road allows cars almost to the summit, where War Memorial Tower affords vistas of the Taconic and Hoosac ranges, far into Vermont and New York. Trails radiate from the parking lot near **Bascom Lodge,** North Main Street off Route 7 in Lanesboro ((C) **413/743-1591** or 413/443-0011), a grandly rustic creation of the Civilian Conservation Corps in the New Deal 1930s. Simple dormitory beds and four private rooms are available for rent from mid-May to late October. Dinners are available by reservation.

SHOPPING
In the small downtown shopping district, **Library Antiques,** 70 Spring St. ((C) 413/458-3436), is filled with a wealth of English chess sets, African carvings, Peruvian alpaca sweaters, Turkish kilim, and antique American fishing lures and creels. South of the town center on Route 7, **Saddleback Antiques,** 1395 Cold Spring Rd. ((C) 413/458-5852), features country, wicker, and Victorian furniture and a variety of collectibles. Slightly north of town on Route 7, **Collectors Warehouse,** 105 North St. ((C) 413/458-9686), has a little bit of everything—jewelry, books, dolls, furniture, and glassware.

WHERE TO STAY
This is a college town, so in addition to the usual Berkshires peak periods of July, August, and the October foliage season, accommodations fill up during graduation and on football weekends. The largest lodging in town is the 100-unit **Williams Inn,** 1090 Main St. ((C) **800/828-0133** or 413/458-9371). Despite the name, it is a standard motel, containing a dining room, tavern, and indoor pool. Three miles south of town at Routes 2 and 7 is the brookside **Berkshire Hills Motel** ((C) 413/458-3950), with a heated pool.

Blackinton Manor 🏵🏵   Music informs this 1849 Greek Revival house, hardly surprising since one of the owner/managers is a classical pianist and his wife is an opera singer and invested cantor. They hold a number of chamber concerts at irregular intervals throughout the year, many of them to benefit favorite causes. They don't neglect their hospitality functions for a minute, be assured—this may be the most gracious of inn experiences in the northern Berkshires. Pass a pleasant evening before the living-room fire with a glass of sherry. All of the rooms are grandly furnished, but try to ask for the lavishly appointed ground-floor Music Room, spacious enough to contain its own piano. A typical breakfast consists of a fresh-fruit plate, an herbed omelet, and freshly baked pastries.

1391 Massachusetts Ave., North Adams, MA 01247. © **800/795-8613** or 413/663-5795. www.blackinton-manor.com. 5 units. $95–$125 double. Rates include breakfast. MC, V. Children over 7 welcome. Follow Rte. 2 east from Williamstown into North Adams, turn left on Ashton, and turn right after railroad bridge. **Amenities:** Unheated outdoor pool. *In room:* A/C, TV.

Field Farm Guesthouse 🏵   After an extended vacation of B&B hopping, there may come a time when one more tilted floor or wobbly Windsor chair will send even a devout inn-lover over the edge. Here's an antidote. This pristine example of postwar modern architecture rose in 1948 on a spectacularly scenic 296-acre estate, with 4 miles of trails. The living room is equipped with a telescope to view the beavers and waterfowl on the lake a hundred yards away. Most guest rooms look over meadows to Mount Greylock, most of the Scandinavian Modern furniture was made to order for the house, and three units have decks while two have fireplaces. Breakfasts are hearty meals of waffles and five-cheese omelets utilizing fruits, herbs, and vegetables grown on the property. Well-behaved children are welcome.

554 Sloan Rd., Williamstown, MA 01262. © and fax **413/458-3135**. www.thetrustees.org. 5 units. $100–$165 double. Rates include breakfast. DISC, MC, V. Follow Rte. 7 to Rte. 43 and turn west, then make an immediate right on Sloan Rd. Continue 1 mile to the Field Farm entrance, on the right. **Amenities:** Heated outdoor pool; tennis court. *In room:* Hair dryer.

WHERE TO DINE

Main Street Café 🏵 CREATIVE ITALIAN   This is a sparkling addition to the once largely woebegone local dining scene. The bar, more often used for eating than extended drinking, has a tasty menu of snacks. There are a variety of imaginative pizzas from the brick oven, plus special risottos and raviolis. Ten wines are available by the glass. Meals are served on the deck, beside the flourishing garden.

16 Water St. © **413/458-3210**. Main courses $16.95–$24.95. AE, DC, MC, V. Tues–Sat 11:30am–2:30pm; daily 5–10pm (until 11pm Fri–Sat).

Mezze 🏵🏵 GLOBAL   Mezze traffics in such elevated edibles as "pan-fried oysters with manchego cornmeal bisquit and guajillo aioli." All the menu descriptions go on like that, detailed but without hyperbole. A basket of warm rosemary bread is brought with a bowl of scented oil for dipping. About a third of the dishes are vegetarian, and most of the rest qualify as healthy—the napoleon of sashimi tuna and mizuna greens, for one. Weekends bring occasional live music of all genres, often for dancing. The place attracts hip gays, grad students in black, and young profs in tweed. A deck in back hangs over the Green River.

84 Water St. © **413/458-0123**. Main courses $16–$20. AE, DC, DISC, MC, V. Mon–Thurs 5:30–9:30pm (until 10:30pm Fri–Sat); Sun 10am–2pm and 5:30–9:30pm (bar until 1am Sun–Thurs, until 2am Fri–Sat). Closed last week in Sept.

Wild Amber Grill ⭐ ECLECTIC AMERICAN   Handy walking distance from the Williamstown Theatre Festival is one draw, dining on the porch another, live music some weekend nights yet another. The long low building has been reconfigured, so a pool table and burgers enforce the informal mood of one large room; more ambitious meals in the other appeal to gourmands. The French-trained chef executes twists on continental classics, as with the scallop and smoked mozzarella ravioli with pepper sauce and pesto.

101 North St. ℂ **413/458-4000.** Reservations suggested on weekends. Main courses $15–$33. AE, MC, V. Mon–Sat 5:30–10pm; Sun 5:30–9pm.

WILLIAMSTOWN AFTER DARK

In addition to the Williamstown Theatre Festival, the Williams College Department of Music sponsors diverse concerts and recitals, from choral groups to jazz ensembles. Call its recorded **Concertline** (ℂ **413/597-3146**) to learn of upcoming events. In addition, the Clark Art Institute (see "Art Museums," above) hosts frequent classical-music events.

The Williamstown Theatre Festival ⭐⭐   Williamstown's premier attraction each summer, the festival performs in the **Adams Memorial Theatre.** Staging classic and new plays during its season from late June to August, the festival attracts many top actors and directors, among them Gwyneth Paltrow, Frank Langella, Ethan Hawke, and Bebe Neuwirth. The Main Stage presents works by major playwrights, while the Other Stage often features more experimental productions. The schedule is usually announced by April. It's not too difficult to get tickets, except at the last minute. Prices depend more upon venue and performance date than on casts.

Main St. (P.O. Box 517). ℂ **413/597-3400** for box office, 413/597-3399 for recorded information. www.wtfestival.org. Tickets $18–$39.

9

Connecticut

by Herbert Bailey Livesey

Connecticut resists generalization and confounds spinners of superlatives. It doesn't rank at the top or bottom of any important chart of virtues or liabilities, which makes it impossible to stuff into pigeonholes. The nation's second-smallest state is certainly compact—only 90 miles wide and 55 miles top to bottom—but it is still three times the size of the most diminutive of all, which happens to lie right next door. While parts of it are clogged with humanity (only three states are more congested), some corners are as empty and undeveloped as inland Maine.

By many measures, Connecticut's citizens are as wealthy as any in the country, but dozens of its towns are only shells of their prosperous 19th-century selves, beset by poverty as intractable as it gets. It can boast no dramatic geographical feature, and its highest elevation is only 2,380 feet. Established in 1635 by disgruntled English settlers who didn't like the way things were going at Plymouth Colony, it has long seemed spiritually divorced from the rest of New England—an appendage of New York, or a place to be traversed on the way from there to Boston.

All this might appear to constitute an identity crisis and hardly makes Connecticut seem an appealing vacation destination. But a closer look reveals an abundance of reasons to slow down and linger.

To a great extent, the state owes its existence to the presence of water. In addition to having Long Island Sound along its entire southern coast, several significant rivers and their tributaries slice through the hills and coastal plain—the Housatonic, Naugatuck, Quinnipiac, Connecticut, and Thames. They provided power for the mills along their courses and the towns and cities that grew around them. Industry still drives most of the economy, despite the bucolic image that mention of the state often conjures, and the pollution that industry has caused in the rivers and the sound is being scoured away.

Development, too, appears to have slowed, helping to preserve for a little longer Connecticut's scores of classic colonial villages, from the Litchfield Hills in the northwest to the Mystic coast, in the opposite corner. They are as placid and timeless as they have been for more than three centuries, or as polished and sophisticated as transplanted urbanites can make them. And the state's salty maritime heritage is palpable in the old boat-building and fishing villages at the mouths of its rivers, especially those east of New Haven.

Connecticut is New England's front porch. Pull up a chair and stay awhile.

1 Fairfield County

Mansions, marinas, and luxury apartment blocks elbow for space right up to the deeply indented Long Island Sound shoreline in the southwestern corner of the

Connecticut

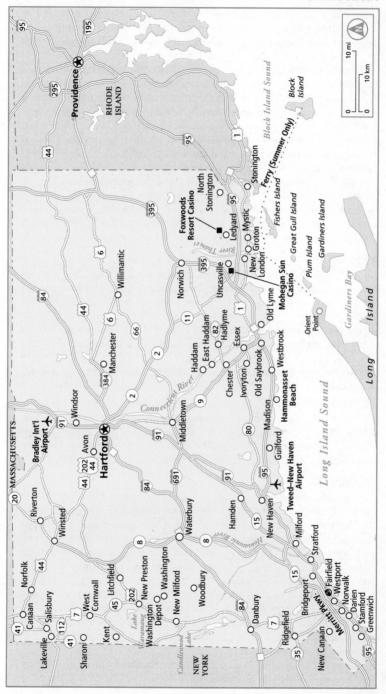

state. This is one of the most heavily developed stretches of the coast, and, in terms of family income, one of the wealthiest. As the land rises slowly inland from the water's edge, woods thicken, roads narrow, and pockets of New England unfold. Yacht country becomes horse country.

The first suburbs began to form in the middle of the last century, when train rails started radiating north and east from New York's Grand Central Terminal into the countryside. This part of the state was made accessible for summertime refugees from the big city, and eventually weekend houses became permanent dwellings. Corporate executives liked the life of the gentry, so after World War II, they started moving their companies closer to their new homes. Stamford became a city; Greenwich, New Canaan, Darien, and Westport were the bedrooms of choice—pricey, haughty, redolent of the good life. (Of course, Fairfield County also contains Bridgeport, a depressed city that once considered filing for bankruptcy.)

But for visitors, the fashionable exurbs and their beaches, restaurants, and upscale shops are the draw, along with the villages farther north, especially Ridgefield, that hint of Vermont, all within 1 1/2 hours of Times Square.

ESSENTIALS

GETTING THERE   From New York and points south, take I-95 or, preferably, the Hutchinson and Merritt parkways. From eastern Massachusetts and northern Connecticut, take I-84 south to Danbury, then Route 7 south into Fairfield County.

The **Metro North** (© **800/223-6052** or 212/532-4900) commuter line has many trains daily to and from New York's Grand Central Terminal, with stops at Greenwich, Stamford, Darien, Norwalk, Westport, and additional stations all the way to New Haven. Express trains make the trip in 45 to 65 minutes, depending upon destination.

VISITOR INFORMATION   An information booklet for the northern part of the county is available from the **Housatonic Valley Tourism District** (© **800/841-4488;** www.housatonic.org), while the **Coastal Fairfield County Convention and Visitor Bureau** (© **800/473-4868;** www.visitfairfieldco.org) can provide materials about the coastal cities and towns.

STAMFORD

A trickle of corporations started moving their headquarters from New York 38 miles northeast to Stamford in the 1960s. That flow became a steady stream by the 1980s, slowed briefly by a recession. Recovery is again evident in much new construction, and more than a dozen Fortune 500 companies continue to direct their operations from here. They have erected shiny mid-rise towers that give the city of 108,000 residents an appearance more like the new urban centers of the Sun Belt than those of the Snow Belt.

One result is a lively downtown that other, less prosperous Connecticut cities surely envy. Roughly contained by Greylock Place, Tresser Boulevard, and Atlantic and Main streets, it has two theaters, tree-lined streets with many shops and a large mall, pocket parks and plazas, and a number of stylish restaurants, sidewalk cafes, and nightclubs.

For further information, contact the **Greater Stamford Convention & Visitors Bureau,** 1 Landmark Sq., Stamford, CT 06902 (© **203/359-4761**).

Whitney Museum of American Art, Fairfield County   This outpost of the parent institution in New York is housed on the ground floor of one of Stamford's office towers. It displays the kind of cutting-edge art that routinely infuriates and amuses critics and art lovers at the mother museum. There is no permanent collection, just traveling exhibitions.

400 Atlantic St. (at Tresser Blvd.). ✆ **203/358-7630** or 203/358-7652. Free admission. Tues–Sat 11am–5pm.

Stamford Museum & Nature Center ✦ *Kids*   About 5 miles north of the city center is this fine family-oriented resource. The center has a large lake with mallards and Canada geese, an open pen with a pair of river otters, and a real, not re-created, farm of weathered barns housing goats, sheep, chickens, dairy cattle, and peacocks. May and June mark the arrival of newborn chicks, kids, calves, and lambs. On the grounds are a country store, nature trails, an imaginative playground, a small planetarium, and an oddball Tudor-Gothic house with galleries of art, natural history, and Indian lore.

39 Scofieldtown Rd. ✆ **203/322-1646.** Admission $5 adults, $4 seniors and children 5–13. Mon–Sat and holidays 9am–5pm; Sun 1–5pm. Feeding time is 9am. The center is 1 mile north of Exit 35 of the Merritt Parkway (Rte. 15).

OUTDOOR PURSUITS

Recreational sailors might want to consider the bare-boat charters at **Yacht Haven,** Washington Boulevard (✆ **203/359-4500**), while less experienced folk may prefer joining the crew of the *Sound Waters* (✆ **203/323-1978**), an 80-foot three-masted schooner. The 3-hour sailing trips are intended as educational sojourns on the ecology of the sound. There are also a handful of sunset dinner cruises and singles sails. Fees are $10 to $25.

SHOPPING

United House Wrecking ✦   Dedicated antiques hounds will want to make time for this sprawling emporium of oddments. The name may not sound promising, but the company got its start selling architectural remnants salvaged from demolitions. Hankering for a 1930s gas pump? A stone pig? A pagoda? They've all been seen here. Open Monday through Saturday from 9:30am to 5:30pm, Sunday from noon to 5pm. (It's tough to find. From Exit 9 of I-95, pick up Route 1, then Route 106 north; make a left on Glenbrook Road, which becomes Church Street, and turn right on Hope Street. Be sure you have a map or detailed directions.) 535 Hope St. ✆ **203/348-5371.**

WHERE TO STAY

Westin Stamford ✦✦   This outpost of the always reliable international chain does nothing to diminish the expectations of business travelers. Everything is in place, from the executive floors with a club lounge to an airport shuttle van.

1 Stamford Place (Exit 7, I-95), Stamford, CT 06902. ✆ **800/937-8461** or 203/967-2222. Fax 203/351-1910. www.westin.com. 481 units. $199–$319 double. AE, DC, DISC, MC, V. **Amenities:** Restaurant (international); heated indoor pool; tennis court; health club; concierge; business center; 24-hour room service; same-day dry cleaning/laundry service. *In room:* A/C, TV, dataport, coffeemaker, hair dryer, iron, safe.

WHERE TO DINE

Beacon ✦ AMERICAN   Chef Waldy Malouf gathered acclaim at three New York restaurants for championing the use of regional ingredients and uncomplicated cooking methods, especially as they related to the Hudson River

Valley. His new exurban outpost was receiving hosannas from reviewers within days of its initial shakedown period. What you get here is a multi-tiered space with outdoor decks directly over the water, accompanied by substantial platters of fish, fowl, and beef subjected to "open-fire cooking"—that is, grilled, smoked, and/or wood-roasted. Tasty, the food certainly is, and simple. It arrives suspiciously fast, and the bill comes before it is requested. Cocktails are good, but skimpy. Think of this not for romantic interludes but rather for groups who don't want to be distracted by inventive formulations meant to push the gastronomic envelope.

183 Harbor Dr. ℂ 203/327-4600. Reservations strongly advised. Main courses $18–$29. AE, DC, MC, V. Tues–Thurs 5:30–10pm; Fri noon–2:30pm and 5:30–11pm; Sat 5:30–11pm; Sun noon–2:30pm and 5–9pm. Take Exit 8 from I-95 north, merging with State St. Turn right on Elm St., right again on Jefferson St., left on Magee Ave., and right on Harbor Dr.

La Hacienda/La Estancia 🟌 TEX-MEX/MEXICAN/ARGENTINE   There aren't any surprises on the menus of these conjoined restaurants, but aficionados of mainstream Mexican cookery and Argentinean steak aren't necessarily looking for invention. Specialties in La Hacienda are *camarones en salsa bruja* (shrimp in a spicy "witch's" sauce) and *puerco en salsa chipotle* (pork in a smoked jalapeño sauce). A tantalizing starter is *ceviche del día*. Skip the ordinary combination plates. La Estancia has a short menu listing grilled fish and slabs of charred beef.

222 Summer St. (north of Main St.). ℂ 203/324-0577. Reservations suggested on weekends. Main courses $12.50–$25.95. AE, DC, DISC, MC, V. La Hacienda Mon–Thurs 11:30am–2:30pm and 5–10pm; Fri 11:30am–2:30pm and 5–11pm; Sat noon–11pm; Sun 1–9pm. La Estancia Tues–Thurs 4:30–10:30pm; Fri–Sat 4:30pm–midnight Sun 5–9pm.

Oceans 211 🟌🟌 NEW AMERICAN/SEAFOOD   First, know that the hands-on owner put in his apprenticeship at the venerable Oyster Bar in New York's Grand Central Terminal. It shows: The ground-floor bar has a Manhattan sheen, with a curving black marble bar and a long display case of featured wines (mostly from California). The menu is deceptively plain, the entrees listed in boldface caps only by their central ingredients—HALIBUT, MAHI-MAHI, SHRIMP. The delights come with what shows up on the plate. TILAPIA, for example, arrives with an olive-and-fig vinaigrette, sweet sausage, orzo, oyster mushrooms, and other vegetables. You might have trouble getting past the delectable appetizers—the curried shrimp quesadilla with annato cream, for one. Upstairs is a less cozy dining room that seats up to 70.

211 Summer St. ℂ 203/973-0494. Reservations suggested on weekends. Main courses $23–$28. Mon–Fri noon–2:30pm and 5:30–9:30pm; Sat 5:30–10:30pm.

Smokey Joe's BARBECUE   This used to be called Buster's, but apart from a paint job and a new sign, nothing much has changed. Smack on the Stamford-Darien line, it wouldn't pass an Amarillo authenticity test, but it's close enough. Upstairs is a down-and-dirty bar with pool table patronized by large men who linger over after-work beers. Downstairs is a classic barbecue joint. Stand in the cafeteria line and select from confusing lists of ribs, brisket, pulled pork, sausage, and birds. Pump sauces of varying hotness on your food, then retire to the oil-clothed picnic tables to gorge.

1308 E. Main St. (Rte. 1). ℂ 203/406-0605. Main courses $9.95–$24.50. Mon–Thurs 11:30am–9:30pm; Fri–Sat 11:30am–10:30pm; Sun 11:30am–9pm.

STAMFORD AFTER DARK

Community and corporate leaders have long supported the cultural and popular performing arts in the city, which also gives rise to commercial performance spaces and nightclubs. The **Rich Forum/Stamford Center for the Arts,** Atlantic Street and Tresser Boulevard (© **203/325-4466;** www.onlyatsca.com), presents professional productions, with name actors, of successful Broadway and off-Broadway plays, while the **Palace Theatre,** 61 Atlantic St. (© **203/ 325-4466;** www.onlyatsca.com), offers musicals; rotating appearances by the Stamford Symphony Orchestra, the Connecticut Grand Opera and Orchestra, and the Connecticut Ballet; and one-night stands by solo acts and traveling troupes like Lily Tomlin, Willie Nelson, and the Alvin Ailey Dance Theater.

Among the handful of downtown clubs is the long-standing **Art Bar,** 84 W. Park Place (© **203/973-0300**), which features a subterranean maze of lounging rooms, a bar, and a DJ. A dress code is enforced. Open Thursday through Sunday nights. The full Wednesday-through-Sunday schedule at the **Terrace Club,** 1938 W. Main St. (© **203/961-9770**), alternately features live acts and DJ nights—country, salsa, and ballroom dancing all get their turn. The aptly named **Next Door Cafe,** 1990 W. Main St. (© **203/961-9770**), has DJs most nights, spiced with open-mike and special one-time events—male strippers on Super Bowl Sunday was one. In summer, there's live Latin music on the patio.

NORWALK

Given the despair that grips many New England cities, the continuing betterment of this city's once notorious South Norwalk neighborhood gladdens the heart. The rehabilitation of several blocks of 19th-century row houses is transforming the waterfront district into a trendy precinct that has come to be called, inevitably, "SoNo." The transformation is far from complete, but new shops, restaurants, and nightspots open monthly. The opening of the Maritime Aquarium was a prime motivation, and the district, bounded roughly by Washington, Water, and North and South Main streets, is readily accessible from the South Norwalk railroad station.

The Maritime Aquarium at Norwalk 🎔🎔 This facility remains the centerpiece of revitalized SoNo. The present name isn't inclusive, since part of the complex includes a section of boat-builders at work as well as exhibits of model ships and full-size vessels, including the *Tango,* which was *pedaled* across the Atlantic. The main attractions, though, are the marine creatures and mammals on view. Five harbor seals are fed at 11:45am, 1:45pm, and 3:45pm, when they wriggle up on the rocks and all but rest their heads in their handler's lap. Additional exhibits include a pair of river otters, an open pool of cow-nosed rays, and tanks alive with creatures found in sound waters. A new sea-turtle exhibit opened in spring 2001. And to make sure no one's expectations are unmet, there's a large tank of tiger sand sharks, swimming silently and eerily in unending circles. Finally, a giant IMAX screen shows nature films that aren't necessarily confined to the seven seas.

10 N. Water St. © 203/852-0700. www.maritimeaquarium.org. Admission $8.75 adults, $8 seniors, $7.25 children 2–12; IMAX $6.75 adults, $5.75 seniors, $5 children; combination packages $12.50 adults, $11 seniors, $9.75 children. July to Labor Day daily 10am–6pm; early Sept to June 10am–5pm.

Lockwood-Mathews Mansion Museum Erected in 1864, this granite mansion in the Second Empire style is covered with peaked and mansard slate roofs and has 50 rooms arranged around a stunning skylit octagonal rotunda.

Marble, gilt, intricately carved wood, marquetry, etched glass, and frescoes were commissioned and incorporated with abandon.

295 West Ave. ✆ **203/838-1434.** Admission $8 adults, $5 seniors, free for children under 12. Visits are by 1-hour guided tour only. Mid-Mar to New Year's Day Wed–Sun noon–5pm. From I-95 southbound, take Exit 15; from I-95 northbound, take Exit 14.

CRUISES
Excursions to **Sheffield Island** and its historic lighthouse are offered by the **M/V Island Girl** (✆ **888/547-6863** or 203/838-9444), a 60-passenger vessel that departs from Hope Dock, near the Maritime Aquarium. Weather permitting, the boat sets out two to four times daily, on Saturdays and Sundays from Memorial Day weekend to late September and Monday through Friday from late June to Labor Day. The round-trip takes about 1½ hours, with a 15-minute layover on the island. Fares are $9 for adults, $8 for seniors, and $7 for children under 12. Special outings include Thursday clambakes and occasional Sunday picnics. Call ahead.

Similarly, the oyster sloop *Hope* has "creature cruises" in winter to spot seals and bird life, as well as marine study cruises at other times, a service of the Maritime Aquarium. Fares are $15 per person. Inquire and reserve ahead by calling ✆ **203/852-0700,** ext. 206.

SHOPPING
Serious shoppers have several choices, primarily among the boutiques and galleries along Washington and Main streets. One shop that may produce a bargain or at least a surprise is **Saga,** 119 Washington St. (✆ **203/855-1900**). It specializes in folk arts and crafts as well as jewelry and furnishings from the southwestern United States, Mexico, and points south.

WHERE TO DINE
Amberjacks Coastal Grill ✿ CONTEMPORARY AMERICAN   The chef/owner used to run a restaurant in Key West, and this room looks as if he trucked it up intact from Duval Street. The bar is shaped like the prow of a boat, while maritime paintings adorn the walls. The food is boldly flavored, with liberal use of tropical fruits and Asian spices. Examples are a yellowfin tuna burger with ginger and mango-papaya "ketchup" on a Portuguese onion roll at lunch, and a popular seafood stew at dinner. Jazz, blues, and local bands appear Thursday, Friday, and some Saturdays. The lively Friday happy hour draws 30-ish singles who move out onto the outdoor deck in summer.

99 Washington St. (between Broad and Main sts.). ✆ **203/853-4332.** Main courses $16–$25. AE, DC, MC, V. Mon–Sat noon–3pm and 5:30–10pm (until 11pm Fri–Sat); Sun noon–10pm.

Barcelona ✿✿ MEDITERRANEAN   Tapas are the featured attraction at this place. The kitchen isn't doctrinaire about recipes, which range all over the Mediterranean and even down to South America for inspiration, from antipasti to meze. The day's delectables might include empanadas of spiced beef, *boquerones* (marinated anchovies), or piquillo peppers stuffed with saffron rice, tuna, and tomato. There's usually a *paella royale* for two at night, along with ostrich steaks and baked halibut.

63-65 N. Main St. (north of Washington St.). ✆ **203/899-0088.** Tapas $3.50–$7.50. Main courses $16–$24. AE, MC, V. Daily 5pm–1am.

WESTPORT

After World War II, the housing crunch had young couples scouring the metropolitan area for affordable housing lying along the three main routes of what is now known as the Metro North transit system. Some of them wound up in this pretty village beside the Saugatuck River, several miles inland from Long Island Sound (47 miles northeast of New York City, 29 miles southwest of New Haven). Most of the new commuter class found Westport to be too far away from Manhattan (1 to 1½ hours each way on the train), and it was deemed the archetype of the far-out bedroom communities that were dubbed the "exurbs"—beyond suburban.

Notable for its large contingent of people in the creative crafts, primarily commercial artists, advertising copywriters, art directors, and their fellows, the town was also appealing to CEOs and higher-level executives, many of whom solved their commuting problem by moving their offices to nearby Stamford. The result is a bustling community with surviving elements of its rural New England past wrapped in a sheen of Big Apple panache.

For further information, contact the **Westport Chamber of Commerce,** 180 Post Rd. E. (© **203/227-9234**).

OUTDOOR PURSUITS

Sherwood Island State Park, Green Farms (© **203/566-2305**), has two long swimming beaches separated by a grove of trees sheltering dozens of picnic tables with grills. Surf fishing is a possibility from designated areas, and the park has concession stands, rest rooms, and an amateurish "nature center." The park is open Memorial Day to Labor Day, daily from 8am to sunset. Pets are not allowed. By car, take Exit 18 off I-95 or U.S. 1, following the road called the Sherwood Island Connector. Admission for out-of-state cars is $8 Monday through Friday, $12 Saturday and Sunday.

You can get to Sherwood Island by taking a train to Westport and a taxi from the station to the park. If you don't have a car, you might prefer to use that method to get to **Compo Beach,** the long municipal strand not far from downtown.

West of the town center is the **Nature Center for Environmental Activities,** 10 Woodside Lane (© **203/227-7253**). Its 62 acres offer several walking trails, a wildlife rehab center, and a building with live animals and an aquarium. Open Monday through Saturday from 9am to 5pm, Sunday from 1 to 4pm. Admission is $1 for adults, 50¢ for children 3 to 14; donations are welcome.

The Nature Conservancy oversees **Devil's Den Preserve,** Old Route 7 (© **203/226-4991**), in Weston, north of Westport (take Route 7 to Old Route 7). An undeveloped, undisturbed tract of more than 1,500 acres of wetlands, woods, and rocky hillocks in the heart of densely populated Fairfield County, this is a refuge of rare value. It has 15 miles of trails beside ponds and waterways rich with birds and other wildlife. Cross-country skiing is permitted, but there are no picnic or toilet facilities. Open daily from sunrise to sunset. Admission is free, but donations are welcome.

Rent a sailboat or arrange a lesson at the **Longshore Sailing School,** Longshore Club Park, 260 S. Compo Rd. (© **203/226-4646**), about 2 miles south of the Boston Post Road (U.S. 1).

SHOPPING

Window-shopping along Main Street is diverting, although stores increasingly are outlets of the chains seen in malls, including **Brooks Brothers, Talbots, J. Crew, Williams-Sonoma,** and **Crabtree & Evelyn.**

Circa Antiques Here is as eclectic a selection as two owners from Ontario and west Texas might contrive. They unload containers from France every 3 months or so, most of it furniture from the 19th and early 20th centuries. Biedermeier pieces are increasingly evident. 11 Riverside Ave. © **203/222-8642.**

Lillian August Less conventional than other Westport stores, Lillian August displays a large collection of paintings, rugs, overstuffed chairs, and related accessories. Owing allegiance to no specific style, it looks as if it were conceived by Laura Ashley on speed. 17 Main St. © **203/629-1539.**

The Stuart Collection On the west end of the bridge over the Saugatuck is a row of fetching shops. This one trumpets its taste for dazzlingly colorful ceramics and blown glassware, most of it Italian, such as the ornate Venetian chandeliers. 11 Winter St. © **203/221-7102.**

WHERE TO STAY

Inn at National Hall ★★★ A playful elegance is on display throughout this riverside hotel, starting as soon as you enter the elevator, which turns out to be a *trompe l'oeil* representation of an estate library. The 1873 brick building has finally realized its destiny as an exquisitely decorated hotel. Voluptuous furnishings, antiques, and canopied beds fill the public rooms and duplex suites—it's improbable that you've seen anything like this elsewhere. Adding to its luster, Boston superchef Todd English took over direction of the restaurant, renamed Miramar.

2 Post Rd. (at west end of Saugatuck Bridge), Westport, CT 06880. © **800/628-4255** or 203/221-1351. Fax 203/221-0276. www.innatnationalhall.com. 15 units. $255–$485 double; $495–$660 suite. Rates include breakfast. AE, DC, MC, V. Valet parking $20. **Amenities:** Restaurant (Mediterranean); lounge; concierge; 24-hour room service; in-room massage; baby-sitting; same-day dry cleaning/laundry service. *In room:* A/C, TV, dataport, minibar.

WHERE TO DINE

In addition to the following choices, consider **Miramar,** at the Inn at National Hall (see above).

Acqua ★ MEDITERRANEAN/SEAFOOD Anticipate food with a light touch that does wonders with such immaculately fresh ingredients as sea bass, crab, skate, and clams. Presentations are marvelously inviting, yet without the appearance of excessive pushing and prodding in the kitchen. The bi- decor consists of murals depicting cherubim and Renaissance musicians, aged-looking decorative tiles, and a bar arching around the wood-burning oven, used for pizzas and the customer favorite, roasted chicken.

43 Main St. (near east end of Saugatuck Bridge). © **203/222-8899.** Reservations recommended on weekends. Main courses $15–$28. AE, DC, MC, V. Mon–Thurs noon–2:30pm and 5:30–10pm; Fri–Sat noon–2:30pm and 5:30–10:30pm; Sun noon–3pm and 5:30–9:30pm.

Tavern on Main ★ AMERICAN BISTRO Westporters don't come in too many different ages, sizes, or colors, but most of them mount the Tavern's front steps with regularity. Local merchants, widows who lunch, executives working at home, and young moms crowd into the clubby bar to wait for a table. The main room has fragments of the building's earliest years—hand-hewn beams and a brick fireplace. Beyond that is a covered terrace. Menu items suffer from neither gushing elaboration nor daring. But the kitchen toys with convention, as with the trademark lobster roll: The center of a seeded roll is scooped out, the cavity filled with warm (not cool) buttery chunks and shreds of the crustacean. Similar turns are taken with coconut shrimp, five-vegetable couscous, and potato-wrapped sea bass.

146 Main St. (€ 203/7222. Reservations recommended. Main courses $7.50–$13.95 lunch; $16.95–$24.95 dinner. AE, MC, V. Daily 11:30am–3pm and 5:30–10pm.

WESTPORT AFTER DARK

One of the oldest theaters on the straw-hat circuit, the **Westport Country Playhouse,** 25 Powers Ct. (€ 203/227-4177), has passed its 70th year. Revitalized under the leadership of Joanne Woodward and other new administrators, the theater produces comedies, dramas, and musicals June through August. Famous or at least vaguely familiar actors appear in almost every production. The **White Barn Theatre,** Newtown Avenue (€ 203/227-3768), is a respected venue with a slightly shorter summer season than the Playhouse. From late June to August, outdoor musical performances are given at **Levitt Pavilion,** off Jesup Green near the center of town (€ 203/226-7600); many of the more than 50 events each year are free.

RIDGEFIELD

No town in Connecticut has a more imposing main street. Ridgefield's main avenue is almost 100 feet wide, lined with ancient towering elms, maples, and oaks, and bordered by massive 19th-century houses. Impressive at any time of the year, it is in its glory during the brief blaze of the October foliage season. Only a little over an hour from New York City (58 miles northeast), the town is nonetheless a true evocation of the New England character.

Aldrich Museum of Contemporary Art ★★   This superb collection of paintings and sculptures from the second half of the 20th century was begun by the eponymous founder decades ago and continues to grow. The original white clapboard structure has more than doubled in size with a harmonious addition. A professional curator now oversees the permanent holdings and organizes three major exhibitions a year, as well as jazz concerts, films, lectures, and other events. The outdoor sculptures set up in the side- and backyards can be viewed even when the museum itself is closed.

258 Main St. (near the intersection of Rtes. 35 and 33 at the south end of Main St.). (€ 203/438-4519. www.aldrichart.org. Admission $5 adults, $2 seniors and students, free for children under 12. Tues–Sun noon–5pm (until 8pm Fri). Hours fluctuate with the season and current exhibitions. Free guided tours Sun 2pm.

Keeler Tavern   This 1713 stagecoach inn was providing sustenance to travelers between Boston and New York long before the Revolutionary War, but that conflict provided it with its object of greatest note. A British cannonball is imbedded in one of its walls, presumably fired during the Battle of Ridgefield in 1777. Since 1966, it has been a museum of colonial life. Period furnishings have been installed to set the tone, and costumed guides tell the story. And the tavern has another claim to fame: It was long the summer home of architect Cass Gilbert (1849–1934), who designed the Supreme Court Building in Washington, D.C., and who was a key figure in the construction of the George Washington Bridge in New York.

132 Main St. (€ 203/438-5485. Admission $4 adults, $2 seniors, $1 children. Wed and Sat–Sun 1–4pm.

SHOPPING

Hay Day Market Apart from the usual antiques shops and the strip malls north of town on Route 35, this is a most interesting stop for devoted food lovers. Hidden in a shopping center behind Main Street, it is about as fancy a food market as exists outside of Manhattan. Sections are devoted to excellent produce, prepared foods, baked goods, charcuterie, cheeses, and fresh flowers. 21 Governor St. © 203/431-4400.

WHERE TO STAY & DINE

The Elms Ridgefield's oldest (1799) operating inn has the ambience of a small contemporary hotel with the conveniences most travelers desire, as well as newly decorated guest rooms with canopied four-poster beds. The **dining rooms** (© **203/438-9206**) are now in the hands of celebrated Manhattan chef Brendan Walsh, whose ministrations have freshened the award-winning restaurant and lower-priced tavern without masking their 18th-century origins. His food utilizes regional ingredients, as in the Connecticut seafood stew. Reservations are essential on weekends. A dining porch is inviting in good weather.

500 Main St. (Rte. 35, at the north end of town), Ridgefield, CT 06877. © and fax **203/438-2541**. www.elmsinn.com. 20 units. $150–$210 double. Rates include breakfast. AE, DC, MC, V. **Amenities:** Restaurant (creative American), tavern. *In room:* A/C, TV.

West Lane Inn An inn to fit most images of a romantic country getaway, this also works for businesspeople, as it offers modem jacks, voice mail, laundry service, and express checkout. Some rooms have fireplaces, and all have four-poster beds. The 1849 house sports a fine oak staircase and stands on a property blessed with giant shade trees. You can take breakfast on the terrace in good weather. There is no dining room, but **Bernard's Inn** (© **203/438-8282**), next door, serves lunch and dinner. Reservations are required on weekends, and men are expected to wear jackets at dinner.

22 West Lane (off Rte. 35), Ridgefield, CT 06877. © **203/438-7323**. Fax 203/438-7325. www.westlaneinn.com. 20 units. $110–$180 double. Rates include breakfast. AE, DC, MC, V. Driving north from Wilton on Rte. 33, turn west on Rte. 35 at the edge of town. **Amenities:** Concierge; limited room service; laundry service; dry cleaning. *In room:* A/C, TV/VCR, dataport, fridge, coffeemaker, hair dryer.

2 The Litchfield Hills

When the Hamptons got too pricey, too visible, and too chichi back in the 1980s, a lot of stockbrokers, CEOs, and celebs started discovering the Litchfield Hills, arguably the most fetchingly rustic yet sophisticated part of Connecticut.

The topography and, to an extent, the microculture of the region are defined by the river that runs through it, the Housatonic. Broad but not deep enough for vessels larger than canoes, it waters farms and villages and forests along its course, provides opportunities for recreational angling and float trips, and, over the millennia, has helped to shape these foothills, which merge with the Massachusetts Berkshires.

Men in overalls and CAT caps still stand on the porches of general stores, their breath steaming in the bracing autumn air. Others wade into the river, working the riffs and rills with long looping casts of trout flies hand-tied over the winter. Churches hold pancake-breakfast fundraisers; neighbors squabble about development. That's one side of these bucolic hills, less than 2 hours from Times Square.

The Litchfield Hills

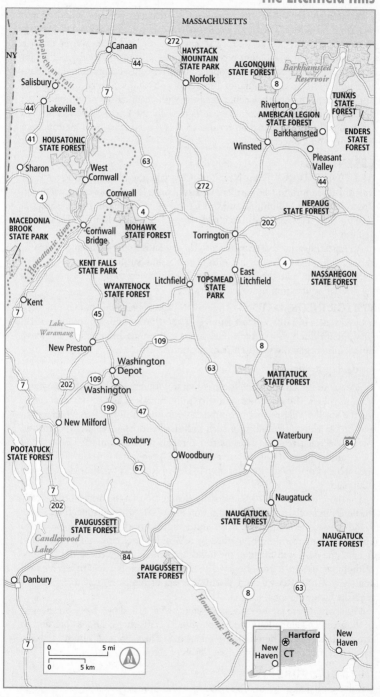

339

Increasingly, the other side is fashioned by refugees, permanent and temporary, from New York. These chic seekers of tranquility and real estate fled to pre-Revolutionary saltboxes and Georgian colonials on Litchfield's warren of back roads and brought Manhattan-bred expectations with them. Boutiques fragrant with designer coffees and cachets opened in spaces once occupied by luncheonettes and feed stores. Restaurants discovered sushi and sun-dried tomatoes and just how much money they could get away with charging the newcomers.

Compromises and city-country conflicts aside, the Litchfield Hills remain a satisfying all-season destination for day trips and overnights from metropolitan New York and Connecticut.

ESSENTIALS

GETTING THERE   From New York City, take the Hutchinson River Parkway to I-684 north to I-84 east, taking Exit 7 onto Route 7 north. Continue on Route 7 for New Milford, Kent, West Cornwall, and Canaan. For Washington Depot, New Preston, and Litchfield, branch off onto Route 202 at New Milford.

An especially attractive entrance into the region is Route 44 from the Taconic Parkway, through Millerton and into Lakeville and Salisbury.

From Boston, take the Massachusetts Turnpike west to the Lee exit, picking up Route 7 south from nearby Stockbridge.

VISITOR INFORMATION   A useful 40-page *Unwind* brochure is produced by the **Litchfield Hills Visitors Bureau** (© **860/567-4506;** fax 860/567-5214; www.litchfieldhills.com). Additional sources of online information are **www.housatonic.org** and **www.litchfieldcty.com**.

NEW MILFORD

A gateway to the Litchfield Hills, this town was founded in 1703 by immigrants from the older Milford, down on the coast. It functions as a commercial center for the smaller villages that surround it—Roxbury, Bridgewater, Washington, and Brookfield—and as host for such industrial entities as Kimberly-Clark and Nestlé. Several rivers and streams run through it, and dammed Candlewood Lake (notorious for daredevil water-skiers and speedboats) is nearby. It is also at the high end of a long stretch of overdeveloped Route 7, which is clogged with minimalls.

For those reasons, New Milford is a welcome stop on the drive north, if only for lunch and a short stroll. Turn right on Route 202 where it splits from Route 7 and crosses the Housatonic River and a railroad track. Up on the left is one end of the long town green, marked by a World War II tank and a bandstand. A 1902 fire destroyed many of the buildings around the green, so this isn't one of those picture-book New England settings. Rather, it is a mix of late Victoriana, early Greek Revival, and Eisenhower-era architecture, not to ignore the requisite Congregational Church.

Otherwise, there are no obligatory sights, so a walk down Bank Street, west of the green and along Railroad Street, with its crafts shops, a bookstore, and an Art Moderne movie house, won't take long. There are also almost a dozen family-friendly restaurants of various levels of accomplishment.

OUTDOOR PURSUITS

Candlewood Lake (© **860/354-6928**) is the third-largest man-made lake in the eastern United States. It has a finger that pokes into New Milford, but the area with the most recreational facilities is a few miles to the west. From New

Milford, drive north on Route 7 about 2½ miles, turn west on Route 37 toward and through Sherman, then south on Route 39 to the unfortunately named **Squantz Pond State Park** (© **860/424-3200**). With over 170 acres along the lakeshore, it offers swimming, ice-skating, fishing, hiking and cycling trails, picnic grounds, rental canoes, and a boat launch.

WHERE TO STAY

There are good reasons for families to consider making New Milford their base for exploring the Litchfield Hills. Inns in the towns farther north typically exclude smokers, pets, and children, and their rates fluctuate wildly according to day and season. The following establishment is more tolerant and relatively inexpensive.

Heritage Inn *(Kids)*   This sky-blue building started life as a tobacco warehouse in 1870, but after the conversion to an inn over a century later, it looks more like a railroad hotel in the Old West, with its high ceilings and a long central hall. The heavy old beams were left exposed, a nice touch, for the decor is otherwise uninspired, though perfectly comfortable. The somewhat more spacious upstairs rooms pull together better visually. Breakfast goes well beyond the minimalist usual, with French toast and made-to-order omelets. While the inn stands next to the railroad tracks, only an occasional freight train rumbles past, since commuter service was ended years ago.

34 Bridge St. (opposite Railroad Station), New Milford, CT 06776. © **800/311-6294** or 860/354-8883. Fax 860/350-5543. www.bedandbreakfast.com. 20 units. $110–$125 double. Rates include breakfast. Children under 5 stay free in parents' room; older kids sharing parents' room pay $15. AE, DC, DISC, MC, V. **Amenities:** Coin-op washers and dryers; dry cleaning. *In room:* A/C, TV, dataport.

WHERE TO DINE

There are many dining choices along Bank and Railroad streets and out on nearby Route 7.

The Cookhouse *(★)* SOUTHERN/BARBECUE   Inexplicably, Connecticut has been home to some thumpingly good barbecue joints. This is the current champ. It's set, appropriately enough, in a converted barn on often tacky Route 7. Ribs, chicken, pulled pork, and beef brisket are slow-smoked over hardwood for 10 hours or more. Heaping portions come with two sides—among the choices, baked beans, collard greens, and horseradish mashed potatoes. There's also sweet potato pie, Louisiana meat pie, and the no-doubt heart-healthy fried catfish po'boy sandwich. Iced tea or the draft Cookhouse Pale Ale go best with all this.

31 Danbury Rd. (Rte. 7). © **860/355-4111**. Main courses $12.95–$19.95. AE, MC, V. Mon–Thurs 11:30am–10pm; Fri–Sat 11:30am–11pm.

WOODBURY *(★)*

The chief distinction of this attractive town strung along several miles of Route 6, west of Waterbury, is its number of high-end antiques stores—at least 40, by rough count. On weekends in good weather, the main road is clogged with cars trolling for treasures, and progress can be slow.

ANTIQUING

Shoppers are drawn here for antiques and collectibles of every sort, from funky to obscure to elegant, with a few contemporary crafts thrown in. To winnow down the list, pick up a copy of the directory of shops produced by the **Woodbury Antiques Dealers Association** *(★★)* (www.antiqueswoodbury.com) at one of the member stores.

Start off slowly in the building at 289 Main St., at the intersection of Routes 6 and 317, which contains **Jennings & Rohn Antiques** (© 203/263-3775). European paintings and furnishings from the 16th century to 1960 are on view, as well as lighting fixtures and some Art Deco. The offerings at **Rosebush Farm** (© 203/266-9114) are sufficiently wide-ranging to include African masks, dollhouses, decoys, garden statuary, and harlequin paintings. At **Martell & Suffin Antiques** (© 203/263-1913), the owners favor 18th- and early-19th-century European furniture as well as Asian works of art, largely Chinese in origin.

Drive south on Main Street (Route 6) to the notable **Wayne Pratt Antiques,** 346 Main St. (© 203/263-5676), which specializes in 18th-century American furniture, much of it Chippendale and Queen Anne. Here are museum-level pieces that cost from the low five figures to nearly half a million dollars. Some items are within reach for the rest of us, like the keepsake Chinese porcelain boxes for $12.

Of similar high order are the offerings at **Country Loft Antiques,** 557 Main St. (© 203/266-4500), largely 19th-century French furnishings and *objets* displayed in a fine old barn. Wares run from biscuit tins to deeply carved armoires, bolts of fabric to 18th-century dining tables. Be sure to look into the basement, outfitted as a wine cellar.

On most Saturdays in decent weather, the **Woodbury Antiques & Flea Market** (© 203/263-2841) sets up in a parking lot at the south end of town.

SEEING THE SIGHTS

Glebe House   About the only scrap of surviving history worth mentioning is this 1750 house of an Episcopal bishop, a quarter mile west of Route 6 on a street of fine 18th-century houses. A *glebe* was a property given to a preacher as partial compensation for his services. Inside are furnishings true to the period; outside is the **Gertrude Jekyll Garden** (see "The Living Legacy of Gertrude Jekyll," below).

Hollow Rd. © 203/263-2855. Admission $4 adults, $1 children under 12. Apr–Oct Wed–Sun 1–5pm; Nov Sat–Sun 1–4pm.

Flanders Nature Center   North of Woodbury on Route 6, watch for Flanders Road forking to the left. Three miles along, on the right, is the office building for this nature center. The organization that runs it is also a land trust, keeping 1,300 acres in four different towns out of the hands of developers. Trail maps of the various properties are available here.

Church Hill and Flanders Rd. © 203/263-3711. Office Mon–Fri 9am–5pm; trails daily dawn to dusk. Free admission.

WHERE TO STAY

Longwood Country Inn ★   South of the town center, this two-century-old house has been a B&B since 1951, until recently known as Merryvale. One of the current owners is an architect and the other worked in fashion, accounting for the spare good taste evident throughout. The considerably upgraded accommodations include spacious room 3, with a four-poster bed and a sitting area with fireplace, and the smaller but country-elegant room 2, with fireplace and a whirlpool bath for two. In addition, the owners have pushed out the walls for a new 48-seat restaurant. Meals are contemporary in execution, but with "historic colonial inspiration."

1204 Main St. (Rte. 6), Woodbury, CT 06798. © 203/266-0800. Fax 203/263-4479. www.litchfieldcty.com/lodging/merryvale. 5 units. $115–$250 double. Rates include breakfast. AE, DC, MC, V. **Amenities:** Restaurant (American Regional). *In room:* A/C, TV.

Finds **The Living Legacy of Gertrude Jekyll**

Perhaps the most influential gardener of the 20th century, Gertrude Jekyll developed the foundations of modern-day garden design. In 1926, the famed English landscapist and writer was commissioned to plan a garden on the grounds of the 1740 Glebe House. The planting was delayed, and Jekyll died in 1932 without ever seeing her work come to fruition. In fact, the garden wasn't planted until 1987, when the yellowed plans were discovered in an archive. The result is a small gem—a downscaled version of the elaborate English landscapes she once created. Annuals and perennials typical of 18th-century arrangements are laid out in mixed border and foundation plantings. This remains the only one of three gardens of her design still in existence in the United States.

WHERE TO DINE

Another option is the **Longwood Country Inn,** described above.

Good News Café ★★ NEW AMERICAN   This is a fun spot, with a cheery young staff and rooms doused in blazing primary colors. The food? Make it Europe meets Asia, touching down in various parts of the Americas along the way. The results are spirited and joyful, but never bizarre. Examples: spiced venison loin with wilted spinach, yucca croquettes, multi-pepper salsa, and plantain chips. Most of the entrees qualify as heart-healthy, and stars on the menu mark ingredients purchased from local organic farmers. Desserts, however, tend to be rich, gooey, and caloric. Saturday nights feature live jazz, and there's outdoor dining in summer.

694 Main St. (Rte. 6). ✆ 203/266-4663. Reservations recommended on weekends. Main courses $15–$29. AE, DC, MC, V. Wed–Mon 11:30am–10pm.

WASHINGTON ★★ & WASHINGTON DEPOT

Settled in 1734, its name changed in 1779 to honor the first American president, Washington occupies the crown of a hill beside Route 47. Its village green, with the impressive 1802 Congregational Meeting House surrounded by uniformly white buildings with black shutters and sheltered by towering shade trees, is an example of a municipal arrangement found all over New England—but rarely to such near-perfection. The village is home to the exclusive Gunnery School and the renowned Mayflower Inn. The traveling series of musical events known as the **Armstrong Chamber Concerts** (✆ 860/868-0522) usually alights in Washington on four Sunday afternoons in spring and fall (other appearances are in Greenwich, Conn., and Lenox, Mass.). Performances are in the Congregational Church.

Adjacent Washington Depot, down the hill beside the Shepaug River, serves as the commercial center, with a bank and a small cluster of shops. Stop in at the beguiling **Hickory Stick Bookshop**, 2 Greenhill Rd. (✆ 860/868-0525).

Nearby **Steep Rock Reservation** (✆ 860/868-9131) is a lovely spot for hiking, fly-fishing, or cross-country skiing. (Unfortunately for pet owners, dogs must now be leashed.)

Institute for American Indian Studies   A worthwhile detour takes drivers down Curtis Road to this small repository of Native American crafts and artifacts. They are presented with sensitivity and, for the most part, without polemics. A soundtrack of birdsong and running water plays in the galleries of permanent and temporary exhibits, which tell the story of American Indians who lived and still live in this region. Down a nearby path is a re-creation of an Algonquian village.

Rte. 199. ℭ **860/868-0518.** Admission $4 adults, $2 children 6–16. Mon–Sat 10am–5pm; Sun noon–5pm (closed Mon–Tues Jan–Mar).

WHERE TO STAY

Mayflower Inn ★★ Galaxies of stars and diamonds have already been showered upon this, one of the state's courtliest manor inns. While the main building is almost entirely new, some elements survive from the original 1894 structure, the most delightful of which is the richly paneled library. Porches look out across manicured lawns to deep woods. The Mayflower makes available everything that a superior urban hotel might offer. Most bedrooms have fireplaces, the bathrooms are done with tapestry rugs and mahogany wainscoting— all is as close to perfection as such an enterprise is likely to be, *almost* justifying the breathtaking prices. The clientele can't be described as youthful.

118 Woodbury Rd. (Rte. 47), Washington, CT 06793. ℭ **860/868-9466.** Fax 860/868-1497. inn@mayflowerinn.com. 25 units. $365–$1,050 double. AE, MC, V. Take Rte. 202 north 2 miles past New Preston, turn south on Rte. 47 through Washington Depot and up the hill past Washington Common. The entrance is on the left. Children over 12 welcome. **Amenities:** Restaurant (eclectic), pub; heated outdoor pool; nearby golf course; tennis court; health club with classes and extensive equipment; sauna; bike rental; massage; same-day dry cleaning/laundry service. *In room:* A/C, TV, fax, dataport, minibar, hair dryer.

WHERE TO DINE

One dining option is the restaurant at the **Mayflower Inn** (see above). For a more casual meal, put together a picnic from the delectable array of quiches, pizzas, and salads at **The Pantry,** 5 Titus Rd., Washington Depot (ℭ **860/ 868-0258**).

G. W. Tavern ★ ECLECTIC AMERICAN The atmospheric bar in front has booths and a fireplace, offering comfort on a rainy day, while the simulated attached barn is airier, with a deck that looks down on Bee Brook. Apart from an occasional digression like mulligatawny, the kitchen is dedicated to interpretations of such robust Americana as Cobb salad and burgers. There are spins on convention, though, in the roasted garlic mashed potatoes and in the sourdough used for the clam fritters. Weekend brunches are popular with stylish locals, including a large gay contingent.

Rte. 47 (north of Washington Depot shopping center). ℭ **860/868-6633.** Main courses $8.50–$23. AE, MC, V. Daily 11:30am–2:30pm and 5:30–10pm (Fri–Sat until 11pm).

NEW PRESTON & LAKE WARAMAUG ★★

Never more than a few houses and retailers at the junction of two country roads, the hamlet of New Preston long served primarily as a supplier for locals and, starting in the mid–19th century, the families who summered on nearby Lake Waramaug. More recently, New Preston's small grocery and hardware stores have been converted to antiques emporia of high order, and they find themselves surrounded on weekends by BMWs and Volvos.

EXPLORING THE LAKE WARAMAUG AREA

At the northwest tip of the L-shaped lake, 95-acre **Lake Waramaug State Park,** Lake Waramaug Road (ℭ **860/868-0220**), gives the public access to a beautiful body of water that is otherwise monopolized by the private homes and inns that border it. Canoes and paddleboats are for rent, and there's a swimming beach as well as picnic tables, food concessions, and a total of almost 80 camping and RV sites.

Hopkins Vineyard A former dairy farm on a promontory above Lake Waramaug was converted in 1979 into a vineyard and winery. Headquartered in a 19th-century barn across the street from the Hopkins Inn (see "Where to Stay & Dine," below), it produces 11 bottlings ranging from a sparkling white to hard cider. It won't make anyone forget the Napa Valley, but prices are fair. A wine bar overlooks the lake and serves pâté and cheese.

25 Hopkins Rd. ℰ 860/868-7954. Jan–Feb Sat 10am–5pm, Sun 11am–5pm; Mar–Apr Wed–Sat 10am–5pm, Sun 11am– 5pm; May–Dec Mon–Sat 10am–5pm, Sun 11am–5pm.

SHOPPING
In no time, the intersecting streets that form the center of the village have gone from sleepy to spiffy. Notable among the shops are **J. Seitz & Co.,** Main Street/East Shore Road (ℰ 860/868-0119), featuring Indian blankets and clothing. Next door is **Del Mediterraneo,** selling pottery and home furnishings. **The Trumpeter,** across the street (ℰ 860/868-9090), specializes in English antiques, including silver candlesticks, leather valises, and huge model sailboats.

WHERE TO STAY & DINE
The Birches Inn ✿ Enthusiastic reviews were lavished upon the latest refiguring of the in-house restaurant before the paint was dry. Less remarked upon were the restored bedrooms, five of them in the main house, up a slope from the road, and another three in the lakeside cottage. Comfort prevails over quaintness, and the results are superior to those found in most nearby lodgings (except the Boulders, described below). Most have water views, sure to inspire pushing off in the canoe available to guests or bicycling on the winding shore road. Take in the vista from the **dining room** ✿✿ or deck, almost a match for the venturesome food. The French-born chef/owner marries often disparate ingredients with cunning and panache.

233 West Shore Rd., New Preston, CT 06777. ℰ 888/590-7945 or 860/868-1735. Fax 860/868-1815. www.thebirchesinn.com. 8 units. May–Oct $125–$300 double; Nov–Apr $95–$225. Rates include breakfast. AE, MC, V. Drive to the left of the town beach on West Shore Rd. about a mile. *In room:* A/C, TV.

The Boulders ✿✿ This once rustic lakeside inn, with access to a swimming beach, has scrambled steadily upward in both price and quality. Part of the improvement lies with the outlying "guest houses," four new buildings with two spacious units each. All enjoy private decks, fireplaces, whirlpool tubs, and refrigerators. These have contemporary furnishings, while the tone of the bedrooms in the 1895 main house is set by antiques and reproductions of country styles. Five rooms have TVs. Plates of cookies await arriving guests, and a serious wine cellar complements the acclaimed cuisine. Guests are encouraged to take the MAP rates, which are a bargain.

E. Shore Rd. (Rte. 45), New Preston, CT 06777. ℰ 800/552-6853 or 860/868-0541. Fax 860/868-1925. www.bouldersinn.com. 17 units. $260–$320 double. Rates are $50 lower midweek Nov–Apr, $60 higher Fri–Sat Memorial Day to Oct. Rates include breakfast. MAP costs $50 more than B&B rate. AE, MC, V. Drive north from New Preston about 2 miles on Rte. 45. **Amenities:** Restaurant (regional American); golf course nearby; tennis court; canoes and rowboats (free). *In room:* A/C, hair dryer.

Hopkins Inn A family named Hopkins started farming this land in 1787, and its descendants were still around in 1979, when they turned the farm into a vineyard and winery. The yellow frame farmhouse sits atop a hill with the best views of Lake Waramaug. A terrace takes maximum advantage of the lake view. Food is the main event, since most of the guest rooms are on the spartan side, with phones and television only in the two-bedroom suite in the annex. Dishes from the Swiss and Austrian Alps are served in hefty portions by waitresses in uniforms hinting of the Tyrol.

22 Hopkins Rd., New Preston, CT 06777. ℂ **860/868-7295.** Fax 860/868-7464. www.thehopkinsinn.com. 13 units (11 with private bathroom). $77–$180 double. AE, DISC, MC, V. From New Preston, take Rte. 45 north about 2½ miles and look for the sign on the left. **Amenities:** Restaurant (closed Jan to late Mar). *In room:* A/C.

LITCHFIELD ★★

Possessed of a long common with stately trees reconfigured around the turn of the 20th century by the Frederick Law Olmsted landscaping firm (designers of New York's Central Park), Litchfield is testimony to the taste and affluence of the Yankee entrepreneurs who built it up in the late 18th and early 19th centuries from a colonial farm community to an industrial center. The factories and mills were dismantled toward the end of the 19th century, and the men who built them settled back to enjoy their riches. Their uncommonly large homes, either authentic Federals and Greek Revivals or later remodeled to look that way, are set well back from the streets. The commercial district is a block of late-19th-century houses facing the common, with gaudier enterprises kept to the outskirts.

In recent decades, the town was discovered by fashionable New Yorkers, who find it less frenetic than the Hamptons. Their influence is seen both in the quality of store merchandise and restaurant fare and in the lofty prices houses command.

A WALK THROUGH HISTORY

Litchfield's houses and broad tree-lined streets reward leisurely strollers. From the stores and restaurants along West Street, walk east (to the right when facing the common), and then turn right on South Street. On the opposite corner is the **Litchfield History Museum,** at South and East streets (ℂ **860/567-4501**), containing an eclectic collection of local historical artifacts, including the world's largest collection of works by the 18th-century portraitist Ralph Earl, an amazing collection of miniatures, and the endearing personal effects of girls who attended the old Litchfield Female Academy. It's open mid-April to November, Tuesday through Saturday from 11am to 5pm and Sunday from 1 to 5pm. Admission is $5 for adults, $3 for seniors, and free for children under 14.

Walking down South Street, on the right behind a white picket fence, are the **Tapping Reeve House and Law School** (ℂ **860/567-4501**). One of the few historic houses regularly open to the public, the Reeve house was built in 1773, while the adjacent 1784 building was the earliest American law school, established before independence. It counted among its students Aaron Burr, Noah Webster, and three Supreme Court justices. Visitors to the museum move through the interactive exhibits as newly enrolled "law students." Hours are the same as those of the Litchfield History Museum, which maintains it; one ticket buys admission to both museums.

When the street starts to peter out into more modern houses, walk back toward the common and cross over to the north side. Over here on the right is the magisterial **First Congregational Church,** built in 1828. Turn left, then right on North Street, where the domestic architecture matches the quiet splendor of South Street.

OUTDOOR PURSUITS

The **White Memorial Foundation,** Route 202 (② **860/567-0857**), is a 4,000-acre wildlife sanctuary and nature conservancy about 3 miles southwest of Litchfield. It has campsites and 35 miles of trails for hiking, cross-country skiing, and horseback riding. On the grounds is a small museum of natural history with nature exhibits, stuffed native animals, and a gift shop. The Holbrook Bird Observatory looks out on a landscape specially planted to attract birds.

This is horse country, so consider a canter across the meadows and along the wooded trails of **Topsmead State Park,** Buell Road (② **860/567-5694**). The park has a wildlife preserve and a Tudor-style mansion that can be toured the second and fourth weekends of each month from June through October. To get here, follow Route 118 for a mile east of town. The grounds are open from 8am to sunset. Horses can be hired nearby at **Lee's Riding Stables,** 57 East Litchfield Rd., off Route 118 (② **860/567-0785**).

SHOPPING

Most of the interesting shops are in the row of late-19th-century brick buildings on the south side of the town green. In the front of **Barnidge & McEnroe,** 7 West St. (② **860/567-4670**), is a coffee bar for muffins and lattes, which will keep you going as you browse through its entertaining three floors of books, gifts, and ceramics.

NEARBY ATTRACTIONS

Haight Vineyard   Chardonnays and merlots don't spring to mind as likely Connecticut products, but this establishment corrects that impression. Established in 1978, it has grown and prospered, presently offering 11 drinkable bottlings, including a respectable Riesling, a couple of sturdy picnic-style reds, and a traditional apple wine. The tasting room is open year-round. There's a second winery in Mystic.

29 Chestnut Hill Rd. ② **860/567-4045**. Mon–Sat 10:30am–5pm; Sun noon–5pm.

WHERE TO STAY

Tollgate Hill Inn ★★   Three barn-red buildings on 10 wooded acres, including the 1745 tavern that is the main house, constitute the liveliest, most atmospheric lodging in Litchfield. The bedrooms are comfortable, with most of the modern conveniences that might be needed. The busy restaurant may have wavy wide-board floors and high-backed wooden booths in its oldest room, but the food is entirely of this moment. The popular Sunday brunch is an all-you-can-eat buffet for $14.95. From mid-June to October, jazz combos perform on Saturday nights and at Sunday brunch.

Rte. 202 (Tollgate Rd., 2½ miles northeast of Litchfield), Litchfield, CT 06759. ② **800/445-3903,** 860/567-4545, or 860/567-3821. Fax 860/567-8397. 21 units. Mid-May to Dec $110–$175 double; Jan to mid-May $90–$150. Rates include breakfast. AE, DC, DISC, MC, V. **Amenities:** Restaurant, bar. *In room:* A/C, TV.

WHERE TO DINE

The restaurant at the **Tollgate Hill Inn** (see above) is another option.

The County Seat ECLECTIC   Not easy to describe, but a pleasure to experience, the County Seat has a store in front selling kitchenware, coffee beans, and espresso machines. In back is a soda fountain, and in between is a coffee bar/lunch counter offering soups, sandwiches, salads, and light meals. One featured sandwich was grilled lamb with sautéed mushrooms and onions on a Kaiser roll. There's table service, and upholstered chairs and sofas are available for lounging and chatting. Live music of many kinds is featured Friday and Saturday nights, with a modest cover.

3 West St. (on the green). ⓒ 860/567-8069. Main courses $6–$15. AE, MC, V. Mon–Thurs 7am–9pm (until 11pm in summer); Fri 7am–midnight; Sat 8am–midnight; Sun 8am–9pm (until 11pm in summer).

West Street Grill ⭐ NEW AMERICAN   Known as an incubator for some of Connecticut's best chefs, several of whom have gone off to open their own places, this sprightly contemporary bistro rarely misses a step, despite the frequent changes. Entrees tend toward fusion renditions of meats, fowl, and grilled fish, little of which knocks your socks off—it just looks and tastes good. The trendiest spot for miles, it attracts the weekend celebrity set.

43 West St. (on the green). ⓒ 860/567-3885. Reservations necessary for dinner, essential on weekends. Main courses $18–$25. AE, MC, V. Mon–Thurs 11:30am–3pm and 5:30–9pm; Fri–Sat 11:30am–4pm and 5:30–10:30pm; Sun 11:30am–4pm.

LITCHFIELD AFTER DARK

No one goes to Litchfield for its nightlife, but movie lovers might consider the **Bantam Cinema** (ⓒ 860/567-0006), in the otherwise unremarkable village of Bantam, about 3 miles southeast on Route 209. Don't expect the latest Schwarzenegger action flick, since the managers usually concentrate on independent and foreign films that don't get wide distribution.

In early August, the 3-day **Litchfield Jazz Festival** (ⓒ 860/567-4162) is held under a tent on the Goshen Fairgrounds. At other times, drop by the **County Seat** (see above) for one of its weekend musicals.

KENT

A prominent prep school of the same name, a history as an iron-smelting center, and a continuing reputation as a gathering place of artists and writers define this town of fewer than 2,000. Noted 19th-century landscape painter George Inness helped establish that assessment, and several galleries represent the works of his creative descendants. They are joined by a multiplicity of antiques shops and bookstores, most of them strung along Route 7. South of town on the same road is the hamlet of Bull's Bridge, named for one of the two remaining covered bridges in the state that can be crossed by cars.

Four miles northeast of Kent is the handily accessible **Kent Falls State Park,** on Route 7 (ⓒ 860/927-3849). Its centerpiece, a 250-foot cascade, is clearly visible from the road, and picnic tables are set about the grounds. A path mounts the hill beside the falls, and there are a total of 295 wooded acres to explore. Rest rooms are available. A parking fee of $8 per out-of-state car ($5 per Connecticut car) is charged on Saturdays, Sundays, and holidays between June and October. Serious hikers have a greater challenge nearby, should they choose to undertake it: On the opposite side of Route 7, the Appalachian Trail follows a stretch of the Housatonic River north toward Cornwall Bridge and West Cornwall and all the way into Massachusetts.

Sloane-Stanley Museum   Fans of the books of illustrator/author Eric Sloane, who celebrated the work and crafts of rural America, will enjoy this replica of his studio, exhibits of tools he depicted, and the drawings and paintings that adorn the walls. On the grounds are the ruins of one of the many iron furnaces that were active in the Kent area in the 19th century.

Rte. 7, north of Kent center (near Kent Falls). ⓒ 860/927-3849. Mid-May to Oct Wed–Sun 10am–4pm. Admission $3.50 adults, $2.50 seniors, $2 children.

WEST CORNWALL

Not to be confused with Cornwall, about 4 miles to the southeast, nor Cornwall Bridge, about 7 miles to the south, this tiny village is best known for its picturesque covered bridge, one of only two in the state that still permit the passage of cars. The bridge connects Routes 7 and 128, crossing the Housatonic. With a state forest to the north and a state park to its immediate south, West Cornwall enjoys a piney seclusion that remains welcoming to passersby.

Housatonic Meadows State Park, on Route 7 (*C* **860/672-6772** in summer, or 860/927-3238 the rest of the year), is comprised of 452 acres bordering both sides of the Housatonic River immediately south of West Cornwall. It offers access to fishing, canoeing, and picnicking.

A couple of outfitters provide equipment and guidance. **Housatonic Anglers,** Route 7 (*C* **860/672-4457**; www.housatonicanglers.com), offers float trips, fly-fishing schools, lodging in two streamside cottages ($100 to $125), and guided fishing trips ($175 for ½-day, $225 for 1-day, both with lunch). **Clarke Outdoors,** 163 Rte. 7, Cornwall (*C* **860/672-6365**; www.adventuresports.com), offers rentals of river craft, including kayaks and rafts, as well as instruction and guided canoe and raft trips.

Just outside Cornwall proper, off Route 4, is **Mohawk Mountain Ski Area,** 46 Great Hollow Rd. (*C* **800/895-5222** or 860/672-6100). "Mountain" is an overstatement, but this is the state's oldest ski resort, with five lifts, 23 trails, snowmakers, and night skiing. The base lodge has a fireplace and outdoor deck. Rentals and instruction are provided. Adult lift tickets are $32.

SHARON

Early on, this attractive hamlet near the New York border established a reputation for its manufactures, which included mousetraps and cannon shells. Those industries no longer exist, and Sharon is now primarily residential, a picturesque village with many houses made of brick or fieldstone in a region where wood-frame houses prevail.

Sharon Audubon Center The 758-acre nature preserve has herb and flower gardens, a shop and interpretive center, and 11 miles of hiking and nature trails. Injured birds are brought to the center for rehabilitation, and there are usually several raptors (birds of prey) recuperating in house.

Rte. 4. *C* **860/364-0520.** Trails $3 adults, $1.50 seniors and children. Main building, Mon–Sat 9am–5pm, Sun 1–5pm; grounds dawn to dusk.

LAKEVILLE & SALISBURY

These two attractive villages share a common history and a main street lined with 19th-century houses stretching along Route 44. The "lake" in question is Wononscopomuc, slightly south of the town center.

In Salisbury, you might want to stop by the **Salisbury Antiques Center,** 46 Library St. (*C* **860/435-0424**), which deals in exalted forms of English and American furniture and accessories.

The discovery in the area of a particularly pure iron ore led to the development of mines and forges as early as the mid-1700s. One of the ironworkers was the eccentric Ethan Allen, later to become the leader of the Green Mountain Boys and a hero for his capture of Fort Ticonderoga from the British in 1775. The forges of the area supplied Washington's army with many cannons in the critical early years of the Revolution.

Holley-Williams House   One wealthy forge owner and manufacturer, John Milton Holley, bought a 1768 mansion and doubled its size in 1808. The result is a Federal and Greek Revival mix. One of the few historic houses in the area open to the public, it contains furnishings assembled by Holley and his descendants over the continuous 173 years the family lived there.

15 Millerton Rd., Rte. 44. ℂ 860/435-2878. Free admission; guided tours $3 adults, $2 seniors and students, free for children under 5. Memorial Day–Labor Day, Sat–Sun and holidays noon–5pm.

Lime Rock Park   Not far from Lakeville center (south on Route 41, then east on Route 112) is one of the premier auto-racing courses in the Northeast. It garnered even greater attention when Paul Newman, a Connecticut resident, started piloting his own car around the turns. There are also special races with vintage vehicles and NASCAR stock cars, and the famous **Skip Barber Racing School** (ℂ **800/221-1131**) is located here.

Rte. 112. ℂ **860/435-2571**. Races held late Apr to early Nov, Sat and Mon holidays.

WHERE TO STAY

White Hart ✴   This inn's fortunes have fluctuated in its 180-plus years, but lately the white clapboard lodging at the end of Salisbury's main street is on the rise. The front porch is a prime summertime perch. Apart from the three suites and the large Ford Room, most of the guest rooms are on the small side. Unlike most country inns, there is ramp access to all rooms. Both dining room and wine cellar have received excellent notices; duos perform Wednesday nights in the Tap Room.

Village Green (P.O. Box 545), Salisbury, CT 06068. ℂ **800/832-0041** or 860/435-0030. Fax 860/435-0040. www.whitehartinn.com. 26 units. Apr–Nov $119–$249 double; Dec–Mar $109–$229. AE, DC, DISC, MC, V. Pets allowed ($10). **Amenities:** Restaurant, cafe, bar. *In room:* A/C, TV, hair dryer.

WHERE TO DINE

You may also want to consider a meal at the **White Hart,** reviewed above.

West Main at Pocketknife Square ✴ FUSION   The team that started out together in a more modest setting in Sharon picked up and moved here a couple of years ago. Judging by the filled tables, Lakeville is grateful to have them. This is a far more attractive venue, with the big beams and old stones of a former barn fitted out with what they claim is the longest bar in the state, two dining rooms, and a sitting area beside a striking fireplace. The food merges Southwestern, Asian, and Mediterranean themes. Such items as turkey and goat cheese chimichanga, sensational *frites* with aioli, and spicy Shandong noodles have caused a lot of oohing and cross-table sampling.

8 Holley Place, Lakeville ℂ **860/435-1450**. Main courses $15–$21. AE, MC, V. Mon and Wed–Sat noon–2:30pm and 5:30–9pm (until 10pm Fri–Sat); Sun 5:30–9pm.

NORFOLK

Founded in 1758, Norfolk was long popular as a vacation destination for industrialists who owned mills and factories along Connecticut's rivers. At the least, drive into the center for a look at the village green. It is highlighted by a monument that involved the participation of two of the late 19th century's most celebrated creative people—sculptor Augustus Saint-Gaudens and architect Stanford White.

At the opposite corner is the 90-year-old "Music Shed," a closed auditorium on the Ellen Battell Stoeckel Estate that is the venue for an eagerly awaited series of summer events, the **Norfolk Chamber Music Festival** ✴. Held from late June to late August, it hosts evening performances by such luminaries as the

Tokyo String Quartet and the Vermeer Quartet. These are augmented by morning recitals by young professional musicians. June through August, call © **860/542-3000** or write to the Ellen Battell Stoeckel Estate, Routes 44 and 272, Box 545, Norfolk, CT 06058-0545; September through May, call © **203/432-1966** or write to 435 College St., P.O. Box 208246, New Haven, CT 06520-8246.

Two prime recreational areas are near each other on Route 272, north of town. A mile from the village green is **Haystack Mountain State Park,** Route 272 (© **860/482-1817**). Its chief feature is a short trail leading from the parking lot to a stone tower at the 1,715-foot crest. On clear days, the views from the top take in a panorama stretching from the Catskill Mountains in New York to the Long Island Sound. Picnicking is allowed.

Another 5 miles farther north, on the Massachusetts border, enjoy this abundance of streams, rapids, and cascades at **Campbell Falls,** Route 272 (© **860/482-1817**). Fishing is a possibility, as are hiking and picnicking.

WHERE TO STAY

Manor House ⭐   This gabled 1898 manse doesn't fit into a stylistic cubbyhole; just call it "Late Victorian Bavarian Tudor." Inside, it manages to be both stately and homey, with authentic Tiffany windows and fireplaces in the main salon, dining room, and four bedrooms. There's a sun porch, as well as a small bar where guests can help themselves to beverages and snacks. Breakfasts often feature omelets, orange waffles, or blueberry pancakes. The most desirable rooms are on the second floor, notably the English Room, with a king-size bed, sitting area, and two-person whirlpool; and the Lincoln Room, with half-canopied antique queen bed, fireplace, and sitting area. The least expensive room is on the third floor (no elevator), tucked under the eaves—when the owner tells you it's very small, believe her.

69 Maple Ave., Norfolk, CT 06058. © **860/542-5690**. Fax 860/542-5690. www.manorhouse-norfolk.com. 9 units. $100–$225 double. Rates include breakfast. AE, DISC, MC, V. *In room:* No phone.

3 New Haven

The approach to New Haven via Interstate 95 isn't a paean to positive urban planning. At the waterfront are acres of railroad switchyards, storage tanks, and warehouses. Inland are a few half-hearted mid-rise office buildings reached by streets that radiate a sense of hope unfulfilled. It is easy to decide to drive on by.

That would be shortchanging both the city and yourself. For while New Haven suffers the afflictions of most of Connecticut's cities—nearly a quarter of its citizens live at or below the poverty line—it also has a great deal to offer the leisure traveler. Ready and waiting to fill a weekend are four performing-arts centers and theaters, three outstanding small museums, autumn renewals of college football rivalries that date back over 120 years, and a variety of ethnic restaurants that will drive foodies mad with choices.

Much of what is worthwhile about New Haven can be credited to the presence of one of the world's most prestigious universities. Yale both enriches its community and exacerbates the usual town-gown conflicts—a paradox with which the institution and civic authorities have struggled since the colonial period. But there can be no denying that the city would wallow in urban malaise were the university to disappear.

Relatively little serious history has happened here, but there are a number of amusing "firsts" that boosters love to trumpet. The first hamburger was allegedly made and sold here, as was—even less certainly—the first pizza. Noah Webster compiled his first dictionary in New Haven, and Eli Whitney perfected his cotton gin here.

ESSENTIALS

GETTING THERE   Interstate 95 between New York and Providence skirts the shoreline of New Haven; I-91 from Springfield, Mass., and Hartford ends here. Connections can also be made from the south along the Merritt and Wilbur Cross parkways. Downtown traffic isn't too congested, except at the usual rush hours, and there are ample parking lots and garages near the green and Yale University, where most visitors spend their time.

   Tweed–New Haven Airport receives feeder flights connecting with several major airlines, including **Continental** (© **800/525-0280**), **United** (© **800/ 241-6522**), and **US Airways** (© **800/428-4322**). It's located southeast of the city, near Exits 50 and 51 off I-95.

   Amtrak (© **800/USA-RAIL;** www.northeast.amtrak.com) has several trains daily that run between Boston and New York and stop in New Haven. To or from New York takes 1½ hours; to or from Boston, about 3 hours. **Metro North** (© **800/METRO-INFO**) commuter trains make many daily trips between New Haven and New York. Metro-North tickets are much cheaper than Amtrak's, but its trains take longer.

VISITOR INFORMATION   The **Greater New Haven Convention & Visitors Bureau** maintains an attended office at 1 Long Wharf Dr. (© **203/ 777-8550**), visible and easily reached from Exit 46 off I-95. It's open from Memorial Day to Labor Day. An especially useful detailed map of New Haven that even points out restaurants and store locations is *Professor Pathfinder's Yale University & New Haven,* available in bookstores.

SPECIAL EVENTS   Important seasonal events are the new **International Festival of Arts & Ideas** (www.artidea.org), held at many sites around the city in late June, and a free **jazz festival** on the green from late July to early August. Call the visitors bureau for additional details.

EXPLORING YALE & NEW HAVEN

The major attractions are all associated with Yale University, and, except for the Peabody Museum, are within walking distance of one another near the **New Haven Green,** which is bounded by Elm, Church, Chapel, and College streets.

   The flat green, about a third the size of Boston Common, is divided into two unequal parts by north-south Temple Street. It was set aside by town elders in the earliest colonial days as a place for citizens to graze their livestock, bury their dead, and spend leisure hours strolling its footpaths. Government and bank buildings, including the Gothic Revival City Hall, border it on the east, a retail district on the south, and some older sections of the vast Yale campus to the north and west.

   Facing Temple Street are three historic churches, all dating from the early 19th century. Next to Chapel Street is **Trinity Episcopal Church,** a brownstone Gothic Revival structure, the Georgian **First Church of Christ/Center Congregational Church,** and the essentially Federal-style **United Congregational.** The First Church of Christ is of greatest interest, built atop a crypt with tombstones inscribed as early as 1687. Tours are conducted Tuesday through Friday between 10:30am and 2:30pm.

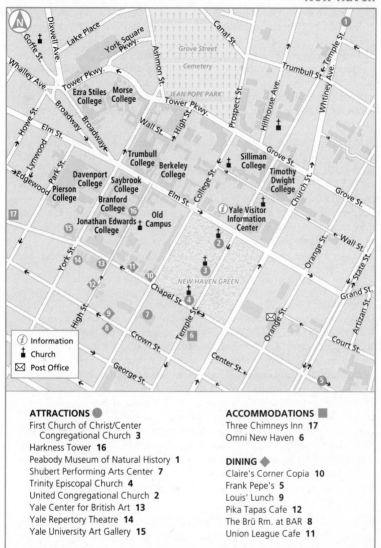

The oldest house in New Haven is now the **Yale University Visitor Information Center,** a colonial facing the north side of the green at 149 Elm St., near College Street (📞 **203/432-2300**). While its primary mission is to familiarize prospective students and their parents with an hour-long **guided walking tour,** the center also has an introductory video and maps for self-guided tours. It's open Monday through Friday from 9am to 4:45pm, Saturday and Sunday from 10am to 4pm. Guided tours are available Monday through Friday at 10:30am and 2pm, Saturday and Sunday at 1:30pm.

It is impossible to imagine New Haven without Yale, so pervasive is its physical and cultural presence. After all, it helped educate our most recent three presidents, as well as Gerald Ford, William Howard Taft, Noah Webster, Nathan Hale, and Eli Whitney. Established in 1702 in the shoreline town now known as Clinton, the young college was eventually moved here in 1718 and named for Elihu Yale, who made a major financial contribution.

The most evocative quadrangle of the sprawling institution is the **Old Campus,** which can be entered from College, High, or Chapel streets. Inside, the mottled green is enclosed by Federal and Victorian Gothic buildings and dominated by **Harkness Tower,** a 1920 Gothic Revival campanile that looks much older.

Yale Center for British Art ★★
What looks like a parking garage from outside is a great deal more impressive inside. The museum, designed by Louis Kahn, claims to be the most important repository of British art outside the United Kingdom, with holdings of more than 1,400 paintings and sculptures and tens of thousands of drawings and prints. Most of the paintings in the permanent collection are from the 16th through the early 19th century. It's a dazzling array, with about 250 canvases on view at any one time, by such luminaries as Hogarth, Gainsborough, Joshua Reynolds, and the glorious Turner.

1080 Chapel St. (at High St.). ✆ 203/432-2800. www.yale.edu/ycba. Free admission. Tues–Sat 10am–5pm; Sun noon–5pm.

Yale University Art Gallery ★★
The artworks of many epochs and regions are on display, but the museum is most noted for its collections of French Impressionists and American realists of the late 19th and early 20th centuries. It's a satisfying collection for connoisseurs, and won't test the patience of reluctant museum-goers. Architect Louis I. Kahn, responsible for the nearby Center for British Art, also designed the larger of these two buildings. Take the elevator to the fourth floor and work your way down. Asian arts and crafts command the top floor. The tiny Netsuke ivories at the center bear close examination. On the third floor are 14th- to 18th-century Gothic ecclesiastical panels, mainly tempera on wood with prodigious amounts of gilt, and 16th-century Italian and Dutch portraits and allegorical scenes, among them paintings by Rubens and Frans Hals. In sharp contrast are adjoining galleries of avant-garde 20th-century Americans of the Abstract Expressionist school—Rothko and Rauschenberg as well as Europeans Braque, Picasso, Mondrian, and Mirí.

1111 Chapel St. (at York St.). ✆ 203/432-0600. www.yale.edu/artgallery. Free admission ($5 suggested donation). Tues–Sat 10am–5pm; Sun 1–6pm.

Peabody Museum of Natural History ★
Head to the third floor and work your way down, especially if a school group has just entered. Up at the top are dioramas with stuffed animals in various environments: bighorn sheep, Alaskan brown bears, bison, musk oxen, and the assorted birds, snakes, and rodents with which they share their natural settings. On the same floor is a small but illuminating collection of ancient Egyptian artifacts. The second floor doesn't hold much of general interest, but down on the first is a "bestiary" of large stuffed animals, which leads logically into the Great Hall of Dinosaurs. Its assembled fossils range from a pea-brained stegosaurus to mastodons and a fearsome brontosaurus.

170 Whitney Ave. (at Sachem St.). ✆ 203/432-5050. Admission $5 adults, $3 seniors and children 3–15, free for children under 3. Mon–Sat 10am–5pm; Sun noon–5pm.

SHOPPING

Atticus Bookstore & Cafe   It might as easily be listed under "Where to Dine," for half of this store consists of a lunch counter and take-out section. Famous for its scones, the cafe also sells crusty loaves of bread, soups, and hero sandwiches. The New Orleans–style muffaletta is especially good. The rest of the space is devoted to what many call the best bookstore in town. It's open daily from 8am to midnight. 1082 Chapel St. ℂ **203/776-4040.**

WHERE TO STAY

New Haven lodgings are both limited and, with one notable exception, devoid of either charm or distinctiveness. Still, its motels and hotels fill up far in advance for football weekends, alumni reunions, and graduation.

Among the chains in town are the **Holiday Inn,** 30 Whalley Rd. (ℂ **203/777-6221**); **Grand Chalet Inn & Suites,** 400 Sargent Dr. (ℂ **203/562-1111**); and **Residence Inn,** 3 Long Wharf Dr. (ℂ **203/777-5337**). The visitors bureau has a **hotel reservation service** (ℂ **800/332-7829**).

Omni New Haven 🎇🎇   The result of an extensive renovation of a hotel that had been derelict for years, this is a conventional member of the reliable chain. Its location couldn't be improved, next to the green and within walking distance of the theaters, much of the university campus, business and government offices, and two of the Yale museums. Rates jump for special-event days at Yale, true of all local lodgings. Galileo's, the 19th-floor restaurant, offers fine views of the green and surrounding cityscape.

155 Temple St. (south of Chapel St.), New Haven, CT 06510. ℂ **800/THE-OMNI** or 203/772-6664. Fax 203/974-6780. www.omnihotels.com. 305 units. $97–$189 double. AE, DC, DISC, MC, V. **Amenities:** Restaurant, bar; exercise room; concierge; full-service business center; limited room service; same-day dry cleaning/laundry service. *In room:* A/C, TV, dataport, minibar, coffeemaker, hair dryer.

Three Chimneys Inn 🎇🎇   Once known as the Inn at Chapel West, this 1870 mansion is the favorite inn of Yalies and their parents. All guest rooms are outfitted with custom-made armoires (to hide the TVs) and mahogany four-poster beds, three of which have drapes that can be drawn completely. In winter, gas fires burn in the dining room and parlor, where a tray of cordials is set out. Businesspeople are more in evidence than is usual at inns, many of them here to interview Yale students for jobs.

1201 Chapel St. (between Park and Howe sts.), New Haven, CT 06511. ℂ **800/443-1554** out of state, or 203/789-1201. Fax 203/776-7363. www.threechimneysinn.com. 11 units. $180 single or double. Rates include breakfast and afternoon tea. AE, DISC, MC, V. Children over 6 welcome. **Amenities:** Access to nearby health club; same-day dry cleaning. *In room:* A/C, TV, dataport, hair dryers.

WHERE TO DINE

The Brü Rm. at BAR 🎇 PIZZA   Yes, those spellings and capitalizations are correct. This is a 1996 brewpub tacked onto a slightly older nightclub ("BAR"). It's also a naked challenge in the eternal New Haven pizza wars. If Frank Pepe's is the champ (see below), as consensus insists, this whippersnapper is a leading contender. Start with the house salad, a concoction of pears and pecans atop mixed greens with crumbled blue cheese. The chrome and copper vats on the ground floor and open mezzanine produce five beers and ales, from the BAR Blonde to the Damn Good Stout.

254 Crown St. (between High and College sts.). ℂ **203/495-1111.** Pizzas $5–$12. AE, DC, DISC, MC, V. Mon–Tues 5pm–1am; Wed–Thurs 11:30am–2:30pm and 5pm–1am; Thurs–Fri 11:30am–1am; Sat 5pm–2am; Sun 5pm–1am.

Claire's Corner Copia VEGETARIAN   Few college towns are without at least one low-cost vegetarian restaurant. This one has ruled in New Haven since 1975, more than enough time for the founder to produce three cookbooks, all available for purchase. Options include curried couscous, eggplant rollatini, and a number of Mexican entrees, but the stars might well be the veggie burgers and pizzettes. The operators aren't vegans, to be sure, offering lox platters and alba-core melt sandwiches. Breakfast brings a bounty of plump scones and massive muffins.

1000 Chapel St. (at College St.). ℂ **203/562-3888**. Main courses $5.25–$9.50. No credit cards. Sun–Thurs 8am–9pm; Fri–Sat 8am–10pm.

Frank Pepe's ⊕ PIZZA   On the scene for most of this century, Pepe's has long claimed the local pizza crown while fighting off perpetual challenges. In exchange for super, almost unimaginably thin-crusted pies, pilgrims put up with long lines, a nothing decor, and a sullen staff.

If the wait looks to be especially long, you can do about as well at **Sally's** ⊕, 237 Wooster St. (ℂ **203/624-5271**), just down the street.

157 Wooster St. (between Olive and Brown sts.). ℂ **203/865-5762**. Pizzas $4.95–$10. No credit cards. Mon and Wed–Thurs 4–10:30pm, Fri–Sat 11:30am–midnight; Sun 2:30–10:30pm.

Louis' Lunch ⊕ SANDWICHES   Here's history on a shingle. The claim, unprovable but gaining strength as the decades roll on, is that America's very first hamburger was sold in 1900 at this boxy little brick luncheonette. It moved from its original location a few years ago to escape demolition, but not much else has changed. The tiny wooden counter and tables are carved with the initials of a century of patrons. The beef is freshly ground each day, thrust into gas-fired ovens almost as old as the building, and then served (medium rare, usually) on two slices of white toast. The only allowable garnishes are slices of tomato, onion, or cheese. There's no mustard and no ketchup, so don't even ask. And no fries, either, just potato chips.

261–263 Crown St. (between High and College sts.). ℂ **203/562-5507**. Burgers $3–$4.50. No credit cards. Tues–Wed 11am–4pm; Thurs–Sat noon–2am.

Pika Tapas Cafe ⊕ SPANISH   Among the most common tapas are the *tortilla,* a firm potato-and-onion omelet; *pan Catalan,* thick slices of bread rubbed with tomato pulp and draped with Serrano ham and Manchego cheese; and *gambas al ajillo,* shrimp sautéed with garlic. These and another dozen or so are set out on the big semicircular bar at this sprightly enterprise. Keep it in mind for light meals before or after curtains at the nearby theaters.

39 High St. (south of Chapel St.). ℂ **203/865-1933**. Main courses $10.50–$16.75, tapas $4.75–$9.75. AE, DC, MC, V. Sun and Tues 5–10pm; Wed–Sat 11:30am–2:30pm and 5–10pm (until 11pm Fri–Sat).

Union League Café ⊕⊕ CREATIVE FRENCH   These grand salons with high arched windows retain an air of their aristocratic origins, which date back to 1854. Even the name fairly shrieks of its former status as a bastion of WASP privilege, the Union League Club. It has loosened up considerably, and jeans-clad Yalies, their doting parents, philosophizing profs, and deal-making execs are all equally comfortable here. With waiters in aprons and tables covered with butcher paper, the atmosphere is now closer to an updated brasserie than to that of a gentlemen's sanctuary. The chef routinely tinkers with Gallic culinary tradition, although that is the foundation from which he works. Entrees on the order of duck breast with potato and white truffle gnocchi and Grenache sauce seem both familiar and fresh.

1032 Chapel St. (between High and College sts.). (C) 203/562-4299. Main courses $16.50–$23.75. AE, DC, MC, V. Mon–Fri 11:30am–2:30pm; Mon–Thurs 5:30–9:30pm; Fri–Sat 5:30–10pm.

NEW HAVEN AFTER DARK

The presence of Yale and a highly educated faction of the general population ensures a cultural life equal to that in many larger cities. A reliable source of information about cultural events and nightlife is the free weekly newspaper, the *New Haven Advocate* (www.newhavenadvocate.com).

THE PERFORMING ARTS   Within a couple of blocks of the green, the **Shubert Performing Arts Center,** 247 College St. (© **800/228-6622** or 203/562-5666), presents musical plays, opera, cabaret, miscellaneous concerts, and such touring troupes as Mummenschanz and the Alvin Ailey Dance Theater. A deconsecrated church west of the green is the home of the well-regarded **Yale Repertory Theatre,** Chapel and York streets (© **203/432-1234**), which mounts an October-to-May season of modern productions as well as classics by Shakespeare and George Bernard Shaw.

Away from downtown, but worth the cab fare, is the prestigious **Long Wharf Theatre,** 222 Sargent Dr. (© **203/787-4282**), known for its success in producing new plays that often make the jump to Off-Broadway and even Broadway itself. The season runs from October to June. The Long Wharf spawned the smaller **Stage II.**

Several venues on the Yale campus, including **Sprague Memorial Hall,** 470 College St., and **Woolsey Hall,** College and Grove streets, host the performances of many resident organizations, including the New Haven Symphony Orchestra, New Haven Civic Orchestra, Yale Concert Band, Yale Glee Club, Yale Philharmonia, and Yale Symphony Orchestra. For upcoming events, call the **Yale Concert Information Line** (© **203/432-4157**).

THE CLUB & MUSIC SCENE   A newish venue for blues, jazz, and Latin soul, **The Blues,** 71 Whitney Ave. (© **203/498-2583**), keeps the scheduling and inducements fresh. There are jam sessions, open-mike nights, salsa dance classes, and a generous—and free!—happy-hour buffet.

The biggest and best venue for live rock and pop is **Toad's Place,** 300 York St. (© **203/621-TOAD**), which has welcomed the likes of the Rolling Stones, U2, Phoebe Snow, and Bob Dylan. Covers can get up to $15 or more for the top acts, but are much lower most of the time. The club usually features live music Wednesday through Sunday, with dancing (to a band or DJ) most Saturday nights.

For something less frenetic, the popular **BAR,** 254 Crown St. (© **203/ 495-1111**), has a lounge in front—open to the street on warm nights—and a pool table, a terrace, and a dance floor with another bar in back. Connected to BAR is the Brü Rm., described above under "Where to Dine."

4 Hartford

Connecticut's capital and second-largest city endures a drooping uneasiness it hasn't been able to shake. There was hope for revival a few years ago when it appeared that the governor had persuaded the New England Patriots to move to downtown Hartford. A new stadium was to have been the centerpiece of a

$1-billion 35-acre riverfront development. At the last contractual minute, the Patriots exercised an escape clause, choosing to remain in the Boston area. While it is possible that parts of the plan will yet be realized, there was a great whoosh of despair when the balloon burst.

It was uncertain that even the ambitious original scheme would have reversed decades of decline. Hartford continues to point gamely to its grand edifices—the divinely overwrought gold-domed capitol, the High Victorian Mark Twain House, the august Wadsworth Atheneum. Worthwhile as these sites certainly are, they don't prevent visitors from noticing the miles of distressed housing, weed-strewn lots, and hollow-eyed office and industrial structures that radiate out from the center. The bedrock insurance business has been in the doldrums, and poverty and its attendant malignancies are persistent thorns in the civic hide.

It isn't as if efforts haven't been made to heal the wounds. A civic center was completed in 1975 in an attempt to attract business downtown, and a flyway connects it with the newer 39-story CityPlace. Both venues offer concerts and art exhibits, and the 489-seat Hartford Stage Company has a 10-month theatrical season in its own 1977 building cater-corner from the center. A block away, the gracious Old State House enjoyed a 4-year renovation. Across Main Street, a shed has been provided for a daily farmers' market; a local paper sponsors noontime rock concerts in summer. All these efforts have encouraged the establishment of a few cosmopolitan restaurants and a couple of good hotels, so most of a day trip or overnight visit can be contained within only a few square blocks.

Dissidents, fleeing the rigid religious dictates of the Massachusetts Bay Colony, founded Hartford in 1636. Three years later, they drafted what were called the "Fundamental Orders," the basis of a subsequent claim that Connecticut was the first political entity on earth to have a written constitution, hence the nickname "Constitution State."

ESSENTIALS

GETTING THERE   Interstates 84 and 91 intersect in central Hartford, halfway between New York and Boston (115 miles northeast of New York, 103 miles southwest of Boston). Downtown Hartford has plenty of convenient parking, including the garage of the Civic Center.

Several major U.S. airlines provide direct or feeder-line service to **Bradley International Airport,** in Windsor Locks, about 12 miles north of the city. Buses, cabs, and limousines shuttle passengers into the city and to other points in the state. Major airlines serving Hartford include **American** (✆ **800/ 433-7300**), **Continental** (✆ **800/525-0280**), **Delta** (✆ **800/221-1212**), **Northwest** (✆ **800/225-2525**), **Southwest** (✆ **800/435-9792**), **United** (✆ **800/241-6522**), and **US Airways** (✆ **800/247-8786**).

Amtrak (✆ **800/USA-RAIL**) has several trains daily following the inland route between New York City and Boston, stopping at Hartford and Windsor Locks. The trip to either New York or Boston takes about 2½ hours.

VISITOR INFORMATION   An information counter on the main floor of the Civic Center, at Trumbull, Asylum, and Church streets, is staffed by members of the **Hartford Guides.** Highly knowledgeable about their city, they not only provide information about sightseeing, shopping, restaurants, and hotels, but also conduct walking tours and can provide escort service for women and seniors from lodgings or restaurants to their cars or buses. To obtain their assistance or suggestions, call ✆ **860/293-8105.**

Hartford

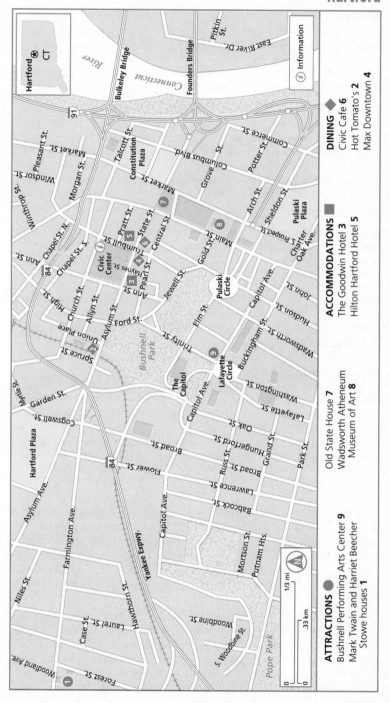

ATTRACTIONS ●
Bushnell Performing Arts Center **9**
Mark Twain and Harriet Beecher
Stowe houses **1**

Old State House **7**
Wadsworth Atheneum
Museum of Art **8**

ACCOMMODATIONS ■
The Goodwin Hotel **3**
Hilton Hartford Hotel **5**

DINING ◆
Civic Cafe **6**
Hot Tomato's **2**
Max Downtown **4**

ⓘ Information

SPECIAL EVENTS   Hartford makes the most of its association with one of America's most beloved authors, Mark Twain. His image is seen everywhere, and the city puts on three **Mark Twain Days** in mid-August, with such relevant events as frog jumping, fence painting, riverboat rides, and performances of plays based on Twain's life or works. Most activities are free. In late July, there's a **Festival of Jazz** with free performances at the pavilion in **Bushnell Park.**

SEEING THE SIGHTS

The Old State House   After a 4-year, $12-million restoration, the 1796 State House opened in time to celebrate its bicentennial. Costumed interpreters stand ready to answer questions. Upstairs on the right is the Senate chamber, with a full-length painting of the first president by the indefatigable Washington portraitist Gilbert Stuart. These days, the building is used for temporary art exhibitions, changed two or three times yearly.

800 Main St. (at Asylum Ave.). ℂ 860/522-6766. Free admission. Mon–Fri 10am–4pm; Sat 11am–4pm.

Mark Twain House ✪✪   This 19-room house is a fascinating example of the late-19th-century style sometimes known as "Picturesque Gothic," with several steeply peaked gables and brick walls whose varying patterns are highlighted by black or orange paint.

Samuel Clemens, whose pseudonym was a term used by Mississippi River pilots to indicate a water depth of 2 fathoms, lived here from 1873 to 1897. The High Victorian interior was the work of distinguished designers of the time, including Louis Comfort Tiffany, who provided both advice and stained glass. Twain's enthusiasm for newfangled gadgets—*Tom Sawyer* is said to be the first novel written on a typewriter—led to the installation of a primitive telephone in the entrance hall.

A guided tour takes about an hour and eventually leads to the top floor and the writer's main workroom, a large space that also has a pool table. Twain would often walk across the hall in the middle of the night and wake up his butler to play a few games.

351 Farmington Ave. ℂ 860/247-0998. www.marktwainhouse.org. Admission $9 adults, $8 seniors, $7 children 13–18, $5 children 6–12. May 1–Oct 31 and Dec Mon–Sat 9:30am–4pm; Sun noon–4pm. Rest of the year, closed Tues. Visits by guided tour only; last tour begins at 4pm. Take Exit 46 off I-84, turn right onto Sisson Ave., then right onto Farmington Ave. The house is on the right. From downtown, drive west on Asylum St., bearing left on Farmington Ave. The house is on the left.

Harriet Beecher Stowe House   On the adjacent property, about 60 yards across the lawn from the Twain residence, this is a smaller version of its neighbor, built in 1871. Stowe, the author of the antislavery novel *Uncle Tom's Cabin*, lived here for most of the time Twain resided in his house.

73 Forest St. ℂ 860/525-9317. Admission $9 adults, $8 seniors, $5 children 6–12. Memorial Day to Oct 15 and Dec Mon–Sat 9:30am–5pm; Sun 11am–5pm. Rest of the year Sun noon–5pm; closed Tues. Visits by guided tour only; last tour begins at 4pm.

Wadsworth Atheneum Museum of Art ✪✪✪   Opened in 1842, this was the first public art museum in the United States and remains a repository with few equals in New England. The strength of the collection lies primarily in its American paintings, spanning the period from landscape artists of the first half of the 19th century through luminaries of the New York School of the mid–20th to provocative work from some of today's young artists.

For an overview, take the elevator to the top floor. In a far corner is a room devoted to Thomas Cole, a leader among artists of the Hudson River School; adjacent galleries contain works by his contemporaries Frederick Church and the flamboyant Albert Bierstadt. On the balcony outside are more Americans—Frederic Remington, Andrew Wyeth, Ben Shahn, Reginald Marsh, Milton Avery, Norman Rockwell. Watch for the shadow box by Joseph Cornell. These lead to a room of American Impressionists.

Second-floor rooms display early Connecticut furniture, most of it elaborately carved in a form of utilitarian folk art. On the first floor is the MATRIX Gallery, full of rule-bending multimedia works, as well as rooms of large canvases by Abstract Expressionists and pop and op artists of the 1950s and 1960s like de Kooning, Rauschenberg, and Kline. Also on this floor is the **Museum Cafe,** which has surprisingly good light items and tables out on the terrace in fair weather.

600 Main St. (1 block west of the Old State House). ℂ **860/278-2670.** Admission $7 adults, $5 seniors and students, $3 children 6–17 (free all day Thurs and 11am–noon on Sat); surcharges for some special exhibitions. Tues–Sun 11am–5pm (until 8pm first Thurs of month).

WHERE TO STAY

The Goodwin Hotel ✪   This quiet hostelry opposite the Civic Center is housed in a Queen Anne–style Victorian built in 1881 as a residence for J. P. Morgan, 19th-century industrialist and railway tycoon. Its understated public areas are attractive, while the cautiously decorated bedrooms are fully equipped. Valet parking is often slow at checkout time, but still a blessing along this crowded block. The in-house restaurant has an erratic reputation, but some of the city's best dining options are short walks away

1 Haynes St. (at Asylum St.), Hartford, CT 06103. ℂ **800/922-5006** or 860/246-7500. Fax 860/244-2669. www.goodwinhotel.com. 124 units. $99–$247 double; $250–$750 suite. Weekend packages available. AE, DC, DISC, MC, V. Valet parking $15. **Amenities:** Restaurant, lounge; modest health club; concierge; business center; limited room service; same-day dry cleaning. *In room:* A/C, TV, VCR on request, dataport, hair dryer, iron.

Hilton Hartford Hotel ✪✪   This 22-story slab used to be a Sheraton. Guests will enjoy the results of the $4 million expended on largely cosmetic renovations. The hotel connects with the Civic Center and is readily visible to drivers entering the city from I-84.

315 Trumbull St., Hartford, CT 06103. ℂ **860/728-5151.** Fax 860/240-7246. www.hilton.com/hotels. 390 units. $155–$189 double. AE, DC, DISC, MC, V. **Amenities:** Restaurant, bar; indoor pool; fully equipped health club; whirlpool; sauna; limited room service; same-day dry cleaning/laundry service. *In room:* A/C, TV, dataport, coffeemaker, hair dryer, iron, Nintendo.

WHERE TO DINE

Civic Cafe ✪ ECLECTIC   Young execs and lawyers frequent this place, which looks like it belongs in a hipper city. Air-conditioning is glacial, and so, sometimes, is the service. No one seems to mind, so busy are they observing or partaking in the ritual collisions of egos. Suits dominate at lunch, when the raw bar is a big draw, and at happy hour, when patrons gather around the bar. The food itself gets your attention, not least for the gobs of salsas and dustings of herbs cast over each plate.

150 Trumbull St. (near Asylum St.). ℂ **860/493-7412.** Main courses $17.95–$24.95. AE, DC, DISC, MC, V. Mon–Fri 11–1am; Sat 5pm–2am.

Hot Tomato's ★ ITALIAN   The renovation of Union Station spawned this popular trattoria in one wing. Dine in the glass-sided dining room or on the terrace. A casually dressed crowd tucks into big bowls of garlicky pasta. Especially spicy dishes are marked with a star; two such are shrimp fra diavolo and ziti tossed with grilled chicken strips and bitter broccoli rabe.

1 Union Place (corner of Asylum St.). (© 860/249-5100. Reservations advised for patio and on weekends. Main courses $13–$32. AE, DISC, DC, MC, V. Mon–Fri 11:30am–11pm; Sat–Sun 4pm–midnight.

Max Downtown ★★ CONTEMPORARY AMERICAN   Hartford's prime-time power and event epicenter has a crowd that looks essentially interchangeable with the one that frequents the Civic (see above), albeit with a few more suits and fading hairlines at midday and a lot of air-kissing at night. The tavern is a jump-off for office parties and deals-in-progress. Too bad no one seems to pay much attention to the bar menu, for its treats are along the lines of mulligatawny and mahi-mahi with mango-papaya sauce. Over 12 wines are available by the glass. The main room has banquettes and booths arrayed behind expanses of glass, with a flashy mural on the back wall. Patrons are indulged with hefty chophouse favorites—thick veal chops and strip steaks—and flightier efforts, such as coconut-crusted shrimp.

185 Asylum St. (opposite City Center). (© 860/522-2530. Reservations advised on weekends. Main courses $14.95–$28.95. AE, DC, MC, V. Mon–Fri 11:30am–2:30pm and 5–10:30pm (until 11:30pm Fri); Sat 5–11:30pm; Sun 4:30–10pm.

HARTFORD AFTER DARK

The free weekly *Hartford Advocate* (www.hartfordadvocate.com) provides useful information on cultural, sports, and musical events.

The **Bushnell Performing Arts Center,** 166 Capitol Ave. (© 860/987-5900; www.bushnell.org), is the venue for the **Hartford Symphony,** the **Connecticut Opera,** and the **Hartford Pops,** when it isn't hosting visiting symphony orchestras or road companies of Broadway plays like *Ragtime, Company,* and *Titanic.* The **Hartford Stage,** 50 Church St. (© 860/527-5151; www.hartfordstage.org), mounts a variety of mainstream plays.

Several downtown clubs host live bands, usually Thursday through Saturday. Assuming they're still in operation, check out the **Arch Street Tavern,** 85 Arch St. (© 860/246-7610), where nationally known bands of the second magnitude have appeared from time to time; and **bar with no name,** 115 Asylum St. (© 860/522-4646), which buzzes with young singles playing pool and attending to both live and recorded alternative, techno, and house music. The **Brickyard Cafe,** 113–115 Allyn St. (© 860/249-2112), contains a street-level bar, a dance floor one flight up, and a sports bar with pool tables up on the third floor.

Now 10 years old, **Hartford Brewery,** 35 Pearl St. (© 860/246-2337), was the city's first brewery. It serves food that goes right with the home brews, and sometimes hosts rock and jazz bands. For beer by the pint or pitcher along with Monday Night Football or the Final Four, where better than **Coach's,** 187 Allyn St. (© 860/522-6224), a place founded by the UConn basketball coach himself? It has 32 TVs, bar snacks like chili in scooped-out loaves of bread, and live music Thursday through Saturday.

5 From Guilford to Old Saybrook

Usually ignored by vacationers anxious to get on to Mystic and Essex and the casinos, the stretch of coast between New Haven and the Connecticut River, known simply as the Shoreline, has its gentle pleasures, enough to justify a short detour for lunch, a walk on a beach, a spell of shopping, or even a proper British high tea (in Madison). When lodgings are difficult to find at the better-known destinations, the Shoreline's inns and resorts are logical alternatives within easy driving distance.

ESSENTIALS

GETTING THERE   The Shoreline can be reached from Exit 57 off I-95. Pick up Route 1 (a.k.a. the Boston Post Road), which serves as the main street of several Shoreline towns.

Several daily **Amtrak** (✆ **800/USA-RAIL**) trains stop at Old Saybrook. The **Shoreline East** (✆ **800/255-7433**) commuter line uses the same tracks to service towns between here and New Haven, but only Monday through Friday.

VISITOR INFORMATION   Informational materials can be obtained in advance from the **Connecticut River Valley and Shoreline Visitors Council,** 393 Main St., Middletown (✆ **800/486-3346** or 860/347-0028).

GUILFORD

One of the state's oldest colonial settlements (1639), this village, 13 miles east of New Haven, is embraced by the West and East rivers and has an uncommonly large green bordered by churches, shops, and public buildings.

There are dozens of historic houses to see in town, most of them privately owned and a few others open to the public on a limited seasonal basis, typically Memorial Day weekend to Labor Day. **Hyland House,** 84 Boston St. (✆ **203/453-9477**), built around 1660, and the **Thomas Griswold House,** 171 Boston St. (✆ **203/453-3176**), from 1774, are two of these.

Henry Whitfield State Museum   The Whitfield Museum's billing as "the oldest house in Connecticut and the oldest stone house in New England" is misleading. Apart from undergoing frequent alterations over the years, the house was devastated by a major fire in 1860 that left little more than the granite walls. It was reconstructed and occupied until the turn of the century, but by the 1930s had deteriorated from neglect and had to be rebuilt once again. Most of what you see now, including the leaded windows, dates from the second reconstruction and not from the mid-1600s. It is presented as a museum, not a historic home. The furnishings are authentic to the period, and there are displays of powder horns, flintlock rifles, and a loom.

248 Old Whitfield St. ✆ 203/453-2457. Admission $3.50 adults, $2.50 seniors, $2 children 6–17. Feb 1–Dec 14 Wed–Sun 10am–4:30pm; Dec 15–Jan 30 by appointment only.

WHERE TO DINE

The Bistro on the Green ✿ NEW AMERICAN   This popular spot hews to the conventions that the word "bistro" suggests. Butcher paper is laid over white tablecloths under vases of fresh flowers; escargot and cassoulet are among the frequent offerings. But the new chef is pushing the edges, so there's a bruschetta du jour, as well as various pastas and eclectic dishes like pistachio-crusted salmon.

25 Whitfield St. ✆ 203/458-9059. Dinner main courses $12–$21. MC, V. Mon–Thurs 11am–9pm; Fri–Sat 11am–10pm; Sun 10am–9pm.

MADISON

Madison, 19 miles east of New Haven, is home to a historic architectural district that stretches west of the business district along the Boston Post Road, from the main green to the town line, and contains many examples of 18th- and 19th-century domestic styles and few commercial intrusions.

The well-to-do town has completed the transition from colony to seaside resort to year-round community, a process begun when the first house was built in 1651. Today, there are two dwellings from the early years that can be visited on limited summer schedules. **Deacon John Grave House,** 581 Boston Post Rd. (✆ **203/245-4798**), dates from 1685, and the **Allis-Bushnell House,** 853 Boston Post Rd. (✆ **203/245-4567**), from 1785.

Off the Boston Post Road east of the town center, also reached from Exit 62 off I-95, is **Hammonasset Beach State Park** (✆ **203/245-1817**), a 900-plus-acre peninsula jutting into Long Island Sound that has the only public swimming beach in the area. The park also has a nature center, picnic areas, and campgrounds, and offers boating, too. Cars with Connecticut license plates get in for $5 Monday through Thursday and $7 Saturday and Sunday; out-of-state plates pay $8 and $12, respectively.

SHOPPING

Madison's commercial district may look ordinary at first glance, but several shops along Boston Post Road and intersecting Wall Street provide entertaining browsing. They are the remaining holdouts against the monster outlet malls recently opened in neighboring Clinton and Westbrook.

One of the most active stores in the community is **R. J. Julia Booksellers,** 768 Boston Post Rd. (✆ **203/245-3959**), which holds frequent author readings and poetry slams.

The British Shoppe, 45 Wall St. (✆ **203/245-4521**), a plum-colored 1690 saltbox, stocks such English favorites as kippers, bangers, pork pies, teas, and sublime cheeses. Gifts and housewares of British origin are on sale, and lunches and afternoon teas are served in the Front Parlor. Classic ploughman's lunches of cheese, bread, tomato, lettuce, and pickled onions recall those in English pubs (tough licensing requirements don't allow for pints of English beer, but you can bring your own).

Exit 63 off I-95 west leads directly to **Clinton Crossing,** 20-A Killingsworth Turnpike (✆ **860/664-0700**), a substantial new "premium" outlet mall with more than 80 shops. Clothing by such designers as Anne Klein, Calvin Klein, Donna Karan, Geoffrey Beene, Perry Ellis, Ralph Lauen, Versace, and Tommy Hilfiger are augmented by Coach leather goods and Le Creuset cookware.

WHERE TO STAY

All rooms in the 9-unit **Tidewater Inn,** 949 Boston Post Rd. (✆ **203/ 245-8457;** fax 203/318-0265), have air-conditioning, TVs, and phones.

The Inn at Lafayette ★**/Cafe Allegre** ★★   The stately Greek Revival portico in the middle of the business district promises a touch of elegance, and the interior delivers. Since 1998, the ground floor has housed Cafe Allegre, a soothing setting for northern Italian food of considerable accomplishment. No thin tomato sauces or high-rise architectural presentations here—flavors are full but exquisitely balanced. The bar in front is a low-key gathering place, popular for lunch, with a piano player on Thursday and Friday nights. The new owners haven't done much with the guest rooms upstairs, but they were already comfortable enough, with marble baths and king- or queen-size beds.

725 Boston Post Rd., Madison, CT 06443. ✆ 203/245-7773. Fax 203/245-6256. www.allegrecafe.net. 5 units. Late May to mid-Oct $125–$175 double; mid-Oct to mid-May $95–$150. AE, DC, MC, V. Children over 12 welcome. **Amenities:** Restaurant (Italian), bar. *In room:* A/C, TV, dataport, hair dryer.

WHERE TO DINE

See above for a review of **Cafe Allegre.**

Lenny & Joe's Fish Tale ☆ SEAFOOD   At this rough-and-ready fish shack, fish rules, most of it fried. And while it is sure to elevate triglyceride counts, the nutty, crunchy coating on super-fresh whole clams, oysters, shrimp, and calamari is hard to resist, especially on a summer evening. The menu is printed daily to reflect market prices and availability. There's another branch at 1301 Boston Post Rd. (✆ **860/245-7289**).

86 Boston Post Rd., Westbrook ✆860/669-0767. Main courses $11.95–$15.95. Daily 11am–10pm (until 9pm Sun).

OLD SAYBROOK

Its location at the mouth of the Connecticut River (35 miles east of New Haven, 26 miles west of Mystic) is this otherwise nondescript town's principal lure. Get off Route 1 to see it at its best. Pick up Route 153 south at the western edge, following the nearly circular route as it touches the shore and passes through the hamlets of Knollwood and Fenwick and across the causeway to Saybrook Point before ending up back in the main business district.

WHERE TO DINE

Cuckoo's Nest ☆ MEXICAN/CAJUN/CREOLE   Sticklers for gastronomic verisimilitude can look elsewhere. The rest of us can have a good time at this raffish roadhouse, which comes with beat-up wooden chairs and tables that have been on site since the 1976 opening. Old advertising signs adorn the walls, pierced-tin lamps hang over some tables, and fans rotate lazily overhead. A jazz duo performs Thursday nights, a pianist on Sundays. As for the food, pasta jambalaya with shrimp, chicken, and sausage is hardly Creole, nor is the chicken and rice with jalapeños precisely Mexican, but they taste mighty good. The Sunday all-you-can-eat brunch is only $10.95. Start off with a mango margarita, out on the terrace if it's warm.

1712 Boston Post Rd. (Rte. 1). ✆ 860/399-9060. Main courses $13.95–$16.95. AE, DC, DISC, MC, V. Mon–Thurs 11:30am–10pm; Fri–Sat 11:30am–11pm; Sun 11am–10pm.

6 The Connecticut River Valley

New England's longest river originates in the far north near the Canadian border, 407 miles from Long Island Sound. It separates Vermont from New Hampshire, splits Massachusetts in half, then takes a 45-degree turn at Middletown, south of Hartford, to make its final run to the sea.

Native Americans of the region called the river *Quinnetukut,* which, to the tin ears of the English settlers, sounded like "Connecticut." The colonists encroached upon Indian territory as far north as present-day Windsor, which ignited a brief war with the Pequot, who occupied the land.

Since the river was navigable by relatively large ships as far as Hartford, the sheltered lower Connecticut became important for boat-building and industries associated with the international clipper trade. The Connecticut River retains that nautical flavor, and the valley has miraculously avoided the industrialization, development, and decay that afflicts most of the state's other rivers.

Cruising, boating, and kayaking are obvious attractions, supplemented by rides on a steam-powered train, a selection of worthy B&Bs, antiques shops, a venerable musical theater, even a bizarre castle on a hilltop.

> **Tips** **A Note on Accommodations**
>
> There aren't a great many motels between Haddam and Old Lyme, the southernmost segment of the valley that is of greatest interest to visitors, but there are several excellent full-service inns and many small B&Bs, some of which can be found only through referral agencies. Two such companies are **Bed & Breakfast, Ltd.,** P.O. Box 216, New Haven, CT 06513 (℡ 203/469-3260), and **Nutmeg Bed & Breakfast Agency,** P.O. Box 21117, West Hartford, CT 06127 (℡ 800/727-7592 or 860/236-6698).

ESSENTIALS

GETTING THERE   Limited-access state highway 9 runs parallel to the river, along the west side of the valley, connecting I-91 south of Hartford with I-95 near Old Saybrook. The lower valley is therefore readily accessible from all points in New England and from the New York metropolitan area and points south.

Amtrak (℡ **800/USA-RAIL;** www.northeast.amtrak.com) trains stop at Old Saybrook, at the mouth of the river, several times daily on runs between New York and Boston. In addition, **Shoreline East** (℡ **800/255-7433**) commuter trains operate Monday through Friday between New Haven and Old Saybrook.

VISITOR INFORMATION   The **Connecticut River Valley and Shoreline Visitors Council,** 393 Main St., Middletown (℡ **800/486-3346** or 860/347-0028; www.cttourism.org), is a source of pamphlets, maps, and related materials.

OLD LYME

As quiet a town as the coast can claim, Old Lyme (40 miles east of New Haven, 21 miles west of Mystic) was the favored residence of generations of seafarers and ship captains. Many of their 18th- and 19th-century homes have survived, some as inns and museums. With its many tree-lined streets largely free of traffic, stressless biking is an attractive option.

Florence Griswold Museum   Once the shipbuilding and merchant trade had all but flickered out at the end of the 19th century, artists who came to be known as the "American Impressionists" took a fancy to this area. They received encouragement, patronage, and even food and shelter from Ms. Griswold, the wealthy daughter of a sea captain. Her 1817 Federal-style mansion was the temporary home for a number of painters, most of whom left samples of their work in gratitude, sometimes painting directly on the walls of the dining room. Rotating exhibits are held on the first and second floors; the restored studio of Impressionist William Chadwick is also on view. Work is currently underway to restore the garden and orchard. Visitors can walk across the mansion's 6 acres to the Lieutenant River.

96 Lyme St. (Rte. 1). ℡ 860/434-5542. Admission $5 adults, $4 seniors and students, free for children under 12. Apr–Dec Tues–Sat 10am–5pm; Sun 1–5pm. Jan–Mar Wed–Sun 1–5pm.

OUTDOOR PURSUITS

One of several state parks located at the edge of the Long Island Sound, **Rocky Neck State Park,** Route 156 (℡ 860/739-5471), east of Old Lyme, has a half-mile crescent-shaped beach and over 560 acres for camping, picnicking, fishing, and hiking. Take I-95 to Exit 72 and follow Route 156 south. Open daily from 8am to sunset.

Although headquartered in New York's Hudson Valley, **Atlantic Kayak Tours,** 320 W. Saugerties Rd., Saugerties (© **914/246-2187**), conducts many tours along Connecticut's rivers and shoreline, as well as crossings to Long Island. Most excursions are in the 6- to 14-mile range, with levels of difficulty ranging from beginner to highly advanced. Most tours are $80.

WHERE TO STAY & DINE

Bee and Thistle Inn ★ Situated on more than 5 acres beside the Lieutenant River, the Bee and Thistle has a core structure that dates from 1756, with the usual later wings and additions. Every corner of the place is an enjoyable jumble of antiques and collectibles. A small, detached cottage is the best lodging, with the only in-room TV and fireplace. Year after year, the inn's **dining room** ★★ is voted "best overall" and "most romantic" in the state by reader polls. A skilled professional kitchen staff prepares three creative meals a day, served on tables near fireplaces. Musicians are on hand weekend evenings; jackets are requested for men.

100 Lyme St. (Rte. 1), Old Lyme, CT 06371. © **800/622-4946** or 860/434-1667. Fax 860/434-3402. www.beeandthistleinn.com. 12 units. $79–$189 double; $210 cottage. AE, DC, DISC, MC, V. From the south, take Exit 70 off I-95; turn left, then right on Rte. 1 (Hall Rd.) north. Children over 12 welcome. **Amenities:** Restaurant (creative American). *In room:* A/C.

Old Lyme Inn ★★ This expansive 1850s farmhouse is more a small hotel than a conventional inn. Most of the spacious bedrooms are furnished in part with attractive Victorian pieces, including love seats and four-poster beds. Scrapes and dings aren't allowed to linger. The dining rooms are even more impressive, especially the Grill, which features an antique Victorian bar and marble-mantled fireplace as well as live music on weekends and a raw bar set out at cocktail hour. Admirers of venerable taverns might not want to leave. The Empire and Champlain dining rooms are more formal, but not stuffy. Pets are accepted, a rare policy among New England inns.

85 Lyme St. (Rte. 1), Old Lyme, CT 06371. © **800/434-5352** or 860/434-2600. Fax 860/434-5352. www.old-lymeinn.com. 13 units. $99–$165 double. Rates include breakfast. AE, DC, DISC, MC, V. To get here, follow directions for the Bee and Thistle, above. **Amenities:** 2 restaurants (creative American), bar. *In room:* A/C, TV, hair dryer.

ESSEX ★★

It is difficult to imagine what improvements might be made to bring this dream of a New England town any closer to perfection. In fact, a published survey, *The 100 Best Small Towns in America,* ranks the waterside village number one. Among the criteria were low crime rates, per-capita income, proportion of college-educated residents, and numbers of physicians.

Tree-bordered streets are lined with shops and homes that retain an early-18th-century flavor without the unreal frozen-in-amber quality that often afflicts other towns as postcard-pretty as this. People live and work and play here, and bustle busily along a Main Street that runs down to Steamboat Dock and its flotilla of working vessels and pleasure craft.

Clustered along the harbor end of Main Street are three historic houses that are open to the public on limited seasonal schedules. No. 40 is the **Richard Hayden House,** an 1814 brick Federal that was home to the namesake merchant and shipbuilder. During the War of 1812, British raiders burned Hayden's entire fleet. He was ruined and died soon after, still a young man. Next door, at no. 42, is the **Noah Tooker House,** an 18th-century center-hall colonial that was also the home of a boat-builder. And at no. 51 is the **Robert Lay House,** completed around 1730 and thought to be the oldest original structure in town.

Connecticut River Museum ⭐   Anglers cast lines from the dock while gulls and ducks hang around hoping for a discarded tidbit. Steamboat service was fully operational here from 1823, and the existing dock dates from 1879. Designated a National Historic Site, the museum proper is a converted warehouse, with two floors of intricately detailed model ships, marine paintings, and related artifacts. Rotating exhibits relate the story of shipbuilding in the valley, which began in 1733 and helped make this a center of world trade far into the 19th century. The first American warship constructed for the War of Independence, the *Oliver Cromwell,* was finished here in 1775. The museum usually has walking-tour maps ($1) of Essex, making this a good first stop on a visit.

Steamboat Dock (at foot of Main St.). ℂ 860/767-8269. www.ctrivermuseum.org. Admission $4 adults, $3 seniors, $2 children 6–12. Tues–Sun 10am–5pm.

Essex Steam Train   Steam locomotives from the 1920s chug along a route from this station on the road between Essex center and Ivoryton to a boat landing in the hamlet of Deep River, a mildly engrossing excursion of about an hour. It can be combined with an optional cruise on the river. Special events include a Halloween "ghost" train, a Christmas express with Santa Claus, an Easter express, and a jazz festival in June.

1 Railroad Ave. (Rte. 154). ℂ 860/767-0103. www.essexsteamtrain.com. Train and boat $18.50 adults, $9.50 children 3–11; train only $10.50 adults, $5.50 children 3–11. Daily trips mid-June to Labor Day, less frequently Sept–Apr.

WHERE TO STAY & DINE

Griswold Inn ⭐⭐   Gloss over the assertion that "the Griz" is the oldest inn in America (there are other claimants). What's more important is that local people have rescued the inn from outside buyers. That's a relief, for it is difficult to imagine this corner of New England without the Griz. Rumpled, cluttered, folksy, and forever besieged by drop-in yachtspeople, anglers, locals, and tourists, the main building dates to 1776. The atmospheric taproom started life as a schoolhouse and was moved here in 1800. There's live entertainment every night, be it a Dixieland band or just a man with a banjo. The colorful dining rooms are named for their displays of books, antique weapons, or marine paintings. The food is hearty, no-foolin' victuals—turkey with stuffing, roast loin of pork, mixed grill with sauerkraut. The too-often plain and unadorned bedrooms scattered through six buildings are slowly being upgraded. Viva Griz!

36 Main St. (center of town), Essex, CT 06426. ℂ 860/767-1776. Fax 860/767-0481. www.originalinns.com. 30 units. $90–$195 double. Rates include breakfast. AE, MC, V. **Amenities:** Restaurant (American), bar. *In room:* A/C.

IVORYTON

Once a center for the ivory trade, where factories fabricated piano keys and hair combs, Ivoryton has since subsided into a residential quietude. A virtual suburb of the only slightly larger Essex, a few miles east, the town perks up a bit in summer, when the **Ivoryton Playhouse** (ℂ 860/767-3075) opens its June-to-August theatrical season. The playhouse's repertoire runs to revivals of Broadway and off-Broadway comedies and mysteries.

WHERE TO STAY & DINE

Copper Beech Inn ★★ Despite comparisons with the Griswold Inn in nearby Essex, these are two very different animals. Where the Griz is decidedly populist and perennially busy, the stately Copper Beech has much less traffic, without a single figurative hair out of place. The rooms in the converted barn have ample elbowroom, cushy chairs, expensive reproductions of 19th-century furniture, TVs, whirlpool tubs, and sun decks. The rooms in the 19th-century main building have most of the character, with original bathroom fixtures and plenty of antiques. These have phones but no TVs, and staying here can be as nostalgic as a visit to Aunt Edna's. The Copper Beech is also home to one of the most honored restaurants in the region, where French techniques are applied to high-quality ingredients. Service in the three formal dining areas is seamless, the wine list impressive.

46 Main St., Ivoryton, CT 06442. ℂ 888/809-2056 or 860/767-0330. www.copperbeechinn.com. 13 units. $115–$185 double. Rates include breakfast. AE, DC, MC, V. Take Exit 3 from Rte. 9 and head west on Main St. Children over 10 welcome. **Amenities:** Restaurant (creative French), bar. *In room:* A/C.

CHESTER

Hardly more than a 3-block business center with a few side streets that straggle off into the countryside, Chester can be dismissed easily enough. But pause a moment, for this is a riverside hamlet that deserves savoring. Along Main Street are antiques shops and galleries, a post office, a library, and several eateries that range from sandal informal to dressy casual.

Downtown Chester doesn't have a whole lot of room for shops, but it squeezes in at least a couple that deserve a closer look. **Naturally, Books and Coffee,** 16 Main St. (℃ 860/526-3212), offers a small selection of books, an espresso bar, outdoor tables on warm days, and live acoustic jazz, folk, and pop performers on weekends. **Ceramica,** 36–38 Main St. (℃ 860/526-9978), an outlet of a small chain with branches in SoHo (Manhattan), West Hartford, Westport, and Scarsdale, N.Y., carries a line of uniformly gorgeous hand-painted bowls, pitchers, vases, and teapots.

WHERE TO DINE

The Wheatmarket (℃ 860/526-9347), next door to Fiddlers (see below), will make up picnic baskets for $9.50 to $16 per person, or you can put together your own from the appetizing array of breads, cheeses, pâtés, cold cuts, soups, salads, and sandwiches.

Fiddlers ✿ SEAFOOD Have your fish any way you want—poached, sautéed, broiled, baked, or grilled over mesquite—or leave it up to the skillful kitchen staff, for they can come up with some eye-openers. If "lobster au pêché" (fat chunks of lobster meat married to peach nubbins, shallots, mushrooms, cream, and peach brandy) is still on the menu, go for it. Not for lobster purists, certainly, but a revelatory example of what an imaginative chef can do. The dining rooms are cheerfully unremarkable, with bentwood chairs, marine prints, and ruffled curtains.

4 Water St. (behind Main St.). ℂ 860/526-3210. Main courses $13.95–$21.95. DC, MC, V. Tues–Thurs 11:30am–2pm and 5:30–9pm; Fri 11:30am–2pm and 5:30–9:30pm; Sat 5:30–10pm; Sun 4–9pm.

EAST HADDAM

Hadlyme (a jurisdiction of the town of East Haddam), being hardly more than a wide spot in a country road surrounded by woods and meadows, wouldn't have attracted much attention at all if a wealthy thespian hadn't decided to build his hilltop redoubt here.

To get here, take the **Chester-Hadlyme Ferry,** at the end of Route 148, slightly less than 2 miles from Chester. A ferry has operated here since 1769, and the current version takes both cars and pedestrians ($2.25 for vehicles plus $1.50 for trailers, 75¢ for walk-on passengers). It operates (when it feels like it) from 7am to 6:45pm in the warmer months. If it's closed down, there will be a sign posted out at the intersection of Routes 148 and 154, in which case you'll have to drive north on Route 154 to Haddam and take the bridge.

Gillette Castle State Park ★   William Gillette was a successful actor and playwright known primarily for his theatrical portrayals of Sherlock Holmes. He took the money and ran to this hill rearing above the Connecticut River, where he had his castle built. It's difficult to believe that he really thought the result resembled the Norman fortresses that allegedly were his inspiration. Rock gardens by roadside eccentrics in South Dakota or Death Valley are closer relations. Gillette felt it necessary, for one example, to design a dining-room table that slid into the wall, an inexplicable space-saving effort by a bachelor rattling around in 24 oddly shaped rooms.

But whatever Gillette's deficiencies as an architect and designer, no one can argue with his choice of location. The castle sits atop a hill above the east bank, with superlative vistas upriver and down. Nowhere else is the blessed underdevelopment of the estuary more apparent.

The 184-acre grounds have picnic areas, nature trails, and fishing sites. Since the terrace of the "castle" can be entered for free, many visitors just come to take in those **views** ★★ and avoid the fees for entering the interior. *Note:* The castle itself has been closed the last 2 years for renovations. Inquire locally whether it has reopened. The grounds have remained open to visitors.

67 River Rd. (© 860/526-2336. www.cttourism.org. Admission $4 adults, $2 children 6–11. Grounds daily 8am–sunset; castle Memorial Day to Labor Day Fri–Sun 10am–5pm.

RIVER CRUISES

A voyage on the river is an irresistible outing. Cruises of a variety of lengths, times, and themes are offered by **Camelot Cruises,** 1 Marine Park (© 800/522-7463; www.camelotcruises.com). The pride of its fleet is the M/V *Camelot,* a 160-foot vessel carrying as many as 500 passengers. In addition to dinner and mystery cruises, there are summer and fall excursions to Sag Harbor, Long Island.

A competing company, **Mark Twain Cruises,** River Street, Deep River (© 877/658-9246), uses six boats for winter eagle spotting, fall foliage, fireworks, birding, meal, and jazz cruises. Embarkations are from State Street and Charter Oak Landings in Hartford as well as from Saybrook Point and other ports along the river.

EAST HADDAM AFTER DARK

From Gillette State Park, turn north on Route 82 and make the short drive to East Haddam proper. The dominant building is a restored six-story Victorian of splendid proportions that was completed in 1877 and is now the **Goodspeed Opera House** ★★, Goodspeed Landing (© 860/873-8668; www.goodspeed. org). A century ago, it presented such productions as *All Is Not Gold That Glitters.* Now, it mostly stages revivals of Broadway musicals on the order of *Man of La Mancha,* but always makes room for more experimental or original shows that have eventually made it all the way to the Big Apple. The season is usually April through October. Tours are given June through October, Monday from 1 to 3pm and Saturday from 11am to 1:30pm; these cost $2 for adults and $1 for children.

7 Mystic & the Southeastern Coast

This section of the shoreline is studded with towns that still bear the stamp of their maritime pasts, a string of fishing ports and inlets that segues into the mainland beach resorts of Rhode Island. Inland are a number of still semi-rural villages, but their futures are unpredictable due to the presence of two enormously successful and steadily expanding Indian casino complexes, Foxwoods and Mohegan Sun. They produce gushers of money that threaten to alter forever the character of this region.

The town of Mystic and its twin attractions, Mystic Aquarium and the living museum that is Mystic Seaport, are the prime reasons for a stay—the Seaport alone can easily occupy most of a day, and the two-part town itself sustains a nautical air, with fun shops and restaurants to suit most tastes.

But that's not a complete list of the region's charms. The tranquil neighboring village of Stonington is home to an active commercial fishing fleet, the last in the state; nearby Groton, on the Thames River, offers tours of the world's first nuclear submarine; there are several enchanting inns in the area; and many companies offer their vessels for whale watching, dinner cruises, and deep-sea fishing excursions. And yes, for those with a taste for the adrenaline rush of a winning streak, there are those casinos.

If at all possible, avoid July, August, and weekends from May to Columbus Day, when the crowds are oppressive, restaurants are packed, and rooms are booked months in advance at very high rates.

ESSENTIALS

GETTING THERE   From New York City, take I-95 to Exit 84 (New London), Exit 86 (Groton), Exit 90 (Mystic), or Exit 91 (Stonington). Or, to avoid the heavy truck and commercial traffic of the western segment of I-95, use the Hutchinson River Parkway, which becomes the Merritt Parkway (Route 15) and merges with the Wilbur Cross Parkway. Continue to Exit 54, connecting with I-95 for the rest of the trip. From Boston, take the Massachusetts Turnpike to I-395 south to Exit 75, then south on Route 32 to New London and I-95.

Amtrak (© **800/USA-RAIL;** www.northeast.amtrak.com) runs several trains daily on its Northeast Direct route between New York, Providence, and Boston, with intermediate stops at New Haven, Old Saybrook, New London, and Mystic.

The regional bus company, **SEAT** (© **860/886-2631**), connects the more important towns and villages of the district, except for North Stonington.

A new way to get from the metropolitan New York region to New London, and from there to the Foxwoods casino complex, are the super-fast tri-catamaran **ferries** operated by **Fox Navigation** (© **888-724-5369;** www.foxnavigation.com). Embarkation is at Glen Cove, on the north shore of Long Island, and the trip takes about 2 hours 15 minutes at speeds exceeding 50 miles an hour. Pass the time on reclining airline-type seats with on-board movies and food service. Passengers debark at the State Pier in New London and are transported from there to Foxwoods. There are four round-trips on four days per week.

VISITOR INFORMATION   **Mystic Coast & Country** (© **800/692-6278;** www.mycoast.com) can provide vacation planning kits. If the many motels off I-95 aren't for you, ask for the folder describing the loosely affiliated **Bed & Breakfasts of Mystic Coast,** which lists 23 establishments in the area, including four just across the Rhode Island state line.

NEW LONDON

Founded in 1646 and first known by the Pequot name *Nameaug,* New London's protected deep-draft harbor at the mouth of the Thames River was responsible for its long and influential history as a whaling port. That heritage lingers, but its years of great prosperity are behind it.

Possessed of an architecturally interesting but largely somnolent downtown district, New London, which lies 46 miles east of New Haven and 45 miles southeast of Hartford, is of note to travelers primarily because it's a transit point for three ferry lines connecting Block Island, R.I., and Long Island, N.Y., with the mainland, as well as the new high-speed ferries connecting with Martha's Vineyard and Glen Cove, Long Island. **Connecticut College** has a large campus at the northern edge of the city, along Route 32 and Williams Street. The **U.S. Coast Guard Academy** is also here, but while it welcomes visitors, it is of interest mainly to alumni and prospective students. In July 2000, New London was a host for **Op Sail,** which drew a million visitors to see the largest tall ship and maritime event in history.

An attended **information booth** is located in downtown New London at the corner of Eugene O'Neill Drive and Golden Street (© **860/444-7264**). It's open June through August, daily from 10am to 4pm; May, September, and October, Friday through Sunday from 10am to 4pm.

Coast Guard Academy   Visitors to the base are directed to a pavilion overlooking the Thames. It doesn't offer much except views of the river and shores. A full-rigged sailing vessel, the *Eagle,* is the academy's principal attraction, with boarding allowed on a very limited basis, usually only in April and May. It was built as a training ship for German Naval cadets in 1936 and taken as a war prize after World War II.

15 Mohegan Ave. (off Williams St., north of Exit 84 off I-95). © **860/444-8611.** Free admission. Grounds daily 9am–5pm; Visitors Pavilion May–Oct daily 10am–5pm, Apr Sat–Sun 10am–5pm. Pavilion closed Nov–Mar.

Lyman Allyn Museum of Art   This neoclassical granite pile stands on a hill looking across Route 32 toward the Coast Guard Academy. Its holdings are the results of the enthusiasms of private collectors and therefore stick to no specific curatorial vision. The various parts are interesting, however, even if they don't belong to a harmonious whole. The basement contains detailed room settings of Victorian dollhouse furniture, right down to tiny ladles on the kitchen counter. On the main floor are colonial American paintings and furnishings, including landscapes by Hudson River School artists Frederic Edwin Church, George Inness, and Albert Bierstadt. Upstairs are galleries with exhibits as diverse as Asian temple castings and Japanese lacquerware.

625 Williams St. © **860/443-2545.** Admission $4 adults, $3 seniors and students, free for children under 6. Tues–Sat 10am–5pm; Sun 1–5pm. From Exit 83 off I-95, follow brown signs to museum.

OUTDOOR PURSUITS

Not far from downtown is **Ocean Beach Park,** at the south end of Ocean Avenue (© **800/510-7263** or 860/447-3031), a 40-acre recreational facility with a broad sand beach, boardwalk, 50-meter freshwater pool, miniature-golf course, and water slide. With those facilities, it surpasses most other beaches along this shore, but verges on the honky-tonk in some of its enterprises. Also available are a bathhouse with lockers and showers, concession stands, and a lounge. Live entertainment is scheduled throughout the summer. Open

Memorial Day weekend through Labor Day, daily from 9am to 10pm. The parking fee covers admission for all occupants of the car.

June through September, waterborne excursions run by **Thames River Cruises** (© 860/444-7827) carry passengers up past the *Nautilus* submarine base (see section on Groton, below). The Thames can't be compared to the Rhine or even the lower Connecticut River for scenic diversion, but it's a pleasant enough outing. (The submarine base can also be reached by car.) Daily departures are made hourly from 9am to 5pm; home dock is the City Pier at the foot of State Street, behind the railroad station. The fare is $10 for adults, $6 for children 6 to 13.

The ferries that ply the Long Island Sound from New London have a recreational aspect, as well as simply serving as transport between Block Island and Long Island. **Cross Sound Ferry** (© 860/443-5281 or 516/323-2525; www.longislandferry.com) provides year-round service to Orient Point on Long Island. Departures are every hour or two during the day, and the one-way voyage takes about an hour and 20 minutes. Call ahead to confirm departure times and make reservations, especially when taking a car. The **Fishers Island Ferry** (© 860/443-6851) also has daily departures for Long Island. From mid-June to early September, **Nelseco Navigation Co.** (© 860/442-7891 or 860/442-9553) operates its ferry once a day (with an extra trip Friday evenings) between New London and the Old Harbor on Block Island. The one-way trip takes about 2 hours. An advance reservation for cars is essential, but a call ahead is also important to determine fares and current sailing times.

WHERE TO STAY

Queen Anne Inn   Parents visiting their kids at the area colleges are frequent guests at the 1903 Queen Anne, as are businesspeople who don't like the anonymity of motels. As a result, rates don't fluctuate as much from season to season as they do at many area inns. An oak staircase reaches up three floors (there's no elevator) to the Tower Room, the best of the lot. It's equipped with a TV and phone as well as a kitchen. The new owners are upgrading, but not every room has such appointments, so make your needs known when reserving. A couple of units have fireplaces or fax machines. Breakfast is an extravaganza of quiches, waffles, and French toast, and is complemented by an afternoon tea of coffeecakes and delicate sandwiches.

265 Williams St. (east of Rte. 32), New London, CT 06320. © 800/347-8818 or 860/447-2600. Fax 860/443-0857. www.queen-anne.com. 9 units (7 with private bathroom). $95–$175 double. Rates include breakfast and afternoon tea. AE, DISC, DC, MC, V. *In room:* A/C, TV, dataport.

WHERE TO DINE

Timothy's ★★ NEW AMERICAN   Although you are invited to dip your bread in olive oil, and three or four perky pastas are listed on the menu, this isn't an overtly Italian restaurant. Think of it as a contemporary bistro. The lobster and crabmeat bisque with a splash of sherry is a signature dish, and items like sautéed flounder coated in crushed pecans and the semi-boneless duckling with a berry/cassis/sage demi-glace are regulars. All of it is brightly seasoned, with daring combinations of fresh herbs. Timothy's is located on a fairly active downtown street not far from the Garde Arts Center and the Eugene O'Neill Theater. New London needs more operations like this.

181 Bank St. © 860/437-0526. Main courses $14.95–$24.95. Tues–Fri 11:30am–2:30pm and 5:30–9pm (until 10pm Fri); Sat 5:30–10pm.

GROTON

The future is uncertain for this naval-industrial town on the opposite side of the Thames from New London. It has long been dependent on the presence of the Electric Boat division of General Dynamics and the Navy's submarine base, and cutbacks in military budgets have adversely affected both. Whatever happens, the principal tourist attraction remains the USS *Nautilus,* the world's first nuclear-powered vessel.

After a visit to the submarine museum, history buffs may wish to stop for a stroll around **Fort Griswold Battlefield State Park,** Monument Street and Park Avenue (© **860/445-1729** or 860/449-6877). It was here, in 1781, that the traitor Benedict Arnold led a British force against American defenders, ruthlessly ordering the massacre of his 88 prisoners after they had surrendered. The free museum is open from Memorial Day to Labor Day, daily from 10am to 5pm; and from Labor Day to Columbus Day, Saturday and Sunday from 10am to 5pm.

Submarine Force Museum   Outside the museum are battered minisubs used by the Axis powers in World War II. The entry hall and adjoining galleries display models of submarines, torpedoes, missiles, deck guns, periscopes, and a full-scale cross-section of Bushnell's *Turtle,* the "first submersible ever used in a military conflict," in 1776. A $4-million addition has doubled exhibition space. Continuing out the back and across a set of railroad tracks, the USS *Nautilus* itself stands at its mooring, ready for inspection. The somewhat claustrophobic walk through the control rooms, attack center, galley, and sleeping quarters is aided by listening devices handed out to each visitor. The self-guided tour takes about 10 minutes.

Naval Submarine Base, 1 Crystal Lake Rd. © **800/343-0079** or 860/694-3174. www.submarinemuseum. Free admission. May 15–Oct 31 Wed–Mon 9am–5pm, Tues 1–5pm; Nov 1–May 14 Wed–Mon 9am–4pm. Take Exit 86 from I-95, drive north on Rte. 12, and follow signs to the USS *Nautilus.*

FISHING TRIPS

A number of companies offer full- and half-day fishing trips. Typical of the party boats is the 114-foot *Hel-Cat II,* 181 Thames St. (© **860/535-2066** or 860/ 535-3200), operating from its own pier about 2 miles south of Exit 85 north or Exit 86 south off I-95.

Both charter and party boats are available from the **Sunbeam Fleet,** based at **Captain John's Sport Fishing Center,** 15 First St., Waterford (© **860/ 443-7259;** www.sunbeamfleet.com). Fishing party boats sail twice daily Friday through Sunday in June; Thursday through Tuesday from July to Labor Day. The same firm has whale-watching voyages three times a week in July and August. Nature cruises go eagle watching in February and March and search for harbor seals from March through May. A substantial variety of fishing trips is offered. Waterford is the town immediately south of New London; the dock is next to the Niantic River Bridge.

WHERE TO STAY

While there are no distinctive lodgings in Groton itself—most visitors settle in nearby towns—there are motels near the I-95 exits.

Clarion Inn *(Kids*   A solid possibility for families planning to spend a few days in the region, 34 of these units have minimally equipped kitchens, and most are suites that sleep up to four people.

156 Kings Hwy., Groton, CT 06340. © **800/252-7466** or 860/446-0660. Fax 860/445-4082. 69 units. $78-$189 double. Lower rates Nov-May. AE, DC, DISC, MC, V. **Amenities:** Restaurant, bar; heated indoor pool; exercise room; sauna. *In room:* A/C, TV.

MYSTIC ✸✸✸

The spirit and texture of the maritime life and history of New England are captured in many ports along its indented coast, but nowhere more cogently than beside the Mystic River estuary and its harbor, nearly stoppered by Mason Island. This was a furiously active whaling and shipbuilding center during the colonial period and into the last century, but the discontinuation of the first industry and the decline of the second haven't adversely affected the community. No derelict barges or rotting piers degrade the views and waterways (or at least not many).

Mystic and West Mystic are stitched together by a drawbridge, the raising of which, mostly for sailboats, causes traffic stoppages at a quarter past every hour but rarely shortens tempers, except for visitors who don't leave their urban impatience behind. There are complaints by some that the two-part town has been commercialized, but the incidence of T-shirt shops and related tackiness is limited, and the more garish motels and attractions have been restricted to the periphery, especially up near Exit 90 off I-95.

The town is home to one of New England's most singular attractions, the Mystic Seaport museum village. Far more than the single building the name might suggest, it is a re-created seaport of the mid-1800s, with dozens of buildings and watercraft of that romantic era of clipper ships and the China Trade. The spidery webs of full-rigged sailing ships and the briny tang of the ocean air beckon visitors almost as soon as they leave the highway.

A **visitor information center** is located in Building 1D of the Olde Mistick Village shopping center, at Route 27 and Coogan Boulevard, near the Interstate (© **860/536-1641**). Mystic is 55 miles east of New Haven.

SEEING THE SIGHTS

The Mystic Places SuperTicket offers reduced-price admission to two or three of the principal area attractions—Mystic Seaport, Mystic Aquarium, and the Mashantucket Pequot Museum. Depending on the combination chosen, the tickets cost $21 to $27 for adults, $12 to $16 for children.

Mystic Seaport ✸✸✸   Few visitors fail to be enthralled by this evocative museum village. It encompasses an entire waterfront settlement, more than 60 buildings on and near a 17-acre peninsula poking into the Mystic River. With all there is to see and do, and considering the hefty admission charges, plan to set aside at least 2 or 3 hours for a visit. In fact, you could easily fill an entire day here, especially if you're one of those people who thrill at the sight of full-rigged tall ships standing at their wharves as if readying for voyages to the Spice Islands. A useful map guide is available at the ticket counter in the **visitor center** in the building opposite the museum stores (which stay open later than the village most of the year, so make them your last stop).

We recommend exiting the visitor center and bearing right along the path leading between the Galley Restaurant and the village green. It bends to the left, intersecting with a street of shops, public buildings, and houses. At that corner is an 1870s hardware and dry-goods store.

Turning right here, you'll pass a one-room schoolhouse, a chapel, and a furnished 1830s home. Stop at the **children's museum,** which invites youngsters to play games characteristic of the seafaring era. It faces a small square that is the starting point for **horse-drawn wagon tours** of the village (daily from 11am to 5pm; $3 for short rides, $4 for long).

From here, the three-masted barque *Charles W. Morgan,* one of the proudest possessions of the Seaport fleet of over 400 craft, is only a few steps away. It was built in 1841, a whaler that called New Bedford home.

If you're a fan of scrimshaw and intricate ship models, continue along the waterfront to the right until you reach the **Stillman Building,** which contains fascinating exhibits of both. Otherwise, head left toward the lighthouse. Along the way, you'll encounter a tavern, an 1833 bank with an upstairs shipping office, a house with a garden, a cooperage (where barrels and casks were made), a print shop, and other shops and services that did business with the whalers and clipper ships that put in at ports such as this.

The friendly docents in the village are highly competent at the crafts they demonstrate and are always ready to impart as much information as visitors care to absorb. The fact that they aren't dressed in period costumes paradoxically enhances the village's feeling of authenticity by avoiding the contrived air of many such enterprises.

The next vessel encountered is the iron-hulled square-rigger *Joseph Conrad,* which dates from 1881 and has spent most of its life as a training ship. Up ahead at the point of the peninsula is a small **lighthouse,** which looks out across the water toward the large riverside houses that line the opposite shore. Round the horn, go past the boat sheds, fishing shacks, and the ketches and sloops that are moored along here in season until you come to the dock for the perky 1908 **SS** *Sabino.* This working ship gives half-hour river rides from mid-May to early October, daily from 11am to 4pm ($3.50 for adults, $2.50 for children 6 to 15), and 1½-hour evening excursions Monday through Thursday leaving at 5pm, Friday and Saturday at 7pm ($8.50 for adults, $7 for children). A few steps away is the 1921 fishing schooner *L. A. Dunton.*

And still the village isn't exhausted. A few steps south is the **Henry B. Du Pont Preservation Shipyard,** where the hundreds of boats in the collection are painstakingly restored and the work can be observed in progress. One of its recent projects was the re-creation of the schooner *Amistad.*

Also on the grounds are the **Gallery Restaurant,** which serves pretty good fish-and-chips, fried clam strips, and lobster rolls during Seaport hours; and **Sprouter's Tavern,** which offers snacks and sandwiches from 11am to 4pm.

When you exit for the day, ask the gatekeeper to validate your ticket so you can come back the next day for free.

Across the brick courtyard with the giant anchor is a building containing several **museum stores** as well as an art gallery. These superior shops stock books dealing with every aspect of seafaring; kitchenware, including enameled metal plates and cups that are perfect for the deck or picnics; fresh-baked goods and coffee; nautical prints and paintings; and ship models, both crude and inexpensive or exquisite and costly.

75 Greenmanville Ave. (Rte. 27). © **888/9-SEAPORT** or 860/572-5315. www.mysticseaport.org. Admission $16 adults, $8 children 6–12 (second day included with validation). AE, MC, V. Apr–Oct daily 9am–5pm; Nov–Mar daily 10am–4pm (ships and exhibits), 9am–5pm (grounds). Closed Christmas. Take Exit 90 off I-95, going about 1 mile south on Rte. 27 toward Mystic. Parking lots are on the left, the entrance on the right.

Mystic Aquarium ★★ *Kids*   If you've never seen a dolphin or orca show, this is the place. Less gimmicky than similar commercial enterprises in Florida and California, the show illuminates as it entertains, and at 15 minutes in length, doesn't test very young attention spans. The adorable mammals squawk, click, roll up onto the apron of their pool, tail walk, joyously splash the nearer rows of spectators, and pick out toys in the water when blindfolded—all of this is at the command of their trainers.

While the rest of the exhibits necessarily fall in the shadow of the stars, they are enough to occupy at least another hour. Near the entrance is a tank of fur seals, and out back are sea lions and a flock of African black-footed penguins. A $52-million expansion program was completed in 1999 under the direction of the legendary undersea explorer Robert Ballard, who discovered the sunken *Titanic*. It includes a 1-acre outdoor habitat called the Alaskan Coast, which contains a 750,000-gallon pool for resident white beluga whales and harbor seals. Visitors are practically eye to eye with such remarkable marine creatures as scorpion fish and sea horses propelled on gossamer fins; billowing, translucent jellyfish; and the pugnacious yellow-head jaw fish, which spends its hours digging fortifications in the sand.

55 Coogan Blvd. (at Exit 90 off I-95). © 860/572-5955. www.mysticaquarium.org. Admission $15 adults, $14 seniors, $10 children 3–12. July to Labor Day daily 9am–6pm; Labor Day to June daily 9am–5pm.

OUTDOOR PURSUITS

For a change from salt air and ship riggings, drive inland to the **Denison Pequotsepos Nature Center,** 109 Pequotsepos Rd. (© 860/536-1216), a 125-acre property with more than 7 miles of trails. The center building has a thrown-together quality, with stuffed birds next to plaster snakes and dog-eared books beside the live boa constrictor and worm farm. Younger children are nonetheless fascinated. Outside are picnic tables and flight cages of rehabilitating raptors. There are five marked nature trails, none of which merit special effort—but they can serve as gentle diversion for a half hour or so. Admission is $4 for adults, $3 for seniors, and $2 for children 12 and under. Open Monday through Saturday from 9am to 5pm, Sunday from 1 to 5pm (closed Sundays January through April, Mondays September through April).

Across the road is the **Denison Homestead** (© 860/536-9248), a 1717 farmhouse that sheltered 11 generations of Denisons and is filled with that family's antique furnishings. Admission is $4 for adults, $1 for children under 16. Open from mid-May to mid-October, Friday through Monday from 10am to 4pm.

To get to the Nature Center and Homestead, take Route 27 north from Mystic, make a right on Mistuxet Avenue, and turn left on Pequotsepos Road.

Several operators offer **sailing and fishing cruises.** One of the most convenient is the ***Argia*** (© 860/536-0416), which docks 100 feet south of the drawbridge in downtown Mystic. Morning sails on this 81-foot replica of a 19th-century schooner are from 10am to 1pm, afternoon sails are from 2 to 5pm, and evening cruises are from 5:30 to 7:30pm. Fares are $32 to $34 for adults, $22 to $24 for children under 18. For longer trips, outings on the windjammer ***Mystic Whaler*** (© 800/697-8420; fax 860/536-4219; www.mysticwhaler.com) include 3-hour lobster dinner sails, day trips, and extended cruises that can last 2, 3, or 5 days. Corresponding rates go from as little as $65 to $735. Voyages set out from a pier at 7 Holmes St., off Route 27, 1 mile south of Mystic Seaport.

SHOPPING

Downtown Mystic has limited shopping, a situation made worse by a fire in March 2000 that destroyed a 19th-century building with eight storefronts next to the famous drawbridge. Of the survivors, an engaging choice is **Bank Square Books,** 53 W. Main St. (✆ **860/536-3795**).

Olde Mistick Village, Route 27 and Coogan Boulevard (✆ **860/536-4941**), out near the I-95 exits, is a conventional mall housed in buildings that simulate a colonial village. It has more than 60 shops and restaurants, including two banks, cinemas, and a winery.

WHERE TO STAY

There are plenty of ho-hum but adequate area motels that can soak up the traffic at all but peak periods, meaning weekends from late spring to early fall plus weekdays in July and August, when it is necessary to have reservations. Pick of the litter may be the **Best Western Sovereign,** north of Exit 90 (✆ **800/ 528-1234**), with a pool, sauna, restaurant, and in-room fridges. Nearby competitors with similar facilities are the **Comfort Inn** (✆ **800/228-5150** or 860/ 572-8531), **Days Inn** (✆ **800/325-2525** or 860/572-0574), and **Residence Inn** (✆ **800/331-3131** or 860/536-5150).

Hilton Mystic ★★ Unlike the motels clustered around the I-95 interchange, this is a full-service hotel, providing the amenities expected of its big-city cousins, if not much personality. The front desk is often willing to negotiate prices according to season and demand. A pianist entertains many evenings in the fireplace lounge. The hotel is owned by the Pequot tribe, so it's no surprise that there are posters announcing coming attractions at Foxwoods Casino and a shuttle van to take you there.

20 Coogan Blvd., Mystic, CT 06355. ✆ **800/445-8667** or 860/572-0731. Fax 860/572-0328. www. hilton.com. 183 units. $95–$250 double. AE, DC, DISC, MC, V. Free valet parking. Take Exit 90 off I-95 and drive south, following signs to the Aquarium; the hotel is opposite. **Amenities:** Restaurant (continental), lounge; heated indoor pool; fitness room; bike rental; limited room service; same-day dry cleaning/laundry service. *In room:* A/C, TV, dataport, coffeemaker, hair dryer, iron.

The Inn at Mystic ★★ A variety of lodgings and rates are on offer at this property occupying 13 hillside acres overlooking Long Island Sound. The complex also incorporates one of the area's best restaurants, Flood Tide (see "Where to Dine," below). At the crest of the hill is the impressive inn, a 1904 Classical Revival mansion with rooms as grand as the exterior, enhanced by whirlpool baths, fireplaces, and canopied beds. Down the hill is the intimate Gatehouse, similarly accoutered and furnished with a scattering of antiques. Some of the units in the new motel sections are equally well appointed, including a few with balconies; others are modest and conventional. Don't miss the bounteous breakfasts.

Rtes. 1 and 27, Mystic, CT 06355. ✆ **800/237-2415** or 860/536-9604. www.innatmystic.com. 67 units. $85–$250 motel double; $160–$295 mansion and gatehouse double. Packages available. Rates include afternoon tea. AE, DC, DISC, MC, V. Pets accepted in six units ($10). **Amenities:** Restaurant (continental), bar; outdoor pool; 2 putting greens; tennis court; access to nearby health club; free use of kayaks and boats; limited room service; same-day dry cleaning/laundry service. *In room:* A/C, TV, dataport, fridge, coffeemaker, hair dryer.

Steamboat Inn ★★ Mystic's most appealing lodging is easily overlooked from land, but readily apparent from the river. Perched on the riverbank, the yellow clapboard structure has apartment-size downstairs bedrooms, with double whirlpool baths, wet bars, and some kitchen facilities, while the upstairs units have smaller whirlpools and wood-burning fireplaces. Every room is decorated uniquely, but they are uniformly attractive—Laura Ashley must have been a muse—and all but one have water views. Sherry is left out all day for guests to pour themselves. The inn commissioned the 97-foot luxury yacht, *Valiant*, that is moored at its dock. The staterooms can be rented when the yacht isn't chartered.

73 Steamboat Wharf, Mystic, CT 06355. ℂ **860/536-8300.** Fax 860/536-9528. www.visitmystic.com/ steamboat. 10 units. Late May to Nov $175–$285 double; Dec to late May $110–$230. Rates include break-fast. AE, DISC, MC, V. Parking in a gated lot; the inn validates. Look for a sign pointing down an alley on the west bank of the Mystic River, just before the drawbridge. Children over 9 welcome. *In room:* A/C, TV, data-port, fridge, coffeemaker, hair dryer, iron.

Taber Inne 🍴 Not quite an inn but more than a motel, this place has some-thing to suit most tastes and budgets, with seven immaculate buildings contain-ing both simple units and hedonistic two-bedroom suites with whirlpool baths and fireplaces. Some accommodations have decks; others have canopied beds. A new cottage with a cathedral ceiling has two bedrooms, a sitting room, and a kitchen; it sleeps up to six. The ever-energetic owner has erected a new building with an indoor pool.

66 Williams Ave. (Rte. 1; 2 blocks east of the intersection with Rte. 27), Mystic, CT 06355. ℂ **860/536-4904.** Fax 860/572-9140. www.taberinne.com. 25 units. Mid-Apr to Nov $125–$145 double, $210–$340 suite; Nov to mid-Apr $95–$125 double, $195–$310 suite. AE, MC, V. **Amenities:** Heated indoor pool; access to nearby health club with tennis court; fitness center. *In room:* A/C, TV, dataport, coffeemaker, hair dryer.

WHERE TO DINE

Abbott's Lobster in the Rough 🍴 SEAFOOD   It's as if a wedge of the Maine coast had been punched into the Connecticut shore. This is a nitty-gritty lobster shack with plenty of picnic tables and not a frill to be found. While there are many options, including hot dogs and chicken (but no fried foods), the clas-sic shore dinner rules. That means clam chowder, boiled shrimp in the shell, steamed mussels, and a tasty lobster, with coleslaw, chips, and drawn butter thrown in. Dessert can be cheese- or carrot cake. Bring your own beer.

117 Pearl St., Noank. ℂ **860/536-7719.** Main courses $15–$23 (lobster dinners $18–$30). AE, MC, V. First Fri in May to Memorial Day Fri–Sun noon–7pm; Memorial Day to Labor Day weekend daily noon–9pm; after Labor Day weekend to Columbus Day weekend Fri–Sun noon–7pm. From downtown Mystic, go south on Rte. 215 and cross a railroad bridge. At Main St. in Noank, turn left, and take an immediate right on Pearl St. Be prepared to ask for directions anyway.

Flood Tide 🍴🍴 CONTINENTAL   Peel back about three decades: They still do tableside preparations here, like Caesar salad, beef Wellington, and rack of lamb, carved showily before your eyes. The retro performance reminds us why we used to relish this celebratory stuff in the days before Nouvelle-Pan-Asian-Italo-Fusion food was invented. Flood Tide even has a pianist plinking at the baby grand nightly and at Sunday brunch. Lunch is cheaper and less fussy, and breakfast is a particular treat, with such offerings as eggs Benedict with lobster and grilled chicken sausage with apple and sage. The two dining rooms look out over the sound, so ask for a window table.

The Inn at Mystic, Rtes. 1 and 27. ℂ **860/536-8140.** Reservations recommended. Main courses $24–$36. AE, DC, DISC, MC, V. Daily 7pm–midnight.

Go Fish 🍴 SEAFOOD   Brash and boisterous, Go Fish is dominated by a sprawling black-granite bar. To one side are the young smokers; on the other, non-puffing older folks and families. At the bar, choose from a generous list of sushi and raw oysters or clams. Otherwise, ask for fish cooked just about any way possible—baked, roasted, grilled, deep-fried, or pan-blackened. Entrees are abundant, so you might want to skip appetizers, enticing though they are (the creamy bisque, for one). Stick to the less complex dishes. Wines are served by the glass, in sizes "full," "half," or "taste."

Olde Mistick Village, at Exit 90 off I-95. ☎ **860/536-2662.** Reservations not accepted. Main courses $14.95–$23.95. AE, DC, DISC, MC, V. Sun–Thurs 11:30am–9:30pm; Fri–Sat 11:30am–10:30pm.

STONINGTON & NORTH STONINGTON

Not much seems to happen in these slumbering villages, only lightly brushed by the 21st century despite all the thrashing about in heavily touristed Mystic. That suits the residents just fine, explaining why most of them are not thrilled by the continual rumors of projected expansions of the nearby Foxwoods complex. It is difficult to imagine what the flexing of that gambling empire will do eventually to inland North Stonington, as peaceful a New England retreat as can be found, with hardly any commercialization beyond a couple of inns. Soundside Stonington has a pronounced maritime flavor, sustained by the presence of the state's only remaining (albeit dwindling) fishing fleet. Its two lengthwise streets are lined with well-preserved Federal-style and Greek Revival homes.

EXPLORING THE AREA

For an introduction, drive south to **Cannon Square** along Stonington's **Water Street,** which has most of the town's shops and restaurants. Standing in the raised grassy main square are two 18-pound cannons that were used to fight off an attack by British warships during the War of 1812. Opposite is a lovely old granite house and, on the corner, a neoclassical bank.

Continue south to the end of Water Street, where there's a parking lot and small **town beach** (admission $2 to $3, or $5 to $6 per family). The misty blue headland directly south across the sound is Montauk Point, the eastern extremity of New York's Long Island. Return along Main Street, which is almost exclusively residential except for a few government buildings.

You might check out the **Old Lighthouse Museum,** 7 Water St. (☎ **860/535-1440**). Built of stone in 1823, it was moved here from a hundred yards away and deactivated. Most of its exhibits relate to the maritime past of the area, with scrimshaw tusks, a whalebone wool-winding wheel, a tortoise-shell serving dish, and the export porcelain that constituted much of the 19th-century China Trade. Most interesting is the carved ivory pagoda. Climb the tower for a view of coast and sea. Admission is $4 for adults, $2 for children 6 to 12. Open May, June, September, and October, Tuesday through Sunday from 10am to 5pm; July and August, daily from 10am to 5pm.

Duffers who feel overwhelmed by all the nautical activity can retreat to the **Pequot Golf Club,** on Wheeler Road in Stonington (☎ **860/535-1898**). It has a par 70, 18-hole course and is fully open to the public, including the restaurant. Cart and club rentals are available. Call ahead to reserve weekend tee times. Take Exit 91 from I-95 north to Taugwonk Road, turn west on Summers Lane, and go south on Wheeler Road.

One of the Nutmeg State's handful of earnest wineries, **Stonington Vineyards,** 523 Taugwonk Rd., Stonington (☎ **860/535-1222**), has a tasting room in a barn beside its vineyard. There are usually six or seven pressings to be sampled, with a chardonnay leading the pack. Open daily from 11am to 5pm, with a cellar tour at 2pm. To get here, take Exit 91 off I-95 and drive north 2½ miles.

WHERE TO STAY

Antiques & Accommodations ✦   Gardens, porches, and patios invite lounging at this converted 1820 farmhouse and 1861 Victorian. Rooms and suites vary substantially. One unit has two bedrooms sharing a kitchen and sitting room, while the "bridal suite" has a canopied bed. Three rooms have working fireplaces, and three have phones with dataports, so make your needs known at the outset. The four-course candlelit breakfast brings such surprises as cantaloupe soup, turkey hash, and walnut-and-banana waffles. Guests who take a liking to any of the antique silver or crystal pieces or furnishings will be pleased to know that just about everything is for sale.

32 Main St., North Stonington, CT 06359. ✆ **800/554-7829** or 860/535-1736. Fax 860/535-2613. www. visitmystic.com/antiques. 8 units. May 1–Jan 1 $129–$199 double, $149–$229 suite; Jan 2–Apr $99–$169 double, $129–$199 suite. Rates include breakfast. MC, V. Sometimes closed Jan. Take Exit 92 off I-95, drive west on Rte. 2 for 2½ miles, and turn right onto Main St. at the sign. *In room:* A/C, TV.

High Acres Set upon the highest elevation of a 150-acre farm, this B&B utilizes a 1743 farmhouse and outbuildings from the mid–19th century. Apart from the fine views, guests over 10 years old can enjoy guided 1½-hour rides ($30) on gentle horses along 3 miles of trails. Bedrooms are modest in size, but are furnished with king- or queen-size beds, with a canopied four-poster here, an iron bedstead there. There are no private TVs or phones, but both are available in the common rooms. Future expansions include a two-bedroom apartment with full kitchen and deck over the garage. The substantial breakfasts feature fruit, omelets, pancakes, and bacon.

222 Northwest Corner Rd., North Stonington, CT 06359. ✆ **860/887-4355**. www.visitmystic.com/highacres. 10 units. $125–$169 double. Rates include breakfast. AE, MC, V. Take Exit 92 off I-95, head north on Rte. 2 about 5 miles, go right on Rte. 201 about 2½ miles, and turn left on Northwest Corner Rd. for 2 miles. Children welcome. *In room:* A/C, hair dryer, no phone.

Randall's Ordinary The oldest structure on this 27-acre estate dates from 1685. The three bedrooms upstairs have fireplaces and are charmingly furnished with four-poster and canopied beds, though without TVs and phones. Those conveniences are provided in the rooms in the nearby barn, which was moved here from upstate New York and converted for this purpose. Meals in the farmhouse are cooked at an open hearth and served by a staff in period costumes. Considering the primitive circumstances under which the food is prepared, it is always hearty, if simple and under-seasoned. Go for the romantic setting, not gastronomy.

Rte. 2, North Stonington, CT 06359. ✆ **860/599-4540**. Fax 860/599-3308. www.randallsordinary.com. 18 units. $140–$250 double. AE, MC, V. Take Exit 92 off I-95 and head north on Rte. 2. *In room:* A/C.

WHERE TO DINE

Boom NEW AMERICAN With past Stonington restaurants closing abruptly, a travel writer can get gun-shy. But this one looks to have the necessaries for a decent life span. It's a companionable, underdecorated little room looking out over a marina of working and pleasure boats. There are irresistible lightly battered fried oysters with chipotle aioli among the appetizers, and entrees of scallops with wasabi-spiked mashed potatoes and wilted Asian greens or grilled vegetable ravioli with toasted pignoli-tomato cream and chevre. In good weather, tables are set up outside with a raw bar. Local purveyors are employed for seafood, and the restaurant moves a lot of lobster in summer. Help keep it around a while.

At the Dodson Boatyard, 194 Water St. ✆ **860/535-2588**. Main courses $15.50–$21.50. AE, MC, V. Tues–Sat 11:30am–3pm; Sun 10am–3pm; Tues–Sun 5:30–9:30pm. Closed Mar.

Stonecroft ECLECTIC This 1807 inn is home to Drew Egy, a gifted young chef who blazes no new trails but works wonders with dishes that have become familiar in the past two decades of America's food revolution. His realm is the lower level of a converted barn with linen-dressed tables and couches

A Casino in the Woods

What has been wrought in the woodlands north of the Mystic coast is nothing less than astonishing. There was very little here when the Mashantucket Pequot tribe received clearance to open a gambling casino on their ancestral lands in rural Ledyard. Virtually overnight, the tribal bingo parlor was expanded into a full-fledged casino, and a hotel was built.

That was in 1992. Within 3 years, it had become the single most profitable gambling operation in the world, with a reported 40,000 visitors a day. Money cascaded over the Pequot (pronounced *Pee*-kwat) in a seemingly endless torrent. Expansion was immediate—another hotel, then a third, more casinos, golf courses, and the $139-million **Mashantucket Pequot Museum and Research Center,** devoted to Native American arts and culture. The tribe bought up adjacent lands and at least four nearby inns and hotels, then opened a shipworks to build high-speed ferries. All that hasn't sopped up the floods of profit, and the tribe has made major contributions to the Mystic Aquarium and Smithsonian Museum of the American Indian.

All this prosperity came to a tribe of fewer than 520 acknowledged members, nearly all of them of mixed ethnicity. Residents of surrounding communities were ambivalent, to put the best face on it. When it was learned that one of the tribe's corporate entities was to be called Two Trees Limited Partnership, a predictable query was, "Is that all you're going to leave us? Two trees?"

But while there is a continuing danger of damage to the fragile character of this authentically picturesque corner of Connecticut, it is also a fact that because of the recent development, thousands of non-Pequots have found employment in their various enterprises.

The complex is reached through forested countryside of quiet hamlets that give little hint of the behemoth rising above the trees in Ledyard township. There are no signs screaming "Foxwoods." Instead,

around a fireplace. Warm focaccia with caramelized onion butter is a nice elevation over the usual rolls. Wine is generously poured in anticipation of such specials as the red pepper and tomato bisque swirled into a tangy black bean soup. A favorite entree is pan-roasted salmon with trendy lemon froth. Other dishes come in a remarkable variety of colors, textures, and ingredients—a touch too many, in some cases—but it's unlikely that you won't be delighted with most choices.

There are also 10 rooms at the inn, many with fireplaces, a few with whirlpool tubs; rates are $135 to $250 double.

515 Pumpkin Hill Rd., Ledyard. ✆ 860/572-0771. www.stonecroft.com. Reservations recommended on weekends. Main courses $16–$25. AE, DC, MC, V. Wed–Sun 6–10pm. Take Exit 89 north from I-95, onto Cow Hill Rd., which shortly becomes Pumpkin Hill Rd.

FOXWOODS RESORT CASINO

This casino-hotel complex (✆ **860/885-3000**) is a moving target, forever changing, adding, renovating, expanding. There are, in fact, several cavernous watch for plaques with the symbols of tree, wolf, and fire above the word RESERVATION. As you enter the property, platoons of attendants point the way to parking and hotels. Ongoing construction surrounds the glassy, turquoise-and-violet towers of the hotels and sprawling casino. Though busy and bustling, it doesn't look like Vegas from the outside—happily, there are no sphinxes, no fake volcanoes, and no 20-story neon palm trees.

Inside, the glitz gap narrows, but it is still relatively restrained as such temples to chance go. The gambling rooms have windows, for example, even though the prevailing wisdom among casino designers is that they should not give customers any idea of what time of day or night it is.

And no one is allowed to forget that this whole eye-popping affair is owned and operated by Native Americans. Prominently placed around the main buildings are larger-than-life sculptures by artists of Chiricahua and Chippewa descent, depicting Amerindians in a variety of poses and artistic styles. One other Indian-oriented display is *The Rainmaker,* a glass statue of an archer shooting an arrow into the air. Every hour on the hour, he is the focus of artificial thunder, wind-whipped rain, and lasers pretending to be lightning bolts, the action described in murky prose by a booming voice-of-Manitou narrator. That's as close as the chest thumping gets to going over the top, although some visitors might reflect upon the political correctness of the non-Indian cocktail waitresses outfitted in skimpy Pocahontas minidresses with feathers in their hair.

The pace of all this is slowing somewhat, at least temporarily. The Pequots are watching closely as the Mohegan Sun Resort, barely 6 miles away as the crow flies, continues to crowd in on their territory.

Two dozen bus companies provide daily service to Foxwoods from Boston, Hartford, Providence, New York, Philadelphia, and Albany, among many other cities—too many to list here. For information about transit from particular destinations, call (C) **860/885-3000.**

gambling rooms, one of the most popular being the hall containing 4,500 slot machines. A high-tech horse parlor with tote boards and live feeds from tracks around the country is a dazzler. All the usual methods of depleting wallets are at hand—blackjack, bingo, chuck-a-luck, keno, craps, baccarat, roulette, acey-deucy, money wheel, and several variations of poker. To keep players at tables, there's food service in the poker parlor, and complimentary drinks served at craps and blackjack tables.

SEEING THE SIGHTS

Mashantucket Pequot Museum and Research Center ★★ A $135-million trickle of the floods of cash washing over southeastern Connecticut and its resurgent Indian Nation has been diverted to create this museum. Opened in 1998 to substantial fanfare, it has justified the hoopla with a carefully conceived mix of film, murals, models, dioramas, and re-creations of scenes of Native American life before and after the arrival of European settlers. The most effective of the exhibits is the walk-around Pequot Village, complete with wig-wams and life-size figures shown fishing, hunting, cooking, growing corn, butchering game, and making baskets and ceramics. A 175-foot **observation tower** supplies views of the forested reservation. Lunch and snacks are served from 11am to 5:30pm in the large restaurant, and there's a museum shop with books, jewelry, crafts, and related items.

110 Pequot Trail. ℂ 860-411-9671. Admission $10 adults, $8 seniors 55 and over, $6 children 6–15. Wed–Mon 10am–7pm.

WHERE TO STAY

The resort has three hotels, the newest and most luxurious of which became operational in 1998, more than doubling Foxwoods' housing capacity to 1,400 rooms. Unlike Las Vegas and other gambling centers, rates aren't kept artificially low as an inducement to gamblers, although that policy may change depending upon competitive pressures from the rival Mohegan Sun Resort.

To get to the resort from Boston, take I-95 south to Exit 92 onto Route 2 west. From New Haven and New York, take I-95 to I-395 north to Exit 79A onto Route 2A east, picking up Route 2 east. Don't bother trying to park your car in the huge garage. It takes forever, and the valet parking at the front door is swift and free.

Grand Pequot Tower 🐸🐸   The Grand Pequot Tower handily takes its place among New England's elite resort hotels. The newest of Foxwoods' hotels (so far) is the grandest in space and concept, yet it is also the most tasteful of the three. Polished granite and imported woods and marbles feature extensively in the handsome lobby. The tower's main restaurants, Fox Harbour and Al Dente, surpass all the resort competition. Live piano music accompanies cocktails in the lobby lounge. In back is a 50,000-square-foot casino, containing a plush Club Newport International open only to big-money players.

Rte. 2, Mashantucket, CT 06339. ℂ **800/369-9663** or 860/885-3000. Fax 860/312-7474. www.foxwoods. com. 824 units. July to Labor Day $220–$295 double, from $400 suite; Sept–June $195–$270 double, from $400 suite. AE, DC, DISC, MC, V. Free valet parking. **Amenities:** 2 restaurants (seafood, Italian), bars; indoor pool; golf course on property; health club and spa; video arcade; shopping arcade; concierge; 24-hour room service; baby-sitting; same-day dry cleaning/laundry service. *In room:* A/C, TV, dataport, hair dryer.

Great Cedar Hotel 🐸   Well maintained despite the heavy foot traffic, this hotel has eight floors adjoining the casinos. Guest rooms are colorful, but not too gaudy (except for the suites for high rollers on the top floor), and are out-fitted with the usual gadgets and technology.

Rte. 2, Mashantucket, CT 06339. ℂ **800/369-9663** or 860/885-3000. Fax 860/885-4040. www.foxwoods. com. 312 units. July to Labor Day $170–$222 double, $500 suite; Sept–June $195–$265 double, $500 suite. AE, DC, DISC, MC, V. Free valet parking. **Amenities:** Restaurant, bars; indoor pool; golf course on the property; health club and spa; video arcade; shopping arcade; limited room service; baby-sitting; same-day dry cleaning/laundry service. *In room:* A/C, TV, dataport.

Two Trees Inn   This was the first Foxwoods lodging, built in less than 3 months, now a short shuttle-bus ride or 10-minute walk from the casino complex. A conventional motor hotel, it attracts large numbers of bus tours. Free coffee and juice in the small lobby provide the opportunity to contemplate your fellow guests' taste in white shorts and pastel tops . . . in January.

240 Lantern Hill Rd. (off Rte. 2), Mashantucket, CT 06339. ℂ **800/369-9663** or 860/312-3000. Fax 860/ 885-4050. www.foxwoods.com. 280 units. July–Nov $160–$195 double, $185–$220 suite; Sept–June $135–$160 double, $160–$185 suite. AE, DC, DISC, MC, V. **Amenities:** Restaurant, bar; heated indoor pool; fitness room; sauna; same-day dry cleaning/laundry service. *In room:* A/C, TV.

(Kids **For a Break from Gambling . . .**

If you want to temporarily escape the whirring of slots and the insistent chatter of the croupiers, or simply need to occupy underage kids, check out **Cinetropolis,** an entertainment center that looks like a cleaned-up futuristic Gotham. This is the electronic age at its most playfully frantic. **Turbo Ride** lets you pretend you're experiencing the rumbling takeoffs and powerful G-forces of jets taking off, this by way of giant films and machinery that makes your seat rock and roll as if in a cockpit. **Fox Giant Screen Theatre** is an IMAX-like production that features front-row rock concerts and exploding volcanoes, and **Virtual Adventures** lets you take control of an undersea vessel slipping past the dangers of the ocean depths. Once all that is exhausted, the **Fox Arcade** has pinball and video games that might seem a little pallid after the rest of these diversions.

WHERE TO DINE

Twenty-four sit-down restaurants and fast-food operations situated throughout the hotel-casino complex cover the most popular options. Only a couple aspire to even moderately serious culinary achievement.

Cedars Steak House (© 860/885-3000, ext. 4252) grills beef and seafood that are supplemented by a raw bar; **Al Dente** (ext. 4090) does designer pizzas and pastas; and **Fox Harbour** (ext. 2445) specializes in seafood. All three expect their guests to be dressed at least a notch better than tank tops and jeans. They are the only ones that accept reservations.

The most popular dining room is the **Festival Buffet** (ext. 3172), which charges $10 for an all-you-can-eat spread that usually includes five or six main courses plus soups, salads, sides of vegetables and starches, and desserts. Other self-explanatory possibilities are **Han Garden** (ext. 4093), **Pequot Grill** (ext. 2690), and **The Deli** (ext. 5481).

FOXWOODS AFTER DARK

Just as in Vegas and Atlantic City, big showbiz names are whisked onto the premises, usually on weekends. Even Wayne Newton makes the scene, as do the likes of Regis Philbin, Tony Bennett, Paul Anka, Reba McEntire, Bill Cosby, the Dixie Chicks, and Jay Leno. For information about current headliners, call © 800/200-2882.

UNCASVILLE & THE MOHEGAN SUN CASINO

About halfway between New London and Norwich, this blue-collar town once hardly provided sufficient reason even to downshift your car. That's changed, for good.

In October 1996, the barely extant Mohegan tribe opened its gambling casino, **Mohegan Sun,** Mohegan Sun Boulevard (© 888/226-7711). Sitting in the middle of a potential $1-billion annual market, it was drawing 20,000 gamblers a day away from Foxwoods within a few weeks of opening. Obviously, the initial outlay of over $300 million for land and construction paid off handsomely, for the tribe announced soon after its inauguration that it was committing another $400 million for a new 1,200-room hotel, a marina, and nongambling entertainment facilities. That projected expenditure was soon doubled, and now includes a 10,000-seat sports arena, a second casino, and a

Which Casino?

When Mohegan Sun first opened, it seemed unlikely to mount a serious challenge to Foxwoods. It was, after all, only a single building, with no big-name entertainment, hotel, or facilities to occupy children. But it is easier to reach, just off I-395, a major highway between Boston and New York, and the essentially childless environment no doubt made it appealing to resolute gamblers. Now a hotel, marina, sports arena, and planetarium are underway, and the headliners in the showroom are of Vegas stature.

Mohegan Sun has a less frantic environment than Foxwoods, comparatively speaking, but it is smaller, with fewer choices in games and restaurants, and until current construction is completed, it has no significant nongambling attraction, while Foxwoods has its heralded museum of Pequot life.

planetarium, all to be completed by 2002. The area under construction triples the size of the existing development.

In the meantime, the original casino building is bulging with eager gamblers. It is circular, with four entrances named for the seasons. The core of 150,000 square feet is devoted to the games, everything from blackjack and baccarat to craps and Pai Gow poker, supplemented by 3,000 slot machines. In the center is a nightclub, the Wolf Den, featuring weekend headliners on the order of Chick Corea, Seal, and Crystal Gayle and nightly entertainers of lounge-act stature. Overhead are simulated log constructions meant to suggest ancient lodge houses. It's an aesthetically pleasing space, as casinos go, although few of the avid players seem to notice. They can even park their kids in the child-care center.

Of the several dining options circling the gambling, the relatively ambitious **Longhouse** proffers mostly prime beef and seafood, while other eateries feature Asian, Italian, deli, and just-about-everything-else chow. The quality of the food is unexpectedly good.

The casino is right off I-395, Exit 79A, which makes for easy on/off access for gamblers who don't want to deal with that onerous 20-minute drive to Foxwoods before emptying their bank accounts.

NORWICH

There is tourist potential here, where the Yantic and Shetucket rivers converge to form the Thames. Blocks of Broadway and Union Street are lined with substantial mansions from the city's golden era, in styles ranging from the Federal and Classical Revival of the first half of the 19th century to the Italianate, French Second Empire, and various Victorian conceits of the second half. There is no pretending, however, that this historic old mill town isn't in the doldrums, and so far, the presence of the nearby Mohegan Sun casino hasn't had much spillover effect. Until efforts to reverse that decline take hold, the principal reason for a visit is the fine lodging described below.

WHERE TO STAY & DINE

The Spa at Norwich Inn ✫✫✫   Reopened after extensive renovations, this is now an even more desirable property. The complex is set among gardens and woods on 40 acres, the main building augmented by outlying "villas" with 160 condo units, about half of which are suites available to overnight guests. A typical suite has a fully equipped kitchen, a large sitting area with logs placed in the fireplace, two double beds in the separate bedroom, and a deck overlooking the woods and a pond. Inn rooms aren't as large and don't have fireplaces, but they are hardly spartan. The dining room features a versatile kitchen staff capable of producing meals either conventional or fitness-minded. The property is owned by the Pequot tribal organization, and its Foxwoods Casino is about 15 minutes away, making this inn a soothing and convenient respite from the glitz.

607 W. Thames St. (Rte. 32), Norwich, CT 06360. © **800/267-4772** or 860/886-2401. Fax 860/886-9483. www.thespaatnorwichinn.com. 103 units. May–Oct $175–$375 double; Nov–Apr $125–$325. AE, DC, MC, V. From New Haven, take Exit 76 off I-95 onto I-395 north, Exit 79A onto Rte. 2A east, then exit onto Rte. 32 north and drive 1½ miles to the inn. **Amenities:** Restaurant, bar; 2 outdoor pools; 1 indoor pool; golf course on property; fully equipped health club and spa (with exercise classes, steam rooms, sauna, and massage); concierge; limited room service; baby-sitting; same-day dry cleaning/laundry service. *In room:* A/C, TV, dataport, fridge, coffeemaker, hair dryer, iron.

Rhode Island

by Herbert Bailey Livesey

Water defines "Little Rhody" as much as mountain peaks characterize Colorado. The Atlantic thrusts all the way to the Massachusetts border, cleaving the state into unequal halves and filling the geological basin that is Narragansett Bay. That leaves 400 miles of coastline and several large islands.

A string of coastal towns runs in a northeasterly arc from the Connecticut border up to Providence, the government and business capital, which lies at the point of the bay, 30 miles from the open ocean. It was here that Roger Williams, banned from the Massachusetts Bay Colony in 1635 for his outspoken views on religious freedom, established his colony. Little survives from that first century, but a large section of the city's East Side is composed almost entirely of 18th- and 19th-century dwellings and public buildings.

Another group of Puritan exiles established their settlement a couple of years after Providence, on an island known to the Narragansett tribe as "Aquidneck." Settlers thought their new home resembled the Isle of Rhodes in the Aegean, so the official name became "Rhode Island and Providence Plantations," a moniker that was subsequently applied to the entire state, and remains the official name.

The most important town on Aquidneck is Newport, and it's the best reason for an extended visit to the state. Its first era of prosperity was during the colonial period, when its ships not only plied the new mercantile routes to China but also engaged in the reprehensible "Triangular Trade" of West Indies molasses for New England rum for African slaves. Their additional skill at smuggling and evading taxes brought them into conflict with their British rulers, whose occupying army all but destroyed Newport during the Revolution. After the Civil War, the town began its transformation from commercial outpost to resort, with the arrival of the millionaires whose lives spawned what Mark Twain sneeringly described as the "Gilded Age." They built astonishingly extravagant mansions, their contribution to Newport's bountiful architectural heritage. Winning the America's Cup and subsequent defenses of yachting's most famous trophy made the town into a recreational sailing center with a packed summer cultural calendar. As a result, travelers who want nothing more than a deep tan by Monday can coexist with history buffs and music-lovers, who come to attend concerts held against a seductive backdrop of waves hissing across packed sand.

Finally, there is Block Island, which is a 1-hour ferry ride from Point Judith. A classic summer resort, it has avoided the imposition of Martha's Vineyard chic and Provincetown clutter. It has also sidestepped history (even though it was first settled in 1661), so there are few mandatory sights. That leaves visitors free simply to explore its lighthouses, hike its cliffside trails, and hit the beach.

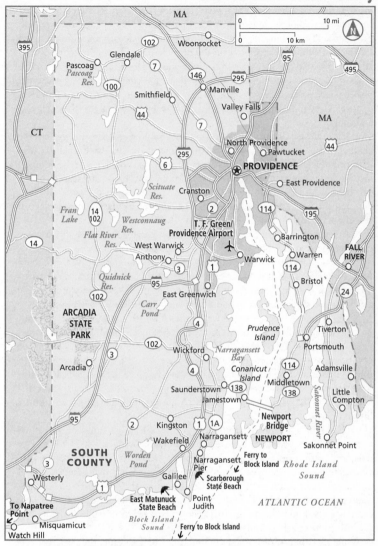

1 Providence ★★

45 miles S of Boston, 55 miles NE of New London

Providence delights in its new sobriquet, "Renaissance City," and is absolutely beside itself over the success of the TV series named for it. No question, this city is moving on up, counter to the trend of so many small and mid-sized New England cities. *Money* magazine even declared it "The Best Place to Live in the East." Revival is in the air and prosperity is returning, especially evident in the resurgent "downcity" business district. Rivers have been uncovered to form canals and waterside walkways, gondolas and kayaks glide beneath graceful bridges, distressed buildings of the last century have been reclaimed, and continued construction includes a new Marriott behind Union Station, along with Providence Place, a monster mall that brings national department stores to town for the first time. Advance buzz on the new Heritage Harbor Museum, Rhode Island's first state history museum, is tremendous. This affiliate of the venerable Smithsonian Institution, being developed on the sprawling site of a former power plant, is scheduled to open in 2002. Aside from a rich trove of artifacts on display, the museum will feature restaurants, shops, festival and theater space, and shops.

Much of the credit for Providence's boom, grudging or exuberant, goes to the ebullient four-terms-and-counting mayor, Vincent A. "Buddy" Cianci, Jr., who even peddles bottles of his own marinara sauce on the side. Despite the airing of some incriminating taped phone conversations, Cianci has so far escaped the net cast by an FBI probe into the bribery of local officials. Called Operation Plunder Dome, the investigation has revived Providence's reputation for tolerance of corruption at high levels.

Still, the local pride in the city's revitalization is palpable, and Buddy is given much of the credit. A burgeoning dining scene includes ambitious new restaurants that are nearly always less expensive than their counterparts in Boston and New York. College Hill is one of only 26 National Historic Districts, the calendar is full of concerts and special events, and the presence of the young people attending the city's 12 colleges and universities guarantees a lively nightlife.

Roger Williams knew what he was doing. Admired for his fervent advocacy of religious and political freedom in the early colonial period, he obviously had good instincts for town building as well. He planted the seeds of his settlement on a steep rise overlooking a swift-flowing river at the point where it widened into a large protected harbor. That part of the city, called the East Side and dominated by the ridge now known as College Hill, remains the most attractive district of a New England city second only to Boston in the breadth of its cultural life and rich architectural heritage.

College Hill is so named because it is the site of Rhode Island College, which started life in 1764 and was later renamed Brown University. The Hill is further enhanced by the presence of the highly regarded Rhode Island School of Design, whose buildings are wrapped around the perimeter of the Brown campus. In and around these institutions are several square miles of 18th- and 19th-century houses, colonial to Victorian, lining often gaslit streets. At the back of the Brown campus is the funky shopping district along Thayer Street, while at the foot of the Hill is the largely commercial Main Street.

While most points of interest are found on the East Side, the far larger collection of neighborhoods west of the river has its own attractions. The level downtown area is the center for business, government, and entertainment, with City Hall, a new convention center, the two best large hotels, some small parks and historic buildings, and several venues for music, dance, and theatrical productions. To its north, across the Woonasquatucket River, is the imposing State House and the Amtrak railroad station. And to its west, on the other side of Interstate 95, is Federal Hill, a residential area bearing a strong ethnic identity, primarily Italian, but increasingly leavened by numbers of more recent immigrant groups.

ESSENTIALS

GETTING THERE   I-95, which connects Boston and New York, runs right through the city. From Cape Cod, pick up I-195 west.

Providence

ATTRACTIONS ●
Brown University **8**
First Unitarian Church **12**
Gov. Henry Lippitt
  House Museum **5**
John Brown House
  Museum **14**
Museum of Art, Rhode Island
  School of Design **6**
The Providence Athenaeum **7**
Rhode Island State House **2**
Roger Williams Park Zoo **15**

ACCOMMODATIONS ■
C.C. Ledbetter **13**
Courtyard by Marriott **9**
Marriott **3**
The Old Court **4**
Providence Biltmore **11**
State House Inn **1**
Westin Providence **10**

T. F. Green/Providence Airport (© 888/268-7222 or 401/737-8222; www.
pvdairport.com) in Warwick, south of Providence (Exit 13, I-95), handles all
national flights. Major airlines serving this airport include **American** (© **800/
433-7300**), **Continental** (© **800/525-0280**), **Delta** (© **800/221-1212**),
Northwest (© **800/225-2525**), **Southwest** (© **800/435-9792**), **United**
(© **800/241-6522**), and **US Airways** (© **800/428-4322**). The Rhode Island
Public Transit Authority (RIPTA) provides transportation between the airport and
the city center. Taxis are also available, costing about $20 for the 20-minute trip.

Amtrak (© **800/USA-RAIL**) runs several trains daily along the shore route
between Boston and New York, stopping at the attractive new station at 100
Gaspee St., near the State House.

GETTING AROUND   Traffic on local streets isn't bad, even at rush hour, so
by all means drive if you wish. Taxis are not easy to come by, with few to be
found outside even the largest hotels. They can take 15 minutes or more when
called from restaurants.

VISITOR INFORMATION   For advance information, contact the **Providence Warwick Convention & Visitors Bureau,** 1 West Exchange St. (© **800/
233-1636** or 401/274-1636; www.providencecvb.com). In town, consult the
new visitor information center in the Rhode Island Convention Center at 1
Sabin St, or check with the helpful park rangers at the visitor center of the Roger
Williams National Park, at the corner of Smith and North Main streets, open
daily from 9am to 4:30pm.

EXPLORING PROVIDENCE
STROLLING AROUND THE HISTORIC NEIGHBORHOODS
This is a city of manageable size—the population is about 170,000—that can
easily occupy 2 or 3 days of a Rhode Island vacation. Two leisurely walks, one
short, another longer, pass most of the prominent attractions and offer up a
sense of the city's evolution from a colony of dissidents to a contemporary center of commerce and government.

Downtown, chart a route from the 1878 City Hall on Kennedy Plaza along
Dorrance Street 1 block to Westminster. Turn left, then right in 1 block, past the
Arcade (see "Quick Bites," below), then left on Weybosset.

To extend this into a longer walk, follow Weybosset until it joins Westminster and continue across the Providence River. Turn right on the other side,
walking along South Water Street as far as James Street, just before the I-195
overpass. Turn left, cross South Main, then turn left on Benefit Street. This is
the start of the so-called **Mile of History** ★★. Lined with restored or carefully
preserved 18th- and 19th-century houses, it is a feast for aficionados of Early
American domestic architecture, enhanced by gas streetlamps and sections of
brick herringbone sidewalks. Along the way are opportunities to visit, in
sequence, the 1786 **John Brown House,** the **First Unitarian Church** (1816),
the **Providence Athenaeum,** and the **Museum of Art, Rhode Island School of
Design.**

SEEING THE SIGHTS
Boosters are understandably proud of their new **Waterplace Park & Riverwalk** ★★, which encircles a tidal basin and borders the Woonasquatucket River
down past where it joins the Moshassuck to become the Providence River. It incorporates an amphitheater, boat landings, landscaped walkways with benches and
trees, and vaguely Venetian bridges that cross to the East Side. Summer concerts

and other events are held here, among them the enormously popular **WaterFires** ★★ (✆ **401/272-3111**), when 97 bonfires are set ablaze in the basin of Waterplace Park and along the river on New Year's Eve and on more than 20 other dates July through October, their roar accentuated by amplified music.

Nearby, in Kennedy Plaza, the new **Fleet Skating Center** has an ice rink twice the size of the one in New York's Rockefeller Center, fully utilized almost every winter evening. Skate rentals, lockers, and a snack bar are available.

Brown University   The nation's seventh-oldest college was founded in 1764 and has a reputation as the most experimental institution among its Ivy League brethren. The evidence of its pre-Revolutionary origins is seen in **University Hall,** built in 1771 and a makeshift barracks for American and French troops in the war against the British. Tours of the campus are intended primarily for prospective students, but anyone can join (call ahead).

Office of Admissions, 45 Prospect St. (corner of Angell St.). ✆ **401/863-1000**. Free admission. Tours late Nov to early Sept Mon–Fri at 10am, 11am, 1pm, 3pm, and 4pm (11am and 3pm only during Christmas and spring vacations); mid-Sept to mid-Nov Sat 10am, 11am, and noon.

Gov. Henry Lippitt House Museum ★   This house is as magnificently true to its grandiose Victorian era as any residence on the Continent. Its style is technically Renaissance Revival—which means that the architect brought to bear any motif or notion that took his fancy. Meticulously detailed stenciling, expanses of stained glass, ornately framed mirrors, inlaid floors, and wood intricately carved or made to look like marble combine to make this mansion one of the treasures of College Hill. The governor and his descendants lived in the house until 1981, which helped enormously in its preservation. Visits to the museum are by guided tour only.

199 Hope St. (at Angell St.). ✆ **401/453-0688**. Admission $4 adults, $2 seniors and students. Tours Apr–Dec Tues–Fri 11am–3pm on the hour; Sat–Sun and Jan–Mar by appointment only.

John Brown House Museum   Quite unlike the fiery 19th-century abolitionist of the same name, *this* John Brown was an 18th-century slave trader who amassed a fortune as a master of the China Trade. He and his descendants contributed much of that fortune to the university that bears the family name. The style of his 1786 brownstone and brick mansion is Georgian, although after the Revolution, Brown no doubt preferred to think of it as Federal-style. Brown's widow, children, and grandchildren lived here until 1846. Subsequent owners made additions and redecorated in the Victorian fashion. Their efforts were reversed after the house was bequeathed in 1941 to the Rhode Island Historical Society, which restored it to its original condition. Visits are by guided tour, which last about 45 minutes.

52 Power St. (at Benefit St.). ✆ **401/331-8575**. Admission $6 adults, $4.50 seniors and students, $3 children 7–17. Mar–Dec Tues–Sat 10am–5pm; Sun noon–4pm. Jan–Feb Fri–Sat 10am–5pm; Sun noon–4pm.

Museum of Art, Rhode Island School of Design ★★   Prestigious RISD (pronounced *Riz*-dee) supports this ingratiating center, which houses the 65,000 artworks of the permanent collection and temporary exhibitions, including biennial shows of the faculty. A broad collection includes Chinese terra cotta, Greek statuary, French Impressionist paintings, and Early American decorative arts. Probably of greatest interest are the works by such masters as Monet, Cézanne, Rodin, Picasso, and Matisse. But allow time for the American wing, which contains not only fine antiques but also paintings by Gilbert Stuart, John Singleton Copley, and John Singer Sargent.

224 Benefit St. (between Waterman and College sts.). ℭ **401/454-6100.** Admission $5 adults, $4 seniors, $2 college students with ID, $1 children 5–18; free to all last Sat of month and Thurs 5–9pm. Tues–Sun 10am–5pm (Thurs until 9pm).

The Providence Athenaeum

The Providence Athenaeum, a learned society founded in 1753, commissioned this granite 1838 Greek Revival building to house its lending library, the fourth oldest in the United States and an innovative concept at the time. Edgar Allan Poe courted Sarah Whitman, his "Annabel Lee," between these shelves. Random glances through the old card catalog reveal handwritten cards dating well back into the 1800s. Bibliophiles will lose themselves in this marvelous place. Rotating exhibits of rare books and works by local artists are additional attractions.

251 Benefit St. (at College St.). ℭ **401/421-6970.** Free admission. Mon–Thurs 10am–8pm; Fri–Sat 10am–5pm; Sun 1–5pm. Closed Sat–Sun in summer.

Roger Williams Park Zoo ★★

Situated in a 430-acre park that also contains a museum of natural history and a planetarium, the zoo is divided into three principal habitats: Tropical America, the Farmyard, and the Plains of Africa. A new exhibit is devoted to Australasia, with tree kangaroos and the zoo's first saltwater aquarium. Ongoing renovations have removed the prisonlike structures of the Victorian era during which the zoo was created, replacing them with concealed moats and hidden fences so that the animals can be viewed with less obvious barriers. The museum of natural history has a planetarium, a carousel, and a boathouse. Every 20 minutes, a trolley ($1) carries passengers on a circuit of those attractions.

1000 Elmwood Ave. (at Exit 17 off I-95). ℭ **401/941-3510.** www.rwpzoo.org. Admission $6 adults, $3.50 seniors and children 3–12. 1-day pass including all sites and trolley $10.25 adults, $8.25 seniors, $6.75 children. Apr–Oct Mon–Fri 9am–5pm, Sat–Sun 9am–6pm; Nov –Mar daily 9am–4pm. Driving south on I-95, take exit 17; driving north, take exit 16.

Rhode Island State House

Constructed of Georgian marble that blazes in the sun, the 1900 capitol building dominates the city center by virtue of its hilltop location and superior aesthetic. This near-flawless example of neoclassical governmental architecture (by McKim, Mead & White, 1891–92) is given room to flaunt, with open space all around. Its self-supported dome is one of the largest in the world, reminding many viewers of the one on St. Peter's Cathedral in Rome. The gilded figure on top represents "Independent Man," the state symbol. Inside, a portrait of George Washington is given pride of place, one of many depictions of the father of his country painted by Gilbert Stuart, a Rhode Island native son.

82 Smith St. (between Francis and Hayes sts.). ℭ **401/277-2357.** Free admission. Guided tours by appointment Mon–Fri 8:30am–noon.

WHERE TO STAY

Assuming charm and character aren't your paramount criteria in lodging, the clusters of motels around most of the exits from I-95 and I-195 are routinely comfortable and offer decent value. Among these possibilities are the **Ramada Inn,** 940 Fall River Ave., Seekonk, Mass. (ℭ **508/336-7300**), and the **Days Hotel,** 220 India St., Providence (ℭ **401/272-5577**).

Alternatives are provided by B&B referral agencies, such as **Bed & Breakfast of Rhode Island** (ℭ **800/828-0000** or 401/849-1298). These are rooms in private homes, so sometimes quirky rules and limitations apply. Remember, too, that they are rarely as inexpensive as local branches of motel chains. Lodgings in the historic districts are required to provide off-street parking, and it's free at the three East Side inns (C. C. Ledbetter, the Old Court, and the State House Inn) recommended below. There's a charge for parking at the big downtown hotels. Rates at most area inns and motels go up on alumni and parents' weekends and graduation weeks.

C. C. Ledbetter   There's no sign out front, as Ms. Ledbetter doesn't want to bother her neighbors. Look for the 1780 clapboard building with the olive-green exterior. Things are more colorful inside, with lots of books and contemporary artwork. One bedroom might be the only one in the state to contain a rowing machine. A hearty continental breakfast is served around a common table downstairs, where the two resident dogs usually linger. While the owner isn't enthusiastic about accepting children and pets, she'll consider both. It's only a couple of blocks from Brown and RISD, so graduation weekends are already booked deep into this new century.

326 Benefit St. (between Charlesfield and Power), Providence, RI 02903. (C) and fax **401/351-4699.** 5 units (3 with private bathroom). $85–$130 double. Rates include breakfast. MC, V. *In room:* A/C, TV, hair dryer, no phone.

Courtyard by Marriott ⭐   This new addition to the downcity lodging scene is welcome for both its lower rates and for the extra rooms provided in a city still short of accommodations. As a mid-priced entry designed primarily for businesspeople, its rooms are equipped with two-line phones, high-speed Internet access, and well-lit desks; four meeting rooms are available. It is just as comfortable for leisure travelers, with several of our recommended restaurants, the new Providence Place mall, WaterFires, and Fleet Skating Center only minutes away. Cribs can be provided.

32 Exchange Terrace, Providence, RI 02903. (C) **800/321-2211** or 401/272-1191. Fax 401/272-1416. www. courtyard.com. 222 units. $149–$169 double. AE, DC, DISC, MC, V. **Amenities:** Cafe/bar (breakfast and light fare); indoor pool with whirlpool; exercise room; business center; laundry; dry cleaning. *In room:* A/C, TV, dataport, coffeemaker, hair dryer, iron.

Marriott   This busy but conventional motor hotel is popular with both business and leisure travelers. It's north of downtown, but within a 10-minute drive of most of the city's attractions. A 24-hour shuttle service to and from the airport and the bus and train stations can be arranged when booking. At off-times, bargaining often results in a lower rate.

1 Orms St., Providence, RI 02904. (C) **800/937-7768** or 401/272-2400. Fax 401/273-2686. www.marriotthotels. com/pvdri. 351 units. $119–$219 double. AE, DC, DISC, MC, V. **Amenities:** Restaurant; bar; indoor/outdoor pool; modest exercise room with whirlpool and sauna; concierge; business center; limited room service; dry cleaning. *In room:* A/C, TV, dataport, coffeemaker, hair dryer.

The Old Court   This was once a rectory, built in 1863, and the furnishings reflect that use and period. There are examples of rococo-revival and Eastlake styles, secretaries embellished with marquetry, and Oriental rugs on bare floors, as well as more familiar Victoriana. Most traces of its tenure as a boardinghouse for college students have been expunged. Breakfast is a production, always with a hot entree. Families or longer-term visitors may be interested in the apartment across the street. Admittedly a little dowdy, it's nonetheless spacious, with a separate bedroom, living room, and full kitchen with dining nook.

144 Benefit St., Providence, RI 02903. (C) **401/751-2002** or 401/351-0747. Fax 401/272-4830. www. oldcourt.com. 10 units. $145–$165 double. Rates include breakfast. AE, DISC, MC, V. No children under 12 accepted. *In room:* A/C, TV, VCR available.

Providence Biltmore ★★ A grand staircase beneath the stunning Deco bronze ceiling dates the centrally located building to the 1920s, and a plaque in the lobby shows the nearly 7-foot-high water level of the villainous 1938 hurricane. From the lobby, the dramatic glass elevator literally shoots skyward, exiting outdoors to scoot up the side of the building. Most guest rooms are large, half of them with more than 600 square feet of floor space; some of the 23 suites have kitchenettes. The entire property has received more than $10 million of overdue attention over the last 3 years, and another 50 rooms are being added.

Kennedy Plaza, Providence, RI 02903. ✆ **800/294-7709** or 401/421-0700. Fax 401/455-3050. info@ providencebiltmore.com. 289 units. $159–$309 double; $259–$380 suite. AE, DC, MC, V. Valet parking $15. **Amenities:** Restaurant, bar; fitness center; concierge; business center; limited room service; baby-sitting; laundry; dry cleaning. *In room:* A/C, TV, VCR available, dataport, coffeemaker, hair dryer.

State House Inn The neighborhood isn't the best (though downtown restaurants are only minutes away), but the owners compensate with lower rates and hotel conveniences, including access to a fax and copier. Some rooms have canopy beds or fireplaces, and new and antique furnishings have been added in the last couple years, part of the ongoing primping. Breakfast is substantial, with at least one hot dish. Children are welcome.

43 Jewett St., Providence, RI 02908. ✆ **401/351-6111.** Fax 401/351-4261. www.providence-inn.com. 10 units. $99–$159 double. Ask about lower weekday corporate rates. Rates include breakfast. AE, DISC, MC, V. From the State House, drive west on Smith St., over I-95, then left on Holden and right on Jewett. *In room:* A/C, TV, VCR available, dataport, hair dryer.

Westin Providence ★★★ The city's best hotel by far, this property does nothing to diminish the solid reputation of the Westin chain, and even with a luxurious interior and downtown location, the rates are considerably lower than those of its siblings in Boston and New York. Guest rooms come equipped with Nintendo PlayStations, while skyways connect the hotel with the new Providence Place mall and the convention center. The architectural grandeur of the lobby rotunda and other public spaces doesn't seem to dampen the sunny dispositions of the staff. Off the lobby rotunda is a lounge with the buffed glow of an exclusive men's club.

1 West Exchange St., Providence, RI 02903. ✆ **800/937-8401** or 401/598-8000. Fax 401/598-8200. www. westin.com. 363 units. $190–$330 double. Valet parking $15. AE, DC, MC, V. **Amenities:** 2 restaurants, 2 bars; indoor pool; fully equipped health club with whirlpool and sauna; concierge; business center; limited room service; baby-sitting; same-day dry-cleaning/laundry service. *In room:* A/C, TV w/ pay movies, VCR available, dataport, minibar, coffeemaker, hair dryer, iron.

WHERE TO DINE

Providence has a sturdy Italian heritage, resulting in a profusion of tomato-sauce and pizza joints, especially on Federal Hill, the district west of downtown and I-95. Since they are so obvious, the suggestions below focus on restaurants that have broken away from the red-gravy imperative.

One fruitful strip to explore for dining options is that part of **Thayer Street** that borders the Brown University campus; it counts Thai, Tex-Mex, barbecue, Indian, and even Egyptian restaurants among its possibilities.

Cafe Nuovo ★★★ MEDITERRANEAN FUSION This spacious room of glass, marble, and burnished wood occupies part of the ground floor of a downtown office tower that overlooks the confluence of the Moshassuck and Woonasquatucket rivers. Its reputation as a place to see and be seen shortchanges the skill of its capable chef, who honed his craft at upscale Manhattan restaurants. The fare is grounded in the Italian repertoire, but skips lightly among other inspirations, too—Thai, Greek, and Portuguese, among them. That culinary restlessness leads to dishes like duck with cranberry chutney and persimmon pudding, or ginger-crusted salmon with Key lime beurre blanc and jasmine rice. Afterward, consider the remarkable crème brûlée, gussied up with gold leaf and tiered with spun sugar. There's music on weekends and outdoor dining in warm weather. This is the hottest observation point for the nearly two dozen WaterFire events.

1 Citizens Plaza (access is from the Steeple St. bridge). ⓒ 401/421-2525. Reservations advised. Main courses $15.95–$29.95. AE, DC, DISC, MC, V. Mon–Fri 11:30am–4pm; Mon–Thurs 5–10:30pm; Fri–Sat 5–11pm. Closed first week in Jan.

Cafe Paragon ⭐ ECLECTIC AMERICAN Located in the heart of the shopping and eating street edging the Brown campus, this spot is understandably popular with university faculty, students, and neighbors. In deference to a core clientele with neither fat salaries nor expense accounts, management has kept prices within reason, yet still manages to serve food that equals that served in many downtown emporia. There are burgers and pastas, of course, but also full menus of some imagination, from soups and bruschettas to such daily specials as roast mahi-mahi with a tomato-caper-onion salsa. Portions are ample—the individual deep-dish pizzas fill 12-inch plates, and the salads are meal-sized.

234 Thayer St. (at Angell St.). ⓒ 401/421-2525. Main courses $9–$18. AE, DISC, MC, V. Sun–Thurs 11am–1am; Fri-Sat 11am–2am.

CAV ⭐⭐ ECLECTIC No corporate design drudge had a hand in *this* warehouse interior, another Jewelry District pioneer. CAV is an acronym for "Coffee/Antiques/Victuals," and patrons are surrounded by tribal rugs, primitive carvings, and assorted antiques (most for sale). Your server is likely to be a hunk taking a break from auditions. He brings dishes prepared by folks more accomplished at their craft than he, selected from such strenuous menu swings as Peking dumplings to the overkill seafood risotto packed with shrimp, scallops, salmon, tuna, haddock, mussels, and sausage. Pastas arrive in prodigious portions, too; one of the best is lobster ravioli. The small stage has an open mike on Mondays and live jazz or blues on Friday and Saturday nights. On those nights, there's a $5 cover.

14 Imperial Place (near corner of Basset St.). ⓒ 401/751-9164. Main courses $13–$24. DISC, MC, V. Mon–Thurs 11:30am–10pm; Fri–Sat 11:30am–1am; Sun 10am–10pm.

The Gatehouse ⭐⭐ NEW AMERICAN Step into a refined taproom with a green marble bar on the left, a working fireplace and elegantly set tables over to the right. Downstairs is a candlelit lounge and an outdoor deck perched above the Seekonk River. Jazz pianists or duos perform down here Wednesday through Saturday nights, and a pub menu offers burgers and pastas. Service and cuisine are more polished on the main floor. Imagine just this one signature appetizer: duck confit wrapped in towers of phyllo husk combined with the tastes of quince preserve and a foie gras cream sauce. Unlikely as it may sound, it's a perfect marriage of flavors. Many of the entrees are grilled, such as the hickory-smoked pork porterhouse smothered with collard greens. There are daily pasta and fish selections. Presentation is careful but not fussy. Sunday brunch is extremely popular.

4 Richmond Sq. (east end of Pitman St.). ⓒ 401/521-9229. Reservations recommended on weekends. Main courses $19–$29. AE, MC, V. Daily 5:30pm–10pm (bar until 1am).

Pot au Feu �, TRADITIONAL FRENCH   If English weren't being spoken all around, you'd think this restaurant was on a village square in Provence. Dishes like *escargot a la Bourguignonne* are exactly as they should be, reminders of what made Gallic cooking memorable long before the excesses of the food revolution set in. Unless you simply must have a tablecloth, there's no reason not to head straight downstairs, especially at dinner, when the price gap widens between the fancier salon and the basement bistro. The brick floors and overhead pipes do nothing to muffle the din down here, but that earthy food comes from the same kitchen, in operation for 30 years.

44 Custom House St. (off Weybosset St.). ℂ 401/273-8953. Main courses $22–$29 salon, $14–$21 bistro. AE, DC, MC, V. Salon Tues–Fri noon–1:30pm and 6–9pm; Sat 6–9:30pm. Bistro Mon–Fri 11:30am–2pm; Mon–Thurs 5:30–9pm; Fri–Sat 5:30–10pm; Sun 4–9pm. Closed Sun July–Aug.

Prov �, ECLECTIC   This is one of a growing number of enterprises helping to transform the distressed Jewelry District into Providence's SoHo. In this case, the Atomic Grill has been re-tooled into a more upscale version of its former self. Lunch has been dropped, unfortunately, but the environment has been slicked down, made warmer, less frantic, the better to attract a slightly older professional group rather than the slacker set that once dominated. In the kitchen, the culinary-arts grads of the nearby Johnson & Wales University haven't gotten timid, and nothing that arrives at the table looks or tastes exactly as it does anywhere else. Prices remain moderate, and live entertainment is provided several nights a week.

99 Chestnut St. (at Clifford St.). ℂ 401/621-8888. Main courses $13–$25. AE, DC, DISC, MC, V. Dining room Wed–Sat 5–10pm (until 11pm Fri–Sat); bar Mon–Thurs 5pm–1am, Fri–Sat 5pm–2am, Sun 8pm–1am.

QUICK BITES

A bona fide National Historic Landmark is an unlikely venue for snarfing up cookies, salads, souvlaki, doughnuts, and egg rolls. But **The Arcade,** 65 Weybosset St. (ℂ **401/598-1199**), is a 19th-century progenitor of 20th-century shopping malls, an 1828 Greek Revival structure that runs between Weybosset and Westminster streets. Its main floor is given over largely to fast-food stands and snack counters of the usual kinds—yes, the Golden Arches, too—while the upper floor is primarily clothing and jewelry boutiques and souvenir shops. It's open daily.

Another local culinary institution arrives in Kennedy Plaza on wheels every afternoon around 4:30pm. The grungy aluminum-sided **Haven Bros.** (ℂ **401/861-7777**) is a food tractor-trailer with stools inside and good deals on decent burgers and even better fries sold from its parking space next to City Hall. No new frontiers here, except that it hangs around until way past midnight to dampen the hunger pangs of clubgoers, lawyers, night people, and workaholic pols (the mayor is a regular).

SHOPPING

Thayer Street, the main commercial district for the university, has the recently expanded official **Brown Bookstore,** at no. 244 (at the corner of Olive Street), open daily, but not in the evenings, and the **College Hill Bookstore,** at no. 252, funkier and wider-ranging in its selections and open daily until midnight. Also in the vicinity are **Silverberry's,** at no. 220, with dressy and casual clothes as well as jewelry for college-age women, and **Hillhouse,** no. 135, long in the business of providing male Brownies with Ivy dress-up clothes for interview weeks and parents' days.

PROVIDENCE AFTER DARK

This being a college town, there is no end of music bars, small concert halls, and pool pubs. A good source of information about who's appearing where is the free weekly, the *Providence Phoenix*, or its website, www.providencephoenix.com.

THE PERFORMING ARTS The **Ocean State Lyric Opera** (✆ 401/331-6060) stages two or three productions a season at various locations, including the Lincoln School Theatre and Veterans Memorial Auditorium. The **Rhode Island Philharmonic** (✆ 401/831-3123) usually appears at the Providence Performing Arts Center. Big-ticket touring musicals on the order of *Cabaret* and *Fosse*, as well as traveling dance companies, comedians, and other attractions, are showcased at the **Providence Performing Arts Center,** 220 Weybosset St. (✆ 401/421-ARTS), while new plays share space with Ibsen and Shakespeare at the **Trinity Repertory Company,** 201 Washington St. (✆ 401/351-4242).

THE CLUB & MUSIC SCENE The southern end of Water and Main streets, known as India Point, has several bar/restaurants functioning essentially as nightspots. **The Hot Club,** 575 S. Water St. (✆ 401/861-9007), sits out over the water, with two bars and two terraces. It has views of a marina, a power plant, and the Fox Point Hurricane Barrier, all incorporated into scenes for the movie *There's Something About Mary.* It's open from noon until well past midnight. Other nearby possibilities include **Fish Company,** 515 S. Water St. (✆ 401/769-2220), popular primarily with 20-somethings.

South of downtown, in the Jewelry District, **The Complex** ⚓, 180 Pine St. (✆ 401/751-4263), offers four distinctive dance clubs for only one cover: techno at **Liquid Assets,** retro disco at **Polly Esta's,** Top 40 at **Algiers,** and dance rock at **Club Uranus.** It's open Wednesday through Saturday nights, with a cover of $3 to $5. Not far away, sharing a building with Prov (see "Where to Dine," above), is **Snooker's,** 99 Chestnut St. (✆ 401/351-7665), a pool hall with live music Friday and Saturday nights in its **Green Room.** Behind the restaurant is the **Reactor Room,** where a DJ pushes a Latin beat, geared to a somewhat older crowd.

Lupo's Heartbreak Hotel, 239 Westminster St. (✆ 401/272-5876), has live concerts five or six nights a week by tribute bands and alternative, hip hop, techno, and house groups. Tickets are sold around the corner at the **Met Café,** 130 Union St. (✆ 401/828-4889), which has its own stage and frequent performances by local bands.

The Call, 15 Elbow St. (✆ 401/751-2255), showcases mostly regional blues and rock bands, supplemented by single and duo acts in the attached **Century Lounge,** 150 Chestnut St. (same phone). Jazz and indie rock are often staged at **AS220,** 115 Empire St. (✆ 401/831-9327), as are unpredictable artistic tangents, including poetry slams and improvs.

Gay clubs on the scene include **Gerardo's,** 1 Franklin Sq. (✆ 401/274-5560), with dancing Thursday through Sunday, and **MiraBar,** 35 Richmond St. (✆ 401/331-6761).

Many restaurants in the city engage musical groups two or more nights a week, including the Gatehouse, CAV, and the Viva! annex to Cafe Paragon, all described above. At the **Trinity Brewhouse,** 186 Fountain St. (✆ 401/453-2337), live jazz and blues share attention with boutique beers, a pool table, and a warm-weather deck.

MOVIES For art-house films and midnight cult movies, there is the **Avon Repertory Cinema,** 260 Thayer St., near Meeting Street (✆ 401/421-3315).

2 A Bucolic Detour to Sakonnet Point

As a break from the urbanity of Providence or the concentration of sights and activities that is Newport, a side trip down the length of the oddly isolated southeastern corner of the state is a soothing excursion.

No one has thought to throw a bridge or run a ferry across the water between Newport and Sakonnet Point, prospects the reclusive residents would no doubt resist to the last lawsuit. They have been known to steal away with road signs to discourage summer visitors, and there are almost no enterprises geared to attract tourists. Things are quiet in these parts, and they intend to keep it that way.

To get here from Providence or Boston, pick up I-195 east, then Route 24 south, toward Newport. Take Exit 4 for Route 77 south, just before the Sakonnet River Bridge. From Newport, take Route 138 toward Fall River, and exit on Route 77 south immediately after crossing the bridge.

After a welter of small businesses, most of them involved in some way with the ocean, Route 77 smoothes out into a pastoral Brigadoon, not quite rural, but more rustic than suburban. Colonial farmhouses, real or replicated, bear sidings and roofs of weathered shakes the color of wood smoke. They are centered in tidy lawns, with fruit trees and firs as sentinels, bordered by miles of low stone walls assembled with a sculptural sense of balanced shapes and textures. No plastic deer, no tomato plants in front yards, none of those cute little banners hung from porches to herald seasons and holidays. It is as if a requirement of residence was attendance at a school of good taste.

There are a few antiques shops and roadside farm stands along the way, and a cluster of one-of-a-kind stores and other businesses at the little enclave of Tiverton Four Corners, about halfway down the point, but none are commercially intrusive enough to sour the pastoral serenity.

One of the rare good reasons to pull off the road is **Sakonnet Vineyards** ⭐, 162 W. Main Rd. (© **401/635-8486**), with an entrance road on the left, about 3 miles south of Tiverton Four Corners. In operation for more than 20 years, it is one of New England's oldest wineries, and produces 50,000 cases of creditable wines annually. Types range from a popular pinot noir to a dry gewürztraminer. Bring along a picnic lunch, then buy a bottle and retire to one of the tables beside the pond near the tasting room. The hospitality center is open daily from 10am to 6pm in summer, 11am to 5pm in winter.

Continuing south on Route 77, the road skirts Little Compton and heads on to **Sakonnet Point,** where the inland terrain gives way to stony beaches and coastal marshes. There's a wetlands wildlife refuge, a small harbor with working boats, and not much else.

Now head back north on Route 77, watching for the green-and-white sign pointing toward Adamsville (if the natives haven't made off with it). Take the right turn at the triangular traffic island just beyond, onto a road that seems to have neither name nor number. Shortly, it arrives at a T intersection surrounded by a Congregational church, some small shops, a post office, law and real-estate offices, and the Common's restaurant (see below). This is downtown **Little Compton** ⭐. Turn left (north) and you're back in the country before you shift into third gear. In about 4 miles, the road ends at Peckham Road. Turn right, in the faith that you are heading toward **Adamsville;** you'll arrive in about 8 miles. It's here that you'll come across Abraham Manchester's (see below).

> ### (Finds Local Favorite
>
> Pull off into a pebbled driveway, where morning glories spill over fenc-
> ing and fanciful painted metal chairs and tables rest in the shade of a big
> oak tree. Bread is baking in the little roadside cottage with the screened
> door. Get in line—for there almost certainly will be a line at **Olga's Cup
> and Saucer,** 261 West Main Rd., Little Compton (© **401/635-8650**)—to
> indulge in some of the most delicious homemade eats you will find any-
> where. Using their own gardens and Walker's Farm Stand next door as
> inspiration, Olga Bravo and her partner, Becky Wagner, create such orig-
> inal delectables as corn-and-tomato-topped pizza, cornmeal-crusted zuc-
> chini sandwiches, and blueberry-peach clafoutie. A polenta cake is
> fashioned with cornmeal and fine-ground almonds. Olga's is so revered
> that Providence demanded an outpost; an in-town Olga's Cup and Saucer
> opened recently at 103 Point St. (© **401/831-6666**), to near-breathless
> praise. The Providence branch is open year-round, the original location,
> from the end of June to Halloween.

From Adamsville, return to Route 77 via Route 179 to Tiverton Four Corners to get back to Newport, or take Route 81 to Route 24 if returning to Providence or Boston.

WHERE TO STAY ALONG THE WAY

Stone House Club   From the last stop in Sakonnet Point, return along Route
77, and you'll shortly note the entrance to this restaurant/tavern/inn. It's open
to the public, but it must observe the wink-wink subterfuge of proclaiming itself
a private club because it serves spirits and there's a church next door. That means
a $25 membership fee for individuals and $40 for couples, in addition to room
rates. Furnishings are worn and unstylish, but look oddly right for their location.
Two private swimming beaches are available to guests. The cellar Tap Room, a
former speakeasy, and the more formal restaurant upstairs traipse all over the
gastronomic map—traditional, nouvelle, Italian, Asian—with an emphasis on
seafood. They are open Tuesday through Sunday in summer, Friday through
Sunday from October to December and March to April.

122 Sakonnet Point Rd., Little Compton, RI 02837. © **401/635-2222**. Fax 401/635-2822. www.stonehouse.
com. 14 units (4 with shared bathroom). Summer and holidays $68–$125 double, $125–$200 suite; Nov–Apr
$48–$80 double, $90–$150 suite. Rates include breakfast. *Note:* Additional membership fee as noted above.
MC, V. **Amenities:** Restaurant, bar. *In room:* No phone.

WHERE TO DINE ALONG THE WAY

Abraham Manchester's ECLECTIC   Adamsville, birthplace of the famed
Rhode Island Red, is a less pristine hamlet than Little Compton, with a
disheveled aspect and more pickup trucks than SUVs. At its heart is Abraham
Manchester's, which serves as the town's social center. The gregarious owner and
her staff greet almost everyone by name, bantering as old friends do. The building is a former general store, but not much attention is paid the niceties of historic preservation. A mounted stag head and wagon wheel are typical of the
decor. The menu is unexpectedly imaginative, with, for example, a smoked
chicken Alfredo over spinach fettuccine, and a production called the "Manchester Medley Platter," a jumble of shrimp marinated in red wine, blackened swordfish, barbecued chicken, and a slab of tenderloin. Portions are daunting.

Before 11:30am, the owner's daughter runs **Breakfast In The Barn** (© **401/ 635-2985**) on the other side of the parking lot, offering freshly baked breads and pastries with her elaborate breakfasts. It's open Monday through Friday from 6 to 11:30am, Saturday and Sunday from 7am to 12:30pm.

Main Rd. © **401/635-2700**. Main courses $6.85–$21.95. MC, V. Daily 11:30am–9pm (until 10pm Sat–Sun)

Common's REGIONAL AMERICAN The apostrophe in the name is theirs—no one seems to know whether it's a mistake or a joke. Never mind. This is the place to sample a few Rhode Island specialties. There are johnnycakes, lacy pancakes of stoneground cornmeal as thin as playing cards, and stuffies, chopped Quahog (*KWAH*-og or *KOE*-hog) clams mixed with minced bell peppers and bread crumbs and packed into both halves of the shell for baking. A satisfying lunch is the chock-full lobster roll, which comes with Quahog chowder, fries, and fritters for $10.95. Everyone here knows everyone else, filling the place with joshing and laughter.

On the Little Compton Commons. © **401/635-4388**. Main courses $5.95–$11.95. No credit cards. Daily 5am–6pm (until 7pm Fri–Sat).

3 Newport ⊛⊛⊛

75 miles S of Boston, 115 miles NE of New Haven

"City by the Sea" is the singularly unimaginative nickname an early resident unloaded on Newport. At least it was accurate, since for a time during the colonial period it rivaled Boston and even New York as a center of New World trade and prosperity. Newport occupies the southern tip of Aquidneck Island in Narragansett Bay, and is connected to the mainland by three bridges and a ferry.

Wealthy industrialists, railroad tycoons, coal magnates, financiers, and robber barons made respectable by political connections and vast fortunes were drawn to the area in the 19th century, especially between the Civil War and World War I. They bought up property at the ocean's rim to build what they called summer "cottages"—that were in fact mansions of immoderate design and proportions patterned after European palaces.

The principal toys of the Newport elite were equally extravagant yachts meant for pleasure, not commerce, and competition among them established Newport's reputation as a sailing center. In 1851, the schooner *America* defeated a British boat in a race around the Isle of Wight. The prize trophy became known as the America's Cup, which remained in the possession of the New York Yacht Club (with an outpost in Newport) until 1983. In that shocking summer, *Australia II* snatched the Cup away from *Liberty* in the last race of a four-out-of-seven series. An American team regained the cup in 1987, but in 1995 a New Zealand crew won it back. The strong U.S. yachting tradition has endured despite the loss of the Cup, and Newport continues as a bastion of world sailing and a destination for long-distance races.

The perimeter of the city resembles a heeled boot, its toe pointing west, not unlike Italy. About where the laces of the boot would be is the downtown business and residential district. Several wharves push into the bay, providing support and mooring for flotillas of pleasure craft, from stubby little inboards and character boats to graceful sloops and visiting tall ships. Much of the strolling, shopping, eating, quaffing, and gawking is done along this waterfront and its parallel streets: America's Cup Avenue and Thames Street. (The latter used to be pronounced "Tems," in the British manner, but was Americanized to "Thaymz" after the Revolution.)

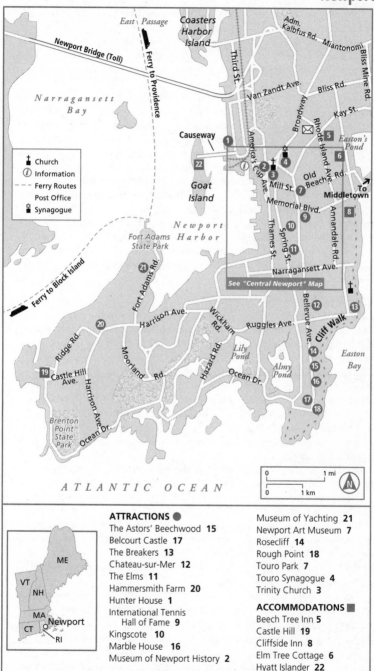

East Passage

Coasters Harbor Island

Newport Bridge (Toll)

Ferry to Providence

Narragansett Bay

Adm. Kalbfus Rd. Miantonomi

Bliss Mine Rd.

Third St.

Van Zandt Ave. Bliss Rd.

Broadway

Rhode Island Ave.

Kay St.

Causeway

1

22

America's Cup Ave.

i

2 **3** **4**

Mill St.

Old Beach Rd.

5 Easton's Pond

6

To **Middletown**

Goat Island

7

Memorial Blvd.

9

Annandale Rd.

8

Newport Harbor

Thames St.

Spring St.

10

11

Fort Adams State Park

21

Narragansett Ave.

See "Central Newport" Map

Church ✝
Information *i*
- - - **Ferry Routes**
Post Office ✉
Synagogue ✡

Ferry to Block Island

Fort Adams Rd.

Harrison Ave.

Wickham Rd.

Ruggles Ave.

Bellevue Ave.

Cliff Walk

12

13

20

Ridge Rd.

Moorland Rd.

Hazard Rd.

Lily Pond

Ocean Dr.

Almy Pond

14

15

16

17

18

Easton Bay

19 Castle Hill Ave.

Harrison Ave.

Brenton Point State Park

Ocean Dr.

ATLANTIC OCEAN

0   1 mi
0   1 km

N

ATTRACTIONS ●

The Astors' Beechwood **15**
Belcourt Castle **17**
The Breakers **13**
Chateau-sur-Mer **12**
The Elms **11**
Hammersmith Farm **20**
Hunter House **1**
International Tennis
 Hall of Fame **9**
Kingscote **10**
Marble House **16**
Museum of Newport History **2**

Museum of Yachting **21**
Newport Art Museum **7**
Rosecliff **14**
Rough Point **18**
Touro Park **7**
Touro Synagogue **4**
Trinity Church **3**

ACCOMMODATIONS ■

Beech Tree Inn **5**
Castle Hill **19**
Cliffside Inn **8**
Elm Tree Cottage **6**
Hyatt Islander **22**

ME

VT
NH

MA
CT Newport

RI

See "Central Newport" map for additional accommodations.

The navy pulled out its battleships, causing a decline in the local economy, but it hasn't proven to be the disaster predicted by some, and Newport has been spared the coarser intrusions that afflict so many coastal resorts. Monster RVs rarely add to the heavy traffic of July and August, and T-shirt emporia have kept within reasonable limits—a remarkable feat, considering that Newport has nearly 4 million visitors a year.

Immediately east and north of the business district are blocks of colonial, Federal, and Victorian houses of the 18th and 19th centuries, many of them restored and bearing plaques designating them National Historic Sites. Happily, they are not frozen in amber but are very much in use as residences, restaurants, offices, and shops. Taken together, they are as visually appealing in their own way as the 40-room cottages of the super-rich. Steven Spielberg found them sufficiently authentic to spend several weeks in town filming *Amistad.*

So, despite Newport's prevailing image as a collection of stupefyingly ornate mansions and regattas of sailing ships inaccessible to all but the rich and famous, the city is, for the most part, middle class and moderately priced. Summer evenings are often cool enough for a cotton sweater. Scores of inns and bed-and-breakfasts assure lodging even during festival weeks, at rates and fixtures from budget to luxury level. In almost every respect, this is the "First Resort" of the New England coast.

ESSENTIALS

GETTING THERE From New York City, take I-95 to the third Newport exit, picking up Route 138 east (which joins briefly with Route 4) and crossing the Newport toll bridge ($2) slightly north of the downtown district. From Boston, take Route 24 through Fall River, picking up Route 114 into town.

T. F. Green/Providence Airport (© 401/737-8222) in Warwick, south of Providence (Exit 13, I-95), handles national flights into the state. Major airlines serving this airport include **American** (© 800/433-7300), **Continental** (© 800/525-0280), **Delta** (© 800/221-1212), **Northwest** (© 800/225-2525), **United** (© 800/241-6522), and **US Airways** (© 800/428-4322). A few of the larger Newport hotels provide shuttle service, as does **Cozy Cab** (© 401/846-2500).

The **Rhode Island Public Transit Authority,** or **RIPTA** (© 800/244-0444 or 401/781-9400; www.ripta.com), runs up to 28 buses a day on the 70-minute ride between Providence's Kennedy Plaza and the Newport Gateway Center. One-way fare is $1.25.

RIPTA has inaugurated a new **ferry service** between Point Street Landing in Providence and Perrotti Park. From mid-April to early October, there are five departures daily; the rest of the year, three departures Monday through Friday only. One-way fare is $4. The operator is Boston Harbor Cruises; call © 617/227-4321 for information.

The **Interstate Navigation Company** (© 401/783-4613) provides ferry service between Providence, Block Island, and Newport's Fort Adams.

VISITOR INFORMATION For advance information available 24 hours, call **visitor information** (© 800/976-5122 outside R.I., or 800/556-2484 in R.I.). In town, stop by the excellent **Newport Gateway Visitors Center,** 23 America's Cup Ave. (© 800/326-6030 or 401/849-8048; www.gonewport.com). Open daily from 9am to 5pm (until 6pm Friday and Saturday), it has attendants on duty, brochures, a lodging-availability service, a cafe, a souvenir stand, rest rooms, and panoramic photos showing the locations of mansions, parks, and other landmarks. The building is shared with the bus station.

PARKING & GETTING AROUND   Most of Newport's attractions, except for the mansions, can be reached on foot, so leaving your car at your hotel or inn is wise. Parking lots and garages aren't cheap, especially at the waterfront, and many streets are too narrow. The metered parking slots along Thames Street are closely monitored by police, and fines are steep (although in the off-season, the meters are hooded and parking is free for up to 3 hours.). Renting or bringing a bicycle is an attractive option.

The **Rhode Island Public Transit Authority,** or **RIPTA** (© 401/781-9400), has a free shuttle bus that follows a roughly circular route through town, making stops at major sights.

SPECIAL EVENTS   Arrive any day between Memorial Day and Labor Day and expect to find at least a half dozen festivals, competitions, or other events in progress. Following is only a partial list of some of the more prominent events. (Specific dates often change from year to year, so call ahead to confirm; © **800/ 263-4636** outside R.I., or 401/848-2000 in R.I.).

While there are a few substantive events in the off-season months, notably the **February Winter Festival** (© 888/976-5122; www.newportevents.com), which focuses on food and winter sports, the pace ratchets up in June, starting with the annual **Great Chowder Cook-Off** at the Newport Yachting Center (© **401/846-1600**; www.newportfestivals.com). In the third week of June, the gardens of the Point section of town are open to visitors during the 3-day **Secret Garden Tour** (© **401/847-0514;** www.secretgardentour.com).

In July, the principal music event is the **Newport Music Festival** (© **401/ 846-1133;** www.newportmusic.org), which offers three classical music concerts daily at various venues during the middle 2 weeks of the month. The second week of July sees the **Hall of Fame Tennis Championships** (© **401/849-6053;** www.tennisfame.org), held on grass. In the third week of the month is the **Black Ships Festival** (© **401/846-5600;** www.newportevents.com), a celebration of all aspects of Japanese culture.

August brings the 3-day **Ben & Jerry's Folk Festival** (www.newportfolk. com) and the 3-day **JVC Jazz Festival** (© **401/847-3700** for both), both held at Fort Adams Park. Things wind down after Labor Day, though there's still the 3-day **Waterfront Irish Festival** (© **401/846-1600;** www.newportfestivals. com) in early September and the annual **Bowen's Wharf Seafood Festival** (© **401/849-2120**) in the third week of October. After Thanksgiving, special decorations and entertainments are featured during **Christmas at the Newport Mansions** (© **401/847-1000;** www.newportmansions.org).

Rosters of scheduled performers for the music festivals are usually released by May. While tickets are often available near concert time, it's wise to purchase them at least a month in advance for the best-known groups and soloists. Newport somehow absorbs the throngs that descend upon it for these events, but lodgings for weekends from Memorial Day to Labor Day should be secured at least 2 months in advance.

THE COTTAGES

That's what wealthy summer people called the almost unimaginably sumptuous mansions they built in Newport in the last decades before the 16th Amendment to the Constitution permitted an income tax.

Say this for the wealthy of the Gilded Age, many of whom obtained their fortunes by less than honorable means: They knew a good place to put down roots when they saw it. These are the same ones, after all, who developed Palm Beach in winter, the Hudson Valley in spring, the Berkshires in autumn, and Newport in summer, sweeping from house to luxurious house with the insouciance of a bejeweled matron dragging her sable down a grand staircase. They were Vanderbilts and Astors and their blue-blooded chums and rivals, and they rarely stayed in any one of their mansions for more than a few weeks a year.

When driving or biking through the cottage district (walking its length is impractical for most people), consider the fact that most of these astonishing residences are still privately owned. That's almost as remarkable as the grounds and interiors of the nine that are open to the public.

Also, resolve to visit only one or two estates per day. The sheer opulence of the mansions can soon become numbing, an effect not unlike touching down in five European countries in a week and touring the most lavish palaces in each.

Each residence requires 45 minutes to an hour for its guided tour. The aptitude and personality of individual docents is generally good, apart from their understandable tendency to take on a robotic tone. If at all possible, go during the week. Weekend foot and vehicular traffic can resemble Times Square at curtain time.

Six of the mansions are maintained by the **Preservation Society of Newport County,** 424 Bellevue Ave. (© **401/847-1000;** www.newportmansions.org), which also operates the 1748 Hunter House, the 1860 Italianate Chepstow villa, the 1883 Shingle-style Isaac Bell House, and the Green Animals Topiary Gardens in Portsmouth. The Society sells a **combination ticket,** good for a year, to any seven of its properties; the cost is $38 for adults, $12 for children 6 to 11. Individual tickets for the Breakers are $12 for adults, $4 for children 6 to 17. Individual tickets for Kingscote, the Elms, Chateau-sur-mer, Marble House, Hunter House, and Rosecliff are $9 for adults, $4 for children 6 to 17. Strip tickets for two to eight mansions are also available. They can be purchased at any of the properties. Credit cards are accepted at most, but not all, of the cottages. Special events, such as the festive Thanksgiving and Christmas celebrations, cost extra. Parking is free at all the Society properties.

The mansions that aren't operated by the Preservation Society but are open to the public are Belcourt Castle, Beechwood, and Rough Point.

Following are descriptions of the cottages in the order in which they're encountered when driving south from Memorial Boulevard along Bellevue Avenue, then west on Ocean Drive.

Kingscote ☆ This mansion (on the right side of the avenue) is a reminder that well-to-do Southern families often had second homes north of the Mason-Dixon line to avoid the sultry summers of the Deep South. Kingscote was built in 1839, nearly 40 years before the Gilded Age (usually regarded as the era between the end of the Civil War and the beginning of World War I). But it is considered one of the Newport Cottages because it was acquired in 1864 by the sea merchant William Henry King, who furnished it with porcelains and textiles accumulated in the China Trade. Architect Richard Upjohn designed the mansion in the same Gothic Revival style he used for Trinity Church in New York. The firm of McKim, Mead & White was commissioned to design the 1881 dining room, notable for its Tiffany glass panels. As you drive down Bellevue, the Isaac Bell House is between Kingscote and the Elms.

Central Newport

ACCOMMODATIONS ■
Admiral Fitzroy Inn **16**
Francis Malbone House **15**
Jailhouse Inn **3**
La Farge Perry House **1**
Mill Street Inn **7**
Pilgrim House **5**
Vanderbilt Hall **6**
The Victorian Ladies **13**

See the "Newport" map for
additional accommodations.

DINING ◆
Asterix & Obelix **19**
Black Pearl **11**
Bouchard **18**
Brick Alley Pub **4**
Cheeky Monkey **12**
Clarke Cooke House **10**
Le Bistro **9**
Rhode Island Quahog Company **8**
Salas **14**
Scales & Shells **17**
White Horse Tavern **2**

Bowery St. (west of Bellevue Ave.). Late Mar to Apr Sat–Sun 10am–5pm; May–Columbus Day daily 10am–5pm. See above for admission details.

The Elms ⭐⭐   Architect Horace Trumbauer is said to have been inspired by the Château d'Asnieres outside Paris, and a first look at the ornate dining room of the Elms, suitable for at least a marquis, buttresses that claim. So, too, do the recently renovated sunken gardens, laid out and maintained in the formal French manner. The owner was a first-generation millionaire, a coal tycoon named Edward J. Berwind. His cottage was completed in 1901, and he filled it with genuine Louis XIV and XV furniture and paintings and accessories true to the late 18th century.

Bellevue Ave. Daily 10am–5pm. Closed Thanksgiving, Christmas Eve, Christmas Day. See above for admission details.

Chateau-sur-mer ⭐   William S. Wetmore was yet another Rhode Island merchant who made his fortune in the lucrative China Trade. The entrance to this "Castle by the Sea" is on the left-hand side of Bellevue, driving south. High Victorian in style, which means it drew from many inspirations (including Italian Renaissance and French Second Empire), the Chateau features a central atrium four stories high with a glass skylight and balconies at every level. A park designed in a style true to the period of the cottage has copper beech and weeping willow trees standing around its garden pavilion.

Bellevue Ave. Late Jan to mid-Mar Sat–Sun and holidays 10am–4pm; late Mar to Apr Sat–Sun 10am–5pm; May–Sept daily 10am[nd5pm; Oct–Nov Sat–Sun and holidays 10am–5pm; late Nov to Jan 3 daily 10am–4pm. See above for admission details.

The Breakers ⭐⭐⭐   After Chateau-sur-mer, turn left on Ruggles Avenue, then left again on Ochre Point Avenue. The Breakers is on the right; a parking lot is on the left.

If you have time to see only one of the cottages, make it this one. Architect Richard Morris Hunt was commissioned to create this replica of a generic Florentine Renaissance palazzo, replacing a wood structure that burned down in 1892. He was unrestrained by cost considerations. The high iron entrance gates alone weigh over 7 tons. The 50-by-50-foot great hall has 50-foot-high ceilings, forming a giant cube, and is sheathed in African and Italian marble. Such mind-numbing extravagance shouldn't really be surprising—Hunt's patron was, after all, Cornelius Vanderbilt II, grandson of railroad tycoon Commodore Vanderbilt and a superstar spender of the Gilded Age.

Had Vanderbilt been European royalty, the Breakers would have provided motive for a peasant revolt. Vanderbilt's small family, their guests, and their staff of 40 servants had 70 rooms in which to roam. The mansion's foundation is approximately the size of a football field, and the Breakers took nearly 3 years to build (1892–95). Platoons of artisans were imported from Europe to apply gold leaf, carve wood and marble, and provide mural-sized baroque paintings. The furnishings on view are original. The bathrooms, far from common at the time, were provided with both fresh and salt running water, hot and cold.

Ochre Point Ave. (east of Bellevue Ave.). © **401/847-1000**. Late Mar to Oct daily 10am–5pm (until 6pm Fri–Sat July–Aug); Dec daily 10am–4pm. See above for admission details.

Rosecliff ⭐   From the Breakers, return to Bellevue Avenue and turn left (south). Rosecliff is on the left.

Stanford White, of McKim, Mead & White, thought the Grand Trianon of Louis XVI at Versailles a suitable model for this 1902 commission for the flamboyant heiress Tessie Fair Oelrichs. With a middling 40 rooms, it doesn't overwhelm, at least not on the scale of the Breakers. But it has the largest ballroom of all the cottages, not to mention a storied heart-shaped grand staircase. All this was made possible by one James Fair, an immigrant who made his fortune after he unearthed the thickest gold and silver vein of Nevada's Comstock Lode and bought this property for his daughters, Theresa and Virginia (aka Tessie and Birdie).

In 1941, the mansion and its contents were sold for $21,000. It was used as a setting for some scenes in the Robert Redford movie of Fitzgerald's *The Great Gatsby* and for a ballroom scene in Arnold Schwarzenegger's *True Lies*.

Bellevue Ave. Late Mar to Oct daily 10am–5pm. See above for admission details.

The Astors' Beechwood ✿✿ Mrs. William Backhouse Astor—*the* Mrs. Astor, as every brochure and guide feels compelled to observe—was, during her active life, the arbiter of exactly who constituted New York and Newport society. "The 400" list of socially acceptable folk was influenced or perhaps even drawn up by her, and that roster bore meaning, in some quarters, well into the second half of the 20th century. Being invited to Beechwood was absolutely critical to a social pretender's sense of self-worth, and elaborate machinations were set in motion to achieve that goal. (It may be of some comfort to the descendants of the failed supplicants that Mrs. Astor spent her last few years at the cottage greeting imaginary guests.)

Rebuilt in 1857 after a fire destroyed the original version, the mansion isn't as large or impressive as some of its neighbors. But unlike those managed by the Preservation Society, it provides a little theatrical pizzazz with a corps of actors who pretend to be friends, children, and servants of Mrs. Astor. Frequent special events are held, often replicating those that took place when she held court, including costume balls and specially decorated banquets with Victorian music and dancing.

580 Bellevue Ave. © 401/846-3772. www.astors-beechwood.com. Admission $10 adults, $8.50 seniors and children 6–12; $30 per family. Mid-May to early Nov daily 10am–5pm (tours every 20 minutes); Christmas events Nov–Dec Wed–Sun (on the hour); Feb to mid-May Fri–Sun 10am–4pm (tours every 30 minutes).

Marble House ✿✿✿ Architect Richard Morris Hunt, another favorite of the cottage builders, outdid himself for his clients William and Alva Vanderbilt. Several types of marble were used both outside and inside, with a lavish hand that rivals the palaces of the Sun King, especially Le Petit Trianon at Versailles. It reaches its apogee in the ballroom, which is encrusted with three kinds of gold.

It cost William $11 million to build and decorate Marble House, but Alva divorced him 4 years after the project was finished. She got the house, which she soon closed after marrying William's friend and neighbor. When her second husband died, Alva discovered the cause of female suffrage, and reopened Marble House in 1913 to hold a benefit for the campaign for women's right to vote. (Dishes in the scullery bear the legend "Votes for Women.")

Bellevue Ave. Late Mar to Oct daily 10am–5pm (until 6pm Fri–Sat); Nov Sat–Sun 10am–4pm; Jan–Mar Sat–Sun and holidays 10am–4pm. See above for admission details.

Belcourt Castle ✿✿ This was the only slightly less grand mansion down the road from Marble House to which Alva Vanderbilt repaired after her second marriage. While the Vanderbilts were avid yachtsmen, her new husband, Oliver Hazard Perry Belmont, was a fanatical horseman. His 60-room house contained extensive stables on the ground floor where his beloved steeds slept under monogrammed blankets (the Belmonts were instrumental in building New York's famed Belmont Racetrack).

Alva and Oliver entertained often, counting among their guests Kaiser Wilhelm and the Duke of Windsor. The castle, intended to resemble a European hunting lodge, has a ponderously masculine character, understandable in that it was designed for the bachelor Belmont before he won over vivacious Alva. It contains artifacts from the medieval era through the 19th century, including collections of stained glass, Oriental carpets, Japanese and Chinese cabinetry, a full-size replica of a gaudy Portuguese coronation carriage, and French Renaissance furniture. Thomas Edison designed the lighting. There are 14 secret doors and a tunnel to the kitchens, which were located 2 blocks away for fear of fire.

The castle sold for a mere $25,000 in the early 1940s to the family of Harold B. Tinney, members of which still live here.

657 Bellevue Ave. (at Lakeview Ave.). ✆ 401/846-0669. Admission $10 adults, $8 seniors and college students, $7 children 13–18, $3.50 children 6–12. Feb–May Sat–Sun and holidays 10am–3pm; Memorial Day to mid-Oct daily 9am–5pm; mid-Oct to Nov daily 10am–4pm; Dec (special tours) 10am–3pm. Closed Jan.

Rough Point ★★   The fabled 1887 Gothic-Tudor home of the late tobacco heiress Doris Duke made its long-awaited opening in May 2000. Of its 105 rooms, only 11 are currently open for viewing, and by only 96 visitors per day. They are likely to be greeted by Chairman Mao, the last of Duke's many pets, which included a pair of camels that were housed in a tent on the property. By the evidence, the heiress had excellent taste in furnishings and the arts. She practiced and composed music at her Steinway two or three hours a day, and her collections include a wealth of large Ming dynasty vases, Flemish and French tapestries, and paintings by Van Dyck and Gainsborough. Watch for the ivory inset side tables bearing the marks of Catherine the Great in what is called the Yellow Room. Her favorite room, reportedly, was the Solarium, enclosed by glass on three sides with an unobstructed view over a bridge of Cliff Walk and the ocean.

While those who knew her reject suggestions that Duke was reclusive or troubled, hers was, at the least, an often darkly eventful life. It was here at Rough Point in 1967 that the story of the tobacco heiress and her interior decorator/companion unfolded. Eduardo Tirella was killed after being crushed against the big iron entrance gates by Duke's station wagon. Duke later claimed that Tirella had gotten out of the car to open the gates when she accidentally hit the accelerator. The police chief declared it "an unfortunate accident," but local tongues wagged, all the more intensely when Duke donated $25,000 to the town toward the restoration of Cliff Walk.

Duke died in 1993, bequeathing Rough Point to the Newport Restoration Foundation, along with all clothing, jewelry, and furniture in the house as well as funds to maintain the property. To get here from Belcourt Castle, continue south on Bellevue. Rough Point is on the left, just before a sharp turn west along what becomes Ocean Drive. Individual visits aren't allowed. The only source for tickets is the Newport Gateway Visitors Center, where parking is also available. Minibuses shuttle visitors to Rough Point; tours take about 70 minutes.

Bellevue Ave. ✆ 401/849-7300. www.newportrestoration.org. Admission $25. By guided tour only, Mid-Apr to early Nov daily at 9:45am, 11:30am, 1:30pm, and 3:30pm.

ADDITIONAL ATTRACTIONS

In addition to checking out the attractions described below, you might want to stroll along **Spring Street** ★ between Memorial Boulevard and Touro Street.

Historic Hill is the large district of colonial Newport that rises from America's Cup Avenue, along the waterfront, to Bellevue Avenue, the beginning of Victorian Newport. Spring Street serves as the Hill's main drag, and it's a treasure trove of colonial, Georgian, and Federal structures serving as residences, inns, and shops. There are no 20th-century architectural intrusions. Chief among its visual delights is the 1725 **Trinity Church** ⚓, at the corner of Church Street. Said to have been influenced by the work of the legendary British architect Christopher Wren, it certainly reflects that inspiration in its belfry and distinctive spire, seen from all over downtown Newport and dominating Queen Anne Square, a greensward that runs down to the waterfront. The church is sheathed in beige clapboard and has two stained-glass windows by Tiffany.

Hammersmith Farm   Built for John W. Auchincloss in 1887, this shingled Victorian mansion was used for the wedding reception of Jacqueline Bouvier (whose mother was married to an Auchincloss), in 1953. Set on a rise with an unimpeded view of Narragansett Bay across 50 acres of lawns and gardens, it subsequently became the unofficial summer White House of the short Kennedy presidency. There is irony in that identity, for a building in the adjoining Fort Adams State Park was the Dwight D. Eisenhower summer White House. It makes concrete the symbolism mentioned by Kennedy in his inaugural address, the passing of power from men born in the 19th century to those born in the 20th.

Hammersmith was sold in 1997 for over $6.6 million to a Chicago businessman who sold it again 2 years later, and it is no longer open to the public. The house can still be seen from the road, however.

Ocean Dr. (past Castle Hill Ave.).

Hunter House ⚓   Another property of the Preservation Society, this 1754 Georgian colonial with its gambrel roof and widow's walk is one of the most impressive dwellings in the lightly touristed neighborhood known as the Point, north of downtown. Above the doorway, within the broken pediment, is a carved wooden pineapple. This symbol of welcome derived from the practice of placing a real pineapple at the door to announce that the sea-captain owner had returned from his long voyage and was ready to receive guests. The interior displays furniture crafted by Newport's famed 18th-century cabinetmakers, Townsend and Goddard.

54 Washington St. (at Elm St.). Ⓒ **401/847-1000**. See "The Cottages," above, for admission details. Late Mar to Apr Sat–Sun 10am–5pm; May–Sept daily 10am–5pm; Apr and Oct Sat–Sun 10am–5pm. Closed Nov to mid-Mar.

International Tennis Hall of Fame   On Bellevue Avenue, there was (and is) an exclusive men's club called the Newport Reading Room. One member was James Gordon Bennett, Jr., the wealthy publisher of the *New York Herald*. He persuaded a friend to ride a horse into the club. The outraged members reprimanded Bennett, who had an instant snit that they hadn't enjoyed his little jest. He went right out and bought a property on the other side of Memorial Boulevard, and ordered a structure built for his own social and sports club.

The New York architectural firm of McKim, Mead & White produced a Shingle-style edifice of lavish proportions, with turrets and verandas and an interior piazza for lawn games, equestrian shows, concerts, and a new game called tennis. It is now given to a permanent grass court cropped down to a carpet of thick emerald fuzz. As Bennett hoped, his Newport Casino swiftly became the premier gathering place of his privileged compatriots.

Now the pavilion hosts professional tournaments, and its courts are open to the public for play (call ahead to make reservations between May and October). The building itself houses the Hall of Fame, recently renovated at a cost of $6 million, containing trophies, memorabilia, and computerized interactive exhibits. The Hall is of interest primarily to fans of the game, but has photographic highlights recognizable to casual observers. A restaurant (Ⓒ **401/847-0418**) serves lunch, sunset dinners, and weekend brunch.

194 Bellevue Ave. (at Memorial Blvd.). Ⓒ **401/849-3990**. www.tennisfame.org. Admission $8 adults, $6 seniors and students, $4 children 16 and under; $20 per family. Daily 9:30am–5pm (except during tournaments).

Museum of Newport History   One of five properties maintained by the Newport Historical Society, this museum is in the refurbished 1772 Brick Market (not to be confused with the nearby shopping mall, Brick Marketplace). The original architect was Peter Harrison, also responsible for the Touro Synagogue (see below). The market has been refurbished and reconfigured to contain this professionally installed illumination of the city's history. The two-floor museum houses boat models, marine charts, paintings, antique silverware, and a ship figurehead, and features videos and audio commentaries on Newport history. A printing press used by Benjamin Franklin's brother James is also on display. At the end of the upper-floor circuit, you can mount a replica of a horse-drawn omnibus, press a button, and enjoy a 10-minute video trip down aristocratic Bellevue Avenue.

127 Thames St (at Touro St.). Ⓒ **401/841-8770**. www.newporthistorical.org. Admission $5 adults, $4 seniors, $3 children 6–18. Mid-May to Oct Mon and Wed–Sat 10am–5pm, Sun 1–5pm; Nov to mid-May Fri–Sat 10am–4pm, Sun 1–4pm.

Newport Art Museum   Across the avenue from Touro Park, this was the first Newport commission of Richard Morris Hunt, who went on to design many of the cottages along Bellevue Avenue. Unlike most of his later Newport houses, this 1862 structure, the former Griswold Mansion, is in the Victorian stick style, a wood construction that had origins in earlier Carpenter Gothic. Now a museum and headquarters of the local art association, it mounts exhibitions of the works of Newport artists, offers classes and lectures, and frequently serves as a venue for concerts.

76 Bellevue Ave. (at Old Beach Rd.). Ⓒ **401/848-8200**. Admission $4 adults, $3 seniors, $2 students, free for children under 6. Only a voluntary donation charged for entrance Sat 10am–noon. Memorial Day to Columbus Day Mon–Sat 10am–5pm, Sun noon–5pm; Columbus Day to Memorial Day Mon–Tues and Thurs–Sat 10am–4pm, Sun noon–4pm.

Touro Park   Opposite the Newport Art Museum, this small park provides a shaded respite from shopping. Its center is the Old Stone Mill. Dreamers like to believe that the eight columns of the roughly circular structure were erected by Vikings. Realists say it was built by Benedict Arnold, a governor of the colony long before his great-great-grandson committed his infamous act of treason during the War for American Independence.

Bellevue Ave. (between Pelham and Mill sts.).

Touro Synagogue   This is the oldest existing synagogue in the United States, dating from 1763. A Sephardic Jewish community, largely refugees from Portugal, lived in Newport from the mid–17th century, over 100 years before this building was erected. It was designed by Peter Harrison, who was also responsible for the Brick Market (see Museum of Newport History, above). The synagogue was closed at the end of its first century for lack of an adequate congregation. It came back into use 100 years later, and was designated a National Historic Site in 1946. On display inside is a 500-year-old Torah.

Next door is the **Newport Historical Society,** 82 Touro St. (© **401/ 846-0813**). In addition to its displays of colonial Newport furnishings and decorative arts, the Society sponsors walking tours (see "Organized Tours & Cruises," below).

85 Touro St. (Spring St.). © **401/847-4794.** Free admission. July 1–Sept 7 Sun–Fri 10am–5pm; Sept 8–June 30 Sun 11am–3pm, Mon–Fri 1–3pm; Nov 1–Apr 30 Sun 11am–3pm, Mon–Fri at 1pm (groups of 10 or more by appointment only). Guided tours only, beginning every ½-hour during open hours.

OUTDOOR PURSUITS: THE BEACH & BEYOND

Fort Adams State Park, Harrison Avenue (© **401/847-2400**), is on the thumb of land that partially encloses Newport Harbor. It can be seen from the downtown docks and reached by driving or biking south on Thames Street and west on Wellington Avenue (a section of Ocean Drive, which becomes Harrison Avenue). The sprawling 1820s fort for which the park is named is under restoration, but can be viewed up close from outside; inquire about tours. Boating, ocean swimming, fishing, and sailing are all available in the park's 105 acres. Open from Memorial Day to Labor Day; admission is $4 per car ($2 for Rhode Islanders and seniors). Tours are conducted from the visitor center during summer, daily from 10am to 4pm. Also on the grounds is the **Museum of Yachting** (© **401/847-1018**), housed in a stone barracks from the early 19th century. Photographs, videos, paintings, and models chart the history of competitive sailing. Open from mid-May to October 31 daily from 10am to 5pm, by appointment the rest of the year. Admission is $4 for adults, $3 for seniors and children under 12.

Farther along Ocean Drive, past Hammersmith Farm, is **Brenton Point State Park** ★★, a dramatically scenic preserve that borders the Atlantic, with nothing to impede the waves rolling in and collapsing on the rock-strewn beach. Scuba divers are often seen surfacing offshore, anglers enjoy casting from the long breakwater, and on a windy day the sky is dotted with colorful, billowing kites. The waves here aren't the towering breakers of the West Coast, but they are usually high enough for rather sedate surfing. (That observation applies to the beach near the end of Ruggles Avenue as well.)

There are other beaches more appropriate for swimming. The longest (over a mile long) and most popular is **Easton's Beach** ★, which lies along Route 138A, the extension of Memorial Boulevard, east of town. It's the best choice for families, since the breakers are usually gentle, and there are plenty of facilities, including a very large bathhouse, eating places, picnic areas, lifeguards, a carousel, and the **Newport Aquarium** (© **401/849-8430**).

On Ocean Drive, less than 2 miles from the south end of Bellevue Avenue, is **Gooseberry Beach** ★, which is privately owned but open to the public. Parking costs $8 Monday through Friday, $12 Saturday and Sunday.

Cliff Walk ★★ skirts the edge of the southern section of town where most of the cottages were built, and provides better views of many of them than can be seen from the street. Traversing its length, high above the crashing surf, is more than a stroll but less than an arduous hike. Think of it as a highly scenic fitness walk. It's lined with marine flora, including rose hips, wild roses, goldenrod, and morning glories. For the full 3½-mile length, start at the access point near the intersection of Memorial Boulevard and Eustis Avenue. For a shorter walk, start at the Forty Steps, at the end of Narragansett Avenue, off Bellevue. Leave the walk at Ledge Road and return via Bellevue Avenue. Figure 2 to 3 hours for the round-trip, and be warned that there are some mildly rugged sections to nego- tiate, no facilities, and no phones. The walk is open from 9am to 9pm.

A new enterprise, the outdoor **Born Family Skating Center,** is set up at the Newport Yachting Center, on America's Cup Avenue (© **401/846-1600**). An oval rink about 40 yards long, it's open from late October into March, depend- ing upon weather. Skate rentals are available.

Biking is one of the best ways to get around town, especially out to the man- sions and along **Ocean Drive** ★★. Among several rental shops are **Firehouse Bicycle,** 25 Mill St. (© **401/847-5700**); **Ten Speed Spokes,** 18 Elm St. (© **401/847-5609**); and **Fun Rentals,** 1 Commercial Wharf (© **401/ 846-3474**). The last firm also rents mopeds.

Adventure Sports Rentals, at the Inn on Long Wharf, 142 Long Wharf (© **401/849-4820**), rents not only bikes and mopeds, but also outboard boats, kayaks, and sailboats; parasailing outings can be arranged.

Guided fly-fishing trips and fly-casting instruction are offered by the **Saltwa- ter Edge,** 561 Lower Thames St. (© **401/842-0062;** www.saltwateredge.com). Anglers are taken out on half- and full-day quests for yellowfin tuna, bluefish, striped bass, and white marlin. Top-flight gear is sold in the pro shop, which is open daily.

ORGANIZED TOURS & CRUISES

Several organizations conduct tours of the mansions and the downtown historic district. Between May 15 and October 15, the **Newport Historical Society,** 82 Touro St. (© **401/846-0813**), offers two itineraries. Tours of Historic Hill leave on Thursday and Friday at 10am and tours of the Point on Saturday at 10am; each takes about 1½ hours. Tours of Cliff Walk leave on Saturday at 10am and take about 2 hours. Tickets cost $7 and can be purchased at the Society or at the Gateway Visitors Center (see "Visitor Information," above).

Newport on Foot (© **401/846-5391**) leaves the Gateway Visitors Center twice daily on 90-minute tours. Call for details and times. Tickets are $7 per person, free for children under 12.

If your car has a cassette deck or you have a portable player, a company called **CCInc Auto Tape Tours** produces a 90-minute recorded tour of the mansions. It has an intelligent narration backed by music and sound effects, although it takes a little while to get the hang of when to turn it on and off. The tapes are available at the Museum Store in the Gateway Visitors Center for $12.95 each or directly from the company at P.O. Box 227, 2 Elbrook Dr., Allendale, NJ 07401 (© **201/236-1666**).

Viking Tours, based at the Gateway Visitors Center (© **401/847-6921**), has narrated bus tours of the mansions and 1- and 2½-hour harbor cruises on the excursion boat *Viking Queen.* Bus tours—daily in summer, Saturdays and Sun- days from November through March—are 1½ to 4½ hours and cost $16 to $34 for adults, $9 to $15 for kids 5 to 11. Boat tours, from late May to mid-Octo- ber, are 1 hour in length and cost $8 for adults, $7 for seniors, and $4 for chil- dren 5 to 11.

Classic Cruises of Newport ★, Bannister's Wharf, schedules narrated cruises on its 72-foot schooner *Madeleine* (© **401/847-0298**) and its classic powerboat *RumRunner II* (© **401/847-0299**). They're offered daily in summer, Saturdays and Sundays in spring and fall.

The *Spirit of Newport* ⚓, 2 Bowen's Wharf (© **401/849-3575**), offers 1½-hour cruises of the bay and harbor. Excursions set out three times daily Monday through Friday, five times daily Saturday and Sunday (weekends only in winter). Another possibility is the *Adirondack* ⚓, a 78-foot schooner that makes 2-hour cruises from the Newport Yachting Center (© **401/846-1600**). Its ticket booth is on America's Cup Avenue at Commercial Wharf; payment and reservations must be made in advance.

The **Old Colony & Newport Railway,** 19 America's Cup Ave. (© **401/624-6951**; www.ocnrr.com), features 80-minute round-trip excursions in vintage trains along the edge of the bay. Take food on board, if you wish. Fares are $6 for adults, $5 for seniors, and $3.50 for children under 14.

SHOPPING
At the heart of the downtown waterfront, **Bannister's Wharf, Bowen's Wharf,** and **Brick Marketplace** have about 60 stores among them, none of them especially compelling.

More interesting, if only for their quirky individuality, are the shops along **Lower Thames Street.** For example, **J. T.'s Ship Chandlery** (no. 364) outfits recreational sailors with sea chests, ship lanterns, boat shoes, and foul-weather gear. **Aardvark Antiques** (no. 475) specializes in salvaged architectural components and larger items rescued from old houses. Books, nautical charts, and sailing videos are offered at **Armchair Sailor** (no. 543); for vintage clothing, visit **Cabbage Rose** (no. 493).

Spring Street is noted for its antiques shops, but purveyors of crafts, jewelry, and folk art are also scattered among them. One of these is **MacDowell Pottery** (no. 140), a studio selling ceramics and gifts by Rhode Island artisans; another, the nearby **J. H. Breakell & Co.** (no. 128), is a good source for handcrafted sterling and gold jewelry. Antique boat models, including mounted half-hulls and miniatures in bottles, are displayed along with marine paintings, charts, and navigational instruments at **North Star Gallery** (no. 105). For a pricey memento of Newport's history, check out **The Drawing Room/The Zsolnay Store** (nos. 152–154), which stocks 19th-century estate furnishings and specializes in Hungarian Zsolnay ceramics. Folk art and furniture are the primary goods at **Liberty Tree** (no. 104), while **The Golden Bear** (69 Mill St.), a half block east of Spring, sells Italian majolica ceramics and table settings as well as European-style furniture.

Spring intersects with **Franklin Street,** which harbors even more antiques shops in its short length, alongside the post office. **Newport China Trade Co.** (no. 8) deals in export porcelain and objects associated with 19th-century China. Take a fat wallet to the **John Gidley House** (no. 22) for European antiques of high order. **Patina** (no. 32) is another dealer in Americana and folk art.

Note that many of these dealers have varying operating hours and may not be open when other stores are; call ahead.

WHERE TO STAY
For those who arrive in town without reservations, the **Gateway Visitors Center** (© **800/976-5122** or 401/849-8040; www.gonewport.com) lists vacancies in motels, hotels, and inns. Most can be called from free direct-line phones located nearby. There's nearly always something available, but less impulsive travelers should reserve in advance, especially on weekends.

Newport Reservations (✆ **800/842-0102** or 401/842-0102) is one free service representing a number of hotels, motels, inns, and B&Bs. **Anna's Victorian Connection** (✆ **800/884-4288** or 401/849-2489) is similar, but charges a fee and doesn't represent hotels or motels. **Bed & Breakfast Newport, Ltd.** (✆ **800/800-8765** or 401/846-5408) claims to offer 350 choices of accommodation.

Many of the better motels are located in Middletown, about 3 miles north of downtown Newport. Possibilities include the **Courtyard by Marriott,** 9 Commerce Dr. (✆ **401/849-8000**); **Newport Ramada Inn,** 936 W. Main Rd. (✆ **401/846-7600**); **Newport Gateway Hotel,** 31 W. Main Rd. (✆ **401/847-2735**); and **Howard Johnson,** 351 W. Main Rd. (✆ **401/849-2000**). Newport itself has a **Marriott,** 25 America's Cup Ave. (✆ **401/849-1000**).

The rates given below generally have very wide ranges depending upon seasonal demand, so a $200 room on weekends in July might be half that in spring. The summer season is usually defined as Memorial Day to Columbus Day, with lower prices in effect the rest of the year.

VERY EXPENSIVE

Castle Hill ★★   The setting—40 beautiful oceanfront acres on a near-island—is the overwhelming attraction of this venerable resort. But now that sorely needed renovations of the 1874 Victorian mansion and its outbuildings are finished, even a visit in foul weather is a treat. The former frumpiness of the bedrooms is history, with the improvements helping to justify the high summer rates. The best values are the Harbor Houses, which have been gutted and over-hauled, with new furniture, whirlpools, and porches overlooking the bay. The handsome taproom offers a riveting view (shared by the dining room, deck, and many of the bedrooms) of sailing ships on Narragansett Bay. Breakfast buffets are expansive. A herd of young drinkers crowds the immense lawn for live jazz on summer Sundays.

590 Ocean Dr., Newport, RI 02840. ✆ **888/466-1355** or 401/849-3800. Fax 401/849-3838. www.castlehillinn. com. 27 units. Summer $225–$395 double, $350–$495 suite; fall–spring $145–$285 double, $225–375 suite. Rates include breakfast. AE, DISC, MC, V. Open weekends only Nov–Apr. Closed Jan. Children under 12 not accepted in main house. **Amenities:** Restaurant (regional); bar; laundry; dry cleaning. *In room:* A/C, TV, hair dryer.

Cliffside Inn ★★★   Assuming that money is no object, this tops the list of places to stay in Newport. It is difficult to imagine what further improvements might be made here, although the tinkering and upgrading continues. Most units have whirlpool baths, and all now have at least one working fireplace. A new lower-level suite in the satellite Seaview Cottage has a bathroom that has to be seen: The Jacuzzi tub features both standard and hand-held showerheads, eight spray nozzles, and a built-in TV and CD player! Antiques and admirable reproductions are generously deployed, including Eastlake and Tiffany originals and Victorian fancies that include (in room 11) an amusing "bird cage" shower from 1890. A favorite unit is the Garden Suite, a duplex with private garden and big double bathroom with radiant heat beneath the Peruvian tile floors. Coffee, juice, and the newspaper of your choice are delivered to your room even before the full breakfast.

The owners recently purchased the **Adele Turner Inn,** 93 Pelham St. (✆ **800/845-1811** or 401/847-1811). There is every reason to believe it will adhere to the exacting standards of the Cliffside—we look forward to hearing what readers think of it.

2 Seaview Ave. (near Cliff Ave.), Newport, RI 02840. ☎ **800/845-1811** or 401/847-1811. Fax 401/848-5850. www.cliffsideinn.com. 16 units. $235–$315 double; $315–$550 suite. Rates include breakfast. AE, DISC, MC, V. No children under 13 accepted. **Amenities:** Limited room service; laundry; dry cleaning. *In room:* A/C, TV/VCR, dataport, hair dryer.

Francis Malbone House ★★   A few years ago, nine modern rooms were added in a wing attached to the original 1760 colonial house. Very nice they are, with king-size beds and excellent reproductions of period furniture. Four of them share two sunken gardens, and three have whirlpool baths built for two. But given a choice, take a room in the old section, where antiques outnumber repros, glowing Oriental rugs adorn buffed wide-board floors, and silks and linens are deployed unsparingly. All but two units enjoy working gas fireplaces. Refreshments are set out every afternoon. The most interesting parts of the waterfront are right outside the door.

392 Thames St. (east of Memorial Blvd.), Newport, RI 02840. ☎ **800/846-0392** or 401/846-0392. Fax 401/848-5956. www.malbone.com. 20 units. Apr–Oct $215–$425 double; Nov–Mar $155–$245. Rates include breakfast and afternoon tea. AE, MC, V. No children under 12 accepted. *In room:* A/C, TV/VCR, CD player, dataport, hair dryer, iron.

La Farge Perry House ★★   The first thing you're likely to notice upon entering this 1852 Federal-style home is the pristine standard of housekeeping, and immediately after, the muted elegance of its superb furnishings, many of them antiques and true to the period of the building. Crystal chandeliers, plush fabrics, and nautical artifacts fill both public and private rooms. That isn't to imply early-19th-century austerity: Unlike many of Newport's lesser B&Bs, no sacrifices in new millennium conveniences are made. All units are suites with poster or sleigh beds; two have double Jacuzzis and one has a working fireplace. Breakfasts are lavishly memorable.

24 Kay St. (at Bull St.), Newport, RI 02840. ☎ **877/736-1100** or 401/847-2223. www.lafargeperry.com. 5 units. May–Oct $300–$350 suite; Nov–Apr $225–$300. Rates include breakfast. AE, MC, V. No children under 12 accepted. *In room:* A/C, TV/VCR, fridge, dataport, hair dryer.

Vanderbilt Hall ★★   After its $11-million renovation, this 1908 Georgian Revival manse gives no hint of its origins as a YMCA. Built with a donation by Alfred Vanderbilt, it would now suit its benefactor as one of his own residences. Serene elegance is the motif here: Public rooms contain antiques and paintings, while Oriental rugs are laid on wall-to-wall carpeting. Bedrooms have armoires instead of closets, fabrics with period patterns, and, in the older wing, 18-foot ceilings. Rosenthal crystal and Wedgwood china set the tone in the acclaimed Alva Restaurant. The less formal Orangery, in a glass conservatory and an adjoining terrace, features three daily meals and afternoon tea (accompanied by live piano music). A nearby Butler's Bar has a snack and dessert menu most of the day. You'll be reminded to watch the sunset from the rooftop deck. An 18% service charge is added to your room and dining bill, so you needn't tip any of the staff.

41 Mary St. (west of Bellevue), Newport, RI 02840. ☎ **401/846-6200.** Fax 401/846-0701. www.vanderbilthall. com. 50 units. Summer $195–$565 double, $445–$795 suite; fall–spring $155–$445 double, $335–$645 suite; winter $95–$365 double, $295–$495 suite. Rates include afternoon tea. AE, DISC, DC, MC, V. No children under 12 accepted. **Amenities:** 2 restaurants, bar; indoor pool; small fitness room with whirlpool and sauna; billiards room. *In room:* A/C, TV, dataport, hair dryer.

EXPENSIVE
Admiral Fitzroy Inn ★   The Admiral Fitzroy attracts Europeans and Australians drawn to the international yachting events and festivals held here.

Despite the current name, the antique barometers, and the ship model at the reception desk, this used to be a nunnery—but that doesn't mean spartan gloom. Many rooms have "peek" harbor views, but you'll get a better look from the roof deck, which offers a 360-degree panorama. Several bathrooms have been renovated, some with new whirlpools. In addition to the breakfast buffet, the kitchen serves a choice of hot dishes each morning. The staff is unfailingly pleasant. Children are accepted here, so lots of families make this home base.

398 Thames St. (south of Memorial Blvd.), Newport, RI 02840. ✆ **866/848-8780** or 401/848-8000. Fax 401/848-8006. www.admiralfitzroy.com. 17 units. May–Oct $110–$225 double; Nov–Apr $85–$165. Rates include breakfast. AE, DISC, MC, V. *In room:* A/C, TV, fridge, coffeemaker, hair dryer.

Beech Tree Inn ⭐   Arrive on a Friday evening, and one of the avuncular innkeepers sits you down to a bowl of chowder and a glass of wine. After that, a lot of guests skip dinner and go straight upstairs to soak in a whirlpool bath. The other big event of the day is the most substantial breakfast served by any B&B in Newport. There are bagels, muffins, pastries, and fruit bowls to pave the way for plates heaped with eggs, waffles, pancakes, sausages, and/or bacon. Lunch becomes irrelevant. Guests are invited to help themselves to brandy and cordials in the parlor. Bedrooms feature king- or queen-size beds and good reading chairs, and many have working fireplaces.

34 Rhode Island Ave., Newport, RI 02840. ✆ **800/748-6565** or 401/847-9794. Fax 401/847-6824. www. beechtreeinn.com. 13 units, 5 rental apartments. May to mid-Nov $109–$275 double; late Nov to Apr $89–$195. Rates include breakfast. AE, DC, MC, V. From downtown, go north on Broadway and turn right on Rhode Island Ave. *In room:* A/C, TV, dataport, hair dryer.

Elm Tree Cottage ⭐   Only a couple of blocks from the beach and the Cliff Walk, this B&B is routinely ranked among Newport's most-loved inns. The flamboyant Victorian manse is a pleasure to behold. Many of the furnishings are French, though they do reflect the Victorian time period, with Louis XV as a central inspiration. All but one of the bedrooms have fireplaces. One of the owners creates stained-glass panels and plays musical instruments in the spare time that only innkeepers seem to be able to find. Look for the bar with silver dollars embedded in its surface in the sitting room, where the owners set out refreshments in the afternoon.

336 Gibbs Ave., Newport, RI 02840. ✆ **888/356-8733** or 401/849-1610. Fax 401/849-2084. www. elmtreebnb.com. 6 units. Spring–summer $225–$295 double, $450 suite; fall–winter $165–$195 double, $325 suite. Rates include breakfast. AE, MC, V. No children under 14 accepted. *In room:* A/C, TV, no phone.

Hyatt Islander ⭐   More than 25 years old (previously a Hilton, a Sheraton, and then a Doubletree), the Hyatt is notable for its complete roster of hotel services, its location on an island at the northern end of Newport Harbor, and its full-service spa, where guests indulge themselves with massages and body wraps. You might expect such a place to be impersonal, but the staff endeavors to be pleasant. There are delightful views of the harbor and town from the restaurant and most of the guest rooms.

1 Goat Island, Newport, RI 02840. ✆ **800/233-1234** or 401/851-1234. Fax 561/845-7210. www.hyatt.com. 264 units. Summer $250–$375 double; winter $99–$225. AE, DC, DISC, MC, V. Valet parking $9. **Amenities:** 2 restaurants (American, regional), bar; indoor freshwater and outdoor saltwater pools; well-equipped health club and spa; 2 tennis courts; airport courtesy van; concierge; business center; limited room service; massage; baby-sitting; laundry; dry cleaning. *In room:* A/C, TV, dataport, coffeemaker, hair dryer.

The Victorian Ladies   The owners of these four small buildings have chosen a version of Victorian decor in keeping with the age of the main house, but updated to suit contemporary tastes. Every room is different, but most have queen beds, often four-posters. Pocket gardens and patios are an added welcome for chats and idles. Full breakfasts include homemade breads and hot entrees. Newport's main shopping district is nearby.

63 Memorial Blvd. (east of Bellevue Ave.), Newport, RI 02840. ℂ 401/849-9960. Fax 401/849-9960. www. victorianladies.com. 11 units. $125–$225 double. Rates include breakfast. MC, V. Closed Jan. Children over 10 welcome. *In room:* A/C, TV, no phone (except in 6 rooms).

MODERATE

Mill Street Inn 🐾   Something different from most Newport inns, this 19th-century sawmill was scooped out and rebuilt from the walls in. Apart from exposed expanses of brick and an occasional wood beam, all of it is new. An all-suite facility, even the smallest unit has a queen-size bed in the bedroom and a convertible sofa in the sitting room, making it a good deal for families. The more expensive duplexes have private balconies, but everyone can use the rooftop decks, where breakfast is served on warm days.

75 Mill St. (2 blocks east of Thames), Newport, RI 02840. ℂ 888/645-5784 or 401/849-9500. Fax 401/ 848-5131. www.millstreetinn.com. 23 units. June–Sept $125–$345 suite; Oct–May $65–$245. Children under 16 stay free in parents' room. Rates include breakfast and afternoon tea. AE, DC, MC, V. Free adjacent parking. *In room:* A/C, TV, minibar, hair dryer.

INEXPENSIVE

Jailhouse Inn   They claim that this was once a colonial jail, although it doesn't look as if it's that old or served that purpose. In any case, the management has toned down the incarceration theme and minimized references to its "prison staff" and the "cell block" rooms. What remains, including the caged reception desk, isn't as cute as someone thinks, but there are compensations— the prices, primarily. Even during a festival week in July, a room can be had here for as little as $85 (the high rate noted below is for a two-bedroom suite), and even lower in off-season.

13 Marlborough St. (east of Thames St., on same block as White Horse Tavern), Newport, RI 02840. ℂ 800/ 427-9444 or 401/847-4638. Fax 401/849-0605. www.historicinnsofnewport.com. 22 units. Summer $85–$250 double; winter $55–$115. Rates include breakfast and afternoon tea. AE, DC, DISC, MC, V. **Amenities:** Access to nearby health club; bike rental; business center; dry cleaning. *In room:* A/C, TV, fridge.

Pilgrim House   This narrow, four-story, elevatorless mid-Victorian has a rooftop deck with unobstructed harbor views, its top selling point. On good days, you can have your "enhanced" continental breakfast out there (also the only place you can smoke). Queen-size beds have been added to several rooms; the common room has a fireplace, a TV, and a VCR.

123 Spring St. (between Mary and Church sts.), Newport, RI 02840. ℂ 800/525-8373 or 401/846-0040. Fax 401/848-0357. www.pilgrimhouseinn.com. 11 units. Summer $90–$220 double; winter $65–$135. Rates include breakfast. MC, V. No children under 12 accepted. *In room:* A/C, no phone.

WHERE TO DINE

There are far too many restaurants in Newport to give full treatment even to only the best among them. Equal in many ways to those recommended below are **Canfield House,** 5 Memorial Blvd. (ℂ **401/847-0416**); **Yesterday's & the Place,** 28 Washington Sq. (ℂ **401/847-0116**); and **The West Deck,** 1 Waites Wharf (ℂ **401/847-3610**).

Winter hours and days of operations are nearly always shorter and fewer than in summer, but adjustments are made repeatedly during the off-season months according to levels of business. Call ahead to avoid disappointment.

EXPENSIVE

Asterix & Obelix ★★ CONTEMPORARY FRENCH   Named for the famous French cartoon characters for no obvious reason, this cheerful place does render classic Gallic bistro dishes. Come and remember how delectable a near-perfect roast herbed chicken or sole meunière can be. To add a note of Lyonnaise authenticity, bluepoints, Wellfleets, and littlenecks are opened to order as starters (only 75¢ each on Friday and Saturday nights). Daily specials, on the other hand, are considerably more venturesome. A short bar menu lists sand-wiches, pizzas, and pastas. What was once a car-repair shop has been given great splashes of color, with a bar installed on the left and an open kitchen in back. Sunday dinners are served to live jazz from 7pm. Breads are provided by the chef/owner's **Boulangerie Obelix**, 382 Spring St. (ⓒ **401/846-3377**).

599 Lower Thames St. ⓒ **401/841-8833**. Reservations recommended on summer weekends. Main courses $18–$27. MC, V. Daily 5–10pm (until 11pm Sat–Sun).

Black Pearl ★ SEAFOOD/AMERICAN   This long building near the end of the wharf has two sections. The Tavern contains an atmospheric bar and a room painted mostly in black with marine charts on the walls. The pricier Com-modore's Room is more formal, with linens and candles. In either setting, most of the preparations of fish, duck, and beef are familiar but of good quality, with an occasional lurch in exotic directions, such as the ostrich fillet in red-wine sauce. In the more popular Tavern, don't miss the definitive Newport chowder, followed by a Pearlburger or one of the other overstuffed sandwiches. In sum-mer, the menu is similar at the dining patio and an open-air bar out on the wharf.

30 Bannister's Wharf. ⓒ **401/846-5264**. Reservations and jackets for men required for dinner in Com-modore's Room. Main courses $13–$23 in Tavern, $17.50–$30 in Commodore's Room. AE, MC, V. Tavern daily 11am–11pm; Commodore daily 11:30am–3pm and 6–10pm. Closed Jan and first 2 weeks in Feb.

Bouchard ★★ CREATIVE FRENCH   Settle in for the evening on comfort-able Empire chairs, while an efficient waiter in apron and black vest takes your coat and your cocktail order. It's a polished performance, under the alert eye of the hostess, wife of the chef, and what issues from the kitchen validates that promise. Presentations are thoughtfully conceived, attractive without voguish excesses. Here come duck breasts redolent with a peppery currant sauce or red snapper in parchment with a delicate Asian sweet-and-sour sauce. You are asked when you place your order if you'll be having the Grand Marnier soufflé. If you do, you won't regret it, and there's enough for two to share. This is dining in a grand tradition.

505 Lower Thames St. ⓒ **401/846-0123**. Reservations recommended in season. Main courses $18.75–$26. AE, DISC, MC, V. Wed–Mon 6–9pm (until 10pm Sat–Sun). Closed first 2 weeks in Jan.

Cheeky Monkey ★★ ECLECTIC   In a town blessed with more than its share of outstanding chefs, James Maxwell is a star. The canny owners of the Gatehouse in Providence brought him on board for this enterprise in 1997. His creations are explosions of flavor—witness the paella with lobster chunks, mus-sels, scallops, and chorizo sausage. You can make a meal of the appetizers—the smoky quesadilla or duck confit spring roll are possibilities. The decor is frisky: Water glasses bear female nudes in relief, and there are leopard-print dadoes and paintings of anthropomorphic simians bearing resemblances to George Burns and Diana Vreeland.

14 Perry Mill Wharf. (C) **401/845-9494.** Reservations recommended in season. Main courses $21–$33. AE, DC, MC, V. June–Sept Wed–Sun noon–2:30pm; May–Oct daily 5:30–10pm (until 11pm Fri–Sat); Nov–May Tues–Sat 5:30–10pm.

Clarke Cooke House ★★★ ECLECTIC   For many, this is the quintessential Newport restaurant. The lovably picturesque 19th-century structure was moved to the wharf from America's Cup Avenue in the 1970s. Most of its several levels are open to the air in summer and glassed-in in winter, with overhead fans dispersing the sea breezes. Several bars lubricate conversation. The one on the main floor has a 5-foot model of a schooner on the back wall and the real thing straining at hawsers right outside.

Up on the formal third floor, the staff sauté your lobster out of the shell while you put away such appetizers as stuffed zucchini blossoms. If that seems too rich, spare the walk upstairs and stop in at the Grille, which wraps around a fireplace and center bar. Opt for the braised lamb shank with black trumpet mushrooms and squash risotto or the four-spice duck confit with potato-leek galette and greens dressed with chevre and raspberries. A welcome menu note asks patrons not to use cell phones.

The main floor, called the Candy Store, serves snacks and drinks, and below that is the Boom Boom Room, with dancing to Top-40 tunes from 9pm to whenever.

Bannister's Wharf. (C) **401/849-2900.** Reservations recommended on summer weekends. Main courses $13–$23 in Candy Store and Grille; $22–$30 in the Porch. AE, DC, DISC, MC, V. Candy Store and Grille daily 11:30am–10:30pm in summer; Fri–Sun 11:30am–10:30pm in winter. Dining rooms open daily 6–10pm in summer; Wed–Sun 6–10pm in winter.

Le Bistro ★ FRENCH   This capable kitchen assembles lightened versions of French country standards, many of them prepared from scratch. A rough country pâté is worth the wait—nibble at crusty bread while checking out the congenial, privileged lot that frequents the place. Rolexes peek out from the cuffs of Ralph Lauren sweatshirts, and it isn't difficult to imagine that all have 50-footers moored in the harbor. Eventually comes the excellent bouillabaisse, the sea scallops paella, the rack of lamb garnished with grilled eggplant and marinated portobello mushrooms. The third-floor wine bar was recently made into a cafe serving lighter, casual fare.

Bowen's Wharf (near America's Cup Ave.). (C) **401/849-7778.** Reservations recommended on summer weekends. Main courses $14–$29. AE, DC, DISC, MC, V. Daily 11am–10pm.

White Horse Tavern ★ NEW AMERICAN   Still going strong after 325 years, the White Horse claims to be the oldest operating tavern in America. Once the residence of a pirate-turned-tavernkeeper, it has undergone many alterations but retains its authenticity. On the ground floor are a bar and two dining rooms, with a big fireplace once used for cooking. Given the setting, the kitchen could have chosen to coast on New England boiled dinners and Indian pudding. But the food is quite good, from the daily lunch specials and sandwiches to the spice-rubbed venison with pears poached with rosemary. About a third of the dishes involve seafood; typical is cod and mussels roasted with potatoes, leeks, and carrots in a spiced blue crab broth. Prices are significantly lower at lunch and on the Tavern menu, available from 5pm Sunday through Thursday.

Marlborough and Farewell sts. (C) **401/849-3600.** Reservations recommended. Jackets required for men at dinner. Lunch specials $12–$16, sandwiches ($9); dinner main courses $26–$35. AE, DC, DISC, MC, V. Sun 11am–2pm; Wed–Mon noon–3pm; daily 6–9:30pm.

MODERATE

Brick Alley Pub ⭐ ECLECTIC   Just so you know what you're getting into, the cab of a Chevy pickup truck is next to the soup-and-salad bar. Walls are covered with old advertising posters, and a room in back has a pool table, pinball machine, and video games. It's loud and good-natured, Newport's favorite hangout. Families, tourists, working stiffs, and yachtsmen squeeze through the doors into the thronged front dining rooms, the bar in the middle, and out onto the tree-shaded terrace in back. The voluminous menu is pub grub squared: stuffed clams, six varieties of Caesar salad, Cajun catfish, nachos, burgers, pizzas, chicken teriyaki, and "triple-hot buffalo shrimp pasta," often carrying the admonition, "No crybabies!"

140 Thames St. ℂ 401/848-5640. Reservations recommended for dinner. Main courses $13.95–$24.95. AE, DC, DISC, MC, V. Mon–Fri 11:30am–midnight; Sat–Sun 11am–midnight.

Rhode Island Quahog Company ⭐ SEAFOOD   This casual temple to the treasured regional clam (pronounced *KOE*-hog) replaced a somnolent Tex-Mex cantina. It retained the terrace facing Thames Street and the sturdy bar; otherwise, brace for prodigious platters of seafood, not fajitas. The $17.95 price may sound steep for a simple plate of fried clams, slaw, and fries, but it will serve two, and the extra-fresh clams still taste of the sea. Filling the chairs Sunday through Thursday are special $9.95 dinners, while Friday and Saturday nights bring live combos playing blues, jazz, or folk-rock. Snack on littlenecks, cherrystones, and oysters from the raw bar, for $1.25 to $1.75 each.

250 Thames St. ℂ 401/848-2330. Main courses $9.95–$24.95. AE, DC, DISC, MC, V. Mon–Thurs noon–3pm and 5:30–10pm; Fri–Sat noon–3pm and 5:30–1am; Sun 11am–9pm.

Scales & Shells ⭐⭐ SEAFOOD   That graceless name reflects the uncompromising character of this clangorous fish house. Diners who insist on a modicum of elegance should head for the less boisterous upstairs room, called Upscales. In summer, avoid a certain wait in line by making a reservation. Myriad fish and shellfish, listed on the blackboard, are offered in guileless preparations that allow the natural flavors to prevail. Substantial, too: The "large" appetizer of fried calamari is enough for four. Swordfish grilled over hardwood and topped with roasted sweet peppers is typical.

527 Lower Thames St. ℂ 401/846-3474 for main floor, 401/847-2000 for Upscales. Reservations accepted May–Sept. Main courses $10.25–$21.25. No credit cards. Sun–Thurs 5–10pm; Fri–Sat 5–11pm. Closed Mon Jan–May and 3 weeks in Dec–Jan.

INEXPENSIVE

Flo's Clam Shack SEAFOOD   Located just past Easton's Beach over the Newport/Middletown line, this old-timer is more than a lopsided strandside shanty—but not *much* more. Step up to the order window, choose from the handwritten menu, and receive a stone with a number painted on it. They'll call you. What you'll get, if you're wise, are clams, on a plate or on a roll. Cooked swiftly to order, they're as tender as any to which you might have set your teeth. All the fish is that way, as if it were netted that morning from the bay out front. This is the place, also, to sample "chowda" and that Rhode Island specialty, stuffies. You can get beef here, but why? Upstairs are a raw bar and deck even more happily ramshackle than below. All entrees are reduced to $9.95 on Sundays, which also feature live music from 2 to 6pm.

4 Wave Ave. ℂ 401/847-8141. Main courses $9.95–$14.95. No credit cards. Apr to mid-May Thurs–Sun 11am–9pm; late May to Aug, daily 11am–10pm; Sept–Jan 1 Thurs–Sun 11am–9pm. Closed Jan–Feb.

Salas ITALIAN   A pure bargain dining establishment, not a wisp of pretense touches this one-flight-up family restaurant. Get this: A standard special gives a choice of lasagna, eggplant or chicken parmigiana, linguine with clams, or mussels marinara, with salad, for $13.95—*for two*. A pound of spaghetti with eight meatballs and garlic bread feeds a family of four—for $12.95. And while none of this will set a gourmet's pulse racing, neither is it the expected runny sauce on flaccid pasta too often encountered. In one choice, eight brightly sauced fresh littlenecks (not canned or chopped) nestle atop a twirled nest of al dente pasta. You'll be hard-pressed to finish it all.

Thames St. ℂ 401/846-8772. Main courses $7.95–$15.95. AE, DC, DISC, MC, V. Daily 5–10pm.

NEWPORT AFTER DARK

The most likely places to spend an evening conversing or listening to music lie along **Thames Street.** Bars are unthreatening and casual. **The Red Parrot,** 348 Thames St., near Memorial Boulevard (ℂ **401/847-3140**), one of the most obvious possibilities, has the look of an Irish saloon and features jazz combos Thursday through Sunday year-round. Have a draft Newport Storm lager at **One Pelham East** , at Thames and Pelham streets (ℂ **401/847-9460**). The place has a cafe to one side, a small dance floor, a pool table and another bar upstairs, and mostly college-age patrons attending to rockers on the stage at front. The gas fixtures behind the bar date to 1872.

Park Place Tavern, at Thames and Church streets above Starbucks (ℂ **401/ 847-1767**), makes room for jazz duos Thursday through Sunday. A full schedule of live music is on the plate at the **Newport Blues Café** , 286 Thames St., at Green St. (ℂ **401/841-5110**), with bands and shouters around 10pm Monday through Saturday in season (Thursday through Saturday off-season) and a Sunday gospel brunch. With its fireplace, dark wood, and massive steel back door that used to guard the safe of this former bank, the cafe has a lot more class than most of the town's music bars. Meals are available nightly in summer, off-season Thursday through Sunday from 6 to 10pm. It might close for 2 or 3 months in winter.

Attracting a younger crowd less attuned to its surroundings, **The Garden,** 206 Thames St. (ℂ **401/849-9300**), has pool, foosball, and live rock 3 to 4 nights a week throughout the year. Folk and rock duos play at **Sully's Pub,** 108 Williams St. (ℂ **401/849-4747**), for under-35 singles more interested in each other than in the music. The pool table stays busy. Upstairs is **Señor Frog's,** a disco with a rudimentary light show and a talkative DJ who spins indie rock 6 nights a week. Frog's liquor license was suspended last year, so check if it's still open.

Several restaurants occasionally offer music, as with the three-piece combo at Asterix and Obelix on Sunday nights at 7pm, disco sounds at the Clarke Cooke House's Boom Boom Room, and jazz, folk, and rock at the Rhode Island Quahog Company (see "Where to Dine," above, for all three).

4 South County: From Wickford to Watch Hill

Narragansett: 32 miles SW of Providence, 14 miles W of Newport

Travelers rushing along the Boston–New York corridor inevitably choose I-95 to get from Providence to the Connecticut border. They either do not have the time for a detour or don't know that the nearby shore has some of the best beaches and most congenial fishing and resort villages of New England. This is called South County, a designation that has no official status, but refers to the coast that is the southerly edge of Bristol County. Bypassed by the inland I-95, it has escaped much of the commercial development that besets many parts of the New England coast, preserving not only long beaches but also small-boat harbors, wetlands, and small state parks.

Rhode Islanders certainly know about the beguilements of South County, though, so try to avoid weekends in July and August, when the crush of day-trippers can turn these two-lane roads into parking lots. Worst of all is arriving on a Friday afternoon and departing on a Sunday evening. If those are your only options, however, lock in lodging reservations well in advance.

Definitions are fuzzy, but for our purposes, South County runs from Wickford, near Providence, to Westerly, nudging Connecticut. See the map on p. 389 to locate towns discussed in this section.

SOUTH COUNTY ESSENTIALS

GETTING THERE   To get to South County from Providence or Boston, take I-95 south, leaving it at Exit 9 to pick up Route 4, also a limited-access highway. In about 7 miles, exit onto Route 102 east, and you'll soon arrive in Wickford. From Newport, cross the Newport and Jamestown bridges on Route 138 to Route 1A north, and follow it to Wickford. Narragansett, at the center of South County's beach country, is 32 miles southwest of Providence and 14 miles west of Newport.

VISITOR INFORMATION   The Chamber of Commerce sponsors the **tourist information office** (© **401/783-7121**), in the landmark Towers on Route 1A in Narragansett. Its attendants can help visitors find lodging. The **South County Tourism Council,** 4808 Tower Hill Rd., Wakefield (© **800/ 548-4662** or 401/789-4422; www.southcountyri.com), is a good source, and on request will mail a useful 48-page brochure, *South County Style.*

WICKFORD

Apart from those crowded summer weekends, a day or two in South County is as stress-free and laid-back as an outing can be. There is nothing that can be regarded as a must-see sight, hardly any museums to speak of, and only a couple of historic houses to divert from serious cafe-sitting, sunbathing, and shopping—and these are the chief pursuits in Wickford, a tidy village that crowds the cusp of a compact harbor.

Sailors and fishermen, artists and craftspeople are among the residents, all of them evident within a block on either side of the **Brown Street** bridge that crosses the narrow neck of the waterway connecting Academy Cove with the harbor, where both working and pleasure boats share the crowded waters of the port. Most of the shopping of interest clusters here, slipping over to adjoining **Main Street.** Buildings in the area are largely survivors from the 18th and 19th centuries. Parking is usually easy to find, for this is the quiet end of South County.

One place that catches the eye is **Nautical Impressions,** 16 W. Main St. (© **401/294-7779**), a second-floor shop that features sextants, boats in bottles, ships' bells, cribbage boards, banded chests, and model yachts. The maritime mood is enhanced by the sea shanties on the tape deck. On the ground floor, around the corner from the shop at the same street address, is **Seaport Tavern** (© **401/294-5771**). Its deck is just the spot for a snack, a light meal, or a glass of iced tea.

Proceed south on Route 1A, known through here as Boston Neck Road. About a mile south of Hamilton, watch for the side street on the right marked for the **Gilbert Stuart Birthplace,** 815 Gilbert Stuart Rd. (✆ **401/294-3001**). This may be the one historic homestead in South County that is worth a detour, and not because the painter famous for his portraits of George Washington was born here. (After all, he left for good in young adulthood, and none of his original art is on display.) Rather, it's the setting and the two preserved buildings that reward a visit. First is a weathered gristmill dating from the late 1600s; second, the Stuart birthplace, built over his father's snuff mill. Admission is $3 for adults, $1 for children 6 to 12; visits are by guided tour only between April and October, Thursday through Monday from 11am to 4pm.

Still on Route 1A, on the right, south of Saunderstown, is the **Casey Farm** (✆ **401/295-1030**). Owned by the Society for the Preservation of New England Antiquities, the working 300-acre farmstead is a handsome 18th-century complex of barns and houses. Free-range chickens hop along the carefully laid stone walls that section the fields. Visits are by guided tour. The farm is open from June 1 to October 15, Tuesday, Thursday, and Saturday from 1 to 5pm. Admission is $3 for adults, $1.50 for children 6 to 12.

NARRAGANSETT & THE BEACHES ✫✫

Continuing south on 1A from the Casey Farm, the pace quickens, at least from late spring to foliage season. After crossing the Narrow River Inlet, the road bends around toward **Narragansett Pier,** the name of which derives from a 19th-century amusement wharf that no longer exists. Along here and several miles on south to Port Judith and Jerusalem are some of the most desirable beaches in New England. They are made so by their swaths of fine sand, relatively clean waters, and summer water temperatures that average about 70°F. Also, shops and food stands facing the water generally avoid honky-tonk excesses.

After a few blocks, Route 1A makes a sharp right turn (west), but stick to the shore, proceeding south on Ocean Road. Straight ahead is the **Towers,** a massive stone structure that spans the road between cylindrical towers with conical roofs. It is all that remains of the Gilded Age Narragansett Casino, which was designed by the New York firm of McKim, Mead & White, but was lost in a 1900 fire. In the seaward tower is the Narragansett **tourist information office** (see "Visitor Information," above).

WHERE TO STAY

Stone Lea   Situated near the crest of a cliff that falls into the ocean, this 1884 McKim, Mead & White commission is an antiques-filled delight to wander through, if a bit formal in tone. The terrace overlooking the sea is a special treat at sunset. Lawn croquet and the mock-antique pool table are other diversions; there's also a TV in the sitting room. Breakfasts are substantial, often including pancakes or quiche.

40 Newton Ave., Narragansett, RI 02882. ✆ 401/783-9546. http://abscn.com. 6 units. $150–$225 double. Rates include breakfast. MC, V. Open weekends only Apr–May and Oct–Nov; closed Dec–Mar. *In room:* No phone.

Village Inn ✫   There are several inns and hotels in the vicinity, many of them looking out over the water across wide lawns. This is one of the largest and most obvious, a couple of blocks from the Towers. Part of a complex that incorporates a three-screen cinema, a gas station, a deli, and a dozen shops, it has an ocean-view deck, ready access to the beach, and modest resort facilities, including extended-stay appliances in the guest rooms.

1 Beach St., Narragansett, RI 02882. ✆ 800/843-7437 or 401/783-6767. Fax 401/782-2220. 62 units. Nov–Mar $70–$90; Apr to mid-May $85–$120; late May to late June and early Sept to late Oct $110–$145; late June to Labor Day $145–$220. Open all year. **Amenities:** One restaurant (Spanish), bar; heated indoor pool with whirlpool. *In room:* A/C, TV, fridge, microwave, coffeemaker, hairdryer, iron.

WHERE TO DINE

Coast Guard House ✿ SEAFOOD/AMERICAN   Adjacent to the Towers is this 1888 former Coast Guard headquarters, now a well-regarded restaurant. It has recovered from a devastating 1991 hurricane, and enjoys unobstructed views of the beach and breakers crashing a few feet below its wraparound picture windows. Despite the venue, the menu features as many meat dishes as seafood, but all are executed with a measure of sophistication. Sample the Rhode Island clam chowder, prepared with broth instead of the traditional milk. There's another bar on the covered deck upstairs.

40 Ocean Rd. ✆ 401/789-0700. Main courses $13–$22. AE, DC, DISC, MC, V. Mon–Thurs 11:30am–3pm and 5–10pm; Fri 11:30am–3pm and 5–11pm; Sat 5–11pm; Sun 10am–2pm and 4–10pm. Closed first 2 weeks in Jan.

Spain ✿✿ SPANISH   South of Scarborough Beach, this restaurant is easily the most popular on this stretch of shore. Partly it's the uniformly congenial staff drawn from Iberia and Latin America, partly the two terraces overlooking the sea. But the greater share of credit goes to the stellar interpretations of the Spanish tapas tradition and such international favorites as *paella Valenciana* and *mariscada salsa verde* (a tumble of five kinds of shellfish in a racy garlic and parsley sauce). If you want to make a meal of tapas, turn right into the bar. For the full treatment, hang a left into the softly lit dining room. Either place, authenticity doesn't head the list of the kitchen's concerns. The irresistible fried calamari are tossed with very un-Spanish hot peppers. Do sample the *espinacas a la Catalana*—spinach sautéed with garlic, raisins, and pine nuts. The nightly land rush suggests that an early arrival is wise.

1144 Ocean Rd. ✆ 401/783-9770. Reservations accepted only for parties of six or more. Main courses $13.95–$18.95. AE, DISC, DC, MC, V. Tues–Sat 4–10pm (bar until midnight); Sun 1–9pm.

FROM NARRAGANSETT TO POINT JUDITH

Follow scenic Ocean Road south from the Towers, soon arriving at **Scarborough State Beach** ✿✿. Noticeably well kept, with a row of modern pavilions for picnicking and changing, it has ample parking and surroundings unsullied by brash commercial enterprises. The beach is largely hard-packed sand, pebbly in streaks and fairly narrow at high tide. While it has a mild surf that makes it good for families with young children, sections of it are often also jammed with frolicking teenagers and college-age folks.

Continuing on Ocean Road to the end, you'll reach the **Point Judith Lighthouse,** 1460 Ocean Rd. (✆ **401/789-0444**). Built in 1816, the brick beacon is a photo op that can be approached but not entered.

GALILEE

Backtrack along Ocean Road, turning left on Route 108, then left again on Sand Hill Cove Road, past the dock of the only year-round ferries to Block Island, and into the Port of Galilee. At the end, past a cluster of restaurants beside the channel connecting Point Judith Pond with the ocean, is the redundantly named **Salty Brine State Beach.** Though small, it is protected by a long breakwater that blunts the waves produced by the passing vessels and is a good choice for families with younger children. On the opposite side of the channel is popular **East**

Matunuck State Beach, where waves break upon the sand at an angle, producing enough action to permit decent surfing on some summer days.

To get a better sense of the area from the water, consider the 1¾-hour tour on the ***Southland*** (© **401/783-2954**), which departs from State Pier in Galilee. It's a renovated Mississippi riverboat that hugs the coast as it moves past fishing villages and beaches. Cruises are on Saturday and Sunday only from Memorial Day to mid-June and after Labor Day until mid-October; there are daily departures from late June to Labor Day. Prices are $7 for adults, $4 for children 4 to 12. Reservations aren't accepted. There's a bar and snack counter on board.

Numerous **party and charter boats** leave for fishing expeditions from Point Judith. Another possible excursion is a **whale-watching cruise** on one of the three boats of the *Frances Fleet*, 2 State St., Point Judith (© **800/662-2824** or 401/783-4988). Cruises are made July 1 to Labor Day, Monday through Saturday from 1 to about 6pm, depending on the location of the whales. It isn't cheap, at $30 for adults, $27 for seniors, and $20 for children under 12, but the sight of a monster humpback leaping from the water is unforgettable.

WHERE TO DINE

George's of Galilee   SEAFOOD/AMERICAN   The impulse to drive as far as you can without winding up in the drink may account for the popularity of George's, in business for over 50 years. It can't be the food, which is ordinary, despite a number of "Best of" magazine awards. Anyway, prices aren't exorbitant, and while it can be brassy on weekends, its decks serve as a good vantage point to watch the boat traffic on the channel. As for food, give the fried smelts, stuffies, fish-and-chips, and clam and cod cakes a thought, perhaps carrying them over to the picnic tables by the beach.

250 Sand Hill Cove Rd. © **401/783-2306**. Main courses $8.95–$29.95 (market prices for lobster). AE, DISC, MC, V. May–Oct daily noon–10pm; Nov–Apr Thurs–Sun noon–2:30pm and 6–9:30pm.

WATCH HILL ⋆⋆

Although much of Westerly township remains peacefully semirural, it contains more than a dozen villages, notably the peninsular resort of Watch Hill, and several contiguous public beaches on slender barrier islands enclosing large saltwater ponds.

A beautiful land's-end village that achieved its resort status during the post–Civil War period, Watch Hill has retained it ever since. It helps that it is the closest of South County's beach towns to New York. Many grand shingled summer mansions and Queen Anne gingerbread houses remain from that time. The north side of the point occupied by the village is the harbor, packed with pleasure boats. Stretching from the eastern edge of Westerly township to the southwesternmost tip of the state at Watch Hill are **Dunes Park Beach** ⋆ and **Atlantic Beach,** followed by **Misquamicut State Beach** ⋆, a gathering place for large numbers of adolescents, and hook-shaped **Napatree Point Barrier Beach** ⋆, a wildlife preserve notable for its abundance of protected seabirds. While you can enter the Napatree preserve for free and walk to its fine dunes and strand, there are no facilities, a reason for its generally sparser crowds. All the beaches are noted for their fine-grained sand and swimming in gentle surf with slow drop-offs, explaining their popularity with families.

To get to Watch Hill from Providence and points north, take Exit 1 off I-95, south on Route 3, which passes through the village of Westerly and continues to Watch Hill. From Connecticut, take Exit 92 from I-95, going south briefly on Route 2, picking up Route 78 (the Westerly Bypass) down along Airport Road into Watch Hill. Free parking in town is extremely limited, so if you arrive after 8am, expect to pay up to $15 in the commercial lot behind the main street.

Amtrak trains from Boston and New York stop in Westerly several times daily. There is a pull-over **information office** on I-95 near the Connecticut border, and a **Chamber of Commerce** office at 74 Post Rd. in Westerly (© **800/ 732-7636**).

WHAT TO SEE & DO
South of town on Watch Hill Road is the picturesque 1856 **Watch Hill Lighthouse.** Open only from 1 to 3pm Tuesday and Thursday, it is otherwise viewable only from outside. Back in town at the small **Watch Hill Beach,** younger kids get a kick out of the nearby **Flying Horse Carousel,** which dates to 1867 and recently was the beneficiary of a 3-year restoration. The meticulously carved horses have leather saddles and horsehair manes, and rather than just pumping up and down, they "fly" out to the sides from overhead cables. There's even a brass ring to catch. Only kids are allowed to ride; tickets are 50¢. The carousel is open daily from mid-June to early September. Parents will have to settle for the more than 50 boutiques that fill the commercial blocks.

WHERE TO STAY
Pleasant View Inn ⚚ Two miles east of Watch Hill at the end of Misquamicut Beach, this is a small resort with a private strand. The front desk can arrange guaranteed tee times at a nearby course. Five categories of rooms are assigned, most of the better ones facing the ocean, with balconies; some have fridges and microwave ovens, while the least expensive are small and overlook the pool or the street.

65 Atlantic Inn. Westerly, RI 02891. © 800/782-3224 or 401/348-8200. www.pvinn.com. 112 units. May–June and Sept–Oct $75–$150; July–Aug $140–$240. AE, MC, V. **Amenities:** 2 restaurants (American), bar; heated outdoor pool and hot tub; fitness room with Jacuzzi and sauna. *In room:* A/C, TV, VCR available.

Shelter Harbor Inn ⚚⚚ If it's time to stop for the night, for dinner, or simply for a spectacular Sunday brunch (reservations essential), watch for the entrance to this venerable inn off U.S. 1, about 6 miles east of Westerly town center. Parts of the main building date to 1810, and a genteel tone prevails. Several of the bedrooms in three buildings have fireplaces, decks, or both. Two paddle-tennis courts and a croquet green are available, and a shuttle takes guests to the private beach a mile away. A creative restaurant and honored wine cellar round out the picture. The inn is more permissive than most: Children are welcome and smoking is allowed.

10 Wagner Rd., Westerly, RI 02891. © 800/468-8883 or 401/322-8883. Fax 401/322-7907. www.shelter harborinn@earthlink.net. 24 units. May–Oct $96–$176 double; Nov–Apr $88–$146. Rates include breakfast. AE, DC, DISC, MC, V. **Amenities:** Restaurant (New American); rooftop whirlpool. *In room:* A/C, TV.

The Villa ⚚ A Dutch colonial manor with many Italianate overlays on Route 1A outside of town, the Villa is most often recommended for its extensive gardens and warm hospitality. The new owners are continuing renovations to both public areas and guest rooms. All units are suites—three have Jacuzzi tubs built for two, and a couple have fireplaces. The buffet-style breakfasts are continental during the week, but enhanced with hot dishes on weekends.

190 Shore Rd., Westerly, RI 02891. © 800/722-9240 or 401/596-1054. Fax 401/596-6268. www. thevillaatwesterly.com. 6 units. Memorial Day–Columbus Day $165–$245 double; Columbus Day–Memorial Day $85–$185. Rates include breakfast. AE, DISC, MC, V. **Amenities:** Outdoor pool with hot tub. *In room:* A/C, TV, fridge, coffeemaker, hair dryer.

Watch Hill Inn ☆   Savor sunsets from the veranda of this big white century-old clapboard lodge. Bedrooms are mostly of good size, with nothing special by way of decor, apart from the four-posters and occasional antiques. There's access to a beach. All three meals are served, largely in the current seafood-and-pasta tradition, but with superb water views. Book two nights between Sunday and Thursday and get a third night free.

38 Bay St., Watch Hill, RI 02891. ✆ **800/356-9314** or 401/348-6300. Fax 401/348-6301. www. watchillinn.com. 16 units. Mid-June to early Sept $165–$250 double; Apr to mid-June and early Sept to Oct 31 $105–$160; Dec–Mar 31 $85–$145. Packages available. Rates include breakfast. MC, V. **Amenities:** Restaurant. *In room:* A/C, TV.

WHERE TO DINE
Additional dining options include the restaurants at the **Pleasant View Inn, Shelter Harbor Inn,** and **Watch Hill Inn** (see above).

Olympia Tea Room ☆ NEW AMERICAN   The genteel tone of Watch Hill is undergirded by the Olympia, long a favorite meet-and-eat retreat. This version of an even older restaurant opened in 1939, and retains its old-timey soda fountains and high-backed wooden booths. The malt-shop atmosphere suggests chicken pot pie and macaroni with cheese, but in fact, the kitchen cranks out pretty imaginative food, with a predilection for fish. Jump for the appetizer of plump, lightly fried oysters on wilted spinach and corn salsa. The "dream stuffies" and lobster rolls are as good as you're likely to enjoy in coastal New England. Despite the name, domestic and imported beers are available. Don't take the hours listed below too literally—weather, business, and simple whim can change them unexpectedly.

74 Bay St. ✆ **401/348-8211.** Reservations not accepted. Main courses $9.95–$17.95. AE, MC, V. June to Columbus Day daily 8am–10pm; mid-Oct to Nov and Apr–May Fri–Sun 11am–9pm. Closed Dec to Easter.

Three Fish ☆ ECLECTIC   What a difference a chef makes! A couple of years ago, this was arguably one of the state's top five dining places, but that was then. That chef left. Now, while the food is workmanlike, no heights are aspired nor achieved. What is left is a converted old woolen mill with a homey pub preceding the large dining room, which is two-tiered to allow water views through the tall glassed wall. It all has a North Woods look, with bare wide-board floors. Despite the name and menu's lean toward seafood, meat-eaters needn't be concerned—more than half the selections use land-based flesh. Eighteen good wines are offered by the glass. Singer-guitarists perform folk-pop-rock on Friday and Saturday nights.

37 Main St., Westerly. ✆ **401/348-9700.** Reservations recommended for dinner. Main courses $14–$23. AE, MC, V. Tues–Fri 11:30am–2:30pm and 5:30–9pm (until 9:30pm Fri); Sat 5:30–9:30pm.

5 Block Island ☆☆
Viewed from above or on a map, Block Island resembles a pork chop with a big bite taken out of the middle. Only 7 miles long and 3 miles wide, it is edged with long stretches of beach lifting at points into dramatic bluffs. The interior is dimpled with undulating hills, only rarely reaching above 150 feet in elevation. Its hollows and clefts cradle 365 sweet-water ponds, some no larger than a backyard swimming pool. That "bite" out of the western edge of the "chop" is **Great Salt Pond,** which almost succeeds in cutting the island in two, but, as it is, serves as a fine protected harbor for fleets of pleasure boats.

The only significant concentration of houses, businesses, hotels, and people is at **Old Harbor,** on the lower eastern shore, where the ferries from the mainland arrive and most of the remaining commercial fishing boats moor.

Named for Adrian Block, a Dutch explorer who briefly stepped ashore in 1641, the island's earliest European settlement was in 1661, and it has since attracted the kinds of people who nurture fierce convictions of independence, fueled in part by the streaks of paranoia that lead them to live on a speck of land with no physical connection to the mainland. In the past, that has meant farmers, pirates, fishermen, smugglers, scavengers, and entrepreneurs, all of them willing to deal with the realities of isolation, lonely winters, and occasional killer hurricanes. Today, that means about 875 permanent residents who tough it out 9 months a year waiting for the sun to stay a while.

The challenges of island living aren't readily apparent to the tens of thousands of visitors who arrive every summer for a day or a season. They aren't likely to worry that the water supply is fragile or that generator-provided electricity is hugely expensive. Vacationers are wont to describe this as paradise, a commendation that seems to be assigned only to islands. And they are correct, at least if sun and sea and zephyrs are paramount considerations. Those elements transformed the island from an offshore afterthought into an accessible summer retreat for the urban middle class after the Civil War, in America's first taste of mass tourism.

Unlike other such regions throughout the country that have lost their sprawling Victorian hotels to fire or demolition, Block Island has preserved many of its buildings from that time. They crowd around Old Harbor, providing most of the lodging base. Smaller inns and B&Bs add more tourist rooms, most in converted houses built at the same time as the great hotels. There are only a handful of establishments that even look like motels, and building stock is marked, with few exceptions, by tasteful Yankee understatement. Angular structures covered in weathered gray shingles prevail. Despite the ominous presence of a few houses that resemble those plunked down in potato fields in hyper-chic precincts of New York's Long Island, development so far remains under control.

Away from the sand and surf, it is an island of peaceful pleasures and gentle observations. Police officers wear Bermuda shorts. Children tend lemonade stands in front of picket fences and low hedges. Old-timers work their morning route along Water Street, barely making it to the other end in time for lunch, so many are the opportunities to exchange views and news.

ESSENTIALS
GETTING THERE   The Interstate Navigation Company, New London, Conn. (ⓒ **860/442-7891,** 860/442-9553, or 401/783-4613), provides most of the surface service, including passenger-only ferries on daily triangular routes between Providence, Newport, and Block Island from late June to early September. Bicycles may be taken on board for a small fee. While reservations aren't required for passengers, get to the dock early, as the boats fill up quickly.

Getting a car to Block Island is something of a hassle and considerably more expensive. Car ferries of the **Nelseco Navigation Company** (same address, phone, and management as above) depart from the Port of Galilee at Point Judith, R.I. Apart from blacked-out days from Christmas to New Year's Day, there are daily departures year-round, as few as one or two a day in winter to as many as 10 a day from early June to late August. Sailing time on the new, larger vessel is usually about 55 minutes. Drivers, be prepared: You are expected to *back* your car into the close quarters of the ferry's main deck.

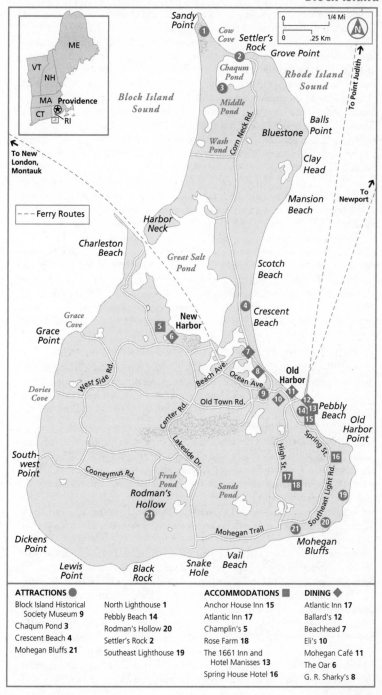

Block Island

0 — 1/4 Mi
0 — .25 Km

N

Block Island Sound

Sandy Point

1 Cow Cove

Settler's Rock

2

Grove Point

Chaqum Pond

3

Middle Pond

Corn Neck Rd.

Rhode Island Sound

Balls Point

Bluestone

To Point Judith

Clay Head

Wash Pond

Mansion Beach

ME
VT
NH
MA Providence
CT
RI

To New London, Montauk

- - - Ferry Routes

Harbor Neck

Charleston Beach

Great Salt Pond

Scotch Beach

To Newport

Grace Cove

Grace Point

5

New Harbor

6

Crescent Beach

4

Dories Cove

West Side Rd.

7

Beach Ave.

Ocean Ave.

8

Old Harbor

9

11

12

13

14

15

Pebbly Beach

Old Harbor Point

Old Town Rd.

10

Center Rd.

South-west Point

Cooneymus Rd.

Lakeside Dr.

Fresh Pond

Sands Pond

High St.

Spring St.

16

17

18

Southeast Light Rd.

19

Rodman's Hollow

21

Dickens Point

Lewis Point

Black Rock

Snake Hole

Vail Beach

Mohegan Trail

21

20

Mohegan Bluffs

ATTRACTIONS ●

Block Island Historical Society Museum **9**
Chaqum Pond **3**
Crescent Beach **4**
Mohegan Bluffs **21**

North Lighthouse **1**
Pebbly Beach **14**
Rodman's Hollow **20**
Settler's Rock **2**
Southeast Lighthouse **19**

ACCOMMODATIONS ■

Anchor House Inn **15**
Atlantic Inn **17**
Champlin's **5**
Rose Farm **18**
The 1661 Inn and Hotel Manisses **13**
Spring House Hotel **16**

DINING ◆

Atlantic Inn **17**
Ballard's **12**
Beachhead **7**
Eli's **10**
Mohegan Café **11**
The Oar **6**
G. R. Sharky's **8**

431

Additional ferries leave New London, Conn., daily from early June to Labor Day at 9am (extra trips at 7:15pm Friday) and return daily at 4:30pm. Sailing time is a little over 2 hours. Since the round-trip fare for a 2- or 3-day weekend for a car, driver, and two passengers can total over $100, consider parking in one of the nearby lots at Point Judith or New London. Block Island is small, rental bikes and mopeds are readily available, cabs can take you longer distances, and most hotels and inns are within a few blocks of the docks. If you intend to take a car anyway, understand that it is important to make ferry reservations well in advance—a month or two isn't too early for weekend departures.

Service is also provided between Block Island and Montauk, at the eastern end of New York's Long Island, by **Viking Ferry Lines** (© 516/668-5709). From mid-May to mid-October, there are daily departures at 9am, returning from Block Island at 4:30pm; the rest of the year, service is provided on Fridays, Saturdays, and Sundays only. Trips take about 1 hour and 45 minutes, landing at the Boat Basin in New Harbor. Only passengers and bicycles can be accommodated; parking is available in Montauk. Reservations aren't required.

Westerly State Airport, near the Connecticut border, is the base for over a dozen regular daily flights to and from Block Island by **New England Airlines** (© **800/243-2460,** 401/596-2460 in Westerly, or 401/466-5881 on Block Island). Flights take 15 minutes and are more frequent in summer. They're supplemented by the June-to-October service of **Action Air** (© **800/243-8623** or 860/448-1646) from Groton, Conn. In either case, make advance reservations and allow for the possibility that not-infrequent coastal fogs will delay or cancel flights.

VISITOR INFORMATION   The new **Block Island Visitor Center,** Old Harbor, Block Island (© **401/466-2982**), is at the edge of the parking lot for the Point Judith ferries. It has racks of brochures, lockers, rest rooms, one of the island's few ATMs, and knowledgeable attendants who can help visitors find lodging. It's open daily year-round. Most useful of the several websites on the area is **www.blockisland.com**.

GETTING AROUND   Cars are allowed on the island, but roads are narrow, winding, and without shoulders, and drivers must contend with groups of hikers, horseback riders, and flocks of bicycles and mopeds, many of which are piloted by inexperienced riders. If you're taking a car to the island, fill up the tank before boarding the ferry. There is only a rudimentary gas station—no signs, nameless pumps—behind the new building at the corner of Corn Neck Road and Ocean Avenue, which also contains a bank with one of the few ATMs on the island.

Our recommendation is to leave your car on the mainland and join the two-wheelers. Several in-town shops and stands rent bikes and/or mopeds, most of them within a couple of blocks of the main ferry dock at Old Harbor. Rates for cruiser or mountain bikes are typically about $28 a day, with widely available discount coupons. Moped rates vary, but are usually about $50 for 4 hours. Prices are lower after Labor Day. **The Moped Man,** 435 Water St. (© **401/ 466-5011**), one convenient source located on the main business street facing the dock, rents bikes and mopeds at the prices mentioned above. Similar outlets are **Island Moped and Bike Rental,** behind the Harborside Inn on Water Street (© **401/466-2700**), and **Esta's Bike Rentals,** on Water Street (© **401/ 466-2651**).

Several inns also rent bicycles, so a possible plan is to take a taxi from the ferry or airport to one of them, drop off luggage, and get around by bike after that. Two such inns are the **Seacrest,** 207 High St. ((C) **401/466-2882**), and **Rose Farm,** on Roslyn Road ((C) **401/466-2034**), but inquire about rentals when making room reservations—most hotels and inns have ready sources.

EXPLORING THE ISLAND

Little on the island distracts from the central missions of sunning, cycling, hiking, lolling, and ingesting copious quantities of lobster, clams, chowder, and alcohol. There is no golf course, and the lone museum takes only about 20 minutes to cover. Add a couple of antique lighthouses, a wildlife refuge, and three topographical features of note, and that's about it, enough to provide destinations for a few leisurely bike trips. A driving tour of every site on that list takes no more than 2 hours.

A couple of miles south of Old Harbor on what starts out as Spring Street is the **Southeast Lighthouse.** A tablet by the road claims that in 1590, the Manisseans, the Indians of Block Island, drove a war-party of 40 Mohegans over the bluffs. An undeniably appealing Victorian structure, built in 1874, the lighthouse's claim for attention lies primarily in the fact that it had to be moved 245 feet back from the eroding precipice a few years ago to save it. That was expensive, and now another $1 million is desperately needed for renovation. That the building was designated a National Historic Landmark in 1997 might help in fundraising. There's a free small exhibit on the ground floor, but the admission fee to the top is as steep as the stairs ($5).

A hundred feet or so farther along the same road is the **Edward S. Payne Overlook,** with paths from the small parking lot that lead out to a promontory with views of the 160-foot-high **Mohegan Bluffs,** cliffs plunging down to the ocean. Pretty, yes; stunning, no.

Continuing in the same direction along the same road, which goes through other names and soon makes a sharp right turn inland, watch for the left (west) turn onto Cooneymus Road. In a few hundred yards, pull over near the sign for **Rodman's Hollow,** a geological dent formed by a passing glacier. Claims of its magnificence pale before the reality of undeveloped acres of low trees laced with walking trails.

Back in Old Harbor, proceed north on Corn Neck Road, skirting Crescent Beach, on the right. The paved road ends at **Settler's Rock** ✦✦✦, with a plaque naming the English pioneers who landed here in 1661. This is one of the loveliest spots on the island, with mirrored **Chaqum Pond** (suitable for swimming) behind the Rock and a scimitar beach curving out to **North Lighthouse,** erected in 1867. In between is a **National Wildlife Refuge** that is of particular interest to birders. The lighthouse, best reached by foot along the rocky beach, is now an interpretive center of local ecology and history, open late June to Labor Day daily from 10am to 5pm.

Back in Old Harbor, the **Block Island Historical Society Museum,** Old Town Road and Ocean Avenue ((C) **401/466-2481**), was an 1871 inn converted to this use in 1945. The ground floor contains a miscellany of photos, ship models, a World War I uniform, a wicker baby carriage, and tools. Upstairs is a room set up to reflect the Victorian period.

Apart from sunbathing, the island's most popular pursuit is **bicycling.** The ferries allow visitors to bring their own bikes (for a small fee), but several local agencies rent bikes as well (see "Getting Around," above).

Use your bike to get to the many beaches. The longest (about 3 miles long) and most popular strand is **Crescent Beach,** which runs over 2 miles along the shore north of Old Harbor and has a pavilion halfway along the beach. (It changes names, to Scotch Beach and then Mansion Beach, as you head farther north from Old Harbor.) Mostly sand, if a little rocky in places, it is lifeguarded and family-oriented, with a bathhouse. The sections nearest Old Harbor are the most crowded, but the more northerly stretches are more secluded, even on July weekends. Other beaches on the island, such as the aptly named **Pebbly Beach** (which is also very crowded because it is just south of the main harbor), are shorter and rockier.

Parasailing has become popular here, and striped chutes can be seen lifting riders up to 1,200 feet above the ocean (600 feet is the more common flight). Athletic ability isn't necessary, and participants take off and land on the deck of a tractor boat. Prices start at $50. Contact **Block Island Parasail,** Old Harbor (© **401/864-2474**).

Fishing, kayaking, and canoeing are hugely popular, and the name to know is **Oceans & Ponds,** at Ocean and Connecticut avenues (© **800/678-4701** or 401/466-5131). Loquacious owner Bruce Johnson possesses an encyclopedic knowledge of his island and doesn't stint on sharing it. His quality stock features Orvis clothing, duffels, and fishing gear. Kayaks and canoes are available for rent, and he can arrange charter trips on three sport-fishing boats as well as surf- and pond fishing trips. Twice a summer, he hosts 1-day fly-fishing schools with Orvis instructors, as well as "mini-schools" for three to five people on Fridays, Saturdays, and Sundays.

Guided trail and beach rides on horseback are another possibility. **Rustic Rides Farm**, on West Side Road (© **401/466-5060**), is the supplier. Reserve in advance.

Much of the island's undeveloped acreage is under the stewardship of the Nature Conservancy. The local branch maintains miles of walking trails on the island; a map is available at the visitor center for $1.50 or by mail for $2 from the **Nature Conservancy,** Box 1287, Block Island, RI 02807.

WHERE TO STAY

Getting off the ferry at Old Harbor, you'll be facing Water Street and its row of Victorian hotels. From left to right, they are the **Harborside Inn** (© **401/466-5504**), the **New Shoreham House** (© **401/466-2651**), the **Water Street Inn** (© **401/466-2605**), the **National** (© **401/466-2901**), and the **Surf** (© **401/466-2241**). Their accommodations range from barely adequate to satisfactory, and they're a logical option for people who arrive without reservations (not a good idea on weekends).

High rates can't be equated with luxury on the island. Just because your room costs $225 for a Saturday night in July, don't expect 24-hour room service, a fitness center, or even a TV. Even in a low-end B&B, a midweek night in high season is likely to cost at least $90. High season is short, roughly from Memorial

---

ⒻTips A Note on Accommodations

If you arrive on Block Island without reservations, here's what to do: Show up at an inn an hour or so after the last ferry has departed, and management will often lower quoted rates if they still have rooms left.

Day to Labor Day, and most inns and hotels are closed from Columbus Day to May. Keep in mind that very few lodgings have air-conditioning, but sea breezes make it unnecessary on all but a few days each summer. Two- or three-day minimum stays apply on weekends.

For help in finding a room, try the visitor center at the edge of the parking lot opposite the ferry docks. Another, more limited, option is **Block Island Reservations** (© 800/825-6254), in the middle of Water Street. Open daily in season, it represents five inns under single ownership.

Camping is not allowed on the island.

Anchor House Inn ✿   A huge anchor out front marks this former eyesore, transformed into a B&B in 1996. Two more units will probably have been added by the time you call; they won't have as many steep stairs to negotiate. Room decor is spare and restful, avoiding froufrou: Quilts on the beds and a few pictures by island artists are about it. All rooms have ceiling fans. Breakfasts are of the hearty continental variety, including fruits, juices, bagels, and fresh muffins. Take your coffee out to one of the rocking chairs lined up on the porch. Parking is limited.

253 Spring St., Block Island, RI 02807. © 800/730-0181 or 401/466-5021. Fax 401/466-8887. www. blockisland.com. 5 units. Mar–Nov $110–$200 double. Rates include breakfast. AE, MC, V. Closed Dec–Feb. No children under 12 accepted. In room: TV.

Atlantic Inn ✿   Perched upon 6 rolling acres south of downtown, this 1879 Victorian hotel beguiles with its long veranda. Drawn by the promise of spectacular sunsets and a menu of Mediterranean nibbles joined with the most diverse beer and wine selection on the island, people start assembling there and on the lawn from 4pm on. The flowers that brighten the public and private rooms are grown on the property. Bedrooms are decorated mostly with antiques, not just reproductions, but the Atlantic shines brightest in its dining room (see "Where To Dine," below.)

High St., Box 188, Block Island, RI 02807. © 800/224-7422 or 401/466-5883. Fax 401/466-5678. www. atlanticinn.com. 21 units. Mid-June to Labor Day and weekends Sept–Nov $150–$240 double; mid-Apr to mid-June and Labor Day–Nov $130–$190. Children under 12 stay free in parents' room. Rates include breakfast. DISC, MC, V. Closed Nov–Apr. **Amenities:** Restaurant (see below), bar; two all-weather tennis courts. In room: Dataport, hair dryer.

Champlin's ✿✿ (Kids)   Families are welcome at this all-inclusive resort, with 225 transient slips in the marina for visiting yachtspeople (for information, call © 800/762-4541). Those who might be put off by the tilted floors and idiosyncratic adornments of Victorian inns will be pleased by the clean lines and muted fabrics of the bedrooms here. There's live music in the bars on weekends, even a theater showing first-run movies. Once you've unpacked, there isn't much to compel you to leave, but a shuttle van is provided for trips to other parts of the island. With all that in its favor, the people in the chaotic reception area are annoyingly distracted and offhanded.

Great Salt Pond, P.O. Box J, Block Island, RI 02807. © 800/762-4541 or 401/466-7777. Fax 401/466-2638. www.champlinsresort.com. 30 units. Summer $150–$325 double; spring and fall $85–$200. AE, MC, V. Closed mid-Oct to early May. From Old Harbor, drive west on Ocean Ave. and turn left on West Side Rd. The entrance road to Champlin's is on the right. The ferry from Long Island docks here. **Amenities:** Restaurant, 2 bars; large outdoor pool; 2 tennis courts; kayak, bumper boat, and paddleboat rentals; moped and bike rentals; game room; car rental; coin-op washers and dryers. In room: A/C, TV, fridge.

Rose Farm ✿   The remodeled 1897 farmhouse that was the original inn is complemented by an additional house across the driveway. Four of the rooms in the new building feature large whirlpool baths and decks. Some have canopied beds, most have ocean views, and their furnishings are often antique, including a handsome Eastlake bedstead. Afternoon refreshments, usually iced tea and pastries, are served.

Roslyn Rd., Box E, Block Island, RI 02807. ✆ **401/466-2034**. Fax 401/466-2053. www.blockisland.com/rosefarm. 19 units (2 with shared bathroom). $99–$250 double. Rates include breakfast. AE, DISC, MC, V. Closed Nov–Mar. From Old Harbor, drive west on High St. and turn left on paved driveway past the Atlantic Inn. Children over 12 welcome. **Amenities:** Bike rental; coin-op washers and dryers.

The 1661 Inn & Hotel Manisses ✸✸✸ Emus, goats, llamas, black swans, and a Scottish Highland ox graze in the meadow behind the Victorian Hotel Manisses, only the most visible part of a small hospitality empire. Other properties include the 1661 Inn & Guest House, up the hill, and the Dodge, Dewey, and Nicholas Ball cottages. (Children are welcome in five of the six buildings; smoking is allowed in one.) Reception personnel at the hotel are aware of vacancies at the other houses. Guest rooms in the hotel utilize oak antiques and lots of wicker. Their sizes vary widely; the corner rooms are largest and have whirlpool tubs. Each unit comes with a tray of soft drinks, cordials, and snacks; some have TVs and/or fireplaces. The median age in the hotel is noticeably grayer than in the other buildings, where families tend to gather. Common rooms host an afternoon "wine and nibble" hour and serve as a dessert parlor in evening, when flaming coffees are featured. The inn is now open year-round, although the restaurants are closed in winter.

1 Spring St., Block Island, RI 02807. ✆ **800/626-4773** or 401/466-2421/2063. Fax 401/466-3162. www.blockisland.com/biresorts. 17 units in hotel, plus 43 (some with shared bathroom) in satellite buildings. $50–$370 double. Rates include breakfast. MC, V. **Amenities:** 2 restaurants, bar; concierge; baby-sitting.

Spring House Hotel ✸ Marked by its red mansard roof and wraparound porch, the island's oldest hotel (1852) has hosted the Kennedy clan, Mark Twain, Ulysses S. Grant . . . and Billy Joel. The young staff is congenial, if occasionally a bit scattered. There are three styles of bedrooms, most of good size, with dusky-rose carpeting, queen-size beds, and pullout sofas. There are no TVs or air-conditioning, but wet bars are standard. A considerable attraction is the all-you-can-eat barbecue lunch next to the bar on the veranda. In the lobby is a sitting area with a fireplace. Swimming is allowed in the freshwater pond on the property.

902 Spring St., P.O. Box 902, Block Island, RI 02807. ✆ **800/234-9263** or 401/466-5844. springhouse@ids.net. 63 units. Summer $175–$375 double; spring and fall $75–$285. Rates include breakfast. AE, MC, V. Closed mid-Oct to March. **Amenities:** Restaurant, bar.

WHERE TO DINE

Apart from a couple of kitchens that aspire to more rarefied levels of achievement, expect boiled or broiled lobsters, lots of fried and grilled fish and chicken, and the routine varieties of burgers and beef cuts. Chowders are usually surefire, especially but not exclusively the creamy New England version. Clam cakes are ubiquitous. (Actually deep-fried fritters containing more dough than clams, clam cakes are still fun eating, especially when dipped in tartar sauce.)

Several inns and hotels have dining rooms worth noting (see "Where to Stay," above), especially the Atlantic Inn and the Hotel Manisses. Even there, neither jackets nor ties are required.

Atlantic Inn ✸✸ ECLECTIC The dining room of the Atlantic Inn has a reputation that travels well beyond the island, a fact that drew President Clinton and his family to an unannounced dinner a few summers ago. Only four-course fixed-price dinners are offered, with choices of six appetizers and six main courses. Ingredients are the freshest available, and presentations are as eye-pleasing as the food is gratifying. The chef might decide on a simple flounder dressed with lime-caraway vinaigrette and bedded with quinoa, then move on to a rack of lamb made memorable by carrot polenta, Swiss chard, and a balsamic red wine jus. Fish, fowl, and vegetables are smoked on premises.

High St. ℂ **401/466-5678.** Reservations essential June–Sept. Fixed-price meals $42. DISC, MC, V. Daily 11:30am–10:30pm. Closed Nov–Apr.

Ballard's AMERICAN/SEAFOOD   Sooner rather than later, everyone winds up at Ballard's. Behind the long porch is a warehouse-like hall, beyond that a ter-race beside a crowded beach. Several bars fuel the late-evening crowd that piles in for frequent live entertainment, afternoon and evening, from rock to that which was in style 50 years ago. The menu is all over the map, with something for everyone. Execution is usually ordinary, but consider the family-style shore dinner for two or more people, which bestows *two* steamed lobsters per person as well as baked potatoes and corn on the cob. In the beachfront cafe, clam chowder comes in a scooped-out sourdough loaf.

Old Harbor. ℂ **401/466-2231.** Main courses $10.95–$25. AE, MC, V. Mon–Thurs 11:30am–10pm; Fri–Sun 1pm–1am. Closed Oct to mid-May.

Beachhead 🔍 *Kids* ECLECTIC   An agreeable, family-friendly place across the road from the town beach, its chef/owner is eager to please all who drop by. Out on the long dining porch, a sushi bar is set up Monday through Wednes-day. On tap are a range of colorful microbrews, Fat Angel, Otter Creek, and Old Buzzard among them. Toad Hollow wines are featured, going well with the Block Island clam chowder. Fish stew and crab cakes are among the other win-ners on the card. Friday and Saturday nights in summer bring rock bands or jazz combos. And, in useful distinction from nearly all its competitors, this place stays open all year.

Corn Neck Rd. ℂ **401/466-2249.** Main courses $9.95–$17. MC, V. Mon–Sat 11:30am–9:30pm; Sun 4–9pm (bar until 11pm).

Eli's 🔍🔍 ITALIAN/AMERICAN   "Eli" was a black Lab, and the place named for him used to be just a spaghetti-and-grinders drop-in. It's evolved into one of the island's most desirable eating places, thronged with mainlanders and natives lusting for its huge servings of quality fish, pasta, and meats. Problem is, only 50 voracious diners can be served at a time, and if you put your name on the host-ess's list, it can be 90 minutes before you get a shot at a seat, even at the bar. Every offering is appetizing and immensely flavorful. Big portions defy anyone to finish—it helps if your room at the inn has a microwave to zap the leftovers. Carpetbagger steak stuffed with lobster and mahi-mahi dredged in macadamia nuts and cilantro are characteristic.

456 Chapel St. ℂ **401/466-5230.** Reservations not accepted. Main courses $16-$35. MC, V. May–Oct Sun–Thurs 5:30–9:30pm, Fri–Sat 5:30–10:30pm; Nov–Dec Sat–Sun 5–10pm. Closed Jan–Apr.

G. R. Sharky's AMERICAN   With its kicked-back atmosphere and pub-style menu, this young entry has a clear kinship with at least a dozen casual eateries on the island. Apart from the expected burger variations and Philly cheesesteak, lunch and dinner entrees run to shrimp fettucine Alfredo, mussels scampi, prime ribs, and their mates. You might choose to have a couple of the more imaginative appetizers instead, such as the fried won tons stuffed with spinach, jalapeños, olives, and two cheeses and doused with red pepper jelly. Live entertainment is offered Thursday nights.

Corn Neck Rd. ℂ **401/466-9900.** Main courses $6.95–$17.95. MC, V. Apr–May and Nov daily 6–8:30pm; June–Columbus Day daily 11:30am–10pm.

Mohegan Café AMERICAN   Walk straight across from the ferry landing into this ever-filled tavern—everyone does. Featured microbrews are listed on the blackboard, and most of the daytime menu is enlightened pub fare, with catfish sandwiches and quesadillas among the highlights. At night, offerings are more ambitious, such as sautéed scallops, walnuts, and asparagus in creamy pesto over ravioli. Faded photos of old island scenes, trophies, and a big model sailboat constitute the haphazard decor. Music on the stereo runs from Louis Armstrong to Metallica.

Water St. ℂ **401/466-5911.** Main courses $13–$22. AE, DISC, MC, V. Summer Sun–Thurs 11:30am–9pm; Fri–Sat 11am–10pm; shorter hours off-season.

The Oar AMERICAN   Locals drop in partly because off-islanders are less likely to find it, but mostly for the dramatic views of storms over the mainland and of the Great Salt Pond and its fleet of pleasure boats. Take it in from either the deck or the cool bar, with its wide picture window. The restaurant's name should be plural, since the ceiling and walls are hung with scores of oars—all of them painted with cartoons, graffiti, names, and assorted messages of obscure or ribald intent. Commemorating races, anniversaries, important events, or simply some really good parties, they provide such idle diversions as "find the oldest" (1965). Once more a good-time bar than eating place, the menu has expanded from Buffalo wings and buckets of fried chicken to codfish cakes with corn salsa and grilled swordfish with roasted leek and tomato vinaigrette.

Block Island Marina, West Side Rd. ℂ **401/466-8820.** Sandwiches and salads $4.25–$12, main courses $7–$20. AE, MC, V. Daily 6:30pm–midnight. Closed late Oct to May.

BLOCK ISLAND AFTER DARK

Nightlife isn't of the rollicking south Florida variety, but bars don't close at sunset, either. Prime candidates for a potential rockin' good time are **Captain Nick's,** on Ocean Avenue (ℂ **401/466-5670**), where pool tables and live bands are supplemented by disco, and the year-round **Yellow Kittens,** on Corn Neck Road (ℂ **401/466-5855**), presenting live bands 4 or 5 nights a week in high season, along with darts, two pool tables, and Ping-Pong to help fill the winter nights.

   Ballard's (see "Where to Dine," above) offers a variety of live music nightly and many afternoons in season, as often of the accordion or big band variety as of rock and pop. Pitchers of beer, pool tables, pinball, and foosball are the regular attractions at **Club Soda,** on Connecticut Avenue (ℂ **401/466-5397**), but there's also live music once or twice a week. Find it under the Highview Inn, up a hill off Ocean Avenue. Another occasional live-music venue is the lounge at the **National Hotel,** on Water Street (ℂ **401/466-2901**).

   Two cinemas show current films: **Oceanwest,** Champlin's Marina, New Harbor (ℂ **401/466-2971**), and the **Empire,** Water Street, Old Harbor (ℂ **401/466-2555**), which also has a video-game room.

Vermont

by Wayne Curtis

Vermont is the Green Mountain State, and the rolling hills, shaggy peaks, and towns clustered along river valleys give the state its distinct sense of place. Still a predominantly rural state, Vermont is filled with dairy farms, dirt roads, and small-scale enterprises. The towns and hills are home to an intriguing mix of old-time Vermonters and back-to-the-landers who showed up in VW microbuses in the 1960s and stayed, many getting involved with municipal affairs.

Without feeling in the least like a theme park, Vermont captures a sense of America as it once was. Vermonters still share a strong sense of community, and they still respect the ideals of thrift and parsimony. They prize their small villages and towns, and they understand what makes them special. Gov. Howard Dean once said that one of Vermont's special traits was in knowing "where our towns begin and end." It seems a simple notion, but that speaks volumes when one considers the erosion of identity that has afflicted many small towns swallowed up by one creeping megalopolis after another.

For travelers, Vermont is a great destination for long country drives, mountain rambles, and overnights at country inns. A good map opens the door to countless back-road adventures. It's not hard to get a taste of Vermont's way of life. You'll find it in almost all of the small towns and villages. And they are small—let the numbers tell the story: Burlington, Vermont's largest city, has just 39,127 residents; Montpelier, the state capital, 8,247; Brattleboro, 8,612; Bennington, 9,532; Woodstock, 1,037; Newfane, 164. The state's entire population is just 608,000—making it one of a handful of states with more senators than representatives in Congress.

Of course, numbers don't tell the whole story. You have to let the people do that. One of Vermont's better-known former residents, Nobel Prize–winning author Sinclair Lewis, wrote more than 70 years ago: "I like Vermont because it is quiet, because you have a population that is solid and not driven mad by the American mania—that mania which considers a town of 4,000 twice as good as a town of 2,000. Following that reasoning, one would get the charming paradox that Chicago would be 10 times better than the entire state of Vermont, but I have been in Chicago and not found it so."

With all respect to readers from Chicago, that still holds true today.

1 Bennington, Manchester & Southwestern Vermont

Southwestern Vermont is the turf of Ethan Allen, Robert Frost, Grandma Moses, and Norman Rockwell. As such, it's likely to seem familiar to you even if you've never been here. Over the decades, it has managed to subtly work itself into America's cultural consciousness.

The region is sandwiched between the Green Mountains to the east and the rolling hills along the Vermont–New York border to the west. If you're coming from Albany or the southwest, the first town you're likely to hit is Bennington, a commercial center that offers up low-key diversions for residents and visitors alike. Northward toward Rutland, the terrain is more intimate than intimidating, with towns clustered in broad valleys along rivers and streams. Former 19th-century summer colonies and erstwhile lumber and marble towns exist side by side, offering pleasant accommodations, delightful food, and—in the case of Manchester Center—world-class outlet shopping.

BENNINGTON

Bennington owes its fame (such as it is) to a handful of eponymous moments, places, and things: like the Battle of Bennington, fought in 1777 during the American War of Independence. And Bennington College, a small but prestigious liberal-arts school. And Bennington pottery, which traces its ancestry back to the first factory here in 1793, and remains prized by collectors for its superb quality.

Today, visitors will find two Benningtons. Historic Bennington with its regal homes sits atop a hill just west of town off Route 9. (Look for the mini–Washington Monument.) Modern downtown Bennington is a pleasant, no-frills commercial center with restaurants and stores that still sell things people actually need. It's not so much a tourist destination as a handy supply depot. (It's actually Vermont's third-largest city.) The downtown is compact, low, and handsome, and boasts a fair number of architecturally striking buildings, including the stern marble Federal building with its six fluted columns, at 118 South St.

ESSENTIALS

GETTING THERE   Bennington is located at the intersection of Routes 9 and 7. If you're coming from the south, the nearest interstate access is via the New York Thruway at Albany, N.Y., about 35 miles away. From the east, I-91 is about 40 miles away at Brattleboro. **Vermont Transit** (© **800/451-3292** or 802/442-4808) offers bus service to Bennington from Albany, Burlington, and other points. Buses arrive and depart from 126 Washington St.

VISITOR INFORMATION   The **Bennington Area Chamber of Commerce,** 100 Veterans Memorial Dr. (© **802/447-3311;** www.bennington.com), maintains an information office on Route 7 North near the veterans complex. The office is open Monday through Friday from 8:30am to 4:30pm year-round; in summer and fall it's also open Saturday and Sunday from 9am to 4pm.

EXPLORING THE TOWN

One of Bennington's claims to history is the fabled Battle of Bennington, which took place on August 16, 1777. This relatively minor skirmish would have major implications for the outcome of the American Revolution. British general John Burgoyne was ordered to attack the settlement of Bennington, where he came upon colonial forces led by Gen. John Stark. After a couple of days playing cat and mouse, Stark ordered the attack on August 16. The battle was over in less than 2 hours—the British and their Hessian mercenaries were defeated, with more than 200 troops killed; the colonials lost but 30 men. This cleared the way for another vital colonial victory at the Battle of Saratoga.

You can't miss the **Bennington Battle Monument** ✦ if you're passing through the surrounding countryside. This 306-foot obelisk of blue limestone

Vermont

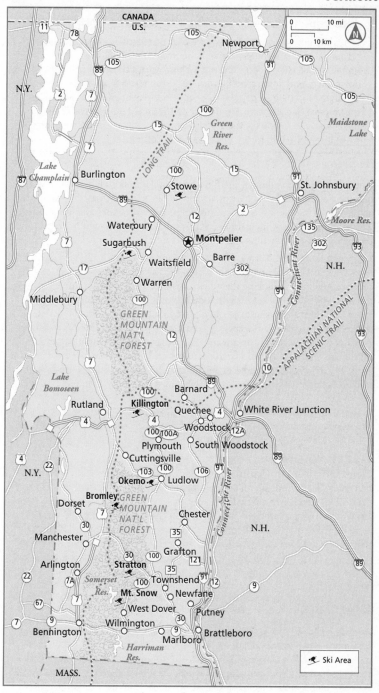

CANADA
U.S.

N.Y.

Newport

Maidstone Lake

Green River Res.

Lake Champlain

Burlington

Stowe

St. Johnsbury

Moore Res.

Waterbury

Montpelier

N.H.

Sugarbush

Waitsfield

Barre

Middlebury

Warren

GREEN MOUNTAIN NAT'L FOREST

Connecticut River

APPALACHIAN NATIONAL SCENIC TRAIL

Lake Bomoseen

Barnard

Rutland

Killington

Quechee

White River Junction

Woodstock

N.Y.

Plymouth

South Woodstock

Cuttingsville

Okemo

Ludlow

Bromley

Dorset

GREEN MOUNTAIN NAT'L FOREST

Chester

N.H.

Manchester

Grafton

Arlington

Stratton

Townshend

Mt. Snow

Newfane

West Dover

Putney

Benjamin

Wilmington

Marlboro

Brattleboro

Somerset Res.

Harriman Res.

MASS.

⚡ Ski Area

10 mi

10 km

441

(*Moments* **"I Had a Lover's Quarrel with the World."**

That's the epitaph on the tombstone of Robert Frost, who's buried with his family in the cemetery behind the impressive 1806 First Congregational Church. (It's where Route 9 makes two quick bends just west of downtown, and down the hill from the Bennington Monument.) Travelers often stop here to pay their respects to the man who many consider the voice of New England. Signs point to the Frost family grave. Closer to the church itself, look for the wondrously carved early tombstones (some with urns and skulls) of the voiceless and forgotten.

---

atop a low rise was dedicated in 1891. It resembles a shorter, paunchier Washington Monument. Note that it's actually about 6 miles from the site of the actual battle; the monument marks the spot where the munitions were stored. The monument's viewing platform, which is reached by elevator, is open April through October, daily from 9am to 5pm. A fee of $1 is charged.

Bennington Museum ★★ This eclectic and intriguing collection traces its roots back to 1875, although the museum has occupied the current stone-and-column building overlooking the valley only since 1928. The expansive galleries feature a wide range of exhibits on local arts and industry, including early Vermont furniture, glass, paintings, and Bennington pottery. Of special interest are the colorful primitive landscapes by Grandma Moses (1860–1961), who lived much of her life nearby. (The museum has the largest collection of Moses paintings in the world.) Look also for the glorious 1925 luxury car called the Wasp, 16 of which were handcrafted in Bennington between 1920 and 1925. A $2-million expansion of the museum in 1999 added new galleries and an expanded gift shop.

W. Main St. (Rte. 9 between Old Bennington and the current town center). © **802/447-1571.** www. benningtonmuseum.com. Admission $6 adults, $5 students and seniors, free for children under 12; $13 per family (with children under 18). Daily 9am–6pm (until 5pm Nov 1–May 31).

WHERE TO STAY

Four Chimneys ★ This striking Colonial Revival building will be among the first to catch your eye as you arrive in Bennington from the west. Set off from Route 7 on an 11-acre, nicely landscaped lot, it's an imposing white three-story structure with—no surprise—four prominent chimneys. The inn, built in 1912, is at the edge of Historic Bennington; the towering Bennington Monument looms over the backyard. Guest rooms are inviting and homey, but the overall sensibility can be mildly offputting, as if you're visiting somebody else's relatives.

21 West Rd., Bennington, VT 05201. © **802/447-3500.** Fax 802/447-3692. www.fourchimneys.com. 11 units. Weekends, holidays, and summer midweek $125–$205 double; winter midweek $100–$180. Rates include breakfast. 2-night minimum stay foliage and holiday weekends. AE, DISC, MC, V. Children 12 and over accepted. **Amenities:** Restaurant (continental). *In room:* A/C, TV, hair dryer.

Paradise Motor Inn ★ *Value* This is Bennington's best motel, with tidy and generously sized accommodations. We'd opt for the North Building, despite its dated 1980s styling—each room here has an outdoor terrace or balcony. The more up-to-date Office Building has a richer Colonial Revival style. The motel is uncommonly clean and well-managed. It's across from the Hemming's gas station, and within walking distance to town.

141 West Main St., Bennington, VT 05201. ☎ **802/442-8351.** Fax 802/447-3889. www.bennington.com/
paradise. 76 units. Summer/winter $65–$100 double (discounts in off-season). DISC, MC, V. **Amenities:** Outdoor heated pool; two hardtop tennis courts. *In room:* A/C, TV.

South Shire Inn 🍂🍂   A locally prominent banking family hired architect
William Bull to design and build this impressive Victorian home in 1880. The
spacious downstairs features leaded glass on the bookshelves and intricate plas-
terwork in the dining room. The guest rooms are richly hued, and most have
canopied beds and working fireplaces (with Duraflame-type logs only). The best
of the bunch is the old master bedroom, which has a king-size canopied bed, a
tile-hearth fireplace, and a beautiful bathroom with hand-painted tile. Four
more modern guest rooms are in the carriage house. The carriage house's downstairs rooms are slightly more formal; the upstairs rooms are more intimate, with
low eaves and skylights over the tubs.

124 Elm St., Bennington, VT 05201. ☎ **802/447-3839.** Fax 802/442-3547. www.southshire.com. 9 units.
$105–$160 double; foliage season $125–$180 double. Rates include breakfast. AE, MC, V. Children over 12
welcome. *In room:* A/C.

WHERE TO DINE

Alldays & Onions ECLECTIC   This casual spot was named after an early-
20th-century British automobile manufacturer. Locals flock here to enjoy the
wholesome, tasty sandwiches, the filling deli salads, and the tasty soups. The
more ambitious dinners offer entrees such as Southwest cowboy steak with skillet corn sauce and soba and stir-fried vegetables. The atmosphere is that of a
small-town restaurant gussied up for a big night out.

519 Main St. ☎ 802/447-0043. Reservations accepted for dinner, but not often needed. Breakfast $2–$8;
sandwiches $2.50–$7.25; dinner $10.95–$19.95. AE, DISC, MC, V. Mon–Tues 7:30am–4pm; Wed–Sat
7:30am–8pm.

Blue Benn Diner 🍂 *Value* DINER   Diner aficionados make pilgrimages to
enjoy the ambience of this 1945 Silk City classic. Blue-plate dinner specials
include vegetables, rice, soup or salad, rolls, and rice pudding for dessert. A bit
incongruously, fancier and vegetarian fare are also available; especially good is
the grilled portobello on sourdough. There's also a great selection of pies, like
blackberry, pumpkin, and chocolate cream.

North St. (Rte. 7). ☎ 802/442-5140. Breakfast $1.50–$5.95; sandwiches and entrees $1.95–$5.75; dinner
specials $7.95–$8.95. No credit cards. Mon–Tues 6am–5pm; Wed–Fri 6am–8pm; Sat 6am–4pm; Sun
7am–4pm.

Geanneli's Restaurant 🍂 AMERICAN   A Frommer's reader tipped us off to
this drive-by restaurant on Main Street, and we're glad he did. It's what neighborhood restaurants used to be—nothing fancy, but with attentive waiters and
a kitchen that cares about quality. Even the plain stuff is great, from the coleslaw
to the tapioca pudding.

520 Main St. ☎ 802/442-9833. Main courses $2.25–$4.75 breakfast, $2.95–$5.85 lunch, $7.75–$12.50
dinner. No credit cards. Daily 7am–8pm (sometimes closed for breakfast in winter; best to call first).

ARLINGTON, MANCHESTER & DORSET

The rolling Green Mountains are rarely out of view from this cluster of hamlets.
And in midsummer, the lush green hereabouts gives Ireland a good run for its
money—verdant hues are found in the forests blanketing the hills, the valley
meadows, and the mosses along the tumbling streams, making it obvious how
these mountains earned their name.

Southern Vermont

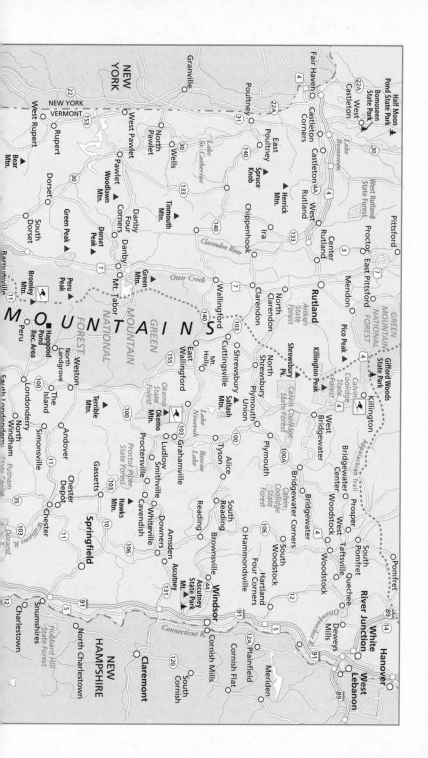

This trio of quintessential Vermont villages makes an ideal destination for romantic getaways, aggressive antiquing, and serious outlet shopping. Each of the towns is worth visiting, and each has its own unique charm. **Arlington** 🏚 has a town center that borders on microscopic; with its auto-body shops and redemption center (remnants of a time when the main highway artery passed through town), it gleams a bit less than its sibling towns to the north.

To the north, **Manchester** 🏚🏚 and **Manchester Center** share a blurred town line, but maintain distinct characters. The more southerly Manchester has an old-world, old-money elegance with a campus-like town centered around the resplendently columned Equinox Hotel. Just to the north, Manchester Center is a major mercantile center with dozens of national outlets offering discounts on brand-name clothing, accessories, and housewares.

A worthy detour off the beaten track is **Dorset** 🏚🏚, an exquisitely preserved town of white clapboard architecture and marble sidewalks.

One caveat: With its proximity to the New York Thruway just 40 miles east at Albany, the area attracts a disproportionate number of affluent weekenders from New York City—so the prices for inns and restaurants tend to be higher throughout this region.

ESSENTIALS
GETTING THERE   Arlington, Manchester, and Manchester Center are located north of Bennington on Historic Route 7A, which runs parallel to and west of the more modern, less scenic Route 7. Dorset is north of Manchester Center on Route 30, which departs from Route 7A in Manchester Center. **Vermont Transit** (📞 **800/451-3292** or 802-362-1226) offers bus service to Manchester.

VISITOR INFORMATION   The **Manchester and the Mountains Chamber of Commerce,** 5046 Main St., Suite 1, Manchester Center (📞 **802/362-2100;** www.manchestervermont.net), maintains a year-round information center in Manchester Center. Hours are Monday through Saturday from 9:30am to 5pm; Memorial Day weekend through October, it's also open Sunday from 9:30am to 5pm.

For information on outdoor recreation, the Green Mountain National Forest maintains a district **ranger office** (📞 **802/362-2307**) in Manchester on Routes 11 and 30 east of Route 7. It's open Monday through Friday from 8am to 4:30pm.

EXPLORING THE AREA
Arlington has long been associated with painter and illustrator Norman Rockwell, who resided here from 1939 to 1953. Arlington residents were regularly featured in Rockwell covers for the *Saturday Evening Post.* A 19th-century Carpenter Gothic–style church in the middle of town, the **Norman Rockwell Exhibit** 🏚 (📞 **802/375-6423;** www.normanrockwellexhibit.com), features a variety of displays, including many of those famous covers, along with photographs of the original models. Summer hours are daily from 9am to 5pm; in the off-season, Monday through Friday from 10am to 4pm, Saturday and Sunday from 10am to 5pm (closed January). Admission is $2 for adults, free for children under 12.

Manchester has long been one of Vermont's more moneyed resorts, attracting prominent summer residents like Mary Todd Lincoln and Julia Boggs Dent, the wife of Ulysses S. Grant. This town is well worth visiting just to wander its quiet streets, bordered by distinguished homes dating from the early Federal period.

It feels a bit like a time warp here, and the cars driving past the green seem strangely out of place. Be sure to note the sidewalks made of irregular marble slabs. The town is said to have 17 miles of such sidewalks, composed of the castoffs from Vermont's marble quarries.

On Route 30, 7 miles north of Manchester, is the village of Dorset. Fans of American architecture owe themselves a visit. While not as grand as Manchester, this quiet town of white clapboard and black and green shutters has a quiet and appealing grace. The elliptical green is fronted by early homes that are modest by Manchester standards, but nonetheless imbued with a subtle elegance. In the right light, Dorset feels more like a Norman Rockwell painting than many Norman Rockwell paintings.

MUSEUMS & HISTORIC HOMES

American Museum of Fly Fishing ★ This is the place for serious anglers interested in the rich history and delicate art of fly-fishing. The museum includes exhibits on the evolution of the fly-fishing reel, paintings and sculptures of fish and anglers, displays of creels, and dioramas depicting fishing at its best. You can see the fly-fishing tackle of some of the nation's more notable anglers, including Herbert Hoover, Andrew Carnegie, and Ernest Hemingway. And, naturally, there are extensive exhibits of beautifully tied flies, displayed in oak and glass cases.

Rte. 7A (1 block north of the Equinox Hotel), Manchester. (C) **802/362-3300.** Admission $3 adults, free for students and children under 12. Jan–Apr Mon–Fri 10am–4pm; May–Dec daily 10am–4pm. (Sometimes closed Sat or Sun in summer; call first.)

Hildene ★★★ Robert Todd Lincoln was the only son of Abraham and Mary Todd Lincoln to survive to maturity. But he's also noted for his own achievements: He earned millions as a prominent corporate attorney, and he served as secretary of war and ambassador to Britain under three presidents. He was president of the Pullman Company (makers of deluxe train cars) from 1897 to 1911, stepping in after the death of company founder George Pullman.

What did one do with millions of dollars in an era when a million bucks was more than chump change? Build lavish summer homes, for the most part. And Lincoln, the son of a man who grew up in famously modest circumstances, was no exception. He summered in this stately, 24-room Georgian Revival mansion between 1905 and 1926 and delighted in showing off its remarkable features, including a sweeping staircase and a 1908 Aeolian organ with 1,000 pipes (you'll hear it played on the tour). Still, it's more regal than ostentatious, and made with an eye to quality. Lincoln had formal gardens designed after the patterns in a stained-glass window and planted on a gentle promontory with outstanding views of the flanking mountains. The home is viewed on group tours that start at an informative visitor center; allow time following the tour to explore the grounds.

Rte. 7A, Manchester. (C) **802/362-1788.** www.hildene.org. Admission $8 adults, $4 children 6–14, free for children under 6. Tours given mid-May through Oct daily, every ½-hour 9:30am–4pm; grounds close at 5:30pm. Special holiday tours Dec 27–29.

Southern Vermont Art Center ★★ This fine art center is well worth the short detour from town. Located in a striking Georgian Revival home surrounded by more than 400 pastoral hillside acres (it overlooks land that once belonged to Charles Orvis of fly-fishing fame), the center features a series of galleries displaying works from its well-regarded collection, as well as frequently changing exhibits of contemporary Vermont artists. A striking modern building across the drive, designed to display more of the 800-piece permanent collection, opened in 2000. Check the schedule before you arrive; you may be able to sign up for an art class while you're in town. Also, leave time to enjoy a light lunch at the Garden Cafe and to wander the grounds, exploring both the sculpture garden and the woods beyond.

West Rd. (P.O. Box 617), Manchester. ℂ 802/362-1405. www.svac.org. Admission $5 adults, $2 students, free for children under 13. Mid-May to Oct Tues–Sat 10am–5pm, Sun noon–5pm. Nov to mid-May Mon–Sat 10am–5pm.

SHOPPING

Manchester Center has the best concentration of high-end outlets in New England. Among the upscale retailers with a presence here are Baccarat, Versace, Giorgio Armani, Coach, and Cole-Haan. Other retailers include Brooks Brothers, Crabtree & Evelyn, Polo/Ralph Lauren, Timberland, Tommy Hilfiger, and J. Crew. The shops are located in tasteful minimall clusters in and around a T intersection in the heart of Manchester Center.

One hometown favorite is worth seeking out if your interests include fishing or rustic, outdoorsy fashion. Orvis has crafted a worldwide reputation for manufacturing top-flight fly-fishing equipment, and happens to be based in Manchester. The **Orvis Catalog Store** (ℂ 802/362-3750) is located between Manchester and Manchester Center and offers housewares, sturdy outdoor clothing, and—of course—fly-fishing equipment. Two small ponds just outside the shop allow prospective customers to try the gear before buying.

Near the middle of Manchester Center, at the intersection of Route 7A and Route 30, is the **Northshire Bookstore** (ℂ 802/362-2200; www.northshire.com), one of the best bookshops in New England. It's not as overwhelmingly large as a chain store, but has an excellent selection of current titles.

SKIING

Bromley Mountain Ski Resort ★   Bromley is a great place to learn to ski. Gentle and forgiving, the mountain also features long, looping intermediate runs that are tremendously popular with families. The slopes are mostly south-facing, which means they receive the warmth of the sun and some protection from the harshest winter winds. (It also means the snow may melt quicker than at other ski resorts.) The base lodge scene is more mellow than at many resorts, and your experience is almost guaranteed to be relaxing.

P.O. Box 1130, Manchester Center, VT 05255. ℂ 800/865-4786 for lodging, or 802/824-5522. www.bromley.com. Vertical drop: 1,334 ft. Lifts: 6 chairlifts (including 1 high-speed detachable quad), 3 surface lifts. Skiable acreage: 175. Lift tickets: $49 Sat–Sun, $42 Mon–Fri.

Stratton ★★   Founded in the 1960s, Stratton labored in its early days under the belief that Vermont ski areas had to be Tyrolean to be successful—hence Swiss chalet architecture, and the overall feel of being Vail's younger, less affluent sibling. In recent years, Stratton has worked to leave the image of Alpine quaintness behind in a bid to attract a younger, edgier set. New owners added $25 million in improvements, mostly in snowmaking, with coverage now up over 80%. The slopes are especially popular with snowboarders, a sport that was invented here when bartender Jake Burton slapped a big plank on his feet and aimed down the mountain. Expert skiers should seek out Upper Middlebrook, a fine, twisting run off the summit.

Stratton Mountain, VT 05155. ℂ 800/843-6867 for lodging, or 802/297-2200. www.stratton.com. Vertical drop: 2,003 ft. Lifts: 1 gondola, 9 chairlifts (including one 6-person high-speed), 2 surface lifts. Skiable acreage: 583. Lift tickets: $60 Sat–Sun and holidays, $55 Mon–Fri.

OTHER OUTDOOR PURSUITS

HIKING & BIKING   Scenic hiking trails ranging from challenging to relaxing can be found in the hills a short drive from town. At the Green Mountain District Ranger Station (see "Visitor Information," above), ask for the free brochure *Day Hikes on the Manchester Ranger District,* which lists 19 hikes easily reached from Manchester.

A scenic drive northwest of Manchester Center will take you to the **Delaware and Hudson Rail-Trail,** approximately 20 miles of which have been built in two sections in Vermont. The southern section of the trail runs about 10 miles from West Pawlet to the state line at West Rupert, over trestles and past vestiges of former industry, such as the old Vermont Milk and Cream Co. Like most rail-trails, this is perfect for exploring by mountain bike. You'll bike sometimes on the original ballast, other times through grassy growth. To reach the trailhead, drive north on Route 30 from Manchester Center to Route 315, then continue north on Route 153. In West Pawlet, park across from Duchie's General Store (a good place for refreshments), then set off on the trail southward from the old D&H freight depot across the street.

CANOEING   For a duck's-eye view of the rolling hills, stop by **Battenkill Canoe Ltd.** in Arlington (© **800/421-5268** or 802/362-2800; www.battenkill. com). This friendly outfit offers daily canoe rentals for exploring the scenic Battenkill and surrounding areas. Trips range from 2 hours to a whole day ($45 per canoe including shuttle), but the firm specializes in 5-day inn-to-inn canoe packages. The shop is open daily in season (May–Oct) from 9am to 5:30pm, and limited hours the remainder of the year.

FLY-FISHING   Aspiring anglers can sign up for fly-fishing classes taught by skilled instructors affiliated with **Orvis** (© **800/548-9548**), the noted fly-fishing supplier and manufacturer. The 2½-day classes include instruction in knot tying and casting; students practice catch-and-release fishing on the company pond and the Battenkill River. Classes are held from mid-April to Labor Day.

WHERE TO STAY

Arlington Inn ★★   This stout, multi-columned Greek Revival house (1848) would be perfectly at home in the Virginia countryside. But it anchors this village well, set back from Historic Route 7A on a lawn bordered with sturdy maples. Inside, the inn boasts a similarly courtly feel, with unique wooden ceilings adorning the first-floor rooms and a tavern that borrows its atmosphere from an English hunt club. If you prefer modern comforts, ask for a room in the 1830 parsonage next door, where you'll find phones and TVs. The quietest units are in the detached carriage house, which is most removed from the sound of Route 7A.

Rte. 7A (P.O. Box 369), Arlington, VT 05250. © **800/443-9442** or 802/375-6532. Fax 802/375-6534. www. arlingtoninn.com. 17 units. $100–$265 double. Rates include breakfast. 2-night minimum stay most weekends. AE, DISC, MC, V. **Amenities:** Restaurant (regional); tennis court; baby-sitting. *In room:* A/C, TV, no phone (except in parsonage rooms).

Barnstead Inn ★   If you're looking for a bit of history with your lodging but are a bit shell-shocked by area room rates, consider this congenial place within walking distance of Manchester. All but two of the guest rooms are located in an 1830s hay barn; many are decorated in a rustic country style, some with exposed beams. Expect vinyl bathroom floors, industrial carpeting, and a mix of motel-modern and antique furniture. Among the more desirable units are room B, which is the largest and most requested, and the two rooms (12 and 13) above the office, each with two double beds and original round beams. Four rooms are priced under $100, and all units offer good value.

Rte. 30 (P.O. Box 988), Manchester Center, VT 05255. © **800/331-1619** or 802/362-1619. www. barnsteadinn.com. 15 units. $70–$200 double. AE, MC, V. Children over 12 welcome. **Amenities:** Heated pool (summer only). *In room:* A/C, TV, dataport, coffeemaker.

Barrows House ★★   Within easy strolling distance of the village of Dorset stands this compound of eight Early American buildings set on 12 nicely land-scaped acres studded with birches, firs, and maples. The main house was built in 1784, and it's been an inn since 1900. The primary distinctions of Barrows House are its historic lineage and the convenience to Dorset; the rooms are more comfortable than elegant, although some have gas or wood fireplaces. A few units have phones—ask in advance if it's important to you. This place will please history buffs; those looking for more pampering may prefer the Equinox or the Inn at Ormsby Hill.

Rte. 30, Dorset, VT 05251. © **800/639-1620** or 802/867-4455. Fax 802/867-0132. www.barrowshouse.com. 28 units. $185–$255 double. Rates include breakfast and dinner. B&B rates also available. Midweek and off-season discounts available. 2-night minimum stay on weekends and some holidays. AE, DISC, MC, V. Pets allowed in 2 cottages. **Amenities:** Restaurant (contemporary New England); outdoor heated pool; 2 tennis courts; sauna; bicycle rental; game room. *In room:* A/C, no phone.

1811 House ★★★   This is one of our favorite inns in New England, and will appeal to anyone who's come here to get a big taste of history. This historic home was built starting in the mid-1770s, and began taking in guests in 1811 (hence the name). And it seems that not much has changed in the intervening cen-turies. The cozy, warren-like common rooms are rich in history—the pine floors are uneven, the doors are out of true, and everything is painted in earthy, colo-nial tones. The antique furniture re-creates the feel of the house during the Fed-eral period, and a delightful English-style pub lies off the entryway, complete with tankards hanging from the beams. Among our favorite units is the Robin-son Room, with a private deck and great view. The chocolate-chip cookies set out each afternoon are quite memorable.

Rte. 7A, Manchester Village, VT 05254. © **800/432-1811** or 802/362-1811. Fax 802/362-2443. www. 1811house.com. 14 units. $120–$230 double. Rates include breakfast. AE, DISC, MC, V. *In room:* A/C.

The Equinox ★★★   The Equinox was purchased in 2000 by Rockresorts, which manages a respected international group of upscale resorts. It remains a blue-blood favorite, with acres of white clapboard behind a long row of stately columns that define lovely Manchester Village. Its roots extend back to 1769, but don't be misled by its lineage: The Equinox is a full-blown modern resort. You'll find extensive sports facilities scattered about its 2,300 acres, four dining rooms, scheduled events (like guided hikes up Mount Equinox), and a sense of settled graciousness. The rooms are tastefully appointed, although not terribly large. Alas, the restaurants don't quite live up to the near-perfection of the inn, so leave nights open to sample other area establishments.

Rte. 7A (P.O. Box 46), Manchester Village, VT 05245. © **800/362-4747** or 802/362-4700. Fax 802/362-1595. www.equinoxresort.com. 183 units. $189–$339 double; $499–$599 suite. Ask about packages. AE, DISC, MC, V. **Amenities:** Four restaurants (contemporary/regional; pub fare); indoor and outdoor pools; three tennis courts; 18-hole golf course; health club; sauna; croquet; concierge; shopping acade; salon; limited room serv-ice; baby-sitting; laundry service; dry cleaning; falconry school. *In room:* A/C, TV, dataport, hair dryer, iron.

Inn at Ormsby Hill ★★   The oldest part of the striking Inn at Ormsby Hill dates to 1764 (the revolutionary Ethan Allen was rumored to have hidden out here). Today, it's a harmonious medley of eras and styles, with inspiring views of the Green Mountains. Guests enjoy those views along with gourmet breakfasts in the dining room, which was built by prominent 19th-century attorney Edward Isham to resemble the interior of a steamship. Among the best units are the Taft Room, with its vaulted wood ceiling, and the first-floor Library, with many of Isham's books still lining the shelves. Nine rooms feature two-person Jacuzzis and fireplaces.

Rte. 7A (near Hildene, south of Manchester Village), Manchester Center, VT 05255. ℂ **800/670-2841** or 802/ 362-1163. Fax 802/362-5176. www. ormsbyhill.com. 10 units. $270–$310 double weekends; $170–$245 weekdays; $315–$370 foliage and holidays. Rates include breakfast. 2-night minimum stay on weekends. DISC, MC, V. Closed briefly in Apr. Children 14 and older welcome. *In room:* A/C, hair dryer.

Palmer House Resort ⭐ This is actually a motel, but several notches above the run-of-the-mill. It's been owned and operated by the same family for nearly 50 years, and the rooms are furnished with antiques and other niceties you might not expect. Ask for one of the somewhat larger rooms in the newer rear building. Added in 2000 were eight spacious suites, each with gas fireplace, wet bar, and private deck overlooking a trout-stocked pond and the mountains beyond. The buildings are set on 22 nicely tended acres, and the motel even has its own small golf course. (There's no charge to play golf or borrow fishing rods.) Rooms tend to book up early in the season, so call far ahead to avoid disappointment.

Rte. 7A, Manchester Center, VT 05255. ℂ **800/917-6245** or 802/362-3600. www.palmerhouse.com. 58 units. Summer $150 double, $220–$230 suite; off-season from $85 double, from $180 suite. 2-night minimum stay some weekends. **Amenities:** Pool; nine-hole golf course; 2 hardtop tennis courts; Jacuzzi; sauna; fishing pond. *In room:* A/C, TV, fridge, coffeemaker, hair dryer.

Wilburton Inn ⭐⭐ This impressive Tudor estate (built in 1902) is sumptuously appointed, the common spaces filled with European antiques, Persian carpets, and even a baby grand. Throughout the brick manor house you'll find works from the modern-art collection amassed by the inn's owners, Albert and Georgette Levis. The guest rooms are divided among the main house and several outbuildings of various vintages, sizes, and styles. In the outbuildings, our favorite unit is spacious room 24, with a private deck with views of Mount Equinox and quirky outdoor sculptures. Three rooms have fireplaces; the units in the mansion lack TVs. One note: The inn hosts weddings virtually every weekend in summer, so travelers looking for quiet are best off booking midweek.

River Rd., Manchester Village, VT 05254. ℂ **800/648-4944** or 802/362-2500. www.wilburton.com. 35 units (1 with private hall bathroom). Weekends $150–$250 double; midweek $125–$205; holidays and foliage $180–$295. Rates include breakfast. 2- to 3-night minimum stay on weekends and holidays. AE, MC, V. **Amenities:** Restaurant (upscale regional); pool; 3 tennis courts. *In room:* A/C, TV.

WHERE TO DINE

Chantecleer ⭐⭐⭐ CONTINENTAL If you like superbly prepared continental fare but are put off by the stuffiness of highbrow Euro-wannabe restaurants, this is the place for you. Rustic elegance is the best description for this century-old dairy barn. The oddly tidy exterior, which looks as if it could house a chain restaurant, doesn't offer a clue to just how pleasantly romantic the interior is. Swiss-born chef Michel Baumann, who's owned and operated the inn since 1981, changes his menu every 3 weeks; he specializes in game and might feature veal with a roasted garlic, sage, and balsamic demi-glaze, or slow-roasted duck with sesame seeds and hoisin sauce. Especially good is the whole Dover sole, which is filleted tableside.

Rte. 7A (3½ miles north of Manchester Center). ℂ **802/362-1616.** Reservations recommended. Main courses $26–$35. AE, MC, V. Wed–Mon 6–9:30pm. Closed Mon–Tues in winter and for 2–3 weeks in both Nov and Apr.

Little Rooster Cafe ✦ CONTEMPORARY/REGIONAL   This appealing spot near the outlets is open only for breakfast and lunch, and it's the best choice in town for either of these meals. Breakfasts include flapjacks served with real maple syrup, a Cajun omelet, and a luscious corned-beef hash (go ahead—your doctor won't know). Lunches feature a creative sandwich selection, such as a commendable roast beef with pickled red cabbage and a horseradish dill sauce.

Rte. 7A South, Manchester Center. ℂ **802/362-3496.** Breakfast items $4.50–$6.75; lunch $6.50–$8.25. No credit cards. Daily 7am–2:30pm (closed Wed in off-season).

Mistral's at Toll Gate ✦✦ FRENCH   The best tables at Mistral's are along the windows, which overlook a lovely creek that's spotlit at night. Located in a tollhouse of a long-since-bypassed byway, the restaurant is a romantic mix of modern and old. The menu changes seasonally, with dishes like salmon cannelloni stuffed with lobster, or grilled filet mignon with Roquefort ravioli. The kitchen is run with great aplomb by chef/owner Dana Markey, who does an admirable job ensuring consistent quality. The restaurant has been recognized with the *Wine Spectator* excellence award since 1994.

Toll Gate Rd. (east of Manchester off Rte. 11/30). ℂ **802/362-1779.** Reservations recommended. Main courses $22–$32. AE, MC, V. July–Oct Thurs–Tues 6–9pm; Nov–June Thurs–Mon 6–9pm.

2 Brattleboro & the Southern Green Mountains

The southern Green Mountains are New England writ large. If you've developed a notion in your head of what New England looks like but haven't ever been here, this may be the place you've envisioned. You half expect to walk into an inn and bump into Bob Newhart, the mild-mannered innkeeper.

The hills and valleys around the bustling town of Brattleboro in Vermont's southeast corner contain some of the state's best-hidden treasures. Driving along the main valley floors—on roads along the West or Connecticut rivers, or on Route 100—tends to be fast and only moderately interesting. To really soak up the region's flavor, turn off the main roads and wander up and over rolling ridges and into the narrow folds in the mountains that hide peaceful villages. If it seems to you that the landscape hasn't changed all that much in the past two centuries, well, you're right. It hasn't.

This region is well known for its pristine and historic villages. You can't help but stumble across them as you explore. A good strategy is to stop for a spell in Brattleboro to stock up on supplies or sample some local food or music. Then head for the southern Green Mountains, settle in at a remote inn, and continue your explorations on foot or by bike. In winter, you can plumb the snowy white hills by cross-country ski or snowshoe.

THE WILMINGTON/MOUNT SNOW REGION

Set high in the hills on the winding mountain highway midway between Bennington and Brattleboro, Wilmington has managed to retain its charm as an attractive village despite its location on two busy roads. It's definitely a town for tourists—if you want to get a light bulb or haircut, you're better off in Bennington or Brattleboro. What Wilmington does have is a nice selection of antiques shops, boutiques, and pizza joints. Except on busy holiday weekends,

---

Tips **Looking for More Information?**

The single best source of information on the region is the **state visitor center** (© 802/254-4593) right off I-91 in Guilford, just south of Brattleboro. The beautiful new building, inspired by Vermont's barns, is filled with maps, brochures, and videos on activities in the region.

---

when visitors driving frightfully large SUVs inundate it, Wilmington still manages to feel like a gracious mountain village untroubled by the times.

From Wilmington, the ski resort of Mount Snow/Haystack is easily accessible to the north via Route 100, which is brisk, busy, and close to impassable on sunny weekends in early October. Heading north, you'll first pass through West Dover, an attractive, classically New England town with a prominent steeple and acres of white clapboard.

ESSENTIALS
GETTING THERE Wilmington is located at the junction of Route 9 and Route 100. Route 9 offers the most direct access. The Mount Snow area is located north of Wilmington on Route 100.

VISITOR INFORMATION The **Mount Snow/Haystack Region Chamber of Commerce** (© **802/464-8092;** info@visitvermont.com) maintains a visitor center at 21 West Main St. in Wilmington. It's open year-round daily from 10am to 5pm. The chamber offers a room booking service, which is especially helpful for smaller inns and B&Bs; call © **877/887-6684.** For on-mountain accommodations, check with **Mount Snow Lodging Bureau and Vacation Service** (© 800/245-7669).

THE MARLBORO MUSIC FESTIVAL ✸✸✸
The renowned Marlboro Music Festival offers classical concerts performed by accomplished masters as well as highly talented younger musicians on weekends from mid-July to mid-August in the agreeable town of Marlboro, east of Wilmington on Route 9. The retreat was founded in 1951 and has hosted countless noted musicians, including Pablo Casals, who participated between 1960 and 1973. Concerts take place in the 700-seat auditorium at Marlboro College, and advance ticket purchases are strongly recommended. Call or write for a schedule and a ticket order form. Ticket prices range from $5 to $25. Between September and June, contact the festival's winter office at Marlboro Music, 135 S. 18th St., Philadelphia, PA 19103 (© **215/569-4690**). In summer, write Marlboro Music, Marlboro, VT 05344, or call the box office (© **802/254-2394**). The website is www.marlboromusic.org.

MOUNTAIN BIKING
Mount Snow was among the first resorts to foresee the appeal of mountain biking, and the region remains one of the leading destinations for those whose vehicle of choice has knobby tires. The first mountain-bike school in the country was established here in 1988. Clinics and guided tours are also available.

The **Mountain Bike Center** ✸ (call Crisports at © **802/464-4040**), open from late May to mid-October at the base of the mountain, offers equipment rentals, maps, and advice. The resort itself has some 45 miles of trails; bikers can also explore an additional 140 miles of trails and abandoned roads that lace the region. For a fee, you can take your bike to the mountaintop by gondola and coast your way down along marked trails, or earn the ride by pumping out the vertical rise to the top. Fanning out from the mountain are numerous abandoned town roads that make for less challenging but no less pleasant excursions.

ALPINE SKIING

Mount Snow ✦   Mount Snow is noted for its widely cut runs on the front face (disparaged by some as "vertical golf courses"), yet remains an excellent destination for intermediates and advanced intermediates. More advanced skiers migrate to the North Face, which is its own little world of bumps and glades. Because it's the closest Vermont ski area to Boston and New York (it's a 4-hour drive from Manhattan), the mountain can be especially crowded on weekends.

Mount Snow's village is attractively arrayed along the base of the mountain. The most imposing structure is the balconied hotel overlooking a small pond, but the overall character is shaped more by the unobtrusive smaller lodges and homes. Once famed for its groovy singles scene, Mount Snow's post-skiing activities have mellowed somewhat and embraced the family market, although 20-somethings will still find a good selection of après-ski activities.

Mount Snow, VT 05356. © **800/245-7669** for lodging, or 802/464-3333. www.mountsnow.com. Vertical drop: 1,700 ft. Lifts: 18 chairlifts (3 high-speed), 5 surface lifts. Skiable acreage: 749. Lift tickets: $55 weekends/holidays, $49 midweek.

CROSS-COUNTRY SKIING

The Mount Snow area offers excellent cross-country ski centers. The 9 miles of groomed trail at **Timber Creek Cross-Country Touring Center** (© **802/464-0999**), in West Dover near the Mount Snow access road, are popular with beginners and hold snow nicely thanks to the high elevation. Tickets are $15. The **Hermitage Ski Touring Center** (© **802/464-3511**) attracts more advanced skiers to its varied terrain and 30 miles of trails. A trail pass here costs $14. The **White House Ski Touring Center** (© **800/541-2135** or 802/464-2135), at the inn by the same name on Route 100, has easy access to the Vermont woods, a good range of terrain, and 25 miles of trails. A pass costs $12. The center also maintains snowshoe trails and offers rentals.

WHERE TO STAY

The Hermitage ✦✦   We love this place not so much for its unpretentious sense of style—the 19th century as interpreted by the 1940s—but for the way it combines the stately with the quirky. The inn is located on 25 acres of meadow and woodland, and feels a bit like one of those British summer estates that P. G. Wodehouse wrote about. Out back are cages filled with game birds, some quite exotic, that are raised for eating, hunting, and show. The guest rooms are designed to satisfy basic comfort more than a thirst for elegance, and some may seem a bit past their prime. But they're still far from shabby—the faded charm is just part of the inn's appeal. The dining room is best known for its wines, but the continental cuisine holds its own quite nicely.

Coldbrook Rd. (P.O. Box 457), Wilmington, VT 05363. © **802/464-3511.** Fax 802/464-2688. www. hermitageinn.com. 15 units. $225–$250 double. Rates include breakfast and dinner. 2- or 3-night minumum stay on weekends/holidays in winter. AE, MC, V. **Amenities:** Restaurant (continental); access to outdoor pool and clay tennis court (1 mile away); cross-country ski center on premises; sporting clays; stocked trout pond; private hunting preserve. *In room:* TV.

Inn at Sawmill Farm ✦✦   The Inn at Sawmill Farm is a Relais & Chateaux property on 28 acres, and one of the first inns in New England to cater to the most affluent travelers. Guest rooms in this old farmhouse, parts of which date back to 1797, are each different, but all share a similar contemporary country styling and colonial reproduction furniture. Among the best are Cider House no. 2, with its rustic beams and oversize canopy bed, and the Woodshed, a quiet cottage with a beautiful brick fireplace and a cozy loft. Some guests report that in recent years the inn has lost a bit of its burnish, and especially given the high room rates, service is no longer as disciplined as it once was.

Crosstown Rd. & Rte. 100 (P.O. Box 367), West Dover, VT 05356. ℂ 800/493-1133 or 802/464-8131. Fax 802/464-1130. www.vermontdirect.com/sawmill. 20 units. Weekdays $360–$470 double; weekends $362–$520. Rates include breakfast and dinner. AE, MC, V. Closed Apr–May. **Amenities:** Restaurant (see review below) outdoor pool; tennis court. *In room:* A/C, hair dryer, iron.

Trail's End ⋆

Trail's End, located a short drive off Route 100 on 10 nicely tended acres, is located in an updated 1960s ski lodge with attractive rooms and plenty of common space. The guest rooms are spotlessly clean, styled in a modern country fashion. Six feature fireplaces, two have Jacuzzis, and the suites and fireplace rooms come with TVs. The two suites are perfect for midwinter cocooning, with microwaves, refrigerators, and VCRs. Our favorite? Room 6, with a lovely fireplace and nice oak accents. Other good places to linger include the main common room with 22-foot stone fireplace, the stone-floored library and game room, and the informal second-floor loft.

5 Trail's End Lane (look for turn between Haystack and Mount Snow), Wilmington, VT 05363. ℂ 800/859-2585 or 802/464-2727. Fax 802/464-5532. www.trailsendvt.com. 15 units. Summer $110–$160 double; fall $120–$180; winter $130–$190. Rates include breakfast. 2- to 3-night minimum stay on weekends and holidays. AE, DISC, MC, V. Children over 7 welcome. **Amenities:** Heated outdoor pool (summer only); clay tennis court; Jacuzzi; game room. *In room:* No phone.

Vintage Motel

This is a good budget choice for those not planning to spend much time in their rooms. It has basic, motel-size rooms with industrial carpeting, durable furniture, and a few nice touches, like quilts on the beds. There's a family room with microwave and VCR. Bathrooms have curious 4-foot-square tubs (with showers), which are weird and appealing at the same time. The place is popular with both snowmobilers and skiers in winter.

195 Rte. 9, Wilmington, VT 05363. ℂ 800/899-9660 or 802/464-8824. www.vintagemotel.com. 18 units. Summer $55[nd[$70 double; winter $65–$95. AE, DISC, MC, V. 2-night minimum stay some weekends. Pets accepted in four rooms. **Amenities:** Outdoor pool. *In room:* TV.

White House of Wilmington ⋆

This grand Colonial Revival mansion sits atop the crest of an open hill just east of Wilmington. Built in 1915 by a lumber baron, the interior features hardwood floors, arched doorways, and nice detailing throughout. It's often a lively and bustling place, especially in winter, with cross-country skiers, snowshoers, and snow tubers (there's a great hill out front) all milling about. The guest rooms are simply furnished in Colonial Revival style; nine have wood fireplaces and four feature whirlpools. Our favorites? Room 1, a corner unit with fireplace and vintage white-tile bathroom, and room 3, which has its own balcony and sitting room with fireplace. The dining room, which serves continental fare, is one of the region's better restaurants.

178 Rte. 9, East Wilmington, VT 05363. ℂ 800/541-2135 or 802/464-2135. Fax 802/464-5222. www. whitehouseinn.com. 23 units. Weekdays $148–$204 double; weekend $162–$262. Rates include breakfast. 2-night minimum stay on weekends. AE, MC, V. Children 8 and older welcome in main inn; all ages welcome in guesthouse. **Amenities:** Outdoor heated pool; indoor pool; tennis courts; Jacuzzi; sauna; steam room; snowshoe rental; 25 miles of groomed cross-country ski trails. *In room:* No phone.

WHERE TO DINE

Dot's ☆ *Value* DINER   Wilmington is justly proud of Dot's, an institution that has stubbornly remained loyal to its longtime clientele, offering good, cheap food in the face of creeping boutique-ification elsewhere in town. (There's a second, more modern Dot's in Dover.) Located right in the village, Dot's is a classic, with pine paneling, swivel stools at the counter, and checkerboard linoleum tile. It's famous for its chili and pancakes, but don't overlook other breakfast fare, like the Cajun skillet—a medley of sausage, peppers, onions, and home fries sautéed and served with eggs and melted Monterey Jack cheese.

West Main St., Wilmington. ☎ 802/464-7284. Breakfast $2.95–$7.25; lunch $2.75–$7.50; dinner $2.75–$12.95. DISC, MC, V. Daily 5:30am–8pm (until 9pm Fri–Sat).

Inn at Sawmill Farm ☆☆ CONTINENTAL   More than 32,000 bottles of wine lurk in the custom-made wine cellar of this inn, which earned a coveted "Grand Award" from *Wine Spectator* magazine. The wine is only one of the reasons the inn consistently attracts well-heeled diners. The food is deftly prepared, with entrees ranging from pheasant breast and roasted salmon to potato-crusted sea bass with wild mushrooms. The converted barn-and-farmhouse atmosphere is romantic and the service superb, although the formality of the servers puts some folks on edge.

Crosstown Rd. & Rte. 100, West Dover. ☎ 802/464-8131. www.vermontdirect.com/sawmill. Reservations recommended. Main courses $27–$38. AE, DC, MC, V. Daily 6–9:30pm. Closed mid-Apr to Memorial Day weekend.

Le Petit Chef ☆☆ FRENCH   Situated in an antique Cape Cod–style farmhouse on Route 100, Le Petit Chef has attracted legions of satisfied customers who flock here to sample Betty Hillman's creative fare. The interior has been updated and modernized at the expense of some historic character, but the quality of the food usually makes diners overlook the made-for-ski-crowds ambience. By all means, start with the signature "Bird's Nest," an innovative mélange of shiitake mushrooms and onions cooked in a cream sauce and served in a deep-fried-potato basket. The main courses include a fillet of salmon baked in a horseradish crust, loin of venison with a fruit marmalade, and fillet of beef with merlot sauce and morels.

Rte. 100, Wilmington. ☎ 802/464-8437. Reservations recommended. Main courses $17–$30 (mostly $24–$26). AE, MC, V. Wed–Thurs and Sun–Mon 6–9pm; Fri–Sat 6–10pm. Closed late fall and early spring.

Maple Leaf Malt & Brewing Co. PUB FARE   This is the place for those nights you don't feel like anything fancy, but Dot's is a bit too, well, authentic for your mood. This neighborly bar, just around the corner from Dot's, features oversize sandwiches, burgers, wraps, and the occasional pasta special. It's all perfectly fine if unexciting, and the food makes a nice accompaniment to the brews crafted on the far side of the glass walls in the downstairs dining room. Expect it to be clamorous and loud on winter weekends.

3 North Main St., Wilmington. ☎ 802/464-9900. Main courses $6.95–$15.95. AE, DISC, MC, V. Daily 11:30am–10pm (sometimes later).

Piero's Trattoria ☆ PASTA/ITALIAN   This appealingly informal spot is located at the Orchard Inn. It's easy to miss as you speed by on Route 100, but it's worth slowing down to seek out. The oddly styleless dining room is small and dim, with just seven tables located off the lobby of the upstairs B&B. Not a promising appearance, but both chefs come from central Italy, the pastas are homemade (a good selection is the smoked salmon and capers tagliatelle), and other entrees might include veal stuffed with prosciutto and mozzarella served over polenta with a Sambuca sage sauce. It's usually open Friday and Saturday nights only, but call ahead and check for possible openings other nights.

53 North Main St. (Rte. 100), Wilmington. © 802/464-7147. www.orchardinn.com. Reservations recommended. Main courses $13.95–$17.95. AE, MC, V. Fri–Sat 5:30–9:30pm.

BRATTLEBORO

Deeply set in a scenic river valley, the commercial center of Brattleboro not only is a good spot for provisioning, but also has a funky, slightly dated charm that's part 19th century, part 1960s. The rough brick texture of this compact, hilly city has aged nicely, its flavor only enhanced since it was adopted by "feral hippies" (as a friend calls them), who live in and around town and operate many of the best local enterprises.

While Brattleboro is very much part of the 20th century, its heritage runs much deeper. In fact, Brattleboro was Vermont's first permanent settlement. (The first actual settlement, which was short-lived, was at Isle La Motte on Lake Champlain in 1666.) Soldiers protecting the Massachusetts town of Northfield built an outpost here in 1724 at Fort Dummer, about 1½ miles south of the current downtown. The site of the fort is now a small state park with a campground. In later years, Brattleboro became a center of trade and manufacturing, and was the home of the Estey Organ Co., which once supplied countless home organs carved in ornate Victorian style to families across the nation.

Brattleboro is the commercial hub of southeastern Vermont, located at the junction of I-89, Routes 5 and 9, and the Connecticut River. It's also the most convenient jumping-off point for those arriving from the south via the interstate. If you're looking for supplies, a strip-mall area with grocery and department stores is just north of town along Route 5. For more interesting shopping, take the time to explore downtown.

Brattleboro has long seemed immune from the vexations of modern life, but one modern inconvenience has made a belated appearance: traffic jams. Lower Main Street (near the bridge from New Hampshire) can back up heading into town, leading to honking horns and frustration. It's the source of considerable local grousing.

ESSENTIALS

GETTING THERE   From the north or south, Brattleboro is easily accessible by car via Exits 1 and 2 on I-91. From the east or west, Brattleboro is best reached via Route 9. Brattleboro is also a stop on the **Amtrak** (© **800/ 872-7245**) line from Boston to northern Vermont.

VISITOR INFORMATION   The **Brattleboro Chamber of Commerce,** 180 Main St. (© **802/254-4565;** www. brattleboro.com), dispenses travel information year-round, Monday through Friday between 8:30am and 5pm.

EXPLORING THE TOWN

Here's a simple, straightforward strategy for exploring Brattleboro: Park. Walk.

The commercially vibrant downtown is blessedly compact, and strolling around is the best way to appreciate its human scale and handsome commercial architecture. It's a town of cafes, bookstores, antiques stores, and outdoor-recreation shops, and it invites browsing. Shops of note include **Sam's Outdoor Outfitters,** 74 Main St. (© **802/254-2933**), which is filled to the eaves with camping and fishing gear. **Tom and Sally's Handmade Chocolates,** 55 Elliot St. (© **802/258-3065**), is a boutique chocolate shop with delicious handmade confections. Of note is the chocolate body-paint kit, which comes complete with two brushes.

Enjoyable for kids and curious adults is the **Brattleboro Museum & Art Center** (© 802/257-0124), at the Union Railroad Station. Wonderful exhibits highlight the history of the town and the Connecticut River valley. The museum is open mid-May through October, Tuesday through Sunday from noon to 6pm. It's located downtown near the bridge to New Hampshire. Admission is $3 for adults, $2 for seniors and college students, and free for children under 18.

OUTDOOR PURSUITS

Vermont Canoe Touring Center (© 802/257-5008) is located at the intersection of Route 5 and the West River north of town. This is a fine spot to rent a canoe or kayak to poke around for a couple of hours ($10 for two people), half a day ($15), or a full day ($20). Explore locally, or arrange for a shuttle upriver or down. The owners are exceedingly helpful about providing information and maps to keep you on track. Among the best spots, especially for birders, are the marshy areas along the lower West River and a detour off the Connecticut River locally called "the Everglades." Get a lunch to go at the Brattleboro Co-op (see "Where to Dine," below) and make a day of it.

Bike rentals and advice on day-trip destinations are available at the **Brattleboro Bicycle Shop,** 165 Main St. (© 800/272-8245 or 802/254-8644). Hybrid bikes ideal for exploring area back roads can be rented by the day ($20) or week ($100).

WHERE TO STAY

Several chain motels flank Route 5 north of Brattleboro. The top choice is **Quality Inn & Suites,** 1380 Putney Rd. (© 802/254-8701; www.qualityinnbrattleboro. com), which features a restaurant and indoor/outdoor pools.

Chesterfield Inn ★★   Located a 10-minute drive east of Brattleboro, this attractive inn sits in a field just off a busy state highway, but inside, it's more quiet and refined than you'd imagine from the road. The original farmhouse dates back to the 1780s, but has been expanded and modernized and today has a casual contemporary sensibility augmented by antique touches. Nine guest rooms are located in the main inn, and six in cottages nearby. All are spacious and comfortably appointed with a mix of modern and antique furniture. Eight have wood-burning fireplaces, and two have gas fireplaces. The priciest units feature fireplaces, double Jacuzzis, and a private deck.

Rte. 9, Chesterfield, NH 03443. © 800/365-5515 or 603/256-3211. Fax 603/256-6131. www.chesterfieldinn. com. 15 units. $150–$250 double. 2-night minimum stay foliage and holidays. Pets allowed with advance permission. AE, DC, DISC, MC, V. **Amenities:** Restaurant (New American). *In room:* A/C, TV, fridge.

Colonial Motel & Spa   Operated by the same family since 1975, this sprawling compound is well-maintained and offers the town's best value. Opt for the back building's slightly larger and quieter rooms, which are furnished with armchairs and sofas. The motel's best feature is the 75-foot indoor lap pool in the freestanding spa building.

Putney Rd., Brattleboro, VT 05301. © 800/239-0032 or 802/257-7733. colonial@together.net. 73 units. $65–$82 double. Rates include continental breakfast Mon–Fri. AE, DISC, MC, V. Take Exit 3 off I-91; turn right and proceed ½ mile. **Amenities:** Restaurant (Italian); indoor lap pool; limited fitness equipment; Jacuzzi; sauna. *In room:* A/C, TV.

40 Putney Road ★★   Built in the early 1930s, this compact French chateau–style home features four guest rooms that are attractively appointed with a mix of modern country furnishings and reproductions. (Plans call for adding several rooms within the next 5 years.) Two units feature gas fireplaces. The best of the bunch is room 4, a spacious minisuite. The inn is close enough to town that you can stroll there within a few minutes. The one downside: It's situated along a busy road, which diminishes the pastoral qualities somewhat. Innkeepers Gwen and Dan Pasco added two guest rooms (somewhat smaller) in the carriage house in May 2001; these may be rented separately or together as a suite.

40 Putney Rd., Brattleboro, VT 05301. ✆ **800/941-2413** or 802/254-6268. Fax 802/258-2673. www. putney.net/40putneyrd. 6 units. $110–$170 double; off-season $100–$160. Rates include breakfast. AE, DISC, MC, V. Children over 10 welcome. **Amenities:** Pub. *In room:* A/C, TV/VCR, dataport, fridge, hair dryer, iron.

Hickory Ridge House ★★   This historic Federal home is 10 miles north of Brattleboro, and is worth the detour if you're looking for the Vermont of rolling hills and stately trees. The brick house dates from 1808 and has high ceilings, large windows, wide pine floors, and an eclectic mix of furniture (ranging from colonial to Mission). The decor is simple rather than cluttered, the grounds are a lovely combination of fields and gardens and handsome trees, and the innkeepers place cookies and flowers in the guest rooms. Room 6 is larger than most and our favorite, with a gas woodstove and a great bathroom with a sink fashioned from an old dresser (alas, only a stall shower). All rooms have VCRs, and there's a library of videos to select from. Breakfasts feature homemade baked goods and hand-squeezed orange juice.

53 Hickory Ridge Rd. South, Putney, VT 05346. ✆ **800/380-9218** or 802/387-5709. Fax 802/387-4328. www. hickoryridgehouse.com. 7 units (2 with private hall bathroom). $145–$155 double; $350 cottage (all rates $20 higher in foliage season). Rates include breakfast. 2-night minimum stay on holiday and foliage weekends. AE, MC. V. *In room:* A/C, TV/VCR, dataport.

Latchis Hotel ★   This downtown hotel fairly leaps out in Victorian-brick Brattleboro. Built in 1938 in an understated Art Deco style, the Latchis was once the cornerstone for a small chain of hotels and theaters. It no longer has its own orchestra or commanding dining room (although the theater remains), but it still has an authentic if funky and slightly outdated flair. For the most part, the guest rooms are compact and comfortable, but not luxurious. About two-thirds of the rooms have limited views of the river, but those come with the sounds of cars on Main Street. If you want quiet, you can sacrifice the view and ask for a room in back. From the hotel, it's easy to explore town on foot, or you can wander the first-floor hallways to take in a first-run movie at the historic Latchis Theatre (which has been undergoing renovations since 1999) or quaff a fresh pint at the Windham Brewery.

50 Main St., Brattleboro, VT 05301. ✆ **802/254-6300.** Fax 802/254-6304. www.brattleboro.com/latchis. 30 units. $75–$155 double. AE, MC, V. **Amenities:** Restaurant (eclectic/brewpub); movie theater. *In room:* A/C, TV, fridge, coffeemaker.

WHERE TO DINE
Backside Cafe ★ AMERICAN   A great choice for either breakfast or lunch. There's nothing fancy here, but everything is simple and homemade, and it's less, well, crunchy than the Common Ground (see below). In 2000, the cafe moved into an open, airy second-floor space with wooden booths in the back of a building that once housed a Chrysler dealership. Lunches include familiar favorites like grilled ham and Swiss, spicy chili, homemade soups, and some modest exotica, like spinach, tomato, and roasted red pepper on focaccia. There's a small selection of local beer.

Midtown Mall, 22 High St. (between High and Elliot sts., off public parking lot). ℂ **802/257-5056.** Main courses $1.75–$4.75 breakfast, $3.25–$5.25 lunch. Mon–Fri 7:30am–3:30pm; Sat 8am–3:30pm; Sun 9am–3pm.

Brattleboro Food Co-op DELI   The Co-op has been selling wholesome foods since 1975, and its location, downtown near the New Hampshire bridge with plenty of parking, features a deli counter and seating area. It's a great spot for a quick, filling lunch. The emphasis is on natural foods, although it's not all tofu and sprouts—you can get a smoked turkey and Swiss cheese sandwich, or opt for a crispy salad. Check out the eclectic wine selection and the cheeses, especially the award-winning Vermont Shepherd cheeses, made nearby in Putney.

Brookside Plaza, 2 Main St. ℂ **802/257-0236.** Sandwiches $3.50–$6; prepared foods around $4–$5/pound. Mon–Sat 9am–9pm; Sun 9am–8pm.

The Common Ground VEGETARIAN   The Common Ground opened 2 years after the Woodstock Music Festival, which establishes it both chronologically and spiritually. This culinary landmark occupies a funky, sometimes chaotic space on the second floor of a downtown building. A meal might include grilled tofu with tahini, brown rice with tamari ginger sauce, or a marinated sea-vegetable salad. The Common Ground is a worker-owned cooperative, and service is cordial if not always brisk. One warning: The hours listed below are in effect somewhat arbitrarily; sometimes the staff just can't get it together enough to open the doors. Call ahead, or arrive with a backup plan.

25 Elliot St., #2 ℂ **802/257-0855.** Reservations not accepted. Lunch $3–$7.50; dinner $3.50–$8. No credit cards. Summer Mon–Thurs 11:30am–8pm; Fri–Sat 11:30am–9pm; Sun 11am–2pm and 5–9pm. Rest of year Thurs–Sat 5–9pm; Sun 11am–2pm and 5–9pm; Mon 11am–9pm.

Peter Havens Restaurant ★★REGIONAL/AMERICAN   Chef-owned Peter Havens has been serving up consistently reliable fare since it opened in 1989. Situated downtown in a pleasantly contemporary building, Peter Havens may not bowl you over with its menu, but you will be impressed by what you're served. You're likely to feel instantly at home in this friendly spot, which has just 10 tables. Meals are prepared with choice ingredients and are served with panache. Seafood is the specialty, with such offerings as salmon with a chipotle pepper rémoulade.

32 Elliot St. ℂ **802/257-3333.** Reservations strongly recommended. Main courses $19–$24. MC, V. Tues–Sat 6–9pm.

T. J. Buckley's ★★★ NEW AMERICAN   This is Brattleboro's best restaurant, and one of the better choices in all of Vermont. The lilliputian T. J. Buckley's is housed in a classic old diner on a dim side street. Renovations like slate floors and golden lighting have created an intimate restaurant that seats about 20. There are no secrets between the chef, the sous chef, and the server, all of whom remain within a couple dozen feet of one another (and you) throughout the meal—the entire place is smaller than the kitchen alone at many restaurants. The menu is limited, with just four entrees each night—beef, poultry, shellfish, and fish—but the food has absolutely nothing in common with simple diner fare. The ingredients are fresh and select, the preparation more concerned with melding flavors than dazzling with architectural flourishes. If you want to sample chef Michael Fuller's inventiveness, we'd recommend the fish or shellfish. Vegetarians can request a veggie platter.

132 Elliot St. ℂ **802/257-4922.** Reservations usually essential. Main courses $25–$30. No credit cards. Winter Thurs–Sun 6–9pm; rest of year Wed–Sun 6–9pm (sometimes later on busy nights).

NEWFANE ✰✰✰ & TOWNSHEND

These two valley villages, about 5 miles apart on Route 30, are both picture-perfect Vermont. They're set along the serpentine West River, and both are built around open town greens. They consist of impressive white clapboard homes and public buildings that share the grace and scale of the surrounding homes. Both boast striking examples of Early American architecture, notably Greek Revival. Don't bother looking for strip malls, McDonald's, or garish video outlets hereabouts.

Newfane and Townshend feel as if they've been idled on a sidetrack for decades while the rest of American society steamed blithely ahead. But these villages certainly don't have the somber feel of a mausoleum. On one visit during a breezy autumn afternoon, a swarm of teenagers skateboarded off the steps of the courthouse in Newfane, and a lively basketball game was under way at the edge of the green in Townshend. There's life here.

One intriguing footnote: That handsome gazebo on the village green in Townshend? It looks like it's been here forever, but it dates back only to 1988, when the Chevy Chase movie *Funny Farm* was filmed here. A production crew built it for the movie, but the townspeople liked it well enough to keep it.

For visitors, inactivity is often the activity of choice. Guests find an inn or lodge that suits their temperament, then spend the days strolling the towns, discovering back roads, hunting for antiques at the many shops, or striking off on foot for one of the rounded, wooded peaks that overlook villages and valleys.

ESSENTIALS

GETTING THERE   Newfane and Townshend are located on Route 30 northwest of Brattleboro. The nearest interstate access is off Exit 3 from I-91.

VISITOR INFORMATION   There's no formal information center serving these towns. Brochures are available at the **state visitor center** (✆ **802/254-4593**) on I-91 in Guilford, south of Brattleboro.

EXPLORING THE AREA

Newfane was originally founded on a hill a few miles from the current village in 1774; in 1825 it was moved to its present location on a valley floor. Some of the original buildings were dismantled and rebuilt, but most date from the early to mid–19th century. The **National Historic District** ✰✰ is comprised of some 60 buildings around the green and on nearby side streets. You'll find styles ranging from Federal through Colonial Revival, although Greek Revival appears to carry the day. A strikingly handsome courthouse—where cases are still heard, as they have been for nearly 2 centuries—dominates the shady green. This structure was originally built in 1825; the imposing portico was added in 1853. For more detailed information on area buildings, get a copy of the free walking-tour brochure at the Moore Free Library on West Street or at the Historical Society, below.

Newfane's history is explored at the engaging **Historical Society of Windham County** ✰, located on Route 30 across from the village common. It's housed in a handsome 1930s Colonial Revival brick building. There's an eclectic assemblage of local artifacts (dolls, melodeons, rail ephemera), along with changing exhibits that feature intriguing snippets of local history. It's open from late May to mid-October, Wednesday through Sunday from noon to 5pm; admission is by donation.

More than two dozen **antiques shops** are located on or near Route 30 in the West River Valley. They provide good grazing on lazy afternoons, and are a fine resource for serious collectors. At any of the shops, look for the free brochure *Antiquing in the West River Valley,* which provides a good overview of what's out there. Among the options: the **Riverdale Antiques Center** ✸ (✆ **802/ 365-4616**), a group shop with about 65 dealers selling some country furniture but mostly smaller collectibles, and **Schommer Antiques** ✸✸ (✆ **802/ 365-7777**) on Route 30 in Newfane Village, which carries a good selection of 19th-century furniture and accessories in a shop that's listed on the National Register of Historic Places.

Treasure hunters should time their visit to hit the **Newfane Flea Market** ✸ (✆ **802/365-4000**), which features 100-plus tables of assorted stuff, much of it of the 12-tube-socks-for-5-bucks variety. The flea market is held on Sundays May through October on Route 30 just north of Newfane Village.

On Route 30 between Townshend and Jamaica, you'll pass the **Scott Covered Bridge** ✸ below the Townshend Dam (closed to car traffic). It dates from 1870, and is an example of a Towne lattice-style bridge, with an added arch. At 166 feet long, it has the distinction of being the longest single-span bridge in the state.

WHERE TO STAY & DINE

Four Columns Inn ✸✸   You can't help but notice the Four Columns Inn in Newfane: It's the regal white clapboard building with four Ionic columns just off the green. This perfect village setting hides an appealing inn within. Rooms in the Main House and Garden Wing are larger (and more expensive) than those above the restaurant. Four units have been made over as luxury suites, with double Jacuzzis. The best choice in the house is room 12, with a Jacuzzi, skylight, gas fireplace, sitting area, and private deck with a view of a small pond. Low beams and white damask tablecloths characterize the inn's well-regarded dining room, which features creative New American cooking.

West St. (P.O. Box 278), Newfane, VT 05345. ✆ **800/787-6633** or 802/365-7713. Fax 802/365-0022. www.fourcolumnsinn.com. 15 units. Weekdays $115-$230; weekends $135-$290. Rates include continental breakfast. AE, DISC, MC, V. Pets accepted with prior permission ($10 per pet per night). **Amenities:** Restaurant (New American); outdoor pool; hiking trails on 150 private acres; baby-sitting. *In room:* A/C, hair dryer.

Three Mountain Inn ✸✸   The lovely Three Mountain Inn is located in the middle of the village of Jamaica, housed in a historic white clapboard home. It's benefited from a major upgrading under new innkeepers, who are refurbishing the rooms one by one in a restrained country style. Accommodations range from the cozy and basic to the outright sumptuous, with whirlpools, gas fireplaces, and TV/VCRs. (Four rooms have TVs.) The inn is well located as a base for exploring southern Vermont; in winter, skiing at Stratton is a short drive away. Guests can walk from the inn to Jamaica State Park, where there's a wonderful hike along the river on an old rail bed.

Rte. 30 (P.O. Box 180), Jamaica, VT 05343. ✆ **800/532-9399** or 802/874-4140. Fax 802/874-4745. www. threemountaininn.com. 15 units. $125–$235 double room, $275 cottage; foliage and holidays $145–$255 room, $295 cottage. Rates include breakfast. AE, MC, V. Children over 12 welcome. Pets allowed with restrictions (call first). **Amenities:** Restaurant (New American). *In room:* A/C, dataport, hairdryer.

Windham Hill Inn ✸✸✸   The Windham Hill Inn is about as good as it gets, especially if you're in search of a romantic getaway. Situated on 160 acres at the end of a dirt road in a high upland valley, the inn was originally built in 1823 as a farmhouse and remained in the same family until the 1950s, when it was converted to an inn. The Windham Hill today melds the best of the old and the new. The guest rooms are wonderfully appointed in an elegant country style; six have Jacuzzis or soaking tubs, nine have balconies or decks, 13 have gas fire-places, and all have views. Especially nice are the Jesse Lawrence Room, with a soaking tub and gas woodstove, and Forget-Me-Not, with a soaking tub and four-poster bed. The excellent dining room features creative cooking with a strong emphasis on local ingredients.

Windham Hill Rd., West Townshend, VT 05359. ℂ 800/944-4080 or 802/874-4080. Fax 802/874-4702. www.windhamhill.com. 21 units. $200–$325 double; foliage season $250–$375. Rates include breakfast. AE, DISC, MC, V. 2- to 3-night minimum stay on weekends and some holidays. Closed the week prior to Dec 27. Children over 12 welcome. Turn uphill across from the country store in West Townshend and climb 1¼ miles to a marked dirt road; turn right and continue to end. **Amenities:** Restaurant (New American); heated pool; clay tennis court; game alcove; 6 miles of groomed cross-country ski trails. *In room:* A/C, hair dryer, iron.

GRAFTON ✸✸✸ & CHESTER ✸

One of Vermont's most scenic villages, **Grafton** was founded in 1763 and soon grew into a thriving settlement. By 1850, the town was home to some 10,000 sheep, and boasted a handsome hotel that provided shelter for guests on the stage between Boston and Montréal. A cheese cooperative was organized in 1890. The soapstone industry flourished. But as agriculture and commerce shifted west and to the cities, Grafton became a mere shadow of a town—by the Depression, many of the buildings were derelict; for 3 decades afterwards, much of the town could be purchased for a song.

In 1963, Hall and Dean Mathey of New Jersey created the Windham Foundation. A wealthy relative, who had recently died, had entrusted these two brothers to come up with a worthy cause for her fortune. It took a few years, but they eventually hit on Grafton, where their family had summered, and began purchasing and restoring the dilapidated center of town, including the old hotel. The foundation eventually came to own some 55 buildings and 2,000 acres around the town—even the cheese cooperative was revived. Within time the village again came to life, although it's now teeming with history buffs and tourists rather than farmers and merchants. The Windham Foundation has taken great care in preserving this gem of a village, even to the point of burying utility lines so as not to mar the landscape with wires.

To the north, more commercial **Chester** is less pristine and more lived in. The downtown area has a pleasant neighborly feel; there's also a handful of boutiques and shops along the main road. Chester is a great destination for antiquing, with several good dealers in the area. When heading north of town on Route 103, be sure to slow through the Stone Village, a neighborhood of well-spaced, austere stone homes that line the roadway. Many of these are rumored to have been stopping points on the Underground Railroad.

ESSENTIALS
GETTING THERE   Take I-91 to Bellows Falls (Exit 5 or 6), and follow signs to town via Route 5. From here, take Route 121 west for 12 miles to Grafton. For a more scenic route, take Route 35 north from Townshend.

VISITOR INFORMATION   The **Grafton Information Center** (ℂ 802/843-2255) is located in the Daniels House on Townshend Road, behind the Grafton Inn. For information on Chester, call the **Chester Area Chamber of Commerce** (ℂ 802/875-2939).

EXPLORING GRAFTON
Grafton is best seen at a languorous pace, on foot, when the weather is welcoming. A picnic is a good idea, especially if it involves the excellent local cheddar.

There are no grand historical homes open for tours; it's more a village to be enjoyed with aimless walks outdoors. Don't expect to be overwhelmed by grandeur. Instead, keep a keen eye out for telling historical details.

Start at the **Grafton Village Cheese Co. (C 800/472-3866)**, a small, modern building where you can buy a snack of award-winning cheese and peer through plate-glass windows to observe the cheese-making process. It's open Monday through Friday from 8am to 4pm, Saturday and Sunday from 10am to 4pm.

From here you can follow the trail over the nearby covered bridge, then bear right on the footpath along the cow pasture to the **Kidder Covered Bridge.** Head into town via Water Street, continuing on to Main Street. Toward the village center, white clapboard homes and shade trees abound. This is about as New England as New England gets.

On Main Street, stop by the **Grafton Historical Society Museum (C 802/ 843-2344;** open weekends only) to peruse photographs, artifacts, and memorabilia of Grafton. Afterwards, take a look at the **Old Tavern at Grafton,** the impressive building that anchors the town and has served as a social center since 1801, and partake of a beverage at the rustic Phelps Barn Lounge, or a meal in one of the dining rooms (see below). From here, you can make your way back to the cheese company by wandering on pleasant side streets. If you'd like to see Grafton from a different perspective, inquire at the inn about horse-and-buggy rides.

More active travelers, whether visiting in winter or summer, should head for the **Grafton Ponds Nordic Ski and Mountain Bike Center (C 802/ 843-2400)**, located just south of the cheese factory on Route 35. Managed by the Old Tavern, Grafton Ponds offers mountain-bike rentals and access to a hillside trails system summer and fall. Come winter, it grooms 18 miles of trails and maintains a warming hut near the ponds, where you can sit by a woodstove and enjoy a steaming bowl of soup. The Big Bear loop runs high up the flanks of a hill and is especially appealing; travel counterclockwise so that you can walk up the steep hill and enjoy the rolling descent. Ski and snowshoe rentals are available; a trail pass costs $15 for adults and $5 for children 12 and under (free for ages 6 and under).

WHERE TO STAY & DINE

Fullerton Inn ✮ The Fullerton Inn is more of a hotel than a country inn, located in a tall building (well, relatively speaking) smack in the middle of Chester's one-street downtown. The lobby has the feel of an informal old roadhouse, but with its polished maple floors, a handsome fieldstone fireplace, and a piano, it's a welcoming spot. The eclectically furnished guest rooms on the two upstairs floors vary in size and decor, although most have small bathrooms. There's little soundproofing, so noises from neighbors can carry. Room 17 is quiet, faces the rear of the property, and has a separate sitting area. For the more socially inclined, rooms 8 and 10 have doors onto a balcony that overlooks the street.

40 Common (P.O. Box 589), Chester, VT 05143. (C) 802/875-2444. Fax 802/875-6414. www. fullertoninn.com. 21 units. $99–$149 double. Rates include continental breakfast. 2-night minimum stay foliage and holiday weekends. AE, DISC, MC, V. Children over 12 welcome. **Amenities:** Restaurant (traditional New England). *In room:* No phone.

Hugging Bear Inn ✮ Young kids love this place. It's a turreted, Queen Anne–style home on Chester's Main Street that's filled with teddy bears: There's a 5-foot teddy in the living room and some 250 of them scattered about the inn. And in the attached barn are another *10,000* bears for sale at the Hugging Bear Shoppe, which attracts serious collectors from around the world. The guest rooms are themed around—no surprise—teddy bears. Expect bear sheets, bear light-switch plates, bear shower curtains, and more. "Pandamonium" has a panda theme; the "Winnie the Pooh Room" is all Winnie, all the time.

244 Main St., Chester, VT 05143. **©** 800/325-0519 or 802/875-2412. Fax 802/875-3823. www.huggingbear. com. 6 units. $90–$125 double. Rates include breakfast. AE, DISC, MC, V. *In room:* A/C, no phone.

The Old Tavern at Grafton *★★*   This beautiful, well-managed historic inn seems much more intimate than its 63 guest rooms would suggest, since the rooms are spread throughout the town. Fourteen rooms are in the handsome colonnaded main inn building, which dates from 1801, while another 22 are across the street in the Homestead Cottage. The remaining rooms are scattered among seven historic guesthouses in and around the village. All are decorated with antiques and an upscale-country sensibility; the rooms in the Homestead Cottage (which is actually two historic homes joined together) have a more modern, hotel-like character (if you want more history, ask for the main inn).

Rtes. 35 and 121, Grafton, VT 05146. **©** **800/843-1801** or 802/843-2231. Fax 802/843-2245. www.old-tavern.com. 63 units. Weekdays $135–$195 double, weekends $175–$260 double; suites to $320. Rates include breakfast. 2- to 3-night minimum stay on winter weekends, some holidays, and in foliage season. MC, V. Closed Apr. **Amenities:** Restaurant (updated New England), pub; sand-bottomed swimming pond; Jacuzzi; tennis court; platform tennis (night-lit); bicycle rental; game room; coin-op laundry; cross-country skiing. *In room:* No phone.

LUDLOW *★* & OKEMO

Centered around a former mill that produced fabrics and, later, aircraft parts, **Ludlow** has an unpretentious made-in-mill-town-Vermont character that seems quite distant from the prim grace of white-clapboard Grafton. Low-key and unassuming, it draws skiers by the busload to **Okemo Mountain,** a once-sleepy ski resort that's come to life in recent years. Ludlow is also notable as one of the few ski towns in New England that didn't go through an unfortunate Tyrolean identity crisis. It lacks splashy nightlife and fancy restaurants, and longtime visitors like it that way.

ESSENTIALS

GETTING THERE   Ludlow is situated at the intersection of Routes 193 and 100. The most direct route from an interstate is Exit 6 off I-91; follow Route 103 west to Ludlow. **Vermont Transit** (**©** **800/451-3292**) offers bus service to Ludlow.

VISITOR INFORMATION   The **Ludlow Area Chamber of Commerce** (**©** **802/228-5830;** www.vacationinvermont.com) staffs a helpful information booth at the Okemo Marketplace, at the foot of Mountain Road. It's usually open Tuesday through Sunday from 10am to 4pm, with some seasonal variation.

SKIING

Okemo *★★*   Okemo fans like to point out a couple of things. First, this is one of the few family-owned mountains remaining in Vermont (it's been owned by Tim and Diane Mueller since 1982). Second, with recent improvements, it features more varied and challenging terrain, yet doesn't attract as many yahoos as does Killington to the north. As such, it's first and foremost a mountain for families, who like not only the welcoming slopes, but also the friendly base area built on a scale that isn't too intimidating for kids. Well-maintained halfpipes with music are popular with younger snowboarders. Okemo has plans to expand its slopes on to adjacent Jackson Gore Peak in the next couple years, a move that will also include new base development. Families should note that the mountain offers three levels of ticket prices, with discounts for young adults (ages 13 to 18) and juniors (ages 7 to 12). Children 6 and under ski free.

Ludlow, VT 05149. © 800/786-5366 for lodging or 802/228-4041. www.okemo.com. Vertical drop: 2,150 ft. Lifts: 10 chairlifts (3 high-speed), 4 surface lifts. Skiable acreage: 520. Lift tickets: $56 Sat–Sun, $51 Mon–Fri.

WHERE TO STAY

In ski season, contact the **Okemo Mountain Lodging Service** (© **800/ 786-5366** or 802/228-5571; www.okemo.com) for reservations in slope-side condos.

The Governor's Inn 🕊   This regal village home was built in 1890 by Vermont governor William W. Stickney (hence the name) and is the picture of Victorian elegance. The downstairs lobby and common room (both with gas fireplaces) are richly hued with time-worn hardwood. The guest rooms vary in size (some are quite small), but all are comfortably appointed with antiques; three have gas fireplaces. Dinner in the cozy Victorian dining rooms is served Thursday through Sunday, by reservation only; the fixed-price meal is $45 for inn guests.

86 Main St., Ludlow, VT 05149. © 800/468-3766 or 802/228-8830. Fax 802/228-2961. www.thegovernorsinn. com. 9 units. $95–$195 double; $200-$275 suite. Rates include breakfast. AE, DISC, MC, V. Children over 12 welcome. *In room:* Hair dryer, no phone (except in suite).

The Inn at Water's Edge 🕊   Located a 10-minute drive north of Okemo Mountain, this 150-year-old house on the banks of the Black River, just off Route 100, has been thoroughly renovated and updated in a florid Victorian style. The innkeepers have focused on making this a destination for romantic getaways. The attached barn features a lounge and bar perfect for relaxing, with an oak pool table, a chess set, leather couches, a TV, and a great mahogany bar imported from England. The guest rooms in the barn over the bar tend toward the cozy and dark. Room 11, upstairs in the main house, would be our choice— it's bright and appealingly furnished, with corner windows and wood floors. The dining room serves four-course meals nightly.

45 Kingdom Rd., Ludlow, VT 05149. © 888/706/9736 or 802/228-8143. Fax 802/228-8443. www. innatwatersedge.com. 11 units. $175–$250 double. Rates include breakfast and dinner. AE, MC, V. Children over 12 welcome. **Amenities:** Canoes; bicycles (free). *In room:* A/C, no phone.

WHERE TO DINE

Harry's Cafe 🕊 ECLECTIC   Along a dark stretch of road north of Ludlow, you'll pass a brightly lit roadside cafe with a red neon "Harry's" over the door. At 50 miles an hour, it looks like a hamburger joint. It's not. Rather, it's an appealing family restaurant with a menu that spans the globe. Entrees are a veritable culinary United Nations, with New York sirloin, jerk pork, spicy Thai curry, and fish-and-chips. Your best bet is the Thai fare, the house specialty. On the downside, the restaurant's interior is more blandly efficient than cozy, and service can bog down on busy nights.

Rte. 103 (5 miles north of Ludlow), Mount Holly. © 802/259-2996. Reservations recommended in winter. Main courses $10.95–$16.95. AE, MC, V. Daily 5–10pm.

Nikki's 🕊 NEW ENGLAND   Nikki's is the best choice in town for a pleasant if not overly creative dinner out. It's a popular and friendly local spot that's been serving up tasty meals since 1976, and is divided between an older section with a crackling fireplace and a new addition that's bright and sleekly modern. Think of the fare as updated comfort food, with familiar favorites like grilled sword-fish, Black Angus steak, New England bouillabaisse, and Maine lobster. The wine selection is several notches above the usual ski-resort fare; the restaurant is a winner of an award of excellence from *Wine Spectator* magazine.

Rte. 103, Ludlow. ✆ 802/228-7797. www.nikkisrestaurant.com. Reservations not accepted. Main courses $12.95–$28.95 (most under $20). AE, DC, MC, V. Spring and summer daily 5:30–9:30pm; fall and winter daily 5–9pm (until 10pm Fri–Sat).

3 Woodstock ✶✶✶

For more than a century, the resort community of Woodstock has been considered one of New England's most exquisite villages, and its attractiveness has benefited from the largess of some of the country's affluent citizens. Even the surrounding countryside is by and large unsullied—you simply can't drive to Woodstock on a route that *isn't* pastoral and scenic. Few other New England villages can top Woodstock for sheer grace and elegance. The tidy downtown is compact and neat, populated largely by galleries and boutiques. The superb village green is surrounded by handsome homes, creating what amounts to a comprehensive review of architectural styles of the 19th and early 20th centuries.

Much of the town is on the National Register of Historic Places, and the Rockefeller family has deeded 500 acres surrounding Mount Tom (see below) to the National Park Service. In fact, locals sometimes joke that downtown Woodstock itself could be renamed Rockefeller National Park, given the attention and cash the Rockefeller family have lavished on the town in the interest of preservation. (For starters, Rockefeller money built the faux-historic Woodstock Inn and paid to bury the unsightly utility lines around town.)

Other wealthy summer rusticators were also instrumental in establishing and preserving the character of the village, and today the very wealthy have turned their attention to the handsome farms outside town. Few of these former dairy farms still produce milk; barns that haven't been converted into architectural showcase homes more than likely house valuable collections of cars or antiques.

One caveat: Woodstock's excellent state of preservation hasn't gone unnoticed, and it draws hordes of visitors. During the peak foliage season, the town green is perpetually obscured by tour buses slowly circling around it.

ESSENTIALS
GETTING THERE   Woodstock is 13 miles west of White River Junction on Route 4 (take Exit 1 off I-89). From the west, Woodstock is 20 miles east of Killington on Route 4. **Vermont Transit** (✆ 800/451-3292) offers daily bus service to Woodstock, with connections to Boston and Burlington.

VISITOR INFORMATION   The **Woodstock Area Chamber of Commerce,** 18 Central St. (✆ **888/496-6378** or 802/457-3555; www.woodstockvt. com), staffs an information booth on the green, open June through October daily from 9:30am to 5:30pm.

EXPLORING THE AREA
The heart of the town is the shady, elliptical Woodstock Green. The noted Admiral George Dewey spent his later years in Woodstock, and locals may tell you that the green was laid out in the shape of Dewey's flagship. This is such a fine and believable explanation for the odd, cigar-shaped green that it causes us

a small amount of distress to note that the green was in place by 1830, 7 years before Dewey was born.

To put local history in perspective, stop by the **Woodstock Historical Society** ⭐, 26 Elm St. (📞 **802/457-1822**). Housed in the 1807 Charles Dana House, this beautiful home has rooms furnished in Federal, Empire, and Victorian styles, and offers displays of dolls, costumes, and early silver and glass. The Dana House and adjoining buildings with more exhibits are open late May through October, plus weekends in December. Hours are Monday through Saturday from 10am to 5pm and Sunday from noon to 4pm. Admission is $2.

Billings Farm and Museum ⭐⭐⭐   This remarkable working farm offers a striking glimpse of a grander era, as well as an introduction to the oddly interesting history of scientific farming. This extraordinary spot was the creation of Frederick Billings, who is credited with completing the Northern Pacific Railroad. (Billings, Montana, is named after him.) The 19th-century dairy farm was once renowned for its scientific breeding of Jersey cows and its fine architecture, especially the gabled 1890 Victorian farmhouse. A tour includes hands-on demonstrations of farm activities, exhibits of farm life, a look at an heirloom kitchen garden, and a visit to active milking barns.

Elm St. (about ½ mile north of town on Rte. 12). 📞 **802/457-2355**. www.billingsfarm.org. Admission $8 adults, $7 seniors, $6 children 13–17, $4 children 5–12, $1 children 3–4. May–Oct daily 10am–5pm.

Marsh-Billings-Rockefeller National Historic Park ⭐⭐   The Billings Farm and the National Park Service have teamed up to manage the new Marsh-Billings-Rockefeller National Historic Park, the first and only national park focusing on the history of conservation. You'll learn about the life of George Perkins Marsh, the author of *Man and Nature* (1864), which is considered one of the first and most influential books in the history of the environmental movement. You'll also learn how Woodstock native and rail tycoon Frederick Billings, who read *Man and Nature,* eventually returned and purchased Marsh's boyhood farm, putting into practice many of the principles of good stewardship that Marsh espoused. The property was subsequently purchased by Mary and Laurance Rockefeller, who in 1982 established the nonprofit farm; a decade later they donated more than 500 acres of forest land and their mansion, filled with exceptional 19th-century landscape art, to the National Park Service. Visitors can tour the elaborate Victorian mansion, walk the graceful carriage roads surrounding Mount Tom, and view one of the oldest professionally managed woodlands in the nation. Tours of the mansion accommodate only a limited number of people; advance reservations are recommended.

P.O. Box 178, Woodstock. 📞 **802/457-3368**. www.nps.gov/mabi. Free admission to grounds; mansion tour $6 adults, $3 children 16 and under. Late May to Oct daily 10am–5pm.

NEARBY SIGHTS

Birders and other wildlife aficionados will enjoy a trip to the **Vermont Raptor Center** ⭐ (📞 **802/457-2779**), home to 25 species of birds of prey that have been injured and can no longer survive in the wild. The winged residents typically include bald eagles, great horned owls, peregrine falcons, saw-whet owls, and an array of hawks. The birds are located outside in spacious cages along a horseshoe-shaped walkway set on a hillside. (*Tip:* Start at the top and work down.) Other attractions include an herbarium and nature trails in the Bragdon Nature Preserve. The institute is located 1½ miles southwest of the village on Church Hill Road. (Look for the turn at the west end of the green.) May through October, it's open Monday through Saturday from 9am to 5pm; November through April, Monday through Saturday from 10am to 4pm. Admission is $6 for adults, $3 for children 12 to 18, and $2 for children 5 to 11.

About 5 miles east of Woodstock is the riverside village of **Quechee** ⭐⭐. This picturesque town still revolves spiritually and economically around the restored brick mill building along the falls. **Simon Pearce Glass** ⭐⭐ (© **802/295-2711**) makes exceptionally fine glassware and pottery from the former Downer's Mill, a historic structure that now houses a glassmaking operation, retail store, and well-regarded restaurant (see "Where to Dine," below). Visitors can watch glass blowing take place weekdays and on summer weekends from a downstairs viewing gallery. Hours are daily from 9am to 9pm.

OUTDOOR PURSUITS

Outdoor activities in the Woodstock area aren't as rugged as those you'll find in the Green Mountains to the west, but they'll easily occupy travelers for an afternoon or two.

BIKING   The rolling hilly terrain around Woodstock is ideal for exploring by road bike for those in reasonably good shape. Few roads don't lead to great bike rides; just grab a map and go. Mountain bikes are available for rent ($20 per day) at **Woodstock Sports,** 30 Central St. (© **802/457-1568**).

HIKING   **Mount Tom** is the prominent hill overlooking Woodstock, and its low summit has great views over the village and to the Green Mountains to the west. (It's part of the Marsh-Billings-Rockefeller National Historic Park; see above.) You can ascend the mountain right from the village: Start at Faulkner Park, named after Mrs. Edward Faulkner, who created the park and had the mountain trail built to encourage healthful exercise. To reach the trailhead from the green, cross Middle Covered Bridge and continue straight on Mountain Avenue. The road bends left and soon arrives at the grassy park at the base of Mount Tom.

The trail winds up the hill, employing one of the most lugubrious sets of switchbacks you're ever likely to experience. Designed after the once-popular "cardiac walks" in Europe, the trail makes hikers feel they are walking miles only to gain a few feet in elevation. But persevere. This gentle trail eventually arrives at a clearing overlooking the town. A steeper, rockier, and more demanding trail continues 100 yards or so to the summit. From the top, you can follow the carriage path down to Billings Farm or retrace your steps back to the park and village.

HORSEBACK RIDING   Experienced and aspiring equestrians head to the **Kedron Valley Stables** ⭐ (© **802/457-1480;** www.kedron.com), about 4½ miles south of Woodstock on Route 106. A full menu of riding options is available, ranging from a 1-hour beginner ride ($35, or $30 per person for parties of three or more) to a 5-night inn-to-inn excursion ($1,450 per person including all meals and lodging, double occupancy). Ask also about weekend riding programs. The stables rent horses to experienced riders for local trail rides, offer sleigh and carriage rides, and have an indoor riding ring for inclement weather. It's open every day except Thanksgiving and Christmas. Credit cards are not accepted.

SKIING   The area's best cross-country skiing is at the **Woodstock Ski Touring Center** ⭐⭐ (© **800/448-7900** or 802/457-6674), at the Woodstock Country Club, just south of town on Route 106. The center maintains 36 miles

Overrated **Quechee Gorge**

Five miles east of town, Route 4 crosses Quechee Gorge, a venerable if somewhat disappointing tourist attraction. The sheer power of the glacial runoff that carved the gorge some 13,000 years ago must have been dramatic, but the 165-foot gorge isn't all that impressive today. More impressive is its engineering history: The chasm was first spanned in 1875 by a wooden rail trestle. The current steel bridge was constructed in 1911 for the railroad, but the tracks were torn up in 1933 and replaced by Route 4.

The best view of the bridge is from the bottom of the gorge, which is accessible by a well-graded gravel path that descends south from the parking area on the gorge's east rim. The round-trip requires no more than half an hour. If the day is warm enough, you might also follow the path northward, then descend to the river to splash around in the rocky swimming hole near the spillway.

---

of trails, including 12 miles of trails groomed for skate-skiing. And it's not all flat; the high and low points along the trail system vary by 750 feet in elevation. There's a lounge and restaurant at the ski center and a large health and fitness center accessible via ski trail. Lessons and picnic tours are available. The full-day trail fee is $12.50 for adults and $8.25 for children under 14.

The ski area **Suicide Six** 🎿 (✆ **802/457-6661**) has an intimidating name, but at just 650 vertical feet it doesn't pose much of a threat to either life or limb. Owned and operated by the Woodstock Inn, this venerable family-oriented ski resort (it first opened in 1934) has two double chairs, a complimentary J-bar for beginners, and a modern base lodge. Beginners, intermediates, and families with young children will be content here. Weekend lift tickets are $42 for adults, $26 for seniors and children under 14; midweek, $23 and $19, respectively. The ski area is located 2 miles north of Woodstock on Pomfret Road.

WHERE TO STAY

Jackson House Inn 🎿🎿🎿   This is a truly comfortable and elegant choice located a 5-minute drive west of the village center. The home was built in 1890 by a lumber baron who hoarded the best wood for himself; the cherry and maple floors are so beautiful you'll feel guilty for not taking off your shoes. The guest rooms are well appointed with antiques, although some of the older rooms are rather small. A well-executed addition (1997) created four one-room suites with fireplaces and Jacuzzis. The inn welcomes guests with a series of pleasant surprises, including complimentary evening hors d'oeuvres and champagne and a 3-acre backyard with formal English gardens. This inn deserves three stars for its elegance and attentive service; only its location, a stone's throw off a busy stretch of Route 4, detracts from the graceful tranquility the innkeepers have succeeded in creating.

114-3 Senior Lane, Woodstock, VT 05091. ✆ **800/448-1890** or 802/457-2065. Fax 802/457-9290. www. jacksonhouse.com. 15 units. $165–$220 double; $260–$340 suite. Rates higher in foliage season. Rates include breakfast. 2-night minimum stay most weekends. AE, MC, V. Children 14 and over welcome. **Amenities:** Restaurant (see below); small fitness room; steam room. *In room:* A/C, hair dryer, no phone (except in suites).

Shire Motel ☆ The convenient Shire Motel is located within walking distance of the green and the rest of the village, and with its attractive colonial decor is better appointed than your average motel. The rooms are bright and have more windows than you might expect, with most facing the river that runs behind the property. (The downside: thin sheets and some scuffed walls.) At the end of the second-floor porch is an outdoor kitchen where you can get a cup of coffee in the morning and sit on rockers overlooking the river. The yellow clapboard house next door has three spacious and modern suites, all with gas fireplaces and Jacuzzis.

46 Pleasant St., Woodstock, VT 05091. © **802/457-2211.** www.shiremotel.com. 36 units. Summer $88-$145 double, holidays and foliage $125-$175, off-season $58-$95; suite $150-$250. Rates include continental breakfast. AE, MC, V. *In room:* A/C, TV, fridge.

Three Church St. *Value* This sturdy brick Greek Revival B&B with a white clapboard ell is located just off the west end of the Woodstock green, and is well situated for launching an exploration of the village. It offers excellent value, especially if you don't mind sharing a bathroom and can overlook small imperfections like the occasional water stain on the ceiling. In the back is a lovely porch overlooking the inn's 3 acres, great for enjoying breakfast or sitting quietly. Guest rooms are furnished comfortably and eclectically with country antiques. A night here feels more like staying with a relative than at a fancy inn.

3 Church St., Woodstock VT 05091. © **802/457-1925.** Fax 802/457-9181. 11 units (5 share 2 bathrooms). $80-$115 double. Higher rates during foliage season and Christmas week. Rates include breakfast. MC, V. Closed Apr. Pets allowed. **Amenities:** Pool; tennis court. *In room:* No phone.

Twin Farms ☆☆☆ Twin Farms offers uncommon luxury at an uncommon price. Housed on a 300-acre farm that was once home to Nobel Prize–winning novelist Sinclair Lewis, Twin Farms is a very private, exceptionally tasteful small resort. The compound consists of the main inn, with four guest rooms, and 10 outlying cottages, each with fireplace. The owners are noted art collectors, and some of the work on display includes originals by David Hockney, Roy Lichtenstein, Milton Avery, and William Wegman. Rates include everything, including open bar and use of all recreational equipment.

Barnard, VT 05031. © **800/894-6327** or 802/234-9999. Fax 802/234-9990. www.twinfarms.com. 14 units. $900-$1,050 inn room double; $1,050-$1,500 cottage. Rates include all meals and liquor. AE, MC, V. Closed Apr. No children under 18 accepted. **Amenities:** Restaurant (New American); lake swimming; 2 tennis courts; fitness center; Jacuzzi; canoes; bike rental; game room; concierge; car rental; free shuttle to rail or plane; limited room service; in-room massage. *In room:* A/C, TV, minibar, hair dryer, iron.

Woodstock Inn & Resort ☆☆☆ The Woodstock Inn is central Vermont's best full-scale resort. Located in an imposing brick structure set off the town green, the inn appears to be a venerable and long-established institution at first glance. But it's not—it wasn't built until 1969. The inn adopted a dignified Colonial Revival look well suited for Woodstock. Inside, guests are greeted by a broad stone fireplace and sitting areas tucked throughout the lobby. Guest rooms are tastefully decorated in either country pine or a Shaker-inspired style. The best units, in the wing built in 1991, feature plush carpeting, fridges, and fireplaces.

14 The Green, Woodstock, VT 05091. © **800/448-7900** or 802/457-1100. Fax 802/457-6699. www. woodstockinn.com. 141 units, 3 town houses. $169-$324 double; $339-$545 suite. Ask about packages and off-season rates. AE, MC, V. 2-night minimum stay on weekends. **Amenities:** 2 restaurants (traditionl/ regional, cafe); 2 pools (indoor and outdoor); Robert Trent Jones–designed golf course (at inn-owned Woodstock Country Club); 12 tennis courts (2 indoor); free shuttle to fitness center (squash, racquetball,

steam rooms); bike rental; cross-country ski trails; concierge; limited room service; baby-sitting; laundry service; dry cleaning. *In room:* A/C, TV, hair dryer, iron, safe.

WHERE TO DINE

Right in the village center is **Pane Salute,** 61 Central St. (© **802/457-4882**), a bakery that specializes in delectable Italian breads.

Jackson House Inn ✿✿✿ CONTINENTAL   The Jackson House dining room is a modern addition to the original country inn (see above). Its centerpiece is a 16-foot-high stone fireplace, and it boasts soaring windows offering views of the gardens in back. Men might feel most comfortable in a sports coat, although a jacket is not required. Once settled, you'll sample some of the most exquisite dishes in New England, ingeniously conceived, deftly prepared, and artfully arranged. The three-course meals begin with offerings like Maine crabmeat and field greens with shaved fennel. The main courses do an equally good job combining the earthy with the celestial. Expect dishes like crispy-skin salmon with a shiitake compote, or an Angus fillet with creamy white-corn polenta and a three-onion marmalade. For dessert, the banana-walnut soufflé is surprisingly delicate, and the crème brûlée with a cranberry compote is striking. Expect a meal that lingers in your memory.

114-3 Senior Lane. © **800/448-1890** or 802/457-2065. Reservations highly recommended. Three-course prix-fixe dinner $49 (chef's tasting menu $58). AE, MC, V. Thurs–Mon 6–9pm.

The Prince and the Pauper ✿✿ NEW AMERICAN   It takes a bit of sleuthing to find the Prince and the Pauper, located down Dana Alley (next to the Woodstock Historical Society's Dana House). But it's worth the effort. This is one of Woodstock's more inviting restaurants, with an intimate but informal setting. (It's quite a bit more casual than the Jackson House.) Ease into the evening with a libation in the taproom (open an hour before the restaurant), then move over to the rustic-but-elegant dining room. The menu changes daily, but you might start with a soup of fire-roasted corn and lobster chowder, then move on to pan-roasted red snapper with a horseradish crust or filet mignon with caramelized shallots. The fixed-price dinner menu offers good value; those on a tighter budget should linger in the lounge and order from the bistro menu, with selections like crab cakes, meatloaf, and tasty wood-fired pizzas.

24 Elm St. © **802/457-1818.** www.princeandpauper.com. Reservations recommended. Dinners (appetizer, salad, entree) $38. AE, DISC, MC, V. Sun 11am–1:30pm; Sun–Thurs 6–9pm; Fri–Sat 6–9:30pm. Lounge opens at 5pm.

Simon Pearce Restaurant ✿✿ NEW AMERICAN   The setting can't be beat. Housed in a restored 19th-century woolen mill with wonderful views of a waterfall (it's spotlit at night), Simon Pearce is a collage of exposed brick, pine floorboards, and handsome wooden tables and chairs. Meals are served on Simon Pearce pottery and glassware—if you like your place setting, you can buy it afterward at the sprawling retail shop in the mill. The atmosphere is a wonderful concoction of formal and informal, ensuring that everybody feels comfortable whether in white shirt and tie or (neatly laundered) jeans. Lunch features dishes like crispy calamari with field greens or crab and cod cakes with a red pepper coulis. At dinner, look for entrees such as crispy roast duck with mango chutney or barbecued salmon with roasted corn salad.

The Mill, Quechee. © **802/295-1470.** Reservations recommended for dinner. Lunch items $8.50–$12.50; dinner main courses $16–$25. AE, DC, DISC, MC, V. Daily 11:30am–2:45pm and 6–9pm.

Wild Grass ★ ECLECTIC   Wild Grass is located east of town on Route 4 in a small business complex that lacks the quaintness of much of the rest of Woodstock—yet the food rises above the prosaic surroundings with a menu that contains genuinely creative offerings and good value for this often-overpriced town. Especially appealing are the unique crispy sage leaves with tangy dipping sauces, served as an appetizer. Fish is grilled to perfection here, and sauces are pleasantly zesty. Other entrees include roast duckling with a shallot port sauce, Caribbean pork with a black-bean corn salsa, and, for vegetarians, marinated tempeh served with fried vegetables and a spicy peanut sauce.

Rte. 4 (east of the village). © 802/457-1917. Reservations recommended during peak season. Main courses $14.25–$19.25. DISC, MC, V. Tues–Sat 6–9pm; occasionally open Sun.

4 Killington ★

In 1937, a travel writer described the town near Killington Peak as "a small village of a church and a few undistinguished houses built on a highway three corners." The area was rugged and remote, isolated from the commercial center of Rutland to the west by imposing mountains and accessible only through daunting Sherburne Pass.

That was before Vermont's second-highest mountain was developed as the Northeast's largest ski area. And before a wide, 5-mile-long access road was slashed through the forest to the mountain's base. And before Route 4 was widened and improved, improving access to Rutland. In fact, that early travel writer would be hard-pressed to recognize the region today.

Killington is plainly not the Vermont pictured on calendars and placemats. But the region around the mountain boasts Vermont's most active winter scene, with loads of distractions both on and off the mountain. The area has a frenetic, where-it's-happening feel in winter. (That's not the case in summer, when empty parking lots can trigger mild melancholia.) Those most content here are skiers who like their skiing BIG, singles in search of aggressive mingling, and travelers who want a wide selection of amenities and are willing to sacrifice the quintessential New England charm in exchange for a broader choice of diversions.

ESSENTIALS

GETTING THERE   Killington Road extends southward from Routes 4 and 100 (marked on some maps as Sherburne). It's about 12 miles east of Rutland on Route 4. Many of the inns offer shuttles to the Rutland airport. **Amtrak** (© 800/USA-RAIL) offers service from New York to Rutland, with connecting shuttles to the mountain and various resorts.

The **Marble Valley Regional Transit District** (© 802/773-3244) operates the **Skibus,** offering service between Rutland and Killington ($1).

VISITOR INFORMATION   The **Killington & Pico Areas Association** (© 802/773-4181) supplies information on lodgings and travel packages. The association also staffs an information booth on Route 4 at the base of the access road; it's open Monday through Friday from 9am to 5pm, Saturday and Sunday from 10am to 2pm. For information on accommodations in the area and travel to Killington, contact the **Killington Lodging and Travel Service** (© 800/621-6867).

ALPINE SKIING

Killington ★★   Killington is a love-it or hate-it kind of place. It's New England's largest and most bustling ski area, offering greater vertical drop than any other New England mountain. You'll find the broadest selection of slopes, with trails ranging from long, narrow, old-fashioned runs to killer bumps high on its flanks. Thanks to this diversity, it has long been the destination of choice for serious skiers.

That said, it's also the skier's equivalent of the Mall of America: a huge operation run with bland efficiency and not much of a personal touch. It's not a particularly friendly place. It's easy to get lost and separated from your friends and family, and it seems to attract boisterous groups of young adults. To avoid getting lost, ask about the free tours of the mountain, led by the ski ambassadors based at Snowshed. If you're looking for the big mountain experience, with lots of evening activities and plenty of challenging terrain, it's a good choice. If you're looking for a less overwhelming experience and a more local sense of place, more intimate resorts like Sugarbush, Stowe, and Suicide Six are better options.

Killington, VT 05751. © **800/621-6867** for lodging, or 802/422-3261. www.killington.com. Vertical drop: 3,150 ft. Lifts: 2 gondolas, 30 chairlifts (6 high-speed), 2 surface lifts. Skiable acreage: 1,200. Lift tickets: $58.

CROSS-COUNTRY SKIING

Nearest to the ski area (just east of the Killington Road on Route 100/Route 4) is **Mountain Meadows Cross Country Ski Resort** ⚡ (© **800/221-0598** or 802/775-7077), with 34 miles of trails groomed for both skating and classic skiing. The trails are largely divided into three pods, with beginner trails closest to the lodge, an intermediate area a bit further along, and an advanced 6-mile loop farthest away. Rentals and lessons are available at the lodge. A 1-day pass is $14, a half-day pass $11.

The intricate network of trails at the **Mountain Top Inn** ⚡⚡ (© **802/ 483-6089**) activity center has had a loyal local following for years. The 66-mile trail network runs through mixed terrain with pastoral views and is groomed for both traditional and skate-skiing. The area is often deep with snow owing to its high ridge-top location in the hills east of Rutland, and snowmaking along key portions of the trail ensure that you won't have to walk across bare spots during snow droughts. The resort maintains three warming huts along the way, and lessons and ski rentals are available. The trails have a combined elevation gain of 670 feet. Adults pay $14 for 1-day trail passes, $11 for half-day passes. With more challenging and picturesque terrain, Mountain Top offers the better deal of the two options.

SUMMER OUTDOOR PURSUITS

MOUNTAIN BIKING Mountain biking comes in two forms at Killington—organized on the mountain and on-your-own on the back roads. On Killington's mountain, around 45 miles of trails are open for biking, and one eight-passenger gondola line is equipped to haul bikes and riders to the summit, delivering great views. Riders give their forearms a workout applying brakes while bumping down the slopes. A trail pass is $8; a trail pass with a two-time gondola ride is $20; unlimited gondola rides are $30 per day.

The **Mountain Bike Shop** (© 802/422-6232) is located at the Killington Base Lodge and is open from June to mid-October. Bike rentals (with suspension) start at $25 for 2 hours, up to $45 for a full day. Helmets are required ($3 additional per day).

Better deals and better bikes—along with sound advice on local trails—are available from **True Wheels Bike Shop** (© 802/422-3234), located in the Basin Ski Shop near the top of the Killington Access Road. Rentals range from

$25 a day for a low-end bike to $60 for a bike with rock shocks and disc brakes (half-day rates also available; helmets are included). Bikes are available from April to mid-October; reservations are helpful during holidays and busy times.

HIKING   Area hikers often set their sights on **Deer Leap Mountain** ★★ and its popular 3-hour loop to the summit and back. The trail departs from the Inn at Long Trail off Route 4 at Sherburne Pass. Leave your car across from the inn, then head north through the inn's parking lot onto the Long Trail/Appalachian Trail and into the forest. Follow the white blazes (you'll return on the blue-blazed trail you'll see entering on the left). In half a mile, you'll arrive at a cross-roads. The Appalachian Trail veers right to New Hampshire's White Mountains and Mount Katahdin in Maine; Vermont's Long Trail runs to the left. Follow the Long Trail; after some hiking through forest and rock slab over the next half mile or so, turn left at the signs for Deer Leap Height. Great views of Pico and the Killington area await you in four-tenths of a mile. After a snack break here, continue down the steep, blue-blazed descent back to Route 4 and your car. The entire loop is about 2½ miles.

A HISTORIC SITE

President Calvin Coolidge State Historic Site ★★   When told that Calvin Coolidge had died, literary wit Dorothy Parker is said to have responded, "How can they tell?" Even in his death, the nation's most taciturn president had to fight for respect. A trip to the Plymouth Notch Historic District should at least raise Silent Cal's reputation among visitors, who'll get a strong sense of the president reared in this mountain village, a man shaped by harsh weather, unrelieved isolation, and a strong sense of community and family.

Situated in a high upland valley, the historic district consists of a group of about a dozen unspoiled buildings open to the public and a number of other private residences that may be observed from the outside only. It was at the Coolidge Homestead (open for tours) that in August 1923 Vice President Coolidge, on a vacation from Washington, was awakened in the middle of the night and informed that President Warren Harding had died. His own father, a notary public, administered the presidential oath of office.

Coolidge is buried in the cemetery across the road. He remains the only president to have been born on Independence Day, and every July 4 a wreath is laid at his simple grave in a quiet ceremony.

Be sure to stop by the **Plymouth Cheese Factory** (✆ 802/672-3650), just uphill from the Coolidge Homestead. Founded in the late 1800s as a farmer's cooperative by President Coolidge's father, the business was until the late 1990s owned by the president's son. Excellent cheeses here include a spicy pepper cheddar. Hours are daily from 9:30am to 5pm; in winter, it's best to call ahead.

Rte. 100A, Plymouth. ✆ 802/672-3773. Admission $6 adults, free for children 14 and under. Daily 9:30am–5pm. Closed mid-Oct to late May.

WHERE TO STAY

Visitors headed to Killington for a week or so of skiing should consider the condo option. A number of condo developments spill down the hillside and along the low ridges flanking the access road. These vary in elegance, convenience, and size; all can be booked by calling the number below. **Highridge** features units with saunas and two-person Jacuzzis, along with access to a compact health club. **Sunrise Village** has a more remote setting, along with a health club and easy access to the Bear Mountain lifts. **The Woods at Killington** is farthest from the slopes (free shuttle), but offers access to the most elaborate health club and the access road's best restaurant. Rates fluctuate widely, depending on time of year, number of bedrooms, and number of days you plan to stay. Prices typically range from $100 to $140 per person per day, which includes lift tickets.

You can line up a vacation—or request more information—by contacting the **Killington Lodging and Travel Bureau** (✆ **800/621-6867;** www.killington. com), which also arranges stays at area inns and motels.

Blueberry Hill Inn ⭐⭐⭐   The wonderfully homey Blueberry Hill Inn lies in the heart of the Moosalamoo recreation area, on 180 acres along a quiet road about 45 minutes northwest of Killington (about midway to Middlebury). With superb hiking, biking, canoeing, swimming, and cross-country skiing, it's an extraordinary destination for those inclined toward spending time outdoors and away from the bother of everyday life. (From the inn's brochure: "We offer you no radios, no televisions, no bedside phones to disturb your vacation.") The inn dates to 1813; one graceful addition is the greenhouse walkway, which leads to the cozy guest rooms. Family-style meals are served in a rustic dining room, with a great stone fireplace and homegrown herbs drying from the wooden beams.

Goshen-Ripton Rd., Goshen, VT 05733. ✆ **800/448-0707** or 802/247-6735. Fax 802/247-3983. www. blueberryhillinn.com. 12 units. $200–$260 double. Rates include breakfast and dinner. MC, V. **Amenities:** Lake swimming nearby; sauna; bike rental; cross-country ski trails; baby-sitting. *In room:* No phone.

Butternut on the Mountain Motor Inn   Butternut is a short remove from the access road, just enough to lend a little quiet, although winter guests tend to make up for that with a dose of boisterousness. It's more a recommended budget choice than an especially noteworthy spot. The rooms are motel-size with motel decor, but the inn's unexpected facilities make it a good option. There's a lounge area with fireplace on the second floor and a restaurant with full bar and darts on the first floor. Eleven rooms have air-conditioning.

Killington Rd., Killington, VT 05751. ✆ **800/524-7654** or 802/422-2000. Fax 802/422-3937. butternt@ together.net. 18 units. Winter $70–$132 double. Lower off-season rates. AE, DISC, MC, V. **Amenities:** Restaurant (pub fare); lounge; tiny indoor pool; Jacuzzi; game room; coin-op laundry. *In room:* TV.

Killington Grand ⭐⭐   This is a good (though pricey) choice for travelers seeking contemporary accommodations right on the mountain. More than half of the units have kitchen facilities, and most are quite spacious though decorated in a generic country-condo style. Some units can sleep up to six people, and the resort has placed an emphasis on catering to families. You pay a premium for convenience compared with other spots near the mountain, but that convenience is hard to top during ski season. The helpful service is a notch above that typically experienced at large ski hotels.

228 East Mountain Rd. (near Snowshed base area), Killington, VT 05751. ✆ **802/422-5001.** Fax 802/ 422-6881. www.killington.com. 200 units. Ski season $250 midweek, $300 weekend, $350 holiday. Rest of year $175–$195 double. Ask about packages. 5-night minimum stay during Christmas and school holidays; 2-night minimum stay on weekends. AE, DISC, MC, V. **Amenities:** 2 restaurants (upscale American, cafe); heated outdoor pool (year-round); 2 tennis courts; fitness center; hot tub; sauna; children's programs; concierge; limited room service; massage; coin-op laundry; dry cleaning. *In room:* A/C, TV, coffeemaker, hair dryer, iron.

The Summit Lodge ⭐   Think plaid carpeting and Saint Bernards. Those two motifs seem to set the tone at this inviting spot on a knoll just off the access road. Although built only in the 1960s, the inn has a more historic character, with much of the common space constructed of salvaged barn timbers. The

---

Tips **Budget Choices**

Budget travelers who don't mind a commute to the slopes (you can take the $1 bus) should look into staying in Rutland, a commercial city about 11 miles west of the access road. Here you'll find a cluster of basic road-side motels and chain hotels, mostly on or along Route 7 south of town. Rates at the **Comfort Inn at Trolley Square,** 19 Allen St. (© **800/228-5150** or 802/775-2200), include continental breakfast. The **Holiday Inn,** 476 U.S. Rte. 7 South (© **800/462-4810** or 802/775-1911), has an indoor pool, hot tub, and sauna. Likewise, the **Howard Johnson Rutland,** 401 U.S. Rte. 7 South (© **802/775-4303**), features an indoor pool and sauna, with the familiar orange-roofed restaurant next door. The **Best Western Hogge Penny Inn,** on Route 4 East (© **800/828-3334** or 802/773-3200), has a pool and tennis court.

---

guest rooms are less distinguished, with clunky pine furniture and little ambience, although all have balconies or terraces. You may not spend much time in your room, however, since the numerous common spaces are so inviting. The Summit has more character than most self-styled resorts along the access road, and offers reasonable value.

Killington Rd. (P.O. Box 119), Killington, VT 05751. © **800/635-6343** or 802/422-3535. Fax 802/422-3536. www.summitlodgevermont.com. 45 units. Summer $95 double. Winter $116–$198 double. Winter rates include breakfast. AE, DC, MC, V. Minimum-stay policy on holidays. **Amenities:** Restaurant (resort fare); 2 pools (small outdoor heated pool in winter, larger pool in summer); 5 clay tennis courts; indoor hot tub; game room; limited room service; massage; coin-op laundry; virtual indoor golf. *In room:* TV.

WHERE TO DINE

It's our impression that *every* Killington restaurant serves up chicken wings, and plenty of them. If you love wings, especially free wings, you'll be in heaven. Alas, if you're looking for something more adventurous, the access road is home to an astonishing level of culinary mediocrity—bland pasta, tired pizza, soggy nachos—capped off with indifferent, harried service. For the most part, don't expect much of a dining adventure. A handful of happy exceptions exist:

Choices Restaurant and Rotisserie ☆ BISTRO   One of the locally favored spots for consistently good, unpretentious fare is Choices, located on the access road across from the Outback. Full dinners come complete with salad or soup and bread and will amply restore calories lost on the slopes or the trail. Fresh pastas are a specialty (try the Cajun green peppercorn fettuccine); other inviting entrees include meats from the rotisserie. The atmosphere is nothing to write home about and the prices are higher than at nearby burger joints, but the high quality of the food and care taken in preparation make up for that.

Killington Rd. (at Glazebook Center). © **802/422-4030.** Main courses $12.50–$21.95. AE, MC, V. Sun–Thurs 5–10pm; Fri–Sat 5–11pm; Sun 11am–2:30pm.

Hemingway's ☆☆☆ NEW AMERICAN   Hemingway's is an uncommonly elegant spot and ranks among the six best restaurants in New England. Located in the 1860 Asa Briggs House, a former stagecoach stop, Hemingway's seats guests in three formal areas. The two upstairs rooms are sophisticatedly appointed with damask linen, crystal goblets, and fresh flowers. Diners tend to dress causally but neatly (no shorts or T-shirts). The three- or four-course dinners are offered at a price that turns out to be rather reasonable given the quality of the kitchen and the unassailable service. The menu changes often to reflect available stock. A typical meal might start with a cured salmon on a crispy potato waffle or wild mushroom raviolis. Then it's on to the splendid main course: perhaps duck steaks with autumn slaw and crisp yams in fall, or cod prepared with lobster, corn, and vanilla in summer.

Rte. 4 (between Rte. 100 N. and Rte. 100 S.). ℂ **802/422-3886.** Reservations strongly recommended. Fixed-price menu $60; vegetarian menu $55; wine-tasting menu $90. AE, MC, V. Wed–Thurs and Sun 6–9pm; Fri–Sat 6–10pm. (Also open selected Mon–Tues during ski and foliage seasons; call first.) Closed mid-Apr to mid-May and early Nov.

Mother Shapiro's PUB FARE   Mother's is a great place for breakfast or brunch. You'll find omelets, lox, corned-beef hash, and pancakes. At Sunday brunch, there's a unique Bloody Mary bar—you get a glass with vodka and formulate your own spicy concoction from a lineup of ingredients. It's a fun place that kids adore, done up in a comic-book Victorian vaudeville look. Dinners, by comparison, tend to be so-so, and service more harried.

Killington Rd. ℂ **802/422-9933.** www.mothershapiros.com. Reservations not accepted. Breakfast $3.99–$8.99; sandwiches $5.99–$7.99; dinner entrees $6.95–$17.95. AE, DISC, MC, V. Daily breakfast 7–11am; lunch and munchies 11am–3pm; dinner 4:30–10pm.

Panache ★★ EXOTIC GAME   Panache isn't for everyone. For starters, the restaurant—located at the Woods condo complex—offers giraffe and camel and cobra and other fare that's not likely to show up any time soon at McDonald's (all from game farms). The exotic offerings attract gourmands in search of new flavors, but there's plenty of traditional fare—like filet mignon and veal—for the less adventurous. And once you get beyond the eye-popping menu, you'll discover a superior restaurant with a deft touch and a creative flair. The service is good, the decor colorful and modern, and the presentation excellent. As an added bonus, parents who make reservations can drop off their kids (no infants or toddlers) at a wonderful adjacent game room with air hockey and video games; the staff will keep an eye on them and feed them free pizza.

Killington Access Rd. ℂ **802/422-8622.** Reservations recommended. Main courses $20–$32. AE, DISC, MC, V. Sun–Thurs 6–9pm; Fri–Sat 6–10pm.

KILLINGTON AFTER DARK

Killington has more going on after dark than any other Vermont ski resort, with a variety of dance clubs and live-music venues along the access road. The more popular are listed below.

Mother Shapiro's   This lively, popular restaurant often features live blues on the small stage later in the evening. It's also a good choice for late-night snacking. Killington Rd. ℂ **802/422-9933.**

Outback/Nightspot   The music tends to be mellower here than at the other hot spots in town, with acoustic musicians often heading the lineup. It's the place to go if you want to chat with friends while enjoying music and wood-fired pizza. Note the resourceful beer-mug cooling system. Killington Rd. ℂ **802/ 422-9885.**

Pickle Barrel   The Pickle Barrel is Killington's largest and loudest nightclub, and lures in B-list national acts like Eddie Money, Little Feat, and the Mighty Mighty Bosstones. The cover ranges from a couple of bucks to nearly $20. Killington Rd. ℂ **802/422-3035.** www.picklebarrelnightclub.com.

Wobbly Barn   The Wobbly is best known for its popular happy hour, but it also packs in the crowds for dancing and mingling until late in the evening. Expect bands that play good, hard-driving rock. The American Skiing Company (owners of the mountain) own this pioneer establishment, located in an old barn. Killington Rd. ℂ **802/42-3392.** www.wobblybarn.com.

5 Middlebury ★★

Middlebury is a gracious college town set amid rolling hills and pastoral countryside. The town center is idyllic in a New-England-as-envisioned-by-Hollywood sort of way. All that's lacking is Jimmy Stewart wandering about, muttering confusedly to himself.

The town centers on an irregular sloping green. Above the green is the commanding Middlebury Inn; shops line the downhill slopes. In the midst of the green is a handsome chapel, and the whole scene is lorded over by a fine, white-steepled Congregational church, built between 1806 and 1809. Otter Creek tumbles dramatically through the middle of town and is flanked by a historic district that feature vestiges of former industry. In fact, Middlebury has 300 buildings listed on the National Register of Historic Places. About the only disruption to the historical perfection is the growl of trucks downshifting as they drive along the main routes through town.

Middlebury College, which is within walking distance at the edge of downtown, doesn't so much dominate the village as coexist nicely alongside it. The college has a sterling reputation for its liberal-arts education, but may be best known for its intensive summer language programs. Don't be surprised if you hear folks gabbing uncertainly in exotic tongues while walking through town in summer. Students commit to total immersion, taking the "Language Pledge," which prohibits the use of English while they're enrolled in the program.

ESSENTIALS

GETTING THERE   Middlebury is located on Route 7 about midway between Rutland and Burlington. **Vermont Transit** (ℂ **800/451-3292** or 802-388-4373) offers bus service to town.

VISITOR INFORMATION   The **Addison County Chamber of Commerce,** 2 Court St. (ℂ **800/733-8376** or 802/388-7951; www.midvermont. com), is located in a handsome, historic white building just off the green, facing the Middlebury Inn. Brochures and assistance are available Monday through Friday during business hours, and often on weekends from early June to mid-October as well. Ask for the map and guide to downtown Middlebury, published by the Downtown Middlebury Business Bureau, which lists shops and restaurants around town.

SEEING THE SIGHTS

The best place to begin a tour of Middlebury is the Addison County Chamber of Commerce (see above), where you can request the chamber's self-guided walking-tour brochure.

The **Vermont Folklife Center** ★, 3 Court St. (ℂ **802/388-4964;** www. vermontfolklifecenter.org), is located in the 1823 Masonic Hall, a short walk from the Middlebury Inn. You'll find a gallery of changing displays featuring various folk arts from Vermont and beyond, including music and visual arts. The small gift shop has intriguing items, such as heritage foods and traditional crafts. It's open Tuesday through Saturday from 11am to 4pm. Admission is by donation.

The historic **Otter Creek** ✦✦ district, set along a steep hillside by the rocky creek, is well worth exploring. While here, you can peruse top-flight Vermont crafts at the **Vermont State Crafts Center at Frog Hollow** ✦✦, 1 Mill St. (📞 **802/388-3177;** www.froghollow.org). The center, picturesquely situated overlooking the tumbling stream, is open daily (closed Sundays in winter) and features the work of some 300 Vermont craftspeople, with exhibits ranging from extraordinary carved wood desks to metalwork to glass and pottery. The Middlebury center also features a pottery studio and a resident potter who's often busy at work. The Crafts Center also maintains shops in Manchester Village and at the Church Street Marketplace in Burlington. Visit the center's website for a listing of monthly exhibits.

Located atop a low ridge with beautiful views of both the Green Mountains to the east and farmlands rolling toward Lake Champlain in the west, prestigious **Middlebury College** has a handsome, well-spaced campus of gray limestone and white marble buildings that's best explored on foot. The architecture of the college, founded in 1800, is primarily Colonial Revival, which lends it a rather stern Calvinist demeanor. Especially appealing is the prospect from the marble Mead Memorial Chapel, which was built in 1917 and overlooks the campus green.

At the edge of campus is the **Middlebury College Center for the Arts,** which opened in 1992. This architecturally engaging center houses the small **Middlebury College Museum of Art** ✦ (📞 **802/443-5007**), with a selective sampling of European and American art, both ancient and new. Classicists will savor the displays of Greek painted urns and vases; modern-art aficionados can check out the museum's permanent and changing exhibits. The museum is located on Route 30 (South Main Street) and is open Tuesday through Friday from 10am to 5pm, Saturday and Sunday from noon to 5pm. Admission is free.

A couple of miles outside of Middlebury is the **Morgan Horse Farm** ✦✦ (📞 **802/388-2011**), which dates back to the late 1800s and is now owned and administered by the University of Vermont. Col. Joseph Battell, owner of the farm from the 1870s to 1906, is credited with preserving the Morgan breed, a horse of considerable beauty and stamina that has served admirably in war and exploration. The farm is open for guided tours May through October, daily from 9am to 4pm. There's also a picnic area and gift shop. Admission is $4 for adults, $3 for teens, $1 for children 5 to 12, and free for kids 4 and under. To reach the farm, take Route 125 to Weybridge Street (Route 23 North), head north for three-quarters of a mile, and then turn right at the sign for the farm and continue on approximately 2 miles.

Brewhounds should schedule a stop at the **Otter Creek Brewing Co.** ✦, 793 Exchange St. (📞 **800/473-0727;** www.ottercreekbrewing.com), for a half-hour tour and free samples of the well-regarded beverages, including the flagship Copper Ale and a robust Stovepipe Porter. The visitor center and gift shop are open Monday through Saturday from 10am to 6pm. Tours are given those days at 1, 3, and 5pm.

OUTDOOR PURSUITS

HIKING   The Green Mountains roll down to Middlebury's eastern edge, making for easy access to the mountains. Stop by the **U.S. Forest Service's Middlebury Ranger District office,** south of town on Route 7 (📞 **802/388-4362**), for guidance and information on area trails and destinations. Ask for the brochure listing day hikes in the region.

One recommended walk for people of all abilities—and especially those of poetic sensibilities—is the **Robert Frost Interpretive Trail,** dedicated to the memory of New England's poet laureate. Frost lived in a cabin on a farm across the road for 23 summers. (The cabin is now a National Historic Landmark.) Located on Route 125 approximately 6 miles east of Middlebury, this relaxing loop trail is just a mile long, and excerpts of Frost's poems are placed on signs along the trail. Also posted is information about the trail's natural history. Managed by the Green Mountain National Forest, the trail offers pleasant access to the gentle woods of these lovely intermountain lowlands.

SKIING   Downhill skiers looking for a low-key, low-pressure mountain invariably head to **Middlebury College Snow Bowl** (✆ 802/388-4356), near Middlebury Gap on Route 125 east of town. This historic ski area, founded in 1939, has a vertical drop of just over 1,000 feet served by three chairlifts. The college ski team uses the ski area for practice, but it's also open to the public at rates of about half what you'd pay at Killington. Adult tickets are $30 on weekends, $25 midweek.

There's cross-country skiing nearby at the **Rikert Ski Touring Center** (✆ 802/388-2759), at Middlebury's Bread Loaf Campus on Route 125. The center offers 24 miles of machine-groomed trails through a lovely winter landscape. Adult ski passes are $10, while students and children pay $5. Half-day passes are also available ($6 and $3, respectively).

WHERE TO STAY

The outskirts of Middlebury are home to a handful of motels in addition to several inns. The 1960s-era **Blue Spruce Motel,** 2428 Rte. 7 South (✆ 800/640-7671 or 802/388-4091), has 22 basic rooms; families lingering in the area for a few days should inquire about room 122, a large suite with full kitchen, sleeping loft, and carport. Rates start at $75 ($125 for the suite). The **Greystone Motel,** 1395 Rte. 7 South (✆ 802/388-4935), has 10 very clean rooms with small bathrooms; rates are $75 to $95 in summer, $55 to $75 in winter.

Inn on the Green ✿✿✿   This is one of our favorites in Vermont. It's a handsome village inn occupying a house that dates back to 1803 (it was Victorianized with a mansard tower later in the century). Operating as an inn since 1997, it's both historic and comfortable, and our recommendation for those wishing to be in downtown Middlebury. The rooms are furnished with a mix of antiques and reproductions; lustrous wood floors and boldly colored walls of harvest yellow, peach, and burgundy lighten the architectural heaviness of the house. The suites are naturally the most spacious, but all units offer plenty of elbowroom. Those in the front of the house are wonderfully flooded with afternoon light.

71 South Pleasant St., Middlebury, VT 05753. ✆ 888/244-7512 or 802/388-7512. Fax 802/388-4075. www.innonthegreen.com. 11 units. $125–$225 weekends and summer; $155–$225 foliage season; $90 midweek winter. 2-night minimum stay on weekends. AE, DISC, MC, V. *In room:* A/C, TV, dataport, hair dryer, iron.

Middlebury Inn and Motel ✿   The historic Middlebury Inn traces its roots back to 1827, when Nathan Wood built a brick public house he called the Vermont Hotel. It now contains 75 modern guest rooms equipped with most conveniences. The rooms are on the large side, and most are outfitted with a sofa or upholstered chairs, colonial-reproduction furniture, and some vintage bathroom fixtures. Rooms 116 and 246 are spacious corner units entered via a dark foyer/sitting room. Room 129, while smaller, has a four-poster bed, a view of the village green, and a Jacuzzi. The 10 guest rooms in the Porterhouse Mansion next door also have a pleasant, historic feel. An adjacent motel with 20 units is decorated in an Early American motif, but it feels like veneer—underneath it's just a standard-issue motel. Stick with the main inn if you're seeking a taste of history.

14 Courthouse Sq., Middlebury, VT 05753. © 800/842-4666 or 802/388-4961. www.middleburyinn.com. 75 units. Midweek $86–$195 double; weekends $96–$215 double; $156–$355 suite. Rates include continental breakfast. AE, DC, MC, V. Pets accepted in some rooms. **Amenities:** Restaurant (traditional New England), tavern (pub fare). *In room:* A/C, TV, dataport.

Swift House Inn ★★   The Swift House Inn is a compound of three graceful historic buildings set in a residential area just a few minutes' walk from the town green. The main Federal-style inn dates back to 1814; inside, it's decorated in a simple, historical style that still has a modern crispness. Guest rooms are well appointed with antique and reproduction furnishings. Especially appealing is the Swift Room, with its oversize bathroom, whirlpool, and private terrace. About half of the rooms have fireplaces or whirlpools or both; all but two have TVs; most also have coffeemakers and hair dryers. Light sleepers may prefer the main inn or the Carriage House rather than the Gate House down the hill; the latter is on Route 7, and the truck noise can be a minor irritant at night.

25 Stewart Lane, Middlebury, VT 05753. © 802/388-9925. Fax 802/388-9927. www.swifthouseinn.com. 21 units, 1 with detached bathroom. $100–$235 double ($10 less weekdays). Rates include continental breakfast. 2-night minimum stay some weekends. AE, DISC, MC, V. **Amenities:** Restaurant (eclectic); sauna; limited room service. *In room:* A/C, TV.

WHERE TO DINE

Storm Cafe ★★ NEW AMERICAN   This tiny, casual spot tucked on the ground floor of a stone mill in Frog Hollow is a chef-owned restaurant that's popular with locals and travelers alike. The menu is beguilingly simple, but tremendous care has been taken in the selection of ingredients and the preparation of the dishes; the salads are especially good. Lunches include smoked salmon, jerk chicken, and hummus; at dinnertime, look for sirloin with portobello and oyster mushrooms, penne carbonara, and grilled shrimp.

3 Mill St. © 802/388-1063. Reservations recommended, especially on weekends. Main courses $7–$8.50 lunch, $12.95–$18.95 dinner. MC, V. Tues–Sat 11am–3pm and 5–9pm.

Woody's ★ PUB FARE/PASTA   Woody's is not Ye Olde New Englande. It's a bright and colorful multi-level restaurant overlooking the creek, made all the more appealing by its surprising location down a small, dark alley. It's the kind of fun, low-key, and hip place destined to put you in a good mood the moment you walk in. Angle for a table perched over the creek. Lunches include burgers, sandwiches, and salads, along with burritos and beer-steamed mussels. Dinner is heavy on the pasta selections (the bourbon shrimp with linguine is popular), but also features appetizing selections from the grill, like the mixed seafood grill with fettuccine, and medallions of pork with a ginger, allspice, and sage rub.

5 Bakery Lane (on Otter Creek just upstream from the bridge in the middle of town). © 802/388-4182. Reservations recommended on weekends and during college events. Lunch items $4.50–$8.50; main dinner courses $12.95–$17.95. AE, MC, V. Mon–Sat 11:30am–9:30pm; Sun 10:30am–9:30pm. Light menu only 3–5pm. Closed Tues in winter.

6 Mad River Valley ★★

The Mad River Valley is one of Vermont's better-kept secrets. This scenic valley surrounding the towns of Warren and Waitsfield has something of a Shangri-La quality to it—in places it hasn't much changed since it was first settled in 1789 by Gen. Benjamin Wait and a handful of Revolutionary War veterans, including half a dozen said to have served as Minutemen at the battles of Concord Bridge and Lexington.

Since 1948, ski-related development has competed with the early farms that were the backbone of the region. But the newcomers haven't been too pushy or overly obnoxious, at least so far. Save for a couple of telltale signs, you could drive Route 100 past the sleepy villages of Warren and Waitsfield and not realize that you've passed close to some of the choicest skiing in the state. The region hasn't fallen prey to unbridled condo or strip-mall developers, and the valley seems to have learned the lessons of haphazard development that afflicted Mount Snow and Killington to the south. Other towns could still learn a lot from Waitsfield: Note the Mad River Green, a tidy strip mall disguised as an old barn on Route 100 just north of Route 17. It's scarcely noticeable from the main road. Longtime Vermont skiers say the valley today is like Stowe used to be 25 years ago.

ESSENTIALS

GETTING THERE   Warren and Waitsfield are on Route 100 between Killington and Waterbury. The nearest interstate access is from Exit 10 (Waterbury) on I-89; drive south on Route 100 for 14 miles to Waitsfield.

VISITOR INFORMATION   The **Sugarbush Chamber of Commerce** (© **800/828-4748** or 802/469-3409; www.madrivervalley.com) is at 4601 Main St. (Route 100) in the General Wait House, next to the elementary school. It's open daily from 9am to 5pm; during slow times expect limited hours and days.

SKIING

Sugarbush ★★   Sugarbush is a fine intermediate-to-advanced resort, comprised of two ski mountains linked in 1995 by a 2-mile, 10-minute high-speed chairlift that crosses three ridges (no more irksome shuttle buses!). The addition of high-speed lifts and excellent snowmaking in the past 6 years has put the mountain on the skier's map. While the improved Sugarbush slopes have generated buzz, it has remained a low-key area with great intermediate cruising runs on the north slopes and some challenging, old-fashioned expert slopes on Castlerock. Sugarbush is a good choice if you find the sprawl of Killington overwhelming but don't want to sacrifice great skiing in the search for a quieter and more intimate resort area.

Warren, VT 05674. © **800/537-8427** for lodging, or 802/583-2381. www. sugarbush.com. Vertical drop: 2,650 ft. Lifts: 14 chairlifts (4 high-speed), 4 surface lifts. Skiable acreage: 432. Lift tickets: $55.

Mad River Glen ★★★   Mad River Glen is the curmudgeon of the Vermont ski world. Its motto is "Ski it if you can." High-speed detachable quads? Forget it. The main lift is a 1948 *single*-chair lift that creaks its way 1 mile to the summit. Snowmaking? Don't count on it. Only 15% of the terrain benefits from the fake stuff; the rest is dependent on Mother Nature. Snowboarding? Nope. It's forbidden at Mad River. Mad River's slopes are twisting and narrow and hide some of the steepest drops you'll find in New England (nearly half of the slopes are classified as expert). Mad River Glen long ago attained the status of a cult mountain among serious skiers, and its fans seem bound and determined to keep it that way. Longtime owner Betsy Pratt sold the ski area to a cooperative of about 1,000 Mad River skiers in 1995, making it the only cooperative-owned ski area in the country. The new owners seem especially proud of the mountain's funky traditions (how *about* that single chair?) and say they're determined to maintain the spirit.

Waitsfield, VT 05763. (℃ **802/496-3551.** www.madriverglen.com. Vertical drop: 2,000 ft. Lifts: 4 chairlifts. Skiable acreage: 115. Lift tickets: $29 midweek, $40 weekends, $42 holidays.

OTHER OUTDOOR PURSUITS

An unusual way to explore the region is atop an Icelandic pony. The **Vermont Icelandic Horse Farm** ⋆ ((℃ **802/496-7141;** www.icelandichorses.com) specializes in tours on these small, sturdy, strong horses. Full- and half-day rides are available daily, but to really appreciate both the countryside and the horses, you should sign up for one of the multi-day treks, which range from 1 to 5 nights and include lodging at area inns, all your meals, your mount, and a guide to lead you through the lush hills around Waitsfield and Warren. In winter, there's also **skijoring,** which can best be described as water-skiing behind a horse. Call for pricing information and reservations.

BIKING   A rewarding 14-mile **bike trip** ⋆ along paved roads begins at the village of Waitsfield. Park your car near the covered bridge, then follow East Warren Road past the Inn at Round Barn Farm and up into the hilly, farm-filled countryside. (Don't be discouraged by the unrelenting hill at the outset.) Near the village of Warren, turn right at Brook Road to connect back to Route 100. Return north on bustling but generally safe and often scenic Route 100 to Waitsfield.

   Clearwater Sports, Route 100, Waitsfield, north of the covered bridge ((℃ **802/496-2708**), offers mountain-bike rentals from a blue-and-white Victorian-era house. The staff is helpful with suggestions for other routes and tours.

HIKING   Hikers in search of good exercise and a spectacular view should strike out for **Mount Abraham** ⋆⋆, west of Warren. Drive west up Lincoln Gap Road (it leaves Route 100 just south of Warren Village) and continue until the crest, where you'll cross the intersection with the Long Trail. Park here and head north on the trail; about 2 miles along you'll hit the Battell Shelter. Push on another four-fifths of a mile up a steep ascent to reach the panoramic views atop 4,006-foot Mount Abraham. Enjoy. Retrace your steps back to your car. Allow 4 or 5 hours for the round-trip hike.

   For a less demanding adventure that still yields great views, head *south* from Lincoln Gap Road on the Long Trail. In about three-fifths of a mile, look for a short spur trail to **Sunset Rock** ⋆, with sweeping westward vistas of the farms of the Champlain Valley, along with Lake Champlain and the knobby Adirondacks beyond. A round-trip hike requires a little more than an hour.

WHERE TO STAY

While Sugarbush isn't overrun with condos and lodges, it has its share. Some 200 of the condos nearest the mountain are managed by the **Sugarbush Resort**

Finds **Stop by a Classic**

The **Warren General Store** ((℃ **802/496-3864)** anchors the former bustling timber town of Warren. Set along a tumbling stream, the store has uneven wooden floorboards, a potbellied stove, and shelf stock fully updated for the 21st century with a good selection of gourmet foods and wines. Get coffee or a sandwich at the back deli counter, and enjoy it on the deck overlooking the water. The store is located in Warren Village just off Route 100 south of the Sugarbush Access Road.

(✆ **800/537-8427** or 802/583-3333; www.sugarbush.com), with accommodations ranging from one to four bedrooms. Guests have access to a slew of amenities, including a health club and five pools. The resort also manages the attractive 46-unit Sugarbush Inn, right on the access road. Shuttle buses deliver guests to and from the mountain and other facilities. During major winter holidays, there's a minimum stay of 5 days. Rates vary widely, and most rooms are sold as packages that include lift tickets in winter.

Inn at the Mad River Barn 🎿 *Value*   This classic 1960s-style ski lodge attracts a clientele that's nearly fanatical in its devotion to the place. It's best not to come here expecting anything fancy—carpets and furniture both tend toward the threadbare. Do come expecting to have some fun once you're settled in. It's all knotty pine, with spartan guest rooms and rustic common rooms where visitors feel at home putting their feet up. Accommodations are in the two-story barn behind the white clapboard main house and in the annex building up the lawn, which is better maintained but has less character. In winter, dinners are offered ($15), served in boisterous family style. In summer, the mood is slightly more sedate, but enhanced by a beautiful pool a short walk away in a grove of birches. Most rooms have televisions.

Rte. 17 (R.R. #1; P.O. Box 88), Waitsfield, VT 05673. ✆ **800/631-0466** or 802/496-3310. Fax 802/496-6696. www.madriverbarn.com. 15 units. Summer $74–$95 double; winter $110 double. Midweek discounts available. Rates include breakfast. 2-night minimum stay holiday and winter weekends. AE, DISC, MC, V. **Amenities:** Restaurant (winter only), lounge; outdoor pool; fitness room; game room; sauna. *In room:* No phone.

Inn at Round Barn Farm 🎿🎿   This ranks among our favorite romantic B&Bs in northern New England. You arrive after passing through a covered bridge just off Route 100; a couple of miles later you come upon a regal barn and farmhouse, set on 235 sloping acres with views of fields all around. The centerpiece of the inn is the Round Barn, a strikingly beautiful 1910 structure that's used for weddings, art exhibits, and Sunday church services. Each guest room is furnished with an understated country elegance. The less expensive rooms are in the older part of the house and are comfortable, if small; the larger luxury units in the attached horse barn feature stunning soaring ceilings under old log beams and include extras like steam showers, gas fireplaces, and phones.

1661 E. Warren Rd., Waitsfield, VT 05673. ✆ **802/496-2276.** Fax 802/496-8832. www.innattheroundbarn. com. 11 units. $135–$270 double. Rates include breakfast. 3-night minimum stay and $20 surcharge during holidays and foliage season. AE, DISC, MC, V. Closed Apr 15–30. No children under 15 accepted. **Amenities:** 60-foot indoor lap pool; 18-mile cross-country ski center; game room. *In room:* No phone (except luxury rooms).

The Pitcher Inn 🎿🎿🎿   This Relais & Chateaux property is one of Vermont's finest. Set in the timeless village of Warren, the inn was newly built from the ground up following a fire that leveled a previous home; only the barn is original. But architect David Sellars created an inn that seamlessly blends modern conveniences and whimsy with classic New England styling. The common areas fuse several styles: a little Colonial Revival, a little Mission, and a little Adirondack sporting camp to cap it off. There's not a bad room in the house, and all are designed with such wit that they're more like elegant puzzles. (Our favorite feature: The carved goose in flight on the ceiling of the Mallard Room is attached to a weathervane on the roof, and it rotates to indicates wind direction.) Nine units have fireplaces (seven wood-burning, two gas), and five have steam showers.

275 Main St., Warren, VT 05674. ✆ **888/867-8424** or 802/496-6350. Fax 802/496-6354. www. pitcherinn.com. 11 units. $300–$550 double; $600 suite. Rates include breakfast. Minimum stay applies on

weekends (2 nights), holiday weekends (3 nights), and Christmas (5 nights). Children under 12 accepted in suites only. AE, MC, V. **Amenities:** Restaurant (New American/regional). *In room:* A/C, TV, dataport, hair dryer.

West Hill House ✹ This is among the more casual and relaxed inns in the valley, in part because of its remote location, and in part because of the easy camaraderie among guests. Nestled on a forested hillside along a lightly traveled country road, the inn offers the quintessential New England experience within a few minutes' commute to the slopes at Sugarbush. Built in the 1850s, this farmhouse boasts three common rooms, including a bright, modern addition with a handsome fireplace for warmth in winter and an outdoor patio for summer lounging. The guest rooms are decorated in an updated country style, and all have gas fireplaces or gas woodstoves; three have air-conditioning. The more modern units include steam showers and Jacuzzis. Generous country breakfasts are served around a large dining-room table.

1496 West Hill Rd., Warren, VT 05674. ℂ 800/898-1427 or 802/496-7162. Fax 802/496-6443. www.westhillhouse.com. 7 units. Summer, foliage, and ski season $115–$160 double; spring $100–$140 double. Rates include breakfast. 3-night minimum stay foliage and holiday weekends; 2-night minimum stay on other weekends. AE, DISC MC, V. Children 12 and over welcome. *In room:* TV/VCR, dataport.

WHERE TO DINE

Bass Restaurant ✹✹ *Value* NEW AMERICAN The Bass Restaurant is located in a multi-level former dinner theater with a circular stone fireplace and a handsome blond-wood bar. Light jazz plays in the background, and modern sculpture enlivens the space. The main courses range from crab cakes and garlic-marinated shrimp to braised lamb shank with black-eyed peas. It's a quiet and romantic spot that offers excellent value, delivering more than one would expect for the price.

527 Sugarbush Access Rd., Warren. ℂ **802/583-3100.** www.bassrestaurant.com. Main courses $11.50–$21.50. AE, MC, V. Sun–Thurs 5–10pm; Fri–Sat 5–11pm.

The Den ✹ AMERICAN Good food, decent service, no frills. That's the Den in a nutshell. A local favorite since 1970 for its well-worn, neighborly feel, it's the kind of spot where you can plop yourself down in a pine booth, help yourself to the salad bar while awaiting your main course, then cheer on the Red Sox on the tube over the bar. The menu offers the usual pub fare, including burgers, Reubens, roast-beef sandwiches, meal-size salads, and pork chops with apple sauce and french fries.

Junction of Rtes. 100 and 17, Waitsfield. ℂ **802/496-8880.** Lunch items $4.95–$6.95; dinner main courses $8.95–$13.95. AE, MC, V. Daily 11:30am–11pm.

The Spotted Cow ✹✹ FRENCH-INSPIRED NEW AMERICAN Set on the ground floor of a small, rustic retail complex in Waitsfield, the Spotted Cow is a low-ceilinged, modern, natural-wood spot with cherry banquettes and windows facing out onto a walkway. The place has the comfortably cozy feel of a bistro only locals know about, with a more cultivated than funky air. The inventive lunch menu features brie sandwiches, shiitake soup, and vegetarian pâté. At dinner, the kitchen shines with creative approaches to old favorites. Venison is always on the menu, as is fresh fish. The duck and lamb cassoulet is a good choice, as is the Bermuda fish chowder, made with a splash of black rum. A vegetarian special is always available.

Bridgestreet Marketplace (at corner of Rte. 100 and East Warren Rd.), Waitsfield. ℂ **802/496-5151.** Reservations recommended. Main courses $8.95–$10.95 lunch, $17.95–$23.95 dinner. MC, V. Tues–Sat 11:30am–3pm and 5:30–9pm; Sun 10:30am–3pm and 5:30–9pm.

7 Montpelier ★★ & Barre

Montpelier is the most down-home, low-key state capital in the United States. There's a hint of that in every photo of the glistening gold dome of the capitol. Rising up behind it isn't a bank of mirror-sided skyscrapers, but a thickly forested hill. Montpelier, it turns out, isn't a self-important center of politics, but a small town that happens to be home to state government.

The state capitol is worth a visit, as is the local historical society. But more than that, Montpelier is worth visiting if only to experience a small, clean New England town that's more than a little friendly. Montpelier centers on two main boulevards: State Street, which is lined with state government buildings, and Main Street, where many of the town's shops are located. It's all very compact, manageable, and cordial.

The downtown has two hardware stores next door to each other, well-stocked bookstores, and two movie theaters, including the **Savoy,** 26 Main St. (© **802/ 229-0509**), one of the best art movie houses in northern New England. At the Savoy, a large cup of cider and popcorn slathered with real, unclarified butter cost less than a small popcorn with flavored oil at a mall cinema.

Nearby **Barre** (pronounced "Barry") is more commercial and less charming, but shares an equally vibrant past. Barre has more of a blue-collar demeanor than Montpelier. The historic connection to the thriving granite industry is glimpsed occasionally, from the granite curbstones lining the long Main Street to the signs for commercial establishments carved out of locally hewn rock. Barre attracted talented stone workers from Scotland and Italy (there's even a statue of Robert Burns), who helped give the turn-of-the-20th-century town a lively, cosmopolitan flavor.

ESSENTIALS

GETTING THERE   Montpelier is accessible via Exit 7 off I-89. For Barre, take Exit 8. Waterbury is located at Exit 10 off I-89. For bus service to Montpelier, contact **Vermont Transit** (© **800/451-3292** or 802/223-7112).

For bus service to Waterbury, call **Vermont Transit** (© **802/244-6943**); for train service to Waterbury, contact **Amtrak** (© **800/872-7245;** www.amtrak. com), whose *Vermonter* makes daily departures from New York.

VISITOR INFORMATION   The **Central Vermont Chamber of Commerce** (© **802/229-5711;** www.central-vt.com) is located on Stewart Road off Exit 7 of I-89. Turn left at the first light; it's a half mile on the left. The chamber is open Monday through Friday from 9am to 5pm.

The **Waterbury Tourism Council** (© **802/244-7822**) operates a small, unstaffed booth stocked with helpful brochures on Route 100 just north of I-89. It's open daily from 7am to 10pm.

EXPLORING THE AREA

Start your exploration of Montpelier with a visit to the gold-domed **State House** ★ (© **802/828-2228**), guarded out front by the statue of Ethan Allen. Three capitol buildings have risen on this site since 1809; the present building retained the impressive portico designed during the height of Greek Revival style in 1836. It was modeled after the temple of Theseus in Athens, and is made of Vermont granite. Self-guided tours of the capitol are offered when the building is open, Monday through Friday (except holidays) from 7:45am to 4:15pm; in summer, it's also open Saturday from 11am to 3pm. Guided tours are run between late June and late October, Monday through Friday from 10am to

Central Vermont & the Champlain Valley

Mountain ▲
Ski area
State Park ♠
Unpaved road
Trail

Shelburne Bay
Lake Champlain
Shelburne
Shelburne Falls
Shelburne Pond
Fays Cors
Richmond
Jonesville
Bolton
Long Trail
MT. MANSFIELD STATE FOREST
Camels Hump State Park
North Duxbury

Lake Iroquois
Huntington
Mechanicville
Hinesburg
Camels Hump ▲
Huntington Center
Mt. Ethan Allen ▲

Essex
Charlotte
East Charlotte
Thompson's Point
Cedar Beach
Mt. Philo State Park
North Ferrisburg
Monkton Ridge
Rockville
Hanksville
Starksboro
Camels Hump State Park
Appalachian Gap
Waitsfield

Wadhams
Ferrisburg Station
Kingsland Bay State Park
Monkton Boro
Ferrisburg
East Monkton
HOGBACK MOUNTAINS
116
17
Fayston
Irasville

Westport
Basin Harbor
Button Bay State Park
Vergennes
Panton
22A
Winona Lake
Bristol
South Starksboro
West Lincoln
Mt. Ellen ▲
Mad R.
Warren

ADIRONDACK
New Haven
Rocky Dale
Lincoln
Mt. Abraham ▲
Lincoln Gap
Roxbury State Forest

Port Henry
D.A.R. State Park
Chimney Point State Park
Addison
New Haven Mills
Brooksville
New Haven R.
South Lincoln
100

STATE
22
Weybridge Hill
125
Middlebury
116
Mt. Roosevelt ▲
GREEN
Granville State Park
Granville

Crown Point
Bridport
West Cornwall
Cornwall
East Middlebury
Ripton
Bread Loaf Mtn. ▲
Bread Loaf
Kirby Peak ▲
Lower Granville
Middlebury Gap

PARK
22
22A
West Bridport
74
West Salisbury
Lake Dunmore
125
Hancock
BRAINTREE MTN.

Shoreham
30
Dunmore
Salisbury
Leicester
Branbury State Park
MOUNTAIN
Mt. Horrid ▲
Rochester

Larrabees Point
Shoreham Center
Whiting
Goshen
73
Long Trail
Brandon Gap
100

Fort Ticonderoga
Chipmans Point
Orwell
73
Sudbury
Forest Dale
Brandon
NATIONAL
Mt. Carmel ▲
Pittsfield

Wright
Sunset Lake
Hortonia
Chaffee Mtn. ▲
7
FOREST
Chittenden Reservoir
100

Hague
Putnam
Putnam Station
22
Benson Landing
30
Hubbardton
Florence
Holden
Pittsford
Chittenden
Sherburne Pass

Benson
Half Moon Pond State Park
Bomoseen State Park
Warrior Lakes
West Rutland State Forest
Pittsford Mills
Proctor
East Pittsford
4
Killington

Montpelier
VT

West Haven
West Castleton
Bomoseen
Castleton
Center Rutland
3
Rutland
Mendon
Calvin Coolidge State Forest

Lake George
89
7
22

488

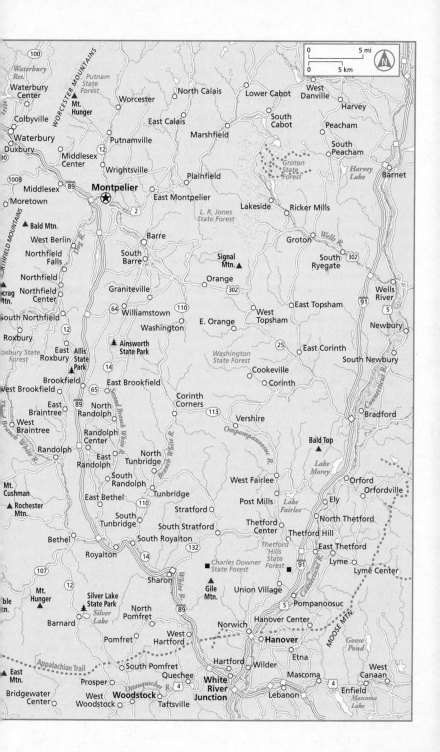

3:30pm and Saturday from 11am to 2:30pm, every half hour. The tour is informative and fun; it's worth your while if you're in the area, but probably not worth a major detour.

A short stroll from the State House is the **Vermont Historical Society** ✴, 109 State St. (© **802/828-2291**). The museum is housed in a replica of the elegant old Pavilion Building, a prominent Victorian hotel, and contains a number of artifacts, including a gun once owned by Ethan Allen. It's open Tuesday through Friday from 9am to 4:30pm, Saturday from 9am to 4pm, and Sunday from noon to 4pm. Admission is $3 for adults, $2 for students and seniors. Starting in October 2001, the museum will be closed for several months for expansion and restoration; call first.

Rock of Ages Quarry ✴✴   When in or around Barre, listen for the deep, throaty hum of industry. That's the Rock of Ages Quarry, set on a rocky hillside high above town near the aptly named hamlet of Graniteville. A free visitor center presents informative exhibits, a video about quarrying, a glimpse of an old granite quarry (no longer active), and a selection of granite gifts. Self-guided tours of the old quarry are free. For a look at the active quarry (the world's largest), sign up for a guided half-hour tour. An old bus groans up to a viewer's platform high above the 500-foot, man-made canyon, where workers cleave huge slabs of fine-grained granite and hoist them out using 150-foot derricks anchored with a spider's web of 15 miles of steel cable. It's an operation to behold.

Graniteville. © 802/476-3119. www.rockofages.com. Guided tours $4 adults, $3.50 seniors, $1.50 children 6–12. Visitor center May–Oct Mon–Sat 8:30am–5pm; Sun noon–5pm (in foliage season, Sun 8:30am–5:30pm). Guided tours given June to mid-Oct, Mon–Fri 9:15am–3pm. Closed July 4. From Barre, drive south on Rte. 14, turn left at lights by McDonald's; watch for signs to quarry.

WHERE TO STAY

Capitol Plaza Hotel ✴   This is the favored hotel of folks coming into town on business with the state government, but is also well located (across from the capitol) to serve visitors exploring the town. The small lobby has a colonial cast to it; the guest rooms on the three upper floors also adopt a light, faux-colonial tone, and more amenities than one might expect. The bottom line: It's nothing fancy, but clean, comfortable, and convenient.

100 State St., Montpelier, VT 05602. © 800/274-5252 or 802/223-5252. Fax 802/229-5427. www.capitolplaza.com. 58 units. $98 double, foliage season from $119 double; $118–$168 suite. AE, DISC, MC, V. **Amenities:** Restaurant (steakhouse). *In room:* A/C, TV, dataport, hair dryer, iron.

Inn at Montpelier ✴   Two historic in-town homes comprise the Inn at Montpelier, and both offer welcoming accommodations and an appeal for those who enjoy historic architecture. The main, cream-colored Federal-style inn, built in 1827, features a mix of historical and up-to-date furnishings, along with a sunny sitting room and deck off the rear of the second floor. (Room 27 is especially pleasant and features a large private deck.) The property is a shade more sparely furnished than other historic inns in the area (you're better off heading to Waitsfield or Warren if you're in search of the quintessential Vermont inn), but it offers comfortable lodging an easy stroll from downtown.

147 Main St., Montpelier, VT 05602. © 802/223-2727. Fax 802/223-0722. www.innatmontpelier.com. 19 units. $104–$163 double (higher during foliage season). Rates include continental breakfast. AE, DISC, MC, V. **Amenities:** Laundry; dry cleaning. *In room:* A/C, TV, dataport.

WHERE TO DINE

Main Street Grill & Bar ✴✴   AMERICAN/ECLECTIC   This modern, comfortable restaurant serves as classroom and ongoing exam for students of the

New England Culinary Institute, which is located just down the block. It's not unusual to see knots of students, toques at a rakish angle, walking between the restaurant and class. You can eat in the first-level dining room, watching street life through the broad windows, or burrow in the homey bar downstairs. Dishes change every 3 months, but might include roasted rabbit paella, pan-seared rainbow trout, or leg of venison with celery root and parsnips. One or two vegetarian dishes are always on the menu.

Also of note is the second-floor **Chef's Table,** which is also owned by the culinary institute but operates on a different schedule. (It's open Monday through Friday for lunch and dinner, and Saturday for dinner only.) This intimate and well-appointed dining room offers more refined fare, like a smoked pork chop with apple-fennel salad, and grilled yellowfin tuna with an olive-caper sauce.

118 Main St., Montpelier. ℂ 802/223-3188. Limited reservations accepted. Lunch items $5.75–$7.95; dinner entrees $11.25–$15.75. AE, DISC, MC, V. Mon–Sat 11:30am–2pm and 5:30–9pm; Sun 10am–2pm and 5:30–9pm.

8 Stowe

Stowe is a wonderful destination, summer, fall, and winter. It was one of Vermont's first winter destination areas, but it has managed the decades-long juggernaut of growth well and with good humor. There are condo developments and strip mall–style restaurants, to be sure. Stowe has more depth and breadth of lodging and restaurants than that offered by comparably sized ski towns—this small town with a year-round population of just 3,400 boasts some 62 lodging establishments and more than 50 restaurants. Still, the village has managed to preserve its essential character nicely, including trademark views of the surrounding mountains and vistas across the fertile farmlands of the valley floor. Thanks to its history and charm, Stowe tends to attract a more affluent clientele than, say, Killington or Okemo.

Stowe is quaint, compact, and home to what may be Vermont's most gracefully tapered church spire, located atop the Stowe Community Church. Because the mountain is a few miles from the village, the town doesn't suffer that woebegone emptiness that many ski villages do come summer. You can actually park your car and enjoyably explore on foot by or bike, which isn't the case at ski resorts that have developed around large parking lots and condo clusters.

Most of the growth in recent decades has taken place along Mountain Road (Route 108), which runs northwest of the village to the base of Mount Mansfield and the Stowe ski area. Here you'll find an array of motels, restaurants, shops, bars, and even a three-screen cinema, with many establishments nicely designed or at least tastefully tucked out of view. The road has all the convenience of a strip-mall area, but with little of the aesthetic blight.

The chief complaint about Mountain Road: traffic. It invariably backs up at the end of the ski day in winter and on foliage weekends, and can make a trip into the village an interesting experiment in blood-pressure management. Fortunately, a free trolley-bus connects the village with the mountain during ski season, so you can let your car get snowed in, and prevent outbreaks of village traffic from getting under your skin.

ESSENTIALS
GETTING THERE   Stowe is located on Route 100 north of Waterbury and south of Morrisville. In summer, Stowe may also be reached via Smugglers Notch on Route 108. This pass, which squeezes narrowly between rocks and is not recommended for RVs or trailers, is closed in winter.

The Saga of Ben & Jerry

The picture of the doleful cows standing amid a bright green meadow that adorns pints of Ben & Jerry's ice cream have almost become a symbol for Vermont. But Ben & Jerry's cows—actually, they're Vermont artist Woody Jackson's cows—have for many become a symbol for friendly capitalism ("hippie capitalism," as some prefer).

The founding of the company is a legend in business circles. Two friends from Long Island, Ben Cohen and Jerry Greenfield, started up their company in Burlington in 1978 with $12,000 and a few mail-order lessons in ice-cream making. The pair experimented with the flavor samples they obtained free from salesmen and sold their products out of an old downtown gas station. Embracing the outlook that work should be fun, they gave away free ice cream at community events, staged free outdoor films in summer, and plowed profits back into the community. Their free-spirited approach, along with the exceptional quality of their product, built a successful corporation with sales rising into the hundreds of millions of dollars.

Still, competition from other gourmet ice-cream makers and a widespread consumer desire to cut back fat consumption made it tougher to have fun and turn a profit at the same time. In April 2000, Ben & Jerry's was bought by Unilever, the British-Dutch company that owns Breyer's ice-cream brands and Good Humor bars, for $326 million. How long the company's heart will remain in Vermont and New England, no one really knows. The hope is that the firm has too much invested in the region to simply walk away.

The main factory in Waterbury, about 10 miles south of Stowe, is among the more popular tourist attractions in Vermont. The plant is located about a mile north of I-89 on Route 100. In peak summer season, crowds mill about waiting for the 30-minute factory tours. Tours are first-come, first-served, and start at 10am; afternoon tours fill up quickly, so arrive early if you want to avoid a long wait. Once you've got your ticket, browse the small ice-cream museum (learn the long, strange history of Cherry Garcia), buy a cone at the scoop shop, or lounge along the promenade, which is scattered with Adirondack chairs and picnic tables. Tours are $2 for adults, $1.75 for seniors, and free for children under 12. (No ice cream is produced on Sundays.)

For kids, there's the "Stairway to Heaven," which leads to a playground, and a "Cow-Viewing Area," which is pretty much self-explanatory. The tours are informative and fun, and conclude with a sample of the day's featured product. For more information, call ✆ **802/244-8687.**

There is no direct train or bus service to Stowe. Travel to Waterbury, 10 miles south of Stowe, via **Vermont Transit** (✆ **800/451-3292** or 802-244-6943) or **Amtrak** (✆ **800/872-7245**), then connect to Stowe via a rental car from **Thrifty** (✆ **802/244-8800**), **Richard's Limousine Service** (✆ **800/698-3176** or 802-253-5600), or a taxi from **Peg's Pick Up** (✆ **800/370-9490** or 802/253-9490).

VISITOR INFORMATION   The **Stowe Area Association** (✆ 877/ 467-8693** or 802/253-7321; www.stoweinfo.com) maintains a handy office on Main Street in the village center. It's open Monday through Friday from 9am to 8pm, Saturday and Sunday from 10am to 5pm (limited hours during slower seasons).

The **Green Mountain Club** (✆ 802/244-7037), a venerable statewide association devoted to building and maintaining backcountry trails, has a visitor center on Route 100 between Waterbury and Stowe.

SPECIAL EVENTS   The weeklong **Stowe Winter Carnival** (✆ 802/ 253-7321) takes place annually at the end of January, as it has since 1921. The fest features a number of wacky events involving skis, snowshoes, and skates, as well as nighttime entertainment in area venues. Don't miss the snow sculpture contest or "turkey bowling," which involves sliding frozen birds across the ice.

ALPINE SKIING

Stowe Mountain Resort ★★★   Stowe was one of the first, one of the classiest, and one of the most noted ski resorts in the world when it opened in the 1930s. Its regional dominance has eroded somewhat in the intervening decades—Killington, Sunday River, and Sugarloaf, among others, have all captured large shares of the New England market. But this historic resort, first developed in the 1930s, still has loads of charm and plenty of excellent runs. It's one of the best places for the full New England ski experience, it's one of the most beautiful ski mountains, and it offers tremendous challenges to advanced skiers with winding, old-style trails. Especially notable are its legendary "Front Four" trails (National, Starr, Lift Line, and Goat) that have humbled more than a handful of skiers attempting to grope their way from advanced intermediate to expert. The mountain has four good, long lifts that go from bottom to top—not the usual patchwork of shorter lifts you find at other ski areas. Beginning skiers can start out across the road at Spruce Peak, which features gentle, wide trails.

Stowe, VT 05672. ✆ 800/253-4754 for lodging, or 802/253-3000. www.stowe.com. Vertical drop: 2,360 ft. Lifts: 1 gondola, 8 chairlifts (1 high-speed), 2 surface lifts. Skiable acreage: 480. Lift tickets: $58 holidays, $56 nonholidays.

CROSS-COUNTRY SKIING

Stowe is an outstanding destination for cross-country skiers, offering no fewer than four groomed ski areas with a combined total of more than 100 miles of trails traversing everything from gentle valley floors to challenging mountain peaks. Note that a single trail pass purchased at any of the four areas listed below is good at all the others, but your car must be parked where you buy your ticket.

The **Trapp Family Lodge Cross-Country Ski Center,** on Luce Hill Road, 2 miles from Mountain Road (✆ 800/826-7000 or 802/253-8511; www. trappfamily.com), was the nation's first cross-country ski center. It remains one of the most gloriously situated in the Northeast, set atop a ridge with views across the broad valley and into the folds of the mountains flanking Mount Mansfield. The center features 27 miles of groomed trails (plus 60 miles of backcountry trails) on its 2,700 acres of rolling forestland. Rates are $14 for a trail pass, $16 for equipment rental, and $14 for a group lesson. A package of all three is $35.

The **Edson Hill Manor Ski Touring Center** (✆ 800/621-0284 or 802/ 253-8954) has 33 miles of wooded trails just off Mountain Road ($10 for a day pass). Also offering appealing ski touring are the **Stowe Mountain Resort**

Cross-Country Touring Center (© 800/253-4754 or 802/253-7311), with 48 miles at the base of Mount Mansfield ($11), and Topnotch Resort (© 800/451-8686 or 802/253-8585), with 24 miles of groomed trails in the forest flanking Mountain Road ($12).

SUMMER OUTDOOR PURSUITS

Stowe's history is linked to winter recreation, but it's also an outstanding fair-weather destination, surrounded by lush, rolling green hills and open farmlands and towered over by craggy Mount Mansfield, at 4,393 feet Vermont's highest peak.

Deciding how to get atop Mount Mansfield is half the challenge. The toll road ☆ (© 802/253-7311) traces its lineage back to the 19th century, when it served horse-drawn vehicles bringing passengers to the old hotel sited near the mountain's crown. (The hotel was demolished in the 1960s.) Drivers now twist their way up this road and park below the summit of Mansfield; a 2-hour hike along well-marked trails will bring you to the top for unforgettable views. The toll road is open from late May to mid-October. The fare is $12 per car with up to six passengers, $2 per additional person. Ascending on foot or by bicycle is free.

Another option is the Stowe gondola ☆ (© 802/253-7311), which whisks visitors to within 1½ miles of the summit at the Cliff House Restaurant. Hikers can explore the rugged, open ridgeline, then descend before twilight. The gondola runs from mid-June to mid-October and costs $10 round-trip for adults, $6 for children 6 to 12.

The budget route up Mount Mansfield (and in our mind the most reward-ing) is on foot, and you have at least nine choices for an ascent. The easiest but least pleasing route is up the toll road. Other options require local guidance and a good map. Ask for information from knowledgeable locals (your inn might be of help), or stop by the Green Mountain Club headquarters, on Route 100 about 4 miles south of Stowe; open Monday through Friday. GMC can also assist with advice on other area trails.

One of the most understated local attractions is the Stowe Recreation Path ☆☆, which winds 5³⁄₁₀ miles from behind the Stowe Community Church up the valley toward the mountain, ending behind the Topnotch Tennis Center. This exceptionally appealing pathway, completed in 1989, is heavily used by locals for transportation and exercise in summer; in winter, it serves as a cross-country ski trail. Connect to the pathway at either end or at points where it crosses side roads that lead to Mountain Road. No motorized vehicles or skateboards are allowed.

All manner of recreational paraphernalia is available for rent at the Mountain Sports & Bike Shop (© 802/253-7919), which is right on the Rec Path. This includes full-suspension demo bikes, baby joggers, and bike trailers. Basic bike rentals are $16 for 4 hours, which is plenty long enough to explore the path. The shop is on Mountain Road (across from the Golden Eagle Resort) and is open from 9am to 6pm daily in summer. (This is also a good spot for cross-country ski and snowshoe rentals in winter.)

Fans of paddle sports should seek out Umiak Outdoor Outfitters, 849 South Main St., in Stowe (© 802/253-2317). The folks here feature a whole slew of guided river trips (flatwater or light rapids) and instruction (learn how to roll that kayak!), which range from 1 hour to 3 days ($20 to $225). Also available are canoe, kayak, and raft rentals ($25 to $35 per day).

WHERE TO STAY

Stowe has a number of basic motels to serve travelers who don't require elaborate amenities. The **Sun and Ski Motor Inn,** 1613 Mountain Rd. (🕿 **800/448-5223** or 802/253-7159), has 26 utilitarian units, all with air-conditioning, phones, TVs, and small fridges. The heated pool is perfect for thawing out after a cold day of skiing. Rates are $67 to $142 double.

Edson Hill Manor ★★   The Edson Hill Manor sits atop a long, quiet drive 2 miles from Mountain Road and has an ineffably quirky charm. The main lodge dates to the 1940s; the four carriage houses just up the hill are of newer vintage. The whole compound is set amid a rolling landscape of lawns, hemlocks, and maples. The comfortable common room in the main house is like a movie set for a country retreat—tapestries, pastels, and oils adorn the walls. Most of the nine guest rooms in the main lodge have pine walls and floors, wood-burning fireplaces, colonial maple furnishings, wingback chairs, and four-poster beds. The 16 carriage house rooms are somewhat larger, but lack the cozy charm of the main inn and feel more like motel units (note that we mean *really* nice motel units). Some units have TVs; manor rooms are air-conditioned.

1500 Edson Hill Rd., Stowe, VT 05672. 🕿 **800/621-0284** or 802/253-7371. www.stowevt.com. 25 units. High season $199–$259 double (including breakfast and dinner); regular season $119–$179 double (including breakfast); off-season (Apr–May and Nov) $75 double midweek, $95 weekend. AE, DISC, MC, V. Pets and young children welcome in carriage house units only. **Amenities:** Restaurant (New American); pool nearby (not on the grounds); riding stables (private lessons available)

Green Mountain Inn ★★★   This handsome historic structure sits right in the village, and it's the best choice for those seeking a sense of New England history along with a bit of pampering. It's a sprawling hostelry with 100 guest rooms spread among several buildings old and new, but it feels far more intimate, with accommodations tastefully decorated in an early-19th-century motif that befits the 1833 vintage of the main inn. More than a dozen units feature Jacuzzis and/or gas fireplaces, and the Mill House has rooms with CD players, sofas, and Jacuzzis that open into the bedroom from behind folding wooden doors. Fall 2000 saw the opening of the luxe Mansfield House, with double Jacuzzis, marble bathrooms, and 36-inch TVs with DVD players. The most expensive rooms are uniformly superb; some of the lower-priced rooms in the main inn feature minor irritants, like balky radiators or views of noisy kitchen ventilators.

Main St. (P.O. Box 60), Stowe, VT 05672. 🕿 **800/253-7302** or 802/253-7301. Fax 802/253-5096. www.greenmountaininn.com. 100 units. $129–$299 double; $299–$409 suite. Discounts available midweek, and in spring and late fall. Ask about packages. 2-night minimum stay summer/winter weekends and in foliage season. AE, DISC, MC, V. Pets allowed in some rooms; ask first. **Amenities:** Restaurant (creative pub fare); heated outdoor pool; well-equipped fitness room; Jacuzzi; sauna; steam room; game room; limited room service in-room massage. *In room:* A/C, TV.

Stowe Motel   This is one of Stowe's best choices for those traveling on a budget. The motel has 60 units spread among three buildings; rooms are basic, but slightly larger than average and a touch more stylish and comfortable with pine furniture, couches, and coffee tables. Efficiency units have two-burner stoves.

2043 Mountain Rd., Stowe, VT 05672. 🕿 **800/829-7629** or 802/253-7629. Fax 802/253-9971 www.stowemotel.com. 30 units. Standard rooms $78–$89 double (winter holidays from $122, foliage from $94); efficiency units $89–$126. Ask about ski packages. Pets accepted in some rooms ($10). **Amenities:** Heated pool (summer only); Jacuzzi; game room; free use of snowshoes. *In room:* A/C, TV, dataport, small fridge.

Topnotch ★★★ A boxy, uninteresting exterior hides a creatively designed interior at this upscale resort and spa. The main lobby is ski-lodge modern, with lots of stone and wood and a huge moose head hanging on the wall. The guest rooms are attractively appointed, most in country pine; renovations completed in 1999 made the accommodations brighter and more cheerful. Ten units have wood-burning fireplaces; 18 have Jacuzzis; and third-floor rooms have cathedral ceilings. The main attractions here are the resort's spa and activities, which range from horseback riding in summer to cross-country skiing and indoor tennis in winter. There are nice touches throughout, like fireplaces in the spa's locker rooms.

4000 Mountain Rd. (P.O. Box 1458), Stowe, VT 05672. © **800/451-8686** or 802/253-8585. Fax 802/253-9263. www.topnotch-resort.com. 92 units. Ski season and midsummer $220–$310 double, $355–$710 suite; off-season $160–$230 double, $280–$550 suite. Higher rates and 6-night minimum stay Christmas week. Town-home accommodations $185–$715 depending on season and size. AE, DC, DISC, MC, V. Pets allowed. **Amenities:** 2 restaurants (continental, family fare); indoor pool; outdoor pool; tennis courts (4 indoor, 10 outdoor); fitness room; full spa; Jacuzzi; sauna; concierge; limited room service; horseback riding. *In room:* A/C, TV, fridge, coffeemaker, hair dryer, iron, safe.

Trapp Family Lodge The Trapp family of *Sound of Music* fame bought this sprawling farm high up in Stowe in 1942, just 4 years after fleeing the Nazi takeover of Austria. The descendants of Maria and Baron von Trapp continue to run this Tyrolean-flavored lodge on 2,700 mountainside acres. It's a comfortable resort hotel, though designed more for efficiency than elegance. The guest rooms are a shade or two better than run-of-the-mill hotel rooms, and most come complete with fine valley views and private balconies. In summer 2000, another 23 modern rooms and suites were added, all with Austrian accents. The restaurant offers well-prepared continental fare (Wiener schnitzel, lamb tenderloin); Sunday concerts are held in the meadow in summer.

700 Trapp Hill Rd., Stowe, VT 05672. © **800/826-7000** or 802/253-8511. Fax 802/253-5740. www.trappfamily.com. 116 units. Winter $140–$235 double ($344–$384 during school vacation, includes meals); summer $98–$235 double. 5-night minimum stay Christmas week; 3-night minimum stay Presidents' week and foliage season. AE, DC, MC, V. Depart Stowe westward on Rte. 108; in 2 miles bear left at fork near white church; continue up hill following signs for lodge. **Amenities:** 2 restaurants (continental, informal Austrian); heated indoor pool; 2 outdoor pools (1 for adults only); 4 clay tennis courts; fitness center; sauna; children's programs; game room; limited room service; in-room massage; baby-sitting; coin-op laundry; dry cleaning. *In room:* TV.

WHERE TO DINE

Blue Moon Cafe ★★★ NEW AMERICAN The delectable crusty bread on the table, Frank Sinatra crooning in the background, and vibrant local art on the walls offer clues that this isn't your typical ski-area pub-fare restaurant. Located a short stroll off Stowe's main street in a contemporary setting in an older home, the Blue Moon serves up the village's finest dining. The menu changes every Friday, but count on lamb, beef, and veggie dishes, plus a couple of seafood offerings. Chef Jack Pickett has superb instincts for spicing and creates inventive dishes like sirloin strip steak with caramelized onions and blue cheese or grilled sea scallops with gumbo sauce. Desserts are simple yet pure delights: profiteroles with espresso ice cream, Belgian chocolate pot, three sorbets with cookies.

35 School St. © 802/253-7006. Reservations recommended. Main courses $16–$24. AE, DISC, MC, V. Daily 6–9:30pm. Usually open weekends only in shoulder seasons; call first.

Miguel's Stowe-Away ★ MEXICAN/SOUTHWEST Located in an old farmhouse midway between the village and the mountain, Miguel's packs in folks looking for the tangiest Mexican and Tex-Mex food in the valley. Start off with a margarita or Vermont beer, then try appetizers like the empanadas or mussels Mexicana. Follow up with sizzling fajitas or one of the filling combo plates. Desserts range from the complicated (apple-mango compote with cinnamon tortilla and ice cream) to the simple (chocolate-chip cookies). Miguel's has grown popular enough to offer its own brand of chips, salsa, and other products, which turn up in specialty shops and grocery stores throughout the Northeast. Expect a loud and boisterous atmosphere on busy nights.

Mountain Rd. ⓒ **800/254-1240** or 802/253-7574. www.miguels.com. Reservations recommended on weekends and in peak ski season. Main courses $8.95–$17.95 (mostly under $14). AE, DISC, MC, V. Daily 5–10pm (from 5:30pm in summer).

Mr. Pickwick's ⭐ BRITISH PUB FARE   Mr. Pickwick's is a pub and restaurant that's part of Ye Old English Inne. It could justly be accused of being a theme-park restaurant, with the theme being, well, ye olde Englande. But it's been run since 1983 with such creative gusto by British expats Chris and Lyn Francis that it's hard not to enjoy yourself here. You can start by admiring the Anglo gewgaws while relaxing at handsome wood tables at the booths (dubbed "pews"). Sample from the 150 beers (many British) before ordering house specialties like bangers and mash (sausages and potatoes), fish-and-chips, and beef Wellington.

433 Mountain Rd. ⓒ **802/253-7558.** Reservations accepted for parties of six or more. Main courses $6.95–$12.95 lunch, $11.95–$22.95 dinner. AE, MC, V. Daily 11am–1am.

9 Burlington

Burlington is a vibrant college town—home to the University of Vermont, known as UVM—that's continually, valiantly resisting the onset of middle age. It's the birthplace of hippies-turned-corporation Ben & Jerry's. (Look for the sidewalk plaque at the corner of St. Paul and College streets commemorating the first store, which opened in 1978.) It elected a socialist mayor in 1981, Bernie Sanders, who's now Vermont's lone representative to the U.S. Congress. Burlington is also home to the eclectic rock band Phish, which for a while was heir to the Grateful Dead hippie-rock tradition.

It's no wonder that Burlington has become a magnet for those seeking alternatives to big-city life with its big-city problems. Burlington has a superb location overlooking Lake Champlain and the Adirondacks of northern New York. To the east, visible on your way out of town, the Green Mountains rise dramatically, with two of the highest points (Mount Mansfield and Camel's Hump) stretching above the undulating ridge.

In the mid–20th century, Burlington turned its back for a time on its spectacular waterfront. Urban redevelopment focused on parking garages and high-rises; the waterfront lay fallow, and was developed for light industry. In recent years, the city has sought to regain a toehold along the lake, acquiring and redeveloping parts for commercial and recreational use. It's been successful in some sections (especially the bike path, discussed below), less so in others.

In contrast, the downtown section is thriving. The pedestrian mall (Church Street), a creation that has failed in so many other towns, works here. New construction has brought large-scale department stores (Filene's, for one) right smack downtown, reversing the flight to the mall that has plagued so many other small cities. The city's scale is pleasantly skewed toward pedestrians—it's best to park your car and walk as soon as you can.

ESSENTIALS

GETTING THERE   Burlington is at the junction of I-89, Route 7, and Route 2. **Burlington International Airport,** about 3 miles east of downtown, is served by **Continental Express** (✆ **800/732-6887**), **Delta** (✆ **800/221-1212**), **Jet Blue** (✆ **800/538-2583**), **United** (✆ **800/241-6522**), and **US Airways** (✆ **800/428-4322**).

The **Amtrak** (✆ **800/872-7245**) *Vermonter* offers daily departures for Burlington from Washington, Baltimore, Philadelphia, New York, New Haven, and Springfield, Mass.

Vermont Transit Lines (✆ **802/864-6811**), with a depot at 345 Pine St., offers bus connections from Albany, Boston, Hartford, New York's JFK Airport, and other points in Vermont, Massachusetts, and New Hampshire.

VISITOR INFORMATION   The **Lake Champlain Regional Chamber of Commerce,** 60 Main St. (✆ **802/863-3489;** www.vermont.org), maintains an information center in a stout 1929 brick building just up from the waterfront and a short walk from Church Street Market. Hours are Monday through Friday from 8:30am to 5pm. On weekends, helpful maps and brochures are left in the entryway for visitors. A summer-only information booth is also staffed on the Church Street Marketplace at the corner of Church and Bank streets (no phone).

Burlington's free weeklies keep residents and visitors informed of local events and happenings. (To confuse matters somewhat, the *Free Press*—the local daily—is the one paper that costs money.) *Seven Days* carries topical and lifestyle articles along with listings. The *Vermont Times* emphasizes local politics. Look for them at downtown stores and restaurants.

EXPLORING BURLINGTON

Shelburne Museum ✫✫✫   Established in 1947 by Americana collector Electra Havenmeyer Webb, the museum contains one of the nation's most singular collections of American decorative, folk, and fine art, occupying some 37 buildings spread over 45 rolling acres 7 miles south of Burlington. The more mundane exhibits include quilts, early tools, decoys, and weather vanes. But the museum also collects and displays *whole* buildings from around New England and New York. These include an 1890 railroad station, a lighthouse, a stagecoach inn, an Adirondack lodge, and a round barn from Vermont. There's even a 220-foot steamship, eerily landlocked on the museum's grounds.

Rte. 7 (P.O. Box 10), Shelburne. ✆ 802/985-3346. www.shelburnemuseum.org. Summer admission (good for 2 consecutive days) $17.50 adults, $10.50 students with ID, $7 children 6–14; winter tours $8.75 adults, $3.50 children. Late May to mid-Oct daily 10am–5pm. Selected buildings only open Apr to late May and mid-Oct to Dec 31; call for information.

Ethan Allen Homestead ✫   A quiet retreat on one of the most idyllic, least developed stretches of the Winooski River, the Ethan Allen Homestead is a shrine to Vermont's favorite son. While Allen wasn't born in Burlington, he settled here later in life on property confiscated from a British sympathizer during the Revolution. The reconstructed farmhouse is an enduring tribute to this Vermont hero; an orientation center offers an intriguing multimedia accounting of Allen's life and other points of regional history. The house is open for tours from mid-October to mid-May by appointment only (a day's notice is required). The grounds are open year-round daily from dawn to dusk. Admission to the park is free.

Burlington

Rte. 127 Beltline
North Ave.
Park St.
N. Champlain St.
North St.
N. Winooski Ave.
N. Union St.
N. Prospect St.
Mansfield Ave.
Riverside Ave.
Winooski River
East Allen St.
Mill St.
Colchester Ave.
Grove St.

■ Ethan Allen Homestead

Pearl St.
Cherry St.
Battery St.
Church St.
S. Winooski Ave.
College St
Main St.
Maple St.
See inset map

University of Vermont ■
University Pl.
East Ave.

BURLINGTON

St. Paul St.
S. Union St.
S. Willard St.
S. Prospect St.
Pine St.
Howard St.
Ledge Rd.

Lake Champlain

Spear St.

89

Patchen Rd.

SOUTH BURLINGTON

Burlington Int'l Airport ✈
Williston Rd.
Hinesburg Rd.
Dorset St.

89

Kennedy Dr.

ACCOMMODATIONS ■
Basin Harbor Club **10**
The Inn at Shelburne Farms **11**
Lang House **7**
Radisson Hotel Burlington **2**
Willard Street Inn **8**

DINING ◆
Al's **9**
Bove's **1**
Daily Planet **5**
Five Spice Cafe **6**
Leunig's Bistro **4**
Penny Cluse Cafe **3**

189

Queen City Park Rd.
Swift St.
7

Burlington ○
★ Montpelier
VT

SOUTH BURLINGTON

0 ___ 1/4 mi
0 ___ 400 m

N

Allen Rd.

Shelburne Museum **10 11**
↓ ↓

Lake St.
Pearl St.
Cathedral Square
Cherry St.
Burlington Square
Bank St.
Burlington Bike Path
Battery St.
College St.
S. Champlain St.
Saint Paul St.
Marketplace
Center St.
Church St.
S. Winooski Ave.
Main St.
Pine St.
King St.
Maple St.

Spirit of Ethan Allen II ■

Ferry Dock

499

Ethan Allen: Patriot & Libertine

In 1749, the governor of New Hampshire began giving away land to settlers willing to brave the howling wilderness of what is now Vermont. Two decades later, the New York State courts decreed those grants void, which opened the door for New York speculators to flood into the region vowing to push the original settlers out of the valleys and up into the Green Mountains.

Not surprisingly, this didn't sit well with those already there. They established a network of military units called the Green Mountain Boys, who promised to drive out the New Yorkers. A hale fellow named Ethan Allen headed up new militia, which launched a series of effective harrying raids against the impudent New Yorkers. Green Mountain Boys destroyed their homes, drove away their livestock, and chased the New York sheriffs back across the border.

The American Revolution soon intervened, and Ethan Allen and the Green Mountain Boys took up the revolutionary cause with vigor. They helped sack Fort Ticonderoga in New York in 1775, rallied to the cause at the famed Battle of Bennington, and continued to make splendid nuisances of themselves to the British effort throughout the war.

Allen's fame grew as word spread about him and his Green Mountain Boys. A hard-drinking, fierce-fighting, large-living sort of guy, Allen became a legend in his own time. He could bite the head off a nail, one story claimed; another said that he was once bit by a rattlesnake, which promptly belched and died.

While Allen's apocryphal exploits lived on following his death in 1789, he also left a more significant legacy. Vermont's statehood in 1791 was due in large part to the independence and patriotism the region showed under Allen. And today you can't drive very far in Vermont without a reminder of Allen's historic presence—parks are named after him, inns boast that he once slept there, and you'll still hear the occasional story about his bawdy doings.

Rte. 127. ✆ **802/865-4556.** Admission $5 adults, $4 seniors, $2.50 children 5–17; $14 per family. Mid-May to mid-June daily 1–5pm. Mid-June to mid-Oct Mon–Sat 10am–5pm; Sun 1–5pm. Take Rte. 127 northward from downtown; look for signs.

Lake Champlain Ferries ★★   Car ferries chug across the often placid, sometimes turbulent waters of Lake Champlain from Burlington to New York State between late spring and foliage season. It's a good way to cut out miles of driving if you're heading west toward the Adirondacks. It's also a great way to see the lake and the mountains on a pleasant, inexpensive cruise. Between June and mid-October a 90-minute narrated lake cruise is also offered; the cost is $7.75 for adults and $3.75 for children. No reservations are accepted; travelers are advised to arrive 20 to 30 minutes in advance of departure.

Ferries also cross Lake Champlain between Grande Isle, Vermont, and Plattsburgh, New York (year-round), and Charlotte, Vermont, and Essex, New York (April to early January). Call the following number for more information.

King St. Dock. ✆ **802/864-9804.** www.ferries.com. $12.75 one-way fare for car and driver from Burlington to Port Kent; $6.50 round-trip for adult passengers; $2.50 children 6–12; free for children under 6. Burlington ferry operates mid-May to mid-Oct. Frequent departures in summer between 7:45am and 7:30pm. Schedule varies in spring, fall, and foliage season; call or check the website for current departure times.

The Spirit of Ethan Allen II ⭐ Accommodating 500 passengers on three decks, the sleek ship offers a more genteel alternative to the ferry. The vistas of Lake Champlain and the Adirondacks haven't changed much since Samuel de Champlain, who first reached here in 1609, explored the area. Food is available on all cruises, including all-you-can-eat buffets at dinner and Sunday brunch. The scenic cruise departs daily every other hour beginning at 10am through 4pm. Parking is available at a small additional cost.

Burlington Boathouse. ✆ **802/862-8300.** Narrated cruises (1½ hours) $8.75 adults, $3.95 children 3–11. Sunset cruises (2½ hours) $9.50 adults, $4.95 children. Specialty cruises (dinner, brunch, mystery theater) priced higher; call for details. Daily late May to mid-Oct.

SHOPPING

The **Church Street Marketplace** is one of the more notable success stories of downtown development. Situated along 4 blocks that extend southward from the austerely elegant 1816 Congregational church, the marketplace buzzes with the sort of downtown energy that makes urban planners everywhere envious. While national chains have discovered this marketplace (Banana Republic, Borders, Pier 1, Urban Outfitters), it still makes room for used-book stores and funky, homegrown shops. In summer, leave time to be entertained by drummers, pan-flutists, buskers, sidewalk vendors, and knots of young folks just hanging out.

OUTDOOR PURSUITS

Burlington is blessed with numerous attractive city parks. Most popular is **Leddy Park** (✆ **802/864-0123**), on North Avenue, with an 1,800-foot beach, tennis courts, ball fields, walking trails, and a handsome indoor skating rink. **North Beach** (✆ **802/862-0942**) also features a long sandy beach, plus a campground for those looking to pitch a tent or park an RV.

On the downtown waterfront, look for the **Burlington Community Boathouse** (✆ **802/865-3377**), a modern structure built with Victorian flair. A lot of summer action takes place at this city-owned structure and along the 900-foot boardwalk. You can rent a sailboat or rowboat, sign up for kayak or sculling lessons, or just wander around and enjoy the sunset.

One of Burlington's hidden but beguiling attractions is the **Burlington Bike Path,** which runs 9 miles on an old rail bed along the picturesque shores of Lake Champlain to the mouth of the Winooski River. It's an easy and quiet trip, passing through parks, past backyards, and along sandy beaches. You can pick it up near the Community Boathouse and head north toward the Winooski River. It's worth packing a picnic lunch and exploring for a few hours on a sunny afternoon.

More exciting still, this is just one segment of an ambitious project to create a 350-mile bikeway around Lake Champlain. Several key links were recently made in the Burlington area, first in fall 2000 when a bike ferry was (briefly) established across the Winooski River.

From the north shore of the Winooski, you can peddle northward, picking up the Causeway Park trail, which is (no surprise) a causeway that lets you seemingly skim across the lake's surface by bike. Also in 2000, a ferry was established (also briefly) across the Colchester Cut, a boater's break in the causeway that prevented bikers from making through-trips. (Burlington Bikeways, a local nonprofit, operated both ferries.) While the ferries were experimental projects, biking advocates hope that these will soon be permanent features for summer bikers. Ask at the Burlington visitor center for the current ferry status, or contact Burlington Parks and Recreation at © **802/864-0123.**

Bike rentals are available downtown at the **Skirack,** 85 Main St. (© **802/ 658-3313**), for $14 to $16 for 4 hours (enough time to do the whole trail), and up to $22 for a whole day. Skirack also rents in-line skates ($10 for 4 hours), which are commonly used on the bike path as well. **North Star Cyclery,** 100 Main St. (© **802/863-3832**), rents bicycles at comparable rates.

WHERE TO STAY

Burlington has benefited from a recent upsurge of chain motels sprouting along Route 7 (Shelburne Road) south of the city. They're a 5- to 10-minute drive from downtown. While they lack any trace of New England charm, they're modern, clean, and reliable.

Among the better choices are these three, which are clustered together: **Holiday Inn Express,** 1712 Shelburne Rd. (© **800/874-1554** or 802/860-1112); **Smart Suites,** 1700 Shelburne Rd. (© **877/862-6800**); and **Howard Johnson,** 1720 Shelburne Rd. (© **800/874-1554** or 802/860-6000).

On and around Route 2 near I-89 (west of downtown, near the airport) are several other chain hotels, including the **Holiday Inn,** 1068 Williston Rd. (© **802/863-6363**); and **Best Western Windjammer Inn,** 1076 Williston Rd. (© **800/371-1125** or 802/863-1125). Our choice for a low-end overnight is the clean, simple **Swiss Host Motel and Village,** 1272 Williston Rd. (© **802/ 862-5734**), which has the excellent good fortune of being across from Al's French Frys.

Basin Harbor Club ⊛⊛⊛   Situated on 700 rolling lakeside acres 30 miles south of Burlington, the Basin Harbor Club offers a detour into a much slower-paced era. Established in 1886, this is the kind of resort where you can spend a week and not get bored—at least if you're a self-starter and don't need a perky recreational director to plan your day. The property also features historic gardens, including the largest collection of annuals in Vermont. Best of all are the trademark Adirondack chairs, which are scattered all over the property and invite the most exquisite indolence (bring books!). Thirty-eight rooms are located in the main lodge. We prefer the rustic cottages, which are tucked along the shore and in shady groves of trees. Nothing's too fancy, yet nothing's too shabby; it's all comfortable in a New England old-money kind of way. (The occasional cobweb and battered Venetian blind seem to add to the charm.) Most rooms have air-conditioning; none have televisions.

Basin Harbor Rd., Vergennes, VT 05491. © **800/622-4000** or 802/475-2311. Fax 802/475-6545. www.basinharbor.com. 105 units. Summer $270–$345 double, to $425 suite (including breakfast, lunch, and dinner); early summer and fall $185–$285 double, to $315 suite (including breakfast and dinner). Closed mid-Oct to mid-May. 2-night minimum stay summer weekends. MC, V. Pets allowed in cottages with additional charge. **Amenities:** 2 restaurants (traditional American, pub fare); heated outdoor pool; 5 tennis courts; 18-hole golf course; aerobics classes; marina with boat rentals (windsurfers, kayaks, canoes, day sailors, outboards); lake cruises; fitness room; bike rental; children's programs (summer); concierge; limited room service; baby-sitting; laundry service; dry cleaning; art workshops; lecture series; airfield.

The Inn at Shelburne Farms ⊛⊛   The numbers behind this elaborate mansion on the shores of Lake Champlain tell the story: 60 rooms, 10 chimneys, 1,400 acres of land. Built in 1899, this sprawling Edwardian "farmhouse" is the place to fantasize about the lifestyles of the *truly* rich and famous. From the first glimpse of the mansion as you come up the winding drive, you'll know you've left the grim world behind. That's by design—noted landscape architect Frederick Law Olmsted had a hand in the shaping the grounds. The 24 guest rooms all vary in terms of decor and upkeep; some are well overdue for a makeover. If you're feeling flush, ask for Overlook, with the great views of the grounds. Among the budget units (with shared bathroom), we like Oak Room with its lake view.

Harbor Rd., Shelburne, VT 05482. ✆ **802/985-8498.** 24 units (7 units share 4 bathrooms). Spring and summer $910–$325 double; fall $105–$365 double. 2-night minimum stay on weekends. Closed mid-Oct to mid-May. AE, DISC, MC, V. **Amenities:** Restaurant (New England regional); lake swimming; tennis court; children's farmyard; baby-sitting; farm tours.

Lang House ✦ This stately white Queen Anne mansion (1881) sits on the hillside between downtown and the University of Vermont. It's not as extravagant as the Willard Street Inn (the owners there are co-owners here), but it's very comfortably appointed and lavish with rich cherry and maple woodwork. Rooms vary, but most have small bathrooms and small TVs. Our favorites are two of the corner units: Room 101, on the first floor, has a wonderfully old-fashioned bathroom with wainscoting, while room 202 has a cozy sitting area tucked in the turret, which gets lots of afternoon light.

360 Main St., Burlington, VT 05401. ✆ **877/919-9799** or 802/652-2500. Fax 802/651-8717. www.langhouse.com. 9 units. $125–$185 double. Rates include breakfast. AE, DISC, MC, V. *In room:* A/C, TV.

Radisson Hotel Burlington ✦✦ The nine-story Radisson offers the best views (if you spend the $20 extra on a lakeside room), as well as the best downtown location. It's a sleek glass box built in 1976, but renovations have kept the weariness at bay. Rooms were all updated in 2000, and the hotel is located between the waterfront and Church Street Marketplace, both of which are a 5-minute walk away. Five cabana rooms, which open up to the pool area, are ideal for families.

60 Battery St., Burlington, VT 05401. ✆ **802/658-6500.** Fax 802/658-4659. 256 units. $119–$209 double. Ask about packages. AE, DISC, MC, V. Parking in attached garage $5 per day. **Amenities:** 2 restaurants (family, New American); indoor pool; small fitness room; Jacuzzi; concierge; free airport shuttle; limited room service; baby-sitting; laundry service; dry cleaning. *In room:* A/C, TV, dataport, coffeemaker, hair dryer, iron, safe.

Willard Street Inn ✦✦ This impressive inn is located in a splendid Queen Anne–style brick mansion a few minutes' walk from the university. The inn has soaring first-floor ceilings, cherry woodwork, and a beautiful window-lined breakfast room. The home was originally built in 1881 by a bank president and served as a retirement home for a time before its conversion to an inn. Among the best units are room 12, which boasts a small sitting area and views of the lake, and the spacious room 4, which has a sizable bathroom and lake views.

349 S. Willard St. (2 blocks south of Main St.), Burlington, VT 05401. ✆ **800/577-8712** or 802/651-8710. Fax 802/651-8714. www.willardstreetinn.com. 14 units (1 with private hall bathroom). $115–$225 double. Rates include breakfast. 2-night minimum stay on weekends. AE, DISC, MC, V. *In room:* A/C, TV.

WHERE TO DINE

Al's ✦ BURGERS & FRIES Al's is where Ben and Jerry (*the* Ben and Jerry) go when they need to sate their french fry cravings. This classic roadside joint is both fun and efficient. The vats of fries draw people back time and again; the other offerings (hamburgers, hot dogs, sloppy-joe-like barbecue on a bun) are okay, but nothing special.

1251 Williston Rd. (Rte. 2, just east of I-89), South Burlington. ✆ **802/862-9203.** Sandwiches 75¢–$3.55. No credit cards. Mon–Wed 10:30am–11pm; Thurs–Sat 10:30am–midnight; Sun 11am–10pm.

Bove's ⚘ ITALIAN   A Burlington landmark since 1941, Bove's is a classic red-sauce-on-spaghetti joint just a couple of blocks from the Church Street Marketplace. The facade is stark black and white, its octagonal windows closed to prying eyes by Venetian blinds. Step through the doors and into a lost era; grab a seat at one of the vinyl-upholstered booths and browse the menu, which offers spaghetti with meat sauce, spaghetti with meatballs, spaghetti with sausage, and . . . well, you get the idea. The red sauce is rich and tangy, while the garlic sauce packs enough garlic to knock you clear out of your booth. Cocktails are inexpensive, and include old chestnuts like stingers, pink ladies, and sloe gin fizzes.

68 Pearl St. ℭ **802/864-6651.** www.boves.com. Sandwiches $1.40–$4.15; dinner items $4.25–$7.70. No credit cards. Tues–Sat 10am–8:45pm.

Daily Planet ⚘ ECLECTIC   This popular spot is often brimming with college students and downtown workers on evenings and weekends. The mild mayhem adds to the charm, enhancing the eclectic, interesting menu. The meals are better prepared than one might expect from a place that takes its cues from a pub. There's a bar menu that features fajitas, grilled eggplant sandwiches, and chicken wings. In the dining room, look for lunch dishes like lamb stew, seafood newburg, and creative salads; at dinner, there's strip steak with a gorgonzola–green peppercorn sauce or rainbow trout with peach–red onion relish.

15 Center St. ℭ **802/862-9647.** Reservations recommended for parties of five or more. Lunch items $5.75–$7.25; dinner main courses $11.25–$19.95. DISC, MC, V. Mon–Fri 11:30am–3pm; Sun–Thurs 5–9:30pm; Fri–Sat 5–10pm. Sept–May Sat–Sun brunch 11am–3pm.

Five Spice Cafe ⚘⚘ PAN-ASIAN   Located upstairs and down in an intimate setting with rough wood floors and aquamarine wainscoting, Five Spice is a popular spot among college students and professors. But customers are drawn here for the exquisite food, not for the scene. The cuisine is multi-Asian, drawing on the best of Thailand, Vietnam, China, and beyond. Try the superb and spicy hot-and-sour soup. Then gear up for Thai red snapper or the robust kung-pao chicken. The dish with the best name on the menu—Evil Jungle Prince with Chicken—is also one of our favorites, made with a light sauce of coconut milk, chilies, and lime leaves.

175 Church St. ℭ **802/864-4045.** Reservations recommended on weekends and in summer. Lunch items $6.95–$9.25; dinner main courses $12.50–$17.95. AE, DISC, MC, V. Mon–Sat 11:30am–10:30pm; Sun 11am–9:30pm.

Leunig's Bistro ⚘⚘ REGIONAL/CONTINENTAL   This boisterous, fun place right on the downtown pedestrian mall has a retro old-world flair, with washed walls, marble bar, crystal chandeliers, and oversize posters. The inventive, large menu features regional foods prepared with a continental touch. There's brunch on weekends; lunch choices include filling sandwiches like turkey cranberry melt. Dinner offerings change seasonally; in summer, there's poached asparagus with smoked salmon or soft-shell crabs with a lemon grass–coconut broth; in fall, look for more hearty fare like pork chops with green-peppercorn apple cider sauce.

115 Church St. ℭ **802/863-3759.** Reservations suggested on weekends and holidays. Dinner $8.95–$22.95. AE, DISC, MC, V. Mon–Thurs 11am–10pm; Fri 11am–midnight; Sat 9am–midnight; Sun 9am–10pm.

Penny Cluse Cafe ⚘⚘ CAFE/LATINO   This gets our vote as the city's best choice for lunch or breakfast. Located a block off the Church Street Marketplace, Penny Cluse is a casual, bright, and popular spot decorated in a vaguely Southwestern motif. Among the better breakfasts: the Zydeco breakfast with eggs, black beans, andouille sausage, and corn muffins. Lunch ranges from salads to sandwiches (the veggie Reuben with mushrooms, spinach, and red onions is excellent) to more elaborate fare like adobo pork chops with a plantain cake. Prices are at the high end of the breakfast/lunch scale, but deliver great value.

169 Cherry St. © 802/651-8834. Breakfast dishes $3.50–$6.50; sandwiches and lunch dishes $6.25–$8. MC, V. Mon–Fri 6:45am–3pm; Sat–Sun 8am–3pm.

BURLINGTON AFTER DARK

Burlington has a thriving local music scene. Check the local weeklies for information on festivals and concerts during your visit, and to find out who's playing at the clubs. Online information about local music and arts events may be found at **www.bigheavyworld.com**.

Nectar's, 188 Main St. (© **802/658-4771**), is an odd amalgam—part funky cafeteria-style restaurant, part no-frills lounge. No wonder this is the place Phish got its start. Live bands play nightly, and there's never a cover. On weekends, it's packed with UVM students and abuzz with a fairly high level of hormonal energy. Look for the revolving neon sign (the last of its kind in Vermont).

Upstairs from Nectar's is **Club Metronome,** 188 Main St. (© **802/865-4563**), a loud and loose nightspot that features a wide array of acts with a heavy dose of world beat. You can dance or shoot a game of pool (or do both at once, as seems popular). This is a good spot to sample some of the local talent, which is actually pretty impressive. The cover is $3 to $15.

For gay nightlife, head to **135 Pearl** (© **802/863-2343**), located naturally enough at 135 Pearl St. It's Burlington's only gay bar. You can get a bite to eat, dance to the DJ, or give karaoke a go. Open Monday through Thursday from 7:30pm to 1am, Friday and Saturday from 5pm to 1am.

10 The Northeast Kingdom

Vermont's Northeast Kingdom has a more wild and remote character than much of the rest of the state. Consisting of Orleans, Essex, and Caledonia counties, the region was given its memorable nickname in 1949 by Sen. George Aiken, who understood the area's allure at a time when few others paid it much heed. What gives this region its character is its stubborn, old-fashioned insularity.

In contrast to the dusky narrow valleys of southern Vermont, the Kingdom's landscape is open and spacious, with rolling meadows ending abruptly at the hard edge of dense boreal forests. The leafy woodlands of the south give way to spiky forests of spruce and fir. Accommodations and services for visitors aren't as plentiful or easy to find here as in the southern reaches of the state, but a handful of inns are tucked among the hills and in the forests.

This section includes a loose, somewhat convoluted driving tour of the Northeast Kingdom, along with some suggestions for outdoor recreation. If your time is limited, make sure you at least stop in St. Johnsbury, which has two of our favorite Vermont attractions—the Fairbanks Museum and St. Johnsbury Athenaeum. The total tour, from Hardwick to St. Johnsbury by way of Newport, Derby Line, and Lake Willoughby, is approximately 90 miles. Allow a full day, or more if you plan to take advantage of hiking and biking in the region.

Visitor information is available from the **Northeast Kingdom Chamber of Commerce,** 357 Western Ave., Suite 2, in St. Johnsbury (© **800/639-6379** or 802/748-3678; www.vermontnekchamber.org). Additional information on Vermont's northern reaches can be found at **www.vtnorthcountry.com**.

Begin at:

① Hardwick

This is a small town with rough edges set along the Lamoille River. It has a compact commercial main street, some quirky shops, and a couple of casual, family-style restaurants.

From here, head north on Route 14 a little over 7 miles to the turnoff toward Craftsbury and

② Craftsbury Common

This uncommonly graceful village is home to a small academy and many historic buildings spread along a sizable green and a broad main street. The town occupies a wide upland ridge and offers sweeping views to the east and west. Be sure to stop by the old cemetery on the south end of town, where you can wander among the historic tombstones of pioneers, which date back to the 1700s. Craftsbury is an excellent destination for mountain biking and cross-country skiing and is home to the region's finest inn (see below).

From Craftsbury, continue north to reconnect to Route 14. You'll wind through the towns of Albany and Irasburg as you head north. At the village of Coventry, veer north on Route 5 to the lakeside town of

③ Newport

This commercial outpost (population 4,400) is set on the southern shores of Lake Memphremagog, a stunning 27-mile-long lake that's just 2 miles wide at its broadest point and the bulk of which lies across the border in Canada. From Newport, continue north on Route 5, crossing under I-91, for about 7 miles to the border town of Derby Line (pop. 2,000). This outpost has a handful of restaurants and antiques shops; you can park and walk across the bridge to poke around the Canadian town of Rock Island with just some simple ID like a driver's license. (That's for U.S. residents; foreign travelers might ask at

the U.S. Customs booth about returning before crossing the line.)

Back in Derby Line, look for the

④ Haskell Free Library and Opera House

Sitting at the corner of Caswell Avenue and Church Street (© 802/873-3022), this handsome neoclassical building contains a public library on the first floor and an elegant opera house on the second that's modeled after the old Boston Opera House. This much-adorned theater opened in 1904 with advertisements promoting a minstrel show featuring "new songs, new jokes, and beautiful electric effects."

What's most curious about the structure, however, is that it's one of few buildings that lies half in Canada and half in the United States. (The Haskell family donated the building jointly to the towns of Derby Line and Rock Island.) A thick black line runs beneath the seats of the opera house, indicating who's in the United States and who's in Canada. Because the stage is set entirely in Canada, apocryphal stories abound from the early days of frustrated U.S. officers watching fugitives perform on stage. More recently, the theater has been used for the occasional extradition hearing.

From Derby Line, retrace your path south on Route 5 to Derby Center and the juncture of Route 5A. Continue south on Route 5A to the town of Westmore on the shores of

⑤ Lake Willoughby

This glacier-carved lake is best viewed from the north, with the shimmering sheet of water pinching between the base of two low mountains at the southern end. There's a distinctive Alpine feel to the whole scene, and this underappreciated lake is certainly one of the most beautiful in the Northeast. Route 5A along the eastern shore is lightly traveled and well suited to biking or walking.

Northern Vermont

Head southwest on Route 16, which departs from Route 5A just north of the lake. Follow Route 16 through the peaceful villages of Barton and Glover. From Glover, continue south through serene farmlands to Lyndonville, where you pick up Route 5 south to

6 St. Johnsbury

This town of 7,600 inhabitants is the largest in the Northeast Kingdom and the region's center of commerce. First settled in 1786, the town enjoyed a buoyant prosperity in the 19th century, largely stemming from the success of platform scales, invented here in 1830 by Thaddeus Fairbanks, which are still manufactured here today. Luckily, the town has not suffered from the depredations of tourist boutiques and brewpubs, and retains an abundance of fine commercial architecture in two distinct areas, which are joined by steep Eastern Avenue. The north end of Main Street is also notable for its grand residential architecture.

At the corner Main and Prospect streets in St. Johnsbury, look for

7 The Fairbanks Museum

In 1889, this imposing Romanesque, red sandstone structure was built at 1302 Main St. (© 802/748-2372; www.fairbanksmsuseum.com), to hold the accumulations of obsessive amateur collector Franklin Fairbanks, the grandson of the inventor of the platform scale. Fairbanks was once described as "the kind of little boy who came home with his pockets full of worms." In adulthood, his propensity to collect continued unabated. His artifacts include four stuffed bears, a huge moose with full antlers, art from Asia, and 4,500 stuffed native and exotic birds. And that's just the tip of the iceberg.

The soaring, barrel-vaulted main hall, reminiscent of an old-fashioned railway depot, embodies Victorian grandeur. Among the assorted clutter, look for the unique mosaics by John Hampson, who crafted scenes of American history—such as Washington bidding his troops farewell—entirely of *mounted insects*. In the

Washington scene, for instance, iridescent green beetles form the epaulets, and the regal great coat is comprised of hundreds of purple moth wings. Words fail us here; you must see these works, which alone are worth the price of admission.

The museum is open Monday through Saturday from 10am to 4pm (to 6pm in July and August), Sunday from 1 to 5pm. Admission is $5 for adults, $4 for seniors, $3 for children 5 to 17, and $12 per family (maximum of three adults).

Also in town, just south of the museum on Main Street, is the

8 St. Johnsbury Athenaeum

The Athenaeum is in an Edward Hopper-esque brick building with a truncated mansard tower and prominent keystones over the windows. This is the town's public library, but it also houses an extraordinary art gallery dating to 1873. It claims to be the oldest unadulterated art gallery in the nation, and we see no reason to question that claim.

Your first view of the gallery is spectacular: After winding through the cozy library with its ticking regulator clock, you round a corner and find yourself gazing across Yosemite National Park. Noted Hudson River School painter Albert Bierstadt created this luminous 10-by-15-foot oil, and the gallery was built specifically to accommodate this work. (Local lore says the small balcony in the gallery was built for Bierstadt to better view his work on subsequent visits.) In 1999, the gallery received the donation of another Bierstadt painting, a 14-by-24-inch work called *The Cove.*

Some 100 other works fill the walls. Most are copies of other paintings (a common teaching tool in the 19th century), but look for originals by other Hudson River School painters, including Asher B. Durand, Thomas Moran, and Jasper Cropsey.

The Athenaeum (© **802/748-8291**) is open Monday and Wednesday from 10am to 8pm; Tuesday, Thursday, and Friday from 10am to 5:30pm; and Saturday from 9:30am to 4pm. Admission is free, but donations are encouraged.

ALPINE SKIING

Jay Peak ★★ Located just south of the Canadian border, Jay is Vermont's best choice for those who prefer to avoid all the modern-day glitz and clutter that seem to plague ski resorts elsewhere. While some new condo development has been taking place at the base of the mountain, Jay still has the feel of a remote, isolated destination, accessible by a winding road through unbroken woodlands. Thanks to its staggering snowfall (an average of 340 inches, more than any other New England ski area), Jay has developed extensive glade skiing; the ski school also specializes in running the glades, making it a fitting place for advanced intermediates to learn how to navigate these exciting, challenging trails.

Rte. 242, Jay, VT 05859. © **800/451-4449** for lodging, or 802/988-2611. www.jaypeakresort.com. Vertical drop: 2,153 ft. Lifts: 1 60-person tram, 4 chairlifts, 2 surface lifts. Skiable acreage: 385 acres. Lift tickets: $49.

OTHER OUTDOOR PURSUITS

CROSS-COUNTRY SKIING The same folks who offer mountain biking at the Craftsbury Outdoor Center (see below) also maintain 61 miles of groomed cross-country trails through the gentle hills surrounding Craftsbury. The forgiving, old-fashioned trails, maintained by **Craftsbury Nordic** ★★ (© **800/729-7751** or 802/586-7767), emphasize pleasing landscapes rather than fast action. Trail passes are $14 for adults, $7 for children 6 to 12, and $9 for seniors. Another option is **Highland Lodge** ★ (© **802/533-2647**), on Caspian Lake, which offers 36 miles of trails (about 10 miles groomed) through rolling woodlands and fields.

HIKING At the southern tip of Lake Willoughby, two rounded peaks rise above the lake's waters. These are the biblically named Mount Hor and Mount Pisgah, both of which lie within Willoughby State Forest. Both summits are accessible via footpaths that are somewhat strenuous but offer excellent views.

For **Mount Pisgah** ★★ (elevation 2,751 feet), look for parking on the west side of Route 5A about 5.7 miles south of the junction with Route 16. The trail departs from across the road and runs 1⁷⁄₁₀ miles to the summit. To hike **Mount Hor** ★ (elevation 2,648 feet), drive 1⅘ miles down the gravel road on the right side of the above-mentioned parking lot, veering right at the fork. Park at the small parking lot, and continue on foot past the lot a short distance until you spot the start of the trail. Follow the trail signs to the summit, a round-trip of about 3½ miles.

MOUNTAIN BIKING The Craftsbury ridge features several excellent variations for bikers in search of easy terrain. Most of the biking is on hard-packed dirt roads through sparsely populated countryside. The views are sensational, and the sense of being well out in the country very strong. The **Craftsbury Outdoor Center at Craftsbury Common** ★★ (© **800/729-7751** or 802/586-7767) rents mountain bikes and is an excellent source for maps and local information on area roads and bike routes. Bike rentals are $25 to $35 per day. A small fee is charged for using bikes on the trail network.

WHERE TO STAY

Comfort Suites ⭐   Newly opened in 2000, the property consists of more than 100 suites and a number of nice touches, like granite vanity counters and high-backed desk chairs. The rooms are pleasantly appointed (more like an inn than a motel), and in the basement are an appealing pool and fitness room, along with a game room outfitted with air hockey and a pool table. The hotel is located just off I-91 about a mile south of downtown St. Johnsbury.

703 Rte. 5 South (off Exit 20 of I-91), St. Johnsbury, VT 05819. ⓒ **800/228-5150** or 802/748-1500. Fax 802/748-1243. 107 units. Summer $109–$169 double; foliage season from $139; off-season from $79. Rates include continental breakfast. AE, DISC, MC, V. **Amenities:** Indoor pool; mid-size fitness room; game room; coin-op laundry. *In room:* A/C, TV, dataport, coffeemaker, hair dryer, iron.

Inn on the Common ⭐⭐⭐   This exceedingly handsome complex of three Federal-style buildings anchors the charming ridge-top village of Craftsbury Common, one of the most quintessential of New England villages. The stunning, comfortable inn offers just the right measures of both history and luxury. It tends to be a rather social place, attracting both families and couples seeking a romantic getaway. Dinner starts with cocktails at 6pm, with guests seated family-style amid elegant surroundings at 7:30pm. The menu changes nightly, but includes well-prepared contemporary American fare. Some deluxe guest rooms feature fireplaces.

Craftsbury Common, VT 05827. ⓒ **800/521-2233** or 802/586-9619. Fax 802/586-2249. www.innonthecommon.com. 16 units. $270–$290 double; foliage season $280–$300 double. Rates include breakfast and dinner. 2-night minimum stay during foliage and Christmas week. AE, MC, V. Pets accepted by prior arrangement ($15 per visit). **Amenities:** Outdoor heated pool (summer only); clay tennis court; croquet; bicycle rental; in-room massage; baby-sitting (by advance arrangement). *In room:* No phone.

12

New Hampshire

by Wayne Curtis

New Hampshire's state symbol is the Old Man of the Mountains, an icon you'll see just about everywhere you look—on state highway signs, on brochures, on state police cars. And it's an apt symbol for a state that relishes its cranky-old-man demeanor. New Hampshire has long been a magnet for folks who speak of government—especially "big government"—in tones normally reserved for bowel ailments. That "Live-Free-or-Die" license plate? It's for real. New Hampshire stands behind its words. This is a state that still regards zoning as a nefarious conspiracy to undermine property rights. Note that New Hampshire does not have a bottle-deposit law, or a law banning billboards. (Heathen Vermont has both, as does its other godless neighbor, Maine.)

New Hampshire savors its reputation as an embattled outpost of plucky and heroic independents fighting the good fight against intrusive laws and irksome bureaucrats. Without a state sales tax or state income tax, it's had to be creative in financing its limited government. Many government services are funded through the "tourist tax" (an 8% levy on meals and rooms at restaurants and hotels) along with a hefty local property tax. In fact, candidates for virtually every office must take "The Pledge," which means they'll vow to fight any effort to impose sales or income tax. To shirk The Pledge is tantamount to political suicide.

Get beyond New Hampshire's affable crankiness, though, and you'll find pure New England. Indeed, New Hampshire may represent the New England ethic distilled to its essence. At its core is a mistrust of outsiders, a premium placed on independence, a belief that government should be frugal above all else, and a laconic acceptance that, no matter what, you just can't change the weather. Travelers exploring the state with open eyes will find these attitudes in spades.

Travelers will also find wonderfully diverse terrain—from ocean beaches to broad lakes to the region's impressive mountains. Without ever leaving the state's borders, you can toss a Frisbee on a sandy beach, ride bikes along quiet country lanes dotted with covered bridges, hike rugged granite hills blasted by some of the most severe weather in the world, and canoe on a placid lake in the company of moose and loons. You'll also find good food and country inns you won't ever want to leave. But most of all, you'll find vestiges of that feisty independence that has defined New England since the first settlers ran up their flag 3½ centuries ago.

1 Portsmouth ★★★

Portsmouth is a civilized seaside city of bridges, brick, and seagulls. Filled with elegant architecture that's more intimate than intimidating, this bonsai-size city projects a strong and proud sense of its heritage without being overly precious about it.

Part of the city's appeal is its variety. Upscale coffee shops and fancy art galleries exist alongside old-fashioned barber shops and tattoo parlors. A steady gentrification in recent years has brought with it some twee shops and businesses, but the town still has a fundamental earthiness that serves as a tangy vinegar for the overly saccharine spots. Portsmouth's humble waterfront must actually be sought out, and when found it's rather understated.

Portsmouth's history runs deep, a fact that is instantly evident on a walk through town. For the past 3 centuries, the city has served as a hub for the region's maritime trade. In the 1600s, Strawbery Banke (it wasn't renamed Portsmouth until 1653) was a center for the export of wood and dried fish to Europe. In the 19th century, it prospered as a center of regional trade. Across the river in Maine, the Portsmouth Naval Shipyard was founded in 1800, and evolved into a prominent base for the building, outfitting, and repair of U.S. Navy submarines. Today, Portsmouth's maritime tradition continues with a lively trade in bulk goods (look for scrap metal and minerals stockpiled along the shores of the Piscataqua River on Market Street). The city's de facto symbol is the tugboat, one or two of which are almost always tied up near the waterfront's picturesque "tugboat alley."

ESSENTIALS

GETTING THERE   Portsmouth is served by Exits 3 through 7 on I-95. The most direct access to downtown is via Market Street (Exit 7), which is the last New Hampshire exit before crossing the river to Maine.

In 2000, discount airline **Pan Am** (© **800/359-7262;** www.flypanam.com) launched operations out of a former military base on Portsmouth's outskirts. The only airline that serves Portsmouth (don't expect onward connections), it has flights to a limited but growing roster of second-tier airports, including Gary, Ind.; Sanford, Fla.; and Allentown, Penn. Call or check the carrier's website for an updated list of airports currently served.

By bus, Portsmouth is served by **Concord Trailways** (© **800/639-3317**) and **Vermont Transit** (© **800/451-3292**).

VISITOR INFORMATION   The **Greater Portsmouth Chamber of Commerce,** 500 Market St. (© **603/436-1118;** www.portcity.org/index), operates an information center between Exit 7 and downtown. From Memorial Day to Columbus Day, it's open Monday through Wednesday from 8:30am to 5pm, Thursday and Friday from 8:30am to 7pm, and Saturday and Sunday from 10am to 5pm. The rest of the year, hours are Monday through Friday from 8:30am to 5pm. In summer, the chamber staffs a second information booth at Market Square in the middle of the historic district.

PARKING   Most of Portsmouth can be easily reconnoitered on foot, so you need park only once. Parking can be tight in and around the historic district in summer. The municipal parking garage costs 50¢ per hour; it's located on Hanover Street between Market and Fleet streets. Strawbery Banke Museum (see below) also offers limited parking for visitors.

A MAGICAL HISTORY TOUR

Portsmouth's 18th-century prosperity is evident in the regal Georgian-style homes that dot the city. Strawbery Banke occupies the core of the historic area, and is well worth visiting. If you don't have the budget, time, or inclination to see Strawbery Banke, a walking tour will bring you past many other significant homes, some of which are maintained by various historical or colonial societies

and are open to the public. A helpful map and brochure, *The Portsmouth Trail: An Historic Walking Tour,* is available free at information centers.

Strawbery Banke Museum ★★★   In 1958, the city planned to raze this venerable neighborhood, first settled in 1653, to make way for urban renewal. A group of local citizens resisted and won, establishing an outdoor history museum that's grown to become one of the largest in New England. Today it consists of 10 downtown acres and 46 historic buildings. Ten of these have been restored with period furnishings; eight others feature exhibits. While Strawbery Banke employs staffers to assume the character of historic residents, the emphasis is more on the buildings, architecture, and historic accoutrement, and less on living history as practiced at Sturbridge Village or Plimoth Plantation in Massachusetts.

The neighborhood surrounds an open lawn and has a settled, picturesque quality to it. At three working crafts shops on the grounds, you can watch coopers, boat builders, and potters at work. The most intriguing home is the split-personality Drisco House, half of which depicts life in the 1790s, and half of which shows life in the 1950s, nicely demonstrating how houses grow and adapt to each era.

Hancock St. ℭ 603/433-1106. www.strawberybanke.org. Admission $12 adults, $11 seniors, $8 children 7–17; $28 per family. Apr 15–Oct 29 daily 10am–5pm. Special events held first 2 weekends of Dec; otherwise closed Nov–Apr. Look for directional signs posted around town.

John Paul Jones House ★★   Revolutionary War hero John Paul ("I have not yet begun to fight") Jones was a boarder in this handsome 1758 home during the Revolutionary War. He was here to oversee the construction of his sloop, *Ranger,* believed to be the first ship to sail under the United States flag (there's a model of it on display). The home has been immaculately restored and maintained by the Portsmouth Historical Society; costumed guides offer tours of 45 minutes to an hour.

43 Middle St. ℭ 603/436-8420. Admission $5 adults, $2.50 children 6–14, free for children under 6. Mon–Sat 10am–4pm; Sun noon–4pm. Closed late Oct to May.

Moffatt-Ladd House ★★   The Moffatt-Ladd House, built for a family of prosperous merchants and traders, is as notable for its elegant garden as for the 1763 home, with its great hall and elaborate carvings throughout. The home belonged to one family between 1763 and 1913, when it became a museum, and many of the furnishings have never left the premises. The house will especially appeal to aficionados of Early American furniture and painting.

154 Market St. ℭ 603/436-8221. Admission $5 adults, $2.50 children under 12. June 15–Oct 15 Mon–Sat 11am–5pm; Sun 1–5pm. Closed mid-Oct to mid-June.

Warner House ★   The Warner House, built in 1716, was the governor's mansion in the mid–18th century when Portsmouth served as state capital. It was a private home until the 1930s, and since then it's been open to the public. This stately brick structure with graceful Georgian architectural elements is a favorite among architectural historians for its wall murals from around 1716 (said to be the oldest murals still in place in the United States), the early wall marbleizing, and the original white pine paneling.

150 Daniel St. ℭ 603/436-5909. Admission $5 adults, $2.50 children 7–12, free for children 6 and under. Tues–Sat 10am–4pm; Sun 1–4pm. Closed Nov to June 1.

Wentworth-Gardner House ★★★   The Wentworth-Gardner is arguably the most handsome mansion in the entire Seacoast region, and is widely considered to be one of the best examples of Georgian architecture in the nation.

Portsmouth

ACCOMMODATIONS ■
Inn at Strawbery Banke **5**
Sise Inn **6**

DINING ◆
Blue Mermaid World Grill **2**
Karen's **3**
Lindbergh's Crossing **1**
Press Room **4**

515

Built in 1760, the home features many of the classic period elements, including very pronounced quoins (the blocks on the building's corners), pedimented window caps, plank sheathing (meant to make the home appear as if made of masonry), and an elaborate doorway featuring Corinthian pilasters, a broken scroll, and a paneled door topped with a pineapple, the symbol of hospitality. The inside is no less impressive, with hand-painted Chinese wallpaper and a vast fireplace in the kitchen.

50 Mechanic St. ℂ **603/436-4406.** Admission $5 adults, $2.50 children 6–14, free for children 5 and under. Tues–Sun 1–4pm. Closed mid-Oct to mid-June.

BOAT TOURS

Portsmouth is especially attractive seen from the water. A small fleet of tour boats ties up at Portsmouth, offering scenic tours of the Piscataqua River and the historic Isle of Shoals throughout the summer and fall.

The **Isle of Shoals Steamship Co.** ★★ (ℂ **800/441-4620** or 603/ 431-5500; www.isleofshoals.com) sails from Barker Wharf on Market Street and is the most established of the tour companies. The firm offers a variety of tours on the 90-foot, three-deck *Thomas Laighton* (a modern replica of a late-19th-century steamship) and the 70-foot *Oceanic,* which was especially designed for whale watching. One of the most popular excursions is to the Isle of Shoals, allowing passengers to disembark and wander about Star Island, a dramatic, rocky island that's part of an island cluster far out in the offshore swells. Reservations are strongly encouraged. Other popular trips include 6-hour whale-watching voyages and a sunset lighthouse cruise. Fares range from $10 to $25 for adults, $6 to $16 for children. Parking is an additional $3 per car.

Portsmouth Harbor Cruises ★ (ℂ **800/776-0915** or 603/436-8084) specializes in tours of the historic Piscataqua River aboard the *Heritage,* a 49-passenger cruise ship with plenty of open deck space. Cruise by five old forts, or enjoy the picturesque tidal estuary of inland Great Bay, a scenic trip upriver from Portsmouth. Trips run daily; reservations are suggested. Fares are $8.50 to $16 for adults, $6 to $9 for children.

ESPECIALLY FOR KIDS

The Children's Museum of Portsmouth ★★ *Kids*   The Children's Museum is a bright, lively arts and science museum that offers a morning's worth of hands-on exhibits of interest to younger artisans and scientists. Among the more popular displays are exhibits on earthquakes, dinosaur digs, and lobstering, along with the miniature yellow submarine and space shuttle cockpit, both of which invite clambering.

280 Marcy St., 2 blocks south of Strawbery Banke. ℂ **603/436-3853.** www.childrens-museum.org. Admission $4 adults and children; free for ages 1 and under. Tues–Sat 10am–5pm; Sun 1–5pm. Also open Mon during summer and school vacations.

SHOPPING

Portsmouth's compact historic district is home to dozens of boutiques offering unique items. A fine contemporary gallery featuring the work of area crafts-people, the **N. W. Barrett Gallery,** 53 Market St. (ℂ **603/431-4262**), offers a classy selection of ceramic sculptures, glassware, lustrous woodworking, and handmade jewelry. The **Robert Lincoln Levy Gallery,** operated by the New Hampshire Art Association, 136 State St. (ℂ **603/431-4230**), has frequently changing exhibits and shows; it's a good destination to view fine art produced by New Hampshire artists.

Antiques stores are scattered around town. Among our favorites is **Victory Antiques,** 96 State St. (© **603/431-3046**), which has a limited yet eclectic selection, often including interesting furniture. About 20 dealers maintain cases here offering a good selection of china and glass.

Paradiza, 63 Penhallow St. (© **603/431-0180**), has an array of very clever greeting cards, along with exotica like soaps and bath products from Israel and Africa. **Macro Polo,** 89 Market St. (© **603/436-8338**), specializes in retro-chic gifts, toys, magnets, and gadgets.

WHERE TO STAY

Portsmouth has a good selection of places to stay within walking distance of the downtown historic area. Less expensive, less stylish options include chain hotels at the edge of town near I-95. Among them are the **Anchorage Inn,** 417 Woodbury Ave. (© **603/431-8111**); **Susse Chalet,** 650 Borthwick Ave. (© **603/436-6363**); and **Holiday Inn of Portsmouth,** 300 Woodbury Ave. (© **603/431-8000**).

In addition to the options listed below, see the Inn at Portsmouth Harbor, on p. 562 in the Maine chapter.

Inn at Strawbery Banke ⟡   This historic inn, located in a home built in the early 1800s on Court Street, is ideally located for exploring Portsmouth. Strawbery Banke is but a block away, and Market Square is just 2 blocks away. The innkeepers have done a nice job taking a cozy antique home and making it comfortable for guests. Rooms are tiny but bright and feature stenciling, wooden shutters, and beautiful pine floors; one has a bathroom down the hall. Common areas include two sitting rooms with TVs and a dining room where a full breakfast is served.

314 Court St., Portsmouth, NH 03801. © 603/436-7242. 7 units. Summer and early fall $120–$130 double; off-season $90–$95 double. Rates include breakfast. 2-night minimum stay Aug and Oct weekends. AE, DISC, MC, V. Children 10 and over welcome. *In room:* A/C, no phone.

Sise Inn ⟡⟡   The Sise Inn is a modern, elegant hotel in the guise of a country inn. This solid Queen Anne–style home was originally built for a prominent merchant in 1881; the hotel addition was constructed in the 1980s. The effect is happily harmonious, with antique stained glass and copious oak trim meshing well with the more contemporary elements. An elevator serves the three floors, and there's modern carpeting throughout, but many of the rooms feature antique armoires and an updated Victorian styling. We like room 406, a suite with a soaking tub and private sitting room, and room 216, with its own sauna and lovely natural light. An elaborate continental breakfast is served in the huge old kitchen and adjoining sunroom. This is a popular hotel for business travelers, but if you're on holiday you won't feel out of place.

40 Court St. (at Middle St.), Portsmouth, NH 03801. © 877-747-3466 or 603/433-1200. Fax 603/433-1200. siseinn@cybertours.com. 34 units. June–Oct $145–$225 double; Nov–May $110–$175 double. Rates include continental breakfast. AE, DISC, MC, V. **Amenities:** Access to health club (within walking distance); laundry. *In room:* A/C, TV, iron.

Three Chimneys Inn ⟡⟡   Located about 20 minutes northwest of Portsmouth at the edge of the pleasant university town of Durham, the Three Chimneys Inn is a wonderful retreat. The main part of the inn dates back to 1649, but later additions and a full-scale renovation in 1997 have given it more of a regal Georgian feel. All units are above average in size and lushly decorated with four-poster or canopied beds, mahogany armoires, and Belgian carpets.

Seventeen rooms have either gas or Duraflame-log fireplaces. Our favorite is the William Randolph Hearst Room, with photos of starlets on the walls and a massive bed that's a replica of one at San Simeon. Note that five rooms are on the ground-floor level beneath the restored barn (all have outside entrances, Jacuzzis, and gas fireplaces), and tend to be a bit more cave-like than the others. The inn is a popular spot for weddings on summer weekends.

17 Newmarket Rd., Durham, NH 03824. ✆ 888/399-9777 (out of state) or 603/868-7800. Fax 603/868-2964. www.threechimneysinn.com. 24 units. May to mid-Nov $179–$209 double ($30 less midweek); off-season $119–$179. Rates include breakfast. 2-night minimum stay on weekends. AE, DISC, MC, V. Children 6 and over welcome. **Amenities:** 2 restaurants (upscale regional, tavern fare). *In room:* A/C, TV, dataport.

WHERE TO DINE

The funky **Ceres Bakery,** 51 Penhallow St. (✆ 603/436-6518), set on a quiet side street, is a tiny space with just a handful of tables, so you might be better off getting a cookie or a slice of cake to go and then walking the few blocks to the waterfront rose gardens. **Cafe Brioche,** 14 Market Sq. (✆ 603/430-9225), is more of a high-profile hangout, often crowded with folks attracted by not only the central location but also the delectable baked goods and buzz-inducing coffees.

Blue Mermaid World Grill ★★ GLOBAL/ECLECTIC   The Blue Mermaid ranks among our favorites in Portsmouth for its good food, good value, and refusal to take itself too seriously. It's a short stroll from Market Square, in a historic area called the Hill. It's not a pretentious place—locals congregate here, Tom Waits drones on in the background, and the service is casual but professional. The menu is adventurous in a low-key global kind of way—you might try lobster and shrimp pad Thai or a Caribbean pan-seared cod served with a coconut cream sauce and rice and beans. There's also seafood, burgers, pasta, and pizza from the wood grill, along with an entertaining drinks menu (think margaritas and mango martinis).

The Hill (at Hanover and High sts. facing the municipal parking garage). ✆ 603/427-2583. www.bluemermaid.com. Reservations recommended for parties of six or more. Lunch items $5.75–$13.95; dinner main courses $10.95–$21.95 (most around $15). AE, DISC, MC, V. Sun–Thurs 11:30am–9pm; Fri–Sat 11:30am–10pm.

Lindbergh's Crossing ★★ BISTRO   If you're in the mood for exotic comfort food, head to this restaurant, which serves what it calls hearty French country fare. Located in an old waterfront warehouse, this intimate, two-story restaurant has a bistro menu that's subtly creative without calling too much attention to itself. The beer-braised lamb shank is served over thyme risotto; another popular dish is the seafood (shrimp, mussels, scallops, and whitefish) served in a tomato broth over couscous. If you don't have reservations, ask about seating in the bar.

29 Ceres St. ✆ 603/431-0887. Reservations recommended. Main courses $14–$24. AE, DC, MC, V. Sun–Thurs 5:30–9:30pm; Fri–Sat 5:30–10pm. Bar opens 4pm daily; light menu available.

Press Room TAVERN FARE   Locals flock here more for the convivial atmosphere and the easy-on-the-budget prices than for creative cuisine. Opened in 1976, the Press Room likes to boast that it was the first in the area to serve Guinness stout, and so it's appropriate that the atmosphere has a Gaelic charm. On cool days, a fire burns in the woodstove and quaffers flex their elbows at darts amid brick walls, pine floors, and heavy wooden beams overhead. Choose your meal from a basic bar menu of inexpensive selections, including a variety of burgers, fish-and-chips, stir-fries, and salads.

77 Daniel St. 🕐 **603/431-5186.** Reservations not accepted. Sandwiches $3.50–$6.50; main courses $7.50–$12.95. AE, DISC, MC, V. Mon 5–11pm; Sun and Tues–Thurs 4–11pm; Fri–Sat 11:30am–11pm.

Roxanne's ⭐ ECLECTIC   Roxanne's is easily overlooked, but it's worth seeking out. You'll find fresh ingredients creatively prepared. For breakfast, indulge in homemade corned-beef hash with poached eggs, or stick with more basic fare like buttermilk pancakes. Lunches get more intriguing: Expect offerings like a tangy smoked seafood chowder or blackened salmon fajita. Dinners include fresh ravioli that changes with the seasons, along with hearty meals like pork tenderloin with red cabbage, turnip, sweet potato, and caramelized pineapple. Roxanne's is the best bet for a visiting vegetarian, offering several dishes nightly for the non-carnivore.

105 Daniel St. 🕐 **603/431-1948.** Reservations strongly recommended for dinner. Main courses $4.95–$7.50 breakfast, $5.95–$7.95 lunch, $14.95–$19.95 dinner. MC, V. Mon–Fri 7:30am–2:30pm; Thurs–Fri 5:30–9:30pm; Sat 8am–2pm and 5:30–9:30pm; Sun 8am–2pm and 4–8pm.

2 Hanover & Environs ⭐⭐⭐

If your idea of New England involves a sweeping green edged with stately brick buildings, be sure to visit Hanover, a thriving university town agreeably situated in the Connecticut River Valley. First settled in 1765, the town was home to early pioneers who were granted a charter by King George III to establish a college. The school was named after the second Earl of Dartmouth, the school's first trustee. Since its founding, Dartmouth College has had a large hand in shaping the community.

This Ivy League school has produced more than its share of celebrated alumni, including poet Robert Frost, Vice President Nelson Rockefeller, former surgeon general C. Everett Koop, and children's-book author Dr. Seuss. Another noted son of Dartmouth was the renowned 19th-century politician and orator Daniel Webster. In arguing for the survival of Dartmouth College in a landmark case before the U.S. Supreme Court in 1816 (when two factions vied for control of the school), Webster offered his famous closing line: "It is a small college, gentlemen, but there are those who love it." This has served as an informal motto for school alumni ever since.

Today, a handsome, oversize village green marks the permeable border between college and town. In summer, the green is an ideal destination for strolling and lounging. The best way to explore Hanover is on foot, so your first endeavor is to park your car, which can be trying during peak seasons. Try the municipal lots west of Main Street.

ESSENTIALS

GETTING THERE   Hanover is north of Lebanon, N.H., and I-89 via Route 10 or Route 120. Amtrak serves White River Junction, Vt., across the river.

VISITOR INFORMATION   Dartmouth College alumni and chamber volunteers maintain an **information center** (🕐 **603/643-3512**) on the green in summer. It's open daily from 10am to 5pm in June and September, daily from 9:30am to 5pm in July and August. In the off-season, head to the **Hanover Chamber of Commerce** (🕐 **603/643-3115**), located on Main Street across from the post office. It's open Monday through Friday from 9am to 4:30pm.

SPECIAL EVENTS   In mid-February, look for the fantastical and intricate ice sculptures of the **Dartmouth Winter Carnival,** held annually; call Dartmouth

College (© **603/646-1110**) for more information on this traditionally beer-soaked event.

EXPLORING HANOVER

Hanover is a superb town to explore on foot, by bike, and even by canoe. Start by picking up a map of the campus, available at the Dartmouth information center on the green or at the Hanover Inn. (Free guided tours are also offered in summer.) The expansive, leafy campus is a delight to walk through.

South of the green next to the Hanover Inn is the modern **Hopkins Center for the Arts** 🎭 (© **603/646-2422;** www.dartmouth.edu/~hop). The center attracts national acts to its 900-seat concert hall and stages top-notch performances at the Moore Theater. Wallace Harrison, the architect who later went on to design New York's Lincoln Center, designed the building.

Dartmouth's **Baker Memorial Library** harbors a wonderful treasure: a set of murals by Latin American painter José Orozco, who painted *The Epic of American Civilization* while teaching here between 1932 and 1934. The huge paintings wrap around a basement study room, and are as colorful as they are densely metaphorical. Ask for the printed interpretation at the front desk.

Hood Museum of Art 🎭   This modern, open building next to the Hopkins Center houses one of the oldest college museums in the nation. Its current incarnation—an austere, three-story modern structure—was built in 1986 and features special exhibits as well as examples from the permanent collection, which includes a superb selection of 19th-century American landscapes.

Wheelock St. © **603/646-2808.** www.dartmouth.edu/~hood. Free admission. Tues, Thurs, and Fri–Sat 10am–5pm; Wed 10am–9pm; Sun noon–5pm.

Ledyard Canoe Club 🎭🎭   An idyllic way to spend a lazy afternoon is to drift along the Connecticut River in a canoe. Dartmouth's historic boating club is located just down the hill from the campus. While much of the club's focus is on competitive racing, it's a good place to get a boat and explore the tree-lined river. Instruction is also available.

Off West Wheelock St. (turn upstream at the bottom of the hill west of bridge; follow signs to the clubhouse). © **603/643-6709.** Canoe and kayak rentals $5 per hour, $15 per day ($25 on weekends). Summer Mon–Fri 10am–8pm; Sat–Sun 9am–8pm. Spring and fall Mon–Fri noon–6pm; Sat–Sun 10am –6pm. Open when river temperature is higher than 50°F.

Montshire Museum of Science 🎭🎭 *(Kids)*   This is not your average New England science museum of musty stuffed animals in a creaky building. Located on the border between New Hampshire and Vermont (hence the name), the Montshire is a modern, architecturally engaging, hands-on museum that draws kids back time and again. It's situated on a beautiful 110-acre property sandwiched between I-91 and the Connecticut River. Exhibits are housed in an open, soaring structure inspired by the region's barns. The museum contains some live animals (don't miss the leaf-cutter ant exhibit on the second floor), but the main emphasis is on fun, interactive exhibits that involve kids. Outside, there's a science park masquerading as a playground, plus four nature trails that wend through this riverside property of tall trees and chirping birds.

Montshire Rd., Norwich, Vt. © **802/649-2200.** www.montshire.net. Admission $5.50 adults, $4.50 children 3–17. MC, V. Daily 10am–5pm. Take Exit 13 off I-91 and head east; look for museum signs almost immediately.

Enfield Shaker Museum 🎭   This cluster of historic buildings on peaceful Lake Mascoma is about a 20-minute drive southeast of Hanover. "The Chosen Vale," as its first inhabitants called it, was founded in 1793; by the mid-1800s it had 350 members and 3,000 acres. From that peak, the community dwindled, and by 1927 the Shakers abandoned the Chosen Vale and sold the village lock, stock, and barrel. Today, much of the property is owned by either the state of New Hampshire or the museum.

Dominating the village is the imposing **Great Stone Dwelling,** an austere but gracious granite structure erected between 1837 and 1841. When constructed, it was the tallest building north of Boston, and it remains the largest dwelling house in any of the Shaker communes. The Enfield Shakers lived and dined here, with as many as 150 Shakers at a time eating at long trestle tables. In 1997, the museum acquired the stone building, and in 1998 a new restaurant and inn opened to the public (see below). The self-guided walking tour of the village is free with admission. The overall historic feel is slightly compromised by a recent condominium development along the lakeshores, although the scale and design of these structures are quite sympathetic to the original village.

Rte. 4A, Enfield. © **603/632-4346.** ww.shakermuseum.org. Admission $7 adults, $6 seniors, $5 students, $3 children 10–18. Memorial Day to Halloween Mon–Sat 10am–5pm; Sun noon–5pm. Winter and spring Sat 10am–4pm; Sun noon–4pm.

WHERE TO STAY

Several hotels and motels are located off the interstate in Lebanon and West Lebanon, about 5 miles south of Hanover. Try the **Airport Economy Inn** (© **800/433-3466** or 603/298-8888), at 45 Airport Rd. (Exit 20 off I-89); **Days Inn** (© **603/448-5070**), at 135 Rte. 120 (Exit 18 off I-89); **Fireside Inn and Suites** (© **603/298-5906**), at 25 Airport Rd. (Exit 20 off I-89); or **Sunset Motor Inn** (© **603/298-8721**), at 305 N. Main St. (Rte. 10, 4 miles off Exit 19 off I-89).

The Hanover Inn ✹✹✹ The Hanover Inn is the Upper Connecticut Valley's most elegant and up-to-date hotel, and is perfectly situated for exploring campus and town. Established in 1780, most of the current five-story inn was added at later dates—1924, 1939, or 1968—and this large, modern hotel now features professional service, tidy rooms, excellent dining, and subterranean walkways to the art museum and performing-arts theater. Yet the inn manages to maintain an appealing old-world graciousness, informed by that mildly starchy neo-Georgian demeanor trendy in the 1940s. Most rooms have canopy or four-poster beds and down comforters; some overlook the green.

Wheelock St. (P.O. Box 151), Hanover, NH 03755. © **800/443-7024** or 603/643-4300. Fax 603/646-3744. www.hanoverinn.com. 92 units. $257–$297 double. AE, DISC, MC, V. Valet parking $12 per day. Pets accepted ($15 per night). **Amenities:** 2 dining rooms (see below); access to Dartmouth's athletic facilities; limited room service; laundry; dry cleaning. *In room:* A/C, TV, dataport, hair dryer, iron.

Mary Keane House ✹ Situated at Lower Shaker Village about 20 minutes from Dartmouth, this is an ideal spot for the gentle recuperation of a harried soul. Built in 1929 (2 years after the Shakers had abandoned the village), this two-story grayish-lavender Georgian Revival doesn't share much with the Shaker village in architecture or spirit—in fact, it's filled with lovely Victorian antiques, which seem to be anathema to the Shaker sensibility. But it's kept immaculately clean and it's smack in the Shaker village, so guests can easily explore the buildings and museum at their leisure.

Rte. 4 (Shaker Village), Enfield, NH 03748. © **888/239-2153** or 603/632-4241. www.marykeanehouse.com. 5 units. $89–$139 double. Rates include breakfast. AE, DISC, MC, V. Pets accepted. **Amenities:** Lake swimming; canoes (free). *In room:* TV, A/C (on request), no phone.

Shaker Inn at the Great Stone Dwelling ✹✹ Part of the Enfield Shaker Museum, the Shaker Inn opened in 1998 and offers a unique destination for those curious about the Shakers and American history. The rooms are spread among the upper floors of the massive stone dwelling house built by the Enfield Shaker community in the late 1830s, when it was the tallest building north of Boston (no elevator). All units are furnished with simple and attractive Shaker reproductions. Some of the rooms have original built-in Shaker cabinets (you can stow your socks in something that would bring five figures at a New York auction house). Room 1 boasts the most original detail (and is also the most expensive). A restaurant in the original dining hall features upscale regional fare that draws on Shaker traditions.

Rte. 4, Enfield, NH 03748. ⒸⒸ 888/707-4257 or 603/632-7810. www.theshakerinn.com. 24 units. $105–$155 double. Rates include breakfast. AE, DISC, MC, V. **Amenities:** Restaurant (Shaker-inspired cuisine); lake swimming. *In room:* No phone.

WHERE TO DINE

Daniel Webster Room ★★ CONTEMPORARY AMERICAN   The Daniel Webster Room of the Hanover Inn will appeal to those looking for fine dining in a formal New England atmosphere. The inn's Colonial Revival dining room is reminiscent of a 19th-century resort hotel, with fluted columns, floral carpeting, and regal upholstered chairs. The dinner menu isn't extensive, but that doesn't make it any less appealing. Produce from the college's organic farm is used seasonally. The changing entrees are eclectic and creative and might include braised rabbit leg with truffled pappardelle. Off the inn's lobby is the more informal Zins, a wine bistro that serves 30 wines by the glass. It's open daily from 11:30am to 10pm.

Hanover Inn, Wheelock St. ⒸⒸ 603/643-4300. Reservations recommended. Breakfast items $4.25–$9.50; lunch items $6.95–$13.50; dinner main courses $17–$26. AE, DISC, MC, V. Mon 7–10:30am and 11:30am–1:30pm; Tues–Fri 7–10:30am, 11:30am–1:30pm, and 6–9pm; Sat 7–10:30am and 6–9pm; Sun 8–10am and 11am–1:30pm.

La Poule à Dents ★★ FRENCH   In the sleepy town of Norwich just across the river from Hanover, this fine restaurant wakes up guests with the valley's most exquisite dining. Housed in a historic 1820 home with a canopied terrace, it has the feel of an intimate French auberge. It's a perfect spot for a romantic meal. The sumptuous meals include an inviting array of appetizers, from a light lobster and saffron broth with a grilled sea scallop to a meaty charcuterie, with three homemade sausages served with fig bread. Entrees include potato-encrusted trout with ratatouille, breast of duck with toasted pumpkin-seed risotto, and scallops baked in puff pastry with black truffle.

Carpenter St. (off Main St. across from the Citgo station), Norwich, Vt. ⒸⒸ 802/649-2922. www.lapoule.com. Reservations recommended. Main courses $18–$27. AE, DISC, MC, V. Daily 6–8:30pm.

Lou's ★ *Value* BAKERY/COMFORT FOOD   Lou's has been a Hanover institution since 1947, attracting hungry crowds for breakfast on weekends and a steady local clientele for lunch throughout the week. The mood is no-frills New Hampshire, with a black-and-white linoleum checkerboard floor, maple-and-vinyl booths, and a harried but efficient crew of waiters. Breakfast is served all day (real maple syrup on your pancakes is $1 extra—go ahead and splurge), and the sandwiches, served on fresh-baked bread, are huge and delicious.

30 S. Main St. ⒸⒸ 603/643-3321. Breakfast items $3–$7; lunch items $4–$7. AE, MC, V. Mon–Fri 6am–3pm; Sat 7am–5pm; Sun 7am–3pm. Bakery open for snacks until 5pm.

3 The Lake Winnipesaukee Region

Lake Winnipesaukee is the state's largest lake, convoluted with coves and dotted with islands. When you're out on the lake, it rarely seems all that huge. That's because the 180-mile shoreline is edged with dozens of inlets, coves, and bays, and further fragmented by 274 islands. As a result, intermittent lake views from the shore give the illusion you're viewing a chain of smaller lakes and ponds rather than one massive body of water that measures 12 by 20 miles at its broadest points.

How to best enjoy the lake? If you're traveling with kids, Weirs Beach is a fun base. If you're looking for isolation, consider renting a lakeside cabin on the eastern shore for a week or so, track down a canoe or sailboat, then explore much the same way travelers did a century ago. If your time is limited, a driving tour around the lake with a few well-chosen stops will give you a nice taste of the region's woodsy flavor.

Lake Winnipesaukee's western shore has a more frenetic, working-class atmosphere than its refined sibling shore across the lake. That's partly for historic reasons—the main stage and rail routes passed along the western shore—and partly for modern reasons: I-93 runs west of the lake, serving as a sluice for harried visitors streaming in from the Boston megalopolis to the south.

WEIRS BEACH ✧

Weirs Beach is a compact, blue-collar resort town with a Victorian heritage that remains evident. Unlike beach towns that sprawl for miles, Weirs Beach clusters in that classic pre-automobile fashion, spread along a boardwalk near a sandy beach. At the heart of the town is a working railroad that still connects to the steamship line—a nice throwback to an era when summer vacationers used mass transportation. The town attracts a mix of visitors, from history and transportation buffs to beach nuts and video-game warriors.

But most of all, it attracts families. Lots of families, many of whom start the morning at sunny Endicott Beach, at the south edge of town, swimming in the clear waters of Winnipesaukee, then taking a train or boat excursion before switching over to afternoon video games at nearby arcades. Weirs Beach hasn't been gentrified—it has a historic authenticity that some find charming, and others find a bit too down-at-the-heels for their tastes.

ESSENTIALS

GETTING THERE   Interstate access to Weirs Beach is from I-93 at Exit 20 or Exit 23. From Exit 20, follow Route 3 north through Laconia to Weirs Beach. From the north, take Exit 23 and drive 9 miles east on Route 104 to Meredith, then head south on Route 3.

VISITOR INFORMATION   The **Greater Laconia/Weirs Beach Chamber of Commerce,** 11 Veterans Sq., Laconia (© **603/524-5531;** www.laconia-weirs.org), maintains a seasonal information booth on Business Route 3 about halfway between Laconia and Weirs Beach. It's open daily in summer from 10am to 6pm. The **Lakes Region Association** (© **800/605-2537;** www.lakesregion.org) has offices at Exit 23 off I-93 and is also happy to send out a handy vacation kit with maps and extensive information on local attractions.

SIGHTSEEING BY LAND & BY LAKE

Scenic train rides leave from town on the **Winnipesaukee Scenic Railroad** ✧ (© **603/279-5253** or 603/745-2135), which offers 1- and 2-hour sightseeing

The White Mountains & Lake Winnipesaukee

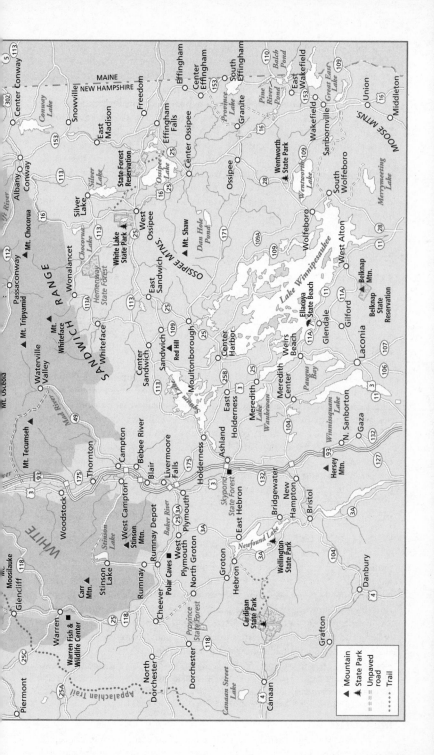

excursions from Weirs Beach in summer. It's a unique way to enjoy great views of lake and forest; kids are provided a hobo lunch packed in a bundle on a stick ($6.95). The 2-hour ride is $8.50 for adults and $6.50 for children 4 to 11. The 1-hour trip is $7.50 for adults and $5.50 for children.

The stately **M/V Mount Washington** ★★ is an exceptionally handsome 230-foot-long vessel with three decks and a capacity of 1,250 passengers (© **603/ 366-2628;** www.cruisenh.com). This ship, by far the largest of the lake tour boats, is our favorite way to tour Winnipesaukee, offering excellent views of the shoreline and the knobby peaks of the White Mountains rising over the lake's northern end. Departing daily from Weirs Beach are a 2-hour tour ($15 for adults, $7 for children 4 to 12) and a 2½-hour excursion ($18 for adults, $9 for children). Occasional summer evening dinner cruises offer different themes, but don't expect alternative rock—most feature classic rock, oldies nights, and country-and-western. The ship also runs tours from other ports around the lake, including Wolfeboro, Alton Bay, Center Harbor, and Meredith (call for details). Excursions run from the end of May to mid-October.

EXPLORING WEIRS BEACH

In addition to the beach, the arcades, and the boat and train rides, Weirs Beach is home to a number of activities that delight young kids and parents desperate to take some of the energy out of them. The **Surfcoaster** (© **603/366-4991**) has a huge assortment of wave pools, water slides, and other wet diversions for most ages. It's on Route 11B just outside of Weirs Beach, and charges $20 for adults, $15 for those under 4 feet tall.

The **Funspot** (© **603/366-4377**) will keep kids occupied with 500-odd games, including video games, candlepin bowling, bingo, and a driving range. There's no charge to enter. Games are priced individually (e.g., bowling is $2.75 per game per person). Also in town on Route 11B is **Daytona Fun Park** (© **603/366-5461**), which has go-carts, minigolf, and batting cages.

Kellerhaus (© **603/366-4466**), located in a storybook-like stone-and-half-timber structure on Route 3, just north of Endicott Beach, features an ice-cream buffet where fanatics can select from a battery of toppings. Open in peak season from 8am to 11pm daily; call for hours in off-season.

Come evening, complete the trip back in time with a movie at the wonderfully old-fashioned **Weirs Drive-In Theater,** on Route 3 (© **603/366-4723**).

WHERE TO STAY

Naswa Resort (Kids)   This old-fashioned (ca. 1936) lakefront resort features motel units, suites, and brightly colored, knotty-pine interior cabins overlooking the lake. Most of the activity revolves around the sandy 1,000-foot beach, which fronts Winnipesaukee and teems with kids throughout the summer. Buildings are crowded in along the beach, and no one would confuse this with a romantic getaway. But it's a good destination for families, with easy access to boating and the activities of nearby Weirs Beach. Guest rooms are mostly motel-sized, furnished comfortably but without much style.

1086 Weirs Blvd., Laconia, NH 03246. © 603/366-4341. Fax 603/366-5731. www.naswaresort.com. 84 units. $69–$139 double midweek; $139–$179 weekend. Discounts available in spring and fall. 2-night minimum stay on weekends. AE, DISC, MC, V. Closed mid-Oct to May. **Amenities:** Restaurant (beach bar/grill); water-sports equipment rental (canoes, powerboats, and jet skis). *In room:* A/C, TV.

MEREDITH ★

The pleasant village of Meredith sits at the northwest corner of Winnipesaukee, with views across lovely Meredith Bay from throughout the town. It lacks both the quaintness and the selection of activities that many travelers seek—a busy road cuts off the tidy downtown from the lakeshore, and small strip malls have intruded—but has good services and is home to several fine inns. Foremost among its appeal is its superb location. We'd choose Meredith as a home base if we were looking to explore the lakes area and the White Mountains, since both are within striking distance for day trips (Franconia Notch is about 50 miles north).

ESSENTIALS

GETTING THERE   Interstate access to Meredith is via Exit 23 off I-93. Drive 9 miles east on Route 104 to Route 3, then turn left down the hill into town.

VISITOR INFORMATION   The **Meredith Area Chamber of Commerce** (© **603/279-6121**) maintains an office in the white house on Route 3 (on the left when driving down the hill from Route 104). It's open daily in summer from 9am to 5pm; closed weekends in winter.

EXPLORING THE AREA

Meredith's attractive if now largely bypassed Main Street runs up the hill from Route 3 at the elbow in the middle of town. A handful of shops, galleries, and boutiques offers low-key browsing. The creative re-adaptation of an early mill at the **Mill Falls Marketplace** ✦ (© **800/622-6455**) features 18 shops, including a well-stocked bookstore. It's connected to the Inns at Mill Falls, at the intersection of Route 3 and Route 25.

An excellent fair-weather trip is an excursion to 112-acre **Stonedam Island** ✦✦, one of the largest protected islands in the lake. The island, owned by the Lakes Region Conservation Trust (© **603/279-3246**), has a trail that winds through wetlands and forest. Located approximately 2½ miles southeast of downtown Meredith, it's an ideal destination for a picnic, although it takes some doing to get here. Rent a canoe or kayak at **Sports & Marine Parafunalia,** Route 25, Meredith Shopping Center (© **603/279-8077**), and make a day of it.

Note also that the **M/V Mt. Washington** (see Weirs Beach, above) makes a stop once weekly in Meredith.

WHERE TO STAY

The Inns at Mill Falls ✦✦   This ever-expanding complex is gradually dominating downtown Meredith, but has managed its growth with considerable elan. The accommodations are spread among three buildings (with a fourth to open in 2002), each of which is subtly different, but all of which are uncommonly well-tended and comfortable. The main inn is located in a former mill complex (a small, tasteful shopping mall is adjacent), and features attractive but less elaborate rooms. All the rooms in the more upscale Chase House have gas fireplaces; most have balconies and porch rockers with views of the lake across Route 3. The Inn at Bay Point is located smack on 2,000 feet of lakefront, and most rooms feature balconies with sensational views of Winnipesaukee. Ten rooms have Jacuzzis. The inn is not especially well suited for kids.

Rte. 3, Meredith, NH 03253. © **800/622-6455** or 603/279-7006. www.millfalls.com. 101 units. Summer $109–$269 double; winter $79–$249. AE, DC, DISC, MC, V. Minimum stay required some weekends. **Amenities:** 5 restaurants (casual dining); small indoor pool; fitness room; shopping arcade; limited room service; massage; baby-sitting; laundry service; dry cleaning. *In room:* A/C, TV, dataport, hair dryer, iron.

Manor on Golden Pond ✦✦✦   This regal stucco-and-shingle mansion, located 9 miles north of Meredith in Holderness, was built between 1903 and

1907 and sits on a low hill overlooking Squam Lake. The Manor is wonderfully situated on 14 landscaped acres studded with white pines. Inside, it has the feel of an English manor house, with rich oak paneling and leaded windows. The larger, more expensive guest rooms are creatively furnished and far more inviting than the motel-sized units along the first-floor wing. Most rooms have wood-burning fireplaces. Among our favorite rooms: Savoy Court, Buckingham, and Stratford, all lavishly appointed. Four recently constructed annex suites have French doors that open onto views of the lake. The top-notch dining room is "dressy casual" (no shorts or jeans).

Rte. 3, Holderness, NH 03245. © 800/545-2141 or 603/968-3348. Fax 603/968-2116. www. manorongoldenpond.com. 27 units. Summer $210–$375 double; winter $150–$375. Rates include breakfast. AE, DISC, MC, V. 2-day minimum stay holidays and foliage season. No children under 12 accepted. **Amenities:** Restaurant (New American); outdoor pool; lake swimming; clay tennis court (night play); canoes and paddleboat (free); croquet; horseshoes; shuffleboard; limited room service; massage. *In room:* A/C, TV, dataport, hair dryer, iron (fridge and coffeemaker in annex rooms).

Red Hill Inn 🎯🎯 This inn is tucked in the rolling hills between Winnipesaukee and Squam Lake, but borrows more of its flavor from the mountains than the lakeshore. Housed in an architecturally austere three-story brick home dating from the turn of the last century, the inn looks down a long meadow toward a small complex of elegant green-and-red shingled farm buildings. Two of these have been converted into well-appointed guest quarters; these are our favorites. Room rates are based on views and size (21 have wood-burning fireplaces), but one of our preferred rooms in the inn, Kearsarge, is one of the less expensive, with a private paneled sitting room and a small bathroom with clawfoot tub. The downside? It's on the third floor of a no-elevator building, and low eaves make it tough for the tall.

Rte. 25B, Box 99M, Center Harbor, NH 03226. © 800/573-3445 or 603/279-7001. Fax 603/279-7003. www.redhillinn.com. 25 units. $115–$195 double; $195 cottage. Rates include breakfast. 2-day minimum stay on weekends. Ask about packages. AE, DISC, MC, V. Children over 5 welcome. From Center Harbor, drive northwest 2⁹⁄₁₀ miles on Rte. 25B. **Amenities:** Restaurant (contemporary regional); outdoor heated pool; outdoor hot tub (year-round). *In room:* A/C, hair dryer, iron.

WHERE TO DINE

Abondante 🎯 ITALIAN/DELI This casual storefront market and deli has a delightful atmosphere—maple floors, copper-topped tables, herbs drying from the joists overhead, classical music. Both table service and to-go orders are available, with a great selection of fresh pastas and rustic breads, not to mention imported chocolates. This is a good spot for a casual dinner, or to pick up a lunch for a boating picnic.

30 Main St., Meredith. © 603/279-7177. Main courses $2.25-$4.50 breakfast, $4.95-$6.95 lunch, $6.95-$14.95 dinner. AE, DISC, MC, V. Summer daily 8am–9pm; off-season Mon–Thurs 8am–5pm, Fri–Sat 8am–9pm.

Hart's Turkey Farm Restaurant TURKEY/AMERICAN Hart's Turkey Farm Restaurant is bad news if you're a turkey. On a typically busy day, this place dishes up more than a ton of America's favorite bird. Judging by name alone, Hart's Farm sounds more rural than it is. In fact, it's in a nondescript building on busy Route 3. Inside, it's comfortable in a faux–Olde New Englande sort of way—a classic family restaurant (founded 1954) that borders on kitsch, but with turkey too good to write off as merely a retro experience. The service is afflicted with that sort of rushed efficiency found in places that attract bus tours. But diners don't return time and again to Hart's for the charm—they come for the turkey.

Tips   Worthwhile Views

For a sweeping view of Winnipesaukee's eastern shore, drive 7 miles north of Wolfeboro on Route 109 to the **Abenaki Tower.** (Look for a parking lot and wooden sign on the right side of the road at the crest of a hill.) From the lot, it's an easy 5-minute hike to the sturdy log tower, which rises about 80 feet high and is ascended by a steep staircase (not a good destination for acrophobes). Those who soldier on to the top are rewarded with excellent views of nearby coves, inlets, and the Belknap Mountains southwest of the lake.

Junction of Rtes. 3 and 104, Meredith. ℭ **603/279-6212.** www.hartsturkeyfarm.com. Main courses $9.50–$21.95 (mostly $13–$15). AE, DISC, MC, V. Summer daily 11:15am–9pm; fall–spring daily 11:15am–8pm.

WOLFEBORO 🐦🐦

The bustling town of Wolfeboro on Lake Winnipesaukee's eastern shore claims to be the first summer resort in the United States. The documentation actually makes a pretty good case for it. In 1763, John Wentworth, the nephew of a former governor, built a summer estate on what's now called Lake Wentworth (just east of Winnipesaukee). The house burned in 1820, and the site now attracts largely archaeologists.

Where western Winnipesaukee tends to be more raucous with the populist attractions of Weirs Beach, Wolfeboro has more of a blue-blood sensibility. You'll find impeccably maintained 19th-century architecture, attractive downtown shops, and a more refined sense of place.

ESSENTIALS

GETTING THERE   Lake Winnipesaukee's east shore is best explored on Route 28 (from Alton Bay to Wolfeboro) and Route 109 (from Wolfeboro to Moultonborough).

VISITOR INFORMATION   The **Wolfeboro Chamber of Commerce** (ℭ **800/516-5324** or 603/569-2200; www.wolfeboroonline.com) offers regional information and advice from its offices in a converted railroad station at 32 Central Ave., a block off Main Street in Wolfeboro. It's open in summer daily from 10am to 5pm, in the off-season Monday through Friday from 10am to 3pm.

EXPLORING THE AREA

Wolfeboro (pop. 2,800) has a vibrant, homey downtown that's easily explored on foot. Park near Depot Square and the Victorian train station, and stock up on brochures and maps at the Chamber of Commerce office inside. Behind the train station, running along the former tracks of the rail line, is the **Russell C. Chase Bridge-Falls Path** 🐦, a rail-trail that runs along Back Bay to a set of small cascades.

Several boat tours depart from docks behind the shops of Main Street. Our favorite option: a wind-in-the-face, half-hour tour on the *Millie B.* 🐦🐦 (ℭ **603/569-5257**), a rare 28-foot mahogany speedboat constructed by Hacker-Craft ($10 for adults, $5 for children under 5). Inquire about the tours at the Wolfeboro Trolley Company, 60 North Main St. (ℭ **800/339-5257** or 603/569-5257).

Also available are 1½-hour excursions on the *Winnipesaukee Belle* 🐦 (ℭ **603/569-3796**), a faux 65-foot steamship with a canopied upper deck, owned and operated by the Wolfeboro Inn. And the impressive **M/V *Mount Washington*** (see Weirs Beach, above) sails out of Wolfeboro four times weekly in summer.

For a self-propelled afternoon, kayak rentals and guided tours are available from **Winnipesaukee Kayak** ✮, 17 Bay St., at Back Bay Marina (✆ **603/569-9926**). On a relatively windless day, little beats exploring by paddle from Wolfeboro Bay to the cluster of islands just to the south.

Quieter lake swimming is available at **Wentworth State Beach** ✮ (✆ **603/569-3699**), which also features a shady picnic area. The park is located 5 miles east of Wolfeboro on Route 109.

Castle in the Clouds ✮✮   About 15 miles north of Wolfeboro is a rather unusual sight. Cranky millionaire Thomas Gustav Plant built an eccentric stone edifice high atop a mountain overlooking Lake Winnipesaukee in 1913, at a cost of $7 million. The home is a sort of rustic San Simeon East, with cliff-hugging rooms, stained-glass windows, and unrivaled views of the surrounding hills and lakes. Visitors drive to the carriage house, where they park and are taken in groups through the house by knowledgeable guides. Even if the castle holds no interest, the 5,200-acre grounds are worth the admission. The long access road is harrowingly narrow and winding, with wonderful vistas and turnouts for stopping along the way. Take your time on the way up; the separate exit road is fast, straight, and uninteresting.

Rte. 171 (4 miles south of Rte. 25), Moultonborough. ✆ 800/729-2468 or 603/476-2352. Admission $12 adults, $8 students, free for children under 6. Grounds only $6 adults, free for children. Mid-May to mid-June Sat–Sun 9am–5pm; mid-June to Labor Day daily 9am–5pm; Labor Day to third week of Oct daily 9am–4pm. Closed Nov–Apr.

New Hampshire Antique and Classic Boat Museum   Winnipesaukee is synonymous with classic wooden powerboats—sleek wooden Cris-Crafts and other icons of a more genteel era. This newly established museum hopes to bring that era to life with a collection of early boats and artifacts. The museum, which opened its doors in 2000, is still shopping for a permanent home; until it finds one, visitors can view displays in an old theater in town. Plan your trip to coincide with one of the summer regattas, which brings boat restorers and aficionados out of the woodwork to show off their obsessions.

397 Center St., Wolfeboro. ✆ 603/569-4554. www.nhacbm.org. Admission $5 adults, $4 seniors, $3 students, free for children under 12. Summer Mon–Sat 10am–4pm, Sun noon–4pm; call for off-seaon hours.

WHERE TO STAY & DINE
Wolfeboro Inn ✮✮   This small, elegant resort hotel strives to mix modern and traditional, and succeeds admirably. Located an easy stroll to downtown Wolfeboro, the inn dates back to 1812 but was extensively expanded and updated in the mid-1980s. The modern lobby features a small atrium with wood beams, a slate floor, and a brick fireplace, but retains an old-world elegance. Most of the comfortable guest rooms are furnished with Early American reproductions and quilts. Deluxe rooms have better views, and a dozen have balconies as well. Rooms 200 and 300 are especially nice, with sofas, fridges, and two balconies. The downside: For an inn of this elegance, it has only a disappointing sliver of lakeshore and just a tiny beach for guests.

90 N. Main St., Wolfeboro, NH 03894. ✆ 800/451-2389 or 603/569-3016. Fax 603/569-5375. www.wolfeboroinn.com. 44 units. Mid-May to Oct $129–$239 double; Nov to mid-May $79–$169 double. Rates include continental breakfast. 2-night minimum stay in peak season. AE, MC, V. **Amenities:** 2 restaurants (steakhouse, pub fare); rowboat; boat tours; concierge; limited room service; baby-sitting; laundry service; dry cleaning. *In room:* A/C, TV, hair dryer, iron.

4 The White Mountains

The White Mountains are northern New England's outdoor-recreation capital. This cluster of ancient mountains is a sprawling, rugged playground that attracts kayakers, mountaineers, rock climbers, skiers, mountain bikers, birdwatchers, and, especially, hikers. (See the map on p. 524 to locate the areas discussed below.)

The **White Mountain National Forest** encompasses some 773,000 acres of rocky, forested terrain, more than 100 waterfalls, dozens of remote backcountry lakes, and miles of clear brooks and cascading streams. An elaborate network of 1,200 miles of hiking trails dates back to the 19th century, when the urban gentry took to the mountains in droves to build character, build trails, and experience nature's sublimity. Trails ranging from easy to demanding lace the hillside forests, run along remote valley rivers, and traverse barren, windswept ridgelines where the weather can change dramatically in less time than it takes to eat your lunch.

The center of the White Mountains—in spirit if not in geography—is its highest point: 6,288-foot **Mount Washington,** an ominous, brooding peak that's often cloud-capped or mantled with snow early and late in the season. This blustery peak is accessible by cog railroad, car, and foot, making it one of the more popular destinations in the region. You won't find wilderness here, but you will find abundant natural drama.

Flanking this colossal peak is the brawny **Presidential Range** of the White Mountains, a series of wind-blasted granite peaks named after U.S. presidents and offering spectacular views. Surrounding these are numerous other rocky

 Guides to Exploring the White Mountains

For serious exploration of the White Mountains, you'll need supplemental guidebooks and maps to keep you on track. Here's a short list of recommended guides, all of which are available at area bookstores:

- *AMC White Mountain Guide* (Appalachian Mountain Club, 1998). This comprehensive 576-page book (complete with maps) is chock-full of helpful information on every hiking trail in the White Mountains. This is the definitive hiker's bible for the region.
- *White Mountains Map Book* (Map Adventures, 2000). This colorful, sharply printed map features 386 hiking trails, distances, and a GPS grid. The text offers an overview of what you'll find on 76 day hikes, along with information on camping. It's a good choice for those planning 2 or 3 days of hiking.
- *50 Hikes in the White Mountains* (Backcountry Publications, 1997). The fifth edition of this popular guide, written by Daniel Doan and Ruth Doan MacDougall, offers a good selection of mountain rambles in the high peaks region around Mount Washington. You'll find descriptions of everything from easy strolls to overnight backpack trips.
- *Ponds & Lakes of the White Mountains* (Backcountry Publications, 1998). The White Mountain high country is studded with dramatic tarns (many left by retreating glaciers). This 350-page guide by Steven D. Smith offers 68 trips to help get you there.

ridges that lure hikers looking for challenges and a place to experience nature at its most elemental.

Travelers whose idea of fun doesn't involve steep cliffs or icy dips in mountain streams can enjoy the mountain scenery via spectacular drives. North of North Conway, Route 302 carries travelers through Crawford Notch to the pleasant towns of Bethlehem and Littleton. Route 16 travels from southern New Hampshire through congested North Conway before twisting up dramatic Pinkham Notch at the base of Mount Washington. Wide and fast, Route 2 skirts the northern edge of the mountains, offering wonderful views en route to the town of Jefferson. I-93 may be the most scenic interstate in northern New England, passing through spectacular Franconia Notch as it narrows to a two-lane road in deference to its natural surroundings (and local political will). The most scenic drive in the Whites, though, is the **Kancamagus Highway,** which links Conway with Lincoln and provides frequent roadside pull-offs for casual explorers to admire cascades, picnic along rivers, and enjoy sweeping mountain views.

Where to base yourself? North Conway is the motel capital of the region, with hundreds of rooms—many quite charmless, but usually available at reasonable rates. The Loon Mountain and Waterville Valley areas have a sort of planned condo-village graciousness that delights some travelers and gives others the creeps. Jackson, Franconia Notch, Crawford Notch, and the Bethlehem-Littleton area are the best destinations for old-fashioned hotels and inns.

BACKCOUNTRY FEES The White Mountain National Forest requires anyone using the backcountry—whether for hiking, mountain biking, picnicking, skiing, or any other activity—to pay a recreation fee. Anyone parking at a trailhead must display a backcountry permit on the dashboard of their car. Those lacking a permit face a fine. Permits are available at ranger stations and many stores in the region. Two permits are sold: an annual permit for $20, and a 7-day pass for $5. For information, contact the **Forest Service's White Mountains office** (© 603/528-8721).

RANGER STATIONS & INFORMATION The Forest Service's **central White Mountains office** is at 719 Main St. in Laconia (© **603/528-8721**), which is near Lake Winnipesaukee. Your best general source of information is the **Saco Ranger Station,** 33 Kancamagus Hwy., 100 yards west of Route 16, Conway (© **603/447-5448**). Other district offices are **Androscoggin Ranger Station,** 300 Glen Rd., Gorham (© **603/466-2713**); **Ammonoosuc Ranger Station,** 660 Trudeau Rd., Bethlehem (© **603/466-2713**); and **Pemigewasset Ranger Station,** Route 175, Holderness, near the Plymouth town line (© **603/ 536-1315**). The **Evans Notch Ranger Station** (© **207/824-2134**), which covers the Maine portion of the White Mountains (about 50,000 acres), is in Bethel at 18 Mayville Rd., off Route 2 just north of town.

Additional information and advice on recreation in the White Mountains are available at the **AMC's Pinkham Notch Camp** (© **603/466-2727**), on Route 16 between Jackson and Gorham. The center is open daily from 6am to 10pm.

CAMPING The White Mountain National Forest maintains 19 drive-in campsites scattered throughout the region, with the number of sites at each ranging from 7 to 176. Campsites are $12 to $16 per night, plus an additional fee if you reserve in advance. Reservations are accepted at about half of these through National Recreation Reservation Service (© **877/444-6777;** www. reserveamerica.com). Most campsites are very basic (some with pit toilets only), but all are well maintained.

Dolly Copp Campground (© 603/466-2713), located near the base of Mount Washington, is the largest and least personal of the campgrounds, but has a superior location and great views from the open sites. Along the Kancamagus Highway, we're partial to the **Covered Bridge Campground** (© 603/447-5448), which is adjacent to an 1858 covered bridge and a short drive to delightful river swimming at the Rocky Gorge Scenic Area.

Backcountry tent camping is free throughout the White Mountains, and no permit is needed. (You will need to purchase a parking permit to leave your car at the trailhead; see above.) Check with one of the ranger stations for current restrictions on camping in the backcountry. Three-sided log lean-tos are also scattered throughout the White Mountain backcountry, providing overnight shelter for campers. Shelters are sometimes free, or sometimes a backcountry manager will collect a small fee. Ask at any ranger station for details and locations.

NORTH CONWAY & ENVIRONS

North Conway is the commercial heart of the White Mountains. Shoppers adore it because of the profusion of outlets, boutiques, and restaurants along Routes 302 and 16. (The two state highways overlap through town.) Outdoor purists abhor it, considering it a garish interloper to be avoided at all costs, except when seeking pizza and beer.

North Conway itself won't strike anyone as nature's wonderland. The shopping strip south of the village is basically one long turn lane flanked with outlet malls, motels, and chain restaurants of every architectural stripe. On rainy weekends and during the foliage season, the road can resemble a linear parking lot.

Sprawl notwithstanding, North Conway is beautifully situated along the eastern edge of the broad and fertile Saco River valley (called the Mount Washington Valley by local tourism boosters). Gentle, forest-covered mountains, some with sheer cliffs that suggest the distant, stunted cousins of Yosemite's rocky faces, border the bottomlands. Northward up the valley, the hills rise in a triumphant crescendo to the blustery, tempestuous heights of Mount Washington.

The village is trim and attractive (if often congested), with an open green, some colorful shops, Victorian frontier-town commercial architecture, and a distinctive train station. It's a good place to park, stretch your legs, and find a cup of coffee or a snack. (*Hint:* There's a Ben & Jerry's ice-cream shop off the green near the train station.)

ESSENTIALS

GETTING THERE   North Conway and the Mount Washington Valley are on Route 16 and Route 302. Route 16 connects to the Spaulding Turnpike, which intersects with I-95 outside of Portsmouth, N.H. Route 302 begins in Portland, Maine. **Concord Trailways** (© 800/639-3317) provides service from points south, including Boston.

Traffic can be vexing in the Mount Washington Valley on holiday weekends in summer and foliage weekends in fall, when backups of several miles aren't uncommon. Try valiantly to plan around these busy times in order to preserve your own sanity.

Another option: Skirt North Conway by taking **West Side Road,** which runs from Conway to just west of Glen. Driving from the south on Route 16, turn north at the light in Conway Village onto Washington Street. In a half mile, bear left on West Side Road. The road passes near two covered bridges in the first half mile, then dips and winds through the broad farmlands of the Saco River Valley.

You'll pass working farms and farm stands, as well as some architecturally distinctive early homes.

VISITOR INFORMATION   The **Mount Washington Valley Chamber of Commerce** (© 800/367-3364 or 603/356-3171; www.4seasonresort.com) operates a seasonal information booth opposite the village green with brochures on attractions and inns. The staff can help arrange local accommodations. It's open in summer daily from 9am to 6pm, in winter on Saturday and Sunday only.

The state of New Hampshire also operates an **information booth** with rest rooms and phones at a vista with fine views of Mount Washington on Routes 16 and 302 north of North Conway.

RIDING THE RAILS
The **Conway Scenic Railroad** ★★ (© 800/232-5251 or 603/356-5251; www.conwayscenic.com) offers mountain excursions in comfortable rail cars (including a dome car) pulled by either steam or early diesel engines. Trips depart from a distinctive 1874 train station just off the village green, recalling an era when tourists arrived from Boston and New York to enjoy the country air for a month or two each summer. The 1-hour excursion heads south to Conway; you're better off signing up for the more picturesque 1¾-hour trip northward to the village of Bartlett. For the best show, select the 5½-hour excursion through dramatic Crawford Notch, with stupendous views of the mountains from high along this beautiful glacial valley. Ask also about the railway's dining excursions.

The train runs from mid-April to mid-December, with more frequent trips scheduled daily in midsummer. Coach and first-class fares are available; first-class passengers sit in "Gertrude Emma," an 1898 parlor car with wicker and rattan chairs, mahogany woodwork, and an observation platform. Tickets are $9.50 to $19 for adults ($33 to $45 for the Crawford Notch trip), $7 to $14 for children ages 4 to 12 ($18 to $30 for Crawford Notch). Kids under 4 ride free on the two shorter trips; there's a charge on the Crawford Notch trip. Reservations are accepted for the dining car and the Crawford Notch train.

SHOPPING
North Conway is one of northern New England's major outlet centers. Some 200 shops are located along the strip, which extends about 3 miles northward from the junction of Route 302 and Route 16 in Conway into to the village of North Conway itself.

The outlet scene has lagged somewhat in recent years—the selection is not as upscale as in Freeport or Kittery, Maine, or in Manchester, Vt. The strip is starting to be plagued by empty storefronts, largely because of the success of one rapidly expanding outlet center, which has absorbed much of the surrounding business into a village-like minimall. That place is **Settler's Green Outlet Village Plus** (© 603/356-7031; www.settlersgreen.com), and shoppers should start here. The center features more than 50 shops, including J. Crew, Harry & David, Nike, Levi's, and Orvis.

Nearby is the popular **L.L.Bean** factory outlet at the Tanger Outlet Center (one of three in North Conway), located just north of Settler's Green. Next to L.L.Bean is **Chuck Roast,** a notable local manufacturer of fleecewear.

Also of note is **Yield House** (© 800/659-2211), the nationally known manufacturer of colonial reproduction furniture. The showroom and discount warehouse is located on Route 3 at the south end of the strip, where it merges with Route 302.

Those drawn to the White Mountains for the tremendous outdoor possibilities don't need to stock up on raingear, tents, and the like before they leave home. Three good equipment suppliers are located in and around North Conway. **International Mountain Equipment** (© 603/356-7013) and **Eastern Mountain Sports** (© 603/356-5433) are both on Main Street, located just north of the green. Our favorite for its good selection and friendly staff advice is **Ragged Mountain Equipment** (© 603/356-3042), 3 miles north of town in Intervale on Routes 16 and 302.

SKIING

Cranmore Mountain Resort ⛷ *Value*   Mount Cranmore is the oldest operating ski area in New England. The slopes are unrepentantly old-fashioned, but the mountain has restyled itself as a snow-sports mecca—look for extensive snow tubing, snow-scooters, ski-bikes, and the Zorb, a 10-foot-diameter ball that participants enter into before being pushed down a gently sloping 700-foot track. The slopes aren't likely to challenge advanced skiers, but the resort will delight beginners and intermediates, as well as those who like a little diversion from the skiing. It's highly recommended for families, thanks to the relaxed attitude, range of activities, and budget ticket prices (kids 6 to 12 pay $15).

North Conway Village, NH 03860. © **603/356-5544**. www.cranmore.com. Vertical drop: 1,200 ft. Lifts: 7 chairlifts (1 high-speed quad), 2 surface lifts. Skiable acreage: 192. Lift tickets: $29.

WHERE TO STAY

Briarcliff Motel   Among North Conway's dozens of roadside motels, the Briarcliff is the best choice. It's a basic U-shaped motel with standard-sized rooms, but all units have recently been redecorated in rich colors, more like B&B rooms. There's a $10 premium for a room with a "porch" and mountain view, but these are a little peculiar—the porches are really a long single enclosed sitting area with each unit separated from its neighbor by cubicle-height partitions. (Save your money.) Get over the traffic noise and the nagging signs, and the Briarcliff offers decent value.

Rte. 16 (P.O. Box 504), ½ mile south of village center, North Conway, NH 03860. © **800/338-4291** or 603/356-5584. www.briarcliffmotel.com. 30 units. Summer $85–$125 double; off-season $59–$89. 2-night minimum stay holidays and foliage. AE, DISC, MC, V. **Amenities:** Small pool. *In room:* A/C, TV, fridge.

The Buttonwood Inn ⛷⛷   Located just a couple minutes' drive from the outlets and restaurants, the Buttonwood has more of a classic country-inn feel than any other North Conway inn. It's set on 17 quiet acres on the side of Mount Surprise in an 1820s-era home, and has a tastefully appointed interior inspired by a simple Shaker style. Most guest rooms tend toward the small and cozy, but two common rooms (one with TV) allow guests plenty of space to unwind. Two units have gas fireplaces, and one of these has a large Jacuzzi as well. Hosts Claudia and Peter Needham are uncommonly helpful with the planning of day trips, no matter what your interests. Peter prepares breakfasts, which tend toward the country-elegant (think cornmeal waffles with strawberry-rhubarb sauce).

Mt. Surprise Rd., North Conway, NH 03860. © **800/258-2625** or 603/356-2625. Fax 603/356-3140. www.buttonwood.com. 10 units (2 with private hall bathroom). $105–$250 double; from $130 foliage season; from $95 off-season. Rates include breakfast. AE, DISC, MC, V. 2- to 3-night minimum stay on weekends and holidays. Closed Apr. Children over 6 welcome. **Amenities:** Pool; cross-country ski trails. *In room:* A/C, dataport.

Comfort Inn & Suites ⛷ *Kids*   This tidy, new chain hotel opened in summer 2000, and features all "suites" (large single rooms, actually) spread among three stories, giving travelers a bit more elbowroom than at most area motels. It's a good choice for families: It's close to the best outlet shopping and has its own elaborate pirate-themed miniature golf course on the property ($1 discount for hotel guests). Four executive suites have separate sitting areas; two rooms have gas fireplaces.

2001 White Mountain Hwy. (Rte. 16), North Conway, NH 03860. © **800/228-5150** or 603/356-8811. Fax 603/356-7770. 58 units. $99–$159 double (executive suites to $249). Rates include continental breakfast. AE, DISC, MC, V. **Amenities:** Small indoor pool; limited fitness room; game room; coin-op laundry. *In room:* A/C, TV, dataport, fridge, coffeemaker, hair dryer, iron.

Cranmore Inn
The Cranmore Inn has the feel of a 19th-century boardinghouse—which is appropriate, since that's what it was. Open since 1863, this three-story Victorian home is a short walk from North Conway's village center. Its heritage—it's the oldest continuously operating hotel in North Conway—adds charm and quirkiness, but comes with drawbacks, like uneven water pressure in the showers. That said, it offers good value thanks to its handy location and the hospitality of the innkeepers. Three new units in the old stable opened in 2000 ($100 to $130).

80 Kearsarge St., North Conway, NH 03860. © **800/526-5502** or 603/356-5502. www.cranmoreinn.com. 18 units (3 with private hall bathroom). Summer $68–$88 double; foliage season and ski weekends $86–$128; off-season $59–$88. Rates include breakfast. AE, DISC, MC, V. 2-night minimum stay weekends, holidays, and foliage season. **Amenities:** Heated outdoor pool (summer only).

The Forest Country Inn ⟨★⟩
Just 10 minutes north of North Conway is a spur road that leads through the village of Intervale, which has several lodges and a feeling removed from the clutter of the outlet shops. The Forest was built in 1850, with a mansard-roofed third floor added in 1890. Typical for the era, the rooms are more cozy than spacious, and today are decorated mostly with reproductions and a smattering of country Victorian antiques. The best units are the two in the nearby stone cottage; ask for the Cottle Room, with its wood-burning fireplace, wing chairs, and small porch with Adirondack chairs.

Rte. 16A (P.O. Box 37), Intervale, NH 03845. © **800/448-3534** or 603/356-9772. Fax 603/356-5652. www. forest-inn.com. 11 units (1 with detached bathroom). July–Oct and mid-Dec to Mar $95–$140 double ($20 surcharge in foliage season); off-season $80–$125. AE, MC, V. Rates include breakfast. 2-night minimum stay most weekends and holidays. Children 6 and over welcome. Closed Apr. **Amenities:** Small pool. *In room:* A/C.

Stonehurst Manor ⟨★⟩
This imposing, architecturally eclectic Victorian stone-and-shingle mansion, originally built for the family that owned Bigelow carpet, is set amid white pines on a rocky knoll above Route 16 a mile north of North Conway. It wouldn't seem at all out of place in either the south of France or the moors of Scotland. One's immediate assumption is that it caters to the stuffy and affluent. But the main focus here is on outdoor adventures, and it attracts a youngish crowd. Request one of the 14 rooms in the regal 1876 mansion (another 10 are in a comfortable but less elegant wing built in 1952).

Rte. 16 (1.2 miles north of North Conway Village; P.O. Box 1937), N. Conway, NH 03860. © **800/525-9100.** Fax 603/356-3217. www.stonehurstmanor.com. 24 units (2 with shared bathroom). $80–$140 double; $106–$166 double with breakfast and dinner included. (7% fuel and energy surcharge in winter; $10 surcharge weekends; $20–$30 surcharge foliage season.) MC, V. 2-night minimum stay on weekends. Pets accepted in limited rooms ($25 per pet per night). **Amenities:** Restaurant (wood-fired pizza/eclectic); outdoor pool; Jacuzzi; tennis court. *In room:* A/C, TV, no phone.

White Mountain Hotel and Resort ⟨★★⟩
This contemporary resort has the best location of any in North Conway. Sited at the base of dramatic White Horse Ledge near Echo Lake State Park amid a new golf-course community, the

White Mountain Hotel was built in 1990, but its style borrows from classic area resorts. Its designers have managed to take some of the more successful elements of a friendly country inn—a nice deck with a view, comfortable seating in the lobby, a clubby tavern area—and incorporate them into a thoroughly contemporary resort. The comfortably appointed guest rooms are a solid notch or two above standard hotel furnishings.

West Side Rd. (5.4 miles west of North Conway), P.O. Box 1828), North Conway, NH 03860. © 800/533-6301 or 603/356-7100. Fax 603/356-7100. www.whitemountainhotel.com. 80 units. Summer $139–$239 double; foliage season $169–$239; winter $79–$179; other times $69–$129. AE, DISC, MC, V. 2-night minimum stay on weekends. **Amenities:** Dining room (continental/regional), tavern; outdoor heated pool; 9-hole golf course; 2 tennis courts; fitness center; Jacuzzi; sauna; game room; limited room service; baby-sitting; coin-op washers and dryers; laundry service; dry cleaning. *In room:* A/C, TV, coffeemaker, hair dryer, iron.

WHERE TO DINE

North Conway is the turf of family-style restaurants, fast-food chains, and bars that happen to serve food. If you're looking for more refined dining, you're best off heading for the Inn at Thorn Hill in Jackson, about 10 minutes north (see below).

Chinook Cafe, 80 Main St. in Conway, south of North Conway (© 603/447-6300), features sinful desserts and healthy fare for breakfast and lunch, with a good selection of vegetarian items. If you're headed from North Conway to the Kancamagus Highway, stop here for a picnic lunch. The chicken wraps are delicious (try one Thai style with peanut sauce), the smoothies nicely sippable while driving, and the homemade baked goods a fitting conclusion to any hike.

Bellini's ★ SOUTHERN ITALIAN   Bellini's has a fun, quirky interior that's more informal than its Victorian exterior might suggest. It's run by the third generation of the Marcello family, who opened their first place in Rhode Island in 1927. The food runs the gamut from fettuccine chicken pesto to *braciola,* and most everything is homemade—soups, breads, pastas, and desserts. Particularly good: the toasted ravioli appetizers.

33 Seavey St., North Conway. © 603/356-7000. www.bellinis.com. Reservations not accepted. Main courses $12–$22. AE, DISC, MC, V. Sun–Mon and Wed–Thurs 5–10pm; Fri–Sat 5–11pm.

Horsefeathers PUB FARE   In a town where pub food is the rule, Horsefeathers has been leading the pack since 1976. Set in the village across from the train station, this popular local hangout is often loud and boisterous, filled with everyone from families to off-duty bartenders. The fare is hard to pin down, ranging from tortilla soup to eggplant ravioli with a red pepper cream sauce, but tends to gather strength in the middle, with burgers, chicken wings, grilled steaks, and the like. The apple-smoked bacon cheddar burger is a good choice, as is the smoked chicken ravioli.

Main St., North Conway. © 603/356-6862. www.horsefeathers.com. Reservations not accepted. Main courses $6.95–$18.95. AE, MC, V. Daily 11:30am–11:45pm.

Moat Mountain Smoke House and Brewing Co. ★ BARBECUE/PUB FARE   Moat Mountain is the place for fresh beer, smoked meat, and wood-fired pizza. It's casual and relaxed, and has a more intriguing variety of eats than most other North Conway beer joints. You can choose from a selection of barbecued meats; several other dishes feature smoked trout and salmon. Other options include burgers, quesadillas, and wraps.

3378 White Mountain Hwy. (Rte. 16), North Conway (about 1 mile north of village). 📞 **603/356-6381.**
Reservations not accepted. Main courses $5.75–$18.95. AE, MC, V. Daily 11:30am–9pm (until 10pm Fri–Sat).

JACKSON & ENVIRONS 🐾🐾

Jackson is a quiet village situated in a picturesque valley just off Route 16 about
15 minutes north of North Conway, approached on a single-lane covered
bridge. The village center is tiny, but touches of old-world elegance remain—
vestiges of a time when Jackson was a favored destination for the East Coast
upper middle class, who fled the summer heat in the cities to relax at rambling
wooden hotels or shingled country homes.

With the Depression and the rise of the motel trade in the 1940s and '50s,
Jackson and its old-fashioned hostelries slipped into a long slumber. Then along
came the 1980s, which brought condo projects sprouting in fields where cows
once roamed, vacation homes flanking the hills, and the resuscitation of the two
vintage wooden hotels that didn't burn or collapse during the dark ages.

Thanks to a revamped golf course and one of the most elaborate and well-
maintained cross-country ski networks in the country, Jackson is again a thriving resort, both in summer and winter. While no longer undiscovered, it still
feels a shade out of the mainstream and is a peaceful spot, especially when compared to commercial North Conway.

ESSENTIALS

GETTING THERE   Jackson is just off Route 16 about 11 miles north of
North Conway. Look for the covered bridge on the right when heading north.

VISITOR INFORMATION   The **Jackson Chamber of Commerce** (📞 **800/
866-3334** or 603/383-9356; www.jacksonnh.com) can answer questions about
area attractions and make lodging reservations.

ASCENDING MOUNT WASHINGTON

Mount Washington, located just north of Jackson amid the national forest, is
home to numerous superlatives. At 6,288 feet, it's the highest mountain in the
Northeast. It's said to have the worst weather in the world outside of the polar
regions. It holds the world's record for the highest surface wind speed ever
recorded—231 miles per hour, in 1934. Winds over 150 miles per hour are routinely recorded every month except June, July, and August, in part the result of
the mountain's location at the confluence of three major storm tracks.

Mount Washington may also be the mountain with the most options for getting to the summit. Visitors can ascend by cog railroad (see the Crawford Notch
section, below), by car, by guide-driven van, or on foot.

Despite the raw power of the weather, the summit of Mount Washington is
not the best destination for those seeking wilderness wild and untamed. The
summit is home to a train platform, a parking lot, a snack bar, a gift shop, a
museum, and a handful of outbuildings, some of which house the weather
observatory, which is staffed year-round. And there are the crowds, which can be
thick on a clear day. Then again, on a clear day the views can't be beat, with vistas extending into four states and to the Atlantic Ocean.

The best place to learn about Mount Washington and its approaches is
the rustic **Pinkham Notch Camp** (📞 **603/466-2721**), operated by the
Appalachian Mountain Club. Located at the crest of Route 16 between Jackson
and Gorham, Pinkham Notch offers overnight accommodations and meals (see
below), maps, a limited selection of outdoor supplies, and plenty of advice from

the helpful staff. A number of hiking trails depart from Pinkham Notch, allowing for several loops and side trips.

About a dozen trails lead to the mountain's summit, ranging in length from 3⅘ to 15 miles. (Detailed information is available at Pinkham Notch Camp.) The most direct and dramatic is the **Tuckerman Ravine Trail** ✹✹✹, which departs from Pinkham Notch. It's a full day's endeavor: Healthy hikers should allow 4 to 5 hours for the ascent, an hour or two less for the return trip. Be sure to allow enough time to enjoy the dramatic glacial cirque of Tuckerman Ravine, which attracts extreme skiers to its snowy chutes and sheer drops as late as June, and often holds patches of snow well into summer.

The **Mount Washington Auto Road** ✹✹ (✆ **603/466-3988;** www.mt-washington.com) opened in 1861 as a carriage road, and has since remained one of the most popular White Mountain attractions. The steep, winding 8-mile road (with an average grade of 12%) is partially paved and incredibly dramatic; your breath will be taken away at one curve after another. The ascent will test your iron will; the descent will test your car's brakes. The trip's not worth doing if the summit is socked in; wait for a clear day.

If you'd prefer to leave the driving to someone else, van tours ascend throughout the day, allowing you to relax, enjoy the views, and learn about the mountain from informed guides. The cost is $20 for adults and $10 for children 5 to 12, including a half-hour stay on the summit.

The Auto Road, which is on Route 16 north of Pinkham Notch, is open from mid-May to late October from 7:30am to 6pm (limited hours early and late in the season). The cost for cars is $16 for vehicle and driver, and $6 for each additional adult ($4 for children). The fee includes audiocassette narration pointing out sights along the way (available in English, French, and German). Management has imposed some curious restrictions on cars; for instance, Acuras and Jaguars with automatic transmissions must show a "1" on the shifter to be allowed on the road, Saturns with automatic transmissions are limited to 300 pounds capacity (passengers and luggage), and no Lincoln Continentals from before 1969 are permitted.

One additional note: The average temperature atop the mountain is 30°F. (The record low was –43°F, and the warmest temperature ever recorded atop the mountain, in August, was 72°F.) Even in summer, visitors should come prepared for blustery, cold conditions.

EXPLORING PINKHAM NOTCH

Pinkham Notch Camp is at the height of land on Route 16. Just south of here, look for signs for **Glen Ellis Falls** ✹✹, a worthwhile 10- to 15-minute stop. From the parking area, you'll pass through a pedestrian tunnel and walk along the Glen Ellis River for a few minutes until it seemingly falls off the face of the earth. The stream plummets 64 feet down a sheer cliff; observation platforms are located at the top and near the bottom of the falls. The whole trip from parking lot to base of the falls is less than a half mile. This is one of the region's most impressive falls after a torrential rain.

From Pinkham Notch Camp, it's about 2⁴⁄₁₀ mile up to **Hermit Lake and Tuckerman Ravine** ✹✹✹ via the Tuckerman Ravine Trail (see above). Even if you're not planning to continue on to the summit, the ravine with its sheer sides and lacey cataracts may be the most dramatic destination in the White Mountains. It's well worth the 2-hour ascent in all but the most miserable weather. The trail is wide and only moderately demanding. Bring a picnic and lunch on the massive boulders that litter the ravine's floor.

Moments **Jackson Falls**

A warm weekday afternoon, a fat book, and Jackson Falls equals a truly memorable combination. This wonderful cascade tumbles down out of Carter Notch just above the village of Jackson (head up Carter Notch Road in front of the Wentworth resort). Park along the road, then find a sunny patch of ledge near the water, with views out to the valley. A few natural pools offer great splashing around. Two caveats: It can be buggy early in the summer, and it can be crowded on weekends all summer long.

In summer, an **enclosed gondola** at Wildcat ski area (see below) hauls passengers up the mountain for a view of Tuckerman Ravine and Mount Washington's summit. The lift operates Saturday and Sunday from Memorial Day to mid-June, then daily through October. The base lodge is just north of Pinkham Notch on Route 16.

CROSS-COUNTRY SKIING

Jackson regularly ranks among the top five cross-country ski resorts in the nation. The reason for that: the nonprofit **Jackson Ski Touring Foundation** (© **603/383-9355;** www.jacksonxc.com), which created and now maintains the extensive trail network of 93 miles (56 of which are regularly groomed). The terrain is wonderfully varied; many of the trails are rated "most difficult," which will keep advanced skiers from getting bored. Novice and intermediate skiers have good options spread out along the valley floor.

Start at the base lodge near the Wentworth Resort in the center of Jackson. There's parking, and you can ski through the village and into the hills. Gentle trails traverse the valley floor, with more advanced trails winding up the flanking mountains. One-way ski trips with shuttles back to Jackson are available; ask if you're interested. Given how extensive and well maintained the trails are, passes are a good value at $14 on Saturday and holidays, $12 all other days. Rentals are available in the ski center ($16 per day). Ticket/rental packages are available, as are snowshoe rentals and trails specifically for snowshoers.

ALPINE SKIING

Black Mountain Dating back to the 1930s, Black Mountain is one of the White Mountains' pioneer ski areas. It remains the quintessential family mountain—modest in size, thoroughly nonthreatening, ideal for beginners—although there's also glade skiing for more advanced skiers. A day here feels a bit as though you're trespassing onto a farmer's unused hayfield, which adds to the charm. The ski area also offers two compact terrain parks for snowboarders, as well as lessons, rentals, a nursery, and a base lodge with cafeteria and pub.

Jackson, NH 03846. © **800/698-4490** or 603/383-4490. www.blackmt.com. Vertical drop: 1,100 ft. Lifts: 2 chairlifts, 2 surface lifts. Skiable acreage: 143. Lift tickets: $32 Sat–Sun, $20 Mon–Fri.

Wildcat Set high within Pinkham Notch, Wildcat Mountain has a rich heritage as a venerable New England ski mountain with the best views of any ski area in the Whites. Wildcat has a bountiful supply of pleasing intermediate trails, as well as some challenging expert slopes. This is skiing as it used to be— there's no base area clutter, just a simple lodge. While that also means there's no on-slope accommodations, there's an abundance of choices within a 15-minute drive. Ask about the occasional midweek specials (such as two-for-one tickets) that can bring down the cost of lift tickets.

Rte. 16, Pinkham Notch, NH 03846. © 800/255-6439 or 603/466-3326. www.skiwildcat.com. Vertical drop: 2,100 ft. Lifts: 4 chairlifts (1 high-speed lift). Skiable acreage: 225. Lift tickets: $49 Sat–Sun and holidays, $39 Mon–Fri.

ESPECIALLY FOR KIDS

Parents with young children (ages 10 and under) can buy peace of mind at **Story-Land** ⭐⭐, situated at the northern junction of Routes 16 and 302 (© **603/383-4293**). This old-fashioned (ca. 1954) fantasy village is filled with 30 acres of improbably leaning buildings, magical rides, fairy-tale creatures, and other enchanted beings. A "sprayground" features a 40-foot water-spurting octopus—if they're so inclined, kids can get a good summer soaking. StoryLand is open from Memorial Day to mid-June, Saturday and Sunday only from 10am to 5pm; mid-June to Labor Day, daily from 9am to 6pm; and Labor Day to Columbus Day, Saturday and Sunday only from 10am to 5pm. Admission is $18 for all visitors 4 and older.

WHERE TO STAY

Covered Bridge Motor Lodge ⭐ This pleasant, family-run motel is situated on 5 acres between Route 16 and the burbling river, virtually next to Jackson's famous covered bridge. Rooms are priced well for this area. The best units

---

Value **Gorham: Budget Beds, Low-Cost Lunches**

White Mountain travelers on a lean budget would do well to look at **Gorham** as a base for mountain explorations. This tidy commercial town 10 minutes north of Pinkham Notch lacks charm, but has a great selection of clean mom-and-pop motels and family-style restaurants that won't break the bank. After all, if you're planning to spend your days hiking or canoeing, where you rest your head at night won't much matter.

The top motel choice is the **Royalty Inn,** 130 Main St. (© **800/437-3529** or 603/466-3312; www.royaltyinn.com), which has a restaurant, larger-than-average if plain rooms, two pools, and a large fitness club; rates are $62 to $88 double in summer. **Top Notch Motor Inn,** 265 Main St. (© **800/228-5496** or 603/466-5496; www.top-notch.com), has an outdoor pool and hot tub and in-room fridges. Rates start at $69 double; small pets are accepted.

For basic family dining, there's **Wilfred's,** 117 Main St. (© **603/466-3315**), serving steaks, chops, and a variety of seafood. For healthier fare, try the **Loaf Around Bakery,** 19 Exchange St. (© **603/466-2706**), which is open for breakfast and lunch (a visit to the extraordinary antique bathroom is mandatory). **Libby's Bistro,** on Main Street (© **603/466-5330**), is located in a handsomely renovated bank building and serves dinners better than anything you'll turn up in North Conway.

Moriah Sports, 101 Main St. (© **603/466-5050**), sells a wide range of sporting equipment (bikes, cross-country skis, raingear) and is a good stop for suggestions on area activities.

have balconies that overlook the river; the noisier rooms facing the road are a bit cheaper. Ask about the two-bedroom apartment units with kitchen and fireplace. While pretty basic, the lodge features lovely gardens and other appealing touches that make this a good value.

Rte. 16, Jackson, NH 03846. ✆ **800/634-2911** or 602/383-9151. www.jacksoncoveredbridge.com. 33 units. Summer $79–$98 double, from $59 off-season. Rates include continental breakfast. AE, DISC, MC, V. **Amenities:** Outdoor pool; Jacuzzi; tennis court. *In room:* A/C, TV.

Eagle Mountain House ★★
The Eagle Mountain House is a handsome relic that happily survived the ravages of time, fire, and the capricious tastes of tourists. Built in 1916 and fully renovated in the 1980s, this five-story gleaming white wooden classic is set in an idyllic valley above Jackson. The guest rooms are furnished in a country pine look with stenciled blanket chests, armoires, and feather comforters. There's a premium for rooms with mountain views, but it's not really worth the extra cash. Just plan to spend your free time lounging on the wide porch with the views across the golf course toward the mountains beyond.

Carter Notch Rd., Jackson, NH 03846. ✆ **800/966-5779** or 603/383-9111. Fax 603/383-0854. www. eaglemt.com. 93 units. Summer $99–$149 double, $139–$179 suite; winter $69–$129 double, $109–$159 suite. Ask about packages. AE, DISC, MC, V. **Amenities:** Dining room (New England), tavern; outdoor pool (summer only); 9-hole golf course; 2 tennis courts (one lit for night play); small health club; Jacuzzi; sauna; game room; massage dry cleaning. *In room:* TV.

Inn at Thorn Hill ★★★
This truly elegant inn is a great choice for a romantic getaway. The classic shingle-style home (alas, now swathed in yellow siding) was designed by famed architect Stanford White in 1895, and sits just outside the village center surrounded by wooded hills. Inside, there's a comfortable Victorian feel. The rooms are luxuriously appointed; you'll rarely want to leave. Our favorites include Catherine's Suite, with a fireplace and two-person Jacuzzi, and Notch View Cottage, with a screened porch and a Jacuzzi with a relaxing view of the forest. The hospitality is warm and top-notch, and the meals are among the best in the Mount Washington Valley.

Thorn Hill Rd. (P.O. Box A), Jackson, NH 03846. ✆ 603/383-4242. www.innatthornhill.com. 19 units. $190–$300 double; foliage season and Christmas $225–$345 double; cottages $275–$300. Rates include breakfast and dinner. 2- to 3-night minimum stay on weekends and some holidays. AE, DISC, MC, V. Children 8 and over welcome. **Amenities:** Restaurant (see below); outdoor pool; hot tub; limited room service; baby-sitting; laundry service. *In room:* A/C, TV.

Joe Dodge Lodge at Pinkham Notch
Guests come to Pinkham Notch Camp more for the camaraderie than the accommodations. Situated spectacularly at the base of Mount Washington and with easy access to numerous hiking and skiing trails, the lodge is operated by the Appalachian Mountain Club like a tightly run youth hostel, with guests sharing spartan bunk rooms, dorm-style bathrooms, and boisterous meals at family-style tables in the main lodge. (Some private rooms offer double beds or family accommodations.) The pluses: a festive atmosphere and an ideal location for outdoor forays.

Rte. 16, Pinkham Notch, NH. (Mailing address: AMC, P.O. Box 298, Gorham, NH 03581.) ✆ 603/466-2727. www.outdoors.org. 108 beds in bunk rooms of 2, 3, and 4 beds; all with shared bathroom. Peak season $49 per adult, $33 per child (discount for AMC members); off-peak $46 per adult, $30 per child. Rates include breakfast and dinner. MC, V. Children 3 and over welcome. **Amenities:** Cafeteria/dining room; weekend activities; outdoor store. *In room:* No phone.

> **Tips Take a Dip**
>
> During the lazy days of summer, the **Saco River**—which runs through the valley—offers several good swimming holes just off the highway. They're unmarked, but watch for local cars parked off the side of the road for no apparent reason, and you should be able to find your way to a good spot for soaking and splashing.

WHERE TO DINE

Inn at Thorn Hill ★★★ NEW AMERICAN   The perfectly romantic Inn at Thorn Hill is a great choice for a memorable meal. The candlelit dining room faces the forested hill behind the inn. Start with a glass of fine wine (the restaurant has won the *Wine Spectator* award of excellence), then browse the menu selections, which change weekly. Appetizers might include a roulade of duck breast with basil and ginger. Entrees feature choices such as toasted cashew and coconut salmon, or pecan-crusted lamb loin with an apple rum demi-glace. If quail's on the menu, it's a great choice.

Thorn Hill Rd., Jackson. ✆ **603/383-4242.** www.innatthornhill.com. Reservations recommended. Main courses $21.95–$27.95. AE, DISC, MC, V. Daily 6–9pm.

Thompson House Eatery ★★ ECLECTIC   This friendly, old-fashioned spot in a 19th-century farmhouse at the edge of Jackson's golf course attracts crowds not only for its uncommonly well-prepared fare, but also for the great prices. There's dining indoor and out, with lunches including six different salads (the curried chicken and toasted almonds is great), knockwurst, frittatas, and basic sandwiches (tuna, grilled cheese). Come dinnertime, there's fresh fish, steak, and several vegetarian entrees. Thompson House has an adjacent ice-cream parlor that's worth a stop.

Rte. 16A, Jackson (near north intersection with Rte. 16). ✆ **603/383-9341.** Reservations recommended for dinner. Main courses $3.95–$6.95 lunch, $6.95–$17.95 dinner. AE, DISC, MC, V. Summer daily 11:30am–3:30pm and 5:30–9pm (until 10pm Fri–Sat); winter Fri–Sun 11:30am–3:30pm, Wed–Mon 5:30pm–9pm. Call for open days/hours in shoulder seasons.

CRAWFORD NOTCH ★★★

Crawford Notch is a wild, rugged mountain valley that angles through the heart of the White Mountains. Within the notch itself is a surplus of legend and history. For years after its discovery by European settlers in 1771, it was an impenetrable wilderness, creating a barrier to commerce by blocking trade between the prosperous upper Connecticut River Valley and commercial harbors in Portland and Portsmouth. This was eventually surmounted by a plucky crew who hauled the first freight through.

Nathaniel Hawthorne immortalized the notch with a short story about a real-life tragedy that struck in 1826. One dark and stormy night (naturally), the Willey family fled its home when they feared an avalanche would roar toward the valley floor. As fate would have it, the avalanche divided above their home and spared the structure; the seven who fled were killed in tumbling debris. You can still visit the site today; watch for signs when driving through the notch.

The notch is accessible via Route 302, which is wide and speedy on the lower sections, becoming steeper as it approaches the narrow defile of the notch itself.

Modern engineering has taken most of the kinks out of the road, so you need to remind yourself to stop from time to time to enjoy the panoramas. The views up the cliffs from the road can be spectacular on a clear day; on an overcast or drizzly day, the effect is foreboding.

ESSENTIALS

GETTING THERE   Route 302 runs through Crawford Notch for approximately 25 miles between the towns of Bartlett and Twin Mountain.

VISITOR INFORMATION   The **Twin Mountain Chamber of Commerce** (© **800/245-8946** or 603/846-5407; www.twinmountain.org) offers general information and lodging referrals at its booth near the intersection of Routes 302 and 3. Open year-round; hours vary.

WATERFALLS & SWIMMING HOLES

Much of the mountainous land flanking Route 302 falls under the jurisdiction of **Crawford Notch State Park** ★★, which was established in 1911 to preserve land that elsewhere had been decimated by overly aggressive logging. The headwaters of the Saco River form in the notch, and what's generally regarded as the first permanent trail up Mount Washington also departs from here. Several turnouts and trailheads invite a more leisurely exploration of the area. The trail network on both sides of Crawford Notch is extensive; consult the *AMC White Mountain Guide* or *White Mountains Map Book* for detailed information.

Up the mountain slopes that form the valley, hikers will spot a number of lovely waterfalls, some more easily accessible than others. Two to start with:

Arethusa Falls ★★ has the highest single drop of any waterfall in the state, and the trail to the falls passes several attractive smaller cascades. These are especially beautiful in the spring or after a heavy rain, when the falls are at their fullest. The trip can be done as a 2⅔-mile round-trip to the falls and back on Arethusa Falls Trail, or as a 4½-mile loop that includes views from Frankenstein Cliffs. (These are named not after the creator of the monster, but after a noted landscape painter.)

If you're arriving from the south, look for signs to the trail parking area shortly after passing the Crawford Notch State Park entrance sign. From the north, the trailhead is a half mile south of the Dry River Campground. At the parking lot, look for the sign and map to get your bearings, then cross the railroad tracks to start up the falls trail.

Continue northward on Route 302 to the trailhead for tumultuous **Ripley Falls** ★. This easy hike is a little more than 1 mile round-trip. Look for the sign to the falls on Route 302 just north of the trailhead for Webster Cliff Trail. (If you pass the Willey House site, you've gone too far.) Park at the site of the Willey Station. Follow trail signs for the Ripley Falls Trail, and allow about a half hour to reach the cascades. The most appealing swimming holes are at the top of the falls.

A HISTORIC RAILWAY

Mount Washington Cog Railway ★★   The cog railway was a marvel of engineering when it opened in 1869, and it remains so today. Part moving museum, part slow-motion roller-coaster ride, the cog railway steams to the summit with a determined "I think I can" pace of about 4 miles per hour. But there's still a frisson of excitement on the way up and back, especially when the train crosses Jacob's Ladder, a rickety-seeming trestle 25 feet high that angles upward at a grade of more than 37%. Passengers enjoy the expanding view on this 3-hour round-trip (there are stops to add water to the steam engine, to check the track switches, and to allow other trains to ascend or descend). There's also a 20-minute stop at the summit to browse around. Be aware that the ride is noisy and sulfurous, and you should dress expecting to acquire a patina of cinder and soot.

Rte. 302, Bretton Woods. ✆ **800/922-8825** or 603/846-5404. Fare $44 adults, $30 children 6–12, free for children 5 and under. MC, V. Runs daily Memorial Day to late Oct, plus weekends in May. Frequent departures; call for schedule. Reservations recommended.

SKIING

Attitash Bear Peak ✿✿ Attitash Bear Peak is a good mountain for families and skiers who are at the intermediate-edging-to-advanced level; look for great cruising runs and a handful of more challenging drops. The ski area includes two peaks, 1,750-foot Attitash and the adjacent 1,450-foot Bear Peak, and is among New England's most scenic ski areas—it's dotted with rugged rock outcroppings, and you'll get sweeping views of Mount Washington and the Presidentials (there's an observation tower on the main summit). The base area tends to be sleepy in the evenings, so those looking for nightlife typically head 15 minutes away to North Conway.

Rte. 302, Bartlett, NH 03812. ✆ **800/223-7669** or 603/374-2368. www.attitash.com. Vertical drop: 1,750 ft. Lifts: 12 chairlifts (including 2 high-speed quads), 3 surface lifts. Skiable acreage: 280. Lift tickets: $49 Sat–Sun, $51 holidays, $42 Mon–Fri.

Bretton Woods ✿ Bretton Woods expanded in 1999 to include the formerly undeveloped West Mountain, doubling the number of chairlifts and skiable acreage (it now has the most skiing terrain in New Hampshire). The new trails and lifts bring a welcome vitality to the mountain, which has long been popular with beginners and families. The trails include glades and wide cruising runs, along with more challenging options for advanced skiers. (Note that the challenge level still doesn't rival the more demanding slopes of Vermont or Maine.) The resort continues to do a great job with kids and offers a pleasantly low-key attitude that families adore. Accommodations are available on the mountain and nearby, notably at the Mount Washington Hotel, but evening entertainment tends to revolve around hot tubs, TVs, and going to bed early. For those so inclined, there's an excellent cross-country ski center nearby.

Rte. 302, Bretton Woods, NH 03575. ✆ **800/232-2972** or 603/278-3307. www.brettonwoods.com. Vertical drop: 1,500 ft. Lifts: 8 chairlifts (including 2 high-speed quads), 2 surface lifts. Skiable acreage: 345. Lift tickets: $51 Sat–Sun and holidays, $42 Mon–Fri.

WHERE TO STAY & DINE

Mount Washington Hotel ✿✿ This five-story resort, with its gleaming white clapboards and cherry-red roof, was built in 1902. In its heyday the resort attracted luminaries like Babe Ruth, Thomas Edison, and Woodrow Wilson. Guest rooms vary in size and decor; many have grand views of the surrounding mountains and countryside. A 900-foot-long veranda makes for relaxing afternoons. Meals are enjoyed in an impressive octagonal dining room. (Men should wear jackets at dinner.) A house orchestra provides entertainment during the meal, and guests often dance between courses. The decor isn't lavish, and while the innkeepers are making overdue improvements, the hotel can feel a bit unfinished in parts. That said, this remains one of our favorite spots in the mountains, partly for the sheer improbability of it all, and partly for its direct link to a lost era.

Rte. 302, Bretton Woods, NH 03575. ✆ **800/258-0330** or 603/278-1000. www.mtwashington.com. 200 units. Midweek $209–$459 double; weekends and holidays $249–$499 double; suites to $1,199. Rates include breakfast and dinner. Minimum stay during holidays. AE, DISC, MC, V. **Amenities:** 2 restaurants (continental, pub fare); indoor and outdoor pools; 2 PGA golf courses (27 holes); 12 clay tennis courts; shuttle to nearby health club; Jacuzzi; sauna; bike rental; summer children's programs; game room; concierge; shopping arcade; room service; baby-sitting; coin-op washers. *In room:* TV.

Notchland Inn ★★ Located off Route 302 in a wild section of Crawford Notch, this inn looks every bit like a redoubt in a Sir Walter Scott novel. Built of hand-cut granite between 1840 and 1862, Notchland is classy yet informal, perfectly situated for exploring the wilds of the White Mountains. All guest rooms are outfitted with antiques, wood-burning fireplaces, high ceilings, and individual thermostats. Three suites have Jacuzzis, while two have soaking tubs. Two units are located in the adjacent schoolhouse; the upstairs room has a wonderful soaking tub. (All but three rooms have air-conditioning.) The inn is also home to two affable Bernese mountain dogs and two llamas. Five-course dinners are included in most rates (the restaurant is closed Monday), and are served in a lively dining room, with a single seating at 7pm.

Rte. 302, Hart's Location, NH 03812. ℭ **800/866-6131** or 603/374-6131. Fax 603/374-6168. www.notchland.com. 13 units. $235–$295 double; foliage season and holidays $285–$345. Rates include breakfast and dinner. (B&B rates from $175.) 2- to 3-night minimum stay on weekends, foliage, and some holidays. AE, DISC, MC, V. Children over 12 welcome. **Amenities:** Restaurant (global fare); river swimming (across road); hot tub; baby-sitting. *In room:* Hair dryer, iron, no phone.

WATERVILLE VALLEY

In the southwestern corner of the White Mountains is Waterville Valley, which occupies a lovely and remote valley at the end of a 12-mile dead-end road. Incorporated as a town in 1829, Waterville Valley became a popular destination for summer visitors during the heyday of mountain travel late in the 19th century. Skiers first started descending the slopes in the 1930s, after the Civilian Conservation Corps and local ski clubs carved a few trails out of the forest. But it wasn't until 1965, when a skier named Tom Corcoran bought 425 acres in the valley, that Waterville began to assume its current air.

Few traces of the village's history remain, and Waterville Valley today has a modern, manufactured character. The "village" is reasonably compact (although you need to drive or take a shuttle to the ski slopes, which are at a higher elevation). Modern lodges, condos, and a handful of restaurants are located within a loop road. In the center is the "Town Square," itself a sort of minor mall complex with a restaurant and a few shops.

Our chief complaint is that Waterville Valley has the unnatural, somewhat antiseptic quality of planned communities everywhere. You don't feel like you're in New England in the least, but rather a sort of 1970s time warp. This is a reasonable choice for a weeklong family vacation—the resort is practiced at planning activities for kids—but those in search of classic New England won't miss anything by not venturing here.

ESSENTIALS

GETTING THERE Waterville Valley is located 12 miles northwest of Exit 28 or Exit 29 off I-93 via Route 49.

VISITOR INFORMATION The **Waterville Valley Chamber of Commerce** (ℭ **800/237-2307** or 603/726-3804; www.watervillevalleyregion.com) staffs a year-round information booth on Route 49 in Campton, just off Exit 28 of I-93.

SKIING

Waterville Valley ★ Waterville Valley is a classic intermediate skier's mountain. The trails are uniformly wide and well-groomed, and the ski area is compact enough that no one will get confused and end up staring down a double-diamond trail. Improvements in recent years have made it a fine place to learn to ski or brush up on your skills. Advanced skiers have a selection of black-diamond trails, but the selection and steepness don't rival that of the larger ski mountains to the north. A new terrain park served by a Poma lift above the base lodge is popular with both advanced and beginning boarders.

Waterville Valley, NH 03215. ☎ 800/468-2553 or 603/236-8311. www.waterville.com. Vertical drop: 2,020 ft. Lifts: 8 chairlifts (2 high-speed), 4 surface lifts. Skiable acreage: 255. Lift tickets: $49 Sat–Sun and holidays, $41 Mon–Fri.

WHERE TO STAY

Snowy Owl Inn 🐦   The Snowy Owl will appeal to those who like the amiable character of a country inn but prefer modern conveniences like in-room hair dryers. A modern, four-story resort project near Town Square, the inn offers a number of nice touches like a towering fieldstone fireplace in the lobby, a handsome octagonal indoor pool, and a rooftop observatory reached via spiral staircase. The rooms are a notch above basic motel-style units in size and decor; five feature kitchens.

Village Rd., Waterville Valley, NH 03215. ☎ 800/766-9969 or 603/236-8383. Fax 603/236-4890. www.snowyowlinn.com. 80 units. Winter $109–$249 double (school holidays from $189), summer $99–$199. Rates include continental breakfast and resort fee. AE, DISC, MC, V. **Amenities:** Indoor and outdoor pools; access to nearby Athletic Club; Jacuzzi; sauna; game room. *In room:* TV, dataport, hair dryer.

The Valley Inn   The Valley Inn is one of the smaller complexes in the valley, and slightly more intimate than its neighbors. Most rooms feature a sitting area and tiny dining table in a bay window as well as a wet bar; suites have kitchenettes. The inn is conveniently located near the village center and within walking distance of the Athletic Club and Town Square. There's a shuttle to the slopes in winter.

Tecumseh Rd. (P.O. Box 1), Waterville Valley, NH 03215. ☎ 800/343-0969 or 603/236-8336. Fax 603/236-4294. www.valleyinn.com. 52 units. Winter weekends $85–$152 double, $272 suite; midweek $75–$128 double, $228 suite; discounts in summer and off-season; premium charged during winter holidays. AE, DISC, MC, V. Minimum stay during certain holidays. **Amenities:** 2 restaurants (American and pub fare); indoor/outdoor heated pool; 2 platform tennis courts; access to valley Athletic Club; Jacuzzi; sauna; game room; limited room service; coin-op laundry. *In room:* A/C, TV.

WHERE TO DINE

The good news is that Waterville Valley's accommodations often include kitchens, so you can prepare your own meals. The bad news? There's a limited selection of restaurants, and no place is outstanding. The Athletic Club has its own restaurant on the second floor, **Wild Coyote Grill** (☎ 603/236-4919), which offers regional favorites like potato-crusted salmon and grilled sirloin with mashed potatoes. Basic pub fare can be enjoyed in the **Red Fox Tavern** (☎ 603/236-8336), located in the basement of the Valley Inn.

LINCOLN, NORTH WOODSTOCK 🐦 & LOON MOUNTAIN

Some 25 miles north of Waterville Valley are the towns of Lincoln and North Woodstock, as well as the Loon Mountain ski resort (located just east of Lincoln). These towns are also the start (or end) of the Kancamagus Highway, a 35-mile route that's one of the White Mountains' most scenic drives.

At the former mill town of Lincoln and the adjacent village of North Woodstock, you'll find mundane stores, fast-food chains, and no-frills motels. Lincoln has embraced strip-mall development; North Woodstock has retained some of its native charm in a vestigial village center. Neither will win any awards for quaintness. Loon Mountain opened in 1966 and was early on criticized for its mediocre skiing, though some upgrading since then has brought the mountain greater respect.

At times it seems that Lincoln underwent not so much a development boom in the 1980s as a development spasm. Clusters of condos now blanket the lower hillsides of this narrow valley. The Loon Mountain base village is usually lively with skiers in winter, but in summer has a post-nuclear-fallout feel to it, with few people in evidence. The ambience is also compromised by that peculiar style of resort architecture that's simultaneously aggressive and bland.

As with Waterville Valley, we think there are other areas of the White Mountains that are more distinctly New England. You're better off pressing on.

ESSENTIALS

GETTING THERE   Waterville Valley is located 12 miles northwest of Exit 29 on I-93 via Route 49. Lincoln is accessible off I-93 on exits 32 and 33.

VISITOR INFORMATION   The **Lincoln-Woodstock Chamber of Commerce** (© **800/227-4191** or 603/745-6621; www.linwoodcc.org) has an information office open daily at Depot Plaza on Route 112 in Lincoln. A better, more comprehensive information source is the **White Mountains Visitor Center** (© **800/346-3687** or 603/745-8720), located just east of Exit 32 on I-93. It's open year-round, daily from 9am to 5pm.

THE KANCAMAGUS HIGHWAY

The Kancamagus Highway—locally called "the Kanc"—is among the White Mountains' most spectacular drives. Officially designated a national scenic byway by the U.S. Forest Service, the 34-mile roadway joins Lincoln and Conway through 2,860-foot Kancamagus Pass. When the highway was built from 1960 to 1961, it opened up 100 square miles of wilderness—a move that irked preservationists but has proven very popular with folks who prefer their sightseeing by car.

The route begins and ends along wide, tumbling rivers on relatively flat plateaus. The two-lane road rises steadily to the pass. Several rest areas with sweeping vistas allow visitors to pause and enjoy the mountain views. The highway also makes a good destination for hikers; any number of day and overnight trips may be launched from the roadside. One simple, short hike along a gravel pathway (it's less than a third of a mile each way) leads to **Sabbaday Falls,** a cascade that's especially impressive after a downpour. Six national forest campgrounds are also located along the highway.

To get the most out of the road, take your time and make frequent stops. Think of it as a scavenger hunt as you look for a covered bridge, cascades with good swimming holes, a historic home with a quirky story behind it, and spectacular mountain panoramas. All of these things and more lie along the route.

SKIING

Loon Mountain ⚑   Located on U.S. Forest Service land, Loon had long been stymied in expansion efforts by environmental concerns regarding land use and water withdrawals from the river. The ski mountain has been slowly reshaped, adding uphill capacity, 15 acres of glade skiing (in 2000), and improved snowmaking. The expansion has reduced some of the congestion of this popular area, but it's still very crowded on weekends. Most of the trails cluster toward the bottom, and most are solid intermediate runs. Experts head to the north peak, which has a challenging selection of advanced trails served by a triple chairlift. For kids, there's a new snow-tubing park off the Little Sister chairlift.

Lincoln, NH 03251. ✆ **800/227-4191** for lodging, or 603/745-8111. www.loonmtn.com. Vertical drop: 2,100 ft. Lifts: 8 chairlifts (1 high-speed), 1 high-speed gondola, 1 surface lift. Skiable acreage: 275. Lift tickets: $49 Sat–Sun, $42 Mon–Fri.

WHERE TO STAY

Mountain Club at Loon 🍴🍴 Set at the foot of Loon Mountain's slopes, the Mountain Club is a contemporary resort of prominent gables and glass built during the real-estate boom of the 1980s. It was managed for several years as a Marriott, and the inoffensive but unexciting decor tends to reflect its chain-hotel heritage. Guest rooms are designed to be rented either individually or as two-room suites. The high rates reflect the proximity to the slopes and the excellent health-club facilities connected to the hotel via covered walkway.

Rte. 112 (R.R. #1; Box 40), Lincoln, NH 03251. ✆ **800/229-7829** or 603/745-2244. Fax 603/745-2317. www. mtnclubonloon.com. 234 units. Winter midweek $169–$399 double; weekend $209–$429 double; summer and off-season $114–$259 double. AE, DISC, MC, V. **Amenities:** 2 restaurants (New England, pub fare); indoor and outdoor pools; 2 tennis courts; fitness center (with basketball court and aerobics); Jacuzzi; sauna; concierge; limited room service; coin-op washers. *In room:* A/C, TV, coffeemaker, hair dryer.

Wilderness Inn 🍴 The Wilderness Inn is located at the southern edge of North Woodstock village—not quite the wilderness that the name suggests. However, it is a friendly, handsome bungalow-style home that dates to 1912. The interior features heavy timbers in classic Craftsman style, a spare mix of antiques and reproductions, and games to occupy an evening. Five rooms have TVs, the second-floor units are air-conditioned, and there's a VCR and TV in the living room. The nearby cottage is a good spot to relax, with a gas fireplace and Jacuzzi. If you're arriving by bus in Lincoln, the innkeepers will pick you up at no charge.

Rte. 3 (just south of Rte. 112), North Woodstock, NH 03262. ✆ **800/200-9453** or 603/745-3890. www. thewildernessinn.com. 8 units. Winter $80–$150 double; off-season $65–$90. Rates include breakfast. AE, MC, V. *In room:* TV, no phone.

Woodstock Inn 🍴 The Woodstock Inn has a Jekyll-and-Hyde thing going on. In the front, it's a white Victorian set in Woodstock's commercial downtown area—one of the few older inns in the land of condos and modern resorts. In the back, it's a modern, boisterous brewpub that serves up hearty fare along with robust ales. The inn's guest rooms are spread among three houses. If you're on a tight budget, go for the shared-bathroom units in the main house and the nearby Deachman house; the slightly less personable Riverside building across the street offers rooms with private bathrooms. Accommodations are individually decorated in a country Victorian style, furnished with both reproductions and antiques. Three units have Jacuzzis.

Main St. (P.O. Box 118), North Woodstock, NH 03262. ✆ **800/321-3985** or 603/745-3951. Fax 603/ 745-3701. www.woodstockinnnh.com. 21 units (8 with shared bathroom). $68–$150 double (shared bathroom from $59.) Rates include breakfast. AE, DISC, MC, V. **Amenities:** 2 restaurants (see below). *In room:* A/C, TV.

WHERE TO DINE

Clement Room Grille/Woodstock Station 🍴 AMERICAN/ PUB FARE Dine in the casually upscale Clement Room on the enclosed porch of the Woodstock Inn, or head to the brewpub out back, housed in an old train station. In the Clement Room, there's an open grill and fare that aspires toward some originality (ostrich quesadilla, bison pot roast). The pub has high ceilings, knotty pine, and a decor that draws on vintage winter recreational gear. The pub menu rounds up the usual suspects, like nachos, chicken wings, burgers, and pasta, none of which is prepared with much creative flair. Better are the porters, stouts, and brown and red ales brewed on the premises.

Main St. (C) **603/745-3951.** Reservations accepted for Clement Room only. Breakfast items $3.95–$9.50; lunch and dinner items $5.49–$22.95. AE, DISC, MC, V. Clement Room daily 7–11:30am and 5:30–9:30pm; Woodstock Station daily 11:30am–10pm.

FRANCONIA NOTCH ★★★

Franconia Notch is rugged New Hampshire writ large. As travelers head north on I-93, the Kinsman Range to the west and the Franconia Range to the east begin to converge, and the road swells upward. Soon, the flanking mountain ranges press in on either side, forming dramatic Franconia Notch, which offers little in the way of civilization and services but a whole lot in the way of natural drama. Most of the notch is included in a well-managed state park that to most travelers will be indistinguishable from the national forest. Travelers seeking the sublime should plan on a leisurely trip through the notch, allowing enough time to get out of the car and explore forests and craggy peaks. Franconia Notch is more developed for recreation (and thus more crowded with daytrippers) than equally rugged Crawford Notch to the northeast (see above).

ESSENTIALS
GETTING THERE I-93 runs through Franconia Notch, gearing down from four lanes to two (where it becomes the Franconia Notch Parkway) in the most scenic and sensitive areas of the park. Several roadside pull-outs and scenic attractions dot the route.

VISITOR INFORMATION Information on the park and surrounding area is available at the **Flume Information Center** ((C) **603/745-8391**), at Exit 1 off the parkway. The center is open in summer daily from 9am to 4:30pm. North of the notch, head to the **Franconia Notch Chamber of Commerce** ((C) **800/237-9007** or 603/823-5661; www.franconianotch.org), on Main Street next to the town hall. It's open spring through fall, Tuesday through Sunday from 10am to 5pm (days and hours often vary).

EXPLORING FRANCONIA NOTCH STATE PARK
Franconia Notch State Park's 8,000 acres, nestled within the surrounding White Mountain National Forest, hosts an array of scenic attractions easily accessible from I-93 and the Franconia Notch Parkway. At the Flume Information Center (see above), there's a free 15-minute video that summarizes the park's attractions. For information on any of the following, contact the park offices ((C) **603/823-8800**).

The most famous park landmark is the **Old Man of the Mountains** ★★, located near Cannon Mountain. From the right spot on the valley floor, this 48-foot-high rock formation bears an uncanny resemblance to the profile of a craggy old man—early settlers said it was Thomas Jefferson. If it looks vaguely familiar, it's because this is the logo you see on all the New Hampshire state highway signs. The profile, which often surprises visitors by just how tiny it is when viewed from far below (bring binoculars), is best seen from the well-marked roadside viewing area at Profile Lake.

The Flume ★★ is a rugged 800-foot gorge through which the Flume Brook tumbles. The gorge, a massively popular attraction in the mid–19th century, is 800 feet long, 90 feet deep, and as narrow as 20 feet at the bottom; visitors explore by means of a network of boardwalks and bridges on a 2-mile walk. Early photos of the chasm show a boulder wedged in overhead; this was swept away in an 1883 avalanche. If you're looking for easy, quick access to natural grandeur, it's worth the money. Otherwise, set off into the mountains and seek your own drama with fewer crowds and less expense. Admission is $7 for adults, $4 for children 6 to 12.

Echo Lake ⚘ is a picturesquely situated recreation area, with a 28-acre lake, a handsome swimming beach, and picnic tables scattered about all within view of Cannon Mountain on one side and Mount Lafayette on the other. A bike path runs alongside the lake and meanders up and down the notch for a total of 8 miles. (Mountain bikes, canoes, and paddleboats may be rented at the park for $10 per hour.) Admission to the park is $2.50 for all visitors over 12.

For a high-altitude view of the region, set off for the alpine ridges on the **Cannon Mountain Tramway** ⚘⚘. The old-fashioned cable car serves skiers in winter; in summer, it whisks up to 80 travelers at a time to the summit of the 4,180-foot mountain. Once at the top, you can strike out on foot along the Rim Trail for superb views. Be prepared for cool, gusty winds. The tramway costs $9 round-trip for adults, $7 for children 6 to 12. It's located at Exit 2 of the parkway.

Looking to save a few dollars? A 1-day park pass ($20 for adults, $16 for children) provides a tram ride, Echo Lake beach access, and 1-hour boat and bike rental.

HIKING

The Franconia Notch area is one of the best destinations for White Mountain hikers. It's easy to plan hikes ranging from gentle valley walks to arduous ascents of blustery granite peaks. Consult the *AMC White Mountain Guide* for a comprehensive directory of area hiking trails, or ask for suggestions at the information center.

Among our recommendations: A pleasant woodland detour of 2 hours or so can be found at the **Basin-Cascades Trail** ⚘⚘ (look for well-marked signs off I-93 about 1½ miles north of the Flume). A popular roadside waterfall and natural pothole, the Basin attracts crowds who come to see pillows of granite scoured smooth by glaciers and water. Relatively few visitors continue to the series of cascades beyond. Look for signs for the trail, then head off into the woods. After about a half mile of easy hiking, you'll reach **Kinsman Falls,** a beautiful 20-foot cascade. Continue another half mile beyond that to **Rocky Glen,** where the stream plummets through a craggy gorge.

SKIING

Cannon Mountain ⚘   One of New England's first ski mountains, Cannon remains famed for its challenging runs and exposed faces, and the mountain still attracts skiers serious about getting down the hill in style. (During skiing's formative years, this state-run ski area was *the* place to ski in the East.) Many of the old-fashioned New England–style trails are narrow and fun (if often icy, scoured by the notch's winds), and the enclosed tramway is an elegant way to get to the summit. There's no base scene to speak of; skiers retire to inns around Franconia or retreat southward to the condo villages of Lincoln.

Franconia Notch Pkwy., Franconia. ⓒ **603/823-8800.** Vertical drop: 2,146 ft. Lifts: 70-person tram, 5 chairlifts, 1 surface lift. Skiable acreage: about 175. Lift tickets: $42 Sat–Sun, $30 Mon–Fri.

A HISTORIC HOME

The Frost Place ⚘   Robert Frost lived in New Hampshire from the time he was 10 until he was 45. The Frost Place is a humble farmhouse, where Frost lived simply with his family. Wandering the grounds, it's not hard to see how his granite-edged poetry evolved at the fringes of the White Mountains. First editions of Frost's works are on display; a nature trail in the woods nearby is posted with excerpts from his poems.

Ridge Rd., Franconia. ℂ **603/823-5510.** www.frostplace.com. Admission $3 adults, $1.50 children 6–15, free for children under 6. Late May to June Sat–Sun 1–5pm; July to mid-Oct Wed–Mon 1–5pm. Head south on Rte. 116 from Franconia 1 mile to Ridge Rd. (gravel); follow signs a short way to the house; park in lot below the house.

WHERE TO STAY & DINE

Franconia Inn ℛ   This pleasant, welcoming inn offers good value. It's set along a quiet road in a bucolic valley 2 miles from the village of Franconia. Built in 1934 after a fire destroyed the original 1886 structure, the inn has an informal feel, with wingback chairs around the fireplace in one common room, and jigsaw puzzles half completed in the paneled library. Guest rooms are appointed in a relaxed country fashion; three feature gas fireplaces, and four have Jacuzzis. The inn is a haven for cross-country skiers—38 miles of groomed trails start right outside the front door.

1300 Easton Rd., Franconia, NH 03580. ℂ **800/473-5299** or 603/823-5542. Fax 603/823-8078. www.franconiainn.com. 32 units. $108–$168 double. Rates include breakfast. MAP rates available. AE, MC, V. 3-night minimum stay on holiday weekends. Closed Apr to mid-May. **Amenities:** Dining room (traditional/New American); heated pool; 4 clay tennis courts; hot tub; sauna; mountain bikes (free); game room; bridle trails and horse rentals; cross-country ski trails. *In room:* No phone.

Sugar Hill Inn ℛℛ   On 16 acres on lovely Sugar Hill, you'll find this classic inn with wraparound porch and sweeping mountain panoramas. It's a welcoming, comfortable spot, and makes for a superb base for exploring the western White Mountains. The rooms are graciously appointed in an antique country style, some influenced by a Shaker sensibility. Most have gas Vermont Castings stoves for heat and atmosphere. The restaurant, featuring upscale regional fare, is one of the area's best.

Rte. 117, Franconia, NH 03580. ℂ **800/548-4748** or 603/823-5621. Fax 603/823-5639. www.sugarhillinn.com. 18 units. $115–$225 double; $225–$325 suite; $125–$250 cottage. Rates include breakfast. AE, MC, V. Closed Apr. Children over 12 welcome. **Amenities:** Restaurant (New England). *In room:* No phone.

BETHLEHEM ℛ & LITTLETON ℛ

More than a century ago, **Bethlehem** was as populous as North Conway to the south, and home to numerous sprawling resort hotels, summer retreats, and even its own semiprofessional baseball team. (Joseph Kennedy, patriarch of the Kennedy clan, once played for the team.) Bethlehem subsequently lost the race for the riches (or won, depending on your view of outlet shopping), and today is again a sleepy town high on a hillside.

Once famed for its lack of ragweed and pollen, Bethlehem teemed with vacationers seeking respite from the ravages of hay fever in the late 19th and early 20th centuries. When antihistamines and air-conditioning appeared on the scene, the sufferers stayed home. Empty resorts burned down one by one until the 1920s, when Hasidim from New York City discovered Bethlehem. They soon arrived in number to spend summers in the remaining boardinghouses. Indeed, that tradition has endured, and it's not uncommon today to see resplendently bearded men in black walking the village streets or rocking on the porches of Victorian-era homes.

Nearby **Littleton,** set in a broad valley along the Ammonoosuc River, is the area's commercial hub, but it still has plenty of bustling small-town charm. The long main street has an eclectic selection of shops—you can buy a wrench, a foreign magazine or literary novel, locally brewed beer, pizza, whole foods, or camping supplies.

Neither town offers much in the way of must-see attractions, but both have good lodging, decent restaurants, and pleasing environs. Either town makes a more economical alternative for travelers seeking to avoid the commercial tourist bustle to the south. Note that some visitors find Bethlehem melancholy and full of unpolished charm; others find it a bit eerie and prefer to push on.

ESSENTIALS

GETTING THERE   Littleton is best reached via I-93; get off at either Exit 41 or 42. Bethlehem is about 3 miles east of Littleton on Route 302. Get off I-93 at Exit 40 and head east. From the east, follow Route 302 past Twin Mountain to Bethlehem.

VISITOR INFORMATION   The **Bethlehem Chamber of Commerce** (© **603/869-3409**) maintains an information booth in summer on Bethlehem's Main Street across from town hall. The **Littleton Area Chamber of Commerce** (© **603/444-6561;** www.littletonareachamber.com) offers information from its office at 120 Main St.

EXPLORING BETHLEHEM

Bethlehem consists of Main Street and a handful of side streets. Several antiques stores clustered in what passes for downtown are worth browsing. Bethlehem once was home to 38 resort hotels; little evidence of them remains today. For a better understanding of the town's rich history, pick up a copy of *An Illustrated Tour of Bethlehem, Past and Present,* available at many shops around town. This informative guide brings to life many of the graceful old homes and buildings of the past.

Just west of Bethlehem on Route 302 is **The Rocks** ✯✯ (© **603/444-6228;** www.therocks.org), a classic Victorian gentleman's farm that today is the headquarters for the Society for the Protection of New Hampshire Forests. Set on 1,200 acres, this 1883 estate contains a well-preserved shingled house, an uncommonly handsome barn, and hiking trails that meander through meadows and woodlands on a gentle hillside. It's a peaceful spot, perfect for a picnic. The society also operates a Christmas-tree farm here. Admission is free; open daily from dawn to dusk.

WHERE TO STAY

Adair ✯✯✯   Adair opened in 1992, yet remains one of New England's better-kept secrets. The peaceful Georgian Revival home dates from 1927 and is set on 200 acres. Its memorable Granite Tap Room is a huge, wonderfully informal, granite-block-lined rumpus room with a VCR, antique pool table, and fireplace. The guest rooms are impeccably well-furnished with a mix of antiques and reproductions; six feature fireplaces. The best of the lot is the Kinsman suite, with a Jacuzzi the size of a small swimming pool, a small library, a gas woodstove, and a petite balcony looking out toward the Dalton Range.

80 Guider Lane (off Exit 40 on Rte. 93), Bethlehem, NH 03574. © **888/444-2600** or 603/444-2600. Fax 603/444-4823. www.adairinn.com. 10 units. $165–$285 double; cottage $345 double. Rates include breakfast, tax, and gratuity. AE, MC, V. 2-night minimum stay weekends and foliage season. Children 12 and over welcome. **Amenities:** Restaurant (see Tim-Bir Alley, below); all-weather tennis court; game room. *In room:* A/C, hair dryer, no phone.

Hearthside Village Cottage Motel ✯ *Kids*   A little weird and a little charming, Hearthside claims to be the first motor court built in New Hampshire. A colony of steeply gabled miniature homes, the village was constructed by a father and son in the 1930s and late 1940s. The six 1940s-era cottages are of somewhat better quality, with warm knotty-pine interiors. Many of the cottages have fireplaces (Duraflame-style logs only), some have kitchenettes, and several are suitable for small families. There's an indoor playroom filled with toys for tots, and another rec room with video games and Ping-Pong for older kids.

Rte. 302 (midway between Bethlehem Village and I-93), Bethlehem, NH 03574. ✆ **603/444-1000.** www.hearthsidevillage.com. 16 cottages. $55–$65 ($10 less in off-season). 2- to 3-night minimum stay in foliage season. MC, V. Closed mid-Oct to mid-May. **Amenities:** Small pool; game rooms. *In room:* TV, coffeemaker (on request), no phone.

Rabbit Hill Inn ☆☆   A short hop across the Connecticut River from Littleton is the lost-in-time Vermont village of Lower Waterford, with its perfect 1859 church and tiny library. Amid this cluster of buildings is the stately Rabbit Hill Inn, constructed in 1795. With its prominent gabled roof and imposing columns, this romantic retreat easily ranks among the most refined structures in the Connecticut River Valley. More than half of the rooms have gas fireplaces, and several feature Jacuzzis. Rates include breakfast and dinner in the creative dining room, where proper attire is expected (jacket and tie are "appropriate," but not required). The inn is halfway between Littleton, N.H., and St. Johnsbury, Vt., allowing guests to easily explore both states.

Rte. 18, Lower Waterford, VT 05848. ✆ **800/762-8669** or 802/748-5168. Fax 802/748-8342. www.rabbithillinn.com. 20 units. $245–$380 double. Rates include breakfast, dinner, afternoon tea, and gratuities. 2-night minimum stay on weekends. AE, MC, V. Closed early Apr and early Nov. From I-93, take Rte. 18 northwest from Exit 44 for approximately 2 miles. Children over 12 welcome. **Amenities:** Swimming pond; golf club membership nearby; in-room massage. *In room:* A/C, coffeemaker, hair dryer, iron.

Thayers Inn ☆ ⓥ*alue*   Thayers may offer the best value of any White Mountains inn. It's a clean, well-run hostelry in an impressive Greek Revival downtown building that dates to 1850. You'll find a mix of rooms furnished comfortably if eclectically with high-quality flea-market furniture. The $50 rooms aren't especially spacious, but are perfectly adequate and comfortable. The top floor is a bit of a hike—but room 47 ($40) is a true bargain for travelers on a budget, with air-conditioning, in-room sink, and shared bathroom. The inn has a free video library of 140 movies. The cupola is worth a visit for the panoramic view of the town.

Main St., Littleton, NH 03561. ✆ **800/634-8179** or 603/444-6469. www.thayersinn.com. 48 units (3 with shared bathroom). $40 double with shared bathroom; $50–$100 double with private bathroom. Rates include continental breakfast. AE, DISC, MC, V. Pets accepted if not left alone in room. **Amenities:** Restaurant (casual dining). *In room:* A/C, TV, no phone.

WHERE TO DINE

Tim-Bir Alley ☆☆ REGIONAL/CONTEMPORARY   The White Mountains' best dining is at Tim-Bir Alley, housed in the area's most gracious country inn. In this romantic setting, owners Tim and Biruta Carr prepare meals from wholesome, basic ingredients. Diners might start with Moroccan sweet-potato soup with spiced almonds, then tuck into a main course of sea scallops with sun-dried tomatoes and capers on pastry. Save room for the superb deserts, which range from peach-blueberry tart to a chocolate-hazelnut pâté. Attentive service isn't a strong suit here, so expect to enjoy a leisurely meal.

Adair Country Inn, Old Littleton Rd., Bethlehem. ✆ 603/444-6142. Reservations required. Main courses $15.95–$19.95. No credit cards. Summer Wed–Sun 5:30–9pm; winter Wed–Sat 5:30–9pm. Closed Apr and Nov.

5 The North Country

New Hampshire's North Country is an ideal destination for those who find the White Mountains too commercialized. The tiny communities of the region—like **Errol,** at a crossroads of two routes to nowhere—regard change with high suspicion, something that held true even during the go-go times of the 1980s. The clean if basic Errol Motel is always here. The Errol Restaurant still serves the best homemade doughnuts north of Boston. And the land surrounding the town remains an outpost of rugged, raw grandeur that has been little compromised.

Of course, the problem with these lost-in-time areas is the nothing-to-see-nothing-to-do syndrome, one that especially seems to afflict young families. You can drive for miles and not see much other than spruce and pine, an infrequent bog, a glimpse of a shimmering lake, and—if you're lucky—a roadside moose chomping on sedges.

But there *is* plenty to do if you're self-motivated and oriented toward the outdoors. There's white-water kayaking on the Androscoggin River, canoeing on Lake Umbagog, and bicycling along the wide valley floors. You can also visit one of the Northeast's grandest, most improbable historic resorts, which continues to thrive despite considerable odds. Some recent advances are encouraging for those who'd like to see the area remain unchanged. The piney shoreline around spectacular Lake Umbagog was protected as a National Wildlife Refuge in the 1990s. The upshot? Umbagog should remain in its more-or-less pristine state for all time.

ESSENTIALS

GETTING THERE   Errol is at the junction of Route 26 (accessible from Bethel, Maine) and Route 16 (accessible from Gorham, N.H.). **Concord Trailways** (© **800/639-3317**) provides service to Berlin from points south, including Boston.

VISITOR INFORMATION   The **Northern White Mountains Chamber of Commerce,** 164 Main St., Berlin (© **800/992-7480** or 603/752-6060; www. northernwhitemountains.com), offers information Monday through Friday between 8:30am and 4:30pm.

OUTDOOR PURSUITS

Dixville Notch State Park 🏔 (© **603/788-2155**) has several hiking trails, including a delightful 2-mile round-trip to Table Rock. Look for the small parking area just east of the Balsams Resort on the edge of Lake Gloriette. The loop hike (it connects with a half-mile return along Route 26) ascends a scraggy trail to an open rock with fine views of the resort and the flanking wild hills.

A great place to learn the fundamentals of white water is at **Saco Bound's Northern Waters** 🏔🏔 (© **603/447-2177**; www.sacobound.com) white-water school, located where the Errol bridge crosses the Androscoggin River. The school offers 2- to 5-day workshops in the art of getting downstream safely, if not dryly. Classes involve videos, dry-land training, and frequent forays onto the river—both at the Class I to III rapids at the bridge and the more forgiving rips downstream. Two-day classes are $170, including equipment and a riverside campsite.

Excellent lake canoeing may be found at Lake Umbagog, which sits between Maine and New Hampshire. The lake, which is home to the **Lake Umbagog Wildlife Refuge** 🏔🏔 (© **603/482-3415**), has some 40 miles of shoreline, most of which is wild and remote. You'll need a boat of some sort to properly see the lake. Canoes and flatwater kayaks are available for rent at Saco Bound's Errol outpost for $27 per day; see above. Saco Bound also offers pontoon boat tours to get a glimpse of the complex river system that feeds both into and out of the lake.

More than 20 primitive **campsites** are scattered around the shoreline and on the lake's islands. Most of these backcountry sites are managed by New Hampshire parks; call ☎ **603/271-3628** for more information.

WHERE TO STAY & DINE

Balsams Grand Resort Hotel ★★★   The Balsams is a grand gem hidden deep in the northern forest. Located on 15,000 acres in a valley surrounded by 800-foot cliffs, it's one of a handful of the great 19th-century New England resorts still in operation, and its survival is all the more extraordinary given its exceedingly remote location. What makes this Victorian grande dame even more exceptional is its refusal to compromise or bend to the trend of the moment. Bathing suits and jeans are prohibited in the public areas, you'll be ejected from the tennis courts or golf course if you're not neatly attired, and men are *required* (not requested) to wear jackets at dinner. The resort has also maintained strict adherence to the spirit of the "American plan"—everything but booze is included in the room rates, from greens fees to boats on Lake Gloriette to evening entertainment in the lounges. Meals are an event—especially the summer luncheon buffet (when did you last gorge on chocolate éclairs?).

Dixville Notch, NH 03576. ☎ **800/255-0600**, 800/255-0800 in N.H., or 603/255-3400. Fax 603/255-4221. www.thebalsams.com. 204 units. Winter $340–$380 double (including breakfast, dinner, and lift tickets); summer $410–$470 double (including all meals, entertainment, golf fees, etc.). AE, DISC, MC, V. 4-night minimum stay on weekends July–Aug. Closed early Apr to late May and mid-Oct to mid-Dec. **Amenities:** Restaurant, 3 lounges; heated outdoor pool; 2 golf courses (18-hole and 9-hole); 6 tennis courts (clay and all-weather); health club; Jacuzzi; sauna; water-sports equipment (free); bike rental; 45 miles of groomed cross-country ski trails; downhill ski area; summer children's programs; game room; concierge; shopping arcade; salon; limited room service; massage; baby-sitting; laundry service; dry cleaning. *In room:* Dataport, iron (TVs in suites).

Philbrook Farm Inn ★★   The Philbrook Farm Inn is a classic New England period piece that traces its lineage to the 19th century, when farmers opened their doors to summer travelers to earn some extra cash. Set on 1,000 acres between the Mahoosuc Range and the Androscoggin River, this country inn has been owned and operated by the Philbrook family since 1853. It has expanded haphazardly, with additions in 1861, 1904, and 1934. As a result, the cozy rooms are eclectic—some have a country farmhouse feel, others a more Victorian flavor. Guests spend their days swimming, playing croquet, exploring trails in the nearby hills, or just reading on the porch. Philbrook Farm is a wonderful retreat, well out of the tourist mainstream, and worthy of protection as a local cultural landmark.

881 North Rd. (off Rte. 2 between Gorham, N.H., and Bethel, Maine), Shelburne, NH 03581. ☎ **603/ 466-3831**. www.nettx.com/philbrook. 24 units (6 with shared bathroom). $120–$150 double, including breakfast and dinner; cottage $700 per week. No credit cards. Closed Apr and Nov–Dec 25. Pets allowed in cottages. **Amenities:** Restaurant (traditional New England) pool; game room; badminton; shuffleboard. *In room:* No phone.

13

Maine

by Wayne Curtis

Professional funny guy Dave Barry once suggested that Maine's state motto should be "Cold, but damp."

Cute, but true. There's spring, which tends to last a few blustery, rain-soaked days. There's November, in which Arctic winds alternate with gray sheets of rain. And then winter brings a character-building mix of blizzards and ice storms to the fabled coast and rolling mountains.

Then there's summer. Summer in Maine brings osprey diving for fish off wooded points, gleaming cumulus clouds building over the steely-blue rounded peaks of the western mountains, and the haunting whoop of loons echoing off the dense forest walls bordering the lakes. It brings languorous days when the sun rises well before most visitors, and by 8am it seems like noontime. Maine summers bring a measure of gracious tranquility, and a placid stay in the right spot can rejuvenate even the most jangled nerves.

The trick comes in finding that right spot. Those who arrive here without a clear plan may find themselves ruing their travel decision. Maine's Route 1 along the coast has its moments, but for the most part it's rather charmless—an amalgam of convenience stores, tourist boutiques, and restaurants catering to bus tours. Acadia National Park can be congested, Mount Katahdin's summit overcrowded, and some of the more popular lakes have become de facto racetracks for jet skis.

But Maine's size works to the traveler's advantage. Maine is roughly as large as the other five New England states combined. It has 3,500 miles of coastline, some 3,000 coastal islands, and millions of acres of undeveloped woodland. In fact, more than half of the state exists as "unorganized territories," where no town government exists, and the few inhabitants look to the state for basic services. With all this space and a little planning, you'll be able to find your piece of Maine.

1 The South Coast

Maine's southern coast runs from the state line at Kittery to about Portland. Thanks to quirks of geography, nearly all of Maine's sandy beaches are located in this 60-mile stretch of coastline. This is the place to head for a relaxing sandy spot amid the lulling sound of the surf. It's not wilderness here—most beaches have beach towns nearby, and these range from classic 19th-century villages to more honky-tonkish resorts. One thing all the beaches share in common: They're washed by the frigid waters of the Gulf of Maine. Swimming sessions tend to be brief and accompanied by shrieks, whoops, and agitated hand-waving—except among the very young, who seem immune to blood-chilling temperatures. These beaches are more suited for early-morning walks than for swimming.

The beach season itself is also brief and intense, running from July 4th to Labor Day. At an increasing number of beach towns, the season is stretching into fall (Columbus Day is generally when the remaining businesses shutter up), and the post–Labor Day pace at these shorefront communities is slower and less frenetic—for some, the perfect atmosphere for a laid-back beachside respite.

KITTERY & THE YORKS

Kittery ✿ is the first town you'll come to if you're driving to Maine from the south. Kittery was once famous nationally for its naval yard (it's still operating), but regionally at least Kittery is now better known for its dozens of factory outlets. Maine has the second-highest number of outlet malls in the nation (second only to California), and Kittery is home to a good many of them.

"The Yorks," just to the north, are comprised of three towns that share a name but little else. In fact, it's rare to find three such well-defined and diverse New England archetypes in such a compact area. **York Village** ✿✿ is redolent with Early American history and architecture. **York Harbor** ✿ reached its zenith during America's late Victorian era, when wealthy urbanites constructed rambling cottages at the ocean's edge. **York Beach** ✿ has an Edwardian beach-town feel, complete with noisy amusements, taffy shops, a modest zoo, and small gabled summer homes set in crowded enclaves near the beach.

ESSENTIALS

GETTING THERE   Kittery is accessible from I-95 or Route 1, with exits well marked. The Yorks are reached most easily from Exit 1 of the Maine Turnpike. From the exit, look for Route 1A just south of the turnpike exit. This route connects all three York towns.

Contact **Amtrak** (© **800/872-7245;** www.amtrak.com) for information on train service from Boston to southern Maine.

VISITOR INFORMATION   The **Kittery Information Center** (© **207/ 439-1319**) is located at a well-marked rest area on I-95. It's open daily from 8am to 6pm in summer, from 9am to 5:30pm the rest of the year.

The **York Chamber of Commerce** (© **207/363-4422**) operates a helpful information center at 571 Rte. 1, a short distance from the turnpike exit. It's open in summer daily from 9am to 5pm (until 6pm Friday); limited days and hours the rest of the year.

GETTING AROUND   A trackless trolley links all three York towns and provides a convenient way to explore without having to hassle with parking. Hop on the trolley at one of the well-marked stops for a 1-hour narrated tour ($4) or get a 1-day pass ($5). Partial trips are $2.

SHOPPING

Kittery's consumer mecca is 4 miles south of York on Route 1. Some 120 **factory outlets** flank the highway, scattered among more than a dozen strip malls. Retailers include Eddie Bauer, Anne Klein, Le Creuset, Calvin Klein, Crate & Barrel, DKNY, Polo/Ralph Lauren, Tommy Hilfiger, and Brookstone.

Navigating the area can be frustrating in summer owing to the four lanes of often heavy traffic and capricious restrictions on turns. (A free shuttle bus links the outlets and lessens some of the frustration.) The selection of outlets is slightly more diverse than in Freeport, a little more than an hour north, which is more clothing oriented. But Freeport's quaint village setting is far more appealing than the congested sprawl zone of Kittery. Information on current

Maine

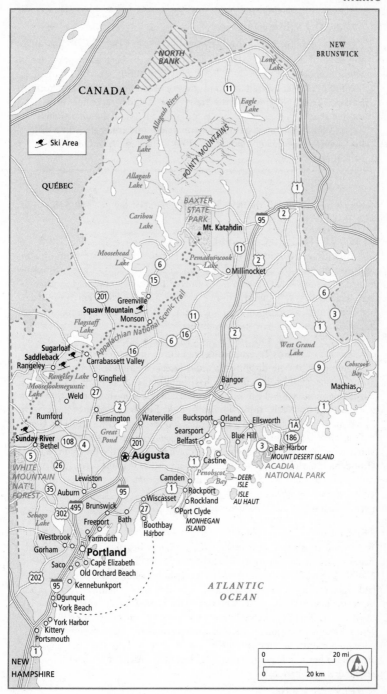

Ski Area

CANADA

NEW BRUNSWICK

NORTH BANK

QUÉBEC

Long Lake

⑪

Eagle Lake

POINTY MOUNTAINS

Allagash River

Long Lake

Allagash Lake

Caribou Lake

BAXTER STATE PARK

▲ Mt. Katahdin

①

②

95

Moosehead Lake

⑥

Pemadumcook Lake

⑪

②

○ Millinocket

⑮

⑥

③

①

West Grand Lake

⑨

Cobscook Bay

⑥

201

○ Greenville

Squaw Mountain

○ Monson

Flagstaff Lake

⑪

⑥ ⑯

Appalachian National Scenic Trail

②

Sugarloaf

Saddleback

Rangeley

Rangeley Lake

⑯

○ Carrabassett Valley

○ Kingfield

Bangor

⑨

Machias

Mooselookmeguntic Lake

27

○ Weld

② Farmington

Great Pond

○ Rumford

108

④

Sunday River

○ Bethel

⑤

○ Waterville

○ Buckbsport ○ Orland

Searsport

Belfast ○

Ellsworth

Blue Hill

1A

186

③ ○ Bar Harbor

MOUNT DESERT ISLAND

ACADIA NATIONAL PARK

WHITE MOUNTAIN NAT'L FOREST

26

201

★ **Augusta**

① ○ Castine

Penobscot Bay

DEER ISLE

ISLE AU HAUT

○ Lewiston

35 ○ Auburn

Sebago Lake

495

302

○ Brunswick

○ Freeport ○ Bath

○ Westbrook

○ Yarmouth

○ Gorham

Portland

Camden ○

① ○ Rockport

○ Rockland

27 ○ Wiscasset

○ Port Clyde

Boothbay Harbor

MONHEGAN ISLAND

○ Saco

202

95

○ Cape Elizabeth

○ Old Orchard Beach

○ Kennebunkport

○ Ogunquit

○ York Beach

○ York Harbor

○ Kittery

Portsmouth

NEW HAMPSHIRE

①

ATLANTIC OCEAN

0   20 mi

0   20 km

Finds **The Wiggly Bridge**

Just west of Route 103 outside of York Harbor, you'll see a tiny bridge at the edge of a marsh. (It's said, not implausibly, to be the smallest suspension bridge in the world.) That's the **Wiggly Bridge,** and it's part of Fisherman's Walk, a lovely footpath that connects York Village and York Harbor. The trail begins near the Stage Neck Inn and tracks upriver past lobster shacks and along lawns leading up to grand shingled homes. Across Wiggly Bridge, it passes into the woods and connects with a dirt lane, which emerges at Lindsay Road near Hancock Wharf. The entire walk is about a mile.

---

outlets is available from the **Kittery Outlet Association** (✆ **888/548-8379;** www.thekitteryoutlets.com).

DISCOVERING LOCAL HISTORY

Old York Historical Society 👫👫   John Hancock is famous for his oversize signature on the Declaration of Independence and the insurance company named after him. What's not so well known is his checkered past as a businessman. Hancock was the proprietor of Hancock Wharf, a failed enterprise that's but one of the intriguing historic sites in York Village, a fine destination for those curious about Early American history.

First settled in 1624, York Village has several homes open to the public. A good place to start is **Jefferds Tavern,** across from the handsome old **burying ground.** Changing exhibits here document various facets of early life. Next door is the **School House,** furnished as it might have been in the last century. A 10-minute walk along Lindsay Road will bring you to **Hancock Wharf,** which is next door to the **George Marshall Store.** Also nearby is the **Elizabeth Perkins House,** with its well-preserved Colonial Revival interiors. Don't miss the intriguing **Old Gaol,** built in 1719 with musty dungeons for criminals. The jail is the oldest surviving public building in the United States. Just down the knoll is the **Emerson-Wilcox House,** built in the mid-1700s. Added to periodically over the years, it's a virtual catalog of architectural styles and early decorative arts.

5 Lindsay Rd., York. ✆ 207/363-4974. Admission $7 adults, $3 children 6–16. Tues–Sat 10am–5pm; Sun 1–5pm (last tour at 4pm). Closed mid-Oct to mid-June.

BEACHES

York Beach consists of two beaches—**Long Sands Beach** 👫 and **Short Sands Beach**—separated by a rocky headland and a small island capped by scenic **Nubble Light** 👫👫. Both offer plenty of room for sunning and throwing Frisbees when the tide is out. When the tide is in, they're both cramped. Short Sands fronts the town of York Beach, with its candlepin bowling and video arcades. It's the better bet for families traveling with kids. Long Sands runs along Route 1A, across from a profusion of motels, summer homes, and convenience stores. Changing rooms, public rest rooms, and metered parking (50¢ per hour) are available at both beaches; other services, including snacks, are provided by local restaurants and vendors.

WHERE TO STAY

York Beach has a proliferation of motels facing Long Sands Beach. Reserve ahead during prime season. Among those offering simple accommodations on

Southern Maine Coast

Bethel
Bryant Pond
(5)
(219)
Livermore
(17)
(26)
Winthrop
(5)
North Waterford
(117)
Turner
South Paris
(118)
Norway
(4)
(11)
(202)
Waterford
(117)
Mechanic Falls
(495)
(201)
Lovell
Lewiston
Richmond
(302)
Bridgton
Long Lake
Auburn
(196)
Lisbon Falls
(95)
Saco R.
Casco
(26)
(136)
Bath
(5)
(117)
Naples
(11)
Gray
Brunswick
Hiram
North Windham
Freeport
(123)
Cornish
Sebago Lake
Yarmouth
Harpswell Peninsula
(209)
(5)
(35)
Orrs Island
(25)
(302)
Bailey Island
Casco Bay
Limerick
Westbrook
(202)
(295)
Hollis Center
(4)
Portland
Shapleigh
(11)
(5)
(95)
South Portland
Alfred
Old Orchard Beach
Cape Elizabeth
(109)
(111)
Saco
Saco Bay
Sanford
Biddeford
(202)
(4)
(109)
(1)
ATLANTIC
Rochester
North Berwick
Kennebunk
OCEAN
Berwick
(95)
Kennebunkport
Somersworth
Wells
MAINE
Ogunquit
Dover
York
Durham
Kittery
(108)
Portsmouth
NEW HAMPSHIRE
(1A)
Rye

Ferry routes - - - -

ME
Augusta
⊛
Portland

0   20 mi
0   20 km

N

or near the beach are the **Anchorage Motor Inn** (*C* 207/363-5112), **Long Beach Motor Inn** (*C* 207/363-5481), and **Nevada Motel** (*C* 207/363-4504).

Dockside Guest Quarters   David and Harriet Lusty established this quiet retreat in 1954, and recent additions haven't changed the friendly, maritime flavor of the place. Situated on a 7-acre peninsula, the inn occupies nicely landscaped grounds shaded with maples and white pines. Five rooms are in the main house (1885), but most of the accommodations are in small, modern town house–style cottages (suites have kitchenettes). These are bright and airy, and all have private decks that overlook the entrance to York Harbor.

Harris Island (P.O. Box 205), York, ME 03909. *C* **207/363-2868**. Fax 207/363-1977. www.docksidegq.com. 25 units (2 with shared bathroom). Mid-June to early Sept $137–$199 double; early summer and late fall $100–$140; winter to spring (open weekends only) $85–$114. DISC, MC, V. 2-night minimum stay July–Sept. Drive south on Rte. 103 from Rte. 1A in York Harbor; after bridge over York River, turn left and follow signs. **Amenities:** Restaurant (traditional New England/seafood); ocean swimming; badminton; croquet; rowboats; bicycle rental; laundry service. *In room:* TV, no phone.

Inn at Portsmouth Harbor 🐾🐾   This 1899 home is just across the river from Portsmouth, N.H., about half a mile away across a bridge (a pleasant walk). Guests here get a taste of small-town life, yet still have access to the restaurants and shopping of Portsmouth. The rooms are tastefully furnished with eclectic antiques, though most are on the small side. Valdra has ruby red walls, antiques, and a bathroom with historic accents; the third-floor Royal Gorge has limited skylight views of the harbor and a cast-iron tub. Breakfasts are flat-out great: fresh-squeezed juice and selections like corn pancakes with smoked salmon.

6 Water St., Kittery, ME 03904. *C* **207/439-4040**. Fax 207/438-9286. www.innatportsmouth.com. 6 units. Apr–Oct $135–$175 double; Nov–Mar $135–$155. Rates include breakfast. 2-night minimum stay summer and holidays. AE, MC, V. Children over 12 welcome. *In room:* A/C, TV, dataport, hair dryer.

Stage Neck Inn 🐾🐾   A hotel in one form or another has been housing guests on this windswept bluff located between the harbor and the open ocean since about 1870. The most recent incarnation was constructed in 1972, and furnished with an understated, country-club-like elegance. Rooms were all renovated in 2000 with fridges and CD players added. The hotel is modern, yet offers an old-fashioned sense of intimacy lacking in other modern resorts. Almost every unit has a view of the water. York Harbor Beach is but a few steps away.

Stage Neck (P.O. Box 70), York Harbor, ME 03911. *C* **800/222-3238** or 207/363-3850. www.stageneck.com. 60 units. June–Labor Day $200–$325 double; early fall $155–$240; winter $125–$175; spring $155–$195. Ask about off-season packages. AE, DISC, MC, V. Head north on Rte. 1A from Rte. 1; make second right after York Harbor post office. **Amenities:** 2 dining rooms (fine dining; pub fare); indoor and outdoor pools; ocean swimming; 2 clay tennis courts; fitness room; Jacuzzi; sauna; limited room service; massage. *In room:* A/C, TV/VCR, dataport, fridge.

WHERE TO DINE

Cape Neddick Inn Restaurant 🐾🐾   CONTEMPORARY AMERICAN This is the best choice for a memorable meal south of Ogunquit. Located in an elegant structure on a relatively quiet stretch of Route 1, the inn has an open dining area that deftly mixes traditional and modern. Summer folks in blazers and floral print dresses flock here to sample the creative menu, which changes seasonally to make the most of local products. Main courses could include chargrilled steak with Vidalia onions and cob-smoked bacon, or salmon glazed with a Sichuan barbecue sauce. Diners can select from more than 100 wines, a selection recognized by a *Wine Spectator* award in 2000.

1233 Rte. 1, Cape Neddick. ℂ **207/363-2899.** Reservations recommended. Main courses $16–$28. DISC, MC, V. Late June to Labor Day daily 5:30–9:30pm; rest of year Wed–Sat (call for hours).

Chauncey Creek Lobster Pier ⭐⭐ LOBSTER POUND   It's not on the wild open ocean, but Chaucey's is one of the best lobster pounds in the state, not least because the Spinney family, which has been selling lobsters here since the 1950s, takes such pride in the place. You reach the pound by walking down a wooden ramp to a broad deck on a tidal inlet, where some 42 festively painted picnic tables await. Lobster is the specialty, of course, but steamed mussels (in wine and garlic) and clams are also available. It's BYOB.

Chauncey Creek Rd. (between Kittery Point and York on Rte. 103; watch for signs), Kittery Point. ℂ **207/ 439-1030.** Reservations not accepted. Lobsters priced to market; other items $1.50–$8.95. MC, V. Daily 11am– 8pm (until 7pm during shoulder seasons); closed Mon after Labor Day. Closed Columbus Day–Mother's Day.

Goldenrod Restaurant ⭐ FAMILY-STYLE   This beach-town classic is the place for local color—it's been a summer institution in York Beach since it first opened in 1896. It's easy to find: Look for visitors gawking through plate-glass windows at the ancient taffy machines hypnotically churning out taffy in volumes enough (9 million candies a year) to make busloads of dentists wealthy. The restaurant is behind the taffy and fudge operation, and is short on gourmet fare, long on atmosphere. Diners sit around a stone fireplace or at the antique soda fountain. The meals are basic and filling, nothing more. Expect waffles, griddle cakes, club sandwiches, and deviled egg and bacon sandwiches.

Railroad Rd. and Ocean Ave., York Beach. ℂ **207/363-2621.** www.thegoldenrod.com. Breakfast $2.65– $5.25; lunch and dinner entrees $2.75–$7.50. MC, V. Memorial Day–Labor Day daily 8am–10pm (until 9pm in June); Labor Day–Columbus Day Wed–Sun 8am–3pm. Closed Columbus Day–Memorial Day.

OGUNQUIT

Ogunquit is a bustling beachside town that has attracted vacationers and artists for more than a century. While notable for its abundant and appealing summer resort architecture, Ogunquit is most famous for its 3½-mile white-sand beach, backed by grassy dunes. The beach serves as the town's front porch, and most everyone drifts over here at least once a day when the sun is shining.

Ogunquit's fame as an art colony dates to around 1890, when Charles H. Woodbury arrived and declared the place an "artist's paradise." He was followed by artists Walt Kuhn, Elihu Vedder, Yasuo Kuniyoshi, and Rudolph Dirks, who was best known for creating the "Katzenjammer Kids" comic strip.

In the latter decades of the 20th century, the town has found quiet fame as a destination for gay travelers, and gay entrepreneurs run many local enterprises. It's low-key compared with the scene at Provincetown, Mass. It's more like an understated family resort, where a good many family members happen to be gay.

Despite the architectural gentility and the overall civility of the place, the town can feel overrun with tourists during the summer, especially on weekends. The teeming crowds are part of the allure for some Ogunquit regulars.

ESSENTIALS

GETTING THERE   Ogunquit is located on Route 1 between York and Wells. It's accessible from either Exit 1 or Exit 2 off the Maine Turnpike.

VISITOR INFORMATION   The **Ogunquit Welcome Center** (ℂ **207/ 646-5533** or 207/646-2939; www.ogunquit.org) is on Route 1 south of the village center. It's open April to Columbus Day, daily from 9am to 5pm (until 8pm during the peak summer season), and the rest of the year, daily from 10am to 2pm.

GETTING AROUND   The village of Ogunquit is centered around an intersection that seems fiendishly designed to cause massive traffic foul-ups in summer. Parking in and around the village is also tight and relatively expensive ($6 per day or more). As a result, Ogunquit is best navigated on foot or by bike.

A number of trackless trolleys run all day from mid-May to Columbus Day between Perkins Cove and the Wells town line to the north, with detours to the sea down Beach and Ocean streets. The cost is $1 per adult, 50¢ per child. It's well worth the small expense to avoid the hassles of driving and parking.

EXPLORING THE TOWN

From the village center—good for an hour or so of browsing among the boutiques—you can walk to scenic Perkins Cove along **Marginal Way** ✪, a mile-long oceanside pathway once used for herding cattle to pasture. Early in the last century, the land was bought by a local developer who deeded the right-of-way to the town. The wide, well-maintained pathway departs across from the Seacastles Resort on Shore Road. It passes tide pools, pocket beaches, and rocky, fissured bluffs, all of which are worth exploring. The seascape can be spectacular (especially after a storm), but Marginal Way can also be spectacularly crowded on fair-weather weekends—head out in the very early morning if possible.

Perkins Cove ✪, accessible either from Marginal Way or by driving south on Shore Road and veering left at the Y intersection, is a small, well-protected harbor that seems custom-designed for a photo opportunity. As such, it attracts visitors by the busload, carload, and boatload, and is often heavily congested. A handful of galleries, restaurants, and T-shirt shops catering to the tourist trade occupies a cluster of quaint buildings between the harbor and the sea. An intriguing pedestrian drawbridge is operated by whoever happens to be handy, allowing sailboats to come and go.

Not far from the cove is the **Ogunquit Museum of American Art** ✪✪, 183 Shore Rd. (© **207/646-4909**), one of the best small art museums in the nation. The engaging modern building is set back from the road in a glen overlooking the shore. The curators have a track record for staging superb shows and attracting national attention. Open July through September, Monday to Saturday from 10:30am to 5pm and Sunday from 2 to 5pm. Admission is $4 for adults, $3 for seniors and students, and free for children under 12.

Excursions Coastal Maine Outfitting Co. ✪, Route 1, Cape Neddick (© **207/363-0181**; www.excursionsinmaine.com), runs 2-hour ($40) and half-day ($65) sea-kayaking tours on rivers and out along the coast three times daily in summer. Ask about sunrise, sunset, and full-moon kayaking trips.

BEACHES

Ogunquit's **main beach** ✪✪ is 3½ miles long, and three paid parking lots ($2 per hour) are located along its length. The beach appeals to everyone—there's a more lively scene at the south end near the town itself, and it's more remote and unpopulated as you head north, where the stretch is backed with dunes and, beyond them, clusters of summer homes. The most popular access point is at the foot of Beach Street, which runs into Ogunquit Village. The beach ends at a sandy spit, where the Ogunquit River flows into the sea; here you'll find a handful of informal restaurants. It's also the most crowded part of the beach. Less congested options are at **Footbridge Beach** (turn on Ocean Avenue off Route 1 north of the village center) and **Moody Beach** (turn on Eldridge Avenue in Wells). Rest rooms and changing rooms are maintained at all access points.

WHERE TO STAY

Just a few steps from Ogunquit's main downtown intersection is the meticulously maintained **Studio East Motel,** 267 Main St. (© **207/646-7297**). It's open from April to mid-November, with peak-season rates running $95 to $119.

Beachmere Inn ⚡ Run by the same family since 1937, the Beachmere Inn sprawls across a grassy 4-acre hillside, and nearly every room has a view northward up Ogunquit's famous beach, which is a 10-minute walk via footpath. Guests choose from two buildings on the main grounds: The Beachmere Victorian dates to the 1890s and is all turrets and porches; next door is the mid-century modern Beachmere South, a motel-like structure with spacious rooms with private balconies or patios. When the main buildings are filled, guests are offered one of five rooms in the Bullfrog Cottage, a short drive away. These units are darker and less impressive, but are spacious and appropriate for families.

Beachmere Rd., Ogunquit, ME 03907. © **800/336-3983** or 207/646-2021. Fax 207/646-2231. www. beachmereinn.com. 53 units. Peak season $85–$210; mid-season $75–$160; off-season $55–$110. Rates include continental breakfast. AE, DC, DISC, MC, V. 3-night minimum stay in summer. Closed mid-Dec to Apr 1. *In room:* A/C, TV.

Marginal Way House This old-fashioned, nothing-fancy compound centers around a mid-19th-century house with summery, basic rooms. Room 7 is among the best, with a private porch and ocean view. The house is surrounded by four outbuildings of more recent vintage, which lack charm and feature motel-style rooms that are generally comfortable. The whole affair is situated on a grassy lot on a quiet cul-de-sac. It's hard to believe that you're smack in the middle of Ogunquit, with both the beach and the village just a few minutes' walk away.

Wharf Lane (P.O. Box 697), Ogunquit, ME 03907. © **207/646-8801,** or 207/363-6566 in winter. www. marginalwayhouse.com. 30 units (1 with private bathroom down hall). Peak season (late June to Aug) $93–$147 double; discounts in off-season. Minimum stay some weekends. MC, V. Closed late Oct to mid-Apr. Pets allowed off-season; advance notice required. *In room:* A/C, TV, fridge, no phone.

Nellie Littlefield House ⚡ The prime location and the handsome Queen Anne architecture are the main draws at this 1889 home near the village center. All rooms feature a mix of modern and antique reproduction furnishings; several have refrigerators. Four units to the rear have private decks, but views are limited (mostly of the unlovely motel next door). Most spacious is the third-floor J. H. Littlefield suite, with two TVs and a Jacuzzi. The most unique? The circular Grace Littlefield room, located in the upper turret and overlooking the street.

9 Shore Rd., Ogunquit, ME 03907. © **207/646-1692.** 8 units. Peak season $150–$210; mid-season $95–$150; off-season $80–$125. Rates include breakfast. 2-night minimum stay on weekends, 3-night minimum on holidays. DISC, MC, V. Closed late Oct to Apr. Children over 12 welcome. **Amenities:** Small fitness room. *In room:* A/C, TV, fridge.

WHERE TO DINE

Arrows ⚡⚡⚡ NEW AMERICAN This restaurant put Ogunquit on the national culinary map by serving up some of the freshest, most innovative cooking in New England. The emphasis is on local products—often very local. The salad greens are grown in gardens on the grounds, and much of the rest is produced or raised locally. The menu changes nightly, but entrees could include lobster tail and sautéed cod with caramelized Belgian endive, leek cream, caviar, and an asparagus and Parmesan custard. Prices are not for the faint-hearted; if you're not an experienced foodie, you'll find better value at Hurricane.

Berwick Rd. (C) **207/361-1100**. www.arrowsrestaurant.com. Reservations recommended. Main courses $36.95–$39.95; tasting menu $75. MC, V. Mid-Apr to Memorial Day weekend Fri–Sun 6–9:30pm; June–Columbus Day Tues–Sun 6–9:30pm; Columbus Day to mid-Dec Fri–Sun 6–9:30pm. Closed mid-Dec to mid-Apr. Turn uphill at the Key Bank in the village; the restaurant is 1.9 miles on your right.

Hurricane ★★ NEW AMERICAN   Tucked away in Perkins Cove is one of southern Maine's classiest and most enjoyable dining experiences. The plain shingled exterior of the building, set along a curving, narrow lane, doesn't hint at what you'll find inside. Hurricane's menu changes daily, and owner Brooks MacDonald is known for his consistently creative concoctions, like the pizza appetizer of grilled boar sausage topped with fresh tomato and provolone. At lunch, look for salmon burgers or seared jerked scallops. At dinner, there's delectable lobster cioppino (the signature dish), a pistachio-coated veal chop, or swordfish topped with a pecan plum sauce. Added bonus: Hurricane has been making the best martinis since well before the current revival.

Oarweed Rd., Perkins Cove. (C) **800/649-6348** in Maine and N.H., or 207/646-6348. www.perkinscove.com. Reservations recommended. Lunch items $7–$15; dinner main courses $16–$28; lobster dishes priced daily (to $39). AE, DC, DISC, MC, V. Daily 11:30am–3:30pm and 5:30–9:30pm (until 10:30pm May–Oct). Closed briefly in Jan (call ahead).

THE KENNEBUNKS

"The Kennebunks" consist of the villages of **Kennebunk** and **Kennebunkport**, both situated along the shores of small rivers, and both claiming a portion of rocky coast. The region was first settled in the mid-1600s and flourished after the American Revolution, when ship captains, ship builders, and prosperous merchants constructed imposing, solid homes. The Kennebunks are famed for their striking historical architecture and expansive beaches.

ESSENTIALS
GETTING THERE   Kennebunk is located off Exit 3 of the Maine Turnpike. Kennebunkport is 3½ miles southeast of Kennebunk on Port Road (Route 35).

VISITOR INFORMATION   The **Kennebunk-Kennebunkport Chamber of Commerce** ((C) **800/982-4421** or 207/967-0857) can answer questions year-round by phone or at its office on Route 9 next to Meserve's Market. The **Kennebunkport Information Center** ((C) **207/967-8600**), operated by an association of local businesses, is off Dock Square (next to Ben & Jerry's) and is open daily throughout summer and fall.

GETTING AROUND   The local trolley ((C) **207/967-3686**)—a bus, really—makes several stops in and around Kennebunkport and also serves the beaches. The fare is $7 per person per day for unlimited trips.

EXPLORING KENNEBUNKPORT ★★
Kennebunkport is the summer home of President George Bush the Elder, whose family has summered here for decades. Given that, it has the appropriately tweedy, upper-crust feel that one might expect. The tiny historic downtown, whose streets were laid out during days of travel by boat and horse, is subject to monumental traffic jams. If the municipal lot off the square is full, head north on North Street a few minutes to the free long-term lot and catch the trolley back into town. Or go about on foot—it's a pleasant walk of about 10 or 15 minutes from the satellite lot to Dock Square.

   Dock Square ★ has a pleasant wharf-like feel to it, with low buildings of mixed vintages and styles, but the flavor is mostly clapboard and shingles. Today it's very touristy, with boutiques featuring some creative arts and crafts and a lot of trinkets. Kennebunkport's real appeal is found in the surrounding blocks, where the side streets are lined with one of the nation's best preserved assortments of Early American homes. The neighborhoods are especially ripe with Federal-style homes; many have been converted to B&Bs (see "Where to Stay," below).

The **Richard A. Nott House** ✿, 8 Maine St., at the head of Spring Street (© 207/967-2751), is an imposing Greek Revival structure built in 1853—a Victorian-era aficionado's dream. It was donated to the local historical society with the stipulation that it remain forever unchanged. It still has the original wallpaper, carpeting, and furnishings. Tours run about 40 minutes; it's open from mid-June to mid-October, Tuesday through Friday from 1 to 4pm and Saturday from 10am to 1pm. Admission is $5 for adults, $2 for children under 18.

A bit further afield, in the affluent neighborhood around the Colony Hotel (about 1 mile east of Dock Square on Ocean Avenue), is a fine collection of homes of the uniquely American shingle style. It's worth a detour on foot or by bike to ogle these icons of the 19th- and early-20th-century leisure class.

Ocean Drive from Dock Square to **Walkers Point** ✿ and beyond is lined with opulent summer homes overlooking surf and rocky shore. You'll likely recognize the former president's home at Walkers Point when you arrive (look for the shingle-style secret service booth at the head of a drive). There's nothing to do here but park for a minute, take a picture of the house, then push on.

The Seashore Trolley Museum ✿✿✿   A short drive north of Kennebunkport is a local marvel: a scrap-yard-masquerading-as-a-museum. This quirky museum was founded in 1939 to preserve a disappearing way of life, and today contains one of the largest collections in the world—more than 200 trolleys, including specimens from Glasgow, Moscow, San Francisco, and Rome. (Naturally, there's a streetcar named "Desire" from New Orleans.) About 40 cars still operate, and admission includes rides on a 2-mile track. The other cars are on display outdoors and in vast storage sheds. Not until visitors are driving away are they likely to realize how much they've learned about how Americans got around before there was a car in every garage.

195 Log Cabin Rd., Kennebunkport. © 207/967-2800. www.trolleymuseum.org. Admission $7 adults, $5 seniors, $4.50 children 6-16; $23 per family. May 29–Oct 21 daily 10am–5pm; May 6–27 and Oct 21–Nov 5 Sat–Sun 10am–5pm. Closed early Nov to early May. Drive north from Kennebunkport on North St. for 1.7 miles; look for signs.

BEACHES

The coastal area around Kennebunkport is home to several of the state's best beaches. Southward across the river (technically this is Kennebunk, although it's much closer to Kennebunkport) are **Gooch's Beach** ✿✿ and **Kennebunk**

ⓘ Tips Beach Parking

Finding a spot is often difficult, and all beaches require a parking permit, which may be obtained at the town offices or from your hotel. You can avoid parking hassles by renting a bike and leaving your car at your inn or hotel. A good spot for rentals is **Cape Able Bike Shop** (© 800/220-0907 or 207/967-4382; www.capeable.com), which offers three-speeds for $10 a day or $40 per week. The bike shop is on North Street north of Kennbunkport at Arundel Road. The local trolley also offers beach access (see above); the fare is $7 per person per day for unlimited trips.

Beach ⭐⭐. Head eastward on Beach Street (from the intersection of Routes 9 and 35) and you'll soon wind into a handsome colony of eclectic shingled summer homes. The narrow road twists past sandy beaches and rocky headlands. It be congested in summer; avoid gridlock by exploring on foot or by bike.

Goose Rocks Beach ⭐⭐⭐ is north of Kennebunkport off Route 9 (watch for signs), and is a good destination for those who like their crowds light and prefer actual beaches to beach scenes. You'll find an enclave of beach homes set amid rustling oaks just off a fine-sand beach. Just offshore is a narrow barrier reef that has historically attracted flocks of geese.

WHERE TO STAY

Beach House Inn ⭐⭐   This is the best choice if you want to be amid the activity of Kennebunk Beach. The inn was built in 1891 but has been extensively modernized and expanded; in 1999, it was purchased and upgraded by the same folks who own the legendary White Barn Inn (see below). The rooms aren't necessarily historic, but most have Victorian furnishings. The main draw is the lovely porch, where you can gaze out at the pebble beach across the road and idly watch bikers and skaters pass by. The inn provides beach chairs and towels.

211 Beach Ave., Kennebunk Beach, ME 04043. ✆ 207/967-3850. Fax 207/967-4719. www.beachhseinn. com. 35 units. Peak season $190–$350; off-season $95–$350. Rates include continental breakfast. AE, MC, V. 2-night minimum stay on weekends. **Amenities:** Bikes (free); canoes (free). *In room:* No phone.

Captain Jefferds Inn ⭐⭐   Fine antiques abound throughout this 1804 Federal home, and guests will need some persuading to come out of their wonderful rooms once they've settled in. Among the best are Manhattan, with a four-poster bed, fireplace, and beautiful afternoon light; and Assisi, with a restful indoor fountain and rock garden (weird, but it works). Winterthur is the only unit with a TV (there's also one in the common room), and Winterthur and Santa Fe both have whirlpools. The price range reflects the varying room sizes, but even the smallest rooms are comfortable. An elaborate breakfast is served before the fire on cool days, and on the terrace when summer weather permits.

5 Pearl St. (P.O. Box 691), Kennebunkport, ME 04046. ✆ 800/839-6844 or 207/967-2311. www. captainjefferdsinn.com. 15 units. $135–$285 double. Rates include breakfast. AE, MC, V. 2-night minimum stay on weekends. Pets allowed by advance reservation ($20). *In room:* A/C, no phone.

Captain Lord ⭐⭐⭐   Housed in a Federal-style home that peers down a shady lawn toward the river, this is one of the most architecturally distinguished inns in New England. You'll know immediately that this is the genuine article once you spot the grandfather clocks and Chippendale highboys in the front hall. The guest rooms are furnished with splendid antiques; all feature gas fireplaces. There's not a single unappealing room (although the Union is a little dark). Among our favorites: Excelsior, a large corner unit with a massive four-poster, a gas fire, and a two-person Jacuzzi; Hesper, the best of the lower priced rooms; and Merchant, a spacious first-floor suite with a large Jacuzzi.

Pleasant St. and Green St. (P.O. Box 800), Kennebunkport, ME 04046. ✆ 207/967-3141. Fax 207/967-3172. www.captainlord.com. 16 units. Summer and fall $199–$399 double; winter and spring from $99 midweek, from $175 weekends. Rates include breakfast. DISC, MC, V. 2- or 3-night minimum stay weekends and holidays. Children 12 and over welcome. *In room:* A/C, hair dryer.

The Colony Hotel ⭐⭐   The Colony is one of the handful of oceanside resorts that has preserved intact the classic New England vacation experience. This mammoth white Georgian Revival (1914) lords over the ocean and the mouth of the Kennebunk River. All rooms in the three-story main inn have been renovated over the last 3 years (but still no air-conditioning). They're bright and cheery, simply furnished with summer cottage antiques. Rooms in two of the three out-buildings carry over the rustic elegance of the main hotel; the exception is the East House, a 1950s-era hotel at the back edge of the property with 20 uninter-esting motel-style rooms. A staff naturalist leads guided coastal ecology tours on Saturdays in July and August; on Fridays, there's a lobster buffet dinner.

140 Ocean Ave. (P.O. Box 511), Kennebunkport, ME 04046. ☎ 800/552-2363 or 207/967-3331. Fax 207/967-8738. www.thecolonyhotel.com/maine. 123 units. $185–$435 double July–Aug; off-season rates available. Rates include breakfast. 3-night minimum stay summer weekends and holidays in main hotel. AE, MC, V. Closed mid-Oct to mid-May. Pets allowed ($25 per night). **Amenities:** Dining room (tradtional resort fare), lounge; heated saltwater pool; putting green; bike rental; shuffleboard court; limited room service; social director.

Franciscan Guest House   This former dormitory on the 200-acre grounds of the St. Anthony's Monastery is a unique budget choice. The rooms are institu-tional, basic, and clean; all have private bathrooms. Guests can stroll the lovely riverside grounds or walk over to Dock Square, about 10 minutes away.

Beach St. (P.O. Box 980), Kennebunk, ME 04046. ☎ 207/967-2011. 60 units. $64–$69 double. No credit cards. Closed mid-Sept to mid-June. *In room:* No phone.

Lodge at Turbat's Creek ☆   The Lodge at Turbat's Creek is a classy, clean motel in a quiet residential neighborhood about a 5-minute drive from Dock Square. The spacious grounds are attractive and scattered with Adirondack chairs. The standard motel-size rooms are decorated with pine furniture and painted a cheerful yellow. Breakfast may be enjoyed on the lawn in pleasant weather.

Turbat's Creek Rd., Kennebunkport, ME 04046. ☎ 207/967-8700. 26 units. June–Aug $119–$129 double; off-season $109–$119. Rates include continental breakfast. AE, MC, V. Closed late-Oct to Apr (open 2 weeks in Dec). Limited pets allowed; ask when booking. From Dock Sq., take Rte. 9 north; turn right on Maine St., left at first fork, right at second. **Amenities:** Heated pool; mountain bikes (free). *In room:* A/C, TV.

White Barn Inn ☆☆☆   Part of the Relais & Chateaux group, the White Barn Inn pampers its guests like no other in Maine. Upon checking in, guests are shown to one of the parlors and offered port or brandy while valets gather lug-gage and park cars. The atmosphere is distinctly European, and the emphasis is on service. The rooms are individually decorated in a refined country style. We're not aware of any other inn of this size that offers as many unexpected niceties, like robes, fresh flowers in the rooms, and turn-down service at night. Nearly half the rooms have wood-burning fireplaces. Guests can avail themselves of the inn's free bikes (including a small fleet of tandems) to head to the beach, or cross the street to explore the grounds of St. Anthony's Franciscan Monastery.

Beach Ave., ¼ mile east of junction of Rtes. 9 and 35 (P.O. Box 560-C), Kennebunkport, ME 04046. ☎ 207/967-2321. Fax 207/967-1100. www.whitebarninn.com. 25 units. $230–$250 double; $365–$550 suite. Rates include continental breakfast and afternoon tea. AE, MC, V. 2-night minimum stay on weekends; 3-night min-imum on holiday weekends. **Amenities:** Restaurant (see below); heated pool; canoes (free); bikes (free); concierge; limited room service; massage. *In room:* A/C, TV/VCR (on request).

WHERE TO DINE

Prices for lobster in the rough tend to be a bit more expensive around Kenne-bunkport than at other casual lobster joints further along the coast. But if you can't wait, **Nunan's Lobster Hut** (☎ 207/967-4362), on Route 9 north of Kennebunkport at Cape Porpoise, is the place. It's a classic lobster shack, often crowded with diners. Open daily for dinner, starting at 5pm in summer.

Grissini ☆ TUSCAN   Run by the folks of the White Barn Inn, Grissini is a handsome trattoria that offers great value. The mood is elegant but rustic Italian writ large: Oversized Italian advertising posters line the walls of the soaring, barn-like space, and burning logs in the handsome stone fireplace takes the chill off a cool evening. The menu changes weekly but includes a wide range of pastas and pizza, served with considerable flair. More far-ranging entrees include osso buco served over garlic mashed potatoes.

27 Western Ave., Kennebunkport. © 207/967-2211. www.restaurantgrissini.com. Reservations recommended. Main courses $7.95–$18.95. AE, MC, V. Sun–Fri 5:30–9:30pm; Sat 5–9pm (closed Wed Jan–Mar).

Seascapes ★★ CONTEMPORARY NEW ENGLAND   A tony restaurant with a wonderful ocean view, Seascapes is decorated in what might be termed traditional country-club bamboo. It's fancy but not fussy, with food several notches above the tried and true. All the fish is fresh (excepting shrimp), and all the breads and desserts are made on the premises. The menu offers traditional favorites along with more adventurous dishes like cashew-crusted Chilean sea bass served with a citrus-tamari sauce. The restaurant has garnered *Wine Spectator*'s award of excellence annually since 1993.

77 Pier Rd., Cape Porpoise, Kennebunkport. © 207/967-8500. www.seascapesrestaurant.com. Reservations recommended. Entrees $19–$25. Daily 12:30–2:30pm and 5–9pm (until 10pm Fri–Sat in peak season). Closed late Oct to Apr.

White Barn Inn ★★★ REGIONAL/NEW AMERICAN   Maine's best restaurant, the White Barn Inn regularly attracts gourmands from New York and Boston. It's pricey, but worth it. The restaurant (attached to an inn; see above) is housed in a rustic barn with a soaring interior and an eclectic collection of country antiques displayed in a hay loft. The setting is magical, the service is astonishingly attentive, and the kitchen rarely produces a flawed dish. The menu changes frequently; you might start with a lobster spring roll with daikon, carrots, snow peas, and cilantro, then graduate to a crab-glazed poached fillet of halibut on sweet-pea puree or pan-seared veal and venison on bacon-roasted butternut squash. Anticipate a meal to remember.

Beach Ave., Kennebunkport. © 207/967-2321. Reservations recommended. Fixed-price dinner $73. AE, MC, V. Daily 6–9pm. Closed 2 weeks in Jan.

2 Portland ★★

Seaside Portland is Maine's largest city. It's easy to drive right through on I-295, admire the skyline as you go, and be on your way to the villages and headlands further up the coast. After all, urban life isn't what one usually thinks of when one thinks of Maine.

But Portland is well worth an afternoon's detour or an overnight. This historic city has plenty of charm—especially the renovated Old Port section with its brick sidewalks and cobblestone streets—but there are also ferries to islands, boutique shops, some top-notch historic homes, and graceful neighborhoods. And there's the food. Portland is blessed with an uncommonly high number of excellent restaurants for a city its size (just 65,000, or roughly half that of Peoria, Ill.), making it a culinary mecca of Maine.

ESSENTIALS
GETTING THERE   Portland is off the Maine Turnpike (I-95). Coming from the south, downtown is most easily reached by taking Exit 6A, then following I-295. Exit at Franklin Street and follow this eastward until you arrive at the waterfront at the Casco Bay Lines terminal. Turn right on Commercial Street and you'll be at the lower edge of the Old Port. Continue several blocks to the visitor center (see below).

Concord Trailways (© 800/639-3317 or 207/828-1151) and **Vermont Transit** (© 800/537-3330 or 207/772-6587) offer bus service to Portland from Boston and Bangor. The Vermont Transit bus terminal is located at 950 Congress St. Concord Trailways, which is slightly more expensive, offers movies and headsets on its trips; its terminal is on Sewall Street (a 35-minute walk from downtown).

The **Portland International Jetport** is served by scheduled flights on **Air Nova** (© 902/873-5000; www.airnova.ca), **American Airlines** (© 800/433-7300; www.im.aa.com), **Delta/Business Express** (© 800/638-7333; www.delta.com), **Continental** (© 800/525-0280; www.continental.com), **Northwest** (© 800/225-2525; www.nwa.com), **US Airways** (© 800/428-4322; www.usairways.com), and **United** (© 800/241-6522; www.ual.com). The airport is located across the Fore River from downtown. Metro buses ($1) connect the airport to downtown; cab fare runs about $12.

VISITOR INFORMATION The **Convention and Visitor's Bureau of Greater Portland,** 305 Commercial St. (© 207/772-5800 or 207/772-4994), stocks a large supply of brochures and is happy to dispense information. The center is open in summer, Monday through Friday from 8am to 6pm and Saturday and Sunday from 10am to 5pm; hours are shorter in the off-season. Ask for the *Greater Portland Visitor Guide* with map. Portland has two free weekly alternative newspapers—*Casco Bay Weekly* and the *Portland Phoenix*—both of which offer listings of local events, films, nightclub performances, and the like.

EXPLORING THE CITY

Any visit to Portland should start with a stroll around the historic **Old Port** ✸✸✸. Bounded by Commercial, Congress, Union, and Pearl streets, this several-square-block area near the waterfront contains the city's most historic commercial architecture, a plethora of fine restaurants, a mess of boutiques, and one of the thickest concentrations of bars on the Eastern Seaboard. (The Old Port tends to transform as night lengthens, with the crowds growing younger and rowdier.) The narrow streets and intricate brick facades reflect the mid-Victorian era; most of the area was rebuilt following a devastating fire in 1866. Leafy, quaint Exchange Street is the heart of the Old Port.

The city's finest harborside stroll is along the **Eastern Prom Pathway** ⭐⭐, which wraps for about a mile along the waterfront beginning at the Casco Bay Lines ferry terminal (corner of Commercial and Franklin streets). The paved pathway is suitable for walking or biking, and offers expansive views out toward the islands and boat traffic on the harbor. The pathway skirts the lower edge of the **Eastern Promenade** ⭐, a 68-acre hillside park with broad, grassy slopes extending down to the water. Tiny East End Beach is located here, but the water is often unhealthy for swimming (look for signs). The pathway continues on to Back Cove Pathway, a 3½-mile loop around tidal Back Cove.

Atop Munjoy Hill (above the Eastern Promenade) is the distinctive **Portland Observatory** ⭐, 138 Congress St. (© **207/774-5561**), a quirky shingled tower dating from 1807 and used to signal the arrival of ships into port. Exhibits provide a quick glimpse of Portland past, but the real draw is the view of city and harbor from the top. Open daily (when flags are flying from the cupola); admission is $3 for adults, $2 for children.

On the other end of the Portland peninsula is the **Western Promenade** ⭐⭐. (From the Old Port, follow Spring Street westward to Vaughan; turn right and then take the first left on Bowdoin Street.) This narrow strip of lawn atop a forested bluff has views across the Fore River, which is lined with less-than-scenic light industry and commercial buildings, with the White Mountains in the distance. A walk through the Western Prom neighborhood reveals the grandest and most imposing houses in the city, in a wide array of architectural styles, from Italianate to shingle to stick.

Portland Public Market ⭐⭐   The Portland Public Market opened in 1998 and features more than two dozen vendors selling fresh foods and flowers, much of which is grown in Maine. The architecturally distinctive building is at once classic and modern, and houses fishmongers, butchers, fresh-fruit dealers, a seafood cafe, a wine shop, and an upscale restaurant called Commissary (see below). The market is a much-recommended spot to see some of the best local food products and to lay in supplies for a picnic or snacks.

25 Preble St. (½ block west of Monument Sq.). © **207/228-2000**. www.portlandmarket.com. Year-round Mon–Sat 9am–7pm; Sun 10am–5pm. Free parking (with validated ticket) at connected garage on the west side of Cumberland Ave.

Children's Museum of Maine ⭐⭐ (Kids)   The centerpiece exhibit is the camera obscura, a room-size "camera" located on the top floor of this stout, columned downtown building next to the art museum. Children gather around a white table in a dark room, where they see magically projected images that include cars driving on city streets, boats plying the harbor, and seagulls flapping by. That's just one attraction; others range from running a supermarket check-out counter to sliding down the firehouse pole.

142 Free St. (next to the Portland Museum of Art). © **207/828-1234**. Admission $5 adults and children, free for children under 1. Mon–Sat 10am–5pm; Sun noon–5pm. Closed Mon–Tues fall through spring. Discounted parking at Spring St. Parking Garage.

Maine Narrow Gauge Railroad Co. & Museum ⭐   In the late 19th century, Maine was home to several narrow-gauge railways, which operated on rails

Downtown Portland

ACCOMMODATIONS ■
The Danforth **10**
The Percy Inn **12**
Pomegranate Inn **11**
Portland Regency Hotel **8**

DINING ◆
Back Bay Grill **1**
Becky's **9**
Benkay **5**
Commissary **3**
Flatbread Company **6**
Fore Street **7**
Natasha's **2**
Silly's **4**

2 feet apart. Most of these versatile trains have disappeared, and this nonprofit organization is dedicated to preserving the examples that remain. The museum itself is free; there's a charge for a short ride on the trains, which chug on a rail line along Casco Bay at the foot of the Eastern Prom. The views of the islands are outstanding; the ride itself is slow-paced and somewhat dull.

58 Fore St. © **207/828-0814.** Free museum admission; train fare $5 adults, $4 seniors, $3 children. Daily 10am–4pm; trains run on the hour from 11am. Closed Jan to mid-Feb. From I-295, take Franklin St. exit and follow to Fore St.; turn left and continue to museum, on right.

Portland Head Light & Museum ⭑⭑⭑ Just a 10-minute drive from downtown Portland is this 1794 lighthouse, easily one of the most picturesque in the nation. The light marks the entrance to Portland Harbor, and was occupied continuously from its construction until 1989, when it was automated and the graceful keeper's house (1891) was converted to a small museum. Still active, the lighthouse is closed to the public, but visitors can stop by the museum, wander the grounds, and watch the sailboats and cargo ships come and go. The park has a pebble beach, grassy lawns, and picnic areas well-suited for informal barbecues.

Fort Williams Park, 1000 Shore Rd., Cape Elizabeth. © **207/799-2661.** www.portlandheadlight.com. Free entrance to park grounds; museum admission $2 adults, $1 children 6–18. Park grounds open year-round, daily from sunrise to sunset (until 8:30pm in summer); museum open June–Oct daily 10am–4pm, spring and late fall Sat–Sun 10am–4pm. From Portland, follow State St. across the Fore River; continue straight on Broadway. At third light, turn right on Cottage Rd., which becomes Shore Rd.; follow until you arrive at the park, on your left.

Portland Museum of Art ★★   This bold, modern museum was designed by
I. M. Pei & Partners in 1983, and features selections from its own fine collections along with touring exhibits. The museum is particularly strong in American artists with Maine connections, including Winslow Homer, Andrew Wyeth,
and Edward Hopper, and has good displays of Early American furniture and
crafts. Colby College and the museum share the Joan Whitney Payson Collection, which includes fine works by Renoir, Degas, and Picasso.

7 Congress Sq. (corner of Congress and High sts.). ☎ 207/775-6148. www.portlandmuseum.org. Admission
$6 adults, $5 students and seniors, $1 children 6-12 (free Fri 5–9pm). Tues–Wed and Sat–Sun 10am–5pm;
Thurs–Fri 10am–9pm; June to mid-Oct also open Mon 10am–5pm. Guided tours daily at 2pm.

Victoria Mansion ★★   Widely regarded as one of the most elaborate brown-
stones ever built in the United States, this mansion (also known as the Morse-
Libby House) is a remarkable display of high Victorian style. Built between
1858 and 1863, the towering home is a prime example of the Italianate style.
Inside, it appears that not a square inch of wall space was left untouched by
craftsmen or artisans (11 painters were hired to create the murals). The decor is
ponderous and somber, but it offers an engaging look at a bygone era.

109 Danforth St. ☎ 207/772-4841. Admission $7 adults, $3 children 6–17. May–Oct Tues–Sat 10am–4pm;
Sun 1–5pm; tours offered at quarter past and quarter of each hour. Closed Nov–Apr, except for holiday tours
from late Nov to mid-Dec. From the Old Port, head west on Fore St., veer right on Danforth St. at light near
Stonecoast Brewing; go 3 blocks to the mansion, at the corner of Park St.

Wadsworth-Longfellow House & Center for Maine History ★   Maine
Historical Society's "history campus" on busy Congress Street includes the aus-
tere brick Wadsworth-Longfellow House (1785), built by Gen. Peleg
Wadsworth, father of poet Henry Wadsworth Longfellow. It's furnished in an
early-19th-century style, with many samples of Longfellow family furniture.
Adjacent is the Maine History Gallery, located in a garish postmodern building.
Changing exhibits here explore the rich texture of Maine history.

489 Congress St. ☎ 207/879-0427. www.mainehistory.com. Gallery and Longfellow house tour $6 adults,
$2 children 6–18. Gallery only $4 adults, $2 children. Longfellow House June–Oct daily 10am–4pm, gallery
daily 10am–5:30pm; Nov–May gallery only Wed–Sat noon–4pm.

BOAT TOURS
Casco Bay Lines ★   Six Casco Bay islands have year-round populations and
are served by scheduled ferries from downtown Portland. Except for Long
Island, the islands are part of the city of Portland. The ferries offer an inexpensive way to view the bustling harbor and get a taste of island life. Trips range
from a 20-minute (one-way) excursion to Peaks Island (the closest thing to an
island suburb with 1,200 year-round residents) to a 5½-hour cruise to Bailey
Island (connected by bridge to the mainland south of Brunswick) and back. All
of the islands are well-suited for walking; Peaks Island has a rocky back shore
that's easily accessible via the island's paved perimeter road (bring a picnic
lunch). Cliff Island is the most remote of the bunch.

Commercial and Franklin sts. ☎ 207/774-7871. www.cascobaylines.com. Fares vary depending on the run
and season, but summer rates typically $5.25–$13.75 round-trip. Frequent departures 6am–10pm.

Eagle Island Tours ★★   Eagle Island was the summer home of famed Arctic
explorer and Portland native Robert E. Peary, who claimed in 1909 to be the
first person to reach the North Pole. (His accomplishments have been the subject of exhaustive debate among Arctic scholars.) In 1904, Peary built a simple
home on a remote, 17-acre island at the edge of Casco Bay; in 1912, he added

flourishes in the form of two low stone towers. After his death in 1920, his family kept up the home before eventually donating it to the state. The home is open to the public, maintained much the way it was when Peary lived here. Eagle Tours offers one trip daily from Portland. The 4-hour excursion includes a 1½-hour stopover on the island.

Long Wharf (Commercial St.). ℂ 207/774-6498. Tour $17.50 adults, $13.50 seniors, $10.50 children under 12 (includes state park fee of $1.50 adults, 50¢ children). One departure daily at 10am.

Old Port Mariner Fleet ★   The *Indian II* offers deep-sea fishing trips far beyond Portland Harbor in search of cod, cusk, hake, pollack, and more. Most are 1-day trips (8am–5pm), but several times each summer, fishing marathons (5am–5pm) are organized for diehards. The *Odyssey* is a cruise boat that offers whale watches from 10am to 4pm as well as evening music parties, including a 2-hour "floating Irish pub" on Saturday and Sunday evenings (departs at 6:30pm).

Commercial St. (Long Wharf and Custom House Wharf). ℂ 207/775-0727. www.marinerfleet.com. Excursions $10–$75. Several departures daily.

WHERE TO STAY

The **Holiday Inn by the Bay** ★, 88 Spring St. (ℂ 207/775-2311), offers great views of the harbor from half the rooms. Peak-season rates are $140. Budget travelers seeking chain hotels can head toward the area around the Maine Mall in South Portland, about a 10-minute drive from downtown. Try **Days Inn** (ℂ 207/772-3450) or **Coastline Inn** (ℂ 207/772-3838).

Black Point Inn ★★★   Located about a 15-minute drive from downtown Portland, the Black Point is a Maine classic. Situated on 9 acres on a point with views along the coast both north and south, the inn was built as a summer resort in 1873 in an area enshrined in some of the work of noted painter Winslow Homer. Sixty rooms are located in the main shingled lodge; the others are spread about four tidy cottages. Even the smaller rooms are generously sized, with enough space for two wing chairs and a writing desk. The cottage units have more of a rustic look; our pick would be the Sprague Cottage, with its flagstone floors in the common area and five rooms with private balconies, some with ocean views. Note that the inn is popular for weddings on summer weekends.

510 Black Point Rd., Prouts Neck, ME 04074. ℂ 800/258-0003 or 207/883-2500. Fax 207/883-9976. www.blackpointinn.com. 80 units. July–Labor Day $345–$470 double; $420–$520 cottage double; spring and fall from $290; winter from $210. Rates include breakfast and dinner. AE, DC, DISC, MC, V. **Amenities:** Restaurant (regional); outdoor pool; small indoor pool; ocean swimming at 2 adjacent beaches; shuttle to 5 area golf courses; fitness room; hot tub; sauna; massage; social director; summer children's programs; limited room service; baby-sitting; laundry service; dry cleaning. *In room:* A/C, TV, VCR (on request), dataport, fridge (on request), hair dryer, iron.

Finds **Play Ball!**

The **Portland Sea Dogs**, a AA team affiliated with the Florida Marlins, plays throughout the summer at Hadlock Field, a compact stadium near downtown that retains an old-time feel despite aluminum benches and other updates. Activities are geared towards families, with lots of entertainment between innings. Tickets are budget priced at $5 to $7 for adults, $3 to $6 for children under 16 and seniors. The season runs from April to Labor Day. For more information, call ℂ 800/936-3647 or 207/879-9500, or check www.portlandseadogs.com.

The Danforth ⭐⭐ Located in an exceptionally handsome brick home constructed in 1821, this is one of Portland's more desirable small inns. Its extra
touches are exceptional throughout, from the working fireplaces in all guest
rooms (except one) to the richly paneled billiards room. Especially appealing is
room 1, with a sitting area and private deck, and room 2, with high ceilings and
superb morning light. The inn is located at the edge of the Spring Street Historic District, a 10-minute walk from downtown. It's popular for weddings, so
if you're in search of a quiet weekend retreat, ask first if anything is planned.

163 Danforth St., Portland, ME 04102. ℂ **800/991-6557** or 207/879-8755. Fax 207/879-8754. www.
danforthmaine.com. 10 units. Summer $139–$329 double; off-season $119–$229. Rates include continental
breakfast. AE, MC, V. Pets sometimes allowed ($10). **Amenities:** Passes to in-town health club; bike rental;
billiards room; in-room massage. *In room:* A/C, TV, dataport, hair dryer, iron.

The Percy Inn ⭐ The Percy Inn, at the edge of Portland's West End, is
housed in a handsome 1830 brick town house in an up-and-coming but not-
quite-there-yet area. It's close to good restaurants and is about a 15-minute walk
to the Old Port. The guest rooms are reached via a narrow and twisting staircase.
The Henry W. Longfellow Room has wonderful random-width floorboards, a
small snack room with fridge, and a corner sitting area with a marble cafe table.
Nice touches abound: All rooms have weather radios, CD players, VCRs, complimentary soft drinks, and coolers with beach blankets for day trips.

15 Pine St., Portland ME 04104. ℂ **207/871-7638.** Fax 207/775-2599. www.percyinn.com. 4 units. June–Oct
$129–$179 double; Nov–May $89–$159. Rates include continental breakfast. MC, V. Limited lot parking plus
street parking. Children over 8 welcome. *In room:* A/C, TV/VCR.

Pomegranate Inn ⭐⭐⭐ This is Portland's most appealing B&B, and one of
the better choices in all of northern New England. Housed in an imposing 1884
Italianate home in the architecturally distinctive Western Prom neighborhood,
the interiors are both whimsical and elegant—a fatally cloying combination
when attempted by anyone without impeccably good taste. Expect bold artwork
and eclectic antique furniture collected by owner Isabel Smiles. Most units have
gas fireplaces; the best of the lot is in the carriage house, which has its own terrace, kitchenette, and fireplace. Tea and wine are served upon arrival, and the
breakfasts are invariably tasty. The inn is well-situated for exploring the West
Prom neighborhood; downtown is a 20-minute walk away.

49 Neal St., Portland, ME 04102. ℂ **800/356-0408** or 207/772-1006. Fax 207/773-4426. www.
pomegranateinn.com. 8 units. Summer and fall $165–$205 double; winter and spring $95–$145. Rates include
breakfast. 2-night minimum stay summer weekends; 4-night minimum Christmas and Thanksgiving. AE, DISC,
MC, V. On-street parking. Children 16 and over welcome. From the Old Port, take Middle St. (which turns into
Spring St.) to Neal St. in the West End (about 1 mile); turn right and proceed to inn. *In room:* A/C, TV.

Portland Regency Hotel ⭐⭐ Centrally located on a cobblestone courtyard
in trendy Old Port, the Regency boasts the city's premier hotel location. Housed
in an 1895 brick armory, the hotel offers attractive rooms appointed with all the
expected amenities. The architects have had to work within the quirky layout of
the building; as a result, the top-floor rooms lack windows but have skylights,
and windows are at knee-height in some other units. For a splurge, ask for room
332 or 336, both corner units with handsome (nonworking) fireplaces and sitting areas. The interior walls can be thin, and on weekends the Old Port revelry
sometimes penetrates even the dense brick outer walls.

20 Milk St., Portland, ME 04101. ℂ **800/727-3436** or 207/774-4200. Fax 207/775-2150. www.theregency.
com. public@theregency.com. 95 units. Summer $199–$249 double; off-season $159–$239. AE, DISC, MC, V.
Valet parking ($8 daily). **Amenities:** Restaurant (contemporary American); extensive health club; Jacuzzi;

sauna; courtesy car to airport; limited room service; massage; baby-sitting; dry cleaning. *In room:* A/C, TV, dataport, minibar, hair dryer, iron.

WHERE TO DINE
EXPENSIVE

Back Bay Grill ★★★ NEW AMERICAN   Back Bay Grill has long been one of Portland's premier restaurants, offering an upscale, contemporary ambience in a rather downscale neighborhood. The innovative menu is revamped seasonally. Diners might start off with the popular terrine of house-cured gravlax and smoked salmon with marinated red onions. Among main courses, look for heavenly dishes like rack of lamb with porcini-infused potato gratin and lavender demi-glace; halibut with a chorizo-saffron sauce; or seared salmon on vanilla-scented Vidalia onions with fresh fava beans and a baby arugula lobster salad.

65 Portland St. ✆ **207/772-8833.** www.backbaygrill.com. Reservations recommended. Main courses $18–$33. AE, DC, DISC, MC, V. Mon–Thurs 5–9pm; Fri–Sat 5–9:30pm.

Commissary ★★ NEW AMERICAN   This new entry, which opened in late 2000, brings an unaccustomed gloss to the Portland restaurant scene. Maine native Matthew Kenney, the author of the cookbook *Matthew Kenney's Mediterranean Cooking* and a pied piper with his three Manhattan restaurants, Matthew's, Mezze, and Monzu, created it. The soaring, spare space is urbane (if noisy), and the menu employs fresh fare from the market and beyond. Among typical offerings: wood-roasted char, chicken stuffed with foie gras and pears, and risotto of wild mushrooms. Side dishes are extra and ambitiously priced ($5 for wilted greens), but the main dishes offer good value.

25 Preble St. (in Portland Public Market). ✆ **207/228-2057.** Reservations recommended. Main courses $17–$23. AE, DC, DISC, MC, V. Tues–Sat 5–10pm; Sun–Mon 5–9pm.

Fore Street ★★ CONTEMPORARY/GRILL   Light floods in through the huge windows at this loft-like space, yet the place never feels empty—the sprawling open kitchen is located in the middle of it all, filled with a team of chefs busy stoking the wood-fired brick oven and grilling fish and meats. The menu changes nightly; for appetizers, look for the likes of local quail roasted in the wood oven, or mussels served with a garlic almond butter. Then move on to the turnspit-roasted Maine rabbit or one of the selection of applewood-grilled dishes, including steak, chicken, duckling, venison, or fresh fish. Meals are consistently well prepared, and the service attentive on all but the busiest nights.

288 Fore St. ✆ **207/775-2717.** Reservations recommended. Main courses $14.95–$25.95. AE, MC, V. Mon–Sat 5:30–10pm; Sun 5:30–9:30pm.

MODERATE

Benkay ★ *Value* JAPANESE/SUSHI   Of Portland's handful of sushi restaurants, Benkay is the hippest. It's usually teeming with a lively crowd lured by good value. Ask about $1 sushi nights (usually weeknights). The $13 regular sushi platter also delivers a lot for the money, although nothing very exotic. Teriyaki and tempura round out the menu. Expect harried service on busy nights.

2 India St. (at Commercial). ✆ **207/773-5555.** Reservations not accepted. Main courses $7.95–$16.95. Mon–Fri 11:30am–2pm; Mon–Sat 5–10pm; Sun noon–9pm.

Flatbread Company ★ PIZZA   This upscale, hippie-chic pizzeria—an offshoot of the original Flatbread Company in Waitsfield, Vt.—may have the best waterfront location in town. It sits on a slip overlooking the Casco Bay Lines terminal, so you can watch fishermen at work while you eat. (There are picnic tables on the deck in fair weather.) The inside brings to mind a Phish concert, with Tibetan prayer flags and long-haired staffers stoking wood-fired ovens and slicing nitrate-free pepperoni and organic vegetables. The laid-back atmosphere makes the place; the pizza is quite good, though the toppings tend to be skimpy.

72 Commercial St. ⊘ **207/772-8777.** Reservations accepted for parties 10 or more. Pizzas $11.25–$14 ($6.50–$8.50 for a half). AE, MC, V. Mon–Tues 5–9pm; Wed–Sun 11:30am–9pm.

Natasha's ☆ ECLECTIC   Located in a down-at-the-heels neighborhood between the main post office and the Portland Public Market, Natasha's combines industrial chic—battered concrete floors, black pew-like benches, white tablecloths topped with butcher's paper—with a menu that's delightfully creative in its simplicity. Starters include a smoked salmon chowder and Maine crab and goat cheese rangoon. Dinner entrees feature the likes of lobster and crab ravioli served with leeks and lemon, pork loin grilled and served with a spicy pepper jam, and a crispy peanut tofu with pad Thai seasoning. Lunch is equally inviting, with original sandwiches (like a grilled vegetarian napoleon with artichoke hearts) and salads. Unfortunately, the service can be frustrating.

40 Portland St. ⊘ **207/774-4004.** Reservations recommended. Main courses $4.50–$8.50 brunch, $4.50–$9.95 lunch, $13–$20 dinner. AE, DISC, MC, V. Mon–Fri 9am–2:30pm; Sat–Sun 8am–2:30pm; Thurs–Sat 5–9:30pm.

INEXPENSIVE

Becky's ☆☆ BREAKFAST/LUNCH   Becky's got a glowing write-up in *Gourmet* magazine in 1999, but it obviously hasn't gone to the proprietor's head. This charmless institution is located in a squat concrete building on the non-quaint end of the waterfront, and has drop ceilings, fluorescent lights, and scruffy booths and tables. It's populated early by local fishermen grabbing a plate o' eggs before setting out; later in the day it attracts students and businessmen. The menu offers about what you'd expect, like inexpensive sandwiches (fried haddock and cheese, corn dogs, tuna melt). It's most noted for breakfast, which includes 13 different omelets. Where else can you find five different types of home fries?

390 Commercial St. ⊘ **207/773-7070.** Breakfast items $3–$6.25; sandwiches $1.75–$4.75. AE, DISC, MC, V. Daily 4am–9pm.

Silly's ☆ ECLECTIC & TAKE-OUT   Silly's is the favored cheap-eats joint among even jaded Portlanders. Situated on a ragged urban street, the interior is bright and funky, with mismatched 1950s dinettes. The menu is creative, and everything made fresh and from scratch. The place is noted for its "fast abdullahs," which consist of tasty fillings rolled up in fresh tortillas. Among our favorites: the shish kebab with feta, and the sloppy "Diesel," made with pulled pork barbecue and coleslaw. The fries are hand cut, and the milkshakes huge.

40 Washington Ave. ⊘ **207/772-0360.** Lunch and dinner items $2.50–$7.50; pizza $7.50–$20. MC, V. Mon–Sat 10am–10pm.

PORTLAND AFTER DARK

Downtown Portland is blessed with three movie theaters, allowing downtown moviegoers to avoid the disheartening slog out to the mall octoplexes. The **Keystone Theatre Cafe,** 504 Congress St. (⊘ **207/871-5500**), offers surprisingly good pub fare and beer while you enjoy second-run films that are more arty than you'll find at the mall. **Nickelodeon Cinemas,** 1 Temple St. (⊘ **207/772-9751**), has six screens showing second-run films at discounted prices. **The Movies,** 10 Exchange St. (⊘ **207/772-9600**), is a compact art-film showcase in the heart of the Old Port.

As for the club and bar scene, Portland is usually lively in the evenings, especially on summer weekends when the testosterone level in the Old Port seems to rocket into the stratosphere—you'll see young men and women prowling the dozens of bars and spilling out onto the streets. Among the Old Port bars favored by locals are **Three-Dollar Dewey's,** at the corner of Commercial and Union streets (try the great fries); **Gritty McDuff's Brew Pub,** on Fore Street near the foot of Exchange Street; and **Brian Ború,** on Center Street. All are casual and pubby, with guests sharing long tables with new companions.

Check one of the two free weekly newspapers, *Casco Bay Weekly* or the *Portland Phoenix,* for current venues, performers, and showtimes.

3 The Mid Coast

Veteran Maine travelers contend this part of the coast is losing its native charm—it's too commercial, too developed, too much like the rest of the country. The grousers have a point, especially regarding Route 1's roadside. But get off the main roads and you'll catch glimpses of another Maine: quiet inland villages, dramatic coastal scenery, and a rich sense of history, especially maritime history.

The best source of information on the region is the **Maine State Information Center** (℃ 207/846-0833), just off I-95, Exit 17 in Yarmouth. This state-run center is stocked with brochures; its helpful staff members can provide information on the entire state.

Just across the road is the **DeLorme Map Store** (℃ 888/227-1656), with a dazzling selection of maps, atlases, and CD-ROMs. What makes the place worth a detour is Eartha, "the world's largest rotating and revolving globe." The 42-foot-diameter globe, which occupies the whole of the atrium lobby, is constructed on a scale of 1:1,000,000, and is the largest satellite image ever produced of the earth.

FREEPORT

If Freeport were a mall (and that's not a far-fetched analogy), **L.L.Bean** would be the anchor store. It's the business that launched Freeport, elevating its status from just another town off the interstate to one of the two outlet capitals of Maine (the other is Kittery). Freeport still has the outward form of a classic coastal village, but it's a village that's been occupied by the national fashion industry. Most of the historic homes have been converted to upscale shops which now sell name-brand clothing and housewares. Banana Republic occupies a handsome brick Federal-style home; even the McDonald's is in a tasteful, understated Victorian farmhouse—you really have to look for the golden arches.

While a number of more modern structures have been built to accommodate the outlet boom, strict planning guidelines have managed to preserve much of the local charm, at least in the village itself. Huge parking lots off Main Street are hidden from view, making this one of the more aesthetically pleasing places to shop. But even with these large lots, parking can be scarce in peak season. Bring a lot of patience, and expect teeming crowds if you come at a busy time.

ESSENTIALS

GETTING THERE   Freeport is on Route 1, but is most commonly reached via I-95 from either Exit 19 or 20.

VISITOR INFORMATION   The **Freeport Merchants Association,** 23 Depot St. (℃ 800/865-1994 or 207/865-1212; www.freeportusa.com), publishes a free map and directory of businesses, restaurants, and accommodations; it's widely available around town.

SHOPPING

Freeport has more than 100 retail shops between Exit 19 of I-95 at the far lower end of Main Street and Mallett Road, which connects to Exit 20. Shops have recently begun to spread south of Exit 19 toward Yarmouth. Get off at Exit 17 and head north on Route 1 if you don't want to miss a single shop. The bargains can vary from extraordinary to "eh?," so plan on racking up some mileage if you're intent on finding outrageous deals. Stores in Freeport are typically open daily from 9am to 9pm during the busy summer season.

Among national chains with a presence in Freeport are the Gap, Burberry's, Levi's, Calvin Klein, Patagonia, North Face, Abercrombie & Fitch, J. Crew, Coach, Chaudier Cookware, Timberland, Maidenform, and many others.

L.L.Bean 🌟🌟🌟 Monster outdoor retailer L.L.Bean traces its roots to the day Leon Leonwood Bean decided that what the world really needed was a good weatherproof hunting shoe. He joined a watertight gum shoe with a laced leather upper. Hunters liked it. The store grew. An empire was born. Today, L.L.Bean sells millions of dollars worth of clothing and outdoor goods to customers nationwide through its catalogs. This modern store is the size of a regional mall, but tastefully done with its own indoor trout pond and lots of natural wood. It's open 365 days a year, 24 hours a day, and it's a popular spot even in the dead of night. Selections include Bean's own trademark clothing, home furnishings, books, shoes, and plenty of outdoor gear. A good place to start is the L.L.Bean factory store, which may have items you're looking for at discounted prices. It's located between Main and Depot streets—ask at the front desk of the main store for directions. Main and Bow sts. ✆ **800/341-4341.** www.llbean.com.

WHERE TO STAY

Harraseeket Inn 🌟🌟 The Harraseeket deftly mixes traditional and modern in a personable property 2 blocks north of L.L.Bean. A late-19th-century home is the soul of the hotel, but most of the rooms are in modern additions. Guests can relax in the well-regarded dining room, read the paper in the common room during afternoon tea, or sip a cocktail in the rustic Broad Arrow Tavern with its wood-fired oven. The guest rooms are large and tastefully appointed with quarter-canopy beds and a mix of contemporary and antique furniture. About a quarter have fireplaces, and more than half feature single or double whirlpools.

162 Main St., Freeport, ME 04032. ✆ **800/342-6423** or 207/865-9377. www.harraseeketinn.com. 84 units. Summer and fall $180–$265 double; spring and early summer $140–$235; winter $110–$215. Rates include breakfast. AE, DC, DISC, MC, V. Take Exit 20 off I-95 to Main St. **Amenities:** 2 restaurants (New American, grill); indoor heated lap pool; concierge; limited room service; laundry service; dry cleaning. *In room:* A/C, TV, dataport, coffeemaker, hair dryer.

Kendall Tavern 🌟 This cheerful yellow farmhouse is out of the bustle of Freeport, but only half a mile from downtown shopping. The rooms are decorated in a bright and airy style with a mix of antique and new furniture. Those facing Route 1 (Main Street) are noisier than others, but the traffic isn't likely to be too disruptive. There's a piano in one of the two parlors, and a hot tub in a spacious private room in the back. Breakfasts are served in the pine-floored dining room.

213 Main St., Freeport, ME 04032. ✆ **800/341-9572** or 207/865-1338. 7 units. $100–$125 double peak season; $75–$95 off-season. Rates include breakfast. AE, DISC, MC, V. **Amenities:** Hot tub. *In room:* No phone.

Maine Idyll Motor Court 🌟 *Value* This 1932 motor court is a classic—20 cottages scattered about a grove of beech and oak trees. Each has a tiny porch, fireplace (birch logs provided), modest kitchen facilities (no ovens), and time-worn furniture. The cabins are not lavishly sized, but are comfortable and clean. The only interruption to an idyll here is the omnipresent sound of traffic: I-95 is just through the trees on one side, Route 1 on the other side.

1411 U.S. Rte. 1, Freeport, ME 04032. © 207/865-4201. www.freeportusa.com/maineidyll. 20 units. $48–$72 double; $68–$90 2- or 3-bedroom cottage. Rates include continental breakfast. No credit cards. Closed early Nov to late Apr. Pets allowed. *In room:* TV, kitchenette, no phone.

WHERE TO DINE

A short walk from L.L.Bean is **Chowder Express & Sandwich Shop,** 2 Mechanic St. (© **207/865-3404**), a hole-in-the-wall with counter seating for about a dozen. Fish, lobster, and clam chowder are served in paper bowls with plastic spoons. It's convenient for a quick bite between shops.

Harraseeket Lunch & Lobster ★★ LOBSTER POUND   Located at a boatyard on the Harraseeket River about a 10-minute drive from Freeport's main shopping district, this lobster pound is a popular destination on sunny days—although with its heated dining room, it's a worthy destination any time. Take in the river view from the dock while waiting for your number to be called. Be prepared for big crowds; a good alternative is to come in late afternoon between the crushing lunch and dinner hordes.

Main St., South Freeport. © 207/865-4888. Lobsters market price (typically $8–$12). No credit cards. Daily 11:30am–8:30pm. Closed mid-Oct to May 1. From I-95, take Exit 17 and head north on Rte. 1; turn right on S. Freeport Rd. at the large Indian statue; continue to stop sign in South Freeport; turn right to waterfront. From Freeport, take South St. (off Bow St.) to Main St. in South Freeport; turn left to water.

Jameson Tavern ★ REGIONAL   Located in a handsome, historic farmhouse literally in the shadow of L.L.Bean, the Jameson Tavern touts itself as the birthplace of Maine. In 1820, the papers legally separating Maine from Massachusetts were signed here. Today, it's a two-part restaurant under single ownership. The historic Tap Room offers fare like crab-cake burgers, lobster croissants, and a variety of build-your-own burgers (sit outside on the brick patio if the weather's good). The other part of the house is the Dining Room, which is more formal in a country-colonial sort of way. Meals here are more sedate and gussied up, with an emphasis on steak and hearty fare.

115 Main St. (just north of L.L.Bean). © 207/865-4196. Reservations encouraged. Tap Room main courses $6.95–$16.95; Dining Room main courses $5.25–$10.95 lunch, $11.95–$22.95 dinner. AE, DC, DISC, MC, V. Tap Room daily 11am–11pm; Dining Room summer daily 11am–10pm, winter daily 11:30am–9pm.

BRUNSWICK ★ & BATH ★

Brunswick and Bath are two handsome, historic towns that share a strong commercial past. **Brunswick** was once home to several mills along the Androscoggin River; these have since been converted to offices and the like, but the town's broad Maine Street still bustles with activity. Brunswick is also home to Bowdoin College. The school was founded in 1794, offered its first classes 8 years later, and has since amassed an illustrious roster of prominent alumni, including Nathaniel Hawthorne, Henry Wadsworth Longfellow, President Franklin Pierce, and Arctic explorer Robert E. Peary.

Eight miles to the east, **Bath** is pleasantly situated on the Kennebec River, and is a noted center of shipbuilding. The first U.S.-built ship was constructed downstream at the Popham Bay colony in the early 17th century; in the years since, shipbuilders have constructed more than 5,000 ships here. Bath shipbuilding reached its heyday in the late 19th century, but the business of shipbuilding continues to this day. Bath Iron Works is one of the nation's preeminent boatyards, constructing and repairing ships for the Navy. The

scaled-down military has left Bath shipbuilders in a somewhat tenuous state, but
it's still common to see the steely gray ships in the dry dock (the best view is
from the bridge over the Kennebec).

ESSENTIALS
GETTING THERE   Brunswick and Bath are both on Route 1. Brunswick is
accessible via Exits 22 and 23 off I-95. If you're bypassing Brunswick and heading north up Route 1 to Bath or beyond, continue up I-95 and exit at the
"coastal connector" exit in Topsham, which avoids some of the slower traffic
going through Brunswick.

For bus service from Portland or Boston, contact **Vermont Transit** (© **800/
451-3292**) or **Concord Trailways** (© **800/639-3317**).

VISITOR INFORMATION   The **Bath-Brunswick Region Chamber of
Commerce,** 59 Pleasant St., near downtown Brunswick (© **207/725-8797** or
207/443-9751), offers information and lodging assistance Monday through Friday from 8:30am to 5pm. The chamber also staffs a summer-only information
center on Route 1 between Brunswick and Bath; open daily from 10am to 7pm.

SEEING THE SIGHTS
Collectors flock to **Cabot Mill Antiques,** 14 Maine St., in downtown
Brunswick (© **207/725-2855;** www.cabotiques.com), located on the ground
floor of a restored textile mill. The emporium features the stuff of 140 dealers.

Bowdoin Museum of Art ★★   This stern, neoclassical building on the Bowdoin campus was designed by the prominent architectural firm of McKim,
Mead & White in 1894. While the collections are relatively small, they include
a number of exceptional paintings from Europe and America, along with early
furniture and artifacts from classical antiquity. The artists include Andrew and
N. C. Wyeth, Marsden Hartley, Winslow Homer, and John Singer Sargent.
Note that construction and expansion plans may disrupt visits into 2002.

Walker Art Building, Bowdoin College, Brunswick. © 207/725-3275. Free admission. Tues–Sat 10am–5pm;
Sun 2–5pm.

Peary-MacMillan Arctic Museum ★   While Admiral Robert E. Peary (class
of 1887) is better known for his accomplishments (he discovered the North Pole
at age 53 in 1909), Donald MacMillan (class of 1898) also racked up an impressive string of achievements in Arctic research and exploration. You can learn
about both men in this highly manageable museum on the Bowdoin campus.
The front room features mounted animals from the Arctic, including impressive
polar bears. A second room outlines Peary's historic 1909 expedition, complete
with excerpts from his journal. The last room includes varied displays of Inuit
arts and crafts, some historic, some modern. This compact museum can be visited in about 20 minutes; the art museum (see above) is just next door.

Hubbard Hall, Bowdoin College, Brunswick. © 207/725-3416. Free admission. Tues–Sat 10am–5pm; Sun
2–5pm.

Maine Maritime Museum & Shipyard ★★   This museum on the banks of
the Kennebec River (just south of the very obvious Bath Iron Works shipyard)
features a wide array of displays and exhibits related to the boat builder's art. It's
sited at the former shipyard of Percy and Small, which built some 42 schooners
in the late 19th and early 20th centuries. The largest wooden ship ever built in
America—the 329-foot *Wyoming*—was constructed on this lot in 1909. The
handsome Maritime History Building houses changing exhibits of maritime art

and artifacts. The 10-acre property contains a fleet of additional displays, including an intriguing exhibit on lobstering and a complete boat-building shop. You can watch wooden boats take shape here in this active program. Kids enjoy the play area, where they can search for pirates from the crow's nest of the play boat. Occasional river cruises ($30) are offered from the riverside dock; these include lighthouse tours and excursions up the river to Merrymeeting Bay.

243 Washington St., Bath. © 207/443-1316. www.bathmaine.com. Admission $8.75 adults, $6 children 6–17; $26 per family. Daily 9:30am–5pm.

BEACHES
This part of Maine is better known for rocky cliffs and lobster pots than swimming beaches, with two notable exceptions.

Popham Beach State Park (© 207/389-1335) is located at the tip of Route 209 (head south from Bath). This handsome park has a long and sandy strand, plus great views of knobby offshore islands such as Seguin Island, capped with a lonesome lighthouse. Parking and basic services, including changing rooms, are available. Admission is $2 for adults, 50¢ for children 5 to 11.

At the tip of the next peninsula to the east is **Reid State Park** (© 207/ 371-2303), an idyllic place to picnic on a summer day. Arrive early enough and you can stake out a picnic table among the wind-blasted pines. The mile-long beach is great for strolling and splashing around. Services include changing rooms and a small snack bar. Admission is $2.50 for adults, 50¢ for children 5 to 11. To reach Reid State Park, follow Route 127 south from Bath and Route 1.

WHERE TO STAY
In Bath
The Kennebec Inn ★★ This imposing 1860 mansion, located on a street of notable homes, was built with bricks shipped from England and looks more like a small bank than a home. The downstairs common rooms have 14-foot ceilings, while the second-floor accommodations make do with 12-foot ceilings. The four larger guest rooms are in the front of the house and were formerly used by the family members. The best of the lot is room 2, with two wing chairs, large windows, pocket shutters, and a great old pedestal sink and Jacuzzi. The rest of the bathrooms range in size from generous to cramped. A breakfast buffet is set out in the butler's pantry; you can dine by candlelight in a formal room with mahogany paneling and tapestry wall coverings.

1024 Washington St., Bath, ME 04530. © 800/822-9393 or 207/443-5202. www.kennebecinn.com. 7 units. $110–$175 double. Ask about off-season rates. Rates include breakfast. AE, DISC, MC, V. 2-night minimum stay on weekends in peak season. Children over 12 welcome. In room: A/C, TV, dataport, hair dryer.

On the Coast
Driftwood Inn & Cottages ★ Value The Driftwood Inn dates back to 1910, and not a lot seems to have changed since then. A family-run rustic retreat on 3 acres at the end of a dead-end road, the inn is a compound of four shingled buildings and a handful of housekeeping cottages on a rocky, oceanside property. The spartan rooms have a simple turn-of-the-last-century flavor that hasn't been gentrified in the least. Most units share bathrooms, but some have private sinks and toilets. Cottages are set along a small cove, and are furnished in a budget style. It's nothing fancy: Expect industrial carpeting, plastic shower stalls, and a few beds that could stand replacing. Bring plenty of books and board games.

Washington Ave., Bailey Island, ME 04003. © 207/833-5461, or 508/947-1066 off-season. 30 units (most share hallways bathrooms). $70–$110 double; weekly $375 per person including breakfast and dinner

(July–Aug only); cottages $550–$600 per week. No credit cards. Open late May to mid-Oct; dining room open late June to Labor Day. **Amenities:** Dining room (traditional New England); ancient saltwater pool. *In room:* No phone.

Grey Havens ★★ This is the inn first-time visitors to Maine fantasize about. Located on Georgetown Island off the beaten track southeast of Bath, this graceful 1904 shingled home with prominent turrets sits on a high, rocky bluff overlooking the sea. Inside, it's all richly mellowed pine paneling; you can relax in a cozy chair in front of the common room's cobblestone fireplace. The guest rooms are simply but comfortably furnished. The oceanfront units command a premium, but are worth it. (Save few dollars by requesting an oceanfront room with private bathroom across the hall.) One caveat: The inn has been only lightly modernized, which is generally good but means rather thin walls.

Seguinland Rd., Georgetown Island, ME 04548. (© 207/371-2616. Fax 207/371-2274. www.greyhavens. com. 13 units (2 with private hall bathrooms). $100–$220 double. Rates include breakfast. MC, V. Closed Nov–May. No children under 12 accepted. From Rte. 1, head south on Rte. 127 and follow signs for Reid State Park; watch for inn on left. **Amenities:** Bikes; canoes (free). *In room:* No phone.

WHERE TO DINE

Five Islands Lobster Co. ★ LOBSTER POUND The drive alone makes this rustic lobster pound a worthy destination. It's located about 12 miles south of Route 1 down winding Route 127, past bogs and spruce forests with glimpses of azure ocean inlets. (Head south from Woolwich, which is just across the bridge from Bath.) Drive until you pass a cluster of clapboard homes, then keep going until you can't go any farther. This is a down-home affair, owned jointly by local lobstermen and the proprietors of the Grey Havens inn (see above). While you're awaiting your lobster, you can wander next door to the Love Nest Snack Bar for extras like soda or (recommended) onion rings. Settle in at one of the picnic tables, or head over to a grassy spot at the edge of the dirt parking lot. Despite its edge-of-the-world feel, the lobster pound can be crowded on weekends.

Rte. 127, Georgetown. (© 207/371-2990. Typically $7–$10 per lobster. MC, V. July–Aug daily 11am–8pm; shorter hours in off-season. Closed Columbus Day to Mother's Day.

Robinhood Free Meetinghouse ★★★ FUSION Chef Michael Gagne's menu features between 30 and 40 entrees, and they're wildly eclectic—from saltimboca to Szechuan swordfish to Wiener schnitzel Viennoise. Ordering from the menu is like playing stump the chef: Let's see you make *this!* And Gagne almost always hits his notes. He has attracted legions of dedicated local followers, who appreciate the extraordinary attention paid to detail, like the foam baffles glued discreetly to the underside of the seats to dampen the echoes in the sparely decorated, immaculately restored 1855 Greek Revival meetinghouse. Even the sorbet served between courses is homemade. While not a budget restaurant, the Meetinghouse offers good value for the price.

Robinhood Rd., Robinhood. (© 207/371-2188. www.robinhood-meetinghouse.com. Reservations encouraged. Main courses $18–$25. AE, DISC, MC, V. May–Oct daily 5:30–9pm; rest of year, limited days (call first).

WISCASSET ★ & THE BOOTHBAYS ★

Wiscasset is a lovely riverside town on Route 1, and it's not shy about letting you know: "The Prettiest Village in Maine" is the boast on the sign at the edge of town and on many brochures. Whether or not you agree, the town *is* attractive (although the sluggish line of traffic snaking through diminishes the charm), and makes a good stop en route to coastal destinations further along.

The Boothbays, 11 miles south of Route 1 on Route 27, consist of several small and scenic villages—**East Boothbay, Boothbay Harbor,** and **Boothbay,** among them—which are closer than Wiscasset to the open ocean.

The former fishing port of Boothbay Harbor was discovered in the 19th century by wealthy rusticators who retreated here each summer. Having embraced the tourist dollar, the harbor-front village never really looked back, and in more recent years it has emerged as one of the premier destinations of travelers in search of classic coastal Maine. This has had an obvious impact: The village is a mandatory stop for bus tours, which have in turn attracted kitschy shops and a slew of mediocre restaurants serving baked stuffed haddock.

If Boothbay Harbor is stuck in a time warp, it's Tourist Trap ca. 1974—bland and boxy motels hem in the harbor, and shops hawk mass-market trinkets. However, if you avoid the touristy claptrap of the downtown harbor area itself, some of the outlying areas are strikingly beautiful.

ESSENTIALS
GETTING THERE   Wiscasset is on Route 1 midway between Bath and Damariscotta. Boothbay Harbor is south of Route 1 on Route 27. Coming from the west, look for signs shortly after crossing the Sheepscot River at Wiscasset.

VISITOR INFORMATION   Wiscasset lacks a tourist information booth, but you can get questions answered by calling the **Wiscasset Regional Business Association** (📞 207/882-9617). The Boothbay area has three visitor centers in and around town, reflecting the importance of the travel dollars to the region. At the intersection of Routes 1 and 27 is a center that's open May through October and is a good place to stock up on brochures. A mile before you reach the village is the seasonal **Boothbay Information Center** on your right, open June through October. The year-round **Boothbay Harbor Region Chamber of Commerce** (📞 207/633-2353) is at the intersection of Routes 27 and 96.

EXPLORING WISCASSET
Aside from enjoying the town's handsome architecture and vaunted prettiness, you'll find a handful of worthwhile shops that range from sparely adorned art galleries to antiques shops cluttered with architectural salvage.

Castle Tucker 🎯   This fascinating mansion overlooking the river at the edge of town was built in 1807, then radically added to in a more ostentatious style in 1860. The home remains more or less in the same state it was when reconfigured by cotton trader Capt. Richard Tucker; his descendant Jane Tucker still lives on the top floor. Tours of the lower floor are offered by the Society of New England Antiquities. The highlight is the detailing; be sure to note the extraordinary elliptical staircase and the painted plaster trim (it's not oak).
Lee and High sts. 📞 207/882-7364. Admission $4 adults, $2 children. July–Aug tours leave on the hour noon–4pm Wed–Sun. Closed Sept–June.

Maine Coast Railroad 🎯   Weary of Route 1 traffic? Hop on the Maine Coast Railroad and enjoy the scenery. The 90-minute excursions are offered to either Bath or Newcastle, and both routes follow along forest and field, offering fleeting glimpses of the Maine of an earlier era. The railcars date from the 1930s.
Rte. 1 (just west of the bridge). 📞 800/795-5404 or 207/882-8000. Fares $10 adults, $5 children 6–12, free for children under 5. Late June to mid-Sept daily 10am and 1pm; mid-Sept to mid-Oct Sat–Sun 10am and 1pm.

Musical Wonder House 🎯🎯   Danilo Konvalinka has been collecting music boxes both grand and tiny for decades, and nothing seems to delight him more

> **Tips** **Escaping the Crowds**
>
> Boothbay Harbor is overrun with summer visitors, but at nearby **Ocean Point,** you can leave most of the crowds behind as you follow a picturesque lane that twists along the rocky shore and past a colony of vintage summer homes. Follow Route 96 southward east of Boothbay Harbor, and you'll pass through the sleepy village of East Boothbay before continuing on toward the point. The narrow road runs through piney forests before arriving at the rocky finger; it's one of a handful of Maine peninsulas with a road edging its perimeter, which allows for fine ocean views. The colorful Victorian-era summer cottages bloom along the roadside like wildflowers. Ocean Point makes for a good **bike loop.** Mountain-bike rentals are available at Tidal Transit (see below).

than to show them off for visitors. The collection ranges from massive music boxes that sound as resonant as an orchestra (an 1870 Girard from Austria) to the tinnier sounds of the smaller contraptions. Music boxes are displayed in four rooms in a stately 1852 home. A full tour is pricey; if you're undecided, try visiting the gift shop and sampling some of the coin-operated 19th-century music boxes in the adjoining hallway. Intrigued? Sign up for the next tour.

18 High St. ✆ 207/882-7163. Tours $15 for full downstairs; $8 for half downstairs; $30 for full house. Late May to mid-Oct daily 10am–5pm. Closed late Oct to late May.

EXPLORING THE BOOTHBAY REGION

Parking in Boothbay Harbor in midsummer will require either persistence or the forking over of a few dollars. A popular local attraction is the long, narrow **footbridge** across the harbor, first built in 1901. It's more of a destination than a link—other than a couple unnotable restaurants and motels, there's not much on the other side. The winding streets that weave through the town are filled with shops that cater to tourists. Don't expect much interesting merchandise.

If dense fog or rain socks in the harbor, bide your time at the vintage **Romar Bowling Lanes** ✦ (✆ 207/633-5721). This log-and-shingle building near the footbridge has a harbor view and has been distracting travelers with the promise of traditional New England candlepin bowling since 1946.

In good weather, stop by one of the Boothbay region information centers (see above) and request a free guide to the holdings of the **Boothbay Region Land Trust** ✦✦ (✆ 207/633-4818). Eight pockets of publicly accessible lands dot the peninsula, and most feature quiet, lightly traveled trails good for a stroll or a picnic. Among the best: the Linekin Preserve, a 95-acre parcel en route to Ocean Point (drive south from Route 1 in Boothbay Harbor on Route 96 for 3.8 miles; look for parking on the left) with 600 feet of riverfront. A hike around the loop trail (about 2.1 miles) will occupy a pleasant hour.

Coastal Maine Botanical Garden This 128-acre waterside garden remains a work in progress, but makes for a peaceable oasis. It's not a fancy, formal garden, but rather a natural habitat that's being coaxed into a more mannered state. Those overseeing this nonprofit organization have blazed several short trails through the mossy forest, good for half an hour's worth of exploring the quiet, lush terrain.

Barters Island Rd., Boothbay (near Hogdon Island). ✆ 207/633-4333. Free admission. Open daylight hours. From Rte. 27 in Boothbay Center, bear right at the monument at the stop sign, then make the first right on Barters Island Rd.; drive 1 mile; look for the stone gate on your left.

Marine Resources Aquarium ⭐ *Kids*   Operated by the state's Department of Marine Resources, this compact aquarium offers context for life in the sea around Boothbay and beyond. Kids will be enthralled by the rare albino and blue lobsters, and can get their hands wet in a 20-foot touch tank. Parking is tight at the aquarium, which is located on a point across the water from downtown Boothbay Harbor, so visitors are urged to use the free shuttle bus (look for the Rocktide trolley) that connects to downtown.

McKown Point Rd., West Boothbay Harbor. ℂ 207/633-9542. Admission $3 adults, $2.50 children 5-18. Daily 10am–5pm. Closed after Columbus Day to just before Memorial Day.

BOAT TOURS

The best way to see the Maine coast around Boothbay is from a boat. Nearly two dozen tour boats berth at the harbor or nearby, offering trips ranging from an hour's outing to a 1-day excursion to Monhegan Island.

Balmy Day Cruises ⭐ (ℂ **800/298-2284** or 207/633-2284) runs several trips from the harbor, including an excursion to Monhegan Island on the 65-foot *Balmy Days II,* which allows passengers about 4 hours to explore the island before returning (see the section on Monhegan Island, below). The cost is $30 for adults, $18 for children. If you'd rather be sailing, ask about the 90-minute cruises on the 15-passenger *Bay Lady* ($18). It's a good idea to make reservations.

A more intimate way to tour the harbor is via sea kayak. **Tidal Transit Kayak Co.** ⭐ (ℂ **207/633-7140**) offers morning, afternoon, and sunset tours of the harbor for $30 (sunset's the best bet). Kayaks may also be rented for $12 per hour or $50 per day. Tidal Transit is open daily in summer (except when it rains); it's located on the waterfront at 47 Townshend Ave. (walk down the alley).

WHERE TO STAY

Five Gables Inn ⭐⭐   This handsome inn sits proudly amid a small colony of summer homes on a quiet road above a peaceful cove. It's nicely isolated from the hubbub of Boothbay Harbor. Room 8 is a corner unit with brilliant morning light; most requested is room 14, with a fine view and a fireplace with marble mantle. (Note that some of the first-floor rooms open onto a common deck and lack privacy.) The breakfast buffet is sumptuous, with offerings like tomato-basil frittata and blueberry-stuffed French toast.

Murray Hill Rd. (P.O. Box 335), East Boothbay, ME 04544. ℂ 800/451-5048 or 207/633-4551. www. fivegablesinn.com. 16 units. $110–$175 double. Rates include breakfast. MC, V. Closed Nov to mid-May. Children 12 and over welcome. Drive through East Boothbay on Rte. 96; turn right after crest of hill on Murray Hill Rd.

The Inn at Lobsterman's Wharf ⭐ *Value*   This is our budget pick for the Boothbay region. A clean, no-frills place located adjacent to a working boatyard, this inn was originally a coal depot and later a boardinghouse. It still has some boardinghouse informality to it (although all rooms now have small private bathrooms), but you get a lot for your money. Seven rooms face the water; Hodgon Suite is the largest, located under the eaves with a view of the boatyard.

Rte. 96, East Boothbay. ℂ 207/633-5481. www.lobstermanswharf.com. 9 units. $56–$85 double. Rates include continental breakfast. MC, V. Limited pets allowed. **Amenities:** Restaurant (see below). *In room:* TV, no phone.

Newagen Seaside Inn ⭐   This small 1940s-era resort has seen more glamorous days, but it's still a superb, low-key establishment offering great ocean views and walks through a seaside spruce forest. The low, wide, white-shingled

Colonial Revival–style inn is furnished simply in country pine. There's a classically austere dining room, narrow hallways with pine wainscoting, and a lobby with a fireplace. The rooms are plain and the inn can be a bit threadbare in spots, but never mind that. Guests return every year to the 85-acre grounds filled with decks, gazebos, and walkways that border on the magical. It's hard to convey the magnificence of the ocean views, which may be the best of any inn in Maine.

Rte. 27 (P.O. Box 68), Cape Newagen, ME 04552. (800/654-5242 or 207/633-5242. www. newagenseasideinn.com. 26 units. $130–$225 double. Ask about off-season discounts. Rates include breakfast. MC, V. Closed mid-Oct to mid-May. Take Rte. 27 from Boothbay Harbor and continue south until tip of Southport Island; look for sign. **Amenities:** Restaurant (traditional New England), freshwater and saltwater pools, tennis court, rowboats, badminton, horseshoes. *In room:* No phone.

Spruce Point Inn ★★ (Kids) The Spruce Point Inn, originally built as a hunting and fishing lodge in the 1890s, evolved into a summer resort in 1912. Those looking for historic authenticity may be disappointed. Those seeking modern facilities with some historic accents will be delighted. (Those who prefer their gentility a bit less glossy should consider the Newagen Seaside Inn, described above.) The rooms in the main inn are basic, mid-size, and comfortable; the newer wings are somewhat more condo-like. This is a great choice for families, and offers plenty of activities to fill each day.

Atlantic Ave. (P.O. Box 237), Boothbay Harbor, ME 04538. (800/553-0289 or 207/633-4152. www. sprucepointinn.com. 93 units. Mid-July to Aug $165–$350 double; fall $140–$250; spring $125–$225; early summer $150–$265. 2-night minimum stay on weekends; 3-night minimum on holidays. AE, DISC, MC, V. Closed mid-Oct to Memorial Day. Pets accepted ($50 deposit, $100 cleaning fee). Turn seaward on Union St. in Boothbay Harbor; go 2 miles to inn. **Amenities:** Restaurant (upscale New England); 2 outdoor pools (1 heated); 2 clay tennis courts; small fitness center; Jacuzzi; game room; concierge; boat tours; free shuttle to downtown Boothbay Harbor; self-service laundry; laundry service; dry cleaning; in-room massage; babysitting; lawn games (shuffleboard, tetherball, croquet, and others). *In room:* TV.

WHERE TO DINE
In Wiscasset
Red's Eats ★ LOBSTER ROLLS/SANDWICHES This roadside stand in downtown Wiscasset has received more than its share of media ink about its famous lobster rolls. (They often crop up in "Best of Maine" surveys.) And they *are* good, consisting of moist chunks of chilled lobster placed in a roll served with a little mayo on the side. Be aware they're at the pricey end of the scale— you can find less expensive (although less meaty) versions elsewhere.

Water St. (Rte. 1 just before the bridge). (207/882-6128. Sandwiches $2–$5.25; lobster rolls vary, but typically around $11. No credit cards. Mon–Thurs 11am–11pm; Fri–Sat 11am–2am; Sun noon–6pm. Closed Oct–Apr.

Sarah's ★ SANDWICHES/TRADITIONAL This hometown favorite overlooks the Sheepscot River and is usually crowded for lunch, with offerings like pita pockets, croissant sandwiches, wraps, burritos, and something called a whaleboat (a two-cheese turnover, like a calzone). The lobsters are fresh, hauled in daily by Sarah's brother and father. This is the best choice for an informal lunch break when motoring up Route 1.

Water St. and Rte. 1 (across from Red's). (207/882-7504. Sandwiches $4.45–$6.25; pizzas $4.95–16.95. AE, DISC, MC, V. Daily 11am–8pm (until 9pm Fri–Sat).

In the Boothbays
In Boothbay Harbor, look for **"King" Brud** and his famous hot-dog cart. Brud started selling hot dogs in 1943, and he's still at it. June through October, he's usually at the corner of McKown and Commercial streets from 10am to 4pm.

Boothbay Region Lobstermen's Co-op SEAFOOD "We are not responsible if the seagulls steal your food," reads the sign at the ordering window of this lobster joint. And that sets the casual tone pretty well. Situated across the harbor from downtown Boothbay, the lobstermen's co-op offers no-frills seafood served at picnic tables on a dock and inside a crude shelter. This is the best pick from among the cluster of lobster-in-the-rough places that line the waterfront. Lobsters are priced to market (figure $8 to $12). The salty atmosphere is the draw here; it's a fair-weather destination that should be avoided in rain or fog.

Atlantic Ave., Boothbay Harbor. ℂ **207/633-4900.** Fried and grilled foods $1.75–$10.25; dinners $7–$11.95. DISC, MC, V. May to mid-Oct daily 11:30am–8:30pm. On foot, cross footbridge and turn right; follow road for ⅓ mile to co-op.

Christopher's Boathouse ★★ CREATIVE AMERICAN/WOOD GRILL Christopher's is the happy exception to the generally unexciting fare found in town. Scenically located at the head of the harbor, the restaurant is bright and modern. (There's also deck dining.) The chef has a deft touch with spicy flavors, and nicely melds the expected with the unexpected (for instance, lobster and mango bisque with spicy lobster won tons). The meals from the grill are excellent, and include an Asian-spiced tuna and a barbecue-spiced flank steak.

25 Union St., Boothbay Harbor. ℂ **207/633-6565.** Reservations recommended in peak season. Main courses $5–$9 lunch, $17–$23 dinner. MC, V. July 4 to mid-Oct daily 11:30am–3pm; July–Sept daily 5:30–9pm; Oct–Dec and Apr–June Wed–Sun 5:30–8:30pm; Jan–Mar Fri–Sun 5:30–8:30pm.

Lobsterman's Wharf ★ SEAFOOD Located on the water in East Boothbay, the Lobsterman's Wharf has the comfortable feel of a popular neighborhood bar, complete with pool table. But it's that rarest of pubs—a place that's popular with the locals, but also serves up a decent meal. If the weather cooperates, sit at a picnic table on the dock and admire the views of a spruce-topped peninsula across the Damariscotta River; you can also grab a table inside amid the festive nautical decor. Entrees include a mixed-seafood grill, a barbecued shrimp-and-ribs platter, and succulent fresh lobster.

Rte. 96, East Boothbay. ℂ **207/633-3443.** Reservations accepted for parties of six or more. Lunch from $4.50–$13.95; dinner $13.95–$22.95 (mostly $14–$16). AE, MC, V. Daily 11:30am–midnight. Closed mid-Oct to mid-May.

MONHEGAN ISLAND ★★★

Monhegan Island is Maine's premier island destination. Visited by Europeans as early as 1497, the wild, remote island was first settled by fishermen attracted to the sea's bounty in offshore waters. Starting in the 1870s, noted artists discovered the island and came to stay for a spell. The roster included Rockwell Kent (the artist most closely associated with the island), George Bellows, Edward Hopper, and Robert Henri. The artists gathered in the kitchen of the lighthouse to chat and drink coffee; it's said that the wife of the lighthouse keeper accumulated a tremendously valuable collection of paintings. Today, Jamie Wyeth, scion of the Wyeth clan, claims the island as his part-time home.

It's not hard to figure out why artists have been attracted to the place: There's a mystical quality to it, from the thin light to the startling contrasts of dark cliffs and foamy white surf. There's also a remarkable sense of tranquility here, which can only help focus one's inner vision. In addition, it's a superb destination for hikers, since most of the island is undeveloped and laced with trails.

Be aware that this is not Martha's Vineyard—no ATMs, few pay phones, even electricity is scarce. That's what repeat visitors like about it. An overnight at one of the several hostelries is strongly recommended. Day trips are easily arranged, but the island's true character doesn't start to emerge until the last day boat sails away and the quiet, rustic appeal of the place percolates to the surface.

ESSENTIALS

GETTING THERE   Access to Monhegan Island is via boat from New Harbor, Boothbay Harbor, or Port Clyde. The wonderfully picturesque trip from Port Clyde is the favored route among longtime island visitors; the boat passes the Marshall Point Lighthouse and through a series of spruce-clad islands before setting out on the open sea.

Two boats make the run to Monhegan from Port Clyde. The *Laura B.,* which takes 70 minutes, is a doughty workboat (building supplies and boxes of food are loaded on first; passengers fill in the available niches on the deck and in the small cabin). The newer, faster (50 minutes), passenger-oriented *Elizabeth Ann* offers a large heated cabin and more seating. You'll need to leave your car behind, so pack light and wear sturdy shoes. The fare is $25 round-trip for adults, $12 for children 2 to 12, and $2 for pets. Reservations are advised; contact **Monhegan Boat Line** (*C* **207/372-8848;** www.monheganboat.com). Parking is available near the dock for $4 per day.

VISITOR INFORMATION   Monhegan Island has no formal visitor center, but it's small and friendly enough that you can ask questions of just about anyone you meet on the island pathways. The clerks at the ferry dock in Port Clyde are also quite helpful. Be sure to buy one of the maps produced by Monhegan Island Associates, which depict the island's hiking trails and lanes. They're available at the ferry office as well as at island inns. *Note:* Because wildfire could destroy this breezy island in short order, smoking is prohibited outside the village.

EXPLORING MONHEGAN

Walking is the chief activity on the island, and it's genuinely surprising how much distance you can cover on these 700 acres (about 1½ miles long and ½ mile wide). The village clusters tightly around the harbor; the rest of the island is mostly wildland, laced with **17 miles of trails** ✵✵✵. Much of the island is ringed with high, open bluffs atop fissured cliffs. Pack a picnic lunch and hike the perimeter trail, and plan to spend much of the day just sitting and reading, or enjoying the surf rolling in against the cliffs.

The inland trails are appealing in a far different way. Deep, dark **Cathedral Woods** ✵✵ is mossy and fragrant; sunlight only dimly filters through the evergreens to the forest floor.

Birding is a popular activity in the spring and fall. Monhegan Island is on the Atlantic flyway, and a wide variety of birds stop at the island along their migration routes.

The sole attraction on the island is the **Monhegan Museum** ✵, located next to the 1824 lighthouse on a high point above the village. The museum, open July through September, has a quirky collection of historic artifacts and provides some context for this rugged island's history. Also near the lighthouse is a small and select art museum featuring the works of Rockwell Kent and other island artists.

The spectacular view from the grassy slope in front of the lighthouse is the real prize. The vista sweeps across a marsh, past one of the island's most historic hotels, past melancholy Manana Island and across the sea beyond. Get here early if you want a good seat for the sunset; it seems most visitors to the island congregate here after dinner to watch the sinking of the sun. (Another popular place

> *Moments* **Quiet Time**
>
> Pack a picnic lunch and an engrossing book and plan to spend a lazy, sunny afternoon lounging on the cliffs that line Monhegan's eastern shore. You haven't experienced utter indolence until you've kicked back a few hours here, relaxing to the calls of seagulls and lulling surf crashing against the rocks. Type A personalities who find this lack of activity unnerving can profitably occupy themselves by scanning the waters for whales, which feed just offshore.

is the island's southern tip, where the wreckage of the *D. T. Sheridan,* a coal barge, washed up in 1948.)

Artists are still attracted here in great number, and many open their **studios** to visitors during posted hours in summer. Stop by and look at their work, chat a bit, and you might find something to bring home. Some of the artwork runs along the lines of predictable seascapes and sunsets, but much of it rises above the banal. Look for the bulletin board along the main pathway in the village for walking directions to the studios and a listing of the days and hours they're open.

WHERE TO STAY & DINE

Monhegan House ⋆   The handsome Monhegan House has been accommodating guests since 1870, and it has the comfortable, worn patina of a venerable lodging house. The rooms at this four-floor walk-up are austere but comfortable; everyone shares clean, dormitory-style bathrooms. The lobby with fireplace is a welcome spot to sit and take the fog-induced chill out of your bones (even August can be cool here), while the front deck is the place to lounge and keep an eye on the comings and goings of the village.

Monhegan Island, ME 04852. ⓒ **800/599-7983** or 207/594-7983. Fax 207/596-6472. 33 units (all with shared bathroom). $100 double. AE, DISC, MC, V. Closed Columbus Day–Memorial Day. **Amenities:** Restaurant (regional). *In room:* No phone.

Trailing Yew ⋆   This friendly, informal place, popular with hikers and birders, has been taking in guests since 1929. Guest rooms are eclectic and simply furnished in a pleasantly dated summer-home style. Only one of the four buildings has electricity (most but not all bathrooms have electricity); those staying in rooms without electricity are provided a kerosene lamp (bring a small flashlight—just in case). Rooms are also unheated, so bring a sleeping bag if the weather's chilly. The Trailing Yew has more of an easy-going, youth-hostel camaraderie; if you're the private type, opt for the Monhegan House.

Monhegan Island, ME 04852. ⓒ **800-592-2520** or 207/596-0440. 37 units (all but 1 share bathrooms). $120 double. Rates include breakfast, dinner, taxes, and tips. No credit cards. Closed mid-Oct to mid-May. Pets allowed. **Amenities:** Restaurant (New England/family-style). *In room:* No phone.

4 Penobscot Bay

Traveling eastward along the Maine coast, those who pay attention to such things will notice they're suddenly heading almost due north around Rockland. The culprit behind this geographic quirk is Penobscot Bay, which takes a sizable bite into the Maine coast, forcing a lengthy northerly detour to cross the head of the bay where the Penobscot River flows in at Bucksport.

You'll find some of Maine's most distinctive coastal scenery in this area, dotted with broad offshore islands and high hills rising above the blue bay.

Penobscot Bay

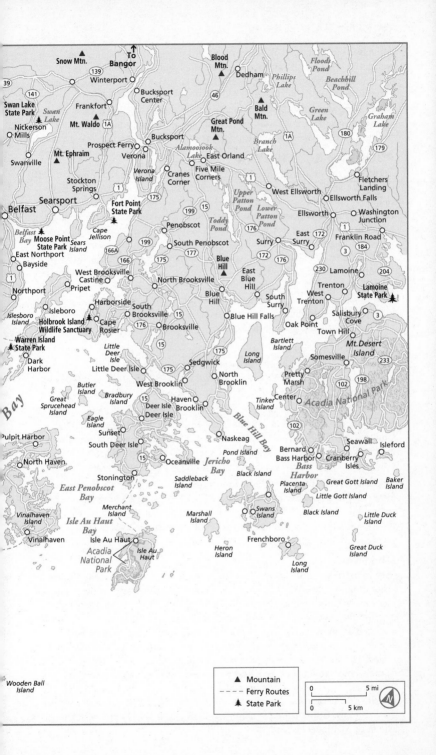

Snow Mtn. ▲

To Bangor ↑

39

141

Winterport

Buckport Center

Blood Mtn. ▲

Dedham

Floods Pond

Beachhill Pond

Phillips Lake

46

Swan Lake State Park ▲

Frankfort

Swan Lake

Mt. Waldo ▲

1A

Bald Mtn. ▲

Great Pond Mtn. ▲

Green Lake

Graham Lake

Branch Lake

1A

180

179

Nickerson Mills

Swanville

Mt. Ephraim ▲

Bucksport

Prospect Ferry

Verona

Alamoosook Lake

East Orland

Five Mile Corners

Fletchers Landing

Washington Junction

Verona Island

Cranes Corner

1

West Ellsworth

Ellsworth Falls

Stockton Springs

1

Upper Patton Pond

Ellsworth

172

Franklin Road

Searsport

Belfast

Fort Point State Park

175

199

15

Lower Patton Pond

176

East Surry

172

184

3

Belfast Bay

Moose Point State Park

Cape Jellison

Penobscot

Toddy Pond

Surry

230

Lamoine

204

Sears Island

199

South Penobscot

177

176

172

176

West Trenton

Lamoine State Park ▲

East Northport

166A

166

175

Blue Hill ▲

East Blue Hill

Trenton

Bayside

Castine

West Brooksville

North Brooksville

South Surry

Town Hill

Salisbury Cove

3

Northport

1

Pripet

Harborside

Blue Hill

Blue Hill Falls

Oak Point

Mt. Desert Island

Islesboro

South Brooksville

15

Bartlett Island

Somesville

233

Islesboro Island

Holbrook Island Wildlife Sanctuary ▲

Cape Rosier

176

Brooksville

Long Island

Pretty Marsh

102

198

Warren Island State Park ▲

Little Deer Isle

15

Sedgwick

175

Center

Acadia National Park

Dark Harbor

Little Deer Isle

West Brooklin

North Brooklin

Tinker Island

Butler Island

Bradbury Island

15

Haven Brooklin

102

Great Sprucehead Island

Eagle Island

Deer Isle

Deer Isle

Seawall

Isleford

Pulpit Harbor

Sunset

Naskeag

Pond Island

Bernard

Bass Harbor

Cranberry Isles

North Haven

South Deer Isle

15

Oceanville

Jericho Bay

Black Island

Bass Harbor

Great Gott Island

Baker Island

Stonington

Saddleback Island

Placenta Island

Little Gott Island

Bay

East Penobscot Bay

Merchant Island

Marshall Island

Swans Island

Black Island

Little Duck Island

Vinalhaven Island

Isle Au Haut Bay

Isle Au Haut

Heron Island

Frenchboro

Great Duck Island

Vinalhaven

Acadia National Park

Isle Au Haut

Long Island

Wooden Ball Island

▲ Mountain

--- Ferry Routes

🌲 State Park

0 _____ 5 mi

0 _____ 5 km

N

593

Although the mouth of Penobscot Bay is occupied by two large islands, its waters can still churn with vigor when the tides and winds conspire.

Penobscot Bay's western shore gets a heavy stream of tourist traffic, especially along Route 1 through the scenic village of Camden. Traffic notwithstanding, it's still a good destination to get a taste of the Maine coast. Services for travelers are abundant, although during peak season a small miracle will be required to find a weekend guest room without a reservation.

ROCKLAND & ENVIRONS

Located on the southwest edge of Penobscot Bay, Rockland has long been proud of its brick-and-blue-collar waterfront town reputation. Built around the fishing industry, Rockland historically dabbled in tourism on the side. But with the decline of the fisheries and the rise of the tourist economy in Maine, the balance has shifted—Rockland has recently been colonized by restaurateurs, innkeepers, and other small-business folks who are painting it with an unaccustomed gloss.

There's a small park on the waterfront, but more appealing than Rockland's harbor is its commercial downtown—basically one long street lined with sophisticated historic brick architecture. If it's picturesque harbor towns you're seeking, head to Camden, Rockport, Port Clyde, or Stonington. But Rockland makes a great base for exploring this beautiful coastal region, especially if you have a low tolerance for trinkets and tourist hordes.

ESSENTIALS

GETTING THERE   Route 1 passes directly through Rockland. Rockland's tiny airport is served by **Colgan Air** (© **800/272-5488** or 207/596-7604), with daily flights from Boston and Bar Harbor. **Concord Trailways** (© **800/ 639-3317**) offers bus service from Rockland to Bangor and Portland.

VISITOR INFORMATION   The **Rockland/Thomaston Area Chamber of Commerce** (© **800/562-2529** or 207/596-0376) staffs an information desk at Harbor Park. It's open from Memorial Day to Labor Day, daily from 9am to 5pm; the rest of the year, Monday through Friday from 9am to 5pm.

SPECIAL EVENTS   The **Maine Lobster Festival** (© **800/562-2529** or 207/ 596-0376) takes place at Harbor Park the first weekend in August (plus the preceding Thursday and Friday). Entertainers and vendors of all sorts of Maine products fill the waterfront parking lot and attract thousands of people. The event includes the Maine Sea Goddess Coronation Pageant.

MUSEUMS

Farnsworth Museum   Rockland, for all its rough edges, has long and historic ties to the arts. Noted sculptor Louise Nevelson grew up here, and in 1935 philanthropist Lucy Farnsworth bequeathed a fortune large enough to establish the Farnsworth Museum, which has since joined the ranks of the most respected art museums in New England. The Farnsworth has a superb collection of paintings and sculptures by renowned American artists with a connection to Maine. This includes not only Nevelson and three generations of Wyeths (N. C., Andrew, and Jamie), but also Rockwell Kent, Childe Hassam, and Maurice Prendergast. In 1998, the museum expanded with the opening of the **Farnsworth Center for the Wyeth Family,** housed in the former Pratt Memorial Methodist Church and containing Andrew and Betsy Wyeth's personal collection of Maine-related art.

Windjammer Tours

During the long transition from sail to steam, captains of the fancy new steamships belittled the old-fashioned sailing ships as "windjammers." The term stuck, and through a curious metamorphosis the name evolved into a term connoting adventure and romance.

Today, **windjammer vacations** ★★★ combine adventure with limited creature comforts. Guests typically bunk in small two-person cabins, which usually offer cold running water and a porthole to let in fresh air, but not much else.

Excursions last from 3 to 7 days, during which these handsome, creaky vessels poke around the tidal inlets and small coves that ring the beautiful bay. Cruises vary from ship to ship and from week to week, depending on the inclination of the captain and the vagaries of the Maine weather. The "standard" cruise often features a stop at one or more spruce-studded Maine islands, hearty breakfasts, and a palpable sense of maritime history.

About a dozen windjammers offer cruises in the Penobscot Bay region during the summer season, with the majority of the fleet berthed in Camden or Rockland. Rates run around $100 to $125 per day per person. The ships vary widely in size and vintage; accommodations range from cramped to reasonably spacious. Contact the **Maine Windjammer Association** (ⓒ 800/807-9463; www.sailmainecoast.com; windjam@acadia.net) to request a packet of brochures and an informative newsletter. If you arrive without reservations, stop by the chamber of commerce at the Rockland waterfront and ask about last-minute berths.

The Farnsworth also owns two other buildings open to the public. The **Farnsworth Homestead,** located behind the museum, offers a glimpse into the life of prosperous coastal Victorians. A 25-minute drive away in the village of Cushing is the **Olson House,** perhaps Maine's most famous home, which was immortalized in Andrew Wyeth's noted painting *Christina's World.* Ask at the museum for directions and information (closed in winter).

52 Main St., Rockland. ⓒ 207/596-6457. www.farnsworthmuseum.org. Admission $9 adults, $8 seniors, $5 students 18 and over, free for ages 17 and under (all prices discounted $1 in winter). Summer daily 9am–5pm; winter Tues–Sat 10am–5pm, Sun 1–5pm.

Owls Head Transportation Museum ★   You don't have to be a car buff or plane nut to enjoy this museum. It has an extraordinary collection of cars, motorcycles, bikes, and planes, displayed in a hangar-like building at the edge of the Knox County Airport. Look for the early Harley-Davidson and the sleek 1929 Rolls-Royce Phantom. The museum is a popular destination for hobbyists, who drive and fly their classic vehicles here for frequent weekend rallies in summer.

Rte. 73 (3 miles south of Rockland), Owls Head. ⓒ 207/594-4418. www.ohtm.org. Admission $6 adults, $5 seniors, $4 children 5–12; $16 per family. Apr–Oct daily 10am–5pm; Nov–Mar daily 10am–4pm.

WHERE TO STAY

Capt. Lindsey House Inn ★★ The three-story brick Capt. Lindsey House (1835) is just a couple minutes' walk from the Farnsworth Museum. Guests enter through a doorway a few steps off Main Street, then pass into an opulent first-floor common area with a well-selected mix of antique and contemporary furniture. The rooms are tastefully decorated in a contemporary country style; bold modern colors meld with traditional design. Even the smaller units (like room 4) are comfortable; the rooms on the third floor feature yellow pine floors and antique Oriental carpets. Rooms facing the street can be noisy.

5 Lindsey St., Rockland, ME 04841. ② **800/523-2145** or 207/596-7950. Fax 207/596-2758. www. rocklandmaine.com. 9 units. Peak season $110–$160 double; Columbus Day–Memorial Day $65–$110. Rates include continental breakfast. AE, DISC, MC, V. **Amenities:** The Water Works Restaurant (American and Indonesian cuisine). *In room:* A/C, TV, hair dryer.

East Wind Inn ★ This low-key inn is located south of Rockland in the sleepy town of Tenants Harbor. It's situated right on the water, with harbor views from all rooms and the long porch. It's a classic seaside hostelry, with simple colonial reproduction furniture and tidy if small rooms. (The 10 rooms across the way at a former sea captain's house have most of the private bathrooms.) The atmosphere is relaxed almost to the point of ennui, and the service good.

P.O. Box 149, Tenants Harbor, ME 04860. ② **800/241-8439** or 207/372-6366. Fax 207/372-6320. www. eastwindinn.com. 26 units (7 with shared bathroom). Summer $138 double ($90 with shared bathroom); $165–$275 suite or apartment. Off-season $72–$126 double. Rates include breakfast. AE, DISC, MC, V. 2-night minimum stay in suites and apartments. Closed Dec–Apr. Pets allowed by reservation ($10). Children 12 and over welcome. **Amenities:** Restaurant (traditional New England). *In room:* No phone.

Samoset Resort ★★ The Samoset is a something of a Maine coast rarity— a modern, self-contained resort that offers contemporary styling, ocean views, and lots of golf. Located on 230 acres at the mouth of Rockland Harbor, the hotel and town houses are surrounded by the handsome 18-hole golf course. The lobby is constructed of massive timbers, and all the guest rooms have balconies or terraces. Golfers love the place—it's been called Pebble Beach East— and families will find plenty of activities for the kids. The resort also has the best sunset stroll in the state—you can ramble across the golf course to a breakwater that leads out to a picturesque lighthouse. The one downside: For the high prices charged, the staff is less polished than you would expect.

Rockport, ME 04856. ② **800/341-1650** or 207/594-2511. www.samoset.com. 250 units. Early July to Labor Day $169–$329 double, $339 suite; fall $159–$259 double, $289 suite; winter $99–$169 double, $189 suite; May to mid-June $129–$219 double, $239 suite; mid-June to early July $179–$289 double, $299 suite. AE, DISC, MC, V. Valet parking available. **Amenities:** 4 restaurants (3 casual/American, 1 continental/fine dining); indoor and outdoor pool; golf course; 4 tennis courts (night play); health club; Jacuzzi; sauna; children's programs; concierge; courtesy car; business center; room service; massage; baby-sitting; laundry service; dry cleaning. *In room:* A/C, TV w/ pay movies, iron.

WHERE TO DINE

Cafe Miranda ★★ WORLD CUISINE Hidden away on a side street, this tiny, contemporary restaurant draws liberally from cuisines from around the globe, and given its wide-ranging culinary inclinations, it comes as something of a surprise just how well-prepared everything is. The char-grilled pork and shrimp cakes with a ginger-lime-coconut sauce are superb. Other creative entrees include barbecued pork ribs with a smoked jalapeño sauce. Cafe Miranda provides the best value for the buck of any restaurant in Maine. Beer and wine are available.

15 Oak St., Rockland. ℂ **207/594-2034.** Reservations recommended. Main courses $9.50–$16.50. DISC, MC, V. Tues–Sat 5:30pm–9:30pm (until 8:30 in winter).

Primo ★★★ MEDITERRANEAN/NEW AMERICAN   Primo opened in 2000 and immediately developed New York–size buzz, with good reason. Executive chef Melissa Kelly trails a string of accolades: She graduated first in her class at the Culinary Institute of America and won the 1999 James Beard Foundation award for "best chef in the Northeast." The restaurant occupies two deftly decorated floors of a century-old home a short drive south of downtown Rockland (no views to speak of). The menu reflects the seasons and draws from local products when available. You might choose from grilled duckling breast on a bed of mashed sweet potatoes with braised cabbage and a caramelized apple jus, or pepper-crusted venison with roasted beets and a pecan wild rice.

2 South Main St. (Rte. 173), Rockland. ℂ **207/596-0770.** www.primorestaurant.com. Reservations recommended. Main courses $16–$28. AE, DISC, MC, V. Thurs–Mon 5:30–9:30pm; call for days and hours in off-season.

CAMDEN ★★

Camden is the quintessential coastal Maine village. Set at the foot of the wooded Camden Hills on a picturesque harbor that no Hollywood movie set could improve upon, the affluent village has attracted the gentry of the Eastern Seaboard for more than a century. Many of their elaborate mansions have been converted into B&Bs, and Camden is still full of grace and sophistication.

Park your car as soon as you can (which may mean driving a block or two off Route 1). The village is ideally explored on foot, which allows a leisurely browsing of boutiques and galleries. Don't miss the hidden town park (look behind the library), which was designed by the firm of Frederick Law Olmsted.

On the downside: Camden attracts a lot of bus tours. The merchandise at the shops seems to be trending downward, and the summer congestion lessens the village's charm. In short, don't come expecting an undiscovered village.

ESSENTIALS

GETTING THERE   Camden is located on Route 1. Travelers driving up Route 1 can shave a few minutes off their trip by turning left on Route 90 6 miles past Waldoboro, bypassing Thomaston and Rockland. The most traffic-free route from southern Maine: Drive to Augusta via the Maine Turnpike, then follow Route 17 to Route 90 to Route 1. **Concord Trailways** (ℂ **800/ 639-3317**) offers bus service from Camden to Bangor and Portland.

VISITOR INFORMATION   The **Rockport-Camden-Lincolnville Chamber of Commerce** (ℂ **800/223-5459** or 207/236-4404) dispenses helpful information from its center at the Public Landing in Camden. It's open year-round, Monday through Friday from 9am to 5pm and Saturday from 10am to 5pm. In summer, it's also open Sunday from 10am to 4pm.

EXPLORING CAMDEN

Camden Hills State Park ★★ (ℂ **207/236-3109**) is located about a mile north of the village center on Route 1. This 6,500-acre park features an oceanside picnic area, 112 campsites, a winding toll road up 800-foot Mount Battie with spectacular views from the summit, and a variety of well-marked hiking trails. The day use fee is $2 for adults, 50¢ for children 5 to 11.

The 57-foot windjammer ***Surprise*** ★★ (ℂ **207/236-4687**), launched in 1918, departs on 2-hour cruises from the Camden Public Landing. Four daily

---

Moments **A Morning in the Park**

Camden Hills State Park attracts plenty of travelers, most of whom list-
lessly drive to the summit of Mount Battie, park for a few moments, then
drive back down. Strive for more than that. The trail up the east side of
Mount Megunticook is often magical early on a still summer morning—
the low sun glints off the waters of Penobscot Bay, Camden Harbor looks
like a perfect diorama, and the hollows of the hills behind you are muf-
fled in low clouds. You're alone with the world.

Here's how you do it: Get up early (*really* early—the summer sun
doesn't dawdle in Maine). Park near the campground and follow the
well-maintained trail to a set of open ledges, which requires only about
30 to 45 minutes' exertion to memorable views.

---

excursions ($25) are offered in July and August, three daily in June, September,
and October. Reservations are recommended; children must be 12 or older.

The *Schooner Lazy Jack* (© **207/230-0602**) has been plying the waters
since 1947, and is modeled after the Gloucester fishing schooners of the late
19th century. There's a maximum of 13 passengers; children must be 10 or
older. The 2-hour tours cost $20 per person.

Maine Sports Outfitters (© **800/722-0826** or 207/236-8797) offers **sea-
kayaking tours** of Camden's scenic harbor. The standard 2-hour excursion
($35) takes paddlers out to Curtis Island at the outer edge of the harbor. This
beginners' tour, offered three times daily, is an easy, delightful way to get a taste
of the area's maritime culture. Longer trips and instruction are also available.
Sign up for the tours either at the store (on Route 1 in Rockport, a few minutes'
drive south of Camden) or at the boathouse, located at the head of the harbor.

WHERE TO STAY

South of the village center are the **Cedar Crest Motel,** 115 Elm St. (© **800/
422-4964** or 207/236-4839), a handsome compound with a shuttle-bus connection downtown ($109 to $132 in peak season); and long-time mainstay
Towne Motel, 68 Elm St. (© **207/236-3377**), within walking distance of the
village ($99 to $115). Also right in town, just across the footbridge, is the **Best
Western Camden Riverhouse Hotel,** 11 Tannery Lane (© **800/755-7483** or
207/236-0500), which has an indoor pool and fitness center ($159 to $209).

Camden Harbour Inn The 1871 Camden Harbour Inn sits in a quiet neighborhood on a rise with a great view of the harbor and mountains beyond. It's
one of the few old-fashioned Victorian-era hotels in town that hasn't been extensively refurbished, and still retains something of a creaky, seaside holiday feel
with lots of floral wallpaper, a mix of simple antiques and ill-advised modern
furnishings, and thin towels. Most rooms have views, eight have balconies or terraces, and six have wood-burning fireplaces. The inn is within walking distance
of downtown Camden and its restaurants.

83 Bayview St., Camden, ME 04843. © **800/236-4266** or 207/236-4200. Fax 207/236-7063. www.
camdenharbourinn.com. 22 units. Peak season $195–$255 double (including breakfast); off-season
$105–$195 (including continental breakfast). 2-night minimum stay in peak season. AE, DISC, MC, V. Children
12 and over welcome. Pets accepted on ground floor. **Amenities:** Restaurant (closed at press time; may
reopen later in 2001).

Camden Windward House ★★   This handsome, intimate inn dating from 1854 features welcoming common rooms decorated with a light Victorian touch; in the library, you'll find a guest refrigerator and afternoon refreshments. The rooms vary in size; four have gas fireplaces, and a new (in 2000) suite features private balcony, cathedral ceilings, and Jacuzzi. Guests choose from seven or eight breakfast entrees, which are served in a pleasant dining room. The property is right on Route 1, but the innkeepers have tamed the traffic noise by adding a sound-muffling facade and installing double windows.

6 High St., Camden, ME 04843. © **207/236-9656.** Fax 207/230-0433. www.windwardhouse.com. 8 units. Peak season $160–$230 double; off-season $99–$160 ($10 less midweek). Rates include breakfast. AE, MC, V. Children 12 and over welcome. *In room:* A/C, TV, dataport.

Inn at Sunrise Point ★★★   This peaceful sanctuary 4 miles north of Camden Harbor is a world apart from the bustling town. The service is helpful, and the setting can't be beat. Situated on the edge of Penobscot Bay down a long, tree-lined road, the inn consists of a cluster of contemporary yet classic shingled buildings. The predominant sounds here are of birds singing and waves lapping at the cobblestone shore. A granite bench and Adirondack chairs on the front lawn allow guests to enjoy the bay view; breakfasts are served in a sunny conservatory. The rooms are spacious, comfortable, and full of amenities, including fireplaces, VCRs, and individual heat controls. The cottages are at the deluxe end of the scale, all featuring double Jacuzzis, fireplaces, wet bars, and private decks.

Rte. 1 (P.O. Box 1344), Camden, ME 04843. © **800/435-6278** or 207/236-7716. Fax 207/236-0820. www.sunrisepoint.com. 7 units. $195–$225 room; $275–$375 cottage. Rates include breakfast. AE, MC, V. Closed Nov to late May. No children permitted.

Maine Stay ★★   The Maine Stay is known for its congenial hospitality. This classic slate-roofed New England home (dating back to 1802 but expanded in 1840) is set in a shady yard within walking distance of both downtown and Camden Hills State Park. All rooms have ceiling fans and antiques; four have TVs as well. The best: the downstairs Carriage House Room, which is away from the buzz of traffic on Route 1 and boasts its own stone patio. Perhaps the most memorable part of a stay here is getting to know the three hosts—Peter Smith; his wife, Donny; and her twin sister, Diana Robson. The trio is genuinely interested in their guests' well-being, and they offer dozens of day-trip suggestions.

22 High St., Camden, ME 04843. © **207/236-9636.** www.mainestay.com. 8 units. $80–$150 double. Rates include breakfast. AE, MC, V. Children over 10 welcome. *In room:* Coffeemaker, hair dryer, no phone.

Norumbega ★★★   This Victorian-era stone castle is big enough to ensure privacy, but also intimate enough to get to know the other guests—mingling often occurs at breakfast and in the afternoon, when the innkeepers put out their famous fresh-baked cookies. Overlooking the bay, the Norumbega has remarkable architectural detailing—extravagant carved-oak woodwork and a stunning oak-and-mahogany inlaid floor. Guest rooms are large and furnished with antiques. Five units have fireplaces, while the three "garden-level rooms" (off the downstairs billiards room) have private decks. Most have TVs. Two rooms rank among the finest in New England—the Library Suite, with interior balcony, and the sprawling Penthouse, with its superlative views.

61 High St., Camden, ME 04843. © **207/236-4646.** Fax 207/236-0824. www.norumbegainn.com. 13 units. July to mid-Oct $160–$475 double; mid-May to June and late Oct $125–375; Nov to mid-May $99–$295. Rates include breakfast. 2-night minimum stay summer, weekends, and holidays. AE, DISC, MC, V. Children 7 and over welcome. *In room:* Dataport, hair dryer.

Whitehall Inn ⭐ The Whitehall is a distinguished and understated New England resort where you half expect to find a young Cary Grant in a blue blazer tickling the ivories on the lobby's 1904 Steinway. Set at the edge of town in a structure that dates to 1834, this three-story inn has a striking architectural integrity with its columns, gables, and long roofline. (Ask for a room away from the Route 1 noise.) Accommodations are simple but appealing. The Whitehall occupies a minor footnote in the annals of American literature—a young local poet recited her poems here for guests in 1912, stunning the audience with her eloquence. Her name? Edna St. Vincent Millay. The inn is quite popular with an older clientele, many of whom have been coming each summer for generations.

52 High St., Camden, ME 04843. ☎ 800/789-6565 or 207/236-3391. Fax 207/236-4427. www.whitehall-inn.com. 50 units (8 units share 4 bathrooms). July to late Oct $165–$190 double with private bathroom, including breakfast and dinner ($150 with breakfast only); $140 double with shared bathroom, including breakfast and dinner ($105 with breakfast only). Discounts available in late May and June. AE, MC, V. Closed late Oct to late May. **Amenities:** Restaurant (traditional New England); tennis court; tour desk; babysitting. *In room:* No phone (except for some units).

WHERE TO DINE

Atlantica ⭐⭐ SEAFOOD/ECLECTIC Atlantica gets high marks for its innovative seafood menu and its consistently well-prepared fare. Located on the waterfront with a small indoor seating area and an equally small outdoor deck, Atlantica features creative fare like pan-seared tuna, served with artichoke and smoked tomatoes, and scallops glazed with ginger and brown sugar. Our recommendation: Start with a cup or bowl of the lobster-corn chowder. The restaurant may reopen for lunch in 2001; it's worth calling ahead to check.

1 Bayview Landing. ☎ 207/236-6011. Reservations recommended. Main courses $16–$28. AE, MC, V. Tues–Sat 5:30–9pm (also Sun June–Aug).

Cappy's Chowder House SEAFOOD/AMERICAN Cappy's is a local institution that's more memorable for its lively atmosphere than for its fare. There's prime rib, a hearty seafood stew flavored with kielbasa, and the famous chowder (which has gotten a nod from *Gourmet* magazine). "Old-time sodas" are a specialty. The Crow's Nest upstairs is a bit quieter.

1 Main St. ☎ 207/236-2254. Main courses $5.95–$13.95. MC, V. Daily 7:30am–midnight.

Peter Ott's ⭐⭐ AMERICAN Peter Ott's opened in 1974 and has satisfied customers ever since with its no-nonsense fare. While it resembles a steakhouse with its wood tables and manly meat dishes (like char-broiled Black Angus), it's

---

Finds **A Special Museum**

Driving eastward from Camden toward Blue Hill or Acadia National Park, look for the engaging **Penobscot Marine Museum** (☎ 207/548-2529) in the low-key town of Searsport. Housed in a cluster of eight historic buildings atop a gentle rise in the tiny downtown, the museum features uncommonly well-organized exhibits on ships, shipbuilding, and the seafaring life. Wandering from building to building induces a keen sense of wonderment at the vast enterprise that was Maine's maritime trade. The museum is open from late May to mid-October, Monday through Saturday from 10am to 5pm and Sunday from noon to 5pm. Admission is $6 for adults, $5 for seniors, and $2 for children 7 to 15.

grown beyond that to satisfy more diverse tastes. In fact, it offers some of the better prepared seafood in town, including grilled salmon with a lemon caper sauce. Leave room for the lemon-almond crumb tart.

16 Bayview St. ⓒ 207/236-4032. Main courses $13.95–$22.95. MC, V. Daily 5:30–9:30pm.

The Waterfront ⭐ SEAFOOD   The Waterfront disproves the theory that "the better the view, the worse the food." Here you can watch yachts and wind-jammers come and go (angle for a seat on the deck), yet still be pleasantly surprised by the food. Look for fried clams, crab cakes, and boiled lobster. On the more adventurous side, you'll find black sesame shrimp salad (served on noodles with a Thai vinaigrette), or seafood linguine with shrimp, mussels, squid, and caramelized balsamic onions. More earthbound fare includes burgers, pitas, and strip steaks. A lighter pub menu is served between 2:30 and 5pm.

Bayview St. on Camden Harbor. ⓒ 207/236-3747. Main courses $6.95–$13.95 lunch; $12.95–$22.95 dinner. AE, MC, V. Daily 11:30am–2:30pm and 5–10pm (closes earlier in off-season).

5 The Blue Hill Peninsula

The Blue Hill Peninsula is a back-roads paradise. If you're in the mood to get lost on country lanes that suddenly dead-end at the sea or inexplicably start to loop back on themselves, this is your place. In contrast to the western shores of Penobscot Bay, the Blue Hill Peninsula has more of a lost-in-time character. The roads are hilly, winding, and narrow, passing through forests and along venerable saltwater farms, and touching on the edge of an azure inlet here or there.

CASTINE & ENVIRONS ⭐⭐

Castine gets our vote for the most gracious village in Maine. It's not so much the stunningly handsome mid-19th-century homes that fill the side streets. Nor is it the location on a quiet peninsula, 16 miles south of RV-clotted Route 1.

No, what lends Castine its charm are the splendid, towering elm trees, approximately 300 of which still overarch many of the village streets. Before Dutch elm disease ravaged the nation's tree-lined streets, much of America once looked like this. Through attentive ministering and a measure of luck, Castine has managed to keep many of its elms alive, and it's worth a detour for these alone.

For American-history buffs, Castine offers much more. This outpost served as a strategic town in various battles among the British, Dutch, French, and feisty colonials in the centuries following its settlement in 1613. Historical figures like Miles Standish and Paul Revere also passed through during one epoch or another.

ESSENTIALS

GETTING THERE   Castine is located 16 miles south of Route 1. Turn south on Route 175 in Orland (east of Bucksport) and follow this to Route 166, which winds its way to Castine. Route 166A offers an alternate route along Penobscot Bay.

VISITOR INFORMATION   Castine lacks a formal information center, but the clerk at the **Town Office** (ⓒ 207/326-4502) is helpful. The Castine Merchants Association publishes an excellent brief history by Elizabeth J. Duff. This handy pamphlet, which also includes a well-planned walking tour of Castine, is entitled *Welcome to Castine* and is widely available at shops in town.

EXPLORING CASTINE

One of the town's more intriguing attractions is the **Wilson Museum** ⭐, on Perkins Street (☎ **207/326-8753** days, or between 5 and 9pm call the curator at 207/326-8545), a quirky anthropological museum constructed in 1921. It contains the collections of John Howard Wilson, an archaeologist and collector of prehistoric artifacts from around the globe. His gleanings are neatly arranged in a staid, classical arrangement that typifies the studied approach to collecting in the late 19th and early 20th centuries. The museum is open from the end of May to the end of September, Tuesday through Sunday from 2 to 5pm; admission is free.

Next door is the **John Perkins House,** Castine's oldest home. The British occupied it during the Revolution and the War of 1812, and a tour features demonstrations of old-fashioned cooking techniques. It's open in July and August, Wednesday and Sunday only from 2 to 5pm. Admission is $2.

The **Maine Maritime Academy** ⭐ (☎ **207/326-4311**) trains sailors for the rigors of life at sea with the merchant marine. The campus is on the western edge of the village, and the 498-foot training vessel T.V. *State of Maine* is often docked in Castine. Free half-hour tours of the ship are offered in summer (assuming the ship is in port) from 10am to noon and 1 to 4pm.

Castine Kayak Adventures ⭐ (☎ **207/326-9045;** www.castinekayak.com) offers 6-hour ($105) and 3-hour ($55) sea-kayak tours departing from Dennett's Wharf restaurant. Both trips are appropriate for those without experience. You'll often spot wildlife, including bald eagles, harbor seals, and ospreys. Ask also about the sunset tours and the nighttime paddles.

Smoke on the water? That's likely to be the 30-foot *Laurie Ellen,* which claims to be "the nation's only wood-powered, steam-driven passenger launch inspected and approved by the U.S. Coast Guard." Capt. Randy Flood's **Castine Steamboat Co.** ⭐⭐ takes 18 passengers on 1-hour tours of the harbor, sailing from Dennett's Wharf. Tickets are $17.50 for adults, $10 for children. Call ☎ **207/374-2536,** or in summer call Randy's cell phone (☎ **207/266-2841**) aboard the boat. Randy's website is www.castinesteamboat.com.

WHERE TO STAY

Castine Harbor Lodge ⭐ *Kids*   Housed in a grand 1893 mansion (the only inn on the water in Castine), this place is run with an informal good cheer that allows kids to feel at home amid the regal architecture. The main parlor is dominated by a pool table, and there's Scrabble and Nintendo for the asking. The front porch, with views that extend across the bay to the Camden Hills, offers one of the best places in the state to unwind. The spacious guest rooms are eclectically appointed with both antiques and modern furnishings. Two of the rooms share an adjoining bathroom—of note to those traveling with children. The family dog is welcome. And if you're not traveling with a family? It's still a great spot if you prefer a well-worn comfort to high-end elegance.

Perkins St. (P.O. Box 215), Castine, ME 04421. ☎ 207/326-4335. www.castinemaine.com. 9 units (2 share 1 bathroom; 1 with private hall bathroom). $75–$150 double. Rates include continental breakfast. DC, DISC, MC, V. Pets allowed ($10 per night). *In room:* No phone.

Castine Inn ⭐   The Castine Inn is a Maine coast rarity—a hotel that was originally built in 1898 as a hotel, not as a residence. This handsome village inn, designed in an eclectic Georgian-Federal–Revival style, has a fine front porch and attractive gardens. Inside, the lobby takes its cue from the 1940s, with wingback chairs and loveseats. The guest rooms on the two upper floors (no elevator) are simply if unevenly furnished in a Colonial Revival style. Note that the innkeepers have revamped several units, adding luxe touches. These are markedly more inviting than the other rooms and are worth a splurge.

Main St. (P.O. Box 41), Castine, ME 04421. © 207/326-4365. Fax 207/326-4570. www.castineinn.com. 19 units. $85–$135 double; $210 suite. Rates include breakfast. 2-night minimum stay July–Aug. MC, V. Closed mid-Dec to May. Children 8 and over welcome. **Amenities:** Restaurant (see below). *In room:* No phone.

Pentagöet Inn ★★   This quirky 1894 structure with its prominent turret is comfortable without being overly fussy, professional without being chilly, personal without being overly intimate. The guest rooms on the upper two floors of the main house are furnished eclectically, with a mix of antiques and collectibles. The five rooms in the adjacent Perkins Street building—a more austere Federal-era house—are furnished simply and feature painted floors. There's no air-conditioning, but all rooms have ceiling or window fans.

Main St. (P.O. Box 4), Castine, ME 04421. © 800/845-1701 or 207/326-8616. Fax 207/326-9382. www. pentagoet.com. 16 units (2 with private hallway bathrooms). $80–$150 double. Rates include breakfast. MC, V. Closed Nov–Apr. Pets accepted by reservation. Older children welcome. **Amenities:** Restaurant (regional and global fare). *In room:* No phone.

WHERE TO DINE

Castine Inn ★★ NEW AMERICAN   At this handsome dining room, you'll find Castine's best fare and some of the better food in the state. Chef/owner Tom Gutow served stints at Bouley and Verbena in New York, and isn't timid about experimenting with local meats and produce. Expect dishes such as lobster with vanilla butter, mango mayonnaise, and tropical-fruit salsa; or lamb loin with eggplant, green lentils, tomatoes, and rosemary jus. One night each week, the restaurant offers a buffet; that night you're better off heading to Dennett's Wharf.

Main St. © 207/326-4365. Reservations recommended. Main courses $15–$26. MC, V. Daily 6–9pm. Closed mid-Dec to May.

Dennett's Wharf PUB FARE   Located in a soaring waterfront sail loft, Dennett's Wharf offers upscale bar food amid a lively setting leavened with a good selection of microbrews. If the weather's decent, there's outdoor dining with superb harbor views. Look for grilled sandwiches, roll-ups, and salads at lunch; dinner includes lobster, stir-fry, and steak teriyaki.

Sea St. (next to the Town Dock). © 207/326-9045. Reservations recommended in summer and for parties of six or more. Lunch $5.50–$17.95; dinner $8.95–$17.95. AE, DISC, MC, V. Daily 11am–midnight. Closed mid-Oct to Apr 30.

DEER ISLE

Deer Isle is well off the beaten path and worth every minute of the long detour off Route 1 if your tastes run to pastoral countryside with a nautical edge. Winding roads cross through forest and farmland, and travelers are rewarded with sudden glimpses of the sun-dappled ocean and mint-green coves.

Deer Isle doesn't cater exclusively to tourists, as many coastal regions do. It's still occupied by fifth-generation fishermen, farmers, long-time rusticators, and artists who prize their seclusion. The village of **Deer Isle** ★ has a handful of inns and galleries, but its primary focus is to serve locals and summer residents, not transients. The village of **Stonington** ★★, on the southern tip, is a rough-hewn sea town. Despite serious incursions over the past 5 years by galleries and enterprises dependent on seasonal tourism, it remains dominated in spirit by fishermen and quarry workers.

ESSENTIALS

GETTING THERE Deer Isle is accessible via several winding country roads from Route 1. Coming from the west, head south on Route 175 off Route 1 in Orland, then connect to Route 15 to Deer Isle. From the east, head south on Route 172 to Blue Hill, where you can pick up Route 15. Deer Isle is connected to the mainland via a high, narrow, and graceful suspension bridge, built in 1938, which can be somewhat harrowing to cross in high winds.

VISITOR INFORMATION The **Deer Isle–Stonington Chamber of Commerce** (© **207/348-6124**) staffs a seasonal information booth just beyond the bridge on Little Deer Isle. The booth is open in summer, daily from 10am to 4pm, depending on volunteer availability.

EXPLORING DEER ISLE

Deer Isle, with its network of narrow roads to nowhere, is ideal for perfunctory rambling. It's a pleasure to explore by car, and is also inviting to travel by bike, although careening fishermen in pickups can make this unnerving at times. Especially tranquil is the narrow road between Deer Isle and Sunshine to the east. Plan to stop and explore the rocky coves and inlets along the way. To get here, head toward Stonington on Route 15 and just south of the village of Deer Isle, turn east toward Stinson Neck, and continue along this scenic byway for about 10 miles over bridges and causeways.

Stonington, at the southern tip of Deer Isle, consists of one commercial street that wraps along the harbor's edge. While B&Bs and boutiques have made inroads here recently, it's still a mostly rough-and-tumble waterfront town. You're likely to observe lots of activity in the harbor as lobstermen come and go. If you hear industrial sounds emanating from just offshore, that's probably the stone quarry on Crotch Island, which has been in operation for more than a century.

Haystack Mountain School of Crafts ⊛ The 40-acre oceanside campus of this respected summer crafts school, established in 1950, is visually stunning. Edward Larrabee Barnes, who set the buildings on a steep hillside overlooking the cerulean waters of Jericho Bay, designed it in the 1960s. Barnes managed to play up the views while respecting the delicate landscape by constructing a series of small structures on pilings that seem to float above the earth. The classrooms and studios are linked by boardwalks, many of which are connected to a wide central staircase, ending at the "Flag Deck," a sort of open-air commons just above the shoreline. The buildings and classrooms are closed to the public, but summer visitors are welcome to walk to the Flag Deck and stroll the nature trail adjacent to the campus. The drive to the campus is outstanding.

Sunshine Rd. © 207/348-2306. www.haystack-mtn.org. Donations appreciated. Summer daily 9am–5pm; tours Wed 1pm. Head south of the village of Deer Isle on Rte. 15; turn left on Greenlaw District Rd. and follow signs to school, approximately 7 miles.

A DAY TRIP TO ISLE AU HAUT ⊛⊛⊛

Rocky and remote Isle au Haut offers the most unusual hiking and camping experience in northern New England. This 6-by-3-mile island, located 6 miles south of Stonington, was originally named Ille Haut—or High Island—in 1604 by French explorer Samuel de Champlain. The name and its pronunciation evolved—today, it's generally pronounced "aisle-a-ho"—but the island itself has remained steadfastly unchanged over the centuries.

About half of the island is owned by the National Park Service and maintained as an outpost of Acadia National Park (see the following section).

A 60-passenger "mailboat" makes a stop in the morning and late afternoon at Duck Harbor, allowing for a solid day of hiking. The National Park Service also maintains a cluster of five Adirondack-style lean-tos at Duck Harbor, available for camping. (Reservations are essential; contact **Acadia National Park,** Bar Harbor, ME 04609, or call © **207-288-3338.**) No day fee is charged.

A network of hiking trails radiates from Duck Harbor. Among the highlights: the trail up 543-foot **Duck Harbor Mountain** (the island's highest point) for exceptional views of the Camden Hills to the west and Mount Desert Island to the east. Also worth hiking are the **Cliff** or **Western Head trails,** which track along high, rocky bluffs and coastal outcroppings capped with damp, tangled fog forests of spruce. The trails periodically descend to cobblestone coves, which issue forth a deep rumble with every incoming wave. A hand pump near Duck Harbor provides drinking water, but be sure to bring food in a daypack.

The other half of the island is privately owned, some by fishermen who can trace their island ancestry back 3 centuries, and some by summer rusticators whose forebears discovered the bucolic splendor of Isle au Haut in the 1880s. The summer population of the island is about 300, with about 50 die-hards remaining year-round. The mailboat also stops at the small harborside village, which has a few old homes, a handsome church, and a tiny schoolhouse, post office, and store. Day-trippers will be better served ferrying straight to Duck Harbor.

Isle au Haut Boat Company (tel] **207-367-6516;** www.isleauhaut.com) operates a ferry to the island; it leaves from the pier at the end of Sea Breeze Avenue in Stonington. From mid-June to mid-September, the *Miss Lizzie* departs for the village of Isle au Haut daily at 7am, 11:30am, and 4:30pm; the *Mink* departs for Duck Harbor daily at 10am and 4:30pm. (Limited trips to Isle au Haut are offered the rest of the year.) The round-trip boat fare to either destination is $26 for adults. Children under 12 pay $12. The crossing takes about 45 minutes to the village, or 1 hour to Duck Harbor. Travelers should arrive at least half an hour before departure. The ferry has been working to set up an online reservations system; check the company's website for current status.

SEA KAYAKING

Old Quarry Charters ★★ (© **207/367-8977;** www.oldquarrycharters.com), just outside the village of Stonington, offers guided kayak tours as well as kayaks for rent. (Old Quarry will rent only to those with prior experience.) Tours range from a 2-hour jaunt ($27) to a 7-hour excursion that weaves through the islands and includes a stop for a swim at an abandoned quarry ($100). Overnight camping trips are also offered. Other services: parking and a launch site for those who've brought their own boats ($5 per boat), sailboat tours and lessons, charter tours aboard a 38-foot lobster boat, accommodations in a three-suite B&B ($160 to $200), and camping ($20 per couple).

WHERE TO STAY

You'll find standard motel rooms at **Eggemoggin Landing,** on Route 15 (© **207/348-6115**), at a great location on the shores of Eggemoggin Reach at the south end of the bridge from the mainland to Little Deer Isle. Open May through October; rates are $69 to $75 in peak season. Pets are allowed in spring and fall. Amenities include a restaurant, kayak and bike rentals, and sailboat cruises.

Goose Cove Lodge ★★ *Kids*   This rustic compound next to a nature preserve is a superb destination for families and lovers of the outdoors. Exploring the grounds offers an adventure every day. You can hike out at low tide to salty Barred Island, or take a guided nature hike on any of five trails. You can mess around in boats in the cove, or borrow a bike for an excursion. Twenty rooms offer fireplaces or Franklin stoves; two modern cottages sleep six and are available through the winter. Our favorites? Elm and Linnea, cozy cabins tucked away in the woods on a rise overlooking the beach. Meals are far above what you would expect to find at the end of a remote dirt road.

Goose Cove Rd. (P.O. Box 40), Sunset, ME 04683. ℂ **207/348-2508.** Fax 207/348-2624. www. goosecovelodge.com. 23 units. Peak season $140–$300 double; off-season $120–$274. Ask about off-season packages. Rates include breakfast. 2-night minimum stay July–Aug (1-week minimum in cottages); some units have 3-person minimum in peak season. MC, V. Closed mid-Oct to mid-May. **Amenities:** Restaurant (New American); canoes, kayaks, bicycles (all free). *In room:* No phone.

Inn on the Harbor ℛ   This quirky waterfront inn has the best location in town—perched over the harbor and right on the main street. This is an ideal spot for resting up before or after a kayak expedition, as well as a good base for a day trip out to Isle au Haut. Ten rooms overlook the harbor; all are nicely appointed with antiques and sisal carpets. Most units have phones. Complimentary sherry and wine are served in the reception room or on the expansive waterfront deck each afternoon. Breakfast includes homebaked muffins and breads. The inn operates a restaurant a short walk away called the **Cafe Atlantic** (ℂ **207/367-6373**), which features seafood, pasta, and beef (prime rib on weekends). Parking is on the street or at nearby lots and can be inconvenient during busy times.

Main St. (P.O. Box 69), Stonington, ME 04681. ℂ **800/942-2420** or 207/367-2420. Fax 207/367-5165. www. innontheharbor.com. 13 units. $105–$135 double; from $80 off-season. Rates include continental breakfast. AE, DISC, MC, V. On-street parking. Children 12 and over welcome. **Amenities:** Espresso bar. *In room:* TV.

Pilgrim's Inn ℛℛ   Set at the edge of the village between an open bay and a millpond, this is a handsomely renovated inn in a lovely setting. The four-story structure, built in 1793, will especially appeal to history buffs. The interior is appointed in a style that's informed by Early Americana, but not beholden to uncomfortable authenticity. The guest rooms are filled with antiques and painted in muted colonial colors; especially intriguing are the rooms on the top floor, with original diagonal beams. Also available are two nearby cottages, which come equipped with TVs, phones, air-conditioning, irons, and coffeemakers.

Deer Isle, ME 04627. ℂ **207/348-6615.** Fax 207/348-7769. www.pilgrimsinn.com. 15 units (3 with shared bathroom). $165 double with shared bathroom; $195 with private bathroom; $220 cottage. Rates include breakfast and dinner. MC, V. Closed mid-Oct to mid-May (cottages open year-round). Pets accepted in cottages. Children 10 and over welcome. **Amenities:** Dining room (regional/fine dining); bicycles. *In room:* No phone.

WHERE TO DINE

For fine dining, **Goose Cove Lodge** and the **Pilgrim's Inn** serve meals to the public; both require reservations (see above.)

Fisherman's Friend ℛ   SEAFOOD   This is a lively and boisterous place where you'll easily get your fill of local color. Simple tables fill a large room, while long-experienced waitresses hustle to keep up with demand. The menu features basic home-cooked meals, with a wide range of fresh fish prepared in a variety of styles. It's justly famous for its lobster stew. Dessert selections, including berry pies and shortcake, are extensive and traditional New England. Bring your own wine, beer, or cocktails.

School St., Stonington. (C) **207/367-2442.** Reservations recommended in peak season and on weekends. Sandwiches $2.50–$6.50; dinner entrees $6.95–$15.95. DISC, MC, V. July–Aug daily 11am–9pm; June and Sept–Oct daily 11am–8pm; Apr–May Tues–Sun 11am–8pm. Closed Nov–Mar. Located up the hill from the harbor past the Opera House.

BLUE HILL ✦

Blue Hill, population 1,900, is fairly easy to find—just look for gently domed Blue Hill Mountain, which lords over the northern end of Blue Hill Bay. Set between the mountain and the bay is the quiet town of Blue Hill, clustered along the bay shore and a burbling stream. There's rarely much going on, and that seems to be exactly what brings visitors back time and again—and may explain why two excellent bookstores are located here. Many old-money families maintain retreats set along the water or in the rolling inland hills. It's a good destination for an escape, and will especially appeal to those deft at crafting their own entertainment.

ESSENTIALS

GETTING THERE   Blue Hill is southeast of Ellsworth on Route 172. Coming from the west, take Route 15 south 5 miles east of Bucksport (it's well marked with road signs).

VISITOR INFORMATION   Blue Hill does not maintain a visitor information booth. Look for the *Blue Hill, Maine* brochure and map at state information centers, or write the **Blue Hill Chamber of Commerce,** P.O. Box 520, Blue Hill, ME 04614.

EXPLORING BLUE HILL

From the open summit of **Blue Hill Mountain** ✦✦ you'll get superb views of the bay and the rocky balds on Mount Desert Island just across the way. To reach the trailhead from the village, drive north on Route 172, then turn west (left) on Mountain Road at the Blue Hill Fairgrounds. Drive four-fifths of a mile and look for the marked trail. An ascent of the "mountain" (elevation 940 feet) is about a mile and requires about 45 minutes. Bring a picnic and enjoy the vistas.

Blue Hill has attracted more than its fair share of artists—especially, it seems, potters. On Union Street, stop by **Rowantrees Pottery** ✦✦ ((C) **207/ 374-5535**), which has been a Blue Hill institution for more than 50 years. The pottery here is richly hued, and the glazes are made from local resources. The family-run **Rackliffe Pottery** ✦, on Ellsworth Road ((C) **207/374-2297**), uses native clay and lead-free glazes. The bowls and vases have a lustrous, silky feel. Visitors are welcome to watch the potters at work. Both shops are open year-round.

The intriguing **Parson Fisher House** ✦ (call Eric Linnell at (C) **207/ 374-2339**) was home to Blue Hill's first permanent minister, who settled here in 1796. He was a rustic Renaissance man: Educated at Harvard, Fisher delivered sermons in six different languages, and was also a gifted writer, painter, and inventor. On a tour of his home, which he built in 1814, you can see a clock with wooden works he made, as well as samples of the books he not only wrote but also published and bound himself. The house is located on Routes 176 and 15 a half mile west of the village. It's open from July to mid-September, Monday through Saturday from 2 to 5 pm. Admission is $2 for adults, free for children under 12.

The **Big Chicken Barn** ((C) **207/667-7308**) is a sprawling antiques shop and bookstore. The first floor features a mix of antiques in dozens of stalls (literally) maintained by local dealers. Upstairs are around 90,000 books, well organized by category. There's also a forest's worth of old magazines in plastic sleeves (great browsing on a rainy afternoon). The shop is on Route 1 between Ellsworth and Bucksport (9 miles west of Ellsworth, 11 miles east of Bucksport).

WHERE TO STAY

Blue Hill Farm Country Inn 🄀   Comfortably situated on 48 acres, this inn's strength is in its common areas. The first floor of a sprawling barn has been converted to a spacious living room for guests. In the adjoining antique farmhouse, you can curl up in the cozy common room, which is amply stocked with a good selection of books. In contrast, the guest rooms are rather small and lightly furnished. The more modern units, upstairs in the barn loft, are nicely decorated in a country farmhouse style, but these are a bit motel-like, with rooms set off a central hallway. The three older rooms in the farmhouse have more character, but share a single bathroom with a small tub and hand-held shower.

Rte. 15, 2 miles north of village (P.O. Box 437), Blue Hill, ME 04614. ℂ **207/374-5126.** 14 units (7 with shared bathroom). June–Oct $80–$95 double; off-season $70–$80 double (no shared bathroom in off-season). Rates include continental breakfast. AE, MC, V. *In room:* No phone.

Blue Hill Inn 🄀🄀   The handsome Blue Hill Inn has been hosting travelers with aplomb since 1840. Situated on one of Blue Hill's main thoroughfares and within walking distance of village attractions, this Federal-style inn is colonial American throughout, with the authenticity enhanced by creaky floors and doorjambs slightly out of true. The guest rooms are furnished with antiques and down comforters; four units feature wood-burning fireplaces. Housed in an adjacent building is a more contemporary luxury suite, which features cathedral ceilings, fireplace, kitchen, and deck.

Union St. (P.O. Box 403), Blue Hill, ME 04614. ℂ **207/374-2844.** Fax 207/374-2829. www.bluehillinn.com. 12 units. $118–$185 double; $220–$255 suite. Rates include breakfast. 2-night minimum stay in summer. Ask about packages that include kayaking, hiking, or sailing. DISC, MC, V. Closed Dec to mid-May. Children 13 and over welcome. **Amenities:** Dining (New American/organic). *In room:* No phone.

WHERE TO DINE

Jean-Paul's Bistro 🄀 UPSCALE SANDWICHES   You get a lot of atmosphere for a moderate price at Jean-Paul's, which serves only lunch and tea . This is an excellent choice on a sunny day; head for the tables and Adirondack chairs on the stone terraces and lawn that overlook the bay. Lunches tend toward quiche, croissant sandwiches, and salads. The walnut tarragon chicken salad is tasty; the delicious desserts make liberal use of local blueberries.

Main St. (at the intersection of Rtes. 172 and 15). ℂ **207/374-5852.** Lunch $6.95–$8.95. MC, V. Daily 11am–5pm. Closed mid-Sept to June.

Jonathan's 🄀🄀 BISTRO   Jonathan's appeals to almost everyone—from a younger, more culinarily adventurous crowd to the blazer-wearing old-money summer denizens. The background music is jazz or light rock, the service brisk and professional, and the wine list extensive. Guests choose between the barn-like back room, with its comfortable knotty-pine feel, or a less elegant space facing Main Street. The kitchen emphasizes locally raised, seasonal dishes—think of it as Maine-meets-Europe, with updated versions of regional classics along with reinterpretations of European fare using Maine ingredients. Expect entrees like the (popular) braised lamb shank with maple barbecue sauce; mixed grill of quail, rabbit, and venison sausage; and poached salmon with dill sauce.

Main St. ℂ **207/374-5226.** Reservations recommended. Main courses $14–$18. MC, V. Mon–Sat 5–9:30pm.

6 Mount Desert Island & Acadia National Park

Mount Desert Island is home to spectacular Acadia National Park, and for many visitors the two places are one and the same. Yet the park holdings are only part of the appeal of this immensely popular island, which is connected to the mainland via a short, two-lane causeway. Beyond the parklands are scenic harborside villages and remote backcountry roads, lovely B&Bs and fine restaurants, oversize 19th-century summer "cottages," and the historic tourist town of Bar Harbor.

Mount Desert (pronounced "de-*sert*") is divided into two lobes separated by Somes Sound, the only legitimate fjord in the continental U.S. (A fjord is a valley carved by a glacier that subsequently filled with rising ocean water.) Most of the parkland is on the east side, although large swaths of park exist on the west as well. The eastern side is more developed, with Bar Harbor the center of commerce and entertainment. The western side has a more quiet, settled air, and teems more with wildlife than tourists. The island isn't huge—it's only about 15 miles from the causeway to the southernmost tip at Bass Harbor Head—yet visitors can do a lot of adventuring in such a compact space. The best plan is to take it slow, exploring whenever possible by foot, bicycle, canoe, or kayak.

ACADIA NATIONAL PARK

It's not hard to fathom why Acadia is one of the biggest draws in the U.S. national park system. The park's landscape offers a rich tapestry of rugged cliffs, restless ocean, and quiet woods. Acadia's terrain, like so much of the rest of northern New England, was carved by glaciers 18,000 years ago. A mile-high ice sheet shaped the land by scouring valleys into distinctive U shapes, rounding many of the once-jagged peaks, and depositing huge boulders around the landscape, including the famous 10-foot-high "Bubble Rock," which appears to be perched precariously on the side of South Bubble Mountain.

The park's more recent roots can be traced back to the 1840s, when noted Hudson River School painter Thomas Cole packed his sketchbooks and easels for a trip to this remote island, then home to a small number of fishermen and boat builders. His stunning renditions of the surging surf pounding against coastal granite were later displayed in New York and triggered an early tourism boom as urbanites flocked to the island to "rusticate." By 1872, national magazines were touting Eden (Bar Harbor's name until 1919) as a desirable summer resort. It attracted the attention of wealthy industrialists, and soon became summer home to Carnegies, Rockefellers, Astors, and Vanderbilts, who erected massive "cottages" with literally dozens of rooms.

By the early 1900s, the popularity and growing development of the island began to concern its most ardent supporters. Boston textile heir and conservationist George Dorr and Harvard president Charles Eliot, aided by the largesse of John D. Rockefeller, Jr., started acquiring large tracts for the public's enjoyment. These parcels were eventually donated to the government, and in 1919 the land was designated Lafayette National Park, the first national park east of the Mississippi. Renamed Acadia in 1929, the park has grown to encompass nearly half the island, with holdings scattered about piecemeal here and there.

Rockefeller purchased and donated about 11,000 acres—about a third of the park. He was also responsible for one of the park's most extraordinary features. Around 1905, a dispute erupted over whether to allow noisy new motorcars on to the island. Resident islanders wanted these new conveniences to aid their mobility; John D. Rockefeller, Jr., whose fortune came from the oil industry (students of irony, take note), strenuously objected, preferring the tranquility of a car-free island. Rockefeller went down to defeat on this issue, and the island was opened to cars in 1913. In response, the multimillionaire set about building an elaborate 57-mile system of private carriage roads, featuring a dozen gracefully handcrafted stone bridges. These roads, open today to pedestrians, bicyclists, and equestrians, are concentrated most densely around Jordan Pond, but also wind through wooded valleys and ascend to some of the most scenic open peaks.

JUST THE FACTS
GETTING THERE   Acadia National Park is reached from the town of Ellsworth via Route 3. *Tip:* If you're driving from southern Maine, avoid the coastal congestion along Route 1 by taking the Maine Turnpike to Bangor, picking up I-395 to Route 1A, then continuing south on Route 1A to Ellsworth. While this looks longer on the map, it's the quickest route in summer and you're not missing much scenery on "coastal" Route 1, which often isn't in sight of the ocean between late May and mid-September.

Daily flights from Boston to the airport in Trenton, just across the causeway from Mount Desert Island, are offered year-round by US Air affiliate **Colgan Air** (© **800/523-3273** or 207/667-7171). In summer, **Concord Trailways** (© **888/741-8686** or 207/942-8686) offers van service between Bangor (including an airport stop), Ellsworth, and Bar Harbor. Reservations are required.

GETTING AROUND   A free islandwide **shuttle bus** service was inaugurated in 1999 as part of an effort to reduce the number of cars on the island's roads. The propane-powered buses, which are equipped with racks for bikes, serve six routes that cover nearly the entire island, and will stop anywhere you request outside the village centers, including trailheads, ferries, small villages, and campgrounds. All routes begin or end at the Village Green in Bar Harbor, but you're encouraged to pick up the bus wherever you're staying, whether at motel or campground, to minimize the number of parked cars in town. Route 3 goes from Bar Harbor along much of the Park Loop, offering easy access to some of the park's best hiking trails. The buses operate from late June to early September.

ENTRY POINTS & FEES   A 1-week park pass, which includes unlimited trips on Park Loop Road, costs $10 per car; no additional charge per passenger. (No daily pass is available.) The main point of entry to Park Loop Road, the park's most scenic byway, is at the visitor center at **Hulls Cove.** Mount Desert Island consists of an interwoven network of park and town roads, allowing visitors to enter the park at numerous points. A glance at a park map (available free at the visitor center) will make these access points self-evident. The entry fee is collected at a toll booth on Park Loop Road a half mile north of Sand Beach.

REGULATIONS   The usual national park rules apply. Guns may not be used in the park; if you have a gun, it must be "cased, broken down, or otherwise packaged against use." Fires and camping are allowed only at designated areas. Pets must be on a leash at all times. Seat belts must be worn in the national park (this is a federal law). Don't remove anything from the park, either man-made or natural; this includes cobblestones from the shore.

VISITOR CENTERS & INFORMATION   Acadia staffs two visitor centers. The **Thompson Island Information Center,** on Route 3 (© **207/288-3411**), is the first you'll pass as you enter Mount Desert Island. The local chambers of commerce maintain this center; park personnel are usually on hand to answer inquiries. It's the best stop for general lodging and restaurant information. Open from mid-May to mid-October.

Mount Desert Island/Acadia National Park

For more detailed information on park attractions, continue on Route 3 to the National Park Service's **Hulls Cove Visitor Center,** about 7½ miles beyond Thompson Island. This attractive stone-walled center includes park service displays, such as a large relief map of the island, natural-history exhibits, and a short film. You can request brochures on trails and carriage roads, or purchase postcards and guidebooks. The center is open mid-April through October.

Information is also available year-round, by phone or in person, from the park's **headquarters** (© **207/288-3338;** www.nps.gov/acad), on Route 233 between Bar Harbor and Somesville.

SEASONS   Summer, of course, is peak season at Acadia. The weather in July and August is perfect for just about any outdoor activity. Most days are warm (in the 70s or 80s), with afternoons frequently cooler owing to ocean breezes. While sun seems to be the norm, come prepared for rain and fog, both frequent visitors to the Maine coast. Once or twice each summer, a heat wave will settle into the area, producing temperatures in the 90s, dense haze, and stifling humidity, but this rarely lasts more than a few days. Sometime during the last 2 weeks of August, a cold wind will blow through at night and you'll smell the approach of autumn, with winter not far behind.

Visit Acadia in September if you can. Between Labor Day and the foliage season of early October, the days are often warm and clear, the nights have a crisp northerly tang, and you can avoid the hassles of congestion, crowds, and pesky

---

(*Tips* **Provisions**

Before you set out to explore the park, pack a picnic lunch and keep it handy. Once you're in the park, there are few places (other than Jordan Pond House) to stop for lunch or snacks. Having drinks and a bite to eat at hand will prevent breaking up your day with backtracking into Bar Harbor or elsewhere to fend off starvation. The more food you bring with you, the more your options for the day will expand.

---

insects. Bus tours seem to proliferate this month, and this can mean periodic crowds at the most popular sites like Thunder Hole. Not to worry: If you walk just a minute or two off the road, you'll have the place to yourself.

Winter is an increasingly popular time to travel here, especially among those who enjoy cross-country skiing on the carriage roads. Be aware, though, that snow along the coast is inconsistent, and services—including most restaurant and many inns—are often closed in winter.

AVOIDING THE CROWDS Early fall is the best time to miss out on the mobs yet still enjoy the weather. If you're here in midsummer, venture out in the early morning or early evening to see the most popular spots, like Thunder Hole or the summit of Cadillac Mountain. Setting off into the woods at every opportunity is also a good strategy. About four out of five visitors restrict their tours to the loop road and a handful of other major attractions, leaving the backcountry open for adventurous spirits. The best guarantee of solitude is to head to the more remote outposts managed by Acadia, especially Isle au Haut and Schoodic Peninsula, located across the bay to the east.

RANGER PROGRAMS Frequent ranger programs are offered throughout the year. These include talks at campground amphitheaters and tours of various island locales and attractions. Examples include the Otter Point nature hike, Mr. Rockefeller's bridges walk, Frenchman Bay cruise (rangers provide commentary on commercial trips), and a discussion of changes in Acadia's landscape. Ask for a schedule of events or more information at a visitor center or campground.

DRIVING TOUR DRIVING THE PARK LOOP ROAD

The 20-mile Park Loop Road ⭐⭐⭐ is to Acadia what Half Dome is to Yosemite—it's the park's premier attraction, and the magnet for the largest crowds. This remarkable roadway starts near the Hulls Cove Visitor Center and follows the high ridges above Bar Harbor before dropping down along the rocky coast. Here, the spires of spruce and fir cap dark granite, and the earthy tones contrast sharply with the frothy white surf and the steely blue sea. After following the picturesque coast and touching on several coves, the road loops back inland along Jordan Pond and Eagle Lake, with a detour to the summit of the island's highest peak.

Ideally, visitors will make two circuits on the loop road. The first is for the sheer exhilaration of it and to discern the lay of the land. On the second trip, plan to stop frequently and poke around on foot by setting off on trails or scrambling along the coastline. Scenic pull-outs are staggered at frequent intervals. The two-lane road is one-way along coastal sections; the right-hand lane is set aside for parking, so you can stop wherever you'd like to admire the vistas.

From about 10am to 4pm in July and August, anticipate large crowds along the loop road, at least on those days when the sun is shining. Parking lots may fill at some of the more popular destinations, including Sand Beach, Thunder Hole, and the Cadillac Mountain summit. Travel early or late. Alternatively, make the best of wet days by donning rain gear and letting the weather work to your advantage. You'll discover that you have the place to yourself.

From the Hulls Cove Visitor Center, the Park Loop initially runs atop

❶ Paradise Hill

The tour will start with sweeping views eastward over Frenchman Bay. You'll clearly see the town of Bar Harbor far below, and just beyond it the Porcupines, a cluster of islands that look like, well, porcupines.

Following the Park Loop Road clockwise, you'll dip into a wooded valley and soon come to

❷ Sieur de Monts Spring

Here you'll find a rather uninteresting natural spring, unnaturally encased, along with a botanical garden with some 300 species showcased in 12 habitats. The original **Abbe Museum** (© **207/288-3519**) is here, featuring a small but select collection of Native American artifacts. Open daily from mid-May to mid-October; admission is $2 for adults, $1 for children. A larger branch of the museum opened in downtown Bar Harbor in 2001, with more exhaustive and better curated displays (see below).

The Tarn is the chief reason to stop here; a few hundred yards south of the springs via footpath, it's a slightly medieval-looking and forsaken pond sandwiched between steep hills. Departing from the south end of the Tarn is the fine **Dorr Mountain Ladder Trail** (see "Hiking," below).

Continue the clockwise trip on the loop road; views eastward over the bay soon resume, almost uninterruptedly.

❸ The Precipice Trail

This is the park's most dramatic trail. It ascends sheer rock faces on the east side of Champlain Mountain. It's only

about four-fifths of a mile to the summit, but it's rigorous, and involves scrambling up iron rungs and ladders in very exposed places (those with a fear of heights or under 5 feet tall should avoid this trail). Alas, the trail is often closed midsummer to protect nesting peregrine falcons. Rangers are often on hand in the trailhead parking lot to point out the birds and suggest alternatives.

Between the Precipice Trail and Sand Beach is a toll booth, where visitors pay the park fee of $10 per car, good for 1 week.

Picturesquely set between the arms of a rocky cove is

❹ Sand Beach

This is the only sand beach on the island. Swimming these cold waters (about 50°F) is best enjoyed on extremely hot days, or by those with a freakishly robust metabolism. When it's sunny out, the sandy strand is usually crowded midday, often with picnickers and urban travelers. *Tip:* The water at the far end of the beach—where a gentle stream enters the cove—is often a few degrees warmer than the end closer to the access stairs.

Two worthwhile hikes depart from near the beach. The **Beehive Trail** overlooks Sand Beach (see "Hiking," below); it starts from a trailhead across the loop road. From the east end of Sand Beach, look for the start of the **Great Head Trail** ⭐⭐, a loop of about 2 miles that follows on the bluff overlooking the beach, then circles back along the shimmering bay before cutting through the woods back to Sand Beach.

About a mile south of Sand Beach is

❺ Thunder Hole

This is a shallow oceanside cavern into which the surf surges, compresses, and bursts out (there's a walking trail along the road if you'd rather leave your car parked at the beach). When the bay is as quiet as a millpond (and it often is during the lulling days of summer), it's a no-star drive-by. You're better off spending time elsewhere.

But on days when the seas are rough and large swells roll in off the Bay of Fundy, it's a must-see, three-star attraction; that's when you can feel the ocean's power and force resonating under your sternum. (*Tip:* The best viewing time is 3 hours before high tide.)

Parents with overly inquisitive toddlers (or teenagers) needn't fear: Visitors walk down to the cusp of Thunder Hole on a path that's girded with stout steel railings; on the most turbulent days, rangers gate off parts of the walkway to keep visitors away from rogue waves.

Just before the road curves around Otter Point, you'll be driving atop

❻ Otter Cliffs

This is a set of 100-foot-high precipices capped with dense spruce that plummet down into roiling seas. Look for whales spouting in summer; in early fall, tens of thousands of eider ducks can sometimes be seen floating in flocks just offshore. A footpath follows the brink of the crags.

At Seal Harbor, the loop road veers north and inland back toward Bar Harbor. Along the route is

❼ Jordan Pond

Jordan Pond is a small but uncommonly beautiful body of water encased by gentle, forested hills. A 3-mile hiking loop follows the pond's shoreline (see "Hiking," below), and a network of splendid carriage roads converge at the pond. After a hike or mountain-bike excursion, spend some time at a table on the lawn of the **Jordan Pond House** restaurant (see "Where to Dine," below).

Shortly before the loop road ends, you'll pass the entrance to

❽ Cadillac Mountain

You can reach this mountain by car by ascending an early carriage road. Among the mountain's claims to fame: At 1,528 feet, it's the highest peak on the Eastern Seaboard between Canada and Brazil. It's also the first place in the United States touched by the sun during much of the year. But because Cadillac Mountain is the only mountaintop in the park accessible by car, and because it's also the island's highest point, the parking lot at the summit can be jammed, and drivers testy. The views are undeniably great, but the shopping-mall-at-Christmas atmosphere puts a serious crimp in one's enjoyment of the place. Some of the lower peaks—like Acadia or Champlain mountains—offer equally excellent views and fewer crowds.

OUTDOOR PURSUITS

HIKING   Acadia National Park has 120 miles of hiking trails, plus 57 miles of carriage roads suitable for walking. The park is studded with low "mountains" (they'd be called hills elsewhere), and almost all have trails with superb views of the open ocean. Many pathways were crafted by experienced stonemasons and others with high aesthetic intent, and thus the routes aren't the most direct—but they're often the most scenic, taking advantage of fractures in the rocks, picturesque ledges, and sudden vistas.

The Hulls Cove Visitor Center offers a brief chart of area hikes; combined with the park map, this is all you'll need to explore the well-maintained, well-marked trails. It's not hard to cobble together loop hikes to make your trips more varied. Coordinate your hiking with the weather; if it's damp or foggy, you'll stay drier and warmer strolling the carriage roads. If it's clear and dry, head for the highest peaks with the best views.

Among our favorite hikes is the **Dorr Mountain Ladder Trail** ✹✹✹, which departs from near the south end of the Tarn, a pond near Sieur de Monts Spring. (Park either at the spring or just off Route 3 south at the Tarn.) This trail begins with a series of massive stone steps that ascend along a vast slab of granite, then passes through crevasses (not for the wide of girth) and up ladders affixed to the rock face. The views east and south are superb. The trip to the summit of Dorr Mountain is three-fifths of a mile; although short, it's quite demanding. Allow about 1½ hours round-trip.

The **Beehive Trail** ✹✹✹ departs from the Park Loop Road just across from Sand Beach. The trail begins with a fairly gentle climb of one-fifth of a mile, then turns right and begins a demanding ascent up a series of vertiginous ledges, some of which are linked with iron ladders set in the rock. (The layers of ledges give the hill its beehive look—and its name, of course.) From the top (a half mile from the road), hikers get splendid views of Sand Beach and the ocean beyond. Those in dubious physical shape or fearful of heights should steer clear. Allow about 45 minutes for a round-trip hike.

The loop around **Jordan Pond** ✹ is more like a long stroll. Depart from the Jordan Pond House. The east side of the pond features a level trail; the west side is edged by a carriage road. The total loop measures just over 3 miles. At the north end of the pond are a pair of oddly symmetrical mounds called **The Bubbles.** Detours to atop these peaks add about 20 minutes each to the loop; look for signs for these spur pathways off the Jordan Pond Shore Trail. Finish up your hike with tea and popovers at the Jordan Pond House (see "Where to Dine," below).

On the island's west side, an ascent and descent of **Acadia Mountain** ✹✹ takes about 1½ hours, but hikers should allow plenty of time for enjoying the view of Somes Sound and the smaller islands off Mount Desert's southern shores. This 2½-mile loop begins off Route 102 at a trailhead 3 miles south of Somesville. Head eastward through rolling mixed forest, then begin an ascent over ledgy terrain. There are two peaks; the east peak has better views.

MOUNTAIN BIKING   The 57 miles of **carriage roads** ✹✹✹ built by John D. Rockefeller, Jr., are among the park's most extraordinary hidden treasures. (See the park introduction, above, for a brief history.) These were maintained by Rockefeller until his death in 1960, after which they became shaggy and overgrown. A major restoration effort was launched in 1990, and the roads today are superbly restored and maintained. With their wide hard-packed surfaces, gentle grades, and extensive directional signs, they make for very smooth biking. Note that bikes are also allowed on the island's free shuttle buses (see "Getting Around," above).

A useful map of the carriage roads is available free at the visitor centers; more detailed guides may be purchased at area bookshops, but they aren't necessary. Where the carriage roads cross private land (generally between Seal Harbor and Northeast Harbor), they are closed to mountain bikes. Mountain bikes are also banned from hiking trails.

Two areas are especially well-suited for launching mountain-bike trips. Near **Jordan Pond,** a number of carriage roads converge, allowing for a series of loops; several famous stone bridges are in this area. Afterward, enjoy tea at the Jordan Pond House, a popular island destination for over a century (see "Where to Dine," below).

At the north end of **Eagle Lake,** there's parking just off Route 223. From here, carriage roads loop around Eagle Lake to the south, with gentle hills and fine views. To the north of this parking area is a wooded loop around Witch Hole Pond; one of the finest stone bridges is located over a small gorge just off the southeast corner of the loop.

To get a taste of mountain biking without having to load rented bikes onto your car, ask the clerk at any one of the Bar Harbor bike-rental shops about the route to **Witch Hole Pond** via West Street. The route is very steep (don't get discouraged!), but relatively traffic-free and relaxing; take your time, and look forward to coasting back into town once you're done.

Mountain bikes may be rented along Cottage Street in Bar Harbor, with rates around $15 to $17 for 1 day. Ask about closing times, since you may be able to get in a couple extra hours of peddling with a later-closing shop. **Bar Harbor Bicycle Shop,** 141 Cottage St. (© 207/288-3886), is the most convenient and friendliest; you might also try **Acadia Outfitters,** 106 Cottage St. (© 207/288-8118), or **Acadia Bike & Coastal Kayak,** 48 Cottage St. (© 207/288-9605).

CANOEING 🎣 Mount Desert's several ponds offer scenic if limited canoeing, and most have public boat access. Canoe rentals are available at the north end of Long Pond (the largest pond on the island at 3 miles long) in Somesville from **National Park Canoe Rentals** (© 207/244-5854). The cost is $22 for 4 hours. Much of the west shore and the southern tip lie within Acadia National Park. Jet skis are banned in the national park. Note that swimming is prohibited in those ponds that serve as public water reservoirs (which include Bubble, Jordan, Eagle, and the south end of Long Pond).

CARRIAGE RIDES 🎣🎣 Carriage rides are offered by **Wildwood Stables** (© 207/276-3622), a park concessionaire located a half mile south of Jordan Pond House. The 1-hour trip departs three times daily and takes in sweeping ocean views; it costs $13.50 for adults, $7 for children 6 to 12, and $4 for children 2 to 5. Longer tours are available, as is a special carriage designed to accommodate handicapped passengers. Reservations are recommended.

ROCK CLIMBING Rock climbing is allowed only at Otter Cliffs, home to spectacular oceanside rock faces that attract experienced climbers as much for the beauty as for the challenge. **Acadia Mountain Guides,** 198 Main St., at the corner of Mount Desert Street (© 207/288-8186; www.acadiamountain-guides.com), offers climbing lessons and guide services, ranging from a half-day introduction to intensive multi-day workshops on self-rescue and instruction on how to lead climbs. It's open from mid-May to mid-October. (In winter, ice climbing is available by special arrangement.)

SEA KAYAKING 🎣🎣 Sea kayaking has boomed around Mount Desert Island in the past decade. Experienced kayakers arrive in droves with their own boats. Novices sign up for guided tours, which are offered by several outfitters. Many new paddlers have found their inaugural experiences gratifying; others have complained that the quantity of paddlers taken out on quick tours in peak season makes the experience a little too much like a cattle drive to truly enjoy.

A variety of options can be found on the island, ranging from a 2½-hour harbor tour to a 7-hour excursion. Details are available from the following outfitters: **Acadia Outfitters,** 106 Cottage St. (© 207/288-8118); **Coastal Kayaking Tours,** 48 Cottage St. (© 800/526-8615 or 207/288-9605); **Island Adventure Kayak Tours & Rentals,** 137 Cottage St. (© 207/288-3886); and **National Park Sea Kayak Tours,** 39 Cottage St. (© 800/347-0940 or 207/

288-0342). Rates range from approximately $35 to $45 per person for a 2- to 3-hour harbor or sunset tour, up to $75 for a 1-day excursion.

Sea-kayak rentals are available from **Loon Bay Kayaks,** located in summer at Barcadia Campground, at the junction of Routes 3 and 102 (✆ **888/786-0676** or 207/288-0099), which will deliver a boat to you, and from **National Park Canoe Rental,** 1 West St., Bar Harbor (✆ **207/288-0007**). Solo kayaks rent for $32 to $35 per day. With unpredictable weather and squirrelly tides, kayakers should have some prior experience before attempting to set out on their own.

CAMPING

The national park itself offers no overnight accommodations other than two campgrounds. (See the "Bar Harbor" and "Elsewhere on the Island" sections, below, for inns, hotels, and motels.) Both campgrounds are extremely popular; in July and August, expect them to fill by early to mid-morning.

Blackwoods (✆ **207/288-3274**), located on the island's eastern side, tends to fill first. It's got a better location—bikers and pedestrians are just off the Park Loop Road and the rocky shore via a short trail—and, more important, it's the only one of the two that accepts reservations (which are required from mid-May to mid-September). On the downside, the sites here are rather gloomy and dour, set in a dense forest of scrappy fir and spruce. No public showers are available, but an enterprising business just outside the campground entrance offers clean showers for a small fee. Blackwoods is open year-round; late fall through spring, sites are easy to come by. You can reserve up to 5 months in advance by calling ✆ **800/365-2267.** (This is a national reservations service whose contract is reviewed from time to time by the park service; if it doesn't work, call the campground directly to ask for the current toll-free reservation number.) Reservations may also be made online, between 10am and 10pm only, at **http://reservations. nps.gov.** Fees are $18 per night.

First-come, first-served **Seawall** (✆ **207/244-3600**) is on the quieter western half of the island, near the fishing village of Bass Harbor. This is a good base for road biking, and several short coastal hikes are within easy striking distance. Many of the tent sites are walk-ins, which require carrying gear a hundred yards or so. Drive-in RV sites are available, but none have hookups. The campground is open late May through September. In general, if you get here by 9 or 10am, you'll have little trouble securing a site, even in midsummer. (This is especially true if you're a tent camper.) No showers are on-site, but they're available nearby. Fees are $12 to $18 per night.

Private campgrounds handle the overflow. The region south of Ellsworth has 14 private campgrounds; the **Thompson Island Information Center** (✆ **207/ 288-3411**) posts up-to-the-minute information on vacancies. In our opinion, two private campgrounds stand above the rest: **Bar Harbor Campground,** Route 3, Salisbury Cove (✆ **207/288-5185**), is on the main route between the causeway and Bar Harbor and doesn't accept reservations, it has 300 wooded and open sites. At the head of Somes Sound is **Mount Desert Campground,** Route 198 (✆ **207/244-3710**); it's especially well suited for tent campers, who should inquire about the walk-in sites at the water's edge.

WHERE TO DINE

Jordan Pond House ★★ AMERICAN   This is the only full-service restaurant within park borders, and it occupies a spectacular location on a grassy lawn looking northward up Jordan Pond. Originally a teahouse on an early farm, the initial birch-bark dining room was destroyed by fire in 1979, replaced by a modern two-level dining room. It's got less charm, but it still has the island's best location. Afternoon tea with popovers is a hallowed Jordan Pond House tradition. Ladies who lunch sit next to mountain bikers, and everyone feasts on huge, tasty popovers and strawberry jam served with a choice of teas or fresh lemonade. The lobster and crab rolls are abundant and filling; the lobster stew is expensive but very, very good. Dinners include classic resort entrees like prime rib, steamed lobster, and baked scallops with a crumb topping.

Park Loop Rd. (near Seal Harbor), Acadia National Park. © 207/276-3316. Advance reservations not accepted; call before arriving to hold table. Lunch $6.50–$12.75; afternoon tea $6.25–$7.25; dinner $13–$18. AE, DISC, MC, V. Mid-May to late Oct daily 11:30am–8pm (until 9pm July–Aug).

BAR HARBOR

Bar Harbor provides most meals and beds to travelers coming to the island, as it has since the grand resort era of the late 19th century. The region was discovered by wealthy rusticators; later, sprawling hotels and boardinghouses cluttered the shores and hillsides as the newly affluent middle class flocked here by steamboat and rail from Eastern Seaboard cities. At its zenith near the turn of the 19th century, Bar Harbor had rooms enough to accommodate 5,000 visitors.

The tourist business continued to grow throughout the early 1900s, then all but collapsed as the Depression and the growing popularity of car travel doomed the era of steamship travel and the extended vacation. Bar Harbor was dealt a further blow in 1947, when a fire leveled many opulent cottages and much of the rest of the town. In all, some 17,000 acres of the island were burned, though downtown Bar Harbor and many in-town mansions along the oceanfront were spared.

After a period of quiet decay, Bar Harbor has been revived and rediscovered by both visitors and entrepreneurs. The less charitable regard Bar Harbor as just another tacky tourist mecca, filled with T-shirt vendors, ice-cream shops, and souvenir palaces; crowds spill off the sidewalk and into the street in midsummer, and the traffic can be appalling. Yet Bar Harbor's history, distinguished architecture, and beautiful location along Frenchman Bay make it a desirable base for exploring the rest of the island, and it offers the most varied selection of lodging, meals, supplies, and services.

ESSENTIALS

GETTING THERE   Bar Harbor is located on Route 3 about 10 miles southeast of the causeway. **Concord Trailways** (© **800/639-3317**) offers seasonal bus service from Boston and Portland. Concord Trailways also operates a seasonal four-times-daily van shuttle between Bar Harbor and the Bangor International Airport; for details, call © **888/741-8686.**

VISITOR INFORMATION   The **Bar Harbor Chamber of Commerce,** 93 Cottage St. (© **207/288-5103;** www.acadia.net/bhcc) stockpiles a huge arsenal of information. Its website is chock-full of information.

EXPLORING BAR HARBOR

The best water views in town are from the foot of Main Street at grassy **Agamont Park,** which overlooks the town pier and Frenchman Bay. From here, set off past the Bar Harbor Inn on the **Shore Path** ★★, a wide, winding trail that follows the shoreline for half a mile along a public right of way. The pathway

Bar Harbor

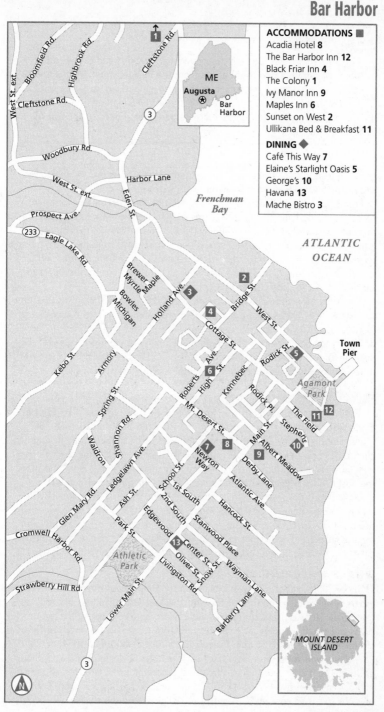

ACCOMMODATIONS ■
Acadia Hotel **8**
The Bar Harbor Inn **12**
Black Friar Inn **4**
The Colony **1**
Ivy Manor Inn **9**
Maples Inn **6**
Sunset on West **2**
Ullikana Bed & Breakfast **11**

DINING ◆
Café This Way **7**
Elaine's Starlight Oasis **5**
George's **10**
Havana **13**
Mache Bistro **3**

Tips **Parking**

If parking spaces are scarce in downtown Bar Harbor, head to the end of Albert Meadow (a side street across from the Village Green). At the end of the road is a small waterfront park with free parking, great views of the bay, and foot access to Shore Path. It's not well marked or well publicized, so you can often find a place to park when much of the rest of town is filled up.

---

passes in front of many elegant summer homes (some converted to inns), offering a superb vantage point to view the area's architecture.

From the path, you'll also have an open view of **The Porcupines,** a cluster of spruce-studded islands just offshore. This is a good spot to witness the powerful force of glacial action. The south-moving glacier ground away at the islands, creating a gentle slope facing north. On the south shore, away from the glacial push (glaciers simply melted when they retreated north), is a more abrupt, clifflike shore. The resulting islands look like a small group of porcupines migrating southward—or so early visitors imagined.

The **Abbe Museum,** 26 Mount Desert St. (© **207/288-3519**), plans to open an extensive 17,000-square-foot gallery showcasing a top-rate collection of Native American artifacts in autumn 2001. (The original museum, next to Sieur de Monts Spring within the park itself, will remain open and unchanged.) The new museum will feature an orientation center and a glass-walled lab where visitors can see archaeologists at work preserving recently recovered artifacts. It will be open in summer, daily from 10am to 5pm; from late fall to Memorial Day, Thursday through Sunday only from 10am to 5pm.

A short stroll around the corner from the Abbe Museum is the **Bar Harbor Historical Society,** 33 Ledgelawn Ave. (© **207/288-0000** or 207/288-3807). Housed in this handsome 1918 former convent are artifacts of life from the resort's glory days. Leave enough time to spend a few minutes thumbing through the scrapbooks about the devastating 1947 fire. The museum is open from mid-June to mid-October, Monday through Saturday from 1 to 4pm; admission is free.

One of downtown's less obvious attractions is the 900-seat **Criterion Theater** ﹖, on Cottage Street (© **207/288-3441**), built in 1932 in Art Deco style. The theater shows first-run movies in summer and is worth the price of admission for the fantastic if somewhat faded interiors. As was the case at most movie palaces in the past, it still costs extra to sit in the more exclusive loges upstairs.

WHALE WATCHING

Humpbacks, finbacks, minke, and (occasionally) right whales migrate to the cool waters offshore each summer to feast on the krill and plankton that well up toward the surface thanks to idiosyncratic ocean bottom topography, vigorous tides, and strong currents. Several operators offer excursions in search of these leviathans. The sleekest is the *Friendship V* ﹖ (© **800/942-5374** or 207/288-2386), which operates from the municipal pier in downtown Bar Harbor. Tours are on a fast, twin-hulled, three-level excursion boat that can hold up to 200 passengers in two heated cabins and on open decks. The tours run 3 hours plus; the cost is $35 per adult. (A puffin and whale-watch tour is offered for $39.) There's free on-site parking, and a money-back guarantee that you'll see whales.

For a slightly more intimate excursion, **Acadian Whale Watcher Co.,** 52 West St. (© **800/421-3307** or 207/288-9794), offers trips on a smaller boat. Ask about puffin and whale combo tours. Rates are comparable to or slightly cheaper than those charged by the *Friendship V.* Free parking is available.

WHERE TO STAY

Bar Harbor is the bedroom community for Mount Desert Island, with hundreds of hotel, motel, and inn rooms. They're invariably filled during the busy days of summer, and even the most basic of rooms can be expensive in July and August. It's essential to reserve as early as possible.

Reputable motels in or near town that offer at least some rooms under $100 in peak season include the conveniently located **Villager Motel,** 207 Main St. (© **207/288-3211**), with 63 rooms; the in-town, pet-friendly **Rockhurst Motel,** 68 Mount Desert St. (© **207/288-3140**); and the smoke-free **Highbrook Motel,** 94 Eden St. (© **800/338-9688** or 207/288-3591).

Expensive

The Bar Harbor Inn 𝕬𝕬   This large and handsome complex is a combination of inn and motel, and has the best location of any lodging in Bar Harbor. Situated on shady waterfront grounds just off downtown Agamont Park and at the start of the Shore Path, it offers both convenience and charm. The rambling shingled inn dates back to the turn of the 19th century and has a settled, old-money feel. Guest rooms in the Oceanfront and Main Inn feature sweeping views of the bay, and many have private balconies; the less expensive Newport building lacks views but is comfortable and up-to-date.

Newport Dr. (P.O. Box 7), Bar Harbor, ME 04609. © 800/248-3351 or 207/288-3351. www. barharborinn.com. 153 units. Peak season $155–$299 double; spring and late fall $75–$205. Rates include continental breakfast. AE, DISC, MC, V. Closed Dec–late Mar. Pets permitted in three rooms ($25 per pet per night). **Amenities:** 2 restaurants (formal dining room, outdoor grill); heated outdoor pool; fitness room; Jacuzzi; limited room service; baby-sitting; laundry service. *In room:* A/C, TV, coffeemaker, hair dryer, iron.

Ivy Manor Inn 𝕬𝕬   Located in a 1940s-era Tudor-style house across from the Village Green, the Ivy Manor offers gracious hospitality with an understated French Victorian style. The rooms are larger than average; most are furnished with antiques. Some units have claw-foot tubs; others have small outdoor sitting decks (none with views). Among our favorites: room 6, a small suite with a private sitting room and small fireplace, and room 1, the honeymoon room with an imposing walnut headboard and matching armoire. Evening cocktails are served up in a cozy first-floor lounge.

194 Main St. Bar Harbor, ME 04609. © 888/670-1997 or 207/288-2138. www.ivymanor.com. 8 units. Peak season $175–$350; off-season $95–$200. Rates include breakfast. AE, DISC, MC, V. 2-night minimum stay on holiday weekends. Closed late Oct to early May. Children over 12 welcome. **Amenities:** Dining room (French/New England). *In room:* A/C, TV.

Sunset on West 𝕬𝕬𝕬   This is precisely what a B&B should be, with gracious hosts, a splendidly renovated 1910 shingled cottage with views of the bay, a good downtown location, and lavish breakfasts. Everything comes together so expertly, you don't notice the lack of usual amenities, like TVs and phones. Common areas include a music room with a baby grand piano and wood-burning fireplace, and a pantry with a guest refrigerator and a selection of teas. Guest rooms feature the plushest towels we've come across, Hammacher Schlemmer robes, down comforters, and VCRs (you can choose from among 200 films in the inn's collection). The Sunset Suite has a sitting room with a gas fireplace and a porch with a water view; Nocturne is a spacious suite perfect for those seeking a getaway. Breakfasts are elaborate, with choices like ricotta hot cakes with blueberries, and crème fraîche scrambled eggs in dill crepes with smoked salmon.

115 West St., Bar Harbor, ME 04609. ✆ **207/288-4242**. Fax 207/288-4545. www.sunsetonwest.com. 4 units. Peak season $175–$275; off-season $150–$235. Rates include breakfast. MC, V. Closed Nov–Mar. Children 16 and over welcome. *In room:* VCR, no phone.

Moderate

Black Friar Inn 🔆 This shingled structure with quirky pediments and an eccentric air offers good value for Bar Harbor. A former owner "collected" interiors and installed them throughout the house. Among them are a replica of the namesake Black Friar Pub in London, complete with elaborate carved-wood paneling (it's now a common room); stamped tin walls in the breakfast room; and a doctor's office (now a guest room). Guest rooms, most of which are quite small, are furnished with a mix of antiques. The least expensive are the two garret rooms on the third floor, each with a detached private bathroom down the hall.

10 Summer St., Bar Harbor, ME 04609. ✆ **207/288-5091**. Fax 207/288-4197. www.blackfriar.com. 7 units (3 with private hall bathrooms). $90–$150 double. Rates include breakfast. DISC, MC, V. 2-night minimum stay mid-June to mid-Oct. Closed Dec–May. Children 12 and over welcome. *In room:* A/C, no phone.

Maples Inn 🔆🔆 This is a popular destination with outdoor enthusiasts. You'll often find guests swapping stories of the day's adventures on the front porch, or lingering over breakfast to compare notes on trails. The architecturally modest (by Bar Harbor standards) farmhouse-style inn is tucked away on a leafy side street among other B&Bs; it's an easy walk downtown. The innkeepers make guests feel comfortable, with board games and paperbacks scattered about. The guest rooms aren't huge, but you're not likely to feel cramped, either. The two-room White Birch has a fireplace and is the largest; White Oak has a private deck. Breakfasts are appropriately filling for a full day outdoors.

16 Roberts Ave., Bar Harbor, ME 04609. ✆ **207/288-3443**. www.maplesinn.com. 6 units (1 with private hall bathroom). Mid-June to mid-Oct $90–$150 double; off-season $60–$95. Rates include breakfast. DISC, MC, V. 2-night minimum stay on holiday weekends. No small children accepted. *In room:* No phone.

Ullikana Bed & Breakfast 🔆 This 1885 Tudor cottage is tucked on a side street near Agamont Park and the Bar Harbor Inn. The 10-bedroom "cottage" is solidly built, and the downstairs with its oak trim and wainscoting is dark in an English-gentleman's-club kind of way. The guest rooms are varied in size, but all are spacious and nicely decorated in a country Victorian mode, some with iron or brass beds. Audrey's Room has a pleasant, storybook feel to it, with pastel colors, high ceilings, and a cozy bathroom with a claw-foot tub. Summery room 6 has a deck with glimpses of the bay, along with a sofa and claw-foot tub for relaxing. Across the lane is the attractive Yellow House, which has six additional rooms simpler in style than the main cottage.

16 The Field, Bar Harbor, ME 04609. ✆ **207/288-9552**. www.ullikana.com. 10 units (2 with detached bathroom), plus 6 across street in Yellow House. $135–$235 double ($185 in Yellow House). Rates include breakfast. MC, V. Closed mid-Oct to early May. Children 8 and over welcome. *In room:* No phone.

Inexpensive

Acadia Hotel 🔆 The Acadia's main advantage is its location: right on the Village Green, easily accessible to in-town activities and free shuttles to everywhere else on the island. This handsome home dating from the late 19th century has a wraparound porch and guest rooms decorated in a country-floral motif that some may find frilly. The rooms vary widely in size and amenities; two have whirlpools, two have phones, and one has a kitchenette. The smaller units offer good value for those who don't plan to spend much time indoors.

20 Mount Desert St., Bar Harbor, ME 04609. (C) **888/876-2463** or 207/288-5721. www.acadiahotel.com. 10 units. Peak season $75–$150 double; off-season $45–$135. MC, V. *In room:* A/C, TV, no phone (except in 2 units).

The Colony (*Value*) This vintage motor court consists of a handful of motel rooms (starting at $95) and a battery of cottages arrayed around a long green. It will be appreciated mostly by those with a taste for the authentically retro; others will prefer accommodations that are more lavishly appointed. The rooms are furnished in a spare 1970s style; many have kitchenettes. It's situated just across Route 3 from a cobblestone beach, and a 10-minute drive from Bar Harbor.

Rte. 3 (P.O. Box 56), Hulls Cove, ME 04644. (C) **800/524-1159** or 207/288-3383. thecolony@acadia.net. 55 units. $65–$105 double (discounts in Oct). AE, DISC, MC, V. Closed mid-Oct to early June. *In room:* A/C, TV.

WHERE TO DINE

Café This Way ★★ NEW AMERICAN   Café This Way has the feel of a casually hip coffeehouse; bookshelves line one wall, and there's a small bar tucked in a nook. The breakfasts are excellent and mildly sinful, with offerings like eggs Benedict with spinach, artichoke, and tomato. The red-skinned potatoes are crispy and delicious; the robust coffee requires two creamers to lighten it. Dinners are equally appetizing, with tasty dishes like butternut-squash ravioli, crab cakes with a tequila-lime sauce, and filet mignon grilled with fresh basil.

14½ Mount Desert St. (C) **207/288-4483.** Reservations recommended for dinner. Main courses $3.25–$5.95 breakfast, $12–$19 dinner. MC, V. Summer Mon–Sat 7–11am and 6–9pm; Sun 8am–1pm.

Elaine's Starlight Oasis ★ VEGETARIAN   Bar Harbor's only fully vegetarian restaurant, Elaine's opened in 1998 and has been happily embraced by herbivorous visitors. Located near the waterfront in a cozy, contemporary space, the menu includes house specialties "beef" burgundy (made with seitan) and a Jamaican jerk tofu served with herb-roasted vegetables. Other offerings on the menu include salads, mushroom lasagna, eggplant casserole, and tempeh Parmesan.

78 West St. (C) **207/288-3287.** Reservations not accepted. Main courses $6.95–$12.95. Wed–Mon 5pm–9:30pm (closes earlier in off-season). Closed Nov–May 1.

George's ★★★ CONTEMPORARY MEDITERRANEAN   For more than 2 decades, this has been a Bar Harbor classic, offering fine dining in elegant yet informal surroundings. Located in a clapboard cottage behind Main Street's First National Bank, George's captures the joyous feel of summer with four smallish dining rooms (and plenty of open windows) and additional seating on the terrace. The service is upbeat, the meals wonderfully prepared. All entrees sell for one price ($25), which includes salad, vegetable, and potato or rice. You won't go wrong with basic choices, like steamed lobster or roast chicken, but you're better off opting for more adventurous fare like lobster strudel or mustard shrimp. The house specialty is lamb in its many incarnations, including char-grilled lamb tenderloin with a rosemary-infused three bean ragout.

7 Stephens Lane. (C) **207/288-4505.** www.georgesbarharbor.com. Reservations recommended. Entrees $25; appetizer, entree, and dessert $37–$40. AE, DISC, MC, V. Daily 5:30–10pm; shorter hours after Labor Day. Closed Nov to early May.

Havana ★★ LATINO/FUSION   Havana established a new creative standard when it opened in 1999 in this town of fried fish and baked stuffed haddock. The spare but sparkling decor in the old storefront is as classy as you'll find in

Lobster Pounds & Shacks

The best lobster restaurants are those right on the water which have few pretensions or frills. The ingredients for a proper feed at a local lobster pound are: a pot of boiling water, a tank of lobsters, some well-worn picnic tables, a good view, and a six-pack of beer, preferably Maine-brewed.

Among the best in the area is **Beal's Lobster Pier,** in Southwest Harbor (✆ **207/244-7178**), which is one of the oldest pounds in the area. **Thurston's Lobster Pound,** in tiny Bernard across the water from Bass Harbor (✆ **207/244-7600**), was atmospheric enough to be used as a backdrop for the Stephen King miniseries *Storm of the Century;* it's a fine place to linger toward dusk.

Abel's Lobster Pound, 5 miles north of Northeast Harbor on Route 198 (✆ **207/276-5827**), overlooks the deep blue waters of Somes Sound; eat at picnic tables under the pines or indoors at the restaurant. (This is the most expensive lobster restaurant on the island; you're paying for atmosphere and better service.)

On the mainland just north of the causeway is the **Oak Point Lobster Pound** (✆ **207/667-6998**). This is off the beaten path (although still popular and often crowded), where you can eat your lobster with a sensational view of the island's rocky hills. To get here, turn west off Route 3 onto Route 230 before crossing the causeway to Mount Desert, then continue 4 miles to the restaurant.

Boston, and the menu could compete in any urban area as well. Expect appetizers like crab and roasted corn cakes with a cilantro sour cream, or sweet potato ravioli with a crabmeat-chipotle béchamel sauce. Recent entrees included ale-roasted rack of lamb; grilled tuna served with a tequila, lime, and habanero glaze; and baked snapper with a mango-chili sauce served over coconut rice.

318 Main St. ✆ 207/288-2822. Reservations recomended. Main courses $12–$28. AE, DC, DISC, MC, V. Daily 5:30–10pm. Closed Jan–Mar.

Mache Bistro ★★ BISTRO   Since opening in 2000, Mache has developed a devoted following among those who know quality food and preparation. The small restaurant (nine tables) with soothing but plain decor hides a sophisticated kitchen. (One wouldn't expect an imported cheese course offered in a place with plywood floors, but that's what you get.) The menu changes monthly; appetizers may include a salad with bleu cheese, apples, and truffle oil. Main courses recently featured a seared steak with black trumpet infused jus, and a Brittany fisherman's soup made with local seafood.

135 Cottage St. ✆ 207/288-0447. Reservations recommended. Main courses $16–$22. AE, MC, V. Daily 6–10pm. Closed Jan–Apr.

ELSEWHERE ON THE ISLAND

There's plenty to explore outside of Acadia National Park and Bar Harbor. Quiet fishing villages, deep woodlands, and unexpected ocean views are among the jewels that turn up when one ventures beyond the usual places.

ESSENTIALS

GETTING AROUND   The east half of the island is best navigated on Route 3, which forms the better part of a loop from Bar Harbor through Seal Harbor and past Northeast Harbor before returning up the eastern shore of Somes Sound. Route 102 and Route 102A provide access to the island's western half. See information on the free islandwide shuttle service under "Getting Around," in the section on Acadia National Park, above.

VISITOR INFORMATION   The best source of information on the island is at the **Thompson Island Information Center** (© 207/288-3411), on Route 3 just south of the causeway connecting Mount Desert Island with the mainland. Another source of local information is the **Mount Desert Chamber of Commerce** (© 207/276-5040).

EXPLORING THE REST OF THE ISLAND

On the tip of the eastern lobe of Mount Desert Island is the staid, prosperous community of **Northeast Harbor** 🏵🏵, long one of the favored retreats among the Eastern Seaboard's upper crust. Those without personal invitations to come as houseguests will need to be satisfied with glimpses of the shingled palaces set in the fragrant spruce forests and along the rocky shore. But the village itself is worth investigating.

One of the best, least publicized places for enjoying views of the harbor is from the understatedly spectacular **Asticou Terraces** 🏵 (© 207/276-5130). Finding the parking lot can be tricky: Head a half mile east (toward Seal Harbor) on Route 3 from the junction with Route 198, and look for the small gravel lot on the water side of the road with a sign reading ASTICOU TERRACES. Park here, cross the road on foot, and set off up a magnificent rock path that ascends the sheer hillside with expanding views of the harbor and town. This pathway, with its precise stonework and the occasional bench and gazebo, is one of the nation's hidden marvels of landscape architecture. Created by Boston landscape architect Joseph Curtis, who summered here for many years prior to his death in 1928, the pathway seems to blend in almost preternaturally with its spruce-and-fir surroundings. Continue on the trail at the top of the hillside and you'll soon arrive at Curtis's cabin (open to the public daily in summer), behind which lies the formal **Thuya Gardens** 🏵🏵, which are as neatly manicured as the terraces are scruffy-natural. These wonderfully maintained gardens attract flower enthusiasts, students of landscape architecture, and folks just looking for a quiet place to rest. It's well worth the trip. A donation of $2 is requested of visitors to the garden; the terraces are free.

From the harbor, visitors can depart on a seaward trip to the beguilingly remote **Cranberry Islands** 🏵🏵. You have a couple of options: Travel with a national park guide to Baker Island, the most distant of this small cluster of low islands, and explore the natural terrain. Or hop one of the ferries to either Great or Little Cranberry islands and explore on your own. On Little Cranberry, there's a small historical museum run by the National Park Service that's worth

---

Tips A Scenic Drive

Sargent Drive is the most scenic route out of Northeast Harbor. This one-way route runs through Acadia National Park lands along the shore of Somes Sound, affording some of the best views of this glacially carved inlet.

a few minutes. Both islands feature a sense of being well away from it all, but neither offers much in the way of shelter or tourist amenities; travelers should head out prepared for the possibility of shifting weather. For ferry information, contact **Beal & Bunker** (ⓒ **207/244-3575**), which departs from Northeast Harbor ($10 round-trip for adults, $5 for children under 12).

WHERE TO STAY

The Claremont ★★ The Claremont offers nothing fancy—just simple, classic New England grace. Early prints of the 1884 building show an austere four-story wooden structure with a single gable overlooking Somes Sound from a grassy rise. And the place hasn't changed much since. It seems appropriate that the state's most combative croquet tournament takes place here annually in early August; all those folks in their whites are right at home. The common areas are appointed in an affable country style. There's a library with rockers, a fireplace, and jigsaw puzzles waiting to be assembled. Most guest rooms are bright and airy, furnished with antiques and some furniture that's simply old; bathrooms are modern. Guests opting for the full meal plan are given preference in reserving rooms overlooking the water; it's almost worth it, although dinners are lackluster.

P.O. Box 137, Southwest Harbor, ME 04679. ⓒ **800/244-5036** or 207/244-5036. www.theclaremonthotel. com. 42 units. July–Labor Day $150 double including breakfast, $225 double including breakfast and dinner, $165–$185 cottage; off-season $89 double including breakfast, $190 double including breakfast and dinner, $100–$150 cottage. 3-day minimum stay in cottages. No credit cards. Closed mid-Oct to early June. **Amenities:** Clay tennis court; rowboats; bicycles (free); baby-sitting. *In room:* No phone.

Lindenwood Inn ★★ The Lindenwood is a refreshing change from the fusty, overly draperied inns along Maine's coast. Housed in a handsome 1902 Queen Anne–style home at the harbor's edge, the rooms are clean and uncluttered, the colors simple and bold. The adornments are few (those that do exist are mostly from the innkeeper's collection of African and Pacific art), but simple lines and bright natural light more than create a relaxing mood. The spacious suite with its great harbor views is especially appealing. If you're on a budget, ask for a room in the annex, housed in an 1883 home just a minute's walk down the block. Its rooms are somewhat smaller and unadorned, but still offer nice touches. Eight rooms feature fireplaces; most also have phones, but ask when you book if this is important to you.

118 Clark Point Rd. (P.O. Box 1328), Southwest Harbor, ME 04679. ⓒ **207/244-5335**. www. lindenwood.com. 23 units. June to mid-Oct $95–$245 double; mid-Oct to June $75–$195. Rates include breakfast. AE, MC, V. **Amenities:** Heated outdoor pool; Jacuzzi; boat dock. *In room:* No phone (except in some units).

WHERE TO DINE

For a quick bite or a picnic lunch, seek out the tiny **Docksider Restaurant,** 14 Sea St. (ⓒ **207/276-38965**), hidden a block off Northeast Harbor's compact downtown. The crab rolls and lobster rolls are outstanding, both made simply and perfectly. There's also lobster dinners, sandwiches, chowder, and grilled salmon.

Keenan's ★ *Value* SEAFOOD Boisterous, inelegant, and fun. That's the short description of this classic seafood shack at a fork in the road far from the water. It's long been one of those local secrets that most travelers zip by. Yet it's worth slowing down for some of the best seafood value for your money on the island. The fried clams are well prepared, and the spicy gumbo packs a kick.

Rte. 102A, Bass Harbor. ⓒ **207/244-3403**. Reservations recommended for parties of five or more. Sandwiches and main courses $5–$17. No credit cards. Summer daily 5–9pm; off-season Sat–Sun 5–9pm.

Restaurant XYZ ★★ AUTHENTIC MEXICAN   Restaurant XYZ doesn't promise much at first: It's on the ground floor beneath a motel, and the interior is adorned with imports from Mexico that might best be described as "stuff." But the food! Drawing on the traditions of central Mexico and the Yucatan, the fare is spicy, earthy, and tangy. Expect a savory mole and a chipotle salsa that sings. Start with one of the stand-out margaritas and peruse the appetizers, which include a seafood cocktail made with octopus, scallops, shrimp, and avocado. Among the more inviting entrees are a pork loin baked in a sauce of ancho, guajillo, and chipotle chilies, and chilies stuffed with corn and cheese. Aficionados of authentic Mexican cooking will be delightfully surprised to find such excellent dining deep behind the lines of boiled lobster and fried clams.

Shore Rd., Manset. © 207/244-5221. Reservations recommended. Main courses $15. MC, V. July–Aug daily 5:30–9pm; June and Sept–Oct Fri–Sat 5:30–9pm. Closed Columbus Day–Memorial Day.

7 The Western Lakes & Mountains

Maine's western mountains create a rugged, brawny region that stretches northeast from the White Mountains to the Carrabassett Valley. It isn't as commercialized as the Maine coast, and the villages aren't as quaint as you'll find in Vermont's Green Mountains. But it has azure lakes, ragged forests of spruce and fir, and rolling hills and mountains that take on a distinct sapphire hue during the summer hiking season.

Cultural amenities are few here, but natural amenities are many. Hikers head for the famed Appalachian Trail, which crosses into Maine in the Mahoosuc Mountains (near where Route 26 enters into New Hampshire) and follows rivers and ridgelines northeast to Bigelow Mountain and beyond. Canoeists and anglers strike for the noted Rangeley Lakes area, a chain of deepwater ponds and lakes. And in winter, skiers can choose among several downhill ski areas, including the two largest in the state, Sunday River and Sugarloaf.

BETHEL ★★

Until the mid-1980s, Bethel was a sleepy resort town with one of those family-oriented ski areas that seemed destined for certain extinction. Then a guy named Les Otten came along. This brash young entrepreneur bought the Sunday River ski area for a song and proceeded to make it into one of New England's most vibrant ski destinations before buying up other major ski areas, including Killington, Attitash, Sugarbush, Sugarloaf, and Mount Snow. (Otten's American Skiing Corp. was planning to merge with a hotel management company at press time, becoming part of the hospitality conglomerate Doral International.)

With the rise of Sunday River, the white-clapboard town of Bethel (located about 7 miles from the ski area) has been dragged into the modern era, although it hasn't yet taken on the artificial, packaged flavor of many other New England ski towns. The village, population 2,500, is still defined by the stoic buildings of the respected prep school Gould Academy, the broad village common, and the Bethel Inn, a sprawling, old-fashioned resort that's managed to stay ahead of the tide by adding condos, but without losing its pleasant, timeworn character.

ESSENTIALS
GETTING THERE   Bethel is located at the intersection of Routes 26 and 2. It's accessible from the Maine Turnpike by heading west on Route 26 from Exit 11. From New Hampshire, drive east on Route 2 from Gorham.

VISITOR INFORMATION The **Bethel Area Chamber of Commerce,** 30 Cross St. (© **800/442-5826** for lodging reservations, or 207/824-2282; www.bethelmaine.com), has offices behind the Casablanca movie theater. It's open year-round, Monday through Friday from 9am to 7pm, Saturday from 10am to 6pm, and Sunday from noon to 5pm.

Across Route 2 from the chamber, the **state tourism office,** 18 Mayville Rd. (© **207/824-4582**), has paired up with the White Mountain National Forest district office. You can stock up on brochures from across the state and get information on activities in the national forest. Open in peak season, daily from 8am to 6pm; in the off-season, Thursday through Tuesday from 8:30am to 5pm.

EXPLORING LOCAL HISTORY

Stately, historic homes ring the **Bethel Common** ⍟⍟, a long, rectangular green created in 1807 atop a low, gentle ridge. The town's **historic district** encompasses some 27 homes, which represent a wide range of architectural styles popular in the 19th century.

The oldest home in the district is the 1813 **Moses Mason House** ⍟, home of the **Bethel Historical Society** (© **207/824-2908**). Mason was a doctor and local civic leader, and was willing to try anything once, including building his Federal-style house on a stone foundation. His compatriots assured him that the house would topple over in a gale. It didn't, and all local houses were soon built on stone foundations. Mason also commissioned an itinerant painter—possibly the renowned landscape artist Rufus Porter—to paint his foyer and stairwell. The result is an engagingly primitive panorama of boats at anchor in a calm harbor. View numerous artifacts of the early 19th century while exploring both the home and the exhibits in an adjacent 1821 home. The house and museum, at 10–14 Broad St., are open in July and August, Tuesday through Sunday from 1 to 4pm. Admission is $2 for adults and $1 for children.

ALPINE SKIING

Sunday River Ski Resort ⍟⍟⍟   Sunday River has grown at stunning speed in recent years, and in our opinion is the best ski mountain in New England for terrain and conditions. (The resort scene, however, sorely lags, and the staff can be surly.) Unlike ski areas that have developed around a single tall peak, Sunday River has expanded along an undulating ridge some 3 miles wide that encompasses seven peaks. Just traversing the resort, stitching runs together with chairlift rides, can take an hour or more. As a result, you'll rarely get bored making the same run time and again. The descents offer something for virtually everyone, from deviously steep bump runs to wide, wonderful intermediate trails. Sunday River is also blessed with plenty of water for snowmaking, and makes tons of the stuff using a proprietary snowmaking system. The superb skiing conditions are, alas, offset by an uninspiring base area. The lodges and condos (total capacity 6,000) tend toward the architecturally dull, and the less-than-delicate landscaping is of the sort created by bulldozers. Sunday River's trails are often crowded on weekends; weekdays you'll have the place to yourself.

P.O. Box 450, Bethel, ME 04217. © 800/543-2754 for lodging, or 207/824-3000. www.sundayriver.com. Vertical drop: 2,340 ft. Lifts: 15 chairlifts (4 high-speed), 3 surface lifts. Skiable acreage: 654. Lift tickets: $51 Sat–Sun, $49 Mon–Fri.

Ski Mt. Abram   Mount Abram is a welcoming intermediate mountain that's perfect for families still ascending skiing's learning curve. It has a friendly, informal atmosphere that sharply contrasts with bustling and impersonal Sunday

River nearby. It's been financially troubled of late; a new owner purchased the mountain at auction at press time and plans (and prices) for the coming year were uncertain.

P.O. Box 120, Locke Mills, ME 04255. © **207/875-5003**. Vertical drop: 1,030 ft. Lifts: 2 chairlifts, 3 T-bars. Skiable acreage: 135. Lift tickets (as of 2000): $32 Sat–Sun, $20 Mon–Fri.

OTHER OUTDOOR PURSUITS

Grafton Notch State Park ✦✦ straddles Route 26 as the road angles northwest from Newry toward Errol, N.H. The picturesque and dramatic 33-mile drive between the two towns is one of our favorites. You initially pass through farmland in a fertile river valley before ascending through bristly forest to a handsome glacial notch hemmed in by cliffs on the towering hillsides above. Foreboding Old Speck Mountain towers to the south; views of Lake Umbagog open to the north as you continue into New Hampshire. This route attracts few crowds, although it's popular with Canadians headed to the Maine coast.

Public access to the park consists of a handful of roadside parking lots near scenic areas. The best of the bunch is **Screw Auger Falls,** where the Bear River drops through several small cascades before tumbling dramatically into a narrow, corkscrewing gorge long ago carved out of granite bedrock by glacial runoff. Picnic tables dot the forested banks upriver of the falls, and kids seem inexorably drawn to splash and swim in the smaller pools on warm days. Admission to the park is $1; look for self-pay stations at the parking lot.

HIKING   The **Appalachian Trail** crosses the Mahoosuc Mountains northwest of Bethel. Many of those who've hiked the entire 2,000-mile trail say this stretch is the most demanding on knees and psyches. The trail doesn't forgive; it generally foregoes switchbacks in favor of sheer ascents and descents. It's also hard to find water along the trail during dry weather. Still, it's worth the knee-pounding effort for the views and the unrivaled sense of remoteness.

One stretch crosses the summit of **Old Speck Mountain** ✦, Maine's third-highest peak. Views from the summit are all but nonexistent since the old fire tower closed a few years back, but an easy-to-moderate spur trail on the lower end of the trail gently ascends an 800-foot cliff called **"The Eyebrow"** ✦✦ and provides an excellent vantage point for Bear River Valley and the rugged terrain of Grafton Notch. Look for the well-signed parking lot where Route 26 intersects the trail in Grafton Notch State Park. Park your car, then head south on the A.T. toward Old Speck; in 0.1 mile you'll intersect the Eyebrow Trail, which you can follow to the overlook.

The Appalachian Mountain Club's *Maine Mountain Guide* is highly recommended for detailed information on other area hikes.

WHERE TO STAY

The Bethel Inn ✦   The Bethel Inn is a classic, old-fashioned resort set on 200 acres in the village. It has a quiet, settled air, which is appropriate since it was built to house patients of Dr. John Gehring, who put Bethel on the map treating nervous disorders through a regimen of healthy country living. (Bethel was once known as "the resting place of Harvard" for the legions of faculty treated here.) The quaint, homey rooms aren't terribly spacious, but they are pleasingly furnished with country antiques. More luxurious are the 16 modern rooms and suites added to the inn in 1998. You give up some of the charm of the old inn, but gain elbowroom. The dining room remains the resort's Achilles' heel—the preparation and service often fail to live up to the promise of the surroundings.

On the Common, Bethel, ME 04217. © **800/654-0125** or 207/824-2175. www.bethelinn.com. 56 units. $198–$318 double; from $358 suite. Rates include breakfast and dinner. 2-night minimum stay summer weekends and ski season; 3-night minimum during winter school vacations. Ski packages available. AE, DISC, MC, V. Pets accepted ($30). **Amenities:** Dining room (continental); outdoor heated pool; nearby lake swimming; modern fitness center; 18-hole golf course; hardtop tennis courts; whirlpool; sauna; cross-country skiing; shuttle to ski areas; baby-sitting; laundry service. *In room:* TV.

Black Bear Bed & Breakfast ★ This 1830s farmhouse in a rural setting is a great choice for those seeking a casual spot to rest up between ski runs or hikes. The rooms vary in size, but are furnished in a simple country style with lots of light streaming through oversize windows. The new upstairs great room is bright and looks out on the hills behind the inn; the downstairs common room is a good spot to chat with other guests. But the chief amenity is the location: It's on 8 acres in a lovely dead-end valley. You can be on the ski slopes at Sunday River within 5 minutes, yet it feels like you're far off in the country by nightfall. In summer, guests splash around in the river or the pool, or set off on mountain-biking and hiking rambles up the valley into the national forest.

Sunday River Rd. (P.O. Box 55), Bethel, ME 04217. © **888/299-5487** or 207/824-0908. www.bbearbandb.com. 6 units. Winter $90–$105 double (including breakfast); summer $80–$90 double. 2-night minimum stay on ski season weekends. AE, MC, V. Closed May. Pets allowed; ask first. **Amenities:** Heated pool (summer only); hardtop tennis court; hot tub. *In room:* No phone.

The Victoria ★★ Built in 1895 and damaged by lightning some years back, the inn was superbly restored in 1998, complete with antique lighting fixtures, period furniture, and the original formidable oak doors. The guest rooms have a luxurious William Morris feel, with richly patterned wallpaper and handmade duvet covers. Room 1 is the luxurious master suite, with a turret window and a sizable bathroom; room 3 is the only unit with wood floors (the others are carpeted), but it has a tiny bathroom. Most intriguing are the four loft rooms in the attached carriage house, each with gas fireplace, Jacuzzi, and soaring ceilings revealing old beams.

32 Main St., Bethel, ME 04217. © **888/774-1235** or 207/824-8060. www.thevictoria-inn.com. 15 units. Winter $178–$298 double; summer $158–$278. Rates include breakfast and dinner. 2-night minimum stay on weekends and holidays. AE, MC, V. **Amenities:** Restaurant (see below). *In room:* A/C, TV, dataport.

WHERE TO DINE

Great Grizzly/Matterhorn ★ STEAKHOUSE/BRICK-OVEN PIZZA These two restaurants share a handsome timber-frame structure a couple of minutes from the ski area. It's casual and relaxed, with pinball, a pool table, and a handsome bar. You'll get two menus after you settle in: Great Grizzly offers mostly steaks, while Matterhorn specializes in wood-fired pizzas, and they're very, very good. The atmosphere is more relaxed and the food significantly better than at the Sunday River Brewing Company down the road, and the beer-on-tap selection doesn't suffer much for not being a brewpub.

Sunday River Rd. © **207/824-6271** or 207/824-6836. Pizzas $7.95 and up; other entrees $6.95–$16.95. MC, V. Daily pizza 3–10pm; steakhouse menu from 5pm. Open only during ski season.

The Victoria ★★ NEW AMERICAN The dining room on the first floor of Bethel's classiest inn happens to serve the town's best dinners. Guests are seated in one of two intimate rooms, where they choose from a delectable menu offering creative fare. House specialties include the New Zealand rack of lamb and a sinful marinated duck, which is maple-roasted and served with an apple-cider-cardamon sauce. This is Bethel's best pick for a romantic dinner out.

32 Main St. ℂ **888/774-1235** or 207/824-8060. www.thevictoria-inn.com. Reservations recommended on weekends. Entrees $17.95–$24.95. AE, MC, V. Wed–Mon 5:30–9pm.

RANGELEY LAKES ★★

Mounted moose heads on the walls, log cabins tucked into spruce forest, and cool August mornings that sometimes require not one sweater but two are the stuff of the Rangeley Lakes region. Although **Rangeley Lake** ★★ and its eponymous town are at the heart of the region, its borders extend much farther, consisting of a series of lakes that feed into and flow out of the main lake.

The town of **Rangeley** ★★ (pop. 1,200) is the regional center for outdoor activities. It offers a handful of motels and restaurants, a bevy of fishing guides, and little else. Attractions in the Rangeley area are few, and most regular tourists and residents seem determined to keep it that way. The wise visitor rents a cabin or takes a room at a lodge, then explores the area with the slow pace that seems custom-made for the region. Rangeley is Maine's highest town at an elevation of 1,546 feet, and usually remains quite cool throughout the summer.

ESSENTIALS

GETTING THERE   Rangeley is 122 miles north of Portland, and 39 miles northwest of Farmington on Route 4.

VISITOR INFORMATION   The **Rangeley Lakes Region Chamber of Commerce** (ℂ **800/685-2537** or 207/864-5364; www.rangeleymaine.com) maintains an information booth in town at a small park near the lake. It's open year-round Monday through Saturday from 9am to 5pm.

MUSEUMS & HISTORIC HOMES

Orgonon ★★★   Among the few historic sites in Maine relating to the 20th century is Orgonon, former home of the controversial Viennese psychiatrist Wilhelm Reich (1897–1957). An associate of Sigmund Freud, Reich took Freud's work a few steps further, building on the hypothesis that pent-up sexual energy resulted in numerous neuroses. Reich settled in Rangeley in 1942, where he developed the science of "orgonomy." According to Reich, living matter was animated by a sort of life force called "orgone," which floated freely in the atmosphere. To cure orgone imbalances, he invented orgone energy boxes, which were said to gather and concentrate ambient orgone. These boxes were just big enough to sit in. Reich was sentenced to federal prison for matters related to the interstate transport of his orgone boxes. He died in prison in 1957. While many dismissed Reich's theories as quackery, he still has dedicated adherents, including those who maintain the museum in his memory.

Orgonon, built in 1948 of native fieldstone, has a spectacular view of Dodge Pond and is designed in a distinctive mid-century modern style, which stands apart from the local rustic-lodge motif. Visitors on the 1-hour guided tour can view the orgone boxes along with other intriguing inventions.

Dodge Pond Rd. (3¹⁄₂ miles west of Rangeley off Rte. 4). ℂ **207/864-3443**. Admission $4 adults, free for children under 12. July–Aug Tues–Sun 1–5pm; Sept Sun 1–5pm.

ALPINE SKIING

Saddleback Ski Area ★   With only two chairlifts, Saddleback qualifies as a small mountain, but it has an unexpectedly big-mountain feel. It offers a vertical drop of just 1,830 feet, but what makes Saddleback so appealing is its rugged Alpine setting (the Appalachian Trail runs across the high, mile-long ridge above the resort) and the old-fashioned trails (the ski area was founded in 1960).

Saddleback offered glade skiing and narrow, winding trails well before the bigger ski areas sought to re-create these old-fashioned slopes. Condos and town houses offer limited on-mountain lodging; the ski mountain is about 7 miles from the village of Rangeley.

P.O. Box 490, Rangeley, ME 04970. ℂ 207/864-5671. www.saddlebackskiarea.com. Vertical drop: 1,830 ft. Lifts: 2 double chairlifts, 3 T-bars. Skiable acreage: 100. Lift tickets: $47 Sat–Sun, $36 Mon–Fri.

OTHER OUTDOOR PURSUITS

CANOEING   The Rangeley Lakes region is a canoeist's paradise. Azure waters, dense forests, and handsome hills are all part of the allure. Rangeley Lake itself is populated along much of the lakeshore, but the cottages are well-spaced, and the lakeshore has a wild aspect to it. **Rangeley Lakes State Park** (ℂ 207/864-3858), on the south shore of the lake, has a cleared area for launching boats; a day-use fee is charged. You can also paddle right from downtown Rangeley, or use the public landing on the far northwest corner of the lake, at the intersection of Routes 16 and 4 near Oquossuc, which also offers easy canoe access to Cupsuptic and Mooselookmeguntic lakes from Haines Landing. For canoe rentals, try **Bald Mountain Camps** (ℂ 207/864-3671) in Oquossoc, or **Dockside Sports Center** (ℂ 207/864-2424) on Main Street in Rangeley.

Vast Mooselookmeguntic Lake suffered an unfortunate period of haphazard lakeshore development in recent years on some of its southeastern coves, but much of the shore, especially along the west shore, is still remote and appealing. Note that capricious winds can come up suddenly, however, so be prepared and strive to stay close to shore. The **Stephen Phillips Wildlife Preserve** (ℂ 207/864-2003) on Mooselookmeguntic Lake rents canoes by the day and is one of the best jumping-off points to explore the wild lakes. A good day trip is out to the tip of Students Island, where there's an open field, spectacular views northwestward up the lake, and a great spot for a picnic.

HIKING   The Appalachian Trail crosses Route 4 about 10 miles south of Rangeley. A strenuous but rewarding hike is along the trail northward to the summit of **Saddleback Mountain** ★★, a 10-mile round-trip that ascends through thick forest and past remote ponds to open, arctic-like terrain with fine views of the surrounding mountains and lakes. Saddleback actually consists of two peaks over 4,000 feet (hence the name). Be prepared for sudden shifts in weather, and for high winds that often rake the open ridgeline.

An easier 2-mile (round-trip) hike may be found at **Bald Mountain** ★, near the village of Oquossuc on the northeast shore of Mooselookmeguntic Lake. (Look for the trailhead 1 mile south of Haines Landing on Bald Mountain Road.) The views have grown over in recent years, but you can still catch glimpses of the clear blue waters from above.

WHERE TO STAY

Rangeley Inn ★★   The architecturally eclectic Rangeley Inn dominates Rangeley's miniature downtown. Parts of this hotel date back to 1877, but the main wing was built in 1907, with additions in the 1920s and the 1940s. A motel annex is behind the inn on Haley Pond, but those looking for creaky floors and a richer sense of local heritage should request a room in the main inn. Some units in the motel have woodstoves, kitchenettes, or whirlpools; in the inn, you'll find a handful of rooms with claw-foot tubs. Phones are offered in motel rooms only. During the heavy tour season (especially fall), expect bus groups.

P.O. Box 160, Rangeley, ME 04907. ℭ **800/666-3687** or 207/864-3341. Fax 207/864-3634. www. rangeleyinn.com. 50 units. $84–$120 double. 2-night minimum stay winter weekends. AE, DISC, MC, V. Pets allowed in one room ($8 per night). **Amenities:** Two restaurants (traditional, pub fare). *In room:* TV, no phone (in main lodge).

Town & Lake Motel and Cottages   This basic, old-fashioned compound offers a wonderful location right on the lake just outside Rangeley. Don't set your expectations too high for the motel rooms, circa 1954—they're worn but clean, and some beds are weary. Motel rooms have optional kitchens ($10 additional per night). The two-bedroom cottages offer better value—all but one are right on the lake, and they feature large windows with lake views, crate-style 1970s-era furnishings, front porches, and full-size kitchens.

112 Main St. (P.O. Box 47), Rangely, ME 04970. ℭ **207/864-3755.** 25 units. $65–$75 motel double; $120–$160 cottage (sleeps up to four). AE, DISC, MC, V. Pets allowed. **Amenities:** Lake swimming; canoes (free); motorboats (extra fee). *In room:* TV, coffeemaker.

CARRABASSETT VALLEY

The region in and around the Carrabassett Valley can be summed up in six words: big peaks, wild woods, deep lakes. The crowning jewel of the region is **Sugarloaf Mountain,** Maine's second-highest peak at 4,237 feet. Distinct from nearby peaks because of its pyramidal shape, the mountain has been developed for top-notch skiing and offers the largest vertical drop in Maine, the best selection of activities, and a wide range of accommodations.

While Sugarloaf draws the lion's share of visitors, it's not the only game in town. Nearby **Kingfield** is an attractive, historic town with a venerable old hotel; it has more of the character of an Old West outpost than of classic New England. Other valley towns offering limited services for travelers include **Eustis, Stratton,** and **Carrabassett Valley.**

Outside the villages and ski resort, it's all rugged hills, tumbling streams, and spectacular natural surroundings. The muscular mountains of the **Bigelow Range** provide terrain for some of the state's best hiking. And **Flagstaff Lake** is the place for flat-water canoeing amid majestic surroundings.

ESSENTIALS

GETTING THERE   Kingfield and Sugarloaf are on Route 27. Skiers debate over the best route from the turnpike. Some exit at Auburn and take Route 4 north to Route 27; others exit in Augusta and take Route 27 straight through. It's a toss-up time-wise, but exiting at Augusta is marginally more scenic. **Maine Tour and Travel** (ℭ **800/649-5071**) offers a private shuttle service from state airports to the mountain.

VISITOR INFORMATION   For information on skiing or summer activities in the Sugarloaf area, contact the resort at ℭ **800/843-5623** or 207/237-2000. A seasonal information booth on Route 27 is staffed in summer and winter.

ALPINE SKIING

Sugarloaf/USA ★★★   Sugarloaf is Maine's big mountain, with the highest vertical drop in New England after Vermont's Killington. And thanks to quirks of geography, it actually feels bigger than it is. From the high, open snowfields or the upper advanced runs like Bubblecuffer or White Nitro, skiers develop vertigo looking down at the valley floor. Sugarloaf attracts plenty of experts to its hard-core runs, but it's also a fine intermediate mountain. Sugarloaf may be the friendliest resort in New England—the staff on the lifts, in the restaurants, and at the hotels all seem genuinely glad you're here. It's also a very friendly family mountain, with lots of activities for kids. The main drawback? Wind. Sugarloaf seems to get buffeted regularly, with the higher lifts often closed because of gusting.

RR #1, Box 5000, Carrabassett Valley, ME 04947. (℃ 800/843-5623 or 207/237-2000. www.sugarloaf.com. Vertical drop: 2,820 ft. Lifts: 13 chairlifts, including 2 high-speed quads; 1 surface lift. Skiable acreage: 1,400 (snowmaking on 475 acres). Lift tickets: $51.

CROSS-COUNTRY SKIING

The **Sugarloaf Outdoor Center** ★ (℃ 207/237-6830) offers 63 miles of groomed trails that weave through the village at the base of the mountain and into the low hills and scrappy woodlands along the Carrabassett River. The trails are impeccably groomed for striding and skating, and wonderful views open here and there to Sugarloaf Mountain and the Bigelow Range. The base lodge is simple and attractive, all knotty pine with a cathedral ceiling, and features a cafeteria, towering stone fireplace, and well-equipped ski shop. Snowshoes are also available for rent. Trail fees are $15 for adults, $10 for seniors and children 12 and under. (Half-day tickets are also available). The center is located on Route 27 about 1 mile south of the Sugarloaf access road. A shuttle bus serves the area in winter.

HIKING

The 12-mile-long Bigelow Range is home to some of the most dramatic high-ridge hiking in the state, a close second to Mount Katahdin. It consists of a handful of lofty peaks, with Avery Peak (the east peak) offering the best views. On exceptionally clear days, hikers can see Mount Washington to the southwest and Mount Katahdin to the northeast. This is terrain for experienced hikers, since it's not that hard to make a wrong turn and end up lost. Bring a compass or GPS.

A strenuous but rewarding excursion for fit hikers is the 10.3-mile loop that begins at the **Fire Warden's Trail.** (The trailhead is at the washed-out bridge on Stratton Brook Pond Road, a rugged dirt road that leaves eastward from Route 27 about 2⅓ miles north of the Sugarloaf access road.) Follow the Fire Warden's Trail up the steep ridge to the junction with the **Appalachian Trail.** Head south on the A.T., which tops the West Peak and South Horn, two open summits with stellar views. A quarter mile past Horns Pond, turn south on **Horns Pond Trail** and descend back to the Fire Warden's Trail to return to your car. Allow about 8 hours for the loop; a topographic map and hiking guide are strongly recommended.

Detailed directions for these hikes and many others in the area may be found in the AMC's *Maine Mountain Guide.*

OTHER OUTDOOR PURSUITS

Sugarloaf's 18-hole **golf course** ★★★ (℃ 207/237-2000) is often ranked number one in the state by experienced golfers, who are lured here by the Robert Trent Jones, Jr., course design and dramatic mountain backdrop. Sugarloaf hosts a well-respected golf school during the season.

Other outdoor activities can be arranged through the **Sugarloaf Outdoor Center** (℃ 207/237-6830): fly-fishing lessons, a mountain-bike excursion, or hiking or white-water rafting in the surrounding mountains and valleys.

WHERE TO STAY & DINE

For convenience, nothing beats staying right on the mountain in winter. Many of the base-area condos are booked through the **Sugarloaf/USA Inn** (℃ 800/843-5623 or 207/237-2000). **Sugarloaf** also operates a lodging reservation service, booking guest rooms and private homes, mostly off mountain; call ℃ 800/843-2732.

Grand Summit Hotel ★★   This is a great choice for skiers who want to be in the thick of it in winter, although it's a bit sleepy during the summer. Located next to the lifts in the heart of the Sugarloaf base area, this attractive, contemporary hotel offers three types of guest rooms. Standard rooms are tucked under sharply angled gables and are a bit dark; the one-bedroom suites (with full kitchens) are divided between two floors, with an upstairs bedroom connected via a narrow spiral staircase. The superior rooms (best value) are brightest and most open, with kitchenettes and small sitting areas. The odd-numbered rooms face the slopes, while even-numbered rooms face across the valley with views of distant hills. The ground floor features a lively pub; a free winter shuttle service connects to other restaurants around the resort.

Sugarloaf base area (RR 1, Box 2299), Carrabassett Valley, ME 04947. ✆ 207/237-2222. Fax 207/237-2874. www.sugarloaf.com. 119 units. Peak ski season $139–$224 double, to $650 suite; off-season from $114. AE, MC, V. Minimum stay required some holiday weekends. **Amenities:** Restaurant (pub fare); 18-hole golf course; health club; Jacuzzi; sauna; bike rental (nearby); baby-sitting. *In room:* A/C, TV, coffeemaker, hair dryer, iron.

The Herbert   The Herbert has the feel of a classic North Woods hostelry—sort of Dodge City by way of Alaska. Built in downtown Kingfield in 1918, the three-story hotel featured all of the finest accoutrements when it was constructed, including fumed oak paneling and incandescent lights in the lobby (look for the original brass fixtures), a classy dining room, and comfortable guest rooms. Under new ownership, the rooms are gradually getting an overdue makeover, and plans are in the works for a new indoor pool and fitness center to be built off the back of the building starting in summer 2001. The Herbert is located about 15 miles from the slopes at Sugarloaf/USA.

Main St. (P.O. Box 67), Kingfield, ME 04947. ✆ 207/265-2000. Fax 207/265-4594. www.mainemountain-inn.com. 27 units. $59 double midweek; $99 weekend; $110 holiday. Rates include continental breakfast. 3-night minimum stay during holidays. AE, DISC, MC, V. Pets allowed; some restrictions apply. **Amenities:** Restaurant (family-style); new indoor pool; fitness room; and Jacuzzi slated for late 2001. *In room:* No phone.

WHERE TO DINE

Hug's ✿ NORTHERN ITALIAN   This is a small place, set just off the highway in a fairy-tale cottage, and the food is better than one would expect for a ski-area Italian restaurant. Dinner is preceded by a tasty basket of pesto bread, and entrees go beyond red sauce, offering a broad selection of pastas. (The wild-mushroom ravioli with walnut-pesto Alfredo is very good.)

Rte. 27 (0.7 miles south of the Sugarloaf access road), Carrabassett Valley. ✆ 207/237-2392. Reservations recommended, especially on weekends. Main courses $11.95–$17.95. DISC, MC, V. Winter daily 5–10pm; summer and fall Wed–Sun 5–10pm. Closed May to late July and mid-Oct to early Dec.

8 Moosehead Lake Region ★★

Thirty-two miles long and 5 miles across at its widest, Moosehead Lake is Maine's largest lake, and the region holds strong appeal for hikers, boaters, and canoeists. The lake was historically the center of the region's logging activity; that history has largely preserved it from second-home development and kept it mostly unspoiled. Timber companies still own much of the lakeside property (although the state has acquired significant amounts recently), and the 350-mile shoreline is unbroken second- or third-growth forest. The second-home building frenzy of the 1980s had an impact on some of the southern reaches of the lake, but the woody shoreline has absorbed most of the boom rather gracefully.

The first thing to know about the lake is that it's not meant to be seen by car. There are some great views from a handful of roads—especially from Route 6/15 as you near Rockwood, and from the high elevations on the way to Lily Bay—but for the most part the roads are a distance from the shores, and offer rather dull driving. To see the lake at its best, you should plan to get out on the water by steamship or canoe. If you prefer your sightseeing by car, you'll find more rewarding drives in the western Maine mountains or along the coast.

Greenville ★ is the de facto capital of Moosehead Lake, scenically situated at the southern tip. Change is creeping into the north woods—what was until recently a rugged outpost town is now orienting itself toward the tourist trade with boutiques and souvenir shops. But it's not a fussy place, and it's a good spot to base yourself for outdoor day excursions.

ESSENTIALS

GETTING THERE   Greenville is 158 miles from Portland. Take the turnpike to the Newport exit (Exit 39) and head north on Route 7/11 to Route 23 in Dexter, following that northward to Route 6/15 near Sangerville. Follow this to Greenville.

VISITOR INFORMATION   The **Moosehead Lake Chamber of Commerce** (𝄞 **207/695-2702;** www.mooseheadarea.com) maintains a helpful information center that's a recommended first stop. Not only will you find a good selection of the usual brochures, but the center also maintains files and bookshelves full of maps, trail information, wildlife guidebooks, and videos that visitors are free to use. From Memorial Day to mid-October, it's open Wednesday through Monday from 10am to 4pm; it's located on your right as you come into Greenville, next to the Indian Hill Trading Post.

EXPLORING MOOSEHEAD LAKE

Northwood Outfitters, on Main Street in Greenville (𝄞 **207/695-3288;** www. maineoutfitter.com), is open daily and can help you plan a trip on the lake or into the woods, as well as load you up with enough equipment to stay out for weeks. It rents complete sets of adventure equipment, including canoe, paddles, life jacket, tent, sleeping bag, pad, camp stove, ax, cook kit, and more. The full kits start at $115 per person for 2 days, up to $325 per person for a week. Shuttle service and individual pieces of equipment are also available for rent, with canoes running $20 a day, mountain bikes from $20 to $30 a day.

Mount Kineo ★★ is that massive cliff that rises from the shores of Moosehead across the lake from the village of Rockwood. This hike begins with a boat trip across the lake; near Rockwood, look for signs advertising boat shuttles to Kineo from the town landing (folks offering this service seem to change from year to year, so ask around; it typically costs about $5). Once on the other side, explore the grounds of the famed old Kineo Mountain House (the grand 500-room hotel was demolished in 1938), then walk across the (active) golf course and follow the shoreline to the trail that leads to the 1,800-foot summit. The views from the cliffs are dazzling. Be sure to continue on the trail to the old fire tower, which you can ascend for a hawk's-eye view of the region.

MOOSE WATCHING ★★

In the past several years, about a half dozen outfitters have cropped up offering excursions along lakeshores and forest trails in search of the wily moose, the region's most noted woodland resident. While you can see moose almost anywhere (keep a sharp lookout when driving!), a guided excursion will get you into some of the most beautiful spots in the region, hidden places you might not see otherwise. The moose-spotting batting average is quite high among all outfitters. Call ahead to reserve. The folks at the visitor information center can provide more information about these tours and can help make arrangements.

Pontoon boats are the most comfortable vehicles to search for moose—a trip is like sitting in an outdoor living room that floats. **The Moose Cruise,** at the Birches Resort in Rockwood (© **207/534-7305**), offers three excursions daily, each lasting a bit over 2 hours. Prices are $25 per adult, $15 per child.

Moose-watching excursions of 4 to 5 hours by canoe are offered by the **Maine Guide Fly Shop,** in Greenville (© **207/695-2266**), and **Ed Mathieu** (© **207/876-4907**). Prices run from $25 for a shorter tour up to $95 for a 5-hour excursion (lunch or snacks included).

WHITE-WATER RAFTING ★★★

Big waves and boiling drops await rafters on the heart-thumping run through Kennebec Gorge at the headwaters of the **Kennebec River,** located southwest of Greenville. Dozens of rafters line up along the churning river below the dam, then await the siren that signals the release. Your guide will signal you to hop in, and you're off, heading off through huge, roiling waves and down precipitous drops with names like Whitewasher and Magic Falls. Most of the excitement is over in the first hour; after that, it's a lazy trip down the river, interrupted only by lunch and the occasional water fight with other rafts. Also nearby is the less thrilling but more technical Dead River, which offers about a half dozen release dates, mostly during early summer.

Commercial white-water outfitters offer trips in summer at a cost of about $85 to $115 per person (usually at the higher end on weekends). **Northern Outdoors** (© **800/765-7238**; www.northernoutdoors.com) is the oldest of the bunch, and offers rock-climbing, mountain-biking, and fishing expeditions as well, plus snowmobiling in winter. Other reputable rafting companies include **Wilderness Expeditions** (© **800/825-9453**), which is affiliated with the rustic Birches Resort, and the **New England Outdoor Center** (© **800/766-7238**).

MOOSEHEAD BY STEAMSHIP ★★

During the lake's golden days of tourism in the late 19th century, visitors would arrive at the lake by train from New York or Washington, then connect with steamship to the resorts and boardinghouses that ringed the lake.

A vestige of that era is found at the **Moosehead Marine Museum** (© **207/695-2716**), in Greenville. A handful of displays suggest the grandeur of life at Kineo Mountain House, a sprawling Victorian lake resort that once defined elegance. But the small museum's showpiece is the S.S. *Katahdin,* a 115-foot steamship that's been cruising Moosehead's waters since 1914. The two-deck ship offers a variety of sightseeing tours, including an excursion up the lake to the site of the former Kineo Mountain House. Fares vary depending on the length of the trip; they range from $12 to $25 for adults, and $6 to $13 for children 6 and over.

WHERE TO STAY & DINE

Blair Hill Inn ★★★   This unexpectedly classy inn amid the wilds occupies an 1891 hilltop Queen Anne mansion with dazzling views of Moosehead Lake and the surrounding hills. It's been sparely and elegantly decorated with a mix of rustic and classic appointments, like Oriental carpets and deer-antler lamps. The bright first-floor common rooms, the drop-dead-gorgeous porch, and the handsome guest rooms invite loafing. All units features terry robes, spring water, and locally made soaps. Room 1 is the best—it's the former master bedroom, featuring a panoramic sunset view and fireplace (Duraflame logs only). All guests can enjoy the outdoor Jacuzzi, Adirondack chairs on the lawn, and a small catch-and-release trout pond (ask about fly-fishing workshops).

Lily Bay Rd. (P.O. Box 1288), Greenville, ME 04441. ⓒ **207/695-0224.** www.blairhill.com. 8 units. June–Oct $175–$265 double; Nov–May $195–$250. Rates include breakfast. DISC, MC, V. 2-night minimum stay on weekends. Closed Nov and Apr. Children over 10 welcome. **Amenities:** Restaurant (fine dining); Jacuzzi. *In room:* Hair dryer, no phone.

Greenville Inn ★★ This handsome 1895 Queen Anne lumber baron's home sits regally on a hilly side street above Greenville's commercial district. The interiors are sumptuous, with wonderful cherry and mahogany woodworking and a lovely stained-glass window over the stairwell. At the handsome small bar, you can order up a cocktail or Maine beer, then sit in front of the fire or retreat to the front porch to watch the evening sun slip over Squaw Mountain and the lake. Six modern cottages on the grounds have TVs and offer more privacy. A European-style breakfast buffet includes homemade breads and pastries.

Norris St., Greenville, ME 04441. ⓒ **888-695-6000** or 207/695-2206. www.greenvilleinn.com. 12 units. Summer $135–$155 double, $165 cottage, $225 suite; off-season $125–$145 double, $155 cottage, $195 suite. Rates include continental breakfast. DISC, MC, V. 2-night minimum stay on holiday weekends. No children under 8 accepted. **Amenities:** Restaurant (continental/regional). *In room:* No phone.

Little Lyford Pond Camps ★ This venerable backwoods logging camp is one of the more welcoming spots in the North Woods—at least for those looking to rough it a bit. Originally built to house loggers in the 1870s, each rustic cabin contains a small woodstove, propane lantern, cold running water, and outhouse. At mealtimes, guests gather in the main lodge, which has books to browse and board games for evenings. During the day, activities aren't hard to find, from fishing for native brook trout (fly-fishing lessons available) and hiking with the lodge's llamas to canoeing at two nearby ponds or wandering on the Appalachian Trail to Gulf Hagas, a scenic gorge 2 miles away. In winter, the cross-country skiing on the lodging's private network is superb, and time spent in the sauna will make you forget the cold weather outside. Access is via rough logging road in summer (ski or snowmobile in winter), so factor in extra time in getting there.

P.O. Box 340, Greenville, ME 04441. ⓒ **207/280-0016** (cell phone). www.littlelyford.com. 8 units. $170 double. Rates include all meals. No credit cards. 2-night minimum stay on weekends and holidays. Pets allowed ($5 per day). **Amenities:** Sauna; canoes (free). *In room:* No phone.

Appendix:
New England in Depth

by Wayne Curtis

Reduced to simplest terms, New England consists of two regions: Boston and Not-Boston.

Boston, of course, is in the same league as other major metropolitan areas, and boasts first-class hotels, elegant historic and modern architecture, and world-class restaurants. Of all U.S. cities, Boston has perhaps the richest history, ranging from the days of America's settlement in the 17th century through the War of Independence in 1776 and on into the nation's cultural renaissance in the mid– and late 19th century. The Boston area is also a national seat of education, with dozens of prestigious colleges and universities including Harvard, MIT, Wellesley, and Boston University. The presence of so many august institutions lends the city a youthful air in contrast to its fusty heritage.

The extensive territory of Not-Boston arcs widely, from the Connecticut and Rhode Island shoreline through the rolling Berkshire Mountains of western Massachusetts on through the Green and White mountains and into the vast state of Maine. The Not-Boston region, while widely spread, traces it roots back to a Puritan ethic, and its longtime residents still tend to display shared traits and values, like a stubborn independence, a respect for thrift, and an almost genetic mistrust of outsiders.

New England's legendary aloofness is important to keep in mind when visiting the area, because getting to know the region requires equal amounts of patience and persistence. New England doesn't wear its attractions on its sleeve. It keeps its best destinations hidden in valleys and on the side streets of small villages. Your most memorable experience might come in cracking open a boiled lobster at a roadside lobster pound marked only with a scrawled paper sign, or exploring a cobblestone Boston alley that's not on the maps. There's no Disneyland or Space Needle or Grand Canyon here. New England is the sum of dozens of smaller attractions, and resists being defined by a few big ones.

Which isn't to say that New England lacks attractions. It has the mansions of Newport, the endless beaches of Cape Cod, the rolling Green Mountains of Vermont, the craggy White Mountains of New Hampshire, and magnificent Acadia National Park on the Maine coast. It has wonderful, lost-in-time towns like New Preston, Conn., and Woodstock, Vt. But attempting to explore New England as a "connect-the-dots" endeavor, linking the major sights with long drives, is a surefire recipe for disappointment. It's better to plan a slower itinerary that allows you to enjoy the desultory trips between destinations, to explore the little villages and quiet byways. What you'll find mostly is an inviting blend of history, both human and natural.

Some writers maintain that New England's character is still informed by a grim Calvinist doctrine, which decrees nothing will change one's fate and that hard work is a moral virtue. The New Englander's dull acceptance that the Boston Red Sox will never be victorious is often trotted out as evidence of the region's enduring Calvinism, as is the inhabitants' perverse celebration of the often brutish climate.

But that's not to say travelers should expect rock-hard mattresses and nutritional but tasteless meals. On the contrary, luxurious country inns and restaurants serving food rivaling what you'll find in Manhattan have become part of the landscape in the past two decades. Be sure to visit these places. But to get the most out of your trip, leave enough time to spend an afternoon rocking and reading on a broad inn porch, or to wander out of town on an abandoned county road with no particular destination in mind.

"There's nothing to do here," an inn manager in Vermont once explained to me. "Our product is indolence." That's an increasingly rare commodity these days. Take the time to savor it.

1 New England Today

It's a common question, so don't be embarrassed about asking it. You might be on Martha's Vineyard, or traveling through a pastoral Vermont valley, or exploring an island off the Maine coast. You'll see houses and people. And you'll wonder: "What do these people do to earn a living?"

As recently as a few decades ago, the answer was probably this: living off the land. They might have fished the seas, harvested timber in the forest, operated a truck farm, or managed a gravel pit. Of course, many still do operate such businesses, but this work is no longer the economic mainstay it once was. Today, scratch a rural New Englander and you're just as likely to find an editor for a magazine that's published in Boston or New York, a farmer who grows specialized produce for gourmet restaurants, or a banking consultant who handles business by fax and e-mail. And you'll find lots of folks dependent on tourism—innkeepers and motel owners and restaurateurs and shopkeepers.

This change in the economy is but one of the tectonic shifts facing the region. The most visible and more wracking change involves development and growth. A region long familiar with economic poverty, the recent prosperity has threatened to bring to New England that curious sort of homogenization that has marked much of the nation. Instead of distinctive downtowns and courthouse squares, the landscape in New England is starting to look a lot like suburbs everywhere—a pastiche of strip malls dotted with fast-food chains and big-box stores like Wal-Mart and Home Depot.

New England towns have long maintained their strong identities in the face of considerable pressure. The region has always taken a quiet pride in its low-key, practical approach to life. In smaller communities, town meetings are still the preferred form of government. Residents gather in a public space in town, usually in the grim season of February or March, and vote on the important issues of the day, like funding for their schools, road improvements, and, at times, symbolic gestures, such as declaring their town a nuclear-free zone. "Use it up, wear it out, make do, or do without" is a well-worn phrase that aptly sums up the attitude of many in New England.

It's as yet unclear how town meetings and that sense of knowing where your town starts and the next one begins will survive the slow but inexorable encroachment of the Wal-Marts. Of course, suburban Connecticut communities in the orbit of New York City and Massachusetts towns just outside of Boston have long since capitulated to sprawl, as have pockets elsewhere in the region—including the areas near Hartford, Conn.; Portland, Maine; and Burlington, Vt.—where little regional identity can be discerned.

But the rest of New England is still figuring out how best to balance the principles of growth and conservation—how to allow the economy to edge into the modern age, without sacrificing those qualities that make New England such a distinctive place.

Development is a hot but not necessarily inflammatory issue—this isn't like the property rights movement in the West, where residents are manning the barricades and taking hostages for the cause. (At least not yet.) Few seem to think that development should be allowed at all costs. And few seem to think that the land should be preserved at all costs.

Pinching off all development means the offspring of longtime New England families will have no jobs, and New England will be fated to spend its days as a sort of quaint theme park. But if development continues unabated, many of the characteristics that make New England unique—and attract tourist dollars—will vanish. Will the Berkshires or the Maine coast be able to sustain their tourism industries if they're blanketed with strip malls and fast-food joints, making them look like every other place in the nation? Not likely. The question is how to respect the conservation ethic while leaving room for growth. And that question won't be resolved in the near future.

New England's heady 5-year economic boom in the late 1980s, which fueled much of the debate over development, slowed in the 1990s, making the issue less urgent but no less critical. Commentators point out that other social changes on the horizon could raise new conflicts. The rise of the information culture will make it increasingly likely that those telecommuters and info-entrepreneurs will settle in remote and pristine villages, running their businesses via modem and satellite. How will these affluent migrants adapt to clear-cutting in the countryside or increasing numbers of tour buses cruising their village greens?

Change doesn't come rapidly to New England. But there's a lot to sort out, and friction will certainly build, one strip mall at a time.

2 History 101

Viewed from a distance, New England's history mirrors that of its namesake, England. The region rose from nowhere to gain tremendous historical prominence, captured a good deal of overseas trade, and became an industrial powerhouse and center for creative thought. And then the party ended relatively abruptly, as commerce and culture sought more fertile grounds to the west and south.

To this day, New England refuses to be divorced from its past. Walking through Boston, layers of a varied history are evident at every turn, from the church steeples that remain powerful icons of colonial times (despite being dwarfed by glass-sided skyscrapers) to verdant parklands that bespeak the refined sensibility of the late Victorian era.

Dateline

- **1000–15** Viking explorers land in Canada, and may or may not have sailed southward to New England. Evidence is spotty.
- **1497** John Cabot, seeking to establish trade for England, reaches the island of Newfoundland in Canada and sails south as far as Maine.
- **1602** Capt. Bartholomew Gosnold lands on the Massachusetts coast. Names Cape Cod, Martha's Vineyard, and other locations.
- **1604** French colonists settle on an island on the St. Croix River between present-day Maine and New Brunswick. They leave after a single miserable winter.
- **1614** Capt. John Smith maps the New England coast, names the Charles River after King Charles I of England, and calls the area a paradise.

continues

History is even more inescapable in off-the-beaten-track New England. Travelers in Downeast Maine, northern New Hampshire, Connecticut's Litchfield Hills, the Berkshires of Massachusetts, and much of Vermont will find clues to what Henry Wadsworth Longfellow called "the irrevocable past" every way they turn, from stone walls running through now-dense woods to spectacular Federal-style homes standing alone in the countryside.

Here's a brief overview of some historical episodes and trends that shaped New England:

INDIGENOUS CULTURE   Native Americans have inhabited New England since about 7000 B.C. While New York's Iroquois Indians had a presence in Vermont, New England was inhabited chiefly by Algonquins known as Abenakis ("people of the dawn"), who lived a nomadic life, moving with the seasons and traveling to areas where food was abundant. What is now Boston was home to several Algonquin tribes, who dwelled along the coast and rivers; Connecticut was home to some 16 Algonquin tribes, who dubbed the region Quinnetukut.

After the arrival of the Europeans, French Catholic missionaries succeeded in converting many Native Americans, and most tribes sided with the French in the French and Indian Wars in the 18th century. Afterward, the Indians fared poorly at the hands of the British, and were quickly pushed to the margins. Today, they are found in greatest concentration at several reservations in Maine, including Indian Island in the Penobscot River, and two Passamaquoddy reservations near the Canadian border in Washington County. The Pequots have established a thriving gaming industry in Connecticut. Other than that, the few clues left behind by Indian cultures have been more or less obliterated by later settlers.

- **1616** Smallpox kills large numbers of Indians between Maine and Rhode Island.
- **1620** The *Mayflower,* carrying some 100 colonists (including many Pilgrims, fleeing religious persecution in England), arrives at Cape Cod.
- **1630** Colonists led by John Winthrop establish the town of Boston, named after an English village.
- **1635–36** Roger Williams is exiled from Massachusetts for espousing liberal religious ideas; he founds the city of Providence, R.I.
- **1636** Harvard College is founded to educate young men for the ministry.
- **1638** America's first printing press is established in Cambridge.
- **1648** First labor unions are established by coopers and shoemakers in Boston.
- **1675–76** Native Americans attack colonists throughout New England in what is known as King Philip's war.
- **1692** The Salem witch trials take place. Twenty people (including 14 women) are executed before the hysteria subsides.
- **1704** America's first regularly published newspaper, the *Boston News Letter,* is founded.
- **1713** The first schooner, a distinctively American sailing ship, is designed and built in Gloucester, Mass.
- **1764** "Taxation without representation" is denounced in reaction to the Sugar Act.
- **1770** Five colonists are killed outside what is now the Old State House in an incident known as the Boston Massacre.
- **1773** British ships are raided by colonists poorly disguised as Indians during the Boston Tea Party. More than 300 chests of tea are dumped into the harbor from three British ships.
- **1775** On April 18, Paul Revere and William Dawes spread the word that the British are marching toward Lexington and Concord. The next day the "shot heard 'round the world" is fired. On June 17, the British win the Battle of Bunker Hill but suffer heavy casualties.

continues

THE COLONIES In 1604, some 80 French colonists spent a winter on a small island at the mouth of the St. Croix River on what today is the Maine–New Brunswick border. They did not care for the harsh weather of their new home, and left in spring to resettle in present-day Nova Scotia. In 1607, 3 months after the celebrated Jamestown, Virginia, colony was founded, a group of 100 English settlers established a community at Popham Beach, Maine. The Maine winter demoralized these would-be colonists as well, and they returned to England the following year, leaving little trace of their sojourn.

The colonization of the region began in earnest with the arrival of the Pilgrims at Plymouth Rock in 1620. The Pilgrims—a religious group that had split from the Church of England—established the first permanent colony, although it came at a hefty price: Half the group perished during the first harsh winter. But the colony took root, and thrived over the years in part thanks to helpful Native Americans.

The success of the Pilgrims lured other settlers from England, who established a constellation of small towns outside of Boston that became the Massachusetts Bay Colony. Roger Williams was expelled from the colony for his religious beliefs; he founded the city of Providence, R.I. Other restless colonists expanded their horizons in search of lands for settlement. Throughout the 17th century, colonists from Massachusetts pushed northward into what is now New Hampshire and Maine, and southward into Connecticut. The first areas to be settled were lands near protected harbors along the coast and on navigable waterways.

The more remote settlements came under attack in the 17th and early 18th centuries in a series of raids by the American Indians against the

- **1783** Treaty of Paris is signed, formally concluding the American Revolution.
- **1788** Connecticut becomes the fifth, Massachusetts the sixth, and New Hampshire the ninth state to formally join the union.
- **1790** Rhode Island becomes the 13th state and the final colony to ratify the constitution.
- **1791** The short-lived Republic of Vermont (1777–91) ends and the state of Vermont joins the union.
- **1812** War of 1812 with England batters New England economy.
- **1814** The nation's first textile mill is built, in Waltham, Mass.
- **1820** Maine, formerly a district of Massachusetts, becomes a state.
- **1835** Samuel Colt of Connecticut develops the six-shooter pistol.
- **1861** Massachusetts Institute of Technology is founded.
- **1892** America's first gasoline-powered automobile is built in Chicopee, Mass.
- **1897** First Boston Marathon is run; Boston completes first American subway.
- **1903** The first World Series is played; Boston Red Sox win.
- **1918** The Red Sox celebrate another World Series victory. For the next eight decades (and counting), they fail to repeat this feat.
- **1930** America's Cup sailing race first held in Newport, R.I.
- **1930s** The Great Depression devastates New England's already reeling industrial base.
- **1938** A major hurricane sweeps into New England, killing hundreds and destroying countless buildings and trees.
- **1942** A fire at Boston's Cocoanut Grove nightclub kills 491 people.
- **1946** John F. Kennedy is elected to Congress to represent Boston's First congressional district.
- **1957** Boston Celtics win their first NBA championship, laying the groundwork for a reign that will eventually include 16 championships.
- **1963** New Hampshire becomes first state to establish a lottery to support education.

continues

British settlers—conducted both independently and in concert with the French. These proved temporary setbacks; colonization continued apace throughout New England into the 18th century.

THE AMERICAN REVOLUTION
Starting around 1765, Great Britain launched a series of ham-handed economic policies to reign in the increasingly feisty colonies in America. These included a direct tax—the Stamp Act—to pay for a standing army

- **1966** Edward Brooke of Massachusetts becomes the first African American elected to the U.S. Senate since Reconstruction.
- **1972** Maine's Indians head to court, claiming the state illegally seized their land in violation of a 1790 act. They settle 8 years later for $81.5 million.
- **1974** In Connecticut, Ella Grasso becomes the first elected woman governor.
- **1991** The Big Dig begins in Boston. Scheduled completion date: 2004.

(created largely to curb the thriving colonial trade in smuggled goods). The crackdown provoked strong resistance. Under the banner of "No taxation without representation," disgruntled colonists engaged in a series of riots, resulting in the Boston Massacre of 1770, when five protesting colonists were fired upon and killed by British soldiers.

In 1773, the most infamous protest took place in Boston. The British had imposed the Tea Act (the right to collect duties on tea imports), which prompted a group of colonists dressed as Mohawk Indians to board three British ships and dump 342 chests of tea into the harbor. This well-known incident was dubbed the Boston Tea Party.

Hostilities reached a peak in April 1775, when the British sought to quell burgeoning unrest in Massachusetts. A contingent of British soldiers was sent to Lexington to seize military supplies and arrest two high-profile rebels—John Hancock and Samuel Adams. The militia formed by the colonists exchanged gunfire with the British, thereby igniting the revolution ("the shot heard 'round the world.").

Notable battles in New England included the Battle of Bunker Hill outside Boston, which the British won but at tremendous cost; and the Battle of Bennington in Vermont, in which the colonists prevailed, thereby ending the British strategy of dividing the colonies and fighting on one front, then the other. Hostilities formally ended in February 1783, and in September, Britain recognized the United States as a sovereign nation.

FARMING & TRADE   As the new republic matured, economic growth in New England followed two tracks. Residents of inland communities survived by clearing the land for farming and trading in furs. Vermont in particular has always been an agrarian state, and remains a prominent dairy producer to this day.

On the coast, boat yards sprang up from Connecticut to Maine, and ship captains made tidy fortunes trading lumber for sugar and rum in the Caribbean. Trade was dealt a severe blow and coastal economies sent into a tailspin following the Embargo Act of 1807 (which sharply limited trade), but commerce eventually recovered, and New England ships could be encountered everywhere around the globe.

The growth of the railroad throughout New England in the mid–19th century was another boon. The train opened up much of the interior, and led to towns springing up overnight, like White River Junction, Vt. The rail lines allowed local resources—such as the fine marbles and granites from Vermont—to be easily shipped to markets to the south.

INDUSTRY   New England's industrial revolution found seed around the time of the embargo of 1807. Barred from importing English fabrics, Americans had to build their own textile mills to obtain cloth. Other common household products were also manufactured domestically, especially shoes, which became an industrial mainstay for decades. Towns like Lowell, Mass.; Lewiston, Maine; and Manchester, N.H., became centers of textile and shoe production. In Connecticut, the manufacture of arms and clocks emerged as lasting and major industries.

Industry no longer plays the prominent role it once did in New England—manufacturing first moved to the southern United States, then overseas. The main manufacturing centers include computer makers around Boston, and paper mills in Maine, but far more New England residents are today employed by service providers and government than by manufacturers.

TOURISM   In the mid– and late 19th century, New Englanders discovered a new cash crop: the tourist. All along the Eastern Seaboard, it became fashionable for the gentry and eventually the working class to set out for excursions to the mountains and the shore. Regions like the White Mountains of New Hampshire, the Berkshires, Vermont's Green Mountains, the southern Maine coast, and Block Island were lifted by the tide of summer visitors. The 19th-century tourism wave crested in the 1890s in Newport, R.I., and Bar Harbor, Maine, both of which were flooded by the affluent who spent time in their extravagant mansions (which were called, not convincingly, "cottages"). Several grand resort hotels from tourism's golden era still host summer travelers in the region.

ECONOMIC DOWNTURN   While the railways allowed New England to thrive in the mid-19th century, the train played an equally central role in undermining its prosperity. The driving of the Golden Spike in 1869 in Utah, linking America's Atlantic and Pacific coasts by rail, was heard loud and clear in New England, and it had a discordant ring. Transcontinental rail meant farmers and manufacturers could ship goods from the fertile Great Plains and California to faraway markets, making it harder for New England's hardscrabble farmers and antiquated, water-powered industries to survive. Likewise, the coastal shipping trade, already in difficult straits, was dealt a fatal blow by this new transportation network. And the tourists set their sights on the Rockies and other stirring sites in the West.

Beginning in the late 19th century and accelerating through much of the early 20th, New England lapsed into an extended economic slumber. Families commonly walked away from their farmhouses (there was no market for resale) and set off for regions with more promising opportunities. The abandoned, decaying farmhouse became almost an icon for New England, and vast tracts of open farmland were reclaimed by forest. With the rise of the automobile, the grand resorts further succumbed, and many closed their doors as inexpensive motels siphoned off their business.

BOOM TIMES   Toward the end of the 20th century, much of New England rode an unexpected wave of prosperity, which peaked in the late 1980s. During that decade, a massive real-estate boom shook the region, driving land prices sky-high as prosperous buyers from New York and Boston—fueled by tremendous growth in the financial-services and tech industries—acquired vacation homes or retired to the most alluring areas, like the Maine coast and regions near ski mountains in Vermont. Tourism also rebounded as harried urbanites of the Eastern Seaboard opted for shorter, more frequent vacations closer to home.

A Literary Legacy

New Englanders have generated whole libraries, from the earliest days of hellfire-and-brimstone Puritan sermons to Stephen King's horror novels set in fictional Maine villages.

Among the more enduring writings from New England's earliest days are the poems of Massachusetts Bay Colony resident **Anne Bradstreet** (1612?–72) and the sermons and essays of **Increase Mather** (1639–1723) and his son, **Cotton Mather** (1663–1728), both of whom sought to reconcile science with religion.

After the American Revolution, Hartford dictionary writer **Noah Webster** (1758–1843) issued a call to American writers: "America must be as independent in literature as she is in politics, as famous for arts as for arms." He struck an early blow for pragmatism by taking the "u" out of British words like "labour" and "honour."

The tales of **Nathaniel Hawthorne** (1804–64) captivated a public eager for a native literature. His most famous story, *The Scarlet Letter*, is a narrative about morality set in 17th-century Boston, but he wrote numerous other books that wrestled with themes of sin and guilt, often set in the emerging republic. Among his best-known works are *The House of the Seven Gables, Twice-Told Tales*, and *The Marble Faun*.

Henry Wadsworth Longfellow (1807–82), the Portland, Maine, poet who settled in Cambridge (his house is a landmark and open to visitors), caught the attention of the public with evocative narrative poems focusing on distinctly American subjects. His popular works included *The Courtship of Miles Standish, Paul Revere's Ride*, and *Hiawatha*. Poetry in the mid–19th century was the equivalent of Hollywood movies today—Longfellow could be considered his generation's Steven Spielberg (apologies to literary scholars).

The zenith of New England literature occurred in the mid– and late 19th century with the Transcendentalist movement. These exalted writers and thinkers included **Ralph Waldo Emerson** (1803–82), **Margaret Fuller** (1813–50), **Bronson Alcott** (1799–1888), and **Henry David Thoreau** (1817–62). They fashioned a way of viewing nature and society that was

Travelers to the more remote regions will discover that many communities never benefited from the boom at all; they're still waiting to rebound from the economic malaise of earlier in the century. Especially hard-hit have been places like northeastern Vermont and far Downeast Maine, where residents still depend on local resources—timber, fisheries, and farmland—to eke out a living.

3 New England Style

You can often trace the evolution of a town by its architecture, as styles evolve from basic structures to elaborate Victorian mansions. The primer below should aid with basic identification.

- **Colonial** (1600–1700): The New England house of the 17th century was a simple, boxy affair, often covered in shingles or rough clapboards. Don't uniquely American. They rejected the rigid doctrines of the Puritans, and found sustenance in self-examination, the glories of nature, and a celebration of individualism. Perhaps the best known work to emerge from this period was Thoreau's *Walden, or, Life in the Woods.*

Among other New England writers who left a lasting mark on American literature was **Emily Dickinson** (1830–86), a native of Amherst, Mass., whose precise and enigmatic poems placed her in the front rank of American poets. **James Russell Lowell** (1819–91), of Cambridge, was an influential poet, critic, and editor. Later poets were imagist **Amy Lowell** (1874–1925), from Brookline, Mass., and **Edna St. Vincent Millay** (1892–1950), from Camden, Maine.

The bestselling *Uncle Tom's Cabin,* the book Abraham Lincoln half-jokingly accused of starting the Civil War, was written by **Harriet Beecher Stowe** (1811–86) in Brunswick, Maine. She lived much of her life as a neighbor of **Mark Twain** (himself an adopted New Englander) in Hartford, Conn. Another bestseller was the children's book *Little Women,* written by **Louisa May Alcott** (1832–88), whose father, Bronson, was part of the Transcendentalist movement.

New England's later role in the literary tradition may best be symbolized by the poet **Robert Frost** (1874–1963). This exceptionally gifted writer, who some believe was the greatest poet of this century, was born in California but lived his life in Massachusetts, New Hampshire, and Vermont. In the New England landscape and community, he found a lasting grace and rich metaphors for life. (Among his most famous lines: "Two roads diverged in a wood, and I—I took the one less traveled by,/And that has made all the difference.")

New England continues to attract writers drawn to the noted educational institutions and the privacy of rural life. Prominent contemporary writers and poets who live in New England at least part of the year include **John Updike, Anne Tyler, Christopher Buckley, P. J. O'Rourke, Bill Bryson, John Irving,** and **Donald Hall.** Maine is also the year-round home of **Stephen King,** who is considered not so much a novelist as Maine's Leading Industry.

look for ornamentation; these homes were designed for basic shelter from the elements, and are often marked by prominent stone chimneys. You can see the very earliest kind of homes at Plimoth Plantation, which features replicas; in Salem, near Boston; another good example is the Sherburne House, at Strawbery Banke in Portsmouth, N.H.

- **Georgian** (1700–1800): Ornamentation comes into play in the Georgian style, which draws heavily on classical symmetry. Georgian buildings were in vogue in England at the time, and were embraced by the affluent colonists. Look for Palladian windows, formal pilasters, and elaborate projecting pediments over the main doorway. Some homes like Portsmouth's impressive Wentworth-Gardner House were made of wood but designed to look like masonry. Deerfield, in the Pioneer Valley, is a good destination for seeing early Georgian homes; Providence, R.I., and Portsmouth, N.H., have abundant examples of later Georgian styles.

- **Federal** (1780–1820): Federal homes (sometimes called Adams homes) may best represent the New England ideal. Spacious yet austere, they are often rectangular or square, with low-pitched roofs and little ornament on the front, although carved swags or other embellishments are frequently seen near the roofline. Look for fan windows and chimneys bracketing the building. Excellent Federal-style homes are found throughout the region in towns like Kennebunkport, Maine.
- **Greek Revival** (1820–60): The most easy-to-identify Greek Revival homes feature a bold projecting portico with massive columns, like a part of the Parthenon grafted onto an existing home. The less dramatic homes may have subtle pilasters, or simply be oriented such that the gable faces the street, accenting the triangular pediment. Greek Revival didn't catch on in New England quite the way it did elsewhere in the South, but some fine examples exist, notably in Newfane, Vt., which is a virtual museum of Greek Revival architecture.
- **Carpenter Gothic** and **Gothic Revival** (1840–80): The second half of the 19th century brought a wave of Gothic Revival homes, which borrowed their aesthetic from the English country home. The 1846 Henry C. Bowen Cottage in Woodstock, Conn., is a superb example; aficionados of this style and its later progeny featuring gingerbread trim owe themselves a trip to Oak Bluffs at Martha's Vineyard, where compact, clustered cottages of a historic Methodist meeting ground are festooned with scrollwork and exuberant architectural flourishes.
- **Victorian** (1860–1900): This is a catchall term for the jumble of mid- to late-19th-century architectural styles that emphasized complexity and opulence. Perhaps the best-known Victorian style—almost a caricature—is the tall and narrow Addams-Family–style house, with mansard roof and prickly roof cresting. You'll find these scattered throughout the region. A notable example of this is author Stephen King's house in Bangor, Maine.

  The Victorian style also includes squarish **Italianate** homes with wide eaves and unusual flourishes; among the best examples are the huge brownstone Victoria Mansion in Portland, Maine, and the domed and pinnacled Samuel Colt House in Hartford, Conn.

  Stretching the definition a bit, Victorian can also include the **Richardsonian Romanesque** style, which was popular for railroad stations and public buildings. The classic Richardsonian building, designed by H. H. Richardson himself in 1872, is Trinity Church in Boston's Copley Square. The influence of the style can be found far and wide; one of the more attractive examples is the 1889 red-sandstone Fairbanks Museum in remote St. Johnsbury, Vt.
- **Shingle Style** (1880–1900): This uniquely New England style arose in the late 19th century, and quickly became the preferred style for vacation homes among the affluent on Cape Cod and the Maine coast. These homes are marked by a profusion of gables, roofs, and porches, and were typically covered with shingles from roofline to foundation.
- **Modern** (1900–present): Outside of Boston, New England has produced little in the way of notable modern architecture.

In the late 1930s, Boston became a center for the stark **International Style** with the appointment of Bauhaus veteran Walter Gropius to the faculty at Harvard. Some of the region's more intriguing experiments in this style are found on the MIT and Harvard campuses, including Gropius's Campus Center and Eero Saarinen's Kresge Auditorium.

4 A Taste of New England

All along the New England coast, you'll be tempted by seafood in its various forms. Fried clams are a filling specialty—you can get them by the bucket at divey clam houses along remote coves and busy highways. They're tasty, but not entirely wholesome if you're watching your waistline. The more upscale seafood restaurants offer fresh fish, grilled or gently sautéed.

Live lobster can be bought literally off the boat at lobster shacks, especially along the Maine coast. The setting is usually rustic—maybe a couple of picnic tables and a shed where huge vats of water are kept at a low boil. A lobster dinner might include corn on the cob or some seafood chowder.

Inland, take time to sample the local products. This includes delectable maple syrup, sold at farmhouses and stands throughout the northern reaches of the region. (Look for the homemade signs tacked to a tree at the end of a driveway.) Check the label for Grade A syrup certification. Cheese is a Vermont specialty, especially the strong cheddar. Look also for Vermont's famed apple cider, and Maine's wild blueberries.

In the summer, small farmers across New England set up stands at the end of their driveways offering fresh produce straight from the garden. Don't pass these by. You can usually find fresh berries, delicious fruits, and sometimes home-baked breads. These stands are rarely tended; just leave your money in the coffee can.

Restaurateurs haven't overlooked New England's bounty. Many chefs throughout the region serve up delicious meals consisting of local ingredients—some places even tend their own gardens for fresh greens and herbs. Some of the fine dishes we've enjoyed while researching this guide include curried pumpkin soup, venison medallions with shiitake mushrooms, and wild boar with juniper berries.

But you don't have to have a hefty budget to enjoy the local foods. A number of regional classics fall under the "road food" category. Here's an abbreviated field guide:

- **Beans:** Boston is forever linked with baked beans (hence the nickname "Beantown"), and the sweet, earthy beans are popular throughout the region. A Saturday-night supper traditionally consists of baked beans and brown bread.
- **Lobster rolls:** Lobster rolls consist of lobster meat plucked from the shell, mixed with just enough mayonnaise to hold it all together, then served on a hot-dog roll.
- **Moxie:** Early in this century, Moxie outsold Coca-Cola. Part of its allure was the fanciful story behind its 1885 creation: A traveler named Moxie was said to have observed South American Indians consuming the sap of a native plant, which gave them extraordinary strength. The drink was "re-created" by Maine native and Massachusetts resident Dr. Augustin Thompson. It's still popular in New England, although some folks liken the taste to a combination of medicine and topsoil.

- **Necco Wafers:** Still made in Cambridge by the New England Confectionery Company, these powdery wafers haven't changed a bit since they were first manufactured in 1847. The factory no longer offers tours, but the candies are available widely throughout the region.
- **Pies:** New Englanders are serious about their pies, and they remain a popular dessert (and sometimes breakfast) throughout the region. Apple, blueberry, and mincemeat are the traditional favorites.

Finally, no survey of comestibles would be complete without mention of something to wash it all down: beer. New England has more microbreweries than any other region outside of the Pacific Northwest. Popular brewpubs that rank high on the list include the Great Providence Brewing Co., the Commonwealth Brewing Co. (Boston's first brewpub), the Portsmouth Brewery, Federal Jack's Brewpub (Kennebunkport), Vermont Pub & Brewery (Burlington), and the Windham Brewery at the Latchis Grille (Brattleboro).

Index

See also Accommodations index, below.

ACCOMMODATIONS

FROMMER'S® COMPLETE TRAVEL GUIDES

Alaska
Amsterdam
Argentina & Chile
Arizona
Atlanta
Australia
Austria
Bahamas
Barcelona, Madrid & Seville
Beijing
Belgium, Holland &
  Luxembourg
Bermuda
Boston
British Columbia & the
  Canadian Rockies
Budapest & the Best of Hungary
California
Canada
Cancún, Cozumel & the
  Yucatán
Cape Cod, Nantucket &
  Martha's Vineyard
Caribbean
Caribbean Cruises & Ports
  of Call
Caribbean Ports of Call
Carolinas & Georgia
Chicago
China
Colorado
Costa Rica
Denmark
Denver, Boulder & Colorado
  Springs
England
Europe

European Cruises & Ports of Call
Florida
France
Germany
Greece
Greek Islands
Hawaii
Hong Kong
Honolulu, Waikiki & Oahu
Ireland
Israel
Italy
Jamaica
Japan
Las Vegas
London
Los Angeles
Maryland & Delaware
Maui
Mexico
Montana & Wyoming
Montréal & Québec City
Munich & the Bavarian Alps
Nashville & Memphis
Nepal
New England
New Mexico
New Orleans
New York City
New Zealand
Nova Scotia, New Brunswick &
  Prince Edward Island
Oregon
Paris
Philadelphia & the Amish
  Country
Portugal

Prague & the Best of the Czech
  Republic
Provence & the Riviera
Puerto Rico
Rome
San Antonio & Austin
San Diego
San Francisco
Santa Fe, Taos & Albuquerque
Scandinavia
Scotland
Seattle & Portland
Shanghai
Singapore & Malaysia
South Africa
Southeast Asia
South Florida
South Pacific
Spain
Sweden
Switzerland
Texas
Thailand
Tokyo
Toronto
Tuscany & Umbria
USA
Utah
Vancouver & Victoria
Vermont, New Hampshire
  & Maine
Vienna & the Danube Valley
Virgin Islands
Virginia
Walt Disney World & Orlando
Washington, D.C.
Washington State

FROMMER'S® DOLLAR-A-DAY GUIDES

Australia from $50 a Day
California from $70 a Day
Caribbean from $70 a Day
England from $70 a Day
Europe from $70 a Day

Florida from $70 a Day
Hawaii from $70 a Day
Ireland from $60 a Day
Italy from $70 a Day
London from $85 a Day

New York from $80 a Day
Paris from $80 a Day
San Francisco from $60 a Day
Washington, D.C.,
  from $70 a Day

FROMMER'S® PORTABLE GUIDES

Acapulco, Ixtapa &
  Zihuatanejo
Alaska Cruises & Ports
  of Call
Amsterdam
Australia's Great Barrier Reef
Bahamas
Baja & Los Cabos
Berlin
Boston
California Wine Country
Charleston & Savannah
Chicago

Dublin
Hawaii: The Big Island
Hong Kong
Houston
Las Vegas
London
Los Angeles
Maine Coast
Maui
Miami
New Orleans
New York City
Paris

Phoenix & Scottsdale
Portland
Puerto Rico
Puerto Vallarta, Manzanillo &
  Guadalajara
San Diego
San Francisco
Seattle
Sydney
Tampa & St. Petersburg
Vancouver
Venice
Washington, D.C.

FROMMER'S® NATIONAL PARK GUIDES

Family Vacations in the
  National Parks
Grand Canyon

National Parks of the American
  West
Rocky Mountain
Yellowstone & Grand Teton

Yosemite & Sequoia/
  Kings Canyon
Zion & Bryce Canyon

FROMMER'S® MEMORABLE WALKS

Chicago	New York	San Francisco
London	Paris	Washington, D.C.

FROMMER'S® GREAT OUTDOOR GUIDES

Arizona & New Mexico	Northern California	Southern New England
New England	Southern California & Baja	Vermont & New Hampshire

FROMMER'S® BORN TO SHOP GUIDES

Born to Shop: France	Born to Shop: Italy	Born to Shop: New York
Born to Shop: Hong Kong,	Born to Shop: London	Born to Shop: Paris
Shanghai & Beijing		

FROMMER'S® IRREVERENT GUIDES

Amsterdam	Los Angeles	Seattle & Portland
Boston	Manhattan	Vancouver
Chicago	New Orleans	Walt Disney World
Las Vegas	Paris	Washington, D.C.
London	San Francisco	

FROMMER'S® BEST-LOVED DRIVING TOURS

America	France	New England
Britain	Germany	Scotland
California	Ireland	Spain
Florida	Italy	Western Europe

THE UNOFFICIAL GUIDES®

Bed & Breakfasts in California	Golf Vacations in the	New Orleans
Bed & Breakfasts in	Eastern U.S.	New York City
New England	The Great Smoky &	Paris
Bed & Breakfasts in the	Blue Ridge Mountains	San Francisco
Northwest	Inside Disney	Skiing in the West
Bed & Breakfasts in Southeast	Hawaii	Southeast with Kids
Beyond Disney	Las Vegas	Walt Disney World
Branson, Missouri	London	Walt Disney World for
California with Kids	Mid-Atlantic with Kids	Grown-ups
Chicago	Mini Las Vegas	Walt Disney World for Kids
Cruises	Mini-Mickey	Washington, D.C.
Disneyland	New England with Kids	World's Best Diving Vacations
Florida with Kids		

SPECIAL-INTEREST TITLES

Frommer's Britain's Best Bed & Breakfasts and
   Country Inns
Frommer's France's Best Bed & Breakfasts and
   Country Inns
Frommer's Italy's Best Bed & Breakfasts and
   Country Inns
Frommer's Caribbean Hideaways
Frommer's Adventure Guide to Australia &
   New Zealand
Frommer's Adventure Guide to Central America
Frommer's Adventure Guide to India & Pakistan
Frommer's Adventure Guide to South America
Frommer's Adventure Guide to Southeast Asia
Frommer's Adventure Guide to Southern Africa
Frommer's Gay & Lesbian Europe
Frommer's Exploring America by RV
Hanging Out in England

Hanging Out in Europe
Hanging Out in France
Hanging Out in Ireland
Hanging Out in Italy
Hanging Out in Spain
Israel Past & Present
Frommer's The Moon
Frommer's New York City with Kids
The New York Times' Guide to Unforgettable
   Weekends
Places Rated Almanac
Retirement Places Rated
Frommer's Road Atlas Britain
Frommer's Road Atlas Europe
Frommer's Washington, D.C., with Kids
Frommer's What the Airlines Never Tell You

Let Us Hear From You!

Dear Frommer's Reader,

You are our greatest resource in keeping our guides relevant, timely, and lively. We'd love to hear from you about your travel experiences—good or bad. Want to recommend a great restaurant or a hotel off the beaten path—or register a complaint? Any thoughts on how to improve the guide itself?

Please use this page to share your thoughts with me and mail it to the address below. Or if you like, send a FAX or e-mail me at frommersfeedback@hungryminds.com. And so that we can thank you—and keep you up on the latest developments in travel—we invite you to sign up for a free daily Frommer's e-mail travel update. Just write your e-mail address on the back of this page. Also, if you'd like to take a moment to answer a few questions about yourself to help us improve our guides, please complete the following quick survey. (We'll keep that information confidential.)

Thanks for your insights.

Yours sincerely,

Michael Spring

Michael Spring, *Publisher*

Name (Optional) _____

Address _____

_____

City _____ **State** _____ **ZIP** _____

Name of Frommer's Travel Guide _____

Comments _____

_____

_____

_____

_____

_____

_____

_____

_____

_____

Age: ( )18-24; ( )25-39; ( )40-49; ( )50-55; ( )Over 55

Income: ( )Under $25,000; ( )$25,000-$50,000; ( )$50,000-$100,000; ( )Over $100,000

I am: ( )Single, never married; ( )Married, with children; ( )Married, without children; ( )Divorced; ( )Widowed

Number of people in my household: ( )1; ( )2; ( )3; ( )4; ( )5 or more

Number of people in my household under 18: ( )1; ( )2; ( )3; ( )4; ( )5 or more

I am ( )a student; ( )employed full-time; ( )employed part-time; ( )not employed at this time; ( )retired; ( )other

I took ( )0; ( )1; ( )2; ( )3; ( )4 or more leisure trips in the past 12 months

My last vacation was ( )a weekend; ( )1 week; ( )2 weeks; ( )3 or more weeks

My last vacation was to ( )the U.S.; ( )Canada; ( )Mexico; ( )Europe; ( )Asia; ( )South America; ( )Central America; ( )The Caribbean; ( )Africa; ( )Middle East; ( )Australia/New Zealand

( )I would; ( )would not buy a Frommer's Travel Guide for business travel

I access the Internet ( )at home; ( )at work; ( )both; ( )I do not use the Internet

I used the Internet to do research for my last trip. ( )Yes; ( )No

I used the Internet to book accommodations or air travel on my last trip. ( )Yes; ( )No

My favorite travel site is ( )frommers.com; ( )travelocity.com; ( )expedia.com;

other_____

I use Frommer's Travel Guides ( )always; ( )sometimes; ( )seldom

I usually buy ( )1; ( )2; ( )more than 2 guides when I travel

Other guides I use include _____

What's the most important thing we could do to improve Frommer's Travel Guides?

_____

_____

_____

_____

Yes, please send me a daily e-mail travel update. My e-mail address is

_____